RON SHANDLER'S **2018**

BASEBALL
FORECASTER

AND ENCYCLOPEDIA OF FANALYTICS

TRIUMPH
B O O K S

Triumph Books and colophon are registered trademarks of Random House, Inc.

This book is available in quantity at special discounts for your group or organization. For further information, contact:

Triumph Books LLC
814 North Franklin Street
Chicago, Illinois 60610
(312) 337-0747
www.triumphbooks.com

Printed in U.S.A.
ISBN: 978-1-62937-481-9

Rotisserie League Baseball is a registered trademark of the Rotisserie League Baseball Association, Inc.

Statistics provided by Baseball Info Solutions

Cover design by Brent Hershey
Front cover photograph by Kelley L Cox/USA TODAY Sports Images
Author photograph by Kevin Hurley

Ron Shandler's
BASEBALL FORECASTER

Editors
Ray Murphy
Brent Hershey

Associate Editor
Brandon Kruse

• • • • •

Technical Wizard
Rob Rosenfeld

Design
Brent Hershey

Data and Charts
Matt Cederholm

Player Commentaries
Ryan Bloomfield
Rob Carroll
Brant Chesser
Alec Dopp
Brent Hershey
Brandon Kruse
Ray Murphy
Stephen Nickrand
Kristopher Olson
Greg Pyron
Joe Pytleski
Brian Rudd
Paul Sporer
Jock Thompson
Rod Truesdell

Research and Articles
Patrick Davitt
Ed DeCaria
Arik Florimonte
David Martin
Paul Petera
Jeff Zimmerman

Prospects
Rob Gordon
Jeremy Deloney
Tom Mulhall
Brian Walton

Injury Chart
Rick Wilton

Acknowledgments

Producing the *Baseball Forecaster* has been a team effort for a number of years now; the list of credits to the left is where the heavy lifting gets done. On behalf of Ron, Brent, and Ray, our most sincere thanks to each of those key contributors.

We are just as grateful to the rest of the BaseballHQ.com staff, who do the yeoman's work in populating the website with 12 months of incredible content: Dave Adler, Andy Andres, Matt Beagle, Dan Becker, Alex Beckey, Bob Berger, Chris Blessing, Derrick Boyd, Brian Brickley, Doug Dennis, Matt Dodge, Greg Fishwick, Neil FitzGerald, Brandon Gavett, Sam Grant, Rick Green, Phil Hertz, Joe Hoffer, Ed Hubbard, Tom Kephart, Brad Kullman, Chris Lee, Bill McKnight, Harold Nichols, Frank Noto, Josh Paley, Nick Richards, Vlad Sedler, Mike Shears, Peter Sheridan, Brian Slack, Skip Snow, Matthew St-Germain, Jeffrey Tomich, Nick Trojanowski, Michael Weddell and Mike Werner.

Thank you to our behind-the-scenes troopers: our technical dynamic duo of Mike Krebs and Rob Rosenfeld.

Thank you to all our industry colleagues, a truly impressive group. They are competitors, but they are also colleagues working to grow this industry, which is never a more evident than at our annual First Pitch Arizona gathering each November.

Thank you to Chris Pirrone, Ryan Bonini, and the team at USA Today Sports Media Group.

Thank you for all the support from the folks at Triumph Books and Action Printing.

And of course, thank *you*, readers, for your interest in what we all have to say. Your kind words, support and (respectful) criticism move us forward on the fanalytic continuum more than you know. We are grateful for your readership.

From Brent Hershey At some point every year in Book Season, during a rare moment when I can catch a breath, I marvel at how *much* this tome contains. It makes me appreciate not only all the names to the left that make the current year's *Baseball Forecaster* posssible, but all of those whose contributions to the 31 annuals past still live on. Ray, thanks for your flexibility and commitment to working together to uphold this tradition and still maintain some semblance of personal balance. Thanks, Ron for holding all the institutional memory of the project and continuing to give us just the right nudge when we need it. And thanks to Lorie, Dillon and Eden for the ways you bring life and energy into our family unit, no matter what the circumstances. There's a lot of history and tradition in our space, too.

From Ray Murphy Assembling this book—with its 280 pages of content, millions of data points and (hopefully) insightful analysis thereof—over the course of about eight weeks, is a major lift. The only reason it gets done is because the team listed at left is supremely talented and just as dedicated. The fact that Ron used to produce this book as a solo project seemingly challenges the laws of physics. It remains a joy to collaborate with him each year. As for Brent, I keep waiting for him to get tired of working with me. Either it hasn't happened yet, or he's hiding it very well. Either way, I am grateful to share the BaseballHQ helm with an ideal partner.

Along with my fantastic wife, Jennifer, and amazing daughters, Bridget and Grace, our family has undertaken major new adventures this fall: new house, new town, new school. (Note to self: don't ever move during Book Season.) I can't wait to see what's next…

From Ron Shandler For me, the annual multi-month gestation that ends with the birth of this book continues to be an immensely gratifying experience. Thanks again to Ray and Brent for shepherding this baby through its early development. Thanks to the BaseballHQ.com staff for pushing the envelope on innovative, high-quality fanalytics. Thanks to all of you for excusing the mixed metaphors.

As always, my eternal gratitude goes to the household of women who have supported me through all 32 editions. Sue, Darielle, Justina and Michele keep me grounded, sane and insane, not necessarily in that order. One day I might get a male dog with whom to watch hockey games.

By time you read this, I will have already reached my six-decade milestone. Wish me a happy birthday. I probably have another decade in me before the fingers give out, but by then we'll all be writing telepathically anyway. All we really crave is immortality, right? Onward…

TABLE OF CONTENTS

Extremes

by Ron Shandler

On August 19, 2017, Los Angeles Dodgers pitcher Yu Darvish was placed on the 10-day disabled list, retroactive to August 17, with "lower back tightness."

As an isolated event, this move was routine and unremarkable. "Lower back tightness" is a common malady and can typically sideline a player for anywhere from a few days to a few weeks, sometimes longer.

The Dodgers would not likely miss him. Analysts suggested that Darvish had not been brought in at the July 31 trading deadline for his contributions in August and September anyway; the Dodgers already had something like a 97-game lead in the NL West. Darvish was primarily acquired for October. As such, they would manage his innings during the stretch run in order to save his arm for the post-season.* This DL stint might have been part of that management program.

Darvish was reinstated on August 27, exactly 10 days after being placed on the list.

The only reason to bring up such an outwardly innocuous event is because this was not the first time the Dodgers used the new 10-day DL to shelve a starting pitcher for right around the 10 day minimum:

Pitcher	On DL	For	Off DL	Days
Rich Hill	7-Apr	blister	16-Apr	9
Hyun-Jin Ryu	1-May	hip contusion	11-May	10
Brandon McCarthy	5-May	sore shoulder	15-May	10
Kenta Maeda	11-May	hamstring	25-May	14
Alex Wood	29-May	SE joint	10-Jun	12
Brandon McCarthy	26-Jun	knee tendinitis	8-Jul	12
Yu Darvish	17-Aug	back tightness	27-Aug	10
Alex Wood	22-Aug	SE joint	3-Sep	12

Some of these stints were seemingly intended to rest the pitcher. Some of them were efforts to avoid further injury, often unsuccessfully. Regardless, the Dodgers made good use of the new rule.

In the olden days of the 15-day DL (and the 21-day DL—remember?), these players would have been forced to sit out for far longer periods before returning to action. So, we'd expect that the effect of this new, shorter disabled list would be to reduce the number of days that players sat on the DL.

That is what appears to have happened:

Year	#Players	DL Days
2010	393	22,911
2011	422	25,610
2012	409	30,408
2013	442	29,551
2014	422	25,839
2015	454	28,982
2016	478	31,329
2017	533	30,913

The number of DL days did decline 1.3%, though it's unclear whether that was wholly the result of the shorter DL. These

---

* Good decision. Bad outcome.

numbers can become muddled because, while it was easier to place a player on the DL, a player could still stay on for as long as a team saw fit. And you can see from the above that a more extreme version of the same phenomenon occurred in 2013.

However, now it seemed that *anyone* could join the pain party. The 11.5% increase in number of players shelved is significant. Those 55 additional players in 2017 can be directly attributed to the lower barrier of entry to the 10 day DL.

Number of players who spent 15 or fewer days on the DL

2015	12
2016	19
2017	84

(excluding 7-day concussion DL)

As a fantasy leaguer, you know the impact this had on our teams. For me personally, the disabled lists in my four public leagues peaked in early June with 37 hobbled players. In my mixed leagues, there were usually some reasonable replacement options but always multiple teams fighting for them. In my AL/NL-only leagues, the free agent pools were mostly devoid of any sign of human life. Frankly, the 10-day DL was a curse.

Beyond all this, the Darvish move had one other important distinction.

On the day he hit the DL, Darvish became the 159th player from the pre-season Top 300 to be disabled, demoted or designated for assignment. *(All ADP data is from the National Fantasy Baseball Championship.)* Prior to this year, the high water mark for Top 300 attrition was 158 players. That total was compiled during the entire 2014 season. Darvish helped break the record this year… on August 19.

By the final day of the regular season, another 16 players would be added to that list, boosting the 2017 attrition rate to a record 58%. Little did you know last March that nearly six out of every 10 players you drafted would be disabled, demoted or DFA'd by year's end.

If there was any saving grace, it was that we did a decent job of drafting around the attrition. We count on the higher-ranked players to be more productive, more reliable and to spend more time on the field. So, we can pat ourselves on the back for this:

ADP	Attrition
Top 100	51%
101-200	57%
201-300	67%

When the best we can be is more than half wrong, it's small consolation.

The splintering of playing time had ripple effects throughout the game, some areas more than others.

Power up

The rise in DL days didn't seem to have any effect on the raw power emanating from major league bats. Players might have been getting shelved more often but the replacements were no less power-enabled.

Year	Tot HR	Players with 20+ HR	30+ HR
2000	5693	102	47
2001	5458	90	41
2002	5059	81	28
2003	5207	86	30
2004	5451	93	37
2005	5017	78	27
2006	5386	91	34
2007	4957	86	26
2008	4878	92	28
2009	5042	87	30
2010	4613	77	18
2011	4552	68	23
2012	4934	79	27
2013	4661	70	14
2014	4186	57	11
2015	4909	64	20
2016	5610	111	35
2017	6105	118	41

Nearly 2,000 more home runs in just three years? Seriously? Perhaps this is the smoking gun:

Year	HR/FB%
2014	9.5%
2015	11.4%
2016	12.8%
2017	13.7%

What has been the cause of all these balls going yard with wanton abandon? Let's put the issue to rest, once and for all:

1. It's not the balls, because Rob Manfred already told us it wasn't and we are always supposed to believe people in authority.

2. It's not the increase in uppercut swings, because baseball's overall flyball rate only rose from 34.6% to 35.5%, and there were four seasons in the past 10 years with still higher rates.

3. It's not performance-enhancing drugs, because the evidence is clear that MLB's drug testing has been working. The recent suspensions of speedsters Dee Gordon and Starling Marte are proof that PEDs have no relationship to power anyway.

Our esteemed rulers want us to believe it's just a random trend that will eventually cycle back around. But even if seams, swings and steroids *are* real (seriously, they are), it doesn't matter. Here's why…

I don't know about you, but for me, home runs are "meh" events. To score a pair of runs, give me a "single, force out, double-thrown-out-at-third, single, triple" over a "walk, home run" any day of the week.

However, in an era when superhero flicks often take up half the screens in multiplexes, home runs are cool displays of brute strength. In an era driven by short attention spans and immediate gratification, home runs take less time to put runs on the board. In an era when football and basketball draw more fantasy leaguers, and daily fantasy is exploding, brute force and quick scoring are immensely popular.

And you have to admit that the 2017 post-season was incredibly exciting baseball, thanks in part to all those home runs.

More eyeballs. More viewers. More clicks. In the end, home runs are *profitable* for MLB. That's all that really matters. That's why they had their collective heads in the sand during the PED era and that's why they are likely tickled pink at all these power

pokes now. You can point your finger at any reason for the surge, but all that matters is that home runs are profitable.

So, if anyone is wondering whether there is going to be much regression, the answer is "not likely." Why would it? If MLB is going to address "the balls" at all, it will less likely be about the barrage of bombs and more likely about the barrage of blisters.

For us fantasy leaguers, this has a huge impact on how we will be constructing our teams. In 2017, there were big sluggers who weren't even drafted, and major power sources who languished in the free agent pool.

30+ HR hitters who were not drafted among the pre-season ADP Top 300

Slugger	HR	'17 ADP
Aaron Judge	52	349
Joey Gallo	41	436
Cody Bellinger	39	445
Logan Morrison	38	517
Justin Smoak	38	541
Ryan Zimmerman	36	406
Travis Shaw	31	305
Scott Schebler	30	387
Steven Souza	30	351
Mark Reynolds	30	512
Lucas Duda	30	352

These 11 represented 27% of the 41 players who hit at least 30 home runs last season. In a 12-team AL/NL league, they would have been players an owner might have speculated on at the bottom of the draft. In a 15-team mixed league, only Shaw, Judge, Souza and Duda might have been deliberate picks by round 23. In a 12-team mixed league, *all of these players would have been left over in the free agent pool!*

If we extend the list to undrafted 20+ HR hitters, we add 23 names to the list. But some of them went *really* late. Here are the 20+ HR hitters who went outside the *Top 400*.

Slugger	HR	'17 ADP
Yonder Alonso	28	550
Eddie Rosario	27	414
Scooter Gennett	27	476
Matt Davidson	26	719
Paul DeJong	25	Not in the top 1000
Matt Joyce	25	480
Trey Mancini	24	593
Matt Olson	24	987
Ian Happ	24	665
Thomas Pham	23	734
Marwin Gonzalez	23	439
Luis Valbuena	22	473
Tim Beckham	22	585
Chris Taylor	21	717
Eduardo Escobar	21	582
Matt Adams	20	468

These 16 hitters would not have been drafted even in an 18-team mixed league (except Rosario, who would have been the final pick at No. 414).

In an off-season poll at RonShandler.com, I asked: *"In your primary league, in what place did the team finish that owned Aaron Judge?"* Almost 30% of Judge owners won their league, nearly 50% finished first or second, and two thirds finished no lower than fourth. This tracks to previous polls about surprise players having a disproportionate impact on the fantasy standings. And if that player is plucked out of the free agent pool in April, it effectively diminishes the value of all that draft prep work we do each spring.

In 2014, you might have been among a handful of owners in a 15-team league without even one 30-HR hitter. In 2017, one of my fantasy teams had *five* 30-HR hitters and I still finished in seventh place. In fact, there were six hitters in 2017 who had more than 20 HRs and still earned *negative rotisserie value.*

So stocking up on power hitters at the draft may not be enough. The rising DL list adds risk to your picks. You'll need to dig deep, perhaps speculating on even more power in your reserves and your farm players. Odds are there is not another Aaron Judge lurking in 2018, but it might not be a bad idea to go an extra buck on the chance that a Ryan McMahon might back into at-bats in Coors Field, or that Victor Robles might stake his claim to a spot in the Washington outfield.

McMahon? Robles? No path to playing time, you say? Today, that's one of fantasy baseball's greatest fallacies.

Last March, I advised readers and attendees to the First Pitch conferences to go all in on Michael Conforto at his prevailing rate (which was less than $5 in most mixed leagues). At the same time, in one of my deeper leagues, I went against my better judgment and passed on Cody Bellinger because I thought, "How is he going to get past Adrian Gonzalez?" I'm so smart.

If there is any benefit to the rise in DL days, it's that it constantly opens up new paths to playing time for other players. Eliminate "no path to playing time" from your vocabulary. And the beauty of it is that playing time speculation has become fantasy baseball's newest undervalued commodity.

Running down

It is unclear whether the increased use of the DL has had any effect on the continuing malaise in stolen base output. Has the rise in DL days resulted in lower motivation to risk injury on the basepaths? Or are there more injuries on the basepaths (not that we can see)? More likely, the tactical question managers asked was, "Why run when the next guy is going to hit a homer anyway?"

But there is one extreme trend worth noting:

| Year | Tot SB | —Players with— | |
		20+ SB	30+ SB
2000	2924	42	13
2001	3103	44	18
2002	2750	33	16
2003	2573	26	11
2004	2589	27	12
2005	2565	27	13
2006	2767	35	19
2007	2918	42	19
2008	2799	37	16
2009	2970	46	17
2010	2959	35	19
2011	3279	50	20
2012	3229	48	23
2013	2693	40	16
2014	2764	39	15
2015	2505	30	7
2016	2537	28	14
2017	2527	29	6

While steals continue to be down, that's not the real problem, at least not from a fantasy standpoint. The critical mass of bags is shifting upward into the legs of fewer players. In 2017, only six baserunners stole 30 bases or more, the lowest number this century.

League-wide, the totals over the past three years have been pretty similar to 2003-2005, another period when power was king. But now there are only about half as many impact burners.

Here were the 30-base stealers of 2017, and few more who just missed the cut-off:

Player	SB	'17 ADP
Dee Gordon	60	50
Billy Hamilton	59	52
Trea Turner	46	10
Whit Merrifield	34	484
Cameron Maybin	33	311
Jose Altuve	32	4
Byron Buxton	29	137
Rajai Davis	29	191
Delino DeShields	29	422
Jarrod Dyson	28	215

These were guys who kept you competitive in the category, or helped you win it outright. And yet, most of them were not drafted very high. Of this group, the only one who had no history of impact speed was Merrifield, and his ADP reflects that. The rest of the lower-drafted players were downgraded due to injury history, unrealized potential, age, or some combination of the three.

However, in 2017, we drafted other players for SBs. The following list contains those 30-bag burners from 2016 for whom we had high expectations, but didn't earn back their draft slot:

| Player | Stolen bases | | ADP |
	2016	2017	
Jonathan Villar	62	23	19
Starling Marte	47	21	23
Eduardo Nunez	40	24	113
Hernan Perez	34	13	188
Juan Segura	33	22	53
Travis Jankowski	30	4	281

There are many speedsters, like Hamilton, DeShields, Perez and Jankowski, whose ADPs are typically depressed because they are essentially "one-trick ponies"—providing stolen bases and little else. That decreases the draftable talent pool even more and, in turn, inflates those players who offer across-the-board skills. Supply and demand.

What often ends up happening is that there is an inclination to chase a Dee Gordon or Trea Turner early so that, once rostered, you can ignore speed for another hour. But given that anyone can get injured (or suspended)—and frequent base-stealers might be more prone—you should think twice about waiting a full hour.

For those who choose, instead, to grab up a bunch of late speed and build the category from the bottom up, there is some risk:

Players with 20+ SB and sub-.300 OBA

Year	No.	Players
2011	5	R.Davis, A.Escobar, A.Hill, I.Desmond, T.Campana
2012	6	C.Gomez, D.Gordon, D.Stubbs, J.Schafer, A.Casilla, A.Ramirez
2013	5	E.Bonifacio, J.Pierre, E.Johnson, A.Escobar, I.Suzuki
2014	6	B.Hamilton, E.Young, J.Jones, M.Upton, K.Wong, J.Segura
2015	3	B.Hamilton, J.Segura, J.Marisnick
2016	1	M.Upton
2017	5	B.Hamilton, R.Davis, J.Villar, J.Peraza, K.Broxton

The trend coming into 2017 seemed to be that teams were finally realizing how damaging one-trick ponies can be. The 2017 regression might have been a blip, but there is never any reason for teams to expose players with poor on-base skills. For us, that ramps up the challenge of finding enough bags without damaging our OBP, or batting average.

Of course, these are all small samples. However, when it comes to impact speedsters, all we have are small samples. With only a handful of impact burners, and leagues with 12 or 15 teams, buying speed has become a scarcity challenge similar to saves, though with lesser risk that the top earners will go belly up.

Splintering innings

Another fallout from the increased number of DL stays is fewer pitchers reaching the 200-inning threshold.

Number of 200-Inning Pitchers

Year	No.
2008	34
2009	36
2010	45
2011	39
2012	31
2013	36
2014	34
2015	28
2016	15
2017	15

It's not only injuries at work here. The increase in bullpen specialization has also been feeding into this trend.

In the past, we felt confident to invest heavily in an anchor starter, a pitcher who would pretty much guarantee 200 innings. These days we still go into our drafts and think, "I need to get one 200-inning, 200-strikeout ace to be my staff's anchor." Over the past decade, how many pitchers have actually reached those dual thresholds?

No. Pitchers with 200 IP and

Year	200+ K	<200 K
2008	9	26
2009	9	27
2010	12	38
2011	11	28
2012	10	21
2013	10	26
2014	11	23
2015	14	14
2016	8	7
2017	10	5

The raw number of 200/200 arms has been fairly stable over the years. About two-thirds of the owners in a 15-team mixed league have been able to roster that caliber of ace pretty consistently. But the number of lesser dominant 200-inning arms has plummeted. When you buy 200 innings, you're now also buying 200 strikeouts whether you like it or not. And that means, you *really* have to pay up.

Look at the earnings for the 200/200 class of 2017:

Pitcher	IP	K	W	ERA	WHIP	R$
Corey Kluber	203.7	265	18	2.28	0.87	$47
Chris Sale	214.3	308	17	2.90	0.97	$40
Max Scherzer	200.7	268	16	2.51	0.90	$42
Zack Greinke	202.3	215	17	3.20	1.07	$27
Carlos Carrasco	200.0	226	18	3.28	1.10	$27
Justin Verlander	206.0	219	15	3.36	1.17	$20
Jacob deGrom	201.3	239	15	3.53	1.19	$19
Carlos Martinez	205.0	217	12	3.64	1.22	$14
Chris Archer	201.0	249	10	4.17	1.26	$9
Jeff Samardzija	207.7	205	9	4.42	1.14	$9

In 2017, 200/200 didn't guarantee you a stud. But here are some honorable mentions; these pitchers struck out over 200 but fell short of 200 innings:

Pitcher	IP	K	W	ERA	WHIP	R$
Clayton Kershaw	175.0	202	18	2.31	0.95	$36
Steven Strasburg	175.3	204	15	2.52	1.02	$30
Luis Severino	193.3	230	14	2.98	1.04	$28
Robbie Ray	162.0	218	15	2.89	1.15	$22
Yu Darvish	186.7	209	10	3.86	1.16	$13
Jose Quintana	188.7	207	11	4.15	1.22	$9

I'm sure that none of the owners of this sextet were complaining about their shortfall in innings. But here's the thing…

We buy roster slots, not players. So the 50 or so innings that you had to backfill when these guys were being rested, skipped a turn or on the shelf would have gone to replacement level arms. Replacement level in a 15-team league in 2017 had a name—Rick Porcello—whose roto output earned a few cents shy of $0 last year.

Let's observe the potential damage of filling up the innings deficiency of one of the core starters with a Porcello-caliber replacement…

Pitcher	IP	K	W	ERA	WHIP	R$
Yu Darvish	186.7	209	10	3.86	1.16	$13
*Replacement	50	44	3	4.65	1.40	
Roster slot total	233.7	253	13	4.08	1.23	$10

* Rick Porcello's stats

…and you've lost $3 in value by replacing an injured player.

Of course, you might have opted to backfill those innings with something other than a replacement level starter. If you were smart, you would have grabbed one of the oft-maligned, typically-overlooked middle relievers out of the pool. But I'm getting ahead of myself.

Finally, Corey Kluber. He led all of baseball with 18 wins in 2017. The last non-strike season that failed to produce even one 19-game winner was… *never*. Yes, you can track all the way back to 1901 and every season, except for strike years 1981 and 1994, boasted at least one 19-game winner. Until now.

If we can't count on wins and we can't count on innings, and the innings shortfalls are putting ERA and WHIP at risk, what can we count on? Of course, strikeouts.

Year	Tot K	Pitchers with 150+ K	200+ K
2000	31,356	35	8
2001	32,404	35	10
2002	31,394	28	7
2003	30,801	33	7
2004	31,828	35	9
2005	30,644	34	8
2006	31,655	39	6
2007	32,189	35	8
2008	32,884	43	10
2009	33,591	40	10
2010	34,306	49	15
2011	34,488	52	14
2012	36,426	53	13
2013	36,710	53	12
2014	37,441	56	13
2015	37,446	56	18
2016	38,982	54	12
2017	40,104	48	16

The consistency in high-K pitchers from 2000 through 2007 is remarkable, which makes the surge over the past 10 years so striking (oooh, a pun!). However, it's the pullback of 150+ K pitchers in 2017 that merits note. That is not a skills regression; it's the impact of the DL eating into innings. Replacement arms tend to be less dominant.

So stock up wherever you can get those strikeouts—at the draft, during the season, and with your keeper league picks.

In the past, a frontline stud could single-handedly account for upward of 15% of your entire staff's innings, making him a worthwhile investment. Now, not so much. Invest in Ks wherever you can get them and let the rest fall where it may.

Seeking relief

You won't find it here. Eleven of the closers drafted back in March ended up on the disabled list; that's not unusual. The overall rate of turnover—from injuries, ineffectiveness, managerial whim, acts of God, etc.—was 53%. It was the second straight year that saw a failure rate topping 50%.

The continuing fallout is that we have been investing less and less in closers each year. As recently as 2014, we'd have to pay a minimum of $10 at the draft table for any frontline closer, no matter how poor his peripherals. Last year in Tout Wars, more than a third of the potential closers were purchased at the auction for less than $10.

Here were the top 11 closers in 2017, ranked by roto earnings:

Closers	Sv	IP	K	ERA	WHIP	15$
Kenley Jansen	41	68.3	109	1.32	0.75	26
Craig Kimbrel	35	69	126	1.43	0.68	26
Corey Knebel	39	76	126	1.78	1.16	19
Felipe Rivero	21	75.3	88	1.67	0.89	17
David Robertson	14	68.3	98	1.84	0.85	17
Roberto Osuna	39	64	83	3.38	0.86	16
Brad Hand	21	79.3	104	2.16	0.93	16
Ken Giles	34	62.7	83	2.30	1.04	14
Alex Colome	47	66.7	58	3.24	1.20	13
Wade Davis	32	58.7	79	2.30	1.14	13
Raisel Iglesias	28	76	92	2.49	1.11	13

What is the significance of showing you the top 11? Well, from $12 earnings on down, you could have owned a middle reliever who would have helped you in more categories, and cost you much less back in March.

The quest for saves is expensive.

The list at the left represents the remaining relievers who recorded at least 20 saves in 2017. That is what you ended up with for all the effort you put into chasing saves. To the right is the same number of non-closing relievers. All are ranked by roto earnings.

Closers	Sv	IP	K	ERA	15$	OTHERS	IP	K	ERA	15$
Holland	41	57	70	3.61	12	C.Green	69	103	1.83	12
E.Diaz	34	66	89	3.27	12	Petit	91	101	2.76	11
Allen	30	67	92	2.94	11	Devenski	81	100	2.68	11
Rodney	39	55	65	4.23	10	A.Miller	63	95	1.44	11
Doolittle	24	51	62	2.81	10	Parker	68	86	2.54	10
Kintzler	29	71	39	3.03	9	Albers	61	63	1.62	10
Neris	26	75	86	3.01	9	Minor	78	88	2.55	9
Chapman	22	50	69	3.22	7	Swarzak	77	91	2.33	9
Ramos	27	59	72	3.99	3	Madson	59	67	1.83	9
Herrera	26	59	56	4.25	3	Neshek	62	69	1.59	9
J.Johnson	22	57	61	5.56	-1	Givens	79	88	2.75	8
Oh	20	59	54	4.10	-1	A.Bradley	73	79	1.73	7
Maurer	22	59	59	6.52	-6	Nicasio	72	72	2.61	6
MEAN		61	67	3.89	6	**MEAN**	72	85	2.17	9
10-19 svs		58	60	3.68	1	Next 16	62	68	2.57	4

(16 pitchers)

As noted, the disparity grows if we include pitchers with at least 10 saves. Their 15$ values ranged from Addison Reed (9) to Sam Dyson (-10).

Looking at just the sampling of those above, you can see the benefit in innings, strikeouts and ERA (WHIP too, though not shown). The cost is in saves. A case could be made that you might have been able to assemble a much more profitable pitching staff by foregoing saves completely. That's crazy, right?

However, of the 32 pitchers drafted back in March for the expectation of saves, only 20 returned positive earnings. By comparison, there were just a handful of non-closing relievers who were drafted last March, yet *40 of them earned positive value.*

One more thing… That group of middle relievers holds even more potential value when you compare their earnings to starting pitchers.

Pop Quiz: How many 150+ inning starters earned less than Juan Nicasio, the $6 arm pulling up the rear of that group of 13 middle relievers above?

Answer: 36.

Yes, 36 starters with at least 150 IP earned less than $6. In fact, 22 of those pitchers were swimming in red.

Given that starting pitchers averaged only 5.5 innings per outing in 2017 (an all-time low) we need to refocus some attention—again—on undervalued middle relievers. They are not only contributing tons of good stats but also gobbling up many of those lost Wins.

These starting pitchers would have been drafted in a 15-team mixed league:

	W	IP	K	ERA	WHIP	15$	'17 ADP
Jon Lester	13	180.7	180	4.33	1.32	$5	34
Julio Teheran	11	188.3	151	4.49	1.37	$0	105
Rick Porcello	11	203.3	181	4.65	1.40	-$1	112
Tanner Roark	13	181.3	166	4.67	1.33	$2	138
Kevin Gausman	11	186.7	179	4.68	1.49	-$4	141
John Lackey	12	170.7	149	4.59	1.28	$3	161
Sean Manaea	12	158.7	140	4.37	1.40	$1	166
Matt Moore	6	174.3	148	5.52	1.53	-$13	171
Marco Estrada	10	186	176	4.98	1.38	-$3	228
Ian Kennedy	5	154	131	5.38	1.32	-$7	236
Ivan Nova	11	187	131	4.14	1.28	$4	253
Mike Foltynewicz	10	154	143	4.79	1.48	-$5	299
Michael Wacha	12	165.7	158	4.13	1.36	$4	301
Jeremy Hellickson	8	164	96	5.43	1.26	-$6	316
Jason Hammel	8	180.3	145	5.29	1.43	-$8	324
Dan Straily	10	181.7	170	4.26	1.30	$4	333
Jordan Zimmermann	8	160	103	6.08	1.55	-$17	337
MEAN	**10**	**175**	**150**	**4.81**	**1.38**	**-$2**	**215**

These middle relievers would *not* have been drafted in a 15-team mixed league:

	W/Sv	IP	K	ERA	WHIP	15$	'17 ADP
Chris Devenski	8/4	80.7	100	2.68	0.94	11	389
Archie Bradley	3/1	73	79	1.73	1.04	7	435
Carl Edwards	5/0	66.3	94	2.98	1.01	5	459
Chad Green	5/0	69	103	1.83	0.74	12	497
Juan Nicasio	5/6	72.3	72	2.61	1.08	6	565
Mychal Givens	8/0	78.7	88	2.75	1.04	8	572
Adam Warren	3/1	57.3	54	2.35	0.87	4	728
Shane Greene	4/9	67.7	73	2.66	1.24	4	825
Brandon Morrow	6/2	43.7	50	2.06	0.92	4	828
Mike Minor	6/6	77.7	88	2.55	1.02	9	988
Pat Neshek	5/1	62.3	69	1.59	0.87	9	995
Yusmeiro Petit	5/4	91.3	101	2.76	0.95	11	997
Blake Parker	3/8	67.3	86	2.54	0.83	10	*
Matt Albers	7/2	61	63	1.62	0.85	10	*
Anthony Swarzak	6/2	77.3	91	2.33	1.03	9	*
Chris Rusin	5/2	85	71	2.65	1.11	6	*
Dominic Leone	3/1	70.3	81	2.56	1.05	5	*
Ryan Tepera	7/2	77.7	81	3.59	1.13	4	*
Joshua Fields	5/2	57	60	2.84	0.96	4	*
MEAN	**5/3**	**70**	**79**	**2.46**	**0.98**	**$7**	**841**

= Not in the Top 1000

Those ratio categories are incredibly alluring, but the trade-off in giving up wins and strikeouts seems too extreme, right? Maybe not. If you wonder at what point the trade-off makes sense, the answer lies in all those positive roto dollars. As you scan the player boxes in this book, it won't take long for you to start craving any pitcher with an ERA under 4.00. There is a very fertile pool of *sub-3.00 ERAs* if you're willing to dip your toes in.

Twenty years ago, the LIMA plan revealed the hidden value of middle relievers. At the time, these inexpensive, under-appreciated arms were intended to fill out the final spots on a 4x4 staff in lieu of poorer-skilled starters. It was the *Moneyball* approach four years before that book came out.

Over time, middle reliever prices began to catch up with their true value. However, the 5x5 game combined with the pitching domination of the past decade shifted the focus to only rostering pitchers who would contribute to the counting categories. Skill was plentiful; ERA and WHIP would take care of themselves.

That effectively pushed those middle relievers off our radar. In 2018, that needs to change.

The Deal

How should fantasy leaguers deal with this new, volatile, higher-risk environment? You have to be willing to make changes. Why?

- Because the 10-day DL is not going anywhere and is a scourge on the fantasy game.
- Because the ripple effects of the burgeoning DL list impact our stat categories and roster construction.
- Because home runs and strikeouts are not likely going away and stolen bases may become more and more irrelevant.
- Because starting pitchers are throwing fewer innings and there is a ton of profit hidden in previously ignored arms.
- Because the environment our game lives in is not likely going to change in the short term, so we need to change to keep up.

If there was any time when it makes sense to reassess everything that you do in advance of draft day, this is the year. (Actually last year might have been better.) The world is changing. Hop on.

Limit DL spots? At First Pitch Arizona in November of 2017, I polled the attendees and was astounded by how many leagues still limit the number of players you can put on the DL. If your league still does this, *just stop it!*

What's the point? Teams are already hurt by losing a player and presumably replacing him with a lesser commodity; why force a choice when the number of shelved players is naturally rising? For those who cite the scarcity of the free agent pool—yes, it's true—however, re-populating it with hurt players does not make it any more fruitful in the short term. In the long-term, it only serves to create artificial FAAB feeding frenzies; do you really want a DL activation to shift the balance of power in a league? And the optimal DL limit is completely arbitrary—three players? Five? Seven?

In 2017, the average team saw more than half its roster turn over during the course of the season. Those particularly snake-bit could have seen 5-7 players on the DL in a typical week. With MLB teams now shuttling players on and off the list willy-nilly, any DL limitations are going to hurt unfortunate owners even more. Just stop it.

Remove the phrase, "but he has no path to playing time" from your vocabulary. I've talked about this already. With more than 50% odds of your player hitting the DL, there is almost always a path to playing time. There are huge potential profits waiting for those who speculate intelligently.

Avoid injuries. Ha! Okay, let's give this a shot. Start by separating all players into two classes.

- **High Risk:** Any player who spent more than 20 days on the disabled list last season or was hurt on Draft Day. (The Injury Log on page 203 is very helpful for this exercise.)
- **Low Risk:** Everyone else.

Had you classified all the players in the pre-season Top 300 last March, you would have ended up with these results:

	No.	DLed	Pct.
Low Risk	171	78	46%
High Risk	129	86	67%
OVERALL	300	164	55%

Avoiding the high risk players back in March 2017 would have given you about a 20% advantage in rostering a healthy human. Still, this would not have helped with many of last year's critical injury losses. Madison Bumgarner, Noah Syndergaard and Freddie Freeman were players in the first two rounds who were not tagged with any elevated risk coming into the season. Similarly, closers Zach Britton and Mark Melancon were also among those low risk players whose DL stints thinned out the talent at an already scarce position.

It's tough to project injuries. However, there are research results in the Encyclopedia showing that the more time a player has spent time on the DL in the past, the more time he is likely to revisit the DL in the future. In the end, the advantage provided by this simple distinction is not huge, but any edge is worthwhile in this volatile environment. If you focus on players in this book with an "A" Health grade, that's a good start. The lists on page 258 can help.

Restructure your pitching staff. Middle relievers have become hidden saviors. We need to start planning this class of pitcher directly into our draft strategy. There are at least three ways.

The first is to start conditioning yourself to think in terms of three types of pitchers—starters, middle relievers and closers. Your pitching staff might be planned to look something like this:

3-5	Starters
2-4	Middle Relievers
2	Closers

Your starters could include one 200-inning stud and 2-4 second tier arms, or you could lean more towards LIMA-esque construction with all mid-level guys. Your 2-4 middle relievers should all be high-skilled pitchers. Closers are closers, but opt for skill over role. Not rocket surgery here, but there needs to be deliberate accommodation for the middle guys.

Another approach is to use middle relievers as your go-to injury replacements when a starter goes down. That has been counterintuitive in the past, but given how valuable they have become, and how damaging a replacement level (*cough* Porcello *cough*) starter can be, this is more logical than it appears.

The final approach might be to finally relent and give middle relievers their own direct value.

Saves are an artificial category. Holds are an artificial category. But together, they represent a reasonable proxy for valuing all bullpen arms. This is not a new argument—heck, it's a standard section in the Encyclopedia—but I think it's time for this to be more than just talk and give serious consideration to officially expanding the category to "Saves plus Holds."

Of the 40 pitchers who had at least 10 saves last year, 31 finished the season with roto earnings in the black. If we expanded to Saves plus Holds, then 73 pitchers would have earned positive value.

Here are the relievers who would have earned double-digit value in 2017 had we used the category of Saves + Holds:

	Sv	Hld	15$
Craig Kimbrel	35	1	26
Kenley Jansen	41	1	25
Felipe Rivero	21	14	19
Corey Knebel	39	11	18
David Robertson	14	8	17
Brad Hand	21	16	17
Chris Devenski	4	24	16
Andrew Miller	2	27	16
Chad Green	0	9	13
Anthony Swarzak	2	27	13
Ryan Madson	2	25	13
Yusmeiro Petit	4	14	12
Pat Neshek	4	23	12
Roberto Osuna	39	0	11
Matt Albers	2	14	11
Archie Bradley	1	25	11
Blake Parker	8	15	10
Mike Minor	6	17	10
Mychal Givens	0	21	10

And remember that increasing the usefulness of middle relievers also helps capture some of the wins that starters are losing, thereby helping to maintain the value of that category.

Change your league parameters to accommodate the game's elevated risk. This idea is only for those ready to take a bold step. Volatile player movement is a problem only because we are limited by our 23-man rosters. If we had more moving pieces to manage, we'd be able to weather the DL storm much easier.

Bold, but simple… Our leagues need to have fewer teams and deeper reserve lists.

Fewer teams means

- It's easier to get a private league together.
- You get to roster at least a few more good players that you like.
- You will likely have tighter standings races (or at least the perception of it).

Deeper reserve lists means

- You'll have more flexibility to keep the best players active.
- There will be less scrounging for injury replacements.
- You'll have more players with which to construct equitable trades.
- There will be more potential to grab game-changing outliers in your draft before they are left over in the free agent pool.

By carefully constructing your new league, you can even maintain the player penetration depth, and draft challenge, of your existing league set-up. Some examples:

AL/NL-only leagues

Current
12 teams x 27 players = 324 (4 reserves)
Population = 375 (15 MLB teams x 25 players)
Penetration = 86%

Possibilities
10 teams x 32 players = 320 (9 reserves)
8 teams x 40 players = 320 (17 reserves)
Both are 85% penetration

12-team mixed leagues

Current

12 teams x 29 players = 348 (6 reserves)
Population = 750 (30 x 25)
Penetration = 46%

Possibilities

10 teams x 35 players = 350 (12 reserves)
8 teams x 44 players = 352 (19 reserves)
Both are 47% penetration

15-team mixed leagues

Current

15 teams x 29 players = 435 (6 reserves)
Penetration = 58%

Possibilities

12 teams x 36 players = 432 (13 reserves)
10 teams x 44 players = 440 (19 reserves)
Both are about 58% penetration

In some of the shallower formats, I might suggest an increase in player penetration, regardless of whether or not you contract teams. A 12-team mixed league that has always drafted to 46%

may resist going deeper, but getting to 55%, 60% or even 70% will take less time and energy than having to comb through the voluminous free agent pool, week after week, for injury replacements.

Granted, these are radical ideas in an industry where mainstream leagues are loath to tinker too much. But the changing environment is causing some fallout.

This past summer, I heard from a handful of readers ready to toss in the towel on playing fantasy baseball. This was not about being lured away by DFS. Their frustration with managing around the interminable roster churn in their full-season leagues had reached a breaking point.

This is a game; it's supposed to be fun. If an existing rules set is causing undue hardship, it's senseless to hold rigid just for the sake of… I don't know—Tradition? Continuity? Fond memories?

Twelve teams in a league is not sacrosanct. Holds are not heresy. Deep reserve lists don't open the gates to hell.

League constitutions should be living documents. Change is not only good; in 2018 it could be necessary.

Welcome to the 32nd Edition

If you are new to the *Baseball Forecaster*, the sheer volume of information in this book may seem a bit daunting. We don't recommend you assessing its contents over a single commute to work, particularly if you drive. But do set aside some time this winter—instead of staring out the window, waiting for baseball to begin again, try immersing yourself in all the wisdom contained in this tome. There's a ton of it, and the payoff—Yoo-Hoo or otherwise—is worth it.

But where to begin?

The best place to start is with the Encyclopedia of Fanalytics, which provides the foundation concepts for everything else that appears in these pages. It's our research archive and collective memory, just as valuable for veterans as it is for rookies. Take a cursory read-through, lingering at any section that looks interesting. You'll keep coming back here frequently.

Then just jump in. Close your eyes, flip to a random page, and put your finger down anywhere. Oh, look—Ian Kinsler, whose 50-point BA dive in 2017 looks like a fluke. With his best plate skills in years, a near-elite HctX and a stable BPX, there's more oomph left in this 36-year-old's bat that what you might think. See, you've learned something already!

What's New in 2018?

Shohei Ohtani: Veteran readers have long known about Ohtani—he first appeared in our International Prospects section in 2013, when he was *still in high school* and we wrote he was "the longest of long shots." Well, every indication is that he'll be suited up for an MLB team come Opening Day. But the questions abound. Could this Japanese import live up to the hype? Will he get his wish and be a two-way player? If so, what does that mean for fantasy roster contruction? Scoring? Commissioner services? We take a crack at all of this by dedicating a page to the Japanese superstar in our Prospects section.

Positive Relative Outcomes (PRO): Converting stats and metrics to figures based entirely on batters faced or plate apperances opens up a whole new way of comparing players. The Research section delves into the specifics, new PRO Scores in the Charts section lays out the results.

Answers to questions, such as: When is a home run truly "deserved"? What goes into the making of a new Starting Pitcher Matchups tool? Does age affect DL stays? Is there a way to predict surprisingly productive years? And much more.

Updates

The Baseball Forecaster page at BaseballHQ.com is at www.baseballhq.com/bf2018. This is your headquarters for all information and updates regarding this book. Here you will find links to the following:

Content Updates: In a project of this magnitude, there are occasionally items that need clarification or correction. You can find them here.

Free Projections Update: As a buyer of this book, you get one free 2018 projections update. This is a set of Excel spreadsheet files that will be posted on or about March 1, 2018. Remember to keep the book handy when you visit as the access codes are hidden within these pages.

Electronic book: The complete PDF version of the *Forecaster*—plus Excel versions of most key charts—is available free to those who bought the book directly through the BaseballHQ.com website. These files will be available in January 2018 for most of you; those who have an annual standing order should have received the PDF just before Thanksgiving. Contact us if you do not receive information via e-mail about access. Information about the e-book version can be found at the above website.

If you purchased the book through an online vendor or book-store, or would like these files earlier, you can purchase them from us for $9.95. Contact us at support@baseballhq.com for more information.

Beyond the Forecaster

The *Baseball Forecaster* is just the beginning. The following companion products and services are described in more detail in the back of the book.

BaseballHQ.com is our home website. It provides regular updates to everything in this book, including daily updated statistics and projections. A subscription to BHQ gets you more than 1,000 articles over the course of a year updated daily from spring training through the end of the regular season, custom-ized tools, access to data going back over a decade, plus much more. Sign up for our free BaseballHQFriday newsletter at www.baseballhq.com/friday.

First Pitch Forums are a series of conferences we run where you can meet top industry analysts and network with fellow fantasy leaguers in your area. We'll be in several cities in February and March. Our big annual symposium at the Arizona Fall League is the first weekend in November.

The 13th edition of the *Minor League Baseball Analyst*, by Rob Gordon and Jeremy Deloney, is the minor league companion to this book, with stat boxes for 1,000-plus prospects, essays on prospects, lists upon lists, and more. It is available in January.

RotoLab is the best draft software on the market and comes pre-loaded with our projections. Learn more at www.rotolab.com.

Even further beyond the Forecaster

Visit us on *Facebook* at www.facebook.com/baseballhq. "Like" the BaseballHQ page for updates, photos from events and links to other important stuff.

Follow us on *Twitter*. Site updates are tweeted from @BaseballHQ and many of our writers share their insights from their own personal accounts. We even have a list to follow: www.twitter.com/BaseballHQ/lists/hq-staff.

But back to baseball. Your winter comfort awaits.

—*Brent Hershey and Ray Murphy*

CONSUMER ADVISORY

AN IMPORTANT MESSAGE FOR FANTASY LEAGUERS
REGARDING PROPER USAGE OF THE *BASEBALL FORECASTER*

This document is provided in compliance with authorities to outline the prospective risks and hazards possible in the event that the Baseball Forecaster is used incorrectly. Please be aware of these potentially dangerous situations and avoid them. The publisher assumes no risk related to any financial loss or stress-induced illnesses caused by ignoring the items as described below.

1. The statistical projections in this book are intended as general guidelines, not as gospel. It is highly dangerous to use the projected statistics alone, and then live and die by them. That's like going to a ballgame, being given a choice of any seat in the park, and deliberately choosing the last row in the right field corner with an obstructed view. The projections are there, you can look at them, but there are so many better places to sit.

We have to publish those numbers, but they are stagnant, inert pieces of data. This book focuses on a live forecasting process that provides the tools so that you can understand the leading indicators and draw your own conclusions. If you at least attempt your own analyses of the data, and enhance them with the player commentaries, you can paint more robust, colorful pictures of the future.

In other words...

If you bought this book purely for the projected statistics and do not intend to spend at least some time learning about the process, then you might as well just buy an $8 magazine.

2. The player commentaries in this book are written by humans, just like you. These commentaries provide an overall evaluation of performance and likely future direction, but 60-word capsules cannot capture everything. Your greatest value will be to use these as a springboard to your own analysis of the data. Odds are, if you take the time, you'll find hidden indicators that we might have missed. Forecaster veterans say that this self-guided excursion is the best part of owning the book.

3. This book does not attempt to tackle playing time. Rather than making arbitrary decisions about how roles will shake out, the focus is on performance. The playing time projections presented here are merely to help you better evaluate each player's talent. Our online preseason projections update provides more current AB and IP expectations based on how roles are being assigned.

4. The dollar values in this book are intended solely for player-to-player comparisons. They are not driven by a finite pool of playing time—which is required for valuation systems to work properly—so they cannot be used for bid values to be used in your own draft.

There are two reasons for this:

a. The finite pool of players that will generate the finite pool of playing time will not be determined until much closer to Opening Day. And, if we are to be brutally honest, there is really no such thing as a finite pool of players.

b. Your particular league's construction will drive the values; a $10 player in a 10-team mixed league will not be the same as a $10 player in a 12-team NL-only league.

Note that book dollar values also cannot be compared to those published at BaseballHQ.com as the online values are generated by a more finite player pool.

5. Do not pass judgment on the effectiveness of this book based on the performance of a few individual players. The test, rather, is on the collective predictive value of the book's methods. Are players with better base skills more likely to produce good results than bad ones? Years of research suggest that the answer is "yes." Does that mean that every high skilled player will do well? No. But many more of them will perform well than will the average low-skilled player. You should always side with the better percentage plays, but recognize that there are factors we cannot predict. Good decisions that beget bad outcomes do not invalidate the methods.

6. If your copy of this book is not marked up and dog-eared by Draft Day, you probably did not get as much value out of it as you might have.

7. This edition of the Forecaster is not intended to provide absorbency for spills of more than 7.5 ounces.

8. This edition is not intended to provide stabilizing weight for more than 18 sheets of 20 lb. paper in winds of more than 45 mph.

9. The pages of this book are not recommended for avian waste collection. In independent laboratory studies, 87% of migratory water fowl refused to excrete on interior pages, even when coaxed.

10. This book, when rolled into a cylindrical shape, is not intended to be used as a weapon for any purpose, including but not limited to insect extermination, canine training or to influence bidding behavior at a fantasy draft.

For new readers...

Everything begins here. The information in the following pages represents the foundation that powers everything we do.

You'll learn about the underlying concepts for our unique mode of analysis. You'll find answers to long-asked questions, interesting insights into what makes players tick, and innovative applications for all this newfound knowledge.

This Encyclopedia is organized into several logical sections:

1. Fundamentals
2. Batters
3. Pitchers
4. Prospects
5. Gaming

Enough talking. Jump in.
Remember to breathe.

For veteran readers...

As we do in each edition, this year's ever-expanding Encyclopedia includes relevant research results we've published over the past year. We've added some of the essays from the Research Abstracts and Gaming Abstracts sections in the 2017 *Forecaster* as well as some other essays from BaseballHQ.com.

And we continue to mold the content to best fit how fantasy leaguers use their information. Many readers consider this their fantasy information bible.

Okay, time to jump-start the analytical process for 2018. Remember to breathe— it's always good advice.

Abbreviations

Fundamentals

What is Fanalytics?

Fanalytics is the scientific approach to fantasy baseball analysis. A contraction of "fantasy" and "analytics," fanalytic gaming might be considered a mode of play that requires a more strategic and quantitative approach to player analysis and game decisions.

The three key elements of fanalytics are:

1. Performance analysis
2. Performance forecasting
3. Gaming analysis

For performance analysis, we tap into the vast knowledge of the sabermetric community. Founded by Bill James, this area of study provides objective and progressive new ways to assess skill. What we do in this book is called "component skills analysis." We break down performance into its component parts, then reverse-engineer it back into the traditional measures with which we are more familiar.

Our forecasting methodology is one part science and one part art. We start with a computer-generated baseline for each player. We then make subjective adjustments based on a variety of factors, such as discrepancies in skills indicators and historical guidelines gleaned from more than 25 years of research. We don't rely on a rigid model; our method forces us to get our hands dirty.

You might say that our brand of forecasting is more about finding logical journeys than blind destinations.

Gaming analysis is an integrated approach designed to help us win our fantasy leagues. It takes the knowledge gleaned from the first two elements and adds the strategic and tactical aspect of each specific fantasy game format.

Component Skills Analysis

Familiar gauges like HR and ERA have long been used to measure skill. In fact, these gauges only measure the outcome of an individual event, or series of events. They represent statistical output. They are "surface stats."

Raw skill is the talent beneath the stats. Players use these skills to create the individual events, or components, that are the building blocks of measures like HR and ERA. Our approach:

1. It's not about batting average; it's about seeing the ball and making contact. We target hitters based on elements such as their batting eye (walks to strikeouts ratio), how often they make contact and the type of contact they make. We then combine these components into an "expected batting average." By comparing each hitter's actual BA to how he should be performing, we can draw conclusions about the future.

2. It's not about home runs; it's about power. From the perspective of a round bat meeting a round ball, it may be only a fraction of an inch at the point of contact that makes the difference between a HR and a long foul ball. When a ball is hit safely, often it is only a few inches that separate a HR from a double. We tend to neglect these facts in our analyses, although the outcomes—the doubles, triples, long fly balls—may be no less a measure of that batter's raw power skill. We must incorporate all these components to paint a complete picture.

3. It's not about ERA; it's about getting the ball over the plate and keeping it in the park. Forget ERA. You want to draft pitchers who walk few batters (Control), strike out many (Dominance) and succeed at both in tandem (Command). You generally want pitchers who keep the ball on the ground (because home runs are bad), though some fly ball pitchers can succeed under the right conditions. All of this translates into an "expected ERA" that you can use to validate a pitcher's actual performance.

4. It's never about wins. For pitchers, winning ballgames is less about skill than it is about offensive support. As such, projecting wins is a very high-risk exercise and valuing hurlers based on their win history is dangerous. Target skill; wins will come.

5. It's not about saves; it's about opportunity first and skills second. While the highest-skilled pitchers have the best potential to succeed as closers, they still have to be given the ball with the game on the line in the 9th inning, and that is a decision left to others. Over the past 15 years, about 40% of relievers drafted for saves failed to hold the role for the entire season. The lesson: Don't take chances on draft day. There will always be saves in the free agent pool.

Accounting for "luck"

Luck has been used as a catch-all term to describe random chance. When we use the term here, we're talking about unexplained variances that shape the statistics. While these variances may be random, they are also often measurable and projectable. To get a better read on "luck," we use formulas that capture the external variability of the data.

Through our research and the work of others, we have learned that when raw skill is separated from statistical output, what's remaining is often unexplained variance. The aggregate totals of many of these variances, for all players, is often a constant. For instance, while a pitcher's ERA might fluctuate, the rate at which his opposition's batted balls fall for hits will tend towards 30%. Large variances can be expected to regress towards 30%.

Why is all this important? Analysts complain about the lack of predictability of many traditional statistical metrics. The reason they find it difficult is that they are trying to project performance using metrics that are loaded with external noise. Raw skills metrics follow better defined trends during a player's career. Then, as we get a better handle on the variances—explained and unexplained—we can construct a complete picture of what a player's statistics really mean.

Baseball Forecasting

Forecasting in perspective

The crystal ball aura of "predicting the future" conceals the fact it is a process. We might define it as "the systematic process of determining likely end results." At its core, it's scientific.

However, the *outcomes* of forecasted events are what is most closely scrutinized, and are used to judge the success or failure of the forecast. That said, as long as the process is sound, the forecast has done the best job it can do. *In the end, forecasting is about analysis, not prophecy.*

Baseball performance forecasting is inherently a high-risk exercise with a very modest accuracy rate. This is because the process involves not only statistics, but also unscientific elements, from random chance to human volatility. And even from within the statistical aspect there are multiple elements that need to be evaluated, from skill to playing time to a host of external variables.

Every system is comprised of the same core elements:

- Players will tend to perform within the framework of past history and/or trends.
- Skills will develop and decline according to age.
- Statistics will be shaped by a player's health, expected role and venue.

While all systems are built from these same elements, they also are constrained by the same limitations. We are all still trying to project a bunch of human beings, each one...

- with his own individual skill set
- with his own rate of growth and decline
- with his own ability to resist and recover from injury
- limited to opportunities determined by other people
- generating a group of statistics largely affected by external noise.

Research has shown that the best accuracy rate that can be attained by any system is about 70%. In fact, a simple system that uses three-year averages adjusted for age ("Marcel") can attain a success rate of 65%. This means all the advanced systems are fighting for occupation of the remaining 5%.

But there is a bigger question... *what exactly are we measuring?* When we search for accuracy, what does that mean? In fact, any quest for accuracy is going to run into a brick wall of paradoxes:

- If a slugging average projection is dead on, but the player hits 10 fewer HRs than expected (and likely, 20 more doubles), is that a success or a failure?
- If a projection of hits and walks allowed by a pitcher is on the mark, but the bullpen and defense implodes, and inflates his ERA by a run, is that a success or a failure?
- If the projection of a speedster's rate of stolen base success is perfect, but his team replaces the manager with one that doesn't run, and the player ends up with half as many SBs as expected, is that a success or a failure?
- If a batter is traded to a hitters' ballpark and all the touts project an increase in production, but he posts a statistical line exactly what would have been projected had he not been traded to that park, is that a success or a failure?
- If the projection for a bullpen closer's ERA, WHIP and peripheral numbers is perfect, but he saves 20 games instead of 40 because the GM decided to bring in a high-priced free agent at the trading deadline, is that a success or a failure?
- If a player is projected to hit .272 in 550 AB and only hits .249, is that a success or failure? Most will say "failure." But wait a minute! The real difference is only two hits per month. That shortfall of 23 points in batting average is because a fielder might have made a spectacular play, or a screaming liner might have been hit right at someone, or a long shot to the outfield might have been held up by the wind... once every 14 games. Does that constitute "failure"?

Even if we were to isolate a single statistic that measures "overall performance" and run our accuracy tests on it, the results will still be inconclusive.

According to OPS, these players are virtually identical:

BATTER	HR	RBI	SB	BA	OBA	SLG	OPS
Mauer,J	7	71	2	.305	.384	.417	.801
Nunez,E	12	58	24	.313	.341	.460	.801
Bell,J	26	90	2	.255	.334	.466	.800

If I projected Bell-caliber stats and ended up with Joe Mauer's numbers, I'd hardly call that an accurate projection, especially if my fantasy team was in dire need of home runs.

According to Roto dollars, these players are also dead-on:

BATTER	HR	RBI	Runs	SB	BA	R$
Turner,T	11	47	75	46	.284	$22
Bellinger,C	39	97	87	10	.267	$22
Rendon,A	25	100	81	7	.301	$22

It's not so simple for someone to claim they have accurate projections. And so, it is best to focus on the bigger picture, especially when it comes to winning at fantasy baseball.

More on this: "The Great Myths of Projective Accuracy"

http://www.baseballhq.com/great-myths-projective-accuracy

Baseball Forecaster's forecasting process

Our approach is to assemble component skills in such a way that they can be used to validate our observations, analyze their relevance and project a likely future direction.

In a perfect world, if a player's raw skills improve, then so should his surface stats. If his skills decline, then his stats should follow as well. But, sometimes a player's skill indicators increase while his surface stats decline. These variances may be due to a variety of factors.

Our forecasting process is based on the expectation that events tend to move towards universal order. Surface stats will eventually approach their skill levels. Unexplained variances will regress to a mean. And from this, we can identify players whose performance may potentially change.

For most of us, this process begins with the previous year's numbers. Last season provides us with a point of reference, so it's a natural way to begin the process of looking at the future. Component skills analysis allows us to validate those numbers. A batter with few HRs but a high linear weighted power level has a good probability of improving his future HR output. A pitcher whose ERA was poor while his command ratio was solid might be a good bet for ERA improvement.

Of course, these leading indicators do not always follow the rules. There are more shades of grey than blacks and whites. When indicators are in conflict—for instance, a pitcher who is displaying both a rising strikeout rate and a rising walk rate—then we have to find ways to sort out what these indicators might be saying.

It is often helpful to look at leading indicators in a hierarchy. A rank of the most important pitching indicators might be: Command (k/bb), Dominance (k/9), Control (bb/9) and GB/FB rate. For batters, contact rate tops the list, followed by power, walk rate and speed.

Assimilating additional research

Once we've painted the statistical picture of a player's potential, we then use additional criteria and research results to help us add some color to the analysis. These other criteria include the player's health, age, changes in role, ballpark and a variety of other factors. We also use the research results described in the following pages. This research looks at things like traditional periods of peak performance and breakout profiles.

The final element of the process is assimilating the news into the forecast. This is the element that many fantasy leaguers tend to rely on most since it is the most accessible. However, it is also the element that provides the most noise. Players, management and the media have absolute control over what we are allowed to know. Factors such as hidden injuries, messy divorces and clubhouse unrest are routinely kept from us, while we are fed red herrings and media spam. *We will never know the entire truth.*

Quite often, all you are reading is just other people's opinions... a manager who believes that a player has what it takes to be a regular or a team physician whose diagnosis is that a player is healthy enough to play. These words from experts have some element of truth, but cannot be wholly relied upon to provide an accurate expectation of future events. As such, it is often helpful to develop an appropriate cynicism for what you read.

For instance, if a player is struggling for no apparent reason and there are denials about health issues, don't dismiss the possibility that an injury does exist. There are often motives for such news to be withheld from the public.

And so, as long as we do not know all the facts, we cannot dismiss the possibility that any one fact is true, no matter how often the media assures it, deplores it, or ignores it. Don't believe everything you read; use your own judgment. If your observations conflict with what is being reported, that's powerful insight that should not be ignored.

Also remember that nothing lasts forever in major league baseball. *Reality is fluid.* One decision begets a series of events that lead to other decisions. Any reported action can easily be reversed based on subsequent events. My favorite examples are announcements of a team's new bullpen closer. Those are about the shortest realities known to man.

We need the media to provide us with context for our analyses, and the real news they provide is valuable intelligence. But separating the news from the noise is difficult. In most cases, the only thing you can trust is how that player actually performs.

Embracing imprecision

Precision in baseball prognosticating is a fool's quest. There are far too many unexpected variables and noise that can render our projections useless. The truth is, the best we can ever hope for is to accurately forecast general tendencies and percentage plays.

However, even when you follow an 80% percentage play, for instance, you will still lose 20% of the time. That 20% is what skeptics use as justification to dismiss prognosticators; they conveniently ignore the more prevalent 80%. The paradox, of course, is that fantasy league titles are often won or lost by those exceptions. Still, long-term success dictates that you always chase the 80% and accept the fact that you will be wrong 20% of the time. Or, whatever that percentage play happens to be.

For fantasy purposes, playing the percentages can take on an even less precise spin. The best projections are often the ones that are just far enough away from the field of expectation to alter decision-making. In other words, it doesn't matter if I project Player X to bat .320 and he only bats .295; it matters that I project .320 and everyone else projects .280. Those who follow my less-accurate projection will go the extra dollar to acquire him in their draft.

Or, perhaps we should evaluate the projections based upon their intrinsic value. For instance, coming into 2017, would it have been more important for me to tell you that Anthony Rizzo was going to hit 30 HRs or that Mike Moustakas would hit 25 HRs (when all other touts predicted fewer)? By season's end, the Rizzo projection would have been more accurate, but the Moustakas projection—even though it was off by 13 HRs—would have been far more valuable. The Moustakas projection might have persuaded you to go an extra buck on Draft Day, yielding far more profit.

And that has to be enough. Any tout who projects a player's statistics dead-on will have just been lucky with his dart throws that day.

Perpetuity

Forecasting is not an exercise that produces a single set of numbers. It is dynamic, cyclical and ongoing. Conditions are constantly changing and we must react to those changes by adjusting our expectations. A pre-season projection is just a snapshot in time. Once the first batter steps to the plate on Opening Day, that projection has become obsolete. Its value is merely to provide a starting point, a baseline for what is about to occur.

During the season, if a projection appears to have been invalidated by current performance, the process continues. It is then that we need to ask... What went wrong? What conditions have changed? In fact, has *anything* changed? We need to analyze the situation and revise our expectation, if necessary. This process must be ongoing.

When good projections go bad

All we can control is the process. We simply can't control outcomes. However, one thing we *can* do is analyze the misses to see *why* they occurred. This is always a valuable exercise each year. It puts a proper focus on the variables that were out of our control as well as providing perspective on those players with whom we might have done a better job.

In general, we can organize these forecasting misses into several categories. To demonstrate, here are all the players whose 2017 Rotisserie earnings varied from projections by at least $10.

The performances that exceeded expectation

Development beyond the growth trend: These are young players for whom we knew there was skill. Some of them were prized prospects in the past who have taken their time ascending the growth curve. Others were a surprise only because their performance spike arrived sooner than anyone anticipated... Josh Bell, Joey Gallo, Avisail Garcia, Scooter Gennett, Zachary Godley, Chad Green, Didi Gregorius, Aaron Judge, Jimmy Nelson, Marcell Ozuna, James Paxton, Thomas Pham, Jose Ramirez, Eddie

Rosario, Domingo Santana, Jonathan Schoop, Luis Severino, Travis Shaw, Justin Smoak, Steven Souza, Michael Taylor.

Skilled players who just had big years: We knew these guys were good too, or at least had an established skill level. We just didn't anticipate they'd be this good... Charlie Blackmon, Yulieski Gurriel, Eric Hosmer, Craig Kimbrel, Corey Kluber, J.D. Martinez, Chris Sale.

Unexpected health: We knew these players had the goods; we just didn't know whether they'd be healthy or would stay healthy all year... Shin-Soo Choo, Logan Morrison, Giancarlo Stanton, Alex Wood, Ryan Zimmerman.

Unexpected playing time: These players had the skills—and may have even displayed them at some time in the past—but had questionable playing time potential coming into this season. Some benefited from another player's injury, a rookie who didn't pan out or leveraged a short streak into a regular gig... Tim Beckham, Cody Bellinger, Delino DeShields Jr., Trey Mancini, Whit Merrifield, Chris Taylor.

Unexpected return to form: This year, just Dee Gordon. After his suspension-shortened 2016, touts hedged their projections for 2017. He rebounded 100%.

Unexpected role: This category is reserved for players who played their way into, or backed into, a larger role than anticipated. For most, there was already some previously demonstrated skill: Michael Clevinger, Marwin Gonzalez, Brad Hand, Greg Holland, Corey Knebel, Brad Peacock, Felipe Rivero, Fernando Rodney.

Unexpected discovery of the Fountain of Youth: These players should have been done, or nearly done, or at least headed down the far side of the bell curve. That's what the trends were pointing to. The trends were wrong... Zack Cozart, Charlie Morton, Blake Parker.

Surprise, yes, but not as good as it looked: These are players whose numbers were pretty, but unsupported by their skills metrics. Enjoy them now, but be wary of next year... Chase Anderson, Elvis Andrus, Gio Gonzalez, Yusmeiro Petit, Robbie Ray, Josh Reddick, Ervin Santana.

Who the heck knows? Maybe there are reasonable explanations, but this year was so far off the charts for Yonder Alonso. After five years topping out at nine HRs, how does he hit 28? Could an uppercut swing alone – with no increase in hard contact – account for a 14% increase in hr/f rate? Rest assured, Rob Manfred says it's not the balls.

The performances that fell short of expectation

The DL denizens: These are players who got hurt, may not have returned fully healthy, or may have never been fully healthy (whether they'd admit it or not)... Brandon Belt, Adrian Beltre, Ryan Braun, Zach Britton, Madison Bumgarner, Matt Bush, Miguel Cabrera, Yoenis Cespedes, Aroldis Chapman, Chris Davis, Ian Desmond, Josh Donaldson, Danny Duffy, Adam Eaton, Jeurys Familia, Adrian Gonzalez, Carlos Gonzalez, Matt Harvey, Kyle Hendricks, Felix Hernandez, Hisashi Iwakuma, Matt Kemp, Clayton Kershaw, Ian Kinsler, Jason Kipnis, Jon Lester,

Sean Manaea, Victor Martinez, Mark Melancon, Dustin Pedroia, Stephen Piscotty, Gregory Polanco, David Price, Addison Russell, Aaron Sanchez, Noah Syndergaard, Jameson Taillon, Yasmany Tomas, Troy Tulowitzki, Ben Zobrist.

Accelerated skills erosion: These are players who we knew were on the downside of their careers or had soft peripherals but who we did not think would plummet so quickly. In some cases, there were injuries involved, but all in all, 2017 might be the beginning of the end for... John Lackey, Hunter Pence.

Inflated expectations: Here are players who we really should not have expected much more than what they produced. Some had short or spotty track records, others had soft peripherals coming into the season, and still others were inflated by media hype. Yes, for some of these, it was "What the heck were we thinking?" For others, we've almost come to expect players to ascend the growth curve faster these days. (You're 23 and you haven't broken out yet? What's the problem??) The bottom line is that player performance trends simply don't progress or regress in a straight line; still, the trends were intriguing enough to take a leap of faith. We were wrong... Chris Archer, Mookie Betts, Robinson Cano, Aledmys Diaz, Todd Frazier, Rougned Odor, Seung-Hwan Oh, Jose Peraza, Rick Porcello, Hanley Ramirez, Trevor Story, Dansby Swanson, Jonathan Villar.

Unexpected loss of role: This category is reserved for players who ended up with a smaller role than expected, perhaps through a bad start, bad luck or bad timing... C.J. Cron, Mallex Smith.

Surprise, yes, but not as bad as it looked: These are players whose numbers were ugly, but supported by better skills metrics. Diss them now, but keep an open mind for next year... Manny Machado, Starling Marte, Masahiro Tanaka.

Who the heck knows? Maybe any one of these players could have been slotted into another category, but they still remain head-scratchers... Johnny Cueto, Kelvin Herrera, Jonathan Lucroy.

About fantasy baseball touts

As a group, there is a strong tendency for all pundits to provide numbers that are publicly palatable, often at the expense of potential accuracy. That's because committing to either end of the range of expectation poses a high risk. Few touts will put their credibility on the line like that, even though we all know that those outliers are inevitable. Among our projections, you will find no .350 hitters or 70-steal speedsters. *Someone* is going to post a sub-2.50 ERA next year, but damned if any of us will commit to that. So we take an easier road. We'll hedge our numbers or split the difference between two equally possible outcomes.

In the world of prognosticating, this is called the *comfort zone.* This represents the outer tolerances for the public acceptability of a set of numbers. In most circumstances, even if the evidence is outstanding, prognosticators will not stray from within the comfort zone.

As for this book, occasionally we do commit to outlying numbers when we feel the data support it. But on the whole, most of the numbers here can be nearly as cowardly as everyone else's. We get around this by providing "color" to the projections in the capsule commentaries, often listing UPside or DOWNside projections. That is where you will find the players whose projection has the best potential to stray beyond the limits of the comfort zone.

As analyst John Burnson once wrote: "The issue is not the success rate for one player, but the success rate for all players. No system is 100% reliable, and in trying to capture the outliers, you weaken the middle and thereby lose more predictive pull than you gain. At some level, everyone is an exception!"

Validating Performance

Performance validation criteria

The following is a set of support variables that helps determine whether a player's statistical output is an accurate reflection of his skills. From this we can validate or refute stats that vary from expectation, essentially asking, is this performance "fact or fluke?"

1. Age: Is the player at the stage of development when we might expect a change in performance?

2. Health: Is he coming off an injury, reconditioned and healthy for the first time in years, or a habitual resident of the disabled list?

3. Minor league performance: Has he shown the potential for greater things at some level of the minors? Or does his minor league history show a poor skill set that might indicate a lower ceiling?

4. Historical trends: Have his skill levels over time been on an upswing or downswing?

5. Component skills indicators: Looking beyond batting averages and ERAs, what do his support ratios look like?

6. Ballpark, team, league: Pitchers going to Colorado will see their ERA spike. Pitchers going to Oakland will see their ERA improve.

7. Team performance: Has a player's performance been affected by overall team chemistry or the environment fostered by a winning or losing club?

8. Batting stance, pitching style/mastery: Has a change in performance been due to a mechanical adjustment?

9. Usage pattern, lineup position, role: Has a change in RBI opportunities been a result of moving further up or down in the batting order? Has pitching effectiveness been impacted by moving from the bullpen to the rotation?

10. Coaching effects: Has the coaching staff changed the way a player approaches his conditioning, or how he approaches the game itself?

11. Off-season activity: Has the player spent the winter frequenting workout rooms or banquet tables?

12. Personal factors: Has the player undergone a family crisis? Experienced spiritual rebirth? Given up red meat? Taken up testosterone?

Skills ownership

Once a player displays a skill, he owns it. That display could occur at any time—earlier in his career, back in the minors, or even in winter ball play. And while that skill may lie dormant after its initial display, the potential is always there for him to tap back into that skill at some point, barring injury or age. That dormant skill can reappear at any time given the right set of circumstances.

Caveats:

1. The initial display of skill must have occurred over an extended period of time. An isolated 1-hit shutout in Single-A ball amidst a 5.00 ERA season is not enough. The shorter the display of skill in the past, the more likely it can be attributed to random chance. The longer the display, the more likely that any reemergence is for real.

2. If a player has been suspected of using performance enhancing drugs at any time, all bets are off.

Corollaries:

1. Once a player displays a vulnerability or skills deficiency, he owns that as well. That vulnerability could be an old injury problem, an inability to hit breaking pitches, or just a tendency to go into prolonged slumps.

2. The probability of a player correcting a skills deficiency declines with each year that deficiency exists.

Contract year performance *(Tom Mullooly)*

There is a contention that players step up their game when they are playing for a contract. Research looked at contract year players and their performance during that year as compared to career levels. Of the batters and pitchers studied, 53% of the batters performed as if they were on a salary drive, while only 15% of the pitchers exhibited some level of contract year behavior.

How do players fare *after* signing a large contract (minimum $4M per year)? Research from 2005-2008 revealed that only 30% of pitchers and 22% of hitters exhibited an increase of more than 15% in BPV after signing a large deal either with their new team, or re-signing with the previous team. But nearly half of the pitchers (49%) and nearly half of the hitters (47%) saw a drop in BPV of more than 15% in the year after signing.

Risk Analysis

Risk management and reliability grades

Forecasts are constructed with the best data available, but there are factors that can impact the variability. One way we manage this risk is to assign each player Reliability Grades. The more certainty we see in a data set, the higher the reliability grades assigned to that player. The following variables are evaluated:

Health: Players with a history of staying healthy and off the DL are valuable to own. Unfortunately, while the ability to stay healthy can be considered skill, it is not very projectable. We can track the number of days spent on the disabled list and draw rough conclusions. The grades in the player boxes also include an adjustment for older players, who have a higher likelihood of getting hurt. That is the only forward-looking element of the grade.

"A" level players would have accumulated fewer than 30 days on the major league DL over the past five years. "F" grades go to those who've spent more than 120 days on the DL. Recent DL stays are given a heavier weight in the calculation.

Playing Time and Experience (PT/Exp): The greater the pool of MLB history to draw from, the greater our ability to construct a viable forecast. Length of service—and consistent service—is important. So players who bounce up and down from the majors to the minors are higher risk players. And rookies are all high risk.

For batters, we simply track plate appearances. Major league PAs have greater weight than minor league PAs. "A" level players would have averaged at least 550 major league PAs per year over the past three years. "F" graded players averaged fewer than 250 major league PA per year.

For pitchers, workload can be a double-edged sword. On one hand, small IP samples are deceptive in providing a read on a pitcher's true potential. Even a consistent 65-inning reliever can be considered higher risk since it would take just one bad outing to skew an entire season's work.

On the flipside, high workload levels also need to be monitored, especially in the formative years of a pitcher's career. Exceeding those levels elevates the risk of injury, burnout, or breakdown. So, tracking workload must be done within a range of innings. The grades capture this.

Consistency: Consistent performers are easier to project and garner higher reliability grades. Players that mix mediocrity with occasional flashes of brilliance or badness generate higher risk projections. Even those who exhibit a consistent upward or downward trend cannot be considered truly consistent as we do not know whether those trends will continue. Typically, they don't. *(See below: Using 3-year trends as leading indicators)*

"A" level players are those whose runs created per game level (xERA for pitchers) has fluctuated by less than half a run during each of the past three years. "F" grades go to those whose RC/G or xERA has fluctuated by two runs or more.

Remember that these grades have nothing to do with quality of performance; they strictly refer to confidence in our expectations. So a grade of AAA for Mike Fiers for instance, only means that there is a high probability he will perform as poorly as we've projected.

Using 3-year trends as leading indicators *(Ed DeCaria)*
It is almost irresistibly tempting to look at three numbers moving in one direction and expect that the fourth will continue that progression. However, for both hitters and pitchers riding positive trends over any consecutive three-year period, not only do most players not continue their positive trend into a fourth year, their Year 4 performance usually regresses significantly. This is true for every metric tested (whether related to playing time, batting skills, pitching skills, running skills, luck indicators, or valuation). Negative trends show similar reversals, but tend to be more "sticky," meaning that rebounds are neither as frequent nor as strong as positive trend regressions.

Reliability and age
Peak batting reliability occurs at ages 29 and 30, followed by a minor decline for four years. So, to draft the most reliable batters, and maximize the odds of returning at least par value on your investments, you should target the age range of 28-34.

The most reliable age range for pitchers is 29-34. While we are forever looking for "sleepers" and hot prospects, it is very risky to draft any pitcher under 27 or over 35.

Evaluating Reliability *(Bill Macey)*
When you head into an upcoming auction or draft, consider the following with regard to risk and reliability:

- Reliability grades do help identify more stable investments: players with "B" grades in both Health and PT/Experience are more likely to return a higher percentage of their projected value.

- While top-end starting pitching may be more reliable than ever, the overall pool of pitchers is fraught with uncertainty and they represent a less reliable investment than batters.

- There does not appear to be a significant market premium for reliability, at least according to the criteria measured by BaseballHQ.com.

- There are only two types of players: risky and riskier. So while it may be worth going the extra buck for a more reliable player, be warned that even the most reliable player can falter—don't go overboard bidding up a AAA-rated player simply due to his Reliability grades.

Normal production variance *(Patrick Davitt)*
Even if we have a perfectly accurate understanding of a player's "normal" performance level, his actual performance can and does vary widely over any particular 150-game span—including the 150-game span we call "a season." A .300 career hitter can perform in a range of .250-.350, a 40-HR hitter from 30-50, and a 3.70/1.15 pitcher from 2.60/0.95 to 6.00/1.55. And all of these results must be considered "normal."

Health Analysis

Disabled list statistics

Year	#Players	3yr Avg	DL Days	3yr Avg
2010	393	408	22,911	25,783
2011	422	408	25,610	24,924
2012	409	408	30,408	27,038
2013	442	419	29,551	28,523
2014	422	424	25,839	28,599
2015	454	439	28,982	28,124
2016	478	451	31,329	28,717
2017	533	488	30,913	30408

D.L. days as a leading indicator *(Bill Macey)*
Players who are injured in one year are likely to be injured in a subsequent year:

% DL batters in Year 1 who are also DL in year 2	38%
Under age 30	36%
Age 30 and older	41%
% DL batters in Year 1 and 2 who are also DL in year 3	54%
% DL pitchers in Year 1 who are also DL in year 2	43%
Under age 30	45%
Age 30 and older	41%
% DL pitchers in Yr 1 and 2 who are also DL in year 3	41%

Previously injured players also tend to spend a longer time on the DL. The average number of days on the DL was 51 days for batters and 73 days for pitchers. For the subset of these players who get hurt again the following year, the average number of days on the DL was 58 days for batters and 88 days for pitchers.

Spring training spin *(Dave Adler)*

Spring training sound bites raise expectations among fantasy leaguers, but how much of that "news" is really "noise"? Thanks to a summary listed at RotoAuthority.com, we were able to compile the stats for 2009. Verdict: Noise.

BATTERS	No.	IMPROVED	DECLINED
Weight change	30	33%	30%
Fitness program	3	0%	67%
Eye surgery	6	50%	33%
Plans more SB	6	17%	33%
PITCHERS	**No.**	**IMPROVED**	**DECLINED**
Weight change	18	44%	44%
Fitness program	4	50%	50%
Eye surgery	2	0%	50%
New pitch	5	60%	40%

In-Season Analysis

April performance as a leading indicator

We isolated all players who earned at least $10 more or $10 less than we had projected in March. Then we looked at the April stats of these players to see if we could have picked out the $10 outliers after just one month.

	Identifiable in April
Earned $10+ more than projected	
BATTERS	39%
PITCHERS	44%
Earned -$10 less than projected	
BATTERS	56%
PITCHERS	74%

Nearly three out of every four pitchers who earned at least $10 less than projected also struggled in April. For all the other surprises—batters or pitchers—April was not a strong leading indicator. Another look:

	Pct.
Batters who finished +$25	45%
Pitchers who finished +$20	44%
Batters who finished under $0	60%
Pitchers who finished under -$5	78%

April surgers are less than a 50/50 proposition to maintain that level all season. Those who finished April at the bottom of the roto rankings were more likely to continue struggling, especially pitchers. In fact, of those pitchers who finished April with a value *under -$10*, 91% finished the season in the red. Holes are tough to dig out of.

The weight of early season numbers

Early season strugglers who surge later in the year often get little respect because they have to live with the weight of their early numbers all season long. Conversely, quick starters who fade late get far more accolades than they deserve.

For instance, take Brandon Drury's month-by-month batting average. The perception is that his .267 BA was a solid follow-up to his rookie year. Not quite. His excellent .318 start inflated his batting average most of the year, but from May 1 on, he batted only .256, and only .241 in the second half.

Month	BA	Cum BA
April	.318	.318
May	.273	.295
June	.272	.287
July	.237	.278
August	.230	.270
Sept-Oct	.254	.267

Courtship period

Any time a player is put into a new situation, he enters into a courtship period. This period might occur when a player switches leagues, or switches teams. It could be the first few games when a minor leaguer is called up. It could occur when a reliever moves into the rotation, or when a lead-off hitter is moved to another spot in the lineup. There is a team-wide courtship period when a manager is replaced. Any external situation that could affect a player's performance sets off a new decision point in evaluating that performance.

During this period, it is difficult to get a true read on how a player is going to ultimately perform. He is adjusting to the new situation. Things could be volatile during this time. For instance, a role change that doesn't work could spur other moves. A rookie hurler might buy himself a few extra starts with a solid debut, even if he has questionable skills.

It is best not to make a decision on a player who is going through a courtship period. Wait until his stats stabilize. Don't cut a struggling pitcher in his first few starts after a managerial change. Don't pick up a hitter who smacks a pair of HRs in his first game after having been traded. Unless, of course, talent and track record say otherwise.

Half-season fallacies

A popular exercise at the midpoint of each season is to analyze those players who are consistent first half to second half surgers or faders. There are several fallacies with this analytical approach.

1. Half-season consistency is rare. There are very few players who show consistent changes in performance from one half of the season to the other.

Research results from a three-year study conducted in the late-1990s: The test groups... batters with min. 300 AB full season, 150 AB first half, and pitchers with min. 100 IP full season, 50 IP first half. Of those groups (size noted):

3-year consistency in	BATTERS (98)	PITCHERS (42)
1 stat category	40%	57%
2 stat categories	18%	21%
3 stat categories	3%	5%

When the analysis was stretched to a fourth year, only 1% of all players showed consistency in even one category.

2. Analysts often use false indicators. Situational statistics provide us with tools that can be misused. Several sources offer up 3- and 5-year stats intended to paint a picture of a long-term performance. Some analysts look at a player's half-season swing over that multi-year period and conclude that he is demonstrating consistent performance.

The fallacy is that those multi-year scans may not show any consistency at all. They are not individual season performances but *aggregate* performances. A player whose 5-year batting average shows a 15-point rise in the 2nd half, for instance, may actually have experienced a BA decline in several of those years, a fact that might have been offset by a huge BA rise in one of the years.

3. It's arbitrary. The season's midpoint is an arbitrary delineator of performance swings. Some players are slow starters and might be more appropriately evaluated as pre-May 1 and post-May 1. Others bring their game up a notch with a pennant chase and might see a performance swing with August 15 as the cut-off. Each player has his own individual tendency, if, in fact, one exists at all. There's nothing magical about mid-season as the break point, and certainly not over a multi-year period.

Half-season tendencies

Despite the above, it stands to reason logically that there might be some underlying tendencies on a more global scale, first half to second half. In fact, one would think that the player population as a whole might decline in performance as the season drones on. There are many variables that might contribute to a player wearing down—workload, weather, boredom—and the longer a player is on the field, the higher the likelihood that he is going to get hurt. A recent 5-year study uncovered the following tendencies:

Batting

Overall, batting skills held up pretty well, half to half. There was a 5% erosion of playing time, likely due, in part, to September roster expansion.

Power: First half power studs (20 HRs in 1H) saw a 10% drop-off in the second half. 34% of first half 20+ HR hitters hit 15 or fewer in the second half and only 27% were able to improve on their first half output.

Speed: Second half speed waned as well. About 26% of the 20+ SB speedsters stole *at least 10 fewer bases* in the second half. Only 26% increased their second half SB output at all.

Batting average: 60% of first half .300 hitters failed to hit .300 in the second half. Only 20% showed any second half improvement at all. As for 1H strugglers, managers tended to stick with their full-timers despite poor starts. Nearly one in five of the sub-.250 1H hitters managed to hit *more than* .300 in the second half.

Pitching

Overall, there was some slight erosion in innings and ERA despite marginal improvement in some peripherals.

ERA: For those who pitched at least 100 innings in the first half, ERAs rose an average of 0.40 runs in the 2H. Of those with first half ERAs less than 4.00, only 49% were able to maintain a sub-4.00 ERA in the second half.

Wins: Pitchers who won 18 or more games in a season tended to pitch *more* innings in the 2H and had slightly better peripherals.

Saves: Of those closers who saved 20 or more games in the first half, only 39% were able to post 20 or more saves in the 2H, and 26% posted fewer than 15 saves. Aggregate ERAs of these pitchers rose from 2.45 to 3.17, half to half.

In-season trends in hitting and pitching *(Bob Berger)*

A study of monthly trends in traditional statistical categories found:

- Batting average, HR/game and RBI/game rise from April through August, then fall in September/October.
- Stolen bases decline in July and August before rebounding in September.
- ERA worsens in July/August and improves in September.
- WHIP gets worse in July/August.
- K/9 rate improves all season.

The statement that hitters perform better in warmer weather seems to be true broadly. For additional new research on monthly HR trends, see our Research Abstracts article on page 68.

Teams

Johnson Effect *(Bryan Johnson)*: Teams whose actual won/loss record exceeds or falls short of their statistically projected record in one season will tend to revert to the level of their projection in the following season.

Law of Competitive Balance *(Bill James)*: The level at which a team (or player) will address its problems is inversely related to its current level of success. Low performers will tend to make changes to improve; high performers will not. This law explains the existence of the Plexiglass and Whirlpool Principles.

Plexiglass Principle *(Bill James)*: If a player or team improves markedly in one season, it will likely decline in the next. The opposite is true but not as often (because a poor performer gets fewer opportunities to rebound).

Whirlpool Principle *(Bill James)*: All team and player performances are forcefully drawn to the center. For teams, that center is a .500 record. For players, it represents their career average level of performance.

Other Diamonds

The Fanalytic Fundamentals

1. This is not a game of accuracy or precision. It is a game of human beings and tendencies.
2. This is not a game of projections. It is a game of market value versus real value.
3. Draft skills, not stats. Draft skills, not roles.
4. A player's ability to post acceptable stats despite lousy support metrics will eventually run out.
5. Once you display a skill, you own it.
6. Virtually every player is vulnerable to a month of aberrant performance. Or a year.
7. Exercise excruciating patience.

Aging Axioms

1. Age is the only variable for which we can project a rising trend with 100% accuracy. (Or, age never regresses.)
2. The aging process slows down for those who maintain a firm grasp on the strike zone. Plate patience and pitching command can preserve any waning skill they have left.
3. Negatives tend to snowball as you age.

Steve Avery List

Players who hang onto MLB rosters for six years searching for a skill level they only had for three.

Balls

The logical variable—independently proven—that explains the sharp increase in batted ball distances and home runs. Refuted by MLB to avoid the appearance of tampering with the game, but that brush-off is tough to believe given the history of MLB financially benefitting from home run surges.

Bylaws of Badness

1. Some players are better than an open roster spot, but not by much.
2. Some players have bad years because they are unlucky. Others have *many* bad years because they are bad... and lucky.

Christie Brinkley Law of Statistical Analysis

Never get married to the model.

Employment Standards

1. If you are right-brain dominant, own a catcher's mitt and are under 40, you will always be gainfully employed.
2. Some teams believe that it is better to employ a player with any experience because it has to be better than the devil they don't know.
3. It's not so good to go *pffft* in a contract year.

Laws of Prognosticating Perspective

- *Berkeley's 17th Law:* A great many problems do not have accurate answers, but do have approximate answers, from which sensible decisions can be made.
- *Ashley-Perry Statistical Axiom #4:* A complex system that works is invariably found to have evolved from a simple system that works.
- *Baseball Variation of Harvard Law:* Under the most rigorously observed conditions of skill, age, environment, statistical rules and other variables, a ballplayer will perform as he damn well pleases.

Brad Fullmer List

Players whose leading indicators indicate upside potential, year after year, but consistently fail to reach that full potential. Players like Devin Mesoraco, Joc Pederson, Jurickson Profar and Jorge Soler are on the list right now.

Good Luck Truism

Good luck is rare and everyone has more of it than you do. That's the law.

The Gravity Principles

1. It is easier to be crappy than it is to be good.
2. All performance starts at zero, ends at zero and can drop to zero at any time.
3. The odds of a good performer slumping are far greater than the odds of a poor performer surging.
4. Once a player is in a slump, it takes several 3-for-5 days to get out of it. Once he is on a streak, it takes a single 0-for-4 day to begin the downward spiral. *Corollary:* Once a player is in a slump, not only does it take several 3-for-5 days to get out of it, but he also has to get his name back on the lineup card.

5. Eventually all performance comes down to earth. It may take a week, or a month, or may not happen until he's 45, but eventually it's going to happen.

Health Homilies

1. Staying healthy is a skill (and "DL Days" should be a Rotisserie category).
2. A $40 player can get hurt just as easily as a $5 player but is eight times tougher to replace.
3. Chronically injured players never suddenly get healthy.
4. There are two kinds of pitchers: those that are hurt and those that are not hurt... yet.
5. Players with back problems are always worth $10 less.
6. "Opting out of surgery" usually means it's coming anyway, just later.

The Health Hush

Players get hurt and potentially have a lot to lose, so there is an incentive for them to hide injuries. HIPAA laws restrict the disclosure of health information. Team doctors and trainers have been instructed not to talk with the media. So, when it comes to information on a player's health status, we're all pretty much in the dark.

The Livan Level

The point when a player's career Runs Above Replacement level has dropped so far below zero that he has effectively cancelled out any possible remaining future value. (Similarly, the Dontrelle Demarcation.)

The Momentum Maxims

1. A player will post a pattern of positive results until the day you add him to your roster.
2. Patterns of negative results are more likely to snowball than correct.
3. When an unstoppable force meets an immovable object, the wall always wins.

Noise

Irrelevant or meaningless pieces of information that can distort the results of an analysis. In news, this is opinion or rumor. In forecasting, this is random variance or irrelevant data. In ballparks, this is a screaming crowd cheering for a team down 12-3 with two outs and bases empty in the bottom of the ninth.

Paradoxes and Conundrums

1. Is a player's improvement in performance from one year to the next a point in a growth trend, an isolated outlier or a complete anomaly?
2. A player can play through an injury, post rotten numbers and put his job at risk... or... he can admit that he can't play through an injury, allow himself to be taken out of the lineup/rotation, and put his job at risk.
3. Did irregular playing time take its toll on the player's performance or did poor performance force a reduction in his playing time?
4. Is a player only in the game versus right-handers because he has a true skills deficiency versus left-handers? Or is his poor performance versus left-handers because he's never given a chance to face them?

5. The problem with stockpiling bench players in the hope that one pans out is that you end up evaluating performance using data sets that are too small to be reliable.

6. There are players who could give you 20 stolen bases if they got 400 AB. But if they got 400 AB, they would likely be on a bad team that wouldn't let them steal.

Paths to Retirement

1. **George Brett:** Get out while you're still putting up good numbers and the public perception of you is favorable. Like Chipper Jones, Mariano Rivera and David Ortiz.

2. **Steve Carlton:** Hang around the majors long enough for your numbers to become so wretched that people begin to forget your past successes. Current players who could be on a similar course include Bartolo Colon, Curtis Granderson, Matt Holliday and Chase Utley.

3. **Johan Santana:** Stay on the disabled list for so long that nobody realizes you haven't officially retired until your name shows up on a Hall of Fame ballot. Also: Cliff Lee. Perhaps: Carl Crawford. Possibly soon: David Wright.

Process-Outcome Matrix *(Russo and Schoemaker)*

	Good Outcome	Bad Outcome
Good Process	Deserved Success	Bad Break
Bad Process	Dumb Luck	Poetic Justice

Quack!

An exclamation in response to the educated speculation that a player has used performance enhancing drugs. While it is rare to have absolute proof, there is often enough information to suggest that, "if it looks like a duck and quacks like a duck, then odds are it's a duck."

Situation Dependent

An event that is affected by the context of team, ballpark, or other outside variables.

RBI: You can't drive in runs if there is nobody on base.

Runs: You can't score a run if no one drives you in.

Wins: You can't win a game unless your offense scores runs, no matter how well you pitch.

Surface Stats

All those wonderful statistics we grew up with that those mean bean counters are telling us don't matter anymore. Home runs, RBIs, batting average, won-loss record. Let's go back to the 1960s and make baseball great again! [EDITOR: No.]

Tenets of Optimal Timing

1. If a second half fader had put up his second half stats in the first half and his first half stats in the second half, then he probably wouldn't even have had a second half.

2. Fast starters can often buy six months of playing time out of one month of productivity.

3. Poor 2nd halves don't get recognized until it's too late.

4. "Baseball is like this. Have one good year and you can fool them for five more, because for five more years they expect you to have another good one." — Frankie Frisch

The Three True Outcomes

1. Strikeouts
2. Walks
3. Home runs

The Three True Handicaps

1. Has power but can't make contact.
2. Has speed but can't hit safely.
3. Has potential but is too old.

Zombie

A player who is indestructible, continuing to get work, year-after-year, no matter how dead his skills metrics are. Like Like Danny Espinosa, Lucas Harrell, Mike Pelfrey and Wily Peralta.

Batters

Batting Eye, Contact and Batting Average

Batting average (BA, or Avg)

This is where it starts. BA is a grand old nugget that has long outgrown its usefulness. We revere .300 hitting superstars and scoff at .250 hitters, yet the difference between the two is one hit every five games. BA is a poor evaluator of performance in that it neglects the offensive value of the base on balls and assumes that all hits are created equal.

Walk rate (bb%)

(BB / (AB + BB))

A measure of a batter's plate patience. BENCHMARKS: The best batters will have levels more than 10%. Those with poor plate patience will have levels of 5% or less.

On base average (OB)

(H + BB + HBP) / (AB + BB + HBP + Sac Flies)

Addressing a key deficiency with BA, OB gives value to events that get batters on base, but are not hits. An OB of .350 can be read as "this batter gets on base 35% of the time." When a run is scored, there is no distinction made as to how that runner reached base. So, two-thirds of the time—about how often a batter comes to the plate with the bases empty—a walk really is as good as a hit. BENCHMARKS: We know what a .300 hitter is, but what represents "good" for OB? That comparable level would likely be .400, with .275 representing the comparable level of futility.

Ground ball, line drive, fly ball percentages (G/L/F)

The percentage of all balls in play that are hit on the ground, as line drives and in the air. For batters, increased fly ball tendency may foretell a rise in power skills; increased line drive tendency may foretell an improvement in batting average. For a pitcher, the ability to keep the ball on the ground can contribute to his statistical output exceeding his demonstrated skill level.

*BIP Type	Total%	Out%
Ground ball	45%	72%
Line drive	20%	28%
Fly ball	35%	85%
TOTAL	*100%*	*69%*

*Data only includes fieldable balls and is net of HRs.

Line drives and luck *(Patrick Davitt)*

Given that each individual batter's hit rate sets its own baseline, and that line drives (LD) are the most productive type of batted ball, a study looked at the relationship between the two. Among the findings were that hit rates on LDs are much higher than on FBs or GBs, with individual batters consistently falling into the 72-73% range. Ninety-five percent of all batters fall between the range of 60%-86%; batters outside this range regress very quickly, often within the season.

Note that batters' BAs did not always follow their LD% up or down, because some of them enjoyed higher hit rates on other batted balls, improved their contact rates, or both. Still, it's

justifiable to bet that players hitting the ball with authority but getting fewer hits than they should will correct over time.

Batting eye (Eye)

(Walks / Strikeouts)

A measure of a player's strike zone judgment. BENCHMARKS: The best hitters have Eye ratios more than 1.00 (indicating more walks than strikeouts) and are the most likely to be among a league's .300 hitters. Ratios less than 0.50 represent batters who likely also have lower BAs.

Batting eye as a leading indicator

There is a correlation between strike zone judgment and batting average. However, research shows that this is more descriptive than predictive:

	Batting Average				
Batting Eye	2013	2014	2015	2016	2017
0.00 - 0.25	.242	.238	.243	.248	.245
0.26 - 0.50	.253	.253	.257	.255	.255
0.51 - 0.75	.265	.268	.267	.271	.270
0.76 - 1.00	.277	.270	.280	.286	.269
1.01 and over	.284	.304	.293	.255	.295

We have been running the above chart for 18 years and have always had large enough samples to make each group statistically significant. But not the past four years. Now, the correlation at some of the cohorts has started to break down because the sample sizes are too small. In 2017, there were only 19 players (min. 100 AB) in the "0.76-1.00" group and only eight in the "1.01 and over" group. All hail the strikeout!

We can create percentage plays for the different levels:

For Eye Levels of	Pct who bat	
	.300+	.250-
0.00 - 0.25	7%	39%
0.26 - 0.50	14%	26%
0.51 - 0.75	18%	17%
0.76 - 1.00	32%	14%
1.01 - 1.50	51%	9%
1.51 +	59%	4%

Any batter with an eye ratio more than 1.50 has about a 4% chance of hitting less than .250 over 500 at bats.

Of all .300 hitters, those with ratios of at least 1.00 have a 65% chance of repeating as .300 hitters. Those with ratios less than 1.00 have less than a 50% chance of repeating.

Only 4% of sub-.250 hitters with ratios less than 0.50 will mature into .300 hitters the following year.

In this study, only 37 batters hit .300-plus with a sub-0.50 eye ratio over at least 300 AB in a season. Of this group, 30% were able to accomplish this feat on a consistent basis. For the other 70%, this was a short-term aberration.

Contact rate (ct%)

((AB - K) / AB)

Measures a batter's ability to get wood on the ball and hit it into the field of play. BENCHMARKS: Those batters with the best contact skill will have levels of 90% or better. The hackers will have levels of 75% or less.

Contact rate as a leading indicator

The more often a batter makes contact with the ball, the higher the likelihood that he will hit safely.

Batting Average

Contact Rate	2013	2014	2015	2016	2017
0% - 60%	.203	.176	.194	.207	.206
61% - 65%	.211	.217	.217	.223	.226
66% - 70%	.232	.230	.236	.232	.244
71% - 75%	.246	.243	.254	.253	.248
76% - 80%	.261	.257	.257	.262	.268
81% - 85%	.268	.266	.268	.271	.270
86% - 90%	.272	.276	.277	.285	.287
Over 90%	.270	.324	.284	.254	.270

Here again, the dearth of players at the higher skill levels has broken the correlation. The "Over 90%" cohort had only 17 players in 2014, 25 players in 2015 and 12 in 2016. In 2017, there were only eight players, and only one with more than 80 AB—Ben Revere. All hail the strikeout!

Contact rate and walk rate as leading indicators

A matrix of contact rates and walk rates can provide expectation benchmarks for a player's batting average:

Walk rate (bb%)

Contact rate (ct%)	0-5	6-10	11-15	16+
65-	.179	.195	.229	.237
66-75	.190	.248	.254	.272
76-85	.265	.267	.276	.283
86+	.269	.279	.301	.309

A contact rate of 65% or lower offers virtually no chance for a player to hit even .250, no matter how high a walk rate he has. The .300 hitters most often come from the group with a minimum 86% contact and 11% walk rate.

HCt and HctX *(Patrick Davitt)*

HCt= hard hit ball rate x contact rate

HctX = Player HCt divided by league average Hct, normalized to 100

The combination of making contact and hitting the ball hard might be the most important skills for a batter. HctX correlates very strongly with BA, and at higher BA levels often does so with high accuracy. Its success with HR was somewhat limited, probably due to GB/FB differences. **BENCHMARKS:** The average major-leaguer in a given year has a HctX of 100. Elite batters have an HctX of 135 or above; weakest batters have HctX of 55 or below.

Balls in play (BIP)

(AB – K)

The total number of batted balls that are hit fair, both hits and outs. An analysis of how these balls are hit—on the ground, in the air, hits, outs, etc.—can provide analytical insight, from player skill levels to the impact of luck on statistical output.

Batting average on balls in play *(Voros McCracken)*

(H – HR) / (AB – HR – K)

Or, BABIP. Also called hit rate (h%). The percent of balls hit into the field of play that fall for hits. **BENCHMARK:** Every hitter

establishes his own individual hit rate that stabilizes over time. A batter whose seasonal hit rate varies significantly from the h% he has established over the preceding three seasons (variance of at least +/- 3%) is likely to improve or regress to his individual h% mean (with over-performer declines more likely and sharper than under-performer recoveries). Three-year h% levels strongly predict a player's h% the following year.

Pitches/Plate Appearance as a leading indicator for BA *(Paul Petera)*

The art of working the count has long been considered one of the more crucial aspects of good hitting. It is common knowledge that the more pitches a hitter sees, the greater opportunity he has to reach base safely.

P/PA	OBA	BA
4.00+	.360	.264
3.75-3.99	.347	.271
3.50-3.74	.334	.274
Under 3.50	.321	.276

Generally speaking, the more pitches seen, the lower the BA, but the higher the OBA. But what about the outliers, those players that bucked the trend in year #1?

	YEAR TWO	
	BA Improved	BA Declined
Low P/PA and Low BA	77%	23%
High P/PA and High BA	21%	79%

In these scenarios, there was a strong tendency for performance to normalize in year #2.

Expected batting average *(John Burnson)*

$xCT\% * [xH1\% + xH2\%]$

where

$$xH1\% = GB\% \times [0.0004\ PX + 0.062\ ln(SX)]$$
$$+ LD\% \times [0.93 - 0.086\ ln(SX)]$$
$$+ FB\% \times 0.12$$

and

$$xH2\% = FB\% \times [0.0013\ PX - 0.0002\ SX - 0.057]$$
$$+ GB\% \times [0.0006\ PX]$$

A hitter's expected batting average as calculated by multiplying the percentage of balls put in play (contact rate) by the chance that a ball in play falls for a hit. The likelihood that a ball in play falls for a hit is a product of the speed of the ball and distance it is hit (PX), the speed of the batter (SX), and distribution of ground balls, fly balls, and line drives. We further split it out by non-homerun hit rate (xH1%) and homerun hit rate (xH2%). **BENCHMARKS:** In general, xBA should approximate batting average fairly closely. Those hitters who have large variances between the two gauges are candidates for further analysis. **LIMITATION:** xBA tends to understate a batter's true value if he is an extreme ground ball hitter (G/F ratio over 3.0) with a low PX. These players are not inherently weak, but choose to take safe singles rather than swing for the fences.

Expected batting average variance

xBA – BA

The variance between a batter's BA and his xBA is a measure of over- or under-achievement. A positive variance indicates the potential for a batter's BA to rise. A negative variance indicates the potential for BA to decline. BENCHMARK: Discount variances that are less than 20 points. Any variance more than 30 points is regarded as a strong indicator of future change.

Power

Slugging average (Slg)
(Singles + (2 x Doubles) + (3 x Triples) + (4 x HR)) / AB

A measure of the total number of bases accumulated (or the minimum number of runners' bases advanced) per at bat. It is a misnomer; it is not a true measure of a batter's slugging ability because it includes singles. Slg also assumes that each type of hit has proportionately increasing value (i.e. a double is twice as valuable as a single, etc.) which is not true. For instance, with the bases loaded, a HR always scores four runs, a triple always scores three, but a double could score two or three and a single could score one, or two, or even three. BENCHMARKS: Top batters will have levels over .500. The bottom batters will have levels less than .300.

Fly ball tendency and power *(Mat Olkin)*
There is a proven connection between a hitter's ground ball/fly ball tendencies and his power production.

1. *Extreme ground ball hitters generally do not hit for much power.* It's almost impossible for a hitter with a ground/fly ratio over 1.80 to hit enough fly balls to produce even 25 HRs in a season. However, this does not mean that a low G/F ratio necessarily guarantees power production. Some players have no problem getting the ball into the air, but lack the strength to reach the fences consistently.

2. *Most batters' ground/fly ratios stay pretty steady over time.* Most year-to-year changes are small and random, as they are in any other statistical category. A large, sudden change in G/F, on the other hand, can signal a conscious change in plate approach. And so...

3. *If a player posts high G/F ratios in his first few years, he probably isn't ever going to hit for all that much power.*

4. *When a batter's power suddenly jumps, his G/F ratio often drops at the same time.*

5. *Every so often, a hitter's ratio will drop significantly even as his power production remains level.* In these rare cases, impending power development is likely, since the two factors almost always follow each other.

Home runs to fly ball rate (hr/f)
The percent of fly balls that are hit for HRs.

hr/f rate as a leading indicator *(Joshua Randall)*
Each batter establishes an individual home run to fly ball rate that stabilizes over rolling three-year periods; those levels strongly predict the hr/f in the subsequent year. A batter who varies significantly from his hr/f is likely to regress toward his individual hr/f mean, with over-performance decline more likely and more severe than under-performance recovery.

Estimating HR rate for young hitters *(Matt Cederholm)*
Over time, hitters establish a baseline hr/f, but how do we measure the HR output of young hitters with little track record?

Since power is a key indicator of HR output, we can look at typical hr/f for various levels of power, as measures by xPX:

xPX	hr/f percentiles				
	10	25	50	75	90
<=70	0.9%	2.0%	3.8%	5.5%	7.4%
71-80	3.3%	5.1%	6.4%	8.1%	10.0%
81-90	3.8%	5.4%	7.4%	9.0%	11.0%
91-100	4.7%	6.6%	8.9%	11.3%	13.0%
101-110	6.6%	8.3%	10.9%	13.0%	16.2%
111-120	7.4%	9.8%	11.9%	14.7%	17.1%
121-130	8.5%	10.9%	12.8%	15.5%	17.4%
131-140	9.7%	11.9%	14.6%	17.1%	20.4%
141-160	11.3%	13.1%	16.5%	19.2%	21.5%
161+	14.4%	16.5%	19.4%	22.0%	25.8%

To predict changes in HR output, just look at a player and project his HR as if his hr/f was at the median for his xPX level. For example, if a player with a 125 xPX exceeds a 12.8% hr/f, we would expect a decline in the following season. The greater the deviation from the mean, the greater the probability of an increase or decline.

Hard-hit flies as a sustainable skill *(Patrick Davitt)*
A study of data from 2009-2011 found that we should seek batters with a high Hard-Hit Fly Ball percentage (HHFB%). Among the findings:

- Avoiding pop-ups and hitting HHFBs are sustainable core power skills.
- Consistent HHFB% performance marks batters with power potential.
- When looking for candidates to regress, we should look at individual past levels of HR/HHFB, perhaps using a three-year rolling average.

Linear weighted power (LWPwr)
((Doubles x .8) + (Triples x .8) + (HR x 1.4)) / (At bats- K) x 100

A variation of the linear weights formula that considers only events that are measures of a batter's pure power. BENCHMARKS: Top sluggers typically top the 17 mark. Weak hitters will have a LWPwr level of less than 10.

Linear weighted power index (PX)
(Batter's LWPwr / League LWPwr) x 100

LWPwr is presented in this book in its normalized form to get a better read on a batter's accomplishment in each year. For instance, a 30-HR season today is much less of an accomplishment than 30 HRs hit in a lower offense year like 2014. BENCHMARKS: A level of 100 equals league average power skills. Any player with a value more than 100 has above average power skills, and those more than 150 are the Slugging Elite.

Expected LW power index (xPX) *(Bill Macey)*
2.6 + 269*HHLD% + 724*HHFB%

Previous research has shown that hard-hit balls are more likely to result in hits and hard-hit fly balls are more likely to end up as HRs. As such, we can use hard-hit ball data to calculate an expected skills-based power index. This metric starts with hard-hit ball data, which measures a player's fundamental skill of making solid contact, and then places it on the same scale as PX (xPX). In the above formula, HHLD% is calculated as the number of hard hit-line drives divided by the total number of balls put in play. HHFB% is similarly calculated for fly balls.

Pitches/Plate Appearance as a leading indicator for PX *(Paul Petera)*
Working the count has a positive effect on power.

P/PA	PX
4.00+	123
3.75-3.99	108
3.50-3.74	96
Under 3.50	84

As for the year #1 outliers:

	YEAR TWO	
	PX Improved	PX Declined
Low P/PA and High PX	11%	89%
High P/PA and Low PX	70%	30%

In these scenarios, there was a strong tendency for performance to normalize in year #2.

Doubles as a leading indicator for home runs *(Bill Macey)*
There is little support for the theory that hitting many doubles in year x leads to an increase in HR in year x+1. However, it was shown that batters with high doubles rates (2B/AB) also tend to hit more HR/AB than the league average; oddly, they are unable to sustain the high 2B/AB rate but do sustain their higher HR/AB rates. Batters with high 2B/AB rates and low HR/AB rates are more likely to see HR gains in the following year, but those rates will still typically trail the league average. And, batters who experience a surge in 2B/AB typically give back most of those gains in the following year without any corresponding gain in HR.

Opposite field home runs *(Ed DeCaria)*
Opposite field HRs serve as a strong indicator of overall home run power (AB/HR). Power hitters (smaller AB/HR rates) hit a far higher percentage of their HR to the opposite field or straight away (over 30%). Conversely, non-power hitters hit almost 90% of their home runs to their pull field.

	Performance in Y2-Y4 (% of Group)		
Y1 Trigger	<=30 AB/HR	5.5+ RC/G	$16+ R$
2+ OppHR	69%	46%	33%
<2 OppHR	29%	13%	12%

Players who hit just two or more OppHR in one season were 2-3 times as likely as those who hit zero or one OppHR to sustain strong AB/HR rates, RC/G levels, or R$ values over the following three seasons.

	Y2-Y4 Breakout Performance (% Breakout by Group, Age <=26 Only)		
	AB/HR	RC/G	R$
Y1 Trigger	>35 to <=30	<4.5 to 5.5+	<$8 to $16+
2+ OppHR	32%	21%	30%
<2 OppHR	23%	12%	10%

Roughly one of every 3-4 batters age 26 or younger experiences a *sustained three-year breakout* in AB/HR, RC/G or R$ after a season in which they hit 2+ OppHR, far better odds than the one in 8-10 batters who experience a breakout without the 2+ OppHR trigger.

In fact, a 2015 Brad Kullman study that examined hard hit balls of all types (flies, liners, and grounders) by hitters with 100 or more plate appearances offered a broader conclusion. His research found that hitters who can effectively use the whole field are more productive in virtually every facet of hitting than those with an exclusively pull-oriented approach.

Home runs in bunches *(Patrick Davitt)*
A study from HR data from 2010-2012 showed that batters hit HRs in a random manner, with game-gaps between HRs that correspond roughly to their average days per HR. Thus, the theory that batters hit HRs in "bunches" is a fallacy. It appears pointless to try to "time the market" by predicting the beginning or end of a drought or a bunch, or by assuming the end of one presages the beginning of the other, despite what the ex-player in the broadcast booth tells you.

Power breakout profile
It is not easy to predict which batters will experience a power spike. We can categorize power breakouts to determine the likelihood of a player taking a step up or of a surprise performer repeating his feat. Possibilities:

- Increase in playing time
- History of power skills at some time in the past
- Redistribution of already demonstrated extra base hit power
- Normal skills growth
- Situational breakouts, particularly in hitter-friendly venues
- Increased fly ball tendency
- Use of illegal performance-enhancing substances
- Miscellaneous unexplained variables

Speed

Wasted talent on the base paths
We refer to some players as having "wasted talent," a high level skill that is negated by a deficiency in another skill. Among these types are players who have blazing speed that is negated by a sub-.300 on base average.

These players can have short-term value. However, their stolen base totals are tied so tightly to their "green light" that any change in managerial strategy could completely erase that value. A higher OB mitigates that downside; the good news is that plate patience can be taught.

In the past, there were always a handful of players who had at least 20 SBs with an OBP less than .300, putting their future SBs at risk. In 2017, there was Billy Hamilton (59 SB, .299 OBP), Rajai Davis (29, .293), Jonathan Villar (23, .293), Jose Peraza (23, .297) and Keon Broxton, (21, .299).

Speed score *(Bill James)*
A measure of the various elements that comprise a runner's speed skills. Although this formula (a variation of James' original version) may be used as a leading indicator for stolen base output,

SB attempts are controlled by managerial strategy which makes speed score somewhat less valuable.

Speed score is calculated as the mean value of the following four elements:

1. Stolen base efficiency = $(((SB + 3)/(SB + CS + 7)) - .4) \times 20$

2. Stolen base freq. = Square root of $((SB + CS)/(Singles + BB)) / .07$

3. Triples rating = $(3B / (AB - HR - K))$ and the result assigned a value based on the following chart:

< 0.001	0	0.0105	6
0.001	1	0.013	7
0.0023	2	0.0158	8
0.0039	3	0.0189	9
0.0058	4	0.0223+	10
0.008	5		

4. Runs scored as a percentage of times on base = $(((R - HR) / (H + BB - HR)) - .1) / .04$

Speed score index (SX)

(Batter's speed score / League speed score) x 100

Normalized speed scores get a better read on a runner's accomplishment in context. A level of 100 equals league average speed skill. Values more than 100 indicate above average skill, more than 200 represent the Fleet of Feet Elite.

Statistically scouted speed (Spd) *(Ed DeCaria)*

$(104 + \{[(Runs–HR+10*age\_wt)/(RBI-HR+10)]/lg\_av*100\} / 5$
$+ \{[(3B+5*age\_wt)/(2B+3B+5)]/lg\_av*100\} / 5$
$+ \{[(SoftMedGBhits+25*age\_wt)/(SoftMedGB+25)]/lg\_av*100\} / 2$
$- \{[Weight (Lbs)/Height (In)^2 * 703]/lg\_av*100\}$

A skills-based gauge that measures speed without relying on stolen bases. Its components are:

- *(Runs – HR) / (RBI – HR)*: This metric aims to minimize the influence of extra base hit power and team run-scoring rates on perceived speed.

- *3B / (2B + 3B)*: No one can deny that triples are a fast runner's stat; dividing them by 2B+3B instead of all balls in play dampens the power aspect of extra base hits.

- *(Soft + Medium Ground Ball Hits) / (Soft + Medium Ground Balls)*: Faster runners are more likely than slower runners to beat out routine grounders. Hard hit balls are excluded from numerator and denominator.

- *Body Mass Index (BMI)*: Calculated as *Weight (lbs) / Height (in)2 * 703*. All other factors considered, leaner players run faster than heavier ones.

In this book, the formula is scaled as an index with a midpoint of 100.

Stolen base opportunity percent (SBO)

(SB + CS) / (BB + Singles)

A rough approximation of how often a baserunner attempts a stolen base. Provides a comparative measure for players on a given team and, as a team measure, the propensity of a manager to give a "green light" to his runners.

Stolen base success rate (SB%)

SB / (SB + CS)

The rate at which baserunners are successful in their stolen base attempts. **BENCHMARK:** It is generally accepted that an 80% rate is the minimum required for a runner to be providing value to his team.

Roto Speed (RSpd)

(Spd x (SBO + SB%))

An adjustment to the measure for raw speed that takes into account a runner's opportunities to steal and his success rate. This stat is intended to provide a more accurate predictive measure of stolen bases for the Mayberry Method.

Stolen base breakout profile *(Bob Berger)*

To find stolen base breakouts (first 30+ steal season in the majors), look for players that:

- are between 22-27 years old
- have 3-7 years of professional (minors and MLB) experience
- have previous steals at the MLB level
- have averaged 20+ SB in previous three seasons (majors and minors combined)
- have at least one professional season of 30+ SB

Overall Performance Analysis

On base plus slugging average (OPS)

A simple sum of the two gauges, it is considered one of the better evaluators of overall performance. OPS combines the two basic elements of offensive production—the ability to get on base (OB) and the ability to advance baserunners (Slg). **BENCHMARKS:** The game's top batters will have OPS levels more than .900. The worst batters will have levels less than .600.

Base Performance Value (BPV)

(Walk rate - 5) x 2)
+ ((Contact rate - 75) x 4)
+ ((Power Index - 80) x 0.8)
+ ((Spd - 80) x 0.3)

A single value that describes a player's overall raw skill level. This is more useful than traditional statistical gauges to track player performance trends and project future statistical output. This formula combines the individual raw skills of batting eye, contact rate, power and speed. **BENCHMARKS:** The best hitters will have a BPV of 50 or greater.

Base Performance Index (BPX)

BPV scaled to league average to account for year-to-year fluctuations in league-wide statistical performance. It's a snapshot of a player's overall skills compared to an average player. **BENCHMARK:** A level of 100 means a player had a league-average BPV in that given season.

Linear weights *(Pete Palmer)*

((Singles x .46) + (Doubles x .8) + (Triples x 1.02)
+ (Home runs x 1.4) + (Walks x .33) + (Stolen Bases x .3)
- (Caught Stealing x .6) - ((At bats - Hits) x Normalizing Factor)

(Also referred to as Batting Runs.) Formula whose premise is that all events in baseball are linear; that is, the output (runs) is directly proportional to the input (offensive events). Each of these events is then weighted according to its relative value in producing runs. Positive events—hits, walks, stolen bases—have positive values. Negative events—outs, caught stealing—have negative values.

The normalizing factor, representing the value of an out, is an offset to the level of offense in a given year. It changes every season, growing larger in high offense years and smaller in low offense years. The value is about .26 and varies by league.

LW is not included in the player forecast boxes, but the LW concept is used with the linear weighted power gauge.

Runs above replacement (RAR)

An estimate of the number of runs a player contributes above a "replacement level" player. "Replacement" is defined as the level of performance at which another player can easily be found at little or no cost to a team. What constitutes replacement level is a topic that is hotly debated. There are a variety of formulas and rules of thumb used to determine this level for each position (replacement level for a catcher will be very different from replacement level for an outfielder). Our estimates appear below.

One of the major values of RAR for fantasy applications is that it can be used to assemble an integrated ranking of batters and pitchers for drafting purposes.

To calculate RAR for batters:

- Start with a batter's runs created per game (RC/G).
- Subtract his position's replacement level RC/G.
- Multiply by number of games played: (AB - H + CS) / 25.5.

Replacement levels used in this book:

POS	NL	AL
CA	4.06	4.14
1B	5.91	5.38
2B	5.02	4.63
3B	5.31	4.86
SS	4.52	4.63
LF	5.26	5.45
CF	5.06	4.75
RF	5.19	4.93
DH		4.87

RAR can also be used to calculate rough projected team won-loss records. *(Roger Miller)* Total the RAR levels for all the players on a team, divide by 10 and add to 53 wins.

Runs created *(Bill James)*

(H + BB − CS) x (Total bases + (.55 x SB)) / (AB + BB)

A formula that converts all offensive events into a total of runs scored. As calculated for individual teams, the result approximates a club's actual run total with great accuracy.

Runs created per game (RC/G)

Runs Created / ((AB - H + CS) / 25.5)

RC expressed on a per-game basis might be considered the hypothetical ERA compiled against a particular batter. Another way

to look at it: A batter with a RC/G of 7.00 would be expected to score 7 runs per game if he were cloned nine times and faced an average pitcher in every at bat. Cloning batters is not a practice we recommend. **BENCHMARKS:** Few players surpass the level of a 10.00 RC/G, but any level more than 7.50 can still be considered very good. At the bottom are levels less than 3.00.

Plate Appearances as a leading indicator *(Patrick Davitt)*

While targeting players "age 26 with experience" as potential breakout candidates has become a commonly accepted concept, a study has found that cumulative plate appearances, especially during the first two years of a young player's career, can also have predictive value in assessing a coming spike in production. Three main conclusions:

- When projecting players, MLB experience is more important than age.
- Players who amass 800+ PAs in their first two seasons are highly likely to have double-digit Rotisserie dollar value in Year 3.
- Also target young players in the season where they attain 400 PAs, as they are twice as likely as other players to grow significantly in value.

Skill-specific aging patterns for batters *(Ed DeCaria)*

Baseball forecasters obsess over "peak age" of player performance because we must understand player ascent toward and decline from that peak to predict future value. Most published aging analyses are done using composite estimates of value such as OPS or linear weights. By contrast, fantasy GMs are typically more concerned with category-specific player value (HR, SB, AVG, etc.). We can better forecast what matters most by analyzing peak age of individual baseball skills rather than overall player value.

For batters, recognized peak age for overall batting value is a player's late 20s. But individual skills do not peak uniformly at the same time:

Contact rate (ct%): Ascends modestly by about a half point of contact per year from age 22 to 26, then holds steady within a half point of peak until age 35, after which players lose a half point of contact per year.

Walk rate (bb%): Trends the opposite way with age compared to contact rate, as batters tend to peak at age 30 and largely remain there until they turn 38.

Stolen Base Opportunity (SBO): Typically, players maintain their SBO through age 27, but then reduce their attempts steadily in each remaining year of their careers.

Stolen base success rate (SB%): Aggressive runners (>14% SBO) tend to lose about 2 points per year as they age. However, less aggressive runners (<=14% SBO) actually improve their SB% by about 2 points per year until age 28, after which they reverse course and give back 1-2 pts every year as they age.

GB%/LD%/FB%: Both GB% and LD% peak at the start of a player's career and then decline as many hitters seemingly learn to elevate the ball more. But at about age 30, hitter GB% ascends toward a second late-career peak while LD% continues to plummet and FB% continues to rise through age 38.

Hit rate (h%): Declines linearly with age. This is a natural result of a loss of speed and change in batted ball trajectory.

Isolated Power (ISO): Typically peaks from age 24-26. Similarly, home runs per fly ball, opposite field HR %, and Hard Hit % all peak by age 25 and decline somewhat linearly from that point on.

Catchers and late-career performance spikes *(Ed Spaulding)*
Many catchers—particularly second line catchers—have their best seasons late in their careers. Some possible reasons why:

1. Catchers, like shortstops, often get to the big leagues for defensive reasons and not their offensive skills. These skills take longer to develop.
2. The heavy emphasis on learning the catching/ defense/ pitching side of the game detracts from their time to learn about, and practice, hitting.
3. Injuries often curtail their ability to show offensive skills, though these injuries (typically jammed fingers, bruises on the arms, rib injuries from collisions) often don't lead to time on the disabled list.
4. The time spent behind the plate has to impact the ability to recognize, and eventually hit, all kinds of pitches.

Spring training Slg as leading indicator *(John Dewan)*
A hitter's spring training Slg .200 or more above his lifetime Slg is a leading indicator for a better than normal season.

Overall batting breakout profile *(Brandon Kruse)*
We define a breakout performance as one where a player posts a Roto value of $20+ after having never posted a value of $10. These criteria are used to validate an apparent breakout in the current season but may also be used carefully to project a potential upcoming breakout:

- Age 27 or younger
- An increase in at least two of: h%, PX or Spd
- Minimum league average PX or Spd (100)
- Minimum contact rate of 75%
- Minimum xBA of .270

In-Season Analysis

Batting order facts *(Ed DeCaria)*
Eighty-eight percent of today's leadoff hitters bat leadoff again in their next game, 78% still bat leadoff 10 games later, and 68% still bat leadoff 50 games later. Despite this level of turnover after 50 games, leadoff hitters have the best chance of retaining their role over time. After leadoff, #3 and #4 hitters are the next most likely to retain their lineup slots.

On a season-to-season basis, leadoff hitters are again the most stable, with 69% of last year's primary leadoff hitters retaining the #1 slot next year.

Plate appearances decline linearly by lineup slot. Leadoff batters receive 10-12% more PAs than when batting lower in the lineup. AL #9 batters and NL #8 batters get 9-10% fewer PAs. These results mirror play-by-play data showing a 15-20 PA drop by lineup slot over a full season.

Walk rate is largely unaffected by lineup slot in the AL. Beware strong walk rates by NL #8 hitters, as much of this "skill" will disappear if ever moved from the #8 slot.

Batting order has no discernable effect on contact rate.

Hit rate slopes gently upward as hitters are slotted deeper in the lineup.

As expected, the #3-4-5 slots are ideal for non-HR RBIs, at the expense of #6 hitters. RBIs are worst for players in the #1-2 slots. Batting atop the order sharply increases the probability of scoring runs, especially in the NL.

The leadoff slot easily has the highest stolen base attempt rate. #4-5-6 hitters attempt steals more often when batting out of those slots than they do batting elsewhere. The NL #8 hitter is a SB attempt sink hole. A change in batting order from #8 to #1 in the NL could nearly double a player's SB output due to lineup slot alone.

DOMination and DISaster rates
Week-to-week consistency is measured using a batter's BPV compiled in each week. A player earns a DOMinant week if his BPV was greater or equal to 50 for that week. A player registers a DISaster if his BPV was less than 0 for that week. The percentage of Dominant weeks, DOM%, is simply calculated as the number of DOM weeks divided by the total number of weeks played.

Is week-to-week consistency a repeatable skill? *(Bill Macey)*
To test whether consistent performance is a repeatable skill for batters, we examined how closely related a player's DOM% was from year to year.

YR1 DOM%	AVG YR2 DOM%
< 35%	37%
35%–45%	40%
46%–55%	45%
56%+	56%

Quality/consistency score (QC)
(DOM% – (2 x DIS%)) x 2)
Using the DOM/DIS percentages, this score measures both the quality of performance as well as week–to-week consistency.

Sample size reliability *(Russell Carleton)*
At what point during the season do stats become reliable indicators of skill? Measured in PA *(unlisted=did not stablize over full season)*:

- 60: Contact rate
- 120: Walk rate
- 160: ISO (Isolated power)
- 170: HR rate
- 320: Slg
- 460: OBP

Measured via balls in play:
- 80: GB%; FB%
- 50: hr/f
- 600: LD%
- 820: hit rate (BABIP)

Projecting RBIs *(Patrick Davitt)*

Evaluating players in-season for RBI potential is a function of the interplay among four factors:

- Teammates' ability to reach base ahead of him and to run the bases efficiently
- His own ability to drive them in by hitting, especially XBH
- Number of Games Played
- Place in the batting order

3-4-5 Hitters:

(0.69 x GP x TOB) + (0.30 x ITB) + (0.275 x HR) – (.191 x GP)

6-7-8 Hitters:

(0.63 x GP x TOB) + (0.27 x ITB) + (0.250 x HR) – (.191 x GP)

9-1-2 Hitters:

(0.57 x GP x TOB) + (0.24 x ITB) + (0.225 x HR) – (.191 x GP)

...where GP = games played, TOB = team on-base pct. and ITB = individual total bases (ITB).

Apply this pRBI formula after 70 games played or so (to reduce the variation from small sample size) to find players more than 9 RBIs over or under their projected RBI. There could be a correction coming.

You should also consider other factors, like injury or trade (involving the player or a top-of-the-order speedster) or team SB philosophy and success rate.

Remember: the player himself has an impact on his TOB. When we first did this study, we excluded the player from his TOB and got better results. The formula overestimates projected RBI for players with high OBP who skew his teams' OBP but can't benefit in RBI from that effect.

Ten-Game hitting streaks as a leading indicator *(Bob Berger)*

Research of hitting streaks from 2011 and 2012 showed that a 10-game streak can reliably predict improved longer-term BA performance during the season. A player who has put together a hitting streak of at least 10 games will improve his BA for the remainder of the season about 60% of the time. This improvement can be significant, on average as much as .020 of BA.

Other Diamonds

Balls

The logical variable—independently proven—that explains the 2017 performances of previously powerless players like Yonder Alonso, Elvis Andrus, Scooter Gennett and Kurt Suzuki.

It's a Busy World Shortcut

For marginal utility-type players, scan their PX and Spd history to see if there's anything to mine for. If you see triple digits anywhere, stop and look further. If not, move on.

Chronology of the Classic Free-Swinger with Pop

1. Gets off to a good start.
2. Thinks he's in a groove.
3. Gets lax, careless.
4. Pitchers begin to catch on.
5. Fades down the stretch.

Errant Gust of Wind

A unit of measure used to describe the difference between your home run projection and mine.

Hannahan Concession

Players with a .218 BA rarely get 500 plate appearances, but when they do, it's usually once.

Mendoza Line

Named for Mario Mendoza, it represents the benchmark for batting futility. Usually refers to a .200 batting average, but can also be used for low levels of other statistical categories. Note that Mendoza's lifetime batting average was actually a much more robust .215.

Old Player Skills

Power, low batting average, no speed and usually good plate patience. Young players, often those with a larger frame, who possess these "old player skills" tend to decline faster than normal, often in their early 30s.

Small Sample Certitude

If players' careers were judged based what they did in a single game performance, then Tuffy Rhodes and Mark Whiten would be in the Hall of Fame.

Esix Snead List

Players with excellent speed and sub-.300 on base averages who get a lot of practice running down the line to first base, and then back to the dugout. Also used as an adjective, as in "Esix-Sneadian."

Pitchers

Strikeouts and Walks

Fundamental skills

The contention that pitching performance is unreliable is a fallacy driven by the practice of attempting to project pitching stats using gauges that are poor evaluators of skill.

How can we better evaluate pitching skill? We can start with the statistical categories that are generally unaffected by external factors. These stats capture the outcome of an individual pitcher versus batter match-up without regard to supporting offense, defense or bullpen:

Walks Allowed, Strikeouts and Ground/Fly Balls

Even with only these stats to observe, there is a wealth of insight that these measures can provide.

Control rate (Ctl, bb/9), or opposition walks per game
BB allowed x 9 / IP

Measures how many walks a pitcher allows per game equivalent. **BENCHMARK:** The best pitchers will have bb/9 of 2.8 or less.

Dominance rate (Dom, k/9), or opposition strikeouts/game
Strikeouts recorded x 9 / IP

Measures how many strikeouts a pitcher allows per game equivalent. **BENCHMARK:** The best pitchers will have k/9 levels of 7.0 or higher.

Command ratio (Cmd)
(Strikeouts / Walks)

A measure of a pitcher's ability to get the ball over the plate. There is no more fundamental a skill than this, and so it is used as a leading indicator to project future rises and falls in other gauges, such as ERA. **BENCHMARKS:** Baseball's best pitchers will have ratios in excess of 3.0. Pitchers with ratios less than 1.0—indicating that they walk more batters than they strike out—have virtually no potential for long-term success. If you make no other changes in your approach to drafting pitchers, limiting your focus to only pitchers with a command ratio of 2.5 or better will substantially improve your odds of success.

Command ratio as a leading indicator

The ability to get the ball over the plate—command of the strike zone—is one of the best leading indicators for future performance. Command ratio (K/BB) can be used to project potential in ERA as well as other skills gauges.

1. Research indicates that there is a high correlation between a pitcher's Cmd ratio and his ERA.

	Earned Run Average				
Command	2013	2014	2015	2016	2017
0.0 - 1.0	5.98	6.81	6.31	7.71	7.24
1.1 - 1.5	4.91	4.97	5.23	5.51	5.50
1.6 - 2.0	4.42	4.37	4.54	4.66	4.84
2.1 - 2.5	3.96	3.80	4.19	4.30	4.62
2.6 - 3.0	3.81	3.78	3.87	4.02	4.13
3.1 - 3.5	3.46	3.43	3.51	3.95	3.85
3.6 - 4.0	3.32	3.16	3.56	3.51	3.68
4.1+	2.86	2.92	3.07	3.30	3.20

We can create percentage plays for the different levels:

For Cmd	% with ERA of	
Levels of	3.50-	4.50+
0.0 - 1.0	0%	100%
1.1 - 1.5	9%	70%
1.6 - 2.0	19%	54%
2.1 - 2.5	33%	41%
2.6 - 3.0	35%	31%
3.1 – 3.5	37%	18%
3.6 – 4.0	56%	15%
4.1 +	61%	11%

Pitchers who maintain a Cmd over 2.5 have a high probability of long-term success. For fantasy drafting purposes, it is best to avoid pitchers with sub-2.0 ratios. Avoid bullpen closers if they have a ratio less than 2.5.

2. A pitcher's Command in tandem with Dominance (strikeout rate) provides even greater predictive abilities.

	Earned Run Average	
Command	-5.6 Dom	5.6+ Dom
0.0-0.9	6.71	n/a
1.0-1.4	5.56	n/a
1.5-1.9	4.78	4.26
2.0-2.4	4.33	4.10
2.5-2.9	4.31	3.74
3.0-3.9	4.10	3.66
4.0+	3.79	3.09

This helps to highlight the limited upside potential of soft-tossers with pinpoint control. The extra dominance makes a huge difference.

Swinging strike rate as leading indicator *(Stephen Nickrand)*

Swinging strike rate (SwK%) measures the percentage of total pitches against which a batter swings and misses. SwK% can help us validate and forecast a SP's Dominance (K/9) rate, which in turn allows us to identify surgers and faders with greater accuracy.

BENCHMARKS: SwK% baselines for SP are 8.0% in AL, 8.4% in NL; Expected Dom (xDom) can be estimated from SwK%; and a pitcher's individual SwK% does not regress to league norms.

The few starters per year who have a 12.0% or higher SwK% are near-locks to have a 9.0 Dom or greater. In contrast, starters with a 7.0% or lower SwK% have nearly no chance at posting even an average Dom. Finally, use an 8.5% SwK% as an acceptable threshold when searching for SP based on this metric; raise it to 9.5% to begin to find SwK% difference-makers.

Fastball velocity and Dominance rate *(Stephen Nickrand)*

It is intuitive that an increase in fastball velocity for starting pitchers leads to more strikeouts. But how much?

Research shows that the vast majority of SP with significant fastball velocity gains

- experience a significant Dom gain during the same season.
- are likely to give back those gains during the following season.
- are likely to increase their Dom the following season, but the magnitude of the Dom increase usually is small.

The vast majority of SP with significant fastball velocity losses

- are likely to experience a significant Dom decrease during the same season.

Those SP with significant fastball velocity losses from one season to the next are just as likely to experience a fastball velocity or Dom increase as they are to experience a fastball or Dom decrease, and the amounts of the increase/decrease are nearly identical.

First-pitch strike rate as leading indicator *(Stephen Nickrand)*
The measurement of a pitcher's rate of first-pitch strikes (FpK%) can help us validate and forecast a pitcher's Control (BB/9) rate. As first-pitch strike rate increases, walks are very likely to go down, and WHIP will follow. As it goes up, walks are likely to increase, as will WHIP. So if you're wondering if a pitcher's newfound good control is likely to hold, check out his FpK%.

The FpK% baseline is 60% for starting pitchers and does not vary significantly by league. Expected Ctl (xCtl) can be estimated from FpK%, and a starting pitcher's individual FpK% does not regress to league norms. BENCHMARKS: Elite pitchers will have a FpK% above 68% and most of them will have a Ctl below 2.0. Avoid pitchers with a FpK% below 55%, as they are likely to have a Ctl at or above 4.0.

First-pitch strikes increase with age *(Ed DeCaria)*
On average, pitchers lose about 0.2 mph per season off their fastballs. Over time, this coincides with decreases in swinging strike rate (SwK%) and overall strikeout rate (K/PA)—the inevitable effects of aging. But one thing that pitchers can do to delay these effects is to throw more first pitch strikes.

Individual pitcher first pitch strike rates (FpK%) increase at a rate of 0.5% per year from age 22 to 26. Pitchers then typically add another 0.5-1.0% as they settle into their respective peak levels. Once pitchers reach their peaks, first pitch strike rate tends not to decline with age—it is a skill that pitchers own until retirement, even as their other physical skills deteriorate.

Younger pitchers (under age 26) with above average SwK% but below average FpK% make for great breakout targets.

Power/contact rating
(BB + K) / IP
Measures the level by which a pitcher allows balls to be put into play. In general, extreme power pitchers can be successful even with poor defensive teams. Power pitchers tend to have greater longevity in the game. Contact pitchers with poor defenses behind them are high risks to have poor W-L records and ERA. BENCHMARKS: A level of 1.13+ describes pure throwers. A level of .93 or less describes high contact pitchers.

Balls in Play

Balls in play (BIP)
(Batters faced − (BB + HBP + SAC)) + H − K
The total number of batted balls that are hit fair, both hits and outs. An analysis of how these balls are hit—on the ground, in the air, hits, outs, etc.—can provide analytical insight, from player skill levels to the impact of luck on statistical output.

Batting average on balls in play *(Voros McCracken)*
(H − HR) / (Batters faced − (BB + HBP + SAC)) + H − K − HR
Abbreviated as BABIP; also called hit rate (H%), this is the percent of balls hit into the field of play that fall for hits. In 2000, Voros McCracken published a study that concluded "there is little if any difference among major league pitchers in their ability to prevent hits on balls hit in the field of play." His assertion was that, while a Johan Santana would have a better ability to prevent a batter from getting wood on a ball, or perhaps keeping the ball in the park, once that ball was hit in the field of play, the probability of it falling for a hit was virtually no different than for any other pitcher.

Among the findings in his study were:

- There is little correlation between what a pitcher does one year in the stat and what he will do the next. This is not true with other significant stats (BB, K, HR).
- You can better predict a pitcher's hits per balls in play from the rate of the rest of the pitcher's team than from the pitcher's own rate.

This last point brings a team's defense into the picture. It begs the question, when a batter gets a hit, is it because the pitcher made a bad pitch, the batter took a good swing, or the defense was not positioned correctly?

BABIP as a leading indicator *(Voros McCracken)*
The league average is 30%, which is also the level that individual performances will regress to on a year to year basis. Any +/- variance of 3% or more can affect a pitcher's ERA.

Pitchers will often post hit rates per balls-in-play that are far off from the league average, but then revert to the mean the following year. As such, we can use that mean to project the direction of a pitcher's ERA.

Subsequent research has shown that ground ball or fly ball propensity has some impact on this rate.

Hit rate *(See Batting average on balls in play)*

Opposition batting average (OBA)
Hits allowed / (Batters faced − (BB + HBP + SAC))
The batting average achieved by opposing batters against a pitcher. BENCHMARKS: The best pitchers will have levels less than .250; the worst pitchers levels more than .300.

Opposition on base average (OOB)
(Hits allowed + BB) / ((Batters faced − (BB + HBP + SAC)) + Hits allowed + BB)
The on base average achieved by opposing batters against a pitcher. BENCHMARK: The best pitchers will have levels less than .300; the worst pitchers levels more than .375.

Walks plus hits divided by innings pitched (WHIP)
Essentially the same measure as opposition on base average, but used for Rotisserie purposes. BENCHMARKS: A WHIP of less than 1.20 is considered top level; more than 1.50 indicative of poor performance. Levels less than 1.00—allowing fewer runners than IP—represent extraordinary performance and are rarely maintained over time.

Ground ball, line drive, fly ball percentage (G/L/F)

The percentage of all balls-in-play that are hit on the ground, in the air and as line drives. For a pitcher, the ability to pitch to a ground ball or fly ball extreme can contribute to his statistical output exceeding his demonstrated skill level.

Ground ball tendency as a leading indicator *(John Burnson)*

Ground ball pitchers tend to give up fewer HRs than do fly ball pitchers. There is also evidence that GB pitchers have higher hit rates. In other words, a ground ball has a higher chance of being a hit than does a fly ball that is not out of the park.

GB pitchers have lower strikeout rates. We should be more forgiving of a low strikeout rate (under 5.5 K/9) if it belongs to an extreme ground ball pitcher.

GB pitchers have a lower ERA but a higher WHIP than do fly ball pitchers. On balance, GB pitchers come out ahead, even when considering strikeouts, because a lower ERA also leads to more wins.

Groundball and strikeout tendencies as indicators

(Mike Dranchak)

Pitchers were assembled into 9 groups based on the following profiles (minimum 23 starts in 2005):

Profile	Ground Ball Rate
Ground Ball	higher than 47%
Neutral	42% to 47%
Fly Ball	less than 42%

Profile	Strikeout Rate (k/9)
Strikeout	higher than 6.6 k/9
Average	5.4 to 6.6 k/9
Soft-Tosser	less than 5.4 k/9

Findings: Pitchers with higher strikeout rates had better ERAs and WHIPs than pitchers with lower strikeout rates, regardless of ground ball profile. However, for pitchers with similar strikeout rates, those with higher ground ball rates had better ERAs and WHIPs than those with lower ground ball rates.

Pitchers with higher strikeout rates tended to strand more baserunners than those with lower K rates. Fly ball pitchers tended to strand fewer runners than their GB or neutral counterparts within their strikeout profile.

Ground ball pitchers (especially those who lacked high-dominance) yielded more home runs per fly ball than did fly ball pitchers. However, the ERA risk was mitigated by the fact that ground ball pitchers (by definition) gave up fewer fly balls to begin with.

Extreme GB/FB pitchers *(Patrick Davitt)*

Among pitchers with normal strikeout levels, extreme GB pitchers (>3–7% of all batters faced) have ERAs about 0.4 runs lower than normal-GB% pitchers but only slight WHIP advantages. Extreme FB% pitchers (32% FB) show no ERA benefits.

Among High-K (>=24% of BF), however, extreme GBers have ERAs about 0.5 runs lower than normal-GB pitchers, and WHIPs about five points lower. Extreme FB% pitchers have ERAs about 0.2 runs lower than normal-FB pitchers, and WHIPs about 10 points lower.

Revisiting flyballs *(Jason Collette)*

The increased emphasis on defensive positioning is often associated with infield shifting, but the same data also influences how outfielders are positioned. Some managers are positioning OFs more aggressively than just the customary few steps per a right- or left-handed swinging batter. Five of the top 10 defensive efficiency teams in 2013 —OAK, STL, MIA, LAA and KC—also had parks among the top 10 in HR suppression.

Before dismissing flyball pitchers as toxic assets, pay more attention to park factors and OF defensive talent. In particular, be a little more willing to roster fly ball pitchers who pitch both in front of good defensive OFs and in good pitchers' parks.

Line drive percentage as a leading indicator *(Seth Samuels)*

The percentage of ball-in-play that are line drives is beyond a pitcher's control. Line drives do the most damage; from 1994-2003, here were the expected hit rates and number of total bases per type of BIP.

	Type of BIP		
	GB	FB	LD
H%	26%	23%	56%
Total bases	0.29	0.57	0.80

Despite the damage done by LDs, pitchers do not have any innate skill to avoid them. There is little relationship between a pitcher's LD% one year and his rate the next year. All rates tend to regress towards a mean of 22.6%.

However, GB pitchers do have a slight ability to prevent LDs (21.7%) and extreme GB hurlers even moreso (18.5%). Extreme FB pitchers have a slight ability to prevent LDs (21.1%) as well.

Home run to fly ball rate (hr/f)

HR / FB

The percent of fly balls that are hit for home runs.

hr/f as a leading indicator *(John Burnson)*

McCracken's work focused on "balls in play," omitting home runs from the study. However, pitchers also do not have much control over the percentage of fly balls that turn into HR. Research shows that there is an underlying rate of HR as a percentage of fly balls of about 10%. A pitcher's HR/FB rate will vary each year but always tends to regress to that 10%. The element that pitchers do have control over is the number of fly balls they allow. That is the underlying skill or deficiency that controls their HR rate.

"Just Enough" home runs as a leading indicator *(Brian Slack)*

Using ESPN's Home Run Tracker data, we analyzed year-to-year consistency of "Just Enough" home runs (those that clear the fence by less than 10 vertical feet or land less than one fence height past the fence). For the 528 starting pitchers who logged enough innings to qualify for the ERA title in consecutive years from 2006 through 2016 season, research showed:

- The percentage of Just Enough home runs that a pitcher gives up gravitates towards league average (32%) the following year.
- There is only a tenuous connection between a pitcher's ability to limit the percentage of Just Enough home runs and a pitcher's HR/FB rate. So we should avoid the

assumption that a pitcher with a high percentage of Just Enough home runs will necessarily improve his HR/FB rate (and presumably ERA) the following year, or vice versa.

- This means be careful not to over-draft a pitcher based solely on the idea of HR/FB improvement in the coming year. Conversely, one should not automatically avoid pitchers with perceived HR/FB downside.

Opposition home runs per game (hr/9)
(HR Allowed x 9 / IP)
Also, expected opposition HR rate = (FB x 0.10) x 9 / IP
Measures how many HR a pitcher allows per game equivalent. Since FB tend to go yard at about a 10% rate, we can also estimate this rate off of fly balls. BENCHMARK: The best pitchers will have hr/9 levels of less than 1.0.

Runs

Expected earned run average (xERA)
Gill and Reeve version: *(.575 x H [per 9 IP]) + (.94 x HR [per 9 IP]) + (.28 x BB [per 9 IP]) – (.01 x K [per 9 IP]) – Normalizing Factor*

John Burnson version (used in this book):
(xER x 9)/IP, where xER is defined as
xER% x (FB/10) + (1-xS%) x [0.3 x (BIP – FB/10) + BB]
where xER% = 0.96 – (0.0284 x (GB/FB))
and
xS% = (64.5 + (K/9 x 1.2) – (BB/9 x (BB/9 + 1)) / 20)
+ ((0.0012 x (GB%^2)) – (0.001 x GB%) - 2.4)
xERA represents the an equivalent of what a pitcher's real ERA might be, calculated solely with skills-based measures. It is not influenced by situation-dependent factors.

Expected ERA variance
xERA – ERA
The variance between a pitcher's ERA and his xERA is a measure of over or underachievement. A positive variance indicates the potential for a pitcher's ERA to rise. A negative variance indicates the potential for ERA improvement. BENCHMARK: Discount variances that are less than 0.50. Any variance more than 1.00 (one run per game) is regarded as a strong indicator of future change.

Projected xERA or projected ERA?
Which should we be using to forecast a pitcher's ERA? Projected xERA is more accurate for looking ahead on a purely skills basis. Projected ERA includes *situation-dependent* events—bullpen support, park factors, etc.—which are reflected better by ERA. The optimal approach is to use both gauges as *a range of expectation* for forecasting purposes.

Strand rate (S%)
(H + BB – ER) / (H + BB – HR)
Measures the percentage of allowed runners a pitcher strands (earned runs only), which incorporates both individual pitcher skill and bullpen effectiveness. BENCHMARKS: The most adept at stranding runners will have S% levels over 75%. Those with

rates over 80% will have artificially low ERAs which will be prone to relapse. Levels below 65% will inflate ERA but have a high probability of regression.

Expected strand rate *(Michael Weddell)*
*73.935 + K/9 - 0.116 * (BB/9*(BB/9+1))*
*+ (0.0047 * GB%^2 - 0.3385 * GB%)*
+ (MAX(2,MIN(4,IP/G))/2-1)
+ (0.82 if left-handed)
This formula is based on three core skills: strikeouts per nine innings, walks per nine innings, and groundballs per balls in play, with adjustments for whether the pitcher is a starter or reliever (measured by IP/G), and his handedness.

Strand rate as a leading indicator *(Ed DeCaria)*
Strand rate often regresses/rebounds toward past rates (usually 69-74%), resulting in Year 2 ERA changes:

% of Pitchers with Year 2 Regression/Rebound			
Y1 S%	RP	SP	LR
<60%	100%	94%	94%
65	81%	74%	88%
70	53%	48%	65%
75	55%	85%	100%
80	80%	100%	100%
85	100%	100%	100%

Typical ERA Regression/Rebound in Year 2			
Y1 S%	RP	SP	LR
<60%	-2.54	-2.03	-2.79
65	-1.00	-0.64	-0.93
70	-0.10	-0.05	-0.44
75	0.24	0.54	0.75
80	1.15	1.36	2.29
85	1.71	2.21	n/a

Starting pitchers (SP) have a narrower range of strand rate outcomes than do relievers (RP) or swingmen/long relievers (LR). **Relief pitchers** with Y1 strand rates of <=67% or >=78% are likely to experience a +/- ERA regression in Y2. **Starters and swingmen/long relievers** with Y1 strand rates of <=65% or >=75% are likely to experience a +/- ERA regression in Y2. Pitchers with strand rates that deviate more than a few points off of their individual expected strand rates are likely to experience some degree of ERA regression in Y2. Over-performing (or "lucky") pitchers are more likely than underperforming (or "unlucky") pitchers to see such a correction.

Wins

Expected Wins (xW) *(Matt Cederholm)*
[(Team runs per game)^1.8]/[(Pitcher ERA)^1.8 + (Team runs per game)^1.8] x 0.72 x GS
Starting pitchers' win totals are often at odds with their ERA. Attempts to find a strictly skill-based analysis of this phenomenon haven't worked, but there is a powerful tool in the toolbox: Bill James' Pythagorean Theorem. While usually applied to team outcomes, recent research has shown that its validity holds up when applied to individual starting pitchers.

One key to applying the Pythagorean Theorem is factoring in no-decisions. Research shows that the average no-decision rate is

28% of starts, regardless of the type or quality of the pitcher or his team, with no correlation in ND% from one season to the next.

Overall, 70% of pitchers whose expected wins varied from actual wins showed regression in wins per start in the following year, making variation from Expected Wins a good leading indicator.

Projecting/chasing wins

There are five events that need to occur in order for a pitcher to post a single win...

1. He must pitch well, allowing few runs.
2. The offense must score enough runs.
3. The defense must successfully field all batted balls.
4. The bullpen must hold the lead.
5. The manager must leave the pitcher in for 5 innings, and not remove him if the team is still behind.

Of these five events, only one is within the control of the pitcher. As such, projecting or chasing wins based on skills alone can be an exercise in futility.

Home field advantage *(John Burnson)*

A 2006 study found that home starting pitchers get credited with a win in 38% of their outings. Visiting team starters are credited with a win in 33% of their outings.

Usage

Batters faced per game *(Craig Wright)*

$((Batters\ faced - (BB + HBP + SAC)) + H + BB) / G$

A measure of pitcher usage and one of the leading indicators for potential pitcher burnout.

Workload

Research suggests that there is a finite number of innings in a pitcher's arm. This number varies by pitcher, by development cycle, and by pitching style and repertoire. We can measure a pitcher's potential for future arm problems and/or reduced effectiveness (burnout):

Sharp increases in usage from one year to the next. Common wisdom has suggested that pitchers who significantly increase their workload from one year to the next are candidates for burnout symptoms. This has often been called the Verducci Effect, after writer Tom Verducci. BaseballHQ.com analyst Michael Weddell tested pitchers with sharp workload increases during the period 1988-2008 and found that no such effect exists.

Starters' overuse. Consistent "batters faced per game" (BF/G) levels of 28.0 or higher, combined with consistent seasonal IP totals of 200 or more may indicate burnout potential, especially with pitchers younger than 25. Within a season, a BF/G of more than 30.0 with a projected IP total of 200 may indicate a late season fade.

Relievers' overuse. Warning flags should be up for relievers who post in excess of 100 IP in a season, while averaging fewer than 2 IP per outing.

When focusing solely on minor league pitchers, research results are striking:

Stamina: Virtually every minor league pitcher who had a BF/G of 28.5 or more in one season experienced a drop-off in BF/G the following year. Many were unable to ever duplicate that previous level of durability.

Performance: Most pitchers experienced an associated drop-off in their BPVs in the years following the 28.5 BF/G season. Some were able to salvage their effectiveness later on by moving to the bullpen.

Protecting young pitchers *(Craig Wright)*

There is a link between some degree of eventual arm trouble and a history of heavy workloads in a pitcher's formative years. Some recommendations from this research:

Teenagers (A-ball): No 200 IP seasons and no BF/G over 28.5 in any 150 IP span. No starts on three days rest.

Ages 20-22: Average no more than 105 pitches per start with a single game ceiling of 130 pitches.

Ages 23-24: Average no more than 110 pitches per start with a single game ceiling of 140 pitches.

When possible, a young starter should be introduced to the majors in long relief before he goes into the rotation.

Overall Performance Analysis

Base Performance Value (BPV)

$((Dominance\ Rate - 5.0)\ x\ 18)$
$+ ((4.0 - Walk\ Rate)\ x\ 27))$
$+ (Ground\ ball\ rate\ as\ a\ whole\ number - 40\%)$

A single value that describes a player's overall raw skill level. This is more useful than traditional statistical gauges to track player performance trends and project future statistical output. The formula combines the individual raw skills of power, control and the ability to keep the ball down in the zone, all characteristics that are unaffected by most external factors. In tandem with a pitcher's strand rate, it provides a more complete picture of the elements that contribute to ERA, and therefore serves as an accurate tool to project likely changes in ERA. **BENCHMARKS:** A BPV of 50 is the minimum level required for long-term success. The elite of the bullpen aces will have BPVs in excess of 100 and it is rare for these stoppers to enjoy long term success with consistent levels under 75.

Base Performance Index (BPX)

BPV scaled to league average to account for year-to-year fluctuations in league-wide statistical performance. It's a snapshot of a player's overall skills compared to an average player. **BENCHMARK:** A level of 100 means a player had a league-average BPV in that given season.

Runs above replacement (RAR)

An estimate of the number of runs a player contributes above a "replacement level" player.

Batters create runs; pitchers save runs. But are batters and pitchers who have comparable RAR levels truly equal in value? Pitchers might be considered to have higher value. Saving an additional run is more important than producing an additional run. A pitcher who throws a shutout is guaranteed to win that game, whereas no matter how many runs a batter produces, his team can still lose given poor pitching support.

To calculate RAR for pitchers:

1. Start with the replacement level league ERA.
2. Subtract the pitcher's ERA. (To calculate projected RAR, use the pitcher's xERA.)
3. Multiply by number of games played, calculated as plate appearances (IP x 4.34) divided by 38.
4. Multiply the resulting RAR level by 1.08 to account for the variance between earned runs and total runs.

Skill-specific aging patterns for pitchers *(Ed DeCaria)*

Baseball forecasters obsess over "peak age" of player performance because we must understand player ascent toward and decline from that peak to predict future value. Most published aging analyses are done using composite estimates of value such as OPS or linear weights. By contrast, fantasy GMs are typically more concerned with category-specific player value (K, ERA, WHIP, etc.). We can better forecast what matters most by analyzing peak age of individual baseball skills rather than overall player value.

For pitchers, prior research has shown that pitcher value peaks somewhere in the late 20s to early 30s. But how does aging affect each demonstrable pitching skill?

Strikeout rate (k/9): Declines fairly linearly beginning at age 25.

Walk rate (bb/9): Improves until age 25 and holds somewhat steady until age 29, at which point it begins to steadily worsen. Deteriorating k/9 and bb/9 rates result in inefficiency, as it requires far more pitches to get an out. For starting pitchers, this affects the ability to pitch deep into games.

Innings Pitched per game (IP/G): Among starters, it improves slightly until age 27, then tails off considerably with age, costing pitchers nearly one full IP/G by age 33 and one more by age 39.

Hit rate (H%): Among pitchers, H% appears to increase slowly but steadily as pitchers age, to the tune of .002-.003 points per year.

Strand rate (S%): Very similar to hit rate, except strand rate decreases with age rather than increasing. GB%/LD%/FB%: Line drives increase steadily from age 24 onward, and outfield flies increase beginning at age 31. Because 70%+ of line drives fall for hits, and 10%+ of fly balls become home runs, this spells trouble for aging pitchers.

Home runs per fly ball (hr/f): As each year passes, a higher percentage of a pitcher's fly balls become home runs allowed increases with age.

Catchers' effect on pitching *(Thomas Hanrahan)*

A typical catcher handles a pitching staff better after having been with a club for a few years. Research has shown that there is an improvement in team ERA of approximately 0.37 runs from a catcher's rookie season to his prime years with a club. Expect a pitcher's ERA to be higher than expected if he is throwing to a rookie backstop.

First productive season *(Michael Weddell)*

To find those starting pitchers who are about to post their first productive season in the majors (10 wins, 150 IP, ERA of 4.00 or less), look for:

- Pitchers entering their age 23-26 seasons, especially those about to pitch their age 25 season.
- Pitchers who already have good skills, shown by an xERA in the prior year of 4.25 or less.
- Pitchers coming off of at least a partial season in the majors without a major health problem.
- To the extent that one speculates on pitchers who are one skill away, look for pitchers who only need to improve their control (bb/9).

Overall pitching breakout profile *(Brandon Kruse)*

A breakout performance is defined here as one where a player posts a Rotisserie value of $20 or higher after having never achieved $10 previously. These criteria are primarily used to validate an apparent breakout in the current season but may also be used carefully to project a potential breakout for an upcoming season.

- Age 27 or younger
- Minimum 5.6 Dom, 2.0 Cmd, 1.1 hr/9 and 50 BPV
- Maximum 30% hit rate
- Minimum 71% strand rate
- Starters should have a H% no greater than the previous year; relievers should show improved command
- Maximum xERA of 4.00

Bounceback fallacy *(Patrick Davitt)*

It is conventional wisdom that a pitcher often or even usually follows a bad year (value decline of more than 50%) with a significant "bounceback" that offers profit opportunity for the canny owner. But research showed the owner is extremely unlikely to get a full bounceback, and in fact, is more likely to suffer a further decline or uselessly small recovery than even a partial bounceback. The safest bet is a $30+ pitcher who has a collapse—but even then, bid to only about half of the previous premium value.

Pitchers crossing leagues *(Bob Berger)*

The AL has higher league-wide ERA and lower K/9 when compared to the NL. Fantasy owners should consider adjusting their ERA, WHIP, and K/9 expectations for pitchers moving to the "other" league. Pitchers moving to the NL may perform better than expected based on their recent career trends; pitchers moving to the AL may perform worse than expected.

Closers

Saves

There are six events that need to occur in order for a relief pitcher to post a single save:

1. The starting pitcher and middle relievers must pitch well.
2. The offense must score enough runs.
3. It must be a reasonably close game.
4. The manager must put the pitcher in for a save opportunity.
5. The pitcher must pitch well and hold the lead.
6. The manager must let him finish the game.

Of these six events, only one is within the control of the relief pitcher. As such, projecting saves for a reliever has less to do with skills than opportunity. However, pitchers with excellent skills may create opportunity for themselves.

Saves conversion rate (Sv%)
Saves / Save Opportunities
The percentage of save opportunities that are successfully converted. BENCHMARK: We look for a minimum 80% for long-term success.

Leverage index (LI) *(Tom Tango)*
Leverage index measures the amount of swing in the possible change in win probability indexed against an average value of 1.00. Thus, relievers who come into games in various situations create a composite score and if that average score is higher than 1.00, then their manager is showing enough confidence in them to try to win games with them. If the average score is below 1.00, then the manager is using them, but not showing nearly as much confidence that they can win games.

Saves chances and wins *(Patrick Davitt)*
Some fantasy owners think that good teams get more saves because they generate more wins. Other owners think that poor teams get more saves because more of their wins are by narrow margins. The "good-team" side is probably on firmer ground, though there are enough exceptions that we should be cautious about drawing broad inferences.

The 2014 study confirmed what Craig Neuman found years earlier: The argument "more wins leads to more saves" is generally correct. Over five studied seasons, the percentage of wins that were saved (Sv%W) was about 50%, and half of all team-seasons fell in the Sv%W range of 48%-56%. As a result, high-saves seasons were more common for high-win teams.

That wins-saves connection for individual team-seasons was much less solid, however, and we observed many outliers. Data for individual team-seasons showed wide ranges of both Sv%W and actual saves.

Finally, higher-win teams do indeed get more blowout wins, but while poorer teams had a higher percentage (73%) of close wins (three runs or fewer) than better teams (56%), good teams' higher number of wins meant they still had more close wins, more save opportunities and more saves, again with many outliers among individual team-seasons.

Origin of closers
History has long maintained that ace closers are not easily recognizable early on in their careers, so that every season does see its share of the unexpected. . Brad Brach, Santiago Casilla, Sean Doolittle, Brad Hand, Greg Holland, Jim Johnson, Corey Knebel, Hector Neris, Bud Norris, Felipe Rivero, Justin Wilson… who would have thought it a year ago?

Accepted facts, all of which have some element of truth:
- You cannot find major league closers from pitchers who were closers in the minors.
- Closers begin their careers as starters.
- Closers are converted set-up men.

- Closers are pitchers who were unable to develop a third effective pitch.

More simply, closers are a product of circumstance.

Are the minor leagues a place to look at all?

From 1990-2004, there were 280 twenty-save seasons in Double-A and Triple-A. Over that period, there were only 13 pitchers ever saved 20 games in the majors and only five who ever posted more than one 20-save season: John Wetteland, Mark Wohlers, Ricky Bottalico, Braden Looper and Francisco Cordero.

More recent data is even more pessimistic:

Year	# with 20 Svs	MLB closers
2006	25	none
2007	22	none
2008	19	none
2009	17	none
2010	14	Craig Kimbrel
2011	16	none
2012	16	A.J. Ramos
2013	16	none
2014	12	none
2015	17	none

That's 177 twenty-save seasons and only two major league closers.

One of the reasons that minor league closers rarely become major league closers is because, in general, they do not get enough innings in the minors to sufficiently develop their arms into big-league caliber.

In fact, organizations do not look at minor league closing performance seriously, assigning that role to pitchers who they do not see as legitimate prospects. The average age of minor league closers over the past decade has been 27.5.

Elements of saves success
The task of finding future closing potential comes down to looking at two elements:

Talent: The raw skills to mow down hitters for short periods of time. Optimal BPVs over 100, but not under 75.

Opportunity: The more important element, yet the one that pitchers have no control over.

There are pitchers that have Talent, but not Opportunity. These pitchers are not given a chance to close for a variety of reasons (e.g. being blocked by a solid front-liner in the pen, being left-handed, etc.), but are good to own because they will not likely hurt your pitching staff. You just can't count on them for saves, at least not in the near term.

There are pitchers that have Opportunity, but not Talent. MLB managers decide who to give the ball to in the 9th inning based on their own perceptions about what skills are required to succeed, even if those perceived "skills" don't translate into acceptable metrics.

Those pitchers without the metrics may have some initial short-term success, but their long-term prognosis is poor and they are high risks to your roster. Classic examples of the short life span of these types of pitchers include Matt Karchner, Heath Slocumb, Ryan Kohlmeier, Dan Miceli, Joe Borowski and Danny Kolb. More recent examples include Tom Wilhelmsen, Kevin Gregg and Jeanmar Gomez.

Closers' job retention *(Michael Weddell)*

Of pitchers with 20 or more saves in one year, only 67.5% of these closers earned 20 or more saves the following year. The variables that best predicted whether a closer would avoid this attrition:

- *Saves history:* Career saves was the most important factor.
- *Age:* Closers are most likely to keep their jobs at age 27. For long-time closers, their growing career saves totals more than offset the negative impact of their advanced ages. Older closers without a long history of racking up saves tend to be bad candidates for retaining their roles.
- *Performance:* Actual performance, measured by ERA+, was of only minor importance.
- *Being right-handed:* Increased the odds of retaining the closer's role by 9% over left-handers.

How well can we predict which closers will keep their jobs? Of the 10 best closers during 1989-2007, 90% saved at least 20 games during the following season. Of the 10 worst bets, only 20% saved at least 20 games the next year.

Closer volatility history

Year	Closers Drafted	Avg R$	Closers Failed	Failure %	New Sources
2008	32	$17.78	10	31%	11
2009	28	$17.56	9	32%	13
2010	28	$16.96	7	25%	13
2011	30	$15.47	11	37%	8
2012	29	$15.28	19	66%	18
2013	29	$15.55	9	31%	13
2014	28	$15.54	11	39%	15
2015	29	$14.79	13	45%	16
2016	33	$13.30	19	58%	17
2017	32	$13.63	17	53%	15

Drafted refers to the number of saves sources purchased in both LABR and Tout Wars experts leagues each year. These only include relievers drafted specifically for saves speculation. *Avg R$* refers to the average purchase price of these pitchers in the AL-only and NL-only leagues. *Failed* is the number (and percentage) of saves sources drafted that did not return at least 50% of their value that year. The failures include those that lost their value due to ineffectiveness, injury or managerial decision. *New Sources* are arms that were drafted for less than $10 (if drafted at all) but finished with at least double-digit saves.

The failed saves investments in 2017 were Cam Bedrosian, Dellin Betances, Zack Britton, Aroldis Chapman, Sam Dyson, Jeurys Familia, Nef-tali Feliz, Jeanmar Gomez, Kelvin Herrera, Jim Johnson, Shawn Kelley, Brandon Maurer, Mark Melancon, Seung-Hwan Oh, AJ Ramos, Francis-co Rodriguez and Tony Watson. The new sources in 2017 were Brad Brach, Matt Bush, Santiago Casilla, Alexander Claudio, Sean Doolittle, Brad Hand, Corey Knebel, Hector Neris, Bud Norris, Felipe Rivero, Trevor Rosenthal, Blake Treinen, Arodys Vizcaino, Justin Wilson and Brad Ziegler. Note that several of these did not finish the season as their team's closer.

The continuing erosion of fantasy bullpen value stabilized slightly in 2017. Owners spent about 33 cents more per pitcher, on average, than 2016. This is insignificant. In 2015, there were five potential closers drafted for less than $10, which used to be the standard floor value for saves speculation. In 2016, that number increased to 10 pitchers. In 2017, there were 11. As MLB managers continue to micro-manage their bullpens, investments in closers will likely continue to be depressed.

Closers and multi-year performance *(Patrick Davitt)*

A team having an "established closer"—even a successful one—in a given year does not affect how many of that team's wins are saved in the next year. However, a top closer (40-plus saves) in a given year has a significantly greater chance to retain his role in the subsequent season.

Research of saves and wins data over several seasons found that the percentage of wins that are saved is consistently 50%-54%, irrespective of whether the saves were concentrated in the hands of a "top closer" or passed around to the dreaded "committee" of lesser closers. But it also found that about two-thirds of high-save closers reprised their roles the next season, while three-quarters of low-save closers did not. Moreover, closers who held the role for two or three straight seasons averaged 34 saves per season while closers new to the role averaged 27.

BPV as a leading indicator *(Doug Dennis)*

Research has shown that base performance value (BPV) is an excellent indicator of long-term success as a closer. Here are 20-plus saves seasons, by year:

		|------------------BPV----------------|	
Year	No.	100+	75+	<75
1999	26	27%	54%	46%
2000	24	25%	54%	46%
2001	25	56%	80%	20%
2002	25	60%	72%	28%
2003	25	36%	64%	36%
2004	23	61%	61%	39%
2005	25	36%	64%	36%
2006	25	52%	72%	28%
2007	23	52%	74%	26%
MEAN	*25*	*45%*	*66%*	*34%*

Though 20-saves success with a 75+ BPV is only a 66% percentage play in any given year, the below-75 group is composed of closers who are rarely able to repeat the feat in the following season:

Year	No. with BPV < 75	No. who followed up 20+ saves <75 BPV
1999	12	2
2000	11	2
2001	5	2
2002	7	3
2003	9	3
2004	9	2
2005	9	1
2006	7	3
2007	6	0

Other Relievers

Projecting holds *(Doug Dennis)*

Here are some general rules of thumb for identifying pitchers who might be in line to accumulate holds. The percentages represent the portion of 2003's top holds leaders who fell into the category noted.

1. Left-handed set-up men with excellent BPIs. (43%)

2. A "go-to" right-handed set-up man with excellent BPIs. This is the one set-up RHer that a manager turns to with a small lead in the 7th or 8th innings. These pitchers also tend to vulture wins. (43%, but 6 of the top 9)

3. Excellent BPIs, but not a firm role as the main LHed or RHed set-up man. Roles change during the season; cream rises to the top. Relievers projected to post great BPIs often overtake lesser set-up men in-season. (14%)

Reliever efficiency percent (REff%)

(Wins + Saves + Holds) / (Wins + Losses + SaveOpps + Holds)

This is a measure of how often a reliever contributes positively to the outcome of a game. A record of consistent, positive impact on game outcomes breeds managerial confidence, and that confidence could pave the way to save opportunities. For those pitchers suddenly thrust into a closer's role, this formula helps gauge their potential to succeed based on past successes in similar roles. BENCHMARK: Minimum of 80%.

Vulture

A pitcher, typically a middle reliever, who accumulates an unusually high number of wins by preying on other pitchers' misfortunes. More accurately, this is a pitcher typically brought into a game after a starting pitcher has put his team behind, and then pitches well enough and long enough to allow his offense to take the lead, thereby "vulturing" a win from the starter.

In-Season Analysis

Pure Quality Starts

Pure Quality Starts (PQS) says that the smallest unit of measure should not be the "event" but instead be the "game." Within that game, we can accumulate all the strikeouts, hits and walks, and evaluate that outing as a whole. After all, when a pitcher takes the mound, he is either "on" or "off" his game; he is either dominant or struggling, or somewhere in between.

In PQS, we give a starting pitcher credit for exhibiting certain skills in each of his starts. Then by tracking his "PQS Score" over time, we can follow his progress. A starter earns one point for each of the following criteria:

1. *The pitcher must go more than 6 innings (record at least one out in the 7th).* This measures stamina.

2. *He must allow fewer hits than innings pitched.* This measures hit prevention.

3. *His number of strikeouts must equal to or more than 5.* This measures dominance.

4. *He must strike out at least three times as many batters as he walks (or have a minimum of three strikeouts if he hasn't walked a batter).* This measures command.

5. *He must not allow a home run.* This measures his ability to keep the ball in the park.

A perfect PQS score is 5. Any pitcher who averages 3 or more over the course of the season is probably performing admirably. The nice thing about PQS is it allows you to approach each start as more than an all-or-nothing event.

Note the absence of earned runs. No matter how many runs a pitcher allows, if he scores high on the PQS scale, he has hurled

a good game in terms of his base skills. The number of runs allowed—a function of not only the pitcher's ability but that of his bullpen and defense—will tend to even out over time.

It doesn't matter if a few extra balls got through the infield, or the pitcher was given the hook in the fourth or sixth inning, or the bullpen was able to strand their inherited baserunners. When we look at performance in the aggregate, those events do matter, and will affect a pitcher's peripherals and ERA. But with PQS, the minutia is less relevant than the overall performance.

In the end, a dominating performance is a dominating performance, whether Chris Sale is hurling a 2-hit shutout or giving up three runs while striking out 12 in 7 IP. And a disaster is still a disaster, whether Chris Tillman gets a 6th inning hook after giving up 5 runs on 11 hits, or "takes one for the team" and gets shelled for 9 runs in 1.1 innings.

Skill versus consistency

Two pitchers have identical 4.50 ERAs and identical 3.0 PQS averages. Their PQS logs look like this:

PITCHER A:	3	3	3	3	3
PITCHER B:	5	0	5	0	5

Which pitcher would you rather have on your team? The risk-averse manager would choose Pitcher A as he represents the perfectly known commodity. Many fantasy leaguers might opt for Pitcher B because his occasional dominating starts show that there is an upside. His Achilles Heel is inconsistency—he is unable to sustain that high level. Is there any hope for Pitcher B?

- If a pitcher's inconsistency is characterized by more poor starts than good starts, his upside is limited.
- Pitchers with extreme inconsistency rarely get a full season of starts.
- However, inconsistency is neither chronic nor fatal.

The outlook for Pitcher A is actually worse. Disaster avoidance might buy these pitchers more starts, but history shows that the lack of dominating outings is more telling of future potential. In short, consistent mediocrity is bad.

PQS DOMination and DISaster rates *(Gene McCaffrey)*

DOM% is the percentage of a starting pitcher's outings that rate as a PQS-4 or PQS-5. DIS% is the percentage that rate as a PQS-0 or PQS-1.

DOM/DIS percentages open up a new perspective, providing us with two separate scales of performance. In tandem, they measure consistency.

Quality/consistency score (QC)

(DOM% – (2 x DIS%)) x 2

Using PQS and DOM/DIS percentages, this score measures both the quality of performance as well as start-to-start consistency.

The predictive value of PQS *(Arik Florimonte)*

Using data from 2010-2015, research showed that PQS values can be used to project future starts. A pitcher who even threw only one PQS-DOM start had a slightly better chance of throwing another DOM in his subsequent start. For a pitcher who posts two, three, or even four PQS-DOMs in a row, the streak does portend better results to come. The longer the streak, the better the results.

Fantasy owners best positioned to take advantage are those who can frequently choose from multiple similar SP options, such as in a DFS league, or streaming in traditional leagues. In either case, make your evaluations as you normally would (e.g. talent first, then matchups, ballpark or by using BaseballHQ. com's Pitcher Matchups Tool)—and then give a value bump to the pitcher with the hot streak.

PQS correlation with Quality Starts *(Paul Petera)*

PQS	QS%
0	8%
1	18%
2	38%
3	63%
4	87%
5	99%

In-season ERA/xERA variance as a leading indicator
(Matt Cederholm)
Pitchers with large first-half ERA/xERA variances will see regression towards their xERA in the second half, if they are allowed (and are able) to finish out the season. Starters have a stronger regression tendency than relievers, which we would expect to see given the larger sample size. In addition, there is substantial attrition among all types of pitchers, but those who are "unlucky" have a much higher rate.

An important corollary: While a pitcher underperforming his xERA is very likely to rebound in the second half, such regression hinges on his ability to hold onto his job long enough to see that regression come to fruition. Healthy veteran pitchers with an established role are more likely to experience the second half boost than a rookie starter trying to make his mark.

Pure Quality Relief *(Patrick Davitt)*
A system for evaluating reliever outings. The scoring :
1. Two points for the first out, and one point for each subsequent out, to a maximum of four points.
2. One point for having at least one strikeout for every four full outs (one K for 1-4 outs, two Ks for 5-8 outs, etc.).
3. One point for zero baserunners, minus one point for each baserunner, though allowing the pitcher one unpenalized runner for each three full outs (one baserunner for 3-5 outs, two for 6-8 outs, three for nine outs)
4. Minus one point for each earned run, though allowing one ER for 8– or 9-out appearances.
5. An automatic PQR-0 for allowing a home run.

Avoiding relief disasters *(Ed DeCaria)*
Relief disasters (defined as ER>=3 and IP<=3), occur in 5%+ of all appearances. The chance of a disaster exceeds 13% in any 7-day period. To minimize the odds of a disaster, we created a model that produced the following list of factors, in order of influence:
1. Strength of opposing offense
2. Park factor of home stadium
3. BB/9 over latest 31 days (more walks is bad)
4. Pitch count over previous 7 days (more pitches is bad)
5. Latest 31 Days ERA>xERA (recent bad luck continues)

Daily league owners who can slot relievers by individual game should also pay attention to days of rest: pitching on less rest than one is accustomed to increases disaster risk.

Sample size reliability *(Russell Carleton)*
At what point during the season do statistics become reliable indicators of skill? Measured in batters faced:
- 60: K/PA
- 120: BB/PA

Measured in balls in play:
- 50: hr/f
- 80: GB%, FB%
- 600: LD%
- 820: h% (or BABIP)

Unlisted stats did not stabilize over a full season of play. *(Note that 150 BF is roughly equivalent to six outings for a starting pitcher; 550 BF would be 22 starts, etc.)*

April ERA as a leading indicator *(Stephen Nickrand)*
A starting pitcher's April ERA can act as a leading indicator for how his ERA is likely to fare during the balance of the season. A study looked at extreme April ERA results to see what kind of in-season forecasting power they may have. From 2010-2012, 42 SP posted an ERA in April that was at least 2.00 ER better than their career ERA. The findings:
- Pitchers who come out of the gates quickly have an excellent chance at finishing the season with an ERA much better than their career ERA.
- While April ERA gems see their in-season ERA regresses towards their career ERA, their May-Sept ERA is still significantly better than their career ERA.
- Those who stumble out of the gates have a strong chance at posting an ERA worse than their career average, but their in-season ERA improves towards their career ERA.
- April ERA disasters tend to have a May-Sept ERA that closely resembles their career ERA.

Using K–BB% to find SP buying opportunities *(Arik Florimonte)*
Research showed that finding pitchers who have seen an uptick in k–bb% over the past 30 days is one way to search for mid-season replacements from the waiver wire. Using 2014-2016 player-seasons and filtering for starting pitchers with ≥ 100 IP, the k–bb% mean is about 13%. The overall MLB mean is approximately 12%, and the top 50 SP tend to be 14% or higher. The findings:
- Last 30 days k–bb% is useful as a gauge of next 30 days performance.
- Pitchers on the upswing are more likely to climb into the elite ranks than other pitchers of similar YTD numbers; pitchers with a larger uptick show a greater likelihood.
- Last-30 k–bb% surgers could be good mid-season pickups if they are being overlooked by other owners in your league.

Second-half ERA reduction drivers *(Stephen Nickrand)*

It's easy to dismiss first-half-to-second-half improvement among starting pitchers as an unpredictable event. After all, the midpoint of the season is an arbitrary cutoff. Performance swings occur throughout the season.

A study of SP who experienced significant 1H-2H ERA improvement from 2010-2012 examined what indicators drove second-half ERA improvement. Among the findings for those 79 SP with a > 1.00 ERA 1H-2H reduction:

- 97% saw their WHIP decrease, with an average decrease of 0.26
- 97% saw their strand (S%) rate improve, with an average increase of 9%
- 87% saw their BABIP (H%) improve, with an average reduction of 5%
- 75% saw their control (bb/9) rate improve, with an average reduction of 0.8
- 70% saw their HR/9 rate improve, with an average decrease of 0.5
- 68% saw their swinging strike (SwK%) rate improve, with an average increase of 1.4%
- 68% saw their BPV improve, with an average increase of 37
- 67% saw their HR per fly ball rate (hr/f) improve, with an average decrease of 4%
- 53% saw their ground ball (GB%) rate improve, with an average increase of 5%
- 52% saw their dominance (k/9) rate improve, with an average increase of 1.3

These findings highlight the power of H% and S% regression as it relates to ERA and WHIP improvement. In fact, H% and S% are more often correlated with ERA improvement than are improved skills. They also suggest that improved control has a bigger impact on ERA reduction than does increased strikeouts.

Pitcher home/road splits *(Stephen Nickrand)*

One overlooked strategy in leagues that allow frequent transactions is to bench pitchers when they are on the road. Research reveals that several pitching stats and indicators are significantly and consistently worse on the road than at home.

Some home/road rules of thumb for SP:

- If you want to gain significant ground in ERA and WHIP, bench all your average or worse SP on the road.
- A pitcher's win percentage drops by 15% on the road, so don't bank on road starts as a means to catch up in wins.
- Control erodes by 10% on the road, so be especially careful with keeping wild SP in your active lineups when they are away from home.
- NL pitchers at home produce significantly more strikeouts than their AL counterparts and vs. all pitchers on the road.
- hr/9, groundball rate, hit rate, strand rate, and hr/f do not show significant home vs. road variances.

Other Diamonds

The Pitching Postulates

1. Never sign a soft-tosser to a long-term contract.
2. Right-brain dominance has a very long shelf life.
3. A fly ball pitcher who gives up many HRs is expected. A GB pitcher who gives up many HRs is making mistakes.
4. Never draft a contact fly ball pitcher who plays in a hitter's park.
5. Only bad teams ever have a need for an inning-eater.
6. Never chase wins.

Balls

The logical variable that explains the 2017 struggles of previously palatable pitchers like Gerrit Cole, Rick Porcello, Masahiro Tanaka and Chris Tillman, who all posted career-worst HR rates.

Dontrelle Willis List

Pitchers with peripherals so horrible that you have to wonder how they can possibly draw a major league paycheck year after year.

Chaconian

Having the ability to post many saves despite sub-Mendoza peripherals and an ERA in the stratosphere.

ERA Benchmark

A half run of ERA over 200 innings comes out to just one earned run every four starts.

Gopheritis (also, Acute Gopheritis and Chronic Gopheritis)

The dreaded malady in which a pitcher is unable to keep the ball in the park. Pitchers with gopheritis have a FB rate of at least 40%. More severe cases have a FB% over 45%.

The Knuckleballers Rule

Knuckleballers don't follow no stinkin' rules.

Brad Lidge Lament

When a closer posts a 62% strand rate, he has nobody to blame but himself.

Vin Mazzaro Vindication

Occasional nightmares (2.1 innings, 14 ER) are just a part of the game.

The Five Saves Certainties

1. On every team, there will be save opportunities and someone will get them. At a bare minimum, there will be at least 30 saves to go around, and not unlikely more than 45.
2. Any pitcher could end up being the chief beneficiary. Bullpen management is a fickle endeavor.
3. Relief pitchers are often the ones that require the most time at the start of the season to find a groove. The weather is cold, the schedule is sparse and their usage is erratic.
4. Despite the talk about "bullpens by committee," managers prefer a go-to guy. It makes their job easier.
5. As many as 50% of the saves in any year will come from pitchers who are unselected at the end of Draft Day.

Soft-tosser land

The place where feebler arms leave their fortunes in the hands of the defense, variable hit and strand rates, and park dimensions. It's a place where many live, but few survive.

Prospects

General

Minor league prospecting in perspective

In our perpetual quest to be the genius who uncovers the next Mike Trout when he's still in high school, there is an obsessive fascination with minor league prospects. That's not to say that prospecting is not important. The issue is perspective:

1. During the 10 year period of 1996 to 2005, only 8% of players selected in the first round of the Major League Baseball First Year Player Draft went on to become stars.

2. Some prospects are going to hit the ground running (Cody Bellinger) and some are going to immediately struggle (Tyler Glasnow), no matter what level of hype follows them.

3. Some prospects are going to start fast (since the league is unfamiliar with them) and then fade (as the league figures them out). Others will start slow (since they are unfamiliar with the opposition) and then improve (as they adjust to the competition). So if you make your free agent and roster decisions based on small early samples sizes, you are just as likely to be an idiot as a genius.

4. How any individual player will perform relative to his talent is largely unknown because there is a psychological element that is vastly unexplored. Some make the transition to the majors seamlessly, some not, completely regardless of how talented they are.

5. Still, talent is the best predictor of future success, so major league equivalent base performance indicators still have a valuable role in the process. As do scouting reports, carefully filtered.

6. Follow the player's path to the majors. Did he have to repeat certain levels? Was he allowed to stay at a level long enough to learn how to adjust to the level of competition? A player with only two great months at Double-A is a good bet to struggle if promoted directly to the majors because he was never fully tested at Double-A, let alone Triple-A.

7. Younger players holding their own against older competition is a good thing. Older players reaching their physical peak, regardless of their current address, can be a good thing too. The Whit Merrifields, Thomas Phams and Zach Godleys can have some very profitable years.

8. Remember team context. A prospect with superior potential often will not unseat a steady but unspectacular incumbent, especially one with a large contract.

9. Don't try to anticipate how a team is going to manage their talent, both at the major and minor league level. You might think it's time to promote Ryan McMahon and give him an everyday role. You are not running the Rockies.

10. Those who play in shallow, one-year leagues should have little cause to be looking at the minors at all. The risk versus reward is so skewed against you, and there is so much talent available with a track record, that taking a chance on an unproven commodity makes little sense.

11. Decide where your priorities really are. If your goal is to win, prospect analysis is just a *part* of the process, not the entire process.

Factors affecting minor league stats *(Terry Linhart)*

1. Often, there is an exaggerated emphasis on short-term performance in an environment that is supposed to focus on the long-term. Two poor outings don't mean a 21-year-old pitcher is washed up.

2. Ballpark dimensions and altitude create hitters parks and pitchers parks, but a factor rarely mentioned is that many parks in the lower minors are inconsistent in their field quality. Minor league clubs have limited resources to maintain field conditions, and this can artificially depress defensive statistics while inflating stats like batting average.

3. Some players' skills are so superior to the competition at their level that you can't get a true picture of what they're going to do from their stats alone.

4. Many pitchers are told to work on secondary pitches in unorthodox situations just to gain confidence in the pitch. The result is an artificially increased number of walks.

5. The #3, #4, and #5 pitchers in the lower minors are truly longshots to make the majors. They often possess only two pitches and are unable to disguise the off-speed offerings. Hitters can see inflated statistics in these leagues.

Minor league level versus age

When evaluating minor leaguers, look at the age of the prospect in relation to the median age of the league he is in:

Low level A	Between 19-20
Upper level A	Around 20
Double-A	21
Triple-A	22

These are the ideal ages for prospects at the particular level. If a prospect is younger than most and holds his own against older and more experienced players, elevate his status. If he is older than the median, reduce his status.

Triple-A experience as a leading indicator

The probability that a minor leaguer will immediately succeed in the majors can vary depending upon the level of Triple-A experience he has amassed at the time of call-up.

	BATTERS		PITCHERS	
	< 1 Yr	Full	< 1 Yr	Full
Performed well	57%	56%	16%	56%
Performed poorly	21%	38%	77%	33%
2nd half drop-off	21%	7%	6%	10%

The odds of a batter achieving immediate MLB success was slightly more than 50-50. More than 80% of all pitchers promoted with less than a full year at Triple-A struggled in their first year in the majors. Those pitchers with a year in Triple-A succeeded at a level equal to that of batters.

Major League Equivalency (MLE) *(Bill James)*

A formula that converts a player's minor or foreign league statistics into a comparable performance in the major leagues. These are not projections, but conversions of current performance. MLEs contain adjustments for the level of play in individual leagues and teams. They work best with Triple-A stats, not quite as well with Double-A stats, and hardly at all with the lower levels. Foreign conversions are still a work in process. James' original formula only addressed batting. Our research has devised conversion formulas for pitchers, however, their best use comes when looking at peripherals, not traditional stats.

Adjusting to the competition

All players must "adjust to the competition" at every level of professional play. Players often get off to fast or slow starts. During their second tour at that level is when we get to see whether the slow starters have caught up or whether the league has figured out the fast starters. That second half "adjustment" period is a good baseline for projecting the subsequent season, in the majors or minors.

Premature major league call-ups often negate the ability for us to accurately evaluate a player due to the lack of this adjustment period. For instance, a hotshot Double-A player might open the season in Triple-A. After putting up solid numbers for a month, he gets a call to the bigs, and struggles. The fact is, we do not have enough evidence that the player has mastered the Triple-A level. We don't know whether the rest of the league would have caught up to him during his second tour of the league. But now he's labeled as an underperformer in the bigs when in fact he has never truly proven his skills at the lower levels.

Bull Durham prospects

There is some potential talent in older players—age 26, 27 or higher—who, for many reasons (untimely injury, circumstance, bad luck, etc.), don't reach the majors until they have already been downgraded from prospect to suspect. Equating potential with age is an economic reality for major league clubs, but not necessarily a skills reality.

Skills growth and decline is universal, whether it occurs at the major league level or in the minors. So a high-skills journeyman in Triple-A is just as likely to peak at age 27 as a major leaguer of the same age. The question becomes one of opportunity—will the parent club see fit to reap the benefits of that peak performance?

Prospecting these players for your fantasy team is, admittedly, a high risk endeavor, though there are some criteria you can use. Look for a player who is/has:

- Optimally, age 27-28 for overall peak skills, age 30-31 for power skills, or age 28-31 for pitchers.
- At least two seasons of experience at Triple-A. Career Double-A players are generally not good picks.
- Solid base skills levels.
- Shallow organizational depth at their position.
- Notable winter league or spring training performance.

Players who meet these conditions are not typically draftable players, but worthwhile reserve or FAAB picks.

Batters

MLE PX as a leading indicator *(Bill Macey)*

Looking at minor league performance (as MLE) in one year and the corresponding MLB performance the subsequent year:

	Year 1 MLE	Year 2 MLB
Observations	496	496
Median PX	95	96
Percent PX > 100	43%	46%

In addition, 53% of the players had a MLB PX in year 2 that exceeded their MLE PX in year 1. A slight bias towards improved performance in year 2 is consistent with general career trajectories.

Year 1 MLE PX	Year 2 MLB PX	Pct. Incr	Pct. MLB PX > 100
<= 50	61	70.3%	5.4%
51-75	85	69.6%	29.4%
76-100	93	55.2%	39.9%
101-125	111	47.4%	62.0%
126-150	119	32.1%	66.1%
> 150	142	28.6%	76.2%

Slicing the numbers by performance level, there is a good amount of regression to the mean.

Players rarely suddenly develop power at the MLB level if they didn't previously display that skill at the minor league level. However, the relatively large gap between the median MLE PX and MLB PX for these players, 125 to 110, confirms the notion that the best players continue to improve once they reach the major leagues.

MLE contact rate as a leading indicator *(Bill Macey)*

There is a strong positive correlation (0.63) between a player's MLE ct% in Year 1 and his actual ct% at the MLB level in Year 2.

MLE ct%	Year 1 MLE ct%	Year 2 MLB ct%
< 70%	69%	68%
70% - 74%	73%	72%
75% - 79%	77%	75%
80% - 84%	82%	77%
85% - 89%	87%	82%
90% +	91%	86%
TOTAL	**84%**	**79%**

There is very little difference between the median MLE BA in Year 1 and the median MLB BA in Year 2:

MLE ct%	Year 1 MLE BA	Year 2 MLB BA
< 70%	.230	.270
70% - 74%	.257	.248
75% - 79%	.248	.255
80% - 84%	.257	.255
85% - 89%	.266	.270
90% +	.282	.273
TOTAL	.261	.262

Excluding the <70% cohort (which was a tiny sample size), there is a positive relationship between MLE ct% and MLB BA.

Pitchers

Skills metrics as a leading indicator for pitching success

The percentage of hurlers that were good investments in the year that they were called up varied by the level of their historical minor league peripherals prior to that year.

Pitchers who had:	Fared well	Fared poorly
Good indicators	79%	21%
Marginal or poor indicators	18%	82%

The data used here were MLE levels from the previous two years, not the season in which they were called up. The significance? Solid current performance is what merits a call-up, but this is not a good indicator of short-term MLB success, because a) the performance data set is too small, typically just a few month's worth of statistics, and b) for those putting up good numbers at a new minor league level, there has typically not been enough time for the scouting reports to make their rounds.

Japanese Baseball *(Tom Mulhall)*

Comparing MLB and Japanese Baseball

The Japanese major leagues are generally considered to be equivalent to Triple-A ball and the pitching is thought to be even better. However, statistics are difficult to convert due to differences in the way the game is played in Japan.

1. While strong on fundamentals, Japanese baseball's guiding philosophy is risk avoidance. Mistakes are not tolerated. Runners rarely take extra bases, batters focus on making contact rather than driving the ball, and managers play for one run at a time. Bunts are more common. As a result, offenses score fewer runs per number of hits, and pitching stats tend to look better than the talent behind them.

2. Stadiums in Japan usually have much shorter fences. This should mean more HRs, but given #1 above, it is the American players who make up the majority of Japan's power elite. No power hitters have made an equivalent transition to the MLB.

3. There are more artificial turf fields, which increases the number of ground ball singles. Only a small number of stadiums have infield grass and a few still use all dirt infields.

4. The quality of umpiring is questionable and even inept. Fewer errors are called, reflecting the cultural philosophy of low tolerance for mistakes and the desire to avoid publicly embarrassing a player. Moreover, umpires are routinely intimidated, even physically.

5. Teams have smaller pitching staffs and use a six-man rotation. Starters usually pitch once a week, typically on the same day since Monday is an off-day for the entire league. Many starters will also occasionally pitch in relief between starts. Moreover, managers push for complete games, no matter what the score or situation. Because of the style of offense, higher pitch counts are common. Despite superior conditioning, Japanese pitchers tend to burn out early due to overuse.

6. The ball is smaller and lighter, and the strike zone is closer to the batter. A new ball was introduced in 2011 with lower-elasticity rubber surrounding the cork, which limited offense and inflated pitching stats. A more hitter-friendly ball was used in 2013 and home runs increased. But continue to exercise some skepticism when analyzing pitching stats and look for possible signs of optimism in hitting stats other than the power categories.

7. Tie games are allowed. If the score remains even after 12 innings, the game goes into the books as a tie.

8. There are 18 fewer games in the Japanese schedule.

Japanese players as fantasy farm selections

When evaluating the potential of Japanese League prospects, the key is not to just identify the best Japanese players—the key is to identify impact players who have the desire and opportunity to sign with a MLB team. With the success of Yu Darvish and Masahiro Tanaka, it is easy to overestimate the value of drafting these players. But since 1995, fewer than 50 Japanese players have made a big league roster, and about half of them were middle relievers. Still, for owners who are allowed to carry a large reserve or farm team at reduced salaries, these players could be a real windfall, especially if your competitors do not do their homework.

A list of Japanese League players who could jump to the majors appears in the Prospects section.

Other Diamonds

Age 26 Paradox

Age 26 is when a player begins to reach his peak skill, no matter what his address is. If circumstances have him celebrating that birthday in the majors, he is a breakout candidate. If circumstances have him celebrating that birthday in the minors, he is washed up.

A-Rod 10-Step Path to Stardom

Not all well-hyped prospects hit the ground running. More often they follow an alternative path:

1. Prospect puts up phenomenal minor league numbers.
2. The media machine gets oiled up.
3. Prospect gets called up, but struggles, Year 1.
4. Prospect gets demoted.
5. Prospect tears it up in the minors, Year 2.
6. Prospect gets called up, but struggles, Year 2.
7. Prospect gets demoted.
8. The media turns their backs. Fantasy leaguers reduce their expectations.
9. Prospect tears it up in the minors, Year 3. The public shrugs its collective shoulders.
10. Prospect is promoted in Year 3 and explodes. Some lucky fantasy leaguer lands a franchise player for under $5.

Some players that are currently stuck at one of the interim steps, and may or may not ever reach Step 10, include Julio Urias, Yoan Moncada and Raul Mondesi.

Balls

The logical variable—independently proven—that explains how prospects Cody Bellinger (pre-season rank #24) and Aaron Judge (#33) became instant superstars in their rookie seasons.

Bull Durham Gardening Tip

Late bloomers have fewer flowering seasons.

Developmental Dogmata

1. Defense is what gets a minor league prospect to the majors; offense is what keeps him there. *(Deric McKamey)*

2. The reason why rapidly promoted minor leaguers often fail is that they are never given the opportunity to master the skill of "adjusting to the competition."

3. Rookies who are promoted in-season often perform better than those that make the club out of spring training. Inferior March competition can inflate the latter group's perceived talent level.

4. Young players rarely lose their inherent skills. Pitchers may uncover weaknesses and the players may have difficulty adjusting. These are bumps along the growth curve, but they do not reflect a loss of skill.

5. Late bloomers have smaller windows of opportunity and much less chance for forgiveness.

6. The greatest risk in this game is to pay for performance that a player has never achieved.

7. Some outwardly talented prospects simply have a ceiling that's spelled "A-A-A."

Rule 5 Reminder

Don't ignore the Rule 5 draft lest you ignore the possibility of players like Jose Bautista, Josh Hamilton, Johan Santana, Joakim Soria, Dan Uggla, Shane Victorino and Jayson Werth. All were Rule 5 draftees.

Trout Inflation

The tendency for rookies to go for exorbitant draft prices following a year when there was a very good rookie crop.

Gaming

Standard Rules and Variations

Rotisserie Baseball was invented as an elegant confluence of base-ball and economics. Whether by design or accident, the result has lasted for more than three decades. But what would Rotisserie and fantasy have been like if the Founding Fathers knew then what we know now about statistical analysis and game design? You can be sure things would be different.

The world has changed since the original game was introduced yet many leagues use the same rules today. New technologies have opened up opportunities to improve elements of the game that might have been limited by the capabilities of the 1980s. New analytical approaches have revealed areas where the original game falls short.

As such, there are good reasons to tinker and experiment; to find ways to enhance the experience.

Following are the basic elements of fantasy competition, those that provide opportunities for alternative rules and experimen-tation. This is by no means an exhaustive list, but at minimum provides some interesting food-for-thought.

Player pool

Standard: American League-only, National League-only or Mixed League.

AL/NL-only typically drafts 8-12 teams (pool penetration of 49% to 74%). Mixed leagues draft 10-18 teams (31% to 55% pene-tration), though 15 teams (46%) is a common number.

Drafting of reserve players will increase the penetration percentages. A 12-team AL/NL-only league adding six reserves onto 23-man rosters would draft 93% of the available pool of players on all teams' 25-man rosters.

The draft penetration level determines which fantasy manage-ment skills are most important to your league. The higher the penetration, the more important it is to draft a good team. The lower the penetration, the greater the availability of free agents and the more important in-season roster management becomes.

There is no generally-accepted optimal penetration level, but we have often suggested that 75% (including reserves) provides a good balance between the skills required for both draft prep and in-season management.

Alternative pools: There is a wide variety of options here. Certain leagues draft from within a small group of major league divisions or teams. Some competitions, like home run leagues, only draft batters.

Bottom-tier pool: Draft only players who posted a Rotisserie dollar value of $5 or less in the previous season. Intended as a test of an owner's ability to identify talent with upside. Best used as a pick-a-player contest with any number of teams participating.

Positional structure

Standard: 23 players. One at each defensive position (though three outfielders may be from any of LF, CF or RF), plus one additional catcher, one middle infielder (2B or SS), one corner infielder (1B or 3B), two additional outfielders and a utility

player/designated hitter (which often can be a batter who quali-fies anywhere). Nine pitchers, typically holding any starting or relief role.

Open: 25 players. One at each defensive position (plus DH), 5-man starting rotation and two relief pitchers. Nine additional players at any position, which may be a part of the active roster or constitute a reserve list.

40-man: Standard 23 plus 17 reserves. Used in many keeper and dynasty leagues.

Reapportioned: In recent years, new obstacles are being faced by 12-team AL/NL-only leagues thanks to changes in the real game. The 14/9 split between batters and pitchers no longer reflects how MLB teams structure their rosters. Of the 30 teams, each with 25-man rosters, not one contains 14 batters for any length of time. In fact, many spend a good part of the season with only 12 batters, which means teams often have more pitchers than hitters.

For fantasy purposes in AL/NL-only leagues, that leaves a disproportionate draft penetration into the batter and pitcher pools:

	BATTERS	PITCHERS
On all MLB rosters	195	180
Players drafted	168	108
Pct.	86%	60%

These drafts are depleting 26% more batters out of the pool than pitchers. Add in those leagues with reserve lists—perhaps an additional six players per team removing another 72 players —and post-draft free agent pools are very thin, especially on the batting side.

The impact is less in 15-team mixed leagues, though the FA pitching pool is still disproportionately deep.

	BATTERS	PITCHERS
On all rosters	381	369
Drafted	210	135
Pct.	55%	37%

One solution is to reapportion the number of batters and pitchers that are rostered. Adding one pitcher slot and elimi-nating one batter slot may be enough to provide better balance. The batting slot most often removed is the second catcher, since it is the position with the least depth.

Beginning in the 2012 season, the Tout Wars AL/NL-only experts leagues opted to eliminate one of the outfield slots and replace it with a "swingman" position. This position could be any batter or pitcher, depending upon the owner's needs at any given time during the season.

Selecting players

Standard: The three most prevalent methods for stocking fantasy rosters are:

Snake/Straight/Serpentine draft: Players are selected in order with seeds reversed in alternating rounds. This method has become the most popular due to its speed, ease of implementation and ease of automation.

In these drafts, the underlying assumption is that value can be ranked relative to a linear baseline. Pick #1 is better than pick #2, which is better than pick #3, and the difference between each pick is assumed to be somewhat equivalent. While a faulty assumption, we must believe in it to assume a level playing field.

Auction: Players are sold to the highest bidder from a fixed budget, typically $260. Auctions provide the team owner with more control over which players will be on his team, but can take twice as long as snake drafts.

The baseline is $0 at the beginning of each player put up for bid. The final purchase price for each player is shaped by many wildly variable factors, from roster need to geographic location of the draft. A $30 player can mean different things to different drafters.

One option that can help reduce the time commitment of auctions is to force minimum bids at each hour mark. You could mandate $15 openers in hour #1; $10 openers in hour #2, etc.

Pick-a-player / Salary cap: Players are assigned fixed dollar values and owners assemble their roster within a fixed cap. This type of roster-stocking is an individual exercise which results in teams typically having some of the same players.

In these leagues, the "value" decision is taken out of the hands of the owners. Each player has a fixed value, pre-assigned based on past season performance and/or future expectation.

Hybrid snake-auction: Each draft begins as an auction. Each team has to fill its first seven roster slots from a budget of $154. Opening bid for any player is $15. After each team has filled seven slots, it becomes a snake draft.

This method is intended to reduce draft time while still providing an economic component for selecting players.

Stat categories

Standard: The standard statistical categories for Rotisserie leagues are:

4x4: HR, RBI, SB, BA, W, Sv, ERA, WHIP

5x5: HR, R, RBI, SB, BA, W, Sv, K, ERA, WHIP

6x6: Categories typically added are Holds and OPS.

7x7, etc.: Any number of categories may be added.

In general, the more categories you add, the more complicated it is to isolate individual performance and manage the categorical impact on your roster. There is also the danger of redundancy; with multiple categories measuring like stats, certain skills can get over-valued. For instance, home runs are double-counted when using the categories of both HR and slugging average. (Though note that HRs are actually already triple-counted in standard 5x5—HRs, runs, and RBIs)

If the goal is to have categories that create a more encompassing picture of player performance, it is actually possible to accomplish more with less:

Modified 4x4: HR, (R+RBI-HR), SB, OBA, (W+QS), (Sv+Hld), K, ERA

This provides a better balance between batting and pitching in that each has three counting categories and one ratio category. In fact, the balance is shown to be even more notable here:

	BATTING	PITCHING
Pure skill counting stat	HR	K
Ratio category	OBA	ERA
Dependent upon managerial decision	SB	(Sv+Hold)
Dependent upon team support	(R+RBI-HR)	(W+QS)

Replacing saves: The problem with the Saves statistic is that we have a scarce commodity that is centered on a small group of players, thereby creating inflated demand for those players. With the rising failure rate for closers these days, the incentive to pay full value for the commodity decreases. The higher the risk, the lower the prices.

We can increase the value of the commodity by reducing the risk. We might do this by increasing the number of players that contribute to that category, thereby spreading the risk around. One way we can accomplish this is by changing the category to Saves + Holds.

Holds are not perfect, but the typical argument about them being random and arbitrary can apply to saves these days as well. In fact, many of the pitchers who record holds are far more skilled and valuable than closers; they are often called to the mound in much higher leverage situations (a fact backed up by a scan of each pitcher's Leverage Index).

Neither stat is perfect, but together they form a reasonable proxy for overall bullpen performance.

In tandem, they effectively double the player pool of draftable relievers while also flattening the values allotted to those pitchers. The more players around which we spread the risk, the more control we have in managing our pitching staffs.

Replacing wins: Using reasons similar to replacing Saves with Saves + Holds, some have argued for replacing the Wins statistic with W + QS (quality starts). This method of scoring gives value to a starting pitcher who pitches well, but fails to receive the win due to his team's poor offense or poor luck.

Keeping score

Standard: These are the most common scoring methods:

Rotisserie: Players are evaluated in several statistical categories. Totals of these statistics are ranked by team. The winner is the team with the highest cumulative ranking.

Points: Players receive points for events that they contribute to in each game. Points are totaled for each team and teams are then ranked.

Head-to-Head (H2H): Using Rotisserie or points scoring, teams are scheduled in daily or weekly matchups. The winner of each matchup is the team that finishes higher in more categories (Rotisserie) or scores the most points.

Hybrid H2H-Rotisserie: Rotisserie's category ranking system can be converted into a weekly won-loss record. Depending upon where your team finishes for that week's statistics determines how many games you win for that week. Each week, your team will play seven games.

*Place	Record	*Place	Record
1st	7-0	7th	3-4
2nd	6-1	8th	2-5
3rd	6-1	9th	2-5
4th	5-2	10th	1-6
5th	5-2	11th	1-6
6th	4-3	12th	0-7

* Based on overall Rotisserie category ranking for the week.

At the end of each week, all the statistics revert to zero and you start over. You never dig a hole in any category that you can't climb out of, because all categories themselves are incidental to the standings.

The regular season lasts for 23 weeks, which equals 161 games. Weeks 24, 25 and 26 are for play-offs.

Free agent acquisition

Standard: Three methods are the most common for acquiring free agent players during the season.

First come first served: Free agents are awarded to the first owner who claims them.

Reverse order of standings: Access to the free agent pool is typically in a snake draft fashion with the last place team getting the first pick, and each successive team higher in the standings picking afterwards.

Free agent acquisition budget (FAAB): Teams are given a set budget at the beginning of the season (typically, $100 or $1000) from which they bid on free agents in a closed auction process.

Vickrey FAAB: Research has shown that more than 50% of FAAB dollars are lost via overbid on an annual basis. Given that this is a scarce commodity, one would think that a system to better manage these dollars might be desirable. The Vickrey system conducts a closed auction in the same way as standard FAAB, but the price of the winning bid is set at the amount of the second highest bid, plus $1. In some cases, gross overbids (at least $10 over) are reduced to the second highest bid plus $5.

This method was designed by William Vickrey, a Professor of Economics at Columbia University. His theory was that this process reveals the true value of the commodity. For his work, Vickrey was awarded the Nobel Prize for Economics (and $1.2 million) in 1996.

Double-Bid FAAB: One of the inherent difficulties in the current FAAB system is that we have so many options for setting a bid amount. You can bid $47, or $51, or $23. You might agonize over whether to go $38 or $39. With a $100 budget, there are 100 decision points. And while you may come up with a rough guesstimate of the range in which your opponents might bid, the results for any individual player bidding are typically random within that range.

The first part of this process reduces the number of decision points. Owners must categorize their interest by bidding a fixed number of pre-set dollar amounts for each player. In a $100 FAAB league, for instance, those levels might be $1, $5, $10, $15, $20, $30, $40 and increasing $10 increments. All owners would set the general market value for free agents in these pre-set levels of interest.

The initial stage of the bidding process serves to screen out those who are not interested in a player at the appropriate market level. That leaves a high potential for tied owners, those who share the same level of interest.

The tied owners must then submit a second bid of equal or greater value than their first bid. These bids can be in $1 increments. The winning owner gets the player; if there is still a tie, then the player would go to the owner lower in the standings.

An advantage of this second bid is that it gives owners an opportunity to see who they are going up against, and adjust. If you are bidding against an owner close to you in the standings,

you may need to be more aggressive in that second bid. If you see that the tied owner(s) wouldn't hurt you by acquiring that player, then maybe you resubmit the original bid and be content to potentially lose out on the player. If you're ahead in the standings, it's actually a way to potentially opt out on that player completely by resubmitting your original bid and forcing another owner to spend his FAAB.

Some leagues will balk at adding another layer to the weekly deadline process; it's a trade-off to having more control over managing your FAAB.

The season

Standard: Leagues are played out during the course of the entire Major League Baseball season.

Split-season: Leagues are conducted from Opening Day through the All-Star break, then re-drafted to play from the All-Star break through the end of the season.

50-game split-season: Leagues are divided into three 50-game seasons with one-week break in between.

Monthly: Leagues are divided into six seasons or rolling four-week seasons.

The advantages of these shorter time frames:

- They can help to maintain interest. There would be fewer abandoned teams.
- There would be more shots at a title each year.
- Given that drafting is considered the most fun aspect of the game, these splits multiply the opportunities to participate in some type of draft. Leagues may choose to do complete re-drafts and treat the year as distinct mini-seasons. Or, leagues might allow teams to drop their five worst players and conduct a restocking draft at each break.

Daily games: Participants select a roster of players from one day's MLB schedule. Scoring is based on an aggregate points-based system rather than categories, with cash prizes awarded based on the day's results. The structure and distribution of that prize pool varies across different types of events, and those differences can affect roster construction strategies. Although scoring and prizes are based on one day's play, the season-long element of bankroll management provides a proxy for overall standings.

In terms of projecting outcomes, daily games are drastically different than full-season leagues. Playing time is one key element of any projection, and daily games offer near-100% accuracy in projecting playing time: you can check pre-game lineups to see exactly which players are in the lineup that night. The other key component of any projection is performance, but that is plagued by variance in daily competitions. Even if you roster a team full of the most advantageous matchups (for instance, Jose Altuve facing A.J. Griffin), Altuve will sometimes go 0-for-4 on that one night.

Single game (Quint-Inning): A game that drafts from the active rosters of two major league teams in a single game. The rules:

1. Start with five owners.

2. Prior to first pitch, conduct a simple snake draft where each owner selects five players. If you're ambitious, auction off the 25 players giving each owner a budget of $50 of real or fake money.

3. Scoring is simple. For batters, singles, walks, hit-by-pitches and stolen bases are one point each. Doubles are 2 points. Triples are 3 points. Home runs are 4 points. Pitchers get one point for each complete inning pitched but lose one point for every run they allow.

4. At the beginning of the 5th inning, each owner has the option of doubling any future points for one player on his roster. We call that player the Quint. Points for all batters are doubled beginning in the 9th inning. That means the Quint's points would be quadrupled.

5. At the end of each inning, you can cut players, claim players from the free agent pool or trade players. You must maintain five players at all times, so all adds, drops and trades must keep your roster square. Free agent claims are done in reverse order of the standings. If two teams are tied and both want the same player, it can be helpful to have a deck of cards handy - the owner who draws high card would get the player.

6. Quint-Inning is a betting game (which makes it technically illegal). Owners need to ante up to play, typically $5, though if you're using a $50 auction budget, that works fine. It then costs $1 per inning to stay in the game for the second through fourth innings. Beginning in the 5th inning, the stakes increase to $2 per inning to stay in the game. You can use higher or lower stakes if you prefer.

7. Owners can fold at any time, forfeiting any monies they contributed to the pot. Their players are released into the free agent pool and are available to the remaining owners in reverse order of the standings.

8. The owner with the most points at the end of the game wins the pot.

Post-season league: Some leagues re-draft teams from among the MLB post-season contenders and play out a separate competition. It is possible, however, to make a post-season competition that is an extension of the regular season.

Start by designating a set number of regular season finishers as qualifying for the post-season. The top four teams in a league is a good number.

These four teams would designate a fixed 23-man roster for all post-season games. First, they would freeze all of their currently-owned players who are on MLB post-season teams.

In order to fill the roster holes that will likely exist, these four teams would then pick players from their league's non-playoff teams (for the sake of the post-season only). This would be in the form of a snake draft done on the day following the end of the regular season. Draft order would be regular season finish, so the play-off team with the most regular season points would get first pick. Picks would continue until all four rosters are filled with 23 men.

Regular scoring would be used for all games during October. The team with the best play-off stats at the end of the World Series is the overall champ.

Snake Drafting

Snake draft first round history

The following tables record the comparison between pre-season projected player rankings (using Average Draft Position data from Mock Draft Central and National Fantasy Baseball

Championship) and actual end-of-season results. The 14-year success rate of identifying each season's top talent is only 35%. Even if we extend the study to the top two rounds, the hit rate is only around 50%.

2010	ADP		ACTUAL = 5
1	Albert Pujols	1	Carlos Gonzalez
2	Hanley Ramirez	2	Albert Pujols (1)
3	Alex Rodriguez	3	Joey Votto
4	Chase Utley	4	Roy Halladay
5	Ryan Braun	5	Carl Crawford (15)
6	Mark Teixeira	6	Miguel Cabrera (9)
7	Matt Kemp	7	Josh Hamilton
8	Prince Fielder	8	Adam Wainwright
9	Miguel Cabrera	9	Felix Hernandez
10	Ryan Howard	10	Robinson Cano
11	Evan Longoria	11	Jose Bautista
12	Tom Lincecum	12	Paul Konerko
13	Joe Mauer	13	Matt Holliday
14	David Wright	14	Ryan Braun (5)
15	Carl Crawford	15	Hanley Ramirez (2)

2011	ADP		ACTUAL = 6
1	Albert Pujols	1	Matt Kemp
2	Hanley Ramirez	2	Jacoby Ellsbury
3	Miguel Cabrera	3	Ryan Braun (10)
4	Troy Tulowitzki	4	Justin Verlander
5	Evan Longoria	5	Clayton Kershaw
6	Carlos Gonzalez	6	Curtis Granderson
7	Joey Votto	7	Adrian Gonzalez (8)
8	Adrian Gonzalez	8	Miguel Cabrera (3)
9	Robinson Cano	9	Roy Halladay (15)
10	Ryan Braun	10	Cliff Lee
11	David Wright	11	Jose Bautista
12	Mark Teixeira	12	Dustin Pedroia
13	Carl Crawford	13	Jered Weaver
14	Josh Hamilton	14	Albert Pujols (1)
15	Roy Halladay	15	Robinson Cano (9)

2012	ADP		ACTUAL = 4
1	Matt Kemp	1	Mike Trout
2	Ryan Braun	2	Ryan Braun (2)
3	Albert Pujols	3	Miguel Cabrera (4)
4	Miguel Cabrera	4	Andrew McCutchen
5	Troy Tulowitzki	5	R.A. Dickey
6	Jose Bautista	6	Clayton Kershaw
7	Jacoby Ellsbury	7	Justin Verlander (8)
8	Justin Verlander	8	Josh Hamilton
9	Adrian Gonzalez	9	Fernando Rodney
10	Justin Upton	10	Adrian Beltre
11	Robinson Cano	11	Alex Rios
12	Joey Votto	12	David Price
13	Evan Longoria	13	Chase Headley
14	Carlos Gonzalez	14	Robinson Cano (11)
15	Prince Fielder	15	Edwin Encarnacion

2013	ADP		ACTUAL = 5
1	Ryan Braun	1	Miguel Cabrera (2)
2	Miguel Cabrera	2	Mike Trout (3)
3	Mike Trout	3	Clayton Kershaw (15)
4	Matt Kemp	4	Chris Davis
5	Andrew McCutchen	5	Paul Goldschmidt
6	Albert Pujols	6	Andrew McCutchen (5)
7	Robinson Cano	7	Adam Jones
8	Jose Bautista	8	Jacoby Ellsbury
9	Joey Votto	9	Max Scherzer
10	Carlos Gonzalez	10	Carlos Gomez
11	Buster Posey	11	Hunter Pence
12	Justin Upton	12	Robinson Cano (7)
13	Giancarlo Stanton	13	Alex Rios
14	Prince Fielder	14	Adrian Beltre
15	Clayton Kershaw	15	Matt Harvey

2014	ADP		ACTUAL = 4
1	Mike Trout	1	Jose Altuve
2	Miguel Cabrera	2	Clayton Kershaw (6)
3	Paul Goldschmidt	3	Michael Brantley
4	Andrew McCutchen	4	Mike Trout (1)
5	Carlos Gonzalez	5	Johnny Cueto
6	Clayton Kershaw	6	Felix Hernandez
7	Chris Davis	7	Victor Martinez
8	Ryan Braun	8	Jose Abreu
9	Adam Jones	9	Giancarlo Stanton
10	Bryce Harper	10	Andrew McCutchen (4)
11	Robinson Cano	11	Miguel Cabrera (2)
12	Hanley Ramirez	12	Carlos Gomez
13	Jacoby Ellsbury	13	Jose Bautista
14	Prince Fielder	14	Dee Gordon
15	Troy Tulowitzki	15	Anthony Rendon

2015	ADP		ACTUAL = 4
1	Mike Trout	1	Jake Arrieta
2	Andrew McCutchen	2	Zack Greinke
3	Clayton Kershaw	3	Clayton Kershaw (3)
4	Giancarlo Stanton	4	Paul Goldschmidt (5)
5	Paul Goldschmidt	5	A.J. Pollock
6	Miguel Cabrera	6	Dee Gordon
7	Jose Abreu	7	Bryce Harper
8	Carlos Gomez	8	Josh Donaldson
9	Jose Bautista	9	Jose Altuve (12)
10	Edwin Encarnacion	10	Mike Trout (1)
11	Felix Hernandez	11	Nolan Arenado
12	Jose Altuve	12	Manny Machado
13	Anthony Rizzo	13	Dallas Keuchel
14	Adam Jones	14	Max Scherzer
15	Troy Tulowitzki	15	Nelson Cruz

2016	ADP		ACTUAL = 7
1	Mike Trout	1	Mookie Betts
2	Paul Goldschmidt	2	Jose Altuve (11)
3	Bryce Harper	3	Mike Trout (1)
4	Clayton Kershaw	4	Jonathan Villar
5	Josh Donaldson	5	Jean Segura
6	Carlos Correa	6	Max Scherzer (15)
7	Nolan Arenado	7	Paul Goldschmidt (2)
8	Manny Machado	8	Charlie Blackmon
9	Anthony Rizzo	9	Clayton Kershaw (4)
10	Giancarlo Stanton	10	Nolan Arenado (7)
11	Jose Altuve	11	Daniel Murphy
12	Kris Bryant	12	Kris Bryant (12)
13	Miguel Cabrera	13	Joey Votto
14	Andrew McCutchen	14	Jon Lester
15	Max Scherzer	15	Madison Bumgarner

2017	ADP		ACTUAL = 5
1	Mike Trout	1	Charlie Blackmon
2	Mookie Betts	2	Jose Altuve (4)
3	Clayton Kershaw	3	Corey Kluber
4	Jose Altuve	4	Max Scherzer (12)
5	Kris Bryant	5	Paul Goldschmidt (7)
6	Nolan Arenado	6	Giancarlo Stanton
7	Paul Goldschmidt	7	Chris Sale
8	Manny Machado	8	Aaron Judge
9	Bryce Harper	9	Dee Gordon
10	Trea Turner	10	Clayton Kershaw (3)
11	Josh Donaldson	11	Nolan Arenado (6)
12	Max Scherzer	12	Jose Ramirez
13	Anthony Rizzo	13	Joey Votto
14	Madison Bumgarner	14	Marcell Ozuna
15	Carlos Correa	15	Elvis Andrus

ADP attrition

Why is our success rate so low in identifying what should be the most easy-to-project players each year? We rank and draft players based on the expectation that those ranked higher will return greater value in terms of productivity and playing time, as well as being the safest investments. However, there are many variables affecting where players finish.

Earlier, it was shown that players spend an inordinate number of days on the disabled list. In fact, of the players projected to finish in the top 300, the number who were disabled, demoted or designated for assignment has been extreme:

Year	Pct. of top-ranked 300 players who lost PT
2009	51%
2010	44%
2011	49%
2012	45%
2013	51%
2014	53%
2015	47%
2016	47%
2017	58%

When you consider that about half of each season's very best players had fewer at-bats or innings pitched than we projected, it shows how tough it is to rank players each year.

The fallout? Consider: It is nearly a foregone conclusion that players like Corey Kluber and Aaron Judge—who finished in the top 15 for the first time last year—will be considerations for first round picks in 2018. The above data provide a strong argument against them returning first-round value.

Yes, they are excellent players, in 2017 anyway. But the issue is not just their skills profiles. Since 2004:

- Two-thirds of players finishing in the Top 15 were not in the Top 15 the previous year. There is a great deal of turnover in the first round, year-to-year.
- Of those who were first-timers, only 14% repeated in the first round the following year.
- Established superstars who finished in the Top 15 were no guarantee to repeat.

As such, the odds are against Kluber or Judge repeating in the first round. In past years, sudden stars like Jonathan Villar, Carlos Gonzalez, Curtis Granderson and Dustin Pedroia have failed to repeat. As talented as these players were, it's not just about skill; it's also about skill relative to the rest of a volatile player pool.

Importance of the early rounds *(Bill Macey)*

It's long been said that you can't win your league in the first round, but you can lose it there. An analysis of data from actual drafts reveals that this holds true—those who spend an early round pick on a player that severely under-performs expectations rarely win their league and seldom even finish in the top 3.

At the same time, drafting a player in the first round that actually returns first-round value is no guarantee of success. In fact, those that draft some of the best values still only win their league about a quarter of the time and finish in the top 3 less than half the time. Research also shows that drafting pitchers in the first round is a risky proposition. Even if the pitchers deliver first-round value, the opportunity cost of passing up on an elite batter makes you less likely to win your league.

How a strong draft contributes to a winning season *(Todd Zola)*

Standings correlation based on draft to final ranges from 0.42 to 0.94 with mean around 0.73. The top hitting counting stat drafted is home runs, stolen bases fewest. The top pitching counting stat drafted is saves, wins fewest. More hitting is acquired at the draft or auction than pitching. Influx of stats is greatest in Mixed Leagues suggesting practicing patience in AL/NL-only formats while being cautiously aggressive in Mixed formats.

Top teams almost always improve ratios from drafted, despite available free agents sporting poorer aggregate ratios. This is most apropos if favoring improving pitching staff as the year progresses; it's easier said than done.

Being top-three in saves is far more important in Mixed leagues than AL/NL only. Most Mixed champions draft the majority of saves while AL/NL only winners often acquire in season.

What is the best seed to draft from?

Most drafters like mid-round so they never have to wait too long for their next player. Some like the swing pick, suggesting that getting two players at 15 and 16 is better than a 1 and a 30. Many drafters assume that the swing pick means you'd be getting something like two $30 players instead of a $40 and $20.

Equivalent auction dollar values reveal the following facts about the first two snake draft rounds:

In an AL/NL-only league, the top seed would get a $44 player (at #1) and a $24 player (at #24) for a total of $68; the 12th seed would get two $29s (at #12 and #13) for $58.

In a mixed league, the top seed would get a $47 and a $24 ($71); the 15th seed would get two $28s ($56).

Since the talent level flattens out after the 2nd round, low seeds never get a chance to catch up:

Dollar value difference between first player selected and last player selected

Round	12-team	15-team
1	$15	$19
2	$7	$8
3	$5	$4
4	$3	$3
5	$2	$2
6	$2	$1
7-17	$1	$1
18-23	$0	$0

The total value each seed accumulates at the end of the draft is hardly equitable:

Seed	Mixed	AL/NL-only
1	$266	$273
2	$264	$269
3	$263	$261
4	$262	$262
5	$259	$260
6	$261	$260
7	$260	$260
8	$261	$260
9	$261	$258
10	$257	$260
11	$257	$257
12	$258	$257
13	$254	
14	$255	
15	$256	

The counter-argument to this focuses on whether we can reasonably expect "accurate projections" at the top of the draft. Given the snake draft first round history, a case could be made

that any seed might potentially do well. In fact, you might even consider the best draft position to be at the 15-16 wheel, which would essentially provide you with two picks from among the top 16 players.

Using ADPs to determine when to select players *(Bill Macey)*

Although average draft position (ADP) data provides a good idea of where in the draft each player is selected, it can be misleading when trying to determine how early to target a player. This chart summarizes the percentage of players drafted within 15 picks of his ADP as well as the average standard deviation by grouping of players.

ADP Rank	% within 15 picks	Standard Deviation
1-25	100%	2.5
26-50	97%	6.1
51-100	87%	9.6
100-150	72%	14.0
150-200	61%	17.4
200-250	53%	20.9

As the draft progresses, the picks for each player become more widely dispersed and less clustered around the average. Most top 100 players will go within one round of their ADP-converted round. However, as you reach the mid-to-late rounds, there is much more uncertainty as to when a player will be selected. Pitchers have slightly smaller standard deviations than do batters (i.e. they tend to be drafted in a narrower range). This suggests that drafters may be more likely to reach for a batter than for a pitcher.

Using the ADP and corresponding standard deviation, we can to estimate the likelihood that a given player will be available at a certain draft pick. We estimate the predicted standard deviation for each player as follows:

$$Stdev = -0.42 + 0.42*(ADP - Earliest\ Pick)$$

(That the figure 0.42 appears twice is pure coincidence; the numbers are not equal past two decimal points.)

If we assume that the picks are normally distributed, we can use a player's ADP and estimated standard deviation to estimate the likelihood that the player is available with a certain pick (MS Excel formula):

$$=1-normdist(x,ADP,Standard\ Deviation,True)$$

where «x» represents the pick number to be evaluated.

We can use this information to prepare for a snake draft by determining how early we may need to reach in order to roster a player. Suppose you had the 8th pick in a 15-team league draft and your target was 2009 sleeper candidate Nelson Cruz. His ADP was 128.9 and his earliest selection was with the 94th pick. This yielded an estimated standard deviation of 14.2. You could have then entered these values into the formula above to estimate the likelihood that he was still available at each of the following picks:

Pick	Likelihood Available
83	100%
98	99%
113	87%
128	53%
143	16%
158	2%

ADPs and scarcity *(Bill Macey)*

Most players are selected within a round or two of their ADP with tight clustering around the average. But every draft is unique and every pick in the draft seemingly affects the ordering of subsequent picks. In fact, deviations from "expected" sequences can sometimes start a chain reaction at that position. This is most often seen in runs at scarce positions such as the closer; once the first one goes, the next seems sure to closely follow.

Research also suggests that within each position, there is a correlation within tiers of players. The sooner players within a generally accepted tier are selected, the sooner other players within the same tier will be taken. However, once that tier is exhausted, draft order reverts to normal.

How can we use this information? If you notice a reach pick, you can expect that other drafters may follow suit. If your draft plan is to get a similar player within that tier, you'll need to adjust your picks accordingly.

Mapping ADPs to auction value *(Bill Macey)*

Reliable average auction values (AAV) are often tougher to come by than ADP data for snake drafts. However, we can estimate predicted auction prices as a function of ADP, arriving at the following equation:

y = -9.8ln(x) + 57.8
where ln(x) is the natural log function, x represents the actual ADP, and y represents the predicted AAV.

This equation does an excellent job estimating auction prices (r2=0.93), though deviations are unavoidable. The asymptotic nature of the logarithmic function, however, causes the model to predict overly high prices for the top players. So be aware of that, and adjust.

The value of mock drafts *(Todd Zola)*

Most assume the purpose of a mock draft is to get to know the market value of the player pool. But even more important, mock drafting is general preparation for the environment and process, thereby allowing the drafter to completely focus on the draft when it counts. Mock drafting is more about fine-tuning your strategy than player value. Here are some tips to maximize your mock drafting experience.

1. Make sure you can seamlessly use an on-line drafting room, draft software or your own lists to track your draft or auction. The less time you spend looking, adding and adjusting names, the more time you can spend on thinking about what player is best for your team. This also gives you the opportunity to make sure your draft lists are complete, and assures all the players are listed at the correct position(s).

2. Alter the positions from which you mock. The flow of each mock will be different, but if you do a few mocks with an early initial pick, a few in the middle and a few with a late first pick, you may learn you prefer one of the spots more than the others. If you're in a league where you can choose your draft spot, this helps you decide where to select. Once you know your spot, a few mocks from that spot will help you decide how to deal with positional runs.

3. Use non-typical strategies and consider players you rarely target. We all have our favorite players. Intentionally passing on those players not only gives you an idea when others may draft them but it also forces you to research players you normally don't consider. The more players you have researched, the more prepared you'll be for any series of events that occurs during your real draft.

Draft preparation with a full-season mindset *(Matt Dodge)*

Each of the dimensions of your league setup—player pool, reserve list depth; type and frequency of transactions, scoring categories, etc.—should impact your draft day plan. But it may also be helpful to look at them in combination.

Sources of additional stats after draft day

League Player Pool		
Reserve List	Mixed 15 team	AL- or NL-only 12 team
Short	free agents	trades, free agents
Long	free agents, trades	trades

Review the prior season's transactions for your league and analyze the successful teams' category contributions from trade acquisitions and free agent pickups. Trades are often necessary to add specific stats in AL/NL-only leagues as the player pool penetration is generally much deeper, and the size of a reserve roster further reduces the help possible from the free agent pool.

Draft strategies related to in-season player acquisition

Trade Activity		
FA Pool	Low	High
Shallow	solid foundation (STR)	tradable commodoties surplus counting stats
Deep	gamble on upside (S&S)	ultimate flexibility

Trading activity is a function of multiple factors. Keeper leagues provide opportunities for owners to contend this year or play for next year. However, those increased opportunities are often controlled by rules to prevent "dump trading." Stratification of the standings in redraft leagues can cause lower ranked owners to lose interest, reducing the number of effective trading partners as the season goes on.

When deep rosters create a shallow free agent pool in a league with little trading, draft day success becomes paramount. In this case, a Spread the Risk strategy designed to accumulate at bats, innings, and saves is recommended. If the free agent pool is deep, the drafter can take more risks with a Stars and Scrubs approach, acquiring "lottery ticket" players with upside, knowing that replacements are readily available if the upside plays don't hit.

In leagues where trading is prevalent, a shallow free agent pool means you should acquire players on draft day with the intent of trading them. This could mean a traditional strategy of acquiring a category surplus (frequently saves and/or steals), and then trading them in-season to shore up other categories. In a keeper league, this includes grabbing a few bargains (to interest those who are rebuilding) or grabbing top performers to flip in trade (if you are already on "the two year plan").

Draft Day Considerations for In-season Roster Management

Reserve List Txn Freq	4 x 4 League Format	5 x 5 League Format
Daily	careful SP management batting platoons positional flexibility	RP (K, ERA, WHIP) batting platoons positional flexibility
Weekly	SP (2 start weeks) cover risky starters	SP (2 start weeks) cover risky starters

Owners must be careful with pitching, due to the negative impact potential of ERA and WHIP. Blindly streaming pitchers on a daily basis can be counter-productive, particularly in 4x4 leagues. In 5x5, the Strikeouts category can make a foundation of high Dom relievers a useful source of mitigation for the invariable starting pitching disappointments.

The degree that these recommendations can be implemented is also dependent on the depth of the reserve list. Those with more reserves can do more than those with fewer, obviously, but the key is deciding up front how you plan to use your reserves, and then tailoring your draft strategy toward that usage.

Draft-day cheat sheet *(Patrick Davitt)*

1. Know what players are available, right to the bottom of the pool.
2. Know what every player is worth in your league format.
3. Know why you think each player is worth what you think he's worth.
4. Identify players you believe you value differently from the other owners.
5. Know each player's risks.
6. Know your opponents' patterns.
7. For sure, know the league rules and its history, and what it takes to win.

Auction Value Analysis

Auction values (R$) in perspective

R$ is the dollar value placed on a player's statistical performance in a Rotisserie league, and designed to measure the impact that player has on the standings.

There are several methods to calculate a player's value from his projected (or actual) statistics.

One method is Standings Gain Points, described in the book, *How to Value Players for Rotisserie Baseball*, by Art McGee (2nd edition available at BaseballHQ.com). SGP converts a player's statistics in each Rotisserie category into the number of points those stats will allow you to gain in the standings. These are then converted back into dollars.

Another popular method is the Percentage Valuation Method. In PVM, a least valuable, or replacement performance level is set for each category (in a given league size) and then values are calculated representing the incremental improvement from that base. A player is then awarded value in direct proportion to the level he contributes to each category.

As much as these methods serve to attach a firm number to projected performance, the winning bid for any player is still highly variable depending upon many factors:

- the salary cap limit
- the number of teams in the league
- each team's roster size
- the impact of any protected players
- each team's positional demands at the time of bidding
- the statistical category demands at the time of bidding
- external factors, e.g. media inflation or deflation of value

In other words, a $30 player is only a $30 player if someone in your draft pays $30 for him.

Roster slot valuation *(John Burnson)*

When you draft a player, what have you bought?

"You have bought the stats generated by this player."

No. You have bought the stats generated by his slot. Initially, the drafted player fills the slot, but he need not fill the slot for the season, and he need not contribute from Day One. If you trade the player during the season, then your bid on Draft Day paid for the stats of the original player plus the stats of the new player. If the player misses time due to injury or demotion, then you bought the stats of whoever fills the time while the drafted player is missing. At season's end, there will be more players providing positive value than there are roster slots.

Before the season, the number of players projected for positive value has to equal the total number of roster slots. However, the projected productivity should be adjusted by the potential to capture extra value in the slot. This is especially important for injury-rehab cases and late-season call-ups. For example, if we think that a player will miss half the season, then we would augment his projected stats with a half-year of stats from a replacement-level player at his position. Only then would we calculate prices. Essentially, we want to apportion $260 per team among the slots, not the players.

Average player value by draft round

Rd	AL/NL	Mxd
1	$34	$34
2	$26	$26
3	$23	$23
4	$20	$20
5	$18	$18
6	$17	$16
7	$16	$15
8	$15	$13
9	$13	$12
10	$12	$11
11	$11	$10
12	$10	$9
13	$9	$8
14	$8	$8
15	$7	$7
16	$6	$6
17	$5	$5
18	$4	$4
19	$3	$3
20	$2	$2
21	$1	$2
22	$1	$1
23	$1	$1

Benchmarks for auction players:

- All $30 players will go in the first round.
- All $20-plus players will go in the first four rounds.
- Double-digit value ends pretty much after Round 11.
- The $1 end game starts at about Round 21.

Dollar values: expected projective accuracy

There is a 65% chance that a player projected for a certain dollar value will finish the season with a value within plus-or-minus $5 of that projection. Therefore, if you value a player at $25, you only have about a 2-in-3 shot of him finishing between $20 and $30.

If you want to raise your odds to 80%, the range becomes +/- $9, so your $25 player has to finish somewhere between $16 and $34.

Dollar values by lineup position *(Michael Roy)*

How much value is derived from batting order position?

Pos	PA	R	RBI	R$
#1	747	107	72	$18.75
#2	728	102	84	$19.00
#3	715	95	100	$19.45
#4	698	93	104	$19.36
#5	682	86	94	$18.18
#6	665	85	82	$17.19
#7	645	81	80	$16.60
#8	623	78	80	$16.19
#9	600	78	73	$15.50

So, a batter moving from the bottom of the order to the clean-up spot, with no change in performance, would gain nearly $4 in value from runs and RBIs alone.

How likely is it that a $30 player will repeat? *(Matt Cederholm)*

From 2003-2008, there were 205 players who earned $30 or more (using single-league 5x5 values). Only 70 of them (34%) earned $30 or more in the next season.

In fact, the odds of repeating a $30 season aren't good. As seen below, the best odds during that period were 42%. And as we would expect, pitchers fare far worse than hitters.

	Total>$30	# Repeat	% Repeat
Hitters	167	64	38%
Pitchers	38	6	16%
Total	205	70	34%
*High-Reliability**			
Hitters	42	16	38%
Pitchers	7	0	0%
Total	49	16	33%
100+ BPV			
Hitters	60	25	42%
Pitchers	31	6	19%
Total	91	31	19%
*High-Reliability and 100+ BPV**			
Hitters	12	5	42%
Pitchers	6	0	0%
Total	18	5	28%

Reliability figures are from 2006-2008

For players with multiple seasons of $30 or more, the numbers get better. Players with consecutive $30 seasons, 2003-2008:

	Total>$30	# Repeat	% Repeat
Two Years	62	29	55%
Three+ Years	29	19	66%

Still, a player with two consecutive seasons at $30 in value is barely a 50/50 proposition. And three consecutive seasons is only a 2/3 shot. Small sample sizes aside, this does illustrate the nature of the beast. Even the most consistent, reliable players fail 1/3 of the time. Of course, this is true whether they are kept or drafted anew, so this alone shouldn't prevent you from keeping a player.

Predicting player value from year 1 performance *(Patrick Davitt)*

Year-1 (Y1, first season >=100AB) batter results predict some— but not all—subsequent-year performance. About half of all Y1players have positive value. Players with higher Y1 value were likelier to get PT in subsequent seasons. Players with –$6 to –$10 in Y1 got more chances than players +$5 to –$5 and performed better. Batters with Y1 value of $16 or more are excellent bets to at least provide positive value in subsequent seasons, and those above $21 in Y1 value play in all subsequent seasons and return an average of $26. But even a $21 batter is only a 50-50 bet to do better in Y2.

How well do elite pitchers retain their value? *(Michael Weddell)*

An elite pitcher (one who earns at least $24 in a season) on average keeps 80% of his R$ value from year 1 to year 2. This compares to the baseline case of only 52%.

Historically, 36% of elite pitchers improve, returning a greater R$ in the second year than they did the first year. That is an impressive performance considering they already were at an elite level. 17% collapse, returning less than a third of their R$ in the second year. The remaining 47% experience a middling outcome, keeping more than a third but less than all of their R$ from one year to the next.

Valuing closers

Given the high risk associated with the closer's role, it is difficult to determine a fair draft value. Typically, those who have successfully held the role for several seasons will earn the highest draft price, but valuing less stable commodities is troublesome.

A rough rule of thumb is to start by paying $10 for the role alone. Any pitcher tagged the closer on draft day should merit at least $10. Then add anywhere from $0 to $15 for support skills.

In this way, the top level talents will draw upwards of $20-$25. Those with moderate skill will draw $15-$20, and those with more questionable skill in the $10-$15 range.

Profiling the end game

What types of players are typically the most profitable in the end-game? First, our overall track record on $1 picks:

Avg Return	%Profitable	Avg Prof	Avg. Loss
$1.89	51%	$10.37	($7.17)

On aggregate, the hundreds of players drafted in the end-game earned $1.89 on our $1 investments. While they were profitable overall, only 51% of them actually turned a profit. Those that did cleared more than $10 on average. Those that didn't—the other 49%—lost about $7 apiece.

Pos	Pct.of tot	Avg Val	%Profit	Avg Prof	Avg Loss
CA	12%	($1.68)	41%	$7.11	($7.77)
CO	9%	$6.12	71%	$10.97	($3.80)
MI	9%	$3.59	53%	$10.33	($4.84)
OF	22%	$2.61	46%	$12.06	($5.90)
SP	29%	$1.96	52%	$8.19	($7.06)
RP	19%	$0.35	50%	$11.33	($10.10)

These results bear out the danger of leaving catchers to the end; only catchers returned negative value. Corner infielder returns say leaving a 1B or 3B open until late.

Age	Pct.of tot	Avg Val	%Profit	Avg Prof	Avg Loss
< 25	15%	($0.88)	33%	$8.25	($8.71)
25-29	48%	$2.59	56%	$11.10	($8.38)
30-35	28%	$2.06	44%	$10.39	($5.04)
35+	9%	$2.15	41%	$8.86	($5.67)

The practice of speculating on younger players—mostly rookies—in the end game was a washout. Part of the reason was that those that even made it to the end game were often the long-term or fringe type. Better prospects were typically drafted earlier.

	Pct.of tot	Avg Val	%Profit	Avg Prof	Avg Loss
Injury rehabs	20%	$3.63	36%	$15.07	($5.65)

One in five end-gamers were players coming back from injury. While only 36% of them were profitable, the healthy ones returned a healthy profit. The group's losses were small, likely because they weren't healthy enough to play.

Realistic expectations of $1 endgamers *(Patrick Davitt)*

Many fantasy articles insist leagues are won or lost with $1 batters, because "that's where the profits are." But are they?

A 2011 analysis showed that when considering $1 players in deep leagues, managing $1 endgamers should be more about minimizing losses than fishing for profit. In the cohort of batters projected $0 to -$5, 82% returned losses, based on a $1 bid. Two-thirds of the projected $1 cohort returned losses. In addition, when considering $1 players, speculate on speed.

Advanced Draft Strategies

Stars & Scrubs v. Spread the Risk

Stars & Scrubs (S&S): A Rotisserie auction strategy in which a roster is anchored by a core of high priced stars and the remaining positions filled with low-cost players.

Spread the Risk (STR): An auction strategy in which available dollars are spread evenly among all roster slots.

Both approaches have benefits and risks. An experiment was conducted in 2004 whereby a league was stocked with four teams assembled as S&S, four as STR and four as a control group. Rosters were then frozen for the season.

The Stars & Scrubs teams won all three ratio categories. Those deep investments ensured stability in the categories that are typically most difficult to manage. On the batting side, however, S&S teams amassed the least amount of playing time, which in turn led to bottom-rung finishes in HRs, RBIs and Runs.

One of the arguments for the S&S approach is that it is easier to replace end-game losers (which, in turn, may help resolve the playing time issues). Not only is this true, but the results of this experiment show that replacing those bottom players is critical to success.

The Spread the Risk teams stockpiled playing time, which led to strong finishes in many counting stats, including clear victories in RBIs, wins and strikeouts. This is a key tenet in drafting philosophy; we often say that the team that compiles the most ABs will be among the top teams in RBI and Runs.

The danger is on the pitching side. More innings did yield more wins and Ks, but also destroyed ERA/WHIP.

So, what approach makes the most sense? **The optimal strategy might be to STR on offense and go S&S with your pitching staff.** STR buys more ABs, so you immediately position yourself well in four of the five batting categories. On pitching, it might be more advisable to roster a few core arms, though that immediately elevates your risk exposure. Admittedly, it's a balancing act, which is why we need to pay more attention to risk analysis and look closer at strategies like the Portfolio3 Plan.

The LIMA Plan

The LIMA Plan is a strategy for Rotisserie leagues (though the underlying concept can be used in other formats) that allows you to target high skills pitchers at very low cost, thereby freeing up dollars for offense. LIMA is an acronym for Low Investment Mound Aces, and also pays tribute to Jose Lima, a $1 pitcher in 1998 who exemplified the power of the strategy. In a $260 league:

1. Budget a maximum of $60 for your pitching staff.
2. Allot no more than $30 of that budget for acquiring saves. In 5x5 leagues, it is reasonable to forego saves at the draft (and acquire them during the season) and re-allocate this $30 to starters ($20) and offense ($10).
3. Ignore ERA. Draft only pitchers with:
   • Command ratio (K/BB) of 2.5 or better.
   • Strikeout rate of 7.0 or better.
   • Expected home run rate of 1.0 or less.
4. Draft as few innings as your league rules will allow. This is intended to manage risk. For some game formats, this should be a secondary consideration.
5. Maximize your batting slots. Target batters with:
   • Contact rate of at least 80%
   • Walk rate of at least 10%
   • PX or Spd level of at least 100

Spend no more than $29 for any player and try to keep the $1 picks to a minimum.

The goal is to ace the batting categories and carefully pick your pitching staff so that it will finish in the upper third in ERA, WHIP and saves (and Ks in 5x5), and an upside of perhaps 9th in wins. In a competitive league, that should be enough to win, and definitely enough to finish in the money. Worst case, you should have an excess of offense available that you can deal for pitching.

The strategy works because it better allocates resources. Fantasy leaguers who spend a lot for pitching are not only paying for expected performance, they are also paying for better defined roles—#1 and #2 rotation starters, ace closers, etc.—which are expected to translate into more IP, wins and saves. But roles are highly variable. A pitcher's role will usually come down to his skill and performance; if he doesn't perform, he'll lose the role.

The LIMA Plan says, *let's invest in skill and let the roles fall where they may.* In the long run, better skills should translate into more innings, wins and saves. And as it turns out, pitching skill costs less than pitching roles do.

In *snake draft leagues,* don't start drafting starting pitchers until Round 10. In *shallow mixed leagues,* the LIMA Plan may not be necessary; just focus on the peripheral metrics. In *simulation leagues,* build your staff around those metrics.

Variations on the LIMA Plan

LIMA Extrema: Limit your total pitching budget to only $30, or less. This can be particularly effective in shallow leagues where LIMA-caliber starting pitcher free agents are plentiful during the season.

SANTANA Plan: Instead of spending $30 on saves, you spend it on a starting pitcher anchor. In 5x5 leagues where you can reasonably punt saves at the draft table, allocating those dollars to a high-end LIMA-caliber starting pitcher can work well as long as you pick the right anchor.

Total Control Drafting (TCD)

On Draft Day, we make every effort to control as many elements as possible. In reality, the players that end up on our teams are largely controlled by the other owners. Their bidding affects your ability to roster the players you want. In a snake draft, the other owners control your roster even more. We are really only able to get the players we want within the limitations set by others.

However, an optimal roster can be constructed from a fanalytic assessment of skill and risk combined with more assertive draft day demeanor.

Why this makes sense

1. Our obsession with projected player values is holding us back. If a player on your draft list is valued at $20 and you agonize when the bidding hits $23, odds are about two chances in three that he could really earn anywhere from $15 to $25. What this means is, in some cases, and within reason, you should just pay what it takes to get the players you want.

2. There is no such thing as a bargain. Most of us *don't* just pay what it takes because we are always on the lookout for players who go under value. But we really don't know which players will cost less than they will earn because prices are still driven by the draft table. The concept of "bargain" assumes that we even know what a player's true value is.

3. "Control" is there for the taking. Most owners are so focused on their own team that they really don't pay much attention to what you're doing. There are some exceptions, and bidding wars do happen, but in general, other owners will not provide that much resistance.

How it's done

1. Create your optimal draft pool.
2. Get those players.

Start by identifying which players will be draftable based on the LIMA or Portfolio3 criteria. Then, at the draft, focus solely on your roster. When it's your bid opener, toss a player you need at

about 50%-75% of your projected value. Bid aggressively and just pay what you need to pay. Of course, don't spend $40 for a player with $25 market value, but it's okay to exceed your projected value within reason.

From a tactical perspective, mix up the caliber of openers. Drop out early on some bids to prevent other owners from catching on to you.

In the end, it's okay to pay a slight premium to make sure you get the players with the highest potential to provide a good return on your investment. It's no different than the premium you might pay for a player with position flexibility or to get the last valuable shortstop. With TCD, you're just spending those extra dollars up front to ensure you are rostering your targets. As a side benefit, TCD almost asssures that you don't leave money on the table.

Mayberry Method

The foundation of the Mayberry Method (MM) is the assertion that we really can't project player performance with the level of precision that advanced metrics and modeling systems would like us to believe.

MM is named after the fictional TV village where life was simpler. MM evaluates skill by embracing the imprecision of the forecasting process and projecting performance in broad strokes rather than with hard statistics.

MM reduces every player to a 7-character code. The format of the code is 5555 AAA, where the first four characters describe elements of a player's skill on a scale of 0 to 5. These skills are indexed to the league average so that players are evaluated within the context of the level of offense or pitching in a given year.

The three alpha characters are our reliability grades (Health, Experience and Consistency) on the standard A-to-F scale. The skills numerics are forward-looking; the alpha characters grade reliability based on past history.

Batting

The first character in the MM code measures a batter's power skills. It is assigned using the following table:

Power Index	MM
0 - 49	0
50 - 79	1
80 - 99	2
100 - 119	3
120 - 159	4
160+	5

The second character measures a batter's speed skills. RSpd takes our Statistically Scouted Speed metric (Spd) and adds the elements of opportunity and success rate, to construct the formula of RSpd = Spd x (SBO + SB%).

RSpd	MM
0 - 39	0
40 - 59	1
60 - 79	2
80 - 99	3
100 - 119	4
120+	5

The third character measures expected batting average.

xBA Index	MM
0-87	0
88-92	1
93-97	2
98-102	3
103-107	4
108+	5

The fourth character measures playing time.

Role	PA	MM
Potential full-timers	450+	5
Mid-timers	250-449	3
Fringe/bench	100-249	1
Non-factors	0-99	0

Pitching

The first character in the pitching MM code measures xERA, which captures a pitcher's overall ability and is a proxy for ERA, and even WHIP.

xERA Index	MM
0-80	0
81-90	1
91-100	2
101-110	3
111-120	4
121+	5

The second character measures strikeout ability.

K/9 Index	MM
0-76	0
77-88	1
89-100	2
101-112	3
113-124	4
125+	5

The third character measures saves potential.

Description	Saves est.	MM
No hope for saves; starting pitchers	0	0
Speculative closer	1-9	1
Closer in a pen with alternatives	10-24	2
Frontline closer with firm bullpen role	25+	3

The fourth character measures **playing time**.

Role	IP	MM
Potential #1-2 starters	180+	5
Potential #3-4 starters	130-179	3
#5 starters/swingmen	70-129	1
Relievers	0-69	0

Overall Mayberry Scores

The real value of Mayberry is to provide a skills profile on a player-by-player basis. I want to be able to see this…

Player A	4455 AAB
Player B	5245 BBD
Player C	5255 BAB
Player D	5155 BAF

…and make an objective, unbiased determination about these four players without being swayed by preconceived notions and baggage. But there is a calculation that provides a single, overall value for each player.

This is the calculation for the overall MM batting score:

MM Score =
(PX score + Spd score + xBA score + PA score)
x PA score

An overall MM pitching score is calculated as:

MM Score =
((xERA score x 2) + K/9 score + Saves score + IP score)
x (IP score + Saves score)

The highest score you can get for either is 100. That makes the result of the formula easy to assess.

BaseballHQ.com analyst Patrick Davitt did some great research about using Reliability Grades to adjust the Mayberry scores. His research showed that "higher-reliability players met their Mayberry targets more often than their lower-reliability counterparts, and players with all "D" or "F" reliability scores underperform Mayberry projections far more often. Those results can be reflected by multiplying a player's MM Score by each of three reliability bonuses or penalties:"

I've taken his work a minor step further and applied slightly different multipliers to each Reliability element.

	Health	Experience	Consistency
A	x 1.10	x 1.10	x 1.10
B	x 1.05	x 1.05	x 1.05
C	x 1.00	x 1.00	x 1.00
D	x 0.90	x 0.95	x 0.95
F	x 0.80	x 0.90	x 0.90

So, let's perform the overall calculations for Player A above, using these Reliability adjustments.

Player A: 4455 AAB
= (4+4+5+5) x 5
= 90 x 1.10 x 1.10 x 1.05
= 114.3

The Portfolio3 Plan (P3)

When it comes to profitability, all players are not created equal. Every player has a different role on your team by virtue of his skill set, dollar value/draft round, position and risk profile. When it comes to a strategy for how to approach a specific player, one size does not fit all.

We need some players to return fair value more than others. A $40/first round player going belly-up is going to hurt you far more than a $1/23rd round bust. End-gamers are easily replaceable.

We rely on some players for profit more than others. First-rounders do not provide the most profit potential; that comes from players further down the value rankings.

We can afford to weather more risk with some players than with others. Since high-priced early-rounders need to return at least fair value, we cannot afford to take on excessive risk. Our risk tolerance opens up with later-round/lower cost picks.

Players have different risk profiles based solely on what roster spot they are going to fill. Catchers are more injury prone. A closer's value is highly dependent on managerial decision. These types of players are high risk even if they have great skills. That needs to affect their draft price or draft round.

For some players, the promise of providing a scarce skill, or productivity at a scarce position, may trump risk. Not always, but sometimes. The determining factor is usually price.

In the end, we need a way to integrate all these different types of players, roles and needs. We need to put some structure to the concept of a diversified draft approach. Thus:

The Portfolio3 Plan provides a three-tiered structure to the draft. Just like most folks prefer to diversify their stock portfolio, P3 advises to diversify your roster with three different types of players. Depending upon the stage of the draft (and budget constraints in auction leagues), P3 uses a different set of rules for each tier that you'll draft from. The three tiers are:

1. Core Players
2. Mid-Game Players
3. End-Game Players

Mayberry scores can be used as proxies for the skills filters. When planning your draft, pretty much all you need to remember is the number "3". That essentially represents "just over league average" and makes it easy to set your targets.

TIER 1: CORE PLAYERS
General Roster Goals

Auction target: Budget a maximum of $160. Any player purchased for $20 or more should meet the Tier 1 skills criteria

Snake draft target: 5-8 players, with an emphasis on those drafted in the earlier rounds

Reliability grades: No worse than "B" for each variable (Health, Experience and Consistency)

Playing time: No restrictions, however, pricier early round players should have more guaranteed playing time

Batter skills: Minimum MM scores of 3 in xBA *plus* either PX or RSpd

Pitcher skills: Minimum MM scores of 3 in xERA *and* K/9

Tier 1 players provide the foundation to your roster. These are your prime contributors and where you will invest the largest percentage of your budget or early round picks. There is no room for risk here, so the majority of these players should be batters.

TIER 2: MID-GAME PLAYERS
General Roster Goals

Auction target: Budget between $50 and $100; players should be under $20

Snake draft target: 7-13 players

Reliability grades: No worse than "B" for Health, no worse than "C" for Experience and Consistency

Playing time: Must have a MM score of 5 for batters (meaning full-time batters) and minimum 3 for pitchers (meaning at least mid-rotation starting pitchers)

Batter skills: Minimum MM scores of 3 in xBA or PX or RSpd

Pitcher skills: Minimum MM score of 3 in xERA or K/9

Tier 1 players are all about skill. Tier 2 is all about accumulating playing time, particularly on the batting side, with lesser regard to skill. This is where you can beef up on runs and RBI. If

a player is getting 500 AB, he is likely going to provide positive value in those categories just from opportunity alone. And given that his team is seeing fit to give him those AB, he is probably also contributing somewhere else.

For pitchers, we use Tier 2 to accumulate arms whose innings provide some level of positive support, either by stockpiling strikeouts or by building your ERA foundation.

TIER 3: END-GAME PLAYERS
General Roster Goals

Auction target: Budget up to $50; players should be under $10

Snake draft target: 5-10 players

Reliability grades: No restrictions, except no "F" Health grades.

Playing time: No restrictions

Batter skills: Minimum MM scores of 3 in xBA plus either PX or RSpd (same as Tier 1)

Pitcher skills: Minimum MM score of 3 in xERA

Tier 3 players are your gambling chips, but every end-gamer must provide the promise of upside. For that reason, the focus must remain on skill and conditional opportunity. MP3 drafters should fill the majority of their pitching slots from this group.

By definition, end-gamers are typically high risk players, but risk is something you'll want to embrace here. If a a Tier 3 player does not pan out, he can be easily replaced.

As such, the best Tier 3 options should possess the MM skill levels noted above, and at least one of the following:

- playing time upside as a back-up to a risky front-liner
- an injury history that has depressed his value (but not chronically injured players)
- solid skills demonstrated at some point in the past
- minor league potential even if he has been more recently a major league bust

A complete list of players in each tier appears in the back of the book starting on page 248. One of the major benefits of the MP3 process is that any player failing to find a home in one of the tiers can be safely ignored. Either his skills are not draft-worthy or his risk-profile too dangerous, regardless of skill. By shrinking the draftable player pool, it makes the roster planning and construction process easier.

Category Targets
The final task is to set MM targets for each category.

If you are in a league with good trading activity, this may not be important—you can always deal away excesses to beef up weak categories. But for those in leagues with little or no trading, drafting a balanced team is critical.

For skills budgeting, here are targets for standard leagues:

BATTING	PX	RSpd	xBA	PA
12-team mixed	41	28	40	66
15-team mixed	41	26	39	64
12-team AL/NL	37	23	32	54

PITCHING	xERA*	K/9*	Sv	IP
12-team mixed	23	33	7	29
15-team mixed	20	30	6	30
12-team AL/NL	17	27	5	25

*Make sure the majority of these points come from starting pitchers.

As you draft, track each MM score and keep a running total of all the categories. With the above goals will allow you to shift your in-draft targets if you see you are falling behind in any area.

Consistency in Head-to-Head leagues *(Dylan Hedges)*

Few things are as valuable to H2H league success as filling your roster with players who can produce a solid baseline of stats, week in and week out. In traditional leagues, while consistency is not as important—all we care about are aggregate numbers—filling your team with consistent players can make roster management easier.

Consistent batters have good plate discipline, walk rates and on base percentages. These are foundation skills. Those who add power to the mix are obviously more valuable, however, the ability to hit home runs consistently is rare.

Consistent pitchers demonstrate similar skills in each outing; if they also produce similar results, they are even more valuable.

We can track consistency but predicting it is difficult. Many fantasy leaguers try to predict a batter's hot or cold streaks, or individual pitcher starts, but that is typically a fool's errand. The best we can do is find players who demonstrate seasonal consistency; in-season, we must manage players and consistency tactically.

Building a consistent Head-to-Head team *(David Martin)*

Teams in head-to-head leagues need batters who are consistent. Focusing on certain metrics helps build consistency, which is the roster holy grail for H2H players. Our filters for such success are:

- Contact rate = minimum 80%
- xBA = minimum .280
- PX (or Spd) = minimum 120
- RC/G = minimum 5.00

Ratio insulation in Head-to-Head leagues *(David Martin)*

On a week-to-week basis, inequities are inherent in the head-to-head game. One way to eliminate your competitor's advantage in the pure numbers game is to build your team's pitching foundation around the ratio categories.

One should normally insulate at the end of a draft, once your hitters are in place. To obtain several ratio insulators, target pitchers that have:

- Cmd greater than 3.0
- Dom greater than 7.5
- xERA less than 3.30

While adopting this strategy may compromise wins, research has shown that wins come at a cost to ERA and WHIP. Roster space permitting, adding two to four insulators to your team will improve your team's weekly ERA and WHIP.

Consistency in points leagues *(Bill Macey)*

Previous research has demonstrated that week-to-week statistical consistency is important for Rotisserie-based head-to-head play. But one can use the same foundation in points-based games. A study showed that not only do players with better skills post more overall points in this format, but that the format caters to consistent performances on a week-to-week basis, even after accounting for differences in total points scored and playing-time.

Therefore, when drafting your batters in points-based head-to-head leagues, ct% and bb% make excellent tiebreakers if you are having trouble deciding between two players with similarly projected point totals. Likewise, when rostering pitchers, favor those who tend not to give up home runs.

In-Season Analyses

The efficacy of streaming *(John Burnson)*

In leagues that allow weekly or daily transactions, many owners flit from hot player to hot player. But published dollar values don't capture this traffic—they assume that players are owned from April to October. For many leagues, this may be unrealistic.

We decided to calculate these "investor returns." For each week, we identified the top players by one statistic—BA for hitters, ERA for pitchers—and took the top 100 hitters and top 50 pitchers. We then said that, at the end of the week, the #1 player was picked up (or already owned) by 100% of teams, the #2 player was picked up or owned by 99% of teams, and so on, down to the 100th player, who was on 1% of teams. (For pitchers, we stepped by 2%.) Last, we tracked each player's performance in the next week, when ownership matters.

We ran this process anew for every week of the season, tabulating each player's "investor returns" along the way. If a player was owned by 100% of teams, then we awarded him 100% of his performance. If the player was owned by half the teams, we gave him half his performance. If he was owned by no one (that is, he was not among the top players in the prior week), his performance was ignored. A player's cumulative stats over the season was his investor return.

The results...

- 60% of pitchers had poorer investor returns, with an aggregate ERA 0.40 higher than their true ERA.
- 55% of batters had poorer investor returns, but with an aggregate batting average virtually identical to the true BA.

Sitting stars and starting scrubs *(Ed DeCaria)*

In setting your pitching rotation, conventional wisdom suggests sticking with trusted stars despite difficult matchups. But does this hold up? And can you carefully start inferior pitchers against weaker opponents? Here are the ERAs posted by varying skilled pitchers facing a range of different strength offenses:

Pitcher (ERA)	OPPOSING OFFENSE (RC/G)				
	5.25+	5.00	4.25	4.00	<4.00
3.00-	3.46	3.04	3.04	2.50	2.20
3.50	3.98	3.94	3.44	3.17	2.87
4.00	4.72	4.57	3.96	3.66	3.24
4.50	5.37	4.92	4.47	4.07	3.66
5.00+	6.02	5.41	5.15	4.94	4.42

Recommendations:

1. Never start below replacement-level pitchers.
2. Always start elite pitchers.
3. Other than that, never say never or always.

Playing matchups can pay off when the difference in opposing offense is severe.

Daily Fantasy Baseball

Daily Fantasy Sports (DFS) is an offshoot of traditional fantasy sports. Many of the same analytic methods that are integral to seasonal fantasy baseball are just as relevant for DFS.

General Format

1. The overwhelming majority of DFS contests are pay-for-play where the winners are compensated a percentage of their entry fee, in accordance with the rules of that game.

2. DFS baseball contests are generally based on a single day's slate of games, or a subset of the day's games (i.e., all afternoon games or all evening games)

3. Most DFS formats are points-based salary cap games.

Most Popular Contests

1. Cash Games: Three variants (50/50, Multipliers, and Head-to-Head) all pay out a flat prize to a portion of the entries.

2. GPP (Guaranteed prize pool) Tournaments: The overall winner earns the largest prize and prizes scale downward.

3. Survivor: A survivor contest is a multiple-slate format where a portion of the entries survives to play the following day.

4. Qualifiers/Satellites: Tournaments where the prize(s) consist of entry tickets to a larger tournament.

DFS Analysis

1. Predicting single-day performance entails adjusting a baseline projection based on that day's match-up. This adjusted expectation is considered in context with a player's salary to determine his potential contributions relative to the other players.

2. Weighted on base average (wOBA) is a souped-up version of OBP, and is a favorite metric to help evaluate both hitters and pitchers. (For more useful DFS metrics, see next section)

3. Pitching: In DFS, innings and strikeouts are the two chief means of accruing points, so they need to be weighed heavily in pitching evaluation.

Tips for Players New to DFS

1. Start slow and be prepared to lose: While cogent analysis can increase your chances of winning, the variance associated with a single day's worth of outcomes doesn't assure success. Short-term losing streaks are inevitable, so start with low cost cash games before embarking on tournament play.

2. Minimize the number of sites you play: The DFS space is dominated by two sites but there are other options. At the beginning, stick to one or two. Once you're comfortable, consider expanding to others.

3. Bankroll management: The recommended means to manage your bankroll is to risk no more than 10% on a given day. Within that portion, the suggested ratio is 80% cash games to 20% GPP tournament action.

4. General Strategies

    A. Cash Games: Conventional wisdom preaches to be conservative in cash games. Upper level starting pitchers make excellent cash game options. For hitters, it's best to spread your choices among several teams. In general, you're looking for players with a high floor rather than a high ceiling.

    B: GPP Tournaments: In tournaments (with a larger number of entrants), a common ploy is to select a lesser priced, though risky, pitcher with a favorable match-up. It's also very common to overload—or stack—several batters from the same team, hoping that squad scores a bunch of runs.

5. Miscellaneous Tips

    A. Pay extra attention to games threatened by weather, as well as players who are not a lock to be in the lineup.

    B. Avoid playing head-to-head against strangers until you're comfortable and have enjoyed some success.

    C. Stay disciplined. The worst thing you can do is eat up your bankroll quickly by entering into tournaments.

    D. Most importantly, have fun. Obviously, you want to win, but hopefully you're also in it for the challenge of mastering the unique skills intrinsic to DFS.

Using BaseballHQ Tools in DFS

Here are some of the additional skill metrics to consider:

Cash Game Metrics

bb%: This simple indicator may receive only a quick glance when building lineups, but it is imperative in providing insight on a batter's underlying approach and plate discipline. Walks also equal points in all DFS scoring structures.

ct%: Another byproduct of good plate discipline, reflecting the percentage of balls put in play. Players with strong contact rates tend to provide a higher floor, and less chance of a negative score from a free swinger with a high strikeout rate.

xBA: Measures a hitter's BA by multiplying his contact rate by the chance that a ball in play falls for a hit. Hitters whose BA is far below their xBA may be "due" for some hits.

Tournament / GPP BPIs

PX / xPX: Home runs are the single greatest multi-point event. Using PX (power index) and xPX (expected power index) together can help identify underperformers who are due in the power category.

Choosing Pitchers in DFS

The criteria for choosing a pitcher(s) may be more narrow than for full-season league, but the skills focus should remain.

Major Considerations

• Overall skills. Look for the following minimums: 2.9 Ctl (bb/9), 7.7 Dom (k/9), 2.6 Cmd (k/bb), and max 1.0 HR/9.

• Home/Away. In 2017, MLB pitchers logged a 4.12 ERA, 8.0 Dom, 2.7 Cmd at home; 4.59 ERA, 8.3 Dom, 2.4 Cmd on the road.

• Is he pitching at Coors Field? (Even the best pitchers are a risky start there.)

Moderate Considerations

• Recent performance. Examine Ks and BBs over last 4-5 starts.

• Strength of opponent. Refer to opposing team's OPS for the season, as well as more recent performance.

Minor Considerations

• L/R issues. Does the pitcher/opponent have wide platoon splits?

• Park. Is the game at a hitter's/pitcher's/neutral park?

• Previous outings. Has he faced this team already this season? If so, how did he fare? (Skills; not just his ERA.)

You will hopefully be left with a tiered list of pitching options, ripe for comparing individual risk/reward level against their price point.

Two-start pitcher weeks *(Ed DeCaria)*

A two-start pitcher is a prized possession. But those starts can mean two DOMinant outings, two DISasters, or anything else in between, as shown by these results:

PQS Pair	% Weeks	ERA	WHIP	Win/Wk	K/Wk
DOM-DOM	20%	2.53	1.02	1.1	12.0
DOM-AVG	28%	3.60	1.25	0.8	9.2
AVG-AVG	14%	4.44	1.45	0.7	6.8
DOM-DIS	15%	5.24	1.48	0.6	7.9
AVG-DIS	17%	6.58	1.74	0.5	5.7
DIS-DIS	6%	8.85	2.07	0.3	5.0

Weeks that include even one DISaster start produce terrible results. Unfortunately, avoiding such disasters is much easier in hindsight. But what is the actual impact of this decision on the stat categories?

ERA and WHIP: When the difference between opponents is extreme, inferior pitchers can be a better percentage play. This is true both for 1-start pitchers and 2-start pitchers, and for choosing inferior one-start pitchers over superior two-start pitchers.

Strikeouts per Week: Unlike the two rate stats, there is a massive shift in the balance of power between one-start and two-start pitchers in the strikeout category. Even stars with easy one-start matchups can only barely keep pace with two-start replacement-level arms in strikeouts per week.

Wins per week are also dominated by the two-start pitchers. Even the very worst two-start pitchers will earn a half of a win on average, which is the same rate as the very best one-start pitchers.

The bottom line: If strikeouts and wins are the strategic priority, use as many two-start weeks as the rules allow, even if it means using a replacement-level pitcher with two tough starts instead of a mid-level arm with a single easy start. But if ERA and/or WHIP management are the priority, two-start pitchers can be very powerful, as a single week might impact the standings by over 1.5 points in ERA/WHIP, positively or negatively.

Six tips on category management *(Todd Zola)*

1. Disregard whether you are near the top or the bottom of a category; focus instead on the gaps directly above and below your squad.
2. Prorate the difference in stats between teams.
3. ERA tends to move towards WHIP.
4. As the season progresses, the number of AB/IF do not preclude a gain/loss in the ratio categories.
5. An opponent's point lost is your point gained.
6. *Most important!* Come crunch time, forget value, forget names, and forget reputation. It's all about stats and where you are situated within each category.

Other Diamonds

Balls

The logical variable—independently proven—that explains why my fantasy team had five 30-HR hitters in 2017 and still finished in 7th place.

Cellar value

The dollar value at which a player cannot help but earn more than he costs. Always profit here.

Crickets

The sound heard when someone's opening draft bid on a player is also the only bid.

Scott Elarton List

Players you drop out on when the bidding reaches $1.

End-game wasteland

Home for players undraftable in the deepest of leagues, who stay in the free agent pool all year. It's the place where even crickets keep quiet when a name is called at the draft.

FAAB Forewarnings

1. Spend early and often.
2. Emptying your budget for one prime league-crosser is a tactic that should be reserved for the desperate.
3. If you chase two rabbits, you will lose them both.

Fantasy Economics 101

The market value for a player is based on the aura of past performance, not the promise of future potential. Your greatest advantage is to leverage the space between market value and real value.

Fantasy Economics 102

The variance between market value and real value is far more important than the absolute accuracy of any individual player projection.

Hope

A commodity that routinely goes for $5 over value at the draft table.

Professional Free Agent (PFA)

Player whose name will never come up on draft day but will always end up on a roster at some point during the season as an injury replacement.

Mike Timlin List

Players who you are unable to resist drafting even though they have burned you multiple times in the past.

Seasonal Assessment Standard

If you still have reason to be reading the boxscores during the last weekend of the season, then your year has to be considered a success.

The Three Cardinal Rules for Winners

If you cherish this hobby, you will live by them or die by them...

1. Revel in your success; fame is fleeting.
2. Exercise excruciating humility.
3. 100% of winnings must be spent on significant others.

Positive Relative Outcomes (PRO): A Better Denominator

by Patrick Davitt

The metrics we use for player evaluation have too many different denominators. Common stats use per 9 IP, Batters Faced (BF), AB and plate appearances (PA). Hardness-of-hit and trajectory metrics use balls-in-play, including HRs, while hit rate (h% or BABIP) uses per ball-in-play, not including HR. And infield flies (IF) are calculated as a percentage of fly balls.

That's seven different denominators (eight, if we count the (AB+BB) denominator used for the BaseballHQ.com batter walk rate). Yet we use these rate stats interchangeably and sometimes in combination to compare and evaluate players. A "common denominator" would let look broadly across multiple outcomes, and combine various outcomes into actionable metrics.

Sticking to percentages—per-BF for pitchers and per-PA for hitters—would be that common denominator and would offer several built-in advantages:

- BF for pitchers is the same as PA for hitters.
- Both PA and BF are based on pitcher-versus-batter, the game's primary interaction.
- It's easy to convert existing metrics, Dom, Ctl and HR/9 to percentages.
- And some commonly cited metrics, like K% and bb%, already use these percentages.

Enter Positive Relative Outcomes (PRO).

Before we get to some results of using BF and PA ratios, we'll set some levels. Starting pitchers reach around 900 batters in a season (2017's leader was Rick Porcello, at 885). The average BF for starters in 2017 was around 520, about 23 BF/G, in a range from 14.5 to 27.0. Elite starters see about the same number of batters per game, but got outs more efficiently and therefore had lower BF/IP and got deeper into games. Ace relievers have 250-300 BF.

Full-time batters at the top of the order will have 725+ PA, mid-order guys roughly 690-710, lower-order guys 650-690. Platoon guys and other part-timers naturally amass fewer PA.

A first step in this PRO study was a general "smell test," comparing player rankings under existing metrics and their percentage-based equivalents. There was general overlap up and down the rankings in all the categories, but at every level, percentages indicated better fantasy performers. For instance, top-10 Dominance (K/9) included Dinelson Lamet and Jacob deGrom. Top-10 K% dropped them in favor of Clayton Kershaw and Stephen Strasburg. The same results emerged with relievers and hitters in all metrics, so the initial smell test came out roses.

Pitchers

The next step in PRO was to focus on pitchers, converting all available outcomes to rates per-BF (which we'll call "percentages" from here on). We further categorized each percentage as "Positive" or "Negative" depending on its effect on the pitcher's results:

- "Positive" outcomes were Ks and IF, which allow neither base hits nor "productive outs" that advance baserunners (Ks, of course, are also a counting stat unto themselves).
- "Positive" outcomes also included soft-and medium-hit groundballs and flyballs, which limit hits and productive outs—the H% is under 10% on soft- and medium-hit FBs and under 20% for soft- and medium-hit GBs.
- "Negative" outcomes were hard-hit GB and FB (hits half or more of the time, and extra-base hits for HHFB), line drives (hits two-thirds or more, including XBH), walks and HBP, all which put runners on and advance them.

Most established regular pitchers are pretty consistent year-to-year in these outcomes. But individual pitchers vary more widely in specific outcome categories. To smooth out the variance and create a broader metric, the next step was to add all the "Positive" outcome percentages into one overall category and all the "Negatives" into an overall category.

For benchmarks in the Positive outcomes, here are the best, worst and average for all starters:

Starters	GB		FB				
	Sft	Med	Sft	Med	K	IF	TOT
Best	15%	26%	12%	18%	36%	7%	73%
Average	7%	17%	4%	11%	21%	2%	62%
Worst	3%	11%	1%	5%	9%	0%	54%

The Top-10 2017 starters (min 10 starts, min 70% starts) by overall Positive percentages:

Starters	GB		FB				
	Sft	Med	Sft	Med	K	IF	TOT
Max Scherzer	4%	13%	6%	12%	34%	3%	73%
Chris Sale	5%	12%	5%	12%	36%	2%	73%
Corey Kluber	9%	14%	4%	8%	34%	2%	72%
Clayton Kershaw	9%	17%	5%	9%	30%	2%	71%
Luis Severino	8%	18%	4%	9%	29%	2%	70%
Marco Estrada	5%	12%	9%	17%	22%	6%	70%
Stephen Strasburg	8%	16%	4%	10%	29%	2%	70%
Luis Castillo	10%	20%	3%	7%	27%	1%	69%
A.J. Griffin	4%	11%	12%	17%	18%	7%	68%
Masahiro Tanaka	9%	19%	4%	9%	26%	3%	68%

The list contains the top of your Cheat Sheet, but also intriguing names like Estrada, Castillo, and Griffin that might be worth further exploration.

And here's the Bottom-10 of lowest Positive pitchers in 2017:

Starters	GB		FB				
	Sft	Med	Sft	Med	K	IF	TOT
Homer Bailey	6%	19%	3%	8%	16%	2%	54%
Daniel Norris	5%	12%	6%	11%	19%	2%	54%
Brett Anderson	14%	16%	2%	6%	15%	1%	54%
Amir Garrett	6%	14%	3%	11%	20%	1%	54%
Chris Tillman	5%	16%	5%	11%	14%	2%	54%
Derek Holland	7%	13%	5%	11%	17%	2%	54%
Edinson Volquez	8%	14%	3%	9%	20%	2%	55%
Kyle Gibson	7%	20%	2%	8%	17%	1%	56%
Adam Conley	6%	14%	6%	10%	16%	4%	56%
Martin Perez	6%	21%	3%	9%	14%	2%	56%

Mostly expected names, but if you've heard early buzz on Kyle Gibson, or a Homer Bailey rebound... well, *caveat emptor.*

We can also flip this metric on its head, and look at pitchers in terms of their Negative outcome rates, rather than Positive outcome rates. The highest (worst) Negative percentages mostly overlapped the low-Positive starters, but included such pitchers as Ian Kennedy, Alex Cobb, and Jake Odorizzi. Pitchers who had low Negative percentages (again, which is a good sign), also mirrored the high-Positives, but you can add Carlos Carrasco, Luke Weaver, Danny Salazar, Lance McCullers and World Series hero Charlie Morton. The full lists appear on page 257.

Next, subtracting every pitcher's Negative percentage from his positive gave a "Net Positive" metric. The gamewide average was +24% (24 points more Positive% outcomes than Negative). Scherzer/Sale/Kluber/Kershaw were all at the top of the list, with Scherzer and Sale at +44%. Also with Net Positive% scores at least 10 points higher than the gamewide level: Estrada, who could be a great bounceback candidate in 2018 after undisclosed personal issues torpedoed his mid-season performance; Nathan Karns, Weaver and Daniels Mengden (+31%) and Duffy (+30%).

Back-testing pitchers

To conclude this section, sorting pitchers by their Net Positive resulted in identifying pitchers worth fantasy consideration at the top and those perhaps worth passing at the bottom. A year ago, this exercise flagged interesting potential in CC Sabathia, Dallas Keuchel, Zack Greinke and Marcus Stroman, all of whom had better 2017 performances than in 2016.

At the bottom of the 2016 table, the lower Net Positive pitchers included 2017 duds like Tillman, Gerrit Cole, Adam Wainwright, John Lackey and Martin Perez. The 2017 low Net Positives include the pitchers named above in the low-Positive and high-Negative lists. The lowest of the low: Chris Tillman, at +6% Net Positive.

Hitters

For hitters, it stood to reason that we could just reverse the outcomes, since what's good for pitchers is bad for hitters, and vice-versa. So, positive hitter outcomes are:

- Hard-hit GB (HHGB) and hard-hit FB (HHFB)
- Line Drives
- HBP and walks

And negative hitter outcomes:

- Strikeouts
- Soft- and medium-hit GB and FB
- And infield flies

Here are the baseline levels on the Positive hitter outcomes:

Batters	|—Hard—|				
	GB	FB	LD	BB	HBP	TOT
Best	12%	16%	23%	19%	5%	54%
Average	6%	9%	14%	9%	1%	34%
Worst	3%	3%	7%	2%	0%	26%

We again totaled Positive and Negative separately, then subtracted Negative from Positive to find hitters who were most successful at having productive plate appearances. We looked at hitters with at least 250 PA in 2017.

Total Positive outcomes averaged 34%, while total Negatives averaged 52%, making the average Net Positive -18% (18 points fewer Positive outcomes than Negative). This sounds bad, but

-18% is actually typical over many seasons and reflects the difficulty of generating positive outcomes. (Remember the adage about good hitters failing 7 times out of 10?)

The leader in Net Positive% was Joey Votto at +8%. Only two other hitters—Justin Turner (+6%) and Matt Carpenter (+1%)—were above zero in Net Positive. All three were also the only hitters above 50% Positive outcomes. The leaders (see page 256 for expanded lists):

Best (Highest) Pos		Best (Lowest) Neg		Best (Highest) Net	
Joey Votto	54%	Joey Votto	46%	Joey Votto	+8%
Justin Turner	54%	Justin Turner	48%	Justin Turner	+6%
Matt Carpenter	50%	Matt Carpenter	50%	Matt Carpenter	+1%
Freddie Freeman	50%	Freddie Freeman	50%	Freddie Freeman	-1%
Mike Trout	49%	Alex Avila	52%	Alex Avila	-3%
Daniel Murphy	49%	Joe Mauer	52%	Miguel Cabrera	-4%
Alex Avila	48%	Miguel Cabrera	52%	Joe Mauer	-4%
Miguel Cabrera	48%	Buster Posey	53%	Mike Trout	-4%
Paul Goldschmidt	48%	Eric Sogard	53%	Buster Posey	-5%
Joe Mauer	48%	Nick Castellanos	53%	Paul Goldschmidt	-6%
Buster Posey	48%	Mike Trout	53%	Aaron Judge	-6%

Worst (Lowest) Pos		Worst (Highest) Neg		Worst (Lowest) Net	
Austin Hedges	33%	Ryan Goins	68%	Hunter Renfroe	-36%
J.J. Hardy	33%	Chris Young	68%	Jarrod Dyson	-36%
Javier Baez	32%	Jake Marisnick	69%	Javier Baez	-36%
Cameron Rupp	32%	Matt Chapman	69%	Kevan Smith	-36%
Guillermo Heredia	32%	Joey Rickard	69%	Cameron Rupp	-36%
Jonathan Villar	32%	Tim Anderson	69%	Joey Rickard	-36%
Kevan Smith	32%	Kennys Vargas	69%	Ryan Goins	-37%
Ryan Goins	32%	Billy Hamilton	69%	M. Maldonado	-37%
Rajai Davis	32%	Mike Napoli	69%	Matt Davidson	-37%

Conclusion

The usual caveats about variability and sample size apply, but it seems that if you can get a player who has more Postive outcomes (and fewer Negatives) than another, you should consider him.

It's important to remember that while these metrics do show some season-to-season stickiness, we haven't fully tested their predictive value, and anomalies suggest further refinement is needed.

Among the lower-ranked guys on the hitter Net-Positive table, for example, we saw hitters like Jonathan Schoop, who was terrific in 2017; Eduardo Nunez, who wasn't as terrific as Schoop but darned useful; and Didi Gregorius, who was likewise excellent.

Schoop's Positive-Negative profile from 2016 to 2017 is interesting and might prove instructive. His K%, IF%, and LD% all stayed the same. He did take more walks, up from 3% to 5% of PA. But the big changes were slight improvements in his hard-hit GB and FB, up a total of five percentage points, with his weaker GB and FB down by a like amount. Considering the difference in H% between hard-hit and non-hard GBs and FBs, Schoop's sudden jump in BA might be explainable (and his RBI surge likewise at least partially explained).

The next step could be to weight the categories, to more accurately reflect actual contributions to success or failure. Maybe Ks would be fully counted or even amplified, with contact types weighted according to their actual relationships with success or failure. Maybe we could regress total bases per BF ... the possibilities abound.

And the future awaits.

Deserved Home Runs

by Arik Florimonte

Introduction

The "Other Diamonds" section of the Encyclopedia of Fanalytics earlier in this book defines "Errant Gust of Wind" as:

A unit of measure used to describe the difference between your home run projection and mine.

While somewhat droll, this definition also contains the core truth: Good or back luck contributes an outsized amount to baseball outcomes in general, and batted ball outcomes in particular. Of perhaps the most interest is the binary outcome that causes the largest swing of all: the home run.

Fortunately, today every batted ball is measured and the results are publicly available via MLB's Statcast™. Using batted ball data, we can compare what actually happened to what usually happens. With focus on home runs, not only can we measure park factors more directly than before, we can also identify pitchers and batters who have benefited or struggled as a result of too many errant gusts of wind.

Methodology

Using batted ball data from 2015-2016, we created a model for expected home run rate given exit velocity (EV) and launch angle (LA). We applied this model to the entire database of batted balls to determine the likelihood that a particular batted ball should have been a home run. This is known as the deserved home run (dHR).

Comparing actual home runs to dHR in aggregate, we calculate the park effects for each ballpark based on the balls that were actually hit there. Finally, for each pitcher or batter, we compare the actual home runs hit or allowed to park-adjusted dHR to find how lucky or unlucky each player was.

Building the Model

For any given LA, we can plot HR per batted ball by EV. We fit a hyperbolic tangent function, offset and normalized so that it goes to 0 as the x-axis approaches -infinity and to +1.0 as the x-axis approaches +infinity. The resulting graph shows the probability of a home run as a function of EV for that launch angle. This example is for the prime HR launch angle of 27 degrees:

Homeruns per Batted Ball
Launch Angle=27°, tanh fit

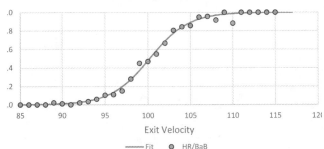

From this fit we extract a midpoint (50% HR probability), and a width (distance between 2% HR probability and 98% HR probability). We repeat this analysis for all launch angles from

16°-46° (those with enough home runs for good statistics). Both the midpoint and width vary across launch angles in a reasonably well-behaved way, and can be modeled themselves. The result is a model that for a given combination of Launch Angle and Exit Velocity, will output the likelihood of that batted ball becoming a home run.

Updated park factors

Reviewing all batted balls from 2015-2017, we simply add up the dHR and compare them to actual HR, by ballpark, by batter handedness, to get dHR park factors (Park Factor = HR/dHR)

LHB are shown on the top graph, and RHB on the bottom. Those with significant deviation from BHQ's existing part factors are noted.

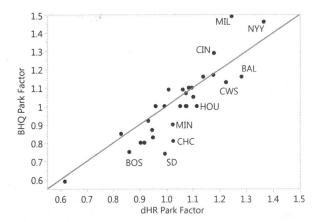

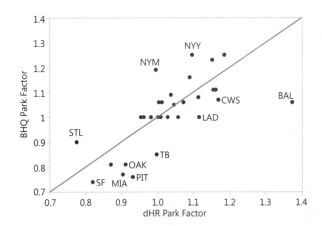

The standard methodology for calculating park factors works on the assumption that the teams ought to produce roughly the same results in different ballparks, so the differences are due to the ballpark. This would likely be true over a very large number of games, but the calculation is done over a relatively small number of games per year, often months apart with different players or different lineups. The result is a highly variable park factor.

The dHR methodology mathematically places objectively measured batted balls into different ballparks, which means that the players and the teams no longer matter (with the underlying assumption that batted-ball direction is not inordinately weighted toward the shorter or deeper parts of the ballpark). The only inputs are the launch angle and the velocity of the ball when it left the bat, so the data set is much, much larger, and we'd expect a much more stable result year to year.

In fact, dHR park factors are reasonably well correlated year to year, with an R2 value of .45, while classic single-year park factors yield and R2 value of .07.

2017's Home Runs

Deserved HR are park-neutral. To get an expected HR output from a list of batted ball attributes, we need to park-adjust dHR. We can't simply multiply by our park factor, because that would result in some batted balls having a dHR probability of greater than 1.0. Instead, we calculate an EV offset (a mathematical construct to raise or lower dHR probability). For each ballpark by handedness, we aggregate all batted balls within the prime HR launch angles, fit a tanh function, and find the midpoint. We compare to league average to get a park-specific EV offset. We then apply that offset to each batted ball in that park then recalculate a park-adjusted dHR probability (PA dHR) for each batted ball.

We created the model from 2015-2016 data, so both dHR and PA dHR necessarily matched HR totals pretty closely. However, we find in 2017 there were 10% more HR hit than would be expected from the EV and LA of batted balls. The way the model is constructed, there are only two possible explanations for more HR than PA dHR. 1) the balls carried farther, or 2) the fences were closer. Using the Carry metric from the Monthly Park Factors article (see page 68), and averaging only over batted balls with a nonzero chance of being a HR, we find that well-struck baseballs in 2017 carried +0.2% farther than 2015, but 0.4% less than 2016.

Could the fences have been closer? Actually, the answer is yes, in a way. Baseballs hit to dead-center need to travel farther to become home runs than those hit down the alleys or the lines. Looking at only hard-hit fly balls, the number of well-struck balls hit to dead center dropped from 47.0% in 2015-2016 to 45.5% in 2017.

Without knowing angular distributions of hard-hit flyballs, we can't say for sure, but it certainly appears that batters have become better at hitting home runs by pulling more of their well-struck batted balls. Recall that in the Monthly Park Factors article, we found that a one-foot increase in distance of a well-struck baseball would lead to approximately a 3.5% increase in HR. By that metric, we can postulate that such baseballs in 2017 were hit to parts of the park that were 3 feet shallower on average.

Predictive Value of Deserved Home runs

It is well-established that HR/FB for pitchers is not sticky from year to year and the best predictor for HR/FB for pitchers is league average HR/FB. We tested whether knowing the prior year's dHR/FB improved our model at all, and the amount of improvement was negligible. Regression to league average HR/FB is still the best predictor.

For batters, HR/FB does not, generally speaking, regress to league averages. According to work done by Joshua Randall:

> *Each batter establishes an individual home run to fly ball rate that stabilizes over rolling three-year periods; those levels strongly predict the hr/f in the subsequent year.*

We tested using 2016's results and found that a one year dHR/FB rate did as well as two years of HR/FB at predicting HR/FB.

2017's dHR Outliers

Despite HR totals exceeding PA dHR by 10% in 2017, we can still evaluate who saw the most impact for the year, either from undeserved HR (uHR) or dHR that were unrealized. Here are the top 25:

Luckiest Pitchers

by unrealized dHR				by unrealized dHR% (min 150 BIP)				
Player	HR	PA dHR	uHR	Player	PA dHR	uHR	uHR/dHR
Nick Vincent	3	7.1	-4.1	Nick Vincent	7.1	-4.1	-58%
Gabriel Ynoa	5	8.7	-3.7	Hunter Strickland	7.5	-3.5	-47%
Danny Duffy	13	16.7	-3.7	Jesse Hahn	7.4	-3.4	-46%
Jerad Eickhoff	16	19.6	-3.6	Scott Alexander	5.0	-2.0	-40%
Hector Neris	9	12.6	-3.6	Eddie Butler	6.7	-2.7	-40%
Hunter Strickland	4	7.5	-3.5	Jared Hughes	6.4	-2.4	-37%
Jesse Hahn	4	7.4	-3.4	Luke Jackson	6.4	-2.4	-37%
Drew Pomeranz	19	22.4	-3.4	Matt Grace	4.8	-1.8	-37%
David Price	8	11.2	-3.2	Od. Despaigne	4.8	-1.8	-37%
Daniel Norris	12	15.1	-3.1	Luis Garcia	4.7	-1.7	-36%
Edinson Volquez	8	11	-3.0	David Hernandez	6.2	-2.2	-35%
Tyler Duffey	9	11.9	-2.9	Alex Colome	6.0	-2.0	-33%
Luis Perdomo	17	19.9	-2.9	Archie Bradley	6.0	-2.0	-33%
Joakim Soria	1	3.8	-2.8	Brett Anderson	7.1	-2.1	-30%
Chad Green	4	6.8	-2.8	David Price	11.2	-3.2	-29%
Ed. Rodriguez	19	21.7	-2.7	Hector Neris	12.6	-3.6	-29%
Eddie Butler	4	6.7	-2.7	Pat Neshek	4.2	-1.2	-28%
Michael Fulmer	13	15.6	-2.6	Randall Delgado	8.3	-2.3	-27%
H. Alvarez	2	4.6	-2.6	Edinson Volquez	11.0	-3.0	-27%
Matt Moore	27	29.5	-2.5	Adam Warren	5.4	-1.4	-27%
S. Strasburg	13	15.5	-2.5	Brandon Kintzler	6.7	-1.7	-26%
Luis Avilan	2	4.5	-2.5	Tyler Duffey	11.9	-2.9	-24%
Dylan Bundy	26	28.5	-2.5	Felipe Rivero	5.2	-1.2	-23%
Craig Kimbrel	6	8.5	-2.5	Dominic Leone	7.8	-1.8	-23%
Bryan Mitchell	2	4.4	-2.4	Joe Kelly	3.9	-0.9	-23%

Unluckiest Pitchers

by most undeserved HR				by highest uHR% (min 150 BIP)			
Player	HR	PA dHR	uHR	Player	HR	uHR	uHR/HR
R.A. Dickey	26	16.0	10.0	Tony Watson	9	4.4	48%
Julio Teheran	31	21.6	9.4	Edwin Diaz	10	4.5	45%
Jharel Cotton	28	19.1	8.9	Chad Bettis	8	3.3	42%
Jake Odorizzi	30	21.3	8.7	George Kontos	9	3.7	41%
Carlos Martinez	27	18.4	8.6	Junichi Tazawa	8	3.2	40%
John Lackey	36	28.0	8.0	Ryan Buchter	10	4.0	40%
Yu Darvish	27	19.1	7.9	Wandy Peralta	8	3.2	40%
Amir Garrett	23	15.3	7.7	Chris Hatcher	10	4.0	40%
Mike Fiers	32	24.5	7.5	R.A. Dickey	26	10.0	38%
Dan Straily	31	23.6	7.4	Danny Barnes	11	4.0	36%
Kenta Maeda	22	14.9	7.1	Kyle Barraclough	5	1.8	36%
J. Hellickson	35	28.1	6.9	Amir Garrett	23	7.7	33%
Jacob deGrom	28	21.2	6.8	Tony Barnette	7	2.3	33%
Ubaldo Jimenez	33	26.3	6.7	Drew Storen	7	2.3	33%
Anibal Sanchez	26	19.4	6.6	Paul Blackburn	5	1.6	33%
Nick Martinez	26	19.7	6.3	Trevor Cahill	16	5.2	32%
Bronson Arroyo	23	16.8	6.2	Dan Otero	6	1.9	32%
Ariel Miranda	37	30.9	6.1	Kenta Maeda	22	7.1	32%
Derek Holland	31	24.9	6.1	Carlos Martinez	27	8.6	32%
Jon Lester	26	20.0	6.0	Jharel Cotton	28	8.9	32%
Tim Adleman	29	23.5	5.5	Lucas Sims	9	2.8	31%
Trevor Cahill	16	10.8	5.2	Julio Teheran	31	9.4	30%
Jeff Samardzija	30	24.9	5.1	Sam Freeman	3	0.9	30%
Ervin Santana	31	26.0	5.0	Blake Wood	8	2.4	30%
Junior Guerra	18	13.0	5.0	Carlos Rodon	12	3.5	29%

Luckiest Batters

by most undeserved HR (uHR)

Player	HR	PA dHR	uHR
Didi Gregorius	25	12.4	12.6
Mike Moustakas	38	25.5	12.5
Kurt Suzuki	19	8.4	10.6
Zack Cozart	24	13.7	10.3
Giancarlo Stanton	59	49.1	9.9
Jose Ramirez	29	19.5	9.5
Max Kepler	19	10.4	8.6
Matt Olson	24	15.5	8.5
Jonathan Schoop	32	23.8	8.2
Scooter Gennett	27	19.0	8.0
Marwin Gonzalez	23	15.3	7.7
Josh Bell	26	19.1	6.9
Paul DeJong	25	18.1	6.9
Logan Morrison	38	31.2	6.8
Eduardo Nunez	12	5.3	6.7
Travis Shaw	31	24.3	6.7
Marcell Ozuna	37	30.4	6.6
Rougned Odor	30	23.5	6.5
Jordy Mercer	14	7.6	6.4
Tommy Joseph	22	15.8	6.2
Maikel Franco	24	17.8	6.2
Eric Hosmer	25	18.8	6.2
Yasmani Grandal	22	15.9	6.1
Yangervis Solarte	18	12.0	6.0
Pat Valaika	13	7.1	5.9

by highest undeserved HR% (min 10 HR)

Player	HR	uHR	uHR/HR
Eduardo Nunez	12	6.7	56%
Kurt Suzuki	19	10.6	56%
Didi Gregorius	25	12.6	50%
Ender Inciarte	11	5.2	47%
Jordy Mercer	14	6.4	46%
Pat Valaika	13	5.9	46%
Max Kepler	19	8.6	45%
Denard Span	12	5.3	44%
Zack Cozart	24	10.3	43%
Jose Reyes	15	5.9	39%
Tyler Flowers	12	4.5	37%
Brandon Phillips	13	4.9	37%
Matt Olson	24	8.5	35%
Josh Harrison	16	5.6	35%
Lorenzo Cain	15	5.1	34%
Yangervis Solarte	18	6.0	34%
Marcus Semien	10	3.3	33%
Marwin Gonzalez	23	7.7	33%
Mike Moustakas	38	12.5	33%
Jose Ramirez	29	9.5	33%
Chris Owings	12	3.9	32%
Wilmer Flores	18	5.8	32%
Manuel Margot	13	4.1	32%
Chris Iannetta	17	5.3	31%
Kevin Kiermaier	15	4.6	31%

Unluckiest Batters

by most undeserved HR (uHR)

Player	HR	PA dHR	uHR
Aaron Judge	52	63.4	-11.4
Avisail Garcia	18	25.4	-7.4
Mitch Moreland	22	28.5	-6.5
Trey Mancini	24	29.2	-5.2
Alex Avila	14	19.2	-5.2
Justin Turner	21	26.2	-5.2
Miguel Cabrera	16	20.8	-4.8
Joe Mauer	7	11.5	-4.5
Nelson Cruz	39	43.3	-4.3
Nick Castellanos	26	30.1	-4.1
Corey Seager	22	25.9	-3.9
Chris Carter	8	11.8	-3.8
Manny Machado	33	36.7	-3.7
Kendrys Morales	28	31.7	-3.7
Logan Forsythe	6	9.6	-3.6
Shin-Soo Choo	22	25.3	-3.3
Hyun-soo Kim	1	4.2	-3.2
Brad Miller	9	12.0	-3.0
Bradley Zimmer	8	11.0	-3.0
Hanley Ramirez	23	25.7	-2.7
Christian Yelich	18	20.7	-2.7
Howie Kendrick	9	11.7	-2.7
Jabari Blash	5	7.7	-2.7
Gorkys Hernandez	0	2.6	-2.6
Jose Martinez	14	16.5	-2.5

by highest undeserved HR% (min 10 HR)

Player	HR	PA dHR	HR/dHR
Joe Mauer	7	11.5	61%
Chris Carter	8	11.8	68%
Avisail Garcia	18	25.4	71%
Alex Avila	14	19.2	73%
Bradley Zimmer	8	11.0	73%
Brad Miller	9	12.0	75%
Miguel Cabrera	16	20.8	77%
Mitch Moreland	22	28.5	77%
Howie Kendrick	9	11.7	77%
Justin Turner	21	26.2	80%
Alex Gordon	9	11.0	82%
Aaron Judge	52	63.4	82%
Trey Mancini	24	29.2	82%
Victor Martinez	10	12.2	82%
Stephen Piscotty	9	10.9	83%
Chase Headley	12	14.3	84%
Jose Martinez	14	16.5	85%
Corey Seager	22	25.9	85%
Jed Lowrie	14	16.5	85%
Hunter Pence	13	15.2	86%
Nick Castellanos	26	30.1	86%
Shin-Soo Choo	22	25.3	87%
Christian Yelich	18	20.7	87%
Kendrys Morales	28	31.7	88%
Cesar Hernandez	9	10.1	89%

Conclusion

The Errant Gust of Wind is real, and it can add up to big shifts in results that make, or ruin a season.

For pitchers, HR/FB should regress to the league average, and this is incorporated in most responsible projection systems. However, biases may linger against pitchers who have "proven" to have acute gopheritis, or in favor of pitchers who managed to avoid surrendering HR. This is another reminder to trust the math, and don't get suckered.

For Batters, HR/FB is a semi-stable ability of the individual. Better hitters consistently exceed league average HR/FB. It's tempting to peruse the batters on the "lucky" list, nod knowingly and think "I wasn't buying that performance anyway"—but the "unlucky" list shows that some of the stars do have room to get even better. With these calculations, we can estimate how much of that performance was earned or unearned, and adjust expectations for 2018.

High Pitch Counts and newPQS

by Paul Petera

One of the more noticeable trends in baseball over the past decade or so has been the conservative approach to starting pitching. Whether it is increased specialization or an attempt to keep starters healthy, pitch counts are at all time lows. Even though starters don't go as long these days, we still want to know if pitch counts have an effect on short-term pitching efficacy. We endeavored to learn whether or not relatively higher pitch counts have any impact on pitching performance from start to start.

In this analysis, we compiled the PQS records for all major league outings from 2014-16 seasons, and studied the pitch counts and PQS data from more than 12,000 pitcher-starts that qualified for analysis. The starts were grouped by pitch count into five cohorts. In order to establish a baseline, for each defined pitch count cohort, we calculated the average PQS for the starts in which those pitch counts occurred as well as the average PQS scores in pitchers' subsequent start:

1st Game Pitches	PQS Avg	Next PQS Avg
25- 89	1.6	2.1
90- 99	2.4	2.3
100-109	2.9	2.5
110-119	3.4	2.8
120+	3.8	3.1
Overall	**2.5**	**2.4**

As you can see, the next start PQS average for individual pitch count cohorts generally gravitates to the overall average. Also as expected, however, pitchers who are throwing more pitches are pitching deeper into games, and those who do that are generally more effective. So as the pitch counts go up, the next start PQS scores are naturally edging higher.

The change in approach to starting pitching in the majors in just the last few years cannot be understated. The percentage of qualifying starts under 100 pitches increased from 49% in the 2010-12 period to 57% in this study. Meanwhile, the percentage of qualifying starts over 110 pitches dropped from 19% to 12%. Between 2010-12, Justin Verlander led all pitchers with 30 starts of 120 pitches or more. No pitcher had more than seven such starts between 2014-16.

Back to the study, in each pitch count category, we reviewed all starts within that pitch count range and how their next start went. The following table shows the percentage of starts in each

PQS score after a certain number of pitches, relative to the PQS distribution for all starts:

PQS	25-89 Pct.	90-99 Pct.	100-09 Pct.	110-19 Pct.	120+ Pct.	All
0	15%	14%	11%	10%	8%	13%
1	21%	20%	18%	15%	13%	19%
2	22%	20%	20%	18%	14%	21%
3	20%	20%	20%	20%	19%	20%
4	14%	17%	18%	20%	22%	17%
5	8%	9%	13%	17%	24%	11%

We see consistent themes across each pitch count. Pitchers who throw a low number of pitches are more apt to pitch poorly in their next start. Pitchers who throw more pitches are typically more successful in their next start. To look at this data another way, we grouped each pitcher in each year of the study by their average pitch count per start, and calculated their respective average PQS scores that year:

Cohort	Count	Avg PC	Avg PQS
25-83	127	74	1.4
84-89	129	87	1.8
90-94	189	92	2.0
95-99	209	97	2.4
100-104	109	101	2.8
105-110	26	107	3.2

So obviously there is a positive correlation between pitch counts and PQS: as one goes up, so does the other. This appears to be primarily a talent or health issue, with pitch counts a symptom of success more so than a reason.

Lastly, we wanted to take this correlation out just a bit more. What about the starts after the first and second start? We looked at the 309 instances over the three years in question where a pitcher threw at least 110 pitches in back-to-back starts.

The average PQS score in the second 110+ pitch start was a hefty 3.6, but it didn't stop there. Even after back-to-back 110+ pitch outings, the third start (immediately after back-to-back 110+ pitch outings) and the fourth start showed average PQS scores were still considerably higher than the overall average.

Start	Avg PQS
2nd	3.6
3rd	3.1
4th	3.0
All	2.4

We believe that pitchers who throw a relatively high number of pitches in a given start are more likely to pitch well in their second. These days, we see fewer pitchers who are given a long enough leash to throw more than 110 pitches. Those who are have proven that it's worth it to keep them out there.

Pitchers with higher pitch counts are safer bets to throw well in their next start (and beyond) than those who throw fewer pitches. Near-term fatigue or other negative symptoms do not appear to be worthy of concern; so do not shy away from these pitchers solely for that reason.

Single Game Outcomes and the New Starting Pitcher Matchup Tool

by Arik Florimonte

Updating the Starting Pitcher Matchup Tool

BaseballHQ.com subscribers will be familiar with the Starting Pitcher Matchup Tool, which lists all projected starting pitchers for the current day, as well as an 8-day scan, along with their opponent and a matchup score. The Matchup Tool was based on the PQS averages of both the starter and the opposing team, and it did a nice job of quantifying the upcoming matchups. It helped fanalytic owners plan their weekly lineups, and certainly helped win a few titles along the way.

When the updated PQS was introduced at the beginning of 2016, it changed the PQS inputs to the SP Matchup Tool, enough so that more research was needed to re-evaluate the matchup index. This work started as a tweak to tame an unruly algorithm, but became a complete overhaul. It still serves the same function—to identify pitchers that should be the best fantasy producers on a given day—and the layout will be similar, but we have stripped down the SP Matchup Tool and built it back up with brand new parts.

Come 2018, this new Matchup system will be fully integrated into BaseballHQ.com.

Methodology

It started with a simple objective: to predict single game outcomes as closely as possible. Specifically, we want to know how each start is likely to influence the statistics in the common starting pitcher categories: Strikeouts, ERA, WHIP, and Wins. Although attempting to predict the outcome of a single game is a fool's errand, existing metrics can help predict tendencies that add up to an advantage over an entire season. Making many decisions to gain small advantages is, after all, what makes a great fanalytic manager.

To project the results of an individual game, we first projected the outcomes in each of the pitcher-batter matchups within the game. We used parameters describing the pitcher, the opposition's offense, and the ballpark to create estimates for four rate parameters—K%, BB%, GB%, and FB%—along with expected number of batters the starter would face. We then created a second tier of formulas that predicted H%, HR/FB, and the efficiency of the pitcher's defense in turning batted balls into outs. Finally, we used those numbers to create a third layer of formulas to predict Strikeouts, ERA, WHIP, and Wins.

For this effort, we used pitching logs from 2010-2016. At each step, we created several versions of formulas to predict the matchup outcomes, and then validated the results. Formulas couldn't just give good results overall. They needed to give good results in each year—for pitchers with a lot of history, or just a little. They had to work in April as well as September.

The First Tier of Matchup Indicators

We began by examining strikeouts, as one only needs to know K% and total batters faced to calculate strikeouts. We worked through several iterations, binning our predictions, examining our results, and adjusting our formulas and assumptions. In the end, our model delivered an expected K% for the matchup of SP and opposition (mK%) that depended on the pitcher's projected K%, 30-day K%, 30-day swinging-strike rate, and opposition 30-day K% (vs. same handedness as our SP), all weighted by total batters the pitcher faced in the last month (TBF_30).

As final validation, we separated the data into seasons, summed over single percentage-point bins, and found excellent correlation, with no R^2 value lower than 0.96 in any season. We also split the data by number of games started by the pitcher in the prior 30 days, and got no R^2 value lower than 0.94.

We used similar methods to compute mBB%, mGB%, and mFB%, again using pitcher's projection, 30-day history, opposition's 30-day history, and TBF_30 to weight the recent results appropriately. We again produced results of similar quality across seasons, and across different amounts of recent history.

Finally, we calculated the expected number of batters faced in a game, mTBF. On average, the results depended both on the pitcher's 30-day games started and mean batters faced per game.

Second Tier of mIndicators

To build the next tier, we needed to understand how often the batted balls went for hits and homeruns. We know that H% depends on batted ball type, ballpark, and how hard the ball is hit, as well as the quality of the defense behind the pitcher. HR/FB also depends on the batted ball type and how hard the ball is hit. We didn't know, however, which of these would have a measurable influence on the outcomes of a single game.

The model for mH% that was most consistent relied on the matchup batted balls rates calculated in the first tier, plus a small adjustment based on a defense's historic efficiency at converting batted balls into outs. Notably, neither park factors nor opposition's hard hit ball rates were included. Park factors are partially baked in to the home team's defensive efficiency numbers, and beyond that neither was predictive enough to be statistically significant.

When modeling expected HR/FB, we note that, despite intuition to the contrary, research at BaseballHQ.com has shown repeatedly that the pitcher has no control over HR/FB. We didn't use the pitcher's history, only data about the opposition's offense. The statistically significant factors were found to be park factors, along with opposition's 30-day hard hit ball rate, opposition's 30-day HR/FB rate (both by pitcher handedness).

The Matchup Ratings

For strikeouts, the inputs are simply mK% * mTBF.

The significant inputs to matchup ERA (mERA) were not surprising: mK%, mBB%, mH%, mHR/FB, and mFB% (the last two both contributing to homeruns).

mWHIP is also found to depend on mK%, mBB%, mH%, mHR/FB, and mFB%.

Finally, for mWins, we used the mERA of both starters and BHQ's equation for expected wins:

$$0.72 * (mERA\_OPP)1.8 / ((mERA\_OPP)1.8 + (mERA)1.8)$$

The new SP Matchup tool will give a rating for each of these matchup statistics, based on the mean and standard deviation of the matchup values over the study period. So, in each category, a zero would be average, i.e the 50th percentile of all SP. +1.0 means they are in the 84th percentile. +2.0 = 98th percentile, etc. The Overall Rating will be a mean of the four ratings.

How to use these numbers

Consider the mean results per start by Overall Rating range, charted below.

Overall Rating	GS	W	IP	HR	BB	K	PQS	ERA	WHIP	BPV
<= -2.0	139	0.31	5.2	0.9	2.1	3.3	1.7	5.19	1.50	25
-2.0 — -1.0	3631	0.27	5.6	0.8	1.9	3.6	1.9	4.90	1.45	41
-1.0 — 0.0	12490	0.33	5.8	0.7	1.9	4.3	2.2	4.38	1.36	60
0.0 — 1.0	10905	0.38	6.1	0.7	1.8	5.2	2.6	3.77	1.25	88
1.0 — 2.0	3480	0.44	6.4	0.6	1.8	6.2	3.1	3.29	1.16	113
2.0 — 3.0	458	0.51	6.7	0.6	1.5	7.2	3.5	2.72	1.01	145
> 3.0	63	0.46	7.0	0.5	1.2	8.6	3.8	2.41	0.91	179

Clearly, any pitcher with rating of 1.0 or higher is a must-start in all but the deepest of leagues. Below -1.0, and those average stats start to look ugly. Aside from the obvious guideline (start the pitcher with the higher rating), owners will need to determine what threshold they care about given layer pool restrictions for their league.

The full version of this research piece is linked to the weekly matchup tool at BaseballHQ.com, and it contains detailed analysis of what ratings play well in different league sizes. For example, in a 12-team "only" league, the median start should have a rating of about 0.2, while the worst rostered SP is around -0.73. In a 15-team mixed, the median start is 0.34 and a top pitcher above +1.

It is worth noting that while much of the value of a SP will come from their inherent ability, the standard deviation in a pitcher's matchup score is 0.5, meaning the SP's single game matchup score will differ from their rating mean by more than 0.5 points about 1/3 of the time. That's the difference between average and unrosterable in a 10-team mixed, or between the 25th percentile and the 75th in a 12-team "only" league.

Conclusion

We now can assess the strength of a starter's matchup from game to game, taking into account the pitcher's inherent ability, recent performance, strength of defense, ballpark, and opposition offense's recent history. We have also built a flexible framework that can evolve as we improve the model in the years that follow.

These matchup ratings will be rolled out for 2018. While matchup scores early in the season will parallel what you'd expect from the projections, divergence will occur as the history accumulates. Additionally, because projections are built in to the matchup scores, if a pitcher's base skills change enough merit a change in projections, that will be reflected in the model, too.

How Age Affects DL Stays

by Jeff Zimmerman

Getting injured is a part of baseball. Pitches hit batters. Hamstrings are pulled. Players collide with walls and each other. You cut your finger repairing your drone. Some acts are random, but some players seem to get more than their fair share.

But for those hitters with the "injury-prone" tag, it only takes one healthy season to make a difference, as any 2017 owner of Giancarlo Stanton will gladly tell you. Is there any method to selecting or targeting "injury prone" players on draft day?

One key is that repeat DL players' chances of getting injured again rise as they get older.

Age 25 and Younger (n=297)			Average	Median
	Count	DL Rate	DL Days	DL Days
Season+1	112	37.7%	49.9	39
Season+2	37	33.0%	61.5	46
Season+3	16	43.2%	64.1	48

Age 26 to 29 (n=524)			Average	Median
	Count	DL Rate	DL Days	DL Days
Season+1	210	40.1%	48.9	34.5
Season+2	86	41.0%	56.3	35.5
Season+3	27	31.4%	57.0	40

Age 30 and older (n=539)			Average	Median
	Count	DL Rate	DL Days	DL Days
Season+1	243	45.1%	53.8	40
Season+2	116	47.7%	62.9	47
Season+3	51	44.0%	69.9	50

Several interesting findings:

1. *If someone in the youngest group goes on the DL once, they aren't as likely to again the next season.* The DL chance increase after two DL seasons is huge, going from 33% to 43%. This is a small sample of hitters, so it could be a sampling error, but the jump could point to young injury-prone players getting weeded out.

2. *The best health is exhibited by the middle group.* They maintain an average to below-average value in all instances. In a small sample, the season three DL chances drop after two straight seasons on the DL. It seems this age is the sweet spot for hitter injuries. The hitters have shown they can hold up to a full season, but their bodies have not started to break down.

3. *Not surprisingly, the oldest group takes longer to heal.* While the middle group players have better than average values, these older players' DL-related stats hover above the league average. On the positive side, the DL rate doesn't increase as a player racks up previous injuries. The disabled list seems to spread the pain around evenly with the plus 30-plus crowd.

Besides this small young group, remember that hitters aren't injury prone—they just age. As they age, their bodies break down more often and for longer periods of time, which may give them the appearance of being injury-prone. As a general overall rule, it's prudent to ignore a hitter's injury history and buy these players at a discount, if possible.

Monthly Park Factors

By Arik Florimonte

Introduction & Methodology

As the baseball season moves from spring to summer, changes in temperature, wind patterns, and humidity affect the travel of batted balls. But how much? Using batted balls from 2015-2017, we calculate how far a batted ball should have carried based on its launch angle and exit velocity, then compare how far fly balls actually did travel relative to the expected value. We'll tabulate this by ballpark, batter handedness, and month to see how park factors change with the calendar.

Batted Ball Carry by Ballpark

We begin with 2015-2017 Statcast data, then filter out batted balls that traveled less than 200 feet or were launched at an angle less than 10 degrees or greater than 60 degrees. We calculate the vertical and horizontal components of exit velocity, and quickly find a model for the distance the ball traveled with a very good correlation, $R^2 = 0.86$.

We then calculate the "Carry"—a term coined by Alan Nathan in his 2009 article titled "The 'Carry' of Fly Ball"—for each ballpark. This is how far the ball went divided by how far it should have been using our model. **Chart 1: Carry by LHB / RHB by ballpark** (facing page) shows the range of monthly carry numbers for both handedness of batters.

We are not surprised to see Colorado and Arizona at the top, nor San Francisco and New York (N) at the bottom, as these fit their reputations. Carry by itself doesn't have tremendous fantasy relevance, at least not directly: these numbers are baked into the park factors already. And while this information might be useful to understand why park factors are what they are, it won't change how we use them.

How Much Carry Matters?

Imagine a section of fence that is 370 feet away, and then consider a fly ball that travels exactly 370 feet. One percent extra carry on that fly would be 3.7 feet. So, using our batted ball data we create bins for flyball distance of size 3.7 feet. We find approximately 750 balls per season in the 370-foot bin (and similar totals in nearby bins) in our sample period. That means 750 fly balls per year that would have been a home run if just given a 1% boost (or 750 home runs that would have fallen just short if given a 1% suppression). That works out to about 13% of all homeruns that were hit in 2016-2017. That means a 1% change in carry can increase/decrease HR output by 13%.

Fantasy Impact of Monthly Park Factors

Using the Carry calculation above, and assigning at 13% change in HR rate for each one percent change in Carry, we tabulated **Adjusted monthly park factors** for each ballpark (Chart 2, facing page). We used BaseballHQ.com's current (2014-2016) 3-year park factors for HR. The shading is darker for increased HR, and lightest for most decreased HR.

As we can see there are some very dramatic changes from month to month, and the best ballparks overall aren't always the best in a given month. For example, New York (AL) and

Chart 1: Carry by LHB / RHB by ballpark

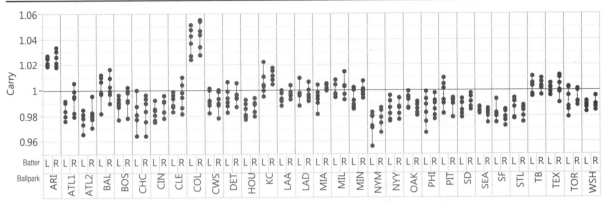

Chart 2: Adjusted monthly ballpark factors

Park	LHB PF	---- Adjusted LHB PF ----						RHB PF	---- Adjusted RHB PF ----					
		Apr	May	Jun	Jul	Aug	Sep		Apr	May	Jun	Jul	Aug	Sep
ARI	9%	5%	11%	19%	13%	5%	1%	8%	4%	10%	18%	12%	4%	0%
ATL*	0%	-3%	-1%	4%	16%	3%	-14%	0%	-3%	-1%	4%	16%	3%	-14%
BAL	16%	-7%	14%	33%	28%	14%	11%	6%	-15%	4%	22%	17%	4%	1%
BOS	-25%	-39%	-27%	-21%	-18%	-21%	-27%	6%	-14%	3%	11%	16%	11%	3%
CHC	-19%	-40%	-17%	-5%	-18%	-12%	-28%	16%	-14%	18%	36%	17%	26%	4%
CIN	29%	14%	22%	43%	33%	32%	27%	11%	-2%	5%	23%	15%	14%	9%
CLE	10%	-6%	8%	25%	17%	13%	1%	5%	-10%	3%	20%	11%	8%	-3%
COL	16%	-2%	-6%	34%	28%	24%	14%	25%	6%	2%	44%	37%	33%	23%
CWS	13%	-6%	7%	24%	24%	13%	10%	7%	-11%	1%	18%	17%	7%	4%
DET	0%	-11%	-7%	10%	13%	0%	-4%	0%	-11%	-7%	10%	13%	0%	-4%
HOU	0%	-5%	3%	9%	4%	-9%	-2%	0%	-5%	3%	9%	4%	-9%	-2%
KC	-20%	-30%	-23%	-11%	-17%	-24%	-18%	-19%	-29%	-22%	-10%	-16%	-23%	-17%
LAA	-13%	-16%	-15%	-8%	-9%	-16%	-15%	0%	-3%	-2%	6%	4%	-3%	-2%
LAD	17%	6%	13%	33%	17%	19%	13%	0%	-10%	-3%	14%	0%	2%	-4%
MIA	-8%	-13%	-7%	-2%	-13%	-7%	-9%	-23%	-28%	-22%	-18%	-27%	-22%	-24%
MIL	49%	40%	48%	68%	48%	53%	33%	11%	4%	10%	25%	10%	14%	-1%
MIN	-10%	-14%	-17%	0%	-6%	-12%	-10%	6%	1%	-3%	18%	11%	3%	5%
NYM	0%	-20%	-5%	9%	9%	7%	-2%	19%	-5%	13%	30%	30%	28%	17%
NYY	46%	29%	44%	64%	59%	47%	34%	25%	10%	23%	40%	36%	26%	15%
OAK	-20%	-22%	-21%	-17%	-22%	-26%	-14%	-19%	-21%	-20%	-15%	-21%	-25%	-13%
PHI	7%	-13%	-4%	20%	20%	11%	3%	23%	0%	10%	38%	38%	28%	19%
PIT	0%	-17%	5%	6%	9%	-3%	-2%	-24%	-37%	-20%	-20%	-17%	-26%	-26%
SD	-26%	-32%	-27%	-21%	-24%	-32%	-23%	6%	-2%	4%	13%	9%	-2%	11%
SEA	10%	9%	4%	9%	13%	12%	13%	0%	-1%	-5%	-1%	3%	1%	3%
SF	-41%	-47%	-40%	-35%	-42%	-42%	-41%	-26%	-33%	-24%	-18%	-27%	-27%	-27%
STL	-15%	-24%	-11%	-10%	-11%	-17%	-18%	-10%	-20%	-6%	-5%	-6%	-12%	-13%
TB	0%	-1%	-3%	9%	3%	-4%	-5%	-15%	-16%	-18%	-7%	-12%	-18%	-19%
TEX	5%	1%	9%	14%	13%	2%	-7%	0%	-4%	4%	9%	8%	-3%	-12%
TOR	9%	16%	3%	20%	19%	0%	-1%	9%	16%	3%	20%	19%	0%	-1%
WSH	-17%	-21%	-18%	-11%	-16%	-17%	-18%	0%	-5%	-2%	7%	1%	-1%	-1%

ATL is presumed to have a neutral park factor, and Carry based on only one year of data

Milwaukee are solid throughout the year, other "hitters' parks" like Colorado, Chicago (NL), Philadelphia, and Baltimore take a while to heat up.

Keep these trends in mind and exploit this knowledge advantage in your roster management and trade negotiations as the season progresses.

A H2H Approach to the Mayberry Method

by David Martin

Introduction

The Mayberry Method ("MM") was created by Ron Shandler in 2010 in an effort to simplify our draft approach and break our reliance on statistical projections. The strategy was designed for use in Rotisserie leagues. However, built into each seven-digit Mayberry code is a skill set analysis about whether a player is head-to-head league material. By "decoding" Mayberry, we can assemble a team that has the characteristics of a successful H2H squad.

MM Basics for H2H Application

If you are unfamiliar with the Mayberry Method, you should take a few minutes to read the summary articles found in the Encyclopedia of Fanalytics section of this book. As a reminder, the seven digit MM code is broken down for hitters as follows:

Skills: Power/Speed/Batting average/Playing time
Reliability: Health/Experience/Consistency

The four skills categories are scored 1-5 and the three reliability components are scored A-F. The corresponding skills index scores and projections that correlate with MM's 1-5 grades can be found on page 55:

Breaking Down MM From a H2H Perspective

In drafting a head-to-head team, we aim to assemble a team of players with similar skill sets, as this creates a more consistent roster. In applying this approach, we've typically used the following filters as a starting point:

ct% > 80%
xBA > .280
PX > 120
RC/G > 5

Due to week-to-week variability in counting statistics, any percentage category (here, batting average) should be prioritized. In reviewing the MM skills scores, we can correlate the power and contact skills as follows:

PX > 4 or 5 = PX of 120 or higher
xBA > 4 or 5 = xBA of .285 or higher

Only full-time players will have an opportunity to produce the counting statistics required, so we need to limit our search to those players who earn a 5 for playing time.

From a reliability standpoint, health grades are critical, particularly early in the draft. Our filter will cull those players with grades of A or B. This creates a top tier H2H Mayberry profile of:

PWR	SPD	BA	PT	HLTH
4/5	N/A	4/5	5	A/B

You may be wondering why the consistency grade is not included above. The consistency grades that are part of the MM scores are based on a year-over-year analysis. For hitters, they look for variations of RC/G between successive years. If a player's RC/G has fluctuated by 2 or more runs, they receive an "F" score. In reviewing consistency grades, it became apparent that players who had improved or breakout years, or a small sample size of at-bats, often had poor consistency grades. Week-to-week consistency is more critical in the H2H game, and therefore, we incorporate quality-consistency scores ("QC scores") as part of our analysis.

Creating Tiers of Players using MM

Top tiered plays in H2H (code listed above) should be sorted by QC scores so that the more consistent players are ranked higher.

Ideally, a homogeneous H2H team should have 6-8 core players with similar skills profiles. Therefore, in order to create a deeper player pool to draft from, we need to modify the code. The strategy here is to protect any percentage categories that are not based on a player's amount of at-bats per week. Therefore, to create the second tier of players, we will lower the power index to 3, but keep all other skill requirements intact:

PWR	SPD	BA	PT	HLTH
3	N/A	4/5	5	A/B

The interplay between tiers is important. This tier of players should be used in conjunction with the higher tier and not simply after the top tier options are exhausted. For instance, if you are picking in the first round and end up drafting someone that has a lower QC score, and the remaining top tier choices in round 2 also have low QC scores, then it might make sense to dip into the second tier if there is a player available with a higher QC score.

Additionally, while our H2H MM codes do not target players based on their speed skills, the second column of the MM codes contains this information. You do not need to punt the steals category. Although we are de-prioritizing the speed skill, you will typically find that the tiers nonetheless contain multiple players with a MM speed score of 3 or higher. These players are categorized as having up to 30-SB potential. Therefore, you can still be competitive in the steal category most weeks applying this approach.

Conclusion

The Mayberry Method may have been designed for the Rotisserie game, but when approached differently it contains all the information we need to determine whether a player is a worthy H2H pick.

Do Overworked Players Wear Down?

by Jeff Zimmerman

Anyone who has owned Salvador Perez has experienced his second half drop-off. Like clockwork, around the All-Star game, Perez transforms from an elite catcher to a normal one. Over the past three seasons, Perez's total is 408 games, 29 more than Yadier Molina. So, does playing an entire season wear down a player? Probably not.

We compared the first- and second-half numbers for batters who played the most games over the entire season. These players are continually run out on the field, and one figures they should start to wear down, just like Salvador Perez. Some might break and go on the DL.

From 2002 to 2016, here are the league-wide average changes in several batting percentages from the first half to second half.

Stat:	Change
AVG:	+.001
OBP:	.000
SLG:	+.002
ISO:	+.002

We started by comparing all hitters who played from 2002 to 2016. Figures below are the changes between the first half and the second half, grouped by the total games played each season:

% of Gms	Min Gms	AVG	OBP	SLG	ISO
80.0%	130	-.004	-.001	-.002	-.002
85.0%	138	-.001	.001	.000	-.002
90.0%	146	-.004	-.004	-.004	-.001
95.0%	154	.000	.001	.003	.002
97.5%	158	.000	.003	.006	.003
98.5%	160	.003	.002	.007	.004

Those numbers don't support the wear-down narrative. The more days a player has off, the lower his production in the second half. Maybe the hitter is hurt and is missing days because of a non-DL injury. Maybe teams don't act like the Royals and quit sending out a worn-down hitter or rest their players once their production drops.

Now, let's look at catchers specifically. We had to drop down the number of games caught, but the results surprised me after knowing the league-wide values.

% of Gms	Min Gms	AVG	OBP	SLG	ISO
50%	81	-0.007	-0.008	-0.011	-0.007
55%	89	-0.007	-0.008	-0.009	-0.007
60%	97	-0.007	-0.008	-0.008	-0.005
65%	105	-0.007	-0.008	-0.008	-0.005
70%	113	-0.006	-0.007	-0.007	-0.001
75%	122	-0.006	-0.008	-0.007	-0.002
80%	130	-0.006	-0.007	-0.007	-0.002
85%	138	0.005	0.006	-0.004	-0.004

Besides some funkiness happening in the last set, catchers see their performance drop from the first to the second half by about the same amount. Fantasy owners need to understand this decline will be coming and not over-react.

If the average position player wears down during the season, it is not seen in their production. If anything, their output improves the more they play. Though this concept goes against how the crowd forms narratives, it is true: If a hitter plays more, the more likely he is healthy and not wearing down.

Surprisingly Productive Years

by Ed DeCaria

When it comes to player valuation, fantasy experts often debate the merits of different methodologies, hitter/pitcher allocations, position scarcity adjustments, and other details. Yet we've always generally agreed on two basic points: 1) avoid players with negative projected values, and 2) ignore valuation once the season starts.

But sometimes we can gain an advantage by zigging when others zag, so at the beginning of the 2017 season, we conducted an experiment at BaseballHQ.com to test these two generally-accepted pieces of advice. We knew from past research that the players we draft initially only deliver 80-85% of the value our fantasy teams accumulate during the season. This means that, collectively, about $500 of what owners in a 12-team AL/NL only league (or about $650 in a 15-team mixed league) pay for players on auction day goes to waste – and players projected to be "worthless" on auction day will be the ones who earn that value.

So instead of pretending all of those undrafted players would really be worth $0 or less all season long, we devised a method to put values on them instead. Our final output was a fascinating list of no-names and new-names and whoa-remember-him-names, including many players that you might say went on to have "surprisingly productive years" (SPYs) in 2017. Which would be true, except … we saw them coming.

Placing value on inherently valueless players required some degree of mind-bending. We couldn't simply take each player's existing projections and value them the same way we did the entire player pool, as that would have ignored the main reason these players could earn value: by outplaying their projections. We also couldn't just re-project each player's rate stats over full playing time, as that would have yielded very unrealistic stat lines and wreaked havoc on our valuation attempt. Instead we decided to embrace the fuzzy nature of skills and playing time projections, while still applying some modest procedural rigor:

1. We considered all batters projected for 50% or less playing time (across all defensive positions), all starting pitchers projected for 10% or less of his team's innings pitched (about 140 IP), and all relief pitchers projected for less than 4% of his team's innings pitched (about 50 IP), according to BaseballHQ.com's playing time projections.

2. We used each player's projected skills—not stats—in the form of his Mayberry scores. This helped us blur out what we (thought we) knew about a player's past fantasy output and focus more on his potential production. For batters, we included only players whose sum of three Mayberry skills (power, speed, and hitting) was 7 or higher (8 or higher for mixed leagues). For pitchers, we included only players whose sum of two Mayberry skills (xERA and strikeout rate) was 4 or higher (5 or higher for mixed leagues). For relievers, we also counted Mayberry's saves potential score, so we included only relievers whose sum of three scores was 7 or higher (8 or higher for mixed leagues).

3. We looked at the specific situation of each player that met our first two criteria and assigned a realistic playing time upside given his skills and injury, consistency, and forecast risk, and that of the player(s) ahead of him on his team's depth chart.

These steps combined to produce lists of batters and pitchers who were projected for far less than full playing time despite good or even great skills.

For each player, we then calculated a single number that measured their "projected skill" over their "potential playing time" to arrive at their "potential value." For hitters, this was calculated as the sum of the player's Mayberry power (P), speed (S), and hitting (H) scores multiplied by his potential playing time (pPT) percentage, or $(P+S+H)*pPT$. This gave us an intermediate measure of value, similar to that used in the standings gain points (SGP) valuation methodology. We then ranked batters by this metric and subtracted the minimum value of the group from all players, so that the least valuable batter had a marginal score (mSCORE) of zero. We then used mSCORE to calculate each player's "share" of the total, and multiplied that by the league's total wasted dollars (using a 65/35 batter/pitcher split) to determine each batter's potential value (pR$).

For pitchers, this was calculated as the sum of 2x his Mayberry xERA score (E) plus his strikeouts (K) and saves (S) scores, multiplied by his potential innings percentage (pPT), or $(2*E+K+S)*pPT$. We then ranked pitchers by this metric, and subtracted the minimum value of the group from all pitchers, so that the least valuable pitcher had a marginal score (mSCORE) of zero. We then used mSCORE to calculate each pitcher's "share" of the total, and multiplied that by the league's total wasted dollars (using a 65/35 batter/pitcher split) to determine each pitcher's potential value (pR$).

The players we identified via this valuation process prior to their 2017 "surprisingly productive years" included:

Batters: Whit Merrifield, Cody Bellinger, Chris Taylor, Scooter Gennett, Tim Beckham, Joey Gallo, Michael Taylor, Gerardo Parra, and Ian Happ.

Pitchers: Alex Wood, Brad Peacock, Chad Green, Blake Parker, Sean Doolittle, Alex Cobb, Carl Edwards, and Josh Fields.

That short list of players alone produced more than $200 in fantasy value in 2017. A well-timed pickup of any one of these players would have been a boon to most fantasy teams' chances of winning their league.

We'll run a similar SPY exercise near Opening Day 2018 at BaseballHQ.com to give those of you with late reserve drafts or in FAAB/transaction leagues yet another leg up on your competition.

The following section contains player boxes for every batter who had significant playing time in 2017 and/or is expected to get fantasy roster-worthy plate appearances in 2018. You will find some prospects here, specifically the most impactful names who we project to play in 2018. For more complete prospect coverage, see our Prospects section.

Snapshot Section

The top band of each player box contains the following information:

Age as of Opening Day 2018.

Bats shows which side of the plate he bats from—(L)eft, (R)ight or (B)oth.

Positions: Up to three defensive positions are listed and represent those for which he appeared a minimum of 20 games in 2017.

Ht/Wt: Each batter's height and weight.

Reliability Grades analyze each batter's forecast risk, on an A-F scale. High grades go to those who have accumulated few disabled list days (Health), have a history of substantial and regular major league playing time (PT/Exp) and have displayed consistent performance over the past three years, using RC/G (Consist).

LIMA Plan Grade evaluates how well a batter would fit into a team using the LIMA Plan draft strategy. Best grades go to batters who have excellent base skills, are expected to see regular playing time, and are in the $10-$30 Rotisserie dollar range. Lowest grades will go to poor skills, few AB and values less than $5 or more than $30.

Random Variance Score (Rand Var) measures the impact random variance had on the batter's 2017 stats and the probability that his 2018 performance will exceed or fall short of 2017. The variables tracked are those prone to regression—h%, hr/f and xBA to BA variance. Players are rated on a scale of –5 to +5 with positive scores indicating rebounds and negative scores indicating corrections. Note that this score is computer-generated and the projections will override it on occasion.

Mayberry Method (MM) acknowledges the imprecision of the forecasting process by projecting player performance in broad strokes. The four digits of MM each represent a fantasy-relevant skill—power, speed, batting average and playing time (PA)—and are all on a scale of 0 to 5.

Commentaries for each batter provide a brief analysis of his skills and the potential impact on performance in 2018. MLB statistics are listed first for those who played only a portion of 2017 at the major league level. Note that these commentaries generally look at performance related issues only. Role and playing time expectations may impact these analyses, so you will have to adjust accordingly. Upside (UP) and downside (DN) statistical potential appears for some players; these are less grounded in hard data and more speculative of skills potential.

Player Stat Section

The past five years' statistics represent the total accumulated in the majors as well as in Triple-A, Double-A ball and various foreign leagues during each year. All non-major league stats have been converted to a major league equivalent (MLE) performance level. Minor league levels below Double-A are not included.

Nearly all baseball publications separate a player's statistical experiences in the major leagues from the minor leagues and outside leagues. While this may be appropriate for official record-keeping purposes, it is not an easy-to-analyze snapshot of a player's complete performance for a given year.

Bill James has proven that minor league statistics (converted to MLEs), at Double-A level or above, provide as accurate a record of a player's performance as major league statistics. Other researchers have also devised conversion factors for foreign leagues. Since these are adequate barometers, we include them in the pool of historical data for each year.

Team designations: An asterisk (*) appearing with a team name means that Triple-A and/or Double-A numbers are included in that year's stat line. Any stints of less than 20 AB are not included (to screen out most rehab appearances). A designation of "a/a" means the stats were accumulated at both AA and AAA levels that year. "for" represents a foreign or independent league. The designation "2TM" appears whenever a player was on more than one major league team, crossing leagues, in a season. "2AL" and "2NL" represent more than one team in the same league. Players who were cut during the season and finished 2017 as a free agent are designated as FAA (Free agent, AL) and FAN (Free agent, NL).

Stats: Descriptions of all the categories appear in the Encyclopedia.

- The leading decimal point has been suppressed on some categories to conserve space.
- Data for platoons (vL, vR), balls-in-play (G/L/F) and consistency (Wk#, DOM, DIS) are for major league performance only.
- Formulas that use BIP data, like xBA and xPX, only appear for years in which G/L/F data is available.

Batting average is presented alongside xBA. On base average and slugging average appear next, and the combined On Base Plus Slugging (OPS). OPS splits vs. left-handed and right-handed pitchers appear after the overall OPS column.

Batting eye and contact skill are measured with walk rate (bb%), contact rate (ct%). Eye is the ratio of walks to strikeouts.

Once the ball leaves the bat, it will either be a (G)round ball, (L)ine drive or (F)ly ball. Hit rate (h%), the also referred to as batting average on balls-in-play (BABIP), measures how often a ball put into play results in a base hit. Hard contact index (HctX) measures the frequency of hard contact, compared to overall league levels. Looking at the ratio of fly balls is a good spring-board to the Power gauges. Linear weighted power index (PX) measures a batter's skill at hitting extra base hits as compared to overall league levels. xPX measures power by assessing how hard the ball is being hit (rather than the outcomes of those hits). And the ratio of home runs to fly balls shows the results of those hits.

To assess speed, first look at on base average (does he get on base?), then Spd (is he fast enough to steal bases?), then SBO (how often is he attempting to steal bases?) and finally, SB% (when he attempts, what is his rate of success?).

In looking at consistency, we use weekly Base Performance Value (BPV) levels. Starting with the total number of weeks the batter accumulated stats (#Wk), the percentage of DOMinating weeks (BPV over 50) and DISaster weeks (BPV under 0) is shown. The larger the variance between DOM and DIS, the greater the consistency.

The final section includes several overall performance measures: runs created per game (RC/G), runs above replacement (RAR), Base performance value (BPV), Base performance index (BPX, which is BPV indexed to each year's league average) and the Rotisserie value (R$).

2018 Projections

Forecasts are computed from a player's trends over the past five years. Adjustments were made for leading indicators and variances between skill and statistical output. After reviewing the leading indicators, you might opt to make further adjustments.

Although each year's numbers include all playing time at the Double-A level or above, the 2018 forecast only represents potential playing time at the major league level, and again is highly preliminary.

Note that the projected Rotisserie values in this book will not necessarily align with each player's historical actuals. Since we currently have no idea who is going to play shortstop for the Orioles, or whether Victor Robles is going to break camp with the Nationals, it is impossible to create a finite pool of playing time, something which is required for valuation. So the projections are roughly based on a 12-team AL/NL league, and include an inflated number of plate appearances, league-wide. This serves to flatten the spread of values and depress individual player dollar projections. In truth, a $25 player in this book might actually be worth $21, or $28. This level of precision is irrelevant in a process that is driven by market forces anyway. So, don't obsess over it.

Be aware of other sources that publish perfectly calibrated Rotisserie values over the winter. They are likely making arbitrary decisions as to where free agents are going to sign and who is going to land jobs in the spring. We do not make those leaps of faith here.

Bottom line… It is far too early to be making definitive projections for 2018, especially on playing time. Focus on the skill levels and trends, then consult BaseballHQ.com for playing time revisions as players change teams and roles become more defined. A free projections update will be available online in March.

Do-it-yourself analysis

Here are some data points you can look at in doing your own player analysis:

- Variance between vLH and vRH OPS
- Growth or decline in walk rate (bb%)
- Growth or decline in contact rate (ct%)
- Growth or decline in G/L/F individually, or concurrent shifts
- Variance in 2017 hit rate (h%) to 2014-2016 three-year average
- Variance between Avg and xBA each year
- Growth or decline in HctX level
- Growth or decline in power index (PX) rate
- Variance between PX and xPX each year
- Variance in 2017 hr/f rate to 2014-2016 three-year average
- Growth or decline in statistically scouted speed (Spd) score
- Concurrent growth/decline of gauges like ct%, FB, PX, xPX, hr/f
- Concurrent growth/decline of gauges like OB, Spd, SBO, SB%
- Trends in DOM/DIS splits

Abreu,Jose

Age: 31 Bats: R Pos: 1B	Health A	LIMA Plan B+	
Ht: 6' 3" Wt: 255	PT/Exp A	Rand Var 0	
	Consist B	MM 4155	

So much for those ominous pre-'17 trends. Premium health, strong consistency, rising contact rate, surging FB rate all make this a near 30-100-.300 lock, especially after thump vR returned in earnest late. Open bidding at $21, push to $25 and jump back in if it stops short of $30. Reliability has value.

Yr	Tm	AB	R	HR	RBI	SB	BA	xBA	OBP	SLG	OPS	vL	vR	bb%	ct%	Eye	G	L	F	h%	HctX	PX	xPX	hr/f	Spd	SBO	SB%	#Wk	DOM	DIS	RC/G	RAR	BPV	BPX	R$
13	for	285	59	10	54	2	320		406	480	886			13	84	0.90				35		103			87	8%	21%				6.76	17.0	72	180	$16
14	CHW	556	80	36	107	3	317	307	383	581	964	1098	919	8	76	0.39	45	23	31	36	120	185	132	27%	72	3%	75%	24	71%	17%	8.09	59.0	94	254	$35
15	CHW	613	88	30	101	0	290	276	347	502	850	658	908	6	77	0.28	47	21	32	33	115	136	116	20%	81	0%	0%	26	54%	31%	6.01	18.2	55	149	$26
16	CHW	624	67	25	100	0	293	263	353	468	820	840	816	7	80	0.38	45	21	33	33	106	103	93	15%	71	1%	0%	27	44%	33%	5.71	14.8	39	111	$22
17	CHW	621	95	33	102	3	304	293	354	552	906	1033	866	5	81	0.29	45	18	36	33	133	134	123	18%	99	2%	100%	27	59%	22%	6.95	26.5	73	221	$28
1st Half		318	49	15	54	0	296	285	345	516	861	1120	782	6	81	0.34	47	19	35	32	133	120	121	17%	84	0%	0%	13	54%	31%	6.30	5.7	61	185	$26
2nd Half		303	46	18	48	3	314	298	364	591	954	948	956	5	80	0.25	44	18	38	34	132	149	125	19%	110	5%	100%	14	64%	14%	7.66	16.4	85	258	$30
18	Proj	**590**	**88**	**30**	**100**	**2**	**295**	**286**	**352**	**523**	**875**	**919**	**862**	**6**	**80**	**0.34**	**46**	**20**	**35**	**33**	**122**	**125**	**116**	**18%**	**90**	**2%**	**63%**				**6.39**	**21.2**	**56**	**169**	**$25**

Acuna,Ronald

Age: 20 Bats: R Pos: OF	Health A	LIMA Plan C	
Ht: 6' 0" Wt: 180	PT/Exp F	Rand Var 0	
	Consist F	MM 1413	

Proof that a prospect can go from good to great in span of one season. This one's emerging power/speed combo gives him immediate multi-category potential, but at age 20, expect early bumps—especially with his marginal pitch recognition. All the makings of a future Braves stud, just don't expect him to be one quite yet.

Yr	Tm	AB	R	HR	RBI	SB	BA	xBA	OBP	SLG	OPS	vL	vR	bb%	ct%	Eye	G	L	F	h%	HctX	PX	xPX	hr/f	Spd	SBO	SB%	#Wk	DOM	DIS	RC/G	RAR	BPV	BPX	R$
13																																			
14																																			
15																																			
16																																			
17	a/a	442	66	16	62	29	306		358	468	826			8	73	0.30				39		94			107	35%	62%				5.60		18	55	$28
1st Half		189	25	6	25	17	297		356	435	791			8	70	0.30				40		86			115	47%	59%				4.83		2	6	$20
2nd Half		253	42	11	38	14	318		367	503	870			7	76	0.32				38		103			122	26%	68%				6.60		40	121	$34
18	Proj	**389**	**54**	**10**	**51**	**19**	**267**	**236**	**321**	**399**	**720**	**720**	**720**	**7**	**74**	**0.30**	**44**	**21**	**35**	**34**		**80**		**10%**	**122**	**29%**	**60%**				**4.14**	**#N/A**	**9**	**27**	**$18**

Adames,Willy

Age: 22 Bats: R Pos: SS	Health A	LIMA Plan D	
Ht: 6' 1" Wt: 180	PT/Exp C	Rand Var 0	
	Consist A	MM 3311	

Upper-tier middle-infield Tampa prospect combines projectable muscle, good wheels, and ability to take a walk into an attractive package. He's another one for whom you'll want to pack your patience though, as underlying skills suggest speed will come before homers, and he's still plenty green. Still, a strong investment.

Yr	Tm	AB	R	HR	RBI	SB	BA	xBA	OBP	SLG	OPS	vL	vR	bb%	ct%	Eye	G	L	F	h%	HctX	PX	xPX	hr/f	Spd	SBO	SB%	#Wk	DOM	DIS	RC/G	RAR	BPV	BPX	R$
13																																			
14																																			
15																																			
16	aa	486	77	9	49	11	249		338	382	720			12	72	0.48				33		93			113	12%	63%				4.29		22	63	$11
17	aaa	506	69	9	58	10	258		339	383	722			11	71	0.42				35		84			109	10%	66%				4.40		7	21	$12
1st Half		289	41	5	32	5	259		349	389	737			12	69	0.45				36		88			141	9%	59%				4.57		15	45	$13
2nd Half		217	28	5	26	6	258		326	375	701			9	73	0.38				33		79			99	13%	72%				4.18		6	18	$11
18	Proj	**125**	**18**	**4**	**14**	**3**	**255**	**232**	**336**	**412**	**748**	**748**	**748**	**11**	**72**	**0.43**	**42**	**18**	**40**	**33**		**100**		**10%**	**122**	**12%**	**68%**				**4.68**	**0.8**	**19**	**59**	**$4**

Adams,Lane

Age: 28 Bats: R Pos: LF	Health A	LIMA Plan F	
Ht: 6' 3" Wt: 220	PT/Exp C	Rand Var -5	
	Consist B	MM 2501	

5-20-.275 with 10 SB in 109 AB at ATL. Flash of pop and speed late will put him on some draft boards, but there's plenty working against him. Plummeting contact rate will be torn apart by MLB pitchers and renders speed moot, and Sept power surge sticks out as an aberration. Speculate only in deepest leagues.

Yr	Tm	AB	R	HR	RBI	SB	BA	xBA	OBP	SLG	OPS	vL	vR	bb%	ct%	Eye	G	L	F	h%	HctX	PX	xPX	hr/f	Spd	SBO	SB%	#Wk	DOM	DIS	RC/G	RAR	BPV	BPX	R$
13	aa	156	23	4	20	12	213		277	333	611			8	69	0.28				29		94			108	32%	100%				3.36		1	3	$4
14	KC *	408	51	8	27	29	229	118	289	355	644	0	0	8	76	0.35	0	0	100	28	0	98	-15	0%	118	41%	74%	4	0%	75%	3.35	-6.0	36	97	$13
15	a/a	488	55	11	47	23	237		290	365	655			7	72	0.27				31		94			100	28%	74%				3.51		9	24	$14
16	a/a	428	48	7	41	32	212		267	303	570			7	65	0.22				31		70			90	38%	84%				2.77		-38	-109	$12
17	ATL *	287	35	10	43	22	227	207	283	381	663	437	937	7	59	0.19	44	22	34	34	94	108	104	20%	129	39%	85%	21	29%	52%	3.70	-11.9	-20	-61	$11
1st Half		175	16	5	25	15	205	202	248	324	572	650	611	5	62	0.15	50	19	31	30	78	79	83	20%	120	48%	85%	7	14%	43%	2.73	-12.1	-41	-124	$10
2nd Half		112	19	5	19	7	261	217	334	470	804	401	1026	10	56	0.25	42	23	35	42	93	158	110	20%	121	28%	85%	14	36%	57%	5.55	2.1	7	21	$12
18	Proj	**162**	**19**	**4**	**18**	**7**	**230**	**211**	**292**	**361**	**653**	**330**	**778**	**8**	**63**	**0.22**	**42**	**23**	**35**	**33**	**84**	**91**	**99**	**12%**	**120**	**24%**	**77%**				**3.46**	**-5.0**	**-24**	**-72**	**$5**

Adams,Matt

Age: 29 Bats: L Pos: 1B	Health C	LIMA Plan D+	
Ht: 6' 3" Wt: 260	PT/Exp D	Rand Var -2	
	Consist C	MM 4033	

Some will still target him for end-draft power, and four 15+ HR seasons in last five confirm he can contribute there. But poor health and yo-yo platoon splits make it impossible to know when to use him, and mediocre plate skills give little hope of anything more. Bid five bucks, and cross fingers and toes.

Yr	Tm	AB	R	HR	RBI	SB	BA	xBA	OBP	SLG	OPS	vL	vR	bb%	ct%	Eye	G	L	F	h%	HctX	PX	xPX	hr/f	Spd	SBO	SB%	#Wk	DOM	DIS	RC/G	RAR	BPV	BPX	R$
13	STL	296	46	17	51	0	284	262	335	503	839	654	876	7	73	0.29	44	19	36	34	123	153	145	22%	71	1%	0%	26	54%	42%	5.93	11.2	52	130	$12
14	STL	527	55	15	68	3	288	265	321	457	779	528	854	5	78	0.23	35	24	41	34	109	124	130	9%	80	4%	60%	26	50%	23%	5.22	15.3	48	130	$19
15	STL	175	14	5	24	1	240	237	280	377	657	499	683	5	77	0.24	41	20	39	29	125	95	120	10%	50	3%	100%	13	38%	31%	3.59	-9.2	10	27	$1
16	STL	297	37	16	54	0	249	252	309	471	780	822	773	8	73	0.31	32	20	48	29	108	142	159	15%	63	2%	0%	25	40%	40%	4.85	-4.2	41	117	$7
17	2 NL	339	46	20	65	0	274	266	319	522	841	583	896	6	74	0.26	39	18	43	32	112	146	123	18%	66	0%	0%	26	50%	38%	5.88	-0.2	47	142	$11
1st Half		194	29	13	39	0	294	266	343	557	899	618	953	7	74	0.30	40	17	43	34	123	148	142	21%	80	0%	0%	13	46%	38%	6.93	6.9	56	170	$15
2nd Half		145	17	7	26	0	248	265	286	476	762	545	815	5	74	0.21	37	20	43	29	97	143	96	15%	55	0%	0%	13	54%	38%	4.64	-4.3	39	118	$5
18	Proj	**263**	**32**	**13**	**46**	**0**	**253**	**257**	**298**	**468**	**766**	**607**	**799**	**6**	**74**	**0.26**	**37**	**20**	**43**	**29**	**111**	**129**	**129**	**15%**	**61**	**1%**	**49%**				**4.75**	**-2.7**	**26**	**77**	**$8**

Adrianza,Ehire

Age: 28 Bats: B Pos: SS	Health F	LIMA Plan D	
Ht: 6' 1" Wt: 170	PT/Exp F	Rand Var -1	
	Consist B	MM 1411	

2-24-.265 with 8 SB in 162 AB at MIN. Years of chronic mediocrity will leave him undrafted in most leagues, but spike in walks combined with that Spd suggest he can be factor on basepaths. That hope is muted by chronic struggles vR, so consider him a dart throw with a one-trick-pony ceiling. UP: 20 SB

Yr	Tm	AB	R	HR	RBI	SB	BA	xBA	OBP	SLG	OPS	vL	vR	bb%	ct%	Eye	G	L	F	h%	HctX	PX	xPX	hr/f	Spd	SBO	SB%	#Wk	DOM	DIS	RC/G	RAR	BPV	BPX	R$
13	SF *	413	41	2	27	12	219	232	286	297	583	583	929	9	78	0.42	42	25	33	28	116	59	152	25%	135	20%	56%	4	50%	0%	2.63	-11.2	17	43	$3
14	SF	97	10	0	5	1	237	226	279	299	578	499	605	5	77	0.23	36	25	39	31	60	63	71	0%	108	9%	50%	15	27%	47%	2.66	-1.4	4	11	-$1
15	SF *	284	22	2	22	7	227	216	295	302	596	517	590	9	77	0.42	53	14	32	29	59	56	59	0%	117	14%	69%	13	23%	54%	2.92	-7.3	7	19	$1
16	SF *	98	7	3	9	1	237	240	263	354	617	853	484	3	82	0.20	41	20	39	27	68	68	62	11%	112	26%	14%	11	36%	36%	2.45	-6.7	23	66	-$1
17	MIN *	199	31	2	27	8	251	234	323	347	669	855	630	9	81	0.56	41	20	39	30	84	57	88	4%	134	18%	78%	21	38%	24%	3.87	-4.4	31	94	$5
1st Half		91	8	0	10	6	230	227	313	274	588	614	666	11	76	0.51	44	24	31	30	51	36	40	0%	111	29%	73%	8	38%	25%	2.91	-4.7	-9	-27	$1
2nd Half		108	23	2	17	2	269	247	325	407	733	913	605	8	85	0.63	39	18	43	30	104	72	110	5%	147	7%	100%	13	38%	23%	4.81	0.7	61	185	$9
18	Proj	**162**	**20**	**2**	**18**	**6**	**248**	**236**	**309**	**344**	**653**	**767**	**586**	**7**	**80**	**0.41**	**42**	**20**	**38**	**30**	**73**	**57**	**72**	**4%**	**125**	**23%**	**66%**				**3.44**	**-5.0**	**16**	**48**	**$5**

Aguilar,Jesus

Age: 28 Bats: R Pos: 1B	Health A	LIMA Plan D+	
Ht: 6' 3" Wt: 250	PT/Exp C	Rand Var -5	
	Consist C	MM 4033	

On surface, a marginal hacker still waiting for a full-time shot with age 30 around the corner. Before you dismiss, there was some legit growth here. Power fully backed by xPX, hit both lefties and righties with authority. Opened up his swing to do it, so he's not for the risk averse. Still... UP: 30 HR

Yr	Tm	AB	R	HR	RBI	SB	BA	xBA	OBP	SLG	OPS	vL	vR	bb%	ct%	Eye	G	L	F	h%	HctX	PX	xPX	hr/f	Spd	SBO	SB%	#Wk	DOM	DIS	RC/G	RAR	BPV	BPX	R$
13	aa	499	49	11	78	0	233		291	352	643			8	75	0.33				29		90			75	1%	0%				3.37		13	33	$6
14	CLE *	460	55	15	62	0	251	242	327	407	733	471	133	10	73	0.41	48	19	33	31	90	125	92	0%	66	0%	0%	8	0%	88%	4.52	4.5	33	89	$11
15	CLE *	529	48	16	81	0	244	281	296	394	690	583	818	7	75	0.29	42	33	25	30	215	107	171	0%	57	0%	0%	4	0%	50%	3.93	-22.5	17	46	$9
16	CLE *	521	50	25	74	0	218	199	278	409	687	0	0	8	78	0.38	80	0	20	23	63	113	125	0%	53	0%	0%	3	0%	33%	3.71	-26.0	35	100	$5
17	MIL	279	40	16	52	0	265	252	331	505	837	889	806	8	66	0.27	41	21	38	34	121	154	165	23%	80	0%	0%	27	44%	48%	5.71	-1.5	30	91	$8
1st Half		151	22	7	25	0	285	273	349	536	886	980	836	7	68	0.24	46	22	32	38	118	169	133	21%	85	0%	0%	13	46%	46%	6.45	3.4	48	145	$8
2nd Half		128	18	9	27	0	242	229	310	469	779	798	766	9	65	0.29	35	21	44	30	125	135	203	24%	71	0%	0%	13	43%	50%	4.92	-2.7	9	27	$8
18	Proj	**290**	**35**	**18**	**49**	**0**	**245**	**261**	**309**	**489**	**798**	**835**	**776**	**8**	**71**	**0.30**	**39**	**21**	**40**	**28**	**122**	**144**	**175**	**23%**	**67**	**0%**	**0%**				**5.03**	**-0.6**	**27**	**82**	**$8**

STEPHEN NICKRAND

Ahmed,Nick

Age: 28	Bats: R	Pos: SS	Health	F	LIMA Plan	D+
Ht: 6' 2"	Wt: 195		PT/Exp	D	Rand Var	-1
			Consist	B	MM	1323

Mid-season pitch off his hand broke a bone—then hit again on the wrist during rehab and broke another bone! Otherwise, decent step up in power presaged by 2016 xPX, so it could stick. Poor SB% hurts, but above-par Spd and history suggest some SB upside. Nothing special, but if health cooperates... UP: 10 HR, 10 SB

Yr Tm	AB	R	HR	RBI	SB	BA	xBA	OBP	SLG	OPS	vL	vR	bb%	ct%	Eye	G	L	F	h%	HctX	PX	xPX	hr/f	Spd	SBO	SB%	#Wk	DOM	DIS	RC/G	RAR	BPV	BPX
13 aa	487	49	4	39	22	223		265	309	574			5	84	0.36				26		59			122	28%	74%				2.69		33	83
14 ARI *	477	45	4	34	9	247	236	286	334	620	428	577	5	84	0.35	42	18	40	29	88	66	85	4%	129	15%	53%	9	22%	56%	3.08	-3.1	41	111
15 ARI	421	49	9	34	4	226	242	275	359	634	803	575	6	81	0.36	46	17	37	26	77	82	78	7%	145	10%	44%	25	28%	28%	3.12	-8.3	47	127
16 ARI	284	26	4	20	5	218	239	265	299	564	633	536	5	80	0.26	48	21	30	26	88	50	92	6%	113	11%	71%	16	19%	50%	2.51	-18.5	4	11
17 ARI	167	24	6	21	3	251	261	298	419	717	1078	568	6	77	0.26	48	20	32	30	99	96	91	15%	125	19%	43%	13	38%	46%	3.84	-3.3	34	103
1st Half	167	24	6	21	3	251	261	298	419	717	1078	568	6	77	0.26	48	20	32	30	99	96	91	15%	125	19%	43%	13	38%	46%	3.84	-3.7	34	103
2nd Half																																	
18 Proj	**264**	**30**	**6**	**24**	**5**	**235**	**250**	**281**	**367**	**647**	**787**	**585**	**6**	**80**	**0.30**	**46**	**19**	**35**	**27**	**87**	**73**	**86**	**9%**	**129**	**16%**	**54%**				**3.24**	**-9.9**	**20**	**61**

Albies,Ozhaino

Age: 21	Bats: B	Pos: 2B	Health	A	LIMA Plan	B
Ht: 5' 9"	Wt: 160		PT/Exp	C	Rand Var	-2
			Consist	A	MM	1525

6-28-.286 with 8 SB in 217 AB at ATL. Terrific debut at age 20. Previous MLEs played up, with solid skills that bounced back across the board after 1st half dip. Sure, the speed is foremost, but this is potentially stat-filling stuff, with xPX suggesting more power upside. And the glove at 2B? Well, he does go by Ozzie, after all.

Yr Tm	AB	R	HR	RBI	SB	BA	xBA	OBP	SLG	OPS	vL	vR	bb%	ct%	Eye	G	L	F	h%	HctX	PX	xPX	hr/f	Spd	SBO	SB%	#Wk	DOM	DIS	RC/G	RAR	BPV	BPX
13																																	
14																																	
15																																	
16 a/a	552	83	6	53	30	272		338	372	710			9	81	0.52				33		59			135	26%	69%				4.30		31	89
17 ATL *	628	95	14	66	27	265	233	317	401	718	926	773	7	78	0.35	41	19	40	32	105	73	113	8%	180	18%	90%	10	60%	20%	4.57	-8.0	41	124
1st Half	309	44	6	31	18	255	230	299	378	677			6	75	0.25				32		68			168	26%	89%				4.07		19	58
2nd Half	319	51	8	34	9	275	246	335	423	758	926	773	8	81	0.47	41	19	40	32	109	78	113	8%	170	11%	90%	10	60%	20%	5.09	2.4	56	170
18 Proj	**548**	**83**	**13**	**55**	**20**	**269**	**240**	**332**	**413**	**745**	**853**	**711**	**8**	**79**	**0.42**	**41**	**19**	**40**	**32**	**106**	**76**	**102**	**7%**	**178**	**17%**	**80%**				**4.76**	**-0.7**	**41**	**123**

Alfaro,Jorge

Age: 25	Bats: R	Pos: CA	Health	A	LIMA Plan	D
Ht: 6' 2"	Wt: 225		PT/Exp	D	Rand Var	-5
			Consist	A	MM	3203

5-14-.318 in 107 AB at PHI, but beware the small sample size. Slashed .241/.291/.358 at AAA, then posted 3/33 BB/K in majors. So heed full-season skills, notably abysmal strike-zone control. Still a baby as catchers go, with a history of decent pop, so there's plenty to hope on. Just don't expect him to arrive in 2018.

Yr Tm	AB	R	HR	RBI	SB	BA	xBA	OBP	SLG	OPS	vL	vR	bb%	ct%	Eye	G	L	F	h%	HctX	PX	xPX	hr/f	Spd	SBO	SB%	#Wk	DOM	DIS	RC/G	RAR	BPV	BPX
13																																	
14 aa	88	10	3	11	0	239		280	393	673			5	72	0.20				29		116			91	0%	0%				3.68		21	57
15 aa	190	17	4	16	2	222		251	369	621			4	66	0.11				32		124			100	9%	59%				2.99		1	3
16 PHI *	420	51	12	50	2	236	226	267	373	640	333	286	4	69	0.13	63	13	25	32	0	94	-24	0%	92	5%	50%	3	0%	100%	3.26	-14.5	-12	-34
17 PHI *	431	41	11	51	1	239	200	267	365	632	500	1054	4	62	0.10	53	16	31	36	61	92	68	22%	107	2%	43%	9	22%	56%	3.23	-10.6	-37	-112
1st Half	254	25	6	32	1	226	196	261	338	599			5	62	0.13				34		80			100	4%	43%				2.86		-46	-139
2nd Half	177	16	6	19	0	256	198	275	405	681	500	1054	3	61	0.07	53	16	31	39	60	111	68	22%	97	0%	0%	9	22%	56%	3.83	-1.4	-31	-94
18 Proj	**337**	**35**	**13**	**38**	**1**	**237**	**226**	**289**	**410**	**699**	**423**	**834**	**4**	**65**	**0.11**	**53**	**16**	**31**	**33**	**54**	**118**	**61**	**20%**	**113**	**4%**	**55%**				**3.61**	**-5.4**	**-19**	**-59**

Alford,Anthony

Age: 23	Bats: R	Pos: LF	Health	C	LIMA Plan	D
Ht: 6' 1"	Wt: 215		PT/Exp	F	Rand Var	-1
			Consist	F	MM	2331

0-0-.125 in 8 AB at TOR. Superb athlete (he played football at Ole Miss) started putting things together in 2017. Nice ct% spike bodes well for BA gains. Skills belie his fine speed, and career 82% SB% shows he knows how to use it. Still relatively inexperienced, so probably gets more minors time. But a future lead-off CF.

Yr Tm	AB	R	HR	RBI	SB	BA	xBA	OBP	SLG	OPS	vL	vR	bb%	ct%	Eye	G	L	F	h%	HctX	PX	xPX	hr/f	Spd	SBO	SB%	#Wk	DOM	DIS	RC/G	RAR	BPV	BPX
13																																	
14																																	
15																																	
16																																	
17 TOR *	265	38	5	22	16	292	274	370	407	777	0	750	11	79	0.60	60	20	20	35	64	74	124	0%	86	22%	83%	2	50%	50%	5.60	6.4	26	79
1st Half	131	15	3	9	8	293	269	360	416	776	0	750	10	77	0.46	60	20	20	36	63	80	124	0%	85	21%	88%	2	50%	50%	5.63	2.7	20	61
2nd Half	134	22	2	12	8	285	248	370	388	758			12	81	0.72				34		67			93	22%	79%				5.23		32	97
18 Proj	**124**	**18**	**3**	**10**	**6**	**278**	**259**	**359**	**420**	**779**	**779**	**779**	**11**	**80**	**0.62**	**46**	**20**	**34**	**33**		**85**		**10%**	**93**	**20%**	**81%**				**5.43**	**3.5**	**36**	**108**

Allen,Greg

Age: 25	Bats: B	Pos: CF	Health	A	LIMA Plan	D
Ht: 6' 0"	Wt: 175		PT/Exp	F	Rand Var	-1
			Consist	B	MM	2521

1-6-.229 with 1 SB in 35 AB at CLE. Another young speedster who runs with success (145 SB, 80% SB% in four pro seasons). Lack of pop hurt BA, but wrist injury may have contributed. Has a history of better, with solid OB skills in the minors. And solid CF defense can only help PT. If AB present themselves... UP: 30 SB

Yr Tm	AB	R	HR	RBI	SB	BA	xBA	OBP	SLG	OPS	vL	vR	bb%	ct%	Eye	G	L	F	h%	HctX	PX	xPX	hr/f	Spd	SBO	SB%	#Wk	DOM	DIS	RC/G	RAR	BPV	BPX
13																																	
14																																	
15																																	
16 aa	145	21	3	11	6	269		342	398	740			10	82	0.60				32		76			122	28%	47%				4.16		46	131
17 CLE *	293	37	3	25	18	240	223	288	329	617	1300	345	6	78	0.32	58	8	35	30	102	61	31	11%	113	28%	89%	6	17%	33%	3.38	-12.0	11	33
1st Half	90	12	1	8	7	244	239	301	326	628			8	81	0.43				29		55			110	30%	100%				3.76		18	55
2nd Half	203	25	2	17	11	238	221	283	330	612	1300	345	6	77	0.27	58	8	35	30	101	63	31	11%	115	27%	83%	6	17%	33%	3.22	-10.4	8	24
18 Proj	**193**	**26**	**5**	**16**	**10**	**251**	**244**	**320**	**395**	**715**	**1487**	**384**	**8**	**80**	**0.44**	**58**	**7.7**	**35**	**29**	**91**	**83**	**28**	**9%**	**129**	**27%**	**74%**				**4.15**	**-2.1**	**39**	**117**

Almora,Albert

Age: 24	Bats: R	Pos: CF	Health	A	LIMA Plan	C+
Ht: 6' 2"	Wt: 190		PT/Exp	C	Rand Var	-4
			Consist	B	MM	2353

Does nothing exceptionally at plate, but does a lot of things well, and age is in his favor. Started season as a lefty-masher, then found footing vR late as CHC pushed him to loft ball more. He delivered, shifting groundballs to LDs and FBs in 2H. If that shift holds and he finds the playing time... UP: 20 HR

Yr Tm	AB	R	HR	RBI	SB	BA	xBA	OBP	SLG	OPS	vL	vR	bb%	ct%	Eye	G	L	F	h%	HctX	PX	xPX	hr/f	Spd	SBO	SB%	#Wk	DOM	DIS	RC/G	RAR	BPV	BPX
13																																	
14 aa	142	16	2	8	0	212		220	312	532			1	83	0.07				24		72			117	5%	0%				2.13		30	81
15 aa	405	56	5	37	7	248		294	361	655			6	87	0.51				27		74			108	12%	63%				3.52		55	149
16 CHC *	432	50	6	47	8	268	280	288	383	672	827	724	3	84	0.17	43	28	29	31	96	72	92	12%	113	12%	70%	12	42%	17%	3.81	-10.5	34	97
17 CHC	299	39	8	46	1	298	273	338	445	782	898	711	6	82	0.36	49	21	30	34	98	85	69	11%	111	1%	100%	27	37%	33%	5.51	3.7	44	133
1st Half	162	22	3	15	0	259	247	330	377	706	1017	554	9	80	0.52	56	17	27	31	87	75	55	9%	110	0%	0%	13	38%	31%	4.27	-3.0	33	100
2nd Half	137	17	5	31	1	343	294	348	526	873	788	939	1	85	0.10	43	24	33	38	111	96	83	13%	117	3%	100%	14	36%	36%	7.25	8.3	58	176
18 Proj	**337**	**42**	**10**	**45**	**3**	**280**	**286**	**306**	**436**	**742**	**805**	**703**	**4**	**84**	**0.25**	**46**	**24**	**30**	**31**	**99**	**86**	**80**	**11%**	**118**	**6%**	**71%**				**4.72**	**2.0**	**38**	**114**

Alonso,Yonder

Age: 31	Bats: L	Pos: 1B	Health	C	LIMA Plan	B
Ht: 6' 1"	Wt: 230		PT/Exp	B	Rand Var	-2
			Consist	D	MM	2125

Opened up swing and went for more FB, and that's all it took. Nothing else. His HctX didn't budge but that one minor adjustment more than tripled his previous career HR high. Right. FB regressed in 2nd half and hr/f still barely budged, but it's NOT THE BALLS. Expect some pullback. Maybe a lot. Just because.

Yr Tm	AB	R	HR	RBI	SB	BA	xBA	OBP	SLG	OPS	vL	vR	bb%	ct%	Eye	G	L	F	h%	HctX	PX	xPX	hr/f	Spd	SBO	SB%	#Wk	DOM	DIS	RC/G	RAR	BPV	BPX
13 SD	334	34	6	45	6	281	247	341	368	710	637	736	9	86	0.68	46	21	33	31	110	57	84	6%	63	6%	100%	19	26%	32%	4.62	0.1	27	68
14 SD	267	27	7	27	6	240	279	285	397	682	607	699	6	87	0.47	43	19	38	25	120	110	121	8%	69	13%	86%	16	44%	13%	3.85	-2.3	69	186
15 SD	354	50	5	31	2	282	269	361	381	742	669	762	10	86	0.88	49	23	28	32	108	65	73	6%	86	6%	29%	19	37%	11%	4.64	-3.0	46	124
16 OAK	482	52	7	56	3	253	268	316	367	683	617	694	8	85	0.61	44	23	33	29	111	76	94	5%	60	3%	75%	27	41%	30%	3.97	-12.4	36	103
17 2 AL	451	72	28	67	2	266	265	365	501	866	679	903	13	74	0.58	34	23	43	30	108	135	124	19%	66	1%	100%	27	44%	33%	6.34	12.4	51	155
1st Half	228	40	17	38	1	281	272	374	561	935	870	953	13	73	0.54	27	22	51	31	108	162	152	20%	70	1%	100%	13	46%	23%	7.43	11.5	71	215
2nd Half	223	32	11	29	1	251	258	355	439	795	441	853	14	74	0.61	41	23	36	29	107	107	97	19%	71	1%	100%	14	43%	43%	5.31	-2.2	34	103
18 Proj	**466**	**68**	**17**	**65**	**3**	**263**	**251**	**347**	**428**	**775**	**633**	**803**	**11**	**75**	**0.51**	**39**	**23**	**39**	**32**	**109**	**99**	**104**	**12%**	**66**	**3%**	**70%**				**5.11**	**0.1**	**21**	**64**

ROD TRUESDELL

Altherr,Aaron

Age: 27	Bats: R	Pos: LF RF	Health F	LIMA Plan B
Ht: 6' 5"	Wt: 215		PT/Exp C	Rand Var -4
			Consist F	MM 3435

Still can't shake injury-prone tag, as bum hamstring caused two DL stints and brought running game to a halt. It's a pity, since a mechanical change to his hand path improved his ct% and coincided with significant growth in HctX, xPX and hr/f. With regular AB, his floor is now higher, but health is still the x-factor.

Yr Tm	AB	R	HR	RBI	SB	BA	xBA	OBP	SLG	OPS	vL	vR	bb%	ct%	Eye	G	L	F	h%	HctX	PX	xPX	hr/f	Spd	SBO	SB%	#Wk	DOM	DIS	RC/G	RAR	BPV	BPX	R$
13																																		
14 PHI *	454	41	12	43	9	201	172	235	337	572	0	0	4	71	0.16	33	0	67	25	103	110	235	0%	98	21%	58%	2	0%	50%	2.40	-24.5	14	38	$3
15 PHI *	570	75	17	74	18	250	260	315	434	750	636	936	9	75	0.39	40	22	38	30	95	128	96	14%	131	19%	74%	8	38%	0%	4.61	-4.1	62	168	$19
16 PHI	198	23	4	22	7	197	222	300	288	587	723	553	10	65	0.33	51	26	22	28	78	67	76	14%	101	17%	78%	11	27%	55%	2.62	-12.9	-32	-91	$1
17 PHI	372	58	19	65	5	272	269	340	516	856	830	867	8	72	0.31	43	19	38	33	106	147	115	19%	109	11%	56%	22	45%	36%	5.77	6.2	56	170	$13
1st Half	248	37	13	41	4	282	265	353	524	877	882	874	8	71	0.31	43	18	39	35	113	149	122	19%	90	13%	50%	13	46%	31%	6.04	7.0	50	152	$18
2nd Half	124	21	6	24	1	250	277	314	500	814	697	851	7	73	0.30	43	22	35	29	94	142	101	19%	139	4%	100%	9	44%	44%	5.25	0.7	66	200	$4
18 Proj	**451**	**62**	**18**	**67**	**10**	**256**	**258**	**329**	**449**	**778**	**760**	**784**	**8**	**71**	**0.30**	**45**	**23**	**32**	**32**	**92**	**118**	**96**	**17%**	**122**	**13%**	**70%**				**4.78**	**4.3**	**31**	**93**	**$14**

Altuve,Jose

Age: 28	Bats: R	Pos: 2B	Health A	LIMA Plan C
Ht: 5' 6"	Wt: 165		PT/Exp A	Rand Var -5
			Consist C	MM 2555

Move to the middle of the order didn't curb SB in the least. Added hr/f for 4th straight season, but xPX and HctX warn of some HR pullback. With a consistent Eye base like this, mid-30s hit rates mean batting titles. Owns one of the most diverse, stable skill sets in MLB. Still just 28; a top 3 superstar.

Yr Tm	AB	R	HR	RBI	SB	BA	xBA	OBP	SLG	OPS	vL	vR	bb%	ct%	Eye	G	L	F	h%	HctX	PX	xPX	hr/f	Spd	SBO	SB%	#Wk	DOM	DIS	RC/G	RAR	BPV	BPX	R$
13 HOU	626	64	5	52	35	283	264	316	363	678	733	656	5	86	0.38	49	23	28	32	94	58	78	3%	109	28%	73%	27	33%	15%	4.05	5.8	36	90	$27
14 HOU	660	85	7	59	56	341	296	377	453	830	1013	775	5	92	0.68	48	23	30	36	95	81	77	4%	131	32%	86%	27	78%	7%	6.86	60.3	84	227	$50
15 HOU	638	86	15	66	38	313	281	353	459	812	973	743	5	89	0.49	47	18	35	33	103	89	92	7%	135	29%	75%	27	67%	19%	5.82	27.2	81	219	$40
16 HOU	640	108	24	96	30	338	311	396	531	928	885	942	8	89	0.86	42	26	32	35	122	104	120	13%	120	20%	75%	27	70%	15%	7.96	55.0	94	269	$46
17 HOU	590	112	24	81	32	346	299	410	547	957	977	952	9	86	0.69	47	20	33	37	98	106	87	15%	132	19%	84%	27	67%	7%	8.75	63.4	87	264	$45
1st Half	306	53	11	40	16	327	300	399	523	922	897	929	10	86	0.77	50	19	31	35	91	107	67	13%	129	19%	84%	13	77%	8%	7.94	25.5	89	270	$41
2nd Half	284	59	13	41	16	366	298	422	574	996	1054	976	8	86	0.60	44	22	34	39	105	105	108	16%	130	20%	84%	14	57%	7%	9.72	35.1	84	255	$50
18 Proj	**614**	**105**	**23**	**80**	**31**	**335**	**301**	**390**	**525**	**915**	**953**	**902**	**8**	**88**	**0.67**	**45**	**22**	**33**	**35**	**105**	**98**	**97**	**13%**	**128**	**20%**	**80%**				**7.79**	**48.7**	**83**	**251**	**$45**

Anderson,Brian

Age: 25	Bats: R	Pos: 3B	Health A	LIMA Plan D+
Ht: 6' 3"	Wt: 185		PT/Exp D	Rand Var +2
			Consist C	MM 2035

0-8-.262 in 84 AB at MIA. Best hitting prospect in a thin org. Does everything well enough, but no standout skill. Power surged at AA/AAA before MLB cup of coffee, but 20ish HR is no longer special. Quality glove should offer full-time opportunity, but upside is limited unless we see on-the-job skill growth.

Yr Tm	AB	R	HR	RBI	SB	BA	xBA	OBP	SLG	OPS	vL	vR	bb%	ct%	Eye	G	L	F	h%	HctX	PX	xPX	hr/f	Spd	SBO	SB%	#Wk	DOM	DIS	RC/G	RAR	BPV	BPX	R$
13																																		
14																																		
15																																		
16 aa	301	34	7	36	0	216		292	315	607			10	78	0.48				26		59			95	0%	0%				2.99		8	23	$0
17 MIA *	513	77	18	80	1	246	273	317	418	735	543	787	9	72	0.38	49	28	23	31	87	105	83	0%	119	2%	28%	6	17%	67%	4.41	-13.6	30	91	$10
1st Half	278	46	11	45	1	235	247	313	406	719			10	74	0.44				28		100			119	3%	46%				4.18		34	103	$11
2nd Half	235	34	8	39	0	267	273	334	450	784	543	787	9	71	0.34	49	28	23	34	85	117	83	0%	118	2%	0%	6	17%	67%	5.13	0.3	32	97	$9
18 Proj	**443**	**61**	**15**	**65**	**0**	**243**	**253**	**312**	**401**	**713**	**634**	**751**	**10**	**74**	**0.41**	**45**	**23**	**32**	**30**	**77**	**94**	**75**	**14%**	**120**	**1%**	**27%**				**4.22**	**-8.9**	**11**	**34**	**$10**

Anderson,Tim

Age: 25	Bats: R	Pos: SS	Health A	LIMA Plan C+
Ht: 6' 1"	Wt: 185		PT/Exp B	Rand Var +1
			Consist A	MM 2535

Does logging just 13 BB in 583 AB qualify as a skill? While pondering ... notice how his 2nd half salvaged his first full season—yet most key metrics declined (LD, FB, HctX, XPX) over the same time frame. Speed is the ticket, but he'll have to improve his MLB-worst Eye ratio for it to matter. Can he? The deep questions persist.

Yr Tm	AB	R	HR	RBI	SB	BA	xBA	OBP	SLG	OPS	vL	vR	bb%	ct%	Eye	G	L	F	h%	HctX	PX	xPX	hr/f	Spd	SBO	SB%	#Wk	DOM	DIS	RC/G	RAR	BPV	BPX	R$
13																																		
14 aa	44	5	1	5	0	326		326	445	771			0	77	0.00				41		97			95	10%	0%				4.88		15	41	$0
15 aa	513	70	5	41	43	287		318	389	707			4	75	0.18				38		69			145	42%	75%				4.37		9	24	$29
16 CHW *	657	89	12	46	19	279	248	300	407	707	797	721	3	72	0.11	54	21	25	37	94	86	86	12%	176	17%	75%	18	28%	50%	4.28	-0.5	17	49	$22
17 CHW	587	72	17	56	15	257	248	276	402	679	811	629	2	72	0.08	53	19	28	33	83	89	68	14%	143	14%	94%	27	15%	59%	3.87	-12.9	10	30	$15
1st Half	285	32	7	24	5	242	233	267	361	628	784	569	3	72	0.11	49	20	31	31	89	75	77	11%	128	8%	100%	13	8%	69%	3.31	-10.7	-6	-18	$8
2nd Half	302	40	10	32	10	272	262	286	440	726	838	686	1	73	0.05	56	18	25	34	77	102	59	18%	147	19%	91%	14	21%	50%	4.44	-1.2	22	67	$22
18 Proj	**580**	**75**	**16**	**49**	**21**	**262**	**253**	**283**	**409**	**692**	**790**	**659**	**3**	**73**	**0.10**	**54**	**20**	**27**	**34**	**87**	**89**	**74**	**14%**	**161**	**22%**	**81%**				**3.99**	**-8.0**	**11**	**32**	**$21**

Andrus,Elvis

Age: 29	Bats: R	Pos: SS	Health A	LIMA Plan D+
Ht: 6' 0"	Wt: 200		PT/Exp A	Rand Var -2
			Consist C	MM 1455

Investors seeking a 20-SB lock were treated to a power surge and a 5-category career year. Doubling of previous hr/f peak drove pop and along with moving to middle of order, boosted his counting stats. Heed xPX - so he won't likely see 20 bombs again - but otherwise it's a remarkably stable profile at a shallow position.

Yr Tm	AB	R	HR	RBI	SB	BA	xBA	OBP	SLG	OPS	vL	vR	bb%	ct%	Eye	G	L	F	h%	HctX	PX	xPX	hr/f	Spd	SBO	SB%	#Wk	DOM	DIS	RC/G	RAR	BPV	BPX	R$
13 TEX	620	91	4	67	42	271	257	328	331	659	698	644	7	84	0.54	56	21	22	32	91	40	54	3%	139	26%	84%	27	30%	44%	3.99	10.1	28	70	$30
14 TEX	619	72	2	41	27	263	268	314	333	647	760	607	7	84	0.48	59	20	21	31	75	59	36	2%	107	25%	64%	27	37%	19%	3.49	5.7	33	89	$19
15 TEX	596	69	7	62	25	258	266	309	357	667	757	618	7	87	0.59	47	21	32	29	104	67	70	4%	106	22%	74%	27	59%	15%	3.81	-10.3	49	132	$19
16 TEX	506	75	8	69	24	302	289	362	439	800	899	771	8	86	0.67	48	24	29	34	95	80	68	6%	140	21%	75%	27	48%	7%	5.77	20.6	69	197	$26
17 TEX	643	100	20	88	25	297	289	337	471	808	845	798	6	84	0.38	49	20	32	33	104	97	80	12%	115	22%	71%	27	52%	26%	5.62	18.0	62	188	$33
1st Half	319	49	11	49	20	301	284	349	473	822	780	834	7	83	0.42	48	21	31	34	101	94	79	13%	114	31%	74%	13	46%	31%	5.88	11.8	56	170	$38
2nd Half	324	51	9	39	5	293	292	326	469	795	905	761	4	86	0.33	49	19	32	32	107	99	80	10%	114	11%	63%	14	57%	21%	5.37	7.2	67	203	$27
18 Proj	**609**	**89**	**13**	**76**	**25**	**289**	**284**	**335**	**430**	**765**	**827**	**745**	**6**	**85**	**0.47**	**49**	**21**	**30**	**32**	**100**	**79**	**72**	**8%**	**119**	**21%**	**73%**				**5.10**	**11.0**	**55**	**168**	**$30**

Aoki,Norichika

Age: 36	Bats: L	Pos: LF RF	Health B	LIMA Plan B
Ht: 5' 9"	Wt: 180		PT/Exp C	Rand Var 0
			Consist B	MM 1453

The aging 4th OF still does a poor man's version of what he's always done: get some base hits and steal some bases. A complete fall off vL the last two seasons is behind the BA decline while dwindling playing time has curbed the SB. His value is limited to deep leagues where even 300 PA can be useful in a final OF slot.

Yr Tm	AB	R	HR	RBI	SB	BA	xBA	OBP	SLG	OPS	vL	vR	bb%	ct%	Eye	G	L	F	h%	HctX	PX	xPX	hr/f	Spd	SBO	SB%	#Wk	DOM	DIS	RC/G	RAR	BPV	BPX	R$
13 MIL	597	80	8	37	20	286	282	356	370	726	781	703	8	93	1.38	60	18	22	30	100	50	69	7%	141	16%	63%	27	56%	4%	4.43	6.4	74	185	$22
14 KC	491	63	1	43	17	285	292	349	360	710	863	658	8	90	0.88	62	21	17	32	73	53	40	1%	135	16%	68%	25	48%	4%	4.34	7.7	61	165	$17
15 SF	355	42	5	26	14	287	294	353	380	733	774	717	8	90	1.20	61	19	20	30	64	52	36	8%	130	17%	74%	17	53%	6%	4.65	-0.6	70	189	$13
16 SEA *	513	75	5	33	10	276	280	328	373	701	557	793	7	88	0.63	61	17	22	31	71	59	32	5%	143	13%	52%	22	50%	23%	4.11	-7.6	57	163	$13
17 3 TM	336	48	5	35	10	277	282	335	393	728	586	756	8	87	0.66	57	17	25	31	83	66	43	7%	107	13%	83%	27	48%	30%	4.71	-5.2	50	152	$10
1st Half	162	15	1	11	4	272	264	313	340	652	520	685	6	86	0.45	61	18	21	31	58	44	2	3%	102	13%	67%	13	31%	38%	3.67	-7.9	25	76	$3
2nd Half	174	33	4	24	6	282	293	355	443	798	671	817	10	87	0.86	54	16	29	30	106	87	82	9%	103	12%	100%	14	64%	21%	5.77	2.0	72	218	$17
18 Proj	**322**	**46**	**4**	**29**	**10**	**280**	**286**	**343**	**386**	**729**	**646**	**750**	**8**	**89**	**0.75**	**59**	**18**	**24**	**31**	**79**	**59**	**44**	**6%**	**121**	**14%**	**73%**				**4.58**	**1.2**	**51**	**156**	**$12**

Arcia,Orlando

Age: 23	Bats: R	Pos: SS	Health A	LIMA Plan B
Ht: 6' 0"	Wt: 165		PT/Exp B	Rand Var -1
			Consist D	MM 1535

Improvement hitting off-speed pitches led to 11 HR/13 SB over final 115 games and resulted in steps forward in HctX and xPX. Speed and position carry value for this elite prospect with more to come, but xPX suggests hr/f must hold to maintain HR output. Prospect growth isn't linear, so no guarantees, but appealing future.

Yr Tm	AB	R	HR	RBI	SB	BA	xBA	OBP	SLG	OPS	vL	vR	bb%	ct%	Eye	G	L	F	h%	HctX	PX	xPX	hr/f	Spd	SBO	SB%	#Wk	DOM	DIS	RC/G	RAR	BPV	BPX	R$
13																																		
14																																		
15 aa	512	67	7	63	23	296		332	432	764			5	85	0.36				34		90			105	24%	73%				5.11		55	149	$25
16 MIL *	605	64	11	56	19	228	250	272	349	621	845	564	6	78	0.27	54	17	29	28	80	74	59	9%	151	21%	68%	10	40%	40%	3.06	-28.9	30	86	$10
17 MIL	506	56	15	53	14	277	259	324	407	731	626	763	7	80	0.36	52	20	29	32	98	70	78	13%	137	15%	67%	26	31%	38%	4.56	0.5	33	100	$17
1st Half	267	31	7	26	5	285	257	326	423	750	664	775	6	80	0.30	51	18	31	33	95	80	78	11%	124	13%	56%	13	23%	38%	4.71	1.0	35	106	$15
2nd Half	239	25	8	27	9	268	260	322	389	711	583	750	8	80	0.43	52	22	26	30	102	59	78	16%	156	17%	75%	13	38%	38%	4.39	-1.3	33	100	$18
18 Proj	**590**	**66**	**16**	**61**	**19**	**268**	**263**	**314**	**404**	**719**	**735**	**713**	**6**	**80**	**0.34**	**53**	**19**	**28**	**31**	**91**	**75**	**70**	**12%**	**148**	**18%**	**69%**				**4.34**	**-2.1**	**25**	**76**	**$22**

PAUL SPORER

Arenado,Nolan

Age: 27	Bats: R	Pos: 3B	Health	A	LIMA Plan	C
Ht: 6' 2"	Wt: 205		PT/Exp	A	Rand Var	-2
			Consist	B	MM	4155

1st half struggles vR were a small sample blip; 2nd half rebound and year-long assault on lefties fueled another elite performance. The upward BA trajectory looks maxed-out from here, but rock-solid HctX and power peripherals point to more of the same. Age, consistency and health keep him a top ten pick.

Yr	Tm	AB	R	HR	RBI	SB	BA	xBA	OBP	SLG	OPS	vL	vR	bb%	ct%	Eye	G	L	F	h%	HctX	PX	xPX	hr/f	Spd	SBO	SB%	#Wk	DOM	DIS	RC/G	RAR	BPV	BPX
13	COL *	552	58	12	65	2	273	284	306	424	730	846	652	4	85	0.32	43	24	34	30	102	103	103	7%	105	3%	47%	23	48%	17%	4.50	7.9	66	165
14	COL	432	58	18	61	2	287	300	328	500	828	973	776	5	87	0.43	38	21	42	30	127	142	134	11%	97	3%	67%	20	80%	10%	5.80	25.3	102	276
15	COL	616	97	42	130	2	287	307	323	575	898	778	931	5	82	0.31	34	22	44	29	133	172	151	19%	97	6%	29%	27	70%	15%	6.46	31.1	107	289
16	COL	618	116	41	133	2	294	290	362	570	932	875	951	10	83	0.66	35	18	47	30	128	146	148	17%	118	3%	40%	27	78%	11%	7.38	41.4	107	306
17	COL	606	100	37	130	3	309	297	373	586	959	1313	843	9	83	0.58	34	21	45	32	123	145	149	16%	118	3%	60%	27	74%	7%	7.99	44.2	102	309
1st Half		324	52	15	61	2	296	283	348	549	898	1273	762	7	81	0.42	31	21	48	33	116	139	142	12%	108	4%	67%	13	69%	8%	6.86	15.9	86	261
2nd Half		282	48	22	69	1	323	312	401	628	1028	1366	931	12	84	0.80	37	21	42	32	130	151	157	22%	121	2%	50%	14	79%	7%	9.39	32.4	117	355
18	**Proj**	**607**	**101**	**39**	**127**	**2**	**301**	**298**	**361**	**577**	**938**	**1092**	**887**	**9**	**83**	**0.57**	**35**	**21**	**44**	**31**	**126**	**142**	**147**	**17%**	**113**	**3%**	**48%**				**7.50**	**43.7**	**87**	**265**

Arroyo,Christian

Age: 23	Bats: R	Pos: 3B	Health	A	LIMA Plan	C+
Ht: 6' 1"	Wt: 180		PT/Exp	F	Rand Var	0
			Consist	A	MM	2143

3-14-.192 in 125 BA at SF. Pedigreed youngster rushed after 66 Triple-A AB, with foreseeable results. Broken hand ended season in early July. Career .300 BA in minors suggests plus hit tool, but sub-par power makes impact questionable. Will have an MLB career, but we have more questions than answers right now.

Yr	Tm	AB	R	HR	RBI	SB	BA	xBA	OBP	SLG	OPS	vL	vR	bb%	ct%	Eye	G	L	F	h%	HctX	PX	xPX	hr/f	Spd	SBO	SB%	#Wk	DOM	DIS	RC/G	RAR	BPV	BPX
13																																		
14																																		
15																																		
16	aa	474	52	2	45	1	261		301	354	655			5	84	0.35				31		67			88	2%	46%				3.65		28	80
17	SF *	216	24	6	28	3	264	264	306	398	704	564	538	6	79	0.29	61	18	21	31	88	81	61	15%	79	9%	58%	6	0%	33%	4.12	-7.4	18	55
1st Half		216	24	6	28	3	264	264	306	398	704	564	538	6	79	0.29	61	18	21	31	88	81	61	15%	79	9%	58%	6	0%	33%	4.12	-6.1	18	55
2nd Half																																		
18	**Proj**	**396**	**44**	**11**	**46**	**4**	**263**	**274**	**308**	**410**	**718**	**757**	**692**	**6**	**81**	**0.32**	**55**	**20**	**25**	**30**	**83**	**87**	**55**	**14%**	**76**	**7%**	**59%**				**4.26**	**-7.3**	**24**	**72**

Asuaje,Carlos

Age: 26	Bats: L	Pos: 2B	Health	A	LIMA Plan	D+
Ht: 5' 9"	Wt: 158		PT/Exp	B	Rand Var	0
			Consist	A	MM	1223

4-21-.270 in 307 AB at SD. Credible surface showing in first extended MLB opportunity. PRO: All-fields hit tool worked vR; Spd looks legit; xPX hints at more in the tank. CON: Futility vL; no sign of a running game despite good speed; punchless in AAA-El Paso launching pad. Average glove points to utility/platoon role for now.

Yr	Tm	AB	R	HR	RBI	SB	BA	xBA	OBP	SLG	OPS	vL	vR	bb%	ct%	Eye	G	L	F	h%	HctX	PX	xPX	hr/f	Spd	SBO	SB%	#Wk	DOM	DIS	RC/G	RAR	BPV	BPX
13																																		
14																																		
15	aa	495	47	6	48	7	226		289	331	620			8	80	0.45				27		71			110	11%	51%				3.04		29	78
16	SD *	559	67	6	47	7	256	246	297	360	657	556	517	5	82	0.32	35	25	40	30	100	65	88	0%	128	9%	52%	2	50%	50%	3.56	-21.6	32	91
17	SD *	535	56	6	43	1	238	237	306	324	630	571	735	9	79	0.46	40	24	36	29	91	53	108	5%	132	2%	22%	17	24%	35%	3.27	-28.1	16	48
1st Half		257	29	2	23	1	203	252	278	278	556	571	686	9	82	0.58	50	23	27	24	72	42	31	0%	143	3%	35%	3	33%	33%	2.43	-19.3	26	79
2nd Half		278	27	4	20	0	270	232	336	367	702	571	738	9	75	0.38	39	24	37	35	90	63	117	5%	120	1%	0%	14	21%	36%	4.19	-5.0	6	18
18	**Proj**	**323**	**35**	**4**	**27**	**2**	**245**	**250**	**305**	**349**	**653**	**532**	**710**	**8**	**80**	**0.41**	**44**	**24**	**33**	**30**	**83**	**62**	**83**	**5%**	**134**	**6%**	**48%**				**3.48**	**-12.7**	**9**	**27**

Avila,Alex

Age: 31	Bats: L	Pos: CA	Health	D	LIMA Plan	D
Ht: 5' 11"	Wt: 210		PT/Exp	D	Rand Var	-5
			Consist	C	MM	3003

1.108 OPS in 100 AB in Apr and June; .709 otherwise. Power plus patience were a given. But it took confluence of career-best HctX, h% luck and rare DL avoidance to generate this. Contact woes say BA might as well be a unicorn, and health remains a risk. Good value in OBP leagues, but still a #2 catching option at best.

Yr	Tm	AB	R	HR	RBI	SB	BA	xBA	OBP	SLG	OPS	vL	vR	bb%	ct%	Eye	G	L	F	h%	HctX	PX	xPX	hr/f	Spd	SBO	SB%	#Wk	DOM	DIS	RC/G	RAR	BPV	BPX
13	DET *	374	43	12	51	0	225	238	316	369	685	455	767	12	66	0.39	42	28	30	31	100	116	138	17%	71	0%	0%	24	25%	42%	3.84	1.6	5	13
14	DET	390	44	11	47	0	218	222	327	359	686	589	720	13	61	0.40	45	25	30	32	105	136	147	15%	63	3%	0%	27	37%	44%	3.68	2.6	2	5
15	DET	178	21	4	13	0	191	207	339	287	626	424	666	18	63	0.61	41	28	32	28	84	77	123	11%	83	2%	0%	19	26%	53%	3.00	-4.5	-22	-59
16	CHW *	193	22	8	13	0	219	203	361	375	736	844	715	18	55	0.49	52	25	23	35	73	129	111	33%	81	0%	0%	19	37%	53%	4.42	0.0	-14	-40
17	2 TM	311	41	14	49	0	264	232	387	447	834	519	876	16	61	0.52	39	28	34	38	121	127	170	22%	78	1%	0%	27	33%	52%	5.91	16.7	6	18
1st Half		164	25	11	28	0	311	267	432	579	1011	322	1061	17	64	0.58	30	28	42	43	148	182	230	25%	71	2%	0%	13	54%	31%	9.02	22.0	59	179
2nd Half		147	16	3	21	0	211	198	335	299	635	603	641	16	59	0.46	48	28	24	34	91	61	97	14%	103	0%	0%	14	14%	71%	3.26	-3.8	-52	-158
18	**Proj**	**233**	**28**	**8**	**27**	**0**	**231**	**218**	**359**	**380**	**739**	**586**	**766**	**17**	**60**	**0.50**	**44**	**27**	**29**	**35**	**98**	**107**	**136**	**21%**	**78**	**1%**	**0%**				**4.48**	**2.4**	**-30**	**-92**

Aybar,Erick

Age: 34	Bats: B	Pos: SS	Health	C	LIMA Plan	D+
Ht: 5' 10"	Wt: 195		PT/Exp	C	Rand Var	+2
			Consist	B	MM	1341

Lost another 6 weeks to DL with fractured foot, but showed he can still swipe a bag when healthy—and plate skills weren't awful. But peak contact-and-speed years are gone, chronic GB% keeps him powerless, and recent HctX trend isn't optimistic. Age, injuries, decreasing SS range point to bench role, not rebound.

Yr	Tm	AB	R	HR	RBI	SB	BA	xBA	OBP	SLG	OPS	vL	vR	bb%	ct%	Eye	G	L	F	h%	HctX	PX	xPX	hr/f	Spd	SBO	SB%	#Wk	DOM	DIS	RC/G	RAR	BPV	BPX
13	LAA	550	68	6	54	12	271	287	301	382	683	723	666	4	89	0.39	50	23	27	29	90	75	63	5%	101	15%	63%	25	52%	20%	3.90	6.3	57	143
14	LAA	589	77	7	68	16	278	282	321	379	700	622	727	6	89	0.58	49	23	28	30	88	69	54	5%	95	16%	64%	27	41%	15%	4.16	14.7	55	149
15	LAA	597	74	3	44	15	270	265	301	338	639	597	657	4	88	0.34	53	21	26	30	88	50	58	2%	98	14%	71%	27	33%	33%	3.51	-4.4	30	81
16	2 TM *	444	36	3	36	5	236	254	288	309	597	532	655	7	84	0.45	57	20	23	28	71	48	39	4%	101	8%	47%	24	29%	38%	2.87	-23.6	19	54
17	SD	333	37	7	22	11	234	264	300	348	648	674	639	8	83	0.49	52	20	29	26	73	65	64	9%	94	18%	73%	22	27%	23%	3.40	-11.3	29	88
1st Half		208	23	6	12	6	226	254	296	351	647	712	625	8	82	0.50	52	17	31	25	76	69	67	12%	86	15%	75%	13	23%	31%	3.37	-7.7	27	82
2nd Half		125	14	1	10	5	248	278	307	344	651	621	664	7	85	0.47	51	24	25	29	67	58	61	4%	99	23%	71%	9	33%	11%	3.45	-4.2	31	94
18	**Proj**	**229**	**25**	**3**	**18**	**6**	**247**	**268**	**301**	**339**	**640**	**613**	**650**	**6**	**85**	**0.45**	**53**	**21**	**26**	**28**	**75**	**55**	**56**	**5%**	**97**	**16%**	**68%**				**3.34**	**-7.8**	**24**	**72**

Bader,Harrison

Age: 24	Bats: R	Pos: CF	Health	A	LIMA Plan	D
Ht: 6' 0"	Wt: 195		PT/Exp	D	Rand Var	-2
			Consist	A	MM	2301

3-10-.235 in 85 AB at STL. Fast-rising 2015 3rd rd pick wasn't overmatched in small-sample MLB audition. Aggressiveness generates less-than-stellar plate skill metrics, but also a .282 career BA and at least average power. Athleticism and plus glove suggest more growth, opportunity. With it... UP: .260 BA, 20 HR.

Yr	Tm	AB	R	HR	RBI	SB	BA	xBA	OBP	SLG	OPS	vL	vR	bb%	ct%	Eye	G	L	F	h%	HctX	PX	xPX	hr/f	Spd	SBO	SB%	#Wk	DOM	DIS	RC/G	RAR	BPV	BPX
13																																		
14																																		
15																																		
16	a/a	465	57	15	47	11	242		287	393	680			6	71	0.21				31		97			112	24%	43%				3.38		7	20
17	STL *	516	71	19	55	14	251	223	295	401	697	1200	496	6	71	0.22	44	16	39	32	97	92	109	13%	112	21%	57%	8	13%	50%	3.80	-19.6	5	15
1st Half		287	38	11	30	3	266	246	300	439	739			5	72	0.18				33		106			101	16%	33%				4.17		16	48
2nd Half		229	33	8	25	11	232	205	290	354	644	1200	496	8	69	0.27	44	16	39	30	95	73	109	13%	112	26%	72%	8	13%	50%	3.36	-10.9	-14	-42
18	**Proj**	**197**	**26**	**6**	**21**	**6**	**244**	**217**	**296**	**382**	**678**	**1214**	**517**	**6**	**70**	**0.23**	**44**	**16**	**39**	**32**	**86**	**85**	**98**	**11%**	**121**	**22%**	**54%**				**3.50**	**-6.1**	**-6**	**-20**

Baez,Javier

Age: 25	Bats: R	Pos: 2B SS	Health	A	LIMA Plan	C+
Ht: 6' 0"	Wt: 190		PT/Exp	C	Rand Var	-3
			Consist	B	MM	3415

PRO: Patience uptick; HR, PX spike; more h% elevation; solid SB%. CON: Sub-par ct%; mediocre HctX; too many GBs; limited SB opps. Mixed signals, but a fine year from a growth stock. Recent hr/f numbers suggest a winter launch-angle project. With a few more FBs and more bb% gains... UP: 30 HR.

Yr	Tm	AB	R	HR	RBI	SB	BA	xBA	OBP	SLG	OPS	vL	vR	bb%	ct%	Eye	G	L	F	h%	HctX	PX	xPX	hr/f	Spd	SBO	SB%	#Wk	DOM	DIS	RC/G	RAR	BPV	BPX
13	aa	218	31	16	43	6	268		317	557	874			7	66	0.21				33		224			79	20%	75%				6.07		81	203
14	CHC *	601	74	26	81	17	209	213	260	393	654	569	546	6	60	0.17	41	14	45	30	81	166	120	17%	97	24%	64%	9	33%	67%	3.17	-4.2	17	46
15	CHC *	357	41	11	51	14	287	249	325	443	768	1082	617	5	69	0.18	37	31	31	39	103	117	121	6%	116	21%	72%	6	33%	67%	5.06	9.1	16	43
16	CHC	421	50	14	59	12	273	241	314	423	737	850	689	3	74	0.14	44	20	36	34	88	95	89	13%	116	16%	80%	26	27%	38%	4.44	-5.1	17	49
17	CHC	469	75	23	75	10	273	247	317	480	796	934	747	6	69	0.21	49	15	36	35	91	129	104	20%	118	12%	77%	27	44%	41%	5.31	3.9	30	91
1st Half		225	30	10	32	3	249	245	290	444	735	859	686	5	72	0.20	48	15	37	30	94	120	102	17%	100	11%	60%	13	46%	38%	4.27	-3.7	25	76
2nd Half		244	45	13	43	7	295	247	341	512	853	1014	800	7	67	0.21	49	16	35	39	88	138	106	23%	132	13%	88%	14	43%	43%	6.40	10.7	34	103
18	**Proj**	**530**	**75**	**21**	**82**	**14**	**273**	**240**	**317**	**451**	**768**	**924**	**712**	**5**	**70**	**0.19**	**45**	**19**	**36**	**35**	**91**	**112**	**105**	**16%**	**117**	**15%**	**77%**				**4.93**	**2.0**	**12**	**36**

JOCK THOMPSON

Bandy,Jett

Age: 28 Bats: R Pos: CA	Health B	LIMA Plan F	
Ht: 6' 4" Wt: 235	PT/Exp F	Rand Var +5	
	Consist A	MM 1011	

6-18-.207 in 169 AB at MIL. Enjoyed a strong April, but posted a .158/.252/.233 from May 1 forward. 2016's ct% gains and fly-ball tilt created some intrigue, but both evaporated in 2017 (albeit in smaller AB sample). LD% keeps a glimmer of hope, but not-quite-average power and deep struggles vR mute any optimism.

Yr Tm	AB	R	HR	RBI	SB	BA	xBA	OBP	SLG	OPS	vL	vR	bb%	ct%	Eye	G	L	F	h%	HctX	PX	xPX	hr/f	Spd	SBO	SB%	#Wk	DOM	DIS	RC/G	RAR	BPV	BPX	R$
13 aa	245	22	3	24	0	213		248	325	573			4	82	0.26				25		83			98	3%	0%				2.55		35	88	-$2
14 aa	312	32	10	34	2	220		281	352	633			8	77	0.37				25		94			83	8%	27%				3.05		25	68	$3
15 LAA *	311	32	8	40	0	229	127	254	358	612	2500	0	3	75	0.13	0	0	100	28	162	93	358	50%	73	0%	0%	2	50%	0%	3.01	-7.5	5	14	$2
16 LAA *	304	32	9	40	2	228	230	259	369	627	696	664	4	80	0.20	27	21	52	26	89	85	101	9%	79	6%	67%	21	52%	29%	3.13	-11.8	20	57	$3
17 MIL *	211	19	8	27	1	214	243	277	357	634	980	570	8	73	0.32	39	25	36	26	95	85	92	14%	68	5%	45%	19	21%	63%	3.14	-5.9	-2	-6	$0
1st Half	160	17	7	24	1	212	250	273	395	668	1232	582	8	73	0.31	38	24	39	24	99	108	95	15%	70	7%	45%	12	33%	58%	3.40	-3.5	16	48	$2
2nd Half	51	1	0	3	0	220	251	289	235	525	444	485	9	73	0.36	47	35	18	30	69	13	77	0%	87	0%	0%	7	0%	71%	2.23	-2.9	-52	-158	-$6
18 Proj	197	15	4	22	1	220	240	285	322	606	661	587	6	75	0.28	37	26	37	27	85	64	91	7%	72	3%	51%				2.81	-8.1	-23	-71	-$1

Barnes,Austin

Age: 28 Bats: R Pos: CA 2B	Health A	LIMA Plan B	
Ht: 5' 10" Wt: 190	PT/Exp D	Rand Var -4	
	Consist F	MM 3453	

Is this a front-line catcher just waiting to emerge? Strong plate skills, above-average speed and no platoon splits in part-time duty. Flash of power growth in 1H didn't quite hold, but that can come late for catchers. Ability to play multiple positions provides an additional path to PT. With 400 AB... UP: 15 HR/15 SB.

Yr Tm	AB	R	HR	RBI	SB	BA	xBA	OBP	SLG	OPS	vL	vR	bb%	ct%	Eye	G	L	F	h%	HctX	PX	xPX	hr/f	Spd	SBO	SB%	#Wk	DOM	DIS	RC/G	RAR	BPV	BPX	R$
13 aa	62	8	1	6	0	307		404	431	835			14	82	0.90				37		73			143	0%	0%				6.40		59	148	$0
14 aa	284	41	7	32	6	245		332	399	730			11	85	0.89				26		105			100	7%	100%				4.60		81	219	$7
15 LA *	321	33	7	32	10	251	269	315	374	689	625	644	8	84	0.59	48	22	30	28	76	79	71	0%	79	14%	80%	9	56%	33%	4.06	2.2	43	116	$8
16 LA *	368	47	5	31	13	231	187	297	337	634	795	297	9	80	0.46	32	9	59	28	70	70	89	0%	120	19%	79%	9	11%	44%	3.37	-11.6	30	86	$6
17 LA	218	35	8	38	4	289	295	408	486	895	886	902	15	80	0.91	45	26	29	33	100	112	94	16%	114	6%	80%	27	56%	22%	6.95	17.7	77	233	$8
1st Half	99	20	4	18	4	293	299	407	535	942	917	965	15	79	0.86	41	26	33	34	98	138	118	15%	125	12%	100%	13	54%	23%	8.08	10.9	96	291	$8
2nd Half	119	15	4	20	0	286	285	410	445	855	862	847	15	82	0.95	48	26	26	32	102	91	74	16%	95	2%	0%	14	57%	21%	6.06	6.6	59	179	$8
18 Proj	308	45	11	43	7	281	294	381	467	848	843	851	12	81	0.73	45	26	29	31	100	103	92	16%	115	10%	79%				6.11	17.2	62	188	$14

Barney,Darwin

Age: 32 Bats: R Pos: 2B 3B	Health A	LIMA Plan D	
Ht: 5' 10" Wt: 180	PT/Exp D	Rand Var +1	
	Consist D	MM 1323	

Continues to find his way into lineup with some regularity, and continues to do little with those opportunities. Speed is only plus skill, long hampered by poor SB%. That improved in 2017, but sample size is tiny and he's long past peak age for SB breakout. Pronounced long-term struggles vR make him safe to ignore.

Yr Tm	AB	R	HR	RBI	SB	BA	xBA	OBP	SLG	OPS	vL	vR	bb%	ct%	Eye	G	L	F	h%	HctX	PX	xPX	hr/f	Spd	SBO	SB%	#Wk	DOM	DIS	RC/G	RAR	BPV	BPX	R$
13 CHC	501	49	7	41	4	208	252	266	303	569	725	515	7	87	0.56	45	19	36	23	74	66	74	4%	94	6%	67%	24	38%	21%	2.53	-18.6	45	113	$0
14 2 NL *	272	27	3	24	1	232	243	281	323	604	707	614	6	85	0.46	43	20	37	26	94	64	79	4%	133	2%	100%	24	38%	21%	3.03	-2.9	46	124	$1
15 2 TM *	374	39	5	25	5	210	219	239	282	522	1111	652	4	84	0.25	44	16	40	24	54	49	74	20%	95	13%	48%	6	33%	0%	2.07	-24.7	13	35	-$1
16 TOR	279	35	4	19	2	269	260	322	373	695	779	649	7	83	0.46	47	22	30	31	93	64	68	6%	126	5%	50%	26	35%	42%	4.11	-4.9	37	106	$4
17 TOR	336	34	6	25	7	232	246	275	327	602	608	595	5	81	0.28	47	21	33	27	62	57	38	7%	107	12%	78%	27	30%	44%	2.97	-16.9	14	42	$3
1st Half	143	11	2	9	3	231	240	272	301	572	568	572	5	81	0.30	46	23	31	27	53	41	15	6%	108	9%	100%	13	23%	54%	2.81	-8.7	2	6	-$2
2nd Half	193	23	4	16	4	233	250	277	347	624	650	609	5	81	0.27	47	19	34	27	69	69	54	8%	105	15%	67%	14	36%	36%	3.07	-10.3	22	67	$7
18 Proj	265	29	4	19	4	237	249	282	332	614	659	589	5	82	0.33	46	21	33	27	76	56	55	6%	110	9%	68%				3.06	-13.9	10	29	$4

Barnhart,Tucker

Age: 27 Bats: B Pos: CA	Health A	LIMA Plan D+	
Ht: 5' 11" Wt: 190	PT/Exp C	Rand Var -1	
	Consist B	MM 1243	

PRO: Sturdy plate discipline and LD% give him a solid BA floor; two-year HctX growth hints at further upside.
CON: Stagnant xPX and low FB% cap HR potential; speed inconsequential. Needs power to pair with BA foundation. 2nd half spike is a tease but support metrics aren't there.

Yr Tm	AB	R	HR	RBI	SB	BA	xBA	OBP	SLG	OPS	vL	vR	bb%	ct%	Eye	G	L	F	h%	HctX	PX	xPX	hr/f	Spd	SBO	SB%	#Wk	DOM	DIS	RC/G	RAR	BPV	BPX	R$
13 aa	339	28	3	40	1	245		326	331	656			11	81	0.64				29		66			86	1%	100%				3.65		28	70	$2
14 CIN *	310	16	2	21	0	202	189	259	258	517	167	568	7	84	0.48	60	7	33	24	79	39	38	7%	107	1%	0%	9	22%	44%	2.10	-13.2	15	41	-$4
15 CIN	242	23	3	18	0	252	245	324	326	650	433	700	9	81	0.56	47	25	28	30	66	52	45	5%	86	1%	0%	24	42%	33%	3.52	-2.0	13	35	$1
16 CIN	377	34	7	51	1	257	270	323	379	702	546	744	9	81	0.50	48	25	28	30	92	79	93	8%	85	1%	100%	27	37%	30%	4.21	-2.1	31	89	$5
17 CIN	370	26	7	44	4	270	281	347	403	750	668	769	10	82	0.62	46	26	28	32	110	80	90	8%	83	4%	100%	27	48%	33%	4.92	9.1	37	112	$7
1st Half	168	11	1	12	1	280	289	332	399	730	433	792	7	83	0.46	44	28	28	33	116	80	107	3%	94	2%	100%	13	54%	23%	4.72	2.9	42	127	$1
2nd Half	202	15	6	32	3	262	274	359	406	765	822	749	13	80	0.73	48	25	27	30	105	80	75	14%	84	5%	100%	14	43%	43%	5.08	5.7	37	112	$12
18 Proj	379	30	7	44	2	267	268	340	387	727	583	763	10	81	0.58	48	24	28	31	96	72	78	8%	84	2%	89%				4.58	4.8	20	60	$8

Barreto,Franklin

Age: 22 Bats: R Pos: SS	Health A	LIMA Plan D+	
Ht: 5' 10" Wt: 190	PT/Exp D	Rand Var -4	
	Consist A	MM 2413	

2-6-.197 in 71 AB at OAK. A career .292/.347/.463 hitter in the minors, but his first taste of MLB action didn't go well. At maturity, combination of moderate power/elite Spd (30 SB in 2016) from MI is appealing. But Eye, SB%, 54% ct% in OAK all say there's a bunch more polishing needed first. A couple years out.

Yr Tm	AB	R	HR	RBI	SB	BA	xBA	OBP	SLG	OPS	vL	vR	bb%	ct%	Eye	G	L	F	h%	HctX	PX	xPX	hr/f	Spd	SBO	SB%	#Wk	DOM	DIS	RC/G	RAR	BPV	BPX	R$
13																																		
14																																		
15																																		
16 a/a	479	57	9	47	26	268		313	390	702			6	80	0.32				32		76			105	36%	59%				3.86		26	74	$19
17 OAK *	540	62	13	51	14	256	196	291	394	685	291	744	5	67	0.15	29	21	50	36	92	88	125	11%	164	19%	62%	8	13%	63%	3.78	-13.6	-1	-3	$13
1st Half	311	34	7	28	3	250	180	289	371	660	650	568	5	65	0.16	36	14	50	36	113	78	152	14%	148	12%	38%	2	50%	50%	3.41	-13.3	-19	-58	$10
2nd Half	229	29	6	22	11	263	210	294	427	721	206	889	4	69	0.14	25	25	50	36	81	101	109	8%	155	29%	77%	6	0%	67%	4.31	-3.5	12	36	$17
18 Proj	332	37	7	29	9	240	227	279	373	652	314	800	5	72	0.19	41	21	38	31	94	81	126	8%	148	20%	60%				3.33	-11.5	2	5	$7

Bauers,Jake

Age: 22 Bats: L Pos: OF	Health A	LIMA Plan D+	
Ht: 6' 1" Wt: 195	PT/Exp B	Rand Var 0	
	Consist B	MM 1321	

A 1B by trade, he spent most of his time in the OF in 2017. Though he doesn't possess a standout skill, his blend of ct%/bb%, gap power, and increased efficiency on the basepaths could be enough to earn a spot as a regular in Tampa. Lack of HR punch caps upside, but there's a broad base of potentially above-average skill here.

Yr Tm	AB	R	HR	RBI	SB	BA	xBA	OBP	SLG	OPS	vL	vR	bb%	ct%	Eye	G	L	F	h%	HctX	PX	xPX	hr/f	Spd	SBO	SB%	#Wk	DOM	DIS	RC/G	RAR	BPV	BPX	R$
13																																		
14																																		
15 aa	257	30	4	30	5	249		297	359	656			6	82	0.39				29		79			83	13%	61%				3.52		32	86	$4
16 aa	493	69	12	68	9	249		336	374	710			12	80	0.65				29		79			86	10%	57%				4.15		33	94	$12
17 aaa	486	74	12	59	19	245		345	379	725			13	74	0.59				31		87			91	14%	85%				4.55		22	67	$15
1st Half	280	48	6	37	10	253		348	386	734			13	74	0.57				32		86			103	13%	91%				4.75		25	76	$18
2nd Half	206	26	5	21	8	234		341	371	712			14	74	0.62				29		89			96	16%	80%				4.29		25	76	$9
18 Proj	216	30	5	27	6	245	249	334	368	702	702	702	12	77	0.59	44	22	34	30		78		8%	98	13%	74%				4.17	#N/A	20	61	$6

Bautista,Jose

Age: 37 Bats: R Pos: RF	Health C	LIMA Plan B	
Ht: 6' 0" Wt: 205	PT/Exp A	Rand Var +3	
	Consist D	MM 3115	

Injuries played a part in disappointing 2016, but 2017 has no such excuse. xBA, xPX, Eye, HctX all say this was every bit as bad as it looks. Lofty FB% has kept HR tally respectable, but the remaining overall package has minimal value in today's game. At his age, it's hard to project any meaningful rebound.

Yr Tm	AB	R	HR	RBI	SB	BA	xBA	OBP	SLG	OPS	vL	vR	bb%	ct%	Eye	G	L	F	h%	HctX	PX	xPX	hr/f	Spd	SBO	SB%	#Wk	DOM	DIS	RC/G	RAR	BPV	BPX	R$
13 TOR	452	82	28	73	7	259	282	358	498	856	910	842	13	81	0.82	41	16	43	26	129	150	138	18%	84	7%	78%	21	67%	5%	6.12	24.2	99	248	$20
14 TOR	553	101	35	103	6	286	290	403	524	928	1079	888	15	83	1.08	40	18	42	29	124	152	121	18%	90	4%	75%	27	81%	7%	7.46	55.4	112	303	$32
15 TOR	543	108	40	114	8	250	285	377	536	913	834	932	17	80	1.04	37	14	49	24	123	168	150	18%	96	6%	80%	27	81%	7%	6.88	33.9	120	324	$26
16 TOR	423	68	22	69	2	234	261	366	452	817	752	834	17	76	0.84	40	19	42	26	126	133	131	16%	70	3%	50%	21	62%	14%	5.42	9.1	66	189	$10
17 TOR	587	92	23	65	6	203	221	308	366	674	629	688	12	71	0.49	38	17	46	24	90	102	112	12%	85	6%	67%	27	26%	44%	3.52	-25.9	18	55	$5
1st Half	295	50	14	37	4	231	228	339	410	749	520	821	13	73	0.57	36	18	47	27	95	105	119	14%	86	7%	67%	13	31%	31%	4.51	-5.0	29	88	$11
2nd Half	292	42	9	28	2	175	213	275	322	597	741	553	12	70	0.43	40	15	45	22	86	99	104	10%	83	5%	67%	14	21%	57%	2.67	-22.7	7	21	-$2
18 Proj	500	79	20	68	4	226	230	329	400	729	708	734	13	73	0.54	39	17	45	27	107	107	123	12%	82	4%	62%				4.26	-6.7	22	67	$10

GREG PYRON

Beckham,Tim

Age: 28	Bats: R	Pos: SS	Health	C	LIMA Plan	C+
Ht: 6' 1"	Wt: 205		PT/Exp	D	Rand Var	-5
			Consist	B	MM	3425

HRs spiked thanks to full-time AB, gains in HctX, xPX, hr/f... and everyone else doin' it. Outlook bleaker for SB. Make no mistake - there is speed skill here. While hamstring injury, SB%, may have played roles in limiting 2H SBO, Spd argues for more chances. Impatient approach, xBA add risk of lower OBP and opps drying up.

Yr	Tm	AB	R	HR	RBI	SB	BA	xBA	OBP	SLG	OPS	vL	vR	bb%	ct%	Eye	G	L	F	h%	HctX	PX	xPX	hr/f	Spd	SBO	SB%	#Wk	DOM	DIS	RC/G	RAR	BPV	BPX
13	TAM *	467	59	3	43	14	247	231	300	341	641	900	667	7	74	0.29	63	13	25	33	39	74	-15	0%	141	18%	64%	2	0%	0%	3.37	-0.7	12	30
14	aaa	62	7	0	3	0	225		245	252	498			3	74	0.10				30		30			101	16%	0%				1.66		-42	-114
15	TAM *	242	28	9	40	5	228	246	279	422	701	725	676	6	66	0.21	50	19	31	30	81	142	87	21%	102	14%	68%	21	48%	38%	3.81	-4.2	25	68
16	TAM	198	25	5	16	2	247	235	300	434	735	792	688	7	66	0.21	46	18	36	35	97	131	97	11%	159	7%	67%	21	38%	43%	4.33	0.1	32	91
17	2 AL	533	67	22	62	6	278	244	328	454	782	760	789	6	69	0.22	49	22	29	37	109	106	111	21%	146	8%	55%	25	28%	48%	5.05	6.4	18	55
1st Half		267	28	10	31	5	277	235	326	431	757	658	796	6	66	0.20	47	26	27	39	123	91	122	21%	156	11%	63%	13	15%	54%	4.78	1.6	-2	-6
2nd Half		266	39	12	31	1	278	254	329	477	806	890	782	6	71	0.24	51	18	32	35	94	120	100	20%	130	5%	33%	12	42%	42%	5.31	5.6	35	106
18	**Proj**	**459**	**58**	**16**	**52**	**6**	**253**	**243**	**304**	**435**	**739**	**758**	**729**	**6**	**68**	**0.21**	**48**	**20**	**32**	**33**	**99**	**113**	**101**	**16%**	**144**	**10%**	**61%**				**4.36**	**-1.5**	**13**	**40**

Bell,Josh

Age: 25	Bats: B	Pos: 1B	Health	A	LIMA Plan	B+
Ht: 6' 2"	Wt: 230		PT/Exp	B	Rand Var	+2
			Consist	A	MM	2145

Despite HR outburst, would be wise to curtail expectations for continued power growth for now, as GB% profile, xPX, add risk of regression. Didn't have to sell out for it, as plate discipline, xBA provide solid BA floor, but without more fly balls, he's a corner option that lacks the raw power to keep pace with 1B player pool.

Yr	Tm	AB	R	HR	RBI	SB	BA	xBA	OBP	SLG	OPS	vL	vR	bb%	ct%	Eye	G	L	F	h%	HctX	PX	xPX	hr/f	Spd	SBO	SB%	#Wk	DOM	DIS	RC/G	RAR	BPV	BPX
13																																		
14	aa	94	10	0	5	3	249		292	268	559			6	86	0.44				29		17			102	15%	73%				2.67		3	8
15	a/a	489	57	5	66	8	285		356	390	747			10	86	0.77				32		65			116	8%	63%				4.89		52	141
16	PIT *	549	71	15	75	3	275	274	362	427	788	515	820	12	82	0.76	50	21	29	31	110	89	96	9%	80	7%	24%	9	56%	22%	5.14	-3.1	50	143
17	PIT	549	75	26	90	2	255	275	334	466	800	758	813	11	79	0.56	51	18	31	28	104	113	95	19%	96	4%	33%	27	56%	26%	5.21	-11.2	57	173
1st Half		270	39	15	38	2	233	280	322	463	785	770	790	11	78	0.58	53	17	30	25	100	124	99	23%	89	4%	67%	13	54%	15%	4.92	-5.9	62	188
2nd Half		279	36	11	52	0	276	271	345	470	815	746	834	10	80	0.54	49	19	32	31	107	103	91	15%	106	4%	0%	14	57%	36%	5.52	-1.0	54	164
18	**Proj**	**503**	**64**	**20**	**72**	**3**	**265**	**276**	**337**	**449**	**785**	**680**	**811**	**10**	**81**	**0.61**	**51**	**19**	**30**	**29**	**106**	**97**	**95**	**16%**	**96**	**6%**	**39%**				**5.13**	**0.4**	**46**	**139**

Bellinger,Cody

Age: 22	Bats: L	Pos: 1B LF	Health	A	LIMA Plan	B+
Ht: 6' 4"	Wt: 210		PT/Exp	D	Rand Var	0
			Consist	F	MM	4435

39-97-.267 with 10 SB in 480 AB at LA. Uppercut swing led to power breakout supported by HctX, FB%, and elite xPX, While hr/f came down to earth in 2H, improved plate discipline bodes well for his future. Raw Spd makes double-digit SB repeat likely, too, and moves him closer to top tier.

Yr	Tm	AB	R	HR	RBI	SB	BA	xBA	OBP	SLG	OPS	vL	vR	bb%	ct%	Eye	G	L	F	h%	HctX	PX	xPX	hr/f	Spd	SBO	SB%	#Wk	DOM	DIS	RC/G	RAR	BPV	BPX
13																																		
14																																		
15																																		
16	a/a	410	56	23	60	7	248		325	458	784			10	75	0.45				28		124			86	8%	76%				5.05		47	134
17	LA *	547	99	43	109	16	272	267	356	579	934	903	948	11	69	0.42	35	18	47	32	120	184	178	25%	122	13%	84%	23	70%	17%	7.25	21.2	84	255
1st Half		304	59	28	68	11	273	272	346	617	963	950	974	10	66	0.33	31	19	50	32	127	215	192	31%	100	17%	92%	10	70%	10%	7.61	17.1	88	267
2nd Half		243	40	15	41	5	272	259	369	531	900	868	917	13	72	0.55	39	16	45	32	114	148	165	19%	141	10%	71%	13	69%	23%	6.77	7.9	79	239
18	**Proj**	**560**	**94**	**36**	**103**	**13**	**268**	**257**	**349**	**521**	**870**	**841**	**884**	**11**	**72**	**0.44**	**37**	**18**	**45**	**31**	**119**	**146**	**176**	**20%**	**123**	**10%**	**80%**				**6.36**	**20.4**	**59**	**180**

Belt,Brandon

Age: 30	Bats: L	Pos: 1B	Health	C	LIMA Plan	B+
Ht: 6' 5"	Wt: 220		PT/Exp	B	Rand Var	+3
			Consist	B	MM	4135

Career-high FB%, hr/f rebound had him on career-best HR pace before season was cut short by concussion, his fourth in four seasons. BA regression was expected, but consistent xBA says he'll rebound to at least league average baseline. Can't ignore the health risk, but with a fresh start in a better park ... UP: 30 HR, finally.

Yr	Tm	AB	R	HR	RBI	SB	BA	xBA	OBP	SLG	OPS	vL	vR	bb%	ct%	Eye	G	L	F	h%	HctX	PX	xPX	hr/f	Spd	SBO	SB%	#Wk	DOM	DIS	RC/G	RAR	BPV	BPX
13	SF	509	76	17	67	5	289	266	360	481	841	755	867	9	75	0.42	34	24	41	35	116	143	132	11%	104	5%	71%	27	56%	22%	6.09	21.5	68	170
14	SF	214	30	12	27	3	243	244	306	449	755	715	772	8	70	0.28	38	18	44	29	90	152	118	18%	108	8%	75%	14	71%	21%	4.54	2.3	52	141
15	SF	492	73	18	68	9	280	257	356	478	834	802	845	10	70	0.38	33	29	38	37	123	145	156	14%	98	9%	75%	24	50%	33%	5.97	8.5	48	130
16	SF	542	77	17	82	0	275	259	394	474	868	883	861	16	73	0.70	26	28	46	35	108	134	163	9%	106	2%	0%	27	59%	30%	6.36	15.9	63	180
17	SF	382	63	18	51	3	241	258	355	469	823	713	879	15	73	0.63	30	23	47	28	113	140	154	14%	95	5%	60%	18	61%	28%	5.49	-4.7	63	191
1st Half		294	43	15	39	3	228	254	339	449	788	650	859	14	73	0.62	33	23	44	26	111	127	148	16%	105	5%	75%	13	54%	31%	5.01	-5.7	56	170
2nd Half		88	20	3	12	0	284	276	406	534	940	929	945	16	72	0.68	18	25	57	37	120	183	173	9%	94	4%	0%	5	80%	20%	7.31	4.2	95	288
18	**Proj**	**482**	**82**	**19**	**67**	**3**	**262**	**258**	**368**	**485**	**853**	**814**	**870**	**14**	**72**	**0.58**	**30**	**22**	**47**	**33**	**114**	**145**	**158**	**12%**	**98**	**5%**	**45%**				**5.98**	**12.4**	**58**	**175**

Beltran,Carlos

Age: 41	Bats: B	Pos: DH	Health	B	LIMA Plan	D+
Ht: 6' 1"	Wt: 215		PT/Exp	B	Rand Var	+2
			Consist	D	MM	2231

Sure looks like age finally caught up to him, as PX slipped below average for first time ever, and OPS, Eye, xBA, and hr/f all hit career lows. Hit .209 with .569 OPS after 8/1, and sharp decline vL (including 71% contact, 0.18 Eye) shows speed of decline. Relegated to end-game status, if he decides to come back at all.

Yr	Tm	AB	R	HR	RBI	SB	BA	xBA	OBP	SLG	OPS	vL	vR	bb%	ct%	Eye	G	L	F	h%	HctX	PX	xPX	hr/f	Spd	SBO	SB%	#Wk	DOM	DIS	RC/G	RAR	BPV	BPX
13	STL	554	79	24	84	2	296	282	339	491	830	729	871	6	84	0.42	35	24	41	32	131	122	128	13%	93	2%	67%	27	63%	11%	6.05	23.7	75	188
14	NYY	403	46	15	49	3	233	258	301	402	703	564	777	8	80	0.46	44	16	39	26	105	120	101	12%	75	4%	75%	23	43%	35%	3.98	-0.8	58	157
15	NYY	478	57	19	67	0	276	276	337	471	808	752	831	8	82	0.53	35	22	43	30	122	125	133	11%	78	0%	0%	25	60%	16%	5.61	2.2	71	192
16	2 AL	552	73	29	93	1	295	284	337	513	850	970	805	6	82	0.35	42	21	37	32	119	124	103	17%	75	1%	100%	27	56%	22%	6.27	11.7	62	177
17	HOU	467	60	14	51	0	231	239	283	383	666	506	721	6	78	0.32	43	16	40	27	107	93	112	9%	73	0%	0%	27	44%	41%	3.59	-18.0	24	73
1st Half		267	37	10	33	0	228	242	284	400	689	577	723	7	77	0.33	43	15	42	26	100	106	122	11%	78	0%	0%	13	46%	31%	3.77	-8.9	33	100
2nd Half		200	23	4	18	0	235	235	281	355	636	422	717	6	80	0.32	43	18	39	28	115	75	100	6%	71	0%	0%	14	43%	50%	3.33	-9.2	13	39
18	Proj																																	

Beltre,Adrian

Age: 39	Bats: R	Pos: 3B DH	Health	B	LIMA Plan	B
Ht: 5' 11"	Wt: 220		PT/Exp	B	Rand Var	-3
			Consist	C	MM	3155

Calf strain in April, hamstring injury in Sept slowed down counting stats for ageless wonder, but HctX, PX/xPX say foundation for 25-30 HR pop remains intact. In addition, plate patience, consistent success vL continue to set high BA floor. With renewed health, these skills are still worth an investment.

Yr	Tm	AB	R	HR	RBI	SB	BA	xBA	OBP	SLG	OPS	vL	vR	bb%	ct%	Eye	G	L	F	h%	HctX	PX	xPX	hr/f	Spd	SBO	SB%	#Wk	DOM	DIS	RC/G	RAR	BPV	BPX
13	TEX	631	88	30	92	1	315	287	371	509	880	948	857	7	88	0.64	38	22	40	32	130	115	127	14%	67	1%	100%	27	63%	7%	6.94	50.6	79	198
14	TEX	549	79	19	77	1	324	286	388	492	879	984	845	9	87	0.77	42	22	36	35	125	111	122	11%	86	1%	50%	26	73%	12%	7.16	50.9	81	219
15	TEX	567	83	18	83	1	287	288	334	453	788	929	715	7	89	0.63	42	23	36	30	130	97	109	10%	96	1%	100%	25	60%	16%	5.45	14.0	76	205
16	TEX	583	89	32	104	1	300	287	358	521	879	1004	842	8	89	0.73	40	18	42	29	128	114	124	15%	71	1%	50%	27	70%	15%	6.68	30.2	84	240
17	TEX	340	47	17	71	1	312	291	383	532	915	1124	862	10	85	0.75	43	20	37	33	124	116	119	16%	62	1%	100%	18	61%	39%	7.57	24.9	72	218
1st Half		104	14	5	22	1	279	293	358	500	858	676	886	11	88	1.00	45	17	38	28	129	116	119	14%	53	3%	100%	5	60%	40%	6.41	3.9	83	252
2nd Half		236	33	12	49	0	326	287	394	547	941	1258	850	10	83	0.67	42	21	37	35	121	115	119	16%	71	0%	0%	13	62%	38%	8.13	19.0	69	209
18	**Proj**	**478**	**68**	**21**	**89**	**1**	**298**	**285**	**362**	**494**	**855**	**987**	**815**	**9**	**87**	**0.73**	**42**	**20**	**38**	**31**	**126**	**101**	**119**	**13%**	**69**	**1%**	**84%**				**6.46**	**20.7**	**63**	**191**

Benintendi,Andrew

Age: 23	Bats: L	Pos: LF CF	Health	A	LIMA Plan	B+
Ht: 5' 10"	Wt: 170		PT/Exp	D	Rand Var	-1
			Consist	A	MM	3345

Met our 2017 UP: HR projection by pairing power skills with impressive plate discipline in first full season. PX/xPX gap, 37% hard contact vR, and age suggest this is only a starting point. Power/speed combo sets a solid floor as he goes to work on struggles vs. LHP and a tepid xBA. Still a pup.

Yr	Tm	AB	R	HR	RBI	SB	BA	xBA	OBP	SLG	OPS	vL	vR	bb%	ct%	Eye	G	L	F	h%	HctX	PX	xPX	hr/f	Spd	SBO	SB%	#Wk	DOM	DIS	RC/G	RAR	BPV	BPX
13																																		
14																																		
15																																		
16	BOS *	342	48	8	50	7	289	288	345	481	826	429	984	8	84	0.53	36	25	39	33	112	117	116	6%	116	19%	47%	8	50%	25%	5.51	12.1	81	231
17	BOS	573	84	20	90	20	271	256	352	424	776	622	813	11	80	0.63	40	21	38	31	112	85	100	11%	110	14%	80%	26	46%	23%	5.24	-3.4	46	139
1st Half		276	38	10	41	9	275	248	351	431	782	665	803	11	82	0.67	39	18	43	30	122	82	120	10%	125	13%	82%	13	54%	15%	5.42	0.5	55	167
2nd Half		297	46	10	49	11	266	265	352	418	770	597	824	11	79	0.59	41	25	34	31	102	88	81	13%	100	15%	79%	13	38%	31%	5.08	-2.4	40	121
18	**Proj**	**568**	**82**	**23**	**87**	**17**	**278**	**277**	**351**	**475**	**825**	**529**	**913**	**10**	**82**	**0.59**	**39**	**22**	**39**	**31**	**111**	**109**	**105**	**12%**	**118**	**15%**	**69%**				**5.73**	**20.9**	**65**	**198**

BRANT CHESSER

Betts,Mookie

Age: 25	Bats: R	Pos: RF	Health	A	LIMA Plan	C
Ht: 5' 9"	Wt: 180		PT/Exp	A	Rand Var	+3
			Consist	D	MM	3455

Solid 1st half metrics were undone by unlucky swing in h%, and from there he started pressing, unraveling his 2nd half even further. But xPX, SBO/SB% provide a solid HR/SB foundation, and ct%/HctX make him elite. After 2016, his owners might have been disappointed, but this is still a core $30 first rounder.

Yr Tm	AB	R	HR	RBI	SB	BA	xBA	OBP	SLG	OPS	vL	vR	bb%	ct%	Eye	G	L	F	h%	HctX	PX	xPX	hr/f	Spd	SBO	SB%	#Wk	DOM	DIS	RC/G	RAR	BPV	BPX	R$
13																																		
14 BOS *	588	106	14	72	34	318	281	392	479	871	843	798	11	86	0.85	41	21	39	35	133	114	116	8%	122	23%	76%	12	67%	8%	7.00	50.0	94	254	$40
15 BOS	597	92	18	77	21	291	277	341	479	820	843	813	7	86	0.56	38	19	42	31	119	114	114	8%	137	18%	78%	26	65%	12%	5.89	18.8	93	251	$30
16 BOS	672	122	31	113	26	318	295	363	534	897	814	917	7	88	0.61	41	19	39	33	120	114	107	13%	128	16%	87%	27	56%	7%	7.40	48.8	98	280	$44
17 BOS	628	101	24	102	26	264	279	344	459	803	928	771	11	87	0.97	40	17	43	27	126	103	110	10%	94	17%	90%	26	81%	4%	5.64	13.0	84	255	$28
1st Half	316	53	13	43	14	278	297	359	487	847	885	838	11	91	1.34	41	17	42	27	134	109	109	11%	92	18%	88%	13	92%	0%	6.31	11.3	102	309	$29
2nd Half	312	48	11	59	12	250	261	329	429	758	959	697	11	84	0.76	40	17	44	27	119	97	111	9%	101	15%	92%	13	69%	8%	5.01	-0.4	68	206	$27
18 Proj	**635**	**106**	**26**	**100**	**25**	**286**	**284**	**352**	**491**	**843**	**901**	**827**	**9**	**87**	**0.78**	**40**	**18**	**42**	**30**	**124**	**107**	**111**	**11%**	**112**	**17%**	**85%**				**6.27**	**28.3**	**91**	**275**	**$33**

Bird,Gregory

Age: 25	Bats: L	Pos: 1B	Health	F	LIMA Plan	B
Ht: 6' 4"	Wt: 220		PT/Exp	F	Rand Var	+5
			Consist	B	MM	4135

9-28-.190 in 147 AB at NYY. Limited to 46 games in last two years due to shoulder, knee, ankle, and foot injuries. In 304 MLB AB, constants have been patience, power, and subpar contact. Still a relative unknown who carries BA and health risk, but elite FB%, xPX point to sizable HR upside, perhaps as early as 2018.

Yr Tm	AB	R	HR	RBI	SB	BA	xBA	OBP	SLG	OPS	vL	vR	bb%	ct%	Eye	G	L	F	h%	HctX	PX	xPX	hr/f	Spd	SBO	SB%	#Wk	DOM	DIS	RC/G	RAR	BPV	BPX	R$
13																																		
14 aa	95	13	6	9	0	230		334	504	838			13	69	0.50				26		218			95	0%	0%				5.58		106	286	$1
15 NYY *	475	65	23	77	1	259	256	329	470	799	752	915	10	75	0.43	27	22	51	30	146	142	203	20%	98	2%	45%	9	78%	22%	5.29	4.8	66	178	$15
16																																		
17 NYY *	194	30	12	34	0	209	248	310	449	759	987	645	13	73	0.54	30	18	52	22	108	140	162	16%	86	0%	0%	12	50%	42%	4.49	-5.2	57	173	$2
1st Half	81	9	1	4	0	105	166	253	201	453	333	457	16	69	0.63	30	11	59	14	117	73	203	5%	98	0%	0%	5	20%	80%	1.44	-11.9	-3	-9	-$11
2nd Half	113	21	11	30	0	284	301	355	627	982	1096	813	10	76	0.46	30	22	48	28	103	183	140	24%	90	0%	0%	7	71%	14%	7.93	7.2	100	303	$11
18 Proj	**464**	**68**	**26**	**75**	**0**	**239**	**255**	**330**	**469**	**799**	**898**	**771**	**12**	**73**	**0.49**	**32**	**20**	**48**	**27**	**124**	**137**	**181**	**16%**	**85**	**1%**	**50%**				**5.12**	**0.3**	**39**	**119**	**$12**

Blackmon,Charlie

Age: 32	Bats: L	Pos: CF	Health	A	LIMA Plan	C
Ht: 6' 3"	Wt: 210		PT/Exp	A	Rand Var	-5
			Consist	D	MM	4455

MLB and fantasy MVP-caliber year for late bloomer after third straight year of OPS gains. 2nd half surge was icing on the cake, but as good as it was, don't let recency bias inflate his value too much. Going forward, his 1st half is probably a more reasonable baseline, but that still means you're gonna have to PAY UP.

Yr Tm	AB	R	HR	RBI	SB	BA	xBA	OBP	SLG	OPS	vL	vR	bb%	ct%	Eye	G	L	F	h%	HctX	PX	xPX	hr/f	Spd	SBO	SB%	#Wk	DOM	DIS	RC/G	RAR	BPV	BPX	R$
13 COL *	503	66	8	44	11	266	268	302	395	697	752	824	5	81	0.27	42	27	31	32	90	90	66	10%	135	15%	64%	16	31%	25%	4.04	-0.8	48	120	$14
14 COL	593	82	19	72	28	288	269	335	440	775	697	801	5	84	0.32	41	22	37	32	103	100	94	10%	102	25%	74%	27	52%	19%	5.02	20.1	57	154	$32
15 COL	614	93	17	58	43	287	266	347	450	797	709	828	7	82	0.41	38	25	37	33	117	100	119	9%	137	34%	77%	27	59%	22%	5.37	18.7	64	173	$36
16 COL	578	111	29	82	17	324	295	381	552	933	843	972	7	82	0.42	34	28	38	35	115	127	129	16%	108	16%	65%	26	62%	23%	7.45	43.9	79	226	$36
17 COL	644	137	37	104	14	331	294	399	601	1000	956	1023	9	79	0.48	41	22	37	37	125	141	141	20%	165	13%	58%	27	56%	7%	8.63	61.7	98	297	$42
1st Half	334	64	17	57	5	311	282	365	575	940	908	957	7	78	0.36	43	18	39	36	109	137	122	17%	178	12%	50%	13	62%	8%	7.34	22.4	92	279	$37
2nd Half	310	73	20	47	9	352	306	434	629	1063	1013	1090	11	80	0.63	38	27	35	39	142	145	162	23%	137	13%	64%	14	50%	7%	10.14	42.3	101	306	$47
18 Proj	**613**	**118**	**34**	**86**	**15**	**321**	**295**	**383**	**573**	**956**	**893**	**983**	**8**	**81**	**0.44**	**39**	**25**	**37**	**35**	**120**	**131**	**131**	**19%**	**142**	**14%**	**66%**				**7.83**	**55.2**	**84**	**253**	**$40**

Blanco,Gregor

Age: 34	Bats: L	Pos: LF CF	Health	B	LIMA Plan	D
Ht: 5' 11"	Wt: 175		PT/Exp	D	Rand Var	-1
			Consist	D	MM	1511

As he has in past, got on base and ran just enough to justify part-time rosterability, though this time it took huge leaps in SBO, SB% to get there. But declining ct% and lack of punch have combined to sink BA, so outside of SB, other value stats are negligible. Advancing mileage doesn't portend late-career renaisssance.

Yr Tm	AB	R	HR	RBI	SB	BA	xBA	OBP	SLG	OPS	vL	vR	bb%	ct%	Eye	G	L	F	h%	HctX	PX	xPX	hr/f	Spd	SBO	SB%	#Wk	DOM	DIS	RC/G	RAR	BPV	BPX	R$
13 SF	452	50	3	41	14	265	250	341	350	690	650	696	10	79	0.55	44	28	28	33	87	60	69	3%	158	16%	61%	27	19%	30%	4.01	-0.6	34	85	$12
14 SF	393	51	5	38	16	260	241	333	374	707	730	697	9	80	0.53	40	21	39	31	93	81	93	4%	140	18%	76%	27	37%	37%	4.27	5.6	49	132	$13
15 SF	327	59	5	26	13	291	268	368	413	781	741	792	11	82	0.68	45	24	30	34	85	83	76	6%	138	17%	72%	23	35%	30%	5.42	6.5	59	159	$14
16 SF	241	28	1	18	6	224	236	309	311	620	686	597	11	79	0.57	46	21	33	28	63	55	41	2%	143	13%	67%	24	21%	54%	3.11	-11.2	26	74	$1
17 ARI	224	43	3	13	15	246	230	337	357	694	525	752	12	74	0.53	43	22	35	32	84	70	90	5%	164	23%	94%	23	39%	43%	4.41	-5.6	26	79	$7
1st Half	128	26	2	8	7	258	242	340	391	731	299	874	11	76	0.52	38	24	37	33	111	81	128	6%	155	21%	88%	9	44%	33%	4.77	-2.2	39	118	$7
2nd Half	96	17	1	5	8	229	213	333	313	646	802	586	14	71	0.54	49	18	32	31	50	53	35	5%	140	25%	100%	14	36%	50%	3.95	-4.1	-3	-9	$7
18 Proj	**155**	**25**	**2**	**11**	**8**	**246**	**238**	**334**	**349**	**683**	**658**	**692**	**12**	**76**	**0.56**	**45**	**22**	**33**	**31**	**75**	**63**	**66**	**4%**	**145**	**19%**	**86%**				**4.12**	**-1.6**	**22**	**67**	**$5**

Blash,Jabari

Age: 28	Bats: R	Pos: RF	Health	B	LIMA Plan	D
Ht: 6' 5"	Wt: 235		PT/Exp	D	Rand Var	-3
			Consist	B	MM	4101

5-16-.213 in 164 AB at SD. Of the Chris Carter mold, immense slugger's game has excessive swing-and-miss that suppresses BA and OBP, particularly against RHP. Has shown ability to work a walk, but mouth-watering PX is still unfulfilled in majors (career 103 PX). And he's not that young. Fear the worst.

Yr Tm	AB	R	HR	RBI	SB	BA	xBA	OBP	SLG	OPS	vL	vR	bb%	ct%	Eye	G	L	F	h%	HctX	PX	xPX	hr/f	Spd	SBO	SB%	#Wk	DOM	DIS	RC/G	RAR	BPV	BPX	R$
13 aa	97	12	7	19	1	279		388	541	929			15	67	0.53				34		188			89	6%	44%				7.19		75	188	$3
14 a/a	289	34	12	40	4	175		253	347	600			9	62	0.27				23		150			86	14%	54%				2.61		13	35	$1
15 a/a	406	56	22	57	6	214		285	430	715			9	62	0.26				28		168			89	8%	82%				4.00		30	81	$8
16 SD *	248	26	10	24	2	188	188	291	350	641	603	627	13	54	0.31	46	16	38	30	83	140	158	21%	80	7%	40%	9	22%	56%	3.09	-12.2	-20	-57	-$1
17 SD *	399	57	17	54	3	212	203	310	386	696	858	544	12	56	0.32	37	22	40	33	96	136	168	13%	83	7%	38%	16	13%	69%	3.74	-19.0	-15	-45	$4
1st Half	212	30	10	30	2	188	192	281	375	656	580	436	11	53	0.28	71	0	29	29	61	150	27	25%	81	9%	45%	5	20%	80%	3.20	-14.7	-19	-58	$3
2nd Half	187	26	7	24	1	239	211	342	399	741	952	558	14	59	0.38	32	26	42	36	107	121	191	11%	89	6%	30%	11	9%	64%	4.40	-5.4	-10	-30	$5
18 Proj	**215**	**28**	**9**	**28**	**2**	**221**	**199**	**325**	**389**	**714**	**835**	**641**	**12**	**58**	**0.33**	**47**	**16**	**37**	**34**	**86**	**127**	**137**	**19%**	**85**	**6%**	**51%**				**3.93**	**-5.1**	**-25**	**-75**	**$4**

Bogaerts,Xander

Age: 25	Bats: R	Pos: SS	Health	A	LIMA Plan	B
Ht: 6' 1"	Wt: 210		PT/Exp	A	Rand Var	0
			Consist	A	MM	1435

Expectations were high after '16 breakout but three-year LD rate, xBA, HctX suggest he's always had a good, not great, skills foundation. Played the 2nd half with a sore wrist after July 6 HBP, which explains away those wretched numbers. His 1st half is a reasonable baseline going forward.

Yr Tm	AB	R	HR	RBI	SB	BA	xBA	OBP	SLG	OPS	vL	vR	bb%	ct%	Eye	G	L	F	h%	HctX	PX	xPX	hr/f	Spd	SBO	SB%	#Wk	DOM	DIS	RC/G	RAR	BPV	BPX	R$
13 BOS *	488	64	12	58	7	277	291	349	427	777	1089	463	10	77	0.48	47	34	19	34	120	107	87	17%	119	7%	67%	7	43%	57%	5.22	25.0	50	125	$16
14 BOS	538	60	12	46	2	240	230	297	362	660	755	621	7	74	0.28	38	21	41	30	110	98	110	7%	99	4%	40%	26	38%	46%	3.47	4.7	21	57	$7
15 BOS	613	84	7	81	10	320	269	355	421	776	892	735	5	84	0.32	53	21	26	37	100	71	60	5%	116	7%	83%	27	33%	22%	5.62	20.0	37	100	$28
16 BOS	652	115	21	89	13	294	262	356	446	802	873	785	8	81	0.47	45	20	35	34	101	91	73	11%	104	9%	76%	27	52%	19%	5.68	24.9	47	134	$29
17 BOS	571	94	10	62	15	273	262	343	403	746	777	739	9	80	0.48	49	21	30	33	101	77	54	7%	134	10%	94%	26	42%	27%	4.91	4.6	40	121	$19
1st Half	303	49	5	39	9	314	279	366	455	821	716	844	7	81	0.39	51	22	27	38	108	85	49	8%	124	11%	90%	13	54%	31%	6.26	13.8	43	130	$25
2nd Half	268	45	5	23	6	228	242	319	343	662	830	616	10	79	0.58	46	19	35	27	94	68	59	7%	138	8%	100%	13	31%	23%	3.67	-7.4	35	106	$12
18 Proj	**610**	**97**	**14**	**71**	**14**	**295**	**260**	**357**	**431**	**789**	**870**	**766**	**8**	**80**	**0.45**	**47**	**20**	**33**	**35**	**101**	**79**	**66**	**9%**	**123**	**9%**	**87%**				**5.59**	**19.1**	**37**	**111**	**$27**

Bonifacio,Jorge

Age: 25	Bats: R	Pos: RF	Health	A	LIMA Plan	D+
Ht: 6' 1"	Wt: 195		PT/Exp	B	Rand Var	-1
			Consist	B	MM	3223

17-40-.255 in 384 AB at KC. If declining ct% countdown (5-4-3-2-1) was in anticipation of power lift-off, inconsistent PX says he's stuck on the pad. But hit tool is still being calibrated for both consistency and exit velocity, and he's young. Hey, at the very least, he's already exceeded brother Emilio's 11-year launch total.

Yr Tm	AB	R	HR	RBI	SB	BA	xBA	OBP	SLG	OPS	vL	vR	bb%	ct%	Eye	G	L	F	h%	HctX	PX	xPX	hr/f	Spd	SBO	SB%	#Wk	DOM	DIS	RC/G	RAR	BPV	BPX	R$
13 aa	93	13	2	16	2	283		348	405	753			9	75	0.39				36		102			88	10%	61%				4.90		27	68	$2
14 aa	505	40	3	42	7	212		270	282	552			7	74	0.31				28		59			105	8%	67%				2.45		-7	-19	$0
15 aa	483	49	13	52	2	218		269	365	634			6	73	0.25				27		109			89	5%	53%				3.16		19	51	$3
16 aaa	495	63	13	66	5	245		299	389	689			7	72	0.27				32		93			110	6%	67%				3.91		10	29	$9
17 KC *	435	60	19	49	1	258	252	320	442	763	713	768	8	71	0.31	39	26	35	32	92	109	98	18%	114	2%	50%	25	24%	40%	4.84	-1.0	23	70	$9
1st Half	262	38	13	36	0	257	269	323	467	791	708	799	9	73	0.37	37	27	36	30	102	121	99	20%	100	0%	0%	11	36%	27%	5.19	1.0	40	121	$13
2nd Half	173	22	6	13	1	260	226	319	405	724	719	725	7	67	0.25	42	24	34	35	80	90	97	15%	129	4%	50%	14	14%	50%	4.33	-3.7	-4	-12	$3
18 Proj	**389**	**49**	**15**	**44**	**3**	**250**	**245**	**309**	**423**	**732**	**701**	**745**	**7**	**71**	**0.28**	**41**	**23**	**35**	**31**	**89**	**105**	**98**	**15%**	**114**	**4%**	**61%**				**4.36**	**-3.8**	**7**	**22**	**$9**

ROB CARROLL

Bour,Justin

Age: 30 Bats: L Pos: 1B	Health D	LIMA Plan B
Ht: 6' 3" Wt: 265	PT/Exp C	Rand Var -4
	Consist C	MM 4045

Ankle, oblique cost him nine weeks; had a career year anyway. PX/xPX growth supports the power spike despite lack of loft, and while he sacrificed some ct%, two years of plus LD%, xBA peg him as a BA asset. Muscled up vL (6 HR, 136 PX in 87 AB), so if that holds and pre-injury 1st half power skills return... UP: 35 HR

Yr	Tm	AB	R	HR	RBI	SB	BA	xBA	OBP	SLG	OPS	vL	vR	bb%	ct%	Eye	G	L	F	h%	HctX	PX	xPX	hr/f	Spd	SBO	SB%	#Wk	DOM	DIS	RC/G	RAR	BPV	BPX
13	aa	317	36	14	47	0	200		263	374	638			8	77	0.38				22		119			79	4%	0%				3.03		45	113
14	MIA *	459	48	11	58	2	246	249	298	372	670	600	734	7	81	0.39	53	16	31	28	127	93	126	6%	61	3%	61%	12	33%	58%	3.73	-6.1	32	86
15	MIA *	460	48	24	77	1	258	254	321	458	779	573	845	8	77	0.40	48	17	35	29	112	128	110	21%	46	1%	100%	25	48%	28%	5.06	-4.1	41	111
16	MIA	280	35	15	51	0	264	276	349	475	824	533	857	12	80	0.68	44	22	35	28	114	117	107	19%	55	0%	0%	18	67%	28%	5.80	3.7	56	160
17	MIA	377	52	25	83	1	289	279	366	536	902	809	929	11	75	0.49	43	23	34	33	118	138	127	26%	41	1%	100%	22	41%	36%	7.09	12.4	46	139
1st Half		237	31	18	52	1	287	276	358	553	911	1098	857	10	74	0.43	45	21	34	32	132	145	147	30%	44	1%	100%	13	38%	31%	7.09	9.6	48	145
2nd Half		140	21	7	31	0	293	285	378	507	885	358	1051	13	76	0.62	41	27	32	34	93	127	93	20%	53	0%	0%	9	44%	44%	7.04	5.4	49	148
18	Proj	**468**	**60**	**28**	**91**	**1**	**272**	**277**	**349**	**503**	**852**	**613**	**902**	**11**	**77**	**0.53**	**44**	**22**	**34**	**30**	**112**	**127**	**113**	**23%**	**45**	**1%**	**77%**				**6.19**	**14.6**	**42**	**128**

Bradley,Jackie

Age: 28 Bats: L Pos: CF	Health A	LIMA Plan B+
Ht: 5' 10" Wt: 200	PT/Exp B	Rand Var 0
	Consist C	MM 3235

We said he'd fall short of repeat last year, and... yeah. Sprained thumb in Aug didn't help, but 2nd half skill collapse—a jump in whiffs, more ground balls, weaker contact (HctX, xPX)—was already in motion. Recent power baseline bodes well for HR rebound, and can chip in SB, but 2016 seems like the high-water mark.

Yr	Tm	AB	R	HR	RBI	SB	BA	xBA	OBP	SLG	OPS	vL	vR	bb%	ct%	Eye	G	L	F	h%	HctX	PX	xPX	hr/f	Spd	SBO	SB%	#Wk	DOM	DIS	RC/G	RAR	BPV	BPX
13	BOS *	415	62	10	37	7	239	268	307	401	708	327	722	9	73	0.36	63	16	22	30	91	130	79	21%	105	16%	49%	11	36%	45%	3.90	-4.2	47	118
14	BOS *	450	50	2	34	8	197	197	252	262	514	640	473	7	69	0.24	46	18	36	28	104	64	119	1%	88	9%	88%	25	16%	68%	2.15	-24.7	-31	-84
15	BOS *	503	75	17	68	6	267	264	337	460	796	918	791	9	76	0.44	48	16	36	32	106	132	133	18%	98	8%	59%	15	53%	47%	5.27	11.2	61	165
16	BOS	558	94	26	87	9	267	270	349	486	835	673	902	10	74	0.44	47	19	34	32	109	133	110	18%	100	7%	82%	27	56%	22%	5.79	22.9	56	160
17	BOS	482	58	17	63	8	245	246	323	402	726	766	713	9	74	0.39	49	18	33	30	100	91	89	15%	97	9%	73%	26	31%	38%	4.24	-7.2	19	58
1st Half		227	30	10	35	4	278	270	365	489	854	1146	772	11	78	0.57	43	19	38	32	117	120	109	15%	91	8%	80%	12	58%	17%	6.22	8.5	58	176
2nd Half		255	28	7	28	4	216	222	285	325	610	477	657	7	71	0.26	55	17	28	27	85	63	71	14%	104	10%	67%	14	7%	57%	2.83	-16.5	-17	-52
18	Proj	**510**	**70**	**22**	**67**	**8**	**253**	**258**	**329**	**444**	**773**	**740**	**786**	**9**	**74**	**0.38**	**49**	**18**	**33**	**30**	**102**	**111**	**100**	**17%**	**100**	**9%**	**70%**				**4.81**	**4.5**	**34**	**103**

Brantley,Michael

Age: 31 Bats: L Pos: LF	Health F	LIMA Plan B
Ht: 6' 2" Wt: 200	PT/Exp D	Rand Var -3
	Consist F	MM 2455

Strong April (.308 BA, 5 HR, 3 SB) preceded right ankle sprains in May, June, AND August. Once-elite ct% slipped a bit, though xBA cements strong BA foundation. SB% prowess injects more value. Sub-average power profile, health woes temper expectations, but versatile production is there if you plan around the risk.

Yr	Tm	AB	R	HR	RBI	SB	BA	xBA	OBP	SLG	OPS	vL	vR	bb%	ct%	Eye	G	L	F	h%	HctX	PX	xPX	hr/f	Spd	SBO	SB%	#Wk	DOM	DIS	RC/G	RAR	BPV	BPX
13	CLE	556	66	10	73	17	284	277	332	396	728	664	757	7	88	0.60	47	23	30	31	89	72	76	7%	109	13%	81%	27	56%	19%	4.74	11.9	57	143
14	CLE	611	94	20	97	23	327	324	385	506	890	826	923	8	91	0.93	46	26	28	34	133	116	105	13%	95	13%	96%	26	85%	4%	7.54	62.1	102	276
15	CLE	529	68	15	84	15	310	308	379	480	859	785	908	10	90	1.18	46	23	32	32	121	107	88	10%	78	10%	94%	26	77%	0%	6.92	36.1	92	249
16	CLE *	67	7	0	8	1	197	258	255	253	508	821	504	7	88	0.64	44	24	32	22	115	43	108	0%	104	7%	100%	3	33%	67%	2.11	-4.5	33	94
17	CLE	338	47	9	52	11	299	288	357	444	801	696	857	8	85	0.62	49	22	28	33	117	81	74	11%	98	12%	92%	20	50%	10%	5.94	4.5	53	161
1st Half		224	25	5	31	7	304	283	367	438	804	704	859	9	83	0.59	49	23	28	35	129	80	81	10%	87	11%	88%	12	50%	17%	5.98	3.9	44	133
2nd Half		114	22	4	21	4	289	295	339	456	795	677	854	7	89	0.69	50	20	30	30	93	81	60	13%	119	13%	100%	8	50%	0%	5.83	1.5	72	218
18	Proj	**418**	**62**	**12**	**67**	**14**	**303**	**299**	**360**	**459**	**818**	**732**	**865**	**8**	**88**	**0.77**	**48**	**23**	**30**	**32**	**113**	**84**	**80**	**11%**	**97**	**12%**	**93%**				**6.21**	**20.1**	**70**	**211**

Braun,Ryan

Age: 34 Bats: R Pos: LF	Health C	LIMA Plan B+
Ht: 6' 2" Wt: 205	PT/Exp B	Rand Var +3
	Consist C	MM 4355

Laundry list of 1H injuries (back, calf, forearm, wrist), career-low h% blocked third straight $30 season, but positive signs remain: xPX, HctX rebounded nicely; xBA held firm despite BA collapse. SB malaise probably permanent now that he's in his mid-30s, and can't ignore bruises, but there's plenty of gas in this tank.

Yr	Tm	AB	R	HR	RBI	SB	BA	xBA	OBP	SLG	OPS	vL	vR	bb%	ct%	Eye	G	L	F	h%	HctX	PX	xPX	hr/f	Spd	SBO	SB%	#Wk	DOM	DIS	RC/G	RAR	BPV	BPX
13	MIL	225	30	9	38	4	298	268	372	498	869	1053	777	11	75	0.48	52	16	32	36	120	142	150	16%	122	13%	44%	14	43%	14%	6.31	14.4	74	185
14	MIL	530	68	19	81	11	266	277	324	453	777	823	760	7	79	0.36	47	20	33	31	115	130	124	14%	118	13%	69%	25	56%	24%	4.94	17.7	70	189
15	MIL	506	87	25	84	24	285	282	356	498	854	957	821	10	77	0.47	50	19	31	33	121	136	139	20%	110	20%	86%	25	52%	28%	6.40	24.1	72	195
16	MIL	511	80	30	91	16	305	303	365	538	903	1010	869	8	81	0.47	56	19	25	33	113	127	97	29%	108	14%	76%	26	58%	23%	7.11	35.0	76	217
17	MIL	380	58	17	52	12	268	291	336	487	823	872	808	9	80	0.50	49	19	32	30	126	124	122	17%	94	17%	75%	21	62%	24%	5.64	4.2	67	203
1st Half		122	23	9	21	4	262	300	338	549	887	963	862	10	75	0.47	49	20	32	28	136	163	139	31%	84	17%	80%	8	63%	13%	6.42	3.8	80	242
2nd Half		258	35	8	31	8	271	286	336	457	793	829	782	9	82	0.52	49	19	32	30	122	107	114	12%	99	17%	73%	13	62%	31%	5.27	-0.6	63	191
18	Proj	**509**	**80**	**25**	**79**	**13**	**281**	**289**	**348**	**501**	**849**	**930**	**822**	**9**	**79**	**0.48**	**51**	**19**	**30**	**31**	**122**	**122**	**121**	**20%**	**101**	**13%**	**71%**				**6.06**	**23.3**	**63**	**192**

Bregman,Alex

Age: 24 Bats: R Pos: 3B SS	Health A	LIMA Plan A
Ht: 6' 0" Wt: 180	PT/Exp D	Rand Var 0
	Consist A	MM 4455

Passed first full season with flying colors thanks to 2nd half surge. More 5-category goodness to come, as contact gains bolstered xBA/BA, took full advantage of green light, and power growth suggests he'll push HR envelope. Shortstop eligibility is just icing on the cake. Enjoy the ride. UP: 30+ HR

Yr	Tm	AB	R	HR	RBI	SB	BA	xBA	OBP	SLG	OPS	vL	vR	bb%	ct%	Eye	G	L	F	h%	HctX	PX	xPX	hr/f	Spd	SBO	SB%	#Wk	DOM	DIS	RC/G	RAR	BPV	BPX
13																																		
14																																		
15																																		
16	HOU *	515	91	25	86	8	273	287	343	504	847	735	813	10	81	0.57	29	28	43	29	106	131	118	13%	124	9%	65%	9	56%	44%	5.96	17.2	89	254
17	HOU	556	88	19	71	17	284	276	352	475	827	974	776	9	83	0.57	38	22	40	32	110	106	102	10%	123	15%	77%	27	56%	26%	5.89	16.2	72	218
1st Half		265	31	8	26	6	245	258	324	396	721	852	678	10	80	0.54	36	24	40	28	99	86	95	9%	105	11%	75%	13	54%	31%	4.25	-6.6	43	130
2nd Half		291	57	11	45	11	320	294	377	546	924	1072	869	8	85	0.60	40	20	40	35	120	124	108	11%	135	18%	79%	14	57%	21%	7.70	20.6	97	294
18	Proj	**573**	**96**	**26**	**85**	**14**	**286**	**285**	**352**	**508**	**860**	**929**	**835**	**9**	**82**	**0.56**	**35**	**24**	**41**	**31**	**109**	**120**	**109**	**13%**	**123**	**13%**	**74%**				**6.32**	**23.3**	**79**	**241**

Brinson,Lewis

Age: 24 Bats: R Pos: LF	Health A	LIMA Plan D+
Ht: 6' 3" Wt: 195	PT/Exp D	Rand Var +1
	Consist C	MM 2331

2-3-.106 with 1 SB in 47 AB at MIL. Top prospect struggled through two mid-season cameos before hamstring strain ended season in August. Toolsy profile highlighted by power/speed blend, and while plate approach, including small sample 57% MLB ct%, says instant success unlikely, he's still a keeper league gem.

Yr	Tm	AB	R	HR	RBI	SB	BA	xBA	OBP	SLG	OPS	vL	vR	bb%	ct%	Eye	G	L	F	h%	HctX	PX	xPX	hr/f	Spd	SBO	SB%	#Wk	DOM	DIS	RC/G	RAR	BPV	BPX
13																																		
14																																		
15	a/a	140	19	6	22	4	291		343	482	825			7	74	0.30				36		131			96	14%	79%				5.95		46	124
16	a/a	393	50	15	50	13	251		280	441	721			4	76	0.17				30		115			108	26%	66%				4.04		39	111
17	MIL *	346	49	13	37	9	260	267	319	446	764	933	314	8	74	0.33	57	17	27	32	100	110	99	25%	121	17%	61%	5	40%	40%	4.70	-3.6	39	118
1st Half		238	35	7	27	7	258	287	315	431	747	347	366	8	70	0.28	61	28	11	34	95	113	57	0%	120	22%	54%	3	0%	67%	4.36	-3.9	24	73
2nd Half		108	14	5	10	2	266	233	326	477	803	1587	182	8	83	0.54	50	0	50	28	112	104	161	33%	129	8%	100%	2	100%	0%	5.52	1.9	74	224
18	Proj	**229**	**31**	**6**	**27**	**5**	**264**	**253**	**330**	**408**	**738**	**976**	**655**	**6**	**77**	**0.30**	**48**	**20**	**32**	**32**	**86**	**85**	**51**	**10%**	**121**	**14%**	**67%**				**4.32**	**-0.9**	**23**	**68**

Broxton,Keon

Age: 28 Bats: R Pos: CF	Health A	LIMA Plan D+
Ht: 6' 3" Wt: 195	PT/Exp C	Rand Var -1
	Consist B	MM 4503

20/20 season, but with an overwhelming wart: plethora of whiffs led to AAA demotion, sporadic 2H playing time; dismal xBA, bb% dip offer little hope for immediate improvement. One of two players with that xPX/Spd combo (min. 100 AB), so counting stat ceiling is high. But if bat-to-ball skills don't improve... DN: More AAA time.

Yr	Tm	AB	R	HR	RBI	SB	BA	xBA	OBP	SLG	OPS	vL	vR	bb%	ct%	Eye	G	L	F	h%	HctX	PX	xPX	hr/f	Spd	SBO	SB%	#Wk	DOM	DIS	RC/G	RAR	BPV	BPX
13	aa	334	34	7	35	5	217		272	338	610			7	63	0.20				32		102			116	8%	82%				3.03		-16	-40
14	aa	407	48	9	37	18	226		295	367	663			9	67	0.30				32		117			120	25%	72%				3.53		16	43
15	PIT *	493	72	7	55	32	233	256	306	360	666	0	0	10	65	0.30	100	0	0	35	0	101	-16	0%	141	40%	64%	2	0%	50%	3.43	-13.6	3	8
16	MIL *	385	48	15	37	35	238	227	324	434	758	916	694	11	58	0.31	45	25	30	37	102	152	139	26%	138	48%	72%	17	29%	53%	4.54	-1.3	20	57
17	MIL *	440	69	21	54	24	225	218	296	422	718	772	701	9	58	0.24	45	20	35	33	83	141	131	24%	146	30%	77%	26	27%	62%	4.10	-13.0	8	24
1st Half		252	45	13	32	14	242	233	312	476	788	786	789	8	58	0.21	41	26	33	36	78	169	120	27%	158	35%	74%	13	38%	38%	4.73	-1.3	31	94
2nd Half		188	24	8	22	10	202	189	287	350	638	746	561	11	58	0.29	51	12	37	30	90	105	147	21%	105	24%	83%	13	15%	85%	3.31	-9.5	-27	-82
18	Proj	**284**	**39**	**13**	**31**	**18**	**236**	**226**	**318**	**437**	**755**	**874**	**700**	**10**	**60**	**0.28**	**46**	**21**	**33**	**34**	**92**	**140**	**137**	**23%**	**137**	**34%**	**73%**				**4.45**	**-0.5**	**13**	**39**

RYAN BLOOMFIELD

Bruce,Jay

Age: 31	Bats: L	Pos: RF	Health	A	LIMA Plan B+
Ht: 6' 3"	Wt: 225		PT/Exp	A	Rand Var 0
			Consist	B	MM 4135

Encore performance of 2016 marked by 3-year growth in HctX, xPX, and career high FB%. Though career 70% ct% and 0.29 Eye vL will cap his batting average, has maintained 150+ PX vR five of last six seasons. There's no more upside here, but will be a valuable 30-HR bat available deep into the draft.

Yr	Tm	AB	R	HR	RBI	SB	BA	xBA	OBP	SLG	OPS	vL	vR	bb%	ct%	Eye	G	L	F	h%	HctX	PX	xPX	hr/f	Spd	SBO	SB%	#Wk	DOM	DIS	RC/G	RAR	BPV	BPX	R$
13	CIN	626	89	30	109	7	262	264	329	478	807	734	841	9	70	0.34	37	24	39	33	102	165	133	17%	81	7%	70%	27	52%	33%	5.40	20.3	58	145	$25
14	CIN	493	71	18	66	12	217	240	281	373	654	556	685	8	70	0.30	45	21	34	27	99	122	109	15%	89	14%	80%	26	35%	46%	3.44	-6.8	21	57	$12
15	CIN	580	72	26	87	9	226	256	294	434	729	666	754	9	75	0.40	37	19	44	26	115	140	144	13%	77	11%	64%	27	48%	22%	4.16	-10.7	55	149	$14
16	2 NL	539	74	33	99	4	250	279	309	506	815	678	872	7	77	0.35	37	22	41	27	119	147	152	19%	95	5%	67%	27	56%	19%	5.25	8.6	70	200	$17
17	2 TM	555	82	36	101	1	254	267	324	508	832	718	883	9	75	0.41	33	21	47	28	122	143	161	18%	78	2%	50%	27	44%	22%	5.59	10.7	58	176	$17
1st Half		296	45	20	55	0	264	271	335	524	859	637	950	10	76	0.45	32	20	48	28	131	146	162	19%	70	1%	0%	13	54%	15%	6.00	8.1	64	194	$20
2nd Half		259	37	16	46	1	243	262	311	490	802	801	802	9	74	0.37	33	22	45	27	112	139	161	18%	92	2%	100%	14	36%	29%	5.14	0.6	53	161	$13
18	Proj	**543**	**76**	**31**	**95**	**2**	**250**	**264**	**316**	**488**	**804**	**712**	**844**	**9**	**75**	**0.38**	**35**	**21**	**44**	**28**	**117**	**135**	**152**	**18%**	**86**	**3%**	**50%**				**5.18**	**7.8**	**46**	**140**	**$16**

Bryant,Kris

Age: 26	Bats: R	Pos: 3B	Health	A	LIMA Plan D+
Ht: 6' 5"	Wt: 230		PT/Exp	A	Rand Var 0
			Consist	B	MM 4345

"Down" year for young slugger? Not so fast: Plate discipline gains (bb%, ct%, Eye), 3-yr trend of outperforming xBA, and above average Spd. Turned HctX and ct% up along with career high xBA in 2nd half. Earnings may have disappointed, but underlying skills, 2nd half surge, age suggest a swift return to $30+ level.

Yr	Tm	AB	R	HR	RBI	SB	BA	xBA	OBP	SLG	OPS	vL	vR	bb%	ct%	Eye	G	L	F	h%	HctX	PX	xPX	hr/f	Spd	SBO	SB%	#Wk	DOM	DIS	RC/G	RAR	BPV	BPX	R$
13																																			
14	a/a	492	91	33	85	12	290		377	559	935			12	63	0.37				40		229			86	11%	72%				7.48		86	232	$32
15	CHC *	587	92	28	107	15	276	233	361	492	854	797	875	12	64	0.38	34	21	45	38	104	165	148	16%	128	11%	78%	26	50%	35%	6.28	26.8	53	143	$29
16	CHC	603	121	39	102	8	292	273	385	554	939	1060	896	11	74	0.49	30	24	46	33	122	158	159	19%	113	7%	62%	27	59%	15%	7.25	38.4	82	234	$31
17	CHC	549	111	29	73	7	295	274	409	537	946	956	943	14	77	0.74	38	20	42	34	102	139	111	16%	123	6%	58%	27	67%	19%	7.61	35.3	85	258	$25
1st Half		273	50	16	32	6	264	262	393	516	910	1060	863	16	74	0.75	34	19	47	30	89	147	110	17%	122	10%	67%	13	69%	15%	6.75	13.3	85	258	$21
2nd Half		276	61	13	41	1	326	286	425	558	983	850	1022	13	79	0.74	41	21	38	37	115	132	111	15%	119	3%	33%	14	64%	21%	8.57	25.7	87	264	$29
18	Proj	**580**	**113**	**31**	**90**	**9**	**294**	**270**	**395**	**534**	**929**	**958**	**919**	**13**	**75**	**0.59**	**36**	**21**	**43**	**34**	**111**	**139**	**133**	**17%**	**118**	**7%**	**65%**				**7.29**	**39.0**	**68**	**206**	**$31**

Buxton,Byron

Age: 24	Bats: R	Pos: CF	Health	B	LIMA Plan B
Ht: 6' 2"	Wt: 190		PT/Exp	C	Rand Var -3
			Consist	A	MM 3515

It was the best of times: Post-leg-kick 2H corresponded with power spike and ct% gains—though h% and hr/f were generous. It was the worst of times: Uh, that entire first half. The glove will keep him in the lineup and the SB will be plentiful, but the plot of A Tale of Two Batters remains unresolved. A page-turner, indeed.

Yr	Tm	AB	R	HR	RBI	SB	BA	xBA	OBP	SLG	OPS	vL	vR	bb%	ct%	Eye	G	L	F	h%	HctX	PX	xPX	hr/f	Spd	SBO	SB%	#Wk	DOM	DIS	RC/G	RAR	BPV	BPX	R$
13																																			
14																																			
15	MIN *	421	61	8	43	20	261	221	310	411	721	318	704	7	74	0.27	43	14	43	34	88	96	104	6%	189	24%	79%	10	20%	70%	4.43	-0.9	45	122	$16
16	MIN *	488	81	20	60	16	250	232	301	469	770	735	704	7	64	0.20	35	22	43	35	70	158	85	14%	174	19%	89%	20	30%	50%	4.90	7.7	48	137	$17
17	MIN	462	69	16	51	29	253	223	314	413	728	792	701	7	68	0.25	39	23	38	34	75	97	85	14%	181	25%	97%	25	24%	48%	4.70	-0.6	19	58	$20
1st Half		230	22	4	14	14	200	193	276	287	563	584	554	9	64	0.28	39	23	38	29	61	60	61	8%	148	26%	93%	13	15%	69%	2.73	-15.8	-30	-91	$6
2nd Half		232	47	12	37	15	306	254	353	539	892	981	853	6	71	0.22	38	24	38	39	90	131	105	20%	183	25%	100%	12	33%	25%	7.35	15.4	57	173	$34
18	Proj	**521**	**83**	**18**	**62**	**30**	**268**	**230**	**323**	**449**	**772**	**770**	**772**	**7**	**67**	**0.23**	**39**	**22**	**39**	**37**	**77**	**113**	**89**	**13%**	**183**	**25%**	**93%**				**5.24**	**11.0**	**26**	**79**	**$27**

Cabrera,Asdrubal

Age: 32	Bats: B	Pos: SS 3B 2B	Health	B	LIMA Plan B
Ht: 6' 0"	Wt: 205		PT/Exp	B	Rand Var -1
			Consist	B	MM 2235

Another year, another boring double-digit R$ (8 of 9 seasons), but accompanied by PX/xPX decline, GB%/FB% flip, and lowest AB total since 2010. History of hr/f makes return to 20 HR improbable, but second half HctX and xPX suggest the bottom hasn't fallen out. Multi-pos eligibility earns him some added value.

Yr	Tm	AB	R	HR	RBI	SB	BA	xBA	OBP	SLG	OPS	vL	vR	bb%	ct%	Eye	G	L	F	h%	HctX	PX	xPX	hr/f	Spd	SBO	SB%	#Wk	DOM	DIS	RC/G	RAR	BPV	BPX	R$
13	CLE	508	66	14	64	9	242	256	299	402	700	639	730	6	78	0.31	36	23	41	29	107	118	138	9%	92	11%	75%	25	32%	24%	3.92	-1.1	47	118	$13
14	2 TM	553	74	14	61	10	241	250	307	387	694	689	696	8	80	0.45	38	19	42	28	118	105	126	8%	108	9%	83%	27	48%	30%	3.97	4.1	56	151	$13
15	TAM	505	66	15	58	6	265	248	315	430	744	725	752	7	79	0.34	36	21	44	31	91	107	107	9%	101	7%	67%	25	48%	28%	4.64	-0.5	46	124	$14
16	NYM	521	65	23	62	5	280	273	336	474	810	835	803	7	80	0.37	37	23	40	31	119	114	142	14%	79	5%	83%	26	38%	23%	5.54	8.3	51	146	$17
17	NYM	479	66	14	59	3	280	267	351	434	785	946	729	9	83	0.60	43	20	36	31	123	90	115	10%	81	4%	60%	25	44%	28%	5.30	0.0	47	142	$13
1st Half		209	35	8	24	3	268	279	343	435	779	750	789	9	85	0.66	48	20	32	28	116	89	99	14%	92	7%	75%	12	50%	42%	5.07	-0.1	58	176	$12
2nd Half		270	31	6	35	0	289	258	356	433	790	1101	684	10	81	0.57	40	21	39	34	128	91	128	7%	75	1%	0%	13	38%	15%	5.48	3.0	41	124	$15
18	Proj	**450**	**59**	**15**	**54**	**4**	**274**	**265**	**337**	**441**	**779**	**858**	**751**	**8**	**81**	**0.47**	**40**	**21**	**39**	**31**	**116**	**96**	**123**	**11%**	**86**	**5%**	**69%**				**5.15**	**8.8**	**39**	**118**	**$15**

Cabrera,Melky

Age: 33	Bats: B	Pos: LF RF	Health	B	LIMA Plan B+
Ht: 5' 10"	Wt: 210		PT/Exp	A	Rand Var 0
			Consist	C	MM 1055

The Melk Man delivers: Since 2014, has averaged .288-15-74 due to excellent ct%, league-average HctX and ~600 AB each season. Uptick in GB% is concerning given age and league-wide FB trend, but regained his old self in the second half. As a complementary piece, continues to prove that Melk does a roster good.

Yr	Tm	AB	R	HR	RBI	SB	BA	xBA	OBP	SLG	OPS	vL	vR	bb%	ct%	Eye	G	L	F	h%	HctX	PX	xPX	hr/f	Spd	SBO	SB%	#Wk	DOM	DIS	RC/G	RAR	BPV	BPX	R$
13	TOR	344	39	3	30	2	279	255	322	360	682	595	717	6	86	0.49	46	22	31	32	120	57	85	3%	99	4%	50%	15	27%	20%	4.07	0.9	35	88	$7
14	TOR	568	81	16	73	6	301	297	351	458	808	785	817	7	88	0.64	49	21	30	32	116	104	90	11%	94	5%	75%	23	61%	9%	5.84	33.6	80	216	$25
15	CHW	629	70	12	77	3	273	278	314	394	709	600	748	6	86	0.45	46	24	30	30	101	79	66	7%	70	2%	100%	26	35%	19%	4.41	0.3	42	114	$16
16	CHW	591	70	14	86	2	296	289	345	455	800	847	788	7	88	0.68	43	22	35	32	103	92	79	8%	82	1%	100%	27	67%	19%	5.76	24.2	68	194	$20
17	2 AL	620	78	17	85	1	285	284	324	423	746	785	734	5	88	0.49	49	22	29	30	103	71	75	11%	75	2%	33%	27	52%	11%	4.84	-10.6	44	133	$18
1st Half		310	43	8	46	0	284	263	330	400	730	847	688	7	87	0.55	53	19	27	31	109	61	69	11%	72	0%	0%	13	38%	15%	4.72	-5.5	34	103	$18
2nd Half		310	35	9	39	1	287	301	317	445	762	709	777	4	89	0.41	44	25	30	30	97	82	80	11%	77	4%	33%	14	64%	7%	4.94	-3.6	55	167	$18
18	Proj	**592**	**72**	**14**	**79**	**1**	**287**	**286**	**328**	**427**	**755**	**748**	**757**	**6**	**88**	**0.52**	**47**	**23**	**31**	**31**	**104**	**75**	**76**	**9%**	**80**	**2%**	**41%**				**4.99**	**8.9**	**42**	**127**	**$19**

Cabrera,Miguel

Age: 35	Bats: R	Pos: 1B	Health	B	LIMA Plan B
Ht: 6' 4"	Wt: 240		PT/Exp	A	Rand Var +4
			Consist	F	MM 3045

Persistent back issues, diagnosed late in season as two herniated disks in lower back, led to dips in Eye, BA and power. Problems ran deeper as the season progressed, though somehow his elite HctX hardly budged. Combo of age and chronic back issues is a bright red flag. Still, UP: 2014. But, DN: 2017 repeat

Yr	Tm	AB	R	HR	RBI	SB	BA	xBA	OBP	SLG	OPS	vL	vR	bb%	ct%	Eye	G	L	F	h%	HctX	PX	xPX	hr/f	Spd	SBO	SB%	#Wk	DOM	DIS	RC/G	RAR	BPV	BPX	R$
13	DET	555	103	44	137	3	348	317	442	636	1078	1210	1038	14	83	0.96	39	24	37	36	157	170	165	25%	75	1%	100%	26	69%	19%	10.96	90.2	120	300	$46
14	DET	611	101	25	109	1	313	302	371	524	895	900	894	9	81	0.51	40	25	35	35	157	154	163	14%	81	1%	50%	27	70%	15%	7.23	51.0	90	243	$33
15	DET	429	64	18	76	1	338	290	440	534	974	1016	964	15	81	0.94	42	25	33	39	142	126	124	16%	84	1%	50%	21	57%	14%	8.97	45.0	82	222	$25
16	DET	595	92	38	108	0	316	293	393	563	956	926	966	11	81	0.65	42	23	36	34	134	137	144	22%	77	0%	0%	27	52%	22%	8.24	53.9	79	226	$31
17	DET	469	50	16	60	0	249	265	329	399	728	928	675	10	77	0.49	40	27	33	29	132	88	125	13%	68	1%	0%	24	29%	38%	4.39	-13.6	19	58	$7
1st Half		250	29	11	39	0	264	281	358	456	814	877	796	12	76	0.59	40	28	33	31	148	113	138	17%	68	1%	0%	12	42%	25%	5.51	-1.0	43	130	$11
2nd Half		219	21	5	21	0	233	246	295	333	628	988	534	8	77	0.37	40	27	33	28	113	59	110	9%	74	0%	0%	12	17%	50%	3.26	-15.7	-6	-18	$2
18	Proj	**499**	**65**	**21**	**76**	**0**	**285**	**276**	**365**	**467**	**831**	**955**	**796**	**11**	**79**	**0.58**	**41**	**26**	**34**	**33**	**134**	**102**	**132**	**16%**	**73**	**1%**	**36%**				**6.03**	**13.0**	**29**	**89**	**$19**

Cain,Lorenzo

Age: 32	Bats: R	Pos: CF	Health	B	LIMA Plan B
Ht: 6' 2"	Wt: 205		PT/Exp	A	Rand Var -1
			Consist	C	MM 1535

Return to LoCain ca. 2015? Like then, rode career-high AB to big counting numbers, but 2017's power metrics were decidedly below average. Career high Spd, SB% smell like outliers, though .300 BA possible with 80% ct%, steady LD%, and hit-rate history. Stars aligned for this encore, but 2018 curtain call seems a reach.

Yr	Tm	AB	R	HR	RBI	SB	BA	xBA	OBP	SLG	OPS	vL	vR	bb%	ct%	Eye	G	L	F	h%	HctX	PX	xPX	hr/f	Spd	SBO	SB%	#Wk	DOM	DIS	RC/G	RAR	BPV	BPX	R$
13	KC	399	54	4	46	14	251	247	310	348	658	617	676	7	77	0.37	49	22	29	31	78	76	69	4%	125	19%	70%	24	38%	46%	3.61	-7.5	25	63	$11
14	KC	471	55	5	53	28	301	260	339	412	751	827	720	5	77	0.22	51	23	26	38	72	90	68	5%	130	26%	85%	25	28%	28%	5.20	17.1	31	84	$25
15	KC	551	101	16	72	28	307	283	361	477	838	959	777	6	82	0.38	46	23	31	35	114	108	109	11%	138	23%	82%	26	50%	31%	6.22	26.1	71	192	$35
16	KC	397	56	9	56	14	287	257	339	408	747	1016	668	7	79	0.37	47	23	30	35	96	76	79	9%	96	16%	74%	20	35%	30%	4.91	6.2	21	60	$17
17	KC	584	86	15	49	26	300	269	363	440	803	824	797	8	83	0.54	44	23	33	34	104	76	84	9%	150	15%	93%	27	37%	15%	5.99	20.0	56	170	$28
1st Half		294	45	10	27	15	286	271	359	449	808	616	874	10	81	0.58	45	22	33	32	106	88	89	13%	133	17%	100%	13	31%	15%	6.06	9.5	57	173	$28
2nd Half		290	41	5	22	11	314	267	367	431	798	1113	725	7	84	0.49	44	23	33	36	103	64	79	6%	153	14%	85%	14	43%	14%	5.91	8.0	51	155	$28
18	Proj	**551**	**82**	**11**	**59**	**21**	**297**	**265**	**353**	**422**	**775**	**893**	**737**	**7**	**81**	**0.43**	**46**	**23**	**31**	**35**	**101**	**72**	**84**	**8%**	**131**	**15%**	**82%**				**5.42**	**13.9**	**35**	**107**	**$27**

OSEPH PYTLESKI

Calhoun,Kole

Age: 30	Bats: L	Pos: RF	Health	A	LIMA Plan B+
Ht: 5' 10"	Wt: 205		PT/Exp	A	Rand Var +1
			Consist	B	MM 2235

Posted awful .605 OPS through end of May, then was basically his usual self over last four months (.265/.357/.434). Power, ct% are just average, and he didn't hold 2016's FB% gains. Should return to the right side of .250 BA line, but reliable 20 HR guys just aren't that hard to find today. Unremarkable.

Yr Tm	AB	R	HR	RBI	SB	BA	xBA	OBP	SLG	OPS	vL	vR	bb%	ct%	Eye	G	L	F	h%	HctX	PX	xPX	hr/f	Spd	SBO	SB%	#Wk	DOM	DIS	RC/G	RAR	BPV	BPX	R$
13 LAA *	435	58	15	62	8	274	267	335	443	777	889	782	8	81	0.49	41	23	36	31	133	106	131	14%	96	10%	64%	10	70%	20%	5.10	10.2	57	143	$1
14 LAA *	515	94	18	61	5	276	281	326	456	782	710	793	7	79	0.35	44	24	32	32	99	129	94	13%	98	7%	53%	23	39%	13%	5.11	17.9	64	173	$2
15 LAA	630	78	26	83	4	256	248	308	422	731	663	763	7	74	0.27	42	23	35	31	90	109	116	16%	80	3%	80%	27	26%	37%	4.42	-6.4	22	59	$
16 LAA	594	91	18	75	2	271	261	348	438	786	830	770	10	80	0.57	38	22	40	31	115	100	113	9%	82	3%	40%	27	41%	22%	5.20	8.3	47	134	$1
17 LAA	569	77	19	71	5	244	248	333	392	725	687	741	11	76	0.53	44	21	35	29	98	85	91	12%	83	4%	83%	27	26%	37%	4.36	-9.5	22	67	$
1st Half	311	38	10	39	4	244	249	323	376	699	708	696	10	77	0.50	42	24	35	29	95	75	92	12%	72	4%	100%	13	23%	38%	4.15	-8.4	14	42	$
2nd Half	258	39	9	32	1	244	247	346	411	756	666	801	12	75	0.56	47	18	35	29	102	97	89	13%	95	3%	50%	14	29%	36%	4.62	-3.4	33	100	$
18 Proj	**568**	**81**	**20**	**72**	**4**	**256**	**254**	**333**	**418**	**751**	**721**	**763**	**10**	**77**	**0.48**	**42**	**21**	**36**	**30**	**103**	**92**	**102**	**12%**	**88**	**4%**	**66%**				**4.68**	**-0.3**	**27**	**81**	$1

Calhoun,Willie

Age: 23	Bats: L	Pos: LF	Health	A	LIMA Plan B
Ht: 5' 8"	Wt: 187		PT/Exp	D	Rand Var +4
			Consist	C	MM 2253

1-4-.265 in 34 AB at TEX. Glove still an open question, so long-term position not clear yet. But bat looks ready, and high ct% should yield a solid BA right away. Power may take a little longer to come around, but pedigree offers hope for immediate step forward. If so, we could be looking at... UP: .280 BA, 20 HR

Yr Tm	AB	R	HR	RBI	SB	BA	xBA	OBP	SLG	OPS	vL	vR	bb%	ct%	Eye	G	L	F	h%	HctX	PX	xPX	hr/f	Spd	SBO	SB%	#Wk	DOM	DIS	RC/G	RAR	BPV	BPX	R$
13																																		
14																																		
15																																		
16 aa	503	64	24	75	0	233		284	425	709			7	86	0.50				23		103			82	0%	0%				4.01		65	186	$
17 TEX *	520	64	25	75	3	267	316	313	479	792	606	711	6	86	0.48	56	22	22	27	90	103	57	17%	132	4%	58%	3	33%	67%	5.15	-4.4	80	242	$
1st Half	290	38	14	41	2	268	294	307	493	800			5	85	0.39				27		110			121	6%	67%				5.22		79	239	$
2nd Half	230	27	11	34	1	266	306	321	461	782	606	711	7	87	0.60	56	22	22	27	91	95	57	17%	114	3%	41%	3	33%	67%	5.05	-2.0	73	221	$
18 Proj	**360**	**45**	**15**	**53**	**1**	**267**	**279**	**330**	**448**	**778**	**697**	**817**	**6**	**86**	**0.48**	**44**	**20**	**36**	**28**	**82**	**91**	**51**	**13%**	**125**	**2%**	**58%**				**4.86**	**4.2**	**51**	**154**	$

Camargo,Johan

Age: 24	Bats: B	Pos: 3B SS	Health	A	LIMA Plan D+
Ht: 6' 0"	Wt: 160		PT/Exp	D	Rand Var -1
			Consist	D	MM 1233

4-27-.299 in 241 AB at ATL. Solid debut on the surface, but a couple reasons to expect a step back. High h% was a major factor in success, particularly vL (48% in 72 AB); xPX and FB% suggest not reading too much into 2nd half PX gains. Glove is biggest strength, but not a fantasy asset unless he can turn Spd into SB.

Yr Tm	AB	R	HR	RBI	SB	BA	xBA	OBP	SLG	OPS	vL	vR	bb%	ct%	Eye	G	L	F	h%	HctX	PX	xPX	hr/f	Spd	SBO	SB%	#Wk	DOM	DIS	RC/G	RAR	BPV	BPX	R$
13																																		
14																																		
15																																		
16 aa	446	46	4	43	1	236		277	320	597			5	79	0.26				29		52			119	3%	31%				2.91		4	11	
17 ATL *	370	45	7	44	1	278	265	314	422	736	1129	636	5	79	0.25	48	21	31	34	91	89	64	7%	122	1%	100%	18	39%	33%	4.70	1.8	36	109	
1st Half	204	26	3	29	1	265	250	297	394	691	1032	612	4	79	0.21	45	20	34	32	78	77	48	0%	140	2%	100%	8	25%	50%	4.09	-2.9	29	88	
2nd Half	166	19	4	15	0	295	274	335	458	792	1161	650	6	79	0.29	49	22	29	35	98	105	72	11%	111	0%	0%	10	50%	20%	5.54	4.4	48	145	
18 Proj	**332**	**38**	**5**	**35**	**1**	**264**	**256**	**301**	**387**	**688**	**873**	**612**	**5**	**79**	**0.26**	**47**	**21**	**31**	**32**	**90**	**77**	**62**	**6%**	**128**	**2%**	**54%**				**4.03**	**-8.2**	**10**	**31**	

Candelario,Jeimer

Age: 24	Bats: B	Pos: 3B	Health	A	LIMA Plan B
Ht: 6' 1"	Wt: 210		PT/Exp	D	Rand Var 0
			Consist	B	MM 3125

3-16-.283 in 127 AB at CHC/DET. Struggled initially, but halted downward ct% trend in 2nd half, and hit .326 in 92 AB following Sept call-up. A lofty 39% h% fueled late success, though, and xPX is skeptical of the power (in small MLB sample only). Opportunity should be there, but don't expect immediate impact.

Yr Tm	AB	R	HR	RBI	SB	BA	xBA	OBP	SLG	OPS	vL	vR	bb%	ct%	Eye	G	L	F	h%	HctX	PX	xPX	hr/f	Spd	SBO	SB%	#Wk	DOM	DIS	RC/G	RAR	BPV	BPX	R$
13																																		
14																																		
15 aa	158	17	4	20	0	264		339	412	751			10	85	0.77				29		93			94	0%	0%				4.84		66	178	
16 CHC *	485	58	10	61	0	242	215	325	389	714	500	350	11	76	0.50	67	0	33	30	154	101	100	0%	89	2%	0%	1	0%	100%	4.17	-11.6	34	97	
17 2 TM *	534	65	17	80	1	253	256	323	442	765	922	754	9	73	0.39	45	19	36	32	86	121	77	9%	113	1%	100%	10	50%	40%	4.89	0.5	45	136	$
1st Half	257	30	9	40	0	239	243	317	458	774	873	417	10	71	0.39	29	19	52	30	68	144	105	9%	109	0%	0%	3	67%	33%	4.86	-1.8	53	161	
2nd Half	277	35	7	40	1	267	257	330	427	757	938	860	9	76	0.39	50	18	32	33	93	101	69	8%	106	1%	100%	7	43%	43%	4.92	-1.3	35	106	$
18 Proj	**472**	**56**	**12**	**65**	**1**	**253**	**248**	**342**	**418**	**760**	**953**	**715**	**10**	**76**	**0.47**	**41**	**19**	**40**	**31**	**83**	**104**	**83**	**9%**	**112**	**1%**	**43%**				**4.65**	**-3.4**	**27**	**80**	$

Cano,Robinson

Age: 35	Bats: L	Pos: 2B	Health	A	LIMA Plan B
Ht: 6' 0"	Wt: 210		PT/Exp	A	Rand Var 0
			Consist	C	MM 2055

Appeared to be on way to another 30 HR season until mid-year power outage (147 PA without HR). Long-term scan at PX/xPX shows clearly that 2016 HR total was an outlier. Plate skills and HctX continue to ensure a healthy BA floor, and struggles vL not all his fault (23% h%), but probably best to use 2017 as new baseline.

Yr Tm	AB	R	HR	RBI	SB	BA	xBA	OBP	SLG	OPS	vL	vR	bb%	ct%	Eye	G	L	F	h%	HctX	PX	xPX	hr/f	Spd	SBO	SB%	#Wk	DOM	DIS	RC/G	RAR	BPV	BPX	R$
13 NYY	605	81	27	107	7	314	312	383	516	899	788	969	10	86	0.76	44	26	30	33	138	128	115	17%	77	4%	88%	26	65%	19%	7.34	58.9	90	225	$
14 SEA	595	77	14	82	10	314	301	382	454	836	746	891	9	89	0.90	53	23	25	34	109	95	81	11%	81	7%	77%	27	59%	11%	6.38	48.2	75	203	$
15 SEA	624	82	21	79	2	287	285	334	446	779	715	815	6	83	0.40	50	24	25	32	118	100	107	16%	74	5%	25%	27	52%	11%	5.11	14.7	48	130	$
16 SEA	655	107	39	103	0	298	290	350	533	882	770	955	7	85	0.47	46	18	36	30	122	124	96	19%	74	1%	0%	27	59%	7%	6.63	34.3	76	217	$
17 SEA	592	79	23	97	1	280	281	338	453	791	557	891	8	86	0.58	50	19	31	30	128	91	111	15%	65	1%	100%	26	54%	27%	5.39	12.7	52	158	$
1st Half	286	41	16	57	1	283	285	339	497	835	714	885	8	88	0.71	51	16	33	28	136	103	128	19%	61	1%	100%	12	67%	17%	6.04	9.8	70	212	$
2nd Half	306	38	7	40	0	278	276	337	412	749	418	896	7	84	0.48	49	23	28	31	120	80	94	10%	75	0%	0%	14	43%	36%	4.80	-0.2	38	115	$
18 Proj	**584**	**82**	**23**	**91**	**2**	**284**	**286**	**339**	**462**	**801**	**644**	**882**	**7**	**85**	**0.52**	**49**	**21**	**31**	**30**	**124**	**94**	**104**	**15%**	**71**	**2%**	**55%**				**5.48**	**11.2**	**46**	**139**	$

Caratini,Victor

Age: 24	Bats: B	Pos: CA	Health	A	LIMA Plan D
Ht: 6' 1"	Wt: 215		PT/Exp	F	Rand Var 0
			Consist	C	MM 2341

1-2-.254 in 59 AB at CHC. Made transition to Triple-A look easy, with concurrent upticks in contact and power, an always-promising combo. Bat was quiet in small MLB sample, and power still just average, but there's room for further growth. Plus xBA, HctX suggest a solid BA floor. Sneaky upside here, as early as 2018.

Yr Tm	AB	R	HR	RBI	SB	BA	xBA	OBP	SLG	OPS	vL	vR	bb%	ct%	Eye	G	L	F	h%	HctX	PX	xPX	hr/f	Spd	SBO	SB%	#Wk	DOM	DIS	RC/G	RAR	BPV	BPX	R$
13																																		
14																																		
15																																		
16 aa	412	47	5	39	2	259		333	357	691			10	78	0.51				32		68			96	2%	60%				4.08		17	49	
17 CHC *	351	44	9	49	1	286	281	335	449	783	1183	553	7	80	0.36	65	15	20	34	99	98	61	11%	83	1%	100%	14	21%	43%	5.38	12.9	39	118	$
1st Half	252	34	6	42	0	285	274	327	439	766	0	0	6	81	0.33	100	0	0	33	65	91	-26	0%	85	0%	0%	1	0%	100%	5.12	7.2	35	106	$
2nd Half	99	10	3	7	1	290	287	353	474	827	1183	630	9	78	0.45	61	17	22	35	101	116	71	11%	95	3%	100%	13	23%	38%	6.06	5.4	54	164	
18 Proj	**192**	**22**	**5**	**20**	**1**	**267**	**268**	**361**	**423**	**784**	**841**	**765**	**9**	**79**	**0.45**	**50**	**20**	**30**	**32**	**91**	**95**	**64**	**10%**	**92**	**2%**	**85%**				**4.89**	**4.2**	**31**	**95**	

Carpenter,Matt

Age: 32	Bats: L	Pos: 1B	Health	B	LIMA Plan A
Ht: 6' 3"	Wt: 205		PT/Exp	A	Rand Var +2
			Consist	A	MM 4145

Took swing-for-fences approach to new level with NL-high FB%. In 1st half, that yielded a straight HR-for-BA tradeoff, then bum shoulder in 2nd half muddied the waters. If he goes back to line-drive swing, 2015-16 profile should return. If he keeps uppercutting, then BA will stay near .250, but... UP: 35 HR, still.

Yr Tm	AB	R	HR	RBI	SB	BA	xBA	OBP	SLG	OPS	vL	vR	bb%	ct%	Eye	G	L	F	h%	HctX	PX	xPX	hr/f	Spd	SBO	SB%	#Wk	DOM	DIS	RC/G	RAR	BPV	BPX	R$
13 STL	626	126	11	78	3	318	293	392	481	873	820	897	10	84	0.73	39	27	34	36	117	116	103	6%	129	3%	50%	27	63%	11%	6.89	38.8	91	228	$
14 STL	595	99	8	59	5	272	253	375	375	750	722	762	13	81	0.86	41	24	35	32	117	80	97	5%	114	4%	63%	26	50%	27%	4.86	11.5	53	143	$
15 STL	574	101	28	84	4	272	278	365	505	871	752	926	12	74	0.54	30	29	42	32	119	164	166	16%	98	4%	57%	27	59%	26%	6.32	15.7	82	222	$
16 STL	473	81	21	68	0	271	282	380	505	885	809	920	14	77	0.75	31	26	43	31	131	144	174	13%	88	3%	0%	24	63%	21%	6.46	15.4	81	231	$
17 STL	497	91	23	69	2	241	250	384	451	835	664	883	18	75	0.87	27	22	51	28	128	124	169	12%	97	2%	67%	26	58%	12%	5.71	-2.8	65	197	$
1st Half	260	45	14	40	1	231	256	372	458	829	564	903	18	75	0.86	27	22	51	25	134	131	179	14%	80	2%	50%	13	54%	8%	5.52	-1.0	66	200	$
2nd Half	237	46	9	29	1	253	245	397	443	840	771	860	18	75	0.88	27	23	51	30	121	117	159	10%	118	1%	100%	13	62%	15%	5.93	1.9	66	200	$
18 Proj	**502**	**91**	**26**	**69**	**2**	**260**	**267**	**380**	**497**	**877**	**761**	**919**	**16**	**76**	**0.77**	**30**	**23**	**48**	**29**	**125**	**138**	**162**	**14%**	**103**	**2%**	**47%**				**6.35**	**18.4**	**68**	**207**	$

BRIAN RUDD

Carrera,Ezequiel

Age: 31	Bats: L	Pos: LF RF	Health	B	LIMA Plan	D+
Ht: 5' 11"	Wt: 185		PT/Exp	D	Rand Var	-5
			Consist	B	MM	1523

Stats don't necessarily scream "career year," but this might be as good as it gets. Hit rate fueled BA bump; xBA was not impressed. SB% was unprecedented; at 31, can he really pull off that trick again? Plate skills stagnant, and 2nd half ct% even a bit ominous. He's cheap end-game speed, nothing more.

Yr Tm	AB	R	HR	RBI	SB	BA	xBA	OBP	SLG	OPS	vL	vR	bb%	ct%	Eye	G	L	F	h%	HctX	PX	xPX	hr/f	Spd	SBO	SB%	#Wk	DOM	DIS	RC/G	RAR	BPV	BPX	R$
13 2 TM *	433	49	4	26	35	207	198	260	282	542	0	533	7	75	0.28	42	17	42	27	72	56	131	0%	140	49%	71%	5	0%	100%	2.31	-23.2	1	3	$11
14 DET *	443	62	4	32	38	257	239	316	350	666	866	590	8	80	0.44	60	12	29	31	101	66	77	0%	157	44%	70%	10	20%	50%	3.66	-0.4	38	103	$20
15 TOR *	288	42	4	34	7	258	241	309	343	652	782	675	7	77	0.32	61	17	23	32	80	63	75	11%	99	13%	67%	22	18%	59%	3.59	-6.8	5	14	$7
16 TOR	270	47	6	23	7	248	236	323	356	679	824	626	9	74	0.39	58	17	26	31	76	68	53	13%	129	14%	64%	26	27%	58%	3.73	-4.4	9	26	$6
17 TOR	287	38	8	20	10	282	245	356	408	764	334	825	9	74	0.40	48	23	29	36	77	74	96	14%	129	12%	91%	26	35%	46%	5.24	-1.6	14	42	$10
1st Half	174	18	5	15	4	287	242	354	397	751	333	804	9	77	0.43	52	21	27	35	84	55	94	15%	128	8%	80%	12	25%	42%	5.02	-1.6	10	30	$9
2nd Half	113	20	3	5	6	274	245	359	425	784	313	857	10	69	0.37	42	25	33	37	67	107	99	12%	134	18%	100%	14	43%	50%	5.57	0.7	25	76	$10
18 Proj	**320**	**49**	**7**	**24**	**12**	**257**	**243**	**329**	**376**	**705**	**622**	**723**	**9**	**74**	**0.37**	**52**	**20**	**28**	**33**	**78**	**74**	**81**	**11%**	**129**	**17%**	**80%**				**4.21**	**-2.3**	**7**	**21**	**$9**

Carter,Chris

Age: 31	Bats: R	Pos: 1B	Health	A	LIMA Plan	D
Ht: 6' 4"	Wt: 245		PT/Exp	C	Rand Var	0
			Consist	D	MM	4101

8-21-.201 in 184 AB at NYY. Namesake's series, "The X-Files," came back for another season—will he be as lucky? Hard to keep MLB job with sub-60% ct% when power skills wane across board, and post-release "bounce back" in AAA (.869 OPS) still featured poor ct%. The truth is out there, and it hurts: at 31, may be done.

Yr Tm	AB	R	HR	RBI	SB	BA	xBA	OBP	SLG	OPS	vL	vR	bb%	ct%	Eye	G	L	F	h%	HctX	PX	xPX	hr/f	Spd	SBO	SB%	#Wk	DOM	DIS	RC/G	RAR	BPV	BPX	R$
13 HOU	506	64	29	82	2	223	226	320	451	770	782	765	12	58	0.33	31	22	47	32	95	197	171	21%	81	2%	100%	27	44%	37%	4.72	1.8	40	100	$12
14 HOU	507	68	37	88	5	227	252	308	491	799	869	772	10	64	0.31	27	22	51	27	106	210	171	22%	77	6%	71%	26	50%	31%	4.89	11.5	69	186	$18
15 HOU	391	50	24	64	1	199	223	307	427	734	736	733	12	61	0.38	30	18	52	25	99	177	175	19%	66	3%	33%	27	44%	30%	4.03	-11.2	34	92	$5
16 MIL	549	84	41	94	3	222	245	321	499	821	875	803	12	62	0.37	32	20	49	27	103	194	174	24%	72	3%	75%	27	48%	33%	5.18	5.3	52	149	$14
17 NYY *	315	35	14	41	0	196	187	272	366	638	635	657	9	57	0.24	30	20	50	29	79	122	135	15%	105	0%	0%	14	21%	79%	3.16	-21.9	-22	-67	-$1
1st Half	175	20	8	25	0	206	193	284	383	667	634	678	9	58	0.25	29	20	51	30	82	124	137	15%	106	0%	0%	13	23%	77%	3.44	-12.0	-15	-45	$0
2nd Half	140	15	6	16	0	185	189	263	345	608	667	250	10	55	0.24	50	17	33	29	74	120	99	0%	90	0%	0%	1	0%	100%	2.84	-12.6	-37	-112	-$2
18 Proj	**188**	**24**	**11**	**28**	**0**	**205**	**212**	**295**	**424**	**718**	**723**	**716**	**11**	**59**	**0.29**	**30**	**20**	**50**	**28**	**95**	**152**	**162**	**19%**	**88**	**2%**	**63%**				**3.93**	**-6.9**	**-2**	**-7**	**$3**

Castellanos,Nick

Age: 26	Bats: R	Pos: 3B RF	Health	B	LIMA Plan	B
Ht: 6' 4"	Wt: 210		PT/Exp	A	Rand Var	0
			Consist	C	MM	4145

Has teased us with monster half-season before, but this one might stick. For one thing, it was more than a half-season (.303 BA, 22 HR after 6/1), plus HctX was there all year, and return of FB%, rising ct% in 2nd half adds intrigue. Fool us twice? Perhaps. But given that he's just reaching peak age... UP: .290, 35 HR

Yr Tm	AB	R	HR	RBI	SB	BA	xBA	OBP	SLG	OPS	vL	vR	bb%	ct%	Eye	G	L	F	h%	HctX	PX	xPX	hr/f	Spd	SBO	SB%	#Wk	DOM	DIS	RC/G	RAR	BPV	BPX	R$
13 DET *	551	70	15	65	3	258	242	315	408	723	545	571	8	81	0.44	59	6	35	29	60	106	-15	0%	100	3%	76%	5	0%	20%	4.41	2.1	57	143	$13
14 DET	533	50	11	66	2	259	252	306	394	700	693	702	6	74	0.26	35	29	37	33	108	108	135	8%	105	3%	50%	27	33%	41%	4.10	3.1	27	73	$11
15 DET	549	42	15	73	0	255	243	303	419	721	970	656	7	72	0.26	36	23	40	33	103	118	118	9%	98	2%	0%	27	33%	37%	4.26	-8.1	28	76	$9
16 DET	411	54	18	58	1	285	260	331	496	827	656	894	6	73	0.25	31	26	43	35	106	135	166	14%	128	2%	50%	20	50%	35%	5.80	12.6	53	151	$13
17 DET	614	73	26	101	4	272	274	320	490	811	934	775	6	77	0.29	37	25	38	32	135	122	142	14%	124	7%	44%	27	52%	30%	5.30	6.6	57	173	$19
1st Half	300	38	9	40	2	247	264	312	430	742	803	725	8	73	0.31	41	26	33	31	144	112	136	13%	133	6%	50%	13	46%	31%	4.34	-6.4	39	118	$11
2nd Half	314	35	17	61	2	296	286	328	548	876	1054	824	5	81	0.26	34	23	43	32	127	132	148	15%	114	7%	40%	14	57%	29%	6.33	11.2	74	224	$26
18 Proj	**590**	**67**	**27**	**93**	**3**	**277**	**269**	**323**	**498**	**821**	**875**	**804**	**6**	**76**	**0.28**	**35**	**24**	**41**	**33**	**120**	**127**	**144**	**15%**	**117**	**5%**	**42%**				**5.55**	**11.1**	**41**	**123**	**$21**

Castillo,Welington

Age: 31	Bats: R	Pos: CA	Health	B	LIMA Plan	C
Ht: 5' 10"	Wt: 220		PT/Exp	C	Rand Var	-5
			Consist	B	MM	3233

Withstood series of injuries to post new career highs in HR, BA. Though he has history of similar power skills (see 2015), 2nd half hr/f likely unsustainable, and stable multi-year xBA says BA could recede a bit; his plate skills are nothing to write home about, after all. Nonetheless, a solid investment at offense-challenged position.

Yr Tm	AB	R	HR	RBI	SB	BA	xBA	OBP	SLG	OPS	vL	vR	bb%	ct%	Eye	G	L	F	h%	HctX	PX	xPX	hr/f	Spd	SBO	SB%	#Wk	DOM	DIS	RC/G	RAR	BPV	BPX	R$
13 CHC	380	41	8	32	2	274	240	349	397	746	707	758	8	74	0.35	44	22	34	35	112	99	110	8%	66	2%	100%	25	32%	40%	4.68	10.4	15	38	$8
14 CHC	380	28	13	46	0	237	228	296	389	686	855	631	6	73	0.25	41	19	40	29	103	118	121	12%	58	0%	0%	24	38%	33%	3.72	4.5	19	51	$5
15 3 TM	342	42	19	57	0	237	253	296	453	750	778	739	7	73	0.27	42	18	40	27	121	142	152	19%	61	0%	0%	27	37%	37%	4.37	6.5	39	105	$8
16 ARI	416	41	14	68	2	264	250	322	423	745	868	698	7	71	0.27	42	25	33	34	115	110	128	14%	65	2%	100%	25	32%	48%	4.70	10.0	8	23	$10
17 BAL	341	44	20	53	0	282	256	323	490	813	937	767	6	72	0.23	39	24	36	34	113	119	130	22%	64	0%	0%	25	32%	56%	5.65	14.5	15	45	$11
1st Half	180	21	8	25	0	272	251	307	439	746	772	736	5	72	0.18	39	26	35	34	110	97	104	18%	64	0%	0%	12	17%	58%	4.72	3.2	-3	-9	$8
2nd Half	161	23	12	28	0	292	262	341	547	887	1105	801	7	71	0.28	40	22	38	34	116	144	159	27%	71	0%	0%	13	46%	54%	6.79	12.0	37	112	$14
18 Proj	**392**	**46**	**20**	**61**	**1**	**264**	**254**	**315**	**464**	**779**	**897**	**735**	**7**	**72**	**0.25**	**41**	**23**	**36**	**32**	**114**	**118**	**135**	**20%**	**62**	**1%**	**100%**				**5.04**	**10.2**	**6**	**17**	**$13**

Castro,Jason

Age: 31	Bats: L	Pos: CA	Health	A	LIMA Plan	D+
Ht: 6' 3"	Wt: 215		PT/Exp	C	Rand Var	0
			Consist	A	MM	3213

Yanked ct% out of tailspin, but he'll never be mistaken for batting champ, or really, even the .265 hitter he was in 2nd half (see h%). Second-half power outage concerning; if not for double-digit HR, would be little reason to draft. Defense, contract will keep AB coming, but you may not want them as part of YOUR totals.

Yr Tm	AB	R	HR	RBI	SB	BA	xBA	OBP	SLG	OPS	vL	vR	bb%	ct%	Eye	G	L	F	h%	HctX	PX	xPX	hr/f	Spd	SBO	SB%	#Wk	DOM	DIS	RC/G	RAR	BPV	BPX	R$
13 HOU	435	63	18	56	2	276	270	350	485	835	738	864	10	70	0.38	39	25	35	36	109	167	140	17%	85	3%	67%	23	61%	22%	5.96	27.8	62	155	$15
14 HOU	465	43	14	56	1	222	225	286	366	651	619	662	7	68	0.23	45	20	36	30	87	119	110	12%	99	1%	100%	26	35%	54%	3.30	-0.3	10	27	$5
15 HOU	337	38	11	31	0	211	229	283	365	648	512	707	9	66	0.29	37	24	38	28	90	124	121	13%	77	0%	0%	25	32%	44%	3.31	-4.3	5	14	$0
16 HOU	329	41	11	32	2	210	222	307	377	684	478	757	12	63	0.37	46	20	34	30	90	124	102	16%	104	4%	67%	26	31%	46%	3.69	-1.7	7	20	$1
17 MIN	356	49	10	47	0	242	242	333	388	720	737	714	11	70	0.42	42	25	33	32	102	101	112	12%	80	0%	0%	26	38%	50%	4.26	1.2	7	21	$4
1st Half	194	21	6	28	0	222	245	314	381	695	633	719	11	69	0.42	40	25	35	29	106	111	140	13%	68	0%	0%	13	38%	46%	3.88	-1.3	10	30	$2
2nd Half	162	28	4	19	0	265	238	355	395	750	876	707	11	70	0.42	45	24	32	35	96	89	79	11%	101	0%	0%	13	38%	54%	4.75	3.0	7	21	$6
18 Proj	**363**	**48**	**11**	**42**	**1**	**233**	**234**	**319**	**387**	**706**	**646**	**727**	**11**	**67**	**0.37**	**43**	**23**	**34**	**31**	**96**	**106**	**108**	**13%**	**89**	**1%**	**68%**				**4.04**	**-1.1**	**-6**	**-18**	**$6**

Castro,Starlin

Age: 28	Bats: R	Pos: 2B	Health	B	LIMA Plan	B
Ht: 6' 2"	Wt: 230		PT/Exp	B	Rand Var	-5
			Consist	B	MM	2235

16-63-.300 in 443 AB at NYY. Pinstripe park factor poster boy: for 2016-17, .315 BA/25 HR at home, .252/12 away. Only 28, but lack of upside abounds: stagnant Eye, h%-driven BA, HR-capping GB%, non-existent running game. Established mid-teens HR totals for now, but if he escapes Bronx Zoo, really start to worry.

Yr Tm	AB	R	HR	RBI	SB	BA	xBA	OBP	SLG	OPS	vL	vR	bb%	ct%	Eye	G	L	F	h%	HctX	PX	xPX	hr/f	Spd	SBO	SB%	#Wk	DOM	DIS	RC/G	RAR	BPV	BPX	R$
13 CHC	666	59	10	44	9	245	249	284	347	631	619	635	4	81	0.23	51	20	29	29	106	75	99	6%	103	10%	60%	27	33%	41%	3.18	-11.0	24	60	$9
14 CHC	528	58	14	65	4	292	272	339	438	777	788	773	6	81	0.35	45	23	32	34	102	107	105	10%	82	6%	50%	23	43%	26%	5.17	26.3	49	132	$19
15 CHC	547	52	11	69	5	265	251	296	375	671	643	679	4	83	0.23	54	17	29	30	86	70	75	8%	98	8%	50%	27	22%	41%	3.69	-9.3	28	76	$13
16 NYY	577	63	21	70	4	270	267	300	433	734	740	731	4	80	0.20	49	20	30	31	101	97	91	15%	90	3%	100%	25	44%	28%	4.58	-2.5	33	94	$15
17 NYY *	474	69	17	65	2	299	263	333	450	783	836	778	5	79	0.24	52	20	28	35	93	84	69	16%	100	2%	100%	22	41%	32%	5.48	11.0	24	73	$17
1st Half	294	52	12	45	1	313	267	348	486	835	724	864	5	80	0.25	49	19	32	36	105	94	82	16%	102	1%	100%	13	46%	31%	6.28	11.5	36	109	$25
2nd Half	180	17	5	20	1	276	253	310	392	702	995	588	5	78	0.22	58	21	21	33	70	66	42	17%	94	2%	100%	9	33%	33%	4.31	-2.6	3	9	$5
18 Proj	**535**	**62**	**18**	**66**	**3**	**274**	**264**	**311**	**420**	**732**	**805**	**706**	**5**	**80**	**0.24**	**52**	**20**	**28**	**32**	**91**	**81**	**73**	**15%**	**94**	**4%**	**75%**				**4.54**	**-4.0**	**14**	**42**	**$17**

Cervelli,Francisco

Age: 32	Bats: R	Pos: CA	Health	F	LIMA Plan	D+
Ht: 6' 1"	Wt: 210		PT/Exp	C	Rand Var	0
			Consist	B	MM	1223

Recaptured some of 2016's lost HctX, power in 1st half; but by 2nd half, frequent DL trips (concussion, wrist, quad) took toll. Contact rate should rebound, but "F" health grade cautions next nick always right around corner. Owed $21 million through 2019; if not for that, transition to "veteran backup" may have already begun.

Yr Tm	AB	R	HR	RBI	SB	BA	xBA	OBP	SLG	OPS	vL	vR	bb%	ct%	Eye	G	L	F	h%	HctX	PX	xPX	hr/f	Spd	SBO	SB%	#Wk	DOM	DIS	RC/G	RAR	BPV	BPX	R$
13 NYY	52	12	3	8	0	269	300	377	500	877	684	1017	13	83	0.89	30	28	42	28	145	145	148	17%	87	0%	0%	4	100%	0%	6.40	4.0	101	253	$0
14 NYY *	172	19	2	13	1	274	247	328	384	712	735	830	7	73	0.30	44	26	30	36	112	97	126	6%	97	2%	100%	17	47%	35%	4.46	4.9	16	43	$2
15 PIT	451	56	7	43	1	295	249	370	401	771	856	747	9	79	0.49	52	21	27	36	106	69	100	7%	128	1%	50%	27	22%	41%	5.20	17.2	30	81	$13
16 PIT	326	42	1	33	6	264	236	377	322	699	888	663	14	78	0.78	56	20	24	34	86	44	59	2%	99	6%	75%	21	24%	43%	4.18	-2.1	7	20	$6
17 PIT	265	31	5	31	0	249	246	342	370	712	677	722	11	75	0.49	52	21	27	31	100	75	101	9%	106	3%	0%	20	35%	40%	4.02	-0.2	17	52	$2
1st Half	168	20	3	21	0	250	264	345	381	726	623	754	12	80	0.65	48	22	30	30	124	81	127	8%	93	4%	0%	12	50%	17%	4.16	0.3	37	112	$3
2nd Half	97	11	2	10	0	247	216	336	351	687	762	663	9	68	0.32	62	17	22	34	58	62	47	14%	123	0%	0%	8	13%	75%	3.77	-0.9	-21	-64	$1
18 Proj	**312**	**37**	**5**	**32**	**2**	**262**	**242**	**352**	**368**	**720**	**759**	**709**	**11**	**75**	**0.48**	**54**	**20**	**26**	**33**	**92**	**66**	**83**	**8%**	**111**	**3%**	**56%**				**4.30**	**1.4**	**-4**	**-11**	**$7**

RISTOPHER OLSON

Cespedes,Yoenis

Age: 32 Bats: R Pos: LF
Ht: 5' 10" Wt: 220

Health	D	LIMA Plan	B+
PT/Exp	B	Rand Var	-2
Consist	A	MM	4145

Second year in a row that leg injuries cut into AB and SBO, and at his age, odds are against full rebound for either. Extreme FB% should keep power intact as main source of value, though xBA shows that approach could take a bite out of BA. There's enough risk here that you can't assume he'll be a $20 player again.

Yr	Tm	AB	R	HR	RBI	SB	BA	xBA	OBP	SLG	OPS	vL	vR	bb%	ct%	Eye	G	L	F	h%	HctX	PX	xPX	hr/f	Spd	SBO	SB%	#Wk	DOM	DIS	RC/G	RAR	BPV	BPX
13	OAK	529	74	26	80	7	240	244	294	442	737	880	672	6	74	0.27	38	17	46	28	98	136	127	14%	114	12%	50%	24	46%	29%	4.11	0.9	54	135
14	2 AL	600	89	22	100	7	260	255	301	450	751	666	777	5	79	0.27	34	18	48	30	106	134	127	10%	109	7%	78%	27	56%	11%	4.66	15.2	67	181
15	2 TM	633	101	35	105	7	291	289	328	542	870	736	909	5	78	0.23	42	20	38	33	123	160	131	19%	96	9%	58%	27	56%	22%	6.20	26.4	80	216
16	NYM	479	72	31	86	3	280	280	354	530	884	1081	839	9	77	0.47	37	21	41	30	123	145	137	20%	73	3%	75%	24	58%	17%	6.54	25.9	69	197
17	NYM	291	46	17	42	0	292	264	352	540	892	906	886	8	79	0.43	34	16	50	32	135	134	159	15%	94	1%	0%	16	63%	19%	6.71	11.8	70	212
1st Half		132	20	9	19	0	288	260	349	553	902	1026	848	8	81	0.48	30	13	57	30	137	140	168	15%	69	3%	0%	8	75%	13%	6.67	4.9	76	230
2nd Half		159	26	8	23	0	296	267	354	528	883	781	915	8	77	0.39	39	19	43	34	134	128	151	15%	107	0%	0%	8	50%	25%	6.74	6.1	62	188
18	Proj	**485**	**75**	**28**	**77**	**2**	**285**	**269**	**342**	**528**	**870**	**895**	**863**	**8**	**78**	**0.38**	**37**	**18**	**45**	**31**	**127**	**133**	**146**	**16%**	**92**	**3%**	**52%**				**6.32**	**25.5**	**57**	**174**

Chapman,Matt

Age: 25 Bats: R Pos: 3B
Ht: 6' 0" Wt: 210

Health	A	LIMA Plan	B
PT/Exp	D	Rand Var	0
Consist	B	MM	4205

14-40-.234 in 290 AB at OAK. 5th-highest FB% among players w/200+ PA, but more pedestrian hr/f, HctX suggest that he didn't fully tap into elite power potential. All those fly balls and history of poor ct% make BA struggles likely to continue; if you can withstand that hit... UP: 30 HR

Yr	Tm	AB	R	HR	RBI	SB	BA	xBA	OBP	SLG	OPS	vL	vR	bb%	ct%	Eye	G	L	F	h%	HctX	PX	xPX	hr/f	Spd	SBO	SB%	#Wk	DOM	DIS	RC/G	RAR	BPV	BPX
13																																		
14																																		
15																																		
16	a/a	514	77	27	80	6	210		287	434	721			10	64	0.30				27		156			103	10%	57%				3.92		34	97
17	OAK *	465	63	25	64	4	228	233	305	469	774	786	785	10	65	0.32	34	16	51	29	95	159	134	14%	113	11%	34%	16	56%	25%	4.45	-5.8	44	133
1st Half		189	26	11	27	4	218	227	297	450	747	250	697	10	60	0.28	29	29	43	29	104	156	45	0%	111	20%	46%	2	0%	100%	4.02	-6.4	20	61
2nd Half		276	37	14	37	0	236	247	313	482	795	807	790	10	69	0.35	34	16	51	29	100	160	137	14%	107	5%	0%	14	64%	14%	4.76	-2.7	59	179
18	Proj	**536**	**76**	**22**	**78**	**5**	**236**	**221**	**313**	**433**	**747**	**758**	**742**	**10**	**67**	**0.33**	**35**	**17**	**49**	**31**	**90**	**129**	**123**	**13%**	**118**	**10%**	**42%**				**4.30**	**-9.7**	**19**	**56**

Chirinos,Robinson

Age: 34 Bats: R Pos: CA
Ht: 6' 1" Wt: 210

Health	C	LIMA Plan	D+
PT/Exp	F	Rand Var	-3
Consist	D	MM	4113

Skills that led to career-best power outburst were already on display in other seasons, but 2H drops in FB%, xPX, and hr/f were sharp enough to question whether this window of opportunity has already closed. He's 34 and timing is everything. You don't want to be the one who pays peak price for a post-peak performance.

Yr	Tm	AB	R	HR	RBI	SB	BA	xBA	OBP	SLG	OPS	vL	vR	bb%	ct%	Eye	G	L	F	h%	HctX	PX	xPX	hr/f	Spd	SBO	SB%	#Wk	DOM	DIS	RC/G	RAR	BPV	BPX
13	TEX *	293	26	6	27	1	199	194	269	305	574	445	583	9	75	0.37	24	19	57	25	100	77	175	0%	93	2%	100%	8	38%	38%	2.63	-9.9	8	20
14	TEX	306	36	13	40	0	239	259	290	415	705	759	682	5	77	0.24	42	21	37	27	100	126	129	15%	72	2%	0%	26	35%	38%	3.81	4.5	42	114
15	TEX	233	33	10	34	0	232	253	325	438	762	845	717	10	73	0.45	35	19	45	27	89	145	133	13%	86	0%	0%	19	53%	26%	4.57	5.8	58	157
16	TEX *	168	21	9	20	0	206	240	271	432	703	823	791	8	69	0.29	40	14	45	24	111	155	156	19%	68	3%	0%	19	42%	47%	3.65	-1.1	37	106
17	TEX	263	46	17	38	1	255	246	360	506	866	1113	775	11	70	0.43	40	14	46	30	100	150	124	20%	102	1%	100%	26	50%	38%	5.91	13.6	55	167
1st Half		108	24	12	25	0	231	267	325	593	918	930	914	9	70	0.34	32	11	57	20	116	199	183	28%	72	0%	0%	13	62%	31%	5.95	6.0	83	252
2nd Half		155	22	5	13	1	271	233	384	445	829	1234	678	13	70	0.49	46	16	39	36	90	115	84	12%	118	2%	100%	13	38%	46%	5.73	7.2	34	103
18	Proj	**315**	**42**	**15**	**39**	**1**	**246**	**236**	**338**	**453**	**791**	**941**	**739**	**10**	**71**	**0.38**	**40**	**15**	**45**	**30**	**101**	**128**	**134**	**15%**	**88**	**2%**	**56%**				**4.89**	**7.0**	**23**	**69**

Chisenhall,Lonnie

Age: 29 Bats: L Pos: RF
Ht: 6' 2" Wt: 190

Health	C	LIMA Plan	B
PT/Exp	D	Rand Var	-3
Consist	C	MM	4235

12-53-.288 in 236 AB at CLE. With career highs in HctX, FB%, PX/xPX, hr/f, and gains vL, this was his best skill season. While he traded ct% to get there, xBA remained stable, albeit mediocre. Three DL stints kept counting stats from fully reflecting growth, and if xPX is right about power potential... UP: 25 HR

Yr	Tm	AB	R	HR	RBI	SB	BA	xBA	OBP	SLG	OPS	vL	vR	bb%	ct%	Eye	G	L	F	h%	HctX	PX	xPX	hr/f	Spd	SBO	SB%	#Wk	DOM	DIS	RC/G	RAR	BPV	BPX
13	CLE *	394	48	16	58	3	256	262	302	445	747	408	705	6	79	0.31	38	20	42	29	83	130	92	11%	107	3%	100%	22	68%	23%	4.64	7.6	64	160
14	CLE	478	62	13	59	3	280	261	343	427	770	729	782	7	79	0.39	38	24	38	33	83	109	93	9%	100	3%	75%	27	56%	22%	5.06	18.4	51	138
15	CLE *	490	53	9	61	5	245	239	291	371	662	624	676	6	78	0.29	41	20	40	30	80	92	74	7%	93	5%	83%	21	38%	43%	3.67	-10.5	26	70
16	CLE *	408	45	8	60	6	274	257	317	421	738	642	784	6	82	0.35	35	24	41	32	87	90	77	6%	122	6%	100%	25	48%	20%	4.78	5.8	48	137
17	CLE *	279	38	13	56	3	279	253	340	491	831	967	857	8	76	0.39	39	16	46	33	104	125	145	14%	104	7%	58%	18	28%	28%	5.79	2.7	55	167
1st Half		187	26	10	44	3	294	259	355	528	883	1051	903	9	78	0.43	37	15	48	33	103	132	149	16%	113	7%	73%	11	36%	36%	6.73	7.2	70	212
2nd Half		92	11	3	12	0	249	238	309	414	723	769	751	8	73	0.33	43	17	40	31	106	110	134	10%	94	5%	0%	7	14%	14%	4.15	-3.3	27	82
18	Proj	**422**	**51**	**19**	**65**	**4**	**266**	**262**	**322**	**480**	**803**	**783**	**806**	**7**	**77**	**0.34**	**38**	**18**	**44**	**30**	**100**	**124**	**110**	**14%**	**103**	**6%**	**66%**				**5.27**	**7.1**	**46**	**139**

Choo,Shin-Soo

Age: 35 Bats: L Pos: RF DH
Ht: 5' 11" Wt: 210

Health	F	LIMA Plan	B
PT/Exp	B	Rand Var	0
Consist	C	MM	2235

Hit career bests in HR, hr/f despite lowest full-season FB% and second-lowest xPX, but it "wasn't the balls." Posted double-digit SB thanks to second-best SB%. That's a lot going right at an age when things are more likely to go wrong, and you don't have to look beyond this box to see what happens when his health/skills go south.

Yr	Tm	AB	R	HR	RBI	SB	BA	xBA	OBP	SLG	OPS	vL	vR	bb%	ct%	Eye	G	L	F	h%	HctX	PX	xPX	hr/f	Spd	SBO	SB%	#Wk	DOM	DIS	RC/G	RAR	BPV	BPX
13	CIN	569	107	21	54	20	285	273	423	462	885	612	1011	16	77	0.84	49	21	29	34	97	126	101	16%	113	14%	65%	27	59%	15%	6.46	32.0	75	188
14	TEX	455	58	13	40	3	242	236	340	374	714	673	732	11	71	0.44	50	20	30	31	113	104	109	13%	89	5%	43%	21	29%	43%	4.01	-0.5	19	51
15	TEX	555	94	22	82	4	276	267	375	463	838	708	917	12	74	0.52	51	21	28	34	105	130	122	19%	85	3%	67%	27	48%	33%	5.89	6.9	49	132
16	TEX *	209	28	8	21	7	251	250	340	403	743	1016	665	11	74	0.51	47	22	31	31	129	96	127	18%	73	19%	55%	13	23%	62%	4.38	-7.0	19	54
17	TEX	544	96	22	78	12	261	268	357	423	780	752	787	12	75	0.57	49	25	26	31	110	92	107	20%	80	9%	80%	26	35%	38%	5.18	4.9	25	76
1st Half		258	45	12	41	6	256	265	374	426	801	622	847	15	74	0.71	50	25	26	30	111	92	97	24%	87	9%	75%	13	38%	38%	5.42	4.2	30	91
2nd Half		286	51	10	37	6	266	270	341	420	760	856	731	9	76	0.44	48	25	27	32	109	91	116	17%	78	9%	86%	13	31%	38%	4.95	0.7	22	67
18	Proj	**464**	**76**	**18**	**59**	**7**	**262**	**263**	**359**	**427**	**786**	**805**	**779**	**12**	**75**	**0.52**	**49**	**23**	**28**	**32**	**113**	**97**	**115**	**19%**	**80**	**8%**	**68%**				**5.09**	**5.3**	**25**	**74**

Conforto,Michael

Age: 25 Bats: L Pos: LF CF
Ht: 6' 1" Wt: 215

Health	B	LIMA Plan	B+
PT/Exp	C	Rand Var	-2
Consist	D	MM	4145

Shoulder surgery brought curtain down early on breakout season, and casts doubt on whether he'll be ready by Opening Day. He's finally overcome Mets' lack of confidence and has 40 HR upside in his bat, but skills vL (59% contact, 0.20 Eye) and health questions mean 500 AB mark may once again prove elusive.

Yr	Tm	AB	R	HR	RBI	SB	BA	xBA	OBP	SLG	OPS	vL	vR	bb%	ct%	Eye	G	L	F	h%	HctX	PX	xPX	hr/f	Spd	SBO	SB%	#Wk	DOM	DIS	RC/G	RAR	BPV	BPX
13																																		
14																																		
15	NYM *	347	48	13	48	1	277	274	346	479	825	481	872	10	77	0.47	39	23	39	32	137	137	157	17%	95	2%	46%	12	83%	17%	5.80	9.3	69	186
16	NYM *	432	59	19	61	3	257	250	329	459	788	295	804	9	74	0.41	36	19	45	31	121	129	157	12%	71	6%	50%	22	36%	41%	5.06	4.8	42	120
17	NYM	373	72	27	68	2	279	276	384	555	939	729	1012	13	70	0.50	38	24	38	33	117	166	141	27%	86	2%	100%	20	50%	20%	7.39	23.2	65	197
1st Half		221	47	14	41	2	285	272	405	548	953	875	974	15	70	0.57	38	24	38	35	125	162	169	23%	99	3%	100%	13	54%	23%	7.68	16.3	69	209
2nd Half		152	25	13	27	0	270	282	351	566	917	581	1077	11	70	0.41	38	25	37	30	107	171	101	33%	74	0%	0%	7	43%	14%	6.93	8.1	62	188
18	Proj	**467**	**75**	**29**	**75**	**2**	**269**	**271**	**356**	**521**	**877**	**583**	**954**	**11**	**72**	**0.45**	**37**	**22**	**40**	**31**	**120**	**149**	**143**	**21%**	**79**	**3%**	**62%**				**6.33**	**25.2**	**51**	**153**

Contreras,Willson

Age: 26 Bats: R Pos: CA
Ht: 6' 1" Wt: 210

Health	A	LIMA Plan	B
PT/Exp	C	Rand Var	0
Consist	A	MM	4155

Overall, looked like more of the same, but 2H breakout (which was shortened by hamstring injury) adds intriguing skill growth to the mix. Plate discipline, power, .300 BA w/skill support, and a dash of SBO, all from a catcher? You can't go all in on 152 AB, but if you're looking for a reason to go an extra buck, this is it.

Yr	Tm	AB	R	HR	RBI	SB	BA	xBA	OBP	SLG	OPS	vL	vR	bb%	ct%	Eye	G	L	F	h%	HctX	PX	xPX	hr/f	Spd	SBO	SB%	#Wk	DOM	DIS	RC/G	RAR	BPV	BPX
13																																		
14																																		
15	aa	454	56	7	59	3	297		361	422	784			9	84	0.65				34		85			94	5%	41%				5.37		54	146
16	CHC *	456	63	19	67	5	290	276	357	488	845	854	841	9	77	0.45	54	18	28	34	101	121	105	24%	109	9%	43%	17	41%	29%	5.97	20.2	58	166
17	CHC	377	50	21	74	5	276	268	356	499	855	916	828	11	74	0.46	53	17	29	32	106	131	101	26%	77	8%	56%	22	45%	27%	6.03	21.4	47	142
1st Half		225	27	10	40	2	253	252	320	453	773	826	748	8	71	0.31	54	16	30	31	97	128	89	21%	81	6%	67%	13	38%	38%	4.83	4.8	30	91
2nd Half		152	23	11	34	3	309	290	407	566	973	1075	934	14	78	0.76	52	20	28	33	120	134	118	33%	81	11%	50%	9	56%	11%	8.07	16.8	75	227
18	Proj	**436**	**59**	**25**	**76**	**5**	**289**	**285**	**372**	**527**	**899**	**944**	**880**	**11**	**77**	**0.55**	**53**	**18**	**29**	**32**	**107**	**132**	**106**	**26%**	**90**	**9%**	**48%**				**6.69**	**31.6**	**56**	**170**

BRANDON KRUSE

Cordero,Franchy

Age: 23 Bats: L Pos: CF | Ht: 6' 3" Wt: 175

Health A | PT/Exp F | Consist B | LIMA Plan D | Rand Var -2 | MM 3521

3-9-.228 with 1 SB in 92 AB at SD. Reasons to look past the 52% ct% in his MLB debut? Youth, triple-digit xPX and Spd, hope in HctX and hr/f. Of course he'll need to clean up the swing, be more patient, and get caught less on the basepaths. But that's what another year of AAA is for. Raw tools defined; patience required.

Yr	Tm	AB	R	HR	RBI	SB	BA	xBA	OBP	SLG	OPS	vL	vR	bb%	ct%	Eye	G	L	F	h%	HctX	PX	xPX	hr/f	Spd	SBO	SB%	#Wk	DOM	DIS	RC/G	RAR	BPV	BPX	R$
13																																			
14																																			
15																																			
16	a/a	258	25	5	15	9	264		305	387	693			6	70	0.20				36		76			147	24%	59%				3.84		0	0	$6
17	SD *	482	62	14	53	11	264	229	295	453	748	610	718	4	63	0.12	48	19	33	39	99	123	125	19%	188	17%	67%	7	29%	57%	4.52	-7.5	18	55	$13
1st Half		272	34	8	25	6	245	213	287	407	694	610	712	6	60	0.15	49	20	31	38	95	110	118	21%	188	16%	66%	6	17%	67%	3.85	-8.7	-3	-9	$12
2nd Half		210	28	7	28	5	289	196	307	513	820	0	800	2	68	0.08	33	0	67	40	91	139	223	0%	168	18%	68%	1	100%	0%	5.50	3.5	40	121	$16
18	**Proj**	**134**	**16**	**4**	**12**	**3**	**239**	**240**	**273**	**426**	**699**	**595**	**723**	**4**	**67**	**0.14**	**49**	**20**	**31**	**32**	**86**	**115**	**106**	**15%**	**175**	**16%**	**68%**				**3.82**	**-2.8**	**6**	**18**	**$1**

Correa,Carlos

Age: 23 Bats: R Pos: SS | Ht: 6' 4" Wt: 215

Health B | PT/Exp B | Consist C | LIMA Plan B+ | Rand Var -3 | MM 4355

24-84-.315 in 422 AB at HOU. Missed nary a beat after six weeks out with torn thumb ligament. Big leap forward in HctX pushed BA over .300, and fueled better power outcomes even though xPX remained skeptical. Batting cleanup has silenced his speed game, but it's a trade-off worth making. Four-category superstar.

Yr	Tm	AB	R	HR	RBI	SB	BA	xBA	OBP	SLG	OPS	vL	vR	bb%	ct%	Eye	G	L	F	h%	HctX	PX	xPX	hr/f	Spd	SBO	SB%	#Wk	DOM	DIS	RC/G	RAR	BPV	BPX	R$
13																																			
14																																			
15	HOU *	602	85	30	101	28	287	302	352	517	869	899	836	9	80	0.50	49	22	29	32	115	146	103	24%	91	21%	84%	18	67%	6%	6.59	37.4	83	224	$36
16	HOU	577	76	20	96	13	274	275	361	451	811	730	839	11	76	0.54	50	22	27	33	115	113	100	17%	109	9%	81%	26	46%	31%	5.69	22.9	51	146	$22
17	HOU *	446	84	24	88	2	312	283	386	535	921	1077	906	11	78	0.55	48	20	32	35	125	125	108	23%	94	2%	67%	20	60%	20%	7.62	36.1	63	191	$23
1st Half		293	56	17	55	0	311	278	388	543	931	958	923	11	78	0.58	48	19	33	35	127	126	112	22%	94	0%	0%	13	62%	15%	7.79	25.4	66	200	$28
2nd Half		153	28	7	33	2	313	292	381	522	903	1392	867	10	78	0.49	47	25	28	37	120	123	99	24%	101	6%	67%	7	57%	29%	7.30	11.3	62	188	$12
18	**Proj**	**595**	**95**	**28**	**110**	**6**	**295**	**287**	**370**	**509**	**878**	**953**	**854**	**11**	**77**	**0.52**	**49**	**22**	**29**	**34**	**119**	**123**	**103**	**21%**	**100**	**4%**	**86%**				**6.83**	**39.0**	**55**	**167**	**$30**

Cowart,Kaleb

Age: 26 Bats: B Pos: 2B 3B | Ht: 6' 3" Wt: 225

Health A | PT/Exp D | Consist B | LIMA Plan D | Rand Var 0 | MM 2311

3-11-.225 with 4 SB in 102 AB at LAA. Has conquered AAA (.840 OPS in past 3 seasons), but the final ascent is the toughest. Added some pop and positional versatility, though a poor approach is easier to surmount in Salt Lake City than in the majors. Still taking small steps, but the point of diminishing returns is looming.

Yr	Tm	AB	R	HR	RBI	SB	BA	xBA	OBP	SLG	OPS	vL	vR	bb%	ct%	Eye	G	L	F	h%	HctX	PX	xPX	hr/f	Spd	SBO	SB%	#Wk	DOM	DIS	RC/G	RAR	BPV	BPX	R$
13	aa	498	42	5	37	12	201		249	270	520			6	73	0.24				27		57			92	16%	69%				2.14		-19	-48	$0
14	aa	435	42	5	48	23	205		266	293	559			8	75	0.33				26		69			103	30%	75%				2.53		4	11	$7
15	LAA *	266	32	5	35	2	250	204	314	367	680	340	685	9	64	0.26	59	11	30	37	40	98	39	13%	87	6%	52%	7	0%	71%	3.83	-5.8	-19	-51	$4
16	LAA *	499	51	7	51	13	221	224	261	342	603	667	378	5	71	0.19	47	16	37	30	64	90	72	4%	92	19%	74%	9	11%	78%	2.91	-29.1	-2	-6	$5
17	LAA *	469	63	11	50	17	241	240	300	370	670	377	762	8	75	0.33	47	19	34	30	91	82	128	12%	90	22%	68%	12	33%	42%	3.65	-17.2	9	27	$12
1st Half		299	34	5	27	11	250	305	307	359	665	0	2500	8	75	0.33	0	67	33	32	101	74	223	0%	89	24%	61%	1	100%	0%	3.56	-13.9	3	9	$13
2nd Half		170	29	6	23	6	226	246	289	391	680	399	714	8	74	0.34	49	17	34	27	90	96	124	13%	103	18%	86%	11	27%	45%	3.80	-6.7	22	67	$9
18	**Proj**	**195**	**25**	**6**	**22**	**6**	**230**	**235**	**299**	**378**	**678**	**612**	**693**	**7**	**72**	**0.28**	**48**	**17**	**35**	**29**	**80**	**94**	**103**	**11%**	**97**	**18%**	**72%**				**3.54**	**-7.5**	**10**	**30**	**$5**

Cozart,Zack

Age: 32 Bats: R Pos: SS | Ht: 6' 0" Wt: 204

Health D | PT/Exp C | Consist D | LIMA Plan B+ | Rand Var -4 | MM 3345

Has taken skills to a new level the past several seasons, but his body has broken down. Had a 2-DL quad strain in 2017, but still notched career highs in several categories. Expect some BA pullback as h% self-corrects, and HR pullback as 2nd half FB% and hr/f do likewise (maybe). At 32, this was likely his ceiling.

Yr	Tm	AB	R	HR	RBI	SB	BA	xBA	OBP	SLG	OPS	vL	vR	bb%	ct%	Eye	G	L	F	h%	HctX	PX	xPX	hr/f	Spd	SBO	SB%	#Wk	DOM	DIS	RC/G	RAR	BPV	BPX	R$
13	CIN	567	74	12	63	0	254	255	284	381	665	686	658	4	82	0.25	50	18	32	29	80	88	63	8%	110	0%	0%	27	44%	19%	3.73	3.8	42	105	$11
14	CIN	506	48	4	38	7	221	231	268	300	568	702	532	5	84	0.32	45	18	38	26	84	55	77	3%	135	6%	100%	27	26%	33%	2.60	-10.6	33	89	$2
15	CIN	194	28	9	28	3	258	276	310	459	769	931	718	7	85	0.48	39	19	42	26	98	117	118	13%	96	14%	50%	10	60%	10%	4.61	4.9	78	211	$5
16	CIN	464	67	16	50	4	252	266	308	425	732	737	731	7	82	0.44	39	21	40	28	104	102	106	10%	91	5%	80%	23	43%	26%	4.46	-2.1	53	151	$10
17	CIN	438	80	24	63	3	297	285	385	548	933	1059	896	12	82	0.79	38	20	42	32	102	128	102	16%	136	2%	100%	25	64%	16%	7.68	38.2	98	297	$19
1st Half		223	40	9	33	2	323	286	405	561	966	1111	922	13	79	0.68	39	23	38	38	98	132	91	13%	133	3%	100%	12	58%	17%	8.69	24.3	88	267	$19
2nd Half		215	40	15	30	1	270	283	363	535	898	1002	869	12	86	0.97	37	16	46	25	107	124	113	17%	124	2%	100%	13	69%	15%	6.74	13.3	105	318	$18
18	**Proj**	**444**	**71**	**20**	**57**	**4**	**271**	**273**	**341**	**477**	**818**	**909**	**791**	**9**	**83**	**0.61**	**39**	**19**	**41**	**29**	**101**	**107**	**103**	**13%**	**116**	**4%**	**75%**				**5.66**	**15.2**	**66**	**200**	**$16**

Crawford,Brandon

Age: 31 Bats: L Pos: SS | Ht: 6' 2" Wt: 215

Health A | PT/Exp A | Consist B | LIMA Plan B+ | Rand Var 0 | MM 2135

There's value in certainty, and of this we can be certain: 1) League-average pop translates to 10-15 HR; 2) makes enough contact to return a .250-.260 BA; 3) there's very little risk in the profile; 4) a fortunate h% here (2016) or a hr/f swing there (2015) equals profit. A viable next-tier SS choice.

Yr	Tm	AB	R	HR	RBI	SB	BA	xBA	OBP	SLG	OPS	vL	vR	bb%	ct%	Eye	G	L	F	h%	HctX	PX	xPX	hr/f	Spd	SBO	SB%	#Wk	DOM	DIS	RC/G	RAR	BPV	BPX	R$
13	SF	499	52	9	43	1	248	246	311	363	674	546	727	8	81	0.44	49	19	32	29	83	80	78	7%	105	2%	33%	27	41%	44%	3.72	3.2	36	90	$6
14	SF	491	54	10	69	5	246	229	324	389	713	879	637	10	74	0.46	38	20	42	32	91	103	125	6%	128	6%	63%	27	48%	37%	4.26	14.1	39	105	$11
15	SF	507	65	21	84	6	256	274	321	462	782	716	808	7	77	0.33	48	19	34	30	111	137	136	16%	86	9%	60%	27	48%	15%	4.80	15.4	57	154	$16
16	SF	553	67	12	84	7	275	257	342	430	772	713	801	9	79	0.50	43	21	36	33	113	92	114	8%	123	4%	100%	27	41%	30%	5.27	10.2	48	137	$16
17	SF	518	58	14	77	3	253	255	305	403	709	661	727	7	78	0.37	46	19	34	30	103	93	102	10%	71	6%	38%	26	31%	27%	4.11	-6.2	25	76	$10
1st Half		245	24	6	37	2	229	240	270	363	634	780	583	6	78	0.29	47	17	36	27	109	81	116	8%	79	6%	67%	12	17%	33%	3.29	-9.6	13	39	$5
2nd Half		273	34	8	40	1	275	268	337	440	776	567	862	9	79	0.45	46	21	33	32	97	103	89	11%	72	7%	20%	14	43%	21%	4.94	2.9	38	115	$14
18	**Proj**	**534**	**63**	**15**	**79**	**4**	**260**	**259**	**320**	**419**	**739**	**682**	**763**	**8**	**78**	**0.41**	**45**	**20**	**35**	**31**	**105**	**94**	**109**	**10%**	**93**	**6%**	**55%**				**4.54**	**1.2**	**30**	**91**	**$15**

Crawford,J.P.

Age: 23 Bats: L Pos: 3B | Ht: 6' 2" Wt: 180

Health A | PT/Exp B | Consist B | LIMA Plan B | Rand Var +1 | MM 1315

0-6-.214 with 1 SB in 70 AB at PHI. Former first-rounder broke out of his Triple-A malaise at the All-Star break (.898 OPS afterwards) and earned a Sept call-up. Controls the plate, has current gap power, and is a plus defender. Showcased late-season positional versatility, but has SS skills. Bat may take time to develop.

Yr	Tm	AB	R	HR	RBI	SB	BA	xBA	OBP	SLG	OPS	vL	vR	bb%	ct%	Eye	G	L	F	h%	HctX	PX	xPX	hr/f	Spd	SBO	SB%	#Wk	DOM	DIS	RC/G	RAR	BPV	BPX	R$
13																																			
14																																			
15	aa	351	43	5	27	6	240		318	363	681			10	86	0.80				27		77			123	8%	73%				3.87		64	173	$4
16	a/a	472	54	6	37	10	226		315	306	621			12	81	0.68				27		51			97	12%	58%				3.08		19	54	$5
17	PHI *	544	75	14	62	5	223	240	329	364	693	380	790	14	76	0.66	31	27	43	27	44	81	20	0%	142	6%	56%	5	20%	60%	3.87	-10.8	41	124	$5
1st Half		255	32	3	25	2	194	226	301	278	579			13	78	0.71				24		49			140	7%	36%				2.55		24	73	-$5
2nd Half		289	43	12	37	4	248	251	354	440	794	380	790	14	74	0.62	31	27	43	30	43	111	20	0%	138	5%	77%	5	20%	60%	5.29	6.2	55	167	$14
18	**Proj**	**491**	**63**	**14**	**48**	**8**	**241**	**239**	**331**	**384**	**715**	**466**	**835**	**12**	**79**	**0.67**	**39**	**20**	**41**	**28**	**62**	**80**	**18**	**9%**	**136**	**9%**	**61%**				**4.24**	**-9.6**	**31**	**95**	**$11**

Cron,C.J.

Age: 28 Bats: R Pos: 1B | Ht: 6' 4" Wt: 235

Health B | PT/Exp C | Consist B | LIMA Plan B | Rand Var 0 | MM 3125

16-56-.248 in 339 AB at LAA. Stop-and-start year (Apr foot injury; two minor league demotions) at an age where he needs consistent AB. Got them in second half, and though power metrics surged, so did his strikeout numbers, which only muddies his future. Component skills in place; now it's high time to consolidate.

Yr	Tm	AB	R	HR	RBI	SB	BA	xBA	OBP	SLG	OPS	vL	vR	bb%	ct%	Eye	G	L	F	h%	HctX	PX	xPX	hr/f	Spd	SBO	SB%	#Wk	DOM	DIS	RC/G	RAR	BPV	BPX	R$
13	aa	519	48	11	71	7	242		269	372	641			4	82	0.20				28		93			79	11%	60%				3.29		35	88	$10
14	LAA *	432	46	15	57	1	250	255	283	413	697	751	731	4	75	0.18	35	25	40	30	109	123	122	15%	84	3%	50%	20	45%	45%	3.94	-2.5	33	89	$10
15	LAA *	471	47	20	66	3	260	263	290	448	738	672	774	4	79	0.20	45	18	37	29	96	120	107	14%	79	4%	75%	25	44%	32%	4.47	-6.4	45	122	$13
16	LAA	407	51	16	69	2	278	271	325	467	792	674	827	5	82	0.32	41	20	39	31	107	111	106	12%	86	5%	40%	22	41%	32%	5.10	2.8	54	154	$13
17	LAA *	421	46	19	71	4	239	240	284	419	703	790	724	6	73	0.23	33	23	45	29	105	107	129	15%	78	6%	65%	23	30%	39%	3.94	-18.1	13	39	$8
1st Half		193	17	5	26	2	211	234	253	325	578	808	500	5	78	0.25	33	23	43	25	98	69	96	5%	61	7%	62%	9	11%	67%	2.63	-18.1	-3	-9	-$1
2nd Half		228	30	14	45	2	262	247	309	499	808	784	857	6	68	0.22	32	22	46	32	107	144	148	20%	96	6%	67%	14	43%	21%	5.28	-2.4	33	100	$16
18	**Proj**	**465**	**53**	**20**	**76**	**4**	**253**	**253**	**300**	**440**	**740**	**733**	**742**	**5**	**75**	**0.22**	**37**	**22**	**42**	**29**	**104**	**109**	**118**	**14%**	**81**	**6%**	**60%**				**4.31**	**-10.9**	**21**	**63**	**$14**

BRENT HERSHEY

Cruz,Nelson

Age: 38	Bats: R	Pos: DH	Health	A	LIMA Plan	B
Ht: 6' 2"	Wt: 230		PT/Exp	A	Rand Var	0
			Consist	A	MM	4135

Continues to exhibit metronomic consistency as age 40 casts a larger shadow. Even managed to stunt the signs of decline that were sneaking into the picture (HctX). Last four years have traded in a narrow range; still-robust skill set and AAA reliability say he can hold that ground for at least another year.

Yr	Tm	AB	R	HR	RBI	SB	BA	xBA	OBP	SLG	OPS	vL	vR	bb%	ct%	Eye	G	L	F	h%	HctX	PX	xPX	hr/f	Spd	SBO	SB%	#Wk	DOM	DIS	RC/G	RAR	BPV	BPX
13	TEX	413	49	27	76	5	266	264	327	506	833	821	837	8	74	0.32	42	17	41	30	120	162	154	21%	64	6%	83%	20	70%	25%	5.71	14.4	61	153
14	BAL	613	87	40	108	4	271	285	333	525	859	977	823	8	77	0.39	42	17	41	29	119	173	131	20%	91	6%	44%	27	63%	15%	5.91	33.0	92	249
15	SEA	590	90	44	93	3	302	277	369	566	936	1107	866	9	72	0.36	46	20	34	35	113	169	137	30%	87	3%	60%	26	50%	31%	7.49	33.1	70	189
16	SEA	589	96	43	105	2	287	274	360	555	915	1020	864	9	73	0.39	44	18	38	33	108	160	134	26%	87	1%	100%	26	62%	23%	7.07	25.8	67	191
17	SEA	556	91	39	119	1	288	268	375	549	924	834	950	11	75	0.50	40	18	42	32	123	146	150	22%	60	1%	50%	27	52%	26%	7.18	36.0	58	176
1st Half		275	39	14	59	1	287	256	370	502	872	793	890	12	77	0.58	45	15	40	33	111	123	125	16%	67	1%	100%	13	62%	23%	6.67	13.8	54	164
2nd Half		281	52	25	60	0	288	279	380	594	975	866	1012	11	72	0.44	36	21	43	31	136	170	176	28%	55	1%	0%	14	43%	29%	7.67	22.1	65	197
18	**Proj**	**547**	**88**	**37**	**106**	**2**	**284**	**265**	**364**	**532**	**896**	**918**	**887**	**10**	**74**	**0.43**	**42**	**18**	**40**	**32**	**119**	**140**	**146**	**23%**	**71**	**2%**	**61%**				**6.73**	**19.0**	**43**	**131**

Cuthbert,Cheslor

Age: 25	Bats: R	Pos: 3B	Health	B	LIMA Plan	D+
Ht: 6' 1"	Wt: 190		PT/Exp	D	Rand Var	+1
			Consist	C	MM	1223

2-18-.231 in 143 AB at KC. Fell back into a reserve role from Opening Day, then never produced enough to merit more AB. Better 2nd half numbers came mostly during minors rehab of a sprained wrist. Larger opportunities may materialize in 2018, but lack of any plus skill casts doubt on recovering 2016 line.

Yr	Tm	AB	R	HR	RBI	SB	BA	xBA	OBP	SLG	OPS	vL	vR	bb%	ct%	Eye	G	L	F	h%	HctX	PX	xPX	hr/f	Spd	SBO	SB%	#Wk	DOM	DIS	RC/G	RAR	BPV	BPX
13	aa	237	20	4	23	4	196		247	315	563			6	78	0.31				23		93			83	14%	65%				2.43		26	65
14	a/a	446	36	9	49	8	243		297	355	652			7	81	0.41				28		83			82	11%	64%				3.49		33	89
15	KC *	443	51	9	50	4	247	263	300	371	671	636	660	7	83	0.46	46	22	32	28	49	81	38	8%	108	6%	65%	8	25%	25%	3.74	-10.8	47	127
16	KC *	568	60	17	67	2	276	252	324	428	752	819	701	7	80	0.36	48	17	35	32	100	92	74	9%	116	2%	63%	23	39%	30%	4.86	1.0	45	129
17	KC *	202	18	5	25	0	232	240	283	361	644	606	591	7	75	0.28	42	23	35	29	86	80	102	5%	100	0%	0%	22	18%	59%	3.39	-8.9	8	24
1st Half		92	4	1	10	0	196	205	221	272	493	537	456	3	73	0.12	43	21	36	26	88	54	82	4%	95	0%	0%	13	15%	69%	1.90	-9.2	-29	-88
2nd Half		110	14	4	15	0	262	267	331	435	766	899	745	9	76	0.43	39	26	34	31	81	101	138	8%	109	0%	0%	9	22%	44%	4.98	-0.3	39	118
18	**Proj**	**327**	**32**	**7**	**39**	**1**	**246**	**245**	**294**	**367**	**661**	**690**	**650**	**7**	**78**	**0.33**	**44**	**21**	**35**	**30**	**90**	**74**	**98**	**7%**	**106**	**2%**	**67%**				**3.67**	**-11.8**	**3**	**10**

D Arnaud,Travis

Age: 29	Bats: R	Pos: CA	Health	F	LIMA Plan	D+
Ht: 6' 2"	Wt: 210		PT/Exp	D	Rand Var	+2
			Consist	C	MM	2233

Bruised wrist cost him a few weeks in May, but a one-DL-stint year is a drastic improvement. Longer look doesn't change his skills: ct% is nice for this era; power just a tick above average. That's a catcher who won't hurt you, though the replacement you pick up during his DL time probably will.

Yr	Tm	AB	R	HR	RBI	SB	BA	xBA	OBP	SLG	OPS	vL	vR	bb%	ct%	Eye	G	L	F	h%	HctX	PX	xPX	hr/f	Spd	SBO	SB%	#Wk	DOM	DIS	RC/G	RAR	BPV	BPX
13	NYM *	182	18	3	15	0	208	225	315	325	639	298	630	13	74	0.61	47	18	35	26	71	93	74	4%	89	0%	0%	7	29%	43%	3.29	-2.2	27	68
14	NYM *	448	58	18	53	1	252	286	305	447	752	707	722	7	84	0.49	42	20	39	26	122	130	135	10%	85	1%	100%	23	57%	17%	4.66	15.8	83	224
15	NYM *	267	33	12	42	0	260	270	319	461	780	1112	758	8	80	0.43	37	21	42	29	101	127	107	15%	80	0%	0%	16	56%	19%	5.07	9.7	62	168
16	NYM	251	27	4	15	0	247	217	307	323	629	455	682	7	80	0.38	52	17	31	29	105	47	85	6%	90	0%	0%	19	11%	42%	3.28	-8.3	1	3
17	NYM	348	39	16	57	0	244	263	293	443	735	894	681	6	83	0.39	42	17	41	25	109	105	114	13%	74	0%	0%	24	50%	29%	4.35	3.0	53	161
1st Half		155	21	9	27	0	232	274	294	471	765	1311	604	8	81	0.43	40	17	42	23	117	125	130	17%	81	0%	0%	11	55%	27%	4.56	2.2	64	194
2nd Half		193	18	7	30	0	254	250	291	420	711	613	747	5	85	0.34	43	16	40	27	104	89	102	10%	75	0%	0%	13	46%	31%	4.17	0.4	45	136
18	**Proj**	**358**	**40**	**13**	**47**	**0**	**252**	**254**	**308**	**420**	**728**	**774**	**714**	**7**	**82**	**0.41**	**44**	**18**	**38**	**28**	**106**	**91**	**104**	**12%**	**77**	**0%**	**100%**				**4.36**	**2.4**	**25**	**77**

Dahl,David

Age: 24	Bats: L	Pos: DH	Health	D	LIMA Plan	C+
Ht: 6' 2"	Wt: 195		PT/Exp	D	Rand Var	0
			Consist	F	MM	2533

Spring injury to rib cage cost him the first half, then back spasms on rehab assignment ended his season. Last year in this space, we loved the power/speed skills, but worried about BA downside due to shaky plate discipline. Both sides of that coin still hold true, but now a shaky health grade adds another layer of risk.

Yr	Tm	AB	R	HR	RBI	SB	BA	xBA	OBP	SLG	OPS	vL	vR	bb%	ct%	Eye	G	L	F	h%	HctX	PX	xPX	hr/f	Spd	SBO	SB%	#Wk	DOM	DIS	RC/G	RAR	BPV	BPX
13																																		
14																																		
15	aa	288	38	5	20	18	274		296	408	704			3	76	0.13				34		93			123	40%	71%				4.07		24	65
16	COL *	572	99	23	73	19	313	274	370	531	901	728	895	8	73	0.34	45	21	33	39	97	140	100	13%	138	16%	72%	11	27%	27%	7.16	39.7	65	186
17	aaa	70	9	2	10	1	229		252	376	628			3	76	0.13				28		77			140	14%	39%				2.93		14	42
1st Half																																		
2nd Half		70	9	2	10	1	229		252	376	628			3	76	0.13				28		77			149	14%	39%				2.93		17	52
18	**Proj**	**335**	**47**	**10**	**37**	**13**	**268**	**258**	**300**	**440**	**739**	**620**	**772**	**4**	**75**	**0.18**	**45**	**21**	**33**	**33**	**87**	**99**	**90**	**12%**	**154**	**26%**	**68%**				**4.43**	**-10.5**	**34**	**103**

Davidson,Matt

Age: 27	Bats: R	Pos: DH 3B	Health	D	LIMA Plan	D+
Ht: 6' 3"	Wt: 230		PT/Exp	C	Rand Var	0
			Consist	B	MM	4005

Wrist injury cost him a chunk of August. Contact problems are well-established, but PX jumped back to a level that starts to offset that swing-and-miss. Better yet, second half gains nudge ct% toward tolerable levels. PX/xPX slipped during that time, but if he marries 1st half pop with 2nd half contact, we're interested.

Yr	Tm	AB	R	HR	RBI	SB	BA	xBA	OBP	SLG	OPS	vL	vR	bb%	ct%	Eye	G	L	F	h%	HctX	PX	xPX	hr/f	Spd	SBO	SB%	#Wk	DOM	DIS	RC/G	RAR	BPV	BPX
13	ARI *	519	43	14	59	1	236	240	289	392	681	641	833	7	67	0.22	37	27	37	33	97	133	144	16%	94	1%	39%	7	43%	43%	3.75	-3.7	18	45
14	aaa	478	39	15	37	0	163		220	285	505			7	61	0.19				23		109			85	0%	0%				1.91		-27	-73
15	aaa	528	51	20	60	1	175		252	323	575			9	58	0.24				26		126			78	1%	100%				2.52		-23	-62
16	CHW *	286	29	8	37	0	231	413	297	379	676	1000	0	9	63	0.26	0	100	0	33	0	118	-24	0%	74	0%	0%	1	0%	100%	3.73	-9.2	-9	-26
17	CHW	414	43	26	68	0	220	218	260	452	711	759	693	4	60	0.12	36	17	46	29	93	158	147	22%	78	1%	0%	25	32%	48%	3.70	-14.6	1	3
1st Half		224	30	17	38	0	246	218	286	518	804	855	780	5	56	0.12	32	16	52	35	93	196	170	26%	105	2%	0%	13	46%	38%	4.87	-1.5	24	73
2nd Half		190	13	9	30	0	189	211	229	374	603	604	602	4	65	0.11	41	19	41	23	93	121	124	17%	59	0%	0%	12	17%	58%	2.57	-15.2	-15	-45
18	**Proj**	**491**	**47**	**24**	**69**	**0**	**220**	**219**	**277**	**413**	**690**	**659**	**703**	**6**	**62**	**0.18**	**37**	**21**	**42**	**30**	**95**	**134**	**144**	**19%**	**72**	**1%**	**28%**				**3.63**	**-28.1**	**-24**	**-73**

Davis,Chris

Age: 32	Bats: L	Pos: 1B	Health	B	LIMA Plan	B
Ht: 6' 3"	Wt: 230		PT/Exp	A	Rand Var	0
			Consist	C	MM	4005

Missed a month with an oblique strain. A few more strikeouts plus a few fly balls becoming line drives chopped his earnings by more than half. 2013 and 2015 show that a tolerable BA requires an intersection of 200+ PX, 60%+ ct%, and 32%+ h%. More than one of those would be a surprise, let alone all three.

Yr	Tm	AB	R	HR	RBI	SB	BA	xBA	OBP	SLG	OPS	vL	vR	bb%	ct%	Eye	G	L	F	h%	HctX	PX	xPX	hr/f	Spd	SBO	SB%	#Wk	DOM	DIS	RC/G	RAR	BPV	BPX
13	BAL	584	103	53	138	4	286	297	370	634	1004	763	1142	11	66	0.36	32	22	46	34	114	266	199	30%	66	3%	80%	27	78%	11%	8.24	59.5	120	300
14	BAL	450	65	26	72	2	196	235	300	404	704	677	716	11	62	0.35	35	25	41	25	96	174	154	23%	66	3%	67%	22	36%	36%	3.71	-6.1	30	81
15	BAL	573	100	47	117	2	262	271	361	562	923	799	984	13	64	0.40	32	25	43	32	115	224	195	29%	61	3%	40%	27	56%	22%	6.80	31.1	80	216
16	BAL	566	99	38	84	1	221	231	332	459	792	711	828	13	61	0.40	36	20	44	28	100	168	179	25%	79	1%	100%	27	41%	41%	4.91	0.8	32	91
17	BAL	456	65	26	61	1	215	216	309	423	732	619	785	12	57	0.31	37	23	40	31	96	149	152	25%	73	2%	50%	24	17%	67%	4.20	-16.5	-4	-12
1st Half		217	34	14	26	0	226	220	320	461	781	802	769	12	56	0.32	33	24	43	32	86	168	163	26%	87	0%	0%	11	27%	64%	4.85	-5.2	12	36
2nd Half		239	31	12	35	1	205	212	299	389	688	421	797	11	58	0.31	40	23	37	29	105	132	143	23%	68	3%	50%	13	8%	69%	3.65	-14.9	-16	-48
18	**Proj**	**524**	**82**	**31**	**81**	**1**	**225**	**226**	**322**	**445**	**767**	**655**	**819**	**12**	**60**	**0.34**	**37**	**23**	**40**	**31**	**101**	**152**	**167**	**24%**	**70**	**2%**	**55%**				**4.63**	**-7.5**	**2**	**5**

Davis,Khristopher

Age: 30	Bats: R	Pos: LF DH	Health	A	LIMA Plan	B
Ht: 5' 10"	Wt: 195		PT/Exp	A	Rand Var	0
			Consist	B	MM	5235

Answered any questions about whether 2016 was a career year with a full repeat. Now has 107 HR over last 2.5 seasons (1,365 AB). Power is elite, plate skills passable, and both are stable. Career platoon split is negligible. Fine, he doesn't run and BA isn't going much past .250. But you can take the power to the bank.

Yr	Tm	AB	R	HR	RBI	SB	BA	xBA	OBP	SLG	OPS	vL	vR	bb%	ct%	Eye	G	L	F	h%	HctX	PX	xPX	hr/f	Spd	SBO	SB%	#Wk	DOM	DIS	RC/G	RAR	BPV	BPX
13	MIL *	379	51	21	52	7	233	265	294	455	749	1009	918	8	72	0.31	43	20	37	27	135	158	162	29%	87	15%	60%	16	63%	25%	4.30	2.8	58	145
14	MIL	501	70	22	69	4	244	278	299	457	756	777	749	6	76	0.26	39	21	40	28	132	161	157	14%	84	5%	80%	26	54%	27%	4.45	11.3	70	189
15	MIL	392	54	27	66	6	247	260	323	505	828	729	864	10	69	0.36	42	17	40	29	105	174	169	25%	87	8%	75%	22	64%	18%	5.51	12.9	63	170
16	OAK	555	85	42	102	1	247	266	307	524	831	881	815	7	70	0.25	43	17	40	27	111	171	145	27%	85	3%	33%	26	54%	38%	5.25	15.9	58	166
17	OAK	566	91	43	110	4	247	257	336	528	864	786	886	11	66	0.37	38	19	42	30	112	177	174	27%	74	3%	100%	27	56%	26%	6.01	9.4	50	152
1st Half		294	49	22	56	4	252	248	336	524	860	633	910	11	63	0.34	40	18	42	32	114	178	177	28%	77	5%	100%	13	62%	31%	6.07	6.2	43	130
2nd Half		272	42	21	54	0	243	267	335	533	869	904	856	12	68	0.41	37	21	43	27	109	177	171	26%	75	0%	0%	14	50%	21%	5.94	4.8	62	188
18	**Proj**	**556**	**85**	**40**	**102**	**4**	**246**	**261**	**323**	**518**	**842**	**822**	**848**	**10**	**68**	**0.34**	**40**	**19**	**41**	**28**	**112**	**165**	**164**	**26%**	**79**	**4%**	**74%**				**5.57**	**18.4**	**47**	**142**

RAY MURPHY

Davis,Rajai

	Health	A	LIMA Plan	D+
Age: 37 Bats: R Pos: CF LF	PT/Exp	C	Rand Var	0
Ht: 5' 10" Wt: 195	Consist	A	MM	2521

Took a step backward from '16 with the lumber, as ct% continued its steady descent and HctX/xPX bottomed out, especially late. Still runs better than your average 37-year-old, but as 2nd half showed, PT might become an issue moving forward. Without thump in his bat or regular AB, those SB totals are a risky investment.

Yr	Tm	AB	R	HR	RBI	SB	BA	xBA	OBP	SLG	OPS	vL	vR	bb%	ct%	Eye	G	L	F	h%	HctX	PX	xPX	hr/f	Spd	SBO	SB%	#Wk	DOM	DIS	RC/G	RAR	BPV	BPX	R$
13	TOR	331	49	6	24	45	260	241	312	375	687	857	594	6	80	0.31	39	23	38	31	90	81	84	6%	132	61%	88%	23	26%	30%	4.34	1.0	37	93	$23
14	DET	461	64	8	51	36	282	269	320	401	721	939	617	4	84	0.29	50	19	31	32	74	88	58	7%	108	41%	77%	26	46%	19%	4.46	7.6	49	132	$26
15	DET	341	55	8	30	18	258	265	306	440	746	758	738	6	78	0.29	44	22	33	31	95	111	77	9%	182	35%	69%	26	50%	38%	4.39	-1.1	68	184	$13
16	CLE	454	74	12	48	43	249	244	306	388	693	670	708	7	77	0.31	45	19	36	30	82	88	75	10%	109	45%	88%	27	26%	48%	4.22	-2.0	25	71	$25
17	2 AL	336	56	5	20	29	235	236	293	348	641	677	619	7	75	0.33	46	19	35	30	68	74	73	6%	129	45%	81%	26	23%	42%	3.50	-12.8	16	48	$13
1st Half		206	29	2	12	10	214	233	269	320	589	582	588	7	77	0.34	45	18	37	27	76	69	80	3%	119	32%	71%	12	25%	42%	2.77	-13.9	16	48	$8
2nd Half		130	27	3	8	19	269	240	331	392	723	762	687	8	72	0.31	49	20	31	35	56	82	61	10%	115	61%	86%	14	21%	43%	4.88	-0.1	7	21	$21
18	Proj	228	39	5	18	19	252	246	307	385	692	727	669	7	76	0.31	46	20	34	31	75	82	72	8%	128	42%	81%				4.07	-3.0	32	98	$10

DeJong,Paul

	Health	A	LIMA Plan	B+
Age: 24 Bats: R Pos: SS 2B	PT/Exp	D	Rand Var	-1
Ht: 6' 1" Wt: 195	Consist	D	MM	4135

25-65-.285 in 417 AB at STL. Ranked outside the ADP top 1000 last March, he snagged a late-May promotion and ran with his opportunity. There's certainly pop and loft in this bat (see PX, FB%), but aggressive approach, mediocre ct% and lack of legs limit his upside. Over 40 players hit 30 HRs in '17. You can probably add him.

Yr	Tm	AB	R	HR	RBI	SB	BA	xBA	OBP	SLG	OPS	vL	vR	bb%	ct%	Eye	G	L	F	h%	HctX	PX	xPX	hr/f	Spd	SBO	SB%	#Wk	DOM	DIS	RC/G	RAR	BPV	BPX	R$
13																																			
14																																			
15																																			
16	aa	496	52	18	61	3	235		283	403	687			6	69	0.22				30		116			86	5%	53%				3.76		10	29	$7
17	STL *	594	77	35	92	1	279	261	311	517	828	952	835	4	71	0.16	34	23	43	34	104	145	133	20%	88	3%	31%	19	53%	26%	5.60	4.9	36	109	$20
1st Half		280	32	16	43	0	266	255	289	485	775	920	738	3	70	0.11	35	24	41	32	100	132	111	21%	78	4%	0%	5	40%	20%	4.70	-3.2	19	58	$15
2nd Half		314	45	19	49	1	290	268	338	545	883	964	864	6	71	0.21	33	23	43	35	106	156	141	20%	99	1%	100%	14	57%	29%	6.48	12.2	52	158	$25
18	Proj	563	68	34	80	2	263	261	306	504	810	927	780	5	70	0.19	34	24	42	32	104	147	129	20%	93	3%	51%				5.21	12.1	26	80	$19

Delmonico,Nick

	Health	A	LIMA Plan	D+
Age: 25 Bats: L Pos: LF	PT/Exp	C	Rand Var	+2
Ht: 6' 2" Wt: 230	Consist	B	MM	3333

9-23-.262 in 141 AB at CHW. Kid's debut was intriguing, posting near-average BPX by way of quality bb%, Eye and solid foundational marks in HctX/xPX with OPS vL/R harmony. That hr/f likely isn't repeatable, but has skills for some sneaky BA upside. Not an impact bat yet, but worth tracking.

Yr	Tm	AB	R	HR	RBI	SB	BA	xBA	OBP	SLG	OPS	vL	vR	bb%	ct%	Eye	G	L	F	h%	HctX	PX	xPX	hr/f	Spd	SBO	SB%	#Wk	DOM	DIS	RC/G	RAR	BPV	BPX	R$
13																																			
14																																			
15	aa	223	23	3	23	2	210		285	342	626			9	73	0.39				28		114			82	6%	61%				3.11		29	78	-$1
16	a/a	402	45	14	48	2	243		305	424	728			8	69	0.28				32		129			88	3%	100%				4.38		22	63	$6
17	CHW *	519	67	19	58	5	233	249	314	389	703	894	844	10	77	0.51	40	22	37	27	91	86	104	23%	104	5%	69%	8	38%	25%	4.04	-12.8	31	94	$8
1st Half		297	33	9	30	2	235	250	306	383	689			9	78	0.48				27		84			95	6%	50%				3.82		30	91	$6
2nd Half		222	34	10	28	3	231	246	324	397	721	894	844	12	75	0.55	40	22	37	26	89	89	104	23%	108	4%	100%	8	38%	25%	4.34	-5.0	31	94	$9
18	Proj	316	39	12	36	3	233	253	315	414	729	775	715	10	73	0.40	40	22	37	28	80	110	94	14%	97	4%	81%				4.24	-2.1	24	73	$6

Descalso,Daniel

	Health	B	LIMA Plan	D+
Age: 31 Bats: L Pos: 2B LF	PT/Exp	D	Rand Var	0
Ht: 5' 10" Wt: 190	Consist	D	MM	2323

Set career-high in HR by way of increased launch angle and more fly balls, but as backup OF, his chance for impact was limited from the start. Could be worth a bench spot in deep OBP formats given his solid bb% history and positional flexibility, but the ceiling is pretty low here overall.

Yr	Tm	AB	R	HR	RBI	SB	BA	xBA	OBP	SLG	OPS	vL	vR	bb%	ct%	Eye	G	L	F	h%	HctX	PX	xPX	hr/f	Spd	SBO	SB%	#Wk	DOM	DIS	RC/G	RAR	BPV	BPX	R$
13	STL	328	43	5	43	6	238	262	290	366	656	529	684	6	83	0.39	48	18	34	27	102	96	85	5%	90	13%	67%	27	41%	30%	3.44	-0.5	50	125	$6
14	STL	161	20	0	10	1	242	220	333	311	644	899	575	11	80	0.61	43	17	39	30	72	68	50	0%	98	8%	25%	26	27%	42%	3.19	-0.4	26	70	$0
15	COL	185	22	5	22	1	205	223	283	324	607	468	628	10	76	0.44	44	19	36	24	68	71	75	10%	123	6%	33%	27	30%	48%	2.83	-5.4	17	46	-$1
16	COL	250	38	8	38	3	264	264	349	424	773	732	782	12	78	0.61	44	24	32	31	92	96	99	13%	90	4%	100%	22	32%	36%	5.25	4.6	40	114	$7
17	ARI	344	47	10	51	4	233	231	332	395	727	588	767	12	74	0.54	39	18	43	29	111	95	153	9%	113	4%	100%	27	37%	33%	4.36	-1.6	32	97	$5
1st Half		160	23	5	28	1	244	241	349	413	762	539	828	13	74	0.55	42	19	39	30	109	100	145	11%	107	2%	100%	13	31%	23%	4.75	0.8	34	103	$4
2nd Half		184	24	5	23	3	223	223	316	380	696	631	715	12	74	0.53	36	17	47	27	113	91	161	8%	115	6%	100%	14	43%	43%	4.03	-3.0	31	94	$6
18	Proj	279	38	8	39	3	236	240	326	387	713	627	734	11	76	0.54	41	20	39	29	98	87	120	9%	107	5%	79%				4.20	-5.1	27	80	$6

DeShields Jr.,Delino

	Health	A	LIMA Plan	C
Age: 25 Bats: R Pos: LF CF	PT/Exp	C	Rand Var	-5
Ht: 5' 9" Wt: 200	Consist	D	MM	1505

Bounced back marginally after putrid 2016 campaign, but these skills are mostly the same. BA lift was largely aided by h% despite poor ct%/HctX marks, and while he added a few more fly balls, PX/xPX says there wasn't much muscle behind them. Rebound in SB% perhaps the most welcome sign.

Yr	Tm	AB	R	HR	RBI	SB	BA	xBA	OBP	SLG	OPS	vL	vR	bb%	ct%	Eye	G	L	F	h%	HctX	PX	xPX	hr/f	Spd	SBO	SB%	#Wk	DOM	DIS	RC/G	RAR	BPV	BPX	R$
13																																			
14	aa	411	58	9	44	41	206		288	309	598			10	69	0.38				28		81			105	51%	73%				2.85		-3	-8	$17
15	TEX *	451	85	2	39	25	262	237	340	374	714	765	693	10	76	0.50	47	19	34	34	72	80	56	2%	167	24%	76%	25	32%	48%	4.43	-1.0	41	111	$18
16	TEX *	389	64	6	26	24	218	218	295	307	602	541	614	10	69	0.35	55	17	28	30	57	66	51	12%	105	33%	69%	18	22%	50%	2.90	-18.1	-17	-49	$10
17	TEX	376	75	6	22	29	269	218	347	367	714	751	696	10	71	0.40	45	20	35	36	69	65	68	7%	168	30%	78%	27	22%	52%	4.52	-2.4	8	24	$19
1st Half		181	37	1	12	18	282	207	345	354	698	739	678	9	67	0.30	50	19	32	42	67	61	74	3%	128	38%	82%	13	8%	62%	4.59	-1.6	-25	-76	$19
2nd Half		195	38	5	10	11	256	228	348	379	728	760	711	12	75	0.53	41	21	38	32	71	68	62	10%	181	23%	73%	14	36%	43%	4.46	-2.6	34	103	$18
18	Proj	470	86	9	32	33	248	226	329	356	686	691	682	10	71	0.41	49	19	32	33	65	70	60	8%	156	32%	75%				3.96	-7.1	7	21	$22

Desmond,Ian

	Health	C	LIMA Plan	C+
Age: 32 Bats: R Pos: LF 1B	PT/Exp	A	Rand Var	-2
Ht: 6' 3" Wt: 215	Consist	C	MM	2425

Exhibit A on how debilitating hand injuries can be. Missed April with fractured left paw and never quite regained his mojo, topping far more balls, resulting in HctX/xPX declines after big 2nd half swoon in 2016. Spd, SB% say there's still SB value here, and as long as his address is Coors, there is reason to speculate on more.

Yr	Tm	AB	R	HR	RBI	SB	BA	xBA	OBP	SLG	OPS	vL	vR	bb%	ct%	Eye	G	L	F	h%	HctX	PX	xPX	hr/f	Spd	SBO	SB%	#Wk	DOM	DIS	RC/G	RAR	BPV	BPX	R$
13	WAS	600	77	20	80	21	280	265	331	453	784	766	789	7	76	0.30	43	22	34	34	101	126	100	13%	99	18%	78%	26	50%	31%	5.26	11.6	49	123	$28
14	WAS	593	73	24	91	24	255	247	313	430	743	771	734	7	69	0.25	50	18	32	33	97	136	107	18%	108	20%	83%	27	41%	37%	4.60	7.1	34	92	$26
15	WAS	583	69	19	62	13	233	229	290	384	674	757	653	7	68	0.24	53	16	31	31	83	113	91	15%	113	14%	72%	27	26%	48%	3.65	-30.3	12	32	$13
16	TEX	625	107	22	86	21	285	264	335	446	782	880	753	6	74	0.28	53	21	26	35	92	101	81	18%	119	16%	78%	26	46%	38%	5.28	-1.0	29	83	$30
17	COL	339	47	7	40	15	274	244	326	375	701	663	715	6	74	0.28	63	16	21	35	82	61	60	13%	113	19%	79%	18	11%	61%	4.29	-15.7	-4	-12	$13
1st Half		219	30	5	26	10	283	242	315	388	703	726	695	4	73	0.15	63	17	20	37	87	63	60	16%	112	24%	71%	9	11%	67%	4.21	-9.0	-16	-48	$16
2nd Half		120	17	2	14	5	258	245	345	350	695	567	750	11	78	0.56	62	16	22	32	73	58	61	10%	109	13%	100%	9	11%	56%	4.37	-4.5	13	39	$7
18	Proj	551	79	17	68	20	267	252	325	410	735	725	739	7	74	0.31	56	18	26	33	85	86	75	16%	113	17%	82%				4.65	3.1	13	40	$23

Devers,Rafael

	Health	A	LIMA Plan	B
Age: 21 Bats: L Pos: 3B	PT/Exp	F	Rand Var	-2
Ht: 6' 0" Wt: 195	Consist	F	MM	3135

10-30-.284 in 222 AB at BOS. Top prospect had AA/AAA breakout and held his own in debut. xBA isn't optimistic of a near-.300 hitter in '18, but he set a solid foundation in HctX/xPX as a 20-year-old pup. Will need to trim those ground balls before seeing short-term HR returns, but still, a kid to stash for the future.

Yr	Tm	AB	R	HR	RBI	SB	BA	xBA	OBP	SLG	OPS	vL	vR	bb%	ct%	Eye	G	L	F	h%	HctX	PX	xPX	hr/f	Spd	SBO	SB%	#Wk	DOM	DIS	RC/G	RAR	BPV	BPX	R$
13																																			
14																																			
15																																			
16																																			
17	BOS *	544	81	27	83	3	298	273	355	523	877	1074	743	8	78	0.40	49	15	36	34	109	129	98	17%	102	5%	42%	11	45%	18%	6.56	25.7	63	191	$22
1st Half		268	35	13	43	0	296	293	351	544	895			8	80	0.42				33		138			102	5%	0%				6.59		79	239	$20
2nd Half		276	44	13	37	3	292	252	349	483	832	1074	743	8	75	0.35	49	15	36	35	105	113	98	17%	97	5%	75%	11	45%	18%	6.05	7.5	39	118	$24
18	Proj	515	76	22	75	3	284	263	342	485	827	1094	746	8	77	0.38	49	15	36	33	95	117	88	16%	103	5%	50%				5.79	13.1	41	124	$21

ALEC DOPP

Diaz,Aledmys

Age: 27	Bats: R	Pos: SS	Health	B	LIMA Plan D+
Ht: 6' 1"	Wt: 195		PT/Exp	C	Rand Var +1
			Consist	F	MM 2233

7-20-.259 in 286 AB at STL. As surprising as his 2016 breakout was, this uber-regression may have been even more so. Hard contact (and thus BA) disappeared, walk rate dropped by half, and with those went most of his value. History and peak age point to a slight rebound. But don't bid expecting 2016 redux.

Yr	Tm	AB	R	HR	RBI	SB	BA	xBA	OBP	SLG	OPS	vL	vR	bb%	ct%	Eye	G	L	F	h%	HctX	PX	xPX	hr/f	Spd	SBO	SB%	#Wk	DOM	DIS	RC/G	RAR	BPV	BPX
13																																		
14	aa	117	11	2	14	5	251		260	381	642			1	77	0.06				31		103			95	33%	67%				3.22		24	65
15	a/a	425	43	9	37	4	225		269	349	618			6	80	0.31				26		85			91	13%	38%				2.89		31	84
16	STL	404	71	17	65	4	300	284	369	510	879	725	941	9	85	0.68	46	16	39	32	109	118	108	13%	139	7%	50%	22	55%	14%	6.57	21.9	97	277
17	STL *	456	45	10	40	6	240	246	273	362	635	602	700	4	83	0.27	46	17	38	27	79	71	69	8%	113	11%	58%	16	44%	38%	3.22	-17.8	34	103
1st Half		280	31	7	21	4	259	258	292	398	690	613	706	4	85	0.31	45	17	38	28	81	79	74	8%	114	8%	80%	13	46%	38%	4.02	-4.6	48	145
2nd Half		176	15	3	19	2	209	218	241	306	547	0	583	4	80	0.22	58	8	33	24	81	57	-26	0%	105	17%	38%	3	33%	33%	2.17	-13.4	9	27
18	Proj	**299**	**35**	**9**	**34**	**4**	**252**	**257**	**293**	**411**	**704**	**605**	**735**	**5**	**82**	**0.31**	**45**	**16**	**38**	**28**	**92**	**89**	**88**	**10%**	**125**	**13%**	**50%**				**3.89**	**-5.2**	**36**	**110**

Diaz,Elias

Age: 27	Bats: R	Pos: CA	Health	D	LIMA Plan D
Ht: 6' 1"	Wt: 215		PT/Exp	F	Rand Var +1
			Consist	B	MM 0111

1-19-.223 in 188 AB at PIT. Production right in line with MLEs. In this case, that means we expected little, and got just that. Rule of thumb: When write-ups tout a prospect's excellent defense first, that's a fanalytic red flag, unless you play in a sim league.

Yr	Tm	AB	R	HR	RBI	SB	BA	xBA	OBP	SLG	OPS	vL	vR	bb%	ct%	Eye	G	L	F	h%	HctX	PX	xPX	hr/f	Spd	SBO	SB%	#Wk	DOM	DIS	RC/G	RAR	BPV	BPX
13																																		
14	a/a	359	33	4	40	2	261		305	343	648			6	82	0.36				31		66			79	6%	39%				3.49		20	54
15	PIT *	327	28	3	40	1	235	102	287	324	612	0	0	7	84	0.45	0	0	100	27	363	59	732	0%	101	7%	15%	2	0%	50%	2.92	-8.8	29	78
16	PIT *	105	3	0	10	1	224	249	248	249	497	0	0	3	80	0.16	33	33	33	28	0	21	-24	0%	82	3%	100%	1	0%	100%	2.07	-7.4	-30	-86
17	PIT *	406	34	3	41	3	225	238	260	300	560	646	557	5	80	0.24	52	18	30	27	84	52	70	2%	66	4%	100%	15	27%	53%	2.61	-17.8	-5	-15
1st Half		196	18	3	28	2	250	224	277	345	623	554	737	4	79	0.19	52	13	34	30	111	63	105	5%	80	4%	100%	7	29%	57%	3.30	-4.6	2	6
2nd Half		210	16	0	13	2	202	245	245	257	502	739	452	5	81	0.30	52	21	27	25	66	43	46	0%	67	4%	100%	8	25%	50%	2.05	-13.5	-7	-21
18	Proj	**200**	**14**	**1**	**20**	**2**	**229**	**231**	**264**	**292**	**556**	**621**	**535**	**5**	**81**	**0.26**	**52**	**18**	**30**	**28**	**84**	**44**	**70**	**2%**	**74**	**5%**	**73%**				**2.56**	**-9.6**	**-14**	**-44**

Diaz,Yandy

Age: 26	Bats: R	Pos: 3B	Health	A	LIMA Plan D+
Ht: 6' 2"	Wt: 185		PT/Exp	B	Rand Var -3
			Consist	A	MM 1343

0-13-.263 in 156 AB at CLE. Some things to like here, with consistently excellent plate control foremost. No, he doesn't have the power you'd like at a corner, and BA likely to dip. But a decent BA floor, outstanding OBP, and some latent speed skills all add value. Finding AB his biggest issue, so watch spring role closely.

Yr	Tm	AB	R	HR	RBI	SB	BA	xBA	OBP	SLG	OPS	vL	vR	bb%	ct%	Eye	G	L	F	h%	HctX	PX	xPX	hr/f	Spd	SBO	SB%	#Wk	DOM	DIS	RC/G	RAR	BPV	BPX
13																																		
14																																		
15	a/a	495	54	6	49	8	286		371	368	739			12	85	0.89				33		51			112	9%	50%				4.71		39	105
16	a/a	444	53	8	47	9	287		370	398	768			12	80	0.67				34		70			99	8%	72%				5.25		31	89
17	CLE *	465	69	4	39	3	293	264	385	379	764	727	648	13	80	0.74	59	22	19	36	106	56	60	0%	120	3%	54%	11	27%	55%	5.22	4.6	28	85
1st Half		213	30	2	15	0	263	264	351	331	681	417	514	12	80	0.66	63	25	13	32	155	40	42	0%	124	0%	0%	4	0%	100%	4.02	-6.6	13	39
2nd Half		252	39	2	24	3	319	265	414	420	833	864	763	14	80	0.81	57	20	23	39	74	70	72	0%	117	5%	54%	7	43%	29%	6.38	8.8	41	124
18	Proj	**306**	**41**	**4**	**29**	**4**	**278**	**272**	**369**	**375**	**745**	**811**	**703**	**12**	**81**	**0.74**	**59**	**22**	**19**	**33**	**106**	**60**	**60**	**8%**	**122**	**6%**	**65%**				**4.83**	**-0.5**	**20**	**61**

Dickerson,Corey

Age: 29	Bats: L	Pos: LF DH	Health	B	LIMA Plan B+
Ht: 6' 1"	Wt: 200		PT/Exp	B	Rand Var -1
			Consist	C	MM 4145

On the surface, 2017 looks like a rebound season. But here's why it wasn't: 1) 1st half BA hit-rate driven; 2) power skills took another step back; 3) OPS fell in every month; 4) 2nd half skills took a massive tumble; 5) full-season skill metrics (e.g., RAR, BPV, BPX) all continue trending the wrong way. Likely to be overvalued.

Yr	Tm	AB	R	HR	RBI	SB	BA	xBA	OBP	SLG	OPS	vL	vR	bb%	ct%	Eye	G	L	F	h%	HctX	PX	xPX	hr/f	Spd	SBO	SB%	#Wk	DOM	DIS	RC/G	RAR	BPV	BPX
13	COL *	509	68	12	47	6	296	287	337	492	829	581	819	6	81	0.33	40	26	34	34	109	124	107	10%	160	16%	29%	14	64%	21%	5.42	19.8	87	218
14	COL	436	74	24	76	8	312	298	364	567	931	724	985	8	77	0.37	37	27	36	36	123	176	135	20%	122	13%	53%	25	60%	24%	7.33	43.8	102	276
15	COL *	252	32	11	33	0	296	293	325	514	839	662	938	4	76	0.18	38	30	32	35	123	149	135	19%	118	2%	0%	16	44%	25%	5.94	8.5	69	186
16	TAM	510	57	24	70	0	245	256	293	469	761	589	807	6	74	0.25	38	17	45	29	95	144	119	14%	90	2%	0%	27	52%	33%	4.52	3.7	51	146
17	TAM	588	84	27	62	4	282	265	325	490	815	820	813	6	74	0.23	42	22	36	34	101	122	106	17%	117	5%	57%	27	37%	37%	5.53	1.4	42	127
1st Half		320	60	17	40	2	325	286	367	569	936	913	946	6	78	0.27	40	22	37	38	110	136	107	18%	128	6%	40%	13	62%	15%	7.55	18.8	72	218
2nd Half		268	24	10	22	2	231	240	274	396	669	657	673	6	70	0.20	44	22	34	29	90	103	105	16%	98	4%	100%	14	14%	57%	3.64	-13.8	4	12
18	Proj	**528**	**67**	**24**	**62**	**3**	**271**	**267**	**314**	**482**	**796**	**711**	**822**	**6**	**74**	**0.24**	**40**	**23**	**37**	**32**	**103**	**125**	**115**	**16%**	**111**	**5%**	**47%**				**5.17**	**10.9**	**33**	**100**

Dietrich,Derek

Age: 28	Bats: L	Pos: 3B	Health	B	LIMA Plan D+
Ht: 6' 0"	Wt: 205		PT/Exp	C	Rand Var 0
			Consist	B	MM 3123

PRO: Career-best .306 BA vL; strong late-season surge (.950 OPS, .317 xBA in Sept). CON: The counterpoint—a .236 BA vR; consistently mediocre year-to-year skills. Tempting to wish on that late-season power surge, but the longer term trends agree—we need to see it for more than two months.

Yr	Tm	AB	R	HR	RBI	SB	BA	xBA	OBP	SLG	OPS	vL	vR	bb%	ct%	Eye	G	L	F	h%	HctX	PX	xPX	hr/f	Spd	SBO	SB%	#Wk	DOM	DIS	RC/G	RAR	BPV	BPX
13	MIA *	433	61	17	54	3	226	256	285	414	699	786	644	7	72	0.29	40	25	35	28	90	136	114	16%	115	4%	100%	12	42%	33%	3.93	-1.6	46	115
14	MIA *	240	41	9	28	2	235	246	281	399	680	372	762	6	75	0.26	43	19	38	28	99	114	100	11%	105	3%	100%	12	42%	42%	3.78	0.0	38	103
15	MIA *	442	58	15	46	0	241	243	297	422	719	519	864	7	74	0.30	37	20	43	30	112	125	159	12%	110	5%	0%	18	39%	39%	4.03	-9.1	44	119
16	MIA	351	39	7	42	1	279	245	374	425	798	556	852	8	76	0.38	40	22	38	35	86	93	99	7%	109	1%	100%	26	46%	31%	5.12	4.8	29	83
17	MIA	406	56	13	53	0	249	252	334	424	758	816	744	8	76	0.37	37	23	41	30	98	102	106	10%	115	1%	0%	26	42%	42%	4.41	-10.1	37	112
1st Half		190	23	3	21	0	237	245	316	363	679	1060	602	5	81	0.30	42	19	39	28	101	75	90	5%	113	0%	0%	13	23%	46%	3.38	-11.2	29	88
2nd Half		216	33	10	32	0	259	256	349	477	826	639	875	10	72	0.41	31	26	43	32	96	128	122	15%	112	2%	0%	13	62%	38%	5.42	0.4	46	139
18	Proj	**355**	**47**	**11**	**44**	**1**	**254**	**249**	**339**	**427**	**767**	**674**	**788**	**8**	**75**	**0.33**	**38**	**22**	**40**	**31**	**97**	**102**	**114**	**10%**	**114**	**2%**	**35%**				**4.51**	**-4.0**	**23**	**70**

Difo,Wilmer

Age: 26	Bats: R	Pos: SS 2B	Health	A	LIMA Plan C
Ht: 5' 11"	Wt: 200		PT/Exp	D	Rand Var -1
			Consist	A	MM 1533

5-21-.271 with 10 SB in 332 AB at WAS. That 38% 2nd half hit rate won't repeat, so heed xBA there. With that caveat out of the way, the seeds of a decent SB source are present: rising OBP and Spd (the latter edging into elite territory) with excellent SB%. While he'll need full-time AB, there's 25-SB upside here.

Yr	Tm	AB	R	HR	RBI	SB	BA	xBA	OBP	SLG	OPS	vL	vR	bb%	ct%	Eye	G	L	F	h%	HctX	PX	xPX	hr/f	Spd	SBO	SB%	#Wk	DOM	DIS	RC/G	RAR	BPV	BPX
13																																		
14																																		
15	WAS *	370	41	2	32	22	251	253	271	335	606	0	500	3	76	0.12	56	22	22	33	73	66	12	0%	99	29%	95%	8	0%	25%	3.34	-9.0	-4	-11
16	WAS *	473	66	6	43	28	240	266	297	324	621	774	725	8	83	0.48	59	20	22	28	95	51	52	10%	112	32%	69%	10	40%	50%	3.16	-24.8	24	69
17	WAS *	372	51	5	22	10	258	256	310	351	661	848	637	7	78	0.35	51	24	25	32	73	53	54	8%	158	11%	91%	27	26%	48%	3.85	-12.6	19	58
1st Half		134	14	1	6	1	179	226	236	244	480	400	533	7	79	0.36	59	14	27	22	65	39	44	5%	122	7%	50%	13	15%	54%	1.75	-13.4	1	3
2nd Half		238	37	4	16	9	303	266	347	412	759	943	685	7	78	0.34	48	28	24	38	75	61	58	9%	161	12%	100%	14	36%	43%	5.56	4.8	24	73
18	Proj	**327**	**44**	**5**	**24**	**14**	**255**	**262**	**304**	**356**	**660**	**765**	**620**	**7**	**80**	**0.34**	**55**	**21**	**24**	**31**	**81**	**58**	**52**	**8%**	**133**	**20%**	**80%**				**3.75**	**-6.9**	**16**	**49**

Donaldson,Josh

Age: 32	Bats: R	Pos: 3B	Health	B	LIMA Plan B+
Ht: 6' 1"	Wt: 210		PT/Exp	A	Rand Var 0
			Consist	A	MM 4255

Slow to get rolling after lingering calf strain, but closed strong, with a .302 BA and 22 HR in Aug/Sept. Only skills red flag is a spike in K's, although that improved some late as well. Nagging injuries first cropped up in 2016; that's the biggest risk as he moves deeper into his 30s. Otherwise, still among the top 3B options.

Yr	Tm	AB	R	HR	RBI	SB	BA	xBA	OBP	SLG	OPS	vL	vR	bb%	ct%	Eye	G	L	F	h%	HctX	PX	xPX	hr/f	Spd	SBO	SB%	#Wk	DOM	DIS	RC/G	RAR	BPV	BPX
13	OAK	579	89	24	93	5	301	282	384	499	883	1042	813	11	81	0.69	44	21	36	34	107	132	99	14%	109	4%	71%	27	48%	19%	6.92	47.4	87	218
14	OAK	608	93	29	98	8	255	264	342	456	798	1007	727	11	79	0.58	45	13	41	28	118	138	126	15%	98	5%	100%	27	56%	30%	5.35	29.8	78	211
15	TOR	620	122	41	123	6	297	297	371	568	939	1024	919	10	79	0.55	45	17	38	32	129	170	140	22%	92	3%	100%	27	74%	19%	7.71	53.6	100	270
16	TOR	577	122	37	99	7	284	290	404	549	953	932	960	16	79	0.92	38	21	41	30	130	148	135	20%	110	4%	88%	27	74%	7%	7.84	49.3	102	291
17	TOR	415	65	33	78	2	270	272	385	559	944	1051	917	15	73	0.68	41	17	42	29	108	164	132	26%	65	3%	50%	21	62%	24%	7.38	30.2	76	230
1st Half		142	15	8	20	1	254	262	361	486	847	960	819	14	72	0.58	42	21	37	30	111	142	116	21%	70	2%	100%	8	50%	38%	5.98	3.7	52	158
2nd Half		273	50	25	58	1	278	276	397	597	994	1090	967	16	74	0.75	40	15	45	29	106	174	140	27%	69	3%	33%	13	69%	15%	8.16	24.0	90	273
18	Proj	**511**	**89**	**35**	**92**	**4**	**278**	**279**	**383**	**544**	**927**	**1005**	**906**	**14**	**76**	**0.69**	**41**	**18**	**41**	**30**	**117**	**148**	**131**	**22%**	**83**	**3%**	**74%**				**7.28**	**34.7**	**73**	**222**

ROD TRUESDELL

Dozier,Brian

Age: 31 Bats: R Pos: 2B
Ht: 5' 11" Wt: 200

Health	A	LIMA Plan	B+
PT/Exp	A	Rand Var	-1
Consist	C	MM	4435

5% fewer fly balls with stable hr/f led to 8 fewer HR, but that's just noise. Shouldn't worry about widening platoon splits as they were mostly driven by h% (36% vL, 28% vR) which should regress. R$ repeat seems likely, and given that 72% of his 2016-17 HR were solo, may even be some RBI upside.

Yr Tm	AB	R	HR	RBI	SB	BA	xBA	OBP	SLG	OPS	vL	vR	bb%	ct%	Eye	G	L	F	h%	HctX	PX	xPX	hr/f	Spd	SBO	SB%	#Wk	DOM	DIS	RC/G	RAR	BPV	BPX	R$
13 MIN	558	72	18	66	14	244	256	312	414	726	978	649	8	78	0.43	38	21	41	28	89	118	99	10%	121	16%	67%	27	48%	37%	4.19	7.8	63	158	$16
14 MIN	598	112	23	71	21	242	257	345	416	762	804	743	13	78	0.69	37	20	43	27	95	124	97	11%	102	16%	75%	27	44%	19%	4.77	24.9	71	192	$24
15 MIN	628	101	28	77	12	236	261	307	444	751	762	746	9	76	0.41	33	23	44	27	100	138	129	13%	102	12%	75%	26	58%	19%	4.48	3.7	66	178	$18
16 MIN	615	104	42	99	18	268	276	340	546	886	965	862	9	78	0.44	36	16	48	28	109	159	137	18%	123	14%	90%	26	65%	15%	6.47	30.8	94	269	$30
17 MIN	617	106	34	93	16	248	264	357	496	853	1057	790	11	77	0.55	38	19	43	30	106	124	138	17%	116	13%	70%	27	63%	22%	5.98	24.2	67	203	$26
1st Half	306	37	13	37	10	248	256	334	431	766	965	711	11	79	0.57	39	19	41	28	107	104	128	13%	93	18%	67%	13	54%	31%	4.70	-1.2	50	152	$17
2nd Half	311	69	21	56	6	289	270	380	559	939	1132	873	12	76	0.54	37	19	44	32	106	144	148	21%	133	9%	75%	14	71%	14%	7.43	22.8	83	252	$36
18 Proj	**596**	**103**	**33**	**95**	**15**	**263**	**265**	**345**	**499**	**844**	**973**	**801**	**10**	**77**	**0.50**	**37**	**19**	**44**	**29**	**105**	**129**	**133**	**16%**	**114**	**13%**	**76%**				**5.83**	**17.9**	**68**	**205**	**$26**

Drury,Brandon

Age: 25 Bats: R Pos: 2B
Ht: 6' 2" Wt: 210

Health	A	LIMA Plan	B
PT/Exp	B	Rand Var	0
Consist	C	MM	3045

Second baseman's second full season was second year in a row he's posted double-digit HR with xPX that calls power output into question. Also second straight season with huge home/away splits: for 2016-17, .915 OPS at home, .639 elsewhere. So if you're having second thoughts about his value, we second that opinion.

Yr Tm	AB	R	HR	RBI	SB	BA	xBA	OBP	SLG	OPS	vL	vR	bb%	ct%	Eye	G	L	F	h%	HctX	PX	xPX	hr/f	Spd	SBO	SB%	#Wk	DOM	DIS	RC/G	RAR	BPV	BPX	R$
13																																		
14 aa	105	10	3	11	0	272		309	435	744			5	80	0.27				31		119			87	0%	0%				4.71		55	149	$1
15 ARI *	580	51	6	53	3	260	267	291	362	653	913	434	4	84	0.27	56	21	23	30	106	75	109	18%	71	9%	25%	5	20%	40%	3.40	-13.2	27	73	$8
16 ARI	461	59	16	53	1	282	271	329	458	786	804	779	6	78	0.31	50	20	30	33	105	111	97	15%	99	2%	50%	27	44%	37%	5.28	5.4	46	131	$13
17 ARI	445	41	13	63	1	267	275	317	447	764	738	775	6	77	0.27	49	22	29	32	99	114	87	13%	88	2%	50%	27	41%	30%	4.80	-2.7	39	118	$9
1st Half	258	26	8	38	1	283	280	329	461	790	637	839	5	76	0.23	49	24	26	34	100	112	77	15%	91	3%	50%	13	38%	38%	5.18	2.6	35	106	$13
2nd Half	187	15	5	25	0	246	265	300	428	728	831	669	7	78	0.33	48	18	34	29	97	116	100	10%	89	0%	0%	14	43%	21%	4.32	-2.8	46	139	$4
18 Proj	**429**	**43**	**13**	**56**	**1**	**270**	**274**	**317**	**443**	**759**	**822**	**730**	**6**	**79**	**0.29**	**50**	**21**	**29**	**32**	**102**	**106**	**96**	**13%**	**89**	**3%**	**36%**				**4.76**	**-0.5**	**27**	**80**	**$11**

Duda,Lucas

Age: 32 Bats: L Pos: 1B DH
Ht: 6' 4" Wt: 255

Health	F	LIMA Plan	B
PT/Exp	C	Rand Var	+4
Consist	C	MM	4035

Freed from 2016's back issues, he restored power to match career-high in HR, but h% didn't get the message, so low average and RBI total killed his value. Consistent xBA insists he has skills to fare better, though only to "BA that doesn't hurt you" level; if you're going to pursue those homers, do it on the cheap.

Yr Tm	AB	R	HR	RBI	SB	BA	xBA	OBP	SLG	OPS	vL	vR	bb%	ct%	Eye	G	L	F	h%	HctX	PX	xPX	hr/f	Spd	SBO	SB%	#Wk	DOM	DIS	RC/G	RAR	BPV	BPX	R$
13 NYM *	380	50	15	38	1	222	221	333	388	721	610	831	14	68	0.52	32	20	48	29	119	130	181	14%	67	3%	16%	18	33%	33%	4.12	-5.4	25	63	$4
14 NYM	514	74	30	92	3	253	263	349	481	830	516	915	12	74	0.51	31	20	49	29	132	165	181	16%	47	4%	60%	27	56%	15%	5.55	21.3	66	178	$20
15 NYM	471	67	27	73	0	244	263	352	486	838	878	823	12	71	0.48	27	22	51	29	120	174	167	16%	58	2%	0%	25	52%	32%	5.44	7.0	65	176	$13
16 NYM	153	20	7	23	0	229	259	302	412	714	454	776	9	76	0.42	37	24	39	25	102	110	110	15%	61	0%	0%	10	40%	40%	4.05	-3.6	32	91	$1
17 2 TM	423	50	30	64	0	217	264	322	496	818	658	867	12	68	0.44	30	21	49	24	116	176	155	21%	33	0%	0%	25	56%	32%	5.09	-3.6	49	148	$6
1st Half	187	24	14	30	0	257	295	365	572	937	798	974	14	70	0.54	31	24	45	29	132	200	159	24%	49	0%	0%	11	73%	27%	7.06	7.7	84	255	$7
2nd Half	236	26	16	34	0	186	239	287	436	723	567	777	11	67	0.38	30	19	52	20	103	157	153	20%	37	0%	0%	14	43%	36%	3.81	-13.8	27	82	$5
18 Proj	**434**	**57**	**26**	**72**	**0**	**234**	**257**	**329**	**474**	**803**	**651**	**848**	**11**	**71**	**0.44**	**32**	**22**	**47**	**27**	**113**	**147**	**148**	**18%**	**43**	**1%**	**26%**				**5.04**	**-0.8**	**33**	**99**	**$11**

Duffy,Matt

Age: 27 Bats: R Pos: DH
Ht: 6' 2" Wt: 170

Health	F	LIMA Plan	D
PT/Exp	D	Rand Var	0
Consist	D	MM	1441

Multiple setbacks from off-season Achilles heel surgery limited him to 8 AB in Single-A rehab stint. Probably best to put 2015 out of your mind, as power skills and BA potential were already waning before the injury, and we have no idea what surgery will do to his speed. He's end-game flyer material, for now.

Yr Tm	AB	R	HR	RBI	SB	BA	xBA	OBP	SLG	OPS	vL	vR	bb%	ct%	Eye	G	L	F	h%	HctX	PX	xPX	hr/f	Spd	SBO	SB%	#Wk	DOM	DIS	RC/G	RAR	BPV	BPX	R$
13																																		
14 SF *	427	48	2	59	16	291	267	347	379	726	888	300	8	79	0.41	41	33	26	36	80	72	56	0%	124	17%	75%	11	18%	55%	4.74	17.5	29	78	$17
15 SF	573	77	12	77	12	295	276	334	428	762	642	803	5	83	0.31	53	21	27	34	103	83	90	9%	137	8%	100%	27	44%	26%	5.24	13.3	52	141	$24
16 2 TM	333	41	5	28	8	258	263	310	357	668	702	654	6	84	0.43	50	21	29	29	90	59	67	6%	137	15%	62%	17	35%	24%	3.65	-6.4	39	111	$7
17																																		
1st Half																																		
2nd Half																																		
18 Proj	**229**	**28**	**2**	**30**	**5**	**267**	**269**	**326**	**364**	**690**	**812**	**617**	**7**	**82**	**0.39**	**47**	**26**	**27**	**32**	**89**	**58**	**68**	**5%**	**130**	**11%**	**67%**				**3.93**	**-10.5**	**17**	**52**	**$7**

Duvall,Adam

Age: 29 Bats: R Pos: LF
Ht: 6' 1" Wt: 215

Health	A	LIMA Plan	B+
PT/Exp	A	Rand Var	0
Consist	A	MM	4125

Another year, another second half with drastic drop in performance. No injuries, but does have Type 1 diabetes—could that be wearing him down? Can't rule out pitchers exploiting poor plate discipline as well. Regardless, PX/xPX gap, BPX regression put a damper on this 30-HR bat.

Yr Tm	AB	R	HR	RBI	SB	BA	xBA	OBP	SLG	OPS	vL	vR	bb%	ct%	Eye	G	L	F	h%	HctX	PX	xPX	hr/f	Spd	SBO	SB%	#Wk	DOM	DIS	RC/G	RAR	BPV	BPX	R$
13 aa	385	43	11	41	1	203		251	350	601			6	78	0.29				23		102			106	4%	55%				2.78		40	100	$0
14 SF *	432	51	18	63	1	219	243	258	395	653	525	629	5	72	0.19	38	21	42	26	105	132	155	14%	82	2%	100%	11	27%	45%	3.34	-5.8	29	78	$7
15 CIN *	561	62	31	77	4	224	248	265	444	709	498	895	5	70	0.18	29	24	47	26	111	153	128	28%	76	5%	77%	6	50%	50%	3.86	-14.6	36	97	$11
16 CIN	552	85	33	103	6	241	256	297	498	795	795	795	7	70	0.25	34	19	47	28	111	163	155	18%	111	11%	55%	27	44%	33%	4.77	2.3	60	171	$17
17 CIN	587	78	31	99	5	249	247	301	480	782	924	737	6	71	0.23	33	18	49	30	91	143	116	15%	87	7%	63%	27	37%	37%	4.75	-8.7	39	118	$16
1st Half	296	45	19	58	5	287	282	331	571	902	1092	849	6	74	0.26	35	21	44	33	104	169	120	19%	89	11%	71%	13	54%	23%	6.70	11.3	71	215	$26
2nd Half	291	33	12	41	0	210	210	272	388	660	782	616	6	68	0.21	32	15	53	26	78	114	111	11%	85	2%	0%	14	21%	50%	3.18	-19.7	4	12	$5
18 Proj	**559**	**73**	**29**	**90**	**4**	**241**	**243**	**295**	**462**	**757**	**748**	**760**	**6**	**71**	**0.22**	**33**	**19**	**48**	**29**	**99**	**135**	**131**	**15%**	**90**	**6%**	**60%**				**4.38**	**-1.3**	**29**	**89**	**$16**

Dyson,Jarrod

Age: 33 Bats: L Pos: CF
Ht: 5' 10" Wt: 165

Health	B	LIMA Plan	C
PT/Exp	D	Rand Var	0
Consist	B	MM	0533

Yet another slugger raises FB% and posts career high in HR... (Sadly, most of this is true.) Those extra fly balls cost him nearly 30 points of xBA, and only fluky 10 HBP kept OBP from similar fate. Recent slides in Spd, SBO have quietly eaten into SB upside, and after season-ending sports hernia surgery... DN: 200 AB, 15 SB

Yr Tm	AB	R	HR	RBI	SB	BA	xBA	OBP	SLG	OPS	vL	vR	bb%	ct%	Eye	G	L	F	h%	HctX	PX	xPX	hr/f	Spd	SBO	SB%	#Wk	DOM	DIS	RC/G	RAR	BPV	BPX	R$
13 KC *	265	36	2	18	37	231	248	293	324	617	531	741	8	78	0.39	58	17	25	29	70	66	68	5%	150	64%	86%	21	33%	33%	3.52	-5.8	26	65	$14
14 KC	260	33	1	24	36	269	233	324	327	651	604	663	8	80	0.42	63	14	23	33	56	37	39	2%	169	52%	84%	27	19%	48%	4.09	1.5	18	49	$17
15 KC	200	31	2	18	26	250	278	311	380	691	578	715	6	82	0.38	54	23	23	30	68	77	28	6%	169	60%	90%	26	42%	38%	4.29	-1.2	53	143	$12
16 KC *	321	51	1	26	33	275	280	335	378	713	1006	698	8	86	0.65	56	20	24	32	60	57	32	2%	161	42%	82%	25	52%	24%	4.66	2.8	57	163	$18
17 SEA	346	56	5	30	28	251	251	324	350	674	375	730	7	84	0.51	47	19	34	29	54	54	41	5%	145	37%	80%	21	38%	24%	3.78	-10.1	40	121	$15
1st Half	241	44	4	21	19	253	260	331	369	700	377	764	8	83	0.49	46	21	33	29	55	66	43	6%	134	37%	83%	13	38%	15%	4.07	-6.1	42	127	$19
2nd Half	105	12	1	9	9	248	227	307	305	612	369	653	7	87	0.57	49	16	36	28	52	26	38	3%	150	39%	75%	8	38%	38%	3.15	-5.6	29	88	$5
18 Proj	**259**	**38**	**2**	**22**	**24**	**256**	**259**	**320**	**351**	**671**	**536**	**694**	**7**	**84**	**0.51**	**52**	**19**	**29**	**30**	**58**	**49**	**38**	**4%**	**166**	**40%**	**84%**				**3.95**	**-4.3**	**43**	**131**	**$14**

Eaton,Adam

Age: 29 Bats: L Pos: CF
Ht: 5' 8" Wt: 185

Health	B	LIMA Plan	B
PT/Exp	B	Rand Var	-2
Consist	B	MM	2445

ACL and meniscus tears wiped away peak age season, so we didn't get to see if he'd build on power skill growth from 2H of 2016 (123 HctX, 116 xPX, 14% hr/f). All indications are he'll be ready for spring training, so hope is that he'll pick up where he left off, as a consistent power-speed asset with 20/20 potential.

Yr Tm	AB	R	HR	RBI	SB	BA	xBA	OBP	SLG	OPS	vL	vR	bb%	ct%	Eye	G	L	F	h%	HctX	PX	xPX	hr/f	Spd	SBO	SB%	#Wk	DOM	DIS	RC/G	RAR	BPV	BPX	R$
13 ARI *	285	43	4	25	5	235	261	282	341	623	708	665	6	81	0.35	57	19	25	28	84	71	63	6%	129	11%	71%	13	31%	23%	3.19	-7.8	35	88	$4
14 CHW	486	76	1	35	15	300	278	362	401	763	724	778	8	83	0.52	60	20	20	36	87	74	44	1%	156	16%	63%	23	43%	30%	5.05	16.7	56	151	$19
15 CHW	610	98	14	56	18	287	267	361	431	792	648	847	8	79	0.44	51	22	27	35	91	93	69	11%	142	14%	69%	26	38%	38%	5.29	17.0	50	135	$26
16 CHW	619	91	14	59	14	284	276	362	428	790	726	812	9	81	0.55	54	21	26	33	104	83	90	11%	129	10%	74%	27	48%	15%	5.33	11.9	51	146	$22
17 WAS	91	24	2	13	3	297	273	393	462	854	594	890	13	80	0.78	53	15	32	35	101	99	87	9%	136	13%	75%	4	50%	0%	6.52	3.7	69	209	$3
1st Half	91	24	2	13	3	297	273	393	462	854	594	890	13	80	0.78	53	15	32	35	101	99	87	9%	136	13%	75%	4	50%	0%	6.52	4.1	69	209	$3
2nd Half																																		
18 Proj	**538**	**96**	**12**	**56**	**13**	**286**	**276**	**363**	**438**	**801**	**672**	**837**	**10**	**81**	**0.55**	**54**	**19**	**27**	**34**	**95**	**86**	**74**	**10%**	**147**	**12%**	**68%**				**5.46**	**14.6**	**50**	**151**	**$23**

BRANDON KRUSE

Ellsbury,Jacoby

Age: 34 Bats: L Pos: CF | Ht: 6' 1" Wt: 195

Health C | LIMA Plan C+ | PT/Exp B | Rand Var 0 | Consist B | MM 1543

Concussion in May cost him a month, cutting short a quietly productive season. Struggles vs. LHP (0.26 Eye in 117 PA) also cost him AB, though stable plate skills with LD% stroke should keep BA afloat, and yield more running opps. But with no power to speak of, you're paying for bags on 34-year-old legs. That's risky.

Yr	Tm	AB	R	HR	RBI	SB	BA	xBA	OBP	SLG	OPS	vL	vR	bb%	ct%	Eye	G	L	F	h%	HctX	PX	xPX	hr/f	Spd	SBO	SB%	#Wk	DOM	DIS	RC/G	RAR	BPV	BPX	R$
13	BOS	577	92	9	53	52	298	276	355	426	781	641	863	7	84	0.51	51	21	28	34	107	85	78	7%	137	33%	93%	25	56%	20%	5.90	26.6	62	155	$39
14	NYY	575	71	16	70	39	271	276	328	419	747	828	711	8	84	0.53	42	25	34	30	103	98	87	10%	109	28%	89%	25	60%	16%	5.06	19.4	64	173	$31
15	NYY	452	66	7	33	21	257	248	318	345	663	652	669	7	81	0.41	45	24	31	30	79	58	56	6%	132	24%	70%	21	24%	43%	3.61	-12.1	26	70	$15
16	NYY	551	71	9	56	20	263	267	330	374	703	618	744	9	85	0.64	46	23	31	30	91	64	67	6%	114	17%	71%	27	30%	22%	4.22	-2.3	44	126	$17
17	NYY	356	65	7	39	22	264	273	348	402	750	637	795	10	82	0.65	46	23	31	30	87	78	62	8%	126	24%	88%	22	59%	23%	4.96	2.2	52	158	$16
1st Half		156	25	4	16	9	276	270	343	410	753	626	806	9	82	0.54	51	20	29	31	79	74	58	11%	109	24%	82%	9	56%	11%	5.01	0.5	40	121	$11
2nd Half		200	40	3	23	13	255	274	352	395	747	646	787	12	83	0.74	42	25	33	30	93	81	65	6%	132	24%	93%	13	62%	31%	4.93	0.1	59	179	$20
18	**Proj**	**349**	**56**	**6**	**36**	**19**	**264**	**269**	**339**	**389**	**728**	**646**	**765**	**9**	**83**	**0.61**	**46**	**23**	**31**	**30**	**89**	**70**	**65**	**7%**	**124**	**23%**	**83%**				**4.62**	**1.2**	**49**	**148**	**$14**

Encarnacion,Edwin

Age: 35 Bats: R Pos: DH 1B | Ht: 6' 1" Wt: 230

Health A | LIMA Plan B+ | PT/Exp A | Rand Var 0 | Consist A | MM 4145

Superb HR consistency, but with some warning signs? Contact rate, xBA declines continued steadily, taking BA down with 'em; PX, BPV in similar spirals; R$ dipped in an age when HR aren't as valuable. Uber-stable, he'll flirt with 40 HR again, and 2nd half plate skills look fine, but peak roto value is likely in the rearview.

Yr	Tm	AB	R	HR	RBI	SB	BA	xBA	OBP	SLG	OPS	vL	vR	bb%	ct%	Eye	G	L	F	h%	HctX	PX	xPX	hr/f	Spd	SBO	SB%	#Wk	DOM	DIS	RC/G	RAR	BPV	BPX	R$
13	TOR	530	90	36	104	7	272	311	370	534	904	859	916	13	88	1.32	35	22	43	25	135	150	152	18%	68	5%	88%	25	84%	8%	6.95	37.1	122	305	$28
14	TOR	477	75	34	98	2	268	300	354	547	901	870	909	11	83	0.76	36	16	47	26	137	176	153	18%	76	2%	100%	22	68%	14%	6.75	36.9	120	324	$24
15	TOR	528	94	39	111	3	277	297	372	557	929	836	950	12	81	0.79	36	19	45	27	129	166	142	20%	54	3%	60%	27	81%	4%	7.17	25.9	101	273	$28
16	TOR	601	99	42	127	2	263	284	357	529	886	902	881	12	77	0.63	38	20	41	28	118	155	137	22%	55	1%	100%	27	78%	7%	6.54	18.1	75	214	$24
17	CLE	554	96	38	107	2	258	269	377	504	881	857	891	16	76	0.78	37	21	42	27	116	131	136	21%	62	1%	100%	27	52%	19%	6.52	26.7	60	182	$20
1st Half		281	48	17	43	1	260	252	373	473	846	891	821	15	73	0.63	40	21	39	30	113	119	128	21%	61	1%	100%	13	31%	31%	6.02	9.4	36	109	$16
2nd Half		273	48	21	64	1	256	285	381	535	916	816	959	17	79	0.98	34	21	44	25	118	142	144	22%	68	1%	100%	14	71%	7%	7.05	17.4	86	261	$23
18	**Proj**	**570**	**98**	**37**	**109**	**2**	**263**	**277**	**370**	**507**	**877**	**843**	**888**	**14**	**78**	**0.77**	**37**	**21**	**42**	**28**	**120**	**130**	**140**	**20%**	**60**	**2%**	**87%**				**6.48**	**16.2**	**64**	**195**	**$24**

Engel,Adam

Age: 26 Bats: R Pos: CF | Ht: 6' 2" Wt: 210

Health A | LIMA Plan D | PT/Exp D | Rand Var +1 | Consist B | MM 2501

6-21-.166 with 8 SB in 301 AB at CHW. Known for his wheels, the speed skills played well at MLB level along with... little else. BA was stifled by 2nd half ct% that questions ability to stick, and couldn't hold uncharacteristic 1st half power spike. It's a long path to relevance and he's already 26; that usually doesn't turn out well.

Yr	Tm	AB	R	HR	RBI	SB	BA	xBA	OBP	SLG	OPS	vL	vR	bb%	ct%	Eye	G	L	F	h%	HctX	PX	xPX	hr/f	Spd	SBO	SB%	#Wk	DOM	DIS	RC/G	RAR	BPV	BPX	R$
13																																			
14																																			
15																																			
16	a/a	455	58	6	32	30	215		279	337	616			8	68	0.28				30		85			138	45%	65%				2.86		1	3	$11
17	CHW *	466	49	12	35	11	172	191	228	316	544	647	467	7	62	0.19	41	14	45	25	64	104	98	8%	136	20%	71%	19	11%	79%	2.20	-39.0	-13	-39	-$3
1st Half		221	27	8	18	7	208	229	269	395	663	929	721	8	65	0.23	44	18	38	28	81	129	115	13%	115	25%	67%	5	20%	80%	3.31	-11.2	13	39	$2
2nd Half		245	22	4	17	4	139	165	210	245	455	566	415	6	59	0.16	41	12	47	21	57	79	93	6%	146	14%	80%	14	7%	79%	1.40	-29.1	-44	-133	-$8
18	**Proj**	**207**	**23**	**3**	**15**	**7**	**187**	**192**	**266**	**311**	**577**	**751**	**506**	**7**	**64**	**0.22**	**42**	**15**	**44**	**27**	**67**	**87**	**102**	**6%**	**143**	**29%**	**64%**				**2.31**	**-14.9**	**-15**	**-46**	**$1**

Ervin,Phillip

Age: 25 Bats: R Pos: CF | Ht: 5' 10" Wt: 207

Health A | LIMA Plan D+ | PT/Exp D | Rand Var -2 | Consist A | MM 3411

3-10-.259 with 4 SB in 58 AB at CIN. Rocky path to majors for 2013 first-rounder, but made good use of first shot in small sample. SB ceiling is the draw and it comes with some pop, but career-low batting Eye tempers overall outlook. At the very least, HR/SB upside makes him viable deep-league dart throw.

Yr	Tm	AB	R	HR	RBI	SB	BA	xBA	OBP	SLG	OPS	vL	vR	bb%	ct%	Eye	G	L	F	h%	HctX	PX	xPX	hr/f	Spd	SBO	SB%	#Wk	DOM	DIS	RC/G	RAR	BPV	BPX	R$
13																																			
14																																			
15	aa	51	6	2	7	3	216		358	381	739			18	66	0.65				29		130			94	38%	51%				3.83		34	92	$0
16	aa	419	65	13	41	33	221		320	374	694			13	76	0.60				26		95			108	37%	75%				3.93		39	111	$16
17	CIN *	421	45	9	42	22	226	205	284	343	627	944	689	8	73	0.30	33	19	49	29	67	75	107	14%	102	30%	74%	10	30%	30%	3.20	-24.3	0	0	$10
1st Half		244	23	4	19	11	201	233	266	294	559	1000	0	8	70	0.29	100	0	0	27	0	63	-26	0%	85	28%	71%	2	50%	0%	2.47	-19.1	-25	-76	$6
2nd Half		177	22	5	23	11	260	224	311	411	722	915	723	7	77	0.31	29	20	51	32	74	91	114	14%	108	34%	77%	8	25%	38%	4.40	-2.7	27	82	$16
18	**Proj**	**222**	**29**	**8**	**23**	**11**	**230**	**231**	**313**	**401**	**714**	**866**	**648**	**10**	**75**	**0.41**	**34**	**19**	**47**	**27**	**67**	**101**	**103**	**11%**	**105**	**30%**	**70%**				**3.92**	**-4.1**	**30**	**92**	**$8**

Escobar,Alcides

Age: 31 Bats: R Pos: SS | Ht: 6' 1" Wt: 185

Health A | LIMA Plan B+ | PT/Exp A | Rand Var 0 | Consist A | MM 1435

Played all 162 for third time in four years, but SB% collapse wrecked his R$. Spd says wheels are still there, ct% recovery drove 2nd half BA gains, so there is hope for some rebound. At best, a Professional Free Agent, but in OBP leagues, he has often been the only 600-AB player to remain unrostered all year.

Yr	Tm	AB	R	HR	RBI	SB	BA	xBA	OBP	SLG	OPS	vL	vR	bb%	ct%	Eye	G	L	F	h%	HctX	PX	xPX	hr/f	Spd	SBO	SB%	#Wk	DOM	DIS	RC/G	RAR	BPV	BPX	R$
13	KC	607	57	4	52	22	234	250	259	300	559	620	532	3	86	0.23	46	23	31	27	75	45	60	3%	140	17%	100%	26	23%	27%	2.74	-12.5	31	78	$11
14	KC	579	74	3	50	31	285	265	317	377	694	784	663	4	86	0.28	44	24	32	33	82	70	62	2%	139	25%	84%	27	41%	22%	4.31	18.7	50	135	$25
15	KC	612	76	3	47	17	257	255	293	320	614	653	598	4	88	0.35	48	22	30	29	80	41	53	2%	137	14%	77%	27	37%	22%	3.18	-22.0	35	95	$14
16	KC	637	57	7	55	17	261	256	292	350	642	584	660	4	85	0.28	50	20	30	30	77	52	49	4%	136	13%	81%	27	44%	48%	3.55	-14.0	32	91	$14
17	KC	599	71	6	54	4	250	252	272	357	629	720	602	2	83	0.15	41	22	37	29	90	65	90	3%	124	9%	36%	27	33%	41%	3.11	-27.1	28	85	$7
1st Half		309	31	2	24	2	227	230	245	311	555	654	524	2	80	0.10	41	20	39	28	84	55	77	2%	126	7%	50%	13	23%	62%	2.41	-20.4	9	27	$1
2nd Half		290	40	4	30	2	276	276	300	407	707	800	682	3	86	0.22	40	24	36	31	96	76	103	4%	118	11%	29%	14	43%	21%	3.97	-5.1	48	145	$13
18	**Proj**	**576**	**65**	**5**	**51**	**11**	**258**	**258**	**285**	**354**	**638**	**679**	**625**	**3**	**85**	**0.22**	**44**	**22**	**34**	**30**	**85**	**56**	**73**	**3%**	**128**	**13%**	**66%**				**3.36**	**-18.8**	**23**	**71**	**$13**

Escobar,Eduardo

Age: 29 Bats: B Pos: 3B DH | Ht: 5' 10" Wt: 185

Health A | LIMA Plan B | PT/Exp C | Rand Var 0 | Consist D | MM 3235

Streaky season ended with 9 HR explosion in Sept, but also featured three months of sub-20 BPV. He's flashed plus power before, and while the added FB% lifts his HR ceiling, stagnant xBA offers little room for BA growth. May be more peaks than valleys thanks to prime age, but set 2017 repeat as your ceiling.

Yr	Tm	AB	R	HR	RBI	SB	BA	xBA	OBP	SLG	OPS	vL	vR	bb%	ct%	Eye	G	L	F	h%	HctX	PX	xPX	hr/f	Spd	SBO	SB%	#Wk	DOM	DIS	RC/G	RAR	BPV	BPX	R$
13	MIN *	331	39	6	30	4	251	244	300	383	683	655	619	7	77	0.31	42	21	37	31	77	97	94	6%	129	11%	51%	18	33%	44%	3.76	3.3	40	100	$5
14	MIN	433	52	6	37	1	275	264	315	406	721	877	654	5	79	0.26	41	24	35	34	99	110	93	5%	109	2%	50%	27	41%	26%	4.44	15.6	47	127	$10
15	MIN	409	48	12	58	2	262	267	309	445	754	789	737	6	79	0.33	42	19	39	31	101	125	118	10%	105	6%	40%	27	44%	30%	4.62	2.7	62	168	$10
16	MIN	352	32	6	37	1	236	241	280	338	618	552	648	6	80	0.29	39	24	37	28	86	63	73	6%	82	5%	25%	25	36%	44%	3.03	-13.5	6	17	$2
17	MIN	457	62	21	73	5	254	250	309	449	758	730	773	7	79	0.34	34	21	45	28	100	102	114	13%	114	6%	83%	27	33%	37%	4.68	0.7	45	136	$12
1st Half		187	22	8	26	1	273	269	318	444	762	934	658	6	83	0.39	33	24	43	29	110	89	85	12%	76	2%	100%	13	46%	38%	4.96	2.1	42	127	$5
2nd Half		270	40	13	47	4	241	239	303	452	755	574	847	7	75	0.31	34	19	47	27	93	111	137	13%	139	8%	80%	14	21%	36%	4.49	-0.7	48	145	$17
18	**Proj**	**492**	**59**	**21**	**67**	**4**	**251**	**259**	**301**	**441**	**742**	**729**	**748**	**6**	**79**	**0.31**	**37**	**22**	**41**	**28**	**95**	**103**	**103**	**13%**	**105**	**6%**	**60%**				**4.42**	**-6.9**	**36**	**109**	**$13**

Escobar,Yunel

Age: 35 Bats: R Pos: 3B | Ht: 6' 2" Wt: 215

Health D | LIMA Plan C | PT/Exp B | Rand Var 0 | Consist B | MM 1033

Lights dimmed on late-career BA bonanza, as injuries (May hamstring, August oblique), fewer LDs, and h% erosion crashed the party. And xBA never bought into him as a .300 hitter anyway. With softer ratio cushion, no power/speed, and health woes in mid-30s, you start looking elsewhere for value.

Yr	Tm	AB	R	HR	RBI	SB	BA	xBA	OBP	SLG	OPS	vL	vR	bb%	ct%	Eye	G	L	F	h%	HctX	PX	xPX	hr/f	Spd	SBO	SB%	#Wk	DOM	DIS	RC/G	RAR	BPV	BPX	R$
13	TAM	508	61	9	56	4	256	266	332	366	698	750	674	10	86	0.78	53	19	27	28	117	76	98	8%	90	5%	50%	27	59%	19%	4.07	1.8	52	130	$10
14	TAM	476	33	7	39	1	258	244	324	340	664	689	656	8	87	0.72	49	20	31	28	105	57	75	6%	74	1%	50%	25	56%	20%	3.72	0.7	36	97	$6
15	WAS	535	75	9	56	2	314	275	375	415	790	760	800	8	87	0.64	55	22	23	35	105	65	72	8%	102	2%	50%	26	46%	19%	5.61	15.0	48	130	$20
16	LAA	517	68	5	39	0	304	271	355	391	745	852	714	7	87	0.60	58	21	21	34	96	56	64	5%	103	2%	0%	26	42%	23%	4.94	2.0	40	114	$14
17	LAA	350	43	7	31	1	274	270	333	397	730	832	689	8	85	0.57	58	18	24	30	105	70	75	10%	100	5%	20%	17	35%	24%	4.40	-4.5	45	136	$6
1st Half		253	31	5	23	1	289	280	350	415	765	882	718	8	86	0.64	59	19	22	32	106	72	69	10%	104	7%	20%	11	27%	9%	4.88	-1.5	50	152	$9
2nd Half		97	12	2	8	0	237	245	288	351	639	704	611	6	85	0.40	56	15	29	26	104	65	90	8%	86	0%	0%	6	50%	50%	3.30	-5.2	30	91	-$2
18	**Proj**	**403**	**48**	**7**	**33**	**1**	**278**	**265**	**334**	**383**	**717**	**783**	**693**	**7**	**86**	**0.55**	**56**	**19**	**25**	**31**	**103**	**61**	**76**	**8%**	**95**	**3%**	**25%**				**4.36**	**-6.0**	**21**	**64**	**$10**

RYAN BLOOMFIELD

Espinosa,Danny

Age: 31 Bats: B Pos: 2B
Ht: 6' 0" Wt: 205

Health	A	LIMA Plan	F
PT/Exp	C	Rand Var	+2
Consist	C	MM	2201

Contact rate and vR have always been terrible, but power/speed combo and success vL have historically allowed him to carve out some value. Now, all of those skills have come crashing down as well. Perhaps he can jump Lines from Espinosa (.173) to Mendoza, but that's not a reason to keep him on your radar.

Yr Tm	AB	R	HR	RBI	SB	BA	xBA	OBP	SLG	OPS	vL	vR	bb%	ct%	Eye	G	L	F	h%	HctX	PX	xPX	hr/f	Spd	SBO	SB%	#Wk	DOM	DIS	RC/G	RAR	BPV	BPX	R$
13 WAS *	441	33	4	27	6	169	173	199	245	444	529	448	4	63	0.10	51	10	39	26	70	74	95	7%	76	11%	83%	10	40%	50%	1.52	-30.9	-55	-138	-$7
14 WAS	333	31	8	27	8	219	215	283	351	634	859	532	5	63	0.15	44	22	34	32	100	115	134	12%	107	14%	89%	26	27%	54%	3.04	-3.5	-9	-24	$4
15 WAS	367	59	13	37	5	240	242	311	409	719	753	709	8	71	0.31	45	18	37	30	86	124	113	14%	100	8%	71%	24	33%	42%	4.12	-1.6	32	86	$8
16 WAS	516	66	24	72	9	209	214	306	378	684	712	675	9	66	0.31	39	18	43	26	90	111	130	17%	75	9%	82%	27	26%	44%	3.49	-19.8	-3	-9	$8
17 3 AL	266	30	6	31	4	173	171	245	278	523	499	537	7	59	0.19	42	14	44	26	76	82	109	9%	83	18%	44%	22	18%	64%	1.87	-24.3	-56	-170	-$3
1st Half	218	27	6	29	3	165	179	243	284	527	515	533	8	61	0.22	43	13	44	24	76	88	110	11%	77	17%	43%	13	8%	69%	1.88	-21.5	-46	-139	-$2
2nd Half	48	3	0	2	1	208	136	255	250	505	453	564	4	52	0.09	40	16	44	40	76	50	104	0%	107	20%	50%	9	33%	56%	1.81	-4.6	-109	-330	-$8
18 Proj	**229**	**25**	**7**	**22**	**4**	**203**	**191**	**272**	**334**	**606**	**572**	**624**	**7**	**61**	**0.18**	**42**	**16**	**42**	**30**	**82**	**96**	**114**	**12%**	**96**	**14%**	**59%**				**2.66**	**-15.5**	**-42**	**-127**	**$0**

Fisher,Derek

Age: 24 Bats: L Pos: LF
Ht: 6' 3" Wt: 205

Health	A	LIMA Plan	D
PT/Exp	D	Rand Var	+2
Consist	A	MM	2323

5-17-.212 with 3 SB in 146 AB at HOU. PRO: contact rate on the rise at Triple-A in 1st half; second straight year with above average power and speed. CON: 63% ct% in MLB; bb% slippage; low FB% caps HR upside; SB% took turn for the worse. Still a long-term asset, but a lot to overcome for a 2018 breakout.

Yr Tm	AB	R	HR	RBI	SB	BA	xBA	OBP	SLG	OPS	vL	vR	bb%	ct%	Eye	G	L	F	h%	HctX	PX	xPX	hr/f	Spd	SBO	SB%	#Wk	DOM	DIS	RC/G	RAR	BPV	BPX	R$
13																																		
14																																		
15																																		
16 a/a	478	59	18	63	23	228		323	394	717			12	63	0.38				32		120			105	23%	75%				4.20		4	11	$15
17 HOU *	489	62	19	60	14	241	266	298	416	714	644	668	7	70	0.27	54	24	21	31	108	110	101	26%	113	25%	48%	13	15%	54%	3.76	-25.5	20	61	$13
1st Half	304	34	14	38	10	247	275	294	445	739	0	1450	6	72	0.24	50	25	25	30	158	121	119	67%	90	35%	43%	2	50%	0%	3.78	-15.0	28	85	$17
2nd Half	185	29	5	22	4	232	245	304	368	672	799	576	9	67	0.31	55	24	21	32	96	91	99	19%	130	12%	67%	11	9%	64%	3.66	-9.6	0	0	$5
18 Proj	**255**	**34**	**8**	**32**	**7**	**234**	**242**	**315**	**387**	**702**	**856**	**667**	**9**	**68**	**0.31**	**50**	**22**	**28**	**31**	**96**	**98**	**89**	**17%**	**128**	**19%**	**56%**				**3.68**	**-6.1**	**1**	**3**	**$7**

Flores,Wilmer

Age: 26 Bats: R Pos: 3B 1B
Ht: 6' 3" Wt: 205

Health	A	LIMA Plan	B+
PT/Exp	C	Rand Var	-1
Consist	B	MM	3045

Lefty masher shook off slow start and was showing some encouraging signs before broken nose ended season in early Sept. Previous year's FB% held up, and power metrics surged across the board. Much of the damage was done vs RHP, too, which bolsters chances for regular role. If that's the case... UP: .280 BA, 30 HR

Yr Tm	AB	R	HR	RBI	SB	BA	xBA	OBP	SLG	OPS	vL	vR	bb%	ct%	Eye	G	L	F	h%	HctX	PX	xPX	hr/f	Spd	SBO	SB%	#Wk	DOM	DIS	RC/G	RAR	BPV	BPX	R$
13 NYM *	519	53	11	69	1	246	269	276	384	660	447	591	4	81	0.22	51	22	27	28	70	98	47	5%	80	4%	16%	8	50%	50%	3.48	-17.1	36	90	$9
14 NYM *	479	54	14	64	1	250	256	283	393	676	382	749	4	84	0.28	40	20	40	27	101	95	103	7%	110	3%	30%	20	40%	35%	3.71	-6.8	54	146	$11
15 NYM	483	55	16	59	0	263	267	295	408	703	955	637	4	87	0.30	42	21	37	27	109	86	95	10%	92	1%	0%	26	46%	23%	4.06	-18.2	54	146	$11
16 NYM	307	38	16	49	1	267	274	319	469	788	1093	642	7	84	0.48	33	22	45	27	93	108	107	14%	96	3%	50%	21	48%	29%	5.14	-1.7	68	194	$9
17 NYM	336	42	18	52	1	271	271	307	488	795	862	765	5	84	0.31	36	18	46	28	120	111	127	14%	96	3%	50%	21	52%	10%	5.17	-7.0	65	197	$9
1st Half	200	26	7	25	1	285	262	313	460	773	778	771	4	86	0.31	37	18	45	30	121	93	118	9%	116	2%	100%	12	50%	8%	5.21	-2.4	62	188	$10
2nd Half	136	16	11	27	0	250	281	297	529	827	1002	756	6	82	0.32	35	19	47	23	120	138	142	21%	74	4%	0%	9	56%	11%	5.08	-2.3	72	218	$9
18 Proj	**504**	**60**	**25**	**79**	**1**	**263**	**269**	**304**	**463**	**767**	**917**	**706**	**5**	**84**	**0.35**	**36**	**20**	**44**	**27**	**108**	**102**	**115**	**14%**	**89**	**3%**	**34%**				**4.77**	**-1.8**	**41**	**125**	**$16**

Flowers,Tyler

Age: 32 Bats: R Pos: CA
Ht: 6' 4" Wt: 260

Health	B	LIMA Plan	D+
PT/Exp	D	Rand Var	-2
Consist	C	MM	3013

1st half BA was a little fluky given the sky high h%, but year-long jumps in ct% and LD% a sign that some of his recent BA gains are sustainable. Power skills fully rebounded in 2nd half, and second straight year with a lot of hard contact hints at the potential for a HR spike. Give him 400 AB and... UP: 20 HR.

Yr Tm	AB	R	HR	RBI	SB	BA	xBA	OBP	SLG	OPS	vL	vR	bb%	ct%	Eye	G	L	F	h%	HctX	PX	xPX	hr/f	Spd	SBO	SB%	#Wk	DOM	DIS	RC/G	RAR	BPV	BPX	R$
13 CHW	256	24	10	24	0	195	208	247	355	603	455	661	5	63	0.15	42	17	41	26	86	133	106	15%	64	2%	0%	22	32%	59%	2.62	-8.7	-8	-20	-$1
14 CHW	407	42	15	50	0	241	222	297	396	693	732	679	6	61	0.16	48	24	29	36	82	137	88	21%	68	1%	0%	26	31%	62%	3.74	3.4	-12	-32	$7
15 CHW	331	21	9	39	0	239	194	295	356	652	751	627	6	69	0.20	47	17	36	32	93	88	85	11%	66	1%	0%	26	27%	54%	3.34	-4.6	-21	-57	$2
16 ATL	281	27	8	41	0	270	217	357	420	777	767	781	9	68	0.32	42	19	39	37	120	113	153	11%	80	0%	0%	22	36%	45%	4.97	4.5	5	14	$5
17 ATL	317	41	12	49	0	281	255	378	445	823	829	821	8	74	0.38	42	24	33	35	111	99	99	15%	64	1%	0%	27	30%	33%	5.37	11.8	14	42	$9
1st Half	179	28	6	26	0	318	257	413	458	872	733	887	9	77	0.41	42	25	33	39	111	80	72	13%	83	0%	0%	13	31%	31%	6.47	11.3	17	52	$12
2nd Half	138	13	6	23	0	232	254	333	428	761	875	714	9	70	0.34	42	23	34	29	112	127	138	18%	48	3%	0%	14	29%	36%	4.16	0.3	18	55	$4
18 Proj	**354**	**36**	**12**	**51**	**0**	**250**	**233**	**336**	**408**	**744**	**764**	**736**	**8**	**70**	**0.29**	**43**	**21**	**36**	**32**	**108**	**103**	**117**	**14%**	**62**	**1%**	**0%**				**4.26**	**1.2**	**-14**	**-41**	**$8**

Forsythe,Logan

Age: 31 Bats: R Pos: 2B 3B
Ht: 6' 1" Wt: 205

Health	C	LIMA Plan	D+
PT/Exp	B	Rand Var	0
Consist	B	MM	2223

Got off to rough start with fractured toe in April, and things never got much better. Reverted back to doing nothing vR, and while ultra-patient approach led to solid bb%/OBP, xBA disapproved of the change. Second half HctX/xPX shows there is some pop left in his bat, so minimal investment should yield a small profit.

Yr Tm	AB	R	HR	RBI	SB	BA	xBA	OBP	SLG	OPS	vL	vR	bb%	ct%	Eye	G	L	F	h%	HctX	PX	xPX	hr/f	Spd	SBO	SB%	#Wk	DOM	DIS	RC/G	RAR	BPV	BPX	R$
13 SD *	245	26	7	22	6	221	254	291	360	651	651	593	9	74	0.38	42	28	29	27	100	94	105	13%	107	11%	86%	17	12%	35%	3.49	-1.2	24	60	$2
14 TAM	301	32	6	26	2	223	224	287	329	616	708	536	7	76	0.35	41	19	40	27	83	80	100	6%	103	3%	100%	27	30%	59%	3.08	-2.8	17	46	$2
15 TAM	540	69	17	68	9	281	255	359	444	804	972	728	9	79	0.50	40	20	41	33	108	109	105	10%	106	8%	69%	26	46%	23%	5.44	19.5	57	154	$20
16 TAM	511	76	20	52	6	264	259	333	444	778	775	778	8	75	0.36	42	23	35	32	110	110	115	15%	122	9%	50%	24	50%	25%	4.83	-0.5	43	123	$14
17 LA	361	56	6	36	3	224	225	351	327	678	870	576	16	70	0.63	44	23	33	30	103	74	111	7%	93	4%	60%	23	30%	52%	3.72	-14.2	0	0	$2
1st Half	158	25	2	12	1	247	223	363	329	692	1061	529	15	69	0.55	43	26	31	35	88	61	68	6%	102	2%	100%	9	11%	56%	4.02	-3.8	-14	-42	$0
2nd Half	203	31	4	24	2	207	226	341	325	666	748	617	17	70	0.70	45	21	35	27	115	84	143	8%	86	6%	50%	14	43%	50%	3.51	-8.4	11	33	$4
18 Proj	**368**	**53**	**11**	**38**	**4**	**245**	**244**	**342**	**391**	**733**	**863**	**673**	**12**	**73**	**0.52**	**43**	**22**	**35**	**31**	**105**	**91**	**111**	**12%**	**101**	**6%**	**61%**				**4.39**	**-4.5**	**14**	**42**	**$8**

Fowler,Dexter

Age: 32 Bats: B Pos: CF
Ht: 6' 5" Wt: 195

Health	C	LIMA Plan	B+
PT/Exp	A	Rand Var	0
Consist	B	MM	3535

Nagging injuries (heel, hip, back, wrist, shoulder, quad) held down AB total again, and likely SBO as well, but skills were better than ever. xBA and power reached new heights, xPX hints at further HR upside, while return of SB can't be dismissed given OBP/Spd. Despite age, if he could just stay healthy... UP: 25 HR, 20 SB

Yr Tm	AB	R	HR	RBI	SB	BA	xBA	OBP	SLG	OPS	vL	vR	bb%	ct%	Eye	G	L	F	h%	HctX	PX	xPX	hr/f	Spd	SBO	SB%	#Wk	DOM	DIS	RC/G	RAR	BPV	BPX	R$
13 COL	415	71	12	42	19	263	246	369	407	776	860	741	13	75	0.62	42	23	34	33	81	102	102	11%	135	20%	68%	23	48%	35%	4.99	11.0	49	123	$18
14 HOU	434	61	8	35	11	276	240	375	399	774	887	737	13	75	0.61	44	21	35	35	95	94	107	7%	145	10%	73%	20	45%	40%	5.23	17.4	47	127	$15
15 CHC	596	102	17	46	20	250	245	346	411	757	865	726	12	74	0.55	43	20	36	31	90	109	98	11%	164	15%	74%	26	50%	27%	4.78	8.3	59	159	$19
16 CHC	456	84	13	48	13	276	250	393	447	840	876	827	14	73	0.64	41	24	36	35	90	110	100	11%	143	11%	76%	23	48%	35%	6.06	18.4	53	151	$18
17 STL	420	68	18	64	7	264	269	363	488	851	754	883	13	76	0.62	39	22	38	31	117	124	150	15%	147	8%	70%	24	54%	38%	6.04	12.0	75	227	$14
1st Half	241	40	13	35	3	245	272	336	481	817	686	865	12	76	0.58	39	22	38	27	115	126	151	18%	138	8%	60%	12	67%	25%	5.36	3.3	74	224	$15
2nd Half	179	28	5	29	4	291	265	397	497	894	859	905	14	75	0.68	39	23	38	36	120	120	149	10%	149	8%	80%	12	42%	50%	7.04	10.7	73	221	$13
18 Proj	**455**	**76**	**15**	**57**	**11**	**270**	**257**	**372**	**458**	**830**	**827**	**831**	**13**	**75**	**0.61**	**41**	**22**	**37**	**33**	**104**	**109**	**125**	**12%**	**151**	**11%**	**74%**				**5.85**	**17.6**	**53**	**161**	**$18**

Fowler,Dustin

Age: 23 Bats: L Pos: RF
Ht: 6' 0" Wt: 195

Health	D	LIMA Plan	C+
PT/Exp	D	Rand Var	0
Consist	B	MM	3433

Earned late June call-up with huge 1H, but suffered season-ending knee injury in MLB debut. Before getting hurt, showed off his usual speed, and made significant power gains. Now in OAK and expected to be ready for spring training, he offers sneaky upside, as abbreviated season could leave him flying under the radar.

Yr Tm	AB	R	HR	RBI	SB	BA	xBA	OBP	SLG	OPS	vL	vR	bb%	ct%	Eye	G	L	F	h%	HctX	PX	xPX	hr/f	Spd	SBO	SB%	#Wk	DOM	DIS	RC/G	RAR	BPV	BPX	R$
13																																		
14																																		
15																																		
16 aa	541	63	13	83	24	268		295	434	730			4	83	0.22				30		93			119	31%	67%				4.26		50	143	$22
17 NYY *	297	44	14	38	12	273	276	304	505	810	0	0	4	76	0.19	44	20	36	32	0	129	-26	0%	133	29%	68%	1	0%	100%	5.17	3.6	59	179	$12
1st Half	297	44	14	38	12	273	276	304	505	810			4	76	0.19				32		129		0%	133	29%	68%	1	0%	100%	5.17	2.3	59	179	$12
2nd Half																																		
18 Proj	**370**	**50**	**12**	**51**	**10**	**271**	**257**	**299**	**462**	**761**	**761**	**761**	**4**	**78**	**0.18**	**38**	**21**	**41**	**32**		**107**		**10%**	**134**	**19%**	**66%**				**4.67**	**-0.2**	**45**	**137**	**$15**

BRIAN RUDD

Franco,Maikel

Age: 25 Bats: R Pos: 3B	Health A	LIMA Plan B+
Ht: 6' 1" Wt: 215	PT/Exp B	Rand Var +3
	Consist C	MM 3145

Treading water in mediocrity with below average power and bb%. Consistent ct% keeps BA from Mendoza Line, but subpar h% limits its upside. Second half G/L/F shift and HctX bump leaves door slightly open for further power growth, which is developmental "doggy paddling" at this point.

Yr	Tm	AB	R	HR	RBI	SB	BA	xBA	OBP	SLG	OPS	vL	vR	bb%	ct%	Eye	G	L	F	h%	HctX	PX	xPX	hr/f	Spd	SBO	SB%	#Wk	DOM	DIS	RC/G	RAR	BPV	BPX	R$
13	aa	277	36	12	39	1	305		324	492	816			3	87	0.22				31		109			101	4%	26%				5.67		75	188	$1
14	PHI *	577	55	14	65	2	222	240	253	358	611	277	573	4	82	0.23	49	12	40	25	32	97	26	0%	105	3%	68%	5	0%	60%	2.96	-13.3	46	124	$6
15	PHI *	445	57	18	70	3	291	283	340	492	832	825	844	7	82	0.40	47	18	35	32	105	130	120	16%	91	2%	100%	16	69%	25%	6.06	17.1	74	200	$18
16	PHI	581	67	25	88	1	255	263	306	427	733	860	698	6	82	0.38	44	20	35	27	102	95	91	15%	76	1%	50%	27	48%	26%	4.40	-9.8	41	117	$14
17	PHI	575	66	24	76	0	230	264	281	409	690	657	701	7	83	0.43	45	18	37	24	105	95	86	13%	63	0%	0%	27	52%	22%	3.80	-26.1	44	133	$7
1st Half		287	26	10	38	0	216	259	276	366	642	784	585	8	85	0.55	51	19	30	22	98	79	73	14%	57	0%	0%	13	46%	31%	3.29	-15.8	36	109	$2
2nd Half		288	40	14	38	0	243	265	286	451	737	498	809	6	82	0.33	40	17	44	25	111	111	98	13%	79	0%	0%	14	57%	14%	4.34	-6.4	55	167	$1
18	**Proj**	**557**	**66**	**25**	**78**	**1**	**252**	**269**	**301**	**445**	**746**	**670**	**774**	**6**	**83**	**0.39**	**45**	**18**	**37**	**26**	**97**	**102**	**87**	**15%**	**74**	**1%**	**67%**				**4.53**	**-5.9**	**41**	**125**	**$1**

Frazier,Adam

Age: 26 Bats: L Pos: LF 2B	Health A	LIMA Plan D+
Ht: 5' 9" Wt: 185	PT/Exp C	Rand Var +2
	Consist B	MM 1351

Sneaky speed source? Career high AB in MLB led to double-digit R$, with excellent contact, above average speed, and a bit of pop. Solid LD approach and decent Eye will buoy BA, but value hinges on regular plate appearances and being smart on the base paths. A potential end-game SB flyer.

Yr	Tm	AB	R	HR	RBI	SB	BA	xBA	OBP	SLG	OPS	vL	vR	bb%	ct%	Eye	G	L	F	h%	HctX	PX	xPX	hr/f	Spd	SBO	SB%	#Wk	DOM	DIS	RC/G	RAR	BPV	BPX	R$
13																																			
14																																			
15	aa	377	47	1	24	9	281		328	356	684			7	88	0.57				32		51			115	15%	52%				3.92		41	111	$10
16	PIT *	407	52	2	31	19	306	298	366	400	766	840	753	9	86	0.70	44	33	23	35	110	59	93	7%	135	28%	52%	16	25%	56%	4.79	1.9	53	151	$18
17	PIT	406	55	6	53	9	276	288	344	399	743	676	754	8	86	0.63	48	25	27	31	96	66	59	6%	119	12%	64%	25	44%	24%	4.61	-7.6	50	152	$12
1st Half		214	33	3	28	5	276	281	350	383	733	711	738	9	86	0.70	51	23	26	31	94	59	47	6%	120	14%	56%	11	36%	18%	4.40	-6.0	47	142	$13
2nd Half		192	22	3	25	4	276	295	338	417	755	619	771	7	86	0.56	45	28	28	31	97	74	73	7%	113	10%	80%	14	50%	29%	4.85	-2.8	53	161	$1
18	**Proj**	**226**	**29**	**4**	**23**	**7**	**287**	**286**	**349**	**415**	**765**	**746**	**768**	**8**	**86**	**0.63**	**48**	**24**	**28**	**32**	**101**	**69**	**75**	**7%**	**120**	**16%**	**67%**				**4.98**	**3.4**	**52**	**158**	**$9**

Frazier,Clint

Age: 23 Bats: R Pos: LF	Health A	LIMA Plan D+
Ht: 6' 1" Wt: 190	PT/Exp D	Rand Var 0
	Consist A	MM 3411

4-17-.231 with 1 SB in 134 AB at NYY. Impact in 2018? Power translated to MLB with big July, when he flashed an above average HctX, but poor plate discipline and 2nd half oblique injury limited him late. Profile suggests legitimate power/speed combo, but unless plate approach changes, could spend more time in AAA.

Yr	Tm	AB	R	HR	RBI	SB	BA	xBA	OBP	SLG	OPS	vL	vR	bb%	ct%	Eye	G	L	F	h%	HctX	PX	xPX	hr/f	Spd	SBO	SB%	#Wk	DOM	DIS	RC/G	RAR	BPV	BPX	R$
13																																			
14																																			
15																																			
16	a/a	463	70	18	51	12	253		319	436	755			9	71	0.34				32		120			108	14%	74%				4.72		33	94	$14
17	NYY *	407	57	17	54	9	237	242	305	449	753	771	695	9	71	0.33	38	17	45	29	115	132	158	10%	121	13%	80%	11	36%	36%	4.58	-10.5	44	133	$9
1st Half		277	43	14	38	8	243	230	323	464	788	5000	1000	11	72	0.42	0	33	67	29	97	136	57	50%	107	15%	79%	1	100%	0%	5.06	-2.4	52	158	$15
2nd Half		130	14	3	16	1	223	228	261	415	676	647	686	5	68	0.17	39	17	44	31	111	124	162	8%	144	5%	100%	10	30%	40%	3.62	-6.9	25	76	-$4
18	**Proj**	**222**	**30**	**8**	**27**	**5**	**240**	**236**	**308**	**431**	**739**	**620**	**779**	**9**	**71**	**0.35**	**39**	**17**	**44**	**30**	**107**	**119**	**146**	**11%**	**125**	**11%**	**79%**				**4.50**	**0.3**	**37**	**111**	**$6**

Frazier,Todd

Age: 32 Bats: R Pos: 3B	Health A	LIMA Plan B+
Ht: 6' 3" Wt: 220	PT/Exp A	Rand Var +4
	Consist A	MM 4125

Lowest AB total since 2012, below average HctX, and dropoff in SB led to single-digit R$. But stable G/L/F and power metrics continue to prop up HR count, and if he can hold bb% and Eye gains, BA will recover (but 2016-17 xBA is his likely ceiling). Full rebound depends on AB—but remember everyone hits HR these days.

Yr	Tm	AB	R	HR	RBI	SB	BA	xBA	OBP	SLG	OPS	vL	vR	bb%	ct%	Eye	G	L	F	h%	HctX	PX	xPX	hr/f	Spd	SBO	SB%	#Wk	DOM	DIS	RC/G	RAR	BPV	BPX	R$
13	CIN	531	63	19	73	6	234	251	314	407	721	782	696	8	76	0.40	42	18	40	27	103	121	121	12%	98	9%	55%	27	41%	22%	3.95	0.0	51	128	$12
14	CIN	597	88	29	80	20	273	263	336	459	795	750	807	8	77	0.37	41	22	37	31	114	127	123	17%	93	17%	71%	27	48%	19%	5.24	27.2	54	146	$30
15	CIN	619	82	35	89	13	255	273	309	498	806	908	773	6	78	0.32	33	19	48	28	125	157	155	15%	79	17%	62%	27	63%	30%	5.01	8.2	76	205	$24
16	CHW	590	89	40	98	15	225	245	302	464	767	803	758	10	72	0.39	36	16	49	24	92	142	111	19%	71	15%	75%	27	44%	26%	4.57	-4.0	46	131	$19
17	2 AL	474	74	27	76	4	213	243	344	428	772	883	736	14	74	0.66	34	18	47	23	96	122	122	16%	76	5%	57%	27	44%	30%	4.52	-4.9	46	139	$8
1st Half		247	34	15	39	4	211	251	324	437	761	817	743	14	75	0.66	35	18	47	22	98	127	121	17%	68	10%	57%	13	54%	15%	4.44	-5.0	52	158	$8
2nd Half		227	40	12	37	0	216	234	364	419	782	958	727	16	72	0.67	33	19	48	24	93	115	123	15%	91	0%	0%	14	36%	43%	4.60	-3.4	41	124	$7
18	**Proj**	**500**	**76**	**28**	**79**	**4**	**229**	**246**	**330**	**447**	**777**	**866**	**750**	**12**	**74**	**0.52**	**35**	**18**	**47**	**25**	**100**	**124**	**124**	**16%**	**78**	**6%**	**54%**				**4.63**	**-4.0**	**40**	**120**	**$14**

Freeman,Freddie

Age: 28 Bats: L Pos: 1B	Health C	LIMA Plan C
Ht: 6' 5" Wt: 220	PT/Exp A	Rand Var 0
	Consist C	MM 4255

What might have been: Wrist injury interrupted monster first half, and it took a while to get going again until a big Sept (137 HctX, 159 xPX). Year-long ct% uptick, rising OPS, above average bb%, and elite LD rates could all come together in 2018. With health, this could finally be the year for... UP: 40+ HR, MVP candidate.

Yr	Tm	AB	R	HR	RBI	SB	BA	xBA	OBP	SLG	OPS	vL	vR	bb%	ct%	Eye	G	L	F	h%	HctX	PX	xPX	hr/f	Spd	SBO	SB%	#Wk	DOM	DIS	RC/G	RAR	BPV	BPX	R$
13	ATL	551	89	23	109	1	319	274	396	501	897	764	958	10	78	0.55	38	27	35	38	123	121	152	15%	99	1%	100%	25	60%	16%	7.38	41.0	62	155	$31
14	ATL	607	93	18	78	3	288	283	386	461	847	756	885	13	76	0.62	37	31	32	35	131	134	159	12%	100	4%	43%	27	56%	22%	6.17	33.8	69	186	$24
15	ATL	416	62	18	66	3	276	279	370	471	841	656	912	12	76	0.57	37	28	36	32	130	133	152	16%	82	3%	75%	22	45%	23%	6.01	7.6	62	168	$16
16	ATL	589	102	34	91	6	302	279	400	569	968	902	1001	13	71	0.52	30	29	41	38	125	173	177	20%	110	4%	86%	27	59%	15%	8.21	46.4	83	237	$29
17	ATL	440	84	28	71	8	307	300	403	586	989	880	1032	13	78	0.68	35	24	41	34	119	157	156	20%	101	10%	62%	21	76%	10%	8.33	29.5	97	294	$24
1st Half		135	35	14	25	4	341	337	461	748	1209	1127	1226	17	77	0.87	38	22	40	36	126	222	183	33%	106	15%	57%	7	86%	14%	12.36	24.2	153	464	$17
2nd Half		305	49	14	46	4	292	286	375	515	890	820	925	11	79	0.59	34	26	41	33	116	130	145	14%	100	7%	67%	14	71%	7%	6.79	9.8	74	224	$27
18	**Proj**	**549**	**100**	**32**	**93**	**6**	**303**	**291**	**399**	**563**	**962**	**850**	**1008**	**13**	**76**	**0.61**	**34**	**26**	**39**	**35**	**123**	**151**	**163**	**20%**	**99**	**5%**	**64%**				**8.00**	**43.8**	**75**	**229**	**$30**

Freese,David

Age: 35 Bats: R Pos: 3B	Health B	LIMA Plan D
Ht: 6' 2" Wt: 220	PT/Exp C	Rand Var -2
	Consist A	MM 1013

Has the $10 Freese begun to thaw? Huge dropoff in power metrics obscured outwardly stable stat line from 2016, and xBA scoffed at his small uptick in plate approach. He continues to hit copious amounts of grounders, now with less authority than ever. At his age, loss of AB often follows. Chilly production, especially from a CO slot.

Yr	Tm	AB	R	HR	RBI	SB	BA	xBA	OBP	SLG	OPS	vL	vR	bb%	ct%	Eye	G	L	F	h%	HctX	PX	xPX	hr/f	Spd	SBO	SB%	#Wk	DOM	DIS	RC/G	RAR	BPV	BPX	R$
13	STL	462	53	9	60	1	262	253	340	381	721	811	689	9	77	0.44	55	21	24	32	118	91	97	10%	79	2%	33%	25	36%	28%	4.28	3.8	25	63	$10
14	LAA	462	53	10	55	1	260	253	321	383	704	876	656	7	73	0.31	49	26	26	34	124	101	116	11%	79	3%	25%	25	28%	48%	4.07	4.8	14	38	$10
15	LAA *	445	54	15	60	1	254	250	306	413	719	719	752	7	75	0.29	54	18	28	31	109	114	108	16%	72	2%	50%	22	50%	32%	4.29	-5.0	27	73	$10
16	PIT	437	63	13	55	0	270	232	352	412	764	963	710	9	68	0.32	61	19	20	37	97	104	92	22%	99	0%	0%	26	27%	50%	4.87	-1.3	3	9	$10
17	PIT	426	44	10	52	0	263	225	368	371	739	839	704	12	73	0.50	57	20	23	34	94	68	80	14%	86	1%	0%	26	23%	50%	4.47	-10.3	-3	-9	$7
1st Half		196	26	6	25	0	250	229	371	372	744	825	718	14	76	0.69	57	18	25	30	96	70	79	16%	92	0%	0%	12	25%	50%	4.53	-3.2	16	48	$6
2nd Half		230	18	4	27	0	274	223	365	370	734	847	692	10	70	0.37	57	23	20	37	92	66	82	12%	83	1%	0%	14	21%	50%	4.40	-4.5	-19	-58	$8
18	**Proj**	**378**	**41**	**9**	**44**	**0**	**259**	**229**	**347**	**377**	**725**	**826**	**692**	**10**	**71**	**0.38**	**57**	**20**	**23**	**34**	**97**	**79**	**90**	**15%**	**85**	**1%**	**20%**				**4.27**	**-6.8**	**-23**	**-71**	**$8**

Fuentes,Reymond

Age: 27 Bats: L Pos: CF	Health A	LIMA Plan D
Ht: 6' 0" Wt: 160	PT/Exp D	Rand Var -2
	Consist C	MM 1521

3-9-.235 with 4 SB in 136 AB at ARI. Former first-round pick parlayed career June (.353 with 10 runs) into another mediocre season. He fails to 1) hit LHP; 2) produce power; 3) log an MLB Eye ratio greater than his age. All of which renders his elite Spd irrelevant. Time is running out—if the clock is even still ticking.

Yr	Tm	AB	R	HR	RBI	SB	BA	xBA	OBP	SLG	OPS	vL	vR	bb%	ct%	Eye	G	L	F	h%	HctX	PX	xPX	hr/f	Spd	SBO	SB%	#Wk	DOM	DIS	RC/G	RAR	BPV	BPX	R$
13	SD *	433	61	5	34	30	272	246	337	360	697	333	381	9	74	0.38	60	20	20	36	73	71	69	0%	133	32%	71%	6	0%	100%	4.18	1.0	13	33	$20
14	a/a	327	38	3	23	18	240		291	329	620			7	77	0.31				30		67			124	25%	84%				3.33		14	38	$8
15	aaa	396	56	7	37	23	274		315	368	683			6	80	0.30				33		57			131	27%	77%				4.11		18	49	$18
16	KC *	281	25	0	15	12	232	240	282	283	565	0	705	6	72	0.25	53	28	19	32	18	39	-9	0%	167	28%	61%	6	17%	50%	2.52	-18.5	-13	-37	$3
17	ARI *	311	38	3	18	12	260	238	294	351	645	418	652	5	77	0.22	46	22	31	33	89	53	72	10%	177	18%	85%	15	33%	53%	3.65	-12.7	15	45	$7
1st Half		223	30	1	11	8	287	229	317	376	694	481	668	4	77	0.20	47	19	34	37	71	52	47	4%	198	14%	88%	7	29%	43%	4.39	-3.2	21	64	$10
2nd Half		88	8	2	7	4	192	256	239	287	526	286	621	6	76	0.26	45	29	26	23	129	56	127	25%	106	32%	79%	8	38%	63%	2.21	-7.7	-5	-15	$0
18	**Proj**	**165**	**15**	**3**	**11**	**7**	**240**	**242**	**284**	**340**	**624**	**399**	**665**	**6**	**76**	**0.26**	**48**	**23**	**29**	**30**	**86**	**57**	**95**	**8%**	**136**	**23%**	**72%**				**3.20**	**-6.5**	**-6**	**-17**	**$4**

JOSEPH PYTLESKI

Gallo,Joey

Age: 24 Bats: L Pos: 3B 1B | Health A | LIMA Plan B+
Ht: 6' 5" Wt: 235 | PT/Exp C | Rand Var +4
Consist B | MM 5315

While 2H xBA, aided by shift to more LD%, offers path forward to higher value, it hinges on repeating PX/xPX combo that was highest of any 2017 full-timer. That's a tall order for any hitter, let alone one who strikes out in nearly half his AB. Youth, high bb% help his chances, but know that the sub-Mendoza Line risk is real.

Yr Tm	AB	R	HR	RBI	SB	BA	xBA	OBP	SLG	OPS	vL	vR	bb%	ct%	Eye	G	L	F	h%	HctX	PX	xPX	hr/f	Spd	SBO	SB%	#Wk	DOM	DIS	RC/G	RAR	BPV	BPX	R$
13																																		
14 aa	250	36	17	46	2	211		295	456	750			11	51	0.24				32		242			81	3%	100%				4.38		46	124	$6
15 TEX *	429	49	24	64	5	210	217	303	433	736	477	836	12	52	0.28	35	27	37	33	115	206	185	32%	81	5%	100%	10	40%	50%	4.29	-8.5	23	62	$7
16 TEX *	384	57	21	52	3	204	184	310	434	743	250	374	13	53	0.33	17	17	67	31	36	185	100	25%	120	3%	100%	7	0%	86%	4.33	-6.2	26	74	$4
17 TEX	449	85	41	80	7	209	237	333	537	869	841	878	14	56	0.38	28	18	54	25	106	231	206	30%	109	8%	78%	27	59%	30%	5.57	2.7	73	221	$13
1st Half	243	47	21	41	5	193	227	300	514	814	790	821	12	56	0.31	26	13	61	23	100	233	212	26%	111	11%	100%	13	69%	15%	4.86	-6.0	69	209	$13
2nd Half	206	38	20	39	2	228	251	369	563	932	877	948	17	57	0.47	30	23	47	28	113	230	200	37%	106	7%	50%	14	50%	43%	6.46	5.1	80	242	$13
18 Proj	**484**	**79**	**39**	**80**	**6**	**221**	**231**	**334**	**519**	**853**	**705**	**910**	**14**	**55**	**0.35**	**31**	**22**	**46**	**30**	**111**	**219**	**197**	**32%**	**108**	**6%**	**80%**				**5.56**	**10.0**	**52**	**159**	**$14**

Galvis,Freddy

Age: 28 Bats: B Pos: SS | Health A | LIMA Plan B
Ht: 5' 10" Wt: 185 | PT/Exp A | Rand Var 0
Consist A | MM 1425

2016's hr/f surge was really only half a season, and now that we have three years of subpar xPX marks, that 20 HR power sure looks like a fluke. SBO jumps have been more common, and with bb% gain, can't rule out run at 20 SB, though given overall mediocrity of skills, hard to believe he'll see 600+ AB again.

Yr Tm	AB	R	HR	RBI	SB	BA	xBA	OBP	SLG	OPS	vL	vR	bb%	ct%	Eye	G	L	F	h%	HctX	PX	xPX	hr/f	Spd	SBO	SB%	#Wk	DOM	DIS	RC/G	RAR	BPV	BPX	R$
13 PHI *	446	33	8	38	3	221	218	256	340	596	688	662	5	77	0.21	36	19	46	27	96	83	115	8%	126	5%	74%	18	39%	39%	2.85	-8.9	22	55	$1
14 PHI *	254	30	6	23	2	200	217	248	347	595	496	573	6	76	0.27	41	8	51	24	84	112	117	9%	106	7%	60%	12	25%	50%	2.70	-4.7	40	108	$0
15 PHI	559	63	7	50	10	263	229	302	343	645	602	662	5	82	0.29	41	22	37	31	88	49	89	4%	139	7%	91%	27	22%	41%	3.64	-1.9	19	51	$13
16 PHI	584	61	20	67	17	241	253	274	399	673	544	715	4	77	0.18	40	23	36	28	83	95	80	13%	98	20%	74%	27	37%	30%	3.62	-17.6	22	63	$14
17 PHI	608	71	12	61	14	255	252	309	382	690	638	714	7	82	0.41	37	24	39	29	84	71	85	6%	125	12%	74%	27	44%	30%	3.99	-9.5	37	112	$14
1st Half	287	27	7	31	5	251	262	299	408	707	685	717	6	83	0.39	39	21	40	28	94	86	97	7%	130	9%	83%	13	62%	23%	4.16	-3.5	54	164	$9
2nd Half	321	44	5	30	9	259	245	317	358	675	587	712	7	81	0.42	34	27	39	31	75	58	75	5%	115	15%	69%	14	29%	36%	3.82	-7.1	21	64	$18
18 Proj	**463**	**52**	**11**	**47**	**12**	**249**	**247**	**292**	**380**	**672**	**605**	**699**	**6**	**80**	**0.29**	**38**	**23**	**39**	**29**	**84**	**74**	**87**	**8%**	**120**	**15%**	**78%**				**3.75**	**-9.8**	**25**	**75**	**$12**

Gamel,Ben

Age: 26 Bats: L Pos: LF RF | Health A | LIMA Plan B
Ht: 5' 11" Wt: 185 | PT/Exp B | Rand Var -2
Consist B | MM 1325

11-59-.275 with 4 SB in 509 AB at SEA. Despite h%-fueled hot start, his average ct%, underwhelming power, and difficulty vL (68% contact, 0.11 Eye) paint him as 4th OF. Spd is biggest asset, but sluggish SBO and SB% rates persist. Even with improvement, best-case might be double-digit SB without hurting you elsewhere.

Yr Tm	AB	R	HR	RBI	SB	BA	xBA	OBP	SLG	OPS	vL	vR	bb%	ct%	Eye	G	L	F	h%	HctX	PX	xPX	hr/f	Spd	SBO	SB%	#Wk	DOM	DIS	RC/G	RAR	BPV	BPX	R$
13 aa	67	4	1	4	1	221		259	318	578			5	71	0.18				30		84			96	6%	100%				2.76		-6	-15	-$2
14 aa	544	47	2	41	11	234		273	301	574			5	82	0.30				28		57			93	13%	66%				2.70		14	38	$5
15 aaa	500	68	10	56	11	276		331	427	757			8	76	0.34				35		100			130	13%	67%				4.89		39	105	$17
16 2 AL *	531	81	7	51	17	273	237	330	375	705	1162	404	8	77	0.36	44	22	34	34	80	68	69	9%	115	17%	66%	9	22%	56%	4.23	-0.6	13	37	$18
17 SEA *	569	73	12	65	5	273	247	326	404	730	699	746	7	76	0.34	45	22	33	34	91	79	80	8%	123	4%	69%	24	29%	38%	4.60	-13.8	22	67	$14
1st Half	285	46	5	33	3	323	241	391	448	839	887	876	10	74	0.42	37	27	37	43	96	81	100	7%	137	4%	70%	10	40%	50%	6.57	9.3	22	67	$21
2nd Half	284	27	7	32	2	222	253	258	359	618	558	637	5	79	0.23	51	18	31	26	87	77	65	10%	114	5%	67%	14	21%	29%	3.02	-20.3	23	70	$7
18 Proj	**455**	**58**	**10**	**48**	**8**	**264**	**251**	**316**	**400**	**716**	**674**	**729**	**7**	**77**	**0.33**	**45**	**22**	**33**	**32**	**91**	**80**	**79**	**9%**	**124**	**10%**	**67%**				**4.33**	**-1.7**	**20**	**61**	**$13**

Garcia,Adonis

Age: 33 Bats: R Pos: 3B | Health D | LIMA Plan D+
Ht: 5' 9" Wt: 205 | PT/Exp C | Rand Var +4
Consist C | MM 1241

Behold Adonis, the Greek god of empty contact: After posting 136 PX, 22% hr/f over 191 AB in majors in 2015, fell to 74 PX, 12% hr/f in 705 AB since. Still owns career .822 OPS vL, but even there, PX is only 89, and in age of smaller benches, being on wrong side of platoon isn't exactly a path to job security.

Yr Tm	AB	R	HR	RBI	SB	BA	xBA	OBP	SLG	OPS	vL	vR	bb%	ct%	Eye	G	L	F	h%	HctX	PX	xPX	hr/f	Spd	SBO	SB%	#Wk	DOM	DIS	RC/G	RAR	BPV	BPX	R$
13 aaa	199	13	3	8	3	211		244	294	538			4	87	0.34				23		54			103	20%	39%				2.09		33	83	-$2
14 aaa	342	38	7	30	7	243		268	354	622			3	80	0.17				28		81			98	16%	65%				3.12		24	65	$6
15 ATL *	522	53	12	62	4	243	264	266	364	631	982	706	3	83	0.19	49	22	29	27	113	79	107	22%	53	5%	75%	13	54%	23%	3.26	-21.9	18	49	$8
16 ATL *	605	76	17	79	5	271	272	301	409	710	765	700	4	82	0.24	52	21	27	31	99	84	63	12%	64	6%	58%	25	40%	44%	4.24	-12.8	24	69	$17
17 ATL	173	19	5	19	4	237	257	273	347	620	772	593	4	87	0.30	55	16	29	25	102	54	69	11%	75	10%	100%	14	21%	43%	3.20	-10.8	22	67	$2
1st Half	154	17	4	16	4	247	259	282	351	633	856	607	4	87	0.30	54	17	29	26	107	52	69	10%	79	11%	100%	9	22%	33%	3.40	-7.7	23	70	$3
2nd Half	19	2	1	3	0	158	219	200	316	516	636	347	5	84	0.33	63	6	31	13	64	69	67	20%	70	0%	0%	5	20%	60%	1.91	-2.0	25	76	-$5
18 Proj	**236**	**25**	**7**	**25**	**4**	**247**	**269**	**278**	**379**	**657**	**825**	**609**	**4**	**84**	**0.24**	**52**	**20**	**28**	**27**	**107**	**71**	**83**	**12%**	**75**	**10%**	**74%**				**3.51**	**-9.7**	**22**	**67**	**$5**

Garcia,Avisail

Age: 27 Bats: R Pos: RF | Health C | LIMA Plan B
Ht: 6' 4" Wt: 240 | PT/Exp B | Rand Var -5
Consist D | MM 2245

Feels like former top prospect's talent has been in hibernation forever, which made 2017 seem like the breakout we've all been waiting for. But h%, xBA say it was mostly a dream. Still only 27, and 2nd half did see gains in bb%, ct%, Eye, so maybe this was a tentative step forward. But odds are he doesn't hit .300 again.

Yr Tm	AB	R	HR	RBI	SB	BA	xBA	OBP	SLG	OPS	vL	vR	bb%	ct%	Eye	G	L	F	h%	HctX	PX	xPX	hr/f	Spd	SBO	SB%	#Wk	DOM	DIS	RC/G	RAR	BPV	BPX	R$
13 2 AL *	418	55	13	58	6	309	254	340	453	793	640	770	5	76	0.20	56	18	26	38	107	95	92	15%	140	10%	55%	17	29%	53%	5.49	13.9	34	85	$19
14 CHW *	222	25	8	31	4	253	242	300	405	705	992	620	6	72	0.23	56	15	28	32	81	119	89	19%	77	9%	80%	10	50%	30%	4.17	1.7	19	51	$6
15 CHW	553	66	13	59	7	257	243	309	365	675	759	650	6	75	0.26	49	25	27	32	96	73	90	12%	98	10%	50%	27	33%	48%	3.65	-18.3	0	0	$13
16 CHW	413	59	12	51	4	245	253	307	385	692	677	696	8	72	0.30	55	22	23	31	101	92	77	17%	93	8%	50%	25	36%	40%	3.81	-11.0	7	20	$8
17 CHW	518	75	18	80	5	330	275	380	506	885	1030	837	6	79	0.30	52	20	27	39	112	98	89	16%	135	5%	63%	25	48%	44%	7.04	28.9	47	142	$26
1st Half	289	40	11	51	2	318	283	362	512	875	1059	817	4	77	0.19	52	23	26	38	113	112	96	19%	126	5%	50%	13	46%	38%	6.52	11.4	45	136	$28
2nd Half	229	35	7	29	3	345	265	401	498	899	996	862	8	81	0.45	53	18	30	40	111	83	81	13%	135	5%	75%	12	50%	50%	7.69	15.6	48	145	$23
18 Proj	**556**	**78**	**19**	**75**	**6**	**286**	**266**	**339**	**445**	**783**	**866**	**755**	**7**	**77**	**0.30**	**53**	**21**	**27**	**34**	**105**	**90**	**85**	**16%**	**117**	**7%**	**59%**				**5.17**	**7.6**	**20**	**62**	**$22**

Garcia,Greg

Age: 28 Bats: L Pos: 3B 2B | Health A | LIMA Plan D
Ht: 6' 0" Wt: 190 | PT/Exp D | Rand Var -1
Consist A | MM 1231

If just six of the hits that drove ridiculous h% behind his 2nd half BA had been turned into outs, he'd have hit .242, not .290, and we might not even be talking about him. Trends in ct%, HctX, xPX, and hr/f all agree: there's nothing to see here. Instead, we could use this space for movie reviews. Wind River is excellent.

Yr Tm	AB	R	HR	RBI	SB	BA	xBA	OBP	SLG	OPS	vL	vR	bb%	ct%	Eye	G	L	F	h%	HctX	PX	xPX	hr/f	Spd	SBO	SB%	#Wk	DOM	DIS	RC/G	RAR	BPV	BPX	R$
13 aaa	354	37	2	26	10	228		301	315	616			9	78	0.47				29		71			109	14%	82%				3.20		21	53	$3
14 STL *	411	46	6	30	6	222	229	276	304	580	1167	377	7	71	0.25	100	0	0	30	115	67	-15	0%	109	11%	49%	8	0%	50%	2.63	-9.6	-13	-35	$3
15 STL *	405	41	2	30	11	236	243	312	307	620	1171	688	10	80	0.55	57	18	25	29	103	56	71	13%	94	13%	76%	12	58%	17%	3.24	-11.3	14	38	$5
16 STL *	318	42	3	23	2	256	249	350	334	684	577	806	12	77	0.62	50	25	24	32	74	55	67	8%	108	5%	41%	23	22%	39%	3.89	-9.1	11	31	$4
17 STL	241	27	2	20	2	253	253	365	332	697	342	758	13	73	0.58	48	30	22	34	50	52	41	5%	121	4%	67%	27	30%	48%	3.99	-7.2	0	0	$2
1st Half	117	8	1	6	2	214	267	338	274	612	392	661	14	75	0.66	47	34	18	28	54	41	54	6%	94	5%	100%	13	31%	46%	2.97	-6.7	-8	-24	-$3
2nd Half	124	19	1	14	0	290	241	390	387	778	259	843	13	72	0.51	49	26	25	40	47	62	28	5%	137	2%	0%	14	29%	50%	5.13	1.1	5	15	$6
18 Proj	**185**	**22**	**2**	**15**	**2**	**252**	**254**	**353**	**346**	**699**	**478**	**739**	**12**	**75**	**0.56**	**50**	**26**	**23**	**32**	**66**	**60**	**53**	**7%**	**116**	**6%**	**61%**				**4.00**	**-4.8**	**-3**	**-11**	**$3**

Garcia,Leury

Age: 27 Bats: B Pos: CF LF | Health C | LIMA Plan C+
Ht: 5' 8" Wt: 170 | PT/Exp D | Rand Var -2
Consist B | MM 1433

Finger, thumb injuries kept him out of action for most of June, July, and Sept, so it's hard to know if 2nd half skill collapse was regression or playing at less than 100%. But even if we give him benefit of the doubt, hr/f doesn't have much support from HctX, xPX. Still, if 1st half ct% gains hold, could be some BA/SB upside here.

Yr Tm	AB	R	HR	RBI	SB	BA	xBA	OBP	SLG	OPS	vL	vR	bb%	ct%	Eye	G	L	F	h%	HctX	PX	xPX	hr/f	Spd	SBO	SB%	#Wk	DOM	DIS	RC/G	RAR	BPV	BPX	R$
13 2 AL *	324	38	4	18	19	227	215	273	314	587	566	445	6	68	0.20	46	25	29	32	45	66	44	0%	159	33%	75%	17	12%	65%	2.84	-8.8	-11	-28	$7
14 CHW	145	13	1	6	11	166	190	192	207	399	368	421	3	67	0.10	62	14	24	24	57	38	25	4%	96	48%	92%	26	12%	73%	1.41	-9.4	-64	-173	-$1
15 CHW *	363	47	3	27	26	257	266	293	336	629	533	444	5	77	0.22	100	0	0	33	95	60	-16	0%	126	43%	65%	9	0%	67%	3.15	-12.4	3	8	$14
16 CHW *	358	42	6	33	16	264	238	305	363	668	353	755	6	75	0.24	54	20	26	34	78	59	68	11%	122	28%	61%	5	0%	80%	3.60	-12.1	-3	-9	$11
17 CHW	300	41	9	33	8	270	271	316	423	739	689	759	4	77	0.19	55	21	24	32	83	89	66	16%	107	19%	62%	16	50%	44%	4.25	-3.2	21	64	$9
1st Half	181	28	6	22	6	298	292	345	459	804	705	843	5	81	0.26	53	24	23	34	93	88	88	18%	101	23%	55%	11	64%	36%	5.09	1.4	37	112	$13
2nd Half	119	13	3	11	2	227	240	270	370	640	667	628	3	71	0.11	60	14	26	30	68	92	27	14%	117	10%	100%	5	20%	60%	3.15	-6.0	0	0	$2
18 Proj	**401**	**49**	**9**	**37**	**16**	**264**	**253**	**304**	**391**	**695**	**642**	**721**	**4**	**76**	**0.20**	**53**	**20**	**27**	**32**	**81**	**74**	**41**	**11%**	**115**	**25%**	**67%**				**3.88**	**-7.5**	**11**	**33**	**$15**

BRANDON KRUSE

Garcia,Willy

Age: 25	Bats: R	Pos: RF	Health	A	LIMA Plan	F
Ht: 6' 2"	Wt: 215		PT/Exp	C	Rand Var	-2
			Consist	B	MM	2101

2-12-.238 in 105 AB at CHW. It's a Good Cop/Bad Cop act: Flashed power at times—but tendency to beat ball into the ground has stifled it. Good speed—but mitigated by historically lousy SB%. A 2017 bb% uptick—but swings and misses way too often. Raw tools are there, but need harnessing. For now, not interested.

Yr	Tm	AB	R	HR	RBI	SB	BA	xBA	OBP	SLG	OPS	vL	vR	bb%	ct%	Eye	G	L	F	h%	HctX	PX	xPX	hr/f	Spd	SBO	SB%	#Wk	DOM	DIS	RC/G	RAR	BPV	BPX	R$
13																																			
14	aa	439	44	12	47	6	231		260	379	639			4	65	0.11				33		131			97	13%	57%				3.16		3	8	$7
15	a/a	480	52	12	56	3	245		274	370	644			4	73	0.14				31		84			113	10%	34%				3.23		1	3	$8
16	aaa	462	49	5	40	5	229		275	341	616			6	70	0.21				32		86			102	15%	32%				2.84		-6	-17	$3
17	CHW *	217	30	6	27	1	241	219	321	399	721	786	663	11	65	0.34	50	16	34	34	68	108	76	8%	120	1%	100%	17	29%	53%	4.33	-7.1	3	9	$2
1st Half		144	20	4	18	1	243	219	315	405	720	819	570	9	63	0.29	47	19	34	35	71	110	63	6%	119	2%	100%	11	18%	55%	4.33	-4.4	-2	-6	$3
2nd Half		73	10	2	9	0	235	212	333	388	721	705	909	13	67	0.45	57	9	35	33	59	102	104	13%	113	0%	0%	6	50%	50%	4.31	-2.3	11	33	$0
18	**Proj**	**129**	**16**	**3**	**14**	**1**	**236**	**217**	**295**	**376**	**671**	**686**	**662**	**8**	**68**	**0.27**	**53**	**13**	**34**	**33**	**64**	**94**	**88**	**10%**	**109**	**6%**	**43%**				**3.63**	**-4.1**	**-9**	**-28**	**$0**

Gardner,Brett

Age: 34	Bats: L	Pos: LF CF	Health	A	LIMA Plan	B
Ht: 5' 11"	Wt: 195		PT/Exp	A	Rand Var	0
			Consist	B	MM	1535

Rebounded from 2016 power outage with career-high HR thanks to resurgent xPX/FB% and a touch of hr/f luck. Faded in Aug/Sept (total of 2 HR; xPX of 33 & 44), so expect some pullback. Wheels remain intact and SB% is as strong as ever, though he's at an age where speed tends to decline.

Yr	Tm	AB	R	HR	RBI	SB	BA	xBA	OBP	SLG	OPS	vL	vR	bb%	ct%	Eye	G	L	F	h%	HctX	PX	xPX	hr/f	Spd	SBO	SB%	#Wk	DOM	DIS	RC/G	RAR	BPV	BPX	R$
13	NYY	539	81	8	52	24	273	251	344	416	759	744	767	9	76	0.41	41	23	35	34	80	104	70	6%	141	22%	75%	24	42%	33%	4.89	14.3	50	125	$22
14	NYY	555	87	17	58	21	256	254	327	422	749	687	775	9	76	0.42	42	22	37	31	95	117	91	11%	140	18%	81%	27	48%	30%	4.73	17.0	59	159	$22
15	NYY	571	94	16	66	20	259	247	343	399	742	761	734	10	76	0.50	45	21	34	31	88	94	87	11%	115	15%	80%	27	37%	48%	4.70	5.1	38	103	$22
16	NYY	547	80	7	41	16	261	257	351	362	713	645	745	11	81	0.66	52	21	27	31	84	61	43	6%	128	11%	80%	27	30%	37%	4.38	1.6	34	97	$15
17	NYY	594	96	21	63	23	264	266	350	428	778	590	840	11	79	0.59	44	22	33	30	92	89	79	13%	123	16%	82%	26	38%	46%	5.17	-4.7	49	148	$23
1st Half		291	56	15	40	10	265	270	342	474	817	559	883	11	78	0.55	41	21	38	29	113	115	107	17%	100	13%	91%	13	46%	31%	5.80	3.7	57	173	$27
2nd Half		303	40	6	23	13	264	264	357	383	740	609	794	11	81	0.64	48	23	29	31	72	66	53	9%	137	18%	76%	13	31%	62%	4.60	-6.7	41	124	$20
18	**Proj**	**563**	**87**	**14**	**54**	**19**	**263**	**259**	**348**	**399**	**747**	**646**	**787**	**11**	**79**	**0.57**	**47**	**22**	**32**	**31**	**87**	**77**	**69**	**10%**	**129**	**14%**	**79%**				**4.77**	**5.2**	**37**	**114**	**$21**

Garver,Mitch

Age: 27	Bats: R	Pos: CA	Health	A	LIMA Plan	D
Ht: 6' 1"	Wt: 220		PT/Exp	D	Rand Var	0
			Consist	D	MM	3221

0-3-.196 in 46 AB at MIN. Turned 30 doubles from 2016 into HR in 2017, and power metrics held their own in minute MLB sample. Plate patience a plus, but hefty swing and miss rates provide a challenge at his age. Known for his defense, which may create opportunities, but wait-and-see is the best course of action.

Yr	Tm	AB	R	HR	RBI	SB	BA	xBA	OBP	SLG	OPS	vL	vR	bb%	ct%	Eye	G	L	F	h%	HctX	PX	xPX	hr/f	Spd	SBO	SB%	#Wk	DOM	DIS	RC/G	RAR	BPV	BPX	R$
13																																			
14																																			
15																																			
16	a/a	434	42	10	62	1	241		306	373	679			9	73	0.35				31		94			74	4%	20%				3.71		10	29	$5
17	MIN *	366	55	15	44	2	255	254	344	471	815	762	530	12	70	0.46	45	16	39	32	92	140	95	0%	106	2%	100%	8	13%	50%	5.57	15.3	52	158	$8
1st Half		185	23	6	24	0	255	240	355	436	791			13	69	0.50				34		128			75	0%	0%				5.30		29	88	$5
2nd Half		181	33	9	19	2	255	270	332	508	839	762	530	10	72	0.42	45	16	39	30	94	152	95	0%	130	4%	100%	8	13%	50%	5.82	9.1	73	221	$11
18	**Proj**	**189**	**25**	**6**	**24**	**1**	**248**	**243**	**325**	**430**	**755**	**808**	**710**	**10**	**72**	**0.40**	**45**	**16**	**39**	**31**	**90**	**118**	**86**	**12%**	**96**	**3%**	**63%**				**4.72**	**3.2**	**25**	**75**	**$4**

Gattis,Evan

Age: 31	Bats: R	Pos: CA DH	Health	B	LIMA Plan	C+
Ht: 6' 4"	Wt: 270		PT/Exp	C	Rand Var	+2
			Consist	B	MM	4043

Where did the power go? A spring training shoulder injury may have been a factor. Seemingly compensated with a career high ct%, but the net gain of 9 BA points didn't begin to offset the lost HRs. Track record says the power will come back. If new ct% sticks as well, then he'd really have something.

Yr	Tm	AB	R	HR	RBI	SB	BA	xBA	OBP	SLG	OPS	vL	vR	bb%	ct%	Eye	G	L	F	h%	HctX	PX	xPX	hr/f	Spd	SBO	SB%	#Wk	DOM	DIS	RC/G	RAR	BPV	BPX	R$
13	ATL *	375	45	22	66	0	244	264	285	483	768	808	757	5	77	0.24	41	14	45	26	117	163	136	17%	43	0%	0%	24	54%	21%	4.64	10.5	64	160	$11
14	ATL	369	41	22	52	0	263	259	317	493	810	970	773	5	74	0.23	39	17	45	30	123	163	165	18%	69	0%	0%	24	50%	25%	5.19	19.9	59	159	$13
15	HOU	566	66	27	88	0	246	267	285	463	748	698	775	5	79	0.25	46	17	37	27	110	126	116	16%	115	1%	0%	27	48%	30%	4.40	11.1	63	170	$14
16	HOU *	487	64	36	79	2	254	265	316	517	833	886	795	8	73	0.33	41	18	41	28	96	157	119	24%	61	3%	67%	24	63%	21%	5.56	24.1	53	151	$16
17	HOU	300	41	12	55	0	263	277	311	457	767	728	783	6	83	0.36	37	21	42	28	113	109	82	11%	50	2%	0%	23	61%	22%	4.75	5.3	49	148	$7
1st Half		177	25	6	32	0	277	273	332	458	789	753	803	7	84	0.45	35	21	44	30	112	104	78	9%	53	0%	0%	13	69%	23%	5.27	5.9	49	148	$9
2nd Half		123	16	6	23	0	244	281	279	455	734	695	751	4	83	0.24	39	21	40	25	115	114	89	15%	56	5%	0%	10	50%	20%	4.04	-0.2	50	152	$5
18	**Proj**	**395**	**51**	**21**	**68**	**0**	**260**	**270**	**308**	**483**	**790**	**788**	**791**	**6**	**79**	**0.30**	**40**	**19**	**41**	**28**	**109**	**122**	**105**	**16%**	**62**	**2%**	**24%**				**4.97**	**9.6**	**43**	**129**	**$13**

Gennett,Scooter

Age: 28	Bats: L	Pos: 2B	Health	A	LIMA Plan	B+
Ht: 5' 10"	Wt: 185		PT/Exp	B	Rand Var	-5
			Consist	C	MM	3245

Unlikely HR eruption followed late-spring release from MIL, and was well-backed by a career-high xPX and FB%. Outlying hr/f would be ripe for complete regression if not for the juiced balls, so all bets are off. We'll split the difference. xBA casts doubt on him as a .300 hitter, too. Full repeat unlikely, but skills are there for a soft landing.

Yr	Tm	AB	R	HR	RBI	SB	BA	xBA	OBP	SLG	OPS	vL	vR	bb%	ct%	Eye	G	L	F	h%	HctX	PX	xPX	hr/f	Spd	SBO	SB%	#Wk	DOM	DIS	RC/G	RAR	BPV	BPX	R$
13	MIL *	534	61	8	37	9	275	240	308	381	689	329	946	5	79	0.23	39	24	37	33	116	72	115	10%	145	11%	58%	14	43%	29%	3.99	5.1	29	73	$14
14	MIL	440	55	9	54	6	289	285	320	434	754	253	802	5	85	0.33	41	25	34	32	105	105	92	7%	93	8%	67%	27	52%	19%	4.95	19.3	62	168	$16
15	MIL *	450	50	7	37	1	262	262	285	384	670	310	713	3	82	0.19	49	22	30	30	78	80	77	7%	122	5%	19%	24	38%	25%	3.64	-6.9	38	103	$7
16	MIL	498	58	14	56	8	263	256	317	412	728	708	733	7	77	0.33	44	22	35	32	91	97	90	11%	87	7%	89%	26	42%	38%	4.55	-4.5	28	80	$13
17	CIN	461	80	27	97	3	295	272	342	531	874	691	930	6	75	0.26	41	21	38	34	105	131	125	21%	106	4%	60%	27	44%	41%	6.42	18.0	52	158	$22
1st Half		186	34	12	42	1	301	287	347	575	922	699	973	6	76	0.24	40	21	39	34	122	152	145	22%	112	5%	50%	13	46%	46%	7.01	11.2	71	215	$16
2nd Half		275	46	15	55	2	291	261	339	502	841	687	897	6	75	0.28	42	21	37	34	93	117	112	20%	100	4%	67%	14	43%	36%	6.03	9.3	38	115	$26
18	**Proj**	**502**	**72**	**20**	**75**	**5**	**273**	**266**	**318**	**460**	**778**	**624**	**815**	**6**	**77**	**0.27**	**43**	**22**	**35**	**32**	**98**	**106**	**107**	**15%**	**105**	**6%**	**65%**				**5.01**	**3.0**	**34**	**104**	**$19**

Goins,Ryan

Age: 30	Bats: L	Pos: SS 2B	Health	A	LIMA Plan	D
Ht: 5' 10"	Wt: 180		PT/Exp	C	Rand Var	-1
			Consist	C	MM	1113

He managed to increase his BA by 35 points, nearly doubled HR output, more than tripled RBI tally... and yet the RAR and BPV/BPX columns remain stuck in truly ugly territory. But he successfully pulled the 'hidden ball trick' on Todd Frazier in September, so if HBTs are a category in your league, he's a top choice.

Yr	Tm	AB	R	HR	RBI	SB	BA	xBA	OBP	SLG	OPS	vL	vR	bb%	ct%	Eye	G	L	F	h%	HctX	PX	xPX	hr/f	Spd	SBO	SB%	#Wk	DOM	DIS	RC/G	RAR	BPV	BPX	R$
13	TOR *	496	43	7	43	2	229	231	264	324	588	576	628	5	74	0.19	56	19	25	30	82	78	53	9%	89	8%	28%	7	14%	43%	2.69	-11.1	-2	-5	$2
14	TOR *	544	42	1	38	3	226	232	263	296	559	395	501	5	78	0.22	55	18	26	29	76	59	51	3%	106	7%	35%	13	23%	62%	2.46	-12.0	2	5	$0
15	TOR	376	52	5	45	2	250	242	318	354	672	586	697	9	78	0.47	54	18	28	31	86	71	75	6%	129	3%	67%	26	23%	38%	3.84	-6.1	27	73	$6
16	TOR *	281	21	5	20	1	202	213	244	319	563	384	571	5	73	0.21	53	11	35	26	82	81	77	6%	95	6%	31%	20	30%	55%	2.40	-16.9	-1	-3	-$3
17	TOR	418	37	9	62	3	237	229	286	356	643	607	650	7	77	0.32	50	15	35	29	86	74	70	8%	95	5%	60%	27	30%	44%	3.41	-15.2	11	33	$4
1st Half		179	17	4	27	1	212	231	276	341	616	454	651	8	77	0.38	47	16	37	26	87	78	72	8%	103	3%	100%	13	38%	54%	3.08	-8.3	18	55	-$1
2nd Half		239	20	5	35	2	255	223	295	368	663	736	649	6	77	0.28	53	14	33	31	86	71	69	8%	91	7%	50%	14	21%	36%	3.68	-6.3	7	21	$8
18	**Proj**	**262**	**24**	**5**	**31**	**2**	**230**	**228**	**279**	**343**	**623**	**548**	**640**	**7**	**76**	**0.29**	**52**	**15**	**33**	**29**	**85**	**71**	**71**	**7%**	**103**	**5%**	**50%**				**3.13**	**-10.6**	**-5**	**-16**	**$3**

Goldschmidt,Paul

Age: 30	Bats: R	Pos: 1B	Health	A	LIMA Plan	D+
Ht: 6' 3"	Wt: 225		PT/Exp	A	Rand Var	0
			Consist	C	MM	4355

Battled right elbow inflammation during horrid Sept. (.568 OPS), but no structural damage found. That didn't stop him from regaining 30+ HR level. His ability to restore pre-2016 xPX/FB% without sacrificing ct% or BA sets a sturdy baseline going forward. Expect SBs to settle in the teens as part of this generally superb profile.

Yr	Tm	AB	R	HR	RBI	SB	BA	xBA	OBP	SLG	OPS	vL	vR	bb%	ct%	Eye	G	L	F	h%	HctX	PX	xPX	hr/f	Spd	SBO	SB%	#Wk	DOM	DIS	RC/G	RAR	BPV	BPX	R$
13	ARI	602	103	36	125	15	302	290	401	551	952	986	941	14	76	0.68	44	21	35	35	132	168	164	23%	101	11%	68%	27	67%	19%	7.94	56.1	98	245	$40
14	ARI	406	75	19	69	9	300	297	396	542	938	1115	894	13	73	0.58	45	22	33	37	139	194	173	19%	105	9%	75%	19	58%	16%	7.78	40.4	107	289	$24
15	ARI	567	103	33	110	21	321	284	435	570	1005	1081	984	17	73	0.78	42	23	35	39	132	169	152	22%	95	11%	81%	27	70%	7%	9.42	61.9	93	251	$42
16	ARI	579	106	24	95	32	297	273	411	489	899	1070	850	16	74	0.73	46	25	29	37	112	121	106	19%	98	17%	86%	27	52%	22%	7.48	34.6	56	160	$37
17	ARI	558	117	36	120	18	297	284	404	563	966	1013	952	14	74	0.64	46	19	35	35	132	154	160	25%	105	12%	78%	27	59%	15%	8.14	34.7	80	242	$35
1st Half		292	70	19	66	13	318	290	436	592	1029	810	1090	16	77	0.79	43	19	38	36	150	153	181	22%	104	16%	76%	13	69%	8%	9.35	29.5	94	285	$44
2nd Half		266	47	17	54	5	274	274	367	530	897	1204	791	13	70	0.51	50	18	31	33	113	154	135	28%	101	8%	83%	14	50%	21%	6.92	9.7	63	191	$26
18	**Proj**	**566**	**108**	**32**	**110**	**16**	**299**	**279**	**405**	**537**	**942**	**1062**	**907**	**15**	**73**	**0.66**	**46**	**21**	**33**	**36**	**125**	**141**	**143**	**23%**	**100**	**10%**	**81%**				**7.92**	**44.2**	**69**	**208**	**$35**

GREG PYRON

Gomes, Yan

		Health	C	LIMA Plan	D+
Age: 30	Bats: R	Pos: CA	PT/Exp	D	Rand Var	-1
Ht: 6'2"	Wt: 215		Consist	D	MM	3213

Last three years of xBA, HctX, BPV show he's not the hitter he used to be, though improved patience and steady power skills should continue to make double-digit HR attainable. Tempting to view 2nd half as upside, but xPX, HctX didn't support, and hr/f was big outlier. 15 HR, .250 is the ceiling now.

Yr	Tm	AB	R	HR	RBI	SB	BA	xBA	OBP	SLG	OPS	vL	vR	bb%	ct%	Eye	G	L	F	h%	HctX	PX	xPX	hr/f	Spd	SBO	SB%	#Wk	DOM	DIS	RC/G	RAR	BPV	BPX	R$
13	CLE	293	45	11	38	2	294	261	345	481	826	934	766	6	77	0.27	43	18	39	35	104	131	126	12%	115	3%	100%	26	54%	38%	5.85	17.3	61	153	$11
14	CLE	485	61	21	74	0	278	266	313	472	785	879	745	5	75	0.20	37	24	39	33	101	139	128	14%	101	0%	0%	24	55%	23%	5.21	25.9	54	146	$18
15	CLE	363	38	12	45	0	231	248	267	391	659	545	702	3	71	0.13	34	26	40	29	86	102	101	11%	62	0%	0%	20	40%	40%	3.35	-4.2	9	24	$4
16	CLE	251	22	9	34	0	167	221	201	327	527	740	445	3	73	0.13	39	16	45	19	80	102	99	11%	80	0%	0%	18	33%	33%	1.96	-15.5	4	11	-$4
17	CLE	341	43	14	56	0	232	223	309	399	708	848	644	8	71	0.31	41	17	42	29	84	103	109	14%	73	0%	0%	27	33%	41%	3.91	-2.2	6	18	$4
1st Half		169	19	4	19	0	225	210	311	361	671	831	600	9	70	0.34	42	15	43	30	91	95	124	8%	74	0%	0%	13	31%	54%	3.51	-3.0	0	0	-$1
2nd Half		172	24	10	37	0	238	236	307	436	743	865	688	8	72	0.29	40	20	41	27	76	110	96	20%	83	0%	0%	14	36%	29%	4.32	1.1	16	48	$10
18	Proj	329	38	13	50	0	222	232	279	391	670	790	618	6	72	0.23	39	19	42	27	84	103	106	13%	77	0%	100%				3.45	-6.9	-3	-8	$3

Gomez, Carlos

		Health	C	LIMA Plan	C+
Age: 32	Bats: R	Pos: CF	PT/Exp	C	Rand Var	-2
Ht: 6'3"	Wt: 220		Consist	B	MM	4325

Continued swing and miss has heightened BA risk, though h% hid some of the damage. Home park boosted pop (.939 OPS w/12 HR), gave life to flagging power skills, but SBO continued its descent, perhaps worsened by hamstring injury. With health dragging down AB for third year, be prepared to stock reserve list with backups.

Yr	Tm	AB	R	HR	RBI	SB	BA	xBA	OBP	SLG	OPS	vL	vR	bb%	ct%	Eye	G	L	F	h%	HctX	PX	xPX	hr/f	Spd	SBO	SB%	#Wk	DOM	DIS	RC/G	RAR	BPV	BPX	R$
13	MIL	536	80	24	73	40	284	263	338	506	843	993	797	6	73	0.25	40	21	38	35	113	153	137	16%	151	37%	85%	27	48%	30%	6.07	28.1	73	183	$36
14	MIL	574	95	23	73	34	284	262	356	477	833	828	835	7	75	0.33	38	22	41	34	117	142	132	13%	122	31%	74%	26	54%	27%	5.63	28.8	69	186	$36
15	2 TM	435	61	12	56	17	255	251	314	409	724	646	745	6	71	0.21	43	19	38	31	101	110	99	10%	90	26%	65%	23	22%	35%	4.09	-5.3	37	100	$16
16	2 AL *	444	48	14	55	17	230	227	285	383	668	636	699	7	66	0.23	44	21	35	32	81	110	87	14%	110	25%	52%	25	20%	52%	3.58	-10.6	2	6	$11
17	TEX	368	51	17	51	13	255	238	340	462	802	645	852	7	65	0.24	39	21	40	34	103	141	116	17%	93	21%	72%	22	36%	36%	4.87	1.3	19	58	$13
1st Half		192	31	10	29	7	250	246	330	479	809	601	861	9	63	0.27	39	24	37	34	105	159	138	23%	96	23%	70%	10	50%	40%	5.04	0.8	28	83	$14
2nd Half		176	20	7	22	6	261	228	351	443	794	676	841	6	68	0.21	39	17	44	35	102	124	93	11%	87	20%	75%	12	25%	33%	4.68	-1.2	11	33	$12
18	Proj	423	55	17	55	13	252	240	326	440	765	673	795	7	69	0.24	41	20	39	33	99	123	106	15%	99	19%	71%				4.49	-0.2	19	57	$16

Gonzalez, Adrian

		Health	D	LIMA Plan	D+
Age: 36	Bats: L	Pos: 1B	PT/Exp	B	Rand Var	+3
Ht: 6'2"	Wt: 215		Consist	C	MM	2043

Former model of consistency derailed by elbow and back issues, though PX, BPV were fading even before injuries. While tiny sample 2nd half HctX, xPX suggest power hasn't evaporated, it might not be enough to hold value at 1B. Even if he rebounds a little, increasing struggles vL make platoon/PH role seem like a best-case scenario.

Yr	Tm	AB	R	HR	RBI	SB	BA	xBA	OBP	SLG	OPS	vL	vR	bb%	ct%	Eye	G	L	F	h%	HctX	PX	xPX	hr/f	Spd	SBO	SB%	#Wk	DOM	DIS	RC/G	RAR	BPV	BPX	R$
13	LA	583	69	22	100	1	293	272	342	461	803	747	829	7	83	0.48	38	23	39	32	125	110	140	11%	76	1%	100%	27	63%	15%	5.77	19.1	60	150	$24
14	LA	590	63	27	116	0	276	292	335	483	818	588	903	8	81	0.50	38	24	38	30	136	145	145	15%	56	1%	50%	28	68%	11%	5.74	26.0	77	208	$26
15	LA	571	76	28	90	0	275	290	350	480	830	782	850	10	81	0.58	37	26	37	30	128	127	154	16%	58	0%	0%	27	48%	22%	5.80	7.0	65	176	$20
16	LA	568	69	18	90	0	285	275	349	435	784	602	859	9	79	0.47	46	26	27	33	106	93	94	14%	70	0%	0%	17	35%	33%	5.33	-0.1	32	91	$18
17	LA	231	14	3	30	0	242	250	287	355	642	453	690	6	81	0.33	41	22	37	29	106	75	108	4%	68	0%	0%	17	35%	29%	3.42	-17.1	21	64	$0
1st Half		165	9	1	23	0	255	246	304	339	643	556	669	7	81	0.42	42	23	35	31	94	60	81	2%	76	0%	0%	10	30%	50%	3.49	-10.5	12	36	$1
2nd Half		66	5	2	7	0	212	262	243	394	637	0	735	4	82	0.25	40	18	42	23	138	111	173	9%	47	0%	0%	7	43%	0%	3.14	-5.1	47	142	-$1
18	Proj	325	32	9	46	0	256	272	306	424	730	535	789	7	81	0.40	41	23	36	29	119	99	129	11%	62	1%	7%				4.42	-6.5	26	77	$7

Gonzalez, Carlos

		Health	B	LIMA Plan	B
Age: 32	Bats: L	Pos: RF	PT/Exp	A	Rand Var	0
Ht: 6'1"	Wt: 220		Consist	B	MM	4245

Missed MLB HR trend memo; can he halt the decline? PRO: 2H HctX, xPX, hr/f rebounds give hope; mashes vR; shoulder injury may have zapped July xPX (28), FB% (17%). CON: Falling FB%, .735 OPS on road add risk; little power vL; took 32% hr/f in Sept to salvage HR. VERDICT: Yes, with health, but not a 2016 sequel.

Yr	Tm	AB	R	HR	RBI	SB	BA	xBA	OBP	SLG	OPS	vL	vR	bb%	ct%	Eye	G	L	F	h%	HctX	PX	xPX	hr/f	Spd	SBO	SB%	#Wk	DOM	DIS	RC/G	RAR	BPV	BPX	R$
13	COL	391	72	26	70	21	302	281	367	591	958	875	1004	9	70	0.35	38	22	41	37	112	206	170	24%	123	23%	88%	22	50%	45%	8.09	37.7	102	255	$30
14	COL	260	35	11	38	3	238	256	292	431	723	635	766	7	73	0.27	47	15	38	28	109	146	119	15%	80	6%	100%	15	40%	40%	4.25	1.2	49	132	$6
15	COL	554	89	40	97	2	271	284	325	540	864	530	997	8	76	0.36	41	19	36	29	114	166	126	26%	81	2%	100%	27	63%	19%	6.19	21.0	78	211	$25
16	COL	584	87	25	100	2	298	282	350	505	855	786	883	7	78	0.36	46	21	33	35	116	129	127	17%	84	2%	100%	27	52%	26%	6.34	26.8	57	163	$24
17	COL	470	72	14	57	3	262	257	339	423	762	561	836	10	75	0.47	49	20	31	33	97	105	101	12%	83	2%	28%	15	32%	28%	5.02	-2.2	31	94	$11
1st Half		244	36	6	20	1	221	245	300	348	648	511	699	11	76	0.50	48	20	32	27	89	80	83	10%	86	2%	0%	12	25%	25%	3.49	-11.7	18	55	$4
2nd Half		226	36	8	37	2	305	268	381	504	886	617	982	9	74	0.44	49	19	32	39	104	134	123	17%	84	2%	100%	13	38%	31%	7.09	12.5	48	145	$19
18	Proj	476	73	20	72	4	272	268	339	470	809	632	879	9	75	0.41	47	19	33	32	106	121	119	17%	84	4%	87%				5.61	12.5	40	121	$18

Gonzalez, Erik

		Health	A	LIMA Plan	D
Age: 26	Bats: R	Pos: 2B	PT/Exp	C	Rand Var	0
Ht: 6'3"	Wt: 195		Consist	B	MM	2431

4-11-.255 with 1 SB in 110 AB at CLE. Aggressive plate approach led to career-low contact and plummeting BA, while low OBP, lack of success on basepaths has been curbing speed to handful of SB. There's nothing in his skill history to suggest he can sustain that elite hr/f. He's an afterthought for now.

Yr	Tm	AB	R	HR	RBI	SB	BA	xBA	OBP	SLG	OPS	vL	vR	bb%	ct%	Eye	G	L	F	h%	HctX	PX	xPX	hr/f	Spd	SBO	SB%	#Wk	DOM	DIS	RC/G	RAR	BPV	BPX	R$
13																																			
14	aa	129	17	1	13	5	314		342	404	746			4	79	0.21				39		67			117	16%	81%				5.20		16	43	$5
15	a/a	549	61	8	60	16	237		267	343	610			4	80	0.20				28		70			108	20%	67%				2.99		17	46	$11
16	CLE *	445	53	9	43	10	272	274	299	407	707	533	727	4	78	0.17	75	13	13	33	119	92	7	0%	111	23%	44%	7	0%	100%	3.86	-11.4	28	80	$12
17	CLE *	270	34	9	21	7	236	239	260	385	645	596	736	3	66	0.09	58	21	22	33	85	97	94	25%	144	16%	61%	18	28%	50%	3.23	-11.4	-7	-21	$3
1st Half		173	21	6	12	7	245	241	267	400	667	579	931	4	65	0.08	65	17	17	34	77	97	104	50%	153	10%	67%	6	33%	33%	3.55	-6.6	-8	-24	$4
2nd Half		97	13	3	9	0	220	239	248	358	610	610	662	4	67	0.11	54	27	24	30	90	97	89	17%	114	27%	56%	12	25%	54%	2.71	-6.5	-13	-39	$0
18	Proj	169	21	4	16	4	249	254	274	375	650	574	688	4	73	0.14	58	20	21	32	85	81	95	14%	127	20%	60%				3.36	-7.3	-4	-12	$4

Gonzalez, Marwin

		Health	A	LIMA Plan	B
Age: 29	Bats: B	Pos: LF SS 1B	PT/Exp	B	Rand Var	-3
Ht: 6'1"	Wt: 205		Consist	F	MM	3245

Three reasons he might not sustain breakout: 1) PX/xPX gap, marginal HctX, somewhat fluky 1st half hr/f put HR repeat at risk; 2) "improvement" vR was driven by 37% h%; 3) Multi-position eligibility is great for us, but teams will often opt for a stable regular if one emerges, putting his PT stability at risk. Just be cautious.

Yr	Tm	AB	R	HR	RBI	SB	BA	xBA	OBP	SLG	OPS	vL	vR	bb%	ct%	Eye	G	L	F	h%	HctX	PX	xPX	hr/f	Spd	SBO	SB%	#Wk	DOM	DIS	RC/G	RAR	BPV	BPX	R$
13	HOU *	376	34	5	29	9	221	240	251	307	559	575	570	4	83	0.24	54	15	30	26	93	62	84	8%	99	16%	74%	20	25%	35%	2.53	-16.7	21	53	$2
14	HOU	285	33	6	23	4	277	253	327	400	727	776	719	5	80	0.29	33	92	92	68	9%	91	8%	33%	26	46%	38%	4.26	4.6	32	86	$7
15	HOU	344	44	12	34	4	279	265	317	442	759	843	701	4	78	0.22	44	23	33	33	109	107	100	11%	94	11%	44%	27	48%	44%	4.62	2.2	38	103	$11
16	HOU	484	55	13	51	12	254	253	293	401	694	724	678	4	76	0.19	47	21	32	31	102	94	99	12%	98	17%	67%	27	37%	37%	3.83	-6.4	18	51	$12
17	HOU	455	67	23	90	8	303	283	377	530	907	789	946	10	78	0.49	44	20	36	35	104	132	94	18%	82	8%	73%	27	56%	30%	7.14	21.2	64	194	$23
1st Half		194	33	13	43	3	314	276	402	567	969	858	1006	12	79	0.60	47	16	37	35	137	154	23%	95	8%	60%	13	54%	38%	8.15	14.8	75	227	$21
2nd Half		261	34	10	47	5	295	286	358	502	860	739	900	8	79	0.41	42	23	35	34	112	128	94	14%	76	9%	83%	14	57%	21%	6.43	7.8	58	176	$24
18	Proj	456	60	18	67	8	282	270	338	467	805	773	818	7	78	0.34	46	20	34	33	103	109	94	15%	87	11%	66%				5.40	12.3	37	113	$19

Goodwin, Brian

		Health	B	LIMA Plan	D+
Age: 27	Bats: L	Pos: CF LF	PT/Exp	C	Rand Var	0
Ht: 6'0"	Wt: 205		Consist	C	MM	4321

13-30-.251 with 6 SB in 251 AB at WAS. Former 1st rounder's power/speed combo offers conflicting signals about road ahead. Improved FB%, xPX supported higher HR gear, but MLE PXs say check engine; and while speed skills suggest caution, rising SB%, 2nd half SBO hint at light turning green. Worth a speculative test drive.

Yr	Tm	AB	R	HR	RBI	SB	BA	xBA	OBP	SLG	OPS	vL	vR	bb%	ct%	Eye	G	L	F	h%	HctX	PX	xPX	hr/f	Spd	SBO	SB%	#Wk	DOM	DIS	RC/G	RAR	BPV	BPX	R$
13	aa	457	66	8	32	15	227		305	354	659			10	72	0.40				30		91			158	23%	56%				3.34		29	73	$9
14	aa	275	23	3	24	4	187		282	266	547			12	62	0.35				29		73			111	12%	49%				2.25		-33	-89	-$3
15	aa	429	46	6	37	12	196		250	282	532			7	76	0.29				25		62			103	22%	60%				2.14		-1	-1	$1
16	WAS *	478	46	12	64	13	250	241	312	388	700	750	746	8	71	0.32	59	15	26	33	114	96	105	0%	96	14%	79%	7	14%	43%	4.15	-7.1	10	29	$12
17	WAS *	341	48	14	38	6	240	244	303	445	748	1001	770	8	70	0.30	36	15	49	30	96	135	133	16%	92	12%	64%	14	57%	21%	4.58	-4.8	34	103	$8
1st Half		200	23	7	26	3	240	214	314	418	733	1645	785	10	67	0.32	36	15	49	30	98	127	124	16%	101	7%	68%	7	57%	29%	4.37	-3.2	15	45	$7
2nd Half		141	25	7	12	3	241	279	288	482	770	813	756	6	74	0.24	40	22	38	28	110	153	139	17%	103	22%	100%	7	57%	14%	4.83	-0.3	62	188	$9
18	Proj	225	29	11	24	6	242	252	302	463	764	933	727	8	71	0.30	38	19	43	29	99	136	133	17%	100	16%	78%				4.70	1.3	40	120	$7

BRANT CHESSER

Gordon, Alex

Age: 34	Bats: L	Pos: LF	
Ht: 6' 1"	Wt: 220		

Health	C	LIMA Plan	D+
PT/Exp	C	Rand Var	+5
Consist	C	MM	2115

Followed 2016's fall to the floor with a dive into the sub-basement in 2017 (look at that RAR!). Diminished quality of contact (HctX), massive downgrade in power metrics and notable rise in GB% are equal parts alarming and debilitating. It's tough to see a silver lining here, particularly given his age.

Yr	Tm	AB	R	HR	RBI	SB	BA	xBA	OBP	SLG	OPS	vL	vR	bb%	ct%	Eye	G	L	F	h%	HctX	PX	xPX	hr/f	Spd	SBO	SB%	#Wk	DOM	DIS	RC/G	RAR	BPV	BPX	R$
13	KC	633	90	20	81	11	265	247	327	422	749	877	683	7	78	0.37	40	20	39	31	112	104	125	10%	121	8%	79%	26	42%	38%	4.71	13.5	47	118	$
14	KC	563	87	19	74	12	266	260	351	432	783	787	782	10	78	0.52	43	19	38	31	108	123	118	11%	71	9%	80%	27	48%	26%	5.16	24.0	52	141	$
15	KC *	382	44	14	52	2	276	250	367	435	802	817	805	12	74	0.57	38	25	38	34	107	111	125	13%	76	6%	29%	20	45%	35%	5.39	10.9	33	89	$1
16	KC *	467	64	18	44	8	223	226	306	382	688	665	704	10	67	0.36	38	24	38	30	100	107	147	15%	92	7%	89%	24	17%	46%	3.90	-5.4	3	9	$
17	KC	476	52	9	45	7	208	236	293	315	608	602	608	8	74	0.36	43	24	33	26	87	68	82	8%	88	10%	64%	27	22%	52%	2.77	-40.0	-6	-18	$
1st Half		242	24	4	23	1	194	239	289	293	582	581	581	9	77	0.45	46	22	32	23	94	61	69	7%	79	5%	33%	13	31%	54%	2.43	-22.6	2	6	$
2nd Half		234	28	5	22	6	222	230	298	338	635	629	635	8	70	0.28	38	27	34	30	80	76	96	9%	97	14%	75%	14	14%	50%	3.14	-16.0	-14	-42	$
18	Proj	443	54	12	46	5	229	237	317	363	680	691	675	9	72	0.37	40	24	36	29	95	84	110	11%	88	7%	60%				3.58	-11.8	-3	-9	$

Gordon, Dee

Age: 30	Bats: L	Pos: 2B	
Ht: 5' 11"	Wt: 170		

Health	A	LIMA Plan	D+
PT/Exp	B	Rand Var	-2
Consist	D	MM	0545

Between the 80-game PED suspension and disappointing performance, there was reason for concern heading into 2017. But BA rebounded fully while xBA peaked, thanks largely to LD%/h% bounceback. Speed skills are stable and elite, even as he reaches age 30. Should be good for another 60ish bags.

Yr	Tm	AB	R	HR	RBI	SB	BA	xBA	OBP	SLG	OPS	vL	vR	bb%	ct%	Eye	G	L	F	h%	HctX	PX	xPX	hr/f	Spd	SBO	SB%	#Wk	DOM	DIS	RC/G	RAR	BPV	BPX	R$
13	LA *	468	53	1	28	43	234	224	299	295	594	577	623	8	77	0.41	49	21	30	30	53	45	33	5%	164	44%	74%	12	33%	33%	2.98	-10.0	14	35	$1
14	LA	609	92	2	34	64	289	274	326	378	704	719	699	5	82	0.29	60	21	19	35	62	62	27	2%	190	49%	77%	27	37%	19%	4.39	17.7	48	130	$3
15	MIA	615	88	4	46	58	333	280	359	418	776	823	760	4	85	0.27	60	22	19	39	67	54	40	4%	170	40%	74%	25	44%	24%	5.62	24.5	45	122	$4
16	MIA	360	52	1	16	32	262	256	298	329	627	579	656	5	83	0.31	59	19	23	31	57	36	29	2%	204	40%	82%	15	13%	40%	3.56	-13.9	34	97	$1
17	MIA	653	114	2	33	60	308	281	341	375	716	648	744	4	86	0.27	58	23	20	36	56	37	20	2%	198	39%	79%	27	22%	22%	4.69	-5.9	41	124	$4
1st Half		312	44	0	18	29	285	287	332	349	682	584	721	4	86	0.31	59	24	17	33	58	38	21	0%	153	39%	85%	13	15%	15%	4.20	-5.6	29	88	$3
2nd Half		341	70	2	15	31	328	275	349	399	748	708	764	3	86	0.23	56	22	22	39	54	36	19	3%	222	39%	74%	14	29%	29%	5.17	3.3	47	142	$5
18	Proj	637	102	3	34	59	297	273	330	370	700	662	714	4	84	0.28	58	21	21	35	58	39	26	2%	204	40%	78%				4.44	-6.5	29	88	$4

Grandal, Yasmani

Age: 29	Bats: B	Pos: CA	
Ht: 6' 1"	Wt: 235		

Health	A	LIMA Plan	D+
PT/Exp	B	Rand Var	-1
Consist	A	MM	4025

Abandoned some of his traditional patience, taking fewer walks in favor of more balls in play. xBA didn't like that approach, and 2016's xPX/PX and hr/f now look like outliers. But even regressed power output sets a reasonable valuation floor in the weak catcher pool.

Yr	Tm	AB	R	HR	RBI	SB	BA	xBA	OBP	SLG	OPS	vL	vR	bb%	ct%	Eye	G	L	F	h%	HctX	PX	xPX	hr/f	Spd	SBO	SB%	#Wk	DOM	DIS	RC/G	RAR	BPV	BPX	R$
13	SD *	124	15	1	10	0	221	255	326	327	653	752	635	13	77	0.69	48	24	28	28	114	94	112	5%	76	0%	0%	6	50%	0%	3.49	-0.7	36	90	-$
14	SD	377	47	15	49	0	225	242	327	401	728	512	781	13	69	0.50	43	19	38	28	108	139	132	15%	67	3%	100%	27	41%	44%	4.38	10.6	37	100	$
15	LA	355	43	16	47	0	234	229	353	403	756	794	749	15	74	0.71	46	17	37	27	97	110	117	16%	61	0%	0%	27	37%	52%	4.68	9.2	35	95	$
16	LA	390	49	27	72	1	228	251	339	477	816	780	824	14	70	0.55	45	15	39	25	112	156	156	25%	61	4%	25%	26	46%	31%	5.17	9.1	51	146	$
17	LA	438	50	22	58	0	247	239	308	459	767	668	790	8	70	0.31	44	16	40	34	104	134	125	18%	62	1%	0%	27	48%	33%	4.76	9.1	26	79	$
1st Half		239	28	10	30	0	264	239	317	456	773	552	834	7	72	0.29	48	15	36	33	100	122	104	16%	73	1%	0%	13	38%	38%	5.02	6.3	26	79	$
2nd Half		199	22	12	28	0	226	240	297	462	760	841	741	10	68	0.33	38	18	45	27	108	150	152	20%	57	2%	0%	14	57%	29%	4.47	2.3	30	91	$
18	Proj	439	51	23	63	0	235	241	315	445	759	719	769	10	71	0.40	43	17	39	28	106	128	135	19%	60	2%	21%				4.60	6.1	17	51	$1

Granderson, Curtis

Age: 37	Bats: L	Pos: CF RF LF	
Ht: 6' 1"	Wt: 200		

Health	B	LIMA Plan	C
PT/Exp	A	Rand Var	+4
Consist	A	MM	4223

Once a multi-category contributor, he has now completed the transition into a one-trick pony. While FB% boost was a salve for his HR total, it came at the price of career-low h% and BA. Issues vL threaten PT going forward. In today's game, HR-only options are a dime a dozen.

Yr	Tm	AB	R	HR	RBI	SB	BA	xBA	OBP	SLG	OPS	vL	vR	bb%	ct%	Eye	G	L	F	h%	HctX	PX	xPX	hr/f	Spd	SBO	SB%	#Wk	DOM	DIS	RC/G	RAR	BPV	BPX	R$
13	NYY *	240	33	8	17	8	238	231	322	411	734	792	695	11	69	0.40	34	23	44	31	97	134	135	11%	144	16%	80%	12	42%	33%	4.48	3.0	49	123	$
14	NYM	564	73	20	66	8	227	236	326	388	714	742	703	12	75	0.56	34	19	47	27	105	119	132	10%	93	6%	80%	27	56%	26%	4.15	6.2	49	132	$1
15	NYM	580	98	26	70	11	259	260	364	457	821	558	892	13	74	0.60	31	27	43	31	118	135	154	14%	102	9%	65%	27	44%	19%	5.55	14.2	63	170	$2
16	NYM	545	88	30	59	4	237	265	335	464	799	723	826	12	76	0.57	36	22	42	26	114	131	127	17%	97	4%	67%	27	48%	22%	5.06	7.0	64	183	$1
17	2 NL	449	74	26	64	6	212	250	323	452	775	668	806	13	73	0.58	33	19	49	23	104	140	154	16%	111	7%	75%	26	50%	31%	4.66	-8.3	65	197	$
1st Half		252	40	12	34	3	234	254	331	468	799	790	803	13	75	0.60	31	18	51	26	103	136	156	12%	116	6%	75%	13	54%	31%	5.17	-1.4	73	221	$
2nd Half		197	34	14	30	3	183	246	312	431	743	454	810	15	69	0.56	35	19	46	18	99	146	152	22%	93	8%	75%	13	46%	31%	4.07	-8.1	52	158	$
18	Proj	334	54	18	43	4	223	253	330	449	779	657	817	13	73	0.56	34	21	45	25	108	131	145	17%	106	6%	67%				4.75	2.5	51	154	$

Gregorius, Didi

Age: 28	Bats: L	Pos: SS	
Ht: 6' 3"	Wt: 205		

Health	B	LIMA Plan	B+
PT/Exp	A	Rand Var	-1
Consist	B	MM	2345

Managed to exceed 2016's unexpected HR outbreak, but he had to sell out in order to do it. A meager xPX doesn't support the HR pace, and the combination of increased FB% and a lack of hard hit balls (23% HH%) casts doubt on ability to maintain BA (see 2nd half BA). Don't pay for another 20 HR.

Yr	Tm	AB	R	HR	RBI	SB	BA	xBA	OBP	SLG	OPS	vL	vR	bb%	ct%	Eye	G	L	F	h%	HctX	PX	xPX	hr/f	Spd	SBO	SB%	#Wk	DOM	DIS	RC/G	RAR	BPV	BPX	R$
13	ARI *	388	51	8	29	1	258	245	324	384	708	512	789	9	83	0.58	37	21	42	29	80	83	87	6%	140	5%	24%	23	52%	30%	4.19	7.8	60	150	$
14	ARI *	496	62	8	43	5	239	241	292	362	654	424	706	7	83	0.45	37	20	43	27	101	82	106	6%	135	4%	100%	19	42%	26%	3.59	4.4	55	149	$
15	NYY	525	57	9	56	5	265	252	318	370	688	626	712	6	84	0.39	45	21	34	30	82	68	64	6%	103	6%	63%	27	33%	30%	3.91	-7.4	34	92	$1
16	NYY	562	68	20	70	7	276	271	304	447	751	834	721	3	85	0.30	43	20	40	29	85	96	78	10%	103	7%	88%	27	56%	19%	4.74	6.9	58	166	$1
17	NYY	534	73	25	87	3	287	274	318	478	796	653	848	4	87	0.36	36	20	44	29	81	96	67	12%	96	3%	75%	23	57%	17%	5.42	11.9	64	194	$1
1st Half		226	29	10	36	2	314	287	335	496	830	779	845	3	86	0.19	44	16	40	33	78	92	71	13%	102	5%	67%	10	60%	10%	6.06	9.1	57	173	$1
2nd Half		308	44	15	51	1	266	280	306	464	771	581	851	4	87	0.49	30	23	47	26	84	99	64	12%	94	1%	100%	13	54%	23%	4.92	3.8	70	212	$2
18	Proj	533	68	19	73	4	271	267	309	435	744	664	773	5	86	0.36	38	20	41	29	83	86	72	10%	103	4%	76%				4.64	2.8	44	134	$1

Grichuk, Randal

Age: 26	Bats: R	Pos: LF RF	
Ht: 6' 1"	Wt: 205		

Health	B	LIMA Plan	B
PT/Exp	C	Rand Var	+1
Consist	B	MM	4325

22-59-.238 in 412 AB at STL. Spent most of June in minors, reportedly working to refine his plate approach. It's tough to see where it helped (see 2nd half Eye). Raw power (xPX) and FB% are enticing, but shoddy plate discipline, ct% and low BA temper the enthusiasm. Could continue to earn time on the bench.

Yr	Tm	AB	R	HR	RBI	SB	BA	xBA	OBP	SLG	OPS	vL	vR	bb%	ct%	Eye	G	L	F	h%	HctX	PX	xPX	hr/f	Spd	SBO	SB%	#Wk	DOM	DIS	RC/G	RAR	BPV	BPX	R$
13	aa	500	74	18	56	8	231		266	412	678			4	80	0.24				28		117			125	15%	59%				3.51		62	155	$1
14	STL	546	63	20	59	6	224	231	257	392	649	689	662	4	72	0.16	39	15	46	27	141	127	162	8%	104	14%	43%	11	27%	45%	3.13	-11.1	33	89	$1
15	STL	323	49	17	47	4	276	265	329	548	877	819	907	6	66	0.20	38	21	42	37	107	202	139	19%	138	9%	67%	22	55%	14%	6.12	12.9	81	219	$1
16	STL *	527	75	28	81	6	238	252	278	474	752	806	754	5	70	0.19	41	16	44	28	114	154	142	18%	111	10%	56%	25	48%	32%	4.30	-5.1	50	143	$1
17	STL *	479	63	27	69	6	236	249	279	478	757	662	788	6	67	0.18	36	21	43	29	109	154	152	18%	109	8%	86%	24	29%	29%	4.47	-11.3	37	112	$1
1st Half		261	33	11	35	5	227	246	272	430	702	495	752	6	67	0.19	33	25	42	29	116	139	150	12%	83	13%	83%	10	20%	50%	3.88	-11.7	18	55	$1
2nd Half		218	29	16	33	1	247	256	286	533	819	799	824	5	67	0.17	39	14	43	29	103	171	155	24%	138	3%	100%	14	36%	64%	5.19	-1.1	58	176	$1
18	Proj	430	59	23	62	5	243	248	287	478	765	729	781	5	69	0.18	30			113	147	149	18%	122	9%	69%				4.53	0.9	37	111	$1

Grossman, Robert

Age: 28	Bats: B	Pos: DH RF	
Ht: 6' 0"	Wt: 215		

Health	A	LIMA Plan	D
PT/Exp	C	Rand Var	+2
Consist	D	MM	2123

Perils of small samples: showed signs of emerging as a bad-side platoon option in 2016, but that sample was 125 AB, and then he couldn't hit LH in 2017. Plate patience is a strength, but subpar power and so-so speed puts a hard cap on his value. As if that's not enough in the negative column, poor defense also endangers PT.

Yr	Tm	AB	R	HR	RBI	SB	BA	xBA	OBP	SLG	OPS	vL	vR	bb%	ct%	Eye	G	L	F	h%	HctX	PX	xPX	hr/f	Spd	SBO	SB%	#Wk	DOM	DIS	RC/G	RAR	BPV	BPX	R$
13	HOU *	510	61	6	36	17	254	223	332	339	671	785	669	10	71	0.40	47	23	30	35	85	72	90	7%	109	21%	52%	12	25%	58%	3.56	-10.5	-2	-5	$1
14	HOU *	535	63	9	47	16	247	231	334	355	689	566	703	12	72	0.46	41	24	35	33	63	92	76	7%	85	17%	56%	21	19%	43%	3.82	-1.0	11	30	$1
15	HOU *	396	42	5	29	9	191	176	267	266	534	345	567	9	69	0.34	55	6	39	26	47	61	56	8%	84	19%	49%	6	33%	50%	2.09	-31.2	-28	-76	-$
16	MIN *	453	62	16	49	5	265	249	365	426	792	994	729	14	72	0.58	38	25	39	33	102	107	96	13%	83	6%	56%	21	38%	38%	5.30	12.3	29	83	$1
17	MIN	382	42	9	45	3	246	252	361	380	741	696	762	15	79	0.85	41	25	34	29	99	81	83	9%	90	3%	75%	25	36%	36%	4.61	-1.5	41	124	$
1st Half		208	36	6	23	2	255	267	390	394	784	779	782	17	80	1.17	40	26	34	29	98	80	76	12%	65	4%	100%	13	46%	31%	5.17	1.4	50	147	$
2nd Half		174	26	3	22	1	236	253	325	362	687	595	735	12	78	0.61	34	27	39	29	107	80	100	4%	99	2%	100%	12	25%	42%	3.96	-4.9	32	97	$
18	Proj	244	34	6	26	3	242	247	342	372	714	733	705	13	75	0.60	40	25	35	30	92	82	88	9%	91	7%	57%				4.17	-9.8	15	45	$

GREG PYRON

Gurriel,Yulieski

Age: 34	Bats: R	Pos: 1B	Health A	LIMA Plan A	
Ht: 6' 0"	Wt: 190		PT/Exp D	Rand Var 0	
			Consist F	MM 2155	

Arrived from Cuba in July 2016 with a reputation for having excellent bat-to-ball ability and gap power. That's precisely what we saw in 2017. Borderline elite ct% sets a nice BA foundation (xBA). Racked up 42 doubles; age prevents us from projecting that into HR growth. This is likely as good as it gets... and it's not bad at all.

Yr	Tm	AB	R	HR	RBI	SB	BA	xBA	OBP	SLG	OPS	vL	vR	bb%	ct%	Eye	G	L	F	h%	HctX	PX	xPX	hr/f	Spd	SBO	SB%	#Wk	DOM	DIS	RC/G	RAR	BPV	BPX	R$
13	for	297	61	10	67	9	292		382	491	873			13	90	1.48				30		119			113	19%	50%				6.24	14.1	117	293	$17
14	for	414	84	11	63	13	299		352	480	833			8	87	0.62				32		131			92	14%	85%				6.24	23.7	96	259	$23
15	for	175	39	4	34	10	320		395	511	906			11	90	1.28				34		121			96	22%	82%				7.64	11.8	111	300	$12
16	HOU *	165	15	4	19	1	234	250	262	348	611	537	739	4	85	0.25	42	20	38	26	98	68	74	7%	83	6%	50%	6	67%	0%	2.98	-9.3	27	77	$0
17	HOU	529	69	18	75	3	299	293	332	486	817	695	865	4	88	0.35	46	19	35	31	125	102	99	11%	88	4%	60%	27	67%	15%	5.71	4.9	71	215	$19
1st Half		267	33	9	37	1	285	283	310	461	770	574	847	2	87	0.17	45	19	36	30	129	97	111	11%	95	4%	50%	13	54%	23%	4.87	-5.8	60	182	$16
2nd Half		262	36	9	38	2	313	304	353	511	865	816	883	6	90	0.59	47	18	34	32	122	107	87	11%	81	5%	67%	14	79%	7%	6.64	7.1	82	248	$22
18	**Proj**	**528**	**75**	**15**	**78**	**3**	**288**	**288**	**332**	**460**	**792**	**678**	**839**	**6**	**88**	**0.51**	**45**	**19**	**36**	**30**	**114**	**95**	**88**	**9%**	**92**	**3%**	**61%**				**5.37**	**4.1**	**62**	**187**	**$18**

Guzman,Ronald

Age: 23	Bats: L	Pos: 1B	Health A	LIMA Plan D	
Ht: 6' 5"	Wt: 205		PT/Exp D	Rand Var 0	
			Consist A	MM 1311	

TEX prospect does a good job of making contact, but will he develop enough pop to be a viable option at 1B? After showing more power at Double-A in 2016, that aspect of his game took a step back in 2017 as he moved up to Triple-A. While time is still on his side, a wait-and-see approach is the best short-term play.

Yr	Tm	AB	R	HR	RBI	SB	BA	xBA	OBP	SLG	OPS	vL	vR	bb%	ct%	Eye	G	L	F	h%	HctX	PX	xPX	hr/f	Spd	SBO	SB%	#Wk	DOM	DIS	RC/G	RAR	BPV	BPX	R$
13																																			
14																																			
15																																			
16	a/a	463	50	14	56	2	256		306	411	717			7	76	0.30				31		92			114	3%	44%				4.24		28	80	$9
17	aaa	470	60	9	48	3	264		318	376	694			7	80	0.40				31		64			110	3%	73%				4.14		22	67	$9
1st Half		291	36	7	32	2	282		331	415	746			7	81	0.38				33		73			129	3%	58%				4.83		36	109	$13
2nd Half		179	24	2	15	2	236		297	313	611			8	79	0.42				28		49			109	3%	100%				3.15		8	24	$2
18	**Proj**	**162**	**20**	**4**	**17**	**1**	**255**	**236**	**309**	**390**	**700**	**700**	**700**	**7**	**79**	**0.36**	**38**	**20**	**42**	**30**		**76**		**8%**	**124**	**4%**	**74%**				**4.13**	**-4.6**	**13**	**40**	**$4**

Gyorko,Jedd

Age: 29	Bats: R	Pos: 3B	Health B	LIMA Plan B	
Ht: 5' 10"	Wt: 215		PT/Exp C	Rand Var -3	
			Consist B	MM 3135	

Sept. injury (hamstring) cost him a shot at his first 500 AB season. 1st half skills were a virtual carbon copy of 2016, just with some hr/f regression and a friendlier h%, the latter of which went 'poof' in 2nd half. Pay for the power, but price in some BA regression and loss of multi-position eligibility.

Yr	Tm	AB	R	HR	RBI	SB	BA	xBA	OBP	SLG	OPS	vL	vR	bb%	ct%	Eye	G	L	F	h%	HctX	PX	xPX	hr/f	Spd	SBO	SB%	#Wk	DOM	DIS	RC/G	RAR	BPV	BPX	R$
13	SD	486	62	23	63	1	249	261	301	444	745	829	715	6	75	0.27	38	23	40	29	115	138	140	16%	83	2%	50%	24	50%	29%	4.45	6.5	49	123	$13
14	SD *	424	41	11	54	3	210	239	275	333	608	669	594	8	75	0.36	44	22	35	25	94	93	115	10%	65	5%	60%	20	30%	40%	2.93	-10.3	13	35	$3
15	SD *	482	39	19	63	0	242	231	289	391	679	803	654	6	75	0.26	42	21	37	29	113	96	129	14%	59	2%	0%	25	24%	56%	3.72	-13.8	8	22	$8
16	STL	400	58	30	59	0	243	265	306	495	801	735	836	8	76	0.39	41	19	40	24	107	137	135	24%	86	0%	0%	27	56%	19%	5.11	1.5	58	166	$10
17	STL	426	52	20	67	6	272	257	341	472	813	975	763	10	75	0.45	41	20	39	32	94	114	114	16%	78	7%	75%	24	38%	33%	5.68	4.6	38	115	$14
1st Half		251	32	12	40	4	299	267	363	518	881	920	869	9	77	0.46	40	19	41	35	105	124	136	15%	87	6%	100%	13	46%	31%	6.98	13.1	55	167	$19
2nd Half		175	20	8	27	2	234	241	310	406	716	1048	610	11	73	0.44	42	21	37	28	78	99	81	17%	65	8%	50%	11	27%	36%	4.14	-5.0	12	36	$7
18	**Proj**	**447**	**53**	**24**	**66**	**3**	**250**	**255**	**315**	**452**	**766**	**867**	**729**	**9**	**75**	**0.39**	**41**	**20**	**39**	**28**	**99**	**112**	**117**	**18%**	**72**	**5%**	**62%**				**4.81**	**-1.1**	**24**	**74**	**$13**

Hamilton,Billy

Age: 27	Bats: B	Pos: CF	Health B	LIMA Plan D+	
Ht: 6' 0"	Wt: 160		PT/Exp B	Rand Var 0	
			Consist B	MM 0515	

Fractured thumb limited him in Sept (50 AB). The exciting plate discipline/OBP gains from late-2016 (13% bb% and .376 OBP) didn't stick. The wheels remain elite, but multi-year slippage of SBO plus 2017 dip in SB% are noteworthy. Still good for 60 bags, but last year's UP: 90 is gone.

Yr	Tm	AB	R	HR	RBI	SB	BA	xBA	OBP	SLG	OPS	vL	vR	bb%	ct%	Eye	G	L	F	h%	HctX	PX	xPX	hr/f	Spd	SBO	SB%	#Wk	DOM	DIS	RC/G	RAR	BPV	BPX	R$
13	CIN *	523	72	6	36	76	238	276	285	319	604	0	950	6	77	0.29	50	36	14	30	40	59	-15	0%	164	71%	81%	5	20%	40%	3.25	-13.8	19	48	$34
14	CIN	563	72	6	48	56	250	237	292	355	648	669	641	6	79	0.29	42	21	37	31	70	77	55	4%	168	58%	71%	26	46%	38%	3.37	-8.0	42	114	$28
15	CIN	412	56	4	28	57	226	216	274	289	563	641	532	6	82	0.37	43	20	38	27	69	38	58	3%	165	61%	88%	22	23%	55%	3.01	-16.6	22	59	$23
16	CIN	411	69	3	17	58	260	239	321	343	664	576	696	8	77	0.39	48	22	30	33	60	57	32	3%	184	56%	88%	23	35%	57%	4.27	-4.6	28	80	$28
17	CIN	582	85	4	38	59	247	238	299	335	634	537	673	7	77	0.33	46	24	31	31	50	49	24	3%	199	46%	82%	26	27%	46%	3.60	-25.8	23	70	$29
1st Half		314	50	2	20	33	242	232	295	322	617	463	667	7	76	0.32	45	23	31	31	48	46	27	3%	187	45%	87%	13	23%	54%	3.51	-13.3	15	45	$29
2nd Half		268	35	2	18	26	254	245	304	351	655	604	679	7	78	0.34	46	24	30	32	52	53	20	3%	191	47%	76%	13	31%	38%	3.69	-9.9	27	82	$28
18	**Proj**	**521**	**76**	**4**	**32**	**62**	**248**	**237**	**300**	**333**	**633**	**583**	**653**	**7**	**78**	**0.34**	**45**	**22**	**32**	**31**	**58**	**50**	**34**	**3%**	**188**	**53%**	**83%**				**3.65**	**-13.7**	**20**	**61**	**$31**

Haniger,Mitch

Age: 27	Bats: R	Pos: RF	Health C	LIMA Plan B	
Ht: 6' 2"	Wt: 215		PT/Exp D	Rand Var -1	
			Consist C	MM 4235	

16-47-.282 in 369 AB at SEA. Missed significant time due to injuries (left oblique in 1st half, mouth in 2nd half). Began and ended 2017 scorching hot but scuffled in between. 2nd half skills profile, with upticks in xBA, ct%, xPX, hints at a valuable contributor, but sooner or later we need to see that for more than 200 AB at a time.

Yr	Tm	AB	R	HR	RBI	SB	BA	xBA	OBP	SLG	OPS	vL	vR	bb%	ct%	Eye	G	L	F	h%	HctX	PX	xPX	hr/f	Spd	SBO	SB%	#Wk	DOM	DIS	RC/G	RAR	BPV	BPX	R$
13																																			
14	aa	267	36	8	30	3	232		277	366	643			6	81	0.33				26		89			99	5%	100%				3.42		39	105	$4
15	aa	153	18	1	15	3	250		307	340	648			8	76	0.35				32		73			100	20%	41%				3.22		10	27	$1
16	ARI *	567	68	24	87	9	268	253	341	476	817	583	760	10	75	0.44	39	18	43	32	113	128	135	14%	114	9%	66%	7	57%	14%	5.57	14.7	57	163	$19
17	SEA *	408	63	18	52	5	275	267	334	484	818	734	877	8	76	0.36	44	19	37	32	106	124	120	16%	101	9%	56%	19	53%	32%	5.53	7.1	50	152	$13
1st Half		165	35	7	24	3	290	256	384	485	869	923	893	13	73	0.56	41	22	37	36	104	120	118	16%	123	9%	60%	7	57%	29%	6.54	6.9	52	158	$12
2nd Half		243	27	12	28	2	264	274	296	484	780	649	861	4	78	0.20	46	18	36	30	107	127	121	16%	84	9%	50%	12	50%	33%	4.82	-1.7	49	148	$14
18	**Proj**	**451**	**62**	**20**	**58**	**6**	**265**	**262**	**334**	**472**	**806**	**681**	**849**	**8**	**76**	**0.36**	**42**	**19**	**39**	**31**	**109**	**120**	**126**	**15%**	**104**	**11%**	**54%**				**5.12**	**5.7**	**43**	**131**	**$16**

Hanson,Alen

Age: 25	Bats: B	Pos: 2B RF	Health A	LIMA Plan D	
Ht: 5' 11"	Wt: 170		PT/Exp C	Rand Var +2	
			Consist A	MM 1521	

Blessed with great speed, but can he get on base enough to use it? Just doesn't put the ball in play, or draw walks, enough to showcase those elite wheels. Has the right idea with the GB% profile, and SBO% shows he knows where his bread is buttered. For now, he's just an end-game flyer when you miss your pricier SB target.

Yr	Tm	AB	R	HR	RBI	SB	BA	xBA	OBP	SLG	OPS	vL	vR	bb%	ct%	Eye	G	L	F	h%	HctX	PX	xPX	hr/f	Spd	SBO	SB%	#Wk	DOM	DIS	RC/G	RAR	BPV	BPX	R$
13	aa	137	11	1	8	5	231		264	327	592			4	81	0.24				28		59			156	24%	69%				2.81		27	68	$0
14	aa	482	48	7	43	19	241		274	356	630			4	81	0.23				29		78			127	30%	60%				3.06		33	89	$12
15	aaa	475	58	5	38	31	240		288	342	630			6	80	0.33				29		63			148	38%	70%				3.20		28	76	$16
16	PIT *	463	59	7	31	35	249	272	297	356	653	286	599	6	81	0.36	60	20	20	29	38	61	-14	0%	171	45%	67%	7	14%	43%	3.37	-17.9	39	111	$18
17	2 TM	217	36	4	11	11	221	238	262	346	607	766	578	5	76	0.23	51	16	34	27	66	73	55	7%	172	32%	79%	27	19%	48%	2.99	-11.0	26	79	$4
1st Half		93	18	1	4	3	237	238	283	323	605	490	621	6	85	0.43	53	14	33	27	83	38	72	4%	190	17%	75%	13	15%	46%	3.06	-4.3	41	124	$0
2nd Half		124	18	3	7	8	210	237	246	363	609	899	544	5	69	0.16	49	17	34	28	53	105	39	10%	137	50%	80%	14	21%	50%	2.91	-6.5	14	42	$7
18	**Proj**	**198**	**28**	**4**	**12**	**12**	**232**	**243**	**275**	**361**	**636**	**802**	**605**	**6**	**78**	**0.27**	**50**	**16**	**34**	**28**	**65**	**71**	**52**	**8%**	**167**	**37%**	**72%**				**3.22**	**-9.7**	**29**	**88**	**$6**

Happ,Ian

Age: 23	Bats: B	Pos: CF 2B LF	Health A	LIMA Plan B	
Ht: 6' 0"	Wt: 205		PT/Exp F	Rand Var 0	
			Consist F	MM 4215	

24-68-.253 in 468 AB at CHC. Reasons why the next step isn't forward: 1) xPX casts doubt upon sustainability of lofty hr/f rate; 2) low ct% gives him some BA risk and suggests more growing pains are possible. Future is bright, but more refinement is needed.

Yr	Tm	AB	R	HR	RBI	SB	BA	xBA	OBP	SLG	OPS	vL	vR	bb%	ct%	Eye	G	L	F	h%	HctX	PX	xPX	hr/f	Spd	SBO	SB%	#Wk	DOM	DIS	RC/G	RAR	BPV	BPX	R$
13																																			
14																																			
15																																			
16	aa	248	30	7	27	5	236		286	369	655			7	73	0.26				30		90			87	13%	70%				3.48		5	14	$4
17	CHC *	468	78	31	88	10	254	253	323	513	836	789	863	9	66	0.30	40	20	40	32	87	163	122	25%	100	13%	65%	22	41%	41%	5.53	6.5	44	133	$19
1st Half		259	38	17	43	3	254	259	317	517	834	901	827	8	67	0.28	40	20	40	31	85	168	126	25%	93	8%	55%	8	63%	38%	5.47	4.3	48	145	$17
2nd Half		209	40	14	45	7	254	245	333	507	841	728	893	10	65	0.32	40	20	40	32	88	157	119	25%	114	19%	70%	14	29%	43%	5.60	4.3	41	124	$20
18	**Proj**	**502**	**76**	**23**	**80**	**11**	**244**	**236**	**309**	**438**	**747**	**710**	**762**	**8**	**68**	**0.27**	**40**	**20**	**40**	**31**	**87**	**124**	**122**	**17%**	**94**	**14%**	**69%**				**4.44**	**-1.1**	**18**	**54**	**$18**

GREG PYRON

Hardy,J.J.

Age: 35	Bats: R	Pos: SS	Health	F	LIMA Plan	D+
Ht: 6' 1"	Wt: 200		PT/Exp	C	Rand Var	+3
			Consist	D	MM	1013

4-24-.217 in 254 AB at BAL. Numbers were way down even before June broken wrist sidelined him for three months. Given the small sample and 23% h%, could bounce back vL, but poor health track record and fourth consecutive sub-80 PX vR suggest he's no longer fit for a regular role. Pass.

Yr	Tm	AB	R	HR	RBI	SB	BA	xBA	OBP	SLG	OPS	vL	vR	bb%	ct%	Eye	G	L	F	h%	HctX	PX	xPX	hr/f	Spd	SBO	SB%	#Wk	DOM	DIS	RC/G	RAR	BPV	BPX	R$
13	BAL	601	66	25	76	2	263	267	306	433	738	783	720	6	88	0.52	45	17	38	26	104	101	99	12%	91	2%	67%	27	63%	19%	4.58	20.0	73	183	$1
14	BAL	529	56	9	52	0	268	234	309	372	682	621	702	5	80	0.28	43	19	38	32	104	81	96	6%	97	0%	0%	27	30%	37%	3.98	12.1	27	73	$1
15	BAL	411	45	8	37	0	219	221	253	311	564	494	593	5	79	0.23	49	17	33	26	82	62	69	7%	92	0%	0%	22	23%	50%	2.60	-22.6	3	8	$
16	BAL	405	43	9	48	0	269	254	309	407	716	782	693	6	83	0.38	45	18	36	30	117	89	110	7%	82	0%	0%	22	55%	18%	4.45	1.7	43	123	$
17	BAL *	276	29	5	26	0	213	232	264	321	585	522	604	7	79	0.34	45	18	37	25	81	66	86	5%	81	2%	0%	16	25%	44%	2.70	-16.4	9	27	-$
1st Half		227	19	3	21	0	211	229	248	308	556	536	566	4	81	0.23	44	17	39	25	82	59	80	4%	81	2%	0%	12	17%	42%	2.39	-15.5	6	18	-$
2nd Half		49	10	2	5	0	219	245	345	378	723	432	978	16	71	0.66	59	18	23	27	78	102	133	20%	92	0%	0%	4	50%	50%	4.25	-0.5	26	79	-$
18	**Proj**	**324**	**43**	**7**	**34**	**0**	**236**	**235**	**293**	**354**	**646**	**633**	**652**	**7**	**79**	**0.38**	**46**	**18**	**36**	**28**	**92**	**72**	**104**	**8%**	**86**	**0%**	**15%**				**3.45**	**-9.8**	**2**	**7**	**$**

Harper,Bryce

Age: 25	Bats: L	Pos: RF	Health	C	LIMA Plan	B+
Ht: 6' 3"	Wt: 215		PT/Exp	A	Rand Var	-4
			Consist	F	MM	4255

On pace for near repeat of huge 2015 prior to August knee injury. But skills didn't measure up, as HctX and xPX were closer to to down 2016 season. Lofty hr/f may not be sustainable without HctX rebound, and 2016 SB looks like an aberration. Bat is certainly elite, but only one season over $26 in six tries. Don't overbid on hope.

Yr	Tm	AB	R	HR	RBI	SB	BA	xBA	OBP	SLG	OPS	vL	vR	bb%	ct%	Eye	G	L	F	h%	HctX	PX	xPX	hr/f	Spd	SBO	SB%	#Wk	DOM	DIS	RC/G	RAR	BPV	BPX	R$
13	WAS	424	71	20	58	11	274	281	368	486	854	648	947	12	78	0.65	47	20	33	31	116	142	118	18%	101	12%	73%	22	64%	27%	6.18	19.2	82	205	$2
14	WAS	352	41	13	32	2	273	234	344	423	768	765	769	10	70	0.37	44	22	35	35	92	110	115	15%	131	4%	50%	18	44%	39%	5.02	9.3	30	81	$1
15	WAS	521	118	42	99	6	330	309	460	649	1109	986	1160	19	75	0.95	39	22	39	37	134	208	161	27%	101	5%	60%	27	85%	7%	11.16	87.2	136	368	$4
16	WAS	506	84	24	86	21	243	252	373	441	814	764	833	17	77	0.92	40	17	42	27	106	117	111	14%	91	17%	68%	26	54%	31%	5.48	12.3	65	186	$2
17	WAS	420	95	29	87	4	319	293	413	595	1008	802	1087	14	76	0.69	40	22	38	36	106	155	105	24%	116	4%	67%	21	62%	24%	9.15	44.7	94	285	$2
1st Half		278	61	18	58	2	313	289	422	576	997	822	1058	16	76	0.78	43	21	36	36	101	151	98	24%	116	4%	50%	13	62%	15%	8.84	28.6	93	282	$3
2nd Half		142	34	11	29	2	331	297	394	634	1028	769	1146	10	77	0.50	35	23	41	36	115	162	118	24%	112	5%	100%	8	63%	38%	9.75	17.5	95	288	$1
18	**Proj**	**503**	**103**	**32**	**93**	**6**	**301**	**281**	**401**	**560**	**960**	**806**	**1023**	**14**	**76**	**0.71**	**40**	**21**	**39**	**34**	**112**	**144**	**119**	**21%**	**107**	**6%**	**58%**				**8.07**	**47.1**	**73**	**223**	**$3**

Harrison,Josh

Age: 30	Bats: R	Pos: 2B 3B	Health	C	LIMA Plan	B
Ht: 5' 8"	Wt: 180		PT/Exp	B	Rand Var	0
			Consist	A	MM	2445

First half featured career best on-base skills (including 20 HBP) and return of pop. OBP and SB/SBO soon crashed; broken hand cut season short. But power gains held, and xPX, rising FB% say they may stick, though perhaps at expense of BA. Deserves a pass for SB slide given past consistency, so safe to pay for repeat.

Yr	Tm	AB	R	HR	RBI	SB	BA	xBA	OBP	SLG	OPS	vL	vR	bb%	ct%	Eye	G	L	F	h%	HctX	PX	xPX	hr/f	Spd	SBO	SB%	#Wk	DOM	DIS	RC/G	RAR	BPV	BPX	R$
13	PIT *	356	48	6	40	16	261	276	294	412	705	981	466	4	85	0.31	47	19	35	29	120	103	122	12%	109	34%	66%	18	33%	28%	3.96	3.2	65	163	$1
14	PIT	520	77	13	52	18	315	284	347	490	837	856	832	4	84	0.27	37	24	39	35	116	121	117	8%	133	20%	72%	27	52%	15%	6.15	39.2	84	227	$2
15	PIT	418	57	4	28	10	287	263	327	390	717	761	702	4	83	0.27	41	25	34	34	104	77	96	3%	118	17%	56%	22	36%	27%	4.21	0.5	40	108	$1
16	PIT	487	57	4	59	19	283	250	311	388	699	810	674	3	84	0.24	44	19	36	33	95	63	99	3%	149	19%	83%	23	35%	35%	4.34	-7.3	42	120	$1
17	PIT	486	66	16	47	12	272	260	339	432	771	857	745	5	81	0.31	36	23	41	31	107	89	120	10%	107	14%	75%	22	36%	23%	4.68	-4.6	42	127	$1
1st Half		294	35	9	27	10	289	265	369	449	818	897	795	7	82	0.39	37	24	39	33	107	89	119	10%	110	18%	71%	13	31%	23%	5.33	4.2	46	139	$2
2nd Half		192	31	7	20	2	245	253	289	406	695	800	661	4	81	0.19	36	21	44	27	108	90	121	10%	96	5%	100%	9	44%	22%	3.77	-6.0	35	106	$
18	**Proj**	**468**	**64**	**14**	**47**	**13**	**274**	**266**	**322**	**433**	**755**	**864**	**721**	**5**	**83**	**0.27**	**40**	**22**	**39**	**31**	**105**	**88**	**111**	**9%**	**119**	**16%**	**74%**				**4.62**	**-2.4**	**46**	**139**	**$1**

Hays,Austin

Age: 22	Bats: R	Pos: RF	Health	A	LIMA Plan	D
Ht: 6' 1"	Wt: 195		PT/Exp	F	Rand Var	0
			Consist	F	MM	1111

1-8-.217 in 60 AB at BAL. Began season in Single-A, but clubbing 32 HR across two levels allowed for rapid ascent to majors. Plate skills, particularly a lack of patience, still need some refining, so some growing pains should be expected. He offers an exciting ceiling, but don't count on him making a big impact just yet.

Yr	Tm	AB	R	HR	RBI	SB	BA	xBA	OBP	SLG	OPS	vL	vR	bb%	ct%	Eye	G	L	F	h%	HctX	PX	xPX	hr/f	Spd	SBO	SB%	#Wk	DOM	DIS	RC/G	RAR	BPV	BPX	R$
13																																			
14																																			
15																																			
16																																			
17	BAL *	321	37	15	54	1	273	262	303	460	764	714	506	4	79	0.20	56	16	29	31	99	100	79	8%	97	3%	43%	5	20%	60%	4.84	0.8	34	103	$
1st Half		43	3	3	9	0	327	273	341	549	890			2	92	0.26				31		101			96	0%	0%				7.08		83	252	-$1
2nd Half		278	34	12	45	1	265	257	298	447	745	714	506	4	77	0.20	56	16	29	31	97	100	79	8%	101	3%	43%	5	20%	60%	4.55	-2.9	28	85	$1
18	**Proj**	**169**	**19**	**5**	**25**	**1**	**240**	**229**	**263**	**372**	**635**	**927**	**546**	**4**	**79**	**0.18**	**40**	**18**	**43**	**28**	**87**	**73**	**71**	**9%**	**98**	**3%**	**50%**				**3.30**	**-7.1**	**1**	**4**	**$**

Headley,Chase

Age: 34	Bats: B	Pos: 3B 1B	Health	A	LIMA Plan	C+
Ht: 6' 2"	Wt: 215		PT/Exp	A	Rand Var	-3
			Consist	B	MM	2325

Finished strong, with seven HR in final two months. End result was highest R$ since 2012, but a few reasons to be wary: posted lowest xPX, 2nd lowest HctX of career; h% correction should bring BA back to typical .250 range; at an age where SB and PT could drop off. May have another year at this level, but have a Plan B.

Yr	Tm	AB	R	HR	RBI	SB	BA	xBA	OBP	SLG	OPS	vL	vR	bb%	ct%	Eye	G	L	F	h%	HctX	PX	xPX	hr/f	Spd	SBO	SB%	#Wk	DOM	DIS	RC/G	RAR	BPV	BPX	R$
13	SD	520	59	13	50	8	250	253	347	400	747	764	740	11	73	0.47	46	23	31	32	106	119	107	11%	88	8%	67%	25	48%	28%	4.52	8.8	37	93	$1
14	2 TM	470	55	13	49	7	243	251	328	372	700	721	693	10	74	0.42	41	27	32	30	113	99	120	12%	75	8%	70%	26	35%	42%	3.95	3.9	19	51	$1
15	NYY	580	74	11	62	0	259	252	324	369	693	743	670	8	77	0.38	43	27	30	32	95	80	91	8%	91	1%	0%	27	26%	44%	3.98	-9.8	16	43	$1
16	NYY	467	58	14	51	8	253	247	331	385	716	697	726	10	75	0.43	44	24	32	31	95	83	106	13%	95	7%	80%	26	35%	42%	4.32	-6.5	15	43	$1
17	NYY	512	77	12	61	9	273	252	352	406	758	704	779	10	74	0.45	43	25	32	35	90	86	78	10%	104	7%	82%	27	30%	44%	5.03	2.4	19	58	$1
1st Half		252	32	4	32	6	250	241	344	365	709	478	801	12	72	0.49	46	24	31	33	80	80	63	7%	113	10%	75%	13	31%	46%	4.26	-6.2	12	36	$1
2nd Half		260	45	8	29	3	296	264	361	446	807	920	758	9	77	0.41	42	26	33	36	100	92	91	12%	93	4%	100%	14	29%	43%	5.87	5.6	27	82	$2
18	**Proj**	**474**	**66**	**12**	**53**	**7**	**265**	**252**	**341**	**396**	**737**	**730**	**740**	**10**	**75**	**0.43**	**43**	**25**	**32**	**33**	**95**	**82**	**91**	**11%**	**96**	**6%**	**78%**				**4.65**	**-3.3**	**10**	**30**	**$1**

Healy,Ryon

Age: 26	Bats: R	Pos: DH 1B 3B	Health	A	LIMA Plan	B+
Ht: 6' 5"	Wt: 225		PT/Exp	B	Rand Var	-1
			Consist	D	MM	3035

A tale of two halves. Swung for fences early on, more than making up for ct% dip with all the HR. When ct% rose in 2nd half, FB%, power collapsed. End result similar to 2016, and sets a reasonable baseline for 2018. Since once you display a skill you own it, recapturing and sustaining his 1st half form would lead to ... UP: 35 HR

Yr	Tm	AB	R	HR	RBI	SB	BA	xBA	OBP	SLG	OPS	vL	vR	bb%	ct%	Eye	G	L	F	h%	HctX	PX	xPX	hr/f	Spd	SBO	SB%	#Wk	DOM	DIS	RC/G	RAR	BPV	BPX	R$
13																																			
14																																			
15	aa	507	47	7	46	0	258		290	357	646			4	82	0.25				30		70			85	1%	0%				3.52		21	57	$
16	OAK *	606	85	23	90	1	296	268	336	499	835	886	853	6	77	0.26	42	20	39	35	93	130	102	16%	103	1%	42%	13	54%	31%	6.03	8.9	55	157	$2
17	OAK	576	66	25	78	0	271	246	302	451	754	873	717	4	75	0.16	43	19	38	32	104	106	115	15%	91	1%	0%	27	44%	37%	4.68	-3.0	23	70	$1
1st Half		312	36	19	51	0	276	253	306	516	822	1105	756	4	72	0.14	40	17	42	33	112	144	154	20%	91	2%	0%	13	54%	31%	5.41	4.8	40	121	$2
2nd Half		264	30	6	27	0	265	240	299	375	674	698	663	4	79	0.20	45	21	34	32	93	65	74	8%	96	0%	0%	14	36%	43%	3.83	-7.9	7	21	$
18	**Proj**	**601**	**72**	**25**	**77**	**0**	**277**	**259**	**313**	**467**	**781**	**848**	**758**	**5**	**77**	**0.21**	**43**	**20**	**38**	**32**	**98**	**110**	**105**	**14%**	**99**	**1%**	**28%**				**5.08**	**-7.1**	**21**	**62**	**$1**

Hechavarria,Adeiny

Age: 29	Bats: R	Pos: SS	Health	C	LIMA Plan	B+
Ht: 6' 0"	Wt: 195		PT/Exp	B	Rand Var	-1
			Consist	C	MM	1535

Oblique injury wiped out much of 1H, but he thrived after slow start following trade to TAM in June. Sold out for power late in year, hurting ct% and already low OBP. But pairing HctX, plus speed with jump in FB%, SBO led to 7 HR, 4 SB over final 2 months. Potential for double digit HR/SB at least makes him interesting again.

Yr	Tm	AB	R	HR	RBI	SB	BA	xBA	OBP	SLG	OPS	vL	vR	bb%	ct%	Eye	G	L	F	h%	HctX	PX	xPX	hr/f	Spd	SBO	SB%	#Wk	DOM	DIS	RC/G	RAR	BPV	BPX	R$
13	MIA	543	30	3	42	11	227	240	267	298	565	589	555	5	82	0.31	52	20	28	27	77	46	55	2%	156	16%	52%	26	31%	50%	2.49	-15.8	25	63	$
14	MIA	536	53	1	34	7	276	262	308	356	664	742	645	5	84	0.30	54	22	24	33	99	55	73	1%	173	8%	58%	25	40%	44%	3.80	9.6	43	116	$1
15	MIA	470	54	5	48	7	281	253	315	374	689	912	637	5	83	0.29	51	20	29	33	92	58	83	5%	137	7%	78%	22	27%	32%	4.19	-2.8	32	86	$1
16	MIA	508	52	3	38	1	236	254	283	311	594	570	600	6	86	0.45	48	22	30	27	112	43	86	2%	139	1%	100%	27	30%	26%	2.95	-20.6	33	94	$
17	2 TM	330	37	8	30	4	261	259	289	406	695	747	678	4	80	0.19	49	20	32	31	116	79	74	10%	142	7%	80%	19	32%	47%	4.05	-5.5	34	103	$
1st Half		84	8	1	9	0	310	281	322	405	727	1152	639	2	87	0.18	46	27	27	35	103	50	58	5%	125	0%	0%	6	33%	50%	4.87	0.7	32	97	-$
2nd Half		246	29	7	21	4	244	253	278	407	684	661	694	4	77	0.20	50	17	34	29	120	91	81	11%	139	10%	80%	13	31%	46%	3.80	-5.7	34	103	$
18	**Proj**	**502**	**53**	**7**	**44**	**10**	**261**	**260**	**293**	**369**	**662**	**742**	**639**	**4**	**83**	**0.26**	**49**	**21**	**30**	**30**	**107**	**58**	**76**	**6%**	**143**	**10%**	**79%**				**3.75**	**-10.5**	**23**	**68**	**$1**

BRIAN RUDD

Hedges,Austin

Age: 25	Bats: R	Pos: CA	Health	A	LIMA Plan	D+
Ht: 6' 1"	Wt: 206		PT/Exp	D	Rand Var	-1
			Consist	C	MM	3113

Flexed his muscles with six HR in April, but swing-for-fences approach came with huge drop in ct%, which soon caught up to him. Still owns that track record of higher ct%, but xBA didn't like the BA outlook then any more than it does now. Yet another 2nd catcher who offers some power with an accompanying BA tax.

Yr Tm	AB	R	HR	RBI	SB	BA	xBA	OBP	SLG	OPS	vL	vR	bb%	ct%	Eye	G	L	F	h%	HctX	PX	xPX	hr/f	Spd	SBO	SB%	#Wk	DOM	DIS	RC/G	RAR	BPV	BPX	R$
13 aa	67	3	0	7	3	198		255	235	490			7	85	0.51				23		34			94	23%	70%				1.92		11	28	-$2
14 aa	427	26	5	36	1	196		231	276	507			4	77	0.19				25		63			91	5%	20%				1.95		-4	-11	-$4
15 SD *	208	21	4	21	1	202	226	250	308	558	420	483	6	77	0.28	45	19	36	24	67	74	55	8%	76	2%	100%	23	17%	74%	2.47	-8.7	4	11	-$2
16 SD *	337	39	13	56	1	256	219	275	433	708	1000	148	2	80	0.13	44	6	50	28	109	104	59	0%	78	5%	24%	3	33%	67%	3.96	-4.3	35	100	$7
17 SD	387	36	18	55	4	214	223	262	398	660	600	684	6	68	0.19	37	18	46	26	92	116	114	15%	69	7%	80%	24	38%	54%	3.34	-8.5	0	0	$3
1st Half	226	22	11	36	1	217	224	261	403	664	504	738	5	69	0.19	37	18	45	26	90	114	107	16%	77	5%	50%	13	38%	54%	3.35	-5.3	3	9	$5
2nd Half	161	14	7	19	3	211	220	263	391	654	768	616	6	68	0.19	36	17	46	26	94	117	124	14%	73	10%	100%	11	36%	55%	3.34	-3.8	0	0	$2
18 Proj	400	38	17	53	3	228	237	267	406	673	639	687	5	73	0.19	40	18	42	27	82	106	92	14%	71	6%	73%				3.53	-7.4	5	17	$5

Heredia,Guillermo

Age: 27	Bats: R	Pos: CF LF	Health	A	LIMA Plan	D+
Ht: 5' 10"	Wt: 180		PT/Exp	D	Rand Var	-1
			Consist	A	MM	1123

Held his own in 1st half, but complete lack of power foretold the inevitable: a 2nd half collapse. SB% shows he's not going to put speed to use, and success vL more luck (35% h%) than skill (72 PX). October shoulder surgery shouldn't keep him from being ready next spring, but also won't make him any more fantasy relevant.

Yr Tm	AB	R	HR	RBI	SB	BA	xBA	OBP	SLG	OPS	vL	vR	bb%	ct%	Eye	G	L	F	h%	HctX	PX	xPX	hr/f	Spd	SBO	SB%	#Wk	DOM	DIS	RC/G	RAR	BPV	BPX	R$
13 for	192	38	1	9	4	238		315	336	652			10	89	1.00				27		66			151	15%	45%				3.32	-5.0	75	188	$2
14																																		
15																																		
16 SEA *	435	66	4	50	5	254	241	332	325	657	658	669	10	83	0.70	49	20	31	30	56	43	13	4%	131	8%	43%	10	30%	60%	3.53	-10.9	30	86	$8
17 SEA	386	43	6	24	1	249	233	315	337	652	794	582	6	83	0.42	47	18	35	28	69	52	38	6%	113	6%	17%	26	27%	35%	3.22	-17.6	24	73	$3
1st Half	201	27	5	13	1	284	241	339	378	718	808	673	6	86	0.43	53	16	31	31	68	47	45	10%	122	7%	25%	13	23%	23%	4.11	-4.6	32	97	$7
2nd Half	185	16	1	11	0	211	228	290	292	582	779	484	8	81	0.42	41	19	40	26	69	58	30	2%	103	5%	0%	13	31%	46%	2.42	-14.4	16	48	-$2
18 Proj	321	44	4	25	3	245	244	323	337	660	725	596	8	83	0.53	47	19	34	28	64	54	27	5%	126	8%	35%				3.32	-11.6	15	46	$5

Hernandez,Cesar

Age: 28	Bats: B	Pos: 2B	Health	B	LIMA Plan	C+
Ht: 5' 10"	Wt: 160		PT/Exp	B	Rand Var	-3
			Consist	B	MM	1545

Missed more than a month following June oblique strain; upon return, bb%, ct%, and SB% all surged. High h% and strong OBP are now well-established, and along with his speed, provide solid floor. Downward trending SBO and modest SB% history cap the SB upside, though. Should be good for something close to a repeat.

Yr Tm	AB	R	HR	RBI	SB	BA	xBA	OBP	SLG	OPS	vL	vR	bb%	ct%	Eye	G	L	F	h%	HctX	PX	xPX	hr/f	Spd	SBO	SB%	#Wk	DOM	DIS	RC/G	RAR	BPV	BPX	R$
13 PHI *	522	64	2	38	25	278	243	331	344	674	581	722	7	77	0.34	52	25	23	36	68	49	48	0%	166	23%	68%	7	14%	57%	3.92	3.9	14	35	$19
14 PHI *	373	40	4	22	7	242	246	299	314	613	626	551	7	76	0.34	53	26	21	31	63	54	50	6%	136	15%	44%	16	19%	56%	2.92	-5.3	5	14	$5
15 PHI	405	57	1	35	19	272	257	339	348	687	769	653	9	79	0.47	54	24	22	34	80	58	67	2%	150	19%	79%	24	38%	42%	4.19	0.3	26	70	$14
16 PHI	547	67	6	39	17	294	262	371	393	764	789	756	11	79	0.57	55	24	21	36	83	55	59	7%	186	15%	57%	27	26%	33%	5.01	2.1	38	109	$20
17 PHI	511	85	9	34	15	294	273	373	421	793	810	786	11	80	0.59	53	23	25	35	71	74	61	9%	185	12%	75%	22	41%	18%	5.60	8.3	57	173	$19
1st Half	238	40	5	14	6	277	260	336	399	735	727	738	8	79	0.39	51	22	27	34	65	70	64	10%	173	13%	67%	10	30%	20%	4.61	-1.5	40	121	$14
2nd Half	273	45	4	20	9	308	283	403	440	842	887	824	13	81	0.77	54	23	22	37	77	77	58	8%	177	11%	82%	12	50%	17%	6.53	12.8	65	197	$24
18 Proj	500	73	6	36	17	288	267	367	395	762	788	752	11	79	0.58	54	23	23	35	75	62	60	7%	179	14%	69%				5.09	4.2	25	77	$20

Hernandez,Enrique

Age: 26	Bats: R	Pos: CF LF SS	Health	B	LIMA Plan	D+
Ht: 5' 11"	Wt: 200		PT/Exp	D	Rand Var	+4
			Consist	C	MM	3223

Low h% hid some positive signs in 1st half: back to lefty-mashing ways; bumped ct% back up; another step forward in bb%. However, he was good, not great vL in 2nd half, and remains lost in the woods vR. There's still room for h% recovery, but he's clearly best-suited for short half of platoon. Tough to carve out value in that role.

Yr Tm	AB	R	HR	RBI	SB	BA	xBA	OBP	SLG	OPS	vL	vR	bb%	ct%	Eye	G	L	F	h%	HctX	PX	xPX	hr/f	Spd	SBO	SB%	#Wk	DOM	DIS	RC/G	RAR	BPV	BPX	R$
13 aa	437	42	11	36	4	210		256	328	584			6	82	0.35				23		77			102	8%	55%				2.65		34	85	$1
14 2 TM *	497	55	10	45	4	266	264	313	401	714	581	796	6	87	0.52	38	21	41	29	94	92	115	7%	113	9%	39%	9	56%	22%	4.16	5.4	69	186	$12
15 LA *	261	28	8	29	1	269	261	306	427	733	1215	592	5	76	0.22	46	23	30	33	110	106	98	15%	118	5%	27%	20	45%	40%	4.42	-2.2	37	100	$5
16 LA	216	25	7	18	2	190	211	283	324	607	668	524	11	70	0.44	41	17	42	23	79	89	91	11%	88	4%	100%	23	26%	48%	2.93	-11.6	4	11	-$2
17 LA	297	46	11	37	3	215	259	308	421	729	946	499	12	73	0.51	42	19	40	26	116	132	122	13%	93	4%	100%	27	48%	37%	4.31	-8.6	52	158	$3
1st Half	174	32	8	25	3	224	282	312	477	789	1040	602	12	75	0.52	40	19	41	25	114	160	132	15%	91	9%	100%	13	62%	15%	5.03	-1.7	80	242	$6
2nd Half	123	14	3	12	0	203	223	303	341	644	857	269	13	71	0.50	44	18	38	26	120	89	107	9%	101	0%	0%	14	36%	57%	3.33	-7.8	12	36	-$3
18 Proj	251	32	10	26	2	229	248	310	411	722	889	551	11	74	0.45	42	19	39	27	104	111	107	13%	98	4%	77%				4.23	-2.2	27	81	$4

Hernandez,Gorkys

Age: 30	Bats: R	Pos: LF CF RF	Health	A	LIMA Plan	D
Ht: 6' 1"	Wt: 190		PT/Exp	D	Rand Var	-2
			Consist	A	MM	1311

Tallied more AB than the rest of MLB career combined. Sporting a .460 OPS in late May, went on h%-fueled hot streak for next three months, keeping BA and fantasy value afloat. Offers nothing but league-average speed, as you can disregard small sample 2016 HctX/xPX, and note poor xBA history. Won't ever see 300 AB again.

Yr Tm	AB	R	HR	RBI	SB	BA	xBA	OBP	SLG	OPS	vL	vR	bb%	ct%	Eye	G	L	F	h%	HctX	PX	xPX	hr/f	Spd	SBO	SB%	#Wk	DOM	DIS	RC/G	RAR	BPV	BPX	R$
13 aaa	430	44	4	24	19	225		263	310	573			5	67	0.16				32		69			137	34%	57%				2.45		-22	-55	$7
14 aaa	189	12	0	6	5	174		212	213	426			5	69	0.16				25		45			93	18%	80%				1.44		-46	-124	-$4
15 PIT *	345	40	4	33	14	232	253	297	320	618	0	0	8	73	0.34	100	0	0	31	0	65	-16	0%	106	20%	80%	3	0%	0%	3.23	-15.6	-3	-8	$7
16 SF *	491	59	7	40	14	238	221	297	336	633	788	714	8	78	0.37	39	20	41	29	125	64	152	12%	132	25%	45%	6	67%	33%	2.97	-25.4	18	51	$9
17 SF	310	40	0	22	12	255	237	327	326	652	610	684	9	76	0.42	47	22	31	33	78	56	66	0%	111	18%	75%	27	19%	44%	3.63	-14.9	4	12	$6
1st Half	142	19	0	12	6	225	217	315	289	604	585	618	11	76	0.50	45	19	36	30	90	47	87	0%	118	22%	67%	13	15%	46%	2.89	-10.9	1	3	$3
2nd Half	168	21	0	10	6	280	252	337	357	694	631	737	8	77	0.36	49	24	27	36	69	64	48	0%	103	15%	86%	14	21%	43%	4.36	-4.8	6	18	$10
18 Proj	161	19	2	12	6	243	236	308	341	649	642	657	8	75	0.37	46	21	33	31	88	66	99	5%	113	21%	66%				3.42	-5.0	2	6	$4

Hernandez,Teoscar

Age: 25	Bats: R	Pos: LF	Health	A	LIMA Plan	D+
Ht: 6' 2"	Wt: 180		PT/Exp	C	Rand Var	0
			Consist	C	MM	4333

8-20-.261 in 88 AB at HOU/TOR. PRO: Dramatic power surge capped by eight Sept HR; improving bb% could generate more SBO. CON: ct% regressed, and fell to 59% in MLB; low SB% may reduce green light. All the whiffs make him risky, but with any improvement in that area, impact could be significant. Worth the gamble.

Yr Tm	AB	R	HR	RBI	SB	BA	xBA	OBP	SLG	OPS	vL	vR	bb%	ct%	Eye	G	L	F	h%	HctX	PX	xPX	hr/f	Spd	SBO	SB%	#Wk	DOM	DIS	RC/G	RAR	BPV	BPX	R$
13																																		
14 aa	95	9	3	8	2	252		264	409	673			2	57	0.04				41		146			109	27%	32%				3.12		-16	-43	$1
15 aa	470	70	14	36	25	191		231	310	541			5	69	0.17				24		81			124	37%	76%				2.26		-7	-19	$9
16 HOU *	523	75	12	54	28	262	234	323	404	727	881	632	8	76	0.38	48	12	40	32	102	94	75	14%	134	34%	59%	9	56%	22%	4.12	-2.4	39	111	$21
17 2AL *	488	78	25	81	15	253	246	322	495	817	647	1014	9	69	0.33	28	23	49	32	79	152	139	31%	125	22%	60%	7	57%	43%	5.15	-4.2	56	170	$19
1st Half	223	35	7	28	10	258	245	340	421	761			11	74	0.48				32		95		0%	144	27%	56%	1	0%	100%	4.51	-5.7	40	121	$13
2nd Half	265	43	19	53	5	249	265	306	557	863	647	1014	8	65	0.23	28	23	49	31	74	208	139	31%	112	15%	68%	6	67%	33%	5.68	2.6	76	230	$24
18 Proj	257	39	14	36	7	247	256	306	484	790	727	820	8	71	0.31	39	19	42	29	85	143	113	18%	125	22%	55%				4.76	2.4	49	150	$10

Herrera,Odubel

Age: 26	Bats: L	Pos: CF	Health	A	LIMA Plan	B
Ht: 5' 11"	Wt: 205		PT/Exp	A	Rand Var	0
			Consist	A	MM	2435

Poor 1H followed by strong 2nd half is probably noise; full-season skills ended up mostly in line with historical levels. PRO: while xPX wasn't buying the 2nd half power surge, more ct%, FB%, and hr/f support higher power ceiling. CON: Spd drop, shaky SB%, lower bb% all cap running game. 20 HR more likely than 20 SB.

Yr Tm	AB	R	HR	RBI	SB	BA	xBA	OBP	SLG	OPS	vL	vR	bb%	ct%	Eye	G	L	F	h%	HctX	PX	xPX	hr/f	Spd	SBO	SB%	#Wk	DOM	DIS	RC/G	RAR	BPV	BPX	R$
13 aa	389	32	2	26	13	246		274	323	596			4	82	0.21				30		50			146	20%	71%				2.95		21	53	$6
14 aa	368	37	2	37	10	289		331	359	690			6	79	0.30				36		55			110	16%	55%				4.04		7	19	$12
15 PHI	495	64	8	41	16	297	248	344	418	762	720	776	5	74	0.22	47	23	29	39	85	93	83	8%	129	18%	67%	27	44%	30%	4.94	8.7	21	57	$20
16 PHI	583	87	15	49	25	286	249	361	420	781	599	841	10	77	0.47	46	22	32	35	85	79	88	11%	150	17%	78%	27	26%	26%	5.38	12.2	37	106	$26
17 PHI	526	67	14	56	8	281	265	325	452	778	794	771	6	76	0.25	44	21	35	35	90	110	79	10%	95	11%	62%	25	40%	36%	5.04	-0.2	34	103	$16
1st Half	304	31	5	28	5	250	254	289	388	677	780	633	5	74	0.21	47	21	32	32	94	97	75	7%	83	16%	50%	13	31%	46%	3.59	-12.0	12	36	$11
2nd Half	222	36	9	28	3	324	278	373	541	914	814	952	6	78	0.31	40	21	38	38	85	126	85	14%	111	5%	100%	12	50%	25%	7.59	15.8	62	188	$22
18 Proj	557	75	15	55	14	283	260	335	440	775	703	801	6	77	0.30	45	22	33	35	87	95	84	10%	121	14%	71%				5.09	9.2	31	94	$22

BRIAN RUDD

Herrmann,Chris

Age: 30	Bats: L	Pos: CA LF	Health B	LIMA Plan D	
Ht: 6' 0"	Wt: 200		PT/Exp F	Rand Var +5	
			Consist F	MM 2501	

Extremely low h% hid 1st half skill set that was plenty serviceable, albeit in small sample. 2016's power carried over, while bb%, ct% surged. Skills cratered in equally small-sample 2nd half, but previous power and sneaky speed (12 for 12 in SB last 2 years) keep him on the radar. Decent $1 flyer if you have firm BA foundation.

Yr	Tm	AB	R	HR	RBI	SB	BA	xBA	OBP	SLG	OPS	vL	vR	bb%	ct%	Eye	G	L	F	h%	HctX	PX	xPX	hr/f	Spd	SBO	SB%	#Wk	DOM	DIS	RC/G	RAR	BPV	BPX	R$
13	MIN *	404	38	5	34	2	193	202	257	280	537	545	624	8	70	0.29	43	19	38	26	106	69	156	10%	104	6%	39%	14	29%	43%	2.20	-19.2	-13	-33	-$
14	MIN *	279	31	4	24	4	246	234	295	377	672	544	496	7	75	0.28	49	12	39	31	73	107	55	0%	120	8%	77%	13	8%	54%	3.76	2.5	37	100	$
15	MIN *	176	20	3	15	2	175	211	241	277	518	224	550	8	70	0.29	48	17	35	23	86	78	68	9%	90	7%	100%	20	25%	65%	2.12	-9.6	-10	-27	-$
16	ARI *	171	23	6	30	4	254	230	325	440	765	1071	804	9	68	0.33	44	17	38	34	123	116	206	15%	147	9%	100%	16	31%	50%	5.03	3.1	31	89	$
17	ARI	226	35	10	27	5	181	227	273	345	619	503	645	11	70	0.43	44	18	38	21	98	97	126	16%	94	9%	100%	27	37%	52%	3.06	-7.2	12	36	$
1st Half		124	17	7	21	1	194	248	294	403	697	333	766	13	75	0.58	38	18	44	20	132	117	183	17%	82	3%	100%	13	62%	38%	3.81	-1.1	45	136	$
2nd Half		102	18	3	6	4	167	204	248	275	522	647	484	10	65	0.31	53	17	30	22	56	69	46	15%	118	17%	100%	14	14%	64%	2.24	-6.2	-29	-88	$
18	Proj	**221**	**31**	**8**	**26**	**4**	**220**	**227**	**297**	**380**	**677**	**643**	**685**	**10**	**69**	**0.36**	**46**	**17**	**37**	**28**	**96**	**97**	**123**	**14%**	**120**	**7%**	**97%**				**3.76**	**-2.6**	**8**	**24**	**$**

Heyward,Jason

Age: 28	Bats: L	Pos: RF	Health B	LIMA Plan B	
Ht: 6' 5"	Wt: 240		PT/Exp A	Rand Var 0	
			Consist D	MM 1235	

Power is long gone, and now running game has followed suit. Since June 1 of 2016, has just 7 SB, 7% SBO and 57% SB%. Multiple DL stints may or may not be sign of things to come, but either way, ineptitude vL likely to prevent him from reaching previous lofty AB totals. Barely relevant in mixed leagues anymore.

Yr	Tm	AB	R	HR	RBI	SB	BA	xBA	OBP	SLG	OPS	vL	vR	bb%	ct%	Eye	G	L	F	h%	HctX	PX	xPX	hr/f	Spd	SBO	SB%	#Wk	DOM	DIS	RC/G	RAR	BPV	BPX	R$
13	ATL	382	67	14	38	2	254	272	349	427	776	801	766	11	81	0.66	44	21	35	28	101	116	95	13%	105	6%	33%	20	65%	25%	4.75	1.5	72	180	$1
14	ATL	573	74	11	58	20	271	251	351	384	735	477	820	10	83	0.68	45	19	36	31	95	80	80	6%	116	13%	83%	26	50%	12%	4.75	10.8	53	143	$2
15	STL	547	79	13	60	23	293	288	359	439	797	709	835	9	84	0.62	57	19	23	33	105	94	73	12%	112	16%	88%	27	48%	19%	5.84	14.9	63	170	$2
16	CHC	530	61	7	49	11	230	249	306	325	631	586	647	9	82	0.58	46	21	33	27	88	62	72	5%	89	11%	73%	27	26%	37%	3.25	-23.1	26	74	$
17	CHC	432	59	11	59	4	259	262	326	389	715	662	734	9	84	0.61	47	20	33	29	87	66	70	9%	113	7%	50%	24	33%	17%	4.22	-12.2	44	133	$1
1st Half		198	24	6	29	1	258	259	315	399	714	662	731	7	84	0.48	48	18	34	28	93	70	88	11%	113	6%	33%	10	30%	20%	4.09	-5.7	43	130	$
2nd Half		234	35	5	30	3	261	265	336	380	716	662	735	10	85	0.72	47	21	32	29	82	63	55	8%	109	7%	60%	14	36%	14%	4.32	-5.1	44	133	$1
18	Proj	**477**	**64**	**11**	**56**	**7**	**257**	**264**	**329**	**382**	**711**	**650**	**733**	**9**	**84**	**0.61**	**48**	**20**	**32**	**29**	**91**	**68**	**72**	**8%**	**105**	**8%**	**63%**				**4.21**	**-6.8**	**36**	**109**	**$1**

Hicks,Aaron

Age: 28	Bats: B	Pos: CF LF	Health D	LIMA Plan B	
Ht: 6' 1"	Wt: 202		PT/Exp C	Rand Var -2	
			Consist F	MM 3335	

15-52-.266 with 10 SB in 301 AB at NYY. Oblique woes interrupted long-awaited breakout. Was it legit? Plate skills: check. Speed: got boost from OBP, SBO jumps, but SB% may slow him down. Power: mixed signals, including just 3 road HR. Verdict: solid plate skills create high floor, from there the only question is PT.

Yr	Tm	AB	R	HR	RBI	SB	BA	xBA	OBP	SLG	OPS	vL	vR	bb%	ct%	Eye	G	L	F	h%	HctX	PX	xPX	hr/f	Spd	SBO	SB%	#Wk	DOM	DIS	RC/G	RAR	BPV	BPX	R$
13	MIN *	353	42	8	31	10	192	219	258	328	586	713	566	8	70	0.29	45	17	38	25	90	102	104	11%	139	18%	76%	16	38%	44%	2.68	-17.5	20	50	$
14	MIN *	406	52	5	41	6	235	241	340	330	670	792	512	14	75	0.64	54	20	26	30	78	81	45	3%	103	11%	45%	16	31%	56%	3.57	-4.0	26	70	$
15	MIN *	501	69	13	49	15	268	259	331	418	750	870	661	9	80	0.48	42	23	35	31	90	94	93	11%	125	13%	78%	18	39%	22%	4.84	4.8	52	141	$1
16	NYY	327	32	8	31	3	217	232	281	336	617	484	691	8	79	0.44	46	17	37	25	93	72	104	8%	93	9%	43%	25	32%	36%	2.98	-14.1	21	60	$
17	NYY *	325	60	16	54	11	267	266	370	481	852	903	816	14	78	0.76	44	16	40	30	98	122	119	16%	91	15%	68%	19	47%	26%	6.08	12.7	67	203	$1
1st Half		200	40	10	37	7	290	278	398	515	913	946	897	16	79	0.88	44	17	39	32	97	130	113	16%	86	17%	58%	13	54%	23%	7.04	12.3	79	239	$1
2nd Half		125	20	6	17	4	230	244	319	427	747	841	615	12	77	0.57	44	13	44	25	100	109	131	15%	109	12%	100%	6	33%	33%	4.70	-0.8	53	161	$
18	Proj	**404**	**59**	**18**	**51**	**10**	**256**	**255**	**340**	**447**	**787**	**835**	**761**	**11**	**78**	**0.57**	**44**	**17**	**40**	**29**	**95**	**106**	**109**	**14%**	**106**	**13%**	**71%**				**5.14**	**7.5**	**48**	**146**	**$1**

Hicks,John

Age: 28	Bats: R	Pos: 1B	Health A	LIMA Plan D	
Ht: 6' 2"	Wt: 230		PT/Exp D	Rand Var -4	
			Consist C	MM 2113	

6-22-.266 in 173 AB at DET. Don't read too much into 1st half HctX, xPX, as most of damage was done at Triple-A. PX history and low FB% point to limited ceiling, and awful OBP will make it hard to lock down regular role. Still mildly interesting in leagues where he earned catcher eligibility (18 G in 2017), but that's about it.

Yr	Tm	AB	R	HR	RBI	SB	BA	xBA	OBP	SLG	OPS	vL	vR	bb%	ct%	Eye	G	L	F	h%	HctX	PX	xPX	hr/f	Spd	SBO	SB%	#Wk	DOM	DIS	RC/G	RAR	BPV	BPX	R$
13	aa	296	35	3	26	11	215		262	300	562			6	76	0.26				27		67			98	25%	72%				2.54		1	3	$
14	a/a	290	29	3	33	5	232		278	313	590			6	72	0.23				31		65			100	12%	58%				2.80		-15	-41	$
15	SEA *	330	26	4	24	7	174	197	202	249	451	200	178	3	67	0.11	14	36	50	24	117	63	198	0%	78	20%	67%	6	17%	67%	1.52	-23.9	-46	-124	-$
16	DET *	325	36	8	36	3	255	330	292	392	684	0	3000	5	74	0.20	50	50	0	33	0	95	-24	0%	82	6%	72%	1	100%	0%	3.91	0.4	7	20	$
17	DET *	381	42	12	51	6	244	242	276	396	672	731	784	4	70	0.14	51	20	30	32	99	100	86	17%	67	14%	57%	19	32%	37%	3.55	-6.6	-9	-27	$
1st Half		187	23	7	33	3	279	245	293	464	757	842	842	2	72	0.07	57	10	33	35	134	115	111	19%	73	11%	69%	9	33%	11%	4.75	3.4	8	24	$1
2nd Half		194	19	5	18	3	211	236	260	331	591	629	754	6	68	0.20	47	26	27	29	75	84	70	15%	71	17%	50%	10	30%	60%	2.62	-9.1	-26	-79	$
18	Proj	**267**	**28**	**6**	**30**	**4**	**231**	**236**	**276**	**359**	**635**	**596**	**655**	**5**	**71**	**0.16**	**51**	**20**	**29**	**30**	**99**	**84**	**86**	**12%**	**72**	**12%**	**64%**				**3.10**	**-16.3**	**-14**	**-43**	**$**

Holliday,Matt

Age: 38	Bats: R	Pos: DH	Health F	LIMA Plan D+	
Ht: 6' 4"	Wt: 240		PT/Exp C	Rand Var 0	
			Consist B	MM 3123	

Contact rate was career worst by wide margin; made up for it in 1st half by showing peak level power. June allergic reaction only sidelined him for three weeks, but skills never recovered. Power should rebound from 2nd half disaster. Even as DH, won't make it through season unscathed. Have a backup plan.

Yr	Tm	AB	R	HR	RBI	SB	BA	xBA	OBP	SLG	OPS	vL	vR	bb%	ct%	Eye	G	L	F	h%	HctX	PX	xPX	hr/f	Spd	SBO	SB%	#Wk	DOM	DIS	RC/G	RAR	BPV	BPX	R$
13	STL	520	103	22	94	6	300	288	389	490	879	799	903	11	83	0.80	46	21	34	33	134	123	126	15%	86	4%	86%	25	68%	0%	6.86	33.8	83	208	$2
14	STL	574	83	20	90	4	272	268	370	441	811	1004	751	11	83	0.74	46	17	38	30	140	119	142	11%	71	3%	80%	26	77%	12%	5.49	23.6	71	192	$2
15	STL	229	24	4	35	2	279	265	394	410	804	796	807	14	79	0.80	48	23	28	34	111	96	74	8%	80	4%	67%	17	53%	29%	5.56	0.7	45	122	$
16	STL	382	48	20	62	0	246	264	322	461	782	797	776	8	81	0.49	50	14	36	25	127	120	126	18%	77	0%	0%	21	52%	19%	4.82	-7.6	63	180	$
17	NYY	373	50	19	64	1	231	234	316	432	748	843	719	11	69	0.40	48	15	38	28	89	125	97	19%	69	1%	100%	22	36%	41%	4.52	-3.8	22	67	$
1st Half		233	36	15	47	1	262	247	366	511	877	862	879	14	70	0.52	45	13	41	31	101	153	125	22%	78	1%	100%	12	50%	25%	6.43	10.5	53	161	$1
2nd Half		140	14	4	17	0	179	212	225	300	525	808	422	6	69	0.21	52	17	31	23	71	78	50	13%	62	0%	0%	10	20%	60%	2.13	-12.4	-28	-85	-$
18	Proj	**347**	**43**	**14**	**55**	**1**	**238**	**246**	**319**	**410**	**730**	**815**	**699**	**10**	**75**	**0.44**	**49**	**17**	**34**	**28**	**104**	**102**	**96**	**15%**	**71**	**2%**	**79%**				**4.31**	**-12.4**	**18**	**54**	**$**

Holt,Brock

Age: 30	Bats: L	Pos: 2B	Health F	LIMA Plan D	
Ht: 5' 10"	Wt: 180		PT/Exp D	Rand Var +5	
			Consist C	MM 0321	

0-7-.200 in 140 AB at BOS. Missed most of 1st half due to vertigo symptoms; troubles didn't end there. Previously outstanding LD% crashed, power reached new lows, and he was a non-factor on the bases again. Without any of the BA, steals, and multi-positional eligibilty he used to provide, there's no reason to roster him.

Yr	Tm	AB	R	HR	RBI	SB	BA	xBA	OBP	SLG	OPS	vL	vR	bb%	ct%	Eye	G	L	F	h%	HctX	PX	xPX	hr/f	Spd	SBO	SB%	#Wk	DOM	DIS	RC/G	RAR	BPV	BPX	R$
13	BOS *	350	35	2	29	7	220	221	279	261	540	384	536	8	81	0.44	57	17	26	26	84	31	33	0%	83	11%	67%	8	13%	50%	2.37	-17.1	-7	-18	$
14	BOS *	557	84	5	34	17	280	272	327	384	711	763	682	6	80	0.35	50	26	23	34	97	80	66	5%	144	13%	84%	19	42%	26%	4.53	13.7	42	114	$1
15	BOS	454	56	2	45	8	280	263	349	379	727	807	701	9	79	0.47	53	24	24	35	88	74	62	2%	128	7%	89%	26	31%	35%	4.72	1.9	32	86	$1
16	BOS *	315	47	7	36	4	258	276	325	382	707	342	762	9	80	0.49	54	24	22	30	75	81	50	14%	99	8%	57%	22	41%	32%	4.17	-5.7	33	94	$
17	BOS *	222	28	2	14	2	193	226	275	253	528	680	518	10	77	0.48	60	17	23	24	66	40	18	0%	104	5%	67%	15	33%	53%	2.20	-18.7	-8	-24	-$
1st Half		67	6	1	4	0	166	161	260	244	504	1000	411	11	70	0.42	38	13	50	21	71	47	99	0%	111	0%	0%	3	0%	100%	1.94	-6.9	-25	-76	-$
2nd Half		155	22	1	10	2	205	238	281	257	539	659	534	10	79	0.52	62	17	21	25	68	37	12	0%	103	7%	67%	12	42%	42%	2.32	-13.5	0	0	$
18	Proj	**190**	**24**	**2**	**16**	**2**	**237**	**247**	**312**	**310**	**622**	**636**	**618**	**9**	**78**	**0.47**	**56**	**22**	**23**	**30**	**80**	**49**	**42**	**5%**	**109**	**6%**	**70%**				**3.19**	**-9.2**	**-8**	**-25**	**$**

Hoskins,Rhys

Age: 25	Bats: R	Pos: LF 1B	Health A	LIMA Plan B+	
Ht: 6' 4"	Wt: 225		PT/Exp D	Rand Var +2	
			Consist D	MM 4145	

18-48-.259 in 170 AB at PHI. We knew he owned the elite power, but concurrent bb%/ct% growth is what unleashed him upon callup. Can those stick? Patience looks legit, but contact was quickly fraying by season's end (MLB splits: Aug 82%, Sept 67%). Let someone else take those 170 AB and extrapolate them over 500.

Yr	Tm	AB	R	HR	RBI	SB	BA	xBA	OBP	SLG	OPS	vL	vR	bb%	ct%	Eye	G	L	F	h%	HctX	PX	xPX	hr/f	Spd	SBO	SB%	#Wk	DOM	DIS	RC/G	RAR	BPV	BPX	R$
13																																			
14																																			
15																																			
16	aa	498	71	31	87	6	240		313	470	783			10	71	0.36				28		144			82	8%	64%				4.87		43	123	$1
17	PHI *	571	104	45	126	5	256	287	359	551	910	1006	1016	14	77	0.69	31	24	45	26	143	158	178	32%	85	5%	71%	9	56%	33%	6.75	14.0	88	267	$2
1st Half		287	50	18	54	2	265	294	351	528	879			12	80	0.64				28		139			110	4%	60%				6.37		88	267	$1
2nd Half		284	54	27	72	4	247	291	367	574	941	1006	1016	16	74	0.72	31	24	45	24	137	178	178	32%	66	6%	77%	9	56%	33%	7.13	12.5	90	273	$2
18	Proj	**490**	**76**	**31**	**91**	**6**	**248**	**269**	**348**	**490**	**838**	**773**	**859**	**12**	**74**	**0.54**	**32**	**26**	**42**	**27**	**123**	**136**	**160**	**20%**	**77**	**6%**	**72%**				**5.65**	**17.4**	**53**	**160**	**$1**

BRIAN RUDD

Hosmer,Eric

Age: 28	Bats: L	Pos: 1B	Health A	LIMA Plan B	
Ht: 6' 4"	Wt: 225		PT/Exp A	Rand Var -4	
			Consist D	MM 2255	

He extended 2016's hr/f spike while turning ct% and h% recovery into big BA rebound. But xPX fell to a remarkable low (heck of a testimonial on the league-wide power level). There is a dearth of plus skills here, just a lot of ct% over huge AB totals yielding a ton of balls in play. Don't pay for another 25 HR.

Yr Tm	AB	R	HR	RBI	SB	BA	xBA	OBP	SLG	OPS	vL	vR	bb%	ct%	Eye	G	L	F	h%	HctX	PX	xPX	hr/f	Spd	SBO	SB%	#Wk	DOM	DIS	RC/G	RAR	BPV	BPX	R$
13 KC	623	86	17	79	11	302	287	353	448	801	797	803	8	84	0.51	53	22	25	34	129	96	105	13%	102	8%	73%	26	46%	8%	5.77	20.1	60	150	$28
14 KC	503	54	9	58	4	270	259	318	398	716	676	732	6	82	0.38	51	17	32	32	117	99	100	7%	82	5%	67%	23	35%	26%	4.39	3.6	45	122	$13
15 KC	599	98	18	93	7	297	290	363	459	822	730	885	9	82	0.56	52	24	24	34	116	102	94	15%	107	5%	70%	27	48%	19%	6.00	17.6	62	168	$27
16 KC	605	80	25	104	5	266	263	328	433	761	656	813	9	78	0.43	59	16	25	30	109	97	89	21%	77	5%	63%	26	46%	23%	4.91	0.8	33	94	$19
17 KC	603	98	25	94	6	318	298	385	498	882	760	938	10	83	0.63	56	22	22	35	99	96	65	23%	91	3%	86%	27	70%	7%	7.21	29.6	57	173	$30
1st Half	305	43	11	37	3	305	301	361	475	837	784	861	8	83	0.54	55	24	21	34	99	93	62	20%	94	3%	100%	13	62%	8%	6.41	6.4	53	161	$23
2nd Half	298	55	14	57	3	332	292	408	520	928	736	1018	11	83	0.73	57	20	23	37	99	99	67	25%	93	4%	75%	14	79%	7%	8.08	19.1	62	188	$36
18 Proj	**604**	**93**	**22**	**97**	**6**	**295**	**285**	**359**	**461**	**820**	**712**	**875**	**9**	**81**	**0.54**	**56**	**21**	**24**	**33**	**106**	**91**	**79**	**19%**	**91**	**4%**	**74%**				**5.99**	**15.0**	**40**	**123**	**$25**

Hundley,Nick

Age: 34	Bats: R	Pos: CA	Health B	LIMA Plan D	
Ht: 6' 1"	Wt: 205		PT/Exp D	Rand Var 0	
			Consist B	MM 3123	

Made one of the toughest-possible venue changes between 2016-17, and apparently his plate patience (such as it was) got misplaced in the move. After contact, everything remains stable, just not exciting. He can still be a viable short-term pickup when he picks up stretches of regular playing time.

Yr Tm	AB	R	HR	RBI	SB	BA	xBA	OBP	SLG	OPS	vL	vR	bb%	ct%	Eye	G	L	F	h%	HctX	PX	xPX	hr/f	Spd	SBO	SB%	#Wk	DOM	DIS	RC/G	RAR	BPV	BPX	R$
13 SD	373	35	13	44	1	233	240	290	389	679	553	721	6	74	0.27	43	20	37	28	87	115	99	13%	87	1%	100%	27	37%	48%	3.68	-0.2	28	70	$5
14 2 TM	218	18	6	22	1	243	219	273	358	631	570	641	4	71	0.16	37	23	40	32	98	89	109	10%	77	2%	100%	27	22%	52%	3.35	-0.6	-10	-27	$2
15 COL	366	45	10	43	5	301	267	339	467	807	727	832	5	79	0.28	43	23	34	36	97	108	107	10%	127	12%	45%	23	57%	26%	5.46	16.9	54	146	$14
16 COL	289	30	10	48	0	260	256	320	439	759	923	674	8	78	0.38	46	18	36	30	118	115	109	12%	85	0%	0%	22	50%	32%	4.82	3.4	45	129	$6
17 SF	287	27	9	35	0	244	242	272	418	691	904	584	4	72	0.15	42	19	38	31	98	119	101	11%	76	0%	0%	27	41%	37%	3.87	-1.5	15	45	$2
1st Half	128	14	3	13	0	250	232	274	414	688	880	582	4	69	0.13	41	18	41	34	92	124	99	8%	76	0%	0%	13	38%	46%	3.92	-0.7	6	18	$0
2nd Half	159	13	6	22	0	239	249	271	421	692	926	585	4	74	0.17	43	20	36	29	103	115	103	14%	79	0%	0%	14	43%	29%	3.83	-1.3	23	70	$5
18 Proj	**265**	**26**	**8**	**35**	**1**	**255**	**251**	**295**	**427**	**721**	**867**	**657**	**5**	**75**	**0.22**	**43**	**20**	**37**	**31**	**103**	**109**	**104**	**11%**	**87**	**2%**	**50%**				**4.28**	**1.1**	**12**	**36**	**$6**

annetta,Chris

Age: 35	Bats: R	Pos: CA	Health A	LIMA Plan D+	
Ht: 6' 0"	Wt: 230		PT/Exp D	Rand Var -2	
			Consist C	MM 4013	

Traded off contact and line drives for an uppercut approach and (stop us if you've heard this before) posted his biggest HR total in a decade. But the balls are just the same as always, right? Tempting to extrapolate this line over 400 AB (okay, what the heck: 25 HR), but at 35, that ain't happening anyway.

Yr Tm	AB	R	HR	RBI	SB	BA	xBA	OBP	SLG	OPS	vL	vR	bb%	ct%	Eye	G	L	F	h%	HctX	PX	xPX	hr/f	Spd	SBO	SB%	#Wk	DOM	DIS	RC/G	RAR	BPV	BPX	R$
13 LAA	325	40	11	39	0	225	218	358	372	731	835	663	17	69	0.68	37	19	43	29	97	115	125	11%	71	1%	0%	27	41%	56%	4.34	6.4	26	65	$3
14 LAA	306	41	7	43	3	252	233	373	392	765	880	697	14	70	0.59	38	20	41	34	93	125	100	8%	74	3%	100%	26	46%	35%	4.93	13.2	34	92	$7
15 LAA	272	28	10	34	0	188	196	293	335	628	764	575	13	69	0.49	39	13	48	23	80	105	105	11%	74	1%	0%	26	31%	54%	3.04	-6.7	12	32	-$2
16 SEA	295	23	7	24	0	210	224	303	329	631	740	557	11	72	0.46	41	22	36	27	102	83	94	9%	68	0%	0%	26	27%	58%	3.19	-11.1	0	0	-$2
17 ARI	272	38	17	43	0	254	259	354	511	865	967	823	12	68	0.43	37	20	42	31	98	166	131	22%	65	0%	0%	26	54%	35%	5.99	15.4	50	152	$6
1st Half	117	16	8	23	0	231	262	302	513	815	1158	683	7	67	0.23	40	18	42	27	86	186	124	24%	51	0%	0%	12	50%	50%	4.86	2.7	47	142	$3
2nd Half	155	22	9	20	0	271	258	390	510	900	832	929	15	69	0.58	35	22	43	34	106	152	136	20%	83	0%	0%	14	57%	21%	6.82	12.0	55	167	$9
18 Proj	**338**	**40**	**15**	**44**	**0**	**232**	**237**	**333**	**425**	**758**	**851**	**712**	**12**	**69**	**0.46**	**38**	**20**	**42**	**29**	**96**	**124**	**116**	**16%**	**67**	**0%**	**41%**				**4.59**	**4.6**	**11**	**32**	**$6**

glesias,Jose

Age: 28	Bats: R	Pos: SS	Health D	LIMA Plan B	
Ht: 5' 11"	Wt: 185		PT/Exp B	Rand Var +2	
			Consist B	MM 1255	

Elite contact has long been the lynchpin of his skill set. It slipped a bit in 2017, but more concerning is the multi-year plunge in Spd, combined with the longstanding problems with SB%. With speed package now below average, contact is now this pony's only trick. It's not enough to entice more than marginal passing interest.

Yr Tm	AB	R	HR	RBI	SB	BA	xBA	OBP	SLG	OPS	vL	vR	bb%	ct%	Eye	G	L	F	h%	HctX	PX	xPX	hr/f	Spd	SBO	SB%	#Wk	DOM	DIS	RC/G	RAR	BPV	BPX	R$
13 2 AL *	469	52	6	41	9	272	250	304	357	661	769	716	4	83	0.27	56	18	26	32	68	59	36	4%	135	11%	63%	22	23%	32%	3.71	3.9	31	78	$12
14																																		
15 DET	416	44	2	23	11	300	273	347	370	717	889	663	6	89	0.57	56	21	23	33	65	46	30	2%	140	15%	58%	22	36%	14%	4.40	0.0	49	132	$13
16 DET	467	57	4	32	7	255	271	306	336	643	704	618	5	89	0.56	51	21	28	28	65	53	28	3%	114	9%	64%	26	46%	23%	3.37	-12.9	47	134	$7
17 DET	463	56	6	54	7	255	287	288	369	657	651	659	4	86	0.32	50	23	26	29	99	71	46	6%	82	11%	64%	26	46%	23%	3.56	-14.5	36	109	$9
1st Half	239	29	2	23	4	251	283	281	351	633	675	622	4	85	0.26	51	24	25	29	102	63	26	4%	96	12%	67%	13	46%	31%	3.28	-9.2	30	91	$6
2nd Half	224	27	4	31	3	259	290	295	388	684	627	699	5	87	0.40	49	23	28	28	95	78	68	7%	75	10%	60%	13	46%	15%	3.88	-4.6	43	130	$11
18 Proj	**499**	**59**	**5**	**47**	**6**	**264**	**278**	**306**	**361**	**666**	**709**	**652**	**5**	**87**	**0.40**	**52**	**22**	**26**	**29**	**82**	**59**	**41**	**5%**	**100**	**10%**	**55%**				**3.64**	**-12.0**	**29**	**89**	**$12**

nciarte,Ender

Age: 27	Bats: L	Pos: CF	Health B	LIMA Plan B	
Ht: 5' 11"	Wt: 190		PT/Exp A	Rand Var -3	
			Consist A	MM 1555	

Career year came about with virtually nothing new in the skill set, just a little extra help from hr/f (like every other batter in this book). Good health and MLB-leading AB total spiked the R$ here, but league-wide 40%+ odds of a DL stint means you can't expect a repeat of that. Expect more of the same, just with fewer AB.

Yr Tm	AB	R	HR	RBI	SB	BA	xBA	OBP	SLG	OPS	vL	vR	bb%	ct%	Eye	G	L	F	h%	HctX	PX	xPX	hr/f	Spd	SBO	SB%	#Wk	DOM	DIS	RC/G	RAR	BPV	BPX	R$
13 aa	473	59	4	21	37	264		298	341	639			5	89	0.45				29		50			137	37%	81%				3.64		49	123	$20
14 ARI *	527	68	5	35	23	273	271	314	358	671	646	691	6	85	0.40	52	24	25	31	87	60	51	5%	126	20%	81%	23	43%	22%	4.02	2.9	40	108	$19
15 ARI	524	73	6	45	21	303	284	338	408	747	530	826	5	89	0.45	52	22	26	33	102	66	72	5%	130	21%	68%	23	43%	13%	4.88	8.4	59	159	$24
16 ATL	522	85	3	29	16	291	275	351	381	732	749	726	8	87	0.66	49	24	27	33	80	53	50	2%	158	14%	70%	24	46%	33%	4.71	0.9	55	157	$18
17 ATL	662	93	11	57	22	304	274	350	409	759	712	773	7	86	0.52	47	24	29	34	77	57	54	7%	135	15%	71%	27	44%	30%	5.21	2.7	45	136	$29
1st Half	340	52	6	31	11	303	261	350	400	750	786	742	7	84	0.48	44	24	32	35	88	54	69	7%	125	15%	69%	13	38%	46%	5.07	1.6	33	100	$29
2nd Half	322	41	5	26	11	304	288	350	419	769	666	812	7	88	0.58	50	24	26	34	65	60	39	7%	137	15%	73%	14	50%	14%	5.35	4.0	55	167	$28
18 Proj	**555**	**79**	**7**	**42**	**20**	**297**	**279**	**344**	**398**	**742**	**678**	**764**	**7**	**87**	**0.54**	**49**	**24**	**27**	**33**	**81**	**55**	**54**	**5%**	**142**	**17%**	**72%**				**4.91**	**6.3**	**42**	**128**	**$25**

Jackson,Austin

Age: 31	Bats: R	Pos: LF CF	Health F	LIMA Plan C	
Ht: 6' 1"	Wt: 205		PT/Exp D	Rand Var -5	
			Consist D	MM 2333	

7-35-.318 in 280 AB at CLE. Had never exhibited a pronounced platoon split for his career until this year's 122 AB vL with a 42% hit rate and 136 PX. Bad news: that's flukish. Worse news: there's very little going on against RHP, so even a larger role wouldn't necessarily be good news.

Yr Tm	AB	R	HR	RBI	SB	BA	xBA	OBP	SLG	OPS	vL	vR	bb%	ct%	Eye	G	L	F	h%	HctX	PX	xPX	hr/f	Spd	SBO	SB%	#Wk	DOM	DIS	RC/G	RAR	BPV	BPX	R$
13 DET	552	99	12	49	8	272	263	337	417	754	681	784	8	77	0.40	42	28	31	34	105	103	101	9%	148	8%	67%	22	41%	23%	4.83	13.5	52	130	$18
14 2 AL	597	71	4	47	20	256	238	308	347	655	735	622	7	76	0.33	42	26	33	33	86	75	87	3%	134	16%	77%	27	30%	48%	3.72	0.5	20	54	$16
15 2 TM *	529	58	9	49	18	261	248	303	372	675	770	657	6	73	0.22	51	24	25	34	95	83	76	10%	102	21%	64%	25	32%	60%	3.75	-10.1	3	8	$16
16 CHW	181	24	0	18	2	254	256	318	343	661	411	741	8	78	0.44	37	30	32	32	109	66	97	0%	126	6%	67%	10	40%	40%	3.70	-3.0	23	66	$1
17 CLE *	307	47	8	38	4	314	268	383	480	863	1013	756	10	77	0.49	48	21	31	39	99	102	88	10%	123	6%	82%	22	55%	41%	6.86	11.7	48	145	$12
1st Half	112	13	4	16	0	306	266	388	513	901	1004	714	12	78	0.60	39	19	43	37	120	127	152	9%	97	0%	0%	11	55%	36%	7.32	6.0	67	203	$3
2nd Half	195	34	4	21	4	319	271	380	461	841	1023	772	9	77	0.43	53	22	24	40	87	88	51	12%	134	9%	82%	11	55%	45%	6.61	6.6	37	112	$17
18 Proj	**287**	**40**	**5**	**31**	**5**	**285**	**262**	**347**	**422**	**770**	**850**	**723**	**9**	**77**	**0.41**	**45**	**24**	**31**	**36**	**101**	**87**	**91**	**7%**	**120**	**8%**	**71%**				**5.22**	**6.2**	**25**	**75**	**$10**

Jankowski,Travis

Age: 27	Bats: L	Pos: LF	Health D	LIMA Plan F	
Ht: 6' 2"	Wt: 185		PT/Exp D	Rand Var +2	
			Consist B	MM 0511	

0-1-.187 with 4 SB in 75 AB at SD. Fractured foot in April sidelined him until July, and likely cut into his running game after his return. Contact is shaky and power non-existent; but the speed is elite, the bb% respectable, and the GB% profile ideal. If and when he stumbles into playing time, he's an instant SB asset.

Yr Tm	AB	R	HR	RBI	SB	BA	xBA	OBP	SLG	OPS	vL	vR	bb%	ct%	Eye	G	L	F	h%	HctX	PX	xPX	hr/f	Spd	SBO	SB%	#Wk	DOM	DIS	RC/G	RAR	BPV	BPX	R$
13																																		
14 aa	100	11	0	8	8	207		256	257	513			6	84	0.41				25		39			111	45%	78%				2.22		15	41	$1
15 SD *	469	59	3	30	25	268	236	325	349	674	650	572	8	82	0.47	63	10	27	32	47	52	12	12%	175	28%	65%	8	38%	50%	3.78	-13.1	40	108	$17
16 SD	335	53	2	12	30	245	244	332	313	646	398	727	11	70	0.42	58	26	16	34	68	53	28	6%	153	39%	71%	27	15%	74%	3.47	-11.9	-6	-17	$13
17 SD *	214	23	0	8	9	200	204	269	233	503	347	536	8	71	0.33	62	14	24	28	106	27	45	0%	138	18%	88%	6	17%	83%	2.15	-20.9	-31	-94	$0
1st Half	50	7	0	0	2	160	157	263	180	443	237	506	12	58	0.33	63	13	25	28	91	22	57	0%	143	14%	100%	3	0%	100%	1.61	-6.2	-81	-245	-$8
2nd Half	164	16	0	8	7	213	223	271	250	521	650	590	7	76	0.33	61	17	22	28	102	28	29	0%	121	20%	85%	3	33%	67%	2.32	-15.5	-22	-67	$2
18 Proj	**159**	**20**	**1**	**7**	**12**	**231**	**230**	**309**	**293**	**603**	**477**	**637**	**9**	**73**	**0.36**	**61**	**18**	**21**	**31**	**80**	**42**	**32**	**4%**	**147**	**33%**	**82%**				**3.10**	**-6.6**	**-18**	**-53**	**$6**

AY MURPHY

Jaso,John

Age: 34 Bats: L Pos: RF 1B | Ht: 6' 2" Wt: 202
Health C | PT/Exp D | Consist B
LIMA Plan D+ | Rand Var +5 | MM 3021

Not a lot of jobs out there for punch-and-judy, OBP-only 1Bmen, so he got in on the league-wide Uppercut Craze. Quickest way to double-digit dingers is a 47% flyball rate in tandem with a xPX spike. That worked for awhile but brutal 15% hit rate in the 2nd half killed him. Speculative value here.

Yr Tm	AB	R	HR	RBI	SB	BA	xBA	OBP	SLG	OPS	vL	vR	bb%	ct%	Eye	G	L	F	h%	HctX	PX	xPX	hr/f	Spd	SBO	SB%	#Wk	DOM	DIS	RC/G	RAR	BPV	BPX
13 OAK	207	31	3	21	2	271	247	387	372	759	442	802	15	78	0.84	40	25	35	33	76	80	58	5%	95	4%	67%	17	35%	35%	4.97	2.3	38	95
14 OAK	307	42	9	40	2	264	273	337	430	767	468	793	8	80	0.47	37	26	38	30	105	117	120	10%	101	3%	100%	21	57%	14%	4.89	6.2	64	173
15 TAM	185	23	5	22	1	286	282	380	459	839	911	831	13	79	0.72	53	22	26	34	129	127	115	13%	87	5%	33%	14	64%	29%	6.04	3.5	71	192
16 PIT	380	45	8	42	0	268	270	353	413	766	258	795	10	81	0.61	52	21	27	32	100	92	77	10%	87	4%	0%	27	56%	30%	4.78	-6.1	45	129
17 PIT	256	28	10	35	1	211	246	328	402	730	627	744	13	74	0.61	34	19	47	24	109	121	149	11%	69	3%	50%	27	41%	41%	4.09	-14.4	43	130
1st Half	159	16	6	22	1	252	267	335	459	794	583	825	10	76	0.47	32	21	46	30	112	133	155	11%	72	5%	50%	13	54%	23%	5.03	-2.9	55	167
2nd Half	97	12	4	13	0	144	212	317	309	626	700	615	18	71	0.79	36	16	49	15	103	101	138	12%	82	0%	0%	14	29%	57%	2.79	-9.3	29	88
18 Proj	218	26	7	27	1	253	253	344	420	764	628	778	11	76	0.53	42	20	38	30	107	103	118	11%	81	3%	33%				4.73	0.2	25	77

Jay,Jon

Age: 33 Bats: L Pos: LF CF | Ht: 5' 11" Wt: 195
Health D | PT/Exp D | Consist C
LIMA Plan C | Rand Var -4 | MM 1343

Nothing remarkable in this skill set, except the way he takes a bunch of middling skills and channels them in one very specific direction: he sets a good table. Line drives galore, more walks than you should ever give a guy who can't really hurt you if you throw strikes, scores a lot of runs per AB. End game profit center.

Yr Tm	AB	R	HR	RBI	SB	BA	xBA	OBP	SLG	OPS	vL	vR	bb%	ct%	Eye	G	L	F	h%	HctX	PX	xPX	hr/f	Spd	SBO	SB%	#Wk	DOM	DIS	RC/G	RAR	BPV	BPX
13 STL	548	75	7	67	10	276	270	351	370	721	620	749	8	81	0.50	50	27	23	33	87	70	58	7%	98	9%	67%	27	37%	33%	4.36	4.8	29	73
14 STL	413	52	3	46	6	303	269	372	378	750	859	721	6	81	0.36	52	28	20	37	94	57	63	4%	116	7%	67%	26	19%	50%	4.75	10.9	19	51
15 STL	210	25	1	10	0	210	248	306	257	563	414	596	8	83	0.53	60	22	18	25	84	32	46	3%	110	4%	0%	18	17%	56%	2.18	-16.6	8	22
16 SD	347	49	2	26	2	291	267	339	389	728	752	713	5	78	0.24	55	24	21	37	93	76	65	4%	106	2%	100%	16	25%	44%	4.63	0.0	15	43
17 CHC	379	65	2	34	6	296	266	374	375	749	751	748	9	79	0.46	47	29	24	37	81	52	54	3%	121	6%	75%	27	26%	44%	4.87	-4.0	13	39
1st Half	154	25	1	15	1	305	269	383	396	779	794	774	9	77	0.43	51	28	21	39	80	62	42	4%	108	2%	100%	13	46%	38%	5.38	0.1	11	33
2nd Half	225	40	1	19	5	289	262	369	360	729	720	730	9	80	0.49	45	30	26	36	81	45	62	2%	125	9%	71%	14	7%	50%	4.54	-5.2	13	39
18 Proj	356	54	2	29	4	281	267	353	361	714	712	715	8	79	0.40	51	26	22	35	85	53	56	3%	113	5%	69%				4.28	-1.7	4	12

Jones,Adam

Age: 32 Bats: R Pos: CF | Ht: 6' 2" Wt: 215
Health A | PT/Exp A | Consist A
LIMA Plan B+ | Rand Var -1 | MM 2235

These stats are as steady as they come, so let's do some macroeconomics. Look at his HR column. Now go look at PX/xPX. 2016-17 dips in those index stats show how the league is literally passing him by. 27 HR in 2015 isn't nearly the same as 26 in 2017. Now go over to R$ column, and see how you need to recalibrate value.

Yr Tm	AB	R	HR	RBI	SB	BA	xBA	OBP	SLG	OPS	vL	vR	bb%	ct%	Eye	G	L	F	h%	HctX	PX	xPX	hr/f	Spd	SBO	SB%	#Wk	DOM	DIS	RC/G	RAR	BPV	BPX
13 BAL	653	100	33	108	14	285	284	318	493	811	732	846	4	79	0.18	48	20	32	32	124	137	126	20%	97	12%	82%	26	62%	19%	5.49	23.0	65	163
14 BAL	644	88	29	96	7	281	270	311	469	780	1003	709	3	79	0.14	47	17	36	32	113	127	119	16%	105	6%	88%	27	52%	30%	5.05	21.0	58	157
15 BAL	546	74	27	82	3	269	274	308	474	782	754	792	4	81	0.24	46	18	36	29	109	122	120	17%	97	3%	75%	25	44%	36%	4.96	7.0	62	168
16 BAL	619	86	29	83	2	265	248	310	436	746	580	798	6	81	0.34	43	17	41	28	108	92	110	14%	86	1%	100%	27	48%	26%	4.69	5.7	39	111
17 BAL	597	82	26	73	2	285	271	322	466	787	739	803	4	81	0.24	45	21	34	31	102	97	84	16%	101	2%	67%	26	42%	15%	5.22	7.9	43	130
1st Half	300	39	13	35	1	267	252	303	430	733	621	775	4	79	0.22	42	21	37	30	96	85	81	15%	119	3%	50%	13	31%	23%	4.43	-4.1	31	94
2nd Half	297	43	13	38	1	303	290	341	502	842	890	829	4	83	0.26	48	21	31	33	107	109	86	17%	88	1%	100%	13	54%	8%	6.12	9.9	57	173
18 Proj	596	80	26	80	2	271	265	309	448	757	706	773	4	81	0.24	45	19	36	30	107	95	100	15%	94	2%	72%				4.74	3.9	28	85

Jones,JaCoby

Age: 26 Bats: R Pos: CF | Ht: 6' 2" Wt: 205
Health A | PT/Exp D | Consist B
LIMA Plan D+ | Rand Var +2 | MM 2403

3-13-.170 with 6 SB in 141 AB at DET. Flailed hopelessly in the majors (54% ct), including an extended look in Sept. Minors track record suggests there's an intriguing power/speed blend here, but none of that matters if he only puts the ball in play half the time. Worth a deep league stash or an early pickup if something clicks.

Yr Tm	AB	R	HR	RBI	SB	BA	xBA	OBP	SLG	OPS	vL	vR	bb%	ct%	Eye	G	L	F	h%	HctX	PX	xPX	hr/f	Spd	SBO	SB%	#Wk	DOM	DIS	RC/G	RAR	BPV	BPX
13																																	
14																																	
15 aa	146	22	5	18	9	241		311	408	719			9	63	0.27				35		130			120	33%	73%				4.18		11	30
16 DET *	397	38	6	37	10	228	221	279	358	637	294	909	7	64	0.20	44	25	31	34	97	98	147	0%	144	19%	65%	5	20%	40%	3.21	-14.0	-6	-17
17 DET *	492	65	11	52	17	206	211	264	326	590	562	491	7	63	0.21	51	19	31	30	78	85	90	13%	117	22%	72%	14	14%	79%	2.74	-31.3	-25	-76
1st Half	239	34	6	24	5	206	225	260	344	604	466	489	7	65	0.21	38	29	33	29	73	94	67	13%	122	16%	72%	6	17%	83%	2.85	-15.4	-14	-42
2nd Half	253	30	5	28	11	206	200	267	309	576	654	490	8	62	0.22	57	14	29	31	79	77	101	13%	108	27%	72%	8	13%	75%	2.63	-18.3	-39	-118
18 Proj	324	39	8	34	10	218	220	296	361	656	713	635	8	63	0.22	49	20	31	32	77	99	87	13%	126	21%	69%				3.19	-13.4	-13	-38

Jones,Ryder

Age: 24 Bats: L Pos: 1B | Ht: 6' 3" Wt: 215
Health A | PT/Exp D | Consist C
LIMA Plan D | Rand Var -1 | MM 1301

2-5-.173 in 150 AB at SF. Classic growing pains: tried to focus on plate patience in 1nd half, and walk rate jumped. But contact took a hit along the way. Then got to majors and was overmatched. There's projectable power here given his size, but first he'll have to figure out how to tell balls from strikes. Until then, pass.

Yr Tm	AB	R	HR	RBI	SB	BA	xBA	OBP	SLG	OPS	vL	vR	bb%	ct%	Eye	G	L	F	h%	HctX	PX	xPX	hr/f	Spd	SBO	SB%	#Wk	DOM	DIS	RC/G	RAR	BPV	BPX
13																																	
14																																	
15																																	
16 aa	474	45	11	61	1	229		266	353	619			5	82	0.28				26		77			77	3%	30%				3.05		24	69
17 SF *	387	49	11	42	7	237	219	299	401	700	397	549	8	71	0.31	38	14	47	31	82	105	90	4%	114	8%	100%	12	8%	67%	4.11	-20.8	21	64
1st Half	218	30	7	27	4	245	214	317	426	743	200	170	10	74	0.41	29	12	59	30	35	112	33	0%	102	8%	100%	2	0%	50%	4.67	-6.3	39	118
2nd Half	169	19	4	14	3	227	203	276	369	645	427	611	6	67	0.21	40	15	45	31	87	95	102	6%	126	7%	100%	10	10%	70%	3.44	-11.3	-4	-12
18 Proj	196	22	3	22	2	231	213	295	348	642	495	681	7	75	0.28	40	15	45	29	78	76	92	5%	107	6%	87%				3.27	-10.9	0	1

Joseph,Caleb

Age: 32 Bats: R Pos: CA | Ht: 6' 3" Wt: 180
Health B | PT/Exp D | Consist F
LIMA Plan D | Rand Var -4 | MM 2021

It took until April 29 to get his first RBI, after 132 AB in BAL without one in 2016. That bit of trivia aside, he went back to being a backup catcher out of central casting, with a little bit of pop and a BA that hurts just a little. However, ct% losses and xPX dip suggest there is some hidden peril in owning him. Hold more auditions.

Yr Tm	AB	R	HR	RBI	SB	BA	xBA	OBP	SLG	OPS	vL	vR	bb%	ct%	Eye	G	L	F	h%	HctX	PX	xPX	hr/f	Spd	SBO	SB%	#Wk	DOM	DIS	RC/G	RAR	BPV	BPX
13 aa	518	52	17	68	3	243		281	395	676			5	79	0.24				28		104			83	5%	53%				3.68		34	85
14 BAL *	338	27	10	35	0	205	224	247	340	588	643	603	5	72	0.20	33	22	46	25	93	106	138	11%	87	2%	0%	21	24%	57%	2.66	-6.9	9	24
15 BAL	320	38	11	49	0	234	249	299	394	693	712	683	8	78	0.38	33	23	43	27	104	105	121	10%	100	0%	0%	26	42%	42%	3.85	1.1	41	111
16 BAL *	193	10	1	4	0	184	189	222	213	435	191	494	5	77	0.21	41	19	39	23	68	22	88	0%	123	3%	0%	20	15%	55%	1.42	-15.1	-24	-69
17 BAL	254	31	8	28	0	256	253	287	413	700	787	672	4	72	0.14	46	24	30	33	82	101	74	15%	115	0%	0%	26	42%	46%	4.02	-0.8	11	33
1st Half	132	11	3	14	0	280	254	312	432	743	801	720	4	73	0.14	45	24	31	37	92	100	78	10%	128	0%	0%	12	50%	42%	4.69	2.2	19	58
2nd Half	122	20	5	14	0	230	252	260	393	653	760	626	4	70	0.14	48	24	28	28	72	101	70	21%	97	0%	0%	14	36%	50%	3.38	-2.6	2	6
18 Proj	233	27	8	24	0	236	243	275	384	660	660	659	5	74	0.19	42	23	36	29	82	88	91	13%	108	1%	15%				3.48	-4.6	-8	-24

Joseph,Tommy

Age: 26 Bats: R Pos: 1B | Ht: 6' 1" Wt: 255
Health A | PT/Exp D | Consist F
LIMA Plan B | Rand Var 0 | MM 4035

Half-season splits suggest some in-season experimentation. Was fairly patient in 1st half, hit too many GBs but still posted a worthy followup to 2016 power breakout. Then seemed to sell out for power in 2nd half, swinging more often and uppercutting. It didn't work. 1st half version is at least mildly interesting if it comes back.

Yr Tm	AB	R	HR	RBI	SB	BA	xBA	OBP	SLG	OPS	vL	vR	bb%	ct%	Eye	G	L	F	h%	HctX	PX	xPX	hr/f	Spd	SBO	SB%	#Wk	DOM	DIS	RC/G	RAR	BPV	BPX
13 a/a	78	5	2	12	0	192		230	309	539			5	77	0.22				22		76			93	7%	0%				2.08		9	23
14 aa	78	6	4	14	0	247		282	473	755			5	81	0.26				26		145			97	0%	0%				4.52		79	214
15 aaa	166	7	3	14	0	165		177	260	437			1	77	0.06				20		70			80	0%	0%				1.41		-7	-19
16 PHI *	410	57	27	62	1	270	270	313	518	830	912	774	6	78	0.29	37	18	45	29	116	142	144	19%	53	4%	32%	22	36%	32%	5.54	2.4	56	160
17 PHI	495	51	22	69	1	240	250	289	432	721	692	732	6	74	0.26	42	19	39	28	105	115	109	15%	55	1%	100%	26	38%	54%	4.19	-25.3	19	58
1st Half	265	31	14	42	1	249	259	309	457	766	798	754	8	73	0.31	46	20	33	29	109	122	110	22%	57	2%	100%	13	46%	38%	4.78	-6.8	25	76
2nd Half	230	20	8	27	0	230	236	264	404	669	559	707	5	75	0.19	36	18	46	27	100	106	108	10%	59	0%	0%	13	31%	69%	3.56	-14.5	13	39
18 Proj	464	48	25	61	1	249	256	290	464	754	768	749	5	76	0.23	39	19	42	28	109	122	123	16%	52	2%	49%				4.52	-7.9	24	72

RAY MURPHY

Joyce,Matt

Age: 33 Bats: L Pos: RF LF | Ht: 6' 2" Wt: 205
Health A | PT/Exp C | Consist F
LIMA Plan D+ | Rand Var +1 | MM 4135

Who says old dogs can't learn new tricks? Set career-high in dingers, and his newfound xPX and ct% gains support a solid HR floor moving forward. But remember: 85% of his PA in 2017 came against RHP, and that OPS vL is ... woof! Still, a reliable companion in deep AL-only formats if you need some HR.

Yr Tm	AB	R	HR	RBI	SB	BA	xBA	OBP	SLG	OPS	vL	vR	bb%	ct%	Eye	G	L	F	h%	HctX	PX	xPX	hr/f	Spd	SBO	SB%	#Wk	DOM	DIS	RC/G	RAR	BPV	BPX	R$
13 TAM	413	61	18	47	7	235	259	328	419	747	499	783	12	79	0.68	37	20	43	26	89	124	90	13%	82	9%	70%	27	44%	41%	4.58	3.7	66	165	$11
14 TAM	418	51	9	52	2	254	232	349	383	732	408	758	13	73	0.56	43	19	38	33	99	104	105	8%	105	5%	29%	26	35%	42%	4.40	6.2	36	97	$9
15 LAA *	283	19	6	25	0	182	209	268	299	567	262	592	10	72	0.42	41	18	42	23	78	87	92	7%	89	5%	0%	20	30%	50%	2.38	-21.9	6	16	-$5
16 PIT	231	45	13	42	1	242	255	403	463	866	763	884	20	71	0.88	46	18	36	28	104	138	126	22%	94	2%	50%	27	56%	37%	6.13	9.8	65	186	$6
17 OAK	469	78	25	68	4	243	268	335	473	808	537	855	12	76	0.58	38	19	43	27	93	136	127	16%	69	4%	80%	26	65%	12%	5.37	6.2	59	179	$12
1st Half	229	32	10	31	1	223	242	327	410	738	640	749	14	74	0.61	39	18	43	26	99	113	143	13%	75	3%	50%	13	46%	15%	4.37	-4.8	39	118	$5
2nd Half	240	46	15	37	3	263	291	342	533	875	481	967	11	78	0.56	37	21	42	28	88	157	112	19%	72	5%	100%	13	85%	8%	6.43	9.5	81	245	$18
18 Proj	392	62	19	56	3	236	256	344	443	787	562	822	14	74	0.63	40	19	41	27	93	123	117	16%	81	4%	60%				5.01	3.7	44	133	$8

Judge,Aaron

Age: 26 Bats: R Pos: RF | Ht: 6' 7" Wt: 282
Health A | PT/Exp B | Consist F
LIMA Plan B+ | Rand Var -3 | MM 5235

Three-true-outcomes poster child had ridiculous first half, though the league adjusted and produced far more empty hacks in the second. OBP floor is high, raw power is savage, but expect .250-ish BA given poor ct% and h% correction (see 2nd half). In short, until we see more consistency, let someone else overpay.

Yr Tm	AB	R	HR	RBI	SB	BA	xBA	OBP	SLG	OPS	vL	vR	bb%	ct%	Eye	G	L	F	h%	HctX	PX	xPX	hr/f	Spd	SBO	SB%	#Wk	DOM	DIS	RC/G	RAR	BPV	BPX	R$
13																																		
14																																		
15 a/a	478	55	20	63	6	238		306	422	728			9	66	0.29				31		138			91	7%	74%				4.31		23	62	$11
16 NYY *	436	65	24	68	4	237	215	317	446	763	289	679	10	65	0.33	35	14	51	31	129	142	196	18%	74	5%	82%	6	33%	50%	4.74	0.3	18	51	$11
17 NYY	542	128	52	114	9	284	267	422	627	1049	934	1079	19	62	0.61	35	22	43	36	113	223	175	36%	94	6%	69%	26	58%	23%	9.29	67.0	92	279	$33
1st Half	274	70	27	62	6	325	286	448	686	1134	1199	1117	17	65	0.60	38	24	38	41	127	221	173	40%	112	8%	75%	13	77%	15%	11.39	46.4	107	324	$40
2nd Half	268	58	25	52	3	243	250	397	567	964	709	1039	20	58	0.62	32	19	49	31	99	226	178	32%	69	5%	60%	13	38%	31%	7.49	19.5	77	233	$25
18 Proj	539	100	46	102	7	256	253	366	561	927	711	980	14	63	0.46	34	18	47	31	118	195	184	28%	81	6%	71%				6.94	35.6	64	194	$26

Kelly,Carson

Age: 23 Bats: R Pos: CA | Ht: 6' 2" Wt: 220
Health A | PT/Exp F | Consist A
LIMA Plan D | Rand Var 0 | MM 1021

0-6-.174 in 69 AB at STL. Touted catching prospect spent almost all of 2017 in AAA, with a few big-league stints along the way. Has posted above-average ct% and shown potential for double-digit HR pop at his peak. More stash-worthy than play-worthy at this point, but good hitting catchers are worth waiting on.

Yr Tm	AB	R	HR	RBI	SB	BA	xBA	OBP	SLG	OPS	vL	vR	bb%	ct%	Eye	G	L	F	h%	HctX	PX	xPX	hr/f	Spd	SBO	SB%	#Wk	DOM	DIS	RC/G	RAR	BPV	BPX	R$
13																																		
14																																		
15																																		
16 STL *	342	36	5	27	0	259	210	300	349	649	1667	91	6	80	0.30	64	9	27	31	59	61	-2	0%	93	1%	0%	5	20%	40%	3.55	-8.5	10	29	$3
17 STL *	313	35	8	40	0	236	244	307	360	666	282	487	9	83	0.59	56	16	28	26	110	70	123	0%	67	3%	0%	12	42%	33%	3.57	-4.5	28	85	$2
1st Half	208	26	6	28	0	255	254	326	399	725			10	82	0.57				29		82			81	4%	0%				4.25		37	112	$5
2nd Half	105	9	2	12	0	200	230	268	282	550	282	487	9	85	0.65	56	16	28	22	113	47	123	0%	75	0%	0%	12	42%	33%	2.41	-5.6	21	64	-$4
18 Proj	193	20	4	20	0	237	247	305	351	656	597	666	8	82	0.49	39	22	39	27	102	66	111	7%	70	1%	0%				3.42	-4.2	9	27	$2

Kemp,Matt

Age: 33 Bats: R Pos: LF | Ht: 6' 4" Wt: 210
Health C | PT/Exp A | Consist A
LIMA Plan B+ | Rand Var 0 | MM 3145

Hit .345 with 10 HR though May 31, but steady correction coupled with a July hamstring tweak derailed a fine start. PRO: ct%, HctX held steady from 2016 levels; hr/f remains strong. CON: xPX took a massive step backwards (see: GB%). Enough skills here to project useful power for a few more seasons.

Yr Tm	AB	R	HR	RBI	SB	BA	xBA	OBP	SLG	OPS	vL	vR	bb%	ct%	Eye	G	L	F	h%	HctX	PX	xPX	hr/f	Spd	SBO	SB%	#Wk	DOM	DIS	RC/G	RAR	BPV	BPX	R$
13 LA	263	35	6	33	9	270	237	328	395	723	853	671	8	71	0.29	40	25	35	36	107	103	142	9%	80	13%	100%	14	29%	50%	4.72	5.0	8	20	$9
14 LA	541	77	25	89	8	287	287	346	506	852	781	879	9	73	0.36	43	26	31	35	128	168	139	20%	92	9%	62%	27	67%	15%	6.18	36.7	74	200	$27
15 SD	596	80	23	100	12	265	258	312	443	755	824	736	6	75	0.27	44	21	35	32	135	119	149	14%	94	10%	86%	26	38%	35%	4.82	1.7	39	105	$23
16 2 NL	623	89	35	108	1	268	270	304	499	803	954	761	5	75	0.23	40	20	40	31	109	143	136	18%	70	1%	100%	27	37%	15%	5.37	13.2	48	137	$21
17 ATL	438	47	19	64	0	276	273	318	463	781	684	808	6	77	0.27	49	23	28	32	109	107	104	20%	81	2%	0%	23	35%	30%	5.10	-2.0	33	100	$11
1st Half	266	31	12	38	0	305	283	346	515	861	799	869	6	77	0.28	43	24	32	36	110	126	120	18%	87	3%	0%	12	50%	33%	6.34	7.2	49	148	$17
2nd Half	172	16	7	26	0	233	259	273	384	657	622	676	5	78	0.26	56	21	22	26	107	77	79	23%	91	0%	0%	11	18%	27%	3.50	-9.6	14	42	$3
18 Proj	528	64	24	83	3	265	269	306	457	763	760	764	6	76	0.25	46	22	32	31	113	110	118	19%	80	4%	70%				4.86	6.1	23	69	$18

Kendrick,Howie

Age: 34 Bats: R Pos: LF | Ht: 5' 11" Wt: 220
Health D | PT/Exp B | Consist C
LIMA Plan C+ | Rand Var -5 | MM 1353

Bounced back after a down year, but did anything improve? 1st half H% drove the faux BA foundation. Still a worm-burner, and HctX took a step backward. On the flip side, ct% and xBA are consistent, mashed LHP and has wheels for double-digit SB. Health, age say these skills might decline soon, but still has deep-league BA/SB value.

Yr Tm	AB	R	HR	RBI	SB	BA	xBA	OBP	SLG	OPS	vL	vR	bb%	ct%	Eye	G	L	F	h%	HctX	PX	xPX	hr/f	Spd	SBO	SB%	#Wk	DOM	DIS	RC/G	RAR	BPV	BPX	R$
13 LAA	478	55	13	54	6	297	289	335	439	775	862	745	4	81	0.26	51	27	21	34	115	93	88	16%	107	7%	67%	23	48%	30%	5.19	15.0	43	108	$18
14 LAA	617	85	7	75	14	293	272	347	397	744	834	714	7	82	0.44	60	19	21	35	133	78	88	7%	101	10%	74%	27	26%	22%	4.92	19.6	38	103	$25
15 LA	464	64	9	54	6	295	286	336	409	746	721	753	5	82	0.33	59	24	17	34	108	75	71	14%	92	6%	75%	22	27%	36%	4.94	2.9	30	81	$17
16 LA	487	65	8	40	10	255	272	326	366	691	626	722	9	80	0.52	61	19	20	30	110	72	63	10%	95	9%	83%	26	31%	38%	4.11	-7.4	28	80	$10
17 2 NL	305	40	9	41	12	315	285	368	475	844	901	819	7	78	0.32	58	22	20	38	99	93	84	19%	109	19%	71%	19	37%	37%	6.24	8.2	33	100	$16
1st Half	126	15	2	14	8	349	284	403	476	879	910	866	8	78	0.39	54	27	19	44	108	81	81	11%	96	25%	73%	7	29%	29%	7.33	6.6	23	70	$12
2nd Half	179	25	7	27	4	291	284	344	475	818	892	785	6	78	0.28	60	19	21	34	92	101	87	24%	110	13%	67%	12	42%	42%	5.53	0.9	38	115	$18
18 Proj	325	43	8	38	9	294	282	350	432	781	798	775	7	79	0.37	59	22	20	35	105	80	78	15%	102	13%	73%				5.33	8.0	28	84	$15

Kepler,Max

Age: 25 Bats: L Pos: RF | Ht: 6' 4" Wt: 205
Health A | PT/Exp C | Consist B
LIMA Plan A | Rand Var +1 | MM 3345

Mostly a carbon-copy of 2016, but xPX took a step backward as those 19 HR didn't quite have as much value as they did in '16. Still young with time to adjust, but there are some roadblocks to a breakout: Can't hit LHP, 2nd half dips in HctX/xPX and waning Spd. Until those results improve, his upside is limited.

Yr Tm	AB	R	HR	RBI	SB	BA	xBA	OBP	SLG	OPS	vL	vR	bb%	ct%	Eye	G	L	F	h%	HctX	PX	xPX	hr/f	Spd	SBO	SB%	#Wk	DOM	DIS	RC/G	RAR	BPV	BPX	R$
13																																		
14																																		
15 MIN *	414	58	7	54	14	288	280	365	457	822	0	333	11	83	0.72	75	0	25	33	90	107	-16	0%	130	15%	76%	2	0%	100%	5.96	14.0	81	219	$17
16 MIN *	506	66	18	80	7	243	259	319	426	744	595	792	10	79	0.52	47	16	36	28	106	105	103	15%	112	8%	69%	22	55%	36%	4.54	-2.5	54	154	$12
17 MIN	511	67	19	69	6	243	256	312	425	737	453	828	8	78	0.41	43	18	40	28	104	107	93	12%	93	6%	86%	26	46%	35%	4.41	-7.8	43	130	$10
1st Half	271	39	9	32	3	251	255	320	424	744	418	854	8	78	0.42	40	20	41	29	109	104	105	10%	105	6%	75%	13	46%	31%	4.53	-4.2	45	136	$11
2nd Half	240	28	10	37	3	233	256	303	425	728	495	799	8	78	0.41	47	16	38	26	98	110	81	14%	88	6%	100%	13	46%	38%	4.28	-5.7	43	130	$10
18 Proj	541	71	22	78	9	248	267	320	451	771	550	851	9	79	0.47	45	17	38	28	104	113	96	14%	108	8%	79%				4.85	2.5	57	173	$17

Kiermaier,Kevin

Age: 28 Bats: L Pos: CF | Ht: 6' 1" Wt: 215
Health D | PT/Exp C | Consist A
LIMA Plan C+ | Rand Var -4 | MM 2535

For the second straight year, injury has derailed what could've been a profitable return. And while the overall baseline numbers actually took a step back from 2016, his post-DL self was intriguing, seeing gains in HctX and xPX coupled with decent wheels. If he can stay healthy (a big "if" right now)... UP: 25 HR/25 SB.

Yr Tm	AB	R	HR	RBI	SB	BA	xBA	OBP	SLG	OPS	vL	vR	bb%	ct%	Eye	G	L	F	h%	HctX	PX	xPX	hr/f	Spd	SBO	SB%	#Wk	DOM	DIS	RC/G	RAR	BPV	BPX	R$
13 TAM *	508	72	5	33	17	263	240	312	381	693	0	0	7	81	0.37	44	20	36	32	0	74	-15	0%	175	23%	56%	1	0%	100%	3.83	-6.1	49	123	$15
14 TAM *	459	58	12	46	14	264	270	314	436	750	507	837	7	79	0.34	53	17	31	31	92	116	82	13%	139	18%	73%	22	45%	32%	4.69	10.7	65	176	$16
15 TAM	505	62	10	40	18	263	275	298	420	718	625	754	4	81	0.25	48	23	29	31	88	96	58	8%	148	21%	78%	26	46%	31%	4.31	-2.8	57	154	$16
16 TAM	366	55	12	37	21	246	260	331	410	741	816	718	10	80	0.54	42	21	38	28	102	98	77	11%	96	25%	88%	19	42%	26%	4.62	2.7	48	137	$14
17 TAM	380	56	15	39	16	276	252	338	450	788	682	851	7	74	0.31	50	18	32	34	95	99	70	17%	132	22%	70%	17	18%	29%	5.10	3.9	31	94	$16
1st Half	233	30	7	20	10	258	246	329	408	737	581	819	9	73	0.37	52	18	30	33	88	90	53	14%	124	22%	71%	10	10%	30%	4.47	-3.0	21	64	$15
2nd Half	147	26	8	19	6	306	262	352	517	869	816	907	5	76	0.22	46	19	36	36	106	114	96	20%	130	23%	67%	7	29%	29%	6.21	5.4	45	136	$17
18 Proj	488	72	18	49	21	271	262	330	447	777	718	804	7	77	0.33	47	19	34	32	97	97	76	14%	135	23%	75%				4.98	6.6	42	128	$23

LEC DOPP

Kingery,Scott

Age: 24 Bats: R Pos: 2B | Health A | LIMA Plan D
Ht: 5' 10" Wt: 180 | PT/Exp F | Rand Var 0
Consist F | MM 1423

Breakout PHI prospect mashed upper-minors pitching, setting career bests in BA, HR and SB. Scouts say the wheels are legit, and Spd/SB% tend to agree he'll have quality SB value. Aggressive approach, but has solid ct% history and continues to grow into his power. Stash him while you can.

Yr Tm	AB	R	HR	RBI	SB	BA	xBA	OBP	SLG	OPS	vL	vR	bb%	ct%	Eye	G	L	F	h%	HctX	PX	xPX	hr/f	Spd	SBO	SB%	#Wk	DOM	DIS	RC/G	RAR	BPV	BPX
13																																	
14																																	
15																																	
16 aa	156	12	2	14	3	213		232	282	514			2	73	0.09				28		51			88	18%	58%				2.03		-31	-89
17 a/a	543	89	24	56	25	275		319	478	797			6	77	0.28				32		112			132	24%	82%				5.39		51	155
1st Half	306	59	20	45	18	282		335	559	894			7	77	0.35				30		148			133	30%	84%				6.72		85	258
2nd Half	237	30	4	11	7	265		298	372	670			5	76	0.20				33		65			144	16%	76%				3.84		11	33
18 Proj	268	33	6	24	9	248	244	281	376	657	657	657	4	75	0.19	48	20	32	31		77		10%	118	20%	76%				3.57	-15.4	8	24

Kinsler,Ian

Age: 36 Bats: R Pos: 2B | Health A | LIMA Plan B+
Ht: 6' 0" Wt: 200 | PT/Exp A | Rand Var +4
Consist C | MM 2335

Lowest R$ in quite some time, but blame most of it on that massive h% tumble. Otherwise, BPX says these skills are actually aging well. xPX, HctX still comfortably above-average; bb% and ct% bounced back in lock-step. Regression vRH isn't inspiring, but even at 36, there's a solid HR/SB floor here.

Yr Tm	AB	R	HR	RBI	SB	BA	xBA	OBP	SLG	OPS	vL	vR	bb%	ct%	Eye	G	L	F	h%	HctX	PX	xPX	hr/f	Spd	SBO	SB%	#Wk	DOM	DIS	RC/G	RAR	BPV	BPX
13 TEX	545	85	13	72	15	277	275	344	413	757	814	733	8	89	0.86	37	24	39	29	123	87	109	7%	101	17%	58%	24	75%	8%	4.71	15.5	75	188
14 DET	684	100	17	92	15	275	267	307	420	727	740	722	4	88	0.37	38	20	43	29	92	96	84	7%	117	12%	79%	27	59%	4%	4.50	21.7	76	205
15 DET	624	94	11	73	10	296	265	342	428	770	798	763	6	87	0.54	34	25	41	33	102	81	94	5%	129	9%	63%	26	42%	15%	5.20	16.0	67	181
16 DET	618	117	28	83	14	288	264	348	484	831	893	809	7	81	0.39	32	24	45	32	112	109	122	13%	123	12%	70%	27	56%	15%	5.74	17.7	65	186
17 DET	551	90	22	52	14	236	257	313	412	725	896	680	9	84	0.64	33	21	46	24	126	90	119	10%	109	14%	74%	25	48%	16%	4.17	-7.5	62	188
1st Half	255	48	9	21	6	243	249	330	404	734	735	733	10	86	0.81	31	20	49	25	133	83	119	8%	116	12%	75%	12	50%	8%	4.36	-3.6	67	203
2nd Half	296	42	13	31	8	230	264	298	419	717	1028	633	8	83	0.52	35	22	44	24	120	97	120	12%	97	17%	73%	13	46%	23%	4.01	-7.4	57	173
18 Proj	550	91	20	62	13	269	262	332	441	773	891	737	8	84	0.53	33	22	44	29	117	89	114	10%	114	13%	70%				4.93	2.1	60	181

Kipnis,Jason

Age: 31 Bats: L Pos: 2B | Health D | LIMA Plan B+
Ht: 5' 11" Wt: 195 | PT/Exp B | Rand Var +5
Consist B | MM 3335

12-35-.232 in 336 AB at CLE. Hamstring tweak relegated him to the DL twice; never quite got going. PRO: FB%, quality xPX bode well for HR value; likely due for some h% correction given steady ct%. CON: xBA says .270 might be a best-case scenario; bb% in decline; iffy speed. Iffy health adds some risk here.

Yr Tm	AB	R	HR	RBI	SB	BA	xBA	OBP	SLG	OPS	vL	vR	bb%	ct%	Eye	G	L	F	h%	HctX	PX	xPX	hr/f	Spd	SBO	SB%	#Wk	DOM	DIS	RC/G	RAR	BPV	BPX
13 CLE	564	86	17	84	30	284	264	366	452	818	850	801	12	75	0.53	43	25	32	35	110	125	128	12%	97	21%	81%	27	44%	44%	6.03	28.8	53	133
14 CLE	500	61	6	41	22	240	249	310	330	640	500	710	9	80	0.50	46	23	31	29	92	72	84	5%	94	18%	88%	23	30%	30%	3.58	-4.6	26	70
15 CLE	565	86	9	52	12	303	284	372	451	823	679	908	9	81	0.53	45	27	28	36	109	103	97	7%	119	12%	60%	24	50%	21%	5.87	21.4	62	168
16 CLE	610	91	23	82	15	275	268	343	469	811	790	822	9	76	0.41	39	24	37	33	110	123	122	13%	91	11%	83%	27	52%	26%	5.66	22.6	49	140
17 CLE *	372	44	13	37	6	223	253	278	400	679	632	744	7	78	0.35	36	20	44	25	95	108	122	10%	93	11%	75%	18	44%	28%	3.65	-12.5	42	127
1st Half	257	29	8	27	5	227	248	279	385	665	662	692	7	80	0.37	38	18	44	25	95	94	109	9%	93	13%	71%	11	36%	18%	3.52	-10.9	40	121
2nd Half	115	16	5	10	1	213	265	276	434	710	541	853	8	73	0.32	32	25	44	25	97	143	155	13%	92	5%	100%	7	57%	43%	3.93	-3.5	50	152
18 Proj	513	71	16	54	9	251	264	316	433	749	651	798	8	77	0.39	38	23	39	30	102	112	124	11%	100	10%	74%				4.60	-3.0	45	135

Kivlehan,Patrick

Age: 28 Bats: R Pos: RF | Health A | LIMA Plan D
Ht: 6' 2" Wt: 223 | PT/Exp D | Rand Var +2
Consist B | MM 4111

Rookie campaign was spent entirely as backup OF, a role in which his bat performed forgettably (see: BPX). Perhaps the only intriguing skill here is the power, but xPX can be volatile in small samples. Willing to walk, but poor ct%, HctX and results on the road (.541 OPS) leave a lot to be desired.

Yr Tm	AB	R	HR	RBI	SB	BA	xBA	OBP	SLG	OPS	vL	vR	bb%	ct%	Eye	G	L	F	h%	HctX	PX	xPX	hr/f	Spd	SBO	SB%	#Wk	DOM	DIS	RC/G	RAR	BPV	BPX
13																																	
14 aa	377	44	8	50	7	246		304	382	687			8	75	0.33				31		104			104	12%	58%				3.82		31	84
15 aaa	472	38	14	47	9	195		232	326	558			5	70	0.16				25		96			81	16%	71%				2.37		-7	-19
16 2 NL *	391	34	8	32	3	192	194	225	299	524	722	564	4	64	0.12	40	20	40	28	52	80	51	25%	94	12%	39%	4	25%	50%	2.00	-33.5	-42	-120
17 CIN	178	23	9	26	1	208	224	304	399	703	784	649	11	66	0.36	44	18	38	26	88	117	126	20%	100	7%	33%	27	44%	52%	3.64	-8.6	10	30
1st Half	88	9	5	12	1	227	229	299	409	708	816	636	8	70	0.31	44	19	37	26	78	99	95	22%	85	9%	50%	13	38%	62%	3.80	-3.4	5	15
2nd Half	90	14	4	14	0	189	219	308	389	697	754	660	13	61	0.40	45	16	39	25	97	138	161	18%	108	5%	0%	14	50%	43%	3.48	-4.6	16	48
18 Proj	193	22	10	24	2	204	229	278	402	679	754	630	8	66	0.26	44	17	38	25	89	123	135	20%	98	10%	44%				3.30	-8.6	3	9

Knapp,Andrew

Age: 26 Bats: B Pos: CA | Health B | LIMA Plan D
Ht: 6' 1" Wt: 195 | PT/Exp D | Rand Var -3
Consist F | MM 2301

First taste of the majors was a mixed bag. Revealed elite bb% and potential future OBP value as a #2 CA in deep formats. xBA wasn't a fan, especially considering those poor ct% skills, LD% and that lofty h%. Has respectable xPX and HctX, though, so maybe all he needs is a chance. Though in Double-A, 2015 wasn't that long ago.

Yr Tm	AB	R	HR	RBI	SB	BA	xBA	OBP	SLG	OPS	vL	vR	bb%	ct%	Eye	G	L	F	h%	HctX	PX	xPX	hr/f	Spd	SBO	SB%	#Wk	DOM	DIS	RC/G	RAR	BPV	BPX
13																																	
14																																	
15 aa	214	30	9	43	1	311		361	540	901			7	76	0.33				37		160			86	1%	100%				7.24		74	200
16 aaa	403	49	8	41	2	235		293	349	642			8	68	0.26				32		85			90	4%	44%				3.35		-13	-37
17 PHI	171	26	3	13	1	257	222	368	368	736	623	767	15	67	0.55	59	17	24	37	105	78	102	11%	125	2%	100%	22	23%	50%	4.74	3.4	1	3
1st Half	106	16	3	10	1	255	239	350	406	755	405	851	13	66	0.44	58	20	23	36	102	101	104	19%	124	3%	100%	13	38%	46%	4.95	2.6	10	30
2nd Half	65	10	0	3	0	262	182	395	308	703	971	630	19	69	0.75	61	13	26	38	110	42	99	0%	118	0%	0%	9	0%	56%	4.25	0.3	-15	-45
18 Proj	215	30	4	21	1	263	224	348	382	730	741	727	12	69	0.45	58	16	27	36	107	83	101	11%	111	2%	71%				4.65	3.2	-12	-37

La Stella,Tommy

Age: 29 Bats: L Pos: 2B | Health D | LIMA Plan D
Ht: 5' 11" Wt: 180 | PT/Exp F | Rand Var 0
Consist B | MM 1141

5-22-.288 in 125 AB at CHC. Despite being up-and-down from AAA all season, was relatively productive (.861 OPS) on the ML roster. xBA anticipates a bounce-back given his solid HctX, LD% and bb% track record. Without speed or much power to speak of, though, his impact will obviously be limited.

Yr Tm	AB	R	HR	RBI	SB	BA	xBA	OBP	SLG	OPS	vL	vR	bb%	ct%	Eye	G	L	F	h%	HctX	PX	xPX	hr/f	Spd	SBO	SB%	#Wk	DOM	DIS	RC/G	RAR	BPV	BPX
13 aa	283	27	3	35	6	308		378	423	800			10	86	0.80				35		82			93	7%	84%				5.95		59	148
14 ATL *	486	35	2	47	3	247	257	322	308	630	818	603	10	88	0.94	48	23	29	28	104	47	79	1%	83	3%	55%	19	42%	16%	3.34	-0.7	37	100
15 CHC *	136	13	2	18	2	254	302	306	379	685	0	771	7	91	0.86	38	30	33	27	91	81	74	5%	86	6%	100%	8	63%	13%	4.05	-0.4	72	195
16 CHC *	196	22	3	13	0	261	267	333	382	715	856	748	10	80	0.55	36	28	36	31	105	82	100	5%	92	2%	0%	20	40%	30%	4.30	-3.2	36	103
17 CHC *	235	28	6	26	0	231	249	311	345	656	1000	845	10	81	0.59	43	23	34	27	105	65	95	14%	78	2%	0%	20	55%	20%	3.48	-10.9	20	61
1st Half	143	15	2	7	0	198	238	265	272	537	1000	730	8	79	0.43	55	20	25	24	87	47	87	9%	91	4%	0%	8	75%	13%	2.20	-11.9	-1	-3
2nd Half	92	12	4	19	0	284	274	379	457	836	1000	914	13	83	0.89	35	25	40	31	119	91	101	15%	88	0%	0%	12	42%	25%	6.17	3.5	59	179
18 Proj	158	17	4	19	1	255	273	334	388	723	781	715	10	83	0.65	41	25	34	29	103	76	92	8%	87	2%	54%				4.35	-2.1	29	87

Lagares,Juan

Age: 29 Bats: R Pos: CF | Health F | LIMA Plan D+
Ht: 6' 1" Wt: 215 | PT/Exp D | Rand Var 0
Consist A | MM 1423

3-15-.250 in 252 AB at NYM. Missed PT with a broken left thumb, but these skills have remained subpar for a while. Poor HctX/xPX and sharp uptick in GB% says his HR value will remain null, and now ct% and bb% took a turn for the worse. Can still run, but doesn't get on base enough. What are you investing in?

Yr Tm	AB	R	HR	RBI	SB	BA	xBA	OBP	SLG	OPS	vL	vR	bb%	ct%	Eye	G	L	F	h%	HctX	PX	xPX	hr/f	Spd	SBO	SB%	#Wk	DOM	DIS	RC/G	RAR	BPV	BPX
13 NYM *	470	43	6	40	7	246	228	281	360	641	657	620	4	76	0.20	49	16	36	31	81	84	81	4%	135	13%	52%	24	21%	42%	3.27	-11.6	22	55
14 NYM	416	46	4	47	13	281	249	321	382	703	875	658	4	79	0.23	46	22	32	35	93	81	89	4%	112	16%	76%	22	41%	36%	4.27	5.2	26	70
15 NYM	441	47	6	41	7	259	236	289	358	647	771	599	3	80	0.18	55	14	31	31	107	64	72	6%	127	10%	70%	27	26%	41%	3.48	-10.7	19	51
16 NYM	142	15	3	9	4	239	259	301	380	682	650	715	7	81	0.41	42	22	35	28	71	83	68	7%	125	18%	67%	19	32%	42%	3.66	-4.2	44	126
17 NYM *	281	40	3	15	7	245	251	281	348	629	604	687	5	77	0.22	51	20	29	31	93	68	77	5%	138	16%	70%	18	28%	50%	3.26	-15.1	16	48
1st Half	93	17	2	8	2	269	253	317	409	725	771	701	6	80	0.32	43	20	36	32	119	81	112	7%	128	9%	100%	10	40%	30%	4.59	-0.8	36	109
2nd Half	188	23	1	7	5	233	250	264	318	583	485	680	4	76	0.18	56	21	24	30	78	61	55	4%	128	21%	63%	8	13%	75%	2.70	-12.7	2	6
18 Proj	399	50	6	27	10	249	250	294	362	655	644	662	5	79	0.25	49	20	31	30	90	69	75	6%	134	15%	69%				3.48	-12.2	16	49

ALEC DOPP

Lamb,Jacob

Age: 27 Bats: L Pos: 3B | Ht: 6' 3" Wt: 215
Health A | PT/Exp B | Consist B | LIMA Plan B+ | Rand Var +2 | MM 4235

Carbon copy of 2016, right down to 2nd half swoon. But was it really? July hand injury likely the culprit in 2017, driving his h% collapse. All the while xPX, bb%, ct% and FB% all took steps up. xBA suggests some BA upside. Struggles vL could mean platoon role down the road, but power is bankable even in this context.

Yr Tm	AB	R	HR	RBI	SB	BA	xBA	OBP	SLG	OPS	vL	vR	bb%	ct%	Eye	G	L	F	h%	HctX	PX	xPX	hr/f	Spd	SBO	SB%	#Wk	DOM	DIS	RC/G	RAR	BPV	BPX	R$
13																																		
14 ARI *	518	59	15	70	2	268	258	323	451	774	364	692	8	70	0.27	52	17	31	36	97	153	105	14%	102	3%	71%	9	33%	44%	5.07	20.2	50	135	$15
15 ARI	350	38	6	34	3	263	234	331	386	716	541	743	9	72	0.37	45	23	32	35	115	87	114	7%	124	5%	60%	21	29%	57%	4.37	-3.0	16	43	$6
16 ARI	523	81	29	91	6	249	271	332	509	840	625	898	11	71	0.42	46	17	37	30	113	164	149	21%	112	6%	86%	27	67%	22%	5.73	11.6	70	200	$17
17 ARI	536	89	30	105	6	248	264	357	487	844	557	938	14	72	0.57	41	21	38	29	104	142	125	20%	96	6%	60%	27	48%	26%	5.74	6.9	58	176	$17
1st Half	294	51	18	65	4	282	274	377	544	921	469	1051	13	70	0.52	45	20	34	34	105	157	116	25%	102	8%	57%	13	46%	8%	7.13	17.1	66	200	$26
2nd Half	242	38	12	40	2	207	253	334	417	752	642	793	15	73	0.65	36	21	43	23	102	125	136	16%	92	5%	67%	14	50%	43%	4.32	-5.8	52	158	$7
18 Proj	**555**	**82**	**26**	**92**	**5**	**265**	**257**	**355**	**481**	**836**	**601**	**901**	**12**	**71**	**0.48**	**43**	**20**	**37**	**33**	**107**	**130**	**129**	**17%**	**106**	**5%**	**67%**				**5.84**	**15.2**	**45**	**135**	**$19**

LeMahieu,DJ

Age: 29 Bats: R Pos: 2B | Ht: 6' 4" Wt: 215
Health A | PT/Exp A | Consist F | LIMA Plan B | Rand Var -1 | MM 1355

Hit rate corrected, BA title passed, and what are we left with? It took 57 more AB just to come close to 2016's counting stats. Ugly SB% returned, joined simultaneously with severe Spd drop and sharply declining opportunities. Lock in BA and Runs totals, but you'll need to get the rest of your productivity somewhere else.

Yr Tm	AB	R	HR	RBI	SB	BA	xBA	OBP	SLG	OPS	vL	vR	bb%	ct%	Eye	G	L	F	h%	HctX	PX	xPX	hr/f	Spd	SBO	SB%	#Wk	DOM	DIS	RC/G	RAR	BPV	BPX	R$
13 COL *	547	59	3	41	23	285	286	316	375	692	652	682	4	84	0.28	55	27	18	34	98	64	64	3%	138	22%	71%	20	30%	30%	4.16	7.8	39	98	$20
14 COL	494	59	5	42	10	267	250	315	348	663	669	660	6	80	0.34	56	21	23	32	98	57	84	5%	143	14%	50%	26	27%	46%	3.58	2.7	24	65	$13
15 COL	564	85	6	61	23	301	271	358	388	746	757	743	8	81	0.47	54	26	19	36	95	58	75	7%	136	14%	88%	26	38%	35%	5.26	16.9	29	78	$27
16 COL	552	104	11	66	11	348	303	416	495	911	931	903	10	86	0.83	51	27	23	39	122	84	95	10%	149	9%	61%	26	62%	19%	7.87	43.2	77	220	$32
17 COL	609	95	8	64	6	310	289	374	409	783	961	724	9	85	0.66	56	25	20	35	105	56	60	8%	112	5%	55%	27	37%	30%	5.51	8.1	39	118	$23
1st Half	318	43	3	38	4	302	286	360	381	741	951	667	8	86	0.57	56	26	18	35	99	47	59	6%	87	8%	50%	13	23%	31%	4.77	-0.5	23	70	$21
2nd Half	291	52	5	26	2	320	291	389	440	828	973	783	10	85	0.75	55	24	21	36	113	66	62	9%	136	3%	67%	14	50%	29%	6.38	12.2	56	170	$24
18 Proj	**574**	**93**	**8**	**60**	**9**	**316**	**290**	**378**	**425**	**803**	**892**	**772**	**9**	**84**	**0.62**	**54**	**25**	**21**	**36**	**108**	**61**	**73**	**8%**	**131**	**7%**	**62%**				**5.88**	**16.8**	**36**	**108**	**$26**

Leon,Sandy

Age: 29 Bats: B Pos: CA | Ht: 5' 10" Wt: 225
Health A | PT/Exp D | Consist F | LIMA Plan D | Rand Var +1 | MM 1013

Who could've possibly seen this coming? Oh, that's right... everybody. His solid '16 was fueled by an outrageous h% and unprecedented hr/f. Haplessness vR has rendered switch-hitting useless, and mediocre Eye paired with weak xPX leave him destined for deep-league two-catcher league filler. DN: more AAA time.

Yr Tm	AB	R	HR	RBI	SB	BA	xBA	OBP	SLG	OPS	vL	vR	bb%	ct%	Eye	G	L	F	h%	HctX	PX	xPX	hr/f	Spd	SBO	SB%	#Wk	DOM	DIS	RC/G	RAR	BPV	BPX	R$
13 WAS *	311	28	2	20	0	154	216	241	216	457	0	0	10	80	0.57	44	20	36	19	0	47	-15	0%	82	0%	0%	2	0%	100%	1.57	-21.9	4	10	-$9
14 WAS *	234	26	4	21	1	182	225	254	275	528	511	413	9	74	0.37	53	19	28	23	67	74	38	8%	62	1%	100%	10	20%	70%	2.18	-9.5	-5	-14	-$3
15 BOS *	213	15	1	14	0	209	188	262	248	510	118	569	7	74	0.28	45	19	36	28	45	34	28	0%	69	4%	0%	19	16%	63%	1.99	-11.6	-38	-103	-$4
16 BOS *	367	46	9	46	0	283	253	341	424	765	1062	764	8	75	0.35	45	24	31	36	95	93	80	12%	116	0%	0%	18	39%	39%	5.15	13.2	26	74	$9
17 BOS	271	32	7	39	0	225	239	290	354	644	732	612	8	73	0.34	37	25	38	28	88	84	65	9%	51	0%	0%	26	19%	62%	3.39	-6.1	-7	-21	$1
1st Half	149	20	5	22	0	255	260	300	403	703	717	697	6	78	0.30	37	26	37	30	107	86	76	12%	56	0%	0%	13	23%	46%	4.16	0.3	12	36	$3
2nd Half	122	12	2	17	0	189	214	279	295	574	748	510	11	66	0.37	37	24	39	27	65	82	50	6%	60	0%	0%	13	15%	77%	2.57	-5.9	-27	-82	-$2
18 Proj	**256**	**28**	**5**	**31**	**0**	**226**	**233**	**293**	**341**	**634**	**693**	**611**	**8**	**73**	**0.34**	**41**	**23**	**35**	**29**	**78**	**75**	**58**	**8%**	**72**	**1%**	**13%**				**3.26**	**-6.9**	**-17**	**-51**	**$2**

Lind,Adam

Age: 34 Bats: L Pos: 1B LF | Ht: 6' 2" Wt: 195
Health A | PT/Exp C | Consist F | LIMA Plan C | Rand Var -3 | MM 3243

Hit rate corrected vR and the Platoon God returned. When strictly deployed, BA and power combine for a useful deep league 1B/OF option. Eye, HctX, and xPX lay a strong foundation, but perhaps most important number is one you don't see here: 29; as in the number of AB vLHP in 2017. Future managers, take note.

Yr Tm	AB	R	HR	RBI	SB	BA	xBA	OBP	SLG	OPS	vL	vR	bb%	ct%	Eye	G	L	F	h%	HctX	PX	xPX	hr/f	Spd	SBO	SB%	#Wk	DOM	DIS	RC/G	RAR	BPV	BPX	R$
13 TOR	465	67	23	67	1	288	279	357	497	854	573	924	10	78	0.50	46	21	33	33	131	140	141	19%	93	1%	100%	27	52%	15%	6.40	23.4	73	183	$19
14 TOR	290	38	6	40	0	321	283	381	479	860	223	942	9	83	0.58	47	21	33	37	134	119	123	8%	108	0%	0%	21	62%	19%	6.85	20.5	81	219	$12
15 MIL	502	72	20	87	0	277	264	360	460	820	575	883	12	80	0.66	46	19	35	31	130	120	137	14%	83	0%	0%	27	48%	19%	5.86	6.9	66	178	$18
16 SEA	401	48	20	58	0	239	258	286	431	717	638	729	6	78	0.29	44	20	36	26	114	111	127	18%	66	1%	0%	26	46%	35%	4.09	-15.0	34	97	$7
17 WAS	267	39	14	59	1	303	274	362	513	875	689	898	9	82	0.60	46	18	36	33	131	110	128	17%	85	1%	100%	27	56%	22%	6.97	7.7	64	194	$12
1st Half	105	18	6	27	0	324	275	388	562	950	522	990	11	82	0.68	40	17	43	35	145	128	156	16%	83	0%	0%	13	69%	15%	8.44	7.8	79	239	$8
2nd Half	162	21	8	32	1	290	272	344	481	826	764	835	8	83	0.54	50	18	32	31	122	99	110	18%	92	2%	100%	14	43%	29%	6.10	2.1	57	173	$14
18 Proj	**287**	**40**	**14**	**54**	**1**	**277**	**268**	**336**	**474**	**810**	**607**	**841**	**9**	**81**	**0.50**	**46**	**19**	**36**	**30**	**127**	**107**	**130**	**16%**	**81**	**1%**	**76%**				**5.68**	**4.7**	**39**	**117**	**$11**

Lindor,Francisco

Age: 24 Bats: B Pos: SS | Ht: 5' 11" Wt: 190
Health A | PT/Exp A | Consist A | LIMA Plan D+ | Rand Var +2 | MM 2455

Amped up power via FB rate en route to stunning power campaign. The HR total masked SB and BA drops, though all is sunny on those fronts also: strong SB%, as well as SBO picked up pace as season progressed; and xBA was as pristine as ever. He's all of 24, folks. That second half points to UP: 30 HR, 30 SB, .300

Yr Tm	AB	R	HR	RBI	SB	BA	xBA	OBP	SLG	OPS	vL	vR	bb%	ct%	Eye	G	L	F	h%	HctX	PX	xPX	hr/f	Spd	SBO	SB%	#Wk	DOM	DIS	RC/G	RAR	BPV	BPX	R$
13 aa	76	11	1	6	4	259		351	342	693			12	90	1.40				28		52			119	23%	65%				4.00		64	160	$1
14 a/a	507	61	9	51	23	248		301	342	643			7	79	0.36				30		67			105	29%	57%				3.20		16	43	$16
15 CLE *	619	73	14	71	20	298	275	349	443	793	890	804	7	82	0.45	51	21	29	34	92	92	75	13%	136	17%	68%	17	71%	18%	5.49	19.1	61	165	$28
16 CLE	604	99	15	78	19	301	282	358	435	794	748	816	8	85	0.65	49	22	28	33	95	77	74	10%	117	13%	79%	27	44%	19%	5.78	24.6	57	163	$29
17 CLE	651	99	33	89	15	273	289	337	505	842	891	817	8	86	0.65	39	18	42	28	122	120	122	14%	100	11%	83%	27	74%	7%	5.97	25.0	87	264	$26
1st Half	316	44	14	38	3	250	282	311	462	773	838	736	8	85	0.61	38	19	43	25	118	113	120	12%	92	6%	75%	13	77%	8%	4.87	2.8	78	236	$15
2nd Half	335	55	19	51	12	296	295	361	546	907	949	888	9	86	0.68	40	18	42	30	126	125	123	16%	110	16%	86%	14	71%	7%	7.14	23.9	96	291	$37
18 Proj	**611**	**100**	**23**	**79**	**20**	**283**	**282**	**341**	**467**	**808**	**823**	**800**	**8**	**84**	**0.57**	**45**	**20**	**35**	**30**	**108**	**97**	**98**	**13%**	**117**	**16%**	**77%**				**5.66**	**20.8**	**69**	**209**	**$30**

Longoria,Evan

Age: 32 Bats: R Pos: 3B | Ht: 6' 2" Wt: 210
Health A | PT/Exp A | Consist B | LIMA Plan B+ | Rand Var +1 | MM 3235

Career-year drop-off, or something more? His hr/f snapped back into line, xBA and HctX held steady, and ct% improved. But at his age, considerable FB dip combined with xPX swoon and a few non-DL injuries raises at least an orange flag. Never the cornerstone player he was touted to be; instead a solid mid-round "glue guy."

Yr Tm	AB	R	HR	RBI	SB	BA	xBA	OBP	SLG	OPS	vL	vR	bb%	ct%	Eye	G	L	F	h%	HctX	PX	xPX	hr/f	Spd	SBO	SB%	#Wk	DOM	DIS	RC/G	RAR	BPV	BPX	R$
13 TAM	614	91	32	88	1	269	264	343	498	842	950	799	10	74	0.43	37	19	45	32	127	164	173	16%	84	1%	100%	27	63%	33%	5.98	35.8	73	183	$23
14 TAM	624	83	22	91	5	253	249	320	404	724	824	691	8	79	0.43	39	20	41	29	109	105	118	11%	95	3%	100%	27	44%	19%	4.40	13.3	46	124	$19
15 TAM	604	74	21	73	3	270	254	328	435	764	960	695	8	78	0.39	39	21	40	31	105	111	121	11%	92	3%	75%	27	44%	33%	4.97	6.8	46	124	$18
16 TAM	633	81	36	98	0	273	276	318	521	840	753	864	6	77	0.29	32	21	47	30	113	148	146	16%	101	2%	0%	27	59%	26%	5.71	16.5	72	206	$21
17 TAM	613	71	20	86	6	261	266	313	424	737	678	760	7	82	0.42	43	20	37	29	114	91	91	11%	88	5%	86%	27	37%	19%	4.60	-4.5	44	133	$15
1st Half	319	45	12	48	2	257	269	320	433	753	672	786	9	81	0.48	45	19	35	29	115	101	99	13%	81	3%	100%	13	31%	8%	4.80	-2.6	46	139	$17
2nd Half	294	26	8	38	4	265	263	305	415	720	684	732	5	84	0.34	41	20	39	29	114	82	84	8%	97	7%	80%	14	43%	29%	4.38	-6.0	43	130	$13
18 Proj	**600**	**71**	**23**	**84**	**4**	**266**	**263**	**317**	**449**	**766**	**757**	**770**	**7**	**80**	**0.37**	**39**	**20**	**41**	**30**	**113**	**103**	**114**	**12%**	**92**	**4%**	**73%**				**4.92**	**0.6**	**38**	**115**	**$19**

Lowrie,Jed

Age: 34 Bats: B Pos: 2B | Ht: 6' 0" Wt: 180
Health F | PT/Exp C | Consist C | LIMA Plan D+ | Rand Var -1 | MM 2133

Only the third 500+ AB season and second-highest total of his career made him a solid waiver find for deep leaguers. HctX and PX joined his consistently solid Eye to support the surge, but BPV and health highlight volatility. Quality xPX built more off gap power further muddying his future. A reserve pick at best.

Yr Tm	AB	R	HR	RBI	SB	BA	xBA	OBP	SLG	OPS	vL	vR	bb%	ct%	Eye	G	L	F	h%	HctX	PX	xPX	hr/f	Spd	SBO	SB%	#Wk	DOM	DIS	RC/G	RAR	BPV	BPX	R$
13 OAK	603	80	15	75	1	290	272	344	446	791	772	800	8	85	0.55	33	23	43	32	96	108	99	7%	99	1%	100%	26	69%	8%	5.53	30.3	73	183	$21
14 OAK	502	59	6	50	0	249	250	321	355	676	598	707	9	84	0.65	31	24	44	29	107	79	112	3%	109	0%	0%	25	40%	16%	3.83	6.5	53	143	$7
15 HOU	230	35	9	30	1	222	263	312	400	712	908	641	11	81	0.65	35	21	44	24	128	115	153	11%	88	2%	100%	15	60%	27%	4.04	-1.6	67	181	$2
16 OAK	338	30	2	27	0	263	239	314	322	637	667	627	7	81	0.40	43	25	32	32	92	40	82	2%	112	0%	0%	17	24%	53%	3.53	-11.7	5	14	$3
17 OAK	567	86	14	69	0	277	280	360	448	808	750	825	11	82	0.73	29	27	43	32	115	103	115	7%	100	1%	0%	27	63%	15%	5.64	16.3	67	203	$14
1st Half	289	50	9	28	0	284	277	356	481	837	669	881	10	82	0.58	28	25	47	32	119	117	124	8%	115	0%	0%	13	62%	15%	6.05	9.9	76	230	$16
2nd Half	278	36	5	41	0	270	283	363	414	777	813	764	13	83	0.89	31	29	40	31	111	89	106	5%	89	1%	0%	14	64%	14%	5.21	3.1	59	179	$13
18 Proj	**346**	**45**	**7**	**40**	**0**	**264**	**265**	**338**	**397**	**736**	**751**	**731**	**10**	**82**	**0.63**	**34**	**26**	**40**	**30**	**109**	**81**	**111**	**6%**	**101**	**1%**	**41%**				**4.64**	**-1.6**	**30**	**92**	**$8**

PAUL SPORER

Lucroy,Jonathan

Age: 32	Bats: R	Pos: CA	Health	B	LIMA Plan	B
Ht: 6' 0"	Wt: 200		PT/Exp	B	Rand Var	+2
			Consist	F	MM	1345

Most notable about this disaster? It occured in two of MLB's most hitter-friendly parks, in TEX and COL. Though plate skills held, just about every other metric took a dive—to the extent that news of a hidden injury would not be surprising. Can't rule out rebound given his history, but 2 of last 3 seasons underscore the risk.

Yr	Tm	AB	R	HR	RBI	SB	BA	xBA	OBP	SLG	OPS	vL	vR	bb%	ct%	Eye	G	L	F	h%	HctX	PX	xPX	hr/f	Spd	SBO	SB%	#Wk	DOM	DIS	RC/G	RAR	BPV	BPX
13	MIL	521	59	18	82	9	280	281	340	455	795	859	775	8	87	0.67	39	23	38	29	133	104	134	10%	108	7%	90%	27	48%	7%	5.53	27.0	80	200
14	MIL	585	73	13	69	4	301	298	373	465	837	838	837	10	88	0.93	42	22	36	33	132	119	128	7%	96	5%	50%	27	78%	0%	6.19	44.2	98	265
15	MIL	371	51	7	43	1	264	275	326	391	717	639	743	9	83	0.56	44	26	29	30	124	83	104	8%	95	1%	100%	21	38%	29%	4.48	7.0	45	122
16	2 TM	490	67	24	81	5	292	276	355	500	855	796	874	9	80	0.47	37	24	39	33	114	118	131	16%	105	4%	100%	27	48%	22%	6.44	27.6	64	183
17	2 TM	423	45	6	40	1	265	270	345	371	716	644	741	10	88	0.90	53	19	28	29	80	59	46	6%	103	1%	100%	27	48%	22%	4.35	3.6	51	155
1st Half		224	23	4	20	0	263	263	311	375	686	725	674	5	89	0.54	54	18	28	28	83	63	61	7%	89	0%	0%	13	46%	15%	3.94	-1.0	47	142
2nd Half		199	22	2	20	1	266	266	379	367	746	565	816	14	86	1.22	53	19	27	30	76	53	28	4%	114	1%	100%	14	50%	29%	4.76	3.8	53	161
18	**Proj**	**475**	**57**	**13**	**57**	**3**	**274**	**275**	**348**	**421**	**769**	**692**	**795**	**10**	**85**	**0.70**	**46**	**22**	**33**	**30**	**100**	**79**	**82**	**10%**	**102**	**2%**	**93%**				**5.11**	**13.1**	**45**	**137**

Luplow,Jordan

Age: 24	Bats: R	Pos: RF	Health	A	LIMA Plan	D
Ht: 6' 1"	Wt: 195		PT/Exp	F	Rand Var	-1
			Consist	F	MM	2211

3-11-.205 in 78 AB at PIT. Got a cup of coffee after breakout at AA/AAA. His 0.71 Eye as a minor leaguer highlights solid discipline, while gap power developed further (23 minor league HR) thanks to a more aggressive 2017 approach. xPX says gains stuck in his few MLB at bats, but expect a bumpy road at first.

Yr	Tm	AB	R	HR	RBI	SB	BA	xBA	OBP	SLG	OPS	vL	vR	bb%	ct%	Eye	G	L	F	h%	HctX	PX	xPX	hr/f	Spd	SBO	SB%	#Wk	DOM	DIS	RC/G	RAR	BPV	BPX
13																																		
14																																		
15																																		
16																																		
17	PIT *	492	71	22	60	4	263	242	326	453	779	664	658	8	78	0.42	38	16	46	30	88	105	103	12%	98	8%	44%	8	38%	38%	4.93	-3.6	43	130
1st Half		265	40	13	33	1	259	275	327	465	792			9	80	0.52				28		112			95	6%	21%				4.99		60	182
2nd Half		227	31	9	28	4	268	226	325	439	764	664	658	8	75	0.34	38	16	46	32	85	96	103	12%	115	9%	62%	8	38%	38%	4.87	-1.3	28	85
18	**Proj**	**128**	**18**	**5**	**16**	**2**	**265**	**233**	**338**	**434**	**771**	**749**	**781**	**8**	**77**	**0.40**	**38**	**16**	**46**	**31**	**77**	**96**	**93**	**10%**	**104**	**8%**	**55%**				**4.80**	**0.4**	**25**	**76**

Machado,Dixon

Age: 26	Bats: R	Pos: SS 2B	Health	A	LIMA Plan	D
Ht: 6' 1"	Wt: 170		PT/Exp	C	Rand Var	-3
			Consist	A	MM	0421

Defensive specialist can handle any infield position, which earns him some AB. But do you want them? PRO: Above average contact; raw speed skill. CON: Just about everything else; adept at hitting routine ground balls. VERDICT: Unless his 9% bb% from the MiLB eventually shows up, and the team lets him run ... No.

Yr	Tm	AB	R	HR	RBI	SB	BA	xBA	OBP	SLG	OPS	vL	vR	bb%	ct%	Eye	G	L	F	h%	HctX	PX	xPX	hr/f	Spd	SBO	SB%	#Wk	DOM	DIS	RC/G	RAR	BPV	BPX
13																																		
14	aa	292	33	4	24	6	266		334	379	713			9	87	0.79				29		84			95	14%	51%				4.18		64	173
15	DET *	577	53	3	42	13	230	239	275	288	563	646	567	6	82	0.34	51	21	28	28	75	44	36	0%	94	11%	79%	7	14%	43%	2.66	-30.5	5	14
16	DET *	502	52	3	41	15	235	353	309	314	623	629	167	10	83	0.62	50	50	0	28	112	53	17	0%	118	14%	72%	5	0%	80%	3.24	-16.2	31	89
17	DET	166	17	1	11	1	259	238	302	319	621	437	695	6	81	0.31	57	19	24	32	95	37	48	3%	142	2%	100%	27	26%	59%	3.34	-6.1	8	24
1st Half		63	5	0	4	0	302	213	333	349	683	414	840	5	84	0.30	51	15	34	36	95	24	82	0%	158	0%	0%	13	23%	69%	4.25	-0.6	14	42
2nd Half		103	12	1	7	1	233	250	283	301	584	458	623	6	79	0.32	61	21	18	29	95	45	26	7%	118	4%	100%	14	29%	50%	2.87	-5.3	1	3
18	**Proj**	**195**	**20**	**1**	**14**	**3**	**250**	**246**	**303**	**314**	**617**	**509**	**657**	**7**	**82**	**0.42**	**55**	**19**	**26**	**30**	**87**	**41**	**44**	**2%**	**130**	**8%**	**73%**				**3.24**	**-7.1**	**1**	**2**

Machado,Manny

Age: 25	Bats: R	Pos: 3B	Health	B	LIMA Plan	B+
Ht: 6' 3"	Wt: 185		PT/Exp	A	Rand Var	+2
			Consist	B	MM	3345

Tested our patience in 1st half but xPX kept hope alive despite unlucky h% and ct% dive. Both returned to form in 2nd half as rest of the profile held strong, and there's a glimmer of even more upside. Team context continues to hold SB back (30th in SB 2014-17), but BA/power skills are elite. No SS eligiblity for 2018, but still a star.

Yr	Tm	AB	R	HR	RBI	SB	BA	xBA	OBP	SLG	OPS	vL	vR	bb%	ct%	Eye	G	L	F	h%	HctX	PX	xPX	hr/f	Spd	SBO	SB%	#Wk	DOM	DIS	RC/G	RAR	BPV	BPX
13	BAL	667	88	14	71	6	283	277	314	432	746	762	738	4	83	0.26	47	21	32	32	101	107	73	8%	122	9%	46%	26	62%	12%	4.64	13.2	65	163
14	BAL	327	38	12	32	2	278	262	324	431	755	642	802	6	79	0.29	49	20	31	32	100	106	101	15%	112	2%	100%	16	56%	25%	4.91	11.5	49	132
15	BAL	633	102	35	86	20	286	279	359	502	861	763	894	10	82	0.63	44	18	38	30	119	127	122	18%	113	15%	71%	27	63%	4%	6.30	31.3	87	235
16	BAL	640	105	37	96	0	294	283	343	533	876	919	862	7	81	0.40	37	20	43	31	117	136	118	17%	111	2%	0%	27	63%	4%	6.47	29.8	83	237
17	BAL	630	81	33	95	9	259	266	310	471	782	826	767	7	82	0.43	42	16	42	27	131	112	131	15%	108	9%	69%	27	59%	22%	5.02	3.0	66	200
1st Half		295	33	15	38	4	217	248	289	420	709	803	673	9	77	0.45	43	14	43	23	122	114	133	15%	105	8%	80%	13	54%	23%	3.97	-10.2	52	158
2nd Half		335	48	18	57	5	296	281	330	516	846	852	844	6	86	0.42	41	17	42	30	138	111	129	15%	114	10%	63%	14	64%	21%	6.13	9.8	79	239
18	**Proj**	**617**	**96**	**32**	**92**	**8**	**283**	**273**	**334**	**496**	**830**	**837**	**827**	**7**	**82**	**0.44**	**42**	**18**	**41**	**30**	**123**	**113**	**122**	**15%**	**111**	**8%**	**65%**				**5.82**	**16.3**	**56**	**170**

Mahtook,Mikie

Age: 28	Bats: R	Pos: CF RF	Health	B	LIMA Plan	B
Ht: 6' 1"	Wt: 200		PT/Exp	D	Rand Var	0
			Consist	D	MM	3525

Mahtook advantage of a full-time role in second half with a balanced skills profile, powered by a surge in ct%. More LD amped up the HctX, xPX, and xBA, though GB surge puts burden on hr/f to maintain HR. Consistently strong Spd, burgeoning pop, and a real shot at 500+ AB offer hope for... UP: 25 HR/15 SB.

Yr	Tm	AB	R	HR	RBI	SB	BA	xBA	OBP	SLG	OPS	vL	vR	bb%	ct%	Eye	G	L	F	h%	HctX	PX	xPX	hr/f	Spd	SBO	SB%	#Wk	DOM	DIS	RC/G	RAR	BPV	BPX
13	aa	511	56	5	54	20	218		266	327	593			6	77	0.28				27		80			121	27%	68%				2.77		22	55
14	aaa	489	46	9	56	15	251		305	386	691			7	67	0.24				36		119			101	17%	72%				3.96		9	24
15	TAM *	490	50	12	54	12	225	221	260	367	627	1030	856	5	69	0.15	33	23	44	30	120	109	192	28%	121	18%	74%	12	58%	17%	3.12	-19.2	12	32
16	TAM *	290	30	4	17	4	218	183	262	318	580	678	438	6	66	0.18	38	14	47	31	86	77	94	5%	130	10%	66%	13	15%	85%	2.68	-14.3	-20	-57
17	DET	348	50	12	38	6	276	264	330	457	787	793	783	6	77	0.29	46	20	33	33	119	99	112	13%	159	7%	100%	25	48%	36%	5.27	-1.7	50	152
1st Half		118	11	4	16	1	271	250	295	441	736	770	702	2	77	0.11	40	20	40	32	137	97	154	11%	116	4%	100%	13	38%	38%	4.51	-2.9	28	85
2nd Half		230	39	8	22	5	278	270	346	465	812	815	810	8	77	0.38	49	21	30	33	110	99	90	15%	174	8%	100%	12	58%	33%	5.66	2.0	59	179
18	**Proj**	**496**	**60**	**19**	**49**	**9**	**261**	**247**	**311**	**447**	**759**	**859**	**692**	**6**	**75**	**0.23**	**41**	**19**	**40**	**31**	**109**	**106**	**120**	**13%**	**143**	**10%**	**81%**				**4.68**	**2.4**	**31**	**95**

Maldonado,Martin

Age: 31	Bats: R	Pos: CA	Health	A	LIMA Plan	D+
Ht: 6' 0"	Wt: 230		PT/Exp	D	Rand Var	0
			Consist	B	MM	2003

Maintained power and added to BA in spite of swinging (and often missing) at everything. Extra playing time fostered a career-high in HR, but xPX preaches caution going forward. He's always been a deep-league second catcher, and 2017 did nothing to change that outlook.

Yr	Tm	AB	R	HR	RBI	SB	BA	xBA	OBP	SLG	OPS	vL	vR	bb%	ct%	Eye	G	L	F	h%	HctX	PX	xPX	hr/f	Spd	SBO	SB%	#Wk	DOM	DIS	RC/G	RAR	BPV	BPX
13	MIL	183	13	4	22	0	169	195	236	284	520	446	543	6	71	0.25	42	14	44	21	72	87	101	7%	82	0%	0%	26	27%	65%	1.96	-10.4	-6	-15
14	MIL	111	14	4	16	0	234	223	320	387	707	721	693	9	71	0.34	36	18	46	29	86	119	107	12%	84	0%	0%	26	31%	54%	3.91	2.0	25	68
15	MIL	229	19	4	22	0	210	205	282	293	575	810	503	9	72	0.35	47	20	33	28	91	62	99	8%	53	2%	0%	25	12%	68%	2.61	-8.0	-27	-73
16	MIL	208	21	8	21	1	202	225	332	351	683	677	685	14	73	0.63	44	18	38	24	84	92	90	14%	52	2%	100%	25	44%	40%	3.58	-1.8	11	31
17	LAA	429	43	14	38	0	221	221	276	368	645	632	649	3	72	0.13	49	15	37	27	78	91	78	13%	72	3%	0%	26	19%	50%	2.92	-16.0	-7	-21
1st Half		224	23	8	24	0	250	227	317	411	728	891	670	5	72	0.17	51	14	35	31	90	98	91	15%	83	4%	0%	13	23%	54%	3.82	-1.9	2	6
2nd Half		205	20	6	14	0	190	217	230	322	552	369	625	2	73	0.07	46	16	38	23	65	83	66	11%	63	0%	0%	13	15%	46%	2.09	-13.1	-18	-55
18	**Proj**	**409**	**40**	**13**	**39**	**0**	**209**	**218**	**285**	**346**	**630**	**633**	**630**	**7**	**72**	**0.28**	**46**	**17**	**37**	**26**	**80**	**84**	**86**	**12%**	**60**	**2%**	**33%**				**2.93**	**-15.4**	**-17**	**-52**

Mancini,Trey

Age: 26	Bats: R	Pos: LF 1B	Health	A	LIMA Plan	B
Ht: 6' 4"	Wt: 215		PT/Exp	B	Rand Var	-3
			Consist	F	MM	3335

If it weren't for the judicial one in NY, he might have garnered serious ROY votes. A shocking 1st half blossomed into a full-time role. But heavy GB% means hr/f determines big flies, and 2nd half showed what happens when it's closer to 14% league avg. Heed season xBA and post-June power outage. DN: 15 HR, .260

Yr	Tm	AB	R	HR	RBI	SB	BA	xBA	OBP	SLG	OPS	vL	vR	bb%	ct%	Eye	G	L	F	h%	HctX	PX	xPX	hr/f	Spd	SBO	SB%	#Wk	DOM	DIS	RC/G	RAR	BPV	BPX
13																																		
14																																		
15	aa	326	52	12	49	2	332		368	540	908			5	81	0.30				38		137			94	3%	61%				7.52		73	197
16	BAL *	560	69	20	63	2	243	220	309	392	701	1800	650	9	70	0.31	40	20	40	31	169	94	250	75%	123	3%	43%	2	50%	50%	4.03	-4.1	10	29
17	BAL	543	65	24	78	1	293	263	338	488	826	742	860	6	74	0.24	51	19	30	36	103	112	113	20%	127	1%	100%	27	37%	37%	5.88	6.4	39	118
1st Half		228	28	14	43	1	307	259	352	553	905	757	988	6	70	0.22	50	16	34	39	103	149	143	26%	120	2%	100%	13	46%	38%	7.14	11.1	48	145
2nd Half		315	37	10	35	0	283	265	327	441	769	725	782	5	78	0.26	51	21	27	34	102	89	93	15%	131	0%	0%	14	29%	36%	5.04	-2.8	34	103
18	**Proj**	**556**	**71**	**24**	**74**	**2**	**272**	**258**	**324**	**458**	**783**	**700**	**816**	**7**	**74**	**0.27**	**51**	**19**	**30**	**33**	**102**	**108**	**113**	**19%**	**131**	**2%**	**64%**				**5.11**	**10.4**	**16**	**49**

PAUL SPORER

Margot,Manuel

Age: 23	Bats: R	Pos: CF	Health	B	LIMA Plan	B+
Ht: 5' 11"	Wt: 180		PT/Exp	C	Rand Var	-1
			Consist	B	MM	2545

A game of adjustments, they say—no more evident than in a rookie's first full season. With 2nd half improvements in FB%, HctX, xPX and SB%, good things are in store. Missed a month with calf strain, but returned with lots of LDs, enough current speed and power to come. A multi-category producer with upside.

Yr Tm	AB	R	HR	RBI	SB	BA	xBA	OBP	SLG	OPS	vL	vR	bb%	ct%	Eye	G	L	F	h%	HctX	PX	xPX	hr/f	Spd	SBO	SB%	#Wk	DOM	DIS	RC/G	RAR	BPV	BPX	R$
13																																		
14																																		
15 aa	258	31	2	27	16	263		309	403	712			6	85	0.45				30		98			104	42%	65%				4.02		65	176	$9
16 SD *	554	72	4	41	23	258	301	289	350	639	769	583	4	86	0.32	63	23	13	29	140	53	51	0%	172	27%	65%	3	33%	67%	3.33	-21.8	49	140	$16
17 SD	487	53	13	39	17	263	251	313	409	721	833	683	7	78	0.33	41	23	36	31	80	79	75	9%	166	19%	71%	22	27%	32%	4.34	-10.3	41	124	$14
1st Half	204	21	4	15	9	275	260	324	402	726	760	712	7	78	0.36	48	23	28	33	71	71	43	9%	149	26%	60%	9	33%	33%	4.32	-3.5	32	97	$9
2nd Half	283	32	9	24	8	254	244	304	413	717	897	664	6	78	0.31	35	23	42	30	87	85	98	10%	167	13%	89%	13	23%	31%	4.35	-4.6	45	136	$17
18 Proj	**562**	**66**	**17**	**46**	**21**	**261**	**268**	**303**	**428**	**731**	**849**	**691**	**6**	**82**	**0.33**	**40**	**23**	**37**	**29**	**81**	**87**	**76**	**10%**	**162**	**24%**	**68%**				**4.32**	**-3.1**	**48**	**146**	**$18**

Marisnick,Jake

Age: 27	Bats: R	Pos: CF	Health	A	LIMA Plan	D
Ht: 6' 4"	Wt: 220		PT/Exp	D	Rand Var	-5
			Consist	D	MM	4403

Reminder that the launch angle phenomenon is NOT a cure-all. Produced more loft, and xPX and hr/f cooperated for career-high HR. But the cost was a Gallonian ct% and a continued LD% spiral, while xBA barely budged. Ironic that just as speed skills window is closing, he's learning value of a walk. Answers ain't easy.

Yr Tm	AB	R	HR	RBI	SB	BA	xBA	OBP	SLG	OPS	vL	vR	bb%	ct%	Eye	G	L	F	h%	HctX	PX	xPX	hr/f	Spd	SBO	SB%	#Wk	DOM	DIS	RC/G	RAR	BPV	BPX	R$
13 MIA *	374	43	10	45	12	245	244	285	383	668	431	498	5	73	0.21	42	25	33	31	73	98	55	4%	127	24%	62%	9	22%	67%	3.51	-6.6	22	55	$10
14 2 TM *	564	55	9	46	27	237	223	263	334	597	738	568	3	75	0.14	39	22	39	30	74	75	73	5%	129	31%	74%	12	25%	67%	2.90	-16.0	9	24	$15
15 HOU	339	46	9	36	24	236	223	281	383	665	669	662	5	69	0.17	42	20	38	32	72	107	93	10%	136	47%	73%	25	32%	48%	3.40	-11.6	14	38	$13
16 HOU *	314	42	5	22	11	204	224	245	321	566	701	519	5	70	0.18	45	19	36	28	74	90	68	7%	114	31%	64%	26	19%	50%	2.40	-19.7	-2	-6	$2
17 HOU	230	50	16	35	9	243	227	319	496	815	817	813	8	61	0.22	37	15	48	32	71	171	119	25%	107	26%	69%	24	50%	42%	4.91	1.1	30	91	$9
1st Half	124	26	10	23	5	258	232	336	524	860	669	1002	7	62	0.21	38	16	46	33	77	168	125	29%	112	28%	63%	13	54%	38%	5.29	1.4	33	100	$11
2nd Half	106	24	6	12	4	226	221	299	462	761	1006	601	9	59	0.23	35	15	50	32	63	175	111	20%	101	24%	80%	11	45%	45%	4.47	-1.4	27	82	$7
18 Proj	**262**	**46**	**11**	**30**	**9**	**230**	**224**	**290**	**417**	**707**	**779**	**661**	**6**	**65**	**0.20**	**40**	**18**	**42**	**31**	**71**	**125**	**96**	**15%**	**113**	**25%**	**71%**				**3.78**	**-5.9**	**14**	**41**	**$9**

Markakis,Nick

Age: 34	Bats: L	Pos: RF	Health	A	LIMA Plan	B+
Ht: 6' 1"	Wt: 215		PT/Exp	A	Rand Var	-1
			Consist	A	MM	1035

You Know What You're Getting—The xBA Edition. But will it be renewed? Contact rate slowly eroding, but that's really the only slippage. Power is on life support but steady, and speed is dead but steady, so the real value is in the first number column: AB. He's got another year or two in the ~600 range. And you know what to expect.

Yr Tm	AB	R	HR	RBI	SB	BA	xBA	OBP	SLG	OPS	vL	vR	bb%	ct%	Eye	G	L	F	h%	HctX	PX	xPX	hr/f	Spd	SBO	SB%	#Wk	DOM	DIS	RC/G	RAR	BPV	BPX	R$
13 BAL	634	89	10	59	1	271	259	329	356	685	651	704	8	88	0.72	47	23	31	30	104	56	71	6%	90	2%	33%	27	44%	19%	4.07	-9.8	41	103	$15
14 BAL	642	81	14	50	4	276	258	342	386	729	673	751	9	87	0.74	46	20	34	30	103	74	85	7%	101	3%	67%	27	41%	11%	4.60	9.1	57	154	$18
15 ATL	612	73	3	53	2	296	261	370	376	746	635	795	10	86	0.84	52	21	27	34	97	60	55	2%	93	1%	67%	27	44%	19%	5.00	2.4	44	119	$16
16 ATL	599	67	13	89	0	269	259	346	397	744	613	800	10	83	0.70	43	22	35	31	111	82	105	7%	60	1%	0%	27	44%	19%	4.73	0.9	39	111	$13
17 ATL	593	76	8	76	0	275	260	354	384	738	722	743	10	81	0.62	49	22	29	33	109	71	71	6%	75	1%	0%	27	33%	26%	4.66	-8.8	27	82	$13
1st Half	304	40	3	42	0	289	253	368	388	756	617	788	10	79	0.51	52	22	27	36	110	67	56	5%	86	1%	0%	13	31%	38%	4.94	-1.0	16	48	$14
2nd Half	289	36	5	34	0	260	270	338	381	719	788	688	11	84	0.78	45	23	32	29	109	74	87	6%	67	1%	0%	14	36%	14%	4.39	-5.7	41	124	$11
18 Proj	**597**	**73**	**9**	**73**	**1**	**273**	**262**	**350**	**381**	**731**	**675**	**753**	**10**	**84**	**0.69**	**47**	**22**	**31**	**31**	**107**	**67**	**80**	**6%**	**74**	**1%**	**22%**				**4.60**	**-1.7**	**21**	**63**	**$15**

Marte,Jefry

Age: 27	Bats: R	Pos: 1B	Health	A	LIMA Plan	D
Ht: 6' 1"	Wt: 220		PT/Exp	D	Rand Var	+5
			Consist	B	MM	3231

4-14-.173 in 127 AB at LAA. Dashed the faint hopes of relevance after a 15-HR outburst in 258 AB in LAA in 2016. Just about all his MLB metrics regressed, as xPX and Spd reverted to below average and a 20% h% finished it off. Has far more versatility on defense (3B, 1B, OF) than he has in the batter's box.

Yr Tm	AB	R	HR	RBI	SB	BA	xBA	OBP	SLG	OPS	vL	vR	bb%	ct%	Eye	G	L	F	h%	HctX	PX	xPX	hr/f	Spd	SBO	SB%	#Wk	DOM	DIS	RC/G	RAR	BPV	BPX	R$
13 aa	245	26	1	22	6	243		300	329	630			8	78	0.37				31		73			95	12%	85%				3.41		16	40	$3
14 aa	405	39	7	41	7	222		285	313	598			8	81	0.48				26		67			82	10%	68%				2.90		22	59	$4
15 DET *	437	46	15	60	6	233	266	285	409	694	920	506	7	79	0.35	46	19	35	26	114	115	102	20%	83	13%	52%	11	45%	45%	3.72	-16.2	49	132	$8
16 LAA *	420	54	17	61	4	237	246	293	418	712	783	793	7	76	0.33	46	15	39	27	113	114	109	19%	74	11%	43%	21	48%	29%	3.91	-12.0	33	94	$8
17 LAA *	312	27	10	40	5	191	240	249	325	574	634	515	7	76	0.32	47	19	34	22	85	79	83	13%	62	10%	80%	13	38%	54%	2.56	-27.9	3	9	-$1
1st Half	184	15	6	22	2	165	225	227	281	508	619	531	7	72	0.28	49	21	31	20	78	69	79	13%	72	7%	100%	10	30%	60%	1.99	-22.0	-20	-61	-$3
2nd Half	128	12	4	18	3	229	235	281	390	671	675	0	7	83	0.42	38	13	50	25	105	92	99	13%	67	15%	69%	3	67%	33%	3.56	-8.2	40	121	$3
18 Proj	**130**	**13**	**6**	**17**	**2**	**218**	**265**	**284**	**413**	**697**	**808**	**618**	**7**	**78**	**0.35**	**47**	**19**	**35**	**23**	**101**	**109**	**96**	**17%**	**78**	**12%**	**65%**				**3.62**	**-5.9**	**34**	**102**	**$2**

Marte,Ketel

Age: 24	Bats: B	Pos: SS	Health	A	LIMA Plan	D+
Ht: 6' 1"	Wt: 165		PT/Exp	C	Rand Var	0
			Consist	D	MM	1543

5-18-.260 with 3 SB in 223 AB at ARI. Some elements of future production here, as ct%, HctX and xPX all took solid steps forward. It's more doubles-power than home-run-power, and portions of his SB history and current speed metrics are intriguing. Needs consistent playing time but, with 400 AB ... UP: 10 HR / 20 SB

Yr Tm	AB	R	HR	RBI	SB	BA	xBA	OBP	SLG	OPS	vL	vR	bb%	ct%	Eye	G	L	F	h%	HctX	PX	xPX	hr/f	Spd	SBO	SB%	#Wk	DOM	DIS	RC/G	RAR	BPV	BPX	R$
13																																		
14 a/a	523	59	3	41	22	263		289	347	636			4	83	0.22				31		67			104	27%	66%				3.34		26	70	$16
15 SEA *	487	58	4	39	24	279	266	333	375	708	720	780	7	84	0.50	52	22	26	33	82	66	45	4%	150	23%	71%	11	55%	18%	4.35	8.2	49	132	$19
16 SEA *	465	59	1	35	13	254	253	284	318	602	525	651	4	82	0.23	52	22	26	31	71	47	41	1%	126	16%	72%	22	14%	41%	3.07	-21.3	12	34	$9
17 ARI *	534	70	9	45	8	276	273	332	416	748	721	748	8	86	0.59	45	21	34	31	98	76	77	8%	158	8%	69%	15	53%	7%	4.83	4.8	68	206	$13
1st Half	316	42	4	28	5	286	203	320	431	752	0	567	5	87	0.39	0	25	75	32	88	79	36	0%	154	9%	66%	1	0%	0%	4.87	2.6	69	209	$16
2nd Half	218	28	5	17	3	261	265	349	394	744	721	754	12	84	0.83	46	21	33	29	96	72	78	8%	147	6%	75%	14	57%	7%	4.75	1.1	63	191	$9
18 Proj	**293**	**37**	**5**	**23**	**8**	**267**	**270**	**318**	**392**	**710**	**676**	**731**	**7**	**84**	**0.47**	**48**	**21**	**31**	**30**	**84**	**70**	**56**	**7%**	**146**	**14%**	**71%**				**4.31**	**-1.3**	**39**	**119**	**$9**

Marte,Starling

Age: 29	Bats: R	Pos: LF CF	Health	A	LIMA Plan	D+
Ht: 6' 1"	Wt: 190		PT/Exp	B	Rand Var	0
			Consist	C	MM	1535

7-31-.275 with 21 SB in 309 AB at PIT. Came back in mid-July after serving 80 game suspension. Speed reverted to form, but power did not. Walk rate improved but was still tepid, leaving h% to drive OBP. We're left with a valuable package—but is it as explosive as we were led to believe? Maybe. Longshot UP still: 20 HR, 50 SB

Yr Tm	AB	R	HR	RBI	SB	BA	xBA	OBP	SLG	OPS	vL	vR	bb%	ct%	Eye	G	L	F	h%	HctX	PX	xPX	hr/f	Spd	SBO	SB%	#Wk	DOM	DIS	RC/G	RAR	BPV	BPX	R$
13 PIT	510	83	12	35	41	280	259	343	441	784	1053	724	4	73	0.18	51	22	28	36	98	116	98	12%	192	47%	73%	24	29%	33%	4.73	10.0	53	133	$30
14 PIT	495	73	13	56	30	291	264	356	453	808	781	814	6	74	0.25	47	23	29	37	105	125	113	13%	166	32%	73%	26	50%	35%	5.33	21.8	58	157	$28
15 PIT	579	84	19	81	30	287	283	337	444	780	717	798	4	79	0.22	54	24	23	34	101	103	94	19%	117	28%	75%	27	48%	22%	4.98	4.3	43	116	$32
16 PIT	489	71	9	46	47	311	274	362	456	818	730	837	4	79	0.22	48	23	28	38	111	95	98	8%	147	46%	80%	25	36%	40%	5.79	15.9	46	131	$35
17 PIT *	345	51	8	33	23	275	245	318	376	694	404	808	6	79	0.30	49	21	30	33	84	54	77	10%	141	28%	85%	15	20%	40%	4.39	-8.6	15	45	$16
1st Half	54	7	2	7	2	241	229	288	370	659	180	857	5	69	0.18	50	22	28	31	95	77	119	20%	91	31%	50%	3	0%	67%	3.07	-3.8	-24	-73	-$13
2nd Half	291	44	6	26	21	281	249	324	378	702	466	798	6	81	0.33	49	21	30	33	81	51	69	8%	151	27%	91%	12	25%	33%	4.67	-5.7	24	73	$22
18 Proj	**565**	**82**	**15**	**60**	**36**	**282**	**260**	**335**	**418**	**753**	**518**	**820**	**5**	**77**	**0.23**	**50**	**22**	**28**	**34**	**96**	**79**	**94**	**13%**	**132**	**31%**	**79%**				**4.75**	**4.8**	**22**	**67**	**$32**

Martin,Russell

Age: 35	Bats: R	Pos: CA	Health	B	LIMA Plan	D+
Ht: 5' 10"	Wt: 205		PT/Exp	B	Rand Var	+4
			Consist	A	MM	3023

Season shortened by shoulder, oblique issues; such is the life of a 35-year-old backstop. While xBA approved of new-found Eye trend and LD% gains, h% scoffed loudly. Significant drops in FB%, xPX and 2nd half HctX point to the inevitable. For now hr/f-led punch earns him a roster spot, but he's no longer one-CA league material.

Yr Tm	AB	R	HR	RBI	SB	BA	xBA	OBP	SLG	OPS	vL	vR	bb%	ct%	Eye	G	L	F	h%	HctX	PX	xPX	hr/f	Spd	SBO	SB%	#Wk	DOM	DIS	RC/G	RAR	BPV	BPX	R$
13 PIT	438	51	15	55	9	226	244	327	377	703	610	729	11	75	0.54	51	17	33	27	103	108	104	14%	68	12%	64%	26	38%	35%	3.86	1.9	33	83	$9
14 PIT	379	45	11	67	4	290	255	402	430	832	693	865	13	79	0.76	49	19	32	34	109	102	91	11%	81	6%	50%	23	39%	35%	5.81	26.6	51	138	$16
15 TOR	441	76	23	77	4	240	272	329	458	787	937	747	10	76	0.50	51	16	33	27	97	140	113	21%	89	8%	44%	27	48%	26%	4.77	13.8	65	176	$14
16 TOR	455	62	20	74	2	231	223	335	398	733	700	743	12	67	0.43	46	18	36	30	92	111	128	18%	66	2%	67%	27	37%	44%	4.28	5.7	4	11	$8
17 TOR	307	49	13	35	1	221	256	343	388	731	581	772	14	73	0.60	48	24	28	26	89	98	84	21%	69	3%	33%	22	36%	50%	4.11	-0.2	20	61	$3
1st Half	171	28	7	16	0	216	241	374	374	748	675	769	18	71	0.76	48	22	30	26	90	94	82	19%	87	2%	0%	13	31%	54%	4.24	0.8	24	73	$2
2nd Half	136	21	6	19	1	228	273	300	404	704	443	770	9	75	0.38	49	25	25	26	88	102	86	23%	57	6%	50%	9	44%	44%	3.86	-1.0	18	55	$4
18 Proj	**369**	**56**	**16**	**53**	**2**	**231**	**251**	**334**	**406**	**741**	**654**	**764**	**12**	**73**	**0.50**	**48**	**21**	**31**	**27**	**93**	**104**	**101**	**20%**	**68**	**5%**	**48%**				**4.28**	**1.6**	**15**	**45**	**$8**

BRENT HERSHEY

Martinez,J.D.

Age: 30	Bats: R	Pos: RF	Health	D	LIMA Plan	B+
Ht: 6' 3"	Wt: 220		PT/Exp	B	Rand Var	0
			Consist	D	MM	5255

More DL time (sprained foot ligament) came early and shelved him until mid-May. Subsequent FB% rebound helped elite HctX rise to cartoonish levels. (More than a third of flyballs went yard? Really?) Onslaught vL cemented BA gains. Durability remains a concern, but now even his partial seasons make him a top OF pick.

Yr Tm	AB	R	HR	RBI	SB	BA	xBA	OBP	SLG	OPS	vL	vR	bb%	ct%	Eye	G	L	F	h%	HctX	PX	xPX	hr/f	Spd	SBO	SB%	#Wk	DOM	DIS	RC/G	RAR	BPV	BPX
13 HOU	296	24	7	36	2	250	236	272	378	650	621	664	3	72	0.12	44	22	34	32	102	103	108	9%	83	3%	100%	18	33%	61%	3.57	-9.0	5	13
14 DET *	506	69	30	92	7	308	287	349	568	917	1003	880	6	71	0.22	40	23	37	38	133	196	159	19%	110	9%	71%	24	54%	33%	7.23	43.4	89	241
15 DET	596	93	38	102	3	282	265	344	535	879	915	870	8	70	0.30	34	22	43	34	131	175	182	21%	96	3%	60%	27	56%	30%	6.42	26.2	68	184
16 DET *	496	71	22	72	2	300	265	364	517	881	861	925	9	71	0.35	42	21	36	38	119	147	144	18%	91	3%	47%	21	48%	14%	6.78	28.7	51	146
17 2 TM	432	85	45	104	4	303	305	376	690	1066	1356	985	11	70	0.41	38	19	43	33	140	224	190	34%	97	4%	100%	22	73%	9%	9.65	52.6	114	345
1st Half	161	32	14	30	0	298	299	385	640	1025	1811	843	13	73	0.55	42	19	39	33	151	192	167	30%	114	0%	0%	8	63%	13%	9.05	17.7	107	324
2nd Half	271	53	31	74	4	306	309	371	720	1090	1138	1076	10	69	0.35	36	18	46	33	133	244	205	36%	85	6%	100%	14	79%	7%	9.99	36.3	118	358
18 Proj	**507**	**85**	**38**	**101**	**4**	**297**	**280**	**362**	**594**	**957**	**1084**	**918**	**10**	**71**	**0.36**	**39**	**20**	**41**	**35**	**131**	**177**	**172**	**26%**	**95**	**3%**	**80%**				**7.83**	**43.9**	**70**	**211**

Martinez,Jose

Age: 29	Bats: R	Pos: 1B LF	Health	A	LIMA Plan	B
Ht: 6' 6"	Wt: 215		PT/Exp	D	Rand Var	-2
			Consist	F	MM	3353

Wow. Late bloomer with plate skills won job with fine spring, delivered year-long power surge as a part-timer. Elevated h% factored into .423 BA vL. But skills seem to advance with AB—notably FB% and HctX. Sample size keeps us leery, but final kick—.975 OPS in 84 Sept AB—suggests he's no longer an end-game flyer.

Yr Tm	AB	R	HR	RBI	SB	BA	xBA	OBP	SLG	OPS	vL	vR	bb%	ct%	Eye	G	L	F	h%	HctX	PX	xPX	hr/f	Spd	SBO	SB%	#Wk	DOM	DIS	RC/G	RAR	BPV	BPX
13 aa	431	38	5	32	5	249		300	322	622			7	83	0.41				29		54			86	13%	32%				3.00		15	38
14																																	
15 aaa	341	43	7	45	6	324		388	467	854			9	81	0.55				38		97			95	7%	71%				6.78		51	138
16 STL *	458	40	7	42	8	226	266	271	328	599	1083	750	6	80	0.32	60	20	20	27	152	67	9	0%	88	9%	86%	5	20%	0%	2.97	-23.1	16	46
17 STL	272	47	14	46	4	309	286	379	518	897	1340	773	10	78	0.53	42	27	31	35	117	115	123	21%	113	5%	100%	24	42%	33%	7.41	15.9	60	182
1st Half	115	18	5	17	1	270	284	309	470	779	864	748	6	76	0.25	45	27	27	32	107	114	119	21%	117	4%	100%	10	40%	30%	5.16	-0.6	42	127
2nd Half	157	29	9	29	3	338	288	426	554	980	1818	787	14	80	0.78	40	26	34	38	125	115	126	21%	106	5%	100%	14	43%	36%	9.32	16.2	72	218
18 Proj	**351**	**48**	**18**	**47**	**5**	**285**	**292**	**346**	**498**	**845**	**1291**	**721**	**9**	**80**	**0.48**	**42**	**27**	**31**	**31**	**118**	**115**	**123**	**21%**	**111**	**7%**	**81%**				**6.21**	**10.9**	**52**	**158**

Martinez,Victor

Age: 39	Bats: B	Pos: DH	Health	C	LIMA Plan	D
Ht: 6' 2"	Wt: 210		PT/Exp	B	Rand Var	+1
			Consist	F	MM	1041

PRO: Plate skills still plus if not peak; HctX still elite; xPX still optimistic. CON: BA, FB%, PX all sagged near career lows; more DL time; fast approaching 40. Irregular heartbeat shelved him twice, finished him in Aug and required surgery—but he's expected to be ready. Has rebounded before, but now in uncharted waters.

Yr Tm	AB	R	HR	RBI	SB	BA	xBA	OBP	SLG	OPS	vL	vR	bb%	ct%	Eye	G	L	F	h%	HctX	PX	xPX	hr/f	Spd	SBO	SB%	#Wk	DOM	DIS	RC/G	RAR	BPV	BPX
13 DET	605	68	14	83	0	301	275	355	430	785	735	813	8	90	0.87	42	23	35	32	143	84	126	7%	79	1%	0%	26	65%	8%	5.54	17.2	68	170
14 DET	561	87	32	103	3	335	320	409	565	974	1123	923	11	93	1.67	41	21	38	32	158	135	147	16%	88	3%	60%	26	88%	4%	8.79	69.7	128	346
15 DET	440	39	11	64	0	245	256	301	366	667	870	616	6	88	0.60	40	21	39	26	116	73	110	7%	63	0%	0%	23	43%	26%	3.65	-23.3	45	122
16 DET	553	65	27	86	0	289	276	351	476	826	812	832	8	84	0.56	37	24	39	31	132	100	132	15%	65	0%	0%	27	48%	30%	5.94	6.8	53	151
17 DET	392	38	10	47	0	255	259	324	372	697	626	719	8	84	0.57	42	24	34	28	135	64	117	9%	76	0%	0%	20	35%	35%	4.05	-9.3	28	85
1st Half	233	23	5	29	0	253	248	328	361	689	706	684	9	85	0.69	44	21	35	28	138	60	114	7%	81	0%	0%	12	33%	25%	3.98	-6.1	33	100
2nd Half	159	15	5	18	0	258	277	318	390	708	532	773	7	82	0.43	39	28	33	29	132	71	121	12%	77	0%	0%	8	38%	50%	4.15	-3.3	25	76
18 Proj	**226**	**24**	**7**	**31**	**0**	**269**	**266**	**331**	**410**	**741**	**719**	**749**	**8**	**84**	**0.52**	**40**	**24**	**36**	**29**	**129**	**76**	**122**	**11%**	**75**	**0%**	**44%**				**4.66**	**-5.4**	**19**	**58**

Mauer,Joe

Age: 35	Bats: L	Pos: 1B	Health	B	LIMA Plan	B+
Ht: 6' 5"	Wt: 225		PT/Exp	A	Rand Var	-2
			Consist	B	MM	1255

Just as his .300 BA seasons were fading into our rear-view, season-long ct% surge combined with HctX returned him to 2013 levels. Soaring h% helped fuel the 2nd half jets. GB/LD-heavy mix keeps a lid on his HR output—and minus secondary skills, a full repeat seems doubtful. But that BA floor looks entrenched.

Yr Tm	AB	R	HR	RBI	SB	BA	xBA	OBP	SLG	OPS	vL	vR	bb%	ct%	Eye	G	L	F	h%	HctX	PX	xPX	hr/f	Spd	SBO	SB%	#Wk	DOM	DIS	RC/G	RAR	BPV	BPX
13 MIN	445	62	11	47	0	324	288	404	476	880	882	879	12	80	0.69	47	28	25	39	125	115	113	12%	93	1%	0%	21	57%	29%	7.22	30.9	66	165
14 MIN	455	60	4	55	3	277	269	361	371	732	654	776	12	79	0.63	51	27	22	34	96	79	70	5%	89	2%	100%	22	45%	32%	4.78	8.2	31	84
15 MIN	592	69	10	66	2	265	276	338	380	718	720	718	10	81	0.60	56	24	20	31	108	80	80	10%	85	2%	67%	26	38%	27%	4.47	-7.9	36	97
16 MIN	494	68	11	49	2	261	283	363	389	752	610	793	14	81	0.85	52	27	21	30	103	75	76	13%	104	1%	100%	26	38%	35%	4.90	0.5	45	129
17 MIN	525	69	7	71	2	305	285	384	417	801	754	816	11	84	0.80	51	25	24	35	124	70	70	7%	89	2%	67%	27	44%	22%	5.84	6.6	44	133
1st Half	264	35	4	31	1	288	276	361	398	758	568	812	10	84	0.67	47	25	28	33	117	69	71	7%	84	1%	100%	13	31%	31%	5.13	-3.8	37	112
2nd Half	261	34	3	40	1	322	295	406	437	843	904	820	12	85	0.93	56	25	19	37	132	72	68	7%	95	2%	50%	14	57%	14%	6.61	6.7	51	155
18 Proj	**556**	**73**	**9**	**68**	**2**	**289**	**286**	**373**	**408**	**780**	**731**	**798**	**12**	**83**	**0.76**	**52**	**26**	**22**	**34**	**116**	**72**	**75**	**9%**	**92**	**2%**	**71%**				**5.44**	**5.3**	**30**	**92**

Maxwell,Bruce

Age: 27	Bats: L	Pos: CA	Health	A	LIMA Plan	D+
Ht: 6' 1"	Wt: 250		PT/Exp	D	Rand Var	-2
			Consist	F	MM	1015

3-22-.237 in 219 AB at OAK. Rookie scuffled in extended 2H PT, but wasn't overmatched on either side of the ball. Plate skills and HctX hint at moderate BA upside; xPX suggests power potential currently capped by GB%. Handedness and improving defense give him a chance. Legit FB growth could yield... UP: 15 HR, .260 BA.

Yr Tm	AB	R	HR	RBI	SB	BA	xBA	OBP	SLG	OPS	vL	vR	bb%	ct%	Eye	G	L	F	h%	HctX	PX	xPX	hr/f	Spd	SBO	SB%	#Wk	DOM	DIS	RC/G	RAR	BPV	BPX
13																																	
14 aa	85	6	0	1	0	118		185	148	333			8	59	0.20				20		41			102	8%	0%				0.73		-84	-227
15 aa	338	22	1	34	0	197		258	249	507			7	82	0.45				24		41			78	1%	0%				2.01		1	3
16 OAK *	285	29	8	46	1	273	257	335	424	759	450	815	8	76	0.39	52	20	28	33	126	97	117	5%	55	1%	100%	12	33%	58%	5.00	9.2	18	51
17 OAK *	303	29	4	32	0	236	228	318	343	662	485	693	11	74	0.46	47	20	32	31	105	77	122	6%	45	0%	0%	19	26%	63%	3.65	-4.4	-5	-15
1st Half	129	14	1	12	0	259	272	311	364	675	571	749	7	77	0.33	50	28	22	33	127	75	122	0%	76	0%	0%	6	0%	83%	3.90	-0.8	8	24
2nd Half	174	15	3	20	0	218	210	320	328	648	460	679	13	71	0.54	47	18	35	29	98	78	122	7%	41	0%	0%	13	38%	54%	3.46	-3.4	-11	-33
18 Proj	**412**	**38**	**6**	**51**	**1**	**242**	**240**	**311**	**351**	**662**	**443**	**708**	**9**	**76**	**0.43**	**47**	**22**	**32**	**31**	**116**	**74**	**120**	**6%**	**44**	**1%**	**73%**				**3.70**	**-5.3**	**-7**	**-22**

Maybin,Cameron

Age: 31	Bats: R	Pos: CF LF	Health	F	LIMA Plan	C+
Ht: 6' 3"	Wt: 215		PT/Exp	B	Rand Var	+3
			Consist	B	MM	1533

1st half OBP encore didn't last long. Year-long FB spike eventually helped torpedo h% and BA; more DL time (sprained knee) piled onto 2nd half disaster. In the end, SBO on a scoring-challenged club fueled his value. With fewer FBs, history suggests a BA rebound. But SB, weak contact and injuries are the only real constants here.

Yr Tm	AB	R	HR	RBI	SB	BA	xBA	OBP	SLG	OPS	vL	vR	bb%	ct%	Eye	G	L	F	h%	HctX	PX	xPX	hr/f	Spd	SBO	SB%	#Wk	DOM	DIS	RC/G	RAR	BPV	BPX
13 SD *	97	11	4	8	5	176	252	255	304	560	435	481	9	79	0.51	55	19	26	18	77	79	45	9%	95	31%	68%	5	20%	60%	2.33	-5.5	28	70
14 SD *	304	28	2	18	5	226	242	280	319	599	575	646	7	77	0.33	57	17	26	29	97	72	60	2%	140	11%	60%	20	15%	55%	2.88	-8.4	24	65
15 ATL	505	65	10	59	23	267	266	327	370	697	711	692	8	80	0.44	58	22	20	32	75	67	46	12%	100	19%	79%	26	31%	38%	4.28	-1.6	21	57
16 DET *	434	76	6	51	18	282	270	352	392	744	802	801	10	79	0.52	57	22	22	35	80	69	48	7%	142	18%	71%	19	32%	26%	4.86	7.2	37	106
17 2 AL	395	63	10	35	33	228	254	318	365	683	640	701	11	76	0.54	58	14	28	27	84	83	65	12%	117	38%	80%	24	29%	54%	3.94	-18.4	31	94
1st Half	242	49	6	19	24	260	271	358	405	763	721	781	13	78	0.68	59	16	26	31	94	89	60	13%	118	34%	92%	13	38%	38%	5.47	0.8	47	142
2nd Half	153	14	4	16	9	176	225	253	301	554	512	571	9	73	0.37	56	12	32	21	70	73	74	11%	112	47%	60%	11	18%	73%	2.11	-16.8	5	15
18 Proj	**348**	**49**	**7**	**35**	**20**	**235**	**253**	**313**	**352**	**665**	**639**	**675**	**10**	**77**	**0.47**	**57**	**17**	**26**	**29**	**80**	**69**	**58**	**10%**	**119**	**29%**	**74%**				**3.63**	**-9.4**	**23**	**70**

Mazara,Nomar

Age: 23	Bats: L	Pos: RF LF	Health	A	LIMA Plan	B
Ht: 6' 4"	Wt: 215		PT/Exp	A	Rand Var	+2
			Consist	A	MM	2035

20/100 production/value fueled by durability, plate appearances. Prospect pedigree keeps our interest, but little here hints at a near-term breakout. 2nd half FB plunge neutralized HctX bump; squinting is required to notice bb%, PX upticks. Young, healthy, with two MLB seasons under his belt. But future doesn't appear to be now.

Yr Tm	AB	R	HR	RBI	SB	BA	xBA	OBP	SLG	OPS	vL	vR	bb%	ct%	Eye	G	L	F	h%	HctX	PX	xPX	hr/f	Spd	SBO	SB%	#Wk	DOM	DIS	RC/G	RAR	BPV	BPX
13																																	
14 aa	85	9	3	14	0	293		352	484	837			8	73	0.34				37		152			96	0%	0%				6.16		63	170
15 a/a	490	56	11	57	2	272		333	398	731			8	78	0.42				33		85			91	1%	100%				4.67		27	73
16 TEX	516	59	20	64	0	266	254	320	419	739	548	791	7	78	0.35	49	21	30	30	91	84	77	16%	119	1%	0%	26	38%	35%	4.53	-2.6	32	91
17 TEX	554	64	20	101	2	253	256	323	422	745	603	786	9	77	0.43	47	19	34	29	102	99	87	14%	83	3%	50%	27	33%	19%	4.57	-5.8	32	97
1st Half	279	34	11	51	2	258	258	330	444	775	601	814	9	77	0.42	44	19	37	30	93	106	79	14%	101	4%	67%	13	31%	8%	4.91	-1.2	43	130
2nd Half	275	30	9	50	0	247	249	316	400	716	604	754	9	77	0.44	49	20	31	29	110	92	96	14%	71	1%	0%	14	36%	29%	4.23	-6.8	24	73
18 Proj	**546**	**62**	**21**	**85**	**1**	**259**	**256**	**322**	**424**	**747**	**586**	**792**	**8**	**78**	**0.40**	**47**	**20**	**33**	**30**	**98**	**92**	**84**	**15%**	**95**	**2%**	**39%**				**4.62**	**-1.2**	**16**	**49**

JOCK THOMPSON

McCann,Brian

Age: 34	Bats: L	Pos: CA	Health B	LIMA Plan D+	
Ht: 6' 3"	Wt: 225		PT/Exp B	Rand Var +1	
			Consist A	MM 2233	

Early GB spike, 2nd half swoon, first DL stint in 3 years all hinted at accelerating decline. Sept rebound (5 HR, 47% FB%, .884 OPS) says he's not finished yet. Balky knee a likely 2nd half factor, but age is like that. Stable hr/f and FB% are still pluses; ct% spike looks inconsequential. Health is now the key to his projection.

Yr Tm	AB	R	HR	RBI	SB	BA	xBA	OBP	SLG	OPS	vL	vR	bb%	ct%	Eye	G	L	F	h%	HctX	PX	xPX	hr/f	Spd	SBO	SB%	#Wk	DOM	DIS	RC/G	RAR	BPV	BPX	R$
13 ATL	356	43	20	57	0	256	273	336	461	796	616	869	10	81	0.59	35	22	42	26	119	125	150	16%	73	1%	0%	21	67%	29%	5.13	14.7	69	173	$11
14 NYY	495	57	23	75	0	232	266	286	406	692	850	633	6	84	0.42	33	22	45	23	113	106	127	12%	67	0%	0%	26	58%	23%	3.76	6.5	57	154	$11
15 NYY	465	68	26	94	0	232	248	320	437	756	753	757	10	79	0.54	36	17	47	24	110	120	131	15%	65	0%	0%	27	52%	30%	4.49	10.5	54	146	$12
16 NYY	429	56	20	58	1	242	242	335	413	748	662	770	11	77	0.55	34	21	44	27	111	97	120	14%	71	1%	100%	27	44%	41%	4.56	8.8	30	86	$8
17 HOU	349	47	18	62	1	241	261	323	436	759	737	767	10	83	0.66	41	17	41	24	99	97	98	15%	77	1%	100%	26	50%	12%	4.63	5.1	55	167	$7
1st Half	196	27	10	42	1	265	256	342	459	801	979	744	10	83	0.65	46	15	39	28	107	99	115	16%	62	2%	100%	13	31%	23%	5.44	7.6	51	155	$11
2nd Half	153	20	8	20	0	209	263	299	405	704	497	801	9	84	0.67	35	20	45	20	89	93	76	14%	105	0%	0%	13	69%	0%	3.71	-1.8	64	194	$2
18 Proj	**379**	**51**	**19**	**61**	**1**	**241**	**254**	**324**	**430**	**754**	**689**	**777**	**10**	**81**	**0.57**	**37**	**19**	**44**	**25**	**104**	**96**	**109**	**14%**	**77**	**1%**	**92%**				**4.55**	**4.6**	**36**	**110**	**$8**

McCann,James

Age: 28	Bats: R	Pos: CA	Health B	LIMA Plan D+	
Ht: 6' 2"	Wt: 210		PT/Exp C	Rand Var 0	
			Consist C	MM 2223	

Turned BA around and finished with career-high HR—but approach gives us whiplash. Awful 1st half luck kept lid on soaring HctX and LD rebound until he stopped swinging for the fences. 2nd half trade of FB, HR for more ct%, LD seemed to help, as h% corrected. Volatility, poor splits vR limit his upside. H2Hers should stay away.

Yr Tm	AB	R	HR	RBI	SB	BA	xBA	OBP	SLG	OPS	vL	vR	bb%	ct%	Eye	G	L	F	h%	HctX	PX	xPX	hr/f	Spd	SBO	SB%	#Wk	DOM	DIS	RC/G	RAR	BPV	BPX	R$
13 aa	441	40	6	43	2	246		285	355	639			5	79	0.26				30		84			86	6%	42%				3.32		23	58	$5
14 DET *	429	40	6	42	8	256	323	289	366	655	333	833	4	77	0.20	20	60	20	32	33	95	10	0%	78	11%	78%	3	33%	33%	3.64	4.0	18	49	$9
15 DET	401	32	7	41	0	264	254	297	387	683	916	609	4	78	0.18	50	23	27	33	90	82	63	8%	107	1%	0%	27	33%	44%	3.87	1.6	18	49	$6
16 DET *	366	33	12	50	0	212	204	267	341	607	848	511	7	68	0.23	41	18	41	28	94	83	112	13%	99	1%	0%	25	20%	56%	2.90	-10.9	-14	-40	$1
17 DET	352	39	13	49	1	253	260	318	415	733	928	650	7	75	0.29	38	28	34	30	116	93	101	14%	103	1%	100%	25	32%	28%	4.32	1.9	20	61	$6
1st Half	141	17	8	21	0	199	259	280	404	684	965	544	8	71	0.32	34	27	39	22	121	120	129	20%	87	0%	0%	12	33%	25%	3.42	-3.0	25	76	$0
2nd Half	211	22	5	28	1	289	263	345	422	767	897	717	6	77	0.27	40	29	31	35	111	76	84	10%	113	2%	100%	13	31%	31%	5.03	5.5	17	52	$10
18 Proj	**394**	**39**	**13**	**51**	**1**	**245**	**245**	**299**	**394**	**693**	**900**	**602**	**6**	**74**	**0.25**	**41**	**24**	**35**	**30**	**104**	**88**	**100**	**13%**	**101**	**2%**	**61%**				**3.86**	**-3.3**	**-4**	**-12**	**$7**

McCutchen,Andrew

Age: 31	Bats: R	Pos: CF	Health A	LIMA Plan B+	
Ht: 5' 10"	Wt: 195		PT/Exp A	Rand Var 0	
			Consist D	MM 3245	

Built nicely off 2016 finish. Wire-to-wire uptick was fueled by better health and year-long onslaught vL. BA rebound coincided with improved ct%, hinting that nagging 2016 thumb injury was an issue. HR remained consistent all season and power is still above average. No longer peak, but new benchmark still offers value.

Yr Tm	AB	R	HR	RBI	SB	BA	xBA	OBP	SLG	OPS	vL	vR	bb%	ct%	Eye	G	L	F	h%	HctX	PX	xPX	hr/f	Spd	SBO	SB%	#Wk	DOM	DIS	RC/G	RAR	BPV	BPX	R$
13 PIT	583	97	21	84	27	317	289	404	508	911	1130	864	12	83	0.77	41	24	35	36	138	125	123	12%	127	19%	73%	26	69%	12%	7.44	53.3	94	235	$40
14 PIT	548	89	25	83	18	314	284	410	542	952	912	962	13	79	0.73	40	19	41	36	139	159	155	14%	125	11%	86%	26	58%	12%	8.27	65.9	109	295	$36
15 PIT	566	91	23	96	11	292	268	401	488	889	918	881	14	77	0.74	38	24	38	35	131	132	158	14%	104	8%	69%	27	59%	30%	6.88	41.0	74	200	$28
16 PIT	598	81	24	79	6	256	249	336	430	766	741	772	10	76	0.48	36	22	42	30	111	104	134	13%	105	8%	46%	27	37%	30%	4.73	1.5	41	117	$16
17 PIT	570	94	28	88	11	279	276	363	486	849	1131	769	11	80	0.63	41	22	37	31	114	113	109	16%	89	9%	69%	27	56%	15%	6.13	17.4	60	182	$24
1st Half	287	47	14	47	6	282	274	372	495	866	1218	773	12	80	0.71	39	21	39	31	115	113	120	15%	104	9%	75%	13	69%	8%	6.48	12.9	70	212	$24
2nd Half	283	47	14	41	5	276	276	354	477	831	1052	764	10	79	0.55	42	23	35	31	112	112	98	18%	74	10%	63%	14	43%	21%	5.77	7.1	50	152	$23
18 Proj	**559**	**88**	**27**	**83**	**12**	**278**	**271**	**364**	**484**	**848**	**1004**	**807**	**11**	**78**	**0.59**	**39**	**22**	**38**	**31**	**118**	**114**	**125**	**16%**	**96**	**10%**	**67%**				**6.06**	**24.9**	**56**	**169**	**$26**

McMahon,Ryan

Age: 23	Bats: L	Pos: 1B	Health A	LIMA Plan C	
Ht: 6' 2"	Wt: 185		PT/Exp D	Rand Var -3	
			Consist F	MM 4243	

0-1-.158 in 19 AB at COL. Athletic prospect rewarded for outstanding effort with brief MLB taste. Huge ct% gains fueled .355 BA; led AA/AAA in hits as power held up nicely. Versatility now includes 2B, could accelerate his ascent. If improved bat-to-ball is real, extended MLB opportunity is within reach.

Yr Tm	AB	R	HR	RBI	SB	BA	xBA	OBP	SLG	OPS	vL	vR	bb%	ct%	Eye	G	L	F	h%	HctX	PX	xPX	hr/f	Spd	SBO	SB%	#Wk	DOM	DIS	RC/G	RAR	BPV	BPX	R$
13																																		
14																																		
15																																		
16 aa	466	42	11	64	9	247		316	403	719			9	67	0.30				35		114			99	13%	60%				4.18		8	23	$9
17 COL *	489	59	17	69	8	333	291	380	534	914	200	635	7	80	0.38	86	0	14	39	70	117	81	0%	101	8%	72%	7	14%	71%	7.69	22.9	60	182	$25
1st Half	306	39	12	47	8	344	294	389	570	958			7	80	0.37				40		134			103	10%	100%				8.84		75	227	$33
2nd Half	183	20	5	22	0	315	248	365	474	839	200	635	7	80	0.39	86	0	14	37	69	89	81	0%	117	6%	0%	7	14%	71%	6.00	1.8	42	127	$11
18 Proj	**258**	**27**	**10**	**35**	**4**	**288**	**271**	**344**	**497**	**841**	**841**	**841**	**8**	**75**	**0.34**	**40**	**24**	**36**	**35**		**125**		**15%**	**116**	**10%**	**57%**				**5.94**	**6.1**	**40**	**122**	**$10**

Meadows,Austin

Age: 23	Bats: L	Pos: OF	Health D	LIMA Plan D+	
Ht: 6' 3"	Wt: 200		PT/Exp F	Rand Var 0	
			Consist F	MM 2441	

Highly-regarded PIT prospect now an injury magnet as 2 years of downtime have stalled development. Repeat of 2016 hamstring, oblique issues limited him to just 318 AB (including A-ball). Hit tool seen at lower levels has yet to emerge in Triple-A; power growth has stalled. Off the fast track; health is now the immediate objective.

Yr Tm	AB	R	HR	RBI	SB	BA	xBA	OBP	SLG	OPS	vL	vR	bb%	ct%	Eye	G	L	F	h%	HctX	PX	xPX	hr/f	Spd	SBO	SB%	#Wk	DOM	DIS	RC/G	RAR	BPV	BPX	R$
13																																		
14																																		
15 aa	25	4	0	1	1	340		381	597	979			6	79	0.33				43		150			145	14%	100%				9.08		96	259	-$1
16 a/a	293	44	10	43	15	261		326	514	840			9	77	0.42				31		150			130	33%	74%				5.66		87	249	$12
17 aaa	284	43	3	33	10	236		291	336	627			7	82	0.43				28		66			89	20%	76%				3.28		23	70	$5
1st Half	254	39	3	32	9	234		293	335	628			8	81	0.44				28		65			97	18%	81%				3.33		22	67	$7
2nd Half	30	5	0	1	1	253		275	349	624			3	90	0.30				28		68			113	35%	46%				2.86		55	167	-$9
18 Proj	**160**	**24**	**3**	**22**	**5**	**243**	**268**	**306**	**404**	**710**	**710**	**710**	**8**	**80**	**0.44**	**44**	**22**	**34**	**29**		**94**		**8%**	**126**	**18%**	**72%**				**4.12**	**#N/A**	**51**	**155**	**$5**

Mejia,Francisco

Age: 22	Bats: B	Pos: CA	Health A	LIMA Plan D+	
Ht: 5' 10"	Wt: 180		PT/Exp F	Rand Var 0	
			Consist F	MM 1341	

0-1-.154 in 13 AB at CLE. Floundered during final two months of Double-A jump. But precocious prospect with elite hard contact skills (and 50-game hit streak in 2016) still posted a .297/.346/.490 line in 347 AB. Could cannon arm compensate for raw receiver skills at the MLB level? Even if not, he's worth the wait.

Yr Tm	AB	R	HR	RBI	SB	BA	xBA	OBP	SLG	OPS	vL	vR	bb%	ct%	Eye	G	L	F	h%	HctX	PX	xPX	hr/f	Spd	SBO	SB%	#Wk	DOM	DIS	RC/G	RAR	BPV	BPX	R$
13																																		
14																																		
15																																		
16																																		
17 CLE *	360	44	12	44	6	278	320	319	447	766	333	393	6	85	0.40	50	30	20	30	138	91	49	0%	92	9%	73%	4	0%	50%	5.01	8.9	53	161	$11
1st Half	212	29	8	28	4	325	291	366	526	892			6	84	0.42				36		111			103	11%	66%				7.12		72	218	$17
2nd Half	148	15	4	17	2	212	303	252	334	586	333	393	5	86	0.37	50	30	20	22	139	63	49	0%	91	6%	100%	4	0%	50%	2.77	-6.1	32	97	$2
18 Proj	**232**	**27**	**7**	**28**	**4**	**256**	**270**	**296**	**402**	**698**	**698**	**698**	**5**	**85**	**0.39**	**45**	**20**	**35**	**27**		**79**		**10%**	**96**	**8%**	**81%**				**4.09**	**-0.3**	**37**	**113**	**$6**

Mercer,Jordy

Age: 31	Bats: R	Pos: SS	Health A	LIMA Plan C+	
Ht: 6' 3"	Wt: 210		PT/Exp B	Rand Var 0	
			Consist B	MM 1135	

Near-repeat of 2016 finish might have been better. Season-long HctX uptick soared in 2nd half, but unable to move that BA. PX/xPX, hr/f jumped nicely despite firmly entrenched GB%. Decent plate skills and health suggest a swing-loft project. Age and history say that continued mediocrity will prevail. It's at least food for thought.

Yr Tm	AB	R	HR	RBI	SB	BA	xBA	OBP	SLG	OPS	vL	vR	bb%	ct%	Eye	G	L	F	h%	HctX	PX	xPX	hr/f	Spd	SBO	SB%	#Wk	DOM	DIS	RC/G	RAR	BPV	BPX	R$
13 PIT *	429	41	9	41	5	282	269	330	418	748	1152	654	7	81	0.37	47	23	30	33	113	97	117	10%	111	7%	62%	23	52%	26%	4.83	16.1	50	125	$12
14 PIT	506	56	12	55	4	255	264	305	387	693	803	658	6	82	0.39	48	20	32	29	90	94	89	9%	106	4%	80%	27	37%	33%	4.03	10.9	51	138	$11
15 PIT *	419	36	4	36	3	240	238	288	317	605	738	580	6	81	0.35	49	21	31	29	89	58	87	3%	86	5%	60%	23	26%	52%	3.03	-9.2	11	30	$3
16 PIT	519	66	11	59	1	256	257	328	374	701	829	669	9	84	0.61	49	20	32	29	86	68	60	8%	116	1%	50%	26	31%	15%	4.12	-7.6	45	129	$9
17 PIT	502	52	14	58	0	255	268	326	406	733	723	735	9	82	0.58	48	21	31	28	104	82	87	11%	114	3%	0%	25	48%	20%	4.36	-2.3	50	152	$7
1st Half	271	30	7	29	0	266	265	345	406	751	511	820	11	82	0.69	49	21	30	30	96	74	79	11%	125	5%	0%	13	54%	31%	4.59	0.1	50	152	$8
2nd Half	231	22	7	29	0	242	272	303	407	710	936	630	7	83	0.45	48	20	32	27	113	90	95	11%	99	0%	0%	12	42%	8%	4.07	-3.5	49	148	$6
18 Proj	**515**	**54**	**12**	**57**	**1**	**253**	**263**	**316**	**384**	**701**	**803**	**671**	**8**	**83**	**0.50**	**48**	**20**	**31**	**29**	**98**	**73**	**83**	**9%**	**107**	**3%**	**36%**				**4.04**	**-6.5**	**24**	**73**	**$10**

OCK THOMPSON

Merrifield,Whit

Age: 29 Bats: R Pos: 2B | Ht: 6' 0" Wt: 195

Health A | PT/Exp B | Consist C | LIMA Plan B | Rand Var -1 | MM 2535

19-78-.288 with 34 SB in 587 AB at KC. Seized job in mid-May, surged to otherworldly in 2nd half. Solid bat-to-ball skills growth suggests staying power, speed adds to BA floor. FB% bump fueled HR surge that looks less reliable. Plus running game looks peakish, but that's a quibble. Age, health complete a nice package.

Yr	Tm	AB	R	HR	RBI	SB	BA	xBA	OBP	SLG	OPS	vL	vR	bb%	ct%	Eye	G	L	F	h%	HctX	PX	xPX	hr/f	Spd	SBO	SB%	#Wk	DOM	DIS	RC/G	RAR	BPV	BPX
13	aa	322	24	2	33	13	240		278	345	624			5	81	0.27				29		76			115	30%	62%				3.05		31	78
14	a/a	483	57	6	36	12	269		309	391	700			5	82	0.31				32		96			103	22%	47%				3.86		47	127
15	aaa	544	63	4	29	24	226		266	310	576			5	86	0.39				26		57			122	30%	70%				2.67		39	105
16	KC *	585	76	7	49	22	252	257	293	364	657	891	657	5	77	0.25	45	26	30	32	111	81	87	3%	124	21%	80%	17	24%	47%	3.68	-18.1	22	63
17	KC *	621	84	21	85	35	291	274	323	469	792	800	780	4	85	0.32	38	22	40	31	105	94	111	9%	130	30%	79%	25	44%	12%	5.43	14.1	65	197
1st Half		270	31	8	37	9	287	272	321	463	785	778	752	5	86	0.35	39	20	41	31	115	92	122	7%	128	17%	79%	11	45%	18%	5.33	3.9	66	200
2nd Half		351	53	13	48	26	293	274	329	473	802	817	798	4	85	0.30	37	23	40	32	98	95	103	11%	125	39%	79%	14	43%	7%	5.50	6.8	63	191
18	**Proj**	**599**	**77**	**15**	**64**	**29**	**274**	**264**	**311**	**424**	**734**	**812**	**712**	**5**	**83**	**0.30**	**39**	**22**	**38**	**31**	**107**	**84**	**101**	**8%**	**129**	**27%**	**76%**				**4.56**	**-4.1**	**47**	**142**

Mesoraco,Devin

Age: 30 Bats: R Pos: CA | Ht: 6' 1" Wt: 229

Health F | PT/Exp F | Consist D | LIMA Plan D | Rand Var +1 | MM 1011

6-14-.213 in 141 AB at CIN. Teased briefly before another lost season. After scuffling in April AA rehab, MLB power and patience were looking vintage (.870 OPS through 92 MLB AB) by late June. But back/knee injuries and finally a broken foot limited him to just 50 AB the rest of the way. Yep, health grade is still rock-solid.

Yr	Tm	AB	R	HR	RBI	SB	BA	xBA	OBP	SLG	OPS	vL	vR	bb%	ct%	Eye	G	L	F	h%	HctX	PX	xPX	hr/f	Spd	SBO	SB%	#Wk	DOM	DIS	RC/G	RAR	BPV	BPX
13	CIN	323	31	9	42	0	238	246	287	362	649	874	576	7	81	0.39	45	21	34	27	88	83	78	10%	58	3%	0%	27	41%	37%	3.43	-2.5	24	60
14	CIN	384	54	25	80	1	273	287	359	534	893	925	883	9	73	0.40	34	23	43	31	123	192	165	20%	59	4%	25%	24	54%	25%	6.25	30.9	84	227
15	CIN	45	2	0	2	1	178	192	275	244	519	481	536	10	80	0.56	42	14	44	22	67	40	67	0%	102	9%	100%	7	43%	43%	2.07	-2.4	4	11
16	CIN	50	2	0	1	0	140	214	218	160	378	507	320	9	80	0.50	48	23	30	18	49	17	7	0%	96	9%	0%	4	25%	50%	0.93	-5.9	-16	-46
17	CIN *	195	21	8	20	1	192	227	286	352	638	645	748	11	71	0.45	41	19	39	23	83	93	84	15%	88	2%	100%	16	31%	50%	3.20	-5.2	10	30
1st Half		154	19	7	17	1	214	243	299	402	701	708	880	11	73	0.45	39	20	41	25	93	108	94	19%	92	3%	100%	10	40%	30%	3.94	-0.8	29	88
2nd Half		41	3	1	3	0	119	158	255	183	438	466	304	15	66	0.53	48	16	36	15	53	36	54	0%	75	0%	0%	6	17%	83%	1.35	-3.9	-53	-161
18	**Proj**	**223**	**26**	**5**	**32**	**1**	**239**	**233**	**318**	**354**	**672**	**716**	**651**	**9**	**76**	**0.41**	**44**	**20**	**36**	**29**	**74**	**71**	**69**	**8%**	**74**	**3%**	**40%**				**3.58**	**-3.7**	**-4**	**-11**

Miller,Brad

Age: 28 Bats: L Pos: 2B | Ht: 6' 2" Wt: 215

Health B | PT/Exp B | Consist B | LIMA Plan C+ | Rand Var +2 | MM 2215

We anticipated some HR regression, but not this train-wreck. Blame a 1st half groin injury, in part. More patient approach yielded an OBP bump—but also a ct% drop—as BA went from poor to horrendous. 2nd half power uptick reflects a more expected hr/f pullback, and offers hope for a mild bounce.

Yr	Tm	AB	R	HR	RBI	SB	BA	xBA	OBP	SLG	OPS	vL	vR	bb%	ct%	Eye	G	L	F	h%	HctX	PX	xPX	hr/f	Spd	SBO	SB%	#Wk	DOM	DIS	RC/G	RAR	BPV	BPX
13	SEA *	563	82	17	77	10	269	264	329	424	753	674	767	8	81	0.46	46	22	32	31	96	97	79	10%	130	11%	56%	15	53%	20%	4.70	16.0	58	145
14	SEA	367	47	10	36	4	221	236	288	365	653	542	692	8	74	0.36	42	19	39	27	98	105	105	10%	117	7%	67%	27	37%	52%	3.40	0.1	34	92
15	SEA	438	44	11	46	13	258	254	329	402	730	513	803	9	77	0.47	48	20	31	31	106	97	97	10%	108	14%	76%	27	22%	41%	4.57	3.7	39	105
16	TAM	548	73	30	81	6	243	268	304	482	786	682	812	8	73	0.32	45	19	37	28	104	147	116	20%	99	9%	60%	26	62%	19%	4.81	1.3	56	160
17	TAM	338	43	9	40	5	201	214	327	337	664	679	659	15	67	0.57	47	17	36	27	105	88	94	11%	120	8%	63%	22	32%	45%	3.48	-12.2	9	27
1st Half		139	21	2	14	4	194	203	343	302	645	695	618	19	66	0.68	51	16	33	28	107	65	77	7%	165	10%	80%	9	22%	56%	3.38	-6.4	6	18
2nd Half		199	22	7	26	1	206	217	315	362	677	659	681	13	68	0.49	45	17	38	26	103	103	106	13%	81	5%	33%	13	38%	38%	3.52	-8.2	9	27
18	**Proj**	**432**	**54**	**14**	**53**	**6**	**241**	**236**	**331**	**402**	**733**	**672**	**752**	**12**	**71**	**0.47**	**47**	**18**	**35**	**31**	**104**	**98**	**100**	**13%**	**115**	**8%**	**61%**				**4.40**	**-5.2**	**16**	**49**

Molina,Yadier

Age: 35 Bats: R Pos: CA | Ht: 5' 11" Wt: 205

Health B | PT/Exp B | Consist C | LIMA Plan B | Rand Var 0 | MM 1145

Juiced-ball theorists point to this. But he swapped a touch of ct% and bb% for a more aggressive approach and a FB hike. And the 5-yr outlier HR, hr/f don't top his 2012 marks. HctX says he's a hitter regardless of the adjustment du jour. HR (and SB) repeat doubtful, but age, health still look like the only risks to his value.

Yr	Tm	AB	R	HR	RBI	SB	BA	xBA	OBP	SLG	OPS	vL	vR	bb%	ct%	Eye	G	L	F	h%	HctX	PX	xPX	hr/f	Spd	SBO	SB%	#Wk	DOM	DIS	RC/G	RAR	BPV	BPX
13	STL	505	68	12	80	3	319	301	359	477	836	883	823	6	89	0.55	42	24	34	34	128	109	111	8%	76	4%	60%	26	65%	23%	6.32	35.5	80	200
14	STL	404	40	7	38	1	282	271	333	386	719	795	695	6	86	0.51	51	23	27	31	115	75	95	7%	73	2%	50%	20	45%	25%	4.48	11.6	42	114
15	STL	488	34	4	61	3	270	254	310	350	660	577	689	6	88	0.54	48	20	32	30	99	54	79	3%	77	3%	75%	25	36%	28%	3.87	0.6	32	86
16	STL	534	56	8	58	3	307	282	360	427	787	776	790	7	88	0.62	48	22	30	34	111	75	88	6%	77	3%	60%	27	48%	26%	5.52	16.2	51	146
17	STL	501	60	18	82	9	273	274	312	439	751	850	724	5	85	0.38	42	20	37	29	126	88	118	11%	75	11%	69%	26	42%	23%	4.74	9.9	46	139
1st Half		253	29	9	35	5	273	266	308	419	727	855	694	5	85	0.34	43	21	36	29	118	76	101	11%	70	11%	71%	13	38%	23%	4.48	2.8	33	100
2nd Half		248	31	9	47	4	274	281	316	460	776	843	755	6	85	0.42	42	20	38	29	133	100	136	11%	81	11%	67%	13	46%	23%	5.01	6.5	60	182
18	**Proj**	**461**	**50**	**11**	**66**	**5**	**278**	**275**	**322**	**415**	**736**	**766**	**727**	**6**	**87**	**0.48**	**45**	**21**	**34**	**30**	**118**	**76**	**105**	**8%**	**75**	**7%**	**67%**				**4.65**	**6.8**	**41**	**124**

Moncada,Yoan

Age: 23 Bats: B Pos: 2B | Ht: 6' 2" Wt: 205

Health A | PT/Exp F | Consist B | LIMA Plan B | Rand Var -2 | MM 3505

8-22-.231 and 3 SB in 199 AB at CHW. Elite rookie struggled early in everyday PT after July call-up. Finished nicely (.806 OPS, 5 HR) in 95 Sept AB. Running game fell off from 94 SB over previous two seasons; contact needs work. But speed, PX, bb% point to huge future. If growth accelerates... UP: 25 HR / 25 SB.

Yr	Tm	AB	R	HR	RBI	SB	BA	xBA	OBP	SLG	OPS	vL	vR	bb%	ct%	Eye	G	L	F	h%	HctX	PX	xPX	hr/f	Spd	SBO	SB%	#Wk	DOM	DIS	RC/G	RAR	BPV	BPX
13	for	165	31	2	13	7	254		320	386	707			9	81	0.50				31		84			164	31%	52%				3.77	-0.9	58	145
14																																		
15																																		
16	BOS *	196	33	9	24	7	259	273	339	457	796	500	517	11	60	0.30	71	29	0	39	70	144	11	0%	129	21%	64%	3	0%	67%	5.11	1.8	18	51
17	CHW *	508	78	18	52	17	246	213	339	405	744	641	804	12	63	0.38	46	19	35	36	91	105	112	18%	142	18%	61%	11	36%	36%	4.46	-6.0	4	12
1st Half		267	42	9	25	13	255	212	351	403	753			13	64	0.41				37		96			139	20%	75%				4.84		2	6
2nd Half		241	36	10	27	4	236	214	327	407	733	641	804	12	61	0.35	46	19	35	34	89	116	112	18%	132	15%	37%	11	36%	36%	4.07	-7.6	3	9
18	**Proj**	**528**	**86**	**20**	**56**	**18**	**251**	**225**	**343**	**428**	**772**	**660**	**827**	**11**	**64**	**0.36**	**46**	**19**	**35**	**35**	**80**	**114**	**101**	**16%**	**157**	**20%**	**58%**				**4.63**	**-2.7**	**12**	**38**

Mondesi,Raul

Age: 22 Bats: B Pos: 2B | Ht: 6' 1" Wt: 185

Health A | PT/Exp D | Consist B | LIMA Plan C | Rand Var -2 | MM 3503

1-3-.170 and 5 SB in 53 AB at KC. Toolsy prospect struggled with 58% MLB ct% while flashing plus running game. Triple-A pitchers didn't slow him down, as suggested by .879 OPS, power spike and 73% ct%. But MLBers still exploit his impatient, hyper-aggressive approach. With less twitchiness: UP 15 HR / 30 SB.

Yr	Tm	AB	R	HR	RBI	SB	BA	xBA	OBP	SLG	OPS	vL	vR	bb%	ct%	Eye	G	L	F	h%	HctX	PX	xPX	hr/f	Spd	SBO	SB%	#Wk	DOM	DIS	RC/G	RAR	BPV	BPX
13																																		
14																																		
15	aa	304	30	5	27	16	230		264	344	608			4	71	0.15				31		80			128	35%	71%				2.94		-4	-11
16	KC *	307	41	7	35	28	232	208	275	375	651	434	546	6	68	0.19	49	12	39	32	86	89	137	7%	170	45%	93%	10	20%	80%	3.76	-5.0	7	20
17	KC *	374	47	11	46	22	270	259	302	453	755	462	459	4	70	0.16	34	34	31	36	73	114	120	11%	144	35%	81%	10	10%	70%	4.80	1.8	25	76
1st Half		257	32	6	28	18	263	234	298	428	726	400	299	5	72	0.17	41	18	41	35	73	105	144	11%	133	41%	81%	4	0%	75%	4.47	-0.8	22	67
2nd Half		117	15	4	17	4	283	329	311	505	817	667	1125	4	66	0.12	14	86	0	39	77	136	45	0%	156	21%	79%	6	17%	67%	5.57	3.3	30	91
18	**Proj**	**333**	**42**	**9**	**40**	**17**	**244**	**221**	**284**	**411**	**695**	**745**	**678**	**5**	**68**	**0.16**	**44**	**16**	**40**	**33**	**78**	**101**	**141**	**9%**	**168**	**31%**	**83%**				**3.95**	**-8.6**	**13**	**40**

Morales,Kendrys

Age: 35 Bats: B Pos: DH | Ht: 6' 1" Wt: 225

Health A | PT/Exp A | Consist B | LIMA Plan B | Rand Var 0 | MM 3035

Another fine HR/RBI season even as problematic FB% and PX/xPX ticked south. But hr/f, FB distance growth and more frequent Ks suggest that, like many MLB hitters, he's swinging for the fences more often these days. Tough to bet against more HR in light of HctX history. But .216 BA (430 AB) vR points to growing risk.

Yr	Tm	AB	R	HR	RBI	SB	BA	xBA	OBP	SLG	OPS	vL	vR	bb%	ct%	Eye	G	L	F	h%	HctX	PX	xPX	hr/f	Spd	SBO	SB%	#Wk	DOM	DIS	RC/G	RAR	BPV	BPX
13	SEA	602	64	23	80	0	277	259	336	449	785	794	780	7	81	0.43	49	19	33	31	123	115	134	14%	70	0%	0%	27	56%	30%	5.25	12.7	54	135
14	2 AL	367	28	8	42	0	218	238	274	338	612	661	584	7	81	0.40	49	18	33	25	106	89	102	8%	64	0%	0%	17	41%	41%	2.99	-11.8	32	86
15	KC	569	81	22	106	0	290	282	362	485	847	771	901	9	82	0.56	45	20	35	32	126	126	134	13%	67	0%	0%	27	63%	11%	6.20	11.8	69	186
16	KC	558	65	30	93	0	263	262	327	468	795	930	730	8	78	0.40	44	20	36	29	131	117	140	19%	42	0%	0%	27	37%	26%	5.21	-4.6	38	109
17	TOR	557	67	28	85	0	250	253	308	445	753	1000	680	7	76	0.33	48	18	33	28	117	110	117	20%	57	0%	0%	26	42%	35%	4.59	-4.5	26	79
1st Half		286	38	15	44	0	259	264	306	465	771	898	731	6	76	0.26	50	19	31	29	123	117	122	22%	62	0%	0%	13	46%	31%	4.84	-0.2	31	94
2nd Half		271	29	13	41	0	240	241	309	424	733	1117	628	8	76	0.39	46	18	36	27	111	103	111	17%	58	0%	0%	13	38%	38%	4.33	-4.4	24	73
18	**Proj**	**550**	**65**	**24**	**87**	**0**	**252**	**255**	**314**	**436**	**750**	**884**	**695**	**8**	**78**	**0.38**	**47**	**19**	**34**	**28**	**121**	**103**	**125**	**17%**	**56**	**0%**	**0%**				**4.60**	**-14.5**	**19**	**57**

JOCK THOMPSON

Moran,Colin

Age: 25 Bats: L Pos: 1B
Ht: 6' 4" Wt: 204

Health	B	LIMA Plan	D
PT/Exp	D	Rand Var	+3
Consist	D	MM	2021

1-3-.364 in 11 AB at HOU. Triple-A rebound featured .916 OPS, FB bump and HR spike. Foul off his face after HOU promotion shelved him from late July until final week. Ex-2013 1st-rounder lauded for hit tool; handedness, corner infield versatility are pluses. With more FB gains and opportunity... UP: .275 BA, 20 HR.

Yr Tm	AB	R	HR	RBI	SB	BA	xBA	OBP	SLG	OPS	vL	vR	bb%	ct%	Eye	G	L	F	h%	HctX	PX	xPX	hr/f	Spd	SBO	SB%	#Wk	DOM	DIS	RC/G	RAR	BPV	BPX	R$
13																																		
14 aa	112	9	2	17	0	267		311	358	669			6	77	0.27				34		75			84	4%	0%				3.71		5	14	$1
15 aa	366	36	8	52	1	268		328	399	728			8	75	0.36				34		97			88	1%	100%				4.58		23	62	$8
16 HOU *	482	41	8	57	2	218	263	275	306	581	0	374	7	68	0.24	47	40	13	31	73	65	76	0%	92	4%	51%	4	25%	75%	2.71	-31.0	-33	-94	$1
17 HOU *	313	37	13	43	0	244	259	291	415	706	1400	1095	6	77	0.29	50	20	30	28	94	93	74	33%	113	5%	0%	3	67%	33%	3.86	-9.3	32	97	$4
1st Half	260	28	11	38	0	234	249	277	406	683			6	76	0.25				27		96			100	4%	0%				3.58		25	76	$6
2nd Half	53	10	2	6	0	298	275	356	460	816	1400	1095	8	84	0.55	50	20	30	33	102	78	74	33%	142	7%	0%	3	67%	33%	5.42	0.5	58	176	-$4
18 Proj	**195**	**24**	**8**	**25**	**0**	**259**	**250**	**313**	**434**	**747**	**747**	**747**	**7**	**76**	**0.32**	**38**	**22**	**40**	**30**		**98**		**13%**	**118**	**4%**	**14%**				**4.50**	**-3.5**	**18**	**54**	**$3**

Moreland,Mitch

Age: 32 Bats: L Pos: 1B
Ht: 6' 2" Wt: 230

Health	C	LIMA Plan	B
PT/Exp	B	Rand Var	+2
Consist	C	MM	3035

Produced near-vintage power and authoritative contact in 1st half, and Fenway helped his BA (.267 vs .226 on the road) all year. But playing through broken toe, subsequent 2nd half knee injury combined with already glacial speed eventually took a toll. Consistent production counts for something, but he's still a lower-tier option.

Yr Tm	AB	R	HR	RBI	SB	BA	xBA	OBP	SLG	OPS	vL	vR	bb%	ct%	Eye	G	L	F	h%	HctX	PX	xPX	hr/f	Spd	SBO	SB%	#Wk	DOM	DIS	RC/G	RAR	BPV	BPX	R$
13 TEX	462	60	23	60	0	232	255	299	437	736	701	752	9	75	0.38	43	17	39	26	115	143	138	17%	73	0%	0%	26	50%	27%	4.35	-3.5	54	135	$9
14 TEX	167	18	2	23	0	246	235	297	347	644	374	692	7	74	0.28	45	22	33	32	136	86	143	5%	74	0%	0%	10	30%	60%	3.48	-3.2	3	8	$1
15 TEX	471	51	23	85	1	278	265	330	482	812	681	876	6	76	0.29	46	20	35	32	120	135	131	18%	61	1%	100%	26	38%	38%	5.53	7.9	46	124	$17
16 TEX	460	49	22	60	1	233	252	298	422	720	799	700	7	74	0.30	42	21	37	27	110	116	111	17%	61	1%	100%	26	38%	31%	4.03	-11.4	24	69	$7
17 BOS	508	73	22	79	0	246	264	326	443	769	684	784	10	76	0.48	43	20	36	28	120	118	119	15%	59	1%	0%	26	35%	42%	4.79	-8.8	39	118	$10
1st Half	265	39	12	41	0	264	261	350	468	818	653	848	11	73	0.44	42	22	36	32	132	128	130	17%	63	1%	0%	13	31%	38%	5.49	-1.2	36	109	$13
2nd Half	243	34	10	38	0	226	267	300	416	716	721	715	9	80	0.52	44	19	36	24	108	108	109	14%	62	0%	0%	13	38%	46%	4.09	-11.5	47	142	$7
18 Proj	**481**	**61**	**21**	**73**	**0**	**244**	**259**	**313**	**434**	**747**	**704**	**757**	**8**	**76**	**0.38**	**43**	**20**	**36**	**28**	**117**	**112**	**120**	**16%**	**60**	**1%**	**53%**				**4.49**	**-8.7**	**22**	**68**	**$11**

Moroff,Max

Age: 25 Bats: B Pos: 2B
Ht: 5' 10" Wt: 185

Health	A	LIMA Plan	D
PT/Exp	C	Rand Var	+1
Consist	A	MM	2201

3-21-.200 in 120 AB at PIT. Prototypical infield utility with extreme patience as calling card. Successfully muscled up in 185 Triple-A AB (13 HR, .519 Slg) and flashed pop in extended MLB opportunity. Hasn't developed a running game, and contact / BA shortcomings look entrenched. Just watch for now.

Yr Tm	AB	R	HR	RBI	SB	BA	xBA	OBP	SLG	OPS	vL	vR	bb%	ct%	Eye	G	L	F	h%	HctX	PX	xPX	hr/f	Spd	SBO	SB%	#Wk	DOM	DIS	RC/G	RAR	BPV	BPX	R$
13																																		
14																																		
15 aa	523	65	5	42	14	263		335	358	694			10	78	0.49				33		69			113	18%	50%				3.87		21	57	$13
16 PIT *	423	58	7	42	8	219	211	351	329	680	0	0	17	68	0.63	44	20	36	31	0	79	-24	0%	118	11%	53%	1	0%	100%	3.65	-16.1	6	17	$4
17 PIT *	305	46	14	53	4	217	221	331	401	733	663	612	14	65	0.49	38	19	43	28	77	121	142	9%	85	8%	57%	19	32%	68%	4.24	-7.3	14	42	$5
1st Half	196	27	11	35	3	212	209	318	423	741	463	178	13	66	0.46	36	9	55	26	23	136	42	0%	81	13%	52%	6	33%	67%	4.17	-4.0	28	85	$7
2nd Half	109	19	3	18	1	226	207	354	363	717	840	747	17	63	0.53	38	24	38	33	95	94	182	14%	109	2%	100%	13	31%	69%	4.29	-1.8	-6	-18	$0
18 Proj	**149**	**22**	**4**	**20**	**2**	**228**	**204**	**353**	**362**	**715**	**768**	**691**	**15**	**67**	**0.54**	**37**	**18**	**45**	**31**	**66**	**88**	**126**	**9%**	**104**	**9%**	**55%**				**4.00**	**-3.6**	**-2**	**-7**	**$3**

Morrison,Logan

Age: 30 Bats: L Pos: 1B
Ht: 6' 3" Wt: 245

Health	C	LIMA Plan	B
PT/Exp	B	Rand Var	0
Consist	C	MM	3135

One of the HR-boom poster boys. Combined uncharacteristic DL avoidance, improved patience and a conscious effort to hit more fly balls to generate career-high AB and season to match. Held FB% spike all season, but contact trend, health risk remain troublesome. 2H is your benchmark. DN: More DL time, .230 BA, 15 HR.

Yr Tm	AB	R	HR	RBI	SB	BA	xBA	OBP	SLG	OPS	vL	vR	bb%	ct%	Eye	G	L	F	h%	HctX	PX	xPX	hr/f	Spd	SBO	SB%	#Wk	DOM	DIS	RC/G	RAR	BPV	BPX	R$
13 MIA *	326	36	7	42	0	233	254	316	364	680	491	778	11	81	0.65	48	20	32	27	112	85	97	8%	104	0%	0%	17	41%	41%	3.82	-7.4	48	120	$3
14 SEA *	401	49	13	43	6	257	272	310	407	717	846	695	7	83	0.44	40	24	36	28	113	104	92	11%	62	8%	76%	20	35%	20%	4.33	2.2	49	132	$11
15 SEA	457	47	17	54	8	225	249	302	383	685	500	767	9	82	0.58	45	16	39	24	110	91	120	12%	85	10%	67%	27	48%	37%	3.70	-17.3	48	130	$8
16 TAM	353	45	14	43	4	238	256	319	414	733	739	731	9	75	0.42	44	21	35	28	104	110	100	15%	64	7%	67%	22	41%	50%	4.26	-6.3	27	77	$6
17 TAM	512	75	38	85	2	246	261	353	516	868	761	905	13	71	0.54	33	20	46	27	107	156	144	22%	58	1%	100%	27	56%	26%	6.11	11.1	55	167	$15
1st Half	270	46	24	57	1	256	287	364	581	946	805	994	15	74	0.66	35	19	46	26	131	180	178	26%	71	1%	100%	13	77%	0%	7.27	12.8	93	282	$22
2nd Half	242	29	14	28	1	236	234	339	442	781	710	805	13	67	0.44	31	23	46	29	80	126	101	19%	54	1%	100%	14	36%	50%	4.92	-5.2	14	42	$6
18 Proj	**465**	**60**	**24**	**64**	**4**	**240**	**253**	**332**	**446**	**778**	**689**	**806**	**11**	**74**	**0.50**	**38**	**20**	**41**	**27**	**104**	**117**	**118**	**17%**	**65**	**4%**	**73%**				**4.88**	**-3.1**	**34**	**104**	**$12**

Moss,Brandon

Age: 34 Bats: L Pos: DH
Ht: 6' 1" Wt: 210

Health	B	LIMA Plan	D+
PT/Exp	B	Rand Var	+2
Consist	B	MM	4213

Plus power still intact even with fewer FBs, but the good news ends there. Plate skills are stagnant, both BA and OBP have reached unplayable levels, and AB at a five-year low despite good health. A dream scenario that pairs opportunity with his 2nd half pop could mean more HR, but age makes it an increasingly bad bet.

Yr Tm	AB	R	HR	RBI	SB	BA	xBA	OBP	SLG	OPS	vL	vR	bb%	ct%	Eye	G	L	F	h%	HctX	PX	xPX	hr/f	Spd	SBO	SB%	#Wk	DOM	DIS	RC/G	RAR	BPV	BPX	R$
13 OAK	446	73	30	87	4	256	255	337	522	859	649	904	10	69	0.36	30	18	52	30	114	193	174	19%	95	6%	67%	27	70%	19%	5.86	17.8	79	198	$20
14 OAK	500	70	25	81	1	234	242	334	438	772	792	768	12	69	0.44	30	21	49	29	100	156	136	15%	65	1%	100%	27	44%	41%	4.74	10.4	47	127	$14
15 2 TM	469	47	19	58	0	226	229	304	407	711	717	709	9	68	0.33	33	20	47	29	117	133	156	13%	89	1%	0%	27	48%	37%	3.98	-20.9	28	76	$5
16 STL	413	66	28	67	1	225	241	300	484	784	664	828	8	66	0.28	27	20	53	27	107	172	186	19%	83	1%	100%	24	58%	25%	4.67	-10.4	45	129	$9
17 KC	362	41	22	50	2	207	234	279	428	707	812	682	9	65	0.29	33	22	44	25	98	142	132	21%	51	3%	100%	27	30%	48%	3.89	-10.9	8	24	$3
1st Half	172	21	10	16	1	198	220	268	401	670	1283	574	9	62	0.26	35	21	44	25	84	133	110	21%	69	3%	100%	13	23%	54%	3.47	-7.6	-4	-12	-$1
2nd Half	190	20	12	34	1	216	248	289	453	742	581	795	10	67	0.32	31	23	45	25	110	149	151	21%	57	3%	100%	14	36%	43%	4.30	-3.3	25	76	$7
18 Proj	**349**	**44**	**21**	**52**	**1**	**222**	**236**	**298**	**449**	**746**	**730**	**751**	**9**	**66**	**0.31**	**31**	**21**	**48**	**27**	**105**	**143**	**153**	**19%**	**68**	**2%**	**88%**				**4.34**	**-12.3**	**16**	**50**	**$7**

Motter,Taylor

Age: 28 Bats: R Pos: SS
Ht: 6' 1" Wt: 195

Health	A	LIMA Plan	D
PT/Exp	C	Rand Var	+3
Consist	C	MM	1321

7-26-.198 with 12 SB in 258 AB at SEA. Turned heads for a few weeks in April (5 HR, 137 HctX) before collapsing. Spent most of 2nd half at AAA Tacoma, posting 1.067 OPS in 100 AB. Has athleticism to play everywhere, reasonable plate skills and he can steal a base. If xBA ever translates ... UP: 15 HR / 15 SB.

Yr Tm	AB	R	HR	RBI	SB	BA	xBA	OBP	SLG	OPS	vL	vR	bb%	ct%	Eye	G	L	F	h%	HctX	PX	xPX	hr/f	Spd	SBO	SB%	#Wk	DOM	DIS	RC/G	RAR	BPV	BPX	R$
13																																		
14 aa	452	46	11	47	11	229		271	350	621			5	81	0.31				26		81			100	20%	58%				2.99		33	89	$9
15 aaa	486	59	11	57	21	242		306	384	690			8	76	0.39				30		107			83	26%	68%				3.85		34	92	$15
16 TAM *	430	48	13	48	17	190	232	258	317	575	1030	408	8	77	0.39	47	16	37	22	91	79	100	9%	81	25%	74%	7	43%	43%	2.58	-23.9	13	37	$5
17 SEA *	358	47	12	39	16	220	251	283	374	657	410	650	8	78	0.40	42	20	38	25	98	88	91	9%	90	26%	78%	23	22%	43%	3.48	-12.7	29	88	$8
1st Half	203	23	7	23	9	207	246	274	365	638	505	678	9	74	0.36	38	23	39	24	99	98	109	12%	80	21%	100%	13	31%	38%	3.44	-7.2	17	52	$7
2nd Half	155	24	5	16	7	238	254	294	387	681	228	500	7	84	0.50	54	11	35	25	81	76	34	0%	114	33%	61%	10	10%	50%	3.53	-5.0	48	145	$9
18 Proj	**194**	**24**	**5**	**21**	**8**	**220**	**242**	**282**	**354**	**637**	**671**	**619**	**8**	**79**	**0.40**	**47**	**16**	**37**	**25**	**90**	**78**	**79**	**9%**	**96**	**26%**	**70%**				**3.18**	**-7.8**	**24**	**73**	**$5**

Moustakas,Mike

Age: 29 Bats: L Pos: 3B
Ht: 6' 0" Wt: 215

Health	D	LIMA Plan	A
PT/Exp	C	Rand Var	-1
Consist	B	MM	3055

Career-best HR year can be credited to skill, increased loft, return to health, and nothing else. He was one of my personal sleeper picks last spring and I knew he was going to do this all along. Others may cite THE BALLS but Rob Manfred dismissed that. And he'll do it again because he has the best skill, believe me.

Yr Tm	AB	R	HR	RBI	SB	BA	xBA	OBP	SLG	OPS	vL	vR	bb%	ct%	Eye	G	L	F	h%	HctX	PX	xPX	hr/f	Spd	SBO	SB%	#Wk	DOM	DIS	RC/G	RAR	BPV	BPX	R$
13 KC	472	42	12	42	2	233	241	287	364	651	546	682	6	82	0.39	37	19	45	26	86	91	87	7%	63	6%	33%	26	46%	23%	3.30	-9.2	36	90	$4
14 KC *	488	47	16	57	1	217	258	272	365	638	554	653	7	83	0.46	39	20	41	23	114	100	120	9%	60	1%	100%	26	50%	27%	3.25	-6.2	47	127	$5
15 KC	549	73	22	82	1	284	274	348	470	817	823	814	7	86	0.57	40	19	41	30	117	112	114	11%	69	2%	33%	27	63%	19%	5.55	15.2	71	192	$20
16 KC	104	12	7	13	0	240	301	301	500	801	842	791	8	88	0.69	42	19	40	21	133	134	135	19%	76	5%	0%	7	71%	29%	4.84	0.1	98	280	$1
17 KC	555	75	38	85	0	272	279	314	521	835	763	862	6	83	0.36	35	20	46	27	107	124	120	18%	72	0%	0%	27	59%	15%	5.73	13.8	66	200	$18
1st Half	289	40	22	49	0	270	280	306	547	853	740	892	5	82	0.29	37	17	46	26	110	140	124	20%	65	0%	0%	13	69%	15%	5.84	6.3	71	215	$21
2nd Half	266	35	16	36	0	274	279	323	492	816	783	829	7	84	0.45	32	22	45	27	105	107	115	16%	88	0%	0%	14	50%	14%	5.59	3.8	64	194	$16
18 Proj	**555**	**69**	**33**	**77**	**0**	**269**	**279**	**321**	**495**	**816**	**790**	**825**	**7**	**85**	**0.48**	**37**	**20**	**43**	**27**	**114**	**114**	**121**	**16%**	**70**	**2%**	**15%**				**5.42**	**8.5**	**52**	**159**	**$19**

OCK THOMPSON

Murphy,Daniel

Age: 33	Bats: L	Pos: 2B	Health A	LIMA Plan A
Ht: 6' 1"	Wt: 220		PT/Exp A	Rand Var -2
			Consist F	MM 3255

Terrific 1st half put him on track to match huge 2017 breakout. But nagging hip injury lingered into Aug and sore hamstring in Sept cut into 2nd half AB, despite DL avoidance. Even with physical woes and regression that factored into near-across-the-board-peripheral slide, he's still elite as he enters his mid-30s.

Yr	Tm	AB	R	HR	RBI	SB	BA	xBA	OBP	SLG	OPS	vL	vR	bb%	ct%	Eye	G	L	F	h%	HctX	PX	xPX	hr/f	Spd	SBO	SB%	#Wk	DOM	DIS	RC/G	RAR	BPV	BPX
13	NYM	658	92	13	78	23	286	266	319	415	733	616	790	5	86	0.34	42	21	36	32	112	87	100	6%	98	16%	88%	27	52%	19%	4.84	21.9	52	130
14	NYM	596	79	9	57	13	289	285	332	403	734	695	747	6	86	0.45	42	28	29	33	106	84	89	6%	93	11%	72%	26	50%	23%	4.77	23.1	52	141
15	NYM	499	56	14	73	2	281	299	322	449	770	633	817	6	92	0.82	43	21	36	28	124	101	108	8%	62	3%	50%	24	63%	4%	5.07	12.7	83	224
16	WAS	531	88	25	104	5	347	314	390	595	985	924	1010	6	89	0.61	36	22	42	35	138	135	138	12%	106	6%	63%	26	77%	0%	8.86	54.8	111	317
17	WAS	534	94	23	93	2	322	307	384	543	928	823	960	9	86	0.68	33	28	39	34	123	119	120	13%	86	1%	100%	27	63%	19%	7.84	40.0	83	252
1st Half		299	53	14	55	1	334	322	387	569	956	898	971	8	90	0.81	34	27	39	34	126	119	108	13%	87	1%	100%	13	69%	8%	8.43	28.1	97	294
2nd Half		235	41	9	38	1	306	290	381	511	892	754	944	10	80	0.59	32	28	39	35	120	119	138	12%	86	1%	100%	14	57%	29%	7.13	14.7	65	197
18	Proj	**550**	**88**	**21**	**92**	**3**	**316**	**301**	**369**	**522**	**891**	**793**	**926**	**8**	**87**	**0.61**	**36**	**25**	**39**	**34**	**125**	**111**	**123**	**11%**	**88**	**3%**	**69%**				**7.12**	**34.3**	**75**	**228**

Murphy,Tom

Age: 27	Bats: R	Pos: CA	Health C	LIMA Plan D
Ht: 6' 1"	Wt: 220		PT/Exp F	Rand Var +4
			Consist F	MM 4211

One hit in 24 AB at COL (.042). Entered March with unquestioned power and 8 HR in first 79 MLB AB. Fractured right forearm played into a lost season. Mid-June return was followed by quick demotion and just 4 Triple-A HR in 141 AB. Poor plate skills remain an obstacle, but if he's recovered... UP: 20 HR.

Yr	Tm	AB	R	HR	RBI	SB	BA	xBA	OBP	SLG	OPS	vL	vR	bb%	ct%	Eye	G	L	F	h%	HctX	PX	xPX	hr/f	Spd	SBO	SB%	#Wk	DOM	DIS	RC/G	RAR	BPV	BPX
13	aa	69	7	3	7	0	279		311	469	780			4	77	0.20				33		138			93	0%	0%				5.16		57	143
14	aa	94	12	4	11	0	199		280	378	658			10	70	0.38				23		136			93	0%	0%				3.37		39	105
15	COL *	429	44	19	54	4	232	228	273	433	705	417	1362	5	68	0.18	33	17	50	29	142	146	213	25%	96	9%	51%	4	50%	25%	3.81	0.0	32	86
16	COL *	347	46	20	56	2	297	274	327	584	911	651	1157	4	71	0.16	28	24	48	37	139	184	225	42%	123	4%	60%	6	83%	17%	6.85	23.5	79	226
17	COL *	165	16	3	14	0	196	192	233	320	553	276	0	5	58	0.12	40	20	40	32	47	104	40	0%	86	0%	0%	6	0%	83%	2.36	-8.7	-46	-139
1st Half		53	5	1	6	0	219	208	257	380	637	330	0	5	62	0.13	38	15	46	34	58	128	51	0%	96	0%	0%	3	0%	100%	3.19	-1.5	-8	-24
2nd Half		112	11	2	8	0	185	260	222	291	513	0	0	5	56	0.11	50	50	0	30	0	92	-26	0%	84	0%	0%	3	0%	67%	2.02	-7.5	-66	-200
18	Proj	**232**	**25**	**10**	**27**	**1**	**240**	**235**	**280**	**447**	**727**	**727**	**727**	**5**	**64**	**0.16**	**40**	**20**	**40**	**33**		**143**		**16%**	**99**	**3%**	**62%**				**4.18**	**0.3**	**8**	**24**

Myers,Wil

Age: 27	Bats: R	Pos: 1B	Health B	LIMA Plan B
Ht: 6' 3"	Wt: 205		PT/Exp B	Rand Var 0
			Consist A	MM 4435

Year-long FB hike merged with stable hr/f to bump xPX into territory more supportive of HR output. Running game held up, and he's now almost 1,200 AB removed from last DL stint. Troublesome ct% gets ugly during down h% stretches (see 2nd half BA). But SB scarcity keeps the package valuable, and a repeat seems doable.

Yr	Tm	AB	R	HR	RBI	SB	BA	xBA	OBP	SLG	OPS	vL	vR	bb%	ct%	Eye	G	L	F	h%	HctX	PX	xPX	hr/f	Spd	SBO	SB%	#Wk	DOM	DIS	RC/G	RAR	BPV	BPX
13	TAM *	587	86	24	100	11	275	255	338	463	801	821	834	9	71	0.33	46	20	34	35	115	143	120	15%	99	9%	78%	16	50%	25%	5.50	15.4	46	115
14	TAM *	349	40	8	40	9	221	216	301	329	630	532	649	10	72	0.41	48	16	36	29	98	88	96	7%	106	10%	89%	16	25%	50%	3.33	-9.1	12	32
15	SD	225	40	8	29	5	253	255	336	427	763	793	751	11	76	0.49	48	17	36	30	115	119	107	14%	112	11%	71%	12	50%	33%	4.82	-3.6	54	146
16	SD	599	99	28	94	28	259	263	336	461	797	814	791	10	73	0.43	44	22	34	31	100	125	111	19%	121	21%	82%	27	52%	33%	5.37	0.6	51	146
17	SD	567	80	30	74	20	243	242	328	464	792	790	792	11	68	0.39	38	20	43	30	114	138	144	18%	126	18%	77%	26	46%	31%	5.09	-13.8	45	136
1st Half		299	43	16	42	9	258	240	334	478	813	790	820	10	67	0.34	37	21	42	33	116	140	149	19%	117	16%	69%	13	38%	46%	5.36	-2.5	36	109
2nd Half		268	37	14	32	11	228	245	322	448	769	790	762	12	70	0.45	38	18	44	27	112	136	140	17%	129	19%	85%	13	54%	15%	4.81	-6.9	54	164
18	Proj	**563**	**85**	**29**	**80**	**20**	**256**	**253**	**337**	**473**	**809**	**812**	**808**	**11**	**71**	**0.41**	**42**	**19**	**39**	**31**	**110**	**131**	**126**	**19%**	**119**	**17%**	**80%**				**5.45**	**5.9**	**44**	**134**

Napoli,Mike

Age: 36	Bats: R	Pos: 1B DH	Health A	LIMA Plan D+
Ht: 6' 1"	Wt: 225		PT/Exp B	Rand Var +3
			Consist C	MM 4003

FB boost helped PX/xPX stay intact, hr/f says he can still crush with the best—when he connects. But career-worst contact, h% dug in all season, bb% was less than vintage, and the HctX, BA/xBA trends look abysmal. Mild rebound is likely, but age and all-or-nothing approach will continue to cut into his AB.

Yr	Tm	AB	R	HR	RBI	SB	BA	xBA	OBP	SLG	OPS	vL	vR	bb%	ct%	Eye	G	L	F	h%	HctX	PX	xPX	hr/f	Spd	SBO	SB%	#Wk	DOM	DIS	RC/G	RAR	BPV	BPX
13	BOS	498	79	23	92	1	259	251	360	482	842	899	816	13	62	0.39	37	24	39	37	108	195	156	19%	74	1%	50%	27	56%	41%	5.84	17.8	55	138
14	BOS	415	49	17	55	3	248	235	370	419	789	923	739	16	68	0.59	45	19	36	32	107	139	138	17%	65	3%	60%	23	48%	39%	5.18	12.8	36	97
15	2 AL	407	46	18	50	3	224	233	324	410	734	954	603	12	71	0.48	42	16	42	27	89	131	116	15%	91	6%	50%	26	42%	38%	4.21	-9.0	42	114
16	CLE	557	92	34	101	5	239	233	335	465	800	817	792	12	65	0.40	36	18	45	30	97	152	149	20%	81	4%	83%	27	48%	41%	5.19	5.6	33	94
17	TEX	425	60	29	66	1	193	212	285	428	713	751	701	10	62	0.30	33	15	52	23	89	151	139	21%	70	3%	33%	23	26%	43%	3.67	-23.0	11	33
1st Half		229	29	15	34	0	192	205	272	415	687	781	660	9	62	0.26	37	12	50	23	91	142	141	21%	60	2%	0%	12	17%	58%	3.37	-16.6	1	3
2nd Half		196	31	14	32	1	194	216	300	444	743	722	751	12	61	0.35	28	18	54	23	86	162	136	22%	84	4%	50%	11	36%	27%	4.03	-10.1	24	73
18	Proj	**340**	**49**	**20**	**54**	**1**	**227**	**222**	**323**	**449**	**772**	**842**	**743**	**12**	**64**	**0.37**	**36**	**17**	**48**	**29**	**92**	**142**	**138**	**20%**	**78**	**3%**	**36%**				**4.63**	**-4.9**	**11**	**32**

Naquin,Tyler

Age: 27	Bats: L	Pos: CF	Health A	LIMA Plan D
Ht: 6' 2"	Wt: 195		PT/Exp D	Rand Var +2
			Consist C	MM 2331

0-1-.216 in 37 AB at CLE. A suprising .886 OPS in 2016 has only left questions in its wake. Demoted after 4-for-17 April due to crowded OF and defensive issues, his numbers fell off in Triple-A. His power remains suspect, and plate skills have never been special. Still owns that MLB debut, but now flyer material.

Yr	Tm	AB	R	HR	RBI	SB	BA	xBA	OBP	SLG	OPS	vL	vR	bb%	ct%	Eye	G	L	F	h%	HctX	PX	xPX	hr/f	Spd	SBO	SB%	#Wk	DOM	DIS	RC/G	RAR	BPV	BPX
13	aa	80	7	1	5	1	193		229	254	483			4	69	0.15				27		54			101	26%	19%				1.48		-38	-95
14	aa	304	43	3	24	11	274		324	361	685			7	73	0.28				36		69			123	16%	77%				4.14		1	3
15	a/a	327	44	6	24	11	279		347	416	764			9	76	0.44				35		106			99	16%	77%				5.13		39	105
16	CLE *	391	57	15	50	7	289	253	359	486	845	775	898	10	67	0.34	46	23	30	40	105	133	127	22%	132	11%	56%	26	50%	46%	6.06	18.8	37	106
17	CLE *	332	37	8	41	4	257	261	311	392	703	500	523	7	75	0.31	59	21	21	32	94	82	69	0%	114	10%	46%	9	22%	56%	4.01	-7.1	16	48
1st Half		122	15	4	13	1	270	249	321	430	751	0	572	7	73	0.27	42	25	33	34	98	94	99	0%	126	6%	40%	2	50%	50%	4.67	-0.8	19	58
2nd Half		210	22	4	28	3	250	270	306	370	676	500	472	8	76	0.34	71	18	12	31	91	75	47	0%	107	12%	48%	7	14%	57%	3.67	-7.8	14	42
18	Proj	**192**	**24**	**6**	**22**	**4**	**270**	**257**	**336**	**431**	**767**	**679**	**777**	**8**	**73**	**0.34**	**46**	**23**	**30**	**34**	**95**	**99**	**114**	**14%**	**122**	**11%**	**62%**				**4.86**	**2.0**	**17**	**51**

Narvaez,Omar

Age: 26	Bats: B	Pos: CA	Health A	LIMA Plan D
Ht: 5' 11"	Wt: 215		PT/Exp F	Rand Var -1
			Consist D	MM 0033

Owned plus plate skills in the minors, but zero thump projected a sub-par MLB contributor. Now after 353 MLB AB, he owns a .274 BA, .371 OBP, and a slightly interesting 2nd half HctX-and-PX uptick. Modest upside with a ton to prove. But age, plus defense and health should keep deep OBP-leaguers watching for now.

Yr	Tm	AB	R	HR	RBI	SB	BA	xBA	OBP	SLG	OPS	vL	vR	bb%	ct%	Eye	G	L	F	h%	HctX	PX	xPX	hr/f	Spd	SBO	SB%	#Wk	DOM	DIS	RC/G	RAR	BPV	BPX
13																																		
14																																		
15																																		
16	CHW *	289	27	3	23	0	227	263	289	293	582	947	617	8	85	0.58	40	28	31	26	50	43	40	4%	83	0%	0%	11	36%	27%	2.80	-9.3	17	49
17	CHW	253	23	2	14	0	277	257	373	340	713	668	723	13	82	0.84	44	28	29	33	65	41	27	3%	79	0%	0%	26	23%	35%	4.45	2.2	13	39
1st Half		127	12	0	5	0	244	236	333	268	601	693	580	12	86	0.94	49	23	28	28	50	17	4	0%	89	0%	0%	13	15%	31%	3.01	-4.1	9	27
2nd Half		126	11	2	9	0	310	281	412	413	825	638	864	14	79	0.78	38	33	30	38	80	67	53	7%	80	0%	0%	13	31%	38%	6.22	7.2	22	67
18	Proj	**280**	**26**	**3**	**19**	**0**	**261**	**264**	**342**	**330**	**672**	**747**	**654**	**11**	**83**	**0.73**	**42**	**28**	**30**	**31**	**61**	**44**	**36**	**4%**	**77**	**0%**	**0%**				**3.90**	**-2.0**	**-4**	**-11**

Nimmo,Brandon

Age: 25	Bats: L	Pos: LF	Health C	LIMA Plan D+
Ht: 6' 3"	Wt: 207		PT/Exp C	Rand Var 0
			Consist B	MM 2223

5-21-.260 in 177 AB At NYM. Took launch-angle-plus-patience route in effort to generate more power. It worked to a degree, as power metrics climbed from sub-par to average. But effort also took ct% from average to sub-par, with only 37% h% keeping his MLB BA above water. At 25, you'd hope for more growth by now.

Yr	Tm	AB	R	HR	RBI	SB	BA	xBA	OBP	SLG	OPS	vL	vR	bb%	ct%	Eye	G	L	F	h%	HctX	PX	xPX	hr/f	Spd	SBO	SB%	#Wk	DOM	DIS	RC/G	RAR	BPV	BPX
13																																		
14	aa	240	28	5	19	4	200		280	320	600			10	75	0.43				25		91			116	8%	77%				2.87		28	76
15	a/a	360	35	4	19	4	237		304	324	628			9	76	0.41				30		61			122	11%	37%				3.09		11	30
16	NYM *	465	61	9	47	5	279	261	337	398	735	661	667	8	76	0.36	42	30	28	35	87	76	79	7%	123	10%	33%	10	20%	50%	4.42	-3.4	19	54
17	NYM *	340	42	7	33	2	221	225	335	353	688	530	878	14	65	0.49	43	24	33	32	92	99	106	13%	101	2%	100%	13	31%	69%	3.90	-13.3	0	0
1st Half		156	15	2	13	0	185	202	305	300	605	500	1292	15	64	0.47	40	20	40	27	103	94	124	0%	99	0%	0%	2	50%	50%	2.86	-11.0	-10	-30
2nd Half		184	27	5	20	2	251	231	360	398	758	523	858	15	66	0.50	43	25	32	36	92	103	105	14%	108	3%	100%	11	27%	73%	4.94	-0.6	8	24
18	Proj	**309**	**38**	**7**	**28**	**3**	**237**	**244**	**333**	**372**	**705**	**521**	**744**	**12**	**70**	**0.45**	**42**	**27**	**31**	**32**	**90**	**88**	**95**	**11%**	**114**	**6%**	**53%**				**3.99**	**-4.3**	**1**	**2**

JOCK THOMPSON

Nunez,Eduardo

Age: 31	Bats: R	Pos: 3B 2B	Health	B	LIMA Plan	B
Ht: 6' 0"	Wt: 195		PT/Exp	C	Rand Var	-2
			Consist	A	MM	2455

Running game clicked until late June, when injuries (hamstring, knee) took a toll and cost him six weeks of AB. But SB plunge was offset by career-best BA, fueled by ct% spike and inflated 2nd half h%. Durability may not be his strong suit, but consistent speed/BA/versatility package is worth the extra buck.

Yr Tm	AB	R	HR	RBI	SB	BA	xBA	OBP	SLG	OPS	vL	vR	bb%	ct%	Eye	G	L	F	h%	HctX	PX	xPX	hr/f	Spd	SBO	SB%	#Wk	DOM	DIS	RC/G	RAR	BPV	BPX	R$
13 NYY	304	38	3	28	10	260	250	307	372	679	652	693	6	83	0.39	41	21	38	30	89	78	81	3%	137	17%	77%	20	45%	40%	3.93	-0.1	50	125	$7
14 MIN *	253	32	5	28	10	251	265	274	377	651	586	716	3	83	0.19	56	16	27	29	80	78	42	9%	148	25%	78%	20	40%	40%	3.52	-1.0	47	127	$7
15 MIN	188	23	4	20	8	282	284	327	431	758	649	809	6	85	0.41	57	16	27	32	93	100	68	10%	101	26%	67%	24	50%	25%	4.78	1.1	62	168	$7
16 2 TM	553	73	16	67	40	288	264	325	432	758	750	760	5	84	0.33	50	17	34	32	95	80	85	10%	143	35%	80%	26	50%	31%	5.04	3.8	55	157	$32
17 2 TM	467	60	12	58	24	313	292	341	460	801	751	821	4	88	0.33	53	17	29	33	96	83	67	10%	101	26%	77%	22	55%	14%	5.74	11.4	60	182	$26
1st Half	254	33	4	25	17	299	289	323	413	737	727	741	4	91	0.43	55	17	28	32	88	66	51	6%	103	31%	85%	12	50%	8%	5.06	-0.1	57	173	$25
2nd Half	213	27	8	33	7	329	293	362	516	878	786	909	4	85	0.26	51	18	31	36	105	104	87	14%	98	20%	64%	10	60%	20%	6.61	8.8	64	194	$27
18 Proj	**468**	**60**	**12**	**57**	**22**	**298**	**281**	**333**	**449**	**782**	**720**	**807**	**5**	**86**	**0.34**	**52**	**17**	**31**	**33**	**95**	**83**	**74**	**10%**	**112**	**24%**	**76%**				**5.34**	**5.9**	**53**	**161**	**$24**

O Neill,Tyler

Age: 23	Bats: R	Pos: OF	Health	A	LIMA Plan	D
Ht: 5' 11"	Wt: 210		PT/Exp	C	Rand Var	0
			Consist	D	MM	3301

Second 30+ HR minor league season in three years for athletic prospect who is also willing to take a walk. And 49/13 career SB/CS says he can run a little. But he couldn't sustain Double-A BA spike at the next level, and now owns 300 strikeouts over two seasons in the high minors. 2018 MLB debut in STL is likely, so are growing pains.

Yr Tm	AB	R	HR	RBI	SB	BA	xBA	OBP	SLG	OPS	vL	vR	bb%	ct%	Eye	G	L	F	h%	HctX	PX	xPX	hr/f	Spd	SBO	SB%	#Wk	DOM	DIS	RC/G	RAR	BPV	BPX	R$
13																																		
14																																		
15																																		
16 aa	492	61	22	92	11	272		345	468	813			10	66	0.33				37		135			90	9%	83%				5.70		21	60	$20
17 aaa	495	64	25	79	12	224		288	434	722			8	68	0.28				28		131			94	13%	84%				4.16		25	76	$12
1st Half	292	32	9	33	6	206		281	371	652			9	69	0.33				27		112			90	13%	73%				3.34		13	39	$6
2nd Half	203	32	16	46	6	251		300	525	825			7	68	0.21				29		160			92	14%	100%				5.52		41	124	$20
18 Proj	**160**	**21**	**7**	**29**	**4**	**236**	**222**	**303**	**418**	**720**	**720**	**720**	**9**	**67**	**0.29**	**38**	**18**	**44**	**31**		**117**		**14%**	**92**	**12%**	**88%**				**4.29**	**#N/A**	**11**	**32**	**$5**

Odor,Rougned

Age: 24	Bats: L	Pos: 2B	Health	A	LIMA Plan	B+
Ht: 5' 11"	Wt: 195		PT/Exp	A	Rand Var	+4
			Consist	C	MM	3325

Year-long ct% plunge took BA along for the ride but horrible h% made this look worse than it really was. Power was re-affirmed in 2nd half, but these days that skill with such soft peripheral support is just one in a crowd. xBA indicates some BA rebound, but ct% trend says an intervention is needed.

Yr Tm	AB	R	HR	RBI	SB	BA	xBA	OBP	SLG	OPS	vL	vR	bb%	ct%	Eye	G	L	F	h%	HctX	PX	xPX	hr/f	Spd	SBO	SB%	#Wk	DOM	DIS	RC/G	RAR	BPV	BPX	R$
13 aa	134	18	6	17	4	309		349	529	878			6	82	0.34				34		139			116	19%	69%				6.61		88	220	$5
14 TEX *	515	57	14	62	9	260	249	292	404	695	626	727	4	82	0.24	49	15	36	29	90	90	68	8%	133	16%	47%	22	41%	23%	3.78	6.0	49	132	$15
15 TEX *	534	76	20	77	9	273	277	316	486	802	781	781	6	83	0.37	46	15	40	30	106	126	102	12%	132	14%	51%	22	55%	18%	5.14	13.3	86	232	$21
16 TEX	605	89	33	88	14	271	269	296	502	798	763	811	3	78	0.14	40	18	42	30	112	135	131	17%	89	19%	67%	26	54%	19%	5.00	4.8	53	151	$25
17 TEX	607	79	30	75	15	204	239	252	397	649	452	719	5	73	0.20	42	16	42	23	109	109	116	16%	92	21%	71%	27	30%	41%	3.05	-30.2	20	61	$9
1st Half	323	40	14	35	9	211	243	249	387	636	449	698	4	76	0.16	43	18	40	23	110	97	104	15%	102	24%	69%	13	23%	23%	2.93	-19.2	20	61	$9
2nd Half	284	39	16	40	6	197	233	255	408	663	455	743	6	71	0.23	40	15	46	22	108	122	130	18%	86	17%	75%	14	36%	57%	3.19	-14.8	21	64	$10
18 Proj	**600**	**82**	**29**	**81**	**14**	**238**	**252**	**282**	**443**	**725**	**616**	**768**	**5**	**76**	**0.21**	**42**	**16**	**42**	**27**	**107**	**113**	**115**	**15%**	**104**	**18%**	**66%**				**3.96**	**-15.4**	**42**	**126**	**$19**

Olson,Matt

Age: 24	Bats: L	Pos: 1B	Health	A	LIMA Plan	B
Ht: 6' 5"	Wt: 230		PT/Exp	B	Rand Var	+1
			Consist	C	MM	4235

24-45-.259 in 185 AB at OAK. Plus power often vanished at game-time in previous two seasons. But fewer GBs fueled 23 HR in 294 AB Triple-A repeat. Outburst accelerated in OAK after Aug call-up (20 HR in 138 AB). Clearly his hr/f and contact-challenged BA are due for some regression. But the future looks bright.

Yr Tm	AB	R	HR	RBI	SB	BA	xBA	OBP	SLG	OPS	vL	vR	bb%	ct%	Eye	G	L	F	h%	HctX	PX	xPX	hr/f	Spd	SBO	SB%	#Wk	DOM	DIS	RC/G	RAR	BPV	BPX	R$
13																																		
14																																		
15 aa	466	62	12	57	4	217		331	366	697			15	68	0.54				29		123			81	4%	78%				3.96		28	76	$5
16 OAK *	485	61	13	51	1	207	203	302	359	661	0	527	12	71	0.46	47	6	47	26	51	110	-10	0%	89	1%	100%	4	50%	25%	3.49	-20.6	24	69	$0
17 OAK *	483	78	41	93	2	245	257	325	536	862	758	1081	11	69	0.38	38	16	46	27	113	168	178	41%	79	2%	100%	16	44%	44%	5.93	7.8	58	176	$16
1st Half	258	35	16	44	2	226	227	313	459	772	111	932	11	66	0.38	42	12	46	27	103	147	185	33%	77	4%	100%	5	20%	80%	4.79	-6.7	31	94	$11
2nd Half	225	43	24	50	0	268	285	339	625	964	894	1132	10	72	0.39	37	17	46	26	119	190	176	43%	97	0%	0%	11	55%	27%	7.39	11.3	92	279	$22
18 Proj	**495**	**74**	**34**	**77**	**2**	**234**	**256**	**337**	**497**	**834**	**558**	**916**	**12**	**70**	**0.44**	**39**	**17**	**44**	**26**	**113**	**157**	**180**	**22%**	**78**	**2%**	**92%**				**5.34**	**3.6**	**47**	**143**	**$14**

Osuna,Jose

Age: 25	Bats: R	Pos: RF 1B	Health	A	LIMA Plan	D
Ht: 6' 3"	Wt: 240		PT/Exp	D	Rand Var	+5
			Consist	A	MM	3140

7-30-.233 in 215 AB at PIT. Age, size and 5 spring training HR got folks excited. 1st half xBA and PX kept them intrigued despite meh surface stats. But despite decent contact, historically high GB% and poor bb% have kept a lid on his raw power. Physicality aside, there's nothing here resembling a plus skill.

Yr Tm	AB	R	HR	RBI	SB	BA	xBA	OBP	SLG	OPS	vL	vR	bb%	ct%	Eye	G	L	F	h%	HctX	PX	xPX	hr/f	Spd	SBO	SB%	#Wk	DOM	DIS	RC/G	RAR	BPV	BPX	R$
13																																		
14																																		
15 aa	323	37	6	42	5	253		283	371	654			4	80	0.21				30		83			91	12%	59%				3.48		23	62	$7
16 a/a	473	53	11	60	3	254		300	408	709			6	82	0.37				29		97			93	7%	37%				4.04		47	134	$8
17 PIT *	251	36	7	31	1	231	283	270	416	686	740	660	5	80	0.27	53	18	29	26	96	106	65	14%	97	5%	43%	25	56%	36%	3.66	-11.5	46	139	$2
1st Half	160	26	5	21	1	244	299	289	441	730	690	815	6	83	0.37	48	23	29	27	91	111	66	16%	85	7%	43%	11	82%	18%	4.19	-4.2	59	179	$4
2nd Half	91	10	2	10	0	209	252	232	374	605	793	392	3	76	0.14	60	11	29	25	101	96	63	10%	115	0%	0%	14	36%	50%	2.82	-6.3	23	70	-$2
18 Proj	**67**	**8**	**2**	**8**	**0**	**238**	**275**	**278**	**416**	**694**	**791**	**602**	**5**	**80**	**0.25**	**55**	**16**	**29**	**27**	**97**	**102**	**64**	**12%**	**93**	**6%**	**51%**				**3.76**	**-1.9**	**41**	**123**	**$1**

Owings,Chris

Age: 26	Bats: R	Pos: SS RF 2B	Health	F	LIMA Plan	B
Ht: 5' 10"	Wt: 185		PT/Exp	B	Rand Var	-1
			Consist	B	MM	2535

Stunning 1st half fueled by friendly combo of h%, hr/f. Resulting OBP bump launched running game, putting him on 20/20 pace by the end of June. July slump finished with season-ending finger injury, leaving us wondering but skeptical about that 1st half PX/xPX. But SB, age, versatility all keep him a worthy upside flyer.

Yr Tm	AB	R	HR	RBI	SB	BA	xBA	OBP	SLG	OPS	vL	vR	bb%	ct%	Eye	G	L	F	h%	HctX	PX	xPX	hr/f	Spd	SBO	SB%	#Wk	DOM	DIS	RC/G	RAR	BPV	BPX	R$
13 ARI *	601	72	8	57	15	282	262	305	397	701	250	932	3	80	0.16	47	24	29	34	67	83	63	0%	124	16%	65%	4	50%	25%	4.17	11.5	32	80	$20
14 ARI *	350	38	6	27	10	255	257	287	386	673	829	672	4	78	0.21	45	24	31	31	90	93	77	8%	163	14%	91%	18	33%	50%	3.89	6.1	46	124	$8
15 ARI	515	59	4	43	16	227	227	264	322	587	495	614	5	72	0.18	39	26	34	31	94	76	93	3%	117	19%	80%	27	30%	63%	2.85	-14.4	-4	-11	$7
16 ARI	437	52	5	49	21	277	273	315	416	731	826	700	4	80	0.23	50	23	27	34	97	84	75	5%	159	23%	91%	22	36%	27%	4.72	1.3	46	131	$17
17 ARI	362	41	12	51	12	268	262	299	442	741	685	759	4	76	0.20	43	22	36	32	97	108	109	12%	99	18%	86%	18	28%	28%	4.70	1.9	31	94	$12
1st Half	283	36	11	47	11	297	277	330	498	828	819	831	5	78	0.25	42	22	36	35	104	121	119	14%	101	20%	85%	13	38%	15%	6.11	12.1	51	155	$19
2nd Half	79	5	1	4	1	165	205	185	241	426	118	509	1	70	0.04	45	20	35	22	72	55	69	5%	97	10%	100%	5	0%	60%	1.32	-8.4	-44	-133	-$13
18 Proj	**503**	**52**	**14**	**59**	**18**	**275**	**258**	**308**	**432**	**741**	**637**	**772**	**4**	**77**	**0.19**	**44**	**22**	**34**	**33**	**97**	**92**	**84**	**11%**	**118**	**18%**	**84%**				**4.70**	**3.4**	**28**	**86**	**$20**

Ozuna,Marcell

Age: 27	Bats: R	Pos: LF	Health	A	LIMA Plan	B
Ht: 6' 1"	Wt: 225		PT/Exp	A	Rand Var	-5
			Consist	D	MM	3145

Obviously a remarkable career year, but sustainable breakout? PRO: Eye has never been better; ditto HctX; owned right-handers wire-to-wire. CON: Outlier BA fueled by lofty h%, lacks xBA support; hr/f looks equally suspicious; GB% remains stagnant; xPX is skeptical. The CONs have it. He's good, but not $30 good.

Yr Tm	AB	R	HR	RBI	SB	BA	xBA	OBP	SLG	OPS	vL	vR	bb%	ct%	Eye	G	L	F	h%	HctX	PX	xPX	hr/f	Spd	SBO	SB%	#Wk	DOM	DIS	RC/G	RAR	BPV	BPX	R$
13 MIA *	317	36	7	45	6	270	266	304	426	730	838	647	5	79	0.23	46	21	33	32	106	110	88	4%	120	10%	85%	13	31%	38%	4.56	4.2	51	128	$9
14 MIA	565	72	23	85	3	269	252	317	455	772	728	783	7	71	0.25	49	18	34	34	117	140	133	17%	126	3%	75%	26	42%	38%	5.05	19.7	49	132	$20
15 MIA *	579	64	14	53	3	263	255	310	402	712	888	646	6	77	0.29	48	21	31	32	115	102	106	9%	79	4%	48%	23	30%	43%	4.24	-1.1	26	70	$12
16 MIA	557	75	23	76	0	266	262	321	452	773	923	732	7	79	0.37	44	20	37	30	120	105	121	14%	134	2%	0%	26	38%	31%	4.89	3.8	58	166	$14
17 MIA	613	93	37	124	1	312	275	376	548	924	804	955	9	77	0.44	47	19	34	36	121	130	106	23%	90	2%	25%	27	52%	22%	7.52	40.9	58	176	$31
1st Half	301	46	20	55	0	312	275	373	555	928	882	939	9	76	0.42	48	20	32	35	131	132	111	27%	82	1%	0%	13	54%	23%	7.61	22.0	56	170	$29
2nd Half	312	47	17	69	1	311	273	378	542	919	727	970	10	77	0.47	47	18	35	36	111	129	101	20%	95	3%	33%	14	50%	21%	7.43	21.5	60	182	$32
18 Proj	**579**	**80**	**26**	**96**	**2**	**288**	**267**	**346**	**488**	**835**	**841**	**833**	**8**	**77**	**0.38**	**46**	**20**	**34**	**33**	**118**	**112**	**110**	**17%**	**101**	**3%**	**37%**				**5.95**	**24.3**	**34**	**103**	**$24**

OCK THOMPSON

Panik,Joe

Age: 27	Bats: L	Pos: 2B	Health	C	LIMA Plan	A
Ht: 6' 1"	Wt: 190		PT/Exp	B	Rand Var	-1
			Consist	D	MM	1355

Another concussion-related DL stint had no adverse effects. Avoiding lengthy downtime obviously generated more plate appearances, but LD rebound and h% correction fueled most of this turnaround. Stable bb%, ct% and HctX make this look like a repeat waiting to happen. Now if they'd only let him run more. Skills are there...

Yr	Tm	AB	R	HR	RBI	SB	BA	xBA	OBP	SLG	OPS	vL	vR	bb%	ct%	Eye	G	L	F	h%	HctX	PX	xPX	hr/f	Spd	SBO	SB%	#Wk	DOM	DIS	RC/G	RAR	BPV	BPX
13	aa	522	47	3	42	7	217		277	289	566			8	85	0.56				25		53			104	10%	57%				2.55		32	80
14	SF *	562	64	4	48	2	281	263	323	358	680	839	655	6	87	0.48	50	23	27	32	90	53	51	2%	141	3%	46%	17	24%	24%	4.04	10.3	47	127
15	SF	382	59	8	37	3	312	288	378	455	833	769	852	9	89	0.90	43	23	34	33	115	91	89	7%	111	4%	60%	18	72%	11%	6.24	21.5	82	222
16	SF	464	67	10	62	5	239	270	315	379	695	595	734	10	90	1.06	45	18	37	25	94	73	87	6%	127	4%	100%	24	67%	13%	4.04	-11.3	77	220
17	SF	511	60	10	53	4	288	282	347	421	768	697	799	8	89	0.85	44	22	34	31	94	70	78	6%	121	3%	80%	27	67%	15%	5.23	3.0	68	206
1st Half		277	35	5	26	4	278	274	342	401	743	697	763	9	87	0.74	46	21	33	30	93	67	81	6%	123	5%	100%	13	62%	15%	4.91	0.6	59	179
2nd Half		234	25	5	27	0	299	291	354	444	799	698	841	8	92	1.05	42	23	35	31	96	73	74	7%	117	1%	0%	14	71%	14%	5.63	5.2	79	239
18	**Proj**	**512**	**65**	**9**	**56**	**4**	**277**	**279**	**340**	**407**	**747**	**685**	**772**	**9**	**89**	**0.89**	**45**	**21**	**34**	**29**	**97**	**68**	**79**	**6%**	**123**	**4%**	**73%**				**4.85**	**0.7**	**57**	**172**

Parker,Jarrett

Age: 29	Bats: L	Pos: LF	Health	D	LIMA Plan	D+
Ht: 6' 4"	Wt: 210		PT/Exp	D	Rand Var	+5
			Consist	A	MM	3303

4-23-.247 in 166 AB at SF. Parlayed decent March into April AB, going 3-for-21 before fracturing his clavicle. Didn't distinguish himself in extended PT following Aug return. Raw power flashed early in career now being crippled by GB%. Speed, but no running game; chronically poor contact/BA skills since forever. We'll pass.

Yr	Tm	AB	R	HR	RBI	SB	BA	xBA	OBP	SLG	OPS	vL	vR	bb%	ct%	Eye	G	L	F	h%	HctX	PX	xPX	hr/f	Spd	SBO	SB%	#Wk	DOM	DIS	RC/G	RAR	BPV	BPX
13	aa	444	52	11	41	9	202		273	330	602			9	58	0.23				32		114			121	22%	43%				2.60		-18	-45
14	a/a	442	46	9	48	9	223		286	352	639			8	66	0.26				32		111			108	15%	55%				3.17		4	11
15	SF *	483	64	20	67	15	236	211	308	417	725	1456	1026	9	54	0.22	39	29	32	39	91	165	216	67%	111	20%	61%	7	43%	43%	4.10	-9.1	1	3
16	SF *	321	55	15	40	1	225	227	308	412	720	370	895	11	61	0.31	52	20	28	32	86	132	76	22%	124	4%	25%	16	25%	69%	4.07	-5.4	10	29
17	SF *	278	30	6	29	3	221	214	287	356	643	669	718	8	67	0.28	52	13	35	31	72	96	79	10%	121	8%	55%	11	45%	45%	3.28	-16.9	0	0
1st Half		57	11	1	4	0	163	193	283	258	541	0	501	14	67	0.51	73	0	27	23	74	61	42	0%	145	0%	0%	2	0%	50%	2.22	-5.9	-9	-27
2nd Half		221	19	5	25	3	236	218	289	381	670	719	752	7	67	0.22	50	15	36	33	72	105	83	11%	107	10%	55%	9	56%	44%	3.57	-12.0	-2	-6
18	**Proj**	**379**	**52**	**12**	**42**	**4**	**228**	**217**	**316**	**385**	**701**	**496**	**758**	**10**	**63**	**0.29**	**51**	**17**	**33**	**33**	**78**	**109**	**80**	**15%**	**130**	**8%**	**55%**				**3.78**	**-7.9**	**-11**	**-32**

Parra,Gerardo

Age: 31	Bats: L	Pos: LF RF	Health	C	LIMA Plan	B
Ht: 5' 11"	Wt: 210		PT/Exp	C	Rand Var	-4
			Consist	F	MM	2153

Strained quad cost him June, but didn't slow him down. Big gains vL, LD+FB upticks, improved ct% and HctX, h% inflation all contributed to the surge. But the bottom line? An .872 OPS at home (.708 away) says he became a bona fide Coors Field hitter in his second season with the Rockies. You've been warned.

Yr	Tm	AB	R	HR	RBI	SB	BA	xBA	OBP	SLG	OPS	vL	vR	bb%	ct%	Eye	G	L	F	h%	HctX	PX	xPX	hr/f	Spd	SBO	SB%	#Wk	DOM	DIS	RC/G	RAR	BPV	BPX
13	ARI	601	79	10	48	10	268	283	323	403	726	501	820	7	83	0.48	55	20	25	31	112	97	97	8%	97	13%	50%	27	48%	19%	4.30	4.3	57	143
14	2 NL	529	64	9	40	9	261	266	308	369	677	554	704	6	81	0.32	54	22	24	31	96	76	85	9%	103	12%	56%	28	25%	43%	3.72	-0.9	29	78
15	2 TM	547	83	14	51	14	291	287	328	452	780	658	809	5	83	0.30	47	24	29	33	109	104	97	11%	113	14%	78%	27	44%	22%	5.27	8.5	61	165
16	COL *	394	47	7	41	6	247	271	265	384	649	634	684	2	79	0.12	55	19	26	29	103	90	100	9%	92	14%	60%	19	53%	37%	3.34	-15.1	24	69
17	COL	392	56	10	71	2	309	277	341	452	793	806	788	5	83	0.30	47	23	30	35	117	83	113	10%	76	7%	29%	24	42%	29%	5.43	1.9	32	97
1st Half		148	23	6	28	0	318	294	348	480	828	776	845	4	82	0.22	48	28	24	36	113	86	119	21%	85	10%	0%	10	30%	40%	5.49	0.5	31	94
2nd Half		244	33	4	43	2	303	267	337	434	772	824	754	5	84	0.35	46	20	34	35	119	80	109	6%	72	5%	67%	14	50%	21%	5.39	0.2	33	100
18	**Proj**	**402**	**55**	**10**	**56**	**5**	**291**	**279**	**322**	**438**	**760**	**721**	**773**	**4**	**82**	**0.25**	**50**	**22**	**28**	**33**	**111**	**86**	**105**	**11%**	**87**	**10%**	**50%**				**4.88**	**4.8**	**31**	**95**

Pearce,Steve

Age: 35	Bats: R	Pos: LF	Health	D	LIMA Plan	D+
Ht: 5' 11"	Wt: 200		PT/Exp	D	Rand Var	+2
			Consist	F	MM	3033

13-37-.252 in 313 AB at TOR. Atypical impatience fueled 9-for-54 start before calf injury shelved him for a month. Scuffles vL and poor h% stunted his 2nd half. Previous power never locked in; prior Sept elbow surgery a possible factor. Should rebound some—but age, fragility and inconsistency raise his risk and cap his upside.

Yr	Tm	AB	R	HR	RBI	SB	BA	xBA	OBP	SLG	OPS	vL	vR	bb%	ct%	Eye	G	L	F	h%	HctX	PX	xPX	hr/f	Spd	SBO	SB%	#Wk	DOM	DIS	RC/G	RAR	BPV	BPX
13	BAL	119	14	4	13	1	261	243	362	420	782	802	749	11	79	0.60	39	17	44	30	120	112	129	10%	84	3%	100%	19	47%	37%	5.03	3.6	54	135
14	BAL	338	51	21	49	5	293	294	373	556	930	1109	856	10	78	0.53	35	19	46	32	116	188	130	18%	78	5%	100%	26	62%	35%	7.48	35.5	107	289
15	BAL	294	42	15	40	1	218	252	289	422	711	623	765	7	77	0.33	34	20	46	23	101	129	132	14%	84	3%	50%	22	50%	36%	3.73	-6.0	51	138
16	2 AL	264	35	13	35	0	288	266	374	492	867	1022	798	11	80	0.63	43	19	38	32	112	117	118	16%	115	4%	0%	21	48%	38%	6.23	14.6	71	203
17	TOR *	335	40	13	38	0	241	257	299	414	713	730	767	7	78	0.37	41	21	38	27	109	99	99	14%	80	0%	0%	20	45%	35%	4.15	-12.8	31	94
1st Half		134	16	6	18	0	243	256	285	415	700	901	771	5	74	0.22	43	25	32	29	103	99	87	22%	78	0%	0%	10	50%	40%	3.99	-5.4	10	30
2nd Half		201	24	7	20	0	239	258	311	413	724	597	766	9	81	0.51	40	20	41	26	113	98	105	10%	84	0%	0%	10	40%	30%	4.26	-6.6	46	139
18	**Proj**	**320**	**41**	**15**	**39**	**1**	**247**	**262**	**321**	**445**	**765**	**789**	**754**	**9**	**78**	**0.43**	**40**	**20**	**40**	**27**	**109**	**110**	**111**	**15%**	**89**	**2%**	**33%**				**4.64**	**1.7**	**34**	**104**

Pederson,Joc

Age: 26	Bats: L	Pos: CF	Health	B	LIMA Plan	D+
Ht: 6' 1"	Wt: 220		PT/Exp	C	Rand Var	+5
			Consist	D	MM	4123

11-35-.212 in 273 AB at LA. Improved ct% didn't help, as GB spike cut into power and 2nd half h% fueled freefall. Mid-August Triple-A exile came amid 7-for-70 stretch and defensive lapses. Patience, power history and recent xBAs say he's salvageable, but may need a scenery change. Skills don't usually disappear at his age.

Yr	Tm	AB	R	HR	RBI	SB	BA	xBA	OBP	SLG	OPS	vL	vR	bb%	ct%	Eye	G	L	F	h%	HctX	PX	xPX	hr/f	Spd	SBO	SB%	#Wk	DOM	DIS	RC/G	RAR	BPV	BPX
13	aa	439	73	20	52	28	260		350	456	806			12	72	0.49				32		142			106	28%	76%				5.48		59	148
14	LA *	473	68	22	49	19	239	217	335	416	751	167	561	13	61	0.37	35	24	41	34	73	148	103	0%	95	23%	56%	5	20%	80%	4.34	7.5	18	49
15	LA	480	67	26	54	4	210	225	346	417	763	691	784	16	65	0.54	42	16	42	26	104	152	147	20%	85	7%	36%	27	41%	37%	4.34	0.5	39	105
16	LA	406	64	25	68	6	246	261	352	495	847	469	918	13	68	0.48	40	21	40	30	107	169	134	23%	77	7%	75%	25	56%	36%	5.81	14.0	59	169
17	LA *	338	50	13	42	5	199	258	288	379	667	597	768	11	75	0.50	47	19	34	22	100	110	101	15%	72	10%	61%	23	43%	35%	3.41	-17.6	33	100
1st Half		170	31	10	27	1	239	271	333	473	806	590	860	12	72	0.50	47	21	32	28	97	144	109	22%	84	9%	25%	11	45%	36%	4.95	0.2	53	161
2nd Half		168	20	4	15	4	158	240	242	285	527	600	642	10	79	0.51	46	17	38	18	102	79	90	9%	68	12%	100%	12	42%	33%	2.18	-15.1	20	61
18	**Proj**	**307**	**45**	**15**	**39**	**6**	**234**	**251**	**341**	**439**	**780**	**588**	**821**	**12**	**71**	**0.49**	**43**	**19**	**38**	**28**	**103**	**127**	**118**	**18%**	**77**	**10%**	**66%**				**4.72**	**2.0**	**34**	**102**

Pedroia,Dustin

Age: 34	Bats: R	Pos: 2B	Health	D	LIMA Plan	C
Ht: 5' 9"	Wt: 175		PT/Exp	B	Rand Var	-1
			Consist	B	MM	1253

Series of injuries (ankle, back, wrist) impacted Spd, HctX. But chronic knee issue was the overriding problem, leading to two (of three) DL stints and eventually post-season surgery that will sideline him until at least June. Plate skills / BA intact, but power looks anemic, and now health is a giant question mark.

Yr	Tm	AB	R	HR	RBI	SB	BA	xBA	OBP	SLG	OPS	vL	vR	bb%	ct%	Eye	G	L	F	h%	HctX	PX	xPX	hr/f	Spd	SBO	SB%	#Wk	DOM	DIS	RC/G	RAR	BPV	BPX
13	BOS	641	91	9	84	17	301	284	372	415	787	937	722	10	88	0.97	50	22	28	33	116	80	82	6%	121	10%	77%	26	65%	19%	5.67	34.4	76	190
14	BOS	551	72	7	53	6	278	276	337	376	712	727	707	8	86	0.68	48	24	28	31	112	75	88	5%	94	7%	50%	24	50%	13%	4.37	15.4	53	143
15	BOS	381	46	12	42	2	291	270	356	441	797	834	785	9	87	0.75	50	18	32	31	96	90	92	11%	118	3%	50%	19	58%	16%	5.56	13.7	74	200
16	BOS	633	105	15	74	7	318	295	376	449	825	812	827	9	88	0.84	49	24	27	34	115	75	82	10%	105	5%	64%	27	52%	4%	6.26	26.1	65	186
17	BOS	406	46	7	62	4	293	273	369	392	760	929	729	11	88	1.02	49	22	29	32	92	55	58	7%	85	5%	57%	23	52%	26%	5.14	5.8	45	136
1st Half		242	27	2	31	2	293	260	376	372	748	915	719	12	91	1.45	46	20	34	32	112	47	73	3%	86	6%	40%	13	54%	23%	4.87	0.3	52	158
2nd Half		164	19	5	31	2	293	289	357	421	778	937	744	9	84	0.65	53	26	21	32	64	67	33	17%	88	4%	100%	10	50%	30%	5.53	3.2	37	112
18	**Proj**	**285**	**37**	**7**	**40**	**3**	**288**	**285**	**355**	**414**	**769**	**856**	**748**	**10**	**87**	**0.83**	**50**	**23**	**27**	**31**	**96**	**68**	**67**	**10%**	**97**	**5%**	**65%**				**5.23**	**3.5**	**41**	**126**

Pence,Hunter

Age: 35	Bats: R	Pos: RF	Health	F	LIMA Plan	B
Ht: 6' 4"	Wt: 220		PT/Exp	C	Rand Var	0
			Consist	C	MM	2335

Some BA loss was expected as 2016 h% regressed. But surprising power outage and struggles vR exacerbated the downturn. Chronic hamstring issues shelved him for another month and keep the fork in his running game. Intact plate skills say mild uptick is likely, but the trends aren't healthy. He's in gentle decline mode.

Yr	Tm	AB	R	HR	RBI	SB	BA	xBA	OBP	SLG	OPS	vL	vR	bb%	ct%	Eye	G	L	F	h%	HctX	PX	xPX	hr/f	Spd	SBO	SB%	#Wk	DOM	DIS	RC/G	RAR	BPV	BPX
13	SF	629	91	27	99	22	283	280	339	483	822	976	769	8	82	0.45	47	17	36	31	116	128	112	15%	117	15%	88%	27	48%	15%	5.92	23.2	82	205
14	SF	650	106	20	74	13	277	264	332	445	777	770	779	7	80	0.40	52	14	34	32	97	112	87	11%	164	11%	68%	27	59%	26%	5.11	18.8	76	205
15	SF	207	30	9	40	4	275	279	327	478	806	570	861	7	77	0.33	54	17	29	32	119	135	117	20%	90	10%	80%	11	73%	9%	5.52	3.9	59	159
16	SF *	419	62	15	62	1	290	258	356	460	816	821	802	9	76	0.43	55	17	28	35	93	108	79	15%	104	2%	50%	20	40%	35%	5.84	13.6	44	126
17	SF	493	55	13	67	2	260	239	315	385	701	776	670	7	79	0.39	57	13	29	30	94	66	76	11%	147	4%	40%	24	38%	42%	4.10	-15.6	31	94
1st Half		228	26	5	30	0	263	213	310	364	675	709	657	6	79	0.31	58	11	31	32	105	56	100	9%	123	3%	0%	10	20%	60%	3.74	-8.8	10	30
2nd Half		265	29	8	37	2	257	256	320	404	723	851	680	9	80	0.47	57	15	28	29	85	74	55	14%	150	4%	67%	14	50%	29%	4.42	-5.0	43	130
18	**Proj**	**451**	**58**	**14**	**67**	**4**	**272**	**254**	**330**	**426**	**756**	**783**	**746**	**8**	**78**	**0.40**	**55**	**15**	**29**	**32**	**98**	**86**	**84**	**14%**	**122**	**5%**	**63%**				**4.88**	**2.4**	**24**	**71**

JOCK THOMPSON

Peralta,David

Age: 30	Bats: L	Pos: RF LF	Health D	LIMA Plan B	
Ht: 6' 1"	Wt: 210		PT/Exp C	Rand Var -1	
			Consist F	MM 2345	

Full season of health, career-best ct%, HctX in 1st half led to brief rebound, but power skills never came on board, with 2015 PX/xPX now a distant memory. Extreme GB% isn't helping either. xBA hasn't supported elite BA output, so you're left with OF who doesn't offer enough HR or SB to be more than a mid/late-rounder.

Yr	Tm	AB	R	HR	RBI	SB	BA	xBA	OBP	SLG	OPS	vL	vR	bb%	ct%	Eye	G	L	F	h%	HctX	PX	xPX	hr/f	Spd	SBO	SB%	#Wk	DOM	DIS	RC/G	RAR	BPV	BPX	R$
13																																			
14	ARI *	531	64	13	69	7	271	282	309	430	739	510	848	5	84	0.34	48	21	31	30	110	104	90	10%	110	8%	71%	17	59%	18%	4.61	12.6	64	173	$17
15	ARI	462	61	17	78	9	312	286	371	522	893	686	936	9	77	0.41	52	21	27	38	118	133	115	18%	123	10%	69%	26	46%	15%	7.08	29.8	70	189	$24
16	ARI *	206	28	4	17	2	244	269	281	414	696	717	731	5	76	0.22	51	21	28	30	107	107	99	11%	116	8%	62%	10	40%	30%	3.87	-4.6	36	103	$2
17	ARI	525	82	14	57	8	293	278	352	444	796	711	825	7	82	0.46	55	18	26	34	106	86	80	12%	115	8%	67%	26	46%	23%	5.49	3.3	49	148	$19
1st Half		265	48	8	26	5	317	296	365	483	848	840	849	6	84	0.42	58	19	23	36	127	91	94	15%	120	8%	83%	13	46%	15%	6.54	8.4	59	179	$23
2nd Half		260	34	6	31	3	269	259	339	404	743	644	794	9	80	0.49	52	18	30	32	84	80	65	10%	109	8%	50%	13	46%	31%	4.55	-6.1	38	115	$15
18	**Proj**	**456**	**64**	**12**	**52**	**6**	**279**	**278**	**334**	**447**	**780**	**672**	**815**	**7**	**80**	**0.37**	**52**	**20**	**28**	**33**	**106**	**95**	**89**	**12%**	**123**	**8%**	**66%**				**5.12**	**5.5**	**43**	**131**	**$14**

Peraza,Jose

Age: 24	Bats: R	Pos: 2B SS	Health A	LIMA Plan C+	
Ht: 6' 0"	Wt: 196		PT/Exp C	Rand Var 0	
			Consist B	MM 0533	

Second half Spd, SBO drops were worst in July/Aug, which coincided with part-time role. Then posted a 53% SBO in Sept, so can still run wild when given green light. BA regression was forecast by xBA, and with no power, he's down to empty ct%. 40-SB upside remains but if warts continue to linger... DN: 250 AB, 15 SB

Yr	Tm	AB	R	HR	RBI	SB	BA	xBA	OBP	SLG	OPS	vL	vR	bb%	ct%	Eye	G	L	F	h%	HctX	PX	xPX	hr/f	Spd	SBO	SB%	#Wk	DOM	DIS	RC/G	RAR	BPV	BPX	R$
13																																			
14	aa	185	30	1	14	21	315		336	391	727			3	91	0.35				34		49			130	55%	71%				4.61		50	135	$13
15	LA *	503	54	3	35	30	255	231	276	324	599	779	125	3	90	0.28	37	21	42	28	37	40	37	0%	132	31%	79%	5	40%	20%	3.11	-9.7	38	103	$16
16	CIN *	529	61	5	44	30	292	268	325	378	703	793	754	5	85	0.33	43	28	29	34	73	52	55	5%	145	32%	63%	18	28%	39%	4.14	-7.4	35	100	$24
17	CIN	487	50	5	37	23	259	248	297	324	622	655	609	4	86	0.29	47	22	31	29	74	33	43	4%	150	24%	74%	26	23%	38%	3.21	-18.9	24	73	$14
1st Half		296	29	3	24	15	250	246	276	328	604	585	610	2	84	0.11	47	20	32	29	71	39	44	4%	160	29%	79%	13	23%	46%	2.96	-14.3	22	67	$15
2nd Half		191	21	2	13	8	272	252	329	319	648	748	607	7	87	0.63	47	23	30	30	79	25	41	4%	106	19%	67%	13	23%	31%	3.57	-5.7	18	55	$12
18	**Proj**	**368**	**42**	**4**	**28**	**21**	**271**	**261**	**312**	**347**	**658**	**699**	**645**	**4**	**86**	**0.33**	**46**	**24**	**30**	**31**	**75**	**40**	**47**	**4%**	**139**	**30%**	**70%**				**3.58**	**-13.3**	**22**	**66**	**$16**

Perez,Hernan

Age: 27	Bats: R	Pos: LF 3B RF	Health A	LIMA Plan C+	
Ht: 6' 1"	Wt: 215		PT/Exp C	Rand Var 0	
			Consist C	MM 1423	

Streakiness we mentioned last year isn't limited to power (see 1st half hr/f); SBO/SB ranged from 5%/0 SB in May to 35%/6 SB in June. Rising GB%, tepid xPX make HR repeat unlikely, and low OBP adds risk to running game. This is a volatile skills profile, which is how you can lose half of R$ in one year. Don't bet on a return.

Yr	Tm	AB	R	HR	RBI	SB	BA	xBA	OBP	SLG	OPS	vL	vR	bb%	ct%	Eye	G	L	F	h%	HctX	PX	xPX	hr/f	Spd	SBO	SB%	#Wk	DOM	DIS	RC/G	RAR	BPV	BPX	R$
13	DET *	495	53	3	37	25	266	254	289	356	646	501	388	3	85	0.22	47	20	33	31	66	67	54	0%	118	29%	77%	12	8%	67%	3.59	-6.7	39	98	$17
14	DET *	552	56	5	42	17	258	207	297	363	659	0	833	5	87	0.43	50	0	50	29	189	72	-15	0%	131	18%	72%	4	25%	75%	3.66	-2.0	59	159	$14
15	2 TM	263	14	1	21	5	243	233	257	327	584	635	552	2	78	0.08	43	22	34	31	102	66	98	1%	91	12%	83%	26	23%	58%	2.87	-14.4	-3	-8	$1
16	MIL *	466	57	14	64	35	273	249	303	424	727	787	699	4	77	0.19	43	20	36	33	100	91	97	12%	118	39%	83%	24	33%	29%	4.62	0.0	27	77	$25
17	MIL	432	47	14	51	13	259	263	289	414	704	789	673	4	82	0.25	48	18	34	29	100	83	81	12%	99	18%	76%	27	37%	37%	4.15	-14.0	34	103	$12
1st Half		258	29	10	34	8	264	289	297	453	750	679	774	5	84	0.31	48	21	31	28	109	98	81	15%	98	18%	80%	13	38%	38%	4.70	-4.9	54	164	$16
2nd Half		174	18	4	17	5	253	221	279	356	635	934	517	4	79	0.19	49	14	37	30	88	60	81	8%	92	17%	71%	14	36%	36%	3.39	-10.2	0	0	$7
18	**Proj**	**370**	**38**	**9**	**41**	**15**	**262**	**250**	**289**	**392**	**681**	**769**	**637**	**4**	**80**	**0.20**	**46**	**19**	**35**	**31**	**95**	**74**	**85**	**8%**	**104**	**23%**	**79%**				**3.96**	**-5.4**	**22**	**66**	**$14**

Perez,Roberto

Age: 29	Bats: R	Pos: CA	Health C	LIMA Plan D	
Ht: 5' 11"	Wt: 220		PT/Exp F	Rand Var +1	
			Consist C	MM 3011	

Sub-replacement level CA rides the occasional HR wave, as hr/f surge, mashing LHP contributed to five Sept knocks. 2nd half HctX, xPX cresting above 2014-15 levels confirm sizable pop potential still lurks in the depths. However, low ct% will likely keep BA crashing on Mendoza line rocks. Bid $1, hope for another HR swell.

Yr	Tm	AB	R	HR	RBI	SB	BA	xBA	OBP	SLG	OPS	vL	vR	bb%	ct%	Eye	G	L	F	h%	HctX	PX	xPX	hr/f	Spd	SBO	SB%	#Wk	DOM	DIS	RC/G	RAR	BPV	BPX	R$
13	a/a	280	20	1	26	1	166		271	234	505			13	65	0.41				25		72			81	4%	25%				1.88		-31	-78	-$7
14	CLE *	259	31	7	36	1	257	217	324	397	721	397	786	9	66	0.29	45	17	38	36	85	125	123	5%	80	1%	100%	13	31%	62%	4.42	8.3	7	19	$5
15	CLE	184	30	7	21	0	228	237	348	402	751	841	715	15	65	0.52	53	20	27	31	89	134	121	21%	93	0%	0%	26	38%	50%	4.59	4.7	27	73	$1
16	CLE	153	14	3	17	0	183	213	285	294	579	683	528	13	71	0.52	54	15	31	24	72	75	94	9%	84	0%	0%	15	33%	53%	2.66	-5.8	-2	-6	-$3
17	CLE	217	22	8	38	0	207	222	291	373	664	807	596	10	67	0.37	50	17	32	27	87	112	94	17%	51	2%	0%	26	23%	54%	3.44	-4.7	-2	-6	$0
1st Half		104	12	1	15	0	183	204	271	260	531	644	467	11	70	0.42	50	18	32	25	69	58	48	4%	65	4%	0%	13	15%	69%	2.12	-6.7	-29	-88	-$5
2nd Half		113	10	7	23	0	230	219	310	478	787	980	705	10	65	0.33	51	17	32	29	102	166	143	30%	53	0%	0%	13	31%	38%	4.90	2.7	30	91	$4
18	**Proj**	**217**	**23**	**8**	**32**	**0**	**216**	**229**	**305**	**387**	**692**	**794**	**646**	**12**	**68**	**0.40**	**51**	**17**	**32**	**28**	**84**	**112**	**106**	**18%**	**64**	**1%**	**14%**				**3.82**	**-2.1**	**-3**	**-10**	**$2**

Perez,Salvador

Age: 28	Bats: R	Pos: CA	Health A	LIMA Plan B+	
Ht: 6' 3"	Wt: 240		PT/Exp B	Rand Var 0	
			Consist A	MM 3235	

Posted career-high HR by building on FB%, xPX, HctX gains from 2016, which support continued 25-HR production. Intercostal strain, groin injury cost him a few weeks and some pop in 2nd half. With health, DOM consistency makes him especially valuable in H2H leagues. Bank on overall repeat performance.

Yr	Tm	AB	R	HR	RBI	SB	BA	xBA	OBP	SLG	OPS	vL	vR	bb%	ct%	Eye	G	L	F	h%	HctX	PX	xPX	hr/f	Spd	SBO	SB%	#Wk	DOM	DIS	RC/G	RAR	BPV	BPX	R$
13	KC	496	48	13	79	0	292	272	323	433	757	867	714	4	87	0.33	47	21	33	31	108	88	96	9%	83	0%	0%	25	52%	28%	5.02	17.8	55	138	$17
14	KC	578	57	17	70	1	260	265	289	403	692	632	710	4	85	0.26	39	21	40	28	115	95	106	9%	71	1%	100%	27	52%	15%	3.99	11.1	48	130	$14
15	KC	531	52	21	70	1	260	268	280	426	706	560	775	2	85	0.16	42	21	37	27	88	99	87	12%	63	1%	100%	27	48%	22%	4.08	5.2	43	116	$13
16	KC	514	57	22	64	0	247	246	288	438	725	763	710	4	77	0.18	35	18	47	28	105	116	107	12%	65	0%	0%	27	44%	26%	4.12	3.8	30	86	$9
17	KC	471	57	27	80	1	268	266	297	495	792	788	794	3	80	0.18	33	20	47	28	123	121	142	15%	53	1%	100%	24	63%	29%	5.06	12.4	41	124	$14
1st Half		272	35	16	50	0	290	271	319	529	849	821	860	4	80	0.18	29	20	51	31	138	131	169	14%	53	0%	0%	13	62%	23%	6.00	14.4	49	148	$19
2nd Half		199	22	11	30	1	236	263	267	447	714	742	703	3	80	0.18	39	19	42	24	102	108	104	16%	72	3%	100%	11	64%	36%	3.94	-1.0	36	109	$7
18	**Proj**	**500**	**56**	**24**	**73**	**1**	**261**	**260**	**292**	**458**	**750**	**740**	**754**	**3**	**80**	**0.18**	**37**	**20**	**44**	**28**	**109**	**105**	**115**	**13%**	**61**	**1%**	**100%**				**4.54**	**5.8**	**30**	**92**	**$15**

Peterson,Jace

Age: 28	Bats: L	Pos: LF	Health A	LIMA Plan D	
Ht: 6' 0"	Wt: 215		PT/Exp C	Rand Var +1	
			Consist A	MM 1211	

2-17-.215 with 3 SB in 186 AB at ATL. Showed growth in bb% despite shuttling between AAA and the majors, yet somehow managed to lose ct%, killing already-low BA. And even when he does put bat on ball, result is a ton of weak grounders. Add in falling SBO, and he's like a value black hole; don't let him suck you in.

Yr	Tm	AB	R	HR	RBI	SB	BA	xBA	OBP	SLG	OPS	vL	vR	bb%	ct%	Eye	G	L	F	h%	HctX	PX	xPX	hr/f	Spd	SBO	SB%	#Wk	DOM	DIS	RC/G	RAR	BPV	BPX	R$
13																																			
14	SD *	375	40	2	32	13	227	241	298	316	614	607	168	9	76	0.42	63	14	23	29	80	73	57	0%	92	24%	55%	11	0%	82%	2.90	-5.7	11	30	$5
15	ATL	528	55	6	52	12	239	238	314	335	649	510	682	9	77	0.47	46	22	32	30	87	68	76	5%	106	15%	55%	27	22%	48%	3.35	-13.2	16	43	$8
16	ATL *	447	51	7	34	7	231	252	324	328	652	571	740	12	80	0.70	58	19	24	27	82	60	69	10%	104	10%	47%	23	30%	39%	3.38	-20.4	27	77	$4
17	ATL *	314	31	3	38	8	210	217	314	297	611	529	644	13	74	0.59	58	12	30	27	88	55	80	5%	101	9%	86%	23	22%	35%	3.10	-18.7	0	0	$1
1st Half		185	14	1	24	5	213	215	309	282	591	308	539	12	75	0.56	63	10	26	28	86	46	63	0%	96	9%	100%	11	9%	55%	2.98	-10.6	-8	-24	$0
2nd Half		129	17	3	14	3	207	218	322	320	642	1250	819	15	73	0.63	48	16	36	26	93	69	109	11%	108	9%	68%	12	33%	17%	3.31	-6.2	10	30	$3
18	**Proj**	**154**	**17**	**2**	**15**	**4**	**221**	**234**	**318**	**322**	**641**	**595**	**647**	**12**	**76**	**0.58**	**55**	**16**	**29**	**28**	**87**	**62**	**80**	**7%**	**102**	**12%**	**66%**				**3.30**	**-5.5**	**7**	**22**	**$2**

Pham,Thomas

Age: 30	Bats: R	Pos: LF CF	Health C	LIMA Plan C+	
Ht: 6' 1"	Wt: 210		PT/Exp D	Rand Var -4	
			Consist F	MM 4445	

23-73-.306 with 25 SB in 444 AB at STL. Took full advantage of second chance to showcase power/speed combo. While growing Eye, increased HctX, Spd supported absolutely Phamtastic 2nd half, elevated h% says BA was a stretch. Another 20/20 season is possible, but Consistency grade, xPX advise caution.

Yr	Tm	AB	R	HR	RBI	SB	BA	xBA	OBP	SLG	OPS	vL	vR	bb%	ct%	Eye	G	L	F	h%	HctX	PX	xPX	hr/f	Spd	SBO	SB%	#Wk	DOM	DIS	RC/G	RAR	BPV	BPX	R$
13	a/a	269	24	5	30	6	234		287	357	644			7	71	0.25				31		90			130	17%	55%				3.25		11	28	$3
14	STL *	348	43	7	30	14	259	225	309	376	685	0	0	7	72	0.26	44	20	36	34	0	91	-15	0%	132	18%	85%	4	0%	100%	4.10	2.7	15	41	$11
15	STL *	324	48	9	45	8	262	258	334	427	761	783	833	10	73	0.40	51	21	27	33	120	111	119	16%	112	9%	100%	12	42%	33%	5.09	7.3	35	95	$11
16	STL *	283	39	12	31	8	214	228	301	383	684	734	784	11	62	0.32	45	25	30	30	107	124	126	35%	102	19%	58%	18	33%	56%	3.56	-9.6	0	0	$5
17	STL *	536	107	26	87	29	292	277	384	497	881	964	922	13	73	0.56	52	22	26	36	106	121	104	27%	106	22%	73%	22	55%	23%	6.76	26.1	50	152	$33
1st Half		269	47	12	39	13	262	267	339	440	778	830	842	10	72	0.41	53	24	24	32	100	108	102	30%	82	25%	70%	9	44%	33%	5.01	0.8	20	61	$25
2nd Half		267	60	14	48	16	322	289	437	554	991	1060	973	16	75	0.74	51	21	28	39	111	133	105	25%	122	20%	76%	13	62%	15%	8.84	28.7	77	233	$42
18	**Proj**	**495**	**84**	**25**	**70**	**21**	**267**	**268**	**361**	**480**	**840**	**812**	**851**	**12**	**70**	**0.44**	**49**	**23**	**27**	**33**	**109**	**128**	**114**	**26%**	**117**	**20%**	**71%**				**5.76**	**19.0**	**44**	**134**	**$25**

GRANT CHESSER

Phillips,Brandon

Age: 37	Bats: R	Pos: 2B 3B	Health	A	LIMA Plan	B+
Ht: 6' 0"	Wt: 211		PT/Exp	A	Rand Var	0
			Consist	A	MM	1155

Despite most HR since 2013, career lows in FB%, xPX suggest he's raging against dying of the light. Steals help prop up his value, but even there, we've got fading skills and totals. And while ct%, HctX say bat speed is intact, it's being redirected into more empty ground balls. He's not done yet, just heed the red flags.

Yr	Tm	AB	R	HR	RBI	SB	BA	xBA	OBP	SLG	OPS	vL	vR	bb%	ct%	Eye	G	L	F	h%	HctX	PX	xPX	hr/f	Spd	SBO	SB%	#Wk	DOM	DIS	RC/G	RAR	BPV	BPX
13	CIN	606	80	18	103	5	261	258	310	396	706	746	689	6	84	0.40	46	19	34	29	99	85	92	10%	90	5%	63%	26	58%	23%	4.13	7.0	44	110
14	CIN	462	44	8	51	2	266	258	306	372	678	594	704	5	84	0.31	44	22	34	30	104	79	79	6%	68	4%	40%	22	32%	32%	3.81	5.5	31	84
15	CIN	588	69	12	70	23	294	273	328	395	723	710	727	4	88	0.40	45	25	30	32	94	58	66	8%	92	16%	88%	27	33%	37%	4.78	8.2	38	103
16	CIN	550	74	11	64	14	291	278	320	416	736	654	761	3	88	0.26	46	21	32	32	95	75	66	7%	85	17%	64%	26	38%	23%	4.54	-2.9	44	126
17	2 TM	572	81	13	60	11	285	288	319	416	735	711	741	3	87	0.29	49	22	28	31	90	73	53	9%	78	14%	58%	26	42%	35%	4.43	-3.2	40	121
1st Half		278	41	7	29	7	291	287	334	435	770	653	791	4	86	0.34	47	22	31	32	98	82	67	9%	73	16%	64%	13	38%	31%	4.90	0.6	44	133
2nd Half		294	40	6	31	4	279	290	304	398	702	745	686	3	88	0.23	52	22	26	30	83	65	40	9%	85	12%	50%	13	46%	38%	4.01	-6.9	37	112
18	**Proj**	**506**	**63**	**10**	**57**	**9**	**279**	**279**	**312**	**395**	**707**	**679**	**715**	**4**	**87**	**0.30**	**48**	**22**	**30**	**30**	**93**	**65**	**60**	**7%**	**80**	**12%**	**60%**				**4.14**	**-9.6**	**35**	**105**

Phillips,Brett

Age: 24	Bats: L	Pos: CF	Health	A	LIMA Plan	D
Ht: 6' 0"	Wt: 185		PT/Exp	C	Rand Var	-4
			Consist	B	MM	4513

4-12-.276 with 5 SB in 87 AB at MIL. Top prospect has a lot to like, including PX growth, elite speed, LD stroke, and flashes of patience. Everything except ct%, which, as xBA shows, threatens to undermine the whole package. Might need more time at AAA, but long-term potential makes him worth the wait.

Yr	Tm	AB	R	HR	RBI	SB	BA	xBA	OBP	SLG	OPS	vL	vR	bb%	ct%	Eye	G	L	F	h%	HctX	PX	xPX	hr/f	Spd	SBO	SB%	#Wk	DOM	DIS	RC/G	RAR	BPV	BPX
13																																		
14																																		
15	aa	214	33	1	22	8	285		347	421	768			9	72	0.34				39		103			133	19%	72%				5.15		31	84
16	aa	441	59	18	61	12	230		330	410	740			13	63	0.40				32		124			122	15%	62%				4.35		14	40
17	MIL *	470	65	20	67	11	265	226	324	466	790	311	855	8	61	0.22	38	25	38	39	73	139	101	20%	147	11%	91%	11	18%	64%	5.33	3.6	17	52
1st Half		258	35	11	38	1	241	217	291	453	744	1000	250	7	59	0.17	67	0	33	36	0	151	-26	0%	146	5%	56%	2	0%	50%	4.37	-4.1	16	48
2nd Half		212	30	8	29	10	295	228	363	482	844	125	921	10	64	0.29	36	26	38	43	82	125	109	21%	135	16%	100%	9	22%	67%	6.66	10.3	16	48
18	**Proj**	**257**	**36**	**9**	**35**	**8**	**252**	**227**	**320**	**439**	**759**	**277**	**807**	**8**	**64**	**0.24**	**36**	**26**	**38**	**36**	**74**	**124**	**98**	**15%**	**143**	**16%**	**78%**				**4.69**	**1.4**	**11**	**34**

Pillar,Kevin

Age: 29	Bats: R	Pos: CF	Health	A	LIMA Plan	B+
Ht: 6' 0"	Wt: 205		PT/Exp	A	Rand Var	+2
			Consist	A	MM	1335

Another cautionary tale for not overreacting to early stats: .301 BA/.844 OPS in April, .246/.675 rest of the way, and overall, same exact R$, nearly same skills as 2016. Peak age, consistency should keep value stable, but flip side is there's very little upside in this profile, especially since he's maxed out playing time.

Yr	Tm	AB	R	HR	RBI	SB	BA	xBA	OBP	SLG	OPS	vL	vR	bb%	ct%	Eye	G	L	F	h%	HctX	PX	xPX	hr/f	Spd	SBO	SB%	#Wk	DOM	DIS	RC/G	RAR	BPV	BPX
13	TOR *	607	67	10	56	17	259	237	291	391	682	680	534	4	82	0.25	36	17	47	30	59	96	55	9%	108	26%	52%	8	25%	50%	3.60	-11.6	47	118
14	TOR *	521	64	11	54	22	285	285	312	445	757	783	631	4	84	0.24	51	16	33	32	98	122	82	7%	102	29%	72%	12	17%	50%	4.82	13.9	72	195
15	TOR	586	76	12	56	25	278	261	314	399	713	684	723	4	85	0.33	41	22	37	31	92	78	72	7%	108	20%	86%	27	33%	22%	4.51	0.0	48	130
16	TOR	548	59	7	53	14	266	259	303	376	679	709	668	4	84	0.27	46	20	34	31	92	72	73	5%	101	16%	70%	25	32%	28%	3.83	-8.5	32	91
17	TOR	587	72	16	42	15	256	269	300	404	704	940	628	5	84	0.35	43	20	36	28	93	85	69	9%	104	16%	71%	26	38%	12%	4.03	-12.4	47	142
1st Half		314	43	9	19	11	252	277	304	408	711	998	616	6	84	0.39	43	22	34	28	107	88	81	10%	108	22%	73%	13	38%	15%	4.07	-7.8	52	158
2nd Half		273	29	7	23	4	260	257	297	399	696	870	641	5	84	0.30	43	18	39	29	76	81	55	8%	97	10%	67%	13	38%	8%	3.99	-7.4	41	124
18	**Proj**	**566**	**66**	**13**	**49**	**16**	**264**	**264**	**304**	**399**	**703**	**822**	**661**	**5**	**84**	**0.31**	**44**	**20**	**36**	**30**	**89**	**79**	**69**	**7%**	**101**	**17%**	**72%**				**4.09**	**-7.0**	**38**	**115**

Pina,Manny

Age: 31	Bats: R	Pos: CA	Health	A	LIMA Plan	D+
Ht: 6' 0"	Wt: 215		PT/Exp	D	Rand Var	-5
			Consist	B	MM	2223

Had 87 MLB AB prior to 2017, so 2nd half drop in ct%, PX, and hr/f were likely signs of pitchers making adjustments (though hip injury at end of Aug didn't help). High FB%, decent HctX make xPX a believer in HR potential, but if those fly balls come up short and the 2nd half Ks stick... DN: .215 BA, return to obscurity.

Yr	Tm	AB	R	HR	RBI	SB	BA	xBA	OBP	SLG	OPS	vL	vR	bb%	ct%	Eye	G	L	F	h%	HctX	PX	xPX	hr/f	Spd	SBO	SB%	#Wk	DOM	DIS	RC/G	RAR	BPV	BPX
13	a/a	298	19	5	28	1	190		224	291	514			4	85	0.28				21		71			79	4%	39%				2.01		30	75
14	a/a	213	21	4	20	1	213		260	296	556			6	84	0.40				24		58			85	3%	100%				2.52		23	62
15	aaa	256	20	5	27	1	241		289	356	645			6	84	0.43				27		79			76	2%	100%				3.48		38	103
16	MIL *	308	26	6	39	1	250	224	297	381	678	555	840	6	78	0.31	36	16	48	30	97	88	118	7%	80	4%	22%	10	30%	30%	3.73	-6.1	23	66
17	MIL	330	45	9	43	2	279	245	327	424	751	706	769	6	76	0.25	35	23	42	34	105	92	131	8%	88	2%	100%	25	32%	36%	4.84	7.3	17	52
1st Half		165	26	6	23	0	291	289	337	479	816	835	808	5	82	0.30	38	26	37	33	111	110	121	12%	80	0%	0%	13	54%	15%	5.64	7.1	52	158
2nd Half		165	19	3	20	2	267	201	317	370	686	567	731	6	70	0.22	31	20	48	36	99	72	143	5%	97	5%	100%	12	8%	58%	4.09	0.0	-18	-55
18	**Proj**	**330**	**35**	**10**	**40**	**2**	**257**	**243**	**305**	**414**	**718**	**586**	**777**	**6**	**78**	**0.28**	**35**	**20**	**45**	**30**	**101**	**94**	**128**	**9%**	**88**	**3%**	**75%**				**4.26**	**1.2**	**16**	**48**

Pinder,Chad

Age: 26	Bats: R	Pos: RF SS	Health	B	LIMA Plan	D+
Ht: 6' 2"	Wt: 195		PT/Exp	C	Rand Var	0
			Consist	B	MM	3313

15-42-.238 in 282 AB at OAK. Hard to tease out whether 2nd half was related to late June hamstring injury or simply league figuring him out, though stability of hr/f, growth in ct% were positive signs. More of an average power guy in minors, but 127 xPX in 333 career AB makes him intriguing speculative flyer material.

Yr	Tm	AB	R	HR	RBI	SB	BA	xBA	OBP	SLG	OPS	vL	vR	bb%	ct%	Eye	G	L	F	h%	HctX	PX	xPX	hr/f	Spd	SBO	SB%	#Wk	DOM	DIS	RC/G	RAR	BPV	BPX
13																																		
14																																		
15	aa	477	53	10	64	5	272		302	403	706			4	76	0.18				34		96			85	10%	48%				4.10		18	49
16	OAK *	477	62	11	45	4	226	224	262	360	622	810	448	5	72	0.17	50	13	37	29	132	91	173	7%	113	6%	78%	8	38%	38%	3.11	-23.4	8	23
17	OAK *	346	38	16	44	4	235	231	282	430	712	738	753	6	66	0.19	41	19	40	31	89	127	119	19%	111	8%	62%	18	50%	39%	3.98	-6.7	13	39
1st Half		182	20	9	26	2	243	233	284	456	740	635	833	5	64	0.16	34	20	46	33	96	148	157	20%	82	9%	60%	10	50%	30%	4.29	-2.9	14	42
2nd Half		164	19	7	18	2	227	231	280	402	682	824	660	7	68	0.23	48	18	34	29	81	105	79	19%	145	8%	64%	8	50%	50%	3.66	-5.8	14	42
18	**Proj**	**331**	**39**	**14**	**38**	**3**	**236**	**237**	**280**	**422**	**702**	**771**	**655**	**5**	**70**	**0.19**	**45**	**17**	**38**	**30**	**105**	**116**	**136**	**15%**	**118**	**8%**	**65%**				**3.85**	**-8.4**	**10**	**31**

Pirela,Jose

Age: 28	Bats: R	Pos: LF	Health	A	LIMA Plan	B
Ht: 6' 0"	Wt: 220		PT/Exp	D	Rand Var	-3
			Consist	F	MM	2345

10-40-.288 with 4 SB in 312 AB at SD. Triple-A coaches encouraged him to put more loft in swing and look at those HRs! However... FB% and xPX show no change at all, and Rob Manfred says the balls are the same. So this power display must be... magic. There is no research on how much we can expect magic to regress.

Yr	Tm	AB	R	HR	RBI	SB	BA	xBA	OBP	SLG	OPS	vL	vR	bb%	ct%	Eye	G	L	F	h%	HctX	PX	xPX	hr/f	Spd	SBO	SB%	#Wk	DOM	DIS	RC/G	RAR	BPV	BPX
13	a/a	482	63	9	52	16	244		313	366	679			9	85	0.68				27		80			107	15%	82%				3.93		57	143
14	NYY *	559	69	8	46	11	256	247	292	362	654	2167	488	5	83	0.31	53	16	32	30	108	68	51	0%	153	14%	57%	2	100%	0%	3.48	-5.0	45	122
15	NYY *	315	41	4	24	5	264	263	314	355	669	752	286	7	85	0.50	56	19	25	30	105	62	56	7%	94	9%	69%	14	7%	50%	3.83	-8.1	35	95
16	SD *	176	14	1	10	1	185	201	214	266	480	556	328	4	80	0.19	53	7	40	22	95	53	84	0%	115	10%	22%	4	25%	50%	1.66	-16.8	8	23
17	SD *	493	66	18	66	9	274	282	323	471	794	928	805	7	79	0.35	47	21	32	32	109	112	97	13%	120	14%	57%	16	50%	31%	5.14	-1.6	57	173
1st Half		270	36	11	36	8	259	284	298	452	750	766	848	5	79	0.27	52	20	29	29	102	109	87	16%	106	21%	67%	4	50%	25%	4.51	-6.8	49	148
2nd Half		223	30	7	30	1	291	281	352	493	846	1042	792	9	78	0.44	46	22	33	35	111	116	101	12%	126	7%	25%	12	50%	33%	5.96	3.8	64	194
18	**Proj**	**459**	**55**	**12**	**47**	**7**	**262**	**274**	**308**	**418**	**727**	**802**	**676**	**6**	**81**	**0.35**	**49**	**21**	**30**	**30**	**106**	**88**	**80**	**11%**	**124**	**12%**	**57%**				**4.31**	**-1.9**	**38**	**114**

Piscotty,Stephen

Age: 27	Bats: R	Pos: RF	Health	B	LIMA Plan	B
Ht: 6' 3"	Wt: 210		PT/Exp	B	Rand Var	+1
			Consist	B	MM	2135

9-39-.235 with 3 SB in 341 AB at STL. Mom was diagnosed with ALS in May, so, not a season played under best of conditions. Second year that plate discipline, power went backward in 2nd half, and half-season MLB xBA trend is alarming: .274, .253, .244, .219. Talented enough to bounce back a bit, just not to 2016 levels. Yet.

Yr	Tm	AB	R	HR	RBI	SB	BA	xBA	OBP	SLG	OPS	vL	vR	bb%	ct%	Eye	G	L	F	h%	HctX	PX	xPX	hr/f	Spd	SBO	SB%	#Wk	DOM	DIS	RC/G	RAR	BPV	BPX
13	aa	184	13	4	18	5	259		314	371	684			7	89	0.70				27		71			85	17%	62%				3.86		54	135
14	aaa	500	50	6	50	8	244		288	339	626			6	86	0.45				27		71			81	12%	58%				3.20		40	108
15	STL *	553	69	15	69	6	259	264	326	428	753	887	841	9	76	0.42	45	21	34	31	127	119	136	12%	136	10%	42%	12	50%	33%	4.57	-4.7	61	165
16	STL	582	86	22	85	7	273	264	343	457	800	952	748	8	77	0.38	44	20	36	32	100	114	105	13%	116	8%	58%	27	48%	19%	5.21	8.8	52	149
17	STL *	380	46	12	45	3	235	240	336	384	720	723	704	13	75	0.60	49	18	33	28	99	91	112	11%	84	8%	33%	22	27%	45%	4.09	-12.7	25	76
1st Half		202	27	6	29	3	242	242	356	390	746	518	822	15	78	0.79	45	17	38	28	102	91	137	10%	85	12%	38%	12	33%	42%	4.35	-4.4	41	124
2nd Half		178	19	6	17	0	227	239	311	378	690	974	537	11	71	0.43	55	18	26	28	95	91	76	11%	92	2%	0%	10	20%	50%	3.80	-6.9	10	30
18	**Proj**	**440**	**54**	**14**	**54**	**4**	**255**	**254**	**338**	**416**	**754**	**885**	**716**	**10**	**76**	**0.49**	**48**	**19**	**33**	**30**	**103**	**95**	**107**	**13%**	**98**	**8%**	**44%**				**4.54**	**-2.0**	**24**	**72**

BRANDON KRUSE

Plawecki,Kevin

Age: 27 Bats: R Pos: CA | Ht: 6' 2" Wt: 210
Health A | PT/Exp D | Consist B
LIMA Plan D | Rand Var -1 | MM 1233

3-13-.260 in 100 AB at NYM. Third stint in majors went better than first two, and ended with 0.92 Eye, 18% hr/f, .296 xBA after 8/1. That's still not much to hang his hat on, given long history of subpar skills on display here, but we'll take signs of life where we can get 'em. At peak age, could be worth a flyer at #2 CA.

Yr	Tm	AB	R	HR	RBI	SB	BA	xBA	OBP	SLG	OPS	vL	vR	bb%	ct%	Eye	G	L	F	h%	HctX	PX	xPX	hr/f	Spd	SBO	SB%	#Wk	DOM	DIS	RC/G	RAR	BPV	BPX	R$
13																																			
14	a/a	376	38	8	42	0	246		283	357	641			5	85	0.34				27		80			81	0%	0%				3.42		39	105	$5
15	NYM *	318	23	4	27	0	208	219	252	288	540	411	609	6	77	0.26	46	20	34	26	97	60	88	5%	105	0%	0%	22	27%	55%	2.34	-14.6	0	0	-$3
16	NYM *	322	23	6	36	0	215	232	274	319	592	651	530	7	82	0.45	56	17	27	24	64	64	44	4%	83	2%	0%	15	13%	67%	2.78	-16.1	22	63	-$1
17	NYM *	347	36	10	44	1	255	271	307	392	700	643	805	7	81	0.39	49	24	27	29	97	79	78	13%	79	1%	100%	14	29%	36%	4.14	0.9	26	79	$5
1st Half		153	14	4	20	0	221	246	260	367	627	0	450	5	83	0.31	57	14	29	24	96	84	69	0%	82	0%	0%	6	17%	67%	3.12	-4.6	35	106	$0
2nd Half		194	22	5	23	1	282	271	343	412	755	739	939	9	79	0.44	46	27	27	33	97	75	81	18%	87	2%	100%	8	38%	13%	5.06	5.3	21	64	$10
18	Proj	**261**	**24**	**6**	**30**	**0**	**243**	**256**	**306**	**360**	**666**	**618**	**682**	**7**	**81**	**0.39**	**49**	**22**	**30**	**28**	**89**	**69**	**75**	**9%**	**94**	**1%**	**67%**				**3.57**	**-4.4**	**6**	**17**	**$2**

Plouffe,Trevor

Age: 32 Bats: R Pos: 3B | Ht: 6' 2" Wt: 215
Health C | PT/Exp C | Consist B
LIMA Plan D | Rand Var +2 | MM 1111

9-19-.198 in 283 AB at OAK/TAM. When you lose 12 points of ct% in one year, it might be time to retire. When you get DFA'd by two teams, it might be time to retire. When you post a negative RAR larger than your best positive RAR, it might be time to retire. When we turn your write-up into a bit, it might be time to retire.

Yr	Tm	AB	R	HR	RBI	SB	BA	xBA	OBP	SLG	OPS	vL	vR	bb%	ct%	Eye	G	L	F	h%	HctX	PX	xPX	hr/f	Spd	SBO	SB%	#Wk	DOM	DIS	RC/G	RAR	BPV	BPX	R$
13	MIN	477	44	14	52	2	254	249	309	392	701	826	663	7	77	0.30	39	25	37	30	105	98	113	10%	99	3%	67%	25	44%	36%	4.05	1.4	29	73	$9
14	MIN	520	69	14	80	2	258	266	328	423	751	783	738	9	79	0.49	38	21	40	30	113	127	133	8%	97	2%	67%	24	58%	17%	4.73	16.0	67	181	$15
15	MIN	573	74	22	86	2	244	260	307	435	742	780	727	8	78	0.40	41	18	41	28	115	124	129	12%	93	2%	67%	26	58%	19%	4.46	-1.8	58	157	$13
16	MIN	319	35	12	47	1	260	256	303	420	723	781	705	6	81	0.32	42	20	38	29	109	90	99	12%	79	1%	100%	17	47%	35%	4.39	-3.7	34	97	$7
17	2 AL *	305	34	9	20	1	197	214	273	311	584	661	548	9	69	0.34	47	20	33	25	93	71	71	14%	87	4%	33%	25	24%	52%	2.63	-21.5	-19	-58	-$3
1st Half		202	24	8	15	1	218	228	281	366	647	759	604	8	69	0.29	52	19	29	27	94	90	75	20%	86	6%	33%	13	31%	38%	3.24	-11.6	-7	-21	$0
2nd Half		103	10	1	5	0	155	187	256	201	457	553	281	12	68	0.43	35	24	42	22	91	32	60	4%	90	0%	0%	12	17%	67%	1.56	-12.0	-48	-145	-$8
18	Proj	**192**	**21**	**6**	**20**	**1**	**243**	**233**	**311**	**377**	**688**	**729**	**665**	**9**	**74**	**0.36**	**40**	**22**	**38**	**30**	**102**	**79**	**89**	**11%**	**85**	**2%**	**52%**				**3.89**	**-5.7**	**-8**	**-24**	**$3**

Polanco,Gregory

Age: 26 Bats: L Pos: RF LF | Ht: 6' 5" Wt: 235
Health B | PT/Exp B | Consist C
LIMA Plan A | Rand Var +2 | MM 2245

Recurring hamstring issue pretty much ruined his season, but hidden amongst rubble was best ct% of MLB career, and .387 BA with 28% LD, 125 PX in July. Revisit 2016 skills to be reminded of where he was headed: last year, we forecast a 20/20 season with 30 HR upside; at 26, health willing, that's still within reach.

Yr	Tm	AB	R	HR	RBI	SB	BA	xBA	OBP	SLG	OPS	vL	vR	bb%	ct%	Eye	G	L	F	h%	HctX	PX	xPX	hr/f	Spd	SBO	SB%	#Wk	DOM	DIS	RC/G	RAR	BPV	BPX	R$
13	a/a	252	30	4	33	11	233		311	344	655			10	85	0.76				26		74			101	27%	60%				3.34		52	130	$6
14	PIT *	551	89	12	72	26	258	252	320	377	697	466	727	8	80	0.45	50	19	31	31	84	85	86	10%	101	25%	69%	17	35%	41%	4.05	-0.7	35	95	$24
15	PIT	593	83	9	52	27	256	250	320	381	701	528	747	8	80	0.45	45	20	35	31	103	87	95	6%	116	24%	73%	27	41%	22%	4.14	-12.6	42	114	$20
16	PIT	527	79	22	86	17	258	274	323	463	786	781	786	9	77	0.45	39	24	37	30	112	125	110	14%	84	18%	74%	26	58%	23%	5.13	7.1	55	157	$21
17	PIT	379	39	11	35	8	251	262	305	391	695	586	730	7	84	0.45	42	20	38	27	88	78	77	9%	80	10%	89%	23	39%	26%	4.06	-12.5	38	115	$7
1st Half		232	25	6	20	7	246	260	310	379	689	588	728	8	84	0.57	45	19	36	27	78	76	68	8%	89	14%	88%	13	38%	15%	4.05	-7.0	42	127	$9
2nd Half		147	14	5	15	1	259	265	297	408	705	577	732	4	84	0.26	38	23	40	28	105	80	91	10%	79	3%	100%	10	40%	40%	4.07	-4.2	35	106	$5
18	Proj	**513**	**63**	**20**	**69**	**14**	**254**	**276**	**318**	**436**	**754**	**626**	**789**	**8**	**82**	**0.49**	**40**	**23**	**37**	**28**	**105**	**99**	**91**	**13%**	**84**	**15%**	**76%**				**4.69**	**0.0**	**52**	**156**	**$18**

Polanco,Jorge

Age: 24 Bats: B Pos: SS | Ht: 5' 11" Wt: 200
Health A | PT/Exp B | Consist B
LIMA Plan B+ | Rand Var 0 | MM 2335

Season-long work with new MIN hitting coach kicked in after 8/1: .316 BA, 0.59 Eye, 103 HctX, 112 xPX, 15% hr/f, .292 xBA, and renewed running game to boot. Previous flashes of similar skills (0.63 Eye, 100 HctX, 11% hr/f in 1st half 2016) suggest growth could stick. This might be your last chance to get him cheap.

Yr	Tm	AB	R	HR	RBI	SB	BA	xBA	OBP	SLG	OPS	vL	vR	bb%	ct%	Eye	G	L	F	h%	HctX	PX	xPX	hr/f	Spd	SBO	SB%	#Wk	DOM	DIS	RC/G	RAR	BPV	BPX	R$
13																																			
14	MIN *	152	13	1	16	6	262	252	304	335	639	1000	1262	6	79	0.30	50	25	25	33	86	59	172	0%	104	22%	64%	3	67%	33%	3.40	1.0	10	27	$3
15	MIN *	492	52	5	45	17	266	269	313	350	662	1333	476	6	84	0.43	56	22	22	31	41	56	-16	0%	101	20%	60%	2	50%	50%	3.63	-11.1	27	73	$14
16	MIN *	538	53	12	62	9	272	274	323	428	751	857	718	7	82	0.41	33	30	37	31	80	90	65	5%	102	12%	54%	16	50%	25%	4.66	5.4	45	129	$14
17	MIN	488	60	13	74	13	256	258	313	410	723	669	749	8	84	0.53	38	19	43	28	94	86	89	7%	96	15%	72%	26	54%	23%	4.37	-3.7	51	155	$14
1st Half		240	27	3	29	3	242	240	290	346	636	572	665	7	85	0.50	39	18	43	27	94	63	79	3%	100	9%	60%	12	50%	17%	3.36	-8.7	36	109	$5
2nd Half		248	33	10	45	10	270	274	335	472	806	755	834	8	83	0.55	36	21	43	29	94	109	98	11%	95	21%	77%	14	57%	29%	5.45	6.3	67	203	$23
18	Proj	**553**	**62**	**15**	**73**	**15**	**263**	**264**	**317**	**419**	**735**	**738**	**734**	**7**	**83**	**0.45**	**36**	**24**	**40**	**29**	**90**	**85**	**80**	**8%**	**102**	**17%**	**67%**				**4.46**	**-0.1**	**46**	**141**	**$19**

Pollock,A.J.

Age: 30 Bats: R Pos: CF | Ht: 6' 1" Wt: 195
Health F | PT/Exp C | Consist C
LIMA Plan B+ | Rand Var +3 | MM 3555

Could've made run at 2015 stats if not for groin strain that cost him seven weeks and unlucky 2nd half h% that cost him some BA. Otherwise, plus power, ct% were restored, speed skills held strong, and BPX says he was all the way back. But health risk can't be ignored—since 2014: 356 games played, 289 days on DL.

Yr	Tm	AB	R	HR	RBI	SB	BA	xBA	OBP	SLG	OPS	vL	vR	bb%	ct%	Eye	G	L	F	h%	HctX	PX	xPX	hr/f	Spd	SBO	SB%	#Wk	DOM	DIS	RC/G	RAR	BPV	BPX	R$
13	ARI	443	64	8	38	12	269	262	322	409	730	811	678	7	81	0.40	48	18	34	31	126	98	112	7%	142	14%	80%	27	48%	22%	4.58	6.1	63	158	$14
14	ARI *	314	43	7	29	14	274	281	318	447	764	953	828	6	84	0.40	52	14	34	31	109	116	97	9%	175	23%	82%	15	67%	13%	5.04	11.0	94	254	$13
15	ARI	609	111	20	76	39	315	299	367	498	865	881	860	8	85	0.60	50	21	29	34	128	111	99	13%	128	26%	85%	27	70%	15%	7.02	45.0	86	232	$44
16	ARI	41	9	2	4	4	244	209	326	390	716	425	788	11	80	0.63	42	9	48	26	89	71	119	13%	121	31%	100%	3	33%	33%	4.88	0.3	39	111	$1
17	ARI	425	73	14	49	20	266	299	330	471	801	854	775	8	83	0.49	45	23	32	29	118	113	111	12%	123	27%	77%	21	52%	19%	5.22	2.0	78	236	$18
1st Half		154	26	2	11	11	299	279	337	455	792	789	793	6	81	0.31	50	20	30	36	116	93	122	5%	145	34%	85%	7	57%	29%	5.73	3.6	56	170	$9
2nd Half		271	47	12	38	9	247	311	327	480	806	894	766	9	85	0.62	42	25	33	25	119	124	105	16%	103	23%	69%	14	50%	14%	4.96	0.4	88	267	$23
18	Proj	**486**	**81**	**16**	**53**	**24**	**281**	**295**	**339**	**477**	**815**	**863**	**796**	**7**	**84**	**0.49**	**48**	**21**	**32**	**31**	**120**	**107**	**106**	**12%**	**137**	**25%**	**81%**				**5.68**	**16.3**	**81**	**246**	**$26**

Posey,Buster

Age: 31 Bats: R Pos: CA 1B | Ht: 6' 1" Wt: 215
Health A | PT/Exp A | Consist C
LIMA Plan B+ | Rand Var -3 | MM 1255

While he's outperformed xBA before, this time h% luck helped mask continued declines in HctX, hr/f, and vanishing HR in 2nd half. Overall skills, led by elite Eye, are still strong enough to keep R$ near $20 for at least one more year. But sure looks like he peaked in 2014-15, and catching takes a physical toll.

Yr	Tm	AB	R	HR	RBI	SB	BA	xBA	OBP	SLG	OPS	vL	vR	bb%	ct%	Eye	G	L	F	h%	HctX	PX	xPX	hr/f	Spd	SBO	SB%	#Wk	DOM	DIS	RC/G	RAR	BPV	BPX	R$
13	SF	520	61	15	72	2	294	279	371	450	821	891	792	10	87	0.86	47	20	33	32	118	103	116	10%	83	2%	67%	27	56%	7%	5.95	32.6	75	188	$19
14	SF	547	72	22	89	0	311	298	364	490	854	875	844	8	87	0.68	42	24	34	32	131	113	121	13%	82	1%	0%	27	70%	19%	6.57	46.2	82	222	$27
15	SF	557	74	19	95	2	318	288	379	470	849	854	847	9	91	1.08	44	22	34	33	137	87	113	11%	58	1%	100%	27	63%	11%	6.71	43.1	70	189	$27
16	SF	539	82	14	80	6	288	289	362	434	796	899	752	10	87	0.94	49	22	30	31	128	84	111	10%	91	4%	86%	27	59%	11%	5.68	19.2	67	191	$19
17	SF	494	62	12	67	6	320	285	400	462	861	1019	799	11	87	0.92	44	23	33	35	116	81	113	8%	79	4%	86%	27	52%	11%	6.87	37.2	58	176	$21
1st Half		253	34	10	35	1	340	301	418	522	940	1096	871	11	89	1.03	39	25	36	36	117	94	118	12%	83	1%	100%	13	69%	8%	8.30	27.5	77	233	$24
2nd Half		241	28	2	32	5	299	269	380	398	779	921	729	11	85	0.84	49	21	30	35	115	67	108	3%	78	7%	83%	14	36%	14%	5.55	9.7	40	121	$18
18	Proj	**502**	**66**	**13**	**73**	**5**	**297**	**281**	**372**	**439**	**811**	**919**	**769**	**10**	**87**	**0.90**	**46**	**21**	**33**	**32**	**123**	**79**	**113**	**9%**	**78**	**4%**	**85%**				**5.93**	**24.8**	**54**	**163**	**$21**

Powell,Boog

Age: 25 Bats: L Pos: CF | Ht: 5' 10" Wt: 185
Health A | PT/Exp D | Consist D
LIMA Plan D | Rand Var -5 | MM 1311

3-12-.282 with 0 SB in 117 AB at SEA/OAK. Hit more HR in 2017 than in all other pro seasons combined, but xPX casts serious doubt on any power upside. Likewise, xBA takes the starch out of BA. Patience, Spd might be enough to rack up modest value, but at some point you have to ask: Do you really need steals this badly?

Yr	Tm	AB	R	HR	RBI	SB	BA	xBA	OBP	SLG	OPS	vL	vR	bb%	ct%	Eye	G	L	F	h%	HctX	PX	xPX	hr/f	Spd	SBO	SB%	#Wk	DOM	DIS	RC/G	RAR	BPV	BPX	R$
13																																			
14																																			
15	a/a	444	55	2	33	15	265		341	346	687			10	80	0.57				33		52			144	21%	49%				3.74		27	73	$12
16	aaa	248	32	3	22	8	235		286	307	593			7	80	0.36				28		45			109	23%	55%				2.73		5	14	$4
17	2 AL *	339	61	7	38	9	287	244	358	403	761	795	755	10	81	0.57	46	18	36	34	80	66	43	10%	131	14%	56%	13	31%	54%	4.94	1.9	37	112	$13
1st Half		164	31	2	18	7	269	247	365	363	727	833	460	13	85	1.00	70	5	25	31	47	53	-26	0%	121	22%	55%	6	0%	67%	4.30	-3.0	47	142	$11
2nd Half		175	30	5	20	2	304	241	352	441	793	778	845	7	77	0.32	39	22	39	37	87	78	63	12%	129	5%	61%	7	57%	43%	5.62	3.4	24	73	$14
18	Proj	**192**	**29**	**4**	**19**	**5**	**240**	**238**	**302**	**346**	**648**	**795**	**633**	**9**	**80**	**0.47**	**51**	**16**	**33**	**28**	**71**	**60**	**27**	**7%**	**133**	**19%**	**54%**				**3.33**	**-6.9**	**19**	**57**	**$5**

BRANDON KRUSE

Prado,Martin

Age: 34 Bats: R Pos: 3B	Health F	LIMA Plan B	
Ht: 6' 0" Wt: 215	PT/Exp C	Rand Var +2	
	Consist C	MM 1145	

A lost season, as early hamstring issues gave way to season-ending knee surgery in July. Previously ironclad ct%/LD% combo should drive a BA rebound, though power/speed skills say that's all you're getting. Age magnifies injury risk, but nearly made Sept return, so offseason of rest should yield return to normal.

Yr Tm	AB	R	HR	RBI	SB	BA	xBA	OBP	SLG	OPS	vL	vR	bb%	ct%	Eye	G	L	F	h%	HctX	PX	xPX	hr/f	Spd	SBO	SB%	#Wk	DOM	DIS	RC/G	RAR	BPV	BPX
13 ARI	609	70	14	82	3	282	290	333	417	750	852	716	7	91	0.89	48	22	30	29	112	85	89	8%	76	5%	38%	27	59%	4%	4.81	14.1	72	180
14 2 TM	536	62	12	58	3	282	276	321	412	733	979	668	5	85	0.33	49	22	29	31	102	88	78	9%	109	3%	75%	26	42%	27%	4.61	13.5	55	149
15 MIA	500	52	9	63	1	288	267	338	394	732	856	695	7	86	0.54	47	23	30	32	103	66	69	7%	77	1%	100%	23	43%	30%	4.77	1.2	37	100
16 MIA	600	70	8	75	2	305	288	359	417	775	1068	695	7	89	0.71	47	25	28	33	102	68	67	5%	98	2%	50%	27	52%	19%	5.42	7.2	55	157
17 MIA	140	13	2	12	0	250	256	279	357	636	658	630	4	84	0.27	49	20	31	28	66	67	58	5%	70	0%	0%	9	22%	33%	3.41	-7.7	22	67
1st Half	95	8	2	11	0	295	269	320	421	741	729	744	4	87	0.33	48	21	31	32	76	72	69	8%	72	0%	0%	6	33%	17%	4.92	-0.4	39	118
2nd Half	45	5	0	1	0	156	227	191	222	414	500	389	4	78	0.20	51	17	31	20	45	54	31	0%	76	0%	0%	3	0%	67%	1.28	-5.7	-12	-36
18 Proj	**462**	**48**	**6**	**56**	**1**	**292**	**270**	**333**	**392**	**725**	**874**	**682**	**6**	**87**	**0.48**	**49**	**21**	**30**	**32**	**80**	**58**	**59**	**5%**	**77**	**2%**	**59%**				**4.68**	**-2.8**	**25**	**76**

Presley,Alex

Age: 32 Bats: L Pos: RF	Health B	LIMA Plan D	
Ht: 5' 10" Wt: 195	PT/Exp D	Rand Var -1	
	Consist B	MM 1331	

3-20-.314 with 5 SB in 245 AB at DET. Career journeyman pieced together an impressive second half. Lots of reasons not to believe it: BA spike driven by fluky LD%, h%; no hard contact (a 28 xPX!?); remains a liability against southpaws. At 32, we're not buying that Spd spike, either. Let the journeying continue.

Yr Tm	AB	R	HR	RBI	SB	BA	xBA	OBP	SLG	OPS	vL	vR	bb%	ct%	Eye	G	L	F	h%	HctX	PX	xPX	hr/f	Spd	SBO	SB%	#Wk	DOM	DIS	RC/G	RAR	BPV	BPX
13 2 TM *	527	58	6	34	13	250	256	300	344	644	634	705	7	80	0.35	52	23	25	30	78	64	45	9%	144	18%	54%	14	21%	64%	3.30	-20.8	29	73
14 HOU	254	22	6	19	5	244	238	281	346	628	777	613	5	83	0.30	47	18	35	27	92	65	83	8%	94	10%	83%	20	25%	40%	3.32	-4.3	22	59
15 HOU *	344	30	2	31	9	213	274	252	265	516	2000	432	5	82	0.29	57	29	14	25	51	37	20	0%	89	18%	64%	3	0%	100%	2.11	-28.7	-1	-3
16 2 TM *	322	33	6	24	4	228	248	288	344	632	582	550	8	79	0.41	46	22	32	27	90	68	99	10%	109	17%	28%	12	17%	67%	2.90	-18.2	22	63
17 DET *	412	51	5	27	8	258	265	300	347	647	579	797	6	77	0.27	45	31	23	32	76	53	35	7%	138	10%	77%	17	41%	59%	3.59	-16.1	7	21
1st Half	204	26	3	12	5	191	243	236	272	508	0	675	6	74	0.23	53	24	24	24	147	51	66	11%	120	19%	67%	4	25%	75%	1.99	-20.2	-13	-39
2nd Half	208	25	2	15	3	324	280	363	420	783	619	831	6	81	0.31	44	33	23	40	59	55	28	5%	137	4%	100%	13	46%	54%	5.86	4.4	21	64
18 Proj	**203**	**22**	**4**	**15**	**4**	**248**	**260**	**296**	**356**	**652**	**564**	**668**	**6**	**79**	**0.32**	**47**	**25**	**27**	**30**	**91**	**60**	**63**	**8%**	**119**	**13%**	**57%**				**3.44**	**-7.7**	**8**	**24**

Profar,Jurickson

Age: 25 Bats: B Pos: LF	Health F	LIMA Plan D	
Ht: 6' 0" Wt: 190	PT/Exp C	Rand Var +3	
	Consist A	MM 1231	

0-5-.172 with 1 SB in 58 AB at TEX. We're still waiting. Denied Sept call-up after two shaky MLB cameos. Not a total lost cause—2nd half Eye growth a great sign, h% masked notable contact gains—but post-shoulder power skills look bad (2nd half xPX based on 7 AB) and running game remains absent. The panic level escalates.

Yr Tm	AB	R	HR	RBI	SB	BA	xBA	OBP	SLG	OPS	vL	vR	bb%	ct%	Eye	G	L	F	h%	HctX	PX	xPX	hr/f	Spd	SBO	SB%	#Wk	DOM	DIS	RC/G	RAR	BPV	BPX
13 TEX *	430	52	9	41	7	244	247	313	359	671	541	696	9	80	0.49	41	23	35	29	96	79	88	8%	102	10%	57%	19	26%	37%	3.68	3.3	32	80
14																																	
15																																	
16 TEX *	441	57	9	40	5	244	247	311	350	661	461	728	9	80	0.48	53	19	28	29	78	62	47	8%	121	8%	54%	20	25%	65%	3.59	-9.4	24	69
17 TEX *	385	46	5	39	5	236	274	311	338	649	733	479	10	87	0.83	41	25	34	26	92	62	82	0%	91	6%	83%	7	43%	57%	3.55	-12.5	46	139
1st Half	245	26	2	23	3	232	270	296	324	619	200	435	8	85	0.61	43	24	32	27	91	62	75	0%	94	7%	77%	6	33%	67%	3.19	-10.3	37	112
2nd Half	140	20	4	16	1	243	277	337	363	701	3000	833	12	90	1.39	29	29	43	25	91	61	116	0%	97	3%	100%	1	100%	0%	4.20	-1.6	64	194
18 Proj	**190**	**24**	**3**	**19**	**2**	**242**	**256**	**324**	**333**	**657**	**553**	**688**	**10**	**84**	**0.66**	**45**	**23**	**33**	**28**	**90**	**53**	**73**	**5%**	**105**	**6%**	**66%**				**3.50**	**-5.4**	**19**	**59**

Puig,Yasiel

Age: 27 Bats: R Pos: RF	Health C	LIMA Plan B	
Ht: 6' 2" Wt: 240	PT/Exp C	Rand Var +1	
	Consist B	MM 3235	

Latest chapter in page-turning career intrigues us. SB spike driven by green light, success on basepaths (not speed skill). Career-best plate skills and xBA growth hint at BA gains. HR repeat unlikely—too many GBs, xPX questions hr/f surge. This is a level he can sustain; just with fewer bombs, more hits.

Yr Tm	AB	R	HR	RBI	SB	BA	xBA	OBP	SLG	OPS	vL	vR	bb%	ct%	Eye	G	L	F	h%	HctX	PX	xPX	hr/f	Spd	SBO	SB%	#Wk	DOM	DIS	RC/G	RAR	BPV	BPX
13 LA *	529	89	26	74	22	309	285	368	533	900	1001	897	8	76	0.38	50	19	31	37	119	154	106	22%	126	24%	62%	18	56%	28%	6.82	32.7	81	203
14 LA	558	92	16	69	11	296	272	382	480	863	736	901	10	78	0.54	52	15	33	36	116	134	110	11%	139	11%	61%	28	54%	36%	6.29	34.3	83	224
15 LA	282	30	11	38	3	255	249	322	436	758	924	704	8	77	0.39	44	17	39	30	107	114	89	13%	104	8%	50%	18	39%	22%	4.60	-2.0	47	127
16 LA *	403	54	14	54	5	268	252	316	428	743	784	715	6	79	0.34	48	16	35	31	100	92	90	12%	101	8%	61%	22	27%	32%	4.62	-0.6	35	100
17 LA	499	72	28	74	15	263	277	346	487	833	592	909	11	80	0.64	48	16	36	28	107	119	95	19%	93	15%	71%	27	56%	22%	5.75	8.2	67	203
1st Half	264	37	15	42	9	250	265	329	458	787	559	861	11	79	0.59	52	14	34	26	102	110	93	21%	82	15%	82%	13	46%	23%	5.24	1.4	52	158
2nd Half	235	35	13	32	6	277	288	364	519	883	629	964	12	81	0.70	44	18	38	29	111	128	97	18%	99	15%	60%	14	64%	21%	6.35	8.8	83	252
18 Proj	**538**	**75**	**23**	**75**	**12**	**272**	**264**	**346**	**464**	**811**	**730**	**841**	**10**	**79**	**0.51**	**48**	**17**	**36**	**31**	**107**	**105**	**94**	**15%**	**103**	**12%**	**65%**				**5.44**	**11.7**	**49**	**148**

Pujols,Albert

Age: 38 Bats: R Pos: DH	Health A	LIMA Plan B+	
Ht: 6' 3" Wt: 240	PT/Exp A	Rand Var +1	
	Consist B	MM 1135	

Joined The 600 Club, but there was little else to celebrate. Skills decline litters this once-bulletproof profile: continued xBA, ct% erosion says he deserved the career-low BA; PX, xPX hit new lows and he's hitting fewer FBs. Showed a pulse in 2nd half, so new normal might be a little better than this, but not by much.

Yr Tm	AB	R	HR	RBI	SB	BA	xBA	OBP	SLG	OPS	vL	vR	bb%	ct%	Eye	G	L	F	h%	HctX	PX	xPX	hr/f	Spd	SBO	SB%	#Wk	DOM	DIS	RC/G	RAR	BPV	BPX
13 LAA	391	49	17	64	1	258	270	330	437	767	690	790	9	86	0.73	38	20	42	26	130	109	135	12%	67	2%	50%	17	59%	12%	4.88	4.3	71	178
14 LAA	633	89	28	105	5	272	299	324	466	790	737	807	7	89	0.68	46	19	35	27	139	122	109	14%	59	4%	83%	27	70%	0%	5.29	22.3	86	232
15 LAA	602	85	40	95	5	244	286	307	480	787	753	799	8	88	0.69	42	16	42	22	127	125	130	18%	57	6%	63%	27	70%	11%	4.83	-11.0	86	232
16 LAA	593	71	31	119	4	268	269	323	457	780	811	770	8	87	0.65	44	17	40	26	129	94	132	15%	57	3%	100%	26	50%	23%	5.20	-5.0	59	169
17 LAA	593	53	23	101	3	241	251	286	386	672	608	692	6	84	0.40	43	18	38	25	120	72	105	12%	49	2%	100%	27	30%	22%	3.73	-19.9	23	70
1st Half	304	24	11	52	1	234	232	278	372	650	498	699	6	82	0.36	44	16	39	25	114	72	98	11%	55	1%	100%	13	23%	23%	3.49	-12.6	15	45
2nd Half	289	29	12	49	2	249	268	294	401	696	730	685	6	87	0.46	43	21	37	25	126	73	112	13%	51	3%	100%	14	36%	21%	4.00	-7.4	36	109
18 Proj	**554**	**61**	**24**	**97**	**3**	**252**	**261**	**304**	**414**	**718**	**696**	**725**	**7**	**86**	**0.53**	**43**	**18**	**39**	**25**	**125**	**79**	**118**	**13%**	**53**	**3%**	**87%**				**4.28**	**-19.8**	**39**	**117**

Quinn,Roman

Age: 25 Bats: B Pos: OF	Health D	LIMA Plan D	
Ht: 5' 10" Wt: 170	PT/Exp F	Rand Var 0	
	Consist A	MM 1521	

Vied for MLB role in spring, instead went to AAA where sprained UCL ended season in May. Game-changing speed remains his calling card, but declining ct% means fewer chances to use it. Career-high AB total stuck at 365, so odds of major 2018 impact are slim, but don't rule out short-term SB burst at some point.

Yr Tm	AB	R	HR	RBI	SB	BA	xBA	OBP	SLG	OPS	vL	vR	bb%	ct%	Eye	G	L	F	h%	HctX	PX	xPX	hr/f	Spd	SBO	SB%	#Wk	DOM	DIS	RC/G	RAR	BPV	BPX
13																																	
14																																	
15 aa	232	35	4	12	23	272		314	378	692			6	79	0.30				33		62			165	53%	67%				3.82		29	78
16 PHI *	343	53	5	25	28	246	248	307	357	664	911	633	8	71	0.31	57	22	22	33	51	77	50	0%	170	42%	74%	3	33%	33%	3.67	-10.2	15	43
17 aaa	175	21	2	11	9	242		304	340	644			8	67	0.27				35		67			132	28%	66%				3.35		-19	-58
1st Half	175	21	2	11	9	242		304	340	644			8	67	0.27				35		67			143	28%	66%				3.35		-17	-52
2nd Half																																	
18 Proj	**130**	**18**	**1**	**8**	**10**	**254**	**243**	**327**	**339**	**666**	**897**	**582**	**7**	**73**	**0.28**	**57**	**22**	**22**	**34**	**66**	**54**	**45**	**5%**	**162**	**42%**	**68%**				**3.41**	**#N/A**	**-4**	**-13**

Ramirez,Hanley

Age: 34 Bats: R Pos: DH	Health C	LIMA Plan B	
Ht: 6' 2" Wt: 235	PT/Exp B	Rand Var +2	
	Consist F	MM 3045	

Said a repeat was "wishful thinking" last year; he didn't even come close. Gave back BA gains as PX dipped towards xPX, took xBA down with it. More bad news: offseason shoulder surgery; running game vanished; UT-only in most formats. Minor rebound possible, but warning signs are growing.

Yr Tm	AB	R	HR	RBI	SB	BA	xBA	OBP	SLG	OPS	vL	vR	bb%	ct%	Eye	G	L	F	h%	HctX	PX	xPX	hr/f	Spd	SBO	SB%	#Wk	DOM	DIS	RC/G	RAR	BPV	BPX
13 LA	304	62	20	57	10	345	326	402	638	1040	1142	1001	8	83	0.52	41	22	37	37	160	186	164	21%	97	14%	83%	18	67%	22%	9.94	42.8	128	320
14 LA	449	64	13	71	14	283	281	369	448	817	869	801	11	81	0.67	45	21	34	32	115	124	115	10%	76	14%	74%	25	56%	16%	5.74	21.6	71	192
15 BOS	401	59	19	53	6	249	277	291	426	717	710	720	5	82	0.30	50	20	30	26	111	101	83	19%	88	10%	67%	20	50%	25%	4.09	-16.1	48	130
16 BOS	549	81	30	111	9	286	278	361	505	866	1097	796	10	78	0.50	48	19	33	32	117	127	109	21%	80	8%	75%	27	59%	30%	6.40	13.9	60	171
17 BOS	496	58	23	62	1	242	257	320	429	750	679	769	9	77	0.44	42	21	37	27	109	107	109	16%	54	3%	25%	26	38%	35%	4.41	-6.7	29	88
1st Half	238	33	11	30	1	252	252	348	433	781	701	796	11	78	0.58	43	19	38	28	119	99	116	15%	67	6%	25%	13	31%	31%	4.74	-1.0	36	109
2nd Half	258	25	12	32	0	233	261	293	426	719	661	740	8	75	0.33	41	23	36	26	100	114	103	17%	48	0%	0%	13	46%	38%	4.11	-5.9	23	70
18 Proj	**479**	**62**	**23**	**68**	**2**	**252**	**269**	**323**	**451**	**774**	**807**	**764**	**9**	**78**	**0.44**	**45**	**21**	**35**	**28**	**113**	**110**	**108**	**18%**	**68**	**4%**	**41%**				**4.78**	**-10.2**	**33**	**101**

RYAN BLOOMFIELD

Ramirez,Jose

Age: 25	Bats: B	Pos: 3B 2B	Health	A	LIMA Plan	C
Ht: 5' 9"	Wt: 165		PT/Exp	B	Rand Var	-2
			Consist	F	MM	3455

Laughed in the face of projected regression with dominant encore. HR surge was highlight, backed by HctX and FB boost. xBA/HctX confirm his solid .300+ BA foundation. xPX history questions full power repeat, but with speed skills hanging on, there's support for a five-category redux. Pay up.

Yr	Tm	AB	R	HR	RBI	SB	BA	xBA	OBP	SLG	OPS	vL	vR	bb%	ct%	Eye	G	L	F	h%	HctX	PX	xPX	hr/f	Spd	SBO	SB%	#Wk	DOM	DIS	RC/G	RAR	BPV	BPX	R$
13	CLE *	494	65	2	29	29	240	220	285	302	587	650	1069	6	90	0.66	50	10	40	26	76	39	135	0%	163	37%	61%	4	25%	50%	2.67	-16.3	55	138	$14
14	CLE *	482	57	6	40	25	265	274	312	366	677	676	632	6	86	0.47	47	24	28	30	85	72	71	4%	120	30%	66%	15	47%	27%	3.77	5.5	51	138	$18
15	CLE *	489	76	7	38	23	240	264	306	355	661	574	655	9	90	0.96	48	16	36	25	94	71	69	6%	135	25%	74%	20	35%	20%	3.63	-9.6	77	208	$14
16	CLE	565	84	11	76	22	312	290	363	462	825	841	818	7	89	0.71	41	23	36	34	97	91	77	6%	109	18%	76%	27	81%	7%	6.15	22.1	78	223	$30
17	CLE	585	107	29	83	17	318	320	374	583	957	953	958	8	88	0.75	39	21	40	32	121	138	102	14%	117	15%	77%	27	85%	4%	8.09	54.8	116	352	$35
1st Half		301	55	13	38	9	319	310	373	561	934	829	996	8	87	0.67	38	23	39	33	124	127	113	13%	115	16%	69%	13	85%	8%	7.66	23.2	102	309	$33
2nd Half		284	52	16	45	8	317	331	375	606	980	1091	920	8	89	0.87	39	20	41	31	118	149	90	15%	119	13%	89%	14	86%	0%	8.56	28.5	131	397	$36
18	Proj	**582**	**96**	**21**	**80**	**19**	**308**	**300**	**362**	**515**	**877**	**898**	**867**	**8**	**89**	**0.74**	**40**	**21**	**39**	**32**	**112**	**109**	**86**	**10%**	**117**	**17%**	**75%**				**6.80**	**30.7**	**94**	**286**	**$32**

Ramos,Wilson

Age: 30	Bats: R	Pos: CA	Health	D	LIMA Plan	B
Ht: 6' 1"	Wt: 255		PT/Exp	C	Rand Var	+1
			Consist	F	MM	2045

11-35-.260 in 208 AB at TAM. Off-season knee surgery pushed debut to June; couldn't rekindle 2016 magic. BA plunge the culprit, xBA says he deserved it despite strong ct%. Power skills stifled by GB% stroke, but strong finish (.293 BA, 8 HR after 8/1) and dearth of productive backstops make him a worthy mid-tier option.

Yr	Tm	AB	R	HR	RBI	SB	BA	xBA	OBP	SLG	OPS	vL	vR	bb%	ct%	Eye	G	L	F	h%	HctX	PX	xPX	hr/f	Spd	SBO	SB%	#Wk	DOM	DIS	RC/G	RAR	BPV	BPX	R$
13	WAS	287	29	16	59	0	272	279	307	470	777	700	803	5	85	0.36	57	20	24	27	145	114	109	28%	53	1%	0%	18	61%	17%	4.99	10.5	61	153	$10
14	WAS	341	32	11	47	0	267	263	299	399	698	820	661	5	83	0.30	55	22	23	29	99	86	88	17%	42	0%	0%	22	32%	50%	4.18	8.4	26	70	$9
15	WAS	475	41	15	68	0	229	240	258	358	616	620	615	4	79	0.21	55	20	25	26	93	81	84	16%	48	0%	0%	26	23%	42%	3.10	-9.0	5	14	$5
16	WAS	482	58	22	80	0	307	280	354	496	850	1008	806	7	84	0.44	54	20	25	33	120	105	97	21%	49	0%	0%	26	62%	23%	6.46	33.9	49	140	$20
17	TAM *	236	22	13	39	0	252	258	287	444	731	809	708	5	84	0.31	52	18	30	25	113	94	106	21%	43	0%	0%	15	40%	47%	4.34	1.4	36	109	$4
1st Half		47	6	4	10	0	202	252	244	461	705	500	835	5	89	0.49	44	6	50	16	157	117	208	25%	70	0%	0%	2	50%	50%	3.60	-0.7	82	248	-$6
2nd Half		189	16	9	29	0	265	251	295	439	734	831	694	5	83	0.28	53	19	28	28	108	87	96	20%	42	0%	0%	13	38%	46%	4.54	2.4	25	76	$7
18	Proj	**464**	**48**	**19**	**78**	**0**	**260**	**269**	**297**	**425**	**722**	**790**	**698**	**5**	**84**	**0.35**	**55**	**20**	**26**	**27**	**109**	**85**	**93**	**19%**	**42**	**0%**	**0%**				**4.38**	**3.2**	**22**	**67**	**$13**

Realmuto,Jacob

Age: 27	Bats: R	Pos: CA	Health	A	LIMA Plan	B+
Ht: 6' 1"	Wt: 210		PT/Exp	B	Rand Var	-2
			Consist	B	MM	2445

All-around production like this is rare for a catcher, but expect more of it. Wasn't going to hold 2016's h% spike, but stable ct% kept BA in plus territory. Modest xPX gains support HR bump but won't likely see 20 at this level. Speed skills hint at double-digit SB potential, but needs greener light which might not come.

Yr	Tm	AB	R	HR	RBI	SB	BA	xBA	OBP	SLG	OPS	vL	vR	bb%	ct%	Eye	G	L	F	h%	HctX	PX	xPX	hr/f	Spd	SBO	SB%	#Wk	DOM	DIS	RC/G	RAR	BPV	BPX	R$
13	aa	368	35	4	33	8	221		282	321	603			8	80	0.43				27		75			106	10%	88%				3.03		30	75	$2
14	MIA *	404	54	5	56	14	258	291	313	386	699	2000	563	7	82	0.44	43	33	24	30	101	91	57	0%	127	19%	71%	6	17%	67%	4.10	7.7	56	151	$13
15	MIA	441	49	10	47	8	259	269	290	406	696	791	671	4	84	0.27	45	21	34	29	106	88	105	8%	125	13%	67%	25	44%	16%	3.96	1.8	54	146	$11
16	MIA	509	60	11	48	12	303	261	343	428	771	617	806	5	80	0.28	49	20	30	36	97	82	86	9%	102	11%	75%	26	27%	35%	5.29	12.4	30	86	$21
17	MIA	532	68	17	65	8	278	267	332	451	783	837	768	6	80	0.34	48	18	34	32	108	97	98	12%	126	8%	80%	27	37%	37%	5.17	16.9	50	152	$17
1st Half		250	32	7	30	4	284	260	344	444	788	1070	711	8	82	0.47	48	16	36	32	108	87	104	10%	141	9%	67%	13	38%	46%	5.30	8.5	57	173	$14
2nd Half		282	36	10	35	4	273	272	320	457	778	632	818	5	78	0.25	47	20	33	32	108	107	92	14%	107	6%	100%	14	36%	29%	5.06	7.7	43	130	$19
18	Proj	**528**	**64**	**15**	**59**	**10**	**277**	**268**	**324**	**436**	**760**	**744**	**764**	**6**	**81**	**0.32**	**48**	**19**	**33**	**32**	**104**	**90**	**94**	**11%**	**121**	**10%**	**76%**				**4.89**	**11.3**	**39**	**119**	**$19**

Reddick,Josh

Age: 31	Bats: L	Pos: RF LF	Health	C	LIMA Plan	B+
Ht: 6' 2"	Wt: 195		PT/Exp	B	Rand Var	-5
			Consist	C	MM	2345

Healthy dose of line drives drove h% spike, career-high BA. Strong ct% cements high ratio floor, but there's little else to like: hr/f remained dormant; running game vanished in 2nd half; gains vL unlikely to stick (39% h%). Hit DL (concussion) for fifth straight season, which in itself is enough to raise a red flag.

Yr	Tm	AB	R	HR	RBI	SB	BA	xBA	OBP	SLG	OPS	vL	vR	bb%	ct%	Eye	G	L	F	h%	HctX	PX	xPX	hr/f	Spd	SBO	SB%	#Wk	DOM	DIS	RC/G	RAR	BPV	BPX	R$
13	OAK	385	54	12	56	9	226	240	307	379	686	667	695	10	78	0.53	36	20	44	26	89	106	110	9%	107	11%	82%	24	58%	25%	3.90	-4.4	50	125	$9
14	OAK	363	53	12	54	1	264	250	316	446	763	533	849	7	83	0.44	33	18	50	29	103	115	118	8%	139	2%	50%	21	62%	14%	4.87	10.2	80	216	$11
15	OAK	526	67	20	77	10	272	276	333	449	781	654	826	8	88	0.75	38	21	41	28	99	100	93	11%	113	8%	83%	26	62%	12%	5.29	7.8	83	224	$20
16	2 TM *	423	54	11	38	8	270	259	333	392	725	366	871	9	85	0.63	41	22	37	30	105	70	90	8%	121	9%	73%	22	50%	27%	4.55	-1.9	52	149	$11
17	HOU	477	77	13	82	7	314	275	363	484	847	762	867	8	85	0.60	34	24	42	35	107	95	97	7%	118	7%	70%	26	58%	12%	6.63	22.0	69	209	$23
1st Half		240	50	8	32	7	308	282	358	504	862	721	886	8	86	0.65	31	26	43	33	110	104	101	9%	120	13%	78%	13	69%	8%	6.80	11.5	81	245	$25
2nd Half		237	27	5	50	0	321	266	367	464	832	786	846	8	84	0.55	36	23	41	37	104	85	94	6%	113	1%	0%	13	46%	15%	6.44	8.8	56	170	$20
18	Proj	**449**	**63**	**12**	**67**	**7**	**282**	**267**	**337**	**437**	**773**	**601**	**825**	**8**	**85**	**0.59**	**37**	**22**	**41**	**31**	**104**	**85**	**96**	**8%**	**118**	**7%**	**72%**				**5.26**	**7.2**	**53**	**161**	**$18**

Reed,A.J.

Age: 25	Bats: L	Pos: 1B	Health	A	LIMA Plan	F
Ht: 6' 4"	Wt: 275		PT/Exp	D	Rand Var	0
			Consist	D	MM	3001

0-0-.000 in 6 AB at HOU. Talk about a short leash; hitless two-game cameo was all she wrote. Raw power is MLB ready, as he led PCL in HR. But also finished third in Ks, which drove ct% further south. Struggles vL (.189 BA, 5 HR in 127 AB) another hurdle. Too many questions to warrant enough AB for 2018 relevance.

Yr	Tm	AB	R	HR	RBI	SB	BA	xBA	OBP	SLG	OPS	vL	vR	bb%	ct%	Eye	G	L	F	h%	HctX	PX	xPX	hr/f	Spd	SBO	SB%	#Wk	DOM	DIS	RC/G	RAR	BPV	BPX	R$
13																																			
14																																			
15	aa	205	30	9	36	0	298		364	506	871			9	73	0.38				37		144			90	0%	0%				6.71		54	146	$8
16	HOU *	383	45	15	49	0	227	220	306	411	718	243	572	10	67	0.34	49	12	39	30	87	131	119	10%	67	0%	0%	15	13%	73%	4.16	-8.1	15	43	$4
17	HOU *	482	58	22	67	0	202	174	271	380	652	0	0	9	63	0.25	60	0	40	27	0	121	-26	0%	52	0%	0%	1	0%	100%	3.30	-31.3	-16	-48	$2
1st Half		283	33	8	31	0	188	203	253	322	575			8	62	0.23				27		100			64	0%	0%				2.56		-36	-109	-$2
2nd Half		199	25	14	37	0	223	189	298	464	762	0	0	10	64	0.30	60	0	40	27	0	151	-26	0%	56	0%	0%	1	0%	100%	4.54	-6.7	15	45	$7
18	Proj	**158**	**20**	**6**	**24**	**0**	**228**	**205**	**300**	**389**	**688**	**278**	**746**	**10**	**66**	**0.31**	**49**	**12**	**39**	**31**	**78**	**109**	**107**	**14%**	**70**	**0%**	**0%**				**3.87**	**-5.9**	**-17**	**-52**	**$3**

Rendon,Anthony

Age: 28	Bats: R	Pos: 3B	Health	B	LIMA Plan	B+
Ht: 6' 1"	Wt: 210		PT/Exp	A	Rand Var	-2
			Consist	D	MM	4245

A skill-supported step forward. Career-high BA came with xBA gains, while bb%/ct% growth drove Eye to elite level. Did it without sacrificing power; even added some loft to push HR ceiling. Lack of running game prevents five-category goodness, but with injuries another year in rearview, bid confidently on a repeat.

Yr	Tm	AB	R	HR	RBI	SB	BA	xBA	OBP	SLG	OPS	vL	vR	bb%	ct%	Eye	G	L	F	h%	HctX	PX	xPX	hr/f	Spd	SBO	SB%	#Wk	DOM	DIS	RC/G	RAR	BPV	BPX	R$
13	WAS *	478	55	12	54	2	267	272	343	421	764	830	682	10	79	0.55	41	26	34	32	122	113	114	7%	110	2%	64%	20	45%	20%	5.01	14.0	62	155	$12
14	WAS	613	111	21	83	17	287	279	351	473	824	825	824	8	83	0.56	40	20	40	32	136	126	146	10%	117	12%	85%	27	67%	11%	5.97	38.9	87	235	$32
15	WAS *	335	44	5	25	1	261	238	337	361	698	750	697	10	78	0.52	45	21	33	32	111	76	104	6%	102	3%	33%	16	19%	44%	4.11	-5.5	25	68	$5
16	WAS	567	91	20	85	12	270	258	348	450	797	817	792	10	79	0.56	36	21	44	31	118	111	116	10%	103	11%	67%	26	58%	12%	5.33	5.7	59	169	$21
17	WAS	508	81	25	100	7	301	282	403	533	937	1131	887	14	84	1.02	34	19	47	32	116	127	112	12%	86	5%	78%	27	67%	15%	7.79	34.8	93	282	$25
1st Half		265	43	16	50	4	298	286	399	555	954	1360	875	14	84	1.02	37	17	46	31	115	134	121	15%	99	7%	67%	13	69%	31%	7.92	20.9	103	312	$27
2nd Half		243	38	9	50	3	305	279	408	510	918	968	901	14	84	1.03	31	21	48	33	118	120	102	9%	74	4%	100%	14	64%	0%	7.64	16.9	84	255	$23
18	Proj	**524**	**81**	**25**	**88**	**7**	**285**	**278**	**374**	**506**	**880**	**984**	**852**	**12**	**82**	**0.74**	**35**	**20**	**44**	**31**	**117**	**123**	**112**	**13%**	**90**	**7%**	**72%**				**6.65**	**26.1**	**72**	**219**	**$24**

Renfroe,Hunter

Age: 26	Bats: R	Pos: RF	Health	A	LIMA Plan	B+
Ht: 6' 1"	Wt: 220		PT/Exp	B	Rand Var	0
			Consist	B	MM	4235

26-58-.231 in 445 AB at SD. Made Opening Day roster, but Aug struggles led to AAA demotion. Power came as advertised—PX/xPX, FB% stroke all check out—but woeful plate discipline locks in BA risk, especially vR (0.12 Eye in 331 MLB AB). 2nd half gains hold some optimism, but lefty-mashing power bats don't carry a ton of value.

Yr	Tm	AB	R	HR	RBI	SB	BA	xBA	OBP	SLG	OPS	vL	vR	bb%	ct%	Eye	G	L	F	h%	HctX	PX	xPX	hr/f	Spd	SBO	SB%	#Wk	DOM	DIS	RC/G	RAR	BPV	BPX	R$
13																																			
14	aa	224	14	4	19	2	202		271	301	572			9	73	0.35				26		82			82	5%	60%				2.58		3	8	-$2
15	a/a	511	48	15	57	4	231		271	380	651			5	70	0.18				30		108			97	5%	77%				3.41		6	16	$6
16	SD *	568	72	23	84	3	255	242	275	443	718	1178	1192	3	76	0.11	43	13	43	30	82	116	125	31%	89	6%	59%	3	100%	0%	4.12	-9.2	30	86	$14
17	SD *	500	63	29	70	4	253	251	296	493	789	1077	636	6	70	0.21	38	17	45	30	99	149	131	19%	86	4%	100%	22	41%	36%	5.03	-2.3	40	121	$13
1st Half		293	32	16	39	3	225	247	284	451	734	1025	623	7	71	0.26	42	15	43	26	95	136	127	18%	86	5%	100%	13	46%	23%	4.19	-7.7	36	109	$12
2nd Half		207	31	13	31	1	292	255	321	553	875	1199	661	4	69	0.14	30	20	51	37	106	167	141	20%	88	2%	100%	9	33%	56%	6.42	7.8	46	139	$15
18	Proj	**501**	**60**	**31**	**72**	**3**	**249**	**258**	**303**	**499**	**802**	**1164**	**682**	**6**	**71**	**0.21**	**37**	**19**	**45**	**29**	**102**	**151**	**135**	**19%**	**89**	**5%**	**81%**				**4.95**	**3.8**	**39**	**117**	**$15**

RYAN BLOOMFIELD

Revere,Ben

Age: 30	Bats: L	Pos: LF	Health	B	LIMA Plan C+
Ht: 5' 9"	Wt: 175		PT/Exp	C	Rand Var +2
			Consist	D	MM 0553

Took year and a half, but h% luck finally turned in July, allowing elite ct%, LD% to send BA back where xBA has long said it belongs. And even though speed skills waned, posted highest SBO of his career. Pigeonholed as 4th OF, but 2nd half vR, Eye say he could at least handle strong side of platoon. UP: .300, 30+ SB, still

Yr	Tm	AB	R	HR	RBI	SB	BA	xBA	OBP	SLG	OPS	vL	vR	bb%	ct%	Eye	G	L	F	h%	HctX	PX	xPX	hr/f	Spd	SBO	SB%	#Wk	DOM	DIS	RC/G	RAR	BPV	BPX
13	PHI	315	37	0	17	22	305	277	338	352	691	858	641	5	89	0.44	59	23	17	34	85	32	31	0%	148	30%	73%	15	20%	33%	4.34	3.3	36	90
14	PHI	601	71	2	28	49	306	293	325	361	686	763	653	2	92	0.27	65	21	14	33	64	33	23	3%	170	33%	86%	27	22%	15%	4.51	13.5	51	138
15	2 TM	592	84	2	45	31	306	291	342	377	719	638	747	5	89	0.50	55	26	19	34	72	44	35	2%	154	21%	82%	27	30%	15%	4.83	7.1	50	135
16	WAS	350	44	2	24	14	217	271	260	300	560	550	562	5	90	0.53	55	18	27	24	74	41	56	2%	160	25%	74%	24	38%	29%	2.49	-19.5	53	151
17	LAA	291	37	1	20	21	275	305	308	344	652	340	715	5	91	0.60	56	25	19	30	80	40	36	2%	124	34%	78%	27	30%	22%	3.81	-13.8	47	142
1st Half		151	19	1	8	6	225	296	239	311	550	279	594	2	89	0.19	58	22	20	25	75	46	40	4%	139	25%	86%	13	31%	31%	2.54	-13.0	42	127
2nd Half		140	18	0	12	15	329	315	379	379	758	385	848	8	94	1.33	54	29	17	35	86	34	31	0%	102	39%	75%	14	29%	14%	5.50	0.6	50	152
18	**Proj**	**332**	**43**	**1**	**23**	**22**	**286**	**296**	**323**	**355**	**677**	**531**	**713**	**5**	**91**	**0.59**	**56**	**24**	**20**	**31**	**78**	**37**	**39**	**2%**	**140**	**29%**	**77%**				**4.14**	**-3.0**	**45**	**138**

Reyes,Jose

Age: 35	Bats: B	Pos: SS 3B 2B	Health	B	LIMA Plan B
Ht: 6' 0"	Wt: 195		PT/Exp	C	Rand Var +1
			Consist	A	MM 2533

After raw hit rate luck in 1H and a short 2nd half DL stint, closed with flourish: .317, 6 HR, 10 SB after Aug 26. Still, late-career love affair with long ball (see FB%) seems ill-advised, given PX/xPX, HctX. Days as full-timer may be past, so don't pay too much, but SB, positional flexibility should help keep him relevant.

Yr	Tm	AB	R	HR	RBI	SB	BA	xBA	OBP	SLG	OPS	vL	vR	bb%	ct%	Eye	G	L	F	h%	HctX	PX	xPX	hr/f	Spd	SBO	SB%	#Wk	DOM	DIS	RC/G	RAR	BPV	BPX
13	TOR	382	58	10	37	15	296	275	353	427	780	705	804	8	88	0.72	46	21	33	32	96	84	81	9%	98	18%	71%	17	59%	24%	5.38	18.5	66	165
14	TOR	610	94	9	51	30	287	268	328	398	726	709	732	6	88	0.52	42	23	36	31	89	77	66	5%	132	19%	94%	26	42%	8%	4.93	26.3	67	181
15	2 TM	481	57	7	53	24	274	257	310	378	688	700	683	5	87	0.42	44	20	36	30	73	67	58	5%	104	24%	80%	24	38%	25%	4.20	0.5	45	122
16	NYM *	317	53	9	27	12	251	248	315	408	723	1196	664	9	81	0.51	35	22	43	28	96	88	100	9%	132	18%	78%	12	67%	25%	4.39	-4.4	55	157
17	NYM	501	75	15	58	24	246	258	315	413	728	843	692	9	84	0.63	37	20	43	27	91	87	88	8%	137	24%	80%	26	54%	19%	4.43	-8.8	67	203
1st Half		266	33	6	27	10	207	251	280	350	630	747	596	10	85	0.72	39	18	42	22	91	74	78	6%	126	18%	91%	13	38%	23%	3.30	-12.6	59	179
2nd Half		235	42	9	31	14	289	266	354	485	839	937	805	9	83	0.55	35	21	44	32	92	103	100	10%	138	29%	74%	13	69%	15%	5.97	7.7	75	227
18	**Proj**	**321**	**49**	**9**	**34**	**15**	**258**	**259**	**319**	**413**	**733**	**870**	**689**	**8**	**84**	**0.57**	**38**	**21**	**41**	**28**	**90**	**82**	**87**	**8%**	**129**	**23%**	**79%**				**4.57**	**1.0**	**61**	**186**

Reynolds,Mark

Age: 34	Bats: R	Pos: 1B	Health	A	LIMA Plan C
Ht: 6' 2"	Wt: 220		PT/Exp	B	Rand Var -5
			Consist	B	MM 4123

Best HR total since 2011; of course, Coors helped (.294, 21 HR), so keep that in mind if home park changes. Unsustainable 1st half hr/f came back to earth, 2016 ct% bump now seems like one-shot deal, and success vR last two years was driven by 37% hit rate. Let others overbid on a HR repeat and endure the BA risk.

Yr	Tm	AB	R	HR	RBI	SB	BA	xBA	OBP	SLG	OPS	vL	vR	bb%	ct%	Eye	G	L	F	h%	HctX	PX	xPX	hr/f	Spd	SBO	SB%	#Wk	DOM	DIS	RC/G	RAR	BPV	BPX
13	2 AL	445	55	21	67	3	220	217	306	393	699	725	684	10	65	0.33	39	18	42	29	94	132	125	17%	76	4%	75%	27	44%	48%	3.86	-9.8	12	30
14	MIL	378	47	22	45	5	196	223	287	394	681	573	719	11	68	0.39	38	14	48	22	94	146	155	18%	88	7%	83%	26	46%	42%	3.58	-7.2	38	103
15	STL	382	35	13	48	2	230	229	315	398	713	753	697	10	68	0.36	41	19	40	30	92	126	117	13%	88	5%	40%	27	48%	41%	3.98	-16.1	23	62
16	COL	393	61	14	53	1	282	256	356	450	806	673	865	10	72	0.38	42	26	33	36	84	115	99	15%	92	3%	33%	23	48%	48%	5.53	2.2	27	77
17	COL	520	82	30	97	2	267	245	352	487	839	760	869	12	66	0.39	42	22	36	35	93	138	133	24%	80	2%	67%	26	38%	46%	5.96	0.8	25	76
1st Half		279	45	19	61	1	290	258	378	534	912	603	1034	12	68	0.44	45	21	33	36	91	146	121	30%	76	2%	50%	13	54%	46%	7.17	11.9	40	121
2nd Half		241	37	11	36	1	241	227	322	432	754	949	681	11	64	0.34	38	22	40	33	95	128	148	18%	84	2%	100%	13	23%	46%	4.73	-6.6	7	21
18	**Proj**	**394**	**56**	**19**	**61**	**2**	**251**	**240**	**333**	**444**	**777**	**739**	**792**	**11**	**68**	**0.37**	**41**	**22**	**37**	**32**	**91**	**123**	**125**	**19%**	**85**	**3%**	**56%**				**4.96**	**-1.6**	**9**	**26**

Rickard,Joey

Age: 27	Bats: R	Pos: RF LF CF	Health	C	LIMA Plan D
Ht: 6' 1"	Wt: 185		PT/Exp	D	Rand Var +1
			Consist	C	MM 1423

4-19-.241 with 8 SB in 261 AB at BAL. Picture further crystallized as to who he is, and it's not pretty. Has yet to show he can handle RHP, minor league walk rate and OBP still AWOL, and already-weak power skills managed to get worse. Yes, he can steal a base. But 5th OFers who only start vL are not in high demand.

Yr	Tm	AB	R	HR	RBI	SB	BA	xBA	OBP	SLG	OPS	vL	vR	bb%	ct%	Eye	G	L	F	h%	HctX	PX	xPX	hr/f	Spd	SBO	SB%	#Wk	DOM	DIS	RC/G	RAR	BPV	BPX
13																																		
14	aa	206	26	1	13	7	208		286	252	538			10	78	0.51				26		39			99	20%	62%				2.27		-3	-8
15	a/a	325	43	2	35	16	287		365	406	770			11	77	0.54				37		87			120	20%	78%				5.35		39	105
16	BAL	257	32	5	19	4	268	240	319	377	696	861	618	6	79	0.33	42	21	37	32	83	72	83	7%	129	7%	80%	16	25%	25%	4.19	-0.6	27	77
17	BAL *	308	36	5	22	8	229	237	273	326	599	687	563	6	76	0.25	35	27	38	29	77	65	64	5%	108	13%	89%	24	21%	58%	3.02	-22.6	1	3
1st Half		133	16	3	11	4	256	240	291	383	674	702	644	4	74	0.14	37	25	38	33	86	85	87	8%	103	18%	80%	11	27%	64%	3.74	-6.4	3	9
2nd Half		175	20	2	11	4	208	237	266	283	548	668	495	7	78	0.35	34	28	38	26	65	50	40	3%	112	10%	100%	13	15%	54%	2.53	-15.4	1	3
18	**Proj**	**260**	**32**	**4**	**20**	**7**	**244**	**241**	**304**	**350**	**655**	**751**	**589**	**7**	**77**	**0.34**	**38**	**24**	**38**	**30**	**77**	**68**	**69**	**6%**	**125**	**14%**	**80%**				**3.56**	**-8.8**	**7**	**21**

Riddle,J.T.

Age: 26	Bats: L	Pos: SS	Health	C	LIMA Plan D
Ht: 6' 1"	Wt: 180		PT/Exp	D	Rand Var 0
			Consist	A	MM 0323

3-31-.250 in 228 AB at MIA. What's black, white and red all over? Yes, that's a pretty weak riddle. Want another? After cracking 3 HR in first 66 MLB AB, hit 0 in next 162 AB; no surprise given GB%. Surgery ended season in mid-July. What's got two legs, one healthy shoulder, and belongs nowhere near your roster?

Yr	Tm	AB	R	HR	RBI	SB	BA	xBA	OBP	SLG	OPS	vL	vR	bb%	ct%	Eye	G	L	F	h%	HctX	PX	xPX	hr/f	Spd	SBO	SB%	#Wk	DOM	DIS	RC/G	RAR	BPV	BPX
13																																		
14																																		
15	a/a	176	23	4	16	0	260		294	363	657			5	85	0.31				29		61			109	0%	0%				3.68		32	86
16	a/a	445	45	3	45	5	239		286	314	599			6	78	0.30				30		51			101	6%	81%				3.02		-1	-3
17	MIA *	291	27	4	36	1	247	251	279	362	641	581	657	4	79	0.21	53	18	28	30	106	71	97	6%	114	5%	29%	13	23%	46%	3.32	-10.3	19	58
1st Half		240	23	4	29	1	233	251	260	364	624	501	661	4	79	0.17	53	17	30	28	112	80	109	7%	118	6%	29%	10	30%	40%	3.03	-11.2	24	73
2nd Half		51	4	0	7	0	314	241	357	353	710	1000	643	7	82	0.44	55	24	21	38	85	30	57	0%	111	0%	0%	3	0%	67%	4.77	0.3	3	9
18	**Proj**	**297**	**29**	**2**	**29**	**1**	**253**	**248**	**290**	**324**	**614**	**677**	**596**	**6**	**81**	**0.31**	**54**	**21**	**25**	**31**	**96**	**46**	**78**	**3%**	**118**	**3%**	**66%**				**3.26**	**-10.5**	**-8**	**-25**

Rivera,Rene

Age: 34	Bats: R	Pos: CA	Health	A	LIMA Plan F
Ht: 5' 10"	Wt: 215		PT/Exp	F	Rand Var -4
			Consist	C	MM 2011

On surface, a carbon copy of his 2014 "apex", such that it is. But while resurgent power skills and fly ball rate may linger another year or two, slipping ct% suggests you might pay dearly in batting average to take that gamble. Even as a second catcher, there are safer bets.

Yr	Tm	AB	R	HR	RBI	SB	BA	xBA	OBP	SLG	OPS	vL	vR	bb%	ct%	Eye	G	L	F	h%	HctX	PX	xPX	hr/f	Spd	SBO	SB%	#Wk	DOM	DIS	RC/G	RAR	BPV	BPX
13	SD *	318	26	3	30	0	242	202	270	325	595	529	618	4	76	0.16	48	13	38	31	126	67	144	0%	75	4%	0%	10	10%	50%	2.84	-8.1	-9	-23
14	SD	294	27	11	44	0	252	252	319	432	751	881	684	8	74	0.36	35	21	44	30	106	138	138	11%	68	0%	0%	27	48%	37%	4.63	10.1	46	124
15	TAM	298	16	5	26	0	178	193	213	275	489	457	503	3	71	0.13	38	17	45	23	83	77	117	5%	43	0%	0%	26	12%	62%	1.77	-19.6	-31	-84
16	NYM *	210	14	6	29	0	218	212	277	326	603	943	556	7	72	0.30	47	22	32	27	92	67	98	14%	53	0%	0%	22	23%	55%	2.94	-9.3	-24	-69
17	2 NL	218	23	10	35	0	252	239	305	431	736	753	730	6	68	0.20	36	25	39	33	99	113	139	17%	53	2%	0%	26	35%	50%	4.28	1.4	-7	-21
1st Half		127	11	5	19	0	260	238	296	409	706	921	642	4	69	0.13	35	27	38	34	101	91	141	15%	65	3%	0%	13	23%	54%	3.91	-0.7	-21	-64
2nd Half		91	12	5	16	0	242	242	317	462	778	575	863	9	66	0.29	37	22	42	31	96	145	136	20%	52	0%	0%	13	46%	46%	4.81	1.9	15	45
18	**Proj**	**196**	**18**	**7**	**28**	**0**	**226**	**228**	**282**	**381**	**663**	**693**	**652**	**6**	**70**	**0.23**	**40**	**22**	**39**	**28**	**96**	**97**	**125**	**14%**	**53**	**1%**	**0%**				**3.42**	**-4.3**	**-21**	**-65**

Rivera,T.J.

Age: 29	Bats: R	Pos: 3B 1B	Health	C	LIMA Plan D+
Ht: 6' 1"	Wt: 203		PT/Exp	D	Rand Var 0
			Consist	B	MM 1141

5-27-.290 in 214 AB at NYM. In second MLB stint, late-blooming 2016 PCL batting champ made better, harder contact, and xPX hints at league-average power. Of course, all bets now off after September Tommy John surgery, which is likely to delay start to season. As age 30 draws near, window for full-time work may be closing.

Yr	Tm	AB	R	HR	RBI	SB	BA	xBA	OBP	SLG	OPS	vL	vR	bb%	ct%	Eye	G	L	F	h%	HctX	PX	xPX	hr/f	Spd	SBO	SB%	#Wk	DOM	DIS	RC/G	RAR	BPV	BPX
13																																		
14	aa	201	19	1	19	1	281		307	343	650			4	83	0.22				34		54			85	1%	100%				3.76		9	24
15	a/a	403	45	5	34	1	254		279	349	628			3	85	0.23				29		66			89	2%	36%				3.29		29	78
16	NYM *	510	51	10	67	2	270	259	295	386	680	457	997	3	82	0.20	42	24	34	31	90	72	92	10%	105	5%	31%	8	25%	25%	3.85	-16.6	25	71
17	NYM *	235	29	6	30	1	282	269	311	421	732	696	780	4	85	0.27	35	25	40	31	102	78	101	7%	99	2%	100%	17	41%	47%	4.68	-4.1	40	121
1st Half		177	22	4	21	1	273	261	299	407	706	600	789	4	82	0.21	34	25	40	31	101	78	105	6%	100	3%	100%	13	31%	54%	4.31	-3.9	31	94
2nd Half		58	7	2	9	0	310	293	355	466	820	1194	760	5	91	0.60	38	25	38	31	105	77	92	10%	98	0%	0%	4	75%	25%	5.93	1.3	68	206
18	**Proj**	**202**	**23**	**6**	**25**	**1**	**282**	**275**	**316**	**422**	**738**	**592**	**786**	**4**	**85**	**0.29**	**39**	**24**	**37**	**31**	**98**	**77**	**95**	**9%**	**97**	**2%**	**56%**				**4.62**	**-1.5**	**28**	**85**

KRISTOPHER OLSON

Rizzo,Anthony

Age: 28 Bats: L Pos: 1B	Health A	LIMA Plan A
Ht: 6' 3" Wt: 240	PT/Exp A	Rand Var +2
	Consist B	MM 4155

1st half BA caused "alarm," but it was nothing h% turnaround couldn't fix. Likewise, given age and career-best Eye, PX/xPX dip likely just a blip. Prior success vL suggests 2nd half drop can be ignored. As a bonus, better job picking his spots on basepaths brought back double-digit SB. Really, there are few safer investments.

Yr Tm	AB	R	HR	RBI	SB	BA	xBA	OBP	SLG	OPS	vL	vR	bb%	ct%	Eye	G	L	F	h%	HctX	PX	xPX	hr/f	Spd	SBO	SB%	#Wk	DOM	DIS	RC/G	RAR	BPV	BPX	R$
13 CHC	606	71	23	80	6	233	269	323	419	742	625	796	11	79	0.60	43	20	38	26	112	130	124	13%	68	7%	55%	27	63%	7%	4.34	-4.5	65	163	$13
14 CHC	524	89	32	78	5	286	286	386	527	913	928	907	12	78	0.63	36	22	42	31	106	164	135	19%	74	6%	56%	25	72%	4%	6.90	40.2	91	246	$28
15 CHC	586	94	31	101	17	278	285	387	512	899	881	905	11	82	0.74	35	22	44	29	121	143	131	15%	76	14%	74%	27	70%	15%	6.51	19.1	90	243	$31
16 CHC	583	94	32	109	3	292	294	385	544	928	832	970	11	81	0.69	38	21	41	31	114	145	120	16%	72	5%	38%	27	74%	7%	7.07	28.4	88	251	$26
17 CHC	572	99	32	109	10	273	291	392	507	899	881	906	13	84	1.01	41	20	39	28	117	119	107	17%	69	8%	71%	27	70%	7%	6.58	11.0	81	245	$25
1st Half	294	49	18	50	5	259	289	385	500	885	1039	829	14	86	1.23	39	18	43	25	108	118	101	17%	59	8%	71%	13	77%	8%	6.22	5.0	88	267	$23
2nd Half	278	50	14	59	5	288	293	399	514	914	704	985	13	82	0.84	42	22	35	31	127	120	113	17%	86	8%	71%	14	64%	7%	6.97	10.4	78	236	$27
18 Proj	**584**	**97**	**31**	**108**	**9**	**284**	**289**	**389**	**519**	**908**	**845**	**933**	**12**	**82**	**0.79**	**39**	**21**	**40**	**30**	**117**	**125**	**117**	**16%**	**74**	**8%**	**66%**				**6.77**	**27.7**	**81**	**245**	**$27**

Robertson,Daniel

Age: 24 Bats: R Pos: 2B SS	Health A	LIMA Plan F
Ht: 5' 11" Wt: 200	PT/Exp D	Rand Var -1
	Consist A	MM 1101

5-19-.206 in 218 AB. April-June debut featured high bb%, low ct% and a surprising bit of pop. Then AB got sporadic after month lost to neck injury. Too young to write off entirely; if you squint, you can see potential in league-average xPX. But xBA, uninspiring high-minors output say there's no short-term reason to pursue.

Yr Tm	AB	R	HR	RBI	SB	BA	xBA	OBP	SLG	OPS	vL	vR	bb%	ct%	Eye	G	L	F	h%	HctX	PX	xPX	hr/f	Spd	SBO	SB%	#Wk	DOM	DIS	RC/G	RAR	BPV	BPX	R$
13																																		
14																																		
15 aa	299	40	3	33	2	244		306	361	667			8	78	0.41				30		83			113	7%	33%				3.59		32	86	$3
16 aaa	436	47	5	40	2	242		327	329	656			11	74	0.49				32		61			101	2%	63%				3.61		1	3	$3
17 TAM *	261	28	6	20	1	229	210	313	346	659	646	629	11	69	0.39	46	18	36	31	94	74	100	9%	117	4%	32%	20	15%	70%	3.48	-9.1	-6	-18	$0
1st Half	170	19	5	16	1	224	213	314	365	679	671	683	11	67	0.38	48	17	35	30	98	87	112	13%	121	4%	50%	13	15%	62%	3.64	-6.2	-2	-6	$1
2nd Half	91	9	1	4	0	239	207	320	311	631	495	471	11	72	0.43	38	22	41	32	73	52	60	0%	104	4%	0%	7	14%	86%	3.17	-4.6	-14	-42	-$2
18 Proj	**156**	**17**	**2**	**13**	**1**	**238**	**215**	**333**	**335**	**668**	**694**	**659**	**11**	**73**	**0.44**	**42**	**20**	**38**	**31**	**83**	**64**	**81**	**5%**	**107**	**4%**	**36%**				**3.51**	**-6.1**	**-16**	**-47**	**$2**

Robles,Victor

Age: 21 Bats: R Pos: RF	Health A	LIMA Plan C+
Ht: 6' 0" Wt: 185	PT/Exp F	Rand Var 0
	Consist F	MM 2553

0-4-.250 in 24 AB at WAS. At 20, elite prospect called up from AA in Sept, even served as playoff reserve, a sign of esteem in which he's held. Speed ahead of power for now, but plate skills, Gold-Glove-caliber CF defense say he could hold his own in MLB. Even if he starts in AAA, a call-up could soon prove irresistible.

Yr Tm	AB	R	HR	RBI	SB	BA	xBA	OBP	SLG	OPS	vL	vR	bb%	ct%	Eye	G	L	F	h%	HctX	PX	xPX	hr/f	Spd	SBO	SB%	#Wk	DOM	DIS	RC/G	RAR	BPV	BPX	R$
13																																		
14																																		
15																																		
16																																		
17 WAS *	163	23	3	16	10	298	264	341	455	797	0	833	6	82	0.36	53	12	35	35	105	93	135	0%	133	33%	70%	5	40%	40%	5.43	1.7	56	170	$7
1st Half																																		
2nd Half	163	23	3	16	10	298	264	341	455	797	0	833	6	82	0.36	53	12	35	35	105	93	135	0%	133	33%	70%	5	40%	40%	5.43	2.4	56	170	$7
18 Proj	**298**	**38**	**6**	**26**	**16**	**271**	**281**	**310**	**437**	**747**	**747**	**747**	**5**	**84**	**0.36**	**43**	**22**	**35**	**31**		**93**		**7%**	**135**	**35%**	**71%**				**4.59**	**-1.0**	**66**	**201**	**$13**

Rodgers,Brendan

Age: 21 Bats: R Pos: SS	Health A	LIMA Plan D
Ht: 6' 0" Wt: 180	PT/Exp F	Rand Var 0
	Consist F	MM 1011

COL's top SS prospect started 2017 by crushing High-A pitching (1.078 OPS in 236 PA), then scuffled a bit in first AA exposure as ct% slid from 80s to 70s. But 2nd half PX was encouraging, even though minor quad injury cost him three weeks. A keeper league plum, and if second tour goes better, good chance of in-season call-up.

Yr Tm	AB	R	HR	RBI	SB	BA	xBA	OBP	SLG	OPS	vL	vR	bb%	ct%	Eye	G	L	F	h%	HctX	PX	xPX	hr/f	Spd	SBO	SB%	#Wk	DOM	DIS	RC/G	RAR	BPV	BPX	R$
13																																		
14																																		
15																																		
16																																		
17 aa	150	17	6	15	0	263		295	412	707			4	77	0.20				31		83			96	6%	0%				3.95		14	42	$1
1st Half	35	4	0	1	0	232		250	232	481			2	78	0.11				30		0			121	0%	0%				1.92		-45	-136	-$8
2nd Half	115	13	6	14	0	273		309	466	775			5	77	0.22				31		108			100	8%	0%				4.66		35	106	$4
18 Proj	**167**	**17**	**5**	**18**	**0**	**243**	**238**	**277**	**372**	**648**	**648**	**648**	**5**	**79**	**0.22**	**42**	**20**	**38**	**28**		**73**		**10%**	**98**	**7%**	**0%**				**3.21**	**-6.4**	**-5**	**-16**	**$3**

Rodriguez,Sean

Age: 33 Bats: R Pos: 3B	Health D	LIMA Plan D
Ht: 6' 0" Wt: 200	PT/Exp F	Rand Var +5
	Consist F	MM 3101

5-8-.167 in 132 AB at ATL/PIT. Never got on track after return from shoulder surgery. xPX suggests he's still got power, but unclear whether woeful ct% was aberration or continuation of 2016 trend. $5 million reasons he'll get another chance, and since he's only one year removed from 2016, probably worth a deep flyer.

Yr Tm	AB	R	HR	RBI	SB	BA	xBA	OBP	SLG	OPS	vL	vR	bb%	ct%	Eye	G	L	F	h%	HctX	PX	xPX	hr/f	Spd	SBO	SB%	#Wk	DOM	DIS	RC/G	RAR	BPV	BPX	R$
13 TAM	195	21	5	23	1	246	227	320	385	704	745	545	8	70	0.29	36	23	41	33	83	110	81	9%	88	8%	25%	27	33%	44%	3.76	-1.3	11	28	$2
14 TAM	237	30	12	41	2	211	262	258	443	701	729	666	4	72	0.15	39	17	44	24	108	170	137	16%	109	9%	67%	27	52%	30%	3.44	-1.9	67	181	$4
15 PIT	224	25	4	17	2	246	232	281	362	642	655	634	2	72	0.08	48	20	32	32	81	90	106	8%	104	9%	50%	27	22%	56%	3.10	-10.5	-2	-5	$2
16 PIT	300	49	18	56	2	270	258	349	510	859	934	831	10	66	0.32	40	24	36	35	115	164	167	25%	86	4%	67%	26	46%	46%	6.06	9.3	42	120	$11
17 2 NL *	162	20	5	10	1	144	174	238	252	490	774	431	11	56	0.28	39	22	39	21	80	78	132	17%	85	3%	100%	12	25%	75%	1.81	-19.0	-64	-194	-$5
1st Half																																		
2nd Half	162	20	5	10	1	144	174	238	252	490	774	431	11	56	0.28	39	22	39	21	80	78	132	17%	85	3%	100%	12	25%	75%	1.81	-17.8	-65	-197	-$5
18 Proj	**195**	**25**	**7**	**22**	**1**	**235**	**223**	**304**	**399**	**703**	**778**	**645**	**7**	**66**	**0.22**	**41**	**21**	**38**	**32**	**92**	**108**	**128**	**15%**	**93**	**5%**	**59%**				**3.79**	**-6.5**	**-14**	**-41**	**$4**

Rojas,Miguel

Age: 29 Bats: R Pos: SS	Health C	LIMA Plan D+
Ht: 5' 11" Wt: 195	PT/Exp D	Rand Var -2
	Consist C	MM 1243

Adept at putting ball in play, so when h% cooperates, helpful BA within reach. Eye is growing more discerning, but positives end there. No power nor any inclination to run, despite decent speed. Small rotator cuff tear didn't stop closing flourish (23-for-55), but that, too, was h% driven. Seek excitement elsewhere.

Yr Tm	AB	R	HR	RBI	SB	BA	xBA	OBP	SLG	OPS	vL	vR	bb%	ct%	Eye	G	L	F	h%	HctX	PX	xPX	hr/f	Spd	SBO	SB%	#Wk	DOM	DIS	RC/G	RAR	BPV	BPX	R$
13 aa	420	38	4	27	9	206		264	268	532			7	87	0.59				23		40			108	13%	65%				2.25		28	70	$0
14 LA *	308	32	4	17	4	205	221	243	271	515	283	516	5	82	0.29	68	8	24	24	50	50	34	4%	97	12%	53%	18	6%	56%	2.05	-16.2	10	27	-$1
15 MIA *	391	39	3	35	2	268	290	307	369	676	327	768	5	88	0.47	55	24	21	30	88	64	42	4%	111	9%	19%	16	38%	31%	3.67	-11.6	50	135	$6
16 MIA	194	27	1	14	2	247	267	288	325	613	697	579	5	86	0.41	54	20	26	28	70	55	37	2%	98	7%	67%	27	37%	44%	3.15	-10.5	30	86	$1
17 MIA	272	37	1	26	2	290	285	361	375	736	712	745	9	88	0.84	48	25	27	33	72	52	32	2%	116	3%	67%	18	22%	28%	4.76	-4.1	49	148	$6
1st Half	65	12	0	4	2	338	270	389	400	789	465	937	8	88	0.75	43	26	31	39	54	44	21	0%	125	8%	100%	6	33%	17%	6.34	2.1	42	127	-$1
2nd Half	207	25	1	22	0	275	288	352	367	719	805	689	9	88	0.88	50	25	25	31	78	54	35	2%	106	2%	0%	12	17%	33%	4.33	-4.4	49	148	$8
18 Proj	**358**	**48**	**2**	**29**	**4**	**273**	**275**	**326**	**353**	**680**	**606**	**705**	**7**	**87**	**0.59**	**52**	**22**	**26**	**31**	**70**	**50**	**34**	**2%**	**114**	**6%**	**63%**				**3.97**	**-5.1**	**29**	**88**	**$9**

Romine,Andrew

Age: 32 Bats: L Pos: 2B CF 3B	Health A	LIMA Plan D
Ht: 6' 1" Wt: 200	PT/Exp F	Rand Var +3
	Consist A	MM 1331

On 9/30, became fifth MLB player to play all nine positions in one game, which just means he's more useful in trivia contests than fantasy ones. Given age, declines in Spd and SBO are no surprise, and elite LD% is only thing keeping BA from cratering. Feel free to let him float until FA pool drained of more intriguing options.

Yr Tm	AB	R	HR	RBI	SB	BA	xBA	OBP	SLG	OPS	vL	vR	bb%	ct%	Eye	G	L	F	h%	HctX	PX	xPX	hr/f	Spd	SBO	SB%	#Wk	DOM	DIS	RC/G	RAR	BPV	BPX	R$
13 LAA *	471	44	2	32	10	216	243	264	271	535	667	566	6	76	0.27	57	25	18	28	49	43	12	0%	129	15%	55%	13	15%	62%	2.23	-29.5	-7	-18	$1
14 DET	251	30	2	12	12	227	223	279	275	554	746	502	7	76	0.30	59	18	23	29	54	39	32	5%	111	21%	86%	26	8%	54%	2.67	-9.3	-15	-41	$4
15 DET	184	25	2	15	10	255	229	307	315	622	640	613	5	75	0.24	58	20	22	33	50	44	40	7%	115	29%	67%	27	15%	70%	3.10	-7.8	-16	-43	$5
16 DET	174	21	2	16	8	236	258	304	322	626	611	630	7	78	0.34	52	26	22	29	71	52	53	7%	121	18%	100%	27	30%	59%	3.34	-5.3	6	17	$3
17 DET	318	45	4	25	6	233	264	289	336	625	674	613	6	79	0.33	47	26	27	28	94	65	76	6%	101	14%	60%	27	30%	56%	3.07	-16.3	13	39	$3
1st Half	170	28	3	17	3	229	256	299	353	652	461	695	8	76	0.38	46	25	29	28	98	74	75	8%	117	17%	43%	13	38%	54%	3.15	-9.3	18	55	$4
2nd Half	148	17	1	8	3	236	274	277	318	594	871	513	5	82	0.26	48	28	24	28	89	56	77	3%	82	9%	100%	14	21%	57%	2.97	-8.6	8	24	$2
18 Proj	**230**	**30**	**2**	**18**	**6**	**236**	**257**	**292**	**320**	**612**	**677**	**594**	**6**	**78**	**0.30**	**51**	**25**	**24**	**29**	**77**	**53**	**60**	**5%**	**110**	**14%**	**71%**				**3.01**	**-12.5**	**0**	**0**	**$4**

KRISTOPHER OLSON

Romine,Austin

Age: 29	Bats: R	Pos: CA	Health A	LIMA Plan F	
Ht: 6' 1"	Wt: 220		PT/Exp F	Rand Var 0	
			Consist B	MM 1221	

Unlike many great SS, backup C don't just come from San Pedro de Macoris. They're from all over, this one from Lake Forest, CA, and he played at the HS my sons attended. That's about the best I can come up with here. Poor on-base skills and no pop guarantee free agent pool permanency. But hey, go Chargers!

Yr	Tm	AB	R	HR	RBI	SB	BA	xBA	OBP	SLG	OPS	vL	vR	bb%	ct%	Eye	G	L	F	h%	HctX	PX	xPX	hr/f	Spd	SBO	SB%	#Wk	DOM	DIS	RC/G	RAR	BPV	BPX	R$
13	NYY *	177	19	2	13	1	229	232	275	312	588	576	540	6	71	0.22	55	23	22	31	88	74	61	5%	77	2%	100%	19	26%	47%	2.87	-4.4	-18	-45	-$
14	NYY *	298	25	5	24	1	196	247	240	292	532	3000	333	5	77	0.25	56	22	22	24	184	78	152	0%	74	1%	100%	5	20%	60%	2.24	-10.1	4	11	-$
15	NYY *	340	30	6	39	0	219	355	258	321	579	0	0	5	81	0.28	50	50	0	25	0	70	-16	0%	69	2%	0%	1	0%	0%	2.66	-11.2	13	35	$
16	NYY	165	17	4	26	1	242	260	269	382	650	725	551	4	81	0.23	47	19	33	28	88	90	100	9%	79	3%	100%	26	38%	42%	3.54	-1.5	30	86	$
17	NYY	229	19	2	21	0	218	235	272	293	565	499	586	6	75	0.28	45	25	30	28	84	50	66	4%	83	0%	0%	27	11%	52%	2.57	-10.9	-19	-58	-$
1st Half		139	13	2	17	0	245	244	289	324	613	454	668	7	76	0.29	44	28	29	31	81	51	69	6%	79	0%	0%	13	8%	62%	3.23	-3.6	-18	-55	$
2nd Half		90	6	0	4	0	178	220	245	244	489	571	463	6	74	0.26	47	21	32	24	89	47	61	0%	90	0%	0%	14	14%	43%	1.74	-6.9	-23	-70	-$
18	**Proj**	**232**	**20**	**3**	**24**	**0**	**217**	**241**	**262**	**308**	**571**	**627**	**537**	**6**	**77**	**0.26**	**48**	**22**	**30**	**27**	**87**	**60**	**76**	**5%**	**78**	**1%**	**82%**				**2.61**	**-10.9**	**-15**	**-44**	**-$**

Rosales,Adam

Age: 35	Bats: R	Pos: SS	Health A	LIMA Plan D	
Ht: 6' 2"	Wt: 200		PT/Exp F	Rand Var -1	
			Consist F	MM 3201	

When BA=xBA (.227) in over 1,600 career AB, projecting BA would seem a gimme, but recent ct% drops put even that low bar in jeopardy. While he can still turn on one occasionally, '16 power spike looks like an outlier. Can play anywhere, but only qualifies at SS for now. Future eligibilities might be worth a deep reserve pick.

Yr	Tm	AB	R	HR	RBI	SB	BA	xBA	OBP	SLG	OPS	vL	vR	bb%	ct%	Eye	G	L	F	h%	HctX	PX	xPX	hr/f	Spd	SBO	SB%	#Wk	DOM	DIS	RC/G	RAR	BPV	BPX	R$
13	2 AL *	185	17	5	16	1	182	218	231	298	529	721	401	6	77	0.28	48	15	37	21	73	81	87	12%	83	6%	32%	21	29%	33%	2.08	-8.4	10	25	-$
14	TEX *	436	45	8	44	6	224	220	273	331	604	824	626	6	72	0.25	33	25	42	29	92	86	91	8%	125	8%	74%	14	21%	57%	2.97	-4.3	10	27	$
15	TEX	114	14	3	7	4	228	218	296	342	638	608	684	8	74	0.33	49	15	36	28	80	79	94	10%	112	28%	50%	18	28%	56%	2.95	-2.9	9	24	$
16	SD	214	37	13	35	4	229	235	319	495	814	843	789	12	59	0.33	37	17	46	32	88	200	145	22%	137	8%	100%	27	56%	33%	5.37	4.8	62	177	$
17	2 TM	289	25	7	36	1	225	211	260	353	613	689	563	4	65	0.11	35	22	42	32	81	94	78	9%	90	6%	33%	26	19%	65%	2.85	-14.7	-26	-79	$
1st Half		186	14	4	24	1	231	220	268	349	617	712	584	4	67	0.13	33	26	41	32	77	86	67	8%	91	5%	50%	13	15%	69%	2.99	-8.9	-25	-76	$
2nd Half		103	11	3	12	0	214	197	245	359	605	672	482	3	62	0.08	40	15	45	31	86	111	101	10%	91	6%	0%	13	23%	62%	2.61	-6.3	-28	-85	-$
18	**Proj**	**164**	**19**	**6**	**20**	**2**	**222**	**215**	**277**	**385**	**663**	**706**	**620**	**6**	**65**	**0.20**	**39**	**18**	**43**	**30**	**83**	**112**	**103**	**13%**	**105**	**11%**	**55%**				**3.34**	**-5.7**	**-11**	**-32**	**$**

Rosario,Amed

Age: 22	Bats: R	Pos: SS	Health A	LIMA Plan C+	
Ht: 6' 2"	Wt: 189		PT/Exp F	Rand Var -1	
			Consist D	MM 2525	

4-10-.248 with 7 SB in 165 AB at NYM. Ballyhooed SS prospect showed flashes of what earned him 9C grade in these pages, particularly on the basepaths. Contact and patience issues were not unexpected, and pop may lag until frame fills out, but the tools are real. Full-season impact could be immediate. Invest.

Yr	Tm	AB	R	HR	RBI	SB	BA	xBA	OBP	SLG	OPS	vL	vR	bb%	ct%	Eye	G	L	F	h%	HctX	PX	xPX	hr/f	Spd	SBO	SB%	#Wk	DOM	DIS	RC/G	RAR	BPV	BPX	R$
13																																			
14																																			
15																																			
16	aa	214	33	2	27	5	307		362	422	783			8	72	0.31				42		83			114	11%	71%				5.55		7	20	$
17	NYM *	558	65	10	53	21	267	246	294	381	676	829	617	4	77	0.17	51	20	29	33	75	65	73	12%	169	23%	68%	10	20%	50%	3.79	-11.9	19	58	$1
1st Half		328	36	6	39	10	267	239	302	381	683			5	79	0.23				32		65			135	21%	60%				3.80		19	58	$2
2nd Half		230	29	4	15	11	266	237	283	382	665	829	617	2	74	0.09	51	20	29	34	72	65	73	12%	187	26%	78%	10	20%	50%	3.77	-5.4	11	33	$1
18	**Proj**	**598**	**80**	**13**	**62**	**20**	**273**	**249**	**317**	**412**	**730**	**881**	**686**	**5**	**74**	**0.21**	**49**	**21**	**30**	**35**	**65**	**83**	**66**	**10%**	**168**	**19%**	**71%**				**4.41**	**-0.9**	**16**	**49**	**$2**

Rosario,Eddie

Age: 26	Bats: L	Pos: LF	Health A	LIMA Plan B+	
Ht: 6' 1"	Wt: 180		PT/Exp B	Rand Var -2	
			Consist B	MM 3345	

Something clicked at midway point for noted hacker as he grew much more discerning, earning career bests in Eye, ct% and bb%. Production followed suit as 2nd half jump in FB% was boon to power, especially vR. Entering prime years, there is an expectation of lessons learned. If so... UP: 2017 2nd half x 2.

Yr	Tm	AB	R	HR	RBI	SB	BA	xBA	OBP	SLG	OPS	vL	vR	bb%	ct%	Eye	G	L	F	h%	HctX	PX	xPX	hr/f	Spd	SBO	SB%	#Wk	DOM	DIS	RC/G	RAR	BPV	BPX	R$
13	aa	289	31	3	30	5	254		294	362	656			5	75	0.22				33		87			106	15%	55%				3.49		14	35	$
14	aa	316	32	6	28	6	213		245	347	592			4	77	0.18				26		103			103	20%	59%				2.64		31	84	$
15	MIN *	548	69	15	60	12	259	242	284	438	722	811	727	3	75	0.14	39	20	41	32	96	110	110	10%	173	17%	62%	22	41%	27%	4.13	-4.3	49	132	$1
16	MIN *	495	75	16	54	9	275	257	301	441	742	594	752	3	76	0.15	46	19	34	33	93	106	102	12%	128	14%	63%	18	28%	44%	4.54	3.8	37	106	$1
17	MIN	542	79	27	78	9	290	281	328	507	836	682	906	6	80	0.33	42	20	37	32	103	119	121	16%	107	13%	53%	27	52%	22%	5.79	5.3	63	191	$2
1st Half		244	36	10	25	3	291	264	328	471	799	697	840	5	79	0.27	49	18	33	33	91	96	106	16%	150	11%	43%	13	38%	31%	5.28	-0.5	51	155	$1
2nd Half		298	43	17	53	6	289	295	328	537	865	673	966	7	82	0.38	38	22	41	31	113	137	133	17%	79	15%	60%	14	64%	14%	6.22	7.4	75	227	$3
18	**Proj**	**566**	**79**	**27**	**72**	**10**	**276**	**272**	**309**	**490**	**800**	**676**	**847**	**5**	**78**	**0.24**	**42**	**20**	**38**	**31**	**101**	**119**	**113**	**16%**	**125**	**15%**	**58%**				**5.17**	**11.7**	**50**	**152**	**$2**

Rua,Ryan

Age: 28	Bats: R	Pos: LF 1B	Health B	LIMA Plan F	
Ht: 6' 2"	Wt: 205		PT/Exp F	Rand Var 0	
			Consist D	MM 2401	

3-12-.217 with 2 SB in 129 AB in TEX. First-half fizzle led to demotion, and then produced one RBI in 30 AB in the 2nd half. Chronic swing-and-miss is a definite downer, and nothing in his profile suggests he'll be anything more than a sporadically effective bench bat. That said, he's 0-for-18 lifetime as a pinch-hitter. Ouch.

Yr	Tm	AB	R	HR	RBI	SB	BA	xBA	OBP	SLG	OPS	vL	vR	bb%	ct%	Eye	G	L	F	h%	HctX	PX	xPX	hr/f	Spd	SBO	SB%	#Wk	DOM	DIS	RC/G	RAR	BPV	BPX	R$
13	aa	86	16	3	8	1	218		269	356	625			6	70	0.23				28		94			133	4%	100%				3.17		11	28	-$
14	TEX *	576	58	15	68	5	266	266	313	403	716	922	664	6	78	0.31	52	23	25	32	97	101	86	9%	95	8%	48%	6	33%	33%	4.25	9.3	35	95	$1
15	TEX *	225	24	9	24	2	175	195	234	329	562	658	556	7	63	0.21	51	8	41	23	75	122	92	19%	83	6%	100%	11	27%	55%	2.41	-14.4	-7	-19	-$
16	TEX	240	40	8	22	9	258	233	331	400	731	754	714	8	68	0.28	52	19	28	35	90	94	57	17%	140	14%	100%	27	30%	56%	4.60	2.2	8	23	$
17	TEX *	306	36	9	32	4	217	220	267	351	618	695	567	6	62	0.18	43	27	30	32	93	95	74	13%	101	9%	67%	16	6%	56%	3.02	-22.9	-30	-91	$
1st Half		158	21	4	15	2	210	220	266	328	594	598	635	7	63	0.21	45	28	28	31	88	83	69	19%	99	11%	50%	11	9%	45%	2.70	-13.2	-36	-109	$
2nd Half		148	15	5	16	2	224	213	268	375	644	967	321	6	61	0.16	37	26	37	33	111	107	92	0%	110	7%	100%	5	0%	80%	3.38	-8.9	-25	-76	$
18	**Proj**	**130**	**16**	**3**	**13**	**2**	**226**	**216**	**284**	**349**	**633**	**734**	**541**	**7**	**65**	**0.21**	**46**	**22**	**32**	**32**	**94**	**85**	**78**	**12%**	**108**	**9%**	**84%**				**3.24**	**-4.8**	**-30**	**-89**	**$**

Ruiz,Rio

Age: 24	Bats: L	Pos: 3B	Health A	LIMA Plan D	
Ht: 6' 1"	Wt: 230		PT/Exp C	Rand Var +2	
			Consist A	MM 1003	

4-19-.193 in 150 AB in ATL. That he scuffled in first real opportunity is no surprise. Contact rate has suffered at each new level, and huge PX/xPX gaps say power hasn't been realized. He can work a walk, but dubious hit tool (.261 BA in MiLB) casts doubts. At this point, he's a speculation target for deep leagues only.

Yr	Tm	AB	R	HR	RBI	SB	BA	xBA	OBP	SLG	OPS	vL	vR	bb%	ct%	Eye	G	L	F	h%	HctX	PX	xPX	hr/f	Spd	SBO	SB%	#Wk	DOM	DIS	RC/G	RAR	BPV	BPX	R$
13																																			
14																																			
15	aa	420	43	4	41	2	214		308	295	603			12	75	0.54				28		63			89	3%	45%				2.91		2	5	-$
16	ATL *	472	48	8	58	2	235	242	318	332	650	0	857	11	71	0.42	20	40	40	31	173	64	225	0%	104	4%	30%	2	0%	0%	3.41	-22.5	-9	-26	$
17	ATL *	538	64	17	68	2	199	214	277	335	612	1429	517	10	68	0.33	56	13	30	26	91	87	123	12%	70	3%	45%	12	42%	33%	2.91	-40.6	-15	-45	$
1st Half		260	31	7	27	1	205	214	264	330	594	1350	507	7	67	0.24	66	11	23	28	77	84	85	15%	76	6%	28%	6	33%	33%	2.69	-19.6	-26	-79	-$
2nd Half		278	33	10	40	1	194	215	288	340	628	1458	527	12	69	0.42	46	16	38	24	105	89	161	10%	77	1%	100%	6	50%	33%	3.11	-17.3	-4	-12	$
18	**Proj**	**282**	**31**	**8**	**34**	**1**	**224**	**219**	**304**	**352**	**656**	**763**	**645**	**11**	**70**	**0.40**	**48**	**18**	**34**	**29**	**94**	**79**	**131**	**12%**	**80**	**3%**	**44%**				**3.49**	**-12.1**	**-16**	**-48**	**$**

Rupp,Cameron

Age: 29	Bats: R	Pos: CA	Health A	LIMA Plan D	
Ht: 6' 2"	Wt: 260		PT/Exp D	Rand Var -2	
			Consist B	MM 4111	

The big flies continued, but ct% and paucity of hard hit balls returned to previous lows, stifling production. He's managed to outslug xPX, but with contact issues dragging down BA, he's corralling himself as a one-trick pony—and a lame one if power recedes. Still a passable #2 catcher, but now with a yellow flag.

Yr	Tm	AB	R	HR	RBI	SB	BA	xBA	OBP	SLG	OPS	vL	vR	bb%	ct%	Eye	G	L	F	h%	HctX	PX	xPX	hr/f	Spd	SBO	SB%	#Wk	DOM	DIS	RC/G	RAR	BPV	BPX	R$
13	PHI *	338	27	11	35	1	219	199	259	358	617	650	778	5	67	0.17	56	11	33	29	93	112	152	0%	59	3%	38%	2	0%	50%	2.99	-7.3	-12	-30	$
14	PHI *	254	17	5	19	0	144	155	204	241	444	0	546	7	56	0.17	43	13	45	23	60	104	123	0%	56	0%	0%	6	0%	67%	1.46	-16.9	-61	-165	-$
15	PHI	270	24	9	28	0	233	225	301	374	675	915	597	8	74	0.34	43	19	38	28	92	93	97	12%	72	1%	0%	27	37%	48%	3.62	-1.5	9	24	$
16	PHI	389	36	16	54	1	252	248	303	447	750	993	699	6	71	0.21	48	17	34	32	99	134	108	17%	67	1%	100%	27	37%	33%	4.52	1.2	24	69	$
17	PHI	295	35	14	34	1	217	221	299	417	716	839	657	10	61	0.30	48	16	36	30	76	145	111	22%	61	1%	100%	26	31%	58%	4.06	0.0	2	6	$
1st Half		163	18	5	14	1	209	201	305	350	655	936	504	12	61	0.35	48	17	36	31	69	106	80	14%	68	2%	100%	13	8%	69%	3.44	-3.3	-24	-73	-$
2nd Half		132	17	9	20	0	227	242	292	500	792	684	829	8	61	0.24	49	15	36	29	86	193	149	31%	60	0%	0%	13	54%	46%	4.81	2.9	36	109	$
18	**Proj**	**225**	**24**	**10**	**27**	**0**	**226**	**227**	**292**	**422**	**714**	**821**	**679**	**8**	**66**	**0.25**	**47**	**16**	**37**	**30**	**84**	**133**	**115**	**19%**	**62**	**1%**	**74%**				**4.01**	**-0.9**	**-4**	**-11**	**$**

ROB CARROLL

Russell,Addison

Age: 24	Bats: R	Pos: SS	Health	B	LIMA Plan	B+
Ht: 6' 0"	Wt: 200		PT/Exp	B	Rand Var	+2
			Consist	A	MM	3235

Lost 58 games to plantar fasciitis, putting dent in counting stats and value. Truth is, most skills were league average or below for third straight year in era when 20-HR middle infielders are the norm. At his age, we'd like to see some signs of growth. 2nd half HctX, PX/xPX offer sliver of hope to dream on.

Yr	Tm	AB	R	HR	RBI	SB	BA	xBA	OBP	SLG	OPS	vL	vR	bb%	ct%	Eye	G	L	F	h%	HctX	PX	xPX	hr/f	Spd	SBO	SB%	#Wk	DOM	DIS	RC/G	RAR	BPV	BPX	R$
13																																			
14	aa	241	31	10	35	4	277		316	466	782			5	80	0.29				31		130			89	15%	48%				4.90		64	173	$9
15	CHC *	519	66	14	61	5	246	226	303	393	696	527	746	8	70	0.27	41	18	41	33	83	115	105	10%	96	6%	61%	25	36%	40%	3.98	3.2	17	46	$11
16	CHC	525	67	21	95	5	238	252	321	417	738	801	715	9	74	0.41	41	21	37	28	88	111	94	14%	110	5%	83%	27	44%	33%	4.35	-4.1	39	111	$12
17	CHC	352	52	12	43	2	239	256	304	418	722	821	687	8	74	0.32	40	23	37	29	97	109	83	13%	111	4%	67%	22	32%	41%	4.13	-4.0	34	103	$5
1st Half		239	36	7	29	2	230	253	300	397	698	742	682	8	75	0.34	44	20	36	28	83	99	60	11%	129	6%	67%	13	31%	46%	3.78	-5.7	37	112	$7
2nd Half		113	16	5	14	0	257	272	311	460	772	980	698	7	72	0.28	31	30	40	32	125	131	134	16%	77	0%	0%	9	33%	33%	4.92	1.1	32	97	$1
18	Proj	517	71	21	82	4	247	257	312	437	748	823	722	8	74	0.31	39	23	38	30	97	115	101	14%	95	5%	65%				4.48	0.2	27	82	$12

Saladino,Tyler

Age: 28	Bats: R	Pos: 2B 3B	Health	B	LIMA Plan	D
Ht: 6' 0"	Wt: 200		PT/Exp	D	Rand Var	+5
			Consist	F	MM	1413

In a year when everyone including the groundskeepers hit a HR, he had none. (Not to beat a dead horse, but Madison Bumgarner hit two on Opening Day.) He's not paid to do that, but it would be nice to mix in a little O while toting IF gloves around. And while SBs are his road back to positive value, OBP says, "grab a hose."

Yr	Tm	AB	R	HR	RBI	SB	BA	xBA	OBP	SLG	OPS	vL	vR	bb%	ct%	Eye	G	L	F	h%	HctX	PX	xPX	hr/f	Spd	SBO	SB%	#Wk	DOM	DIS	RC/G	RAR	BPV	BPX	R$
13	aa	424	39	5	44	23	200		277	274	552			10	76	0.45				25		56			95	29%	71%				2.43		1	3	$6
14	aaa	294	27	6	28	5	248		293	373	666			6	79	0.31				29		89			103	8%	79%				3.72		33	89	$5
15	CHW *	432	55	7	43	28	219	257	270	322	592	650	585	7	79	0.33	54	23	23	26	61	63	32	9%	129	32%	86%	14	43%	50%	3.00	-17.0	19	51	$12
16	CHW	298	33	8	38	11	282	257	315	409	725	799	698	4	79	0.21	51	20	29	33	83	79	58	12%	91	21%	69%	25	20%	36%	4.41	-2.6	17	49	$11
17	CHW	253	23	0	10	5	178	198	254	229	484	567	441	8	74	0.34	46	17	37	24	66	37	38	0%	137	16%	56%	21	5%	62%	1.69	-24.3	-16	-48	-$5
1st Half		110	10	0	4	2	200	187	302	273	574	678	532	11	68	0.37	44	16	40	29	68	50	42	0%	157	17%	40%	8	13%	75%	2.27	-9.1	-17	-52	-$6
2nd Half		143	13	0	6	3	161	205	216	196	411	499	358	7	78	0.31	47	17	35	21	65	28	35	0%	99	14%	75%	13	0%	54%	1.31	-16.7	-22	-67	-$4
18	Proj	260	26	3	20	8	214	228	276	297	572	637	544	7	76	0.32	49	19	32	27	71	52	44	5%	118	20%	69%				2.57	-18.2	-7	-22	$3

Sanchez,Gary

Age: 25	Bats: R	Pos: CA	Health	A	LIMA Plan	B
Ht: 6' 2"	Wt: 230		PT/Exp	C	Rand Var	-1
			Consist	B	MM	4155

Missing a month with strained bicep didn't forestall ascent to top fantasy backstop. Mashing against all comers makes him special, and while 2016 hr/f was too absurd to last, 25% is still remarkable. Real challenge is defensive ability, clouding long-term CA outlook. But that's a minor concern if power continues its march.

Yr	Tm	AB	R	HR	RBI	SB	BA	xBA	OBP	SLG	OPS	vL	vR	bb%	ct%	Eye	G	L	F	h%	HctX	PX	xPX	hr/f	Spd	SBO	SB%	#Wk	DOM	DIS	RC/G	RAR	BPV	BPX	R$
13	aa	92	10	2	9	0	232		316	354	670			11	81	0.66				27		89			94	0%	0%				3.71		49	123	-$2
14	aa	429	39	12	53	1	245		303	367	669			8	76	0.35				29		90			78	2%	43%				3.72		18	49	$7
15	NYY *	367	44	18	55	6	255	164	304	459	763	0	0	7	76	0.29	0	0	100	29	0	135	-16	0%	69	10%	74%	2	0%	50%	4.74	10.8	48	130	$12
16	NYY *	485	69	31	87	7	275	288	334	530	864	868	1093	8	78	0.40	49	16	34	30	132	150	159	40%	72	7%	87%	11	45%	36%	6.27	33.2	70	200	$21
17	NYY	471	79	33	90	2	278	275	345	531	876	882	874	8	75	0.33	42	21	37	31	111	140	114	25%	83	3%	67%	23	39%	22%	6.25	28.2	52	158	$20
1st Half		187	36	13	40	2	283	274	371	524	895	636	958	10	74	0.43	43	23	33	32	115	132	99	28%	93	5%	67%	10	40%	20%	6.57	13.1	51	155	$15
2nd Half		284	43	20	50	0	275	273	327	535	862	1005	813	6	75	0.27	41	20	39	30	109	145	125	24%	80	0%	0%	13	38%	23%	6.02	15.5	54	164	$23
18	Proj	484	71	34	92	3	276	281	339	535	875	803	898	8	76	0.35	46	19	35	30	120	143	132	26%	78	4%	71%				6.23	28.9	50	152	$22

Sanchez,Hector

Age: 28	Bats: B	Pos: CA	Health	D	LIMA Plan	D
Ht: 6' 0"	Wt: 235		PT/Exp	F	Rand Var	0
			Consist	C	MM	3011

8-25-.219 in 137 AB at SD. The cruel wrinkle in many fantasy games is the mandatory second CA. This one gets repeated looks because he hit .280 at age 22. Since then: .219 in 534 AB. But last two years of PX, hr/f have given him occasional value. If you gotta bite the bullet, at least he has a glimmer of HR upside.

Yr	Tm	AB	R	HR	RBI	SB	BA	xBA	OBP	SLG	OPS	vL	vR	bb%	ct%	Eye	G	L	F	h%	HctX	PX	xPX	hr/f	Spd	SBO	SB%	#Wk	DOM	DIS	RC/G	RAR	BPV	BPX	R$
13	SF *	214	15	5	26	0	235	247	286	337	623	860	552	7	78	0.33	43	27	31	28	84	71	74	10%	66	0%	0%	19	11%	47%	3.21	-3.0	5	13	$0
14	SF	163	8	3	28	0	196	198	237	301	538	531	540	5	66	0.15	34	21	46	28	95	96	150	6%	59	3%	0%	17	18%	71%	2.16	-6.6	-28	-76	-$2
15	SF *	195	18	3	15	0	205	212	238	302	540	458	533	4	77	0.19	52	14	33	25	62	71	49	7%	63	0%	0%	11	36%	55%	2.31	-9.1	-5	-14	-$3
16	2 TM *	253	20	12	35	0	235	247	283	434	717	286	886	6	74	0.25	33	21	46	27	108	127	91	17%	48	0%	0%	12	42%	42%	4.09	-2.3	26	74	$2
17	SD *	163	15	9	29	0	216	236	244	418	663	660	671	4	69	0.12	35	22	43	25	98	122	100	19%	59	0%	0%	21	33%	52%	3.33	-3.6	0	0	$0
1st Half		54	4	4	11	0	188	220	234	448	682	0	928	6	61	0.15	29	18	53	21	73	168	135	33%	74	0%	0%	7	43%	57%	3.29	-1.4	15	45	-$4
2nd Half		109	11	5	18	0	229	240	248	404	651	804	601	3	72	0.10	36	23	41	27	106	102	92	15%	65	0%	0%	14	29%	50%	3.34	-2.5	-2	-6	$3
18	Proj	167	14	7	25	0	216	230	255	390	646	571	673	5	71	0.18	39	20	41	26	85	106	97	15%	59	0%	0%				3.23	-4.7	-14	-42	$2

Sanchez,Yolmer

Age: 26	Bats: B	Pos: 2B 3B	Health	A	LIMA Plan	D+
Ht: 5' 11"	Wt: 185		PT/Exp	C	Rand Var	-3
			Consist	B	MM	1325

Three times the R$ of 2016, but gains were incremental if not illusory. Despite 2nd half jump in FB% and hr/f, HctX and xPX were still subpar, and rise in BA was driven by h% as much as anything. Meanwhile, Spd score was inflated by career-high eight triples. Not a bad end-of-draft option, just know what you're getting.

Yr	Tm	AB	R	HR	RBI	SB	BA	xBA	OBP	SLG	OPS	vL	vR	bb%	ct%	Eye	G	L	F	h%	HctX	PX	xPX	hr/f	Spd	SBO	SB%	#Wk	DOM	DIS	RC/G	RAR	BPV	BPX	R$
13	aaa	432	41	0	23	13	218		264	267	531			6	81	0.31				27		43			106	21%	64%				2.24		2	5	$2
14	CHW *	537	48	5	45	12	248	240	288	331	619	867	423	5	77	0.25	42	26	32	31	84	64	87	0%	123	13%	69%	8	25%	75%	3.20	-3.1	10	27	$9
15	CHW *	520	54	7	45	6	244	261	276	349	624	606	591	4	78	0.20	54	23	23	30	76	79	48	7%	89	10%	59%	23	22%	57%	3.18	-17.0	12	32	$7
16	CHW *	389	40	11	44	8	217	232	255	362	617	405	662	5	73	0.18	39	21	40	27	67	95	75	9%	102	19%	59%	17	35%	53%	2.88	-22.3	8	23	$4
17	CHW	484	63	12	59	8	267	251	319	413	732	660	755	7	77	0.32	45	22	34	32	75	81	72	9%	160	14%	47%	27	33%	33%	4.28	-4.9	36	109	$13
1st Half		226	31	3	21	4	274	263	335	398	733	680	756	8	78	0.38	47	26	28	34	70	73	63	6%	160	16%	40%	13	31%	31%	4.23	-3.9	35	106	$8
2nd Half		258	32	9	38	4	260	241	305	426	731	630	755	6	76	0.26	43	18	39	31	79	89	79	12%	151	11%	57%	14	36%	36%	4.31	-3.9	36	109	$17
18	Proj	429	49	9	48	8	247	245	294	376	670	618	687	6	76	0.26	44	22	34	31	74	76	71	8%	133	14%	54%				3.54	-16.3	9	28	$10

Sandoval,Pablo

Age: 31	Bats: B	Pos: 3B	Health	F	LIMA Plan	D
Ht: 5' 11"	Wt: 255		PT/Exp	D	Rand Var	0
			Consist	F	MM	1021

9-32-.220 in 259 AB at BOS/SF. Injured and released before being rescued by former employer, Panda is an endangered species. Can still paste one occasionally, but ct% is waning, GB are more frequent, and the usual physique concerns are further complicated by age and health. It's all part of the Circle of Life.

Yr	Tm	AB	R	HR	RBI	SB	BA	xBA	OBP	SLG	OPS	vL	vR	bb%	ct%	Eye	G	L	F	h%	HctX	PX	xPX	hr/f	Spd	SBO	SB%	#Wk	DOM	DIS	RC/G	RAR	BPV	BPX	R$
13	SF	525	52	14	79	0	278	262	341	417	758	686	786	8	85	0.59	41	21	37	31	103	90	92	8%	50	0%	0%	25	44%	20%	4.97	14.5	45	113	$15
14	SF	588	68	16	73	0	279	263	324	415	739	563	824	6	86	0.46	43	21	37	30	114	89	111	9%	72	0%	0%	27	48%	30%	4.75	17.2	49	132	$18
15	BOS	470	43	10	47	0	245	253	292	366	658	465	744	5	84	0.34	49	19	32	27	88	79	68	8%	48	0%	0%	25	36%	32%	3.49	-16.4	27	73	$5
16	BOS	6	0	0	0	0	0	0	143	0	143	0	143	14	33	0.25	0	0	100	0	0	0	-24	0%	67	0%	0%	2	0%	100%	0.00	-1.1	-215	-614	-$2
17	2 TM *	365	35	10	37	0	204	226	250	326	577	391	704	6	79	0.29	47	16	36	23	104	70	87	12%	40	1%	0%	18	22%	33%	2.58	-31.1	-3	-9	-$2
1st Half		149	15	5	15	0	197	241	248	318	567	340	692	6	75	0.28	49	22	29	23	120	70	95	18%	59	3%	0%	8	13%	25%	2.43	-12.6	-11	-33	-$5
2nd Half		216	20	6	22	0	209	217	252	332	584	417	711	5	81	0.30	47	13	41	23	94	70	83	9%	38	0%	0%	10	30%	40%	2.70	-16.0	5	15	$0
18	Proj	198	19	6	22	0	232	247	278	371	649	460	718	6	82	0.33	46	18	35	26	102	76	87	10%	51	1%	0%				3.37	-9.1	11	33	$2

Sano,Miguel

Age: 25	Bats: R	Pos: 3B DH	Health	C	LIMA Plan	B
Ht: 6' 4"	Wt: 260		PT/Exp	C	Rand Var	-5
			Consist	C	MM	5115

On June 1, he was batting .292 despite a 54% contact rate, fully aided by a 46% hit rate. We projected "It has to crash," and from there he batted just .247. But that's still remarkable given the baseline set by xBA. Prodigious power but expect inconsistency, as shown by DOM/DIS split. Even 65% ct% would mean 40 easy HRs.

Yr	Tm	AB	R	HR	RBI	SB	BA	xBA	OBP	SLG	OPS	vL	vR	bb%	ct%	Eye	G	L	F	h%	HctX	PX	xPX	hr/f	Spd	SBO	SB%	#Wk	DOM	DIS	RC/G	RAR	BPV	BPX	R$
13	aa	233	28	14	44	2	213		299	477	776			11	64	0.34				26		209			102	6%	60%				4.57		77	193	$4
14																																			
15	MIN *	520	88	29	89	5	257	249	357	496	853	881	929	13	63	0.43	33	25	42	35	122	188	175	26%	90	5%	70%	15	53%	20%	6.04	22.4	60	162	$20
16	MIN *	462	60	27	68	1	231	224	317	459	776	818	771	11	59	0.31	34	20	46	32	96	173	157	21%	81	1%	100%	24	38%	42%	4.84	0.6	24	69	$9
17	MIN	424	75	28	77	0	264	229	352	507	859	992	817	11	59	0.31	39	21	40	38	107	166	148	27%	103	0%	0%	22	36%	41%	6.10	15.2	25	76	$14
1st Half		269	48	20	58	0	268	240	367	546	913	915	912	14	60	0.39	36	20	44	37	120	187	174	28%	92	0%	0%	13	54%	23%	6.97	14.6	47	142	$21
2nd Half		155	27	8	19	0	258	210	326	439	764	1175	665	7	57	0.18	44	22	33	40	85	128	101	27%	105	0%	0%	9	11%	67%	4.70	-1.8	-20	-61	$2
18	Proj	531	84	33	86	1	249	230	334	484	818	940	781	11	60	0.30	37	21	41	35	101	163	146	25%	99	1%	49%				5.40	8.1	11	33	$17

ROB CARROLL

Santana,Carlos

Age: 32	Bats: B	Pos: 1B	Health	A	LIMA Plan	A
Ht: 5' 11"	Wt: 210		PT/Exp	A	Rand Var	+1
			Consist	C	MM	3245

Couldn't muscle up again, as across-the-board fallback in power skills prevented HR repeat. Volatile h% drove wild 1H/2H swings, but its subpar baseline ultimately caps BA upside. Uber-stable batting Eye, AB totals solidify high-floor, low-ceiling profile. R$ history serves as your narrow range of outcomes.

Yr Tm	AB	R	HR	RBI	SB	BA	xBA	OBP	SLG	OPS	vL	vR	bb%	ct%	Eye	G	L	F	h%	HctX	PX	xPX	hr/f	Spd	SBO	SB%	#Wk	DOM	DIS	RC/G	RAR	BPV	BPX	R$
13 CLE	541	75	20	74	3	268	277	377	455	832	864	815	14	80	0.85	42	22	36	30	106	131	99	13%	72	2%	75%	27	67%	7%	5.95	20.8	76	190	$1
14 CLE	541	68	27	85	5	231	262	365	427	792	864	757	17	77	0.91	40	19	40	25	117	136	125	16%	67	4%	71%	27	56%	22%	5.15	16.4	73	197	$1
15 CLE	550	72	19	85	11	231	253	357	395	752	755	750	16	78	0.89	45	18	37	26	101	108	95	12%	73	8%	79%	27	56%	22%	4.71	-3.8	54	146	$1
16 CLE	582	89	34	87	5	259	281	366	498	865	742	915	14	83	1.00	43	16	41	26	122	129	122	17%	79	4%	71%	27	74%	7%	6.28	24.1	90	257	$2
17 CLE	571	90	23	79	5	259	278	363	455	818	777	844	13	84	0.94	41	20	39	28	112	106	102	12%	86	3%	83%	27	63%	11%	5.64	4.2	73	221	$1
1st Half	305	48	10	43	3	226	271	331	390	721	642	774	13	84	0.90	42	21	37	24	112	90	98	11%	75	4%	100%	13	62%	0%	4.25	-12.9	57	173	$1
2nd Half	266	42	13	36	2	297	287	399	530	929	951	917	14	83	0.98	39	19	42	32	111	124	106	14%	97	3%	67%	14	64%	21%	7.55	14.0	92	279	$2
18 Proj	**569**	**85**	**26**	**82**	**6**	**257**	**274**	**366**	**462**	**828**	**793**	**847**	**14**	**82**	**0.94**	**42**	**19**	**40**	**27**	**113**	**111**	**107**	**14%**	**83**	**4%**	**77%**				**5.77**	**11.2**	**70**	**213**	**$1**

Santana,Domingo

Age: 25	Bats: R	Pos: RF	Health	C	LIMA Plan	C+
Ht: 6' 5"	Wt: 220		PT/Exp	C	Rand Var	-2
			Consist	B	MM	4225

A five-category breakout, but this was a perfect storm. By category: 1) HR likely maxed out, as very few sustain a higher hr/f; not enough FBs. 2) Ditto for BA, which hinges on holding sky-high h% and LD%. 3) SB%, Spd baselines question the running game. Tough to expect even a repeat, let alone any further gains.

Yr Tm	AB	R	HR	RBI	SB	BA	xBA	OBP	SLG	OPS	vL	vR	bb%	ct%	Eye	G	L	F	h%	HctX	PX	xPX	hr/f	Spd	SBO	SB%	#Wk	DOM	DIS	RC/G	RAR	BPV	BPX	R$
13 aa	416	58	21	51	10	228		292	437	728			8	63	0.24				31		170			98	17%	64%				4.09		35	88	$1
14 HOU *	460	47	12	60	4	245	224	317	384	701	100	0	10	60	0.26	33	33	33	38	86	133	235	0%	95	7%	50%	3	0%	100%	4.00	-1.2	-4	-11	$1
15 2 TM *	514	74	21	81	5	271	237	347	457	803	950	681	10	64	0.32	52	19	29	39	92	146	135	28%	114	8%	45%	11	55%	36%	5.33	7.0	29	78	$1
16 MIL	246	34	11	32	2	256	252	345	447	792	937	726	11	63	0.35	44	30	26	36	98	143	107	28%	87	7%	40%	17	29%	47%	5.04	2.6	17	49	$
17 MIL	525	88	30	85	15	278	266	371	505	875	892	870	12	66	0.41	45	27	28	37	106	148	120	31%	96	12%	79%	26	46%	31%	6.54	20.3	38	115	$2
1st Half	267	46	14	43	7	273	263	368	479	847	860	843	12	69	0.45	49	24	26	35	100	129	116	29%	101	12%	70%	13	38%	38%	6.04	7.6	35	106	$2
2nd Half	258	42	16	42	8	283	267	374	531	905	926	897	12	64	0.37	40	31	29	39	112	169	125	33%	92	12%	89%	13	54%	23%	7.08	14.7	43	130	$2
18 Proj	**528**	**80**	**24**	**79**	**10**	**268**	**249**	**356**	**465**	**821**	**913**	**784**	**11**	**64**	**0.36**	**44**	**27**	**29**	**37**	**102**	**135**	**118**	**24%**	**94**	**10%**	**67%**				**5.59**	**13.7**	**11**	**35**	**$2**

Saunders,Michael

Age: 31	Bats: L	Pos: RF	Health	F	LIMA Plan	D+
Ht: 6' 4"	Wt: 225		PT/Exp	D	Rand Var	+3
			Consist	F	MM	3221

6-21-.202 in 218 AB at PHI/TOR. Was batting .271 on 4/20 when he was scratched from game due to "illness." A few weeks later, a groin strain continued downward spiral, leading to June release. Power outage driven by dearth of hard contact; xBA supports BA plunge. No official DL days this year, but health remains biggest obstacle.

Yr Tm	AB	R	HR	RBI	SB	BA	xBA	OBP	SLG	OPS	vL	vR	bb%	ct%	Eye	G	L	F	h%	HctX	PX	xPX	hr/f	Spd	SBO	SB%	#Wk	DOM	DIS	RC/G	RAR	BPV	BPX	R$
13 SEA	406	59	12	46	13	236	241	323	397	720	654	751	12	71	0.46	41	22	37	30	103	123	129	11%	105	16%	72%	25	48%	44%	4.29	0.1	39	98	$1
14 SEA *	286	45	9	40	4	267	246	348	428	776	680	836	11	72	0.45	42	22	36	34	116	121	112	13%	127	10%	44%	18	39%	28%	4.92	8.6	48	130	$1
15 TOR	31	2	0	3	0	194	151	306	194	499	1417	393	14	68	0.50	75	15	10	29	56	0	59	0%	108	0%	0%	3	0%	67%	1.87	-2.7	-66	-178	-$
16 TOR	490	70	24	57	1	253	257	338	478	815	927	783	11	68	0.38	41	22	37	32	103	154	130	20%	90	2%	33%	27	44%	37%	5.36	9.4	45	129	$1
17 2 TM *	364	44	8	31	1	215	228	260	347	607	619	594	6	75	0.24	45	17	39	27	85	82	76	10%	94	3%	45%	18	17%	39%	2.90	-22.7	6	18	-$
1st Half	215	25	6	20	0	195	227	249	339	588	619	616	7	74	0.28	42	17	40	23	82	85	79	10%	95	2%	0%	12	25%	42%	2.61	-16.8	8	24	-$
2nd Half	149	19	2	11	1	244	242	278	358	635	0	417	4	76	0.19	71	7	21	31	109	78	45	0%	108	3%	100%	6	0%	33%	3.38	-7.4	8	24	$
18 Proj	**225**	**30**	**8**	**23**	**2**	**238**	**248**	**299**	**419**	**719**	**676**	**735**	**8**	**72**	**0.32**	**42**	**21**	**38**	**29**	**101**	**112**	**108**	**13%**	**101**	**6%**	**57%**				**4.14**	**-3.8**	**23**	**69**	**$**

Schebler,Scott

Age: 27	Bats: L	Pos: RF	Health	A	LIMA Plan	B+
Ht: 6' 0"	Wt: 225		PT/Exp	C	Rand Var	+4
			Consist	C	MM	4245

30 HR, just $10 in roto value; this is where we are. Played through June shoulder strain that DL'ed him in Aug, could explain 2nd half swoon. Legit pre-injury power came with more contact, and while low BA made its mark, xBA hints he's more than a HR-only bat. Rand Var also hints at gains, especially with off-season R&R.

Yr Tm	AB	R	HR	RBI	SB	BA	xBA	OBP	SLG	OPS	vL	vR	bb%	ct%	Eye	G	L	F	h%	HctX	PX	xPX	hr/f	Spd	SBO	SB%	#Wk	DOM	DIS	RC/G	RAR	BPV	BPX	R$
13																																		
14 aa	489	57	21	51	7	229		273	425	698			6	73	0.23				27		137			124	12%	60%				3.73		54	146	$1
15 LA *	468	48	13	41	13	201	215	249	335	584	200	905	6	74	0.25	52	9	39	24	125	87	136	33%	115	18%	80%	7	43%	43%	2.68	-32.1	14	38	$
16 CIN *	546	69	21	76	4	269	270	313	462	775	608	791	6	76	0.27	53	18	29	32	103	116	78	16%	104	6%	48%	15	47%	27%	4.92	3.9	42	120	$1
17 CIN	473	63	30	67	5	233	268	307	484	791	782	794	7	74	0.31	46	16	38	25	117	144	132	22%	77	9%	63%	26	50%	27%	4.60	-8.3	49	148	$1
1st Half	262	36	20	40	3	256	282	337	531	867	950	835	9	78	0.43	44	17	39	26	125	145	150	25%	66	7%	75%	13	69%	8%	5.80	5.7	67	203	$1
2nd Half	211	27	10	27	2	204	249	269	427	696	576	742	6	68	0.21	48	15	37	25	107	142	106	18%	92	13%	50%	13	31%	46%	3.34	-11.5	29	88	$
18 Proj	**520**	**68**	**30**	**71**	**6**	**248**	**269**	**317**	**491**	**808**	**732**	**830**	**7**	**74**	**0.30**	**45**	**18**	**37**	**28**	**110**	**137**	**106**	**21%**	**96**	**9%**	**59%**				**4.92**	**3.4**	**49**	**149**	**$1**

Schimpf,Ryan

Age: 30	Bats: L	Pos: 3B	Health	A	LIMA Plan	D
Ht: 5' 9"	Wt: 180		PT/Exp	C	Rand Var	+4
			Consist	F	MM	5011

14-25-.158 in 165 AB at SD. Hit 25 HR and earned -$5 in roto value - wow! Fly ball machine whiffed his way down to AAA in June, never made it back. All that loft pairs well with prodigious pop, but it's death to his h%. Even if we assume some ct% rebound, BA risk remains severe. A profile to avoid in any format.

Yr Tm	AB	R	HR	RBI	SB	BA	xBA	OBP	SLG	OPS	vL	vR	bb%	ct%	Eye	G	L	F	h%	HctX	PX	xPX	hr/f	Spd	SBO	SB%	#Wk	DOM	DIS	RC/G	RAR	BPV	BPX	R$
13 aa	442	48	18	46	2	178		270	349	618			11	63	0.34				23		139			101	6%	38%				2.84		19	48	-$
14 a/a	397	49	20	44	2	198		270	410	681			9	65	0.28				25		176			93	5%	66%				3.51		49	132	$
15 a/a	368	44	20	51	2	219		300	449	749			10	75	0.45				24		156			76	7%	31%				4.25		69	186	$6
16 SD *	442	70	29	81	1	236	241	320	524	843	698	907	11	67	0.37	20	16	65	28	108	194	202	18%	90	3%	30%	17	59%	29%	5.48	6.7	73	209	$1
17 SD *	407	50	25	51	0	149	171	238	351	589	716	706	10	50	0.24	20	16	64	20	55	156	144	23%	104	0%	0%	10	40%	30%	2.51	-38.0	-18	-55	-$
1st Half	235	34	18	34	0	169	200	275	417	692	716	706	13	56	0.34	20	16	64	19	61	171	144	23%	100	0%	0%	10	40%	30%	3.52	-12.0	19	58	$
2nd Half	172	16	7	17	0	123	154	185	262	447			7	43	0.13				22		130			106	0%	0%				1.41		-77	-233	-$1
18 Proj	**158**	**20**	**13**	**23**	**0**	**213**	**229**	**303**	**509**	**812**	**738**	**834**	**10**	**62**	**0.29**	**20**	**16**	**64**	**25**	**80**	**193**	**167**	**21%**	**101**	**3%**	**37%**				**4.74**	**-0.7**	**37**	**113**	**$**

Schoop,Jonathan

Age: 26	Bats: R	Pos: 2B	Health	B	LIMA Plan	B
Ht: 6' 1"	Wt: 225		PT/Exp	B	Rand Var	-3
			Consist	C	MM	3135

Breakout season put him among 2B elite. Stable hr/f came with welcome uptick from xPX, which lends hope for 30 HR encore. BA repeat less likely thanks to career-high h% and an xBA that barely budged. Production was significantly AB-driven, suggesting a repeat is stretching it, but the drop will be soft.

Yr Tm	AB	R	HR	RBI	SB	BA	xBA	OBP	SLG	OPS	vL	vR	bb%	ct%	Eye	G	L	F	h%	HctX	PX	xPX	hr/f	Spd	SBO	SB%	#Wk	DOM	DIS	RC/G	RAR	BPV	BPX	R$
13 BAL *	284	30	9	29	1	238	253	268	371	639	1167	750	4	79	0.19	67	17	17	27	137	88	69	50%	79	5%	27%	2	50%	0%	3.22	-4.3	18	45	$
14 BAL	455	48	16	45	2	209	228	244	354	598	529	625	3	73	0.11	49	14	37	25	82	109	95	13%	75	3%	100%	27	33%	44%	2.65	-10.4	10	27	$
15 BAL *	330	36	18	44	2	274	264	295	493	788	573	892	3	74	0.11	43	19	38	32	115	147	123	17%	65	3%	100%	15	47%	27%	5.14	8.1	41	111	$1
16 BAL	615	82	25	82	1	267	266	298	454	752	688	772	3	78	0.15	45	20	35	31	84	116	74	15%	81	2%	33%	27	41%	26%	4.53	-3.5	36	103	$1
17 BAL	622	92	32	105	1	293	270	338	503	841	955	805	5	77	0.25	42	21	37	33	113	120	113	18%	66	1%	100%	27	41%	19%	6.00	23.7	37	112	$2
1st Half	286	45	16	51	0	297	287	352	545	898	915	891	6	76	0.26	39	23	38	34	105	148	118	19%	71	0%	0%	13	54%	0%	6.71	14.8	58	176	$2
2nd Half	336	47	16	54	1	289	253	325	467	792	997	735	5	78	0.23	44	19	36	33	120	96	109	17%	68	1%	100%	14	29%	36%	5.43	5.7	21	64	$2
18 Proj	**603**	**81**	**28**	**89**	**2**	**276**	**261**	**315**	**470**	**785**	**777**	**788**	**4**	**77**	**0.19**	**44**	**20**	**37**	**32**	**103**	**112**	**103**	**16%**	**69**	**2%**	**69%**				**5.08**	**4.9**	**21**	**62**	**$2**

Schwarber,Kyle

Age: 25	Bats: L	Pos: LF	Health	F	LIMA Plan	B
Ht: 6' 0"	Wt: 235		PT/Exp	D	Rand Var	-3
			Consist	F	MM	5125

30-59-.211 in 422 AB at CHC. Power stroke showed no ill effects from year off, as PX, hr/f and FB% swing pave the way for more HR. Ks remain a major issue, especially vL (56% ct% in 138 career AB), which prevents full-time AB. Low BA/power combo is not very shiny in today's game; bid accordingly.

Yr Tm	AB	R	HR	RBI	SB	BA	xBA	OBP	SLG	OPS	vL	vR	bb%	ct%	Eye	G	L	F	h%	HctX	PX	xPX	hr/f	Spd	SBO	SB%	#Wk	DOM	DIS	RC/G	RAR	BPV	BPX	R$
13																																		
14																																		
15 CHC *	489	88	29	82	4	271	247	368	505	873	481	953	13	68	0.48	40	17	42	34	116	164	157	24%	94	4%	56%	14	57%	21%	6.41	23.8	59	159	$2
16 CHC	4	0	0	0	0	0	0	200	0	200	0	200	20	50	0.50	100	0	0	0	203	0	-24	0%	87	0%	0%	1	0%	100%	0.00	-0.6	-131	-374	-$2
17 CHC *	457	74	33	66	1	217	234	315	476	791	648	814	12	64	0.40	38	15	46	25	94	163	125	24%	71	2%	50%	26	42%	23%	4.85	-5.7	35	106	$8
1st Half	248	38	15	35	0	188	217	301	411	712	556	706	14	65	0.47	40	12	47	21	85	142	109	17%	66	0%	0%	12	42%	25%	3.88	-11.7	25	76	$4
2nd Half	209	36	18	31	1	252	249	333	553	886	782	927	11	62	0.32	36	19	46	31	105	190	144	32%	85	4%	50%	14	43%	21%	6.18	5.1	51	155	$1
18 Proj	**428**	**73**	**32**	**66**	**2**	**244**	**245**	**347**	**513**	**860**	**616**	**924**	**13**	**65**	**0.42**	**39**	**17**	**45**	**29**	**104**	**166**	**140**	**25%**	**82**	**3%**	**55%**				**5.81**	**17.3**	**42**	**126**	**$1**

RYAN BLOOMFIELD

Seager,Corey

Age: 24 Bats: L Pos: SS | Ht: 6' 4" Wt: 220

Health A | PT/Exp A | Consist B | LIMA Plan B | Rand Var -1 | MM 4255

Elbow pain may be reason ROY encore petered out, but many reasons to be bullish about future: plethora of line drives, hard contact; steady growth in bb%, FB%; higher PX vL (125) than vR. Okay, so we do have to watch ongoing ct% slide, along with those nagging injuries. But with health... UP: 30 HR

Yr	Tm	AB	R	HR	RBI	SB	BA	xBA	OBP	SLG	OPS	vL	vR	bb%	ct%	Eye	G	L	F	h%	HctX	PX	xPX	hr/f	Spd	SBO	SB%	#Wk	DOM	DIS	RC/G	RAR	BPV	BPX	R$
13																																			
14	aa	148	21	2	21	1	304		337	457	793			5	70	0.17				42		142			98	5%	41%				5.49		36	97	$4
15	LA *	599	86	20	82	5	280	296	328	462	790	926	1028	7	83	0.42	53	20	27	31	168	118	139	19%	92	5%	83%	6	83%	17%	5.39	27.4	69	186	$22
16	LA	627	105	26	72	3	308	290	365	512	877	722	948	8	79	0.41	46	24	29	36	127	122	130	18%	112	3%	50%	27	59%	19%	6.75	36.4	64	183	$27
17	LA	539	85	22	77	4	295	271	375	479	854	916	826	11	76	0.51	42	25	33	35	135	111	136	16%	77	4%	67%	27	52%	33%	6.42	28.5	39	118	$21
1st Half		274	57	13	40	3	299	277	401	511	912	1019	866	14	76	0.67	40	25	35	36	144	127	143	18%	89	4%	75%	13	62%	23%	7.39	21.3	61	185	$26
2nd Half		265	28	9	37	1	291	262	347	445	792	818	780	8	76	0.34	44	25	31	35	126	93	129	14%	74	3%	50%	14	43%	43%	5.46	6.6	17	52	$16
18	Proj	576	87	25	77	4	296	282	360	502	862	831	877	9	77	0.41	44	24	32	35	136	120	134	18%	92	4%	62%				6.44	31.5	43	131	$23

Seager,Kyle

Age: 30 Bats: L Pos: 3B | Ht: 6' 0" Wt: 210

Health A | PT/Exp A | Consist C | LIMA Plan A | Rand Var +1 | MM 3135

Rode the Uppercut Wave like everyone else (52% FBs!), but didn't see the juiced hr/f levels others did, likely due to drop in HctX. Still, xPX remained strong all year so 30+ HRs still in play. But downside of extreme FB lean is BA risk; .280 is now off the table. He's amid peak-age plateau so you pretty much know what you're buying.

Yr	Tm	AB	R	HR	RBI	SB	BA	xBA	OBP	SLG	OPS	vL	vR	bb%	ct%	Eye	G	L	F	h%	HctX	PX	xPX	hr/f	Spd	SBO	SB%	#Wk	DOM	DIS	RC/G	RAR	BPV	BPX	R$
13	SEA	615	79	22	69	9	260	252	338	426	764	690	808	10	80	0.56	34	21	45	29	98	111	106	10%	84	7%	75%	27	56%	26%	4.90	17.0	56	140	$19
14	SEA	590	71	25	96	7	268	268	334	454	788	661	862	8	80	0.44	37	22	41	30	131	124	141	13%	85	8%	58%	27	56%	22%	5.07	23.9	63	170	$23
15	SEA	623	85	26	74	6	266	281	328	451	779	835	747	8	84	0.55	35	24	41	28	122	113	112	12%	81	8%	50%	27	70%	15%	4.95	6.9	70	189	$20
16	SEA	597	89	30	99	3	278	282	359	499	859	728	932	10	82	0.64	36	22	42	30	129	125	135	15%	72	2%	75%	27	67%	11%	6.21	24.0	72	206	$22
17	SEA	578	72	27	88	2	249	251	323	450	773	766	776	9	81	0.53	31	17	52	27	117	110	142	11%	78	2%	67%	27	48%	7%	4.84	-0.3	55	167	$13
1st Half		300	32	10	45	1	260	250	330	427	757	628	803	9	82	0.56	33	19	48	29	123	94	139	8%	85	1%	100%	13	38%	0%	4.83	-2.2	49	148	$11
2nd Half		278	40	17	43	1	237	251	315	475	790	893	744	9	80	0.50	30	15	56	24	111	127	145	14%	74	3%	50%	14	57%	14%	4.82	-2.2	64	194	$15
18	Proj	598	81	29	89	3	259	263	332	464	797	770	810	9	81	0.54	33	19	47	28	120	111	134	12%	77	4%	62%				5.18	5.0	52	158	$19

Segura,Jean

Age: 28 Bats: R Pos: SS | Ht: 5' 10" Wt: 205

Health B | PT/Exp A | Consist F | LIMA Plan B | Rand Var -3 | MM 1545

No surprise he didn't even approach 2016 HR total; GB%, PX/xPX history confirm he's no slugger. And while xBA says he won't hurt your BA, history confirms he's no .300 hitter either, at least not without h% fortune. Pretty much everything went right in ARI; if others want to bet on that happening again, let them.

Yr	Tm	AB	R	HR	RBI	SB	BA	xBA	OBP	SLG	OPS	vL	vR	bb%	ct%	Eye	G	L	F	h%	HctX	PX	xPX	hr/f	Spd	SBO	SB%	#Wk	DOM	DIS	RC/G	RAR	BPV	BPX	R$
13	MIL	588	74	12	49	44	294	282	329	423	752	865	716	4	86	0.30	59	18	23	33	99	76	69	10%	174	37%	77%	26	46%	31%	4.91	24.9	66	165	$35
14	MIL	513	61	5	31	20	246	265	289	326	614	511	643	5	86	0.40	59	18	23	28	79	51	51	5%	160	22%	69%	27	33%	41%	3.07	-1.6	46	124	$12
15	MIL	560	57	6	50	25	257	252	281	336	616	679	594	2	83	0.14	59	17	24	30	71	49	48	5%	128	24%	81%	26	19%	31%	3.21	-19.5	18	49	$17
16	ARI	637	102	20	64	33	319	296	368	499	867	763	900	6	84	0.39	53	19	28	35	101	103	93	14%	143	25%	77%	27	41%	15%	6.63	40.3	75	214	$39
17	SEA	524	80	11	45	22	300	279	349	427	776	819	762	6	84	0.41	54	19	26	34	96	73	66	9%	120	20%	73%	23	35%	22%	5.27	9.3	45	136	$24
1st Half		220	35	5	23	8	327	263	376	450	826	764	841	6	83	0.37	51	19	30	38	103	72	66	9%	102	20%	57%	10	20%	10%	5.85	7.7	33	100	$20
2nd Half		304	45	6	22	14	280	290	329	411	740	850	701	6	85	0.44	57	20	24	31	92	74	65	10%	128	20%	88%	13	46%	31%	4.87	2.5	53	161	$27
18	Proj	564	81	11	50	26	289	278	333	414	747	754	745	5	84	0.35	55	19	26	33	93	70	69	9%	129	23%	76%				4.82	5.6	43	129	$27

Semien,Marcus

Age: 27 Bats: R Pos: SS | Ht: 6' 0" Wt: 195

Health C | PT/Exp B | Consist A | LIMA Plan B+ | Rand Var -1 | MM 2425

Missed three months with early wrist injury; others may think that slowed HR pace, but 2nd half HctX, xPX suggest not to worry. Meanwhile, he's turning into quite the running threat, and recent SB% growth could keep opps coming. xBA says BA is what it is, but... UP: First 20/20 season.

Yr	Tm	AB	R	HR	RBI	SB	BA	xBA	OBP	SLG	OPS	vL	vR	bb%	ct%	Eye	G	L	F	h%	HctX	PX	xPX	hr/f	Spd	SBO	SB%	#Wk	DOM	DIS	RC/G	RAR	BPV	BPX	R$
13	CHW*	587	97	20	61	22	256	249	354	428	782	783	643	13	79	0.71	27	25	48	30	96	118	95	9%	131	16%	74%	5	40%	60%	5.18	30.6	77	193	$24
14	CHW*	534	68	17	62	8	224	245	301	383	684	735	637	10	74	0.42	40	21	39	27	78	119	75	10%	136	8%	77%	15	33%	53%	3.79	10.0	53	143	$10
15	OAK	556	65	15	45	11	257	242	310	405	715	879	653	7	76	0.32	38	23	39	31	98	96	119	9%	138	11%	69%	27	37%	30%	4.24	-2.5	39	105	$14
16	OAK	568	72	27	75	10	238	249	300	435	735	813	707	8	76	0.37	39	17	43	27	88	119	115	15%	110	9%	83%	27	41%	22%	4.40	1.5	49	140	$14
17	OAK	342	53	10	40	12	249	237	325	398	722	670	743	10	75	0.45	37	20	42	30	92	92	110	9%	107	14%	92%	16	38%	38%	4.52	-1.0	28	85	$10
1st Half		35	5	0	1	4	171	206	370	229	598	500	648	22	69	0.91	38	25	38	25	69	53	57	0%	94	29%	100%	2	0%	50%	3.19	-1.6	-9	-27	-$17
2nd Half		307	48	10	39	8	257	241	319	417	736	693	752	8	76	0.38	37	20	43	31	95	96	115	10%	111	11%	89%	14	43%	36%	4.67	0.8	32	97	$13
18	Proj	544	75	17	61	14	248	241	316	404	720	731	716	9	76	0.39	38	21	41	30	88	92	101	10%	113	12%	82%				4.33	-2.2	29	89	$17

Senzel,Nick

Age: 23 Bats: R Pos: 3B | Ht: 6' 1" Wt: 205

Health A | PT/Exp F | Consist F | LIMA Plan C | Rand Var 0 | MM 3243

With some help from h%, CIN top prospect's first stint in AA was going swimmingly before he was waylaid by vertigo, ending season in late August. Power/patience look very promising, and might deliver a few steals on the side. Assuming full recovery, 2016 No. 2 pick should get back on fast track to majors.

Yr	Tm	AB	R	HR	RBI	SB	BA	xBA	OBP	SLG	OPS	vL	vR	bb%	ct%	Eye	G	L	F	h%	HctX	PX	xPX	hr/f	Spd	SBO	SB%	#Wk	DOM	DIS	RC/G	RAR	BPV	BPX	R$
13																																			
14																																			
15																																			
16																																			
17	aa	209	42	12	36	5	345		423	588	1010			12	78	0.61				40		137			98	13%	56%				9.20		75	227	$13
1st Half		32	6	0	5	1	252		379	283	662			17	66	0.60				38		30			100	8%	100%				3.89		-46	-139	-$13
2nd Half		177	36	12	31	4	361		431	642	1074			11	80	0.61				40		153			99	14%	50%				10.35		95	288	$18
18	Proj	284	49	10	42	6	280	273	351	461	812	812	812	10	78	0.50	48	20	32	33		107		14%	100	14%	50%				5.41	4.3	47	143	$13

Severino,Pedro

Age: 24 Bats: R Pos: CA | Ht: 6' 0" Wt: 215

Health A | PT/Exp F | Consist C | LIMA Plan F | Rand Var +1 | MM 0101

0-3-.172 in 29 AB at WAS. Defensive stalwart has yet to develop even a semblance of an offensive game to match. OPS in AAA last two seasons: .653, .623. If your league somehow rewards footwork and arm cannon, maybe he's of interest. Otherwise, pass.

Yr	Tm	AB	R	HR	RBI	SB	BA	xBA	OBP	SLG	OPS	vL	vR	bb%	ct%	Eye	G	L	F	h%	HctX	PX	xPX	hr/f	Spd	SBO	SB%	#Wk	DOM	DIS	RC/G	RAR	BPV	BPX	R$
13																																			
14																																			
15	WAS *	333	29	4	29	1	229	271	265	305	570	0	750	5	84	0.30	33	33	33	26	120	53	233	0%	75	4%	28%	2	50%	50%	2.61	-12.2	11	30	$0
16	WAS *	319	30	4	24	3	263	212	313	345	658	1229	1010	7	84	0.45	60	8	32	30	82	53	76	25%	98	8%	39%	9	56%	33%	3.57	-7.8	24	69	$4
17	WAS *	240	14	4	27	1	207	192	252	275	527	571	390	6	76	0.24	47	16	37	26	64	40	66	0%	79	3%	42%	8	13%	75%	2.19	-13.9	-28	-85	-$2
1st Half		146	7	2	19	0	179	199	219	239	458			5	75	0.20				22		34			82	4%	0%				1.56		-35	-106	-$4
2nd Half		94	7	2	8	1	251	202	303	331	634	571	390	7	76	0.31	47	16	37	31	65	49	66	0%	89	3%	100%	8	13%	75%	3.46	-1.8	-14	-42	$1
18	Proj	197	15	0	18	1	218	199	266	253	520	724	457	6	80	0.32	47	16	37	27	59	28	59	0%	84	5%	51%				2.16	-12.0	-32	-96	$0

Shaw,Travis

Age: 28 Bats: L Pos: 3B | Ht: 6' 4" Wt: 230

Health A | PT/Exp B | Consist C | LIMA Plan B+ | Rand Var -1 | MM 4235

Big question entering 2017: Can he repeat HR outburst? PX/xPX say yes, as does 19 HR away from Miller Park, even if hr/f a bit high. Picked spots well on basepaths, and dispelled bad rap of being unable to hit LHP. Unsustained 1st half ct% suggests BA may have peaked, but otherwise, a solid investment.

Yr	Tm	AB	R	HR	RBI	SB	BA	xBA	OBP	SLG	OPS	vL	vR	bb%	ct%	Eye	G	L	F	h%	HctX	PX	xPX	hr/f	Spd	SBO	SB%	#Wk	DOM	DIS	RC/G	RAR	BPV	BPX	R$
13	aa	444	44	12	38	5	200		293	341	633			12	71	0.46				25		107			108	8%	62%				3.14		29	73	$1
14	a/a	490	61	16	61	6	252		315	415	730			8	78	0.41				30		121			87	7%	62%				4.39		52	141	$14
15	BOS *	515	56	17	61	0	248	237	302	397	699	975	723	7	77	0.34	37	20	43	29	98	98	128	18%	87	2%	0%	16	31%	31%	3.99	-10.5	29	78	$9
16	BOS	480	63	16	71	5	242	240	306	421	726	599	762	8	72	0.32	36	19	45	30	98	123	122	10%	80	6%	83%	26	35%	38%	4.32	-9.3	30	86	$10
17	MIL	538	84	31	101	10	273	274	349	513	862	776	892	10	74	0.43	43	20	38	31	112	141	128	21%	76	7%	100%	26	69%	19%	6.35	16.0	55	167	$23
1st Half		278	42	17	59	7	291	295	357	554	911	757	961	9	77	0.44	45	20	35	32	117	149	125	23%	72	10%	100%	13	77%	15%	7.28	16.9	71	215	$28
2nd Half		260	42	14	42	3	254	251	340	469	809	794	815	11	71	0.43	39	20	41	30	106	131	131	18%	87	4%	100%	13	62%	23%	5.45	2.8	39	118	$18
18	Proj	540	75	27	84	7	255	258	326	469	795	760	808	9	74	0.39	39	20	41	30	104	128	126	16%	81	6%	88%				5.23	5.4	43	130	$19

KRISTOPHER OLSON

Simmons,Andrelton

Age: 28 Bats: R Pos: SS	Health A	LIMA Plan A	
Ht: 6' 2" Wt: 200	PT/Exp A	Rand Var 0	
	Consist B	MM 1355	

The bat finally hung with years of elite glovework; difference was in the counting stats. While AB total certainly helped, PX/xPX gains are enough to sustain double-digit HR, and he took advantage of green light. This was probably his peak, as gravity is a powerful force, but Rand Var, BPV growth agree: a lot of this can stick.

Yr	Tm	AB	R	HR	RBI	SB	BA	xBA	OBP	SLG	OPS	vL	vR	bb%	ct%	Eye	G	L	F	h%	HctX	PX	xPX	hr/f	Spd	SBO	SB%	#Wk	DOM	DIS	RC/G	RAR	BPV	BPX	R
13	ATL	606	76	17	59	6	248	272	296	396	692	692	691	6	91	0.73	42	18	39	25	102	86	89	8%	135	8%	55%	27	56%	7%	3.85	7.7	87	218	$1
14	ATL	540	44	7	46	4	244	250	286	331	617	679	603	6	89	0.53	52	16	31	26	102	56	87	5%	129	7%	44%	26	54%	23%	3.11	-1.1	52	141	$
15	ATL	535	60	4	44	5	265	279	321	338	660	565	683	7	91	0.81	56	22	22	29	92	47	61	4%	106	5%	63%	27	56%	22%	3.67	-11.2	49	132	$1
16	LAA	448	48	4	44	10	281	282	324	366	690	752	671	6	92	0.74	55	20	26	30	87	51	54	4%	107	9%	91%	23	48%	4%	4.30	0.0	53	151	$1
17	LAA	589	77	14	69	19	278	286	331	421	752	690	770	7	89	0.70	50	19	31	30	105	78	82	8%	102	16%	76%	27	56%	15%	4.93	5.0	64	194	$2
1st Half		313	39	9	36	13	281	295	335	431	767	716	781	8	89	0.76	51	20	29	29	114	79	91	11%	105	17%	87%	13	62%	15%	5.28	6.2	68	206	$2
2nd Half		276	38	5	33	6	275	275	326	409	735	662	758	7	88	0.64	48	18	35	30	95	77	72	6%	100	14%	60%	14	50%	14%	4.55	-0.2	60	182	$1
18	Proj	**588**	**71**	**10**	**62**	**13**	**274**	**281**	**323**	**387**	**709**	**684**	**717**	**7**	**90**	**0.71**	**51**	**19**	**29**	**29**	**97**	**62**	**71**	**6%**	**104**	**11%**	**74%**				**4.37**	**-1.7**	**52**	**156**	**$1**

Sisco,Chance

Age: 23 Bats: L Pos: CA	Health A	LIMA Plan F	
Ht: 6' 2" Wt: 195	PT/Exp D	Rand Var -3	
	Consist C	MM 1101	

2-4-.333 in 18 AB at BAL. Org's top prospect got Sept cup of joe, but signs point to more minor league time. Declining ct% magnifies BA risk, PX hints there's not much pop, and he struggled vL (0.20 Eye, .552 OPS in 65 Triple-A AB). Better with the leather and catchers can take a while to hit; keep him off your 2018 draft list.

Yr	Tm	AB	R	HR	RBI	SB	BA	xBA	OBP	SLG	OPS	vL	vR	bb%	ct%	Eye	G	L	F	h%	HctX	PX	xPX	hr/f	Spd	SBO	SB%	#Wk	DOM	DIS	RC/G	RAR	BPV	BPX	R
13																																			
14																																			
15	aa	74	8	2	7	0	248		321	379	700			10	81	0.56				28		87			94	5%	0%				3.89		42	114	-$
16	a/a	426	52	5	46	2	282		370	363	733			12	76	0.59				36		55			91	3%	45%				4.71		3	9	$1
17	BAL *	362	46	8	47	2	237	204	303	349	652	167	1639	9	67	0.28	45	18	36	33	172	79	223	50%	88	4%	45%	5	20%	40%	3.47	-7.2	-24	-73	$
1st Half		222	29	3	26	2	240	195	308	323	631			9	65	0.28				36		65			98	5%	62%				3.31		-40	-121	$
2nd Half		140	17	6	20	0	231	224	295	391	686	167	1639	8	70	0.30	45	18	36	29	180	99	223	50%	93	3%	0%	5	20%	40%	3.70	-1.7	5	15	$
18	Proj	**158**	**20**	**4**	**19**	**1**	**240**	**223**	**315**	**356**	**672**	**672**	**672**	**10**	**71**	**0.38**	**44**	**21**	**35**	**31**		**75**		**10%**	**103**	**3%**	**43%**				**3.70**	**-2.1**	**-19**	**-59**	**$**

Slater,Austin

Age: 25 Bats: R Pos: LF	Health B	LIMA Plan D	
Ht: 6' 2" Wt: 215	PT/Exp D	Rand Var -3	
	Consist B	MM 1123	

3-16-.282 in 117 AB at SF. Held his own after June call-up, but hip injury sent him to DL in July, ended season in Sept. Contact skills held steady, but elevated h% drove wedge between BA and xBA. MLB xPX, PX history suggest the power stroke remains a work in progress. Too many roadblocks on path to relevance.

Yr	Tm	AB	R	HR	RBI	SB	BA	xBA	OBP	SLG	OPS	vL	vR	bb%	ct%	Eye	G	L	F	h%	HctX	PX	xPX	hr/f	Spd	SBO	SB%	#Wk	DOM	DIS	RC/G	RAR	BPV	BPX	R
13																																			
14																																			
15	aa	199	20	0	12	1	279		324	344	668			6	73	0.25				38		58			106	4%	46%				3.87		-14	-38	$
16	a/a	390	47	12	56	7	265		347	413	759			11	74	0.48				33		95			87	12%	46%				4.68		21	60	$1
17	SF *	301	37	6	38	3	277	235	322	391	714	813	709	6	75	0.27	61	14	25	35	73	71	48	14%	112	8%	48%	9	22%	56%	4.29	-8.3	5	15	$
1st Half		258	34	6	34	3	294	250	338	419	758	982	849	6	76	0.28	60	16	24	37	87	78	71	19%	114	9%	48%	5	40%	20%	4.92	-3.2	15	45	$1
2nd Half		43	3	1	4	0	174	132	228	221	449	516	282	7	69	0.23	67	5	29	23	27	25	-26	0%	104	0%	0%	4	0%	100%	1.55	-5.3	-57	-173	-$1
18	Proj	**259**	**30**	**4**	**28**	**3**	**241**	**247**	**303**	**340**	**643**	**768**	**578**	**7**	**74**	**0.31**	**52**	**23**	**25**	**31**	**51**	**66**	**13**	**8%**	**109**	**9%**	**46%**				**3.26**	**-9.4**	**-13**	**-39**	**$**

Smith,Dominic

Age: 23 Bats: L Pos: 1B	Health A	LIMA Plan B+	
Ht: 6' 0" Wt: 239	PT/Exp D	Rand Var -1	
	Consist A	MM 3035	

9-26-.198 in 167 AB at NYM. Couldn't deliver on hype that came with Aug call-up, but skills breed optimism. Made plenty of hard contact despite lack of FBs, and while he traded some contact for it (71% MLB ct%), minor league Eye, 2nd half xBA say he won't hurt you. Keeper outlook is rosy; could deliver quickly.

Yr	Tm	AB	R	HR	RBI	SB	BA	xBA	OBP	SLG	OPS	vL	vR	bb%	ct%	Eye	G	L	F	h%	HctX	PX	xPX	hr/f	Spd	SBO	SB%	#Wk	DOM	DIS	RC/G	RAR	BPV	BPX	R
13																																			
14																																			
15																																			
16	aa	484	56	13	79	2	272		337	410	748			9	82	0.56				31		83			82	2%	61%				4.83		40	114	$1
17	NYM *	624	74	22	82	1	256	242	307	418	725	437	708	7	75	0.30	50	16	34	31	113	98	112	23%	49	1%	40%	9	33%	44%	4.38	-27.9	10	30	$1
1st Half		327	36	6	34	0	269	234	317	381	697			7	78	0.31				33		70			72	1%	0%				4.14		3	9	$
2nd Half		297	38	15	48	1	242	258	297	460	757	437	708	7	73	0.29	50	16	34	28	109	131	112	23%	49	1%	100%	9	33%	44%	4.61	-9.1	28	85	$1
18	Proj	**516**	**61**	**20**	**76**	**1**	**261**	**254**	**321**	**439**	**759**	**565**	**805**	**8**	**76**	**0.36**	**45**	**19**	**36**	**31**	**98**	**104**	**101**	**14%**	**48**	**2%**	**64%**				**4.81**	**-4.3**	**21**	**63**	**$1**

Smith,Kevan

Age: 30 Bats: R Pos: CA	Health A	LIMA Plan D	
Ht: 6' 4" Wt: 230	PT/Exp D	Rand Var -5	
	Consist C	MM 1021	

4-30-.283 in 276 AB at CHW. Former college QB got his shot via part-time role. Made the most of it with plus BA, but it came with little support from xBA, and h% spike casts doubt he'll repeat. Not much else here, as dismal PX, hard-hit metrics say there's no pop. Sack, interception, whatever the parallel; it's not good.

Yr	Tm	AB	R	HR	RBI	SB	BA	xBA	OBP	SLG	OPS	vL	vR	bb%	ct%	Eye	G	L	F	h%	HctX	PX	xPX	hr/f	Spd	SBO	SB%	#Wk	DOM	DIS	RC/G	RAR	BPV	BPX	R
13																																			
14	aa	389	31	8	34	1	235		297	347	643			8	79	0.41				28		83			94	2%	37%				3.39		27	73	$
15	aaa	319	32	5	28	0	211		266	298	565			7	74	0.29				27		62			100	2%	0%				2.52		-8	-22	-$
16	CHW *	199	15	6	18	0	170	199	220	300	520	200	333	6	74	0.24	60	10	30	20	180	82	150	0%	84	0%	0%	5	0%	80%	2.03	-11.8	0	0	-$
17	CHW *	329	30	4	41	0	285	254	313	388	701	615	751	4	82	0.23	57	19	23	34	75	67	43	7%	68	0%	0%	23	26%	39%	4.33	1.7	13	39	$
1st Half		171	19	1	24	0	290	250	313	383	696	555	774	3	80	0.16	58	19	23	36	83	67	62	5%	75	0%	0%	10	20%	40%	4.31	1.0	5	15	$
2nd Half		158	11	3	17	0	278	253	315	392	708	663	735	5	85	0.33	56	20	24	31	70	67	29	9%	69	0%	0%	13	31%	38%	4.34	1.1	25	76	$
18	Proj	**232**	**20**	**3**	**24**	**0**	**240**	**243**	**285**	**333**	**618**	**543**	**667**	**5**	**79**	**0.27**	**57**	**20**	**23**	**29**	**75**	**60**	**42**	**7%**	**75**	**0%**	**26%**				**3.13**	**-7.0**	**-14**	**-43**	**$**

Smith,Mallex

Age: 25 Bats: L Pos: CF LF	Health C	LIMA Plan C	
Ht: 5' 9" Wt: 180	PT/Exp C	Rand Var -1	
	Consist A	MM 1523	

2-12-.270 with 16 SB in 256 AB at TAM. April hammy shelved him for nearly two months, and while top-notch Spd and SBO remained intact, he's a one-trick pony. Mediocre Eye, xBA limit running opps, and BA risk is further magnified vL, which will cut into AB. A legit 30-SB contender, but it'll cost you everywhere else.

Yr	Tm	AB	R	HR	RBI	SB	BA	xBA	OBP	SLG	OPS	vL	vR	bb%	ct%	Eye	G	L	F	h%	HctX	PX	xPX	hr/f	Spd	SBO	SB%	#Wk	DOM	DIS	RC/G	RAR	BPV	BPX	R
13																																			
14																																			
15	a/a	484	75	2	31	51	283		346	353	699			9	80	0.48				35		47			148	41%	78%				4.49		21	57	$3
16	ATL *	220	37	3	26	20	258	253	331	388	719	299	819	10	74	0.42	61	16	23	34	58	79	59	11%	146	45%	68%	15	27%	40%	4.18	-3.0	24	69	$1
17	TAM *	442	56	5	21	35	256	238	315	352	667	603	699	8	74	0.34	50	22	28	34	64	57	29	4%	183	39%	71%	19	21%	47%	3.72	-23.2	15	45	$1
1st Half		232	37	4	12	23	293	252	348	408	756	885	752	8	76	0.35	54	21	25	37	68	64	37	6%	190	49%	66%	7	29%	43%	4.69	-4.6	30	91	$2
2nd Half		210	19	1	9	11	215	223	280	290	570	300	666	8	72	0.32	48	23	29	29	61	48	24	3%	147	25%	84%	12	17%	50%	2.77	-16.9	-11	-33	$
18	Proj	**320**	**45**	**4**	**24**	**27**	**256**	**246**	**322**	**368**	**690**	**448**	**751**	**9**	**75**	**0.37**	**55**	**20**	**26**	**33**	**62**	**65**	**41**	**7%**	**167**	**40%**	**72%**				**3.96**	**-5.3**	**16**	**49**	**$1**

Smith,Seth

Age: 35 Bats: L Pos: RF	Health A	LIMA Plan D+	
Ht: 6' 3" Wt: 210	PT/Exp C	Rand Var 0	
	Consist A	MM 3333	

Not a box of chocolates—you know exactly what you're going to get: platoon AB, average BA, modest HR. Things just as steady under the surface: plate skills, LD% stroke barely budged; ditto for xPX, HctX. "Gains" vL were over just 24 AB, and while slight slide vR worth tracking at 35, he remains useful in daily formats.

Yr	Tm	AB	R	HR	RBI	SB	BA	xBA	OBP	SLG	OPS	vL	vR	bb%	ct%	Eye	G	L	F	h%	HctX	PX	xPX	hr/f	Spd	SBO	SB%	#Wk	DOM	DIS	RC/G	RAR	BPV	BPX	R
13	OAK	368	49	8	40	0	253	243	329	391	721	621	748	10	74	0.41	45	20	35	32	91	113	102	8%	88	0%	0%	27	37%	41%	4.33	0.5	36	90	$
14	SD	443	55	12	48	1	266	281	367	440	807	744	815	13	80	0.79	47	21	32	31	115	126	115	11%	99	1%	50%	27	56%	26%	5.56	21.2	81	219	$1
15	SEA	395	54	12	42	0	248	264	330	443	773	571	801	10	75	0.47	42	20	38	30	118	139	122	11%	100	0%	0%	27	52%	22%	4.93	1.9	64	173	$
16	SEA	378	62	16	63	0	249	257	342	415	758	476	782	11	76	0.54	48	22	30	29	105	99	108	18%	81	0%	0%	26	38%	42%	4.70	0.0	33	94	$
17	BAL	330	50	13	32	2	258	264	340	433	774	808	771	10	76	0.46	43	23	34	30	111	105	115	15%	90	2%	100%	26	50%	31%	4.96	0.3	37	112	$
1st Half		190	30	8	16	2	258	264	333	437	770	957	752	9	74	0.39	45	24	31	31	99	107	113	18%	98	4%	100%	13	46%	31%	4.95	-0.6	32	97	$
2nd Half		140	20	5	16	0	257	262	350	429	779	429	796	11	79	0.57	41	22	37	30	127	102	117	12%	82	0%	0%	13	54%	31%	4.97	-0.4	44	133	$
18	Proj	**376**	**56**	**14**	**45**	**1**	**254**	**263**	**341**	**429**	**770**	**626**	**784**	**11**	**77**	**0.50**	**44**	**22**	**34**	**30**	**112**	**104**	**114**	**14%**	**89**	**1%**	**95%**				**4.90**	**2.2**	**29**	**87**	**$1**

RYAN BLOOMFIELD

Smoak,Justin

Age: 31	Bats: B	Pos: 1B	Health	A	LIMA Plan	B+
Ht: 6' 4"	Wt: 220		PT/Exp	C	Rand Var	0
			Consist	D	MM	4035

Funny, these 2017 skills aren't THAT much different from the rest of his career! Except: made better contact, and more hard contact, but even those weren't significant changes. Tailed off late (.194 BA after 8/15), but a 21% hit rate seems to blame; skills didn't suffer much. Some regression to the mean seems reasonable.

Yr	Tm	AB	R	HR	RBI	SB	BA	xBA	OBP	SLG	OPS	vL	vR	bb%	ct%	Eye	G	L	F	h%	HctX	PX	xPX	hr/f	Spd	SBO	SB%	#Wk	DOM	DIS	RC/G	RAR	BPV	BPX	R$
13	SEA *	475	54	20	51	0	235	234	326	405	731	548	839	12	74	0.51	35	20	46	28	112	120	152	13%	86	0%	0%	25	44%	36%	4.41	-2.7	42	105	$8
14	SEA *	453	46	11	55	0	224	223	292	349	641	618	611	9	73	0.37	42	18	39	28	116	101	145	10%	66	3%	0%	18	33%	44%	3.23	-12.6	14	38	$4
15	TOR	296	44	18	59	0	226	274	299	470	768	839	757	9	71	0.34	43	24	34	26	112	166	141	25%	73	0%	0%	27	52%	33%	4.57	-3.2	58	157	$7
16	TOR	299	33	14	34	1	217	224	314	391	705	621	738	12	63	0.36	30	27	42	29	99	123	144	18%	81	1%	100%	26	27%	58%	3.97	-8.1	-1	-3	$2
17	TOR	560	85	38	90	0	270	277	355	529	883	977	856	11	77	0.57	34	21	44	29	123	141	158	20%	68	1%	0%	27	56%	19%	6.49	17.8	67	203	$19
1st Half		267	45	22	52	0	300	298	368	592	960	1113	909	10	79	0.53	36	24	41	31	125	147	146	25%	83	1%	0%	13	54%	23%	7.82	16.0	82	248	$25
2nd Half		293	40	16	38	0	242	256	343	471	814	825	811	13	75	0.60	33	19	48	27	122	135	170	15%	66	0%	0%	14	57%	14%	5.41	-2.1	56	170	$13
18	Proj	553	75	32	82	0	258	260	343	485	828	823	830	11	73	0.47	35	23	42	30	115	132	152	19%	70	1%	41%				5.67	9.2	31	93	$16

Sogard,Eric

Age: 32	Bats: L	Pos: 2B SS	Health	F	LIMA Plan	D+
Ht: 5' 9"	Wt: 180		PT/Exp	F	Rand Var	0
			Consist	D	MM	0231

3-18-.273 in 249 AB at MIL. Nice little comeback after missing all of 2016 with a knee problem; an ankle strain cost him some 2017 time. Simply hit the ball a bit harder, fueling BA. Walk rate spike helped too. Mind you, most skills are still below par. But a buck spent here is consistently several earned. Deep-league filler.

Yr	Tm	AB	R	HR	RBI	SB	BA	xBA	OBP	SLG	OPS	vL	vR	bb%	ct%	Eye	G	L	F	h%	HctX	PX	xPX	hr/f	Spd	SBO	SB%	#Wk	DOM	DIS	RC/G	RAR	BPV	BPX	R$
13	OAK	368	45	2	35	10	266	256	322	364	686	640	695	7	86	0.53	35	25	40	30	65	73	44	2%	108	16%	67%	27	56%	22%	3.93	4.6	50	125	$9
14	OAK	291	38	1	22	11	223	241	298	268	567	478	581	9	87	0.84	42	24	35	25	65	36	52	1%	91	18%	73%	26	27%	38%	2.66	-5.6	26	70	$4
15	OAK	372	40	1	37	6	247	240	294	304	598	543	609	6	87	0.46	44	22	34	28	63	37	40	1%	114	7%	86%	26	19%	46%	3.05	-7.9	24	65	$5
16																																			
17	MIL *	340	56	5	29	6	265	279	366	378	745	745	771	14	84	1.02	39	29	33	30	90	68	62	4%	94	8%	67%	21	43%	29%	4.77	2.5	49	148	$8
1st Half		221	43	5	25	6	300	293	386	450	837	837	980	12	84	0.87	39	29	32	34	89	92	64	9%	93	11%	75%	8	50%	13%	6.33	10.8	63	191	$15
2nd Half		119	13	0	4	0	202	255	331	244	575	490	578	16	86	1.35	39	29	33	24	91	25	60	0%	109	2%	0%	13	38%	38%	2.50	-7.8	30	91	-$6
18	Proj	219	29	2	17	4	260	262	344	344	688	664	692	11	86	0.84	40	26	34	30	87	49	53	3%	103	8%	68%				4.00	-5.1	30	91	$5

Solarte,Yangervis

Age: 30	Bats: B	Pos: 2B SS 3B	Health	C	LIMA Plan	B
Ht: 5' 11"	Wt: 205		PT/Exp	B	Rand Var	+1
			Consist	B	MM	2245

PRO: Continues to develop power stroke while maintaining near-elite contact. CON: Average vL routinely undercuts value, missed more time with injury. That 24% 2H hit rate looks to be the outlier in these numbers. A simple regression there recovers any lost value, and FB growth suggests he hasn't peaked yet... UP: 25 HR

Yr	Tm	AB	R	HR	RBI	SB	BA	xBA	OBP	SLG	OPS	vL	vR	bb%	ct%	Eye	G	L	F	h%	HctX	PX	xPX	hr/f	Spd	SBO	SB%	#Wk	DOM	DIS	RC/G	RAR	BPV	BPX	R$
13	aaa	526	47	9	53	2	231		270	334	604			5	85	0.35				26		72			79	2%	100%				3.01		33	83	$4
14	2 TM	469	56	10	48	0	260	254	336	369	705	760	673	10	88	0.91	45	19	35	28	99	72	71	7%	81	1%	0%	26	42%	12%	4.23	11.3	54	146	$10
15	SD	526	63	14	63	1	270	280	320	428	748	667	771	6	89	0.61	44	19	37	28	118	94	96	8%	90	1%	100%	27	59%	15%	4.71	8.1	74	200	$13
16	SD	405	55	15	71	1	286	282	341	467	808	772	819	7	84	0.48	41	22	37	31	112	104	91	12%	66	2%	50%	22	45%	18%	5.56	7.8	56	160	$14
17	SD	466	49	18	64	3	255	257	314	416	731	564	794	7	87	0.61	42	16	42	26	109	82	98	10%	71	3%	100%	22	50%	14%	4.46	-7.5	51	155	$10
1st Half		254	28	10	40	2	268	249	349	425	775	621	825	10	87	0.85	43	15	42	27	104	79	104	11%	84	3%	100%	12	50%	8%	5.09	1.9	58	176	$13
2nd Half		212	21	8	24	1	241	264	269	406	675	505	750	4	87	0.32	40	18	42	24	115	86	91	10%	66	2%	100%	10	50%	20%	3.72	-7.0	46	139	$6
18	Proj	497	57	19	68	2	262	271	314	432	747	640	786	7	87	0.52	42	19	39	27	111	88	92	11%	72	2%	85%				4.65	-2.1	47	141	$14

Soler,Jorge

Age: 26	Bats: R	Pos: RF	Health	D	LIMA Plan	F
Ht: 6' 4"	Wt: 215		PT/Exp	D	Rand Var	+5
			Consist	A	MM	2201

2-6-.144 in 97 AB at KC. This, uh, didn't go well. March strained oblique set a dismal tone early. Then showed flashes in the minors after two demotions, but never carried it to KC. Still pre-peak, still hugely talented, still owns that 2014 promise. But also still struggling to put it in play, and 2014 fades further each year.

Yr	Tm	AB	R	HR	RBI	SB	BA	xBA	OBP	SLG	OPS	vL	vR	bb%	ct%	Eye	G	L	F	h%	HctX	PX	xPX	hr/f	Spd	SBO	SB%	#Wk	DOM	DIS	RC/G	RAR	BPV	BPX	R$
13																																			
14	CHC *	264	38	16	59	1	296	312	365	594	960	701	964	10	73	0.41	52	12	36	35	128	230	131	21%	97	3%	47%	6	67%	33%	7.76	26.8	128	346	$14
15	CHC	366	39	10	47	3	262	236	324	399	723	730	720	8	67	0.26	42	28	30	37	110	107	123	14%	104	4%	75%	20	30%	50%	4.43	-3.5	2	5	$8
16	CHC *	264	40	12	33	0	224	215	325	394	719	812	749	13	68	0.47	40	17	43	28	86	112	91	17%	91	0%	0%	19	47%	37%	4.20	-3.7	17	49	$3
17	KC *	370	45	19	52	1	205	217	300	394	694	577	459	12	65	0.39	38	18	44	26	82	122	88	7%	70	1%	100%	13	0%	69%	3.80	-12.9	6	18	$2
1st Half		182	21	10	30	0	240	224	341	450	791	821	498	13	67	0.47	38	17	46	30	91	133	83	9%	74	0%	0%	6	0%	50%	5.15	0.5	27	82	$4
2nd Half		188	24	9	22	1	170	218	259	341	600	77	330	11	63	0.33	38	23	38	21	59	110	108	0%	87	2%	100%	7	0%	86%	2.73	-14.2	-10	-30	$0
18	Proj	124	16	3	18	0	224	210	319	351	671	586	715	11	67	0.38	41	20	40	31	87	87	103	10%	92	1%	80%				3.60	-4.1	-24	-74	$2

Souza,Steven

Age: 29	Bats: R	Pos: RF	Health	C	LIMA Plan	C+
Ht: 6' 4"	Wt: 225		PT/Exp	B	Rand Var	+2
			Consist	B	MM	4315

Stayed on the field for a change, and showed flashes of former upside. But there are serious flaws, notably the still-awful contact rate that's dragging down BA. What's more, xPX, Spd both hint at downside in counting stats—not to mention that he's never stayed healthy before. Don't be surprised if 2017 was his career year.

Yr	Tm	AB	R	HR	RBI	SB	BA	xBA	OBP	SLG	OPS	vL	vR	bb%	ct%	Eye	G	L	F	h%	HctX	PX	xPX	hr/f	Spd	SBO	SB%	#Wk	DOM	DIS	RC/G	RAR	BPV	BPX	R$
13	aa	273	43	12	35	16	265		341	476	817			10	69	0.38				34		168			93	32%	70%				5.43		62	155	$14
14	WAS *	369	48	14	57	19	284	254	356	465	820	2071	105	10	75	0.44	50	13	38	35	121	136	141	33%	80	25%	70%	9	22%	78%	5.72	17.3	54	146	$21
15	TAM	373	59	16	40	12	225	220	318	399	717	730	712	11	61	0.32	45	20	35	32	92	138	100	21%	105	18%	67%	21	24%	48%	3.98	-9.0	11	30	$10
16	TAM	430	58	17	49	7	247	224	303	409	713	664	731	7	63	0.19	41	25	35	35	83	118	112	18%	119	13%	54%	24	25%	58%	3.95	-9.7	-1	-3	$10
17	TAM	523	78	30	78	16	239	246	351	459	810	785	819	14	66	0.47	45	21	34	30	91	139	100	26%	96	13%	80%	27	48%	26%	5.33	6.3	32	97	$17
1st Half		282	44	16	53	3	270	262	373	500	873	699	946	13	67	0.47	41	27	32	35	96	144	103	27%	102	4%	75%	13	54%	23%	6.41	11.0	43	130	$20
2nd Half		241	34	14	25	13	203	226	326	411	737	906	680	14	64	0.47	49	14	37	25	85	132	98	25%	90	24%	81%	14	43%	29%	4.25	-6.2	20	61	$14
18	Proj	467	68	23	59	15	238	236	329	435	765	763	765	11	65	0.36	44	21	35	31	88	129	104	22%	102	17%	72%				4.64	-0.8	15	46	$17

Span,Denard

Age: 34	Bats: L	Pos: CF	Health	C	LIMA Plan	B+
Ht: 6' 0"	Wt: 210		PT/Exp	B	Rand Var	+1
			Consist	C	MM	1355

For the most part, skills continue to hold up. But there are reasons for concern. Defensive metrics are so bad, he's reportedly volunteered to move to LF. With those awful vL splits, a potential platoon would loom large. That might prop up BA some, but set expectations accordingly—it would come over ~400 AB, not 500-600.

Yr	Tm	AB	R	HR	RBI	SB	BA	xBA	OBP	SLG	OPS	vL	vR	bb%	ct%	Eye	G	L	F	h%	HctX	PX	xPX	hr/f	Spd	SBO	SB%	#Wk	DOM	DIS	RC/G	RAR	BPV	BPX	R$
13	WAS	610	75	4	47	20	279	285	327	380	707	539	765	6	87	0.55	54	23	23	31	68	65	41	3%	153	15%	77%	26	46%	12%	4.39	5.0	62	155	$20
14	WAS	610	94	5	37	31	302	288	355	416	771	694	802	7	89	0.77	46	24	30	33	98	80	52	3%	134	21%	82%	27	56%	7%	5.49	28.2	78	211	$30
15	WAS	246	38	5	22	11	301	301	365	431	796	542	880	9	89	0.96	50	24	26	32	95	84	72	9%	103	14%	100%	13	54%	23%	6.07	11.9	76	205	$11
16	SF	572	70	11	53	12	266	282	331	381	712	566	781	8	86	0.67	52	23	25	29	87	64	51	9%	96	11%	63%	27	52%	30%	4.25	-6.6	44	126	$15
17	SF	497	73	12	43	12	272	283	329	427	756	576	804	7	86	0.58	45	21	34	30	88	84	74	8%	116	15%	63%	25	56%	20%	4.73	-4.7	63	191	$15
1st Half		232	33	5	18	4	297	287	348	457	805	674	839	6	87	0.52	43	23	34	33	80	84	68	8%	125	11%	57%	11	64%	18%	5.50	3.8	66	200	$12
2nd Half		265	40	7	25	8	249	278	313	400	713	497	774	8	86	0.63	47	20	34	27	94	84	80	9%	99	18%	67%	14	50%	21%	4.13	-6.2	58	176	$17
18	Proj	452	64	10	39	13	275	287	333	412	745	566	805	8	87	0.64	48	22	29	30	89	74	66	8%	111	15%	72%				4.74	3.0	57	171	$17

Spangenberg,Cory

Age: 27	Bats: L	Pos: 3B LF	Health	F	LIMA Plan	C+
Ht: 6' 0"	Wt: 195		PT/Exp	F	Rand Var	-2
			Consist	B	MM	2435

13-46-.264 with 11 SB in 444 AB at SD. Got a late start after missing most of 2016 with a torn quad, but stayed healthy and with big club after April recall. PRO: Spanks RHP; contributes in several categories. CON: Poor plate skills keep lid on BA; no apparent power upside (see G/F, xPX); a must-sit vL in DFS.

Yr	Tm	AB	R	HR	RBI	SB	BA	xBA	OBP	SLG	OPS	vL	vR	bb%	ct%	Eye	G	L	F	h%	HctX	PX	xPX	hr/f	Spd	SBO	SB%	#Wk	DOM	DIS	RC/G	RAR	BPV	BPX	R$
13	aa	287	30	2	17	16	259		294	325	620			5	75	0.21				34		50			132	37%	57%				2.95		-6	-15	$8
14	SD *	343	38	4	27	15	291	250	320	415	735	667	795	4	75	0.17	45	26	30	38	86	93	113	14%	136	32%	56%	5	20%	40%	4.30	5.9	24	65	$14
15	SD *	341	42	5	24	12	260	262	321	385	706	703	738	8	76	0.38	50	25	25	33	84	86	74	8%	144	17%	75%	20	40%	45%	4.25	-4.2	35	95	$9
16	SD	48	6	1	8	1	229	251	302	354	656	1074	448	8	73	0.31	69	16	16	29	51	72	15	20%	120	8%	100%	3	0%	67%	3.49	-2.1	2	6	-$1
17	SD *	510	62	14	51	13	265	247	314	395	710	487	811	7	73	0.27	49	23	28	34	86	79	76	15%	119	14%	70%	24	17%	58%	4.26	-15.6	6	18	$14
1st Half		254	22	5	22	7	265	230	299	361	660	462	735	5	74	0.19	47	21	31	34	87	61	78	10%	108	16%	67%	10	10%	80%	3.66	-10.6	-11	-33	$9
2nd Half		256	40	9	29	6	266	261	338	430	768	504	867	9	72	0.33	51	24	25	34	85	99	75	20%	125	11%	75%	14	21%	43%	4.89	-1.5	23	70	$19
18	Proj	424	52	11	37	14	267	258	321	411	732	570	782	7	74	0.28	49	24	27	34	85	85	81	13%	140	19%	66%				4.40	-6.1	15	46	$15

ROD TRUESDELL

Springer,George	Health	C	LIMA Plan	B
Age: 28 Bats: R Pos: CF RF	PT/Exp	A	Rand Var	+1
Ht: 6' 3" Wt: 215	Consist	B	MM	4145

Took a while to get rolling after July quad strain (2nd in 3 years), and 2nd half power took a hit. Indeed, shaky health looks like part of this package. But was having a huge season prior, with stunning contact growth—his former Achilles' heel—driving the train. With (perhaps improbable) full health and additional FB ... UP: 40 HR

Yr	Tm	AB	R	HR	RBI	SB	BA	xBA	OBP	SLG	OPS	vL	vR	bb%	ct%	Eye	G	L	F	h%	HctX	PX	xPX	hr/f	Spd	SBO	SB%	#Wk	DOM	DIS	RC/G	RAR	BPV	BPX	R$
13	a/a	492	81	29	82	34	262		346	501	847			11	61	0.34				36		194			102	32%	79%				5.99		56	140	$3
14	HOU *	346	57	22	57	8	239	241	328	475	802	774	811	11	62	0.34	45	15	39	32	105	191	161	28%	130	11%	80%	14	50%	36%	5.23	13.9	63	170	$1
15	HOU	388	59	16	41	16	276	261	367	459	826	936	767	11	72	0.46	45	24	30	35	106	127	112	19%	121	17%	80%	19	58%	32%	5.84	14.8	50	135	$1
16	HOU	644	116	29	82	9	261	260	359	457	815	945	769	12	72	0.49	48	20	31	32	99	122	111	20%	125	10%	47%	27	41%	26%	5.27	17.2	50	143	$2
17	HOU	548	112	34	85	5	283	285	367	522	889	972	860	10	80	0.58	48	18	34	30	119	128	112	23%	99	8%	42%	25	64%	8%	6.38	25.5	73	221	$2
1st Half		305	63	24	52	0	285	290	363	574	936	1096	884	9	75	0.42	48	19	33	31	113	160	138	32%	99	4%	0%	13	62%	8%	6.95	17.7	79	239	$2
2nd Half		243	49	10	33	5	280	277	372	457	829	816	831	12	86	0.91	49	17	34	29	126	93	85	14%	99	12%	56%	12	67%	8%	5.66	5.3	72	218	$1
18	Proj	**560**	**104**	**30**	**83**	**5**	**273**	**269**	**363**	**487**	**850**	**926**	**822**	**11**	**76**	**0.52**	**48**	**19**	**33**	**31**	**112**	**121**	**114**	**21%**	**108**	**8%**	**42%**				**5.79**	**20.8**	**46**	**138**	**$2**

Stanton,Giancarlo	Health	C	LIMA Plan	B+
Age: 28 Bats: R Pos: RF	PT/Exp	B	Rand Var	+1
Ht: 6' 6" Wt: 245	Consist	F	MM	5145

Finally! And no, it wasn't THAT surprising. Power skills nothing new, but health and a notable ct% spike were a surprise. However... He's had better PXs before, and xPX was a career LOW (yes, you read right). 34% hr/f was the driver, which means the BALLS had a role. If they stay juiced and he stays healthy... UP: 60+ HR

Yr	Tm	AB	R	HR	RBI	SB	BA	xBA	OBP	SLG	OPS	vL	vR	bb%	ct%	Eye	G	L	F	h%	HctX	PX	xPX	hr/f	Spd	SBO	SB%	#Wk	DOM	DIS	RC/G	RAR	BPV	BPX	R$
13	MIA	425	62	24	62	1	249	253	365	480	845	1006	789	15	67	0.53	43	18	38	31	109	180	139	22%	82	1%	100%	22	45%	27%	5.90	16.1	68	170	$
14	MIA	539	89	37	105	13	288	278	395	555	950	1075	920	15	68	0.55	41	20	39	36	120	206	145	26%	81	8%	93%	24	75%	13%	7.94	58.0	95	257	$3
15	MIA	279	47	27	67	4	265	282	346	606	952	1172	893	11	66	0.36	35	20	45	30	142	236	209	32%	91	9%	67%	12	75%	25%	7.14	18.5	103	278	$1
16	MIA	413	56	27	74	0	240	243	326	489	815	947	779	11	66	0.36	40	17	43	29	115	167	156	23%	85	0%	0%	24	46%	46%	5.28	7.4	47	134	$1
17	MIA	597	123	59	132	2	281	296	376	631	1007	1213	950	12	73	0.52	45	16	39	29	114	197	131	34%	59	2%	50%	27	74%	15%	8.23	51.4	93	282	$3
1st Half		292	51	21	50	1	267	273	350	538	888	1053	844	11	73	0.44	46	17	37	30	105	156	97	27%	70	1%	100%	13	62%	15%	6.49	12.0	61	185	$2
2nd Half		305	72	38	82	1	295	318	399	721	1120	1358	1053	14	72	0.60	43	15	42	28	124	236	163	41%	59	3%	33%	14	86%	14%	10.07	42.7	127	385	$4
18	Proj	**523**	**94**	**46**	**111**	**3**	**272**	**276**	**365**	**588**	**953**	**1138**	**901**	**12**	**70**	**0.45**	**42**	**17**	**41**	**30**	**120**	**187**	**153**	**30%**	**71**	**3%**	**62%**				**7.38**	**40.3**	**69**	**209**	**$2**

Stassi,Max	Health	B	LIMA Plan	F
Age: 27 Bats: R Pos: CA	PT/Exp	F	Rand Var	-2
Ht: 5' 10" Wt: 200	Consist	B	MM	2101

2-4-.167 in 24 AB at HOU. Has a little power, and might hit a HR or two. Notes of actual interest: Max and his brother Brock are the only Stassis in MLB history. They've raised over $100,000 for charity with an annual event called "Homers for the Hungry," which benefits food banks in their hometown of Yuba, AZ. Very cool!

Yr	Tm	AB	R	HR	RBI	SB	BA	xBA	OBP	SLG	OPS	vL	vR	bb%	ct%	Eye	G	L	F	h%	HctX	PX	xPX	hr/f	Spd	SBO	SB%	#Wk	DOM	DIS	RC/G	RAR	BPV	BPX	R$
13	HOU *	296	32	14	49	1	249	281	286	458	744	400	1167	5	73	0.19	60	20	20	29	61	151	135	0%	84	3%	42%	2	0%	50%	4.39	5.8	52	130	$
14	HOU *	412	37	7	36	1	214	231	243	316	559	1000	765	4	70	0.13	21	36	43	29	86	88	128	0%	89	1%	100%	4	50%	50%	2.50	-10.4	-14	-38	$
15	HOU *	309	29	11	31	1	184	234	230	318	548	667	1278	6	63	0.16	30	40	30	25	74	98	59	33%	101	3%	37%	5	20%	80%	2.25	-14.7	-25	-68	-$
16	HOU *	256	17	5	25	1	187	218	233	298	531	0	200	6	67	0.18	75	13	13	26	34	80	-24	0%	91	2%	100%	6	0%	67%	2.19	-13.6	-26	-74	-$
17	HOU *	274	46	12	30	1	212	199	300	391	690	731	806	11	66	0.37	38	10	52	27	89	118	105	18%	80	3%	37%	6	33%	50%	3.73	-3.4	8	24	$
1st Half		159	26	5	14	1	214	209	293	362	655			10	60	0.28				32		114			92	5%	34%				3.35		-18	-55	$
2nd Half		115	17	6	14	0	194	213	282	393	675	731	806	11	74	0.47	38	10	52	20	99	113	105	18%	79	0%	0%	6	33%	50%	3.51	-2.1	32	97	$
18	Proj	**129**	**15**	**4**	**14**	**0**	**213**	**216**	**276**	**344**	**620**	**620**	**620**	**8**	**68**	**0.27**	**39**	**22**	**39**	**28**		**86**		**11%**	**91**	**2%**	**61%**				**3.06**	**-4.3**	**-27**	**-82**	**$**

Story,Trevor	Health	C	LIMA Plan	B+
Age: 25 Bats: R Pos: SS	PT/Exp	B	Rand Var	-1
Ht: 6' 1" Wt: 210	Consist	D	MM	5325

Not quite the return from injury that most hoped for. Still flashed plus-plus power even with a regression, with nice FB tilt. But ct% slide hurt BA, and, more subtly, keeps lid on HR totals (with fewer balls in play). Better in 2nd half, and counting stats at SS help. But don't look for a full breakout until/unless contact rate improves.

Yr	Tm	AB	R	HR	RBI	SB	BA	xBA	OBP	SLG	OPS	vL	vR	bb%	ct%	Eye	G	L	F	h%	HctX	PX	xPX	hr/f	Spd	SBO	SB%	#Wk	DOM	DIS	RC/G	RAR	BPV	BPX	R$
13																																			
14	aa	205	23	8	16	2	192		269	356	625			10	59	0.26				28		147			108	8%	69%				3.00		8	22	$
15	a/a	512	60	16	58	16	259		309	463	771			7	73	0.26				33		144			116	18%	83%				4.96		56	151	$1
16	COL	372	67	27	72	8	272	259	341	567	909	975	883	8	65	0.27	29	24	47	34	119	199	191	24%	111	15%	62%	17	53%	12%	6.41	19.3	72	206	$1
17	COL	503	68	24	82	7	239	224	308	457	765	1034	668	9	62	0.26	34	18	48	33	101	156	166	16%	116	8%	78%	26	38%	38%	4.69	2.5	27	82	$1
1st Half		232	32	11	31	2	224	202	305	409	715	942	624	10	62	0.30	30	17	52	31	82	129	147	15%	109	3%	100%	12	17%	50%	4.15	-3.0	5	15	$
2nd Half		271	36	13	51	5	251	243	311	498	809	1124	704	8	62	0.22	37	19	44	35	117	178	183	18%	112	13%	71%	14	57%	29%	5.15	4.6	42	127	$1
18	Proj	**513**	**72**	**30**	**80**	**9**	**252**	**242**	**319**	**509**	**828**	**1017**	**759**	**8**	**64**	**0.26**	**32**	**21**	**47**	**33**	**109**	**171**	**177**	**19%**	**118**	**12%**	**72%**				**5.41**	**14.3**	**45**	**137**	**$2**

Suarez,Eugenio	Health	A	LIMA Plan	B+
Age: 26 Bats: R Pos: 3B	PT/Exp	A	Rand Var	-1
Ht: 5' 11" Wt: 213	Consist	B	MM	3125

PRO: Fine bb% spike, climbing LD rate & power skills, improvement vR, superb health grade, just reaching peak age. CON: climbing K rate, only average hard contact. The latter two put lids on BA and HR, which may regress a bit. But together, the rest all mean that the downside risk here is less than the upside potential.

Yr	Tm	AB	R	HR	RBI	SB	BA	xBA	OBP	SLG	OPS	vL	vR	bb%	ct%	Eye	G	L	F	h%	HctX	PX	xPX	hr/f	Spd	SBO	SB%	#Wk	DOM	DIS	RC/G	RAR	BPV	BPX	R$
13	aa	442	43	7	36	7	231		290	347	638			8	77	0.36				29		85			112	18%	38%				3.03		27	68	
14	DET *	442	57	10	50	10	246	231	306	379	685	656	650	8	74	0.33	35	22	43	31	87	107	109	5%	97	13%	70%	17	29%	59%	3.88	2.2	26	70	$1
15	CIN *	575	67	21	69	7	263	248	310	429	739	819	744	6	75	0.28	41	21	38	32	95	111	105	12%	107	9%	54%	18	39%	39%	4.47	-3.4	37	100	$1
16	CIN	565	78	21	70	11	248	241	317	411	728	882	683	8	73	0.33	41	22	38	31	103	104	105	13%	93	11%	69%	27	30%	37%	4.26	-12.0	20	57	$1
17	CIN	534	87	26	82	4	260	258	367	461	828	896	806	13	72	0.57	39	24	37	31	99	118	116	18%	82	5%	44%	27	37%	37%	5.58	4.3	37	112	$1
1st Half		270	45	12	42	3	259	261	363	456	818	926	790	13	73	0.54	46	22	33	31	96	115	109	18%	96	6%	60%	13	38%	31%	5.45	2.9	41	124	$1
2nd Half		264	42	14	40	1	261	258	371	466	837	872	824	15	72	0.60	32	27	41	31	102	122	124	18%	67	5%	25%	14	36%	43%	5.72	4.9	35	106	$1
18	Proj	**562**	**81**	**23**	**76**	**7**	**255**	**249**	**343**	**434**	**776**	**846**	**753**	**11**	**73**	**0.45**	**38**	**23**	**39**	**31**	**99**	**106**	**112**	**15%**	**87**	**8%**	**54%**				**4.87**	**-0.4**	**22**	**67**	**$1**

Sucre,Jesus	Health	D	LIMA Plan	D
Age: 30 Bats: R Pos: CA	PT/Exp	F	Rand Var	-1
Ht: 6' 0" Wt: 200	Consist	C	MM	1121

This is like the ad in the old comic books, where the skinny kid on the beach gets sand kicked in his face until he gets all muscled up by sending in a dollar to Charles Atlas. As in, where did this pop come from? Okay, let's not get carried away; it's not Ruthian power, or even Stantonian. But maybe worth a buck now? Maybe.

Yr	Tm	AB	R	HR	RBI	SB	BA	xBA	OBP	SLG	OPS	vL	vR	bb%	ct%	Eye	G	L	F	h%	HctX	PX	xPX	hr/f	Spd	SBO	SB%	#Wk	DOM	DIS	RC/G	RAR	BPV	BPX	R$
13	SEA *	113	8	0	8	1	229	302	272	252	524	500	405	5	88	0.50	58	35	8	26	43	20	5	0%	73	6%	36%	3	0%	0%	2.18	-5.2	4	10	-$
14	SEA *	236	12	1	15	0	211	224	219	263	482	409	487	1	77	0.05	43	25	32	27	36	44	8	0%	101	3%	0%	12	8%	58%	1.80	-11.1	-20	-54	-$
15	SEA *	150	12	1	8	0	163	204	205	223	428	767	268	5	79	0.25	48	16	36	20	71	47	55	3%	79	0%	0%	21	24%	38%	1.39	-11.5	-10	-27	-$
16	SEA *	124	9	1	13	0	266	272	290	341	632	2800	835	3	80	0.17	50	30	20	33	65	50	63	25%	106	4%	0%	6	33%	33%	3.28	-2.0	1	3	$
17	TAM	176	20	7	29	2	256	254	289	409	699	734	689	4	80	0.20	39	22	39	28	110	82	105	13%	62	5%	100%	26	38%	46%	4.04	-0.4	14	42	$
1st Half		98	11	3	19	1	255	250	279	388	667	495	740	4	82	0.22	38	22	40	29	111	73	96	9%	75	5%	100%	13	38%	46%	3.83	-0.8	17	52	$
2nd Half		78	9	4	10	1	256	258	302	436	738	1417	637	4	78	0.18	41	22	37	28	109	93	116	17%	69	6%	100%	13	38%	46%	4.31	0.5	17	52	$
18	Proj	**168**	**16**	**5**	**20**	**1**	**252**	**244**	**286**	**379**	**665**	**848**	**600**	**4**	**80**	**0.20**	**43**	**21**	**36**	**29**	**85**	**69**	**74**	**10%**	**77**	**4%**	**70%**				**3.62**	**-2.6**	**1**	**2**	**$**

Suzuki,Ichiro	Health	A	LIMA Plan	D
Age: 44 Bats: L Pos: RF	PT/Exp	D	Rand Var	-1
Ht: 5' 11" Wt: 175	Consist	D	MM	0331

For the first time EVER, posted below-average Spd—and didn't add that lonely "1" to the SB column until week 26. Not coincidentally, he also netted a lonely "$1" in the R$ column. Second half shows he can still slap a single, and says he wants to play until he's 50. But with wheels gone, will they let him? DN: Retires in March

Yr	Tm	AB	R	HR	RBI	SB	BA	xBA	OBP	SLG	OPS	vL	vR	bb%	ct%	Eye	G	L	F	h%	HctX	PX	xPX	hr/f	Spd	SBO	SB%	#Wk	DOM	DIS	RC/G	RAR	BPV	BPX	R$
13	NYY	520	57	7	35	20	262	264	297	342	639	753	590	5	88	0.41	52	21	27	29	58	50	34	6%	139	18%	83%	26	38%	27%	3.59	-15.4	45	113	$1
14	NYY	359	42	1	22	15	284	255	324	340	664	807	632	5	81	0.31	58	22	20	35	67	45	22	2%	135	17%	83%	27	22%	48%	4.03	-0.6	14	38	$1
15	MIA	398	45	1	21	11	229	251	282	279	561	723	514	7	87	0.61	58	18	23	26	52	26	28	1%	178	15%	69%	27	22%	44%	2.61	-27.4	39	105	$
16	MIA	327	48	1	22	10	291	286	354	376	730	859	700	8	87	0.71	48	28	24	33	77	51	50	1%	138	12%	83%	27	44%	22%	4.82	1.3	49	140	$1
17	MIA	196	19	3	20	1	255	240	318	332	649	796	603	8	82	0.49	57	19	24	30	62	44	25	8%	89	3%	50%	27	33%	41%	3.52	-9.5	8	24	$
1st Half		102	12	2	8	0	206	218	236	284	520	690	454	4	75	0.16	68	12	20	25	60	45	10	13%	103	5%	0%	13	23%	69%	2.04	-9.7	-22	-67	-$
2nd Half		94	7	1	12	1	309	273	398	383	781	950	739	12	89	1.30	46	25	29	34	64	43	39	4%	85	3%	100%	14	43%	14%	5.63	1.4	44	133	$
18	Proj	**193**	**21**	**2**	**16**	**3**	**268**	**264**	**329**	**345**	**674**	**813**	**635**	**8**	**85**	**0.59**	**54**	**22**	**24**	**31**	**65**	**43**	**33**	**5%**	**117**	**7%**	**69%**				**3.91**	**-4.4**	**15**	**46**	**$**

ROD TRUESDELL

Suzuki,Kurt

Age: 34 Bats: R Pos: CA | Ht: 5' 11" Wt: 205
Health A | PT/Exp C | Consist D | LIMA Plan D+ | Rand Var -1 | MM 2143

Easy to say "juiced ball" and dismiss shocking power outburst. But, out of context, 2nd half skills are those of a star slugger. Of course, it's one thing to say he earned it, and quite another to say he'll repeat it. Second half (and recency bias) say "yes," but small 163-AB sample size, age and 10+ years of history argue against.

Yr Tm	AB	R	HR	RBI	SB	BA	xBA	OBP	SLG	OPS	vL	vR	bb%	ct%	Eye	G	L	F	h%	HctX	PX	xPX	hr/f	Spd	SBO	SB%	#Wk	DOM	DIS	RC/G	RAR	BPV	BPX	R$
13 2 TM	285	25	5	32	2	232	255	290	337	627	653	619	7	88	0.63	37	23	40	25	106	69	100	5%	88	3%	100%	26	38%	31%	3.24	-3.8	48	120	$2
14 MIN	452	37	3	61	0	288	268	345	383	727	810	695	7	90	0.74	44	22	34	32	100	76	82	2%	71	1%	0%	27	56%	15%	4.58	14.2	57	154	$11
15 MIN	433	36	5	50	0	240	230	296	314	610	658	587	6	86	0.49	43	19	38	27	100	50	84	4%	77	0%	0%	26	38%	35%	3.03	-10.0	23	62	$3
16 MIN	345	34	8	49	0	258	270	301	403	704	745	685	5	86	0.38	40	21	39	28	103	88	79	7%	59	0%	0%	26	54%	27%	4.08	-3.2	44	126	$5
17 ATL	276	38	19	50	0	283	284	351	536	887	1191	806	6	86	0.44	35	18	47	27	116	123	124	17%	62	0%	0%	27	56%	33%	6.18	16.5	74	224	$10
1st Half	113	12	4	19	0	230	243	336	381	716	879	688	9	84	0.61	38	18	45	24	94	80	86	9%	65	0%	0%	13	38%	46%	3.76	-1.2	40	121	-$2
2nd Half	163	26	15	31	0	319	313	362	644	1006	1322	899	4	87	0.29	33	19	48	29	132	152	150	22%	68	0%	0%	14	71%	21%	8.28	18.2	100	303	$17
18 Proj	264	30	11	41	0	268	269	327	445	772	903	727	6	86	0.45	38	20	42	28	109	91	104	11%	67	0%	76%				4.81	5.1	41	125	$6

Swanson,Dansby

Age: 24 Bats: R Pos: SS | Ht: 6' 1" Wt: 190
Health A | PT/Exp D | Consist C | LIMA Plan D+ | Rand Var 0 | MM 1315

6-51-.232 in 488 AB at ATL. Elite prospect didn't live up to pre-season hype. Showed flashes of upside (2 months over .300) but also wild inconsistency (2 months under .160). Some nice tidbits in skills (see bb%, Spd) but lots of mediocrity—or worse. Talented, but let's face it, it's going to take some time.

Yr Tm	AB	R	HR	RBI	SB	BA	xBA	OBP	SLG	OPS	vL	vR	bb%	ct%	Eye	G	L	F	h%	HctX	PX	xPX	hr/f	Spd	SBO	SB%	#Wk	DOM	DIS	RC/G	RAR	BPV	BPX	R$
13																																		
14																																		
15																																		
16 ATL *	462	74	10	62	10	258	243	331	382	713	1015	771	10	75	0.44	46	23	31	32	106	75	97	10%	163	9%	82%	8	25%	63%	4.39	-3.0	31	89	$13
17 ATL *	526	63	7	55	4	229	239	314	321	634	741	610	11	75	0.49	47	23	29	29	89	60	73	6%	107	4%	56%	26	19%	38%	3.29	-19.6	5	15	$4
1st Half	280	33	6	35	1	232	244	304	343	646	1047	581	10	75	0.43	51	22	27	29	90	70	67	10%	91	1%	100%	13	15%	31%	3.51	-9.0	6	18	$5
2nd Half	246	30	1	20	3	226	229	321	295	617	529	656	12	75	0.56	43	25	32	30	88	48	80	0%	126	8%	49%	13	23%	46%	3.04	-11.6	3	9	$2
18 Proj	469	64	7	53	6	245	239	322	345	667	739	651	11	75	0.47	46	23	31	31	96	62	84	7%	125	7%	70%				3.77	-9.7	1	2	$10

Tapia,Raimel

Age: 24 Bats: L Pos: RF | Ht: 6' 2" Wt: 160
Health A | PT/Exp D | Consist B | LIMA Plan C+ | Rand Var -3 | MM 2553

2-16-.288 with 5 SB in 160 AB at COL. PRO: Blazing speed, LD stroke, solid contact, consistent playing time mid-season yielded .366 BA over 93 AB. CON: Little power, poor patience. Regression likely: BA drives value, and only a much greener light will bump SB to get him into double-figure R$.

Yr Tm	AB	R	HR	RBI	SB	BA	xBA	OBP	SLG	OPS	vL	vR	bb%	ct%	Eye	G	L	F	h%	HctX	PX	xPX	hr/f	Spd	SBO	SB%	#Wk	DOM	DIS	RC/G	RAR	BPV	BPX	R$
13																																		
14																																		
15																																		
16 COL *	566	79	7	42	22	322	292	349	441	791	500	570	4	88	0.34	37	33	30	36	76	65	59	0%	176	24%	55%	6	0%	67%	5.30	10.6	65	186	$28
17 COL *	423	59	4	37	14	325	283	352	468	820	640	798	4	81	0.22	42	28	29	39	71	85	69	6%	163	16%	76%	19	42%	42%	6.19	10.5	53	161	$20
1st Half	227	37	2	22	11	325	290	359	465	824	786	751	5	82	0.30	46	27	27	39	88	85	112	7%	156	24%	72%	8	38%	38%	6.17	5.0	56	170	$23
2nd Half	196	22	2	15	3	325	280	343	471	814	546	838	3	81	0.13	39	30	31	40	58	86	33	5%	162	6%	100%	11	45%	45%	6.21	4.4	47	142	$16
18 Proj	269	37	4	22	9	291	289	327	438	765	624	819	4	84	0.25	42	29	30	34	70	81	65	6%	168	21%	66%				4.84	1.1	51	154	$11

Tatis Jr.,Fernando

Age: 19 Bats: R Pos: SS | Ht: 6'3" Wt: 185
Health A | PT/Exp F | Consist F | LIMA Plan F | Rand Var 0 | MM 1401

SD prospect's only higher-level MiLB experience is 57 ineffective PA at AA. So a long way from a finished product. But torching the high-A Midwest League with a .910 OPS at age 18 is a good start. Profiles as a multi-category talent (.278, 22 HR, 32 SB overall in 2017). Don't count on much for 2018, but a keeper-league must-own.

Yr Tm	AB	R	HR	RBI	SB	BA	xBA	OBP	SLG	OPS	vL	vR	bb%	ct%	Eye	G	L	F	h%	HctX	PX	xPX	hr/f	Spd	SBO	SB%	#Wk	DOM	DIS	RC/G	RAR	BPV	BPX	R$
13																																		
14																																		
15																																		
16																																		
17 aa	55	6	1	6	3	268		294	341	634			3	71	0.12				36		45			104	21%	100%				3.80		-41	-124	$0
1st Half																																		
2nd Half	55	6	1	6	3	268		294	341	634			3	71	0.12				36		45			99	21%	100%				3.80		-43	-130	$0
18 Proj	136	13	4	13	7	245	211	266	357	623	623	623	3	74	0.11	37	20	43	30		62		10%	95	22%	100%				3.45	-4.1	-22	-68	$5

Taylor,Chris

Age: 27 Bats: R Pos: CF LF 2B | Ht: 6' 1" Wt: 195
Health A | PT/Exp C | Consist D | LIMA Plan B | Rand Var -4 | MM 3535

21-72-.288 with 17 SB in 514 AB at LA. Odd little breakout. After fortunate 1st half HR spike, he actually began earning it later in the year, with FB, HctX growth. So he may not give it ALL back. But given history, xBA and xPX, almost certain to regress some, plus likely to lose some AB. Bank on double-digit thefts though.

Yr Tm	AB	R	HR	RBI	SB	BA	xBA	OBP	SLG	OPS	vL	vR	bb%	ct%	Eye	G	L	F	h%	HctX	PX	xPX	hr/f	Spd	SBO	SB%	#Wk	DOM	DIS	RC/G	RAR	BPV	BPX	R$
13 aa	256	42	1	14	16	273		361	353	713			12	76	0.56				36		64			138	22%	83%				4.67		22	55	$10
14 SEA *	438	59	3	34	15	271	219	324	371	695	699	687	7	71	0.26	41	21	38	38	52	91	62	0%	155	20%	62%	11	18%	55%	4.04	2.7	18	49	$14
15 SEA *	437	47	3	22	14	221	210	285	302	586	635	358	8	75	0.36	32	24	44	29	126	60	161	0%	134	23%	54%	10	10%	70%	2.63	-23.1	8	22	$4
16 2 TM *	365	45	3	35	13	258	243	312	380	693	644	606	7	74	0.30	44	22	33	34	79	87	98	7%	133	21%	69%	12	17%	50%	3.99	-7.0	23	66	$9
17 LA *	557	91	22	76	18	280	263	343	483	826	837	855	9	73	0.36	42	23	36	35	96	123	103	16%	142	17%	73%	25	40%	24%	5.80	11.8	54	164	$25
1st Half	261	46	11	41	11	264	268	350	460	809	907	840	12	71	0.45	46	25	29	33	91	125	78	24%	111	22%	66%	11	45%	27%	5.39	3.7	42	127	$24
2nd Half	296	45	11	35	7	294	262	342	503	845	790	867	6	76	0.26	39	21	40	36	101	122	119	12%	160	11%	88%	14	36%	21%	6.19	10.6	62	188	$25
18 Proj	450	64	15	47	15	266	256	328	448	776	768	780	8	74	0.34	41	23	37	33	92	110	106	12%	145	19%	70%				4.97	6.1	40	122	$18

Taylor,Michael

Age: 27 Bats: R Pos: CF | Ht: 6' 3" Wt: 210
Health A | PT/Exp D | Consist C | LIMA Plan C+ | Rand Var -2 | MM 3515

19-53-.271 with 17 SB in 399 AB at WAS. On the surface, a big career turnaround. But hold on: Plate skills mostly unchanged, HR spike not fully supported, and xBA and 2nd half point to the likely BA regression. Simply doesn't make enough consistently hard contact for those gains to stick. You can only count on the ~20 SB.

Yr Tm	AB	R	HR	RBI	SB	BA	xBA	OBP	SLG	OPS	vL	vR	bb%	ct%	Eye	G	L	F	h%	HctX	PX	xPX	hr/f	Spd	SBO	SB%	#Wk	DOM	DIS	RC/G	RAR	BPV	BPX	R$
13																																		
14 WAS *	467	65	17	52	27	258	240	323	417	739	1095	553	9	63	0.25	55	23	23	38	49	139	65	20%	114	31%	69%	6	17%	50%	4.45	8.7	15	41	$22
15 WAS *	498	52	15	66	18	235	219	290	364	654	667	633	7	66	0.23	46	22	32	33	90	96	115	15%	109	18%	81%	26	19%	54%	3.58	-11.0	-9	-24	$14
16 WAS *	338	43	8	24	20	215	228	269	335	604	755	596	7	66	0.22	44	27	30	30	85	90	81	17%	107	33%	83%	22	18%	64%	3.04	-16.9	-14	-40	$8
17 WAS *	425	57	20	56	19	262	243	311	473	785	849	794	7	66	0.21	43	20	37	35	90	141	109	20%	129	28%	73%	21	38%	43%	4.99	-0.8	29	88	$17
1st Half	229	36	11	33	9	279	252	316	511	826	915	806	5	66	0.16	43	20	37	38	94	157	110	20%	127	25%	75%	12	33%	42%	5.66	5.0	38	115	$20
2nd Half	196	21	9	23	10	241	234	304	430	733	788	776	8	66	0.26	43	21	36	32	85	123	108	20%	122	31%	72%	9	44%	44%	4.28	-3.8	16	48	$14
18 Proj	436	54	16	49	21	243	234	297	414	711	760	692	7	66	0.22	44	23	33	33	88	115	100	17%	118	28%	76%				4.10	-5.5	6	18	$17

Thames,Eric

Age: 31 Bats: L Pos: 1B LF | Ht: 6' 0" Wt: 210
Health A | PT/Exp B | Consist F | LIMA Plan B+ | Rand Var +2 | MM 5235

Another big post-KBO season in 2018? FOR: Power supported by skills and looks repeatable, and he devoured RHP. AGAINST: Slid in 2nd half, ct% fell by 10% after May (72% to 62%), and slashed only .125/.205/.212(!) vs. LHP post-April. Could face stricter platoon. More downside than up in this projection.

Yr Tm	AB	R	HR	RBI	SB	BA	xBA	OBP	SLG	OPS	vL	vR	bb%	ct%	Eye	G	L	F	h%	HctX	PX	xPX	hr/f	Spd	SBO	SB%	#Wk	DOM	DIS	RC/G	RAR	BPV	BPX	R$
13 aaa	352	36	8	34	4	231		291	355	646			8	68	0.26				32		102			95	8%	65%				3.39		0	0	$3
14 for	443	93	22	118	10	320		385	580	965			10	79	0.50				36		175			113	10%	82%				8.38	50.2	110	297	$34
15 for	472	127	28	137	36	355		452	656	1108			15	82	0.96				39		184			104	26%	80%				11.70	80.3	137	370	$54
16 for	436	115	24	118	12	299		383	555	938			12	78	0.61				34		151			101	12%	72%				7.65	31.0	88	251	$30
17 MIL	469	83	31	63	4	247	256	359	518	877	664	936	14	65	0.46	38	20	41	31	110	174	162	25%	98	5%	67%	27	48%	44%	6.12	2.9	59	179	$14
1st Half	257	51	20	40	2	241	266	369	537	906	844	926	16	67	0.57	40	18	42	27	115	182	161	27%	77	4%	67%	13	54%	38%	6.47	6.3	71	215	$18
2nd Half	212	32	11	23	2	255	243	347	495	842	288	945	11	63	0.34	37	23	40	35	103	163	163	21%	120	5%	67%	14	43%	50%	5.70	0.3	42	127	$8
18 Proj	410	74	25	70	6	251	264	354	519	872	582	942	13	68	0.45	38	22	40	31	108	168	162	22%	98	9%	65%				6.00	11.0	65	197	$17

ROD TRUESDELL

Toles,Andrew

Age: 26	Bats: L	Pos: LF	Health F	LIMA Plan D+
Ht: 5' 9"	Wt: 192		PT/Exp F	Rand Var 0
			Consist A	MM 2243

Tore an ACL in May, and we really can't read too much into this 100-ish PA sample. But, as we noted last year, he owns a lot of possible paths to value, with solid BA floor, above-average speed leading the way. Check on health reports this spring, but if those are clear, he's once again well worth a late-round flyer.

Yr	Tm	AB	R	HR	RBI	SB	BA	xBA	OBP	SLG	OPS	vL	vR	bb%	ct%	Eye	G	L	F	h%	HctX	PX	xPX	hr/f	Spd	SBO	SB%	#Wk	DOM	DIS	RC/G	RAR	BPV	BPX
13																																		
14																																		
15																																		
16	LA *	336	46	9	40	12	288	283	325	462	788	692	893	5	79	0.27	48	22	30	34	103	112	90	13%	107	29%	55%	11	27%	45%	4.92	2.8	51	146
17	LA	96	17	5	15	0	271	277	314	458	772	1000	760	5	83	0.31	53	18	29	28	84	93	84	22%	106	4%	0%	6	50%	33%	4.69	-1.5	51	155
1st Half		96	17	5	15	0	271	277	314	458	772	1000	760	5	83	0.31	53	18	29	28	84	93	84	22%	106	4%	0%	6	50%	33%	4.69	-1.8	51	155
2nd Half																																		
18	Proj	266	43	10	38	6	278	277	320	443	763	764	763	5	82	0.29	51	20	29	31	92	90	86	15%	108	17%	55%				4.66	1.6	39	119

Tomas,Yasmany

Age: 27	Bats: R	Pos: LF	Health D	LIMA Plan B
Ht: 6' 2"	Wt: 250		PT/Exp C	Rand Var +2
			Consist C	MM 4155

A lost season. First hurt a hip, then went on the DL in early June with a core muscle injury that eventually needed surgery. Around those woes, flashed more of the big-time power that exploded in 2016. Contact issues worsened, and that's part of the package (and worth monitoring). But he clearly owns that 30-HR upside.

Yr	Tm	AB	R	HR	RBI	SB	BA	xBA	OBP	SLG	OPS	vL	vR	bb%	ct%	Eye	G	L	F	h%	HctX	PX	xPX	hr/f	Spd	SBO	SB%	#Wk	DOM	DIS	RC/G	RAR	BPV	BPX
13	for	277	44	9	59	1	269		335	465	800			9	82	0.56				30		127			114	6%	21%				5.19	9.5	85	213
14	for	241	27	4	35	5	267		317	403	720			7	81	0.38				32		102			102	20%	45%				4.06	2.3	51	138
15	ARI *	427	41	10	50	5	267	250	297	395	692	797	673	4	73	0.16	55	22	23	35	98	92	77	13%	90	7%	71%	25	24%	40%	4.07	-8.0	2	5
16	ARI	530	72	31	83	2	272	279	313	508	820	1112	724	6	74	0.23	48	21	31	31	124	145	129	25%	59	5%	33%	27	44%	37%	5.38	11.5	44	126
17	ARI	166	19	8	32	0	241	261	294	464	758	580	843	7	70	0.26	47	21	32	30	118	141	159	21%	73	0%	0%	9	44%	33%	4.61	-3.1	31	94
1st Half		166	19	8	32	0	241	261	294	464	758	580	843	7	70	0.26	47	21	32	30	118	141	159	21%	73	0%	0%	9	44%	33%	4.61	-3.7	31	94
2nd Half																																		
18	Proj	460	54	25	74	3	262	280	308	498	806	840	793	6	74	0.26	47	21	32	30	112	136	119	23%	81	7%	47%				5.15	9.3	42	128

Tomlinson,Kelby

Age: 28	Bats: R	Pos: 3B 2B	Health A	LIMA Plan D
Ht: 6' 3"	Wt: 180		PT/Exp D	Rand Var 0
			Consist A	MM 0541

1-11-.258 with 9 SB in 194 AB at SF. Has some things going for him—decent plate skills overall, and notably that fine speed, with a growing knowledge of how to use it (see SB% trend). But GB ways, average contact bode ill for BA as well as power (obviously). Key to value is contact rate: 1st half good, 2nd half not so good.

Yr	Tm	AB	R	HR	RBI	SB	BA	xBA	OBP	SLG	OPS	vL	vR	bb%	ct%	Eye	G	L	F	h%	HctX	PX	xPX	hr/f	Spd	SBO	SB%	#Wk	DOM	DIS	RC/G	RAR	BPV	BPX
13	aa	96	9	0	3	2	166		256	211	467			11	69	0.39				24		49			104	14%	66%				1.65		-30	-75
14	aa	433	50	1	25	39	233		292	281	573			8	78	0.38				30		34			151	43%	74%				2.77		3	8
15	SF *	567	74	4	55	22	286	277	333	373	706	913	682	7	81	0.37	56	28	17	35	63	58	27	9%	146	22%	60%	10	50%	40%	4.20	0.5	28	76
16	SF *	291	34	0	21	14	259	269	326	303	629	728	640	9	83	0.59	51	29	20	31	91	32	29	0%	129	20%	76%	15	27%	47%	3.46	-12.0	17	49
17	SF *	302	45	1	17	16	253	250	327	306	632	695	614	10	80	0.54	50	25	24	31	63	33	26	3%	160	20%	82%	22	23%	55%	3.56	-13.1	15	45
1st Half		179	21	0	10	11	248	263	306	281	587	510	612	8	83	0.49	48	29	23	30	54	25	12	0%	129	25%	82%	9	0%	67%	3.07	-9.4	8	24
2nd Half		123	24	1	7	5	260	241	347	341	689	811	615	13	76	0.60	52	23	25	34	66	46	34	4%	175	14%	83%	13	38%	46%	4.31	-1.9	19	58
18	Proj	190	27	1	12	9	265	266	336	328	664	714	617	10	82	0.58	51	27	22	32	72	38	27	3%	148	19%	76%				3.89	-5.6	12	36

Torres,Gleyber

Age: 21	Bats: R	Pos: SS	Health A	LIMA Plan D
Ht: 6' 1"	Wt: 175		PT/Exp F	Rand Var 0
			Consist F	MM 2321

Top prospect suffered through injury-riddled campaign, first via sore shoulder, then TJS on his (non-throwing) elbow. But around that, first tour through the high minors—at age 20—did nothing to eclipse his rising star. Shaky contact may bring struggles early on, but going forward, this is a must-own, multi-skill talent.

Yr	Tm	AB	R	HR	RBI	SB	BA	xBA	OBP	SLG	OPS	vL	vR	bb%	ct%	Eye	G	L	F	h%	HctX	PX	xPX	hr/f	Spd	SBO	SB%	#Wk	DOM	DIS	RC/G	RAR	BPV	BPX
13																																		
14																																		
15																																		
16																																		
17	a/a	201	29	8	32	7	280		372	476	847			13	75	0.59				34		117			100	20%	51%				5.76		52	158
1st Half		201	29	8	32	7	280		372	476	847			13	75	0.59				34		117			116	20%	51%				5.76		57	173
2nd Half																																		
18	Proj	124	16	4	18	4	251	250	338	416	754	754	754	12	78	0.59	37	21	42	29		97		10%	112	20%	54%				4.48	0.0	38	117

Torreyes,Ronald

Age: 25	Bats: R	Pos: 2B SS 3B	Health A	LIMA Plan D+
Ht: 5' 8"	Wt: 151		PT/Exp D	Rand Var -5
			Consist B	MM 1431

Value driven exclusively by a BA that is almost certain to regress (see xBA, h%). Wheels could be an asset, but two SB tries won't cut it. That's not even mentioning the punchless slap-hitting or halved walk rate. His main help to you may be in dynasty leagues—if another owner confuses him with Gleyber Torres.

Yr	Tm	AB	R	HR	RBI	SB	BA	xBA	OBP	SLG	OPS	vL	vR	bb%	ct%	Eye	G	L	F	h%	HctX	PX	xPX	hr/f	Spd	SBO	SB%	#Wk	DOM	DIS	RC/G	RAR	BPV	BPX
13	aa	375	41	2	30	4	244		287	332	619			6	91	0.70				26		57			126	6%	79%				3.23		62	155
14	aaa	460	48	2	34	9	257		286	322	607			4	94	0.62				27		44			115	17%	47%				2.93		53	143
15	LA *	424	51	3	31	4	230	242	268	305	573	0	1100	5	90	0.49	40	20	40	25	0	48	-16	0%	128	9%	48%	4	25%	50%	2.61	-20.1	47	127
16	NYY	155	20	1	12	2	258	280	300	374	680	495	745	6	87	0.50	55	20	26	29	79	63	50	3%	169	8%	67%	25	28%	52%	3.86	-3.9	63	180
17	NYY	315	35	3	36	2	292	251	314	375	689	741	672	3	86	0.26	52	17	30	33	61	49	37	4%	135	2%	100%	27	22%	41%	4.30	-2.8	34	103
1st Half		152	19	2	20	2	289	255	319	382	700	903	660	4	88	0.33	49	18	33	32	76	49	64	4%	138	5%	100%	13	31%	31%	4.42	-1.7	43	130
2nd Half		163	16	1	16	0	294	236	310	368	678	661	686	3	85	0.20	56	17	28	34	47	49	10	3%	129	0%	0%	14	14%	50%	4.20	-2.8	24	73
18	Proj	201	23	2	19	2	270	265	302	359	662	611	679	4	87	0.37	54	18	28	30	67	50	40	3%	144	5%	67%				3.78	-5.9	27	82

Travis,Devon

Age: 27	Bats: R	Pos: 2B	Health F	LIMA Plan D+
Ht: 5' 9"	Wt: 190		PT/Exp F	Rand Var +3
			Consist B	MM 3253

Getting hurt happens, but this staying-hurt thing is now a real problem. This time it was a right knee, first injured way back in the 2016 ALCS, that didn't heal properly. Before that the left shoulder, injured in 2015, took over a year to heal. When he's right, skills are solid. But you can't afford any more two-season injuries.

Yr	Tm	AB	R	HR	RBI	SB	BA	xBA	OBP	SLG	OPS	vL	vR	bb%	ct%	Eye	G	L	F	h%	HctX	PX	xPX	hr/f	Spd	SBO	SB%	#Wk	DOM	DIS	RC/G	RAR	BPV	BPX
13																																		
14	aa	396	49	7	37	11	259		306	391	697			6	84	0.42				29		86			129	17%	67%				4.02		58	157
15	TOR *	260	42	8	36	4	282	277	340	447	787	974	812	8	79	0.42	50	22	28	33	95	116	109	16%	89	7%	79%	12	58%	8%	5.41	8.4	52	141
16	TOR *	432	56	11	53	4	298	261	329	448	777	617	838	4	79	0.22	46	19	34	35	94	98	81	10%	109	5%	80%	20	25%	25%	5.36	7.5	39	111
17	TOR	185	22	5	24	4	259	284	291	438	729	1013	670	4	79	0.18	37	26	36	30	104	115	131	9%	75	19%	67%	10	40%	40%	4.21	-2.2	41	124
1st Half		185	22	5	24	4	259	284	291	438	729	1013	670	4	79	0.18	37	26	36	30	104	115	131	9%	75	19%	67%	10	40%	40%	4.21	-3.3	41	124
2nd Half																																		
18	Proj	264	36	8	33	5	274	279	320	451	771	864	743	6	80	0.31	45	23	33	32	98	106	110	12%	94	11%	71%				4.97	1.3	43	130

Trout,Mike

Age: 26	Bats: R	Pos: CF	Health B	LIMA Plan C
Ht: 6' 2"	Wt: 235		PT/Exp A	Rand Var 0
			Consist B	MM 4455

Even an ill-fated headfirst slide, resulting in a torn thumb ligament and six missed weeks, couldn't keep him from another $30+ season. And that's despite a skills drop-off after he returned. With health, should be fine... and oh, just now reaching peak age. bb% and ct% trends could mean further upside. That's scary.

Yr	Tm	AB	R	HR	RBI	SB	BA	xBA	OBP	SLG	OPS	vL	vR	bb%	ct%	Eye	G	L	F	h%	HctX	PX	xPX	hr/f	Spd	SBO	SB%	#Wk	DOM	DIS	RC/G	RAR	BPV	BPX
13	LAA	589	109	27	97	33	323	287	432	557	988	954	1000	15	77	0.81	41	23	36	38	122	159	133	16%	151	18%	83%	27	74%	11%	9.11	77.6	113	283
14	LAA	602	115	36	111	16	287	272	377	561	939	910	948	12	69	0.45	34	19	47	36	115	209	151	18%	144	10%	89%	27	67%	11%	7.61	62.8	114	308
15	LAA	575	104	41	90	11	299	289	402	590	991	1032	978	13	73	0.58	37	24	38	35	129	190	152	25%	121	10%	61%	27	70%	7%	8.27	60.4	107	289
16	LAA	549	123	29	100	30	315	276	441	550	991	971	996	17	75	0.85	41	22	37	38	127	142	142	19%	117	17%	81%	27	63%	19%	8.99	69.4	85	243
17	LAA	402	92	33	72	22	306	296	442	629	1071	907	1113	19	78	1.04	37	18	45	32	120	173	133	23%	115	17%	85%	22	73%	9%	10.26	61.1	123	373
1st Half		163	36	16	36	10	337	329	461	742	1203	1087	1232	18	74	0.86	37	23	40	37	126	230	159	32%	113	19%	91%	9	89%	11%	13.38	36.2	153	464
2nd Half		239	56	17	36	12	285	272	429	552	981	793	1031	20	80	1.21	36	16	48	29	116	138	116	18%	109	15%	80%	13	62%	8%	8.41	23.9	104	315
18	Proj	550	119	39	97	26	307	288	431	596	1028	946	1051	17	76	0.88	38	20	41	34	123	159	139	22%	120	16%	82%				9.42	74.6	107	324

ROD TRUESDELL

Trumbo,Mark

Age: 32 Bats: R Pos: DH RF | Health B | LIMA Plan B
Ht: 6' 4" Wt: 225 | PT/Exp A | Rand Var 0
Consist C | MM 3215

An expected pullback, as we knew that 2016 hr/f wasn't going to stick. Neither did hard contact, which dragged xPX with it. In the end, he hasn't changed much, which means there's still no predictable baseline to use for him; reference huge annual variation in HRs. 2nd half fade favors pessimism more than hope, so side there.

Yr Tm	AB	R	HR	RBI	SB	BA	xBA	OBP	SLG	OPS	vL	vR	bb%	ct%	Eye	G	L	F	h%	HctX	PX	xPX	hr/f	Spd	SBO	SB%	#Wk	DOM	DIS	RC/G	RAR	BPV	BPX	R$
13 LAA	620	85	34	100	5	234	256	294	453	747	923	685	8	70	0.29	46	17	37	28	105	158	132	21%	87	5%	71%	27	52%	26%	4.43	-1.2	52	130	$19
14 ARI	328	37	14	61	2	235	241	293	415	707	796	679	8	73	0.31	45	15	40	28	111	133	135	14%	90	7%	40%	18	39%	44%	3.94	-1.0	42	114	$8
15 2 TM	508	62	22	64	0	262	244	310	449	759	856	709	7	74	0.27	42	18	40	31	107	124	122	14%	118	0%	0%	27	52%	30%	4.82	-9.2	46	124	$13
16 BAL	613	94	47	108	2	256	268	316	533	850	608	932	8	72	0.30	40	17	43	28	115	166	147	25%	85	2%	100%	27	56%	26%	5.75	4.4	65	186	$22
17 BAL	559	79	23	65	1	234	228	289	397	686	763	658	7	73	0.28	43	16	41	28	90	96	87	14%	87	1%	100%	26	19%	50%	3.82	-17.6	12	36	$8
1st Half	317	49	11	39	1	252	238	313	401	714	676	728	8	77	0.38	42	18	40	30	96	86	79	11%	92	1%	100%	13	15%	46%	4.30	-5.3	22	67	$12
2nd Half	242	30	12	26	0	211	211	256	393	648	897	570	5	69	0.18	46	13	42	25	83	110	98	17%	83	0%	0%	13	23%	54%	3.22	-12.4	0	0	$2
18 Proj	**555**	**76**	**26**	**71**	**1**	**240**	**233**	**293**	**423**	**716**	**747**	**705**	**7**	**72**	**0.26**	**43**	**16**	**41**	**29**	**100**	**108**	**114**	**15%**	**91**	**1%**	**78%**				**4.15**	**-22.3**	**8**	**25**	**$11**

Tulowitzki,Troy

Age: 33 Bats: R Pos: SS | Health F | LIMA Plan D+
Ht: 6' 3" Wt: 205 | PT/Exp C | Rand Var 0
Consist B | MM 1013

Hamstring plagued him early, ankle sidelined him late. In between, was a shell of his former self. Concurrently plummeting LDs, HctX, xPX put 20 HR at risk even if he can stay healthy—and with F health, that ain't happening. xBA last three years gives little hope for rebound there. Stop when bidding hits two digits.

Yr Tm	AB	R	HR	RBI	SB	BA	xBA	OBP	SLG	OPS	vL	vR	bb%	ct%	Eye	G	L	F	h%	HctX	PX	xPX	hr/f	Spd	SBO	SB%	#Wk	DOM	DIS	RC/G	RAR	BPV	BPX	R$
13 COL	446	72	25	82	1	312	288	391	540	931	906	938	11	81	0.67	42	21	38	34	124	148	147	18%	89	1%	100%	24	75%	17%	7.82	52.8	93	233	$25
14 COL	315	71	21	52	1	340	310	432	603	1035	1348	930	13	82	0.88	38	23	39	36	150	170	163	21%	105	2%	50%	16	75%	13%	9.94	55.4	124	335	$23
15 2 TM	486	77	17	70	1	280	254	337	440	777	940	735	7	77	0.33	41	22	37	34	126	110	126	12%	88	1%	100%	25	44%	36%	5.19	10.9	37	100	$17
16 TOR	492	54	24	79	1	254	257	318	443	761	767	759	8	79	0.43	41	19	40	28	109	108	113	15%	77	1%	100%	25	52%	24%	4.77	6.6	45	129	$12
17 TOR	241	16	7	26	0	249	220	300	378	678	479	750	7	83	0.43	52	14	33	27	102	70	68	10%	74	2%	0%	13	46%	15%	3.76	-6.1	27	82	$1
1st Half	168	13	5	19	0	232	232	290	369	659	475	725	7	87	0.59	50	14	36	24	96	72	64	9%	78	0%	0%	9	67%	11%	3.52	-5.3	45	136	$2
2nd Half	73	3	2	7	0	288	189	325	397	722	488	810	5	75	0.22	60	15	25	36	116	63	78	14%	80	5%	0%	4	0%	25%	4.35	-0.5	-12	-36	$0
18 Proj	**390**	**38**	**11**	**51**	**0**	**250**	**235**	**307**	**381**	**688**	**617**	**711**	**7**	**79**	**0.38**	**48**	**18**	**34**	**29**	**114**	**75**	**99**	**11%**	**76**	**2%**	**20%**				**3.87**	**-6.8**	**1**	**4**	**$8**

Turner,Justin

Age: 33 Bats: R Pos: 3B | Health B | LIMA Plan A
Ht: 5' 11" Wt: 205 | PT/Exp B | Rand Var -2
Consist C | MM 3255

Age, production seemingly give him ceiling of a second-tier 3B. However, parallel gains in FBs, HctX, xPX and now-elite plate control paint a pretty picture. Halted prior struggles vL, confirming he can play every day. There's a $30 player lurking here, but at 33, odds of that are maybe 30%. If others are shy, go an extra buck.

Yr Tm	AB	R	HR	RBI	SB	BA	xBA	OBP	SLG	OPS	vL	vR	bb%	ct%	Eye	G	L	F	h%	HctX	PX	xPX	hr/f	Spd	SBO	SB%	#Wk	DOM	DIS	RC/G	RAR	BPV	BPX	R$
13 NYM	200	12	2	16	0	280	257	319	385	704	668	735	5	83	0.32	46	22	32	33	120	80	132	4%	91	2%	0%	22	45%	32%	4.24	1.4	36	90	$1
14 LA	288	46	7	43	6	340	283	404	493	897	911	890	9	80	0.48	49	23	28	41	115	117	105	11%	98	7%	86%	26	46%	31%	7.67	29.6	62	168	$17
15 LA	385	55	16	60	5	294	291	370	491	861	751	904	8	82	0.51	36	28	36	33	113	126	117	14%	75	7%	71%	25	40%	28%	6.23	16.7	68	184	$17
16 LA	556	79	27	90	4	275	283	339	493	832	640	919	8	81	0.45	36	24	40	30	123	125	123	15%	91	4%	80%	27	56%	26%	5.77	12.6	68	194	$20
17 LA	457	72	21	71	7	322	282	415	530	945	1181	837	11	88	1.05	31	21	48	33	138	108	154	11%	68	5%	88%	25	64%	12%	8.01	32.9	82	248	$24
1st Half	209	37	7	31	2	388	300	473	565	1038	1216	940	11	88	1.00	32	28	41	42	138	97	141	9%	82	2%	100%	11	55%	9%	10.75	28.4	78	236	$24
2nd Half	248	35	14	40	5	266	271	367	500	867	1144	761	12	88	1.10	31	15	54	26	138	118	165	12%	60	9%	83%	14	71%	14%	6.20	8.0	89	270	$24
18 Proj	**506**	**74**	**25**	**84**	**6**	**297**	**286**	**378**	**516**	**893**	**948**	**868**	**10**	**85**	**0.72**	**33**	**22**	**45**	**31**	**128**	**115**	**138**	**13%**	**75**	**5%**	**82%**				**6.85**	**27.4**	**75**	**229**	**$25**

Turner,Trea

Age: 25 Bats: R Pos: SS | Health C | LIMA Plan D+
Ht: 6' 1" Wt: 185 | PT/Exp B | Rand Var +1
Consist D | MM 3545

Expected pull-back from electric MLB debut. Broken wrist mid-year certainly played a role, but early mediocre power skills and steep GB tilt confirm 15-HR baseline is level to use. You'll buy him for speed though, and with his acumen on basepaths and continued full green light, that's where to speculate on more. UP: 65 SB

Yr Tm	AB	R	HR	RBI	SB	BA	xBA	OBP	SLG	OPS	vL	vR	bb%	ct%	Eye	G	L	F	h%	HctX	PX	xPX	hr/f	Spd	SBO	SB%	#Wk	DOM	DIS	RC/G	RAR	BPV	BPX	R$
13																																		
14																																		
15 WAS *	494	64	7	48	27	295	248	345	405	750	819	570	7	77	0.33	50	21	29	37	36	79	11	13%	118	24%	76%	8	13%	50%	5.06	18.1	22	59	$25
16 WAS *	638	111	18	71	57	313	276	362	498	860	751	985	7	78	0.36	43	25	32	38	111	109	122	17%	201	36%	87%	14	64%	21%	6.98	41.3	78	223	$49
17 WAS	412	75	11	45	46	284	268	338	451	789	630	836	7	81	0.38	52	15	34	33	87	94	85	10%	180	51%	85%	18	61%	28%	5.59	12.7	67	203	$30
1st Half	294	53	7	32	35	279	264	324	422	746	387	838	6	81	0.33	53	16	31	32	81	77	72	9%	190	54%	85%	12	50%	33%	5.05	4.0	57	173	$37
2nd Half	118	22	4	13	11	297	279	371	525	897	1045	833	9	79	0.48	49	11	40	35	103	136	118	11%	138	43%	85%	6	83%	17%	7.07	8.3	86	261	$13
18 Proj	**551**	**95**	**16**	**60**	**50**	**286**	**270**	**344**	**471**	**815**	**763**	**831**	**7**	**79**	**0.38**	**48**	**18**	**34**	**34**	**101**	**106**	**108**	**11%**	**175**	**42%**	**85%**				**5.91**	**22.7**	**68**	**206**	**$39**

Upton,Justin

Age: 30 Bats: R Pos: LF | Health A | LIMA Plan B
Ht: 6' 2" Wt: 205 | PT/Exp A | Rand Var -2
Consist C | MM 4225

Best season since 2011 got even better after trade. A new baseline? Not so fast. It was entirely driven by mashing lefties; prior OPS vL confirms we can't bank on that sticking. And with marginal-turned-bad Spd, those second half steals seem like an aberration. Bid, but keep .260 BA, 30 HR as your baseline.

Yr Tm	AB	R	HR	RBI	SB	BA	xBA	OBP	SLG	OPS	vL	vR	bb%	ct%	Eye	G	L	F	h%	HctX	PX	xPX	hr/f	Spd	SBO	SB%	#Wk	DOM	DIS	RC/G	RAR	BPV	BPX	R$
13 ATL	558	94	27	70	8	263	254	354	464	818	994	762	12	71	0.47	41	22	38	32	89	145	110	18%	109	5%	89%	27	52%	33%	5.69	27.7	58	145	$22
14 ATL	566	77	29	102	8	270	262	342	491	833	981	794	9	70	0.35	40	20	40	34	115	173	159	18%	95	8%	67%	26	62%	19%	5.77	33.9	67	181	$26
15 SD	542	85	26	81	19	251	240	336	454	790	558	848	11	71	0.43	39	17	44	31	108	140	131	15%	127	16%	79%	26	50%	38%	5.19	12.7	57	154	$23
16 DET	570	81	31	87	9	246	242	310	465	775	754	783	8	69	0.28	39	18	43	30	106	144	127	18%	97	10%	69%	27	44%	48%	4.76	8.1	37	106	$17
17 2 AL	557	100	35	109	14	273	263	361	540	901	1155	828	12	68	0.41	37	20	44	34	112	176	151	21%	74	13%	74%	27	52%	26%	6.72	20.5	59	179	$27
1st Half	270	48	15	52	5	267	247	351	500	851	919	834	11	69	0.39	35	18	46	33	120	150	160	17%	90	11%	63%	13	54%	15%	5.88	4.2	46	139	$22
2nd Half	287	52	20	57	9	279	278	370	578	948	1333	821	13	67	0.43	38	21	41	35	105	202	143	25%	66	15%	82%	14	50%	36%	7.57	18.1	75	227	$32
18 Proj	**562**	**92**	**31**	**95**	**10**	**263**	**251**	**345**	**497**	**842**	**951**	**808**	**11**	**69**	**0.38**	**38**	**19**	**43**	**33**	**108**	**151**	**140**	**19%**	**88**	**9%**	**75%**				**5.86**	**23.1**	**44**	**133**	**$24**

Urena,Richard

Age: 22 Bats: B Pos: SS | Health A | LIMA Plan D+
Ht: 6' 0" Wt: 185 | PT/Exp F | Rand Var +4
Consist A | MM 2051

1-4-.206 in 68 AB at TOR. Young infielder took step back after building prospect profile over prior two seasons. GB/LD stroke in minors makes BA impact much more likely than HR. Problem is, saw big plate discipline regression in Double-A debut, which adds risk. Age is on his side, but he's firmly a work-in-progress.

Yr Tm	AB	R	HR	RBI	SB	BA	xBA	OBP	SLG	OPS	vL	vR	bb%	ct%	Eye	G	L	F	h%	HctX	PX	xPX	hr/f	Spd	SBO	SB%	#Wk	DOM	DIS	RC/G	RAR	BPV	BPX	R$
13																																		
14																																		
15																																		
16 aa	124	12	0	16	0	263		283	389	672			3	84	0.18				31		70			134	8%	0%				3.51		40	114	$0
17 TOR *	578	45	6	57	1	235	292	275	344	619	618	563	5	77	0.24	38	38	23	30	114	76	96	11%	87	2%	49%	6	17%	67%	3.14	-25.9	6	18	$2
1st Half	305	20	3	33	0	225	243	263	334	597			5	80	0.26				27		70			107	2%	0%				2.84		19	58	$0
2nd Half	273	25	3	23	1	245	285	289	355	644	618	563	6	73	0.23	38	38	23	33	109	84	96	11%	82	2%	100%	6	17%	67%	3.49	-8.8	-2	-6	$4
18 Proj	**201**	**17**	**4**	**22**	**0**	**269**	**305**	**301**	**423**	**724**	**793**	**701**	**4**	**79**	**0.22**	**38**	**38**	**23**	**32**	**98**	**90**	**86**	**10%**	**120**	**4%**	**15%**				**4.30**	**-0.9**	**22**	**68**	**$4**

Urshela,Giovanny

Age: 26 Bats: R Pos: 3B | Health A | LIMA Plan D
Ht: 6' 0" Wt: 215 | PT/Exp C | Rand Var +3
Consist A | MM 1031

1-15-.224 in 156 AB at CLE. Couldn't take advantage of opportunities for semi-regular work in 2nd half. With his wobbly skills foundation, it shouldn't have come as a surprise. Plummeting xPX gives him zero power upside. Bat-on-ball aptitude is his only redeemable skill, but it's an empty one without any power or speed.

Yr Tm	AB	R	HR	RBI	SB	BA	xBA	OBP	SLG	OPS	vL	vR	bb%	ct%	Eye	G	L	F	h%	HctX	PX	xPX	hr/f	Spd	SBO	SB%	#Wk	DOM	DIS	RC/G	RAR	BPV	BPX	R$
13 aa	445	32	6	33	1	233		251	325	576			2	88	0.19				25		62			92	2%	41%				2.68		35	88	$1
14 a/a	486	62	14	66	1	244		285	414	699			5	84	0.36				26		118			93	4%	19%				3.86		71	192	$11
15 CLE *	348	35	9	29	0	231	251	274	352	626	677	585	6	80	0.29	42	24	34	27	77	77	74	8%	96	1%	0%	17	18%	41%	3.15	-14.8	22	59	$1
16 aaa	468	44	7	47	0	249		269	346	616			3	87	0.21				27		59			84	0%	0%				3.17		29	83	$4
17 CLE *	453	40	6	41	0	231	254	269	313	582	535	560	5	85	0.35	46	23	31	26	84	48	60	2%	85	0%	0%	14	21%	29%	2.79	-28.2	15	45	$0
1st Half	287	25	5	25	0	229	266	266	318	584	0	0	5	84	0.31	50	25	25	26	85	49	36	0%	84	0%	0%	1	0%	0%	2.80	-19.8	12	36	$1
2nd Half	166	16	1	17	0	232	257	274	304	579	554	571	5	86	0.42	45	23	32	26	85	47	60	2%	83	0%	0%	13	23%	31%	2.77	-11.6	20	61	-$1
18 Proj	**234**	**22**	**3**	**23**	**0**	**237**	**261**	**273**	**330**	**603**	**618**	**596**	**4**	**85**	**0.31**	**44**	**24**	**33**	**27**	**82**	**55**	**66**	**5%**	**89**	**0%**	**20%**				**2.98**	**-13.4**	**7**	**22**	**$2**

STEPHEN NICKRAND

Utley,Chase

Age: 39	Bats: L	Pos: 2B	Health B	LIMA Plan D	
Ht: 6' 1"	Wt: 195		PT/Exp C	Rand Var +2	
			Consist B	MM 2331	

As he nears the big four-oh and career approaches its end, days of double-digit bids are long gone. That said, solid xPX and decent wheels keep double-digit HR, SB on radar—if he can somehow eek out 400 AB. Age, three years of struggles vL tell you to take the under. Still, there's enough here to warrant an end-buck bid.

Yr	Tm	AB	R	HR	RBI	SB	BA	xBA	OBP	SLG	OPS	vL	vR	bb%	ct%	Eye	G	L	F	h%	HctX	PX	xPX	hr/f	Spd	SBO	SB%	#Wk	DOM	DIS	RC/G	RAR	BPV	BPX	R
13	PHI	476	73	18	69	8	284	269	348	475	823	754	855	8	83	0.57	38	20	43	31	121	119	126	11%	119	8%	73%	24	67%	21%	5.80	28.9	84	210	$2
14	PHI	589	74	11	78	10	270	276	339	407	746	682	775	8	86	0.62	39	25	36	30	113	95	106	6%	105	7%	91%	27	67%	22%	4.77	23.3	68	184	$1
15	2 NL	373	37	8	39	4	212	257	286	343	629	557	655	8	83	0.50	44	20	36	24	112	86	106	7%	91	5%	100%	22	45%	45%	3.10	-12.3	45	122	$
16	LA	512	79	14	52	2	252	255	319	396	716	470	768	7	78	0.35	44	22	34	30	119	90	101	11%	101	3%	50%	27	30%	30%	4.09	-11.7	29	83	$1
17	LA	309	43	8	34	6	236	264	324	405	728	661	734	9	82	0.56	43	19	38	27	120	95	134	8%	113	10%	86%	27	52%	26%	4.21	-7.4	56	170	$
1st Half		180	24	5	22	3	228	269	329	400	729	435	755	12	82	0.75	47	18	35	25	112	93	112	9%	107	9%	75%	13	62%	31%	4.21	-3.4	61	185	$
2nd Half		129	19	3	12	3	248	258	317	411	728	1030	705	6	81	0.32	38	19	42	29	132	99	166	7%	119	12%	100%	14	43%	21%	4.19	-2.4	51	155	$
18	**Proj**	**193**	**27**	**5**	**21**	**3**	**258**	**261**	**331**	**414**	**745**	**641**	**764**	**8**	**81**	**0.45**	**42**	**20**	**38**	**30**	**120**	**90**	**125**	**8%**	**108**	**7%**	**85%**				**4.55**	**-1.4**	**42**	**128**	**$**

Valaika,Pat

Age: 25	Bats: R	Pos: SS	Health A	LIMA Plan D+	
Ht: 5' 11"	Wt: 200		PT/Exp C	Rand Var 0	
			Consist C	MM 4131	

13-40-.258 in 182 AB at COL. Sterling MLB debut from a non-prospect. With steep FB tilt and an xPX that fully backed up power, the thump in his bat is real. However, so are the holes in his swing, which grew the more pitchers saw him. Speculate on the power, but know that those plate warts will prevent sustained production.

Yr	Tm	AB	R	HR	RBI	SB	BA	xBA	OBP	SLG	OPS	vL	vR	bb%	ct%	Eye	G	L	F	h%	HctX	PX	xPX	hr/f	Spd	SBO	SB%	#Wk	DOM	DIS	RC/G	RAR	BPV	BPX	R
13																																			
14																																			
15	aa	468	45	7	45	15	225		262	344	606			5	75	0.21				28		84			111	26%	64%				2.84		14	38	$
16	COL *	560	61	13	64	8	245	241	275	401	676	714	750	4	76	0.18	55	9	36	30	169	105	66	25%	104	17%	44%	5	40%	40%	3.47	-19.3	31	89	$1
17	COL *	227	32	14	48	0	255	248	285	501	786	927	729	4	72	0.15	33	17	50	30	99	147	145	20%	80	0%	0%	25	44%	40%	4.88	2.4	38	115	$
1st Half		137	19	6	22	0	225	233	261	435	696	770	669	5	73	0.18	35	12	52	27	81	132	101	15%	87	0%	0%	11	45%	36%	3.74	-3.5	34	103	$
2nd Half		90	13	8	26	0	300	267	323	600	923	1098	786	3	70	0.11	31	21	48	35	116	170	191	27%	82	0%	0%	14	43%	43%	7.05	6.1	49	148	$
18	**Proj**	**202**	**25**	**11**	**31**	**2**	**255**	**257**	**283**	**494**	**778**	**901**	**688**	**4**	**73**	**0.16**	**36**	**19**	**46**	**29**	**102**	**140**	**155**	**17%**	**91**	**11%**	**52%**				**4.66**	**1.1**	**39**	**117**	**$**

Valbuena,Luis

Age: 32	Bats: L	Pos: 3B 1B	Health D	LIMA Plan C	
Ht: 5' 10"	Wt: 215		PT/Exp C	Rand Var +4	
			Consist C	MM 4025	

Dumped in many leagues after horrible 1st half, then resumed righty-mashing ways late. Four straight seasons of elite power and dual 1B/3B eligibility make him a hidden value. He'll never help you in BA, but don't be swayed by pitiful '17 mark, as it was driven by a fluky hit rate. There's $5 of profit embedded in a $5 bid.

Yr	Tm	AB	R	HR	RBI	SB	BA	xBA	OBP	SLG	OPS	vL	vR	bb%	ct%	Eye	G	L	F	h%	HctX	PX	xPX	hr/f	Spd	SBO	SB%	#Wk	DOM	DIS	RC/G	RAR	BPV	BPX	R
13	CHC	331	34	12	37	1	218	239	331	378	708	647	715	14	81	0.84	40	16	45	23	109	104	131	10%	72	5%	20%	22	59%	27%	3.84	-7.9	58	145	$
14	CHC	478	68	16	51	1	249	255	341	435	776	610	811	12	76	0.58	31	20	48	30	120	140	155	9%	87	2%	33%	27	52%	22%	4.94	11.2	69	186	$1
15	HOU	434	62	25	56	1	224	256	310	438	748	581	808	10	76	0.47	34	21	45	24	109	136	147	17%	68	1%	100%	27	41%	33%	4.38	-7.3	54	146	$
16	HOU	292	38	13	40	1	260	250	357	459	816	741	841	13	72	0.54	37	21	42	32	105	129	134	15%	61	2%	50%	17	41%	29%	5.60	6.3	38	109	$
17	LAA	347	42	22	65	0	199	230	294	432	727	423	765	12	69	0.45	38	14	47	21	101	140	144	19%	40	3%	0%	23	30%	39%	3.98	-15.3	28	85	$
1st Half		150	16	5	21	0	187	185	279	313	592	481	603	12	69	0.43	43	12	45	23	93	78	95	11%	62	3%	0%	9	0%	56%	2.69	-14.2	-19	-58	-$
2nd Half		197	26	17	44	0	208	266	306	523	829	394	893	12	70	0.47	35	16	49	20	107	186	181	25%	38	2%	0%	14	50%	29%	5.06	-3.6	67	203	$
18	**Proj**	**400**	**51**	**22**	**64**	**1**	**237**	**241**	**328**	**453**	**781**	**611**	**817**	**12**	**72**	**0.49**	**37**	**17**	**46**	**27**	**105**	**128**	**143**	**17%**	**52**	**2%**	**24%**				**4.89**	**0.0**	**25**	**77**	**$1**

Valencia,Danny

Age: 33	Bats: R	Pos: 1B	Health A	LIMA Plan C+	
Ht: 6' 2"	Wt: 210		PT/Exp C	Rand Var 0	
			Consist B	MM 2225	

On the surface, another part-timer for whom you can write 15 HR and 60 RBI in pen. Problem is, dwindling HctX, xPX, and ct% all increase risk now, as does waning production vs. RHers. And last two xBAs support that .250-ish mark, so don't expect significant upward regression there. Downside outweighs upside now.

Yr	Tm	AB	R	HR	RBI	SB	BA	xBA	OBP	SLG	OPS	vL	vR	bb%	ct%	Eye	G	L	F	h%	HctX	PX	xPX	hr/f	Spd	SBO	SB%	#Wk	DOM	DIS	RC/G	RAR	BPV	BPX	R
13	BAL *	423	48	19	59	1	257	278	291	470	761	1031	672	5	78	0.22	38	22	40	29	119	148	142	15%	97	5%	18%	17	47%	35%	4.53	-0.8	71	178	$1
14	2AL	264	20	4	30	1	258	251	296	371	667	835	540	5	77	0.23	45	24	31	32	111	93	105	6%	91	3%	50%	22	36%	50%	3.72	-3.2	20	54	$
15	2AL	345	59	18	66	2	290	285	345	519	864	834	881	8	77	0.36	53	17	30	33	117	151	110	22%	90	5%	50%	27	63%	26%	6.31	13.3	72	195	$1
16	OAK	471	72	17	51	1	287	257	346	446	792	924	742	8	76	0.36	45	23	32	35	97	99	94	15%	113	1%	50%	25	28%	36%	5.45	7.7	33	94	$1
17	SEA	450	54	15	66	2	256	247	314	411	725	804	693	8	73	0.33	48	21	31	32	88	93	79	14%	118	3%	50%	26	23%	38%	4.40	-12.9	19	58	$
1st Half		263	32	8	40	1	274	249	336	422	758	756	757	9	73	0.36	46	23	31	35	89	88	67	13%	130	4%	33%	13	23%	46%	4.86	-5.9	22	67	$1
2nd Half		187	22	7	26	1	230	244	284	396	679	846	585	7	72	0.29	50	19	31	28	86	99	95	16%	95	2%	100%	13	23%	31%	3.79	-10.5	13	39	$
18	**Proj**	**421**	**56**	**12**	**49**	**2**	**260**	**249**	**315**	**404**	**718**	**814**	**670**	**8**	**74**	**0.31**	**48**	**22**	**31**	**33**	**97**	**89**	**94**	**13%**	**108**	**3%**	**54%**				**4.35**	**-9.3**	**3**	**10**	**$1**

Vargas,Kennys

Age: 27	Bats: B	Pos: 1B DH	Health A	LIMA Plan D	
Ht: 6' 5"	Wt: 290		PT/Exp C	Rand Var -1	
			Consist A	MM 4021	

11-41-.253 in 241 AB at MIN. PRO: Figured out righties, .800+ OPS in three months, solid gains in 2nd half.. CON: Prior GB tilt returned, PX not backed by xPX, still too many Ks. Those warts have produced the inconsistency we've seen from him throughout his career, and they will keep him from sticking as a viable regular.

Yr	Tm	AB	R	HR	RBI	SB	BA	xBA	OBP	SLG	OPS	vL	vR	bb%	ct%	Eye	G	L	F	h%	HctX	PX	xPX	hr/f	Spd	SBO	SB%	#Wk	DOM	DIS	RC/G	RAR	BPV	BPX	R
13																																			
14	MIN *	571	65	22	87	0	256	248	311	418	729	602	899	7	76	0.33	47	19	34	30	101	117	109	17%	60	2%	0%	10	40%	50%	4.38	5.5	31	84	$1
15	MIN *	419	49	15	53	0	242	240	320	384	704	869	514	10	68	0.36	51	26	23	32	83	99	56	18%	58	0%	0%	16	13%	69%	4.13	-16.3	-7	-19	$
16	MIN *	482	62	23	70	1	214	223	324	412	736	1262	654	14	68	0.51	38	15	48	26	115	135	152	22%	55	1%	100%	12	50%	33%	4.34	-17.1	26	74	$
17	MIN *	419	56	19	66	0	241	237	317	428	745	597	819	10	68	0.34	48	19	32	31	78	121	81	21%	53	0%	0%	21	43%	48%	4.56	-3.8	5	15	$
1st Half		218	31	10	38	0	214	231	277	395	671	461	764	8	68	0.27	45	19	36	27	73	114	69	18%	54	0%	0%	10	60%	40%	3.54	-8.9	-4	-12	$
2nd Half		201	24	9	27	0	270	243	358	465	823	817	907	12	67	0.42	54	21	25	36	86	128	105	29%	66	0%	0%	11	27%	55%	5.83	5.5	18	55	$
18	**Proj**	**156**	**20**	**8**	**23**	**0**	**239**	**242**	**325**	**441**	**765**	**816**	**743**	**11**	**68**	**0.39**	**47**	**19**	**33**	**30**	**92**	**126**	**103**	**22%**	**63**	**0%**	**60%**				**4.76**	**-1.6**	**9**	**27**	**$**

Vazquez,Christian

Age: 27	Bats: R	Pos: CA	Health F	LIMA Plan C	
Ht: 5' 9"	Wt: 195		PT/Exp F	Rand Var -4	
			Consist C	MM 1243	

Glove-first backstop finished year strong on surface, combining .300 BA and some pop in 2nd half. Forget that last part though, as GB tilt, lack of HctX eliminate any shot at sustained power. But high LD rate, improving ct% set a sturdy BA floor (see 2-year xBAs). Throw in a few SB, and that's a second catcher with some value.

Yr	Tm	AB	R	HR	RBI	SB	BA	xBA	OBP	SLG	OPS	vL	vR	bb%	ct%	Eye	G	L	F	h%	HctX	PX	xPX	hr/f	Spd	SBO	SB%	#Wk	DOM	DIS	RC/G	RAR	BPV	BPX	R
13	a/a	345	37	4	37	5	262		332	355	687			10	86	0.76				30		67			90	11%	49%				3.90		46	115	$
14	BOS *	419	42	3	36	0	249	230	308	335	643	539	638	8	78	0.39	57	17	26	31	82	77	58	3%	78	1%	0%	12	25%	42%	3.46	1.7	16	43	$
15																																			
16	BOS *	324	38	3	26	2	240	271	291	329	620	804	527	7	77	0.32	60	25	15	30	87	65	53	5%	91	2%	100%	16	13%	56%	3.25	-5.9	4	11	$
17	BOS	324	43	5	32	7	290	268	330	404	735	748	732	5	80	0.27	47	25	28	35	86	70	58	7%	91	10%	78%	27	41%	44%	4.74	5.4	16	48	$1
1st Half		144	13	1	15	3	278	265	318	382	700	813	678	5	80	0.24	47	24	28	34	95	70	79	3%	87	11%	75%	13	46%	38%	4.19	0.4	13	39	$
2nd Half		180	30	4	17	4	300	271	340	422	763	700	775	5	81	0.29	47	26	28	35	79	70	41	10%	97	10%	80%	14	36%	50%	5.21	5.5	20	61	$1
18	**Proj**	**394**	**48**	**4**	**37**	**5**	**269**	**268**	**319**	**366**	**685**	**751**	**670**	**6**	**80**	**0.33**	**53**	**24**	**23**	**33**	**85**	**63**	**55**	**6%**	**86**	**7%**	**73%**				**4.02**	**-1.4**	**9**	**29**	**$1**

Verdugo,Alex

Age: 22	Bats: L	Pos: CF	Health A	LIMA Plan D+	
Ht: 6' 0"	Wt: 205		PT/Exp D	Rand Var 0	
			Consist B	MM 1133	

1-1-.174 in 23 AB at LA. Steady ascent through minors crested with cup of coffee in MLB. Power MIA for now, but as one of youngest at each stop in minors, that shouldn't surprise. Excellent plate discipline in high minors gives him path towards reaching .300 BA, 20/20 ceiling. Just don't expect him to get there in 2018.

Yr	Tm	AB	R	HR	RBI	SB	BA	xBA	OBP	SLG	OPS	vL	vR	bb%	ct%	Eye	G	L	F	h%	HctX	PX	xPX	hr/f	Spd	SBO	SB%	#Wk	DOM	DIS	RC/G	RAR	BPV	BPX	R
13																																			
14																																			
15																																			
16	aa	477	51	12	56	2	256		308	381	688			7	85	0.50				28		73			84	7%	22%				3.81		39	111	$
17	LA *	456	57	6	53	8	279	328	340	387	727	400	583	8	87	0.70	58	32	11	31	74	62	40	50%	90	9%	64%	6	17%	33%	4.59	-6.1	43	130	$1
1st Half		279	41	3	32	7	312	256	370	406	776			8	88	0.74				35		53			112	8%	86%				5.67		45	136	$1
2nd Half		177	16	4	21	1	227	328	293	358	651	400	583	9	86	0.66	58	32	11	25	73	77	40	50%	75	10%	21%	6	17%	33%	3.22	-9.2	47	142	$
18	**Proj**	**290**	**34**	**7**	**38**	**3**	**270**	**262**	**328**	**405**	**732**	**732**	**732**	**8**	**86**	**0.61**	**46**	**18**	**36**	**29**		**75**		**8%**	**88**	**8%**	**46%**				**4.46**	**-0.4**	**38**	**116**	**$**

STEPHEN NICKRAND

Villar,Jonathan

Age: 27	Bats: B	Pos: 2B	Health	A	LIMA Plan	C
Ht: 6' 1"	Wt: 215		PT/Exp	B	Rand Var	0
			Consist	F	MM	2523

Any question which year is the outlier? As h% normalized and modest Spd caught up to him, his elite 2016 evaporated. He's a GB hitter who struggles to put bat on ball, and as such, he won't be able to sustain BA or HR. Young enough to still rebound somewhat, but cap bidding at $10 for any hope of profit.

Yr	Tm	AB	R	HR	RBI	SB	BA	xBA	OBP	SLG	OPS	vL	vR	bb%	ct%	Eye	G	L	F	h%	HctX	PX	xPX	hr/f	Spd	SBO	SB%	#Wk	DOM	DIS	RC/G	RAR	BPV	BPX	R$
13	HOU *	549	63	8	40	42	246	249	308	361	669	673	627	8	68	0.28	66	20	14	35	82	91	54	6%	138	40%	73%	11	18%	64%	3.70	0.7	4	10	$22
14	HOU *	453	55	9	46	34	213	218	279	325	604	644	608	8	67	0.27	51	19	30	30	84	91	108	13%	100	41%	76%	19	21%	47%	2.96	-6.1	-11	-30	$14
15	HOU *	396	58	6	33	31	242	240	293	356	649	761	742	7	70	0.24	57	20	23	33	75	85	44	10%	140	45%	71%	15	33%	40%	3.41	-9.2	5	14	$16
16	MIL	589	92	19	63	62	285	264	369	457	826	930	786	12	70	0.45	56	20	24	38	101	120	103	19%	110	43%	78%	27	44%	48%	6.04	20.1	36	103	$43
17	MIL	403	49	11	40	23	241	240	293	372	665	607	689	7	67	0.23	57	21	22	33	90	89	83	19%	105	32%	74%	25	20%	60%	3.63	-17.0	-12	-36	$13
1st Half		241	31	8	29	15	216	239	281	361	642	573	669	8	67	0.28	62	16	22	29	92	94	91	24%	97	34%	79%	11	18%	45%	3.35	-11.2	-10	-30	$15
2nd Half		162	18	3	11	8	278	245	310	389	699	650	721	5	68	0.15	50	28	22	39	88	82	71	13%	121	29%	67%	14	21%	71%	4.09	-3.5	-15	-45	$10
18	Proj	355	47	9	33	26	257	247	315	392	706	711	704	8	69	0.27	56	21	23	35	90	91	80	16%	117	38%	74%				4.18	-6.6	1	4	$15

Vogelbach,Daniel

Age: 25	Bats: L	Pos: 1B	Health	A	LIMA Plan	D
Ht: 6' 0"	Wt: 250		PT/Exp	C	Rand Var	+2
			Consist	B	MM	3013

0-2-.214 in 28 AB at SEA. Bat-first prospect continues to own a power/patience profile worthy of keeper league investment. Indeed, xPX in tiny MLB sample hints at that upside, as does high rate of hard contact. Finding consistent AB is his hurdle, and it's a big one given his issues on defense. With PT... UP: 20 HR

Yr	Tm	AB	R	HR	RBI	SB	BA	xBA	OBP	SLG	OPS	vL	vR	bb%	ct%	Eye	G	L	F	h%	HctX	PX	xPX	hr/f	Spd	SBO	SB%	#Wk	DOM	DIS	RC/G	RAR	BPV	BPX	R$
13																																			
14																																			
15	aa	254	32	6	31	1	241		356	371	727			15	73	0.66				31		98			91	2%	41%				4.39		29	78	$3
16	SEA *	471	63	19	77	0	246	255	353	417	771	0	258	14	73	0.62	67	17	17	30	0	108	-24	0%	56	0%	0%	4	0%	75%	4.99	1.8	26	74	$10
17	SEA *	487	51	14	69	2	242	273	328	372	701	500	546	11	74	0.49	32	37	32	30	141	81	145	0%	55	2%	67%	7	29%	71%	4.10	-18.4	1	3	$7
1st Half		267	24	7	37	2	232	240	321	342	663	500	466	12	72	0.47	50	25	25	29	146	66	99	0%	60	3%	100%	3	33%	67%	3.70	-15.6	-15	-45	$6
2nd Half		220	28	7	32	0	255	334	337	409	746	0	636	11	75	0.51	0	57	43	31	131	98	223	0%	58	2%	0%	4	25%	75%	4.62	-6.6	22	67	$8
18	Proj	274	33	11	40	1	245	234	343	415	758	758	758	13	74	0.56	44	18	36	29		102		15%	62	1%	52%				4.78	-2.6	14	43	$6

Vogt,Stephen

Age: 33	Bats: L	Pos: CA	Health	B	LIMA Plan	D+
Ht: 6' 0"	Wt: 225		PT/Exp	C	Rand Var	+3
			Consist	B	MM	2033

PRO: BA should rebound with h% regression, HctX and xPX bounce-back confirm he still has thump. CON: Struggles vL deepened, Eye erosion reached new depths in 2nd half, nagging injuries prevent full-time work. Takeaway: should give you a BA you can live with and double-digit HR, but max 400 AB or so.

Yr	Tm	AB	R	HR	RBI	SB	BA	xBA	OBP	SLG	OPS	vL	vR	bb%	ct%	Eye	G	L	F	h%	HctX	PX	xPX	hr/f	Spd	SBO	SB%	#Wk	DOM	DIS	RC/G	RAR	BPV	BPX	R$
13	OAK *	431	53	11	52	0	242	247	296	386	682	667	698	7	80	0.38	30	24	46	28	102	98	111	8%	98	2%	0%	13	38%	46%	3.75	0.7	43	108	$6
14	OAK *	357	37	11	46	2	275	254	315	428	744	647	770	6	86	0.42	33	20	47	30	123	97	144	8%	101	2%	100%	17	53%	35%	4.78	13.4	65	176	$11
15	OAK	445	58	18	71	0	261	259	341	443	783	631	832	11	78	0.58	38	22	40	30	96	115	110	13%	86	2%	0%	25	48%	32%	5.15	17.3	55	149	$12
16	OAK	490	54	14	56	0	251	260	305	406	711	549	748	7	83	0.42	30	23	46	28	90	93	106	7%	69	0%	0%	27	52%	26%	4.16	-3.5	42	120	$7
17	2 TM	279	25	12	40	0	233	255	285	423	708	509	732	7	80	0.38	38	19	44	25	106	105	122	12%	83	2%	0%	23	57%	26%	3.97	-0.7	44	133	$2
1st Half		167	15	6	25	0	228	257	296	395	691	248	733	9	81	0.53	38	21	41	25	103	91	112	11%	85	3%	0%	13	62%	23%	3.80	-1.5	42	127	$2
2nd Half		112	10	6	15	0	241	246	267	464	732	750	729	3	79	0.17	38	15	48	26	111	126	138	14%	82	0%	0%	10	50%	30%	4.17	0.2	48	145	$2
18	Proj	392	40	15	53	0	248	257	298	428	725	601	748	7	81	0.36	36	20	44	27	102	100	120	11%	82	1%	12%				4.28	1.6	28	86	$8

Voit,Luke

Age: 27	Bats: R	Pos: 1B	Health	A	LIMA Plan	D
Ht: 6' 3"	Wt: 225		PT/Exp	D	Rand Var	0
			Consist	B	MM	3031

4-18-.246 in 114 AB at STL. Hit lefties well enough to garner attention in PT role. Problem is, subpar OPS vR, marginal plate skills, and GB tilt all are stacked against him, and those warts got exposed more as the season went along. His only value lies in power vs. LHers. Using him as anything more than a fill-in will hurt you.

Yr	Tm	AB	R	HR	RBI	SB	BA	xBA	OBP	SLG	OPS	vL	vR	bb%	ct%	Eye	G	L	F	h%	HctX	PX	xPX	hr/f	Spd	SBO	SB%	#Wk	DOM	DIS	RC/G	RAR	BPV	BPX	R$
13																																			
14																																			
15																																			
16	aa	482	57	15	60	1	259		318	404	722			8	81	0.45				29		82			105	2%	26%				4.34		39	111	$10
17	STL *	383	45	14	57	1	268	261	320	455	774	797	713	7	76	0.32	48	18	34	32	126	116	142	14%	73	2%	39%	14	36%	50%	5.01	-9.9	35	106	$9
1st Half		264	29	9	37	1	274	263	331	465	796	0	2667	8	77	0.36	50	17	33	33	156	119	223	0%	77	3%	39%	1	100%	0%	5.32	-2.5	43	130	$12
2nd Half		119	17	5	20	0	253	250	295	432	727	986	634	6	75	0.23	48	18	34	30	121	109	136	15%	77	0%	0%	13	31%	54%	4.35	-4.5	22	67	$3
18	Proj	162	20	6	23	0	260	258	325	434	759	1036	673	7	78	0.35	48	18	34	30	109	101	122	14%	87	2%	41%				4.66	-2.1	24	72	$4

Votto,Joey

Age: 34	Bats: L	Pos: 1B	Health	B	LIMA Plan	C
Ht: 6' 2"	Wt: 220		PT/Exp	A	Rand Var	0
			Consist	A	MM	4255

One of the few .300 BA, 30-HR locks in today's game, and this was one of his best seasons yet. Steady-as-they-come underlying skills, including soaring vR OPS, huge reduction in Ks, FB shift... If he was 5 years younger, these would hint at another level yet to come. Even at 34, there's a $40 player lurking in here.

Yr	Tm	AB	R	HR	RBI	SB	BA	xBA	OBP	SLG	OPS	vL	vR	bb%	ct%	Eye	G	L	F	h%	HctX	PX	xPX	hr/f	Spd	SBO	SB%	#Wk	DOM	DIS	RC/G	RAR	BPV	BPX	R$
13	CIN	581	101	24	73	6	305	279	435	491	926	824	977	19	76	0.98	44	27	29	37	120	128	128	18%	110	4%	67%	27	67%	0%	7.80	51.2	80	200	$29
14	CIN	220	32	6	23	1	255	276	390	409	799	969	736	17	78	0.96	41	27	33	30	109	122	146	11%	67	2%	50%	11	64%	18%	5.35	7.5	65	176	$4
15	CIN	545	95	29	80	11	314	285	459	541	1000	1009	997	21	75	1.06	42	25	33	37	126	151	150	22%	81	6%	79%	27	59%	22%	9.20	56.7	89	241	$33
16	CIN	556	101	29	97	8	326	298	434	550	985	861	1033	16	78	0.90	43	27	30	37	123	133	134	22%	84	4%	89%	27	52%	22%	9.13	55.9	79	226	$33
17	CIN	559	106	36	100	5	320	309	454	578	1032	988	1048	19	85	1.61	39	23	38	33	125	130	141	20%	84	2%	83%	27	85%	11%	9.82	58.4	110	333	$32
1st Half		286	60	23	57	3	315	324	428	622	1051	1104	1032	16	87	1.47	39	21	40	30	124	151	156	23%	75	4%	75%	13	92%	0%	9.86	32.6	125	379	$37
2nd Half		273	46	13	43	2	326	293	479	531	1010	883	1066	22	84	1.73	39	25	35	35	126	107	124	16%	96	1%	100%	14	79%	21%	9.63	28.8	95	288	$27
18	Proj	541	101	32	98	5	317	303	446	560	1006	948	1030	19	82	1.27	40	25	35	34	124	128	138	21%	83	3%	80%				9.31	61.3	89	268	$33

Walker,Christian

Age: 27	Bats: R	Pos: 1B	Health	A	LIMA Plan	D
Ht: 6' 0"	Wt: 220		PT/Exp	B	Rand Var	0
			Consist	C	MM	3121

2-2-.250 in 12 AB at ARI. After 30-plus bombs in high air of Triple-A, he'll get some end-game appeal in deep leagues for those desperate for power. Don't follow suit. Sub-.500 Slg on road, mediocre plate discipline, age are all working against him. Best to spend your speculative dollars elsewhere.

Yr	Tm	AB	R	HR	RBI	SB	BA	xBA	OBP	SLG	OPS	vL	vR	bb%	ct%	Eye	G	L	F	h%	HctX	PX	xPX	hr/f	Spd	SBO	SB%	#Wk	DOM	DIS	RC/G	RAR	BPV	BPX	R$
13	aa	62	5	0	1	0	214		269	285	554			7	83	0.43				26		65			103	0%	0%				2.49		29	73	-$3
14	BAL *	550	55	22	72	1	247	267	301	413	715	600	599	7	72	0.27	33	33	33	31	103	124	124	33%	74	2%	57%	2	50%	50%	4.20	0.1	25	68	$13
15	BAL *	543	64	19	70	1	241	274	304	404	708	425	500	8	72	0.32	80	20	0	30	125	118	34	0%	77	3%	22%	4	50%	50%	4.03	-21.7	25	68	$10
16	aaa	504	58	16	58	1	223		278	359	637			7	67	0.23				30		92			94	4%	21%				3.18		-13	-37	$4
17	ARI *	526	66	23	73	3	250	229	301	464	766	1511	400	7	75	0.29	29	14	57	29	174	122	330	50%	111	5%	56%	4	50%	50%	4.70	-18.8	47	142	$12
1st Half		312	39	13	52	2	238	273	282	447	729			6	78	0.28				27		116			106	8%	51%				4.11		50	152	$14
2nd Half		214	27	10	21	1	269	224	329	489	819	1511	400	8	71	0.31	29	14	57	34	164	131	330	50%	121	1%	100%	4	50%	50%	5.64	0.0	44	133	$8
18	Proj	162	19	6	20	1	244	245	299	425	724	724	724	7	72	0.28	40	22	38	30		109		14%	101	3%	49%				4.23	-4.2	13	38	$3

Walker,Neil

Age: 32	Bats: B	Pos: 2B	Health	D	LIMA Plan	B
Ht: 6' 3"	Wt: 210		PT/Exp	B	Rand Var	0
			Consist	B	MM	2135

Another year plagued by nagging injuries, but there's still value here. Steady approach at plate showing no signs of wear. xPX confirms power isn't eroding as much as it appears. Ineptitude vL two of three years plus injury risk makes 400-AB baseline the one to use, but he'll be productive in them.

Yr	Tm	AB	R	HR	RBI	SB	BA	xBA	OBP	SLG	OPS	vL	vR	bb%	ct%	Eye	G	L	F	h%	HctX	PX	xPX	hr/f	Spd	SBO	SB%	#Wk	DOM	DIS	RC/G	RAR	BPV	BPX	R$
13	PIT *	499	62	16	54	1	252	268	322	415	738	518	805	9	82	0.59	39	23	39	28	116	106	115	11%	102	2%	33%	22	50%	27%	4.50	12.3	65	163	$10
14	PIT	512	74	23	76	2	271	282	342	467	809	727	831	8	83	0.51	38	23	39	29	102	126	105	14%	81	3%	50%	26	65%	12%	5.33	28.5	74	200	$20
15	PIT	543	69	16	71	4	269	261	328	427	756	575	793	7	80	0.40	42	21	37	31	112	105	113	10%	96	4%	80%	27	44%	22%	4.83	10.3	48	130	$16
16	NYM	412	57	23	55	3	282	255	347	476	823	1001	766	9	80	0.50	35	21	43	30	116	102	136	16%	100	3%	75%	21	52%	24%	5.87	11.6	50	143	$15
17	2 NL	385	59	14	49	0	265	260	362	439	801	610	854	12	80	0.71	36	22	42	30	106	97	114	11%	95	2%	0%	21	71%	24%	5.33	3.4	53	161	$9
1st Half		222	35	9	33	0	270	271	352	468	820	725	851	10	84	0.72	34	21	45	29	111	104	129	11%	105	2%	0%	11	82%	9%	5.58	4.8	73	221	$12
2nd Half		163	24	5	16	0	258	243	376	399	775	402	857	15	75	0.71	40	23	37	32	99	87	93	11%	84	2%	0%	10	60%	40%	4.95	0.6	26	79	$4
18	Proj	406	58	18	51	1	268	260	352	452	804	698	831	11	79	0.58	37	22	41	30	109	100	116	13%	94	2%	44%				5.40	7.0	37	111	$13

STEPHEN NICKRAND

Werth,Jayson

Age: 39	Bats: R	Pos: LF	Health F	LIMA Plan D+
Ht: 6' 5"	Wt: 235		PT/Exp C	Rand Var +1
			Consist B	MM 3113

Felled by groin, toe, shoulder injuries, all of which contributed to this drop-off. As he nears 40, we can't assume health will improve; even 400 AB is optimistic now. Still has enough thump for double-digit bombs, but it's offset by his average. And with sub-par LD rate fueling eroding xBA, that ain't getting better either.

Yr	Tm	AB	R	HR	RBI	SB	BA	xBA	OBP	SLG	OPS	vL	vR	bb%	ct%	Eye	G	L	F	h%	HctX	PX	xPX	hr/f	Spd	SBO	SB%	#Wk	DOM	DIS	RC/G	RAR	BPV	BPX
13	WAS	462	84	25	82	10	318	281	398	532	931	1092	884	11	78	0.59	36	26	38	36	130	142	142	18%	80	7%	91%	22	64%	14%	8.01	49.0	75	188
14	WAS	534	85	16	82	9	292	262	394	455	849	933	823	13	79	0.73	40	20	40	35	134	123	142	9%	90	5%	90%	26	69%	15%	6.44	39.3	69	186
15	WAS *	354	52	12	46	1	227	240	303	384	687	771	658	10	76	0.45	34	22	44	27	114	107	137	11%	66	2%	43%	16	31%	44%	3.81	-9.7	29	78
16	WAS	525	84	21	69	5	244	238	335	417	752	1031	668	12	74	0.51	41	17	42	29	107	112	116	13%	79	4%	83%	26	46%	35%	4.72	1.4	33	94
17	WAS	252	35	10	29	4	226	230	322	393	715	820	691	12	73	0.51	40	18	42	27	96	98	122	13%	101	10%	57%	15	27%	27%	4.04	-9.4	25	76
1st Half		168	28	8	18	4	262	245	367	446	814	959	789	14	74	0.63	39	21	40	31	87	101	94	16%	122	12%	57%	9	33%	22%	5.41	0.3	45	136
2nd Half		84	7	2	11	0	155	191	226	286	512	671	444	9	69	0.31	41	12	47	20	114	93	181	7%	66	0%	0%	6	17%	33%	1.97	-9.4	-10	-30
18	Proj	311	43	11	40	3	234	231	320	397	717	873	670	11	73	0.47	39	18	43	28	109	100	137	12%	78	5%	67%				4.19	-2.5	17	51

White,Tyler

Age: 27	Bats: R	Pos: 1B	Health A	LIMA Plan D
Ht: 5' 11"	Wt: 225		PT/Exp C	Rand Var -1
			Consist B	MM 3111

3-10-.279 in 61 AB at HOU. The window is closing for him to stake claim to everyday MLB role. PRO: Peak age, power is big-league worthy, no platoon split in Triple-A. CON: Contact going wrong way; you can drive vehicles through holes in this swing. VERDICT: Needs a ton to break right. There are better speculations.

Yr	Tm	AB	R	HR	RBI	SB	BA	xBA	OBP	SLG	OPS	vL	vR	bb%	ct%	Eye	G	L	F	h%	HctX	PX	xPX	hr/f	Spd	SBO	SB%	#Wk	DOM	DIS	RC/G	RAR	BPV	BPX
13																																		
14																																		
15	a/a	403	50	11	70	1	268		363	404	766			13	78	0.67				32		92			81	1%	37%				5.06		37	100
16	HOU *	423	45	18	50	2	210	245	270	387	657	798	591	8	76	0.34	43	18	39	23	96	107	104	11%	75	3%	60%	21	33%	38%	3.35	-19.8	28	80
17	HOU *	497	59	18	65	4	230	217	277	390	668	1333	780	6	70	0.22	26	22	52	29	123	101	185	13%	78	9%	47%	8	38%	50%	3.47	-28.9	-1	-3
1st Half		297	34	8	29	2	223	221	273	350	623			6	70	0.23				29		82			81	7%	42%				3.04		-16	-48
2nd Half		200	24	10	35	2	241	237	284	451	734	1333	780	6	70	0.20	26	22	52	29	124	129	185	13%	72	12%	52%	8	38%	50%	4.14	-9.1	19	58
18	Proj	129	15	5	18	1	246	234	308	420	728	955	664	8	73	0.31	33	20	47	30	113	105	153	12%	78	5%	51%				4.22	-3.4	9	27

Wieters,Matt

Age: 32	Bats: B	Pos: CA	Health C	LIMA Plan D+
Ht: 6' 5"	Wt: 230		PT/Exp C	Rand Var +3
			Consist B	MM 2123

After showing glimpses of former upside again in '16, this was more of the same, and maybe even worse—see sub-.600 OPS in four of six months. Concurrent PX, LD% declines put both HR and BA at further risk, and that OPS vR trend even negates option for platooning. No longer much of a post-hype speculative target.

Yr	Tm	AB	R	HR	RBI	SB	BA	xBA	OBP	SLG	OPS	vL	vR	bb%	ct%	Eye	G	L	F	h%	HctX	PX	xPX	hr/f	Spd	SBO	SB%	#Wk	DOM	DIS	RC/G	RAR	BPV	BPX
13	BAL	523	59	22	79	2	235	256	287	417	704	872	628	7	80	0.41	39	18	44	25	105	122	126	12%	72	2%	100%	26	62%	27%	4.10	6.2	57	143
14	BAL	104	13	5	18	0	308	292	339	500	839	799	849	5	82	0.32	28	30	43	34	138	127	160	14%	84	4%	0%	6	67%	33%	6.11	7.6	66	178
15	BAL	258	24	8	25	0	267	255	319	422	742	728	746	7	74	0.31	43	25	32	33	101	109	113	13%	79	0%	0%	19	53%	37%	4.74	6.8	24	65
16	BAL	423	48	17	66	1	243	261	302	409	711	645	733	7	80	0.38	36	24	40	27	106	94	113	13%	85	1%	100%	27	41%	44%	4.10	-3.7	36	103
17	WAS	422	43	10	52	1	225	239	288	344	632	687	619	8	78	0.40	42	21	36	27	86	72	100	8%	68	1%	100%	27	30%	41%	3.28	-9.9	7	21
1st Half		237	25	7	31	1	249	254	299	388	687	867	656	6	80	0.33	41	22	37	29	99	81	116	10%	80	2%	100%	13	38%	38%	3.93	-1.2	22	67
2nd Half		185	18	3	21	0	195	217	275	286	561	542	567	11	75	0.48	45	20	36	24	70	60	79	6%	64	0%	0%	14	21%	43%	2.54	-9.1	-9	-27
18	Proj	386	40	11	50	1	236	247	296	373	669	676	667	8	78	0.39	40	23	37	28	95	80	106	10%	72	1%	77%				3.70	-5.1	4	12

Williams,Nick

Age: 24	Bats: L	Pos: RF	Health A	LIMA Plan C+
Ht: 6' 3"	Wt: 195		PT/Exp B	Rand Var -3
			Consist C	MM 3325

12-55-.288 in 313 AB at PHI. Toolsy prospect put them to good use in MLB debut. Will it stick? Can't bank on another hr/f like that again, and with his GB stroke, this isn't a place to look for power. Speed is where he'll help you most—but not yet, as overall plate skills remain stuck in the mud. Likely to be overvalued in 2018.

Yr	Tm	AB	R	HR	RBI	SB	BA	xBA	OBP	SLG	OPS	vL	vR	bb%	ct%	Eye	G	L	F	h%	HctX	PX	xPX	hr/f	Spd	SBO	SB%	#Wk	DOM	DIS	RC/G	RAR	BPV	BPX
13																																		
14	aa	62	3	0	3	1	208		229	266	494			3	64	0.07				32		53			115	16%	43%				1.82		-58	-157
15	aa	475	61	15	43	10	270		310	432	742			6	77	0.25				32		106			114	17%	54%				4.42		38	103
16	aaa	497	73	13	60	6	239		265	398	663			3	69	0.11				32		113			106	11%	56%				3.43		7	20
17	PHI *	595	82	26	93	5	270	251	309	466	775	738	838	5	66	0.17	50	23	27	37	90	127	87	20%	131	9%	45%	15	27%	53%	4.83	-7.3	17	52
1st Half		288	38	14	38	4	251	268	288	455	743	0	833	5	63	0.14	40	40	20	35	153	138	74	0%	110	15%	49%	1	0%	100%	4.22	-9.8	7	21
2nd Half		307	44	12	55	1	287	255	334	476	810	738	837	6	69	0.20	50	23	27	38	92	117	88	20%	140	4%	33%	14	29%	50%	5.45	0.8	24	73
18	Proj	500	70	15	68	6	260	249	302	425	727	657	753	5	69	0.16	50	23	27	35	83	106	79	16%	135	10%	50%				4.17	-7.7	2	7

Winker,Jesse

Age: 24	Bats: L	Pos: RF	Health A	LIMA Plan B
Ht: 6' 3"	Wt: 215		PT/Exp C	Rand Var -4
			Consist A	MM 2145

7-15-.298 in 121 AB at CIN. Young OF investment on path to becoming impact bat—torched RHP and, notably, carried good plate skills to MLB. But overall production was fueled by a fluky hr/f. As power history and current GB tilt show, don't expect the HR numbers to continue just yet. Still, a premium stash in keeper leagues.

Yr	Tm	AB	R	HR	RBI	SB	BA	xBA	OBP	SLG	OPS	vL	vR	bb%	ct%	Eye	G	L	F	h%	HctX	PX	xPX	hr/f	Spd	SBO	SB%	#Wk	DOM	DIS	RC/G	RAR	BPV	BPX
13																																		
14	aa	77	12	2	6	0	186		288	316	604			13	68	0.45				25		116			99	0%	0%				2.85		21	57
15	aa	443	60	13	48	7	264		359	407	766			13	78	0.69				31		96			95	8%	62%				4.98		47	127
16	aaa	380	35	3	40	0	280		369	357	726			12	82	0.80				33		55			80	0%	0%				4.67		24	69
17	CIN *	420	48	9	49	3	283	247	355	409	765	354	1042	10	81	0.60	53	16	31	33	118	77	100	23%	80	6%	32%	13	54%	15%	4.95	-2.8	33	100
1st Half		257	21	2	34	1	269	137	338	353	691	3000	500	9	83	0.60	30	0	70	32	134	57	124	0%	79	7%	15%	2	100%	0%	3.90	-8.8	21	64
2nd Half		163	27	7	14	2	306	279	382	498	880	245	1101	11	79	0.60	55	18	26	35	113	110	97	30%	100	5%	65%	11	45%	18%	6.91	8.3	59	179
18	Proj	496	57	18	52	3	283	269	365	452	817	246	969	11	81	0.67	55	18	26	32	102	96	87	17%	82	4%	49%				5.75	14.9	35	105

Wolters,Tony

Age: 26	Bats: L	Pos: CA	Health A	LIMA Plan F
Ht: 5' 10"	Wt: 200		PT/Exp F	Rand Var 0
			Consist D	MM 1111

0-16-.240 in 229 AB at COL. At the right age to take a step up. Problem is, there are no signs his bat wants to cooperate. It got knocked out of his hands even more in sophomore season. With weak contact and no loft in swing, that won't change. And late collapse puts playing time at further risk. A fringe backup at best.

Yr	Tm	AB	R	HR	RBI	SB	BA	xBA	OBP	SLG	OPS	vL	vR	bb%	ct%	Eye	G	L	F	h%	HctX	PX	xPX	hr/f	Spd	SBO	SB%	#Wk	DOM	DIS	RC/G	RAR	BPV	BPX
13																																		
14	aa	341	29	1	28	2	221		279	276	556			7	76	0.33				29		50			95	5%	53%				2.49		-10	-27
15	aa	239	21	2	15	3	198		256	263	518			7	72	0.28				27		49			111	9%	55%				2.09		-21	-57
16	COL	205	27	3	30	4	259	258	327	395	723	579	757	9	74	0.40	48	23	29	34	64	98	72	7%	103	9%	80%	25	36%	44%	4.48	0.4	26	74
17	COL *	283	34	2	22	0	239	236	323	312	635	496	661	11	75	0.50	55	22	24	31	64	51	42	0%	97	2%	0%	24	21%	54%	3.27	-6.6	-5	-15
1st Half		167	28	1	14	0	280	248	369	341	711	694	734	12	78	0.64	53	25	22	36	63	40	34	0%	111	2%	0%	12	8%	42%	4.37	1.3	3	9
2nd Half		116	6	1	8	0	179	213	253	270	523	186	486	9	71	0.34	59	14	27	25	66	67	62	0%	80	5%	0%	12	33%	67%	2.02	-7.9	-18	-55
18	Proj	159	16	1	15	1	227	232	300	307	607	429	658	9	74	0.39	53	20	27	30	64	57	59	3%	98	5%	52%				2.97	-5.7	-17	-53

Wong,Kolten

Age: 27	Bats: L	Pos: 2B	Health B	LIMA Plan B+
Ht: 5' 9"	Wt: 185		PT/Exp C	Rand Var -2
			Consist B	MM 1435

On surface, another season where he fell short of expectation. Truth is, nagging injuries (triceps, back, hip) contributed to marginal results. History of sobering xPX caps HR hopes, but his combo of a surging bb% and top-flight Spd—when healthy—give him more SB upside than you might realize. UP: 25 SB

Yr	Tm	AB	R	HR	RBI	SB	BA	xBA	OBP	SLG	OPS	vL	vR	bb%	ct%	Eye	G	L	F	h%	HctX	PX	xPX	hr/f	Spd	SBO	SB%	#Wk	DOM	DIS	RC/G	RAR	BPV	BPX
13	STL *	471	58	7	35	18	247	272	299	357	656	0	410	7	83	0.44	61	17	22	28	74	72	18	0%	139	16%	94%	8	0%	75%	3.79	1.8	48	120
14	STL *	477	63	14	51	24	257	262	294	395	689	790	656	5	83	0.30	47	19	34	28	93	90	82	11%	106	25%	86%	23	48%	30%	4.10	9.9	47	127
15	STL	557	71	11	61	15	262	262	321	386	707	552	772	6	83	0.38	45	22	33	30	98	80	86	7%	107	17%	65%	27	30%	26%	3.99	-2.9	42	114
16	STL *	341	46	8	31	8	249	253	323	384	707	653	689	9	83	0.63	46	20	34	28	87	67	79	6%	155	8%	100%	26	35%	35%	4.35	-5.1	52	149
17	STL	354	55	4	42	8	285	270	376	412	788	703	810	10	83	0.68	48	20	32	33	95	79	72	4%	112	9%	80%	22	55%	18%	5.33	3.1	51	155
1st Half		153	23	1	19	3	301	286	393	444	838	721	864	11	84	0.76	49	21	30	35	86	92	46	3%	103	9%	75%	10	70%	10%	6.12	5.5	63	191
2nd Half		201	32	3	23	5	274	258	362	388	750	689	768	10	83	0.63	47	19	33	32	101	69	92	5%	117	10%	83%	12	42%	25%	4.77	-0.3	42	127
18	Proj	509	73	7	55	14	269	263	349	389	738	659	759	9	83	0.58	48	20	32	31	92	69	74	5%	124	11%	83%				4.62	-2.7	44	133

STEPHEN NICKRAND

Wright,David

Age: 35 Bats: R Pos: DH | Ht: 6' 0" Wt: 205

Health F | PT/Exp F | Consist B | LIMA Plan D | Rand Var 0 | MM 3221

Shoulder, back issues both resulted in surgeries, adding further doubt to a player who last made it through a full season four years ago. Most recent metrics say he can still hit, but that flunking health will scare most everyone away. October laminotomy has provided most optimistic prognosis in years, so maybe stash him in reserve.

Yr Tm	AB	R	HR	RBI	SB	BA	xBA	OBP	SLG	OPS	vL	vR	bb%	ct%	Eye	G	L	F	h%	HctX	PX	xPX	hr/f	Spd	SBO	SB%	#Wk	DOM	DIS	RC/G	RAR	BPV	BPX	R$
13 NYM	430	63	18	58	17	307	280	390	514	904	1072	836	11	82	0.70	38	23	39	34	124	130	141	13%	147	14%	85%	21	67%	5%	7.40	40.2	99	248	$26
14 NYM	535	54	8	63	8	269	245	324	374	698	921	634	7	79	0.37	40	23	37	33	116	84	113	5%	83	9%	62%	24	42%	46%	4.13	6.4	24	65	$15
15 NYM	152	24	5	17	2	289	247	379	434	814	1023	746	13	76	0.61	37	24	39	35	120	98	132	11%	87	6%	67%	9	22%	44%	5.86	5.1	37	100	$4
16 NYM	137	18	7	14	3	226	228	350	438	788	714	814	16	60	0.47	23	28	49	32	116	165	228	18%	80	12%	60%	8	38%	50%	4.91	-0.2	29	83	$2
17																																		
1st Half																																		
2nd Half																																		
18 Proj	**217**	**28**	**7**	**25**	**4**	**266**	**244**	**352**	**427**	**779**	**900**	**738**	**11**	**73**	**0.48**	**34**	**25**	**41**	**33**	**118**	**100**	**156**	**11%**	**89**	**10%**	**67%**				**5.13**	**-2.3**	**19**	**58**	**$5**

Yelich,Christian

Age: 26 Bats: L Pos: CF | Ht: 6' 3" Wt: 195

Health A | PT/Exp A | Consist B | LIMA Plan B | Rand Var 0 | MM 3445

Continues to make strides towards a full-fledged breakout. Four reasons it might happen in 2018: 1) Steady rise in FB%, especially in 2nd half; 2) exit velocity top 25 in MLB; 3) legs and acumen on basepaths; 4) ascending Eye confirms maturity. With continued shift towards FBs and stronger green light... UP: 25 HR, 25 SB

Yr Tm	AB	R	HR	RBI	SB	BA	xBA	OBP	SLG	OPS	vL	vR	bb%	ct%	Eye	G	L	F	h%	HctX	PX	xPX	hr/f	Spd	SBO	SB%	#Wk	DOM	DIS	RC/G	RAR	BPV	BPX	R$
13 MIA *	433	62	9	41	14	276	276	356	427	782	476	941	11	72	0.44	63	23	14	37	103	114	83	17%	153	15%	73%	10	30%	20%	5.31	15.6	49	123	$16
14 MIA	582	94	9	54	21	284	271	362	402	764	819	747	11	76	0.51	61	21	18	36	113	91	96	12%	137	15%	75%	25	44%	16%	5.16	22.9	43	116	$25
15 MIA	476	63	7	44	16	300	282	366	416	782	703	812	9	79	0.47	62	23	15	37	114	85	82	13%	122	14%	76%	25	48%	32%	5.52	10.6	40	108	$20
16 MIA	578	78	21	98	9	298	289	376	483	859	716	908	11	76	0.52	57	23	20	36	117	118	97	24%	93	7%	69%	27	52%	22%	6.52	30.4	51	146	$25
17 MIA	602	100	18	81	16	282	272	369	439	807	722	837	12	77	0.58	55	19	25	34	110	94	77	15%	109	9%	89%	27	48%	30%	5.83	9.7	42	127	$25
1st Half	288	49	7	37	7	271	264	352	385	738	674	762	11	79	0.56	58	20	22	32	113	67	61	14%	103	8%	100%	13	38%	46%	4.85	-4.2	23	70	$19
2nd Half	314	51	11	44	9	293	278	384	487	871	773	903	13	76	0.61	53	19	29	36	108	120	91	16%	115	11%	82%	14	57%	14%	6.79	12.6	61	185	$30
18 Proj	**590**	**89**	**19**	**79**	**17**	**289**	**278**	**371**	**458**	**829**	**715**	**870**	**11**	**77**	**0.55**	**54**	**21**	**25**	**35**	**112**	**102**	**85**	**17%**	**111**	**11%**	**86%**				**6.18**	**27.6**	**44**	**134**	**$28**

Young,Chris

Age: 34 Bats: R Pos: LF DH | Ht: 6' 2" Wt: 200

Health C | PT/Exp D | Consist B | LIMA Plan D+ | Rand Var 0 | MM 3213

Drafted as a lefty-masher, futility against them dried up at-bats as season went along. Blame three-mph dive in exit velocity for sudden loss of power. PX history favors a bounce-back there, but as someone who has never hit the ball with authority vR for long stretches, his utility to you remains that of an injury fill-in or 5th OF.

Yr Tm	AB	R	HR	RBI	SB	BA	xBA	OBP	SLG	OPS	vL	vR	bb%	ct%	Eye	G	L	F	h%	HctX	PX	xPX	hr/f	Spd	SBO	SB%	#Wk	DOM	DIS	RC/G	RAR	BPV	BPX	R$
13 OAK	335	46	12	40	10	200	231	280	379	659	712	614	10	72	0.39	29	22	50	24	83	131	120	10%	114	19%	77%	26	46%	35%	3.36	-6.5	49	123	$5
14 2 TM *	352	45	13	43	9	229	244	297	403	699	561	720	9	77	0.42	29	20	52	26	94	129	109	8%	103	15%	74%	23	43%	48%	3.93	2.6	62	168	$9
15 NYY	318	53	14	42	3	252	253	320	453	773	972	585	8	77	0.41	36	17	47	29	97	134	105	12%	105	5%	75%	26	50%	35%	4.87	4.4	66	178	$9
16 BOS *	226	31	9	26	4	268	261	332	476	808	999	766	9	74	0.37	25	25	50	32	112	142	127	12%	83	11%	67%	19	47%	32%	5.41	7.4	55	157	$6
17 BOS	243	30	7	25	3	235	234	322	387	709	590	793	11	77	0.55	35	19	46	28	93	88	89	8%	100	8%	60%	27	30%	52%	4.04	-10.3	34	103	$2
1st Half	146	19	4	17	3	260	251	343	397	741	602	815	12	81	0.68	35	23	42	30	118	80	100	8%	79	11%	60%	13	31%	38%	4.61	-3.2	36	109	$5
2nd Half	97	11	3	8	0	196	211	291	371	662	579	747	10	72	0.41	36	13	51	24	54	101	70	8%	123	0%	0%	14	29%	64%	3.27	-6.4	29	88	-$1
18 Proj	**253**	**34**	**9**	**27**	**3**	**236**	**239**	**318**	**418**	**736**	**740**	**732**	**10**	**75**	**0.44**	**32**	**19**	**48**	**28**	**91**	**109**	**100**	**10%**	**100**	**8%**	**67%**				**4.30**	**-1.2**	**36**	**108**	**$6**

Zimmer,Bradley

Age: 25 Bats: L Pos: CF | Ht: 6' 5" Wt: 220

Health A | PT/Exp C | Consist B | LIMA Plan C+ | Rand Var -3 | MM 2505

8-39-.241 with 18 SB in 299 AB at CLE. Former 1st-rounder showed flashes of power/speed combo that made him so coveted. But 3 reasons to expect pull-back in '18: 1) Shaky skills base crumbled late; 2) PX fueled by early fluky hr/f; 3) Still huge holes in swing. Plenty of question marks; don't roster expecting linear growth.

Yr Tm	AB	R	HR	RBI	SB	BA	xBA	OBP	SLG	OPS	vL	vR	bb%	ct%	Eye	G	L	F	h%	HctX	PX	xPX	hr/f	Spd	SBO	SB%	#Wk	DOM	DIS	RC/G	RAR	BPV	BPX	R$
13																																		
14																																		
15 aa	187	22	6	22	11	208		270	354	624			8	70	0.28				27		108			95	33%	83%				3.18		11	30	$4
16 a/a	468	62	13	51	31	230		324	382	706			12	63	0.38				33		115			105	36%	67%				3.91		4	11	$17
17 CLE *	425	58	12	50	25	248	236	309	410	719	624	714	8	66	0.26	48	20	32	35	90	112	83	13%	121	29%	85%	18	17%	61%	4.43	-3.9	9	27	$16
1st Half	247	32	8	33	14	269	262	333	454	787	566	848	9	68	0.29	48	26	26	37	90	129	74	19%	109	30%	76%	7	29%	43%	5.23	2.4	26	79	$20
2nd Half	178	26	4	17	11	219	208	283	348	631	662	621	7	65	0.22	48	16	36	32	89	88	90	10%	138	28%	100%	11	9%	73%	3.45	-8.0	-13	-39	$11
18 Proj	**473**	**63**	**11**	**53**	**29**	**231**	**224**	**313**	**367**	**680**	**612**	**702**	**10**	**66**	**0.32**	**48**	**20**	**32**	**33**	**89**	**96**	**84**	**11%**	**124**	**31%**	**79%**				**3.80**	**-10.3**	**1**	**3**	**$18**

Zimmerman,Ryan

Age: 33 Bats: R Pos: 1B | Ht: 6' 3" Wt: 225

Health D | PT/Exp B | Consist F | LIMA Plan B | Rand Var -5 | MM 3235

Turned back the clock and single-handedly carried owners to titles given 389 ADP at end of draft season. Fact or fluke? Doubling of hr/f, best h% since '10 say to side with latter. We just can't bet those marks will stick, nor can we bank on another 500 AB given health history. Heed 2nd half and expect substantial regression.

Yr Tm	AB	R	HR	RBI	SB	BA	xBA	OBP	SLG	OPS	vL	vR	bb%	ct%	Eye	G	L	F	h%	HctX	PX	xPX	hr/f	Spd	SBO	SB%	#Wk	DOM	DIS	RC/G	RAR	BPV	BPX	R$
13 WAS	568	84	26	79	6	275	267	344	465	809	850	794	9	77	0.45	45	21	34	32	128	127	144	18%	103	4%	100%	25	48%	24%	5.69	17.8	60	150	$23
14 WAS	214	26	5	38	0	280	284	342	449	790	779	794	9	83	0.59	44	21	35	32	121	128	115	8%	77	0%	0%	13	69%	15%	5.52	8.1	77	208	$6
15 WAS	346	43	16	73	1	249	275	308	465	773	1058	672	8	77	0.42	48	17	35	28	124	146	141	16%	73	1%	100%	17	47%	35%	4.97	-3.9	66	178	$10
16 WAS	427	60	15	46	4	218	243	272	370	642	683	632	6	76	0.28	49	17	35	25	106	94	99	13%	86	6%	80%	24	46%	46%	3.24	-27.5	18	51	$4
17 WAS	524	90	36	108	1	303	289	358	573	930	1038	895	8	76	0.35	46	20	34	34	124	152	138	26%	82	1%	100%	27	59%	30%	7.50	22.8	67	203	$26
1st Half	278	50	19	62	1	335	315	375	619	994	1062	976	6	80	0.34	45	23	32	36	132	157	136	26%	85	1%	100%	13	69%	15%	8.97	24.1	85	258	$33
2nd Half	246	40	17	46	0	268	255	338	520	859	1017	794	9	72	0.36	48	16	36	31	116	146	141	27%	80	0%	0%	14	50%	43%	6.09	3.1	47	142	$19
18 Proj	**452**	**69**	**22**	**79**	**2**	**271**	**264**	**327**	**475**	**802**	**928**	**762**	**8**	**76**	**0.34**	**47**	**18**	**35**	**31**	**119**	**119**	**128**	**18%**	**80**	**2%**	**87%**				**5.45**	**4.6**	**33**	**100**	**$17**

Zobrist,Ben

Age: 37 Bats: B Pos: 2B LF RF | Ht: 6' 3" Wt: 210

Health B | PT/Exp B | Consist C | LIMA Plan C | Rand Var +3 | MM 2243

Plagued by early back issues, then missed month with a wrist problem. Both explain nosedive in PX. As he ages, power is relegated to vL; last above-par PX vs. RH was in *2012*. Best hope is for BA rebound, as that h% shouldn't repeat and LD rate was likely impacted by injuries. Still, more likely to return $10 than $20 now.

Yr Tm	AB	R	HR	RBI	SB	BA	xBA	OBP	SLG	OPS	vL	vR	bb%	ct%	Eye	G	L	F	h%	HctX	PX	xPX	hr/f	Spd	SBO	SB%	#Wk	DOM	DIS	RC/G	RAR	BPV	BPX	R$
13 TAM	612	77	12	71	11	275	260	354	402	756	643	812	10	85	0.79	43	20	37	31	103	87	98	6%	105	7%	79%	27	63%	19%	4.98	23.1	64	160	$20
14 TAM	570	83	10	52	10	272	267	354	395	749	873	703	11	85	0.89	49	18	33	30	103	88	89	6%	112	8%	67%	25	60%	16%	4.88	24.5	70	189	$18
15 2 AL	467	76	13	56	3	276	293	359	450	809	926	753	12	88	1.11	49	19	32	29	107	108	85	10%	105	5%	43%	23	61%	9%	5.58	18.9	95	257	$15
16 CHC	523	94	18	76	6	272	288	386	446	831	856	823	15	84	1.17	48	22	30	29	111	99	94	13%	99	5%	60%	27	52%	19%	5.92	15.8	79	226	$18
17 CHC	435	58	12	50	2	232	257	318	375	693	553	737	11	84	0.76	51	16	33	25	109	76	84	10%	108	3%	50%	26	54%	27%	3.90	-14.7	52	158	$4
1st Half	189	21	7	21	0	222	258	319	392	711	612	739	12	83	0.81	51	15	34	23	120	85	102	13%	110	0%	0%	12	58%	17%	4.06	-4.4	59	179	$0
2nd Half	246	37	5	29	2	240	255	317	362	678	514	736	10	84	0.72	51	16	33	27	101	69	70	7%	104	6%	50%	14	50%	36%	3.77	-7.8	45	136	$8
18 Proj	**369**	**56**	**10**	**45**	**3**	**253**	**271**	**343**	**406**	**749**	**716**	**762**	**12**	**85**	**0.89**	**49**	**18**	**33**	**27**	**108**	**83**	**87**	**10%**	**105**	**5%**	**56%**				**4.69**	**-1.2**	**53**	**161**	**$10**

Zunino,Mike

Age: 27 Bats: R Pos: CA | Ht: 6' 2" Wt: 220

Health A | PT/Exp D | Consist D | LIMA Plan C+ | Rand Var -5 | MM 5125

25-64-.251 in 387 AB at SEA. Made annual trip to AAA after slumping, then finished with electric Sept. Given whiff rate, that inconsistency is embedded in his profile. Still, another uptick in LDs gives his BA some footing now, power is firmly elite, and keeps getting better vs. RH. Now's the time to speculate on... UP: 35 HR

Yr Tm	AB	R	HR	RBI	SB	BA	xBA	OBP	SLG	OPS	vL	vR	bb%	ct%	Eye	G	L	F	h%	HctX	PX	xPX	hr/f	Spd	SBO	SB%	#Wk	DOM	DIS	RC/G	RAR	BPV	BPX	R$
13 SEA *	376	49	12	44	1	201	219	256	350	606	650	609	7	67	0.22	43	19	39	26	92	117	108	10%	95	1%	100%	12	33%	67%	2.87	-9.9	6	15	$2
14 SEA	438	51	22	60	0	199	226	254	404	658	722	632	4	64	0.11	34	17	49	25	86	170	143	16%	90	5%	0%	27	30%	37%	2.83	-6.8	28	76	$5
15 SEA *	391	33	13	33	0	183	186	224	315	539	522	534	5	64	0.15	33	17	50	25	81	102	121	10%	79	1%	0%	21	14%	62%	2.17	-19.6	-27	-73	-$4
16 SEA *	444	53	26	76	0	228	227	304	446	749	835	769	10	66	0.32	29	18	53	28	95	146	155	23%	91	1%	0%	14	36%	43%	4.42	7.4	31	89	$8
17 SEA *	428	57	29	72	1	250	245	317	515	832	883	827	9	61	0.25	32	22	46	34	96	186	141	24%	82	1%	100%	24	50%	50%	5.57	18.0	38	115	$11
1st Half	222	29	15	43	0	239	248	296	498	794	913	755	8	62	0.21	32	24	44	31	99	179	134	24%	77	0%	0%	11	36%	64%	4.94	5.6	30	91	$11
2nd Half	206	28	14	29	1	262	245	350	534	884	860	892	10	61	0.30	32	21	47	36	92	194	148	24%	91	2%	100%	13	62%	38%	6.29	13.1	48	145	$12
18 Proj	**417**	**55**	**28**	**70**	**1**	**247**	**242**	**323**	**502**	**825**	**850**	**817**	**8**	**63**	**0.25**	**32**	**21**	**47**	**32**	**92**	**170**	**141**	**23%**	**82**	**1%**	**55%**				**5.24**	**13.6**	**16**	**50**	**$13**

TEPHEN NICKRAND

THE NEXT TIER

The preceding section provided player boxes and analysis for 441 batters. As we know, far more than 441 batters will play in the major leagues in 2018. Many of those additional hitters are covered in the minor league section, but that still leaves a gap: established major leaguers who don't play enough, or well enough, to merit a player box.

This section looks to fill that gap. Here, you will find "The Next Tier" of batters who are mostly past their growth years, but who are likely to see some playing time in 2018. We are including their 2016-17 MLB stats here for reference for you to do your own analysis. This way, if Craig Gentry stumbles into some playing time in June, a quick check would show that his Spd skills were an asset even in 2017. Or if you're looking for a short-term pop, the power skills of Tyler Moore are still intact.

Batter	Yr	B	Age	Pos	AB	R	HR	RBI	SB	BA	xBA	OPS	VL	VR	bb%	ct%	Eye	GLF	HctX	PX	xPX	SPD	SBO	SB%	BPV
Adduci, James	17	L	32	4o	83	14	1	10	1	241	240	720	664	728	11	67	.37	53/16/31	137	115	92	111	10	50	19
Alcantara, Arismendy	16	B	24	o	19	2	0	2	3	211	157	474	333	538	0	58	.00	64/0/36	64	61	112	118	200	50	-81
	17	B	25	o97	105	13	1	7	2	171	193	435	184	575	2	64	.05	59/12/29	49	56	23	124	13	100	-56
Almonte, Abraham	16	B	27	0	182	24	1	22	8	264	271	695	771	649	4	77	.19	48/21/31	96	109	85	64	24	100	24
	17	B	28	0	172	26	3	14	2	233	253	681	561	723	10	73	.43	51/22/27	86	85	84	114	7	67	18
Alvarez, Pedro	16	L	29	4	337	43	22	49	1	249	264	826	654	848	10	71	.38	47/17/36	112	163	120	68	1	100	57
	17	L	30	4o6	32	4	1	4	0	313	212	790	2333	633	6	69	.20	50/18/32	101	82	99	74	0	-	-22
Amarista, Alexi	16	L	27	3	140	9	0	11	9	257	230	567	293	612	5	81	.31	47/25/28	80	12	34	97	26	82	-22
	17	L	28	3	168	22	3	19	1	238	257	620	721	607	4	77	.18	46/24/30	79	77	70	85	3	100	7
Austin, Tyler	16	R	24	45	83	7	5	12	1	241	209	758	1097	621	8	57	.19	43/17/40	78	167	135	78	5	100	1
	17	R	25	543	40	4	2	8	0	225	239	708	1258	429	9	57	.24	28/32/40	93	157	154	77	0	-	-1
Blanco, Andres	16	B	32	o	190	26	4	21	2	253	271	721	551	764	5	78	.27	52/19/29	87	103	68	88	13	40	35
	17	B	33	o978	130	10	3	13	1	192	209	549	531	555	8	74	.35	51/15/34	73	63	64	69	3	100	-14
Bourjos, Peter	16	R	29	2	355	40	5	23	6	251	243	681	695	676	5	74	.19	51/17/32	69	90	66	178	14	60	34
	17	R	30	2	188	27	5	15	5	223	238	655	752	534	6	72	.23	49/16/36	87	101	73	158	24	56	29
Butera, Drew	16	R	32	35o	123	18	4	16	0	285	256	808	555	883	6	71	.22	40/22/38	71	138	95	102	0	-	38
	17	R	33	o978	163	18	3	14	0	227	215	603	596	606	7	75	.29	30/25/45	86	55	90	104	0	-	-9
Canha, Mark	16	R	27	4o	41	4	3	6	0	122	190	481	632	352	0	51	.00	36/18/45	81	167	157	94	50	0	-30
	17	R	28	o745	173	16	5	14	2	208	229	644	581	689	4	68	.13	33/20/47	77	128	75	93	8	100	10
Coghlan, Chris	16	L	31	o	261	35	6	30	2	188	237	608	427	627	12	72	.48	48/21/31	85	87	94	82	5	67	8
	17	L	32	o89	75	7	1	5	0	200	206	566	429	569	10	71	.41	42/23/35	73	47	84	83	0	-	-31
Collins, Tyler	16	L	26	4	136	14	4	15	1	235	220	687	311	780	9	72	.34	41/19/39	86	82	82	135	6	50	14
	17	L	27	465	150	18	5	14	0	193	201	611	382	628	11	63	.33	36/21/43	101	95	121	91	11	0	-19
Drew, Stephen	16	L	33	2	143	24	8	21	0	266	284	864	485	910	10	78	.52	32/22/47	132	155	187	93	3	0	87
	17	L	34	2	95	9	1	17	0	253	232	660	900	646	8	78	.38	34/21/45	98	78	87	66	0	-	11
Ellis, A.J.	16	R	35	o	171	11	2	22	2	216	238	599	566	620	10	82	.61	41/22/36	102	55	92	75	7	67	16
	17	R	36	o7	143	17	6	14	0	210	234	669	532	720	7	80	.41	50/14/37	95	89	89	79	0	-	31
Ethier, Andre	16	L	34	5	24	2	1	2	0	208	201	644	0	671	8	75	.33	39/11/50	68	102	114	81	0	-	23
	17	L	35	54	34	3	2	3	0	235	214	757	0	827	11	71	.40	54/17/29	107	123	119	81	0	-	28
Flaherty, Ryan	16	L	29	o	157	16	3	15	2	217	218	610	717	593	10	69	.35	56/17/27	79	75	54	99	5	100	-10
	17	L	30	o7	38	5	0	4	0	211	183	539	347	590	9	74	.40	54/14/32	43	24	27	90	0	-	-37
Franklin, Nick	16	B	25	2	174	18	6	26	6	270	243	771	554	828	6	76	.29	38/18/44	94	109	101	118	17	86	41
	17	B	26	2	106	9	2	12	2	179	250	552	0	644	8	79	.45	47/23/30	111	59	103	103	9	100	14
Garneau, Dustin	16	R	28	o	68	7	1	6	0	235	221	661	608	694	8	68	.27	30/22/48	94	113	138	88	0	-	6
	17	R	29	o97	112	10	2	9	0	188	222	585	699	453	10	68	.33	30/24/46	64	100	53	71	0	-	-5
Gentry, Craig	16	R	32	2	34	2	0	2	0	147	186	413	459	250	8	82	.50	64/11/25	23	24	29	92	0	-	-4
	17	R	33	2	101	17	2	11	5	257	260	719	786	626	9	76	.46	51/22/27	91	81	78	127	31	56	29
Gimenez, Chris	16	R	33	o	139	17	4	11	0	216	223	602	736	557	7	70	.24	49/21/30	94	75	113	78	0	-	-18
	17	R	34	o79	186	28	7	16	1	220	239	731	699	754	15	68	.55	37/26/37	84	111	99	71	2	100	12
Guyer, Brandon	16	R	30	o	293	39	9	32	3	266	263	795	1013	631	6	81	.35	41/22/38	93	95	80	91	7	60	43
	17	R	31	o7	165	23	2	20	2	236	230	654	691	577	8	74	.35	39/25/36	67	62	59	116	5	100	-1
Heisey, Chris	16	R	31	4o	139	18	9	17	0	216	231	736	764	722	9	68	.30	31/19/50	81	139	124	104	3	0	35
	17	R	32	45o	74	8	1	5	0	162	188	485	667	414	6	70	.23	39/12/49	71	73	116	108	0	-	-12
Kelly, Tyler	17	B	28	o79	89	11	2	14	0	191	243	595	492	642	8	72	.32	42/21/37	70	108	86	81	0	-	15
	16	B	27	o	58	9	1	7	0	241	207	697	974	559	16	84	###	41/12/47	108	51	122	134	0	-	53
Kim, Hyun-Soo	17	L	29	2	212	20	1	14	0	231	238	599	321	620	9	78	.48	47/24/29	89	43	82	101	0	-	14
	16	L	28	2	305	36	6	22	1	302	264	801	217	839	11	83	.71	53/21/27	102	72	78	115	4	25	48

Batter	Yr	B	Age	Pos	AB	R	HR	RBI	SB	BA	xBA	OPS	VL	VR	bb%	ct%	Eye	GLF	HctX	PX	xPX	SPD	SBO	SB%	BPV
Lobaton, Jose	16	B	31	o	99	10	3	8	0	232	255	692	443	737	11	82	.67	46/21/33	96	76	110	115	0	-	46
	17	B	32	8o9	141	11	4	11	0	170	209	525	416	564	9	75	.40	51/17/32	85	62	77	71	0	-	-8
Martin, Leonys	16	L	28	2	518	72	15	47	24	247	224	684	684	684	8	71	.30	43/20/37	85	84	79	133	22	80	10
	17	L	29	2	128	14	3	9	7	172	213	513	857	444	6	74	.24	46/15/39	76	64	100	113	48	64	-3
Mathis, Jeff	16	R	33	2	126	12	2	15	0	238	194	601	845	498	3	71	.11	41/16/43	76	63	101	108	0	-	-22
	17	R	34	2	186	13	2	11	1	215	219	600	677	573	7	67	.23	42/23/35	84	82	94	103	3	100	-18
Montero, Miguel	16	L	32	3o	241	33	8	33	1	216	236	684	439	727	14	76	.66	50/17/33	83	84	115	87	1	100	26
	17	L	33	o	185	24	6	16	1	216	216	656	582	668	11	75	.49	42/16/42	93	79	132	74	2	100	7
Moore, Tyler	17	R	30	o7	187	17	6	30	0	230	218	668	495	778	5	70	.18	36/14/50	94	123	138	69	0	-	11
Nava, Daniel	16	B	33	2	130	11	1	13	0	223	241	590	1167	579	7	77	.33	38/28/34	109	52	97	70	0	-	-12
	17	B	34	o	183	21	4	21	1	301	270	813	581	897	12	79	.68	44/28/29	109	73	94	87	1	100	28
Norris, Derek	16	R	27	o98	415	50	14	42	9	186	212	583	628	565	8	67	.26	35/22/43	93	100	103	49	13	82	-20
	17	R	28	4	179	21	9	24	1	201	241	637	741	605	6	73	.25	27/25/47	108	104	122	53	3	100	6
Orlando, Paulo	16	R	30	465	457	52	5	43	14	302	254	734	817	697	3	77	.12	52/22/26	91	70	67	150	14	82	17
	17	R	31	5	86	9	2	6	1	198	235	527	646	501	1	77	.05	43/22/35	113	65	97	86	15	50	-10
Pennington, Cliff	16	B	32	5	172	18	3	10	1	209	202	573	190	624	7	68	.24	40/22/38	67	64	65	121	3	100	-23
	17	B	33	2	194	23	3	21	3	253	197	635	512	690	7	70	.28	40/19/40	84	54	76	92	7	75	-31
Peralta, Jhonny	16	R	34	2	289	37	8	29	0	260	267	715	541	778	6	81	.36	41/24/35	105	92	103	93	0	-	39
	17	R	35	o	54	3	0	0	0	204	209	462	285	600	7	76	.31	44/27/29	67	0	11	82	0	-	-55
Phegley, Joshua	17	R	29	o987	149	14	3	10	0	201	241	590	600	582	6	83	.35	35/17/48	97	87	91	51	4	0	28
	16	R	28	6	78	11	1	10	0	256	250	686	658	709	6	83	.38	39/20/41	108	80	108	83	0	-	36
Presley, Alex	16	L	30	56	121	12	3	11	0	198	231	558	582	550	8	79	.44	46/22/32	90	50	99	75	7	0	-1
	17	L	31	2	245	30	3	20	5	314	278	770	579	797	6	80	.31	45/31/23	78	61	35	125	7	100	20
Reynolds, Matt	16	R	25	2	89	11	3	13	0	225	252	682	951	565	4	62	.12	55/24/22	75	161	85	85	8	0	12
	17	R	26	45	113	12	1	5	0	230	180	626	615	629	11	67	.38	55/12/33	64	41	24	183	3	0	-19
Ruiz, Carlos	16	R	37	54	201	21	3	15	3	264	246	713	793	668	12	84	.82	46/21/33	115	53	71	68	6	75	23
	17	R	38	o87	125	14	3	11	1	216	235	665	696	653	10	70	.37	44/22/34	92	100	124	70	3	100	1
Rutledge, Josh	16	R	27	o	49	9	0	3	2	265	220	733	859	669	11	61	.32	60/10/30	64	134	42	117	15	100	11
	17	R	28	2	107	10	0	9	1	224	208	558	620	536	8	71	.29	59/18/22	87	26	76	145	3	100	-33
Santana, Daniel	17	B	26	2	168	19	4	23	7	202	258	600	417	657	4	76	.20	54/15/31	103	98	121	103	27	100	23
	16	B	25	o789	233	29	2	14	12	240	246	606	404	658	5	76	.22	53/22/25	93	58	76	129	39	57	3
Stewart, Chris	16	R	34	o	98	10	1	7	0	214	225	604	778	563	11	85	.80	49/17/34	70	46	70	90	0	-	27
	17	R	35	5	131	8	0	4	0	183	236	463	303	513	6	83	.41	41/26/33	105	18	97	141	0	-	4
Szczur, Matthew	17	R	27	65	195	28	3	18	0	226	235	704	702	705	14	77	.77	39/19/43	63	84	72	131	3	0	47
	16	R	26	o	185	30	5	24	2	259	247	712	671	737	7	79	.33	43/20/38	72	86	56	123	13	33	36
Tejada, Ruben	16	R	26	o7	66	9	0	5	0	167	233	489	742	265	10	80	.54	42/20/38	74	63	80	97	0	-	22
	17	R	27	0o	113	17	0	5	0	230	240	576	624	559	6	87	.53	40/21/39	113	40	94	89	0	-	20
Van Slyke, Scott	16	R	29	o78	102	10	1	7	1	225	235	606	739	529	5	76	.21	39/24/37	98	66	102	98	14	33	0
	17	R	30	0	41	6	2	3	1	122	202	543	541	548	15	63	.47	31/19/50	118	114	214	97	11	100	5
Young Jr., Eric	16	B	31	0	1	2	0	0	1	0	0	000	0	0	0	100	.00	0/100/0	406	0	226	99	-	100	32
	17	B	32	0	110	24	4	16	12	264	253	754	596	828	4	72	.16	58/14/27	67	100	45	92		80	5

The following section contains player boxes for every pitcher who had significant playing time in 2017 and/or is expected to get fantasy roster-worthy innings in 2018. You will find some prospects here, specifically the most impactful names who we project to play in 2018. For more complete prospect coverage, see our Prospects section.

Snapshot Section

The top band of each player box contains the following information:

Age as of Opening Day 2018.

Throws right (R) or left (L).

Role: Starters (SP) are those projected to face 20+ batters per game; the rest are relievers (RP).

Ht/Wt: Each batter's height and weight.

Type evaluates the extent to which a pitcher allows the ball to be put into play and his ground ball or fly ball tendency. CON (contact) represents pitchers who allow the ball to be put into play a great deal. PWR (power) represents those with high strikeout and/or walk totals who keep the ball out of play. GB are those who have a ground ball rate more than 50%; xGB are those who have a GB rate more than 55%. FB are those who have a fly ball rate more than 40%; xFB are those who have a FB rate more than 45%.

Reliability Grades analyze each pitcher's forecast risk, on an A-F scale. High grades go to those who have accumulated few disabled list days (Health), have a history of substantial and regular major league playing time (PT/Exp) and have displayed consistent performance over the past three years, using xERA (Consist).

LIMA Plan Grade evaluates how well that pitcher would be a good fit for a team using the LIMA Plan draft strategy. Best grades go to pitchers who have excellent base skills and had a 2017 dollar value less than $20. Lowest grades will go to poor skills and values more than $20.

Random Variance Score (Rand Var) measures the impact random variance had on the pitcher's 2017 stats and the probability that his 2018 performance will exceed or fall short of 2017. The variables tracked are those prone to regression—H%, S%, hr/f and xERA to ERA variance. Players are rated on a scale of −5 to +5 with positive scores indicating rebounds and negative scores indicating corrections. Note that this score is computer-generated and the projections will override it on occasion.

Mayberry Method (MM) acknowledges the imprecision of the forecasting process by projecting player performance in broad strokes. The four digits of MM each represent a fantasy-relevant skill—ERA, strikeout rate, saves potential and playing time (IP)—and are all on a scale of 0 to 5.

Commentaries for each pitcher provide a brief analysis of his skills and the potential impact on performance in 2018. MLB statistics are listed first for those who played only a portion of 2017 at the major league level. Note that these commentaries generally look at performance related issues only. Role and playing time expectations may impact these analyses, so you will have to adjust accordingly. Upside (UP) and downside (DN) statistical potential appears for some players; these are less grounded in hard data and more speculative of skills potential.

Player Stat Section

The past five years' statistics represent the total accumulated in the majors as well as in Triple-A, Double-A ball and various foreign leagues during each year. All non-major league stats have been converted to a major league equivalent (MLE) performance level. Minor league levels below Double-A are not included.

Nearly all baseball publications separate a player's statistical experiences in the major leagues from the minor leagues and outside leagues. While this may be appropriate for official record-keeping purposes, it is not an easy-to-analyze snapshot of a player's complete performance for a given year.

Bill James has proven that minor league statistics (converted to MLEs), at Double-A level or above, provide as accurate a record of a player's performance as major league statistics. Other researchers have also devised conversion factors for foreign leagues. Since these are adequate barometers, we include them in the pool of historical data for each year.

Team designations: An asterisk (*) appearing with a team name means that Triple-A and/or Double-A numbers are included in that year's stat line. Any stints of less than 10 IP are not included (to screen out most rehab appearances). A designation of "a/a" means the stats were accumulated at both AA and AAA levels that year. "for" represents a foreign or independent league. The designation "2TM" appears whenever a player was on more than one major league team, crossing leagues, in a season. "2AL" and "2NL" represent more than one team in the same league. Players who were cut during the season and finished 2017 as a free agent are designated as FAA (Free agent, AL) and FAN (Free agent, NL).

Stats: Descriptions of all the categories appear in the Encyclopedia.

- The leading decimal point has been suppressed on some categories to conserve space.
- Data for platoons (vL, vR), balls-in-play (G/L/F) and consistency (Wk#, DOM, DIS) are for major league performance only.
- Formulas that use BIP data, like xERA and BPV, are used for years in which G/L/F data is available. Where feasible, older versions of these formulas are used otherwise.

Earned run average is presented alongside skills-based xERA. WHIP appears next, followed by opponents' overall OPS (oOPS). OPS splits vs. left-handed and right-handed batters appear to the right of oOPS. Batters faced per game (BF/G) provide a quick view of a pitcher's role—starters will generally have levels over 20.

Basic pitching skills are measured with Control, or walk rate (Ctl), Dominance, or strikeout rate (Dom), and Command, or strikeout-to-walk rate (Cmd). First-pitch strike rate (FpK) and Swinging strikeout rate (SwK) are also presented with these basic skills. Our research shows that FpK serves as a useful tool for validating Ctl, and SwK serves as a similar check on Dom.

Once the ball leaves the bat, it will either be a (G)round ball, (L)ine drive or (F)ly ball.

Random variance indicators include hit rate (H%)—often referred to as batting average on balls-in-play (BABIP)—which tends to regress to 30%. Normal strand rates (S%) fall within the tolerances of 65% to 80%. The ratio of home runs to fly balls (hr/f) is another sanity check; levels far from the league average of 14% are prone to regression.

In looking at consistency for starting pitchers, we track games started (GS), average pitch counts (APC) for all outings (for starters and relievers), the percentage of DOMinating starts (PQS 4 or 5) and DISaster starts (PQS 0 or 1). The larger the variance between DOM and DIS, the greater the consistency.

For relievers, we look at their saves success rate (Sv%) and Leverage Index (LI). A Doug Dennis study showed little correlation between saves success and future opportunity. However, you can increase your odds by prospecting for pitchers who have *both* a high saves percentage (80% or better) *and* high skills. Relievers with LI levels over 1.0 are being used more often by managers to win ballgames.

The final section includes several overall performance measures: runs above replacement (RAR), Base performance value (BPV), Base performance index (BPX, which is BPV indexed to each year's league average) and the Rotisserie value (R$).

2018 Projections

Forecasts are computed from a player's trends over the past five years. Adjustments were made for leading indicators and variances between skill and statistical output. After reviewing the leading indicators, you might opt to make further adjustments.

Although each year's numbers include all playing time at the Double-A level or above, the 2018 forecast only represents potential playing time at the major league level, and again is highly preliminary.

Note that the projected Rotisserie values in this book will not necessarily align with each player's historical actuals. Since we currently have no idea who is going to close games for the Angels, or whether Brent Honeywell is going to break camp with the Rays, it is impossible to create a finite pool of playing time, something which is required for valuation. So the projections are roughly based on a 12-team AL/NL league, and include an inflated number of innings, league-wide. This serves to flatten the spread of values and depress individual player dollar projections. In truth, a $25 player in this book might actually be worth $21, or $28. This level of precision is irrelevant in a process that is driven by market forces anyway. So, don't obsess over it.

Be aware of other sources that publish perfectly calibrated Rotisserie values over the winter. They are likely making arbitrary decisions as to where free agents are going to sign and who is going to land jobs in the spring. We do not make those leaps of faith here.

Bottom line… It is far too early to be making definitive projections for 2018, especially on playing time. Focus on the skill levels and trends, then consult BaseballHQ.com for playing time revisions as players change teams and roles become more defined. A free projections update will be available online in March.

Do-it-yourself analysis

Here are some data points you can look at in doing your own player analysis:

- Variance between vLH and vRH opposition OPS
- Variance in 2017 hr/f rate from 14%
- Variance in 2017 hit rate (H%) from 30%
- Variance in 2017 strand rate (S%) to tolerances (65% - 80%)
- Variance between ERA and xERA each year
- Growth or decline in Base Performance Value (BPV)
- Spikes in innings pitched
- Trends in average pitch counts (APC)
- Trends in DOM/DIS splits
- Trends in saves success rate (Sv%)
- Variance between Dom changes and corresponding SwK levels
- Variance between Ctl changes and corresponding FpK levels

Adams,Chance

Age: 23	Th: R	Role SP	Health A	LIMA Plan C	
Ht: 6' 0"	Wt: 215	Type Pwr FB	PT/Exp D	Rand Var -1	
			Consist C	MM 0100	

NYY prospect began 2017 at AA before quickly ascending to AAA in his second full pro season. While overall ERA/xERA is appealing, the steep 2nd half downturn further confirms that additional minor league seasoning is needed. Still has keeper intrigue, but don't expect a major contribution in 2018.

Yr Tm	W	L	Sv	IP	K	ERA	xERA	WHIP	oOPS	vL	vR	BF/G	Ctl	Dom	Cmd	FpK	SwK	G	L	F	H%	S%	hr/f	GS	APC	DOM%	DIS%	Sv%	LI	RAR	BPV	BPX	R$
13																																	
14																																	
15																																	
16 aa	8	1	0	70	63	2.83	2.13	0.98				20.3	3.3	8.1	2.5						21%	76%								11.7	91	108	$9
17 a/a	15	5	0	150	117	3.41	3.60	1.27				22.8	3.8	7.0	1.9						27%	77%								17.7	60	72	$13
1st Half	10	2	0	88	78	2.56	2.82	1.17				21.8	3.8	8.0	2.1						26%	82%								19.4	82	99	$24
2nd Half	5	3	0	63	39	4.58	4.68	1.42				24.2	3.7	5.6	1.5						28%	71%								-1.7	29	35	-$1
18 Proj	**3**	**1**	**0**	**29**	**23**	**4.32**	**5.02**	**1.39**				**23.1**	**3.6**	**7.2**	**2.0**	**9%**	**59%**	**40**	**18**	**42**	**29%**	**73%**	**11%**	**5**						**0.1**	**51**	**61**	**-$3**

Adleman,Timothy

Age: 30	Th: R	Role RP	Health D	LIMA Plan D+	
Ht: 6' 5"	Wt: 225	Type xFB	PT/Exp C	Rand Var +3	
			Consist A	MM 0100	

Minor-league journeyman found opportunity, and promptly wilted under the bright lights. Reasons to avoid: 1) Relies heavily on a poorly-located fastball that yields lots of fly balls and HR; 2) too many walks; 3) struggles vL (1.5 Cmd). Horrid DOM/DIS%, xERA and BPX underscore downside.

Yr Tm	W	L	Sv	IP	K	ERA	xERA	WHIP	oOPS	vL	vR	BF/G	Ctl	Dom	Cmd	FpK	SwK	G	L	F	H%	S%	hr/f	GS	APC	DOM%	DIS%	Sv%	LI	RAR	BPV	BPX	R$
13																																	
14 aa	3	8	0	79	57	3.53	4.51	1.36				11.0	2.5	6.5	2.6						31%	78%								2.0	61	73	-$1
15 aa	9	10	0	150	91	3.77	4.87	1.57				24.4	3.5	5.5	1.6						33%	77%								3.5	43	51	-$4
16 CIN *	7	5	0	126	76	3.85	4.70	1.33	779	787	773	22.8	2.3	5.4	2.3	65%	10%	36	18	45	29%	77%	14%	13	85	15%	69%			5.3	41	48	$2
17 CIN	5	11	0	122	108	5.52	5.06	1.43	872	939	819	17.7	3.8	7.9	2.1	60%	11%	34	19	47	29%	68%	17%	20	70	5%	65%	0	0.80	-17.5	54	65	-$5
1st Half	5	4	0	74	68	4.62	4.74	1.32	794	808	784	22.3	3.8	8.3	2.2	62%	11%	38	17	46	27%	73%	17%	13	86	8%	62%	0	0.76	-2.4	63	75	$2
2nd Half	0	7	0	48	40	6.89	5.54	1.59	984	1122	870	13.7	3.7	7.4	2.0	58%	11%	30	22	48	31%	63%	18%	7	55	0%	71%	0	0.84	-15.1	41	49	-$16
18 Proj	**2**	**5**	**0**	**58**	**43**	**4.87**	**5.35**	**1.45**	**896**	**953**	**848**	**17.2**	**3.2**	**6.7**	**2.1**	**62%**	**11%**	**34**	**19**	**46**	**30%**	**74%**	**15%**	**10**						**-3.7**	**46**	**55**	**-$5**

Alexander,Scott

Age: 28	Th: L	Role RP	Health B	LIMA Plan B	
Ht: 6' 2"	Wt: 190	Type Pwr xGB	PT/Exp D	Rand Var -1	
			Consist D	MM 3110	

Exceeded expectations and earned some late-season saves. PRO: Led MLB in GB% (min. 10 IP) with everpresent (92% of his pitches!) sinker; SwK/FpK hint at some Dom/Ctl upside. CON: 2nd half Cmd/Ctl slipped; overall Cmd vR (1.9) also worrisome. Elite GB% helps to cover, but flaws will block more Sv opps.

Yr Tm	W	L	Sv	IP	K	ERA	xERA	WHIP	oOPS	vL	vR	BF/G	Ctl	Dom	Cmd	FpK	SwK	G	L	F	H%	S%	hr/f	GS	APC	DOM%	DIS%	Sv%	LI	RAR	BPV	BPX	R$
13 aa	2	0	1	33	32	6.34	5.50	1.91				6.5	5.0	8.7	1.7						42%	63%								-10.1	79	102	-$8
14 a/a	2	4	3	68	38	5.33	4.88	1.50				6.4	3.5	5.1	1.5						31%	65%								-13.3	31	36	-$7
15 KC *	2	3	14	69	42	3.49	3.48	1.24	598	762	533	6.3	2.7	5.4	2.0	48%	8%	78	17	6	28%	74%	0%	0	22			78	0.03	4.1	57	68	$5
16 KC *	2	0	1	49	34	3.64	5.35	1.66	790	761	814	5.6	3.2	6.3	1.9	63%	13%	68	8	23	37%	79%	7%	0	19			25	0.52	3.3	53	63	-$4
17 KC	5	4	4	69	59	2.48	3.26	1.30	647	681	633	4.9	3.7	7.7	2.1	61%	14%	74	15	11	30%	82%	14%	0	18			67	1.38	16.0	92	110	$6
1st Half	0	2	0	29	25	2.15	3.00	1.13	575	831	483	5.8	3.1	7.7	2.5	63%	12%	75	14	11	28%	81%	11%	0	21			0	0.73	8.0	108	130	$2
2nd Half	5	2	4	40	34	2.72	3.46	1.44	697	586	744	4.4	4.1	7.7	1.9	59%	15%	73	17	10	32%	82%	17%	0	17			67	1.72	8.0	80	95	$10
18 Proj	**4**	**2**	**5**	**65**	**50**	**3.41**	**3.55**	**1.43**	**713**	**737**	**704**	**5.4**	**3.5**	**6.9**	**2.0**	**61%**	**14%**	**74**	**15**	**11**	**33%**	**76%**	**12%**	**0**						**7.6**	**82**	**99**	**$1**

Allen,Cody

Age: 29	Th: R	Role RP	Health A	LIMA Plan C+	
Ht: 6' 1"	Wt: 210	Type Pwr FB	PT/Exp A	Rand Var -2	
			Consist A	MM 4530	

Run of dominance continued. Renewed emphasis on getting ahead in count (FpK) paid dividends as Ctl, Cmd and BPX were career-bests. The substantial rise in FB% and the risk it presents in today's HR-happy climate is a concern, but the otherwise elite skill set should keep him in the upper tier of closers.

Yr Tm	W	L	Sv	IP	K	ERA	xERA	WHIP	oOPS	vL	vR	BF/G	Ctl	Dom	Cmd	FpK	SwK	G	L	F	H%	S%	hr/f	GS	APC	DOM%	DIS%	Sv%	LI	RAR	BPV	BPX	R$
13 CLE	6	1	2	70	88	2.43	3.48	1.25	679	691	669	3.9	3.3	11.3	3.4	55%	12%	30	25	45	33%	85%	9%	0	16			50	1.11	12.4	121	158	$7
14 CLE	6	4	24	70	91	2.07	3.08	1.06	601	451	757	3.7	3.4	11.8	3.5	63%	14%	36	15	48	28%	87%	9%	0	15			86	1.43	14.4	135	161	$18
15 CLE	2	5	34	69	99	2.99	3.01	1.17	596	512	676	4.1	3.2	12.9	4.0	60%	14%	33	26	41	36%	73%	3%	0	16			89	1.23	8.3	155	184	$18
16 CLE	3	5	32	68	87	2.51	3.08	1.00	584	677	501	3.9	3.6	11.5	3.2	55%	14%	46	18	36	24%	82%	15%	0	17			91	1.25	14.0	135	160	$21
17 CLE	3	7	30	67	92	2.94	3.50	1.16	649	545	727	4.1	2.8	12.3	4.4	59%	15%	34	20	46	33%	81%	12%	0	17			88	1.26	11.8	158	189	$18
1st Half	0	4	15	32	46	2.81	3.73	1.34	743	589	880	4.3	3.4	12.9	3.8	60%	14%	32	17	51	37%	87%	13%	0	18			94	1.18	6.1	152	182	$16
2nd Half	3	3	15	35	46	3.06	3.30	0.99	560	491	603	3.9	2.3	11.7	5.1	58%	16%	35	23	42	29%	74%	11%	0	16			83	1.32	5.7	162	194	$21
18 Proj	**3**	**6**	**38**	**68**	**90**	**2.78**	**3.37**	**1.11**	**618**	**571**	**657**	**3.8**	**3.1**	**12.1**	**3.9**	**58%**	**15%**	**37**	**21**	**43**	**31%**	**80%**	**11%**	**0**						**13.1**	**149**	**179**	**$22**

Altavilla,Dan

Age: 25	Th: R	Role RP	Health A	LIMA Plan C	
Ht: 5' 11"	Wt: 200	Type Pwr xFB	PT/Exp F	Rand Var -1	
			Consist C	MM 1400	

1-1, 4.24 ERA in 47 IP at SEA. Intriguing ability to miss bats with a nasty fastball/slider combo, but Ctl decayed from "acceptable" in 2016 to "shaky" in 1st half 2017 to "awful" in 2nd half. And FpK tracked it all the way. Add in an extreme FB% and there's reason to be wary. Don't fall in love with the Dom here.

Yr Tm	W	L	Sv	IP	K	ERA	xERA	WHIP	oOPS	vL	vR	BF/G	Ctl	Dom	Cmd	FpK	SwK	G	L	F	H%	S%	hr/f	GS	APC	DOM%	DIS%	Sv%	LI	RAR	BPV	BPX	R$
13																																	
14																																	
15																																	
16 SEA *	7	3	16	69	66	2.08	2.82	1.19	560	552	563	4.8	3.1	8.6	2.8	69%	12%	50	25	25	30%	84%	0%	0	11			76	0.61	17.9	106	126	$14
17 SEA *	3	1	6	70	82	3.44	4.31	1.40	765	687	813	4.8	4.5	10.6	2.3	55%	14%	36	17	47	31%	81%	15%	0	19			55	0.61	7.9	80	97	$4
1st Half	1	1	0	35	42	5.19	5.49	1.47	853	711	929	4.6	4.1	10.7	2.6	59%	13%	36	18	46	33%	72%	21%	0	17			0	0.75	-3.6	60	72	-$3
2nd Half	2	0	6	35	40	1.66	3.10	1.33	592	646	551	5.1	5.0	10.5	2.1	46%	14%	36	15	49	30%	90%	4%	0	22			86	0.29	11.5	103	123	$11
18 Proj	**3**	**1**	**0**	**44**	**47**	**3.89**	**4.50**	**1.31**	**713**	**676**	**738**	**4.8**	**4.0**	**9.8**	**2.4**	**52%**	**14%**	**36**	**16**	**48**	**29%**	**75%**	**12%**	**0**						**2.5**	**82**	**99**	**-$1**

Alvarez,Jose

Age: 29	Th: L	Role RP	Health A	LIMA Plan C	
Ht: 5' 11"	Wt: 190	Type Pwr	PT/Exp D	Rand Var 0	
			Consist A	MM 1200	

Former starter completes transition to a useful reliever. However, his struggles vR actually worsened in 2017 (1.7 Cmd) and threaten to pigeonhole him as a lefty specialist (lifetime 4.6 Cmd vL). He could have some value in deeper leagues that count Holds, but that's likely the extent of his fantasy relevance.

Yr Tm	W	L	Sv	IP	K	ERA	xERA	WHIP	oOPS	vL	vR	BF/G	Ctl	Dom	Cmd	FpK	SwK	G	L	F	H%	S%	hr/f	GS	APC	DOM%	DIS%	Sv%	LI	RAR	BPV	BPX	R$
13 DET *	9	11	1	167	123	4.14	4.33	1.33	866	851	872	19.8	2.3	6.6	2.9	55%	11%	40	23	37	31%	72%	16%	6	50	0%	50%	100	1.22	-5.6	68	89	$1
14 LAA *	0	2	0	31	15	5.64	5.65	1.53	667	0	2000	17.0	3.5	4.3	1.2	67%	20%	50	0	50	29%	67%	0%	0	5			0	1.79	-7.3	0	0	-$7
15 LAA	4	3	0	67	59	3.49	3.74	1.21	642	575	690	4.4	3.1	7.9	2.6	69%	11%	51	19	30	29%	72%	9%	0	16			0	0.89	3.9	88	105	$2
16 LAA	1	3	0	57	51	3.45	4.24	1.50	745	671	811	4.0	2.4	8.0	3.4	64%	10%	44	24	32	38%	78%	7%	0	15			0	0.94	5.2	103	122	-$2
17 LAA	0	3	1	49	45	3.88	4.15	1.27	733	715	749	3.2	2.2	8.3	3.8	60%	11%	39	24	37	32%	75%	13%	0	12			33	1.02	2.8	107	128	-$2
1st Half	0	3	1	30	27	5.40	4.33	1.23	756	781	722	3.1	1.8	8.1	4.5	58%	11%	35	22	43	30%	61%	15%	0	11			33	1.26	-3.9	110	132	-$3
2nd Half	0	0	0	19	18	1.45	3.85	1.34	696	610	793	3.3	2.9	8.7	3.0	64%	11%	45	28	26	34%	92%	7%	0	13			0	0.62	6.7	101	122	$0
18 Proj	**1**	**2**	**0**	**51**	**45**	**3.93**	**4.22**	**1.35**	**743**	**690**	**791**	**3.8**	**2.6**	**8.0**	**3.1**	**63%**	**11%**	**43**	**24**	**33**	**33%**	**74%**	**12%**	**0**						**2.7**	**95**	**115**	**-$2**

Anderson,Brett

Age: 30	Th: L	Role RP	Health F	LIMA Plan D+	
Ht: 6' 3"	Wt: 230	Type xGB	PT/Exp C	Rand Var +4	
			Consist C	MM 1001	

4-4, 6.34 ERA in 55 IP at CHC/TOR. 2013-15 track record featured stretches of effective pitching in between DL stints. Again missed significant time due to injury (back, finger), but skills decline now pairs with significant performance risk. Trend in DOM%/DIS% chronicles the carnage.

Yr Tm	W	L	Sv	IP	K	ERA	xERA	WHIP	oOPS	vL	vR	BF/G	Ctl	Dom	Cmd	FpK	SwK	G	L	F	H%	S%	hr/f	GS	APC	DOM%	DIS%	Sv%	LI	RAR	BPV	BPX	R$
13 OAK	1	4	3	45	46	6.04	3.36	1.61	794	853	774	12.5	4.2	9.3	2.2	58%	9%	63	16	21	37%	63%	18%	5	48	40%	40%	100	0.78	-12.0	94	122	-$7
14 COL	1	3	0	43	29	2.91	3.55	1.32	688	724	675	22.5	2.7	6.0	2.2	62%	9%	61	17	22	32%	77%	3%	8	83	25%	25%			4.5	75	89	-$1
15 LA	10	9	0	180	116	3.69	3.53	1.33	726	698	737	24.2	2.3	5.8	2.5	58%	8%	66	15	19	31%	75%	17%	31	88	13%	39%			6.0	86	103	$5
16 LA	1	2	0	11	5	11.91	6.27	2.56	1208	1267	1178	15.5	3.2	4.0	1.3	67%	6%	50	29	21	44%	56%	36%	3	52	0%	100%	0	0.71	-10.8	14	16	-$9
17 2 TM *	7	7	0	92	52	6.14	6.04	1.75	872	1078	830	20.1	3.4	5.0	1.5	57%	9%	49	29	22	36%	64%	12%	13	69	0%	46%			-20.3	27	33	-$12
1st Half	2	2	0	30	18	7.35	7.43	2.03	986	1304	916	18.2	4.3	5.5	1.3	53%	8%	50	33	17	39%	63%	14%	6	68	0%	33%			-11.1	13	15	-$19
2nd Half	5	5	0	62	33	5.52	5.32	1.61	785	887	763	21.2	2.9	4.8	1.6	61%	10%	49	25	26	35%	65%	11%	7	71	0%	57%			-8.9	36	43	-$9
18 Proj	**5**	**6**	**0**	**87**	**56**	**5.11**	**4.61**	**1.57**	**817**	**888**	**797**	**19.8**	**3.1**	**5.8**	**1.9**	**58%**	**9%**	**57**	**22**	**21**	**34%**	**67%**	**12%**	**15**						**-8.1**	**55**	**66**	**-$7**

GREG PYRON

Anderson,Chase

Age: 30	Th: R	Role SP	Health D	LIMA Plan C
Ht: 6' 1"	Wt: 200	Type Pwr FB	PT/Exp A	Rand Var -3
			Consist B	MM 1205

Enjoyed breakout 2017, but is it sustainable? PRO: SwK/FpK nicely support the Dom/Ctl gains; 2 mph uptick in velocity. CON: hr/f was a far cry from his prior mark (13%) and MLB average; growth vR influenced by low h%. He made real progress, but 2018 truth likely lies near the midpoint of xERA/ERA gap.

Yr Tm	W	L	Sv	IP	K	ERA	xERA	WHIP	oOPS	vL	vR	BF/G	Ctl	Dom	Cmd	FpK	SwK	G	L	F	H%	S%	hr/f	GS	APC	DOM%	DIS%	Sv%	LI	RAR	BPV	BPX	R$
13 aaa	4	7	0	88	63	5.76	5.84	1.67				15.2	3.1	6.4	2.0						36%	66%								-20.6	41	53	-$1
14 ARI *	13	9	0	153	135	3.23	3.79	1.25	779	714	831	23.1	2.7	7.9	2.9	63%	10%	40	24	36	30%	78%	14%	21	90	10%	33%			9.7	82	98	$
15 ARI	6	6	0	153	111	4.30	4.16	1.30	754	746	761	23.7	2.4	6.5	2.8	62%	8%	42	24	34	30%	69%	11%	27	91	11%	26%			-6.4	74	88	$(
16 MIL	9	11	0	152	120	4.39	4.75	1.37	819	664	935	20.9	3.1	7.1	2.3	58%	9%	36	23	41	29%	74%	15%	30	85	13%	47%	0	0.78	-3.8	57	68	$
17 MIL	12	4	0	141	133	2.74	4.11	1.09	647	607	679	22.8	2.6	8.5	3.2	61%	11%	39	18	43	27%	79%	9%	25	90	36%	20%			28.2	99	119	$2
1st Half	6	2	0	90	85	2.89	4.13	1.11	671	620	713	22.7	2.7	8.5	3.1	61%	11%	38	19	43	28%	77%	8%	16	90	38%	19%			16.4	96	115	$2
2nd Half	6	2	0	51	48	2.47	4.06	1.06	607	581	624	22.9	2.5	8.5	3.4	62%	10%	41	17	42	26%	83%	10%	9	90	33%	22%			11.9	105	126	$1
18 Proj	**13**	**9**	**0**	**189**	**162**	**3.61**	**4.46**	**1.24**	**742**	**674**	**794**	**21.4**	**2.7**	**7.7**	**2.8**	**61%**	**10%**	**39**	**20**	**40**	**29%**	**77%**	**13%**	**36**						**17.5**	**83**	**100**	**$1**

Anderson,Tyler

Age: 28	Th: L	Role SP	Health F	LIMA Plan C
Ht: 6' 4"	Wt: 210	Type Pwr	PT/Exp D	Rand Var +4
			Consist A	MM 1203

Two DL stints (knee), culminating in late-June surgery, cost him big chunk of 2017. Flashed enticing skills when healthy, results tarnished by hr/f. Traded some GB% for SwK-supported Dom gains, but xERA was unmoved. Health issues can't be ignored, but with another tweak, there is sub-4.00 upside here.

Yr Tm	W	L	Sv	IP	K	ERA	xERA	WHIP	oOPS	vL	vR	BF/G	Ctl	Dom	Cmd	FpK	SwK	G	L	F	H%	S%	hr/f	GS	APC	DOM%	DIS%	Sv%	LI	RAR	BPV	BPX	R$
13																																	
14 aa	7	4	0	118	83	2.94	3.64	1.38				21.6	3.4	6.3	1.8						31%	78%								11.7	68	81	$
15																																	
16 COL *	7	8	0	141	116	3.48	4.08	1.32	742	607	783	24.4	2.4	7.4	3.1	64%	11%	51	20	29	32%	76%	12%	19	94	16%	11%			12.3	84	100	$
17 COL	6	6	0	86	81	4.81	4.07	1.33	820	740	848	21.3	2.7	8.5	3.1	65%	12%	44	23	33	31%	69%	20%	15	83	13%	33%	0	0.78	-4.8	101	121	$
1st Half	3	5	0	63	63	6.11	4.27	1.55	936	875	958	21.6	3.3	9.0	2.7	64%	13%	44	24	32	34%	66%	25%	12	85	8%	42%	0	0.73	-13.7	94	113	-$
2nd Half	3	1	0	23	18	1.19	3.50	0.71	427	222	489	20.3	1.2	7.1	6.0	68%	11%	44	19	37	21%	87%	5%	3	76	33%	0%	0	0.94	8.9	119	142	$1
18 Proj	**11**	**8**	**0**	**145**	**126**	**4.18**	**4.19**	**1.33**	**791**	**650**	**837**	**22.7**	**2.6**	**7.8**	**3.1**	**65%**	**11%**	**47**	**21**	**33**	**32%**	**73%**	**14%**	**26**						**3.2**	**97**	**117**	**$**

Andriese,Matt

Age: 28	Th: R	Role SP	Health D	LIMA Plan C
Ht: 6' 2"	Wt: 225	Type	PT/Exp C	Rand Var +2
			Consist A	MM 1201

Missed significant time with injuries (groin, hip). Unable to build on late-2016 gains (2nd half: 147 BPV, 9.0 Dom), and FpK/Ctl slip here is problematic. Dom spike dating back to mid-2016 has been offset by big problems with HRs, and righties pounding him. Current approach not working, watch from afar for now.

Yr Tm	W	L	Sv	IP	K	ERA	xERA	WHIP	oOPS	vL	vR	BF/G	Ctl	Dom	Cmd	FpK	SwK	G	L	F	H%	S%	hr/f	GS	APC	DOM%	DIS%	Sv%	LI	RAR	BPV	BPX	R$
13 a/a	11	7	0	135	91	3.36	3.52	1.28				20.4	1.8	6.1	3.4						33%	73%								8.4	97	127	$
14 aaa	11	8	0	162	107	4.83	4.94	1.46				24.8	2.9	5.9	2.1						32%	69%								-21.8	44	53	-$
15 TAM *	6	8	2	131	105	3.59	4.31	1.36	728	785	677	14.4	2.0	7.3	3.7	59%	9%	48	17	35	35%	75%	11%	8	44	13%	50%	100	0.77	6.0	97	115	$
16 TAM *	9	10	1	162	145	4.49	4.24	1.27	720	706	732	19.0	1.8	8.0	4.3	66%	11%	43	19	38	33%	67%	11%	19	68	11%	26%	100	0.81	-6.1	107	127	$
17 TAM	5	5	1	86	76	4.50	4.43	1.37	795	617	931	20.8	2.9	8.0	2.7	61%	11%	45	20	35	31%	74%	17%	17	80	12%	41%	100	0.73	-1.5	87	105	$
1st Half	5	1	0	61	55	3.54	4.29	1.31	754	564	902	21.8	3.1	8.1	2.6	60%	11%	46	20	34	30%	80%	16%	12	86	17%	33%			6.1	87	104	$
2nd Half	0	4	1	25	21	6.84	4.77	1.52	888	741	997	18.8	2.5	7.6	3.0	63%	13%	42	21	37	34%	59%	19%	5	68	0%	60%	100	0.64	-7.7	88	105	-$1
18 Proj	**5**	**8**	**0**	**102**	**86**	**4.30**	**4.41**	**1.38**	**785**	**708**	**848**	**21.2**	**2.4**	**7.6**	**3.2**	**63%**	**11%**	**44**	**20**	**36**	**33%**	**74%**	**14%**	**20**						**0.7**	**95**	**114**	**-$**

Archer,Chris

Age: 29	Th: R	Role SP	Health A	LIMA Plan B
Ht: 6' 2"	Wt: 195	Type Pwr	PT/Exp A	Rand Var +4
			Consist A	MM 3505

Failed to deliver ace results for second consecutive year, despite strong skills. PRO: Punched up Dom to a new level; career-best Cmd; incredibly durable. CON: Continued hr/f problems killed him -join the club. Don't pay for an ace, though there's still one trapped in here somewhere. UP: That nice xERA and beyond

Yr Tm	W	L	Sv	IP	K	ERA	xERA	WHIP	oOPS	vL	vR	BF/G	Ctl	Dom	Cmd	FpK	SwK	G	L	F	H%	S%	hr/f	GS	APC	DOM%	DIS%	Sv%	LI	RAR	BPV	BPX	R$
13 TAM *	14	10	0	179	144	3.64	3.79	1.27	660	801	455	22.1	3.1	7.3	2.4	58%	9%	47	19	34	29%	75%	12%	23	91	26%	30%			5.1	66	87	$1
14 TAM	10	9	0	195	173	3.33	3.68	1.28	650	624	685	25.7	3.3	8.0	2.4	57%	10%	47	22	31	31%	75%	7%	32	99	31%	19%			9.9	79	94	$
15 TAM	12	13	0	212	252	3.23	3.12	1.14	613	604	622	25.5	2.8	10.7	3.8	64%	13%	46	20	34	31%	74%	10%	34	101	44%	15%			19.2	141	168	$2
16 TAM	9	19	0	201	233	4.02	3.50	1.24	703	698	708	25.8	3.0	10.4	3.5	58%	13%	48	18	35	31%	73%	16%	33	103	36%	27%			4.1	133	158	$1
17 TAM	10	12	0	201	249	4.07	3.50	1.26	710	760	666	25.1	2.7	11.1	4.2	62%	14%	42	22	36	34%	72%	14%	34	100	35%	12%			7.0	148	178	$1
1st Half	6	5	0	110	131	3.92	3.51	1.21	683	766	618	26.9	2.7	10.7	4.0	61%	13%	43	22	36	33%	70%	11%	17	106	47%	12%			6.0	140	168	$1
2nd Half	4	7	0	91	118	4.27	3.50	1.32	742	754	730	23.2	2.7	11.7	4.4	64%	14%	41	22	36	36%	74%	18%	17	95	24%	12%			1.0	158	189	$
18 Proj	**12**	**12**	**0**	**203**	**240**	**3.77**	**3.53**	**1.23**	**686**	**707**	**665**	**23.9**	**2.8**	**10.6**	**3.8**	**61%**	**13%**	**44**	**21**	**35**	**32%**	**74%**	**15%**	**34**						**14.8**	**137**	**165**	**$1**

Arrieta,Jake

Age: 32	Th: R	Role SP	Health B	LIMA Plan C
Ht: 6' 4"	Wt: 225	Type Pwr	PT/Exp A	Rand Var 0
			Consist B	MM 1205

Missed a couple weeks in Sept (hamstring). Things aren't quite as rosy as the surface stats would suggest. Three reasons for concern: 1) ERA/xERA are trending in the wrong direction; 2) SwK/FpK suggest Dom/Ctl downside; 3) 2 mph drop in velocity compared to 2016. Full season xERA is your caution indicator.

Yr Tm	W	L	Sv	IP	K	ERA	xERA	WHIP	oOPS	vL	vR	BF/G	Ctl	Dom	Cmd	FpK	SwK	G	L	F	H%	S%	hr/f	GS	APC	DOM%	DIS%	Sv%	LI	RAR	BPV	BPX	R$
13 2 TM *	12	9	0	155	120	5.06	4.43	1.49	718	664	775	22.2	4.4	7.0	1.6	60%	7%	40	25	34	31%	67%	12%	14	90	14%	29%			-22.8	50	65	-$
14 CHC	10	5	0	157	167	2.53	2.79	0.99	535	553	520	24.6	2.4	9.6	4.1	59%	11%	49	22	28	28%	74%	4%	25	97	60%	12%			23.4	136	162	$2
15 CHC	22	6	0	229	236	1.77	2.62	0.86	507	449	557	26.4	1.9	9.3	4.9	60%	11%	56	21	23	25%	81%	8%	33	104	67%	3%			62.0	150	179	$5
16 CHC	18	8	0	197	190	3.10	3.60	1.08	583	612	557	25.6	3.5	8.7	2.5	59%	11%	53	20	28	25%	74%	11%	31	101	42%	19%			26.5	93	111	$2
17 CHC	14	10	0	168	163	3.53	4.03	1.22	716	843	610	23.6	2.9	8.7	3.0	58%	9%	45	21	34	29%	76%	14%	30	91	20%	27%			17.2	100	121	$1
1st Half	7	6	0	89	93	4.67	3.99	1.36	767	843	708	24.0	3.1	9.4	3.0	60%	10%	44	24	32	33%	69%	16%	16	93	19%	25%			-3.4	107	128	$
2nd Half	7	4	0	80	70	2.26	4.07	1.05	654	843	488	23.1	2.7	7.9	2.9	56%	8%	46	17	37	24%	86%	12%	14	90	21%	29%			20.6	94	112	$2
18 Proj	**13**	**10**	**0**	**189**	**171**	**3.75**	**4.13**	**1.26**	**709**	**784**	**645**	**24.4**	**3.4**	**8.2**	**2.4**	**58%**	**10%**	**49**	**20**	**31**	**29%**	**73%**	**13%**	**32**						**14.2**	**82**	**99**	**$1**

Asher,Alec

Age: 26	Th: R	Role RP	Health A	LIMA Plan D+
Ht: 6' 4"	Wt: 230	Type xFB	PT/Exp D	Rand Var +2
			Consist F	MM 0000

2-5, 5.25 ERA in 60 IP at BAL. Came back from a PED suspension in 2016 with five solid September starts, offering hope for 2017. That never happened. While we might still hope for a return to 2016, those soft skills didn't provide much of a foundation anyway. Pass. And if given a chance, pass again.

Yr Tm	W	L	Sv	IP	K	ERA	xERA	WHIP	oOPS	vL	vR	BF/G	Ctl	Dom	Cmd	FpK	SwK	G	L	F	H%	S%	hr/f	GS	APC	DOM%	DIS%	Sv%	LI	RAR	BPV	BPX	R$
13																																	
14 aa	11	11	0	154	102	4.66	4.29	1.26				22.5	1.9	6.0	3.1						30%	66%								-17.5	66	79	-$
15 PHI *	6	16	0	163	110	5.58	6.20	1.55	1019	1075	955	22.9	2.8	6.1	2.2	59%	8%	36	19	45	32%	70%	16%	7	72	14%	86%			-32.4	18	21	-$
16 PHI *	6	3	0	86	47	2.80	2.72	1.01	551	636	439	23.6	1.3	4.9	3.8	56%	6%	35	23	42	26%	75%	3%	5	85	0%	20%			14.8	95	112	$
17 BAL *	5	8	0	110	77	5.86	6.15	1.65	793	683	891	14.5	3.4	6.3	1.9	53%	9%	39	19	42	34%	67%	13%	6	45	33%	50%	0	0.75	-20.4	26	31	-$
1st Half	2	5	0	60	47	5.13	4.67	1.38	795	734	852	11.4	3.2	7.1	2.2	53%	9%	39	19	41	30%	66%	13%	6	47	33%	50%	0	0.83	-5.7	50	60	-$
2nd Half	3	3	0	51	30	6.72	7.88	1.97	768	0	1250	20.2	3.6	5.3	1.5	50%	6%	33	13	53	39%	68%	13%	0	29			0	0.21	-14.7	-1	-1	-$
18 Proj	**2**	**3**	**0**	**44**	**28**	**5.06**	**5.43**	**1.48**	**789**	**725**	**848**	**18.5**	**2.6**	**5.8**	**2.2**	**53%**	**9%**	**39**	**19**	**41**	**32%**	**69%**	**10%**	**9**						**-3.8**	**50**	**60**	**-**

Baez,Pedro

Age: 30	Th: R	Role RP	Health C	LIMA Plan A
Ht: 6' 0"	Wt: 230	Type Pwr FB	PT/Exp C	Rand Var -5
			Consist B	MM 2410

Nudged ERA below 3.00, but this wasn't a growth year. First-half skills plunge was a warning sign for second half collapse. Ctl/FpK deteriоriation plus return of prior FB% lean is combustible combo, producing massive xERA/ERA gap. Still a big arm, but lost some luster in Holds leagues, and Saves are further away than ever.

Yr Tm	W	L	Sv	IP	K	ERA	xERA	WHIP	oOPS	vL	vR	BF/G	Ctl	Dom	Cmd	FpK	SwK	G	L	F	H%	S%	hr/f	GS	APC	DOM%	DIS%	Sv%	LI	RAR	BPV	BPX	R$
13 aa	1	1	0	23	19	5.47	6.30	1.71				6.6	3.2	7.3	2.3						37%	71%								-4.6	41	53	
14 LA *	2	1	12	66	49	3.28	3.40	1.16	537	578	501	4.4	2.2	6.7	3.0	61%	10%	37	15	49	28%	75%	9%	0	18			100	0.46	3.7	81	97	
15 LA	4	2	0	51	60	3.35	3.27	1.14	693	735	678	4.0	1.9	10.6	5.5	66%	16%	38	19	44	34%	72%	7%	0	16			0	1.20	3.8	154	184	
16 LA	3	2	0	74	83	3.04	3.39	1.00	615	553	649	4.0	2.7	10.1	3.8	63%	15%	43	20	38	25%	78%	16%	0	16			0	1.02	10.5	130	155	
17 LA	3	6	0	64	64	2.95	4.82	1.33	728	678	763	4.2	4.1	9.0	2.2	58%	16%	35	22	43	29%	84%	11%	0	18			0	1.00	11.1	65	78	
1st Half	2	1	0	34	33	1.32	4.59	1.18	616	701	562	4.2	4.0	8.7	2.2	61%	17%	39	20	41	26%	95%	8%	0	17			0	0.85	12.7	67	80	
2nd Half	1	5	0	30	31	4.80	5.07	1.50	847	654	1001	4.3	4.2	9.3	2.2	54%	16%	30	24	46	32%	74%	15%	0	18			0	1.16	-1.6	62	74	
18 Proj	**3**	**5**	**1**	**65**	**70**	**3.57**	**4.11**	**1.22**	**707**	**646**	**744**	**4.0**	**3.2**	**9.6**	**3.0**	**60%**	**16%**	**37**	**21**	**42**	**29%**	**76%**	**13%**	**0**						**6.3**	**101**	**121**	

GREG PYRON

Bailey,Homer

Age: 32 | Th: R | Role: SP | Ht: 6' 4" | Wt: 225 | Type: Pwr
Health: F | PT/Exp: D | Consist: F
LIMA Plan: C | Rand Var: +5 | MM: 1203

2nd year back from TJS, missed most of 1st half following surgery to remove bone chips from elbow. Surface stats were unsightly, but his velocity, SwK and FpK returned to near pre-injury level as he clawed his way back to form (Sept: 4.08 ERA, 68 BPV). Major health risk, but worthy of an end-game flyer.

Yr Tm	W	L	Sv	IP	K	ERA	xERA	WHIP	oOPS	vL	vR	BF/G	Ctl	Dom	Cmd	FpK	SwK	G	L	F	H%	S%	hr/f	GS	APC	DOM%	DIS%	Sv%	LI	RAR	BPV	BPX	R$
13 CIN	11	12	0	209	199	3.49	3.29	1.12	660	746	575	26.5	2.3	8.6	3.7	64%	11%	46	19	34	29%	72%	10%	32	103	38%	22%			9.7	115	150	$16
14 CIN	9	5	0	146	124	3.71	3.46	1.23	703	750	666	26.3	2.8	7.7	2.8	62%	11%	51	21	29	29%	73%	13%	23	99	35%	26%			0.6	92	109	$5
15 CIN	0	1	0	11	3	5.56	5.64	1.76	1009	1424	707	25.5	3.2	2.4	0.8	63%	7%	52	17	31	31%	76%	23%	2	86	0%	100%			-2.2	-13	-15	-$6
16 CIN *	3	6	0	51	44	7.51	9.32	2.13	816	968	706	18.0	3.7	7.7	2.1	54%	10%	45	30	25	43%	69%	11%	6	76	17%	33%			-20.9	-1	-1	-$15
17 CIN	6	9	0	91	67	6.43	5.19	1.69	875	817	931	23.3	4.2	6.6	1.6	61%	10%	45	27	28	35%	62%	13%	18	88	6%	61%			-23.2	30	36	-$12
1st Half	0	2	0	5	4	27.00	9.28	3.64	1524	1205	1675	16.5	9.6	7.7	0.8	52%	13%	45	32	23	50%	21%	60%	2	66	0%	100%			-13.0	-98	-118	-$26
2nd Half	6	7	0	86	63	5.32	5.00	1.59	824	798	851	24.2	3.9	6.6	1.7	62%	10%	45	27	29	34%	67%	10%	16	90	6%	56%			-10.2	37	44	-$11
18 Proj	**8**	**9**	**0**	**145**	**121**	**4.44**	**4.50**	**1.43**	**809**	**844**	**775**	**23.5**	**3.2**	**7.5**	**2.3**	**63%**	**11%**	**47**	**22**	**31**	**32%**	**72%**	**14%**	**22**						**-1.4**	**73**	**87**	**$0**

Barnes,Daniel

Age: 28 | Th: R | Role: RP | Ht: 6' 1" | Wt: 195 | Type: Pwr xFB
Health: A | PT/Exp: D | Consist: F
LIMA Plan: B+ | Rand Var: -3 | MM: 1300

First extended MLB action was a tale of two halves. 1st half skills, though aided by some H%/S% fortune, were sturdy. Things disintegrated in 2nd half, despite continued favorable H% and healthy FpK/SwK. Overall, extreme FB% makes him HR prone, and xERA urges caution. Unless 1st half Dom returns, just a guy.

Yr Tm	W	L	Sv	IP	K	ERA	xERA	WHIP	oOPS	vL	vR	BF/G	Ctl	Dom	Cmd	FpK	SwK	G	L	F	H%	S%	hr/f	GS	APC	DOM%	DIS%	Sv%	LI	RAR	BPV	BPX	R$
13																																	
14																																	
15 aa	3	2	4	61	61	3.99	5.81	1.67				6.8	3.1	9.0	2.9						40%	79%								-0.2	76	91	-$4
16 TOR *	3	1	6	75	74	1.62	1.12	0.76	700	633	743	5.1	1.4	8.9	6.2	60%	12%	38	18	44	23%	83%	0%	0	20			100	0.69	23.8	188	224	$16
17 TOR	3	6	0	66	62	3.55	4.60	1.09	646	518	728	4.4	3.3	8.5	2.6	62%	12%	32	16	52	23%	75%	12%	0	18			0	1.20	6.6	74	89	$4
1st Half	1	2	0	35	39	2.57	4.10	0.97	546	427	606	4.9	2.8	10.0	3.5	62%	13%	29	16	55	24%	80%	8%	0	21			0	0.93	7.7	111	133	$6
2nd Half	2	4	0	31	23	4.65	5.23	1.23	758	591	887	4.0	3.8	6.7	1.8	62%	11%	36	16	49	22%	71%	16%	0	15			0	1.43	-1.1	32	38	$0
18 Proj	**3**	**3**	**0**	**58**	**55**	**4.14**	**4.55**	**1.18**	**716**	**571**	**812**	**4.9**	**2.7**	**8.5**	**3.2**	**62%**	**12%**	**33**	**16**	**51**	**28%**	**71%**	**11%**	**0**						**1.6**	**91**	**110**	**$0**

Barnes,Jacob

Age: 28 | Th: R | Role: RP | Ht: 6' 2" | Wt: 220 | Type: Pwr GB
Health: B | PT/Exp: D | Consist: D
LIMA Plan: A | Rand Var: +2 | MM: 2400

Generates lots of strikeouts and groundballs with combination of 97 mph fastball and elite slider (26% SwK, 59% GB%). He also made strides vL, doubling his K% against them while allowing just 1 HR in 2017. FpK implies some Ctl upside, and if it materializes, he could take the next step forward... in results and role.

Yr Tm	W	L	Sv	IP	K	ERA	xERA	WHIP	oOPS	vL	vR	BF/G	Ctl	Dom	Cmd	FpK	SwK	G	L	F	H%	S%	hr/f	GS	APC	DOM%	DIS%	Sv%	LI	RAR	BPV	BPX	R$
13																																	
14 aa	2	6	0	106	63	5.25	4.56	1.43				19.5	3.5	5.4	1.6						30%	64%								-19.6	35	42	-$9
15 aa	4	5	0	75	68	4.85	5.20	1.73				8.7	4.1	8.2	2.0						39%	70%								-8.2	74	88	-$8
16 MIL *	2	2	2	52	48	2.09	2.62	1.11	612	820	437	4.3	2.4	8.3	3.5	62%	16%	49	21	31	30%	83%	5%	0	15			67	0.55	13.4	120	142	$5
17 MIL	3	4	2	72	80	4.00	3.68	1.25	664	686	645	4.2	4.1	10.0	2.4	60%	16%	53	20	27	28%	71%	16%	0	17			29	1.10	3.2	100	120	$2
1st Half	1	1	2	37	42	3.93	3.56	1.28	673	669	677	3.9	3.9	10.3	2.6	61%	15%	53	20	27	31%	72%	16%	0	16			67	1.09	1.9	111	133	$2
2nd Half	2	3	0	35	38	4.08	3.80	1.22	656	702	615	4.4	4.3	9.7	2.2	59%	16%	53	19	28	26%	69%	16%	0	17			0	1.11	1.2	89	106	$3
18 Proj	**3**	**4**	**0**	**65**	**69**	**3.64**	**3.72**	**1.30**	**690**	**739**	**649**	**5.0**	**3.7**	**9.5**	**2.6**	**60%**	**16%**	**53**	**19**	**27**	**32%**	**74%**	**11%**	**0**						**5.8**	**104**	**125**	**$1**

Barnes,Matt

Age: 28 | Th: R | Role: RP | Ht: 6' 4" | Wt: 210 | Type: Pwr
Health: A | PT/Exp: D | Consist: C
LIMA Plan: A | Rand Var: +2 | MM: 2400

Beneath the near-4.00 ERA lies some interesting peripherals. The groundball lean is a nice asset, especially in today's game. Pair it with a double-digit Dom and you have our attention. A look under the hood also tells us a 36% H% obscured progress vL (2.9 Cmd). FpK/Ctl isn't ideal, but he's a solid option in Holds leagues.

Yr Tm	W	L	Sv	IP	K	ERA	xERA	WHIP	oOPS	vL	vR	BF/G	Ctl	Dom	Cmd	FpK	SwK	G	L	F	H%	S%	hr/f	GS	APC	DOM%	DIS%	Sv%	LI	RAR	BPV	BPX	R$
13 a/a	6	10	0	113	119	5.01	5.09	1.59				20.0	3.8	9.4	2.5						38%	70%								-16.0	78	101	-$8
14 BOS *	8	9	0	137	93	4.98	4.57	1.50	861	1000	762	21.1	3.3	6.1	1.8	67%	13%	31	21	48	33%	66%	7%	0	31			0	0.27	-21.0	54	64	-$9
15 BOS *	4	5	0	81	72	5.68	6.34	1.77	887	800	959	7.6	4.5	8.1	1.8	58%	10%	39	22	40	37%	71%	16%	2	25	0%	100%	0	0.88	-17.1	37	44	-$12
16 BOS	4	3	1	67	71	4.05	4.03	1.40	711	741	693	4.6	4.2	9.6	2.3	58%	11%	46	21	33	32%	72%	10%	0	19			50	1.08	1.1	84	99	$0
17 BOS	7	3	1	70	83	3.88	3.41	1.22	655	792	577	4.1	3.6	10.7	3.0	57%	13%	49	23	28	31%	71%	14%	0	17			33	0.95	4.1	122	147	$5
1st Half	5	2	0	37	46	3.68	3.48	1.25	641	806	546	4.1	4.7	11.3	2.4	58%	13%	48	26	25	29%	72%	14%	0	18			0	0.93	3.1	104	124	$6
2nd Half	2	1	1	33	37	4.09	3.35	1.18	670	776	609	4.1	2.5	10.1	4.1	57%	12%	49	20	31	32%	69%	15%	0	16			50	0.97	1.1	143	171	$3
18 Proj	**5**	**3**	**0**	**65**	**73**	**3.64**	**3.78**	**1.34**	**705**	**762**	**669**	**4.9**	**3.7**	**10.1**	**2.7**	**58%**	**12%**	**48**	**22**	**30**	**33%**	**76%**	**14%**	**0**						**5.8**	**107**	**128**	**$1**

Barnette,Tony

Age: 34 | Th: R | Role: RP | Ht: 6' 1" | Wt: 190 | Type: Pwr
Health: B | PT/Exp: C | Consist: C
LIMA Plan: C | Rand Var: +5 | MM: 1310

Second year back from a six-season stint in Japan didn't go nearly as well as the first, but BPV/BPX actually says he was the same guy both years. History of shaky Ctl implies that this is his baseline, and even with added Dom, Cmd hovers around average. Trouble vL also keeps him from a high-leverage role.

Yr Tm	W	L	Sv	IP	K	ERA	xERA	WHIP	oOPS	vL	vR	BF/G	Ctl	Dom	Cmd	FpK	SwK	G	L	F	H%	S%	hr/f	GS	APC	DOM%	DIS%	Sv%	LI	RAR	BPV	BPX	R$
13 for	1	8	7	40	59	7.55	4.95	1.56				3.7	5.3	13.2	2.5						37%	52%								-18.2	91	119	-$7
14 for	1	2	14	32	40	4.19	4.67	1.33				4.0	3.8	11.2	2.9						31%	77%								-1.8	79	94	$3
15 for	3	1	41	63	53	1.42	1.59	1.00				4.1	3.4	7.6	2.3						23%	87%								19.8	104	124	$25
16 TEX	7	3	0	60	49	2.09	3.83	1.16	638	777	523	4.6	2.4	7.3	3.1	57%	12%	46	25	29	29%	85%	8%	0	17			0	1.16	15.6	91	108	$7
17 TEX	2	1	2	57	57	5.49	4.44	1.50	809	898	764	5.0	3.5	8.9	2.6	60%	13%	41	22	36	35%	65%	11%	0	21			33	0.94	-8.0	87	104	-$5
1st Half	1	1	0	24	24	7.23	4.42	1.69	914	794	987	4.7	3.4	9.1	2.7	62%	14%	47	21	32	39%	58%	17%	0	19			0	1.15	-8.4	97	117	-$11
2nd Half	1	0	2	34	33	4.28	4.44	1.37	729	994	616	5.3	3.5	8.8	2.5	59%	13%	36	23	40	33%	70%	8%	0	22			100	0.76	0.3	79	95	-$1
18 Proj	**3**	**2**	**1**	**58**	**56**	**4.06**	**4.21**	**1.34**	**720**	**816**	**661**	**4.6**	**3.3**	**8.7**	**2.6**	**59%**	**13%**	**43**	**24**	**33**	**32%**	**72%**	**11%**	**0**						**2.1**	**88**	**106**	**$0**

Barraclough,Kyle

Age: 28 | Th: R | Role: RP | Ht: 6' 3" | Wt: 225 | Type: Pwr
Health: B | PT/Exp: D | Consist: B
LIMA Plan: B+ | Rand Var: -3 | MM: 2521

Shoulder impingment cost him first half of August. ERA and Dom have the look of being closer-worthy, but don't be fooled. There are serious concerns: 1) Far too many walks, and FpK doesn't buy the improved 2nd half Ctl; 2) 2nd half LD% coincided with 1.3 mph velocity drop from 2016. Heed the xERA warning.

Yr Tm	W	L	Sv	IP	K	ERA	xERA	WHIP	oOPS	vL	vR	BF/G	Ctl	Dom	Cmd	FpK	SwK	G	L	F	H%	S%	hr/f	GS	APC	DOM%	DIS%	Sv%	LI	RAR	BPV	BPX	R$
13																																	
14																																	
15 MIA *	4	1	10	53	59	3.12	2.74	1.44	563	656	497	4.3	6.9	10.1	1.5	48%	15%	32	26	42	28%	77%	5%	0	19			83	1.15	5.5	102	122	$4
16 MIA	6	3	0	73	113	2.85	2.87	1.22	538	584	492	4.1	5.4	14.0	2.6	57%	14%	52	21	27	32%	75%	3%	0	18			0	1.21	12.0	135	160	$7
17 MIA	6	2	1	66	76	3.00	4.27	1.38	638	581	702	4.3	5.2	10.4	2.0	56%	12%	43	23	34	30%	80%	9%	0	18			20	0.95	11.1	68	81	$4
1st Half	4	1	0	36	40	3.22	4.89	1.43	635	528	757	4.4	6.2	9.9	1.6	58%	12%	43	17	39	28%	80%	8%	0	18			0	0.72	5.1	33	39	$4
2nd Half	2	1	1	30	36	2.73	3.56	1.31	643	647	638	4.2	3.9	10.9	2.8	54%	13%	42	30	27	33%	81%	10%	0	18			25	1.23	6.0	111	133	$4
18 Proj	**6**	**2**	**12**	**73**	**90**	**3.79**	**3.90**	**1.35**	**631**	**631**	**631**	**4.1**	**5.3**	**11.2**	**2.1**	**56%**	**13%**	**47**	**23**	**30**	**30%**	**73%**	**10%**	**0**						**5.1**	**81**	**98**	**$7**

Bauer,Trevor

Age: 27 | Th: R | Role: SP | Ht: 6' 1" | Wt: 190 | Type: Pwr
Health: A | PT/Exp: A | Consist: A
LIMA Plan: B | Rand Var: +4 | MM: 2305

Long-time tinkerer found a winning formula in 2nd half; can it stick? Narrowed pitch mix, relying heavily on four-seamer (39%) and curve (32%) while re-incorporating a nasty slider (21% SwK). 2nd half SwK/FpK implies some Cmd pullback, but there's enough there for... UP: sub-3.50 ERA.

Yr Tm	W	L	Sv	IP	K	ERA	xERA	WHIP	oOPS	vL	vR	BF/G	Ctl	Dom	Cmd	FpK	SwK	G	L	F	H%	S%	hr/f	GS	APC	DOM%	DIS%	Sv%	LI	RAR	BPV	BPX	R$
13 CLE *	7	9	0	138	104	5.04	5.44	1.72	840	908	778	24.2	5.7	6.8	1.2	57%	7%	35	20	45	32%	73%	13%	4	88	0%	50%			-20.1	30	40	-$14
14 CLE *	9	9	0	199	181	3.77	3.97	1.33	737	729	744	25.0	3.3	8.2	2.5	56%	9%	35	23	41	31%	74%	9%	26	100	31%	38%			-0.7	77	91	$4
15 CLE	11	12	0	176	170	4.55	4.21	1.31	713	705	721	24.0	4.0	8.7	2.2	59%	10%	39	20	41	28%	68%	12%	30	93	40%	27%	0	0.76	-12.8	64	77	$2
16 CLE	12	8	0	190	168	4.26	4.11	1.31	712	690	732	23.2	3.3	8.0	2.4	60%	9%	49	20	31	30%	69%	12%	28	88	25%	39%	0	0.74	-1.7	81	96	$7
17 CLE	17	9	0	176	196	4.19	3.72	1.37	774	839	717	23.4	3.1	10.0	3.3	57%	9%	46	22	32	34%	74%	16%	31	98	19%	23%	0	0.77	3.8	121	146	$11
1st Half	7	6	0	88	96	5.24	3.84	1.38	783	790	776	23.4	3.3	9.9	3.0	56%	9%	48	19	33	33%	65%	18%	16	100	19%	31%			-9.5	115	137	$3
2nd Half	10	3	0	89	100	3.15	3.60	1.35	766	890	662	23.4	2.8	10.2	3.6	57%	10%	45	24	31	35%	82%	15%	15	96	20%	13%	0	0.78	13.3	129	154	$19
18 Proj	**14**	**9**	**0**	**189**	**190**	**3.89**	**4.04**	**1.31**	**735**	**765**	**708**	**22.8**	**3.2**	**9.1**	**2.9**	**58%**	**10%**	**45**	**21**	**34**	**31%**	**74%**	**14%**	**34**						**10.8**	**101**	**121**	**$11**

REG PYRON

Bedrosian,Cam

Age: 26 | Th: R | Role: RP | Ht: 6' 0" | Wt: 230 | Type: Pwr
Health: F | PT/Exp: D | Consist: C
LIMA Plan: A | Rand Var: +2 | MM: 2420

Opened season with brief stint as closer, then hit DL for eight weeks with groin injury. More slider-heavy approach explains uptick in SwK, but batters teed off on lower velocity fastball, and Ctl wavered in 2nd half. Has flashed closer-worthy skills at times, but 2nd half metrics and health show the risk he carries.

Yr Tm	W	L	Sv	IP	K	ERA	xERA	WHIP	oOPS	vL	vR	BF/G	Ctl	Dom	Cmd	FpK	SwK	G	L	F	H%	S%	hr/f	GS	APC	DOM%	DIS%	Sv%	LI	RAR	BPV	BPX
13																																
14 LAA *	2	2	17	59	78	3.66	2.05	1.10	801	1055	531	4.2	4.0	11.9	3.0	61%	11%	41	21	38	29%	66%	9%	0	24			81	0.67	0.6	139	166
15 LAA *	2	1	3	69	70	3.99	4.18	1.52	833	1047	719	5.2	4.1	9.1	2.2	55%	7%	43	23	34	36%	73%	9%	0	19			60	0.73	-0.3	90	107
16 LAA	2	0	1	40	51	1.12	2.94	1.09	532	583	485	3.6	3.1	11.4	3.6	62%	11%	49	21	29	32%	91%	4%	0	15			50	0.78	15.3	147	175
17 LAA	6	5	6	45	53	4.43	3.91	1.30	705	778	639	4.0	3.4	10.7	3.1	61%	13%	43	17	40	33%	68%	10%	0	16			55	1.12	-0.4	121	145
1st Half	2	0	3	12	18	2.25	2.63	1.00	642	642	641	3.9	1.5	13.5	9.0	65%	15%	37	22	41	36%	82%	9%	0	18			60	1.71	3.1	218	261
2nd Half	4	5	3	33	35	5.23	4.46	1.41	726	827	636	4.0	4.1	9.6	2.3	59%	12%	45	15	40	32%	64%	11%	0	15			50	0.92	-3.5	85	101
18 Proj	**4**	**3**	**18**	**58**	**65**	**3.30**	**3.81**	**1.25**	**640**	**743**	**565**	**4.1**	**3.6**	**10.2**	**2.8**	**60%**	**12%**	**45**	**20**	**35**	**31%**	**76%**	**9%**	**0**						**7.6**	**108**	**131**

Belisle,Matt

Age: 38 | Th: R | Role: RP | Ht: 6' 3" | Wt: 230 | Type:
Health: F | PT/Exp: D | Consist: A
LIMA Plan: B+ | Rand Var: -1 | MM: 1220

1st half was a disaster, but after 11 scoreless innings in July, inherited closer role post-deadline and ran with it. Dom gains unlikely to stick, FB% continued to soar, and he had a lot of help from H% and S%. Role in spring will obviously be key, but 37-year-olds don't suddenly sprout elite, sustainable closer skills.

Yr Tm	W	L	Sv	IP	K	ERA	xERA	WHIP	oOPS	vL	vR	BF/G	Ctl	Dom	Cmd	FpK	SwK	G	L	F	H%	S%	hr/f	GS	APC	DOM%	DIS%	Sv%	LI	RAR	BPV	BPX
13 COL	5	7	0	73	62	4.32	3.27	1.25	707	750	679	4.2	1.8	7.6	4.1	67%	11%	49	26	25	33%	66%	11%	0	16			0	1.16	-4.0	115	149
14 COL	4	7	0	65	43	4.87	4.13	1.44	757	813	711	4.3	2.6	6.0	2.3	68%	8%	46	25	29	33%	66%	8%	1	16	0%	100%	0	0.82	-9.0	60	72
15 STL	1	1	0	34	25	2.67	4.40	1.46	690	784	639	4.4	4.0	6.7	1.7	67%	9%	51	20	28	32%	81%	3%	0	17			0	1.08	5.4	41	49
16 WAS	0	0	0	46	32	1.76	3.93	1.09	611	443	736	4.7	1.4	6.3	4.6	68%	10%	47	22	31	30%	85%	5%	0	17			0	0.71	13.8	101	120
17 MIN	2	2	9	60	54	4.03	4.35	1.16	662	595	696	4.0	3.3	8.1	2.5	67%	11%	41	21	38	26%	68%	11%	0	15			64	1.17	2.5	75	91
1st Half	0	1	0	32	23	6.25	5.73	1.61	817	778	833	4.3	4.8	6.5	1.4	69%	10%	41	24	35	31%	62%	11%	0	15			0	1.21	-7.4	6	7
2nd Half	2	1	9	29	31	1.57	3.04	0.66	451	413	475	3.6	1.6	9.7	6.2	63%	12%	41	16	44	18%	88%	11%	0	15			82	1.13	9.9	151	182
18 Proj	**2**	**2**	**12**	**58**	**48**	**3.49**	**4.33**	**1.21**	**689**	**629**	**725**	**4.1**	**2.6**	**7.5**	**2.9**	**67%**	**10%**	**43**	**21**	**37**	**29%**	**74%**	**9%**	**0**						**6.2**	**85**	**102**

Bell,Chadwick

Age: 29 | Th: L | Role: RP | Ht: 6' 3" | Wt: 200 | Type: Pwr
Health: A | PT/Exp: D | Consist: B
LIMA Plan: D+ | Rand Var: +5 | MM: 0100

0-3, 6.93 ERA in 62 IP at DET. Opened with 2.21 ERA across 20 1st half IP, but soft skills soon caught up to him. Ctl was a problem for second straight year, and he ranked in top 10 in hard contact against. Even the 2nd half Dom bump wasn't supported by fading SwK. Nothing to see here.

Yr Tm	W	L	Sv	IP	K	ERA	xERA	WHIP	oOPS	vL	vR	BF/G	Ctl	Dom	Cmd	FpK	SwK	G	L	F	H%	S%	hr/f	GS	APC	DOM%	DIS%	Sv%	LI	RAR	BPV	BPX
13																																
14																																
15 aa	7	13	0	141	92	5.70	5.56	1.64				23.4	2.9	5.9	2.0						36%	65%								-30.2	45	53
16 aaa	11	4	0	98	66	4.68	5.15	1.71				13.5	4.5	6.1	1.3						35%	72%								-5.9	45	54
17 DET *	2	7	0	97	80	6.34	6.61	1.77	906	817	944	12.7	4.0	7.4	1.8	57%	9%	45	21	34	37%	66%	17%	4	42	0%	75%	0	0.40	-23.6	29	35
1st Half	1	4	0	50	37	3.98	4.94	1.49	641	646	638	14.3	3.3	6.8	2.1	52%	10%	48	25	27	33%	76%	19%	0	37			0	0.24	2.3	51	61
2nd Half	1	3	0	47	42	8.83	8.37	2.07	1015	904	1057	11.5	4.8	8.1	1.7	59%	9%	44	19	37	41%	59%	17%	4	45	0%	75%	0	0.47	-25.9	9	11
18 Proj	**3**	**4**	**0**	**58**	**43**	**5.30**	**5.19**	**1.59**	**776**	**705**	**807**	**13.2**	**4.1**	**6.7**	**1.6**	**57%**	**9%**	**46**	**21**	**33**	**33%**	**68%**	**11%**	**6**						**-6.8**	**33**	**40**

Berrios,Jose

Age: 24 | Th: R | Role: SP | Ht: 6' 0" | Wt: 185 | Type: Pwr
Health: A | PT/Exp: C | Consist: C
LIMA Plan: C+ | Rand Var: 0 | MM: 1203

14-8, 3.89 ERA in 146 IP at MIN. With sub-3.00 ERA and 9.0 Dom in first nine starts, appeared he may have figured things out. There's still work to do, though. Posted 1.4 Cmd vL in 2nd half, while GB%, SwK and Ctl also took turn for the worse. Long-term upside is huge, so you will have to ride out the occasional bumps.

Yr Tm	W	L	Sv	IP	K	ERA	xERA	WHIP	oOPS	vL	vR	BF/G	Ctl	Dom	Cmd	FpK	SwK	G	L	F	H%	S%	hr/f	GS	APC	DOM%	DIS%	Sv%	LI	RAR	BPV	BPX
13																																
14 a/a	3	5	0	44	27	5.36	3.71	1.35				20.2	3.0	5.5	1.9						31%	58%								-8.7	61	73
15 a/a	14	5	0	166	147	3.41	3.11	1.14				24.4	2.0	7.9	4.0						30%	72%								11.4	118	140
16 MIN *	13	12	0	170	152	5.05	4.36	1.40	932	837	1034	23.1	3.8	8.0	2.1	55%	9%	38	22	40	30%	66%	16%	14	82	7%	50%			-18.0	61	72
17 MIN *	17	8	0	185	170	3.43	3.28	1.18	693	783	616	23.2	2.8	8.3	3.0	59%	10%	39	21	40	29%	74%	9%	25	92	32%	32%	0	0.78	21.3	95	114
1st Half	10	2	0	105	96	2.79	2.74	1.04	641	733	556	25.4	2.4	8.3	3.5	64%	11%	44	15	41	26%	78%	11%	10	102	50%	30%			20.3	107	128
2nd Half	7	6	0	80	74	4.26	4.63	1.36	732	825	659	22.0	3.2	8.3	2.6	55%	9%	36	25	39	32%	70%	8%	15	85	20%	33%	0	0.80	1.0	75	90
18 Proj	**14**	**10**	**0**	**174**	**161**	**3.63**	**4.30**	**1.21**	**685**	**693**	**678**	**22.3**	**2.9**	**8.3**	**2.9**	**58%**	**10%**	**39**	**22**	**40**	**29%**	**74%**	**11%**	**29**						**15.6**	**88**	**106**

Betances,Dellin

Age: 30 | Th: R | Role: RP | Ht: 6' 8" | Wt: 265 | Type: Pwr
Health: A | PT/Exp: C | Consist: B
LIMA Plan: A | Rand Var: -1 | MM: 5510

Was typical dominant self early on, but while velocity and ERA held strong, other signs of trouble emerged. FpK was way down all year; in 2nd half, SwK on curve plummeted, and FB% jumped. Perhaps a hidden injury is at play? We'll have to wait and see, but absent an explanation, just exercise a bit more caution.

Yr Tm	W	L	Sv	IP	K	ERA	xERA	WHIP	oOPS	vL	vR	BF/G	Ctl	Dom	Cmd	FpK	SwK	G	L	F	H%	S%	hr/f	GS	APC	DOM%	DIS%	Sv%	LI	RAR	BPV	BPX
13 NYY *	6	4	5	89	98	4.16	3.25	1.40	965	1339	804	8.5	5.0	9.9	2.0	65%	9%	36	36	29	32%	69%	25%	0	20			100	0.28	-3.3	98	127
14 NYY	5	0	1	90	135	1.40	2.03	0.78	442	405	482	4.9	2.4	13.5	5.6	66%	13%	47	20	33	26%	85%	7%	0	20			20	1.19	26.0	203	242
15 NYY	6	4	9	84	131	1.50	2.43	1.01	510	454	558	4.5	4.3	14.0	3.3	59%	15%	48	21	32	27%	90%	12%	0	19			69	1.42	25.5	163	194
16 NYY	3	6	12	73	126	3.08	2.09	1.12	577	634	532	4.1	3.5	15.5	4.5	61%	16%	54	19	27	38%	74%	13%	0	17			71	1.19	10.0	218	260
17 NYY	3	6	10	60	100	2.87	3.21	1.22	538	441	623	4.0	6.6	15.1	2.3	52%	13%	49	13	38	28%	77%	8%	0	17			77	1.09	11.0	119	143
1st Half	3	3	6	26	48	3.12	2.89	1.35	517	364	639	4.0	7.3	16.6	2.3	53%	17%	50	23	27	34%	76%	8%	0	17			75	1.19	4.0	131	157
2nd Half	0	3	4	34	52	2.67	3.44	1.13	554	496	610	3.9	6.1	13.9	2.3	51%	10%	48	7	46	23%	78%	7%	0	17			80	1.00	7.0	110	132
18 Proj	**3**	**5**	**5**	**66**	**108**	**2.70**	**2.83**	**1.15**	**548**	**500**	**591**	**4.0**	**5.2**	**14.7**	**2.8**	**56%**	**14%**	**50**	**16**	**34**	**30%**	**78%**	**10%**	**0**						**13.5**	**152**	**183**

Bettis,Chad

Age: 29 | Th: R | Role: RP | Ht: 6' 1" | Wt: 200 | Type:
Health: F | PT/Exp: C | Consist: C
LIMA Plan: C | Rand Var: +1 | MM: 0003

2-4, 5.05 ERA in 46 IP at COL. Learned in March that cancer had spread, and spent most of season recovering. Once healthy, skills were flat: Dom dipped but SwK slightly improved, GB tilt remained intact. Skill set doesn't look impressive, except when considered in context of beating cancer twice.

Yr Tm	W	L	Sv	IP	K	ERA	xERA	WHIP	oOPS	vL	vR	BF/G	Ctl	Dom	Cmd	FpK	SwK	G	L	F	H%	S%	hr/f	GS	APC	DOM%	DIS%	Sv%	LI	RAR	BPV	BPX
13 COL *	4	7	0	108	82	5.46	5.75	1.54	859	812	906	16.8	2.9	6.9	2.4	61%	8%	47	21	32	34%	69%	12%	8	49	0%	63%	0	0.91	-21.2	38	49
14 COL *	3	6	3	80	56	5.37	4.87	1.58	1020	901	1138	8.6	3.5	6.3	1.8	50%	6%	46	24	30	35%	65%	14%	0	24			60	0.70	-16.1	53	64
15 COL *	11	8	0	157	125	4.29	4.79	1.46	771	737	806	24.1	3.2	7.1	2.3	58%	10%	49	22	28	33%	73%	11%	20	94	20%	40%			-6.4	58	69
16 COL	14	8	0	186	138	4.79	4.31	1.41	775	694	854	25.4	2.9	6.7	2.3	63%	9%	51	22	27	32%	68%	14%	32	95	19%	44%			-13.8	72	86
17 COL *	2	7	0	70	42	5.62	5.95	1.53	828	797	856	20.2	2.5	5.4	2.1	60%	10%	48	19	33	32%	67%	16%	9	82	11%	44%			-10.8	22	26
1st Half																																
2nd Half	2	7	0	70	42	5.62	5.95	1.53	828	797	856	20.2	2.5	5.4	2.1	60%	10%	48	19	33	32%	67%	16%	9	82	11%	44%			-10.8	22	26
18 Proj	**8**	**11**	**0**	**160**	**113**	**4.88**	**4.63**	**1.44**	**818**	**770**	**865**	**17.3**	**2.8**	**6.4**	**2.3**	**60%**	**10%**	**49**	**21**	**30**	**32%**	**69%**	**14%**	**29**						**-10.3**	**67**	**81**

Biagini,Joe

Age: 28 | Th: R | Role: RP | Ht: 6' 5" | Wt: 240 | Type: GB
Health: A | PT/Exp: D | Consist: B
LIMA Plan: C | Rand Var: +4 | MM: 1101

3-13, 5.34 ERA in 120 IP at TOR. Transition to starting role didn't go so well (5.73 ERA), but skills out of pen took a step back as well (7.7 Dom, 3.4 Ctl). Sure, he was very unlucky on fly balls in 2nd half and has GB tilt working in his favor. But until he can get SwK back up, he's safe to ignore, regardless of role.

Yr Tm	W	L	Sv	IP	K	ERA	xERA	WHIP	oOPS	vL	vR	BF/G	Ctl	Dom	Cmd	FpK	SwK	G	L	F	H%	S%	hr/f	GS	APC	DOM%	DIS%	Sv%	LI	RAR	BPV	BPX
13																																
14																																
15 aa	10	7	0	130	70	3.35	3.89	1.38				23.8	2.6	4.8	1.8						31%	75%								9.8	55	66
16 TOR	4	3	1	68	62	3.06	3.75	1.30	678	725	644	4.9	2.5	8.2	3.3	69%	12%	52	21	26	34%	76%	6%	0	19			33	0.91	9.4	110	131
17 TOR *	4	14	1	137	108	5.31	4.64	1.41	752	788	724	12.1	3.2	7.1	2.2	64%	9%	56	18	27	31%	64%	15%	18	44	17%	39%	33	1.22	-16.1	54	64
1st Half	2	7	1	68	56	4.50	3.88	1.22	666	748	606	11.9	2.4	7.4	3.1	67%	9%	58	14	28	31%	63%	9%	10	43	20%	30%	33	1.48	-1.2	105	126
2nd Half	2	7	0	69	52	6.11	5.84	1.59	860	837	876	12.7	4.1	6.8	1.7	60%	8%	52	22	26	31%	65%	24%	8	45	13%	50%	0	0.90	-14.9	22	26
18 Proj	**4**	**6**	**0**	**87**	**69**	**4.32**	**4.22**	**1.38**	**728**	**759**	**705**	**8.2**	**3.0**	**7.1**	**2.4**	**65%**	**10%**	**54**	**20**	**26**	**32%**	**70%**	**11%**	**0**						**0.4**	**80**	**96**

BRIAN RUDD

Bibens-Dirkx,Austin

Age: 33	Th: R	Role RP		Health A		LIMA Plan D+	
Ht: 6' 1"	Wt: 210	Type Con		PT/Exp D		Rand Var 0	
				Consist B		MM 0000	

5-2, 4.67 ERA in 69 IP at TEX. Minor league journeyman finally got the call, though BPV history says it was unearned. Lucky H% helped keep him above water in 1st half, then waves overtook him. Given his inability to miss bats, his fly ball tilt, and 0.8 Cmd vL, sequel is likely to be worse than the long-delayed premiere.

Yr Tm	W	L	Sv	IP	K	ERA	xERA	WHIP	oOPS	vL	vR	BF/G	Ctl	Dom	Cmd	FpK	SwK	G	L	F	H%	S%	hr/f	GS	APC	DOM%	DIS%	Sv%	LI	RAR	BPV	BPX	R$
13 aa	3	4	0	66	44	2.44	2.96	1.17				21.9	2.5	6.1	2.4						28%	81%								11.5	78	102	$3
14 a/a	8	6	1	113	71	4.93	6.00	1.51				14.4	2.1	5.6	2.6						33%	73%								-16.7	31	37	-$7
15 a/a	7	9	0	114	79	6.40	6.98	1.81				21.2	3.1	6.2	2.0						38%	67%								-34.3	23	27	-$20
16 aaa	3	2	0	85	44	6.17	6.48	1.70				22.6	3.2	4.7	1.5						34%	66%								-20.8	4	4	-$13
17 TEX *	5	4	0	93	52	4.56	5.36	1.41	803	782	818	13.1	2.7	5.1	1.8	61%	9%	40	21	39	29%	74%	15%	6	49	0%	50%	0	0.74	-2.3	16	19	-$2
1st Half	3	2	0	66	37	4.10	4.77	1.25	723	703	738	16.8	2.4	5.1	2.2	62%	9%	39	18	42	26%	76%	17%	5	68	0%	40%	0	0.71	2.1	22	27	$1
2nd Half	2	2	0	27	15	5.67	6.04	1.81	908	875	936	9.2	3.7	5.0	1.4	59%	9%	41	26	34	36%	71%	12%	1	35	0%	100%	0	0.76	-4.4	10	12	-$11
18 Proj	**3**	**3**	**0**	**51**	**29**	**5.38**	**5.62**	**1.62**	**874**	**847**	**896**	**16.3**	**3.0**	**5.2**	**1.7**	**60%**	**9%**	**40**	**23**	**37**	**33%**	**70%**	**13%**	**8**						**-6.4**	**29**	**35**	**-$7**

Blach,Ty

Age: 27	Th: L	Role SP		Health A		LIMA Plan D+	
Ht: 6' 2"	Wt: 200	Type Con		PT/Exp C		Rand Var 0	
				Consist D		MM 0003	

Soft-tosser walked fine line all year, and late struggles eventually cost him rotation spot. Has yet to allow a HR vL, but that and pitcher-friendly home park have been all he's had going for him. On the road, posted 5.55 ERA, with .972 OPS vR. There aren't enough LHB in majors to make him useful as a starter.

Yr Tm	W	L	Sv	IP	K	ERA	xERA	WHIP	oOPS	vL	vR	BF/G	Ctl	Dom	Cmd	FpK	SwK	G	L	F	H%	S%	hr/f	GS	APC	DOM%	DIS%	Sv%	LI	RAR	BPV	BPX	R$
13																																	
14 aa	8	8	0	141	76	3.53	4.20	1.41				23.9	2.5	4.9	1.9						32%	75%								3.7	54	65	$0
15 aaa	11	12	0	165	77	4.82	4.94	1.46				26.2	1.7	4.2	2.5						34%	67%								-17.5	49	58	-$7
16 SF *	15	7	0	180	101	3.89	3.56	1.28	445	374	495	24.5	2.3	5.0	2.2	65%	6%	58	9	33	30%	69%	7%	2	60	50%	50%	0	0.40	6.7	65	77	$9
17 SF	8	12	0	164	73	4.78	5.20	1.36	766	592	831	20.4	2.4	4.0	1.7	62%	7%	47	21	32	29%	66%	10%	24	74	8%	38%	0	0.72	-8.6	33	40	-$1
1st Half	5	5	0	86	41	4.60	5.06	1.35	779	585	850	18.2	2.1	4.3	2.1	62%	7%	47	20	33	30%	67%	8%	13	66	15%	23%	0	0.72	-2.6	46	55	$0
2nd Half	3	7	0	78	32	4.98	5.37	1.36	752	600	810	23.4	2.7	3.7	1.4	61%	6%	46	23	31	28%	65%	11%	11	85	0%	55%	0	0.72	-6.0	19	23	-$3
18 Proj	**8**	**8**	**0**	**131**	**63**	**4.61**	**5.07**	**1.36**	**774**	**599**	**839**	**22.6**	**2.3**	**4.3**	**1.9**	**61%**	**6%**	**47**	**22**	**32**	**30%**	**68%**	**10%**	**21**						**-4.0**	**41**	**49**	**-$1**

Blackburn,Paul

Age: 24	Th: R	Role SP		Health C		LIMA Plan D+	
Ht: 6' 1"	Wt: 195	Type Con xGB		PT/Exp D		Rand Var 0	
				Consist A		MM 0001	

3-1, 3.22 ERA in 59 IP at OAK. Held his own in 10 starts before wrist bruise ended season in late August. Looks like he did it with smoke and mirrors, though. Awful FpK suggests Ctl will rise again, and MLB worst K% leaves no hope for Dom surge. GB tilt alone won't be enough to survive. DN: 5.00 ERA

Yr Tm	W	L	Sv	IP	K	ERA	xERA	WHIP	oOPS	vL	vR	BF/G	Ctl	Dom	Cmd	FpK	SwK	G	L	F	H%	S%	hr/f	GS	APC	DOM%	DIS%	Sv%	LI	RAR	BPV	BPX	R$
13																																	
14																																	
15																																	
16 aa	9	5	0	143	87	4.00	4.14	1.37				23.0	2.2	5.5	2.5						32%	71%								3.3	66	78	$2
17 OAK *	8	7	0	138	67	3.43	3.78	1.29	686	585	773	22.8	2.7	4.3	1.6	48%	6%	56	19	25	28%	75%	10%	10	94	0%	50%			15.9	41	50	$7
1st Half	5	6	0	86	49	3.33	3.54	1.27	390	538	182	21.9	2.8	5.1	1.8	63%	8%	50	11	39	28%	75%	0%	1	96	0%	0%			10.9	55	66	$10
2nd Half	3	1	0	53	18	3.59	4.92	1.33	719	591	824	23.8	2.6	3.1	1.2	46%	5%	57	20	23	28%	75%	12%	9	93	0%	56%			5.0	21	25	$1
18 Proj	**2**	**4**	**0**	**73**	**37**	**4.45**	**4.66**	**1.33**	**648**	**537**	**739**	**23.1**	**2.5**	**4.6**	**1.8**	**46%**	**6%**	**57**	**20**	**23**	**30%**	**67%**	**9%**	**13**						**-0.8**	**50**	**60**	**-$3**

Bleier,Richard

Age: 31	Th: L	Role RP		Health A		LIMA Plan B+	
Ht: 6' 3"	Wt: 215	Type Con xGB		PT/Exp D		Rand Var -5	
				Consist B		MM 1000	

Quietly put together solid ratios, thanks to combo of elite GB% and stellar Ctl, plus some good fortune. Now owns 1.98 ERA in 86 1/3 career MLB innings, but xERA is more than two runs higher (4.02). Complete lack of whiffs is eventually going to catch up with him, so heed xERA's warning before it's too late.

Yr Tm	W	L	Sv	IP	K	ERA	xERA	WHIP	oOPS	vL	vR	BF/G	Ctl	Dom	Cmd	FpK	SwK	G	L	F	H%	S%	hr/f	GS	APC	DOM%	DIS%	Sv%	LI	RAR	BPV	BPX	R$
13 a/a	6	6	4	81	38	4.56	5.48	1.59				8.5	2.5	4.2	1.7						34%	73%								-6.9	25	33	-$5
14 a/a	6	5	1	87	36	5.45	7.39	1.67				11.1	1.3	3.8	3.0						35%	73%								-18.2	10	12	-$11
15 a/a	14	5	0	172	48	3.66	4.63	1.42				26.0	1.0	2.5	2.6						33%	73%								6.4	49	59	$1
16 NYY *	2	3	1	81	32	4.74	5.31	1.61	586	409	740	10.2	1.9	3.5	1.8	60%	10%	54	24	22	36%	69%	0%	0	15			100	0.28	-5.5	37	44	-$8
17 BAL	2	1	0	63	26	1.99	4.25	1.18	671	678	666	4.6	1.8	3.7	2.0	59%	9%	69	11	20	27%	88%	14%	0	16			0	0.69	18.5	64	76	$4
1st Half	1	1	0	26	12	1.75	4.86	1.40	677	669	678	5.3	3.2	4.2	1.3	59%	9%	68	11	21	29%	91%	11%	0	18			0	0.79	8.2	37	44	$0
2nd Half	1	0	0	38	14	2.15	3.85	1.04	666	680	653	4.2	1.0	3.3	3.5	59%	9%	69	12	19	25%	86%	17%	0	15			0	0.63	10.3	82	98	$7
18 Proj	**2**	**2**	**0**	**58**	**23**	**3.86**	**4.38**	**1.37**	**757**	**746**	**765**	**5.7**	**1.8**	**3.5**	**2.0**	**59%**	**9%**	**69**	**11**	**20**	**31%**	**73%**	**11%**	**0**						**3.6**	**63**	**75**	**-$3**

Blevins,Jerry

Age: 34	Th: L	Role RP		Health F		LIMA Plan A	
Ht: 6' 6"	Wt: 190	Type Pwr		PT/Exp D		Rand Var 0	
				Consist B		MM 2500	

Changed up his repertoire, throwing more curves than fastballs. Strategy paid off in some ways—LHB managed just one XBH in 132 PA, and Dom, SwK reached new heights. But Cmd fell to 1.2 vR, and they teed off, while WHIP rose to 1.74 over final 40 outings. Decent strikeout source for a RP, but ERA is headed north.

Yr Tm	W	L	Sv	IP	K	ERA	xERA	WHIP	oOPS	vL	vR	BF/G	Ctl	Dom	Cmd	FpK	SwK	G	L	F	H%	S%	hr/f	GS	APC	DOM%	DIS%	Sv%	LI	RAR	BPV	BPX	R$
13 OAK	5	0	0	60	52	3.15	4.00	1.07	651	741	581	3.7	2.6	7.8	3.1	58%	10%	31	19	50	25%	75%	8%	0	15			0	0.97	5.3	81	105	$4
14 WAS	2	3	0	57	66	4.87	3.37	1.24	623	419	821	3.8	3.6	10.4	2.9	68%	12%	39	24	37	32%	59%	6%	0	15			0	0.94	-8.0	106	126	-$2
15 NYM	1	0	0	5	4	0.00	1.77	0.00	0	0	0	2.1	0.0	7.2	0.0	67%	9%	55	36	9	0%	0%	0%	0	8			0	1.50	2.4	163	194	-$2
16 NYM	4	2	2	42	52	2.79	3.46	1.21	627	636	611	2.4	3.2	11.1	3.5	61%	11%	46	17	37	33%	81%	10%	0	10			67	1.31	7.3	138	164	$3
17 NYM	6	0	1	49	69	2.94	3.64	1.37	652	455	993	2.9	4.4	12.7	2.9	55%	13%	41	21	38	36%	81%	9%	0	12			13	1.34	8.6	128	154	$3
1st Half	4	0	0	28	39	2.60	3.50	1.27	607	374	1053	2.8	4.2	12.7	3.0	58%	14%	44	15	42	34%	82%	8%	0	11			0	1.46	6.0	136	163	$5
2nd Half	2	0	1	21	30	3.38	3.82	1.50	705	560	929	3.0	4.6	12.7	2.7	52%	12%	38	27	35	39%	80%	11%	0	13			25	1.19	2.6	119	142	$1
18 Proj	**3**	**2**	**0**	**51**	**65**	**3.63**	**3.73**	**1.30**	**650**	**536**	**817**	**2.8**	**3.8**	**11.5**	**3.0**	**58%**	**12%**	**41**	**21**	**39**	**34%**	**74%**	**9%**	**0**						**4.6**	**121**	**146**	**$0**

Bowman,Matthew

Age: 27	Th: R	Role RP		Health A		LIMA Plan B+	
Ht: 6' 0"	Wt: 175	Type xGB		PT/Exp D		Rand Var 0	
				Consist C		MM 1100	

Sinkerballer generated a few more swings and misses in 1st half. 2nd half Ctl erosion was really just one bad week, and FpK, track record both say it's nothing to worry about. Ability to keep the ball down and handle LHB already makes him serviceable option, and if he can get back to 1st half Dom, even offers some upside.

Yr Tm	W	L	Sv	IP	K	ERA	xERA	WHIP	oOPS	vL	vR	BF/G	Ctl	Dom	Cmd	FpK	SwK	G	L	F	H%	S%	hr/f	GS	APC	DOM%	DIS%	Sv%	LI	RAR	BPV	BPX	R$
13																																	
14 a/a	10	8	0	135	108	2.85	3.51	1.26				22.9	2.1	7.2	3.5						33%	78%								14.9	104	124	$8
15 aaa	7	16	0	140	65	5.35	5.96	1.71				22.6	3.0	4.2	1.4						35%	69%								-24.0	18	21	-$17
16 STL	2	5	0	68	52	3.46	3.63	1.17	623	570	651	4.8	2.7	6.9	2.6	62%	10%	62	19	19	28%	71%	10%	0	18			0	0.81	6.1	93	110	$2
17 STL	3	6	2	59	46	3.99	4.11	1.19	659	623	687	3.3	2.8	7.1	2.6	64%	10%	55	17	29	29%	67%	8%	0	13			40	1.32	2.7	85	103	$1
1st Half	1	3	1	35	30	4.15	3.65	1.10	637	563	693	3.6	2.3	7.8	3.3	62%	11%	56	16	28	28%	63%	11%	0	15			50	1.34	0.9	111	133	$2
2nd Half	2	3	1	24	16	3.75	4.80	1.33	689	701	678	2.9	3.4	6.0	1.8	65%	10%	53	17	30	30%	71%	4%	0	11			33	1.30	1.8	48	58	$1
18 Proj	**3**	**5**	**0**	**58**	**43**	**3.91**	**4.15**	**1.31**	**700**	**666**	**723**	**4.4**	**3.0**	**6.7**	**2.3**	**63%**	**10%**	**57**	**18**	**25**	**31%**	**70%**	**8%**	**0**						**3.2**	**77**	**92**	**-$1**

Boxberger,Brad

Age: 30	Th: R	Role RP		Health F		LIMA Plan A	
Ht: 6' 2"	Wt: 205	Type Pwr FB		PT/Exp C		Rand Var +1	
				Consist D		MM 4510	

Missed 1st half with back injury, and shaky skills from 2016 carried over initially. But lights out down the stretch, with 13.1 Dom, 1.8 Ctl in last 19 outings. Health, iffy Ctl history work against him, but with closer experience, regaining 9th inning gig may still be attainable. UP: 3.00 ERA, 20 saves

Yr Tm	W	L	Sv	IP	K	ERA	xERA	WHIP	oOPS	vL	vR	BF/G	Ctl	Dom	Cmd	FpK	SwK	G	L	F	H%	S%	hr/f	GS	APC	DOM%	DIS%	Sv%	LI	RAR	BPV	BPX	R$
13 SD *	2	5	6	79	100	3.24	3.28	1.27	760	495	948	5.4	3.4	11.3	3.3	62%	13%	42	17	40	35%	76%	14%	0	22			75	0.66	6.1	125	163	$4
14 TAM	5	2	2	65	104	2.37	2.08	0.84	538	402	659	3.9	2.8	14.5	5.2	67%	15%	41	17	42	24%	82%	19%	0	17			40	1.23	11.0	204	243	$11
15 TAM	4	10	41	63	74	3.71	3.98	1.37	703	657	759	3.9	4.6	10.6	2.3	56%	13%	36	21	43	30%	78%	13%	0	17			87	1.58	1.9	81	96	$17
16 TAM	4	3	0	24	22	4.81	5.64	1.73	728	750	711	4.2	7.0	8.1	1.2	58%	10%	48	15	37	30%	74%	12%	0	17			0	1.15	-1.9	-17	-21	-$4
17 TAM	4	4	0	29	40	3.38	3.34	1.16	665	584	753	4.0	3.4	12.3	3.6	59%	13%	42	16	42	31%	77%	14%	0	17			0	1.14	3.6	150	180	$0
1st Half	0	0	0	1	3	0.00	0.00	0.00	0	0	0	3.0	0.0	27.0	0.0	67%	15%	0	0	0	0%	0%	0%	0	13			0	0.22	0.5	464	556	-$11
2nd Half	4	4	0	28	37	3.49	3.53	1.20	684	594	782	4.1	3.5	11.8	3.4	59%	13%	42	16	42	31%	77%	14%	0	17			0	1.17	3.0	137	164	$1
18 Proj	**5**	**5**	**2**	**58**	**80**	**3.42**	**3.35**	**1.17**	**653**	**565**	**745**	**4.1**	**3.8**	**12.4**	**3.3**	**61%**	**13%**	**44**	**15**	**41**	**30%**	**76%**	**15%**	**0**						**6.7**	**144**	**174**	**$5**

BRIAN RUDD

Boyd,Matt

Age: 27	Th: L	Role SP		Health	A	LIMA Plan	C
Ht: 6' 3"	Wt: 215	Type Pwr FB		PT/Exp	C	Rand Var	0
				Consist	B	MM	0103

6-11, 5.27 ERA in 135 IP at DET. Kept the ball down early on, but previously consistent Cmd collapsed, leading to June demotion. Upon return, looked a lot like pitcher we saw in 2nd half of 2016, where strong SwK, Dom were offset by heavy fly ball lean. xERA says that both versions are risky investments.

Yr	Tm	W	L	Sv	IP	K	ERA	xERA	WHIP	oOPS	vL	vR	BF/G	Ctl	Dom	Cmd	FpK	SwK	G	L	F	H%	S%	hr/f	GS	APC	DOM%	DIS%	Sv%	LI	RAR	BPV	BPX	R
13																																		
14	aa	1	4	0	43	39	8.72	7.05	1.82				19.8	2.8	8.2	2.9						42%	51%								-26.2	56	67	-$1
15	2 AL *	10	8	0	172	128	3.84	3.77	1.17	979	1134	913	21.5	2.5	6.7	2.6	59%	9%	32	16	52	26%	73%	18%	12	77	0%	50%	0	0.74	2.6	63	74	$
16	DET *	8	10	0	161	127	3.95	4.39	1.31	765	598	800	21.5	2.7	7.1	2.6	63%	10%	38	17	45	30%	75%	13%	18	84	22%	44%	0	0.87	4.8	60	72	$
17	DET *	9	14	0	186	151	4.97	5.03	1.46	826	712	847	23.4	3.3	7.3	2.2	59%	10%	38	22	40	32%	69%	11%	25	91	12%	48%	0	0.74	-14.0	50	60	-$
1st Half		5	6	0	92	67	4.89	5.35	1.53	879	670	910	23.4	3.5	6.6	1.9	59%	8%	44	23	33	32%	71%	11%	11	89	9%	73%			-6.0	36	43	-$
2nd Half		4	8	0	94	84	5.04	4.71	1.39	787	735	798	23.4	3.1	8.0	2.6	59%	12%	33	22	45	32%	67%	10%	14	92	14%	29%	0	0.72	-8.0	64	76	-$
18	**Proj**	**8**	**11**	**0**	**160**	**130**	**4.76**	**4.92**	**1.38**	**783**	**739**	**793**	**23.6**	**3.0**	**7.3**	**2.5**	**60%**	**10%**	**37**	**20**	**44**	**31%**	**70%**	**12%**	**28**						**-7.9**	**67**	**80**	**-$**

Brach,Brad

Age: 32	Th: R	Role RP		Health	A	LIMA Plan	C+
Ht: 6' 6"	Wt: 215	Type Pwr		PT/Exp	C	Rand Var	-2
				Consist	A	MM	2410

Received boost in value when he slid into closer role in April, where he converted 18 of 22 chances. But now a few causes for concern: SwK decline paired with FpK, Ctl troubles in 2nd half; significant drop in K% vR. He should be good again, but may no longer be a top LIMA option nor clear Plan B in pen.

Yr	Tm	W	L	Sv	IP	K	ERA	xERA	WHIP	oOPS	vL	vR	BF/G	Ctl	Dom	Cmd	FpK	SwK	G	L	F	H%	S%	hr/f	GS	APC	DOM%	DIS%	Sv%	LI	RAR	BPV	BPX	R
13	SD *	5	3	3	75	67	2.95	4.72	1.52	819	647	972	5.0	3.9	8.0	2.1	54%	9%	38	23	39	34%	84%	9%	0	19			100	0.62	8.5	63	83	$
14	BAL *	10	2	1	86	86	3.47	3.63	1.30	640	776	543	5.6	3.3	9.1	2.7	58%	13%	36	19	45	32%	75%	8%	0	23			50	0.82	2.9	95	113	$
15	BAL	5	3	1	79	89	2.72	3.61	1.20	627	534	729	5.2	4.3	10.1	2.3	58%	14%	45	19	36	27%	81%	10%	0	21			50	0.99	12.1	88	105	$
16	BAL	10	4	2	79	92	2.05	3.34	1.04	578	784	399	4.4	2.8	10.5	3.7	60%	15%	41	21	38	28%	85%	10%	0	18			29	1.05	20.8	131	155	$1
17	BAL	4	5	18	68	70	3.18	4.03	1.13	620	559	675	4.1	3.4	9.3	2.7	58%	13%	42	19	39	27%	76%	10%	0	18			75	1.06	9.9	94	113	$1
1st Half		2	1	15	36	36	2.72	3.72	0.91	543	434	638	3.8	2.7	8.9	3.3	66%	13%	44	13	42	21%	76%	11%	0	17			79	1.21	7.3	109	131	$2
2nd Half		2	4	3	32	34	3.69	4.39	1.39	699	685	712	4.5	4.3	9.7	2.3	51%	12%	40	24	36	32%	76%	10%	0	19			60	0.90	2.6	77	92	$
18	**Proj**	**5**	**4**	**7**	**65**	**70**	**3.04**	**3.96**	**1.18**	**634**	**641**	**627**	**4.4**	**3.5**	**9.7**	**2.7**	**57%**	**13%**	**42**	**20**	**38**	**28%**	**78%**	**10%**	**0**						**10.6**	**98**	**118**	**$**

Bradley,Archie

Age: 25	Th: R	Role RP		Health	D	LIMA Plan	B
Ht: 6' 4"	Wt: 225	Type Pwr		PT/Exp	D	Rand Var	-5
				Consist	B	MM	3411

Had no problem adjusting to life in the pen. Relying on two-pitch arsenal, velocity soared, and Ctl improved significantly. Did give back some of those gains in 2nd half, only to be saved by S% and hr/f. ERA is sure to rise, but if he can just limit the walks, could quickly emerge as top-end late inning option.

Yr	Tm	W	L	Sv	IP	K	ERA	xERA	WHIP	oOPS	vL	vR	BF/G	Ctl	Dom	Cmd	FpK	SwK	G	L	F	H%	S%	hr/f	GS	APC	DOM%	DIS%	Sv%	LI	RAR	BPV	BPX	R
13	aa	12	5	0	123	103	2.60	3.41	1.38				24.7	4.4	7.5	1.7						30%	82%								19.3	74	97	$
14	a/a	3	7	0	79	60	4.76	3.83	1.53				20.2	5.0	6.8	1.3						31%	66%								-9.9	66	78	-$
15	ARI *	3	3	0	57	40	4.70	4.90	1.57	768	587	985	20.8	4.2	6.3	1.5	55%	6%	58	14	28	32%	71%	10%	8	81	0%	63%			-5.2	41	49	-$
16	ARI *	13	10	0	182	182	4.42	4.29	1.47	802	936	666	23.7	4.2	9.0	2.1	57%	9%	45	25	30	34%	71%	13%	26	99	15%	38%			-5.2	78	92	$
17	ARI	3	3	1	73	79	1.73	3.32	1.04	567	579	556	4.6	2.6	9.7	3.8	59%	11%	48	23	29	29%	86%	7%	0	18			14	1.29	23.7	131	158	$1
1st Half		3	1	0	37	43	1.23	2.78	0.90	538	466	586	4.7	1.7	10.6	6.1	60%	11%	51	21	28	28%	93%	12%	0	19			0	1.38	14.2	172	206	$1
2nd Half		0	2	1	36	36	2.23	3.92	1.18	595	667	519	4.5	3.5	8.9	2.6	58%	11%	45	25	30	30%	81%	3%	0	18			17	1.21	9.5	90	108	$
18	**Proj**	**4**	**4**	**8**	**73**	**78**	**2.86**	**3.59**	**1.23**	**655**	**690**	**621**	**5.6**	**3.0**	**9.7**	**3.2**	**58%**	**11%**	**48**	**23**	**29**	**32%**	**78%**	**9%**	**0**						**13.4**	**119**	**143**	**$**

Brebbia,John

Age: 28	Th: R	Role RP		Health	A	LIMA Plan	B+
Ht: 6' 1"	Wt: 185	Type Pwr xFB		PT/Exp	F	Rand Var	-5
				Consist	F	MM	0210

0-0, 2.44 ERA in 52 IP at STL. Showed improvement at Triple-A early on, earning May call-up. PRO: Ctl gains supported by healthy FpK; more whiffs as season progressed. CON: Turned into extreme fly ball pitcher; short track record of success. Ratios will regress, but given 2nd half Dom surge, he's worth a flyer.

Yr	Tm	W	L	Sv	IP	K	ERA	xERA	WHIP	oOPS	vL	vR	BF/G	Ctl	Dom	Cmd	FpK	SwK	G	L	F	H%	S%	hr/f	GS	APC	DOM%	DIS%	Sv%	LI	RAR	BPV	BPX	R
13																																		
14																																		
15																																		
16	a/a	5	5	2	68	52	6.31	6.72	1.76				7.2	2.6	6.9	2.6						39%	65%								-17.8	43	51	-$1
17	STL *	1	1	3	78	73	2.37	2.59	0.94	640	737	575	4.5	1.9	8.3	4.4	71%	13%	25	19	56	24%	84%	10%	0	16			75	0.68	19.3	121	146	$1
1st Half		1	1	3	41	30	2.32	1.95	0.84	498	733	391	5.6	1.6	6.5	4.0	84%	12%	38	10	53	21%	79%	10%	0	17			100	0.64	10.3	111	133	$1
2nd Half		0	0	0	37	43	2.41	4.17	1.04	691	736	655	4.1	2.2	10.4	4.8	67%	14%	20	22	58	28%	88%	11%	0	15			0	0.69	9.0	126	151	$
18	**Proj**	**2**	**2**	**2**	**58**	**53**	**3.68**	**4.71**	**1.22**	**733**	**777**	**699**	**5.2**	**2.0**	**8.2**	**4.0**	**64%**	**14%**	**27**	**22**	**50**	**30%**	**78%**	**11%**	**0**						**4.9**	**97**	**117**	**$**

Bridwell,Parker

Age: 26	Th: R	Role RP		Health	A	LIMA Plan	D+
Ht: 6' 4"	Wt: 185	Type FB		PT/Exp	D	Rand Var	0
				Consist	B	MM	0003

10-3, 3.64 ERA in 121 IP at LAA. Made transition back to starting role following April trade. Behind respectable ERA, not much to get excited about: Dom is weak, and trending in wrong direction; serves up a lot of fly balls; 1.7 Cmd vL indicates they'll soon fare better against him. Odds are stacked against a repeat.

Yr	Tm	W	L	Sv	IP	K	ERA	xERA	WHIP	oOPS	vL	vR	BF/G	Ctl	Dom	Cmd	FpK	SwK	G	L	F	H%	S%	hr/f	GS	APC	DOM%	DIS%	Sv%	LI	RAR	BPV	BPX	R
13																																		
14																																		
15	aa	4	5	0	97	76	5.43	5.41	1.64				24.1	3.8	7.0	1.9						36%	67%								-17.5	49	58	-$1
16	BAL *	2	1	1	69	47	5.98	5.95	1.67	1186	1800	856	12.9	4.6	6.1	1.3	80%	14%	20	20	60	32%	67%	33%	0	30			100	0.17	-15.2	14	17	-$1
17	LAA *	12	7	0	161	104	4.29	4.64	1.29	720	763	680	20.7	2.2	5.8	2.6	63%	9%	38	21	41	29%	72%	12%	20	84	30%	40%	0	0.86	1.4	45	55	$
1st Half		4	5	0	68	45	5.30	6.31	1.53	917	979	861	18.4	2.3	5.9	2.6	61%	10%	39	22	39	33%	72%	20%	4	78	0%	75%	0	1.14	-7.9	25	30	-$
2nd Half		8	2	0	94	59	3.56	4.84	1.12	661	699	627	23.6	2.2	5.7	2.6	64%	9%	38	21	41	25%	73%	10%	16	86	38%	31%			9.3	58	70	$1
18	**Proj**	**8**	**5**	**0**	**145**	**98**	**4.99**	**5.28**	**1.45**	**812**	**866**	**764**	**19.2**	**3.1**	**6.1**	**2.0**	**62%**	**10%**	**38**	**21**	**40**	**31%**	**69%**	**12%**	**27**						**-11.3**	**42**	**51**	**-$**

Britton,Zach

Age: 30	Th: L	Role RP		Health	D	LIMA Plan	A
Ht: 6' 3"	Wt: 195	Type Pwr xGB		PT/Exp	B	Rand Var	-1
				Consist	B	MM	5230

April forearm strain sidelined him for nearly three months, and he never fully returned to form. Had MRI on knee in August, which may help explain 7.4 Ctl for the month. Clearly some risk now, but velocity and GB-inducing sinker are fine. That means odds of rebound look good, pending health check in March.

Yr	Tm	W	L	Sv	IP	K	ERA	xERA	WHIP	oOPS	vL	vR	BF/G	Ctl	Dom	Cmd	FpK	SwK	G	L	F	H%	S%	hr/f	GS	APC	DOM%	DIS%	Sv%	LI	RAR	BPV	BPX	R
13	BAL *	8	8	0	143	77	5.48	5.89	1.81	837	849	832	24.6	4.2	4.8	1.1	54%	7%	58	20	22	36%	69%	13%	7	83	14%	71%	0	0.75	-28.5	23	31	-$1
14	BAL	3	2	37	76	62	1.65	2.44	0.90	500	386	559	4.0	2.7	7.3	2.7	55%	13%	75	13	12	22%	85%	17%	0	15			90	1.41	19.7	111	133	$2
15	BAL	4	1	36	66	79	1.92	1.75	0.99	547	325	636	4.0	1.9	10.8	5.6	64%	17%	79	11	9	31%	82%	20%	0	14			90	1.17	16.5	200	238	$2
16	BAL	2	1	47	67	74	0.54	2.03	0.84	430	495	410	3.7	2.4	9.9	4.1	56%	18%	80	11	9	24%	95%	7%	0	15			100	1.31	30.2	172	204	$3
17	BAL	2	1	15	37	29	2.89	3.74	1.53	690	717	680	4.2	4.3	7.0	1.6	56%	12%	73	19	8	33%	80%	11%	0	15			88	1.05	6.7	60	72	$
1st Half		0	0	5	9	7	1.00	4.13	1.78	753	333	834	4.9	4.0	7.0	1.8	54%	12%	61	25	14	39%	94%	0%	0	17			100	1.26	3.7	57	68	-$
2nd Half		2	1	10	28	22	3.49	3.60	1.45	669	790	621	4.1	4.4	7.0	1.6	57%	13%	76	18	6	31%	75%	20%	0	15			83	0.99	3.0	60	72	$
18	**Proj**	**3**	**2**	**38**	**65**	**61**	**2.43**	**2.83**	**1.17**	**577**	**555**	**586**	**4.3**	**3.1**	**8.4**	**2.7**	**58%**	**14%**	**76**	**14**	**10**	**30%**	**79%**	**9%**	**0**						**15.5**	**120**	**145**	**$2**

Buchter,Ryan

Age: 31	Th: L	Role RP		Health	A	LIMA Plan	B
Ht: 6' 4"	Wt: 258	Type Pwr xFB		PT/Exp	D	Rand Var	-5
				Consist	B	MM	1300

1st half a near mirror image of 2016, from shaky Ctl, to sky high FB%, to low H%. Working in cutter/slider more often in 2nd half had neutral effect—better Ctl was offset by Dom dip. Induced a lot of infield flies again, which may help him continue to outpitch peripherals. But can't bank on another sub-3.00 ERA.

Yr	Tm	W	L	Sv	IP	K	ERA	xERA	WHIP	oOPS	vL	vR	BF/G	Ctl	Dom	Cmd	FpK	SwK	G	L	F	H%	S%	hr/f	GS	APC	DOM%	DIS%	Sv%	LI	RAR	BPV	BPX	R
13	aaa	4	0	5	62	84	3.44	3.68	1.58				5.3	7.9	12.2	1.5						30%	80%								3.3	97	126	$
14	ATL *	4	3	1	64	52	3.76	4.42	1.60	333	1000	0	5.7	6.0	7.4	1.2	67%	8%	100	0	0	30%	78%	0%	0	12			20	2.46	-0.2	53	63	-$
15	aaa	2	0	3	51	48	2.24	3.11	1.43				5.0	4.9	8.5	1.7						32%	83%								10.8	95	113	$
16	SD	3	0	1	63	78	2.86	4.02	1.03	559	489	597	3.7	4.4	11.1	2.5	55%	10%	21	21	58	23%	74%	5%	0	17			50	0.92	10.4	80	95	$
17	2 TM	4	3	1	65	65	2.89	4.59	1.07	642	618	656	3.8	3.6	9.0	2.5	59%	11%	33	14	54	22%	82%	11%	0	15			33	0.87	11.8	75	91	$
1st Half		3	3	1	30	36	3.00	4.37	1.17	664	745	615	3.8	4.5	10.8	2.4	58%	11%	32	15	53	24%	83%	13%	0	16			33	1.02	5.0	83	99	$
2nd Half		1	0	0	35	29	2.80	4.78	0.99	623	497	690	3.8	2.8	7.4	2.6	59%	11%	34	12	54	21%	80%	9%	0	15			0	0.74	6.8	69	83	$
18	**Proj**	**3**	**1**	**0**	**58**	**61**	**3.64**	**4.62**	**1.25**	**706**	**653**	**735**	**4.0**	**4.1**	**9.4**	**2.3**	**57%**	**11%**	**33**	**18**	**49**	**28%**	**75%**	**9%**	**0**						**5.1**	**69**	**83**	**$**

BRIAN RUDD

Buehler,Walker

Age: 23	Th: R	Role RP	Health A	LIMA Plan C+
Ht: 6' 2"	Wt: 175	Type Pwr	PT/Exp F	Rand Var +5
			Consist F	MM 2500

1-0, 7.71 ERA in 9 IP at LA. Prized prospect was handled with care, but dominance in minors eventually led to brief MLB trial. In all, struck out 34% of batters faced, while displaying strong GB tilt at all levels. An obvious keeper league gem, and if given opportunity, could make immediate splash in majors as well.

Yr Tm	W	L	Sv	IP	K	ERA	xERA	WHIP	oOPS	vL	vR	BF/G	Ctl	Dom	Cmd	FpK	SwK	G	L	F	H%	S%	hr/f	GS	APC	DOM%	DIS%	Sv%	LI	RAR	BPV	BPX	R$
13																																	
14																																	
15																																	
16																																	
17 LA *	4	3	1	82	97	4.79	3.90	1.33	932	503	1270	10.9	3.5	10.6	3.1	59%	10%	67	17	17	34%	65%	50%	0	24			100	0.33	-4.4	105	126	$0
1st Half	2	2	0	41	44	3.34	3.59	1.14				18.0	2.0	9.7	4.8						31%	76%	0%	0						5.2	129	155	$5
2nd Half	2	1	1	41	53	6.33	4.30	1.54	932	503	1270	8.1	5.0	11.6	2.3	59%	10%	67	17	17	37%	57%	50%	0	24			100	0.33	-9.9	102	122	-$5
18 Proj	**2**	**2**	**0**	**51**	**59**	**3.93**	**3.83**	**1.34**				**19.3**	**4.1**	**10.5**	**2.6**	**60%**	**11%**	**47**	**20**	**33**	**32%**	**73%**	**12%**	**8**						**2.7**	**105**	**127**	**-$1**

Bumgarner,Madison

Age: 28	Th: L	Role SP	Health D	LIMA Plan B+
Ht: 6' 5"	Wt: 250	Type Pwr	PT/Exp A	Rand Var 0
			Consist A	MM 3305

Shoulder sprain, suffered in April dirt bike accident, knocked him out for nearly three months. Swing-and-miss stuff was lacking immediately upon return, but SwK got back to 12% in final 10 starts, while Ctl never blinked. New FB% a mild concern, but he appears to be back in ace condition. (Less sure about the bike.)

Yr Tm	W	L	Sv	IP	K	ERA	xERA	WHIP	oOPS	vL	vR	BF/G	Ctl	Dom	Cmd	FpK	SwK	G	L	F	H%	S%	hr/f	GS	APC	DOM%	DIS%	Sv%	LI	RAR	BPV	BPX	R$
13 SF	13	9	0	201	199	2.77	3.25	1.03	577	487	602	25.9	2.8	8.9	3.2	60%	11%	47	18	35	26%	76%	8%	31	103	48%	6%			27.2	110	144	$26
14 SF	18	10	0	217	219	2.98	3.08	1.09	653	539	684	26.5	1.8	9.1	5.1	66%	12%	44	20	36	31%	76%	10%	33	102	48%	15%			20.4	137	163	$23
15 SF	18	9	0	218	234	2.93	3.10	1.01	612	539	627	27.2	1.6	9.6	6.0	64%	13%	42	23	36	30%	75%	10%	32	104	59%	6%			27.9	150	179	$32
16 SF	15	9	0	227	251	2.74	3.48	1.03	619	513	645	26.8	2.1	10.0	4.6	65%	12%	40	19	41	28%	79%	11%	34	105	56%	9%			40.5	140	166	$34
17 SF	4	9	0	111	101	3.32	3.99	1.09	704	530	740	26.5	1.6	8.2	5.1	67%	11%	41	18	41	28%	77%	13%	17	98	53%	12%			14.2	123	147	$10
1st Half	0	3	0	27	28	3.00	3.54	1.07	629	364	697	28.0	1.3	9.3	7.0	65%	11%	46	18	36	32%	74%	7%	4	101	50%	0%			4.5	156	187	-$4
2nd Half	4	6	0	84	73	3.43	4.13	1.10	729	599	753	26.0	1.7	7.8	4.6	67%	10%	39	18	43	27%	78%	14%	13	97	54%	15%			9.6	112	134	$14
18 Proj	**12**	**10**	**0**	**203**	**204**	**3.04**	**3.67**	**1.06**	**653**	**505**	**686**	**25.7**	**1.8**	**9.0**	**5.1**	**65%**	**11%**	**42**	**19**	**39**	**29%**	**77%**	**11%**	**31**						**33.0**	**134**	**162**	**$26**

Bundy,Dylan

Age: 25	Th: R	Role SP	Health C	LIMA Plan C+
Ht: 6' 1"	Wt: 200	Type Pwr xFB	PT/Exp C	Rand Var 0
			Consist A	MM 1305

Burst out of gate with sub-2.00 ERA in first six starts, but skills lagged behind (5.7 Dom). Showed some encouraging signs later in season, even as ERA climbed: significant 2nd half step forward in SwK/Dom; suddenly solved LHers; 6.8 Cmd in Aug/Sept. Durability caveats remain, but... UP: 3.50 ERA, 200 K.

Yr Tm	W	L	Sv	IP	K	ERA	xERA	WHIP	oOPS	vL	vR	BF/G	Ctl	Dom	Cmd	FpK	SwK	G	L	F	H%	S%	hr/f	GS	APC	DOM%	DIS%	Sv%	LI	RAR	BPV	BPX	R$
13																																	
14																																	
15 aa	0	3	0	22	21	4.91	3.74	1.39				11.6	2.1	8.5	4.0						38%	61%								-2.6	131	156	-$5
16 BAL	10	6	0	110	104	4.02	4.51	1.38	766	756	776	13.2	3.4	8.5	2.5	61%	11%	36	22	42	31%	77%	13%	14	54	14%	43%	0	0.82	2.3	75	89	$3
17 BAL	13	9	0	170	152	4.24	4.55	1.20	721	773	674	24.9	2.7	8.1	3.0	60%	12%	33	20	47	28%	69%	11%	28	101	25%	29%			2.4	83	100	$12
1st Half	8	7	0	103	80	4.02	4.88	1.24	774	825	729	24.8	2.9	7.0	2.4	58%	11%	31	22	47	27%	75%	13%	17	103	18%	24%			4.3	57	69	$14
2nd Half	5	2	0	67	72	4.59	4.06	1.13	642	699	589	25.2	2.4	9.7	4.0	62%	14%	35	17	48	30%	61%	9%	11	97	36%	36%			-1.9	123	147	$8
18 Proj	**14**	**10**	**0**	**189**	**182**	**3.98**	**4.45**	**1.26**	**725**	**752**	**698**	**21.7**	**3.0**	**8.7**	**3.0**	**61%**	**12%**	**35**	**20**	**45**	**30%**	**74%**	**12%**	**31**						**8.8**	**90**	**108**	**$13**

Bush,Matt

Age: 32	Th: R	Role RP	Health B	LIMA Plan A
Ht: 5' 9"	Wt: 180	Type Pwr	PT/Exp D	Rand Var 0
			Consist F	MM 2410

Ascended to closer role mid-April, could only hold the gig for two months. Swing and miss stuff still evident, but FpK and FB% took a turn for the worse, indicating Ctl, HR issues may linger. Off-season shoulder surgery further clouds the outlook for 2018. In all, an uphill battle to gain more 9th inning opps.

Yr Tm	W	L	Sv	IP	K	ERA	xERA	WHIP	oOPS	vL	vR	BF/G	Ctl	Dom	Cmd	FpK	SwK	G	L	F	H%	S%	hr/f	GS	APC	DOM%	DIS%	Sv%	LI	RAR	BPV	BPX	R$
13																																	
14																																	
15																																	
16 TEX *	7	4	6	79	74	2.84	2.24	0.96	525	636	458	4.3	2.2	8.4	3.9	66%	13%	42	25	32	25%	74%	8%	0	16			67	1.10	13.1	123	146	$12
17 TEX	3	4	10	52	58	3.78	4.51	1.45	750	824	699	4.2	3.3	10.0	3.1	55%	13%	37	20	43	36%	78%	10%	0	17			67	0.98	3.7	106	128	$3
1st Half	2	4	10	29	31	4.03	4.57	1.55	797	893	713	4.5	3.1	9.6	3.1	59%	12%	37	22	41	37%	80%	14%	0	17			67	1.21	1.2	104	125	$6
2nd Half	1	0	0	23	27	3.47	4.43	1.33	690	700	685	3.9	3.5	10.4	3.0	51%	14%	38	16	46	34%	76%	6%	0	16			0	0.73	2.6	110	132	$0
18 Proj	**4**	**3**	**2**	**58**	**61**	**3.52**	**4.01**	**1.24**	**668**	**753**	**615**	**4.0**	**2.9**	**9.4**	**3.3**	**59%**	**13%**	**40**	**21**	**39**	**31%**	**75%**	**10%**	**0**						**6.0**	**110**	**133**	**$3**

Butler,Eddie

Age: 27	Th: R	Role SP	Health B	LIMA Plan D
Ht: 6' 2"	Wt: 180	Type Con	PT/Exp D	Rand Var -2
			Consist C	MM 0000

4-3, 3.95 ERA in 55 IP at CHC. Escaping Coors Field helped him improve ERA, but skills remained as uninspiring as ever. K-BB% was second worst in majors (min. 50 IP), and GB% is trending in wrong direction. If and when hr/f normalizes, it could get ugly in a hurry. Safe to avoid in all formats.

Yr Tm	W	L	Sv	IP	K	ERA	xERA	WHIP	oOPS	vL	vR	BF/G	Ctl	Dom	Cmd	FpK	SwK	G	L	F	H%	S%	hr/f	GS	APC	DOM%	DIS%	Sv%	LI	RAR	BPV	BPX	R$
13 aa	1	0	0	28	20	0.90	0.70	0.80				16.7	2.1	6.5	3.2						21%	88%								10.1	127	165	$2
14 COL *	7	11	0	129	57	5.08	5.24	1.52	973	1310	760	25.5	3.0	4.0	1.3	49%	5%	52	25	23	31%	68%	13%	3	86	0%	100%			-21.4	16	19	-$11
15 COL *	5	16	0	143	72	6.21	6.32	1.77	952	1073	831	24.3	4.3	4.5	1.1	57%	7%	50	22	28	33%	66%	17%	16	85	0%	69%			-39.5	3	4	-$24
16 COL *	10	8	0	153	73	6.76	6.49	1.68	944	894	977	21.5	3.0	4.3	1.5	58%	8%	46	25	30	34%	62%	20%	9	63	11%	67%	0	0.78	-48.6	0	0	-$21
17 CHC *	6	3	0	100	54	3.31	4.21	1.48	715	665	748	20.5	3.6	4.9	1.3	60%	7%	44	22	33	31%	78%	7%	11	71	0%	64%	0	0.65	13.0	44	52	$1
1st Half	5	3	0	78	42	3.08	3.46	1.36	708	727	694	21.7	3.7	4.8	1.3	60%	7%	45	22	32	28%	77%	6%	10	79	0%	60%			12.3	51	61	$5
2nd Half	1	0	0	22	13	4.10	6.81	1.89	757	298	1099	17.5	3.3	5.1	1.5	62%	7%	38	23	38	39%	80%	10%	1	43	0%	100%	0	0.26	0.7	22	27	-$11
18 Proj	**3**	**3**	**0**	**58**	**30**	**4.96**	**5.50**	**1.62**	**868**	**919**	**826**	**20.5**	**3.4**	**4.7**	**1.4**	**58%**	**8%**	**47**	**23**	**30**	**33%**	**71%**	**10%**	**13**						**-4.3**	**19**	**22**	**-$7**

Cahill,Trevor

Age: 30	Th: R	Role RP	Health F	LIMA Plan C
Ht: 6' 4"	Wt: 240	Type Pwr xGB	PT/Exp D	Rand Var +5
			Consist A	MM 1201

Back in rotation, quickly achieved must-own status by pairing elite GB% with more whiffs than ever. May shoulder strain put breakout on hold, and soon after return, the wheels fell off, both in terms of skills and luck. Ended up back in pen with another sub-2.0 Cmd. That electric 1H says he may deserve one last shot.

Yr Tm	W	L	Sv	IP	K	ERA	xERA	WHIP	oOPS	vL	vR	BF/G	Ctl	Dom	Cmd	FpK	SwK	G	L	F	H%	S%	hr/f	GS	APC	DOM%	DIS%	Sv%	LI	RAR	BPV	BPX	R$
13 ARI *	8	12	0	163	112	4.18	4.16	1.43	745	769	719	23.9	4.0	6.2	1.5	60%	8%	56	20	24	29%	72%	12%	25	91	16%	36%	0	0.85	-6.3	47	61	-$3
14 ARI *	5	14	1	139	126	5.21	4.77	1.58	791	929	657	16.1	4.8	8.2	1.7	57%	11%	48	24	27	33%	67%	10%	17	60	18%	35%	50	0.67	-25.2	60	72	-$11
15 2 NL *	2	6	0	80	55	5.72	4.86	1.55	725	684	751	9.4	3.9	6.2	1.6	59%	10%	63	19	18	32%	63%	17%	3	26	0%	100%	0	0.63	-17.3	44	52	-$11
16 CHC *	4	7	0	85	85	3.35	4.38	1.49	621	660	594	6.6	5.1	9.0	1.8	54%	12%	57	22	22	31%	82%	18%	1	23	0%	0%	0	0.70	8.8	65	77	$1
17 2 TM	4	3	0	84	87	4.93	4.28	1.62	850	767	915	18.1	4.8	9.3	1.9	60%	12%	56	18	26	33%	75%	25%	14	73	21%	29%	0	0.66	-5.9	72	86	-$6
1st Half	3	2	0	41	51	3.27	3.14	1.21	606	451	715	24.7	3.7	11.1	3.0	62%	14%	60	14	26	31%	74%	11%	7	98	29%	0%			5.6	138	166	$5
2nd Half	1	1	0	43	36	6.54	5.55	2.02	1061	1008	1106	14.9	5.9	7.6	1.3	58%	9%	52	21	26	35%	75%	35%	7	60	14%	57%	0	0.60	-11.5	7	9	-$15
18 Proj	**4**	**5**	**0**	**87**	**81**	**4.48**	**4.30**	**1.53**	**798**	**776**	**815**	**15.2**	**4.6**	**8.4**	**1.8**	**58%**	**11%**	**57**	**20**	**24**	**31%**	**75%**	**23%**	**22**						**-1.3**	**62**	**74**	**-$4**

Carrasco,Carlos

Age: 31	Th: R	Role SP	Health C	LIMA Plan C
Ht: 6' 3"	Wt: 212	Type Pwr	PT/Exp A	Rand Var 0
			Consist A	MM 4405

March elbow soreness provided a scare, but skills didn't miss a beat on his way to first 200-IP season. SwK/Dom peaked in 2nd half, and he posted 1.82 ERA in last 10 starts. Track record shows heavy workload isn't something we can bank on, but if he can stay healthy again... UP: sub-3.00 ERA, 250 K

Yr Tm	W	L	Sv	IP	K	ERA	xERA	WHIP	oOPS	vL	vR	BF/G	Ctl	Dom	Cmd	FpK	SwK	G	L	F	H%	S%	hr/f	GS	APC	DOM%	DIS%	Sv%	LI	RAR	BPV	BPX	R$
13 CLE *	4	5	1	118	94	5.15	4.76	1.50	864	980	745	16.5	3.1	7.2	2.3	67%	9%	50	22	28	35%	66%	9%	7	52	14%	71%	100	0.59	-18.8	64	83	-$9
14 CLE	8	7	1	134	140	2.55	2.73	0.99	543	516	566	13.2	1.9	9.4	4.8	63%	14%	53	20	28	29%	75%	7%	14	49	43%	0%	100	0.63	19.6	148	176	$17
15 CLE	14	12	0	184	216	3.63	2.75	1.07	646	639	651	24.3	2.1	10.6	5.0	67%	14%	51	19	30	31%	69%	13%	30	93	57%	20%			7.6	163	194	$19
16 CLE	11	8	0	146	150	3.32	3.41	1.15	711	739	688	24.0	2.1	9.2	4.4	62%	13%	49	20	31	30%	78%	16%	25	90	32%	20%			15.7	137	162	$15
17 CLE	18	6	0	200	226	3.29	3.24	1.10	674	727	629	24.9	2.1	10.2	4.9	63%	14%	45	22	33	31%	74%	12%	32	96	50%	13%			26.5	150	180	$28
1st Half	9	3	0	98	103	3.50	3.45	1.05	661	724	614	24.2	2.4	9.5	4.0	60%	13%	45	21	34	27%	71%	14%	16	95	50%	19%			10.3	129	154	$27
2nd Half	9	3	0	102	123	3.08	3.04	1.13	685	729	645	25.7	1.8	10.8	6.2	66%	15%	46	22	32	34%	76%	11%	16	96	50%	6%			16.2	171	205	$30
18 Proj	**15**	**8**	**0**	**189**	**207**	**3.38**	**3.33**	**1.12**	**679**	**717**	**647**	**24.5**	**2.1**	**9.9**	**4.7**	**64%**	**13%**	**48**	**21**	**32**	**31%**	**74%**	**13%**	**29**						**22.6**	**147**	**177**	**$22**

BRIAN RUDD

Cashner,Andrew

Cashner,Andrew				Health	F	LIMA Plan	C+
Age: 31	Th: R	Role	SP	PT/Exp	A	Rand Var	-4
Ht: 6' 6"	Wt: 235	Type		Consist	B	MM	0003

Drastic changes in pitch mix, including the elimination of his slider (lifetime 17% SwK), addition of a cutter and return of his 2014-15 sinker-heavy approach yielded a pretty picture. However, the puny Dom/SwK, cratering BPV, horrid DOM/DIS% and giant ERA/xERA chasm show that it's a mirage. Heed BPX trend.

Yr Tm	W	L	Sv	IP	K	ERA	xERA	WHIP	oOPS	vL	vR	BF/G	Ctl	Dom	Cmd	FpK	SwK	G	L	F	H%	S%	hr/f	GS	APC	DOM%	DIS%	Sv%	LI	RAR	BPV	BPX	R$
13 SD	10	9	0	175	128	3.09	3.56	1.13	639	703	578	22.8	2.4	6.6	2.7	60%	9%	53	19	29	28%	74%	8%	26	87	31%	15%	0	0.73	16.8	84	110	$14
14 SD	5	7	0	123	93	2.55	3.60	1.13	623	675	573	26.6	2.1	6.8	3.2	63%	8%	48	20	31	29%	79%	6%	19	95	32%	26%			18.1	91	108	$10
15 SD	6	16	0	185	165	4.34	3.95	1.44	772	896	669	25.9	3.2	8.0	2.5	62%	9%	47	23	30	34%	72%	12%	31	100	23%	26%			-8.6	83	99	-$4
16 2 NL	5	11	0	132	112	5.25	4.65	1.53	849	903	794	21.0	4.1	7.6	1.9	55%	8%	46	20	33	32%	68%	15%	27	85	11%	37%	0	1.05	-17.3	51	61	-$8
17 TEX	11	11	0	167	86	3.40	5.24	1.32	692	701	683	25.1	3.5	4.6	1.3	58%	6%	49	19	32	27%	77%	9%	28	94	7%	43%			19.7	17	21	$10
1st Half	3	7	0	74	36	3.87	5.52	1.48	740	740	740	24.5	4.0	4.4	1.1	58%	6%	50	20	30	29%	74%	7%	13	92	0%	46%			4.4	-2	-2	-$2
2nd Half	8	4	0	92	50	3.02	5.02	1.19	652	665	640	25.7	3.0	4.9	1.6	59%	7%	48	19	34	25%	79%	10%	15	96	13%	40%			15.2	32	38	$19
18 Proj	**9**	**12**	**0**	**167**	**113**	**4.30**	**4.88**	**1.38**	**745**	**791**	**704**	**23.5**	**3.4**	**6.1**	**1.8**	**58%**	**7%**	**48**	**20**	**32**	**30%**	**71%**	**10%**	**30**						**1.1**	**43**	**52**	**$1**

Casilla,Santiago

Casilla,Santiago				Health	C	LIMA Plan	B
Age: 37	Th: R	Role	RP	PT/Exp	B	Rand Var	0
Ht: 6' 0"	Wt: 210	Type	Pwr	Consist	B	MM	2310

Longtime closer finally displayed closer-worthy skills in 2016, but they left as quickly as they came. Issues vL (1.4 Cmd), shoddy FpK/Ctl downside and sharp decline in GB% are worrisome. All of that contributed to his worst xERA since 2009. His days of closing out games appear to be over.

Yr Tm	W	L	Sv	IP	K	ERA	xERA	WHIP	oOPS	vL	vR	BF/G	Ctl	Dom	Cmd	FpK	SwK	G	L	F	H%	S%	hr/f	GS	APC	DOM%	DIS%	Sv%	LI	RAR	BPV	BPX	R$
13 SF	7	2	2	50	38	2.16	4.03	1.28	627	652	611	3.6	4.5	6.8	1.5	54%	10%	54	17	29	26%	84%	5%	0	14			67	1.66	10.5	34	44	$4
14 SF	3	3	19	58	45	1.70	3.07	0.86	493	539	461	4.0	2.3	6.9	3.0	57%	11%	56	15	29	21%	83%	7%	0	16			83	1.37	14.7	96	115	$15
15 SF	4	2	38	58	62	2.79	3.51	1.28	680	841	531	3.6	3.6	9.6	2.7	57%	11%	46	24	30	31%	82%	13%	0	14			86	1.47	8.4	101	120	$18
16 SF	2	5	31	58	65	3.57	3.46	1.19	710	849	622	3.9	2.9	10.1	3.4	54%	11%	48	16	36	30%	75%	15%	0	15			78	1.79	4.4	128	152	$14
17 OAK	4	5	16	59	57	4.27	4.46	1.36	757	803	724	4.1	3.4	8.7	2.6	55%	12%	40	22	38	31%	72%	12%	0	16			70	0.94	0.6	84	101	$6
1st Half	1	3	14	29	27	3.99	4.59	1.33	699	724	680	4.3	3.7	8.3	2.3	56%	11%	41	22	36	30%	72%	10%	0	17			82	1.15	1.3	69	83	$10
2nd Half	3	2	2	30	30	4.55	4.34	1.38	813	875	767	4.0	3.0	9.1	3.0	54%	14%	39	21	40	33%	72%	14%	0	15			33	0.74	-0.7	99	119	$2
18 Proj	**4**	**4**	**4**	**58**	**58**	**3.98**	**4.08**	**1.28**	**722**	**810**	**659**	**3.8**	**3.3**	**9.0**	**2.8**	**55%**	**12%**	**44**	**20**	**36**	**30%**	**73%**	**13%**	**0**						**2.7**	**97**	**117**	**$2**

Castillo,Luis

Castillo,Luis				Health	A	LIMA Plan	C+
Age: 25	Th: R	Role	SP	PT/Exp	D	Rand Var	+2
Ht: 6' 2"	Wt: 190	Type	Pwr xGB	Consist	F	MM	3305

3-7, 3.12 ERA in 89 IP at CIN. Utilized a 98 mph fastball, hard slider, sinker and vastly improved change-up (23% SwK, 59% GB%) to great success in 2017. His ability to marry an extreme GB% with lots of strikeouts and respectable Ctl is immensely appealing (see 2nd half) and gives him ... UP: 3.25 ERA, 200 K.

Yr Tm	W	L	Sv	IP	K	ERA	xERA	WHIP	oOPS	vL	vR	BF/G	Ctl	Dom	Cmd	FpK	SwK	G	L	F	H%	S%	hr/f	GS	APC	DOM%	DIS%	Sv%	LI	RAR	BPV	BPX	R$
13																																	
14																																	
15																																	
16																																	
17 CIN *	7	11	0	170	166	3.70	3.70	1.22	638	630	646	23.6	2.6	8.8	3.4	57%	13%	59	12	29	31%	73%	17%	15	99	40%	20%			13.8	100	120	$12
1st Half	4	4	0	91	82	4.23	4.88	1.42	905	737	1066	24.1	2.4	8.1	3.4	50%	14%	67	4	29	35%	73%	43%	2	100	0%	50%			1.4	83	100	$5
2nd Half	3	7	0	79	84	3.09	3.22	0.99	601	614	591	24.1	2.7	9.6	3.5	58%	13%	58	13	29	25%	73%	14%	13	99	46%	15%			12.3	135	161	$20
18 Proj	**10**	**12**	**0**	**189**	**189**	**3.55**	**3.53**	**1.16**	**649**	**658**	**642**	**23.5**	**2.6**	**9.0**	**3.5**	**58%**	**13%**	**58**	**13**	**29**	**30%**	**73%**	**13%**	**32**						**18.7**	**128**	**154**	**$16**

Castro,Miguel

Castro,Miguel				Health	B	LIMA Plan	D+
Age: 23	Th: R	Role	RP	PT/Exp	D	Rand Var	0
Ht: 6' 7"	Wt: 205	Type	xGB	Consist	F	MM	0001

3-3, 3.53 ERA in 66 IP at BAL. Once labeled a "closer of the future," he has yet to live up to it. The 2nd half line, amassed entirely in MLB, was dreadful, as xERA, Cmd and BPV were all downright ugly. SwK hints at some Dom potential, and at his age, there's still time. But he's a long way from fantasy relevance.

Yr Tm	W	L	Sv	IP	K	ERA	xERA	WHIP	oOPS	vL	vR	BF/G	Ctl	Dom	Cmd	FpK	SwK	G	L	F	H%	S%	hr/f	GS	APC	DOM%	DIS%	Sv%	LI	RAR	BPV	BPX	R$
13																																	
14																																	
15 2 TM *	3	6	4	51	43	4.57	5.75	1.67	937	920	952	5.4	5.0	7.5	1.5	58%	11%	33	24	43	32%	77%	17%	0	16			36	1.04	-3.9	30	35	-$5
16 COL *	2	3	0	30	24	10.27	8.39	1.84	880	1111	772	4.0	3.7	7.1	1.9	42%	10%	54	19	27	35%	46%	23%	0	13			0	1.27	-22.7	-17	-21	-$12
17 BAL *	6	3	0	91	48	4.05	3.59	1.26	682	848	573	8.2	3.4	4.7	1.4	58%	10%	49	17	34	25%	70%	12%	1	26	0%	100%	0	0.90	3.4	38	45	$
1st Half	4	0	0	37	17	4.86	4.46	1.37	857	922	824	10.3	2.8	4.1	1.4	62%	11%	44	21	36	29%	66%	21%	0	22			0	0.86	-2.3	25	30	-$
2nd Half	2	3	0	54	31	3.50	5.03	1.19	641	833	507	7.3	3.8	5.2	1.3	57%	10%	51	16	33	23%	73%	9%	1	28	0%	100%	0	0.92	5.7	18	22	$
18 Proj	**5**	**5**	**0**	**73**	**48**	**5.49**	**5.27**	**1.56**	**840**	**1116**	**650**	**5.6**	**3.7**	**6.0**	**1.6**	**57%**	**10%**	**51**	**16**	**33**	**31%**	**69%**	**15%**	**0**						**-10.1**	**36**	**44**	**-$7**

Cecil,Brett

Cecil,Brett				Health	D	LIMA Plan	A
Age: 31	Th: L	Role	RP	PT/Exp	D	Rand Var	0
Ht: 6' 3"	Wt: 235	Type	Pwr	Consist	B	MM	3400

Strong BPX and xERA history establishes him as a reliable reliever. Though his Dom tumbled, SwK points to a rebound. Regained prior form vR, but ran into trouble vL thanks largely to 40% H% and woeful Cmd (1.7; career: 3.7). Overall package is showing signs of age, but still useful at back end of staff.

Yr Tm	W	L	Sv	IP	K	ERA	xERA	WHIP	oOPS	vL	vR	BF/G	Ctl	Dom	Cmd	FpK	SwK	G	L	F	H%	S%	hr/f	GS	APC	DOM%	DIS%	Sv%	LI	RAR	BPV	BPX	R$
13 TOR	5	1	1	61	70	2.82	2.96	1.10	594	458	736	4.2	3.4	10.4	3.0	58%	12%	51	20	29	28%	76%	9%	0	15			33	0.89	7.8	124	161	$
14 TOR	2	3	5	53	76	2.70	2.68	1.37	627	714	569	3.5	4.6	12.8	2.8	54%	17%	54	25	22	37%	80%	7%	0	14			71	1.22	6.8	140	167	$
15 TOR	5	5	5	54	70	2.48	2.49	0.96	562	539	576	3.4	2.2	11.6	5.4	60%	15%	52	19	29	30%	77%	11%	0	13			63	1.01	9.9	181	215	$
16 TOR	1	7	0	37	45	3.93	3.14	1.28	742	673	799	2.9	2.0	11.0	5.6	66%	13%	42	28	30	36%	76%	20%	0	10			0	1.08	1.2	166	197	-$
17 STL	2	4	1	67	66	3.88	3.83	1.23	714	936	561	3.8	2.1	8.8	4.1	61%	14%	43	22	36	33%	71%	11%	0	14			14	1.06	4.0	122	147	$
1st Half	1	2	0	32	31	3.69	4.07	1.26	713	982	487	3.3	3.1	8.8	2.8	55%	15%	48	15	37	30%	75%	13%	0	12			0	1.33	2.6	100	120	$
2nd Half	1	2	1	36	35	4.04	3.61	1.21	715	886	617	4.4	1.3	8.8	7.0	67%	14%	39	27	35	35%	68%	9%	0	15			33	0.72	1.4	142	170	$
18 Proj	**2**	**5**	**0**	**51**	**57**	**3.58**	**3.44**	**1.20**	**689**	**767**	**634**	**3.4**	**2.2**	**10.1**	**4.5**	**62%**	**14%**	**45**	**23**	**32**	**33%**	**73%**	**13%**	**0**						**4.9**	**144**	**174**	**$**

Cedeno,Xavier

Cedeno,Xavier				Health	F	LIMA Plan	C+
Age: 31	Th: L	Role	RP	PT/Exp	D	Rand Var	+5
Ht: 5' 11"	Wt: 210	Type	Pwr	Consist	F	MM	3300

Missed five months with forearm tightness. His cutter/curve combo has proven to be deadly vL (career .584 oOPS; 4.0 Cmd). There's some value here in Holds leagues, but specialist role holds down his IP and counting stats/Ks. R$ column demonstrates how this profile barely moves the value needle.

Yr Tm	W	L	Sv	IP	K	ERA	xERA	WHIP	oOPS	vL	vR	BF/G	Ctl	Dom	Cmd	FpK	SwK	G	L	F	H%	S%	hr/f	GS	APC	DOM%	DIS%	Sv%	LI	RAR	BPV	BPX	R$
13 2 TM *	2	0	4	47	43	2.90	3.55	1.43	811	603	1039	3.6	4.7	8.3	1.8	62%	10%	60	15	25	31%	80%	0%	0	14			57	0.61	5.5	80	105	$
14 WAS *	5	1	4	46	47	3.05	2.82	1.09	833	1067	600	4.1	2.5	9.1	3.6	47%	8%	38	33	29	28%	75%	14%	0	12			57	0.94	3.9	117	139	$
15 2 TM	4	1	1	46	47	2.35	3.16	1.17	614	490	768	2.9	2.7	9.2	3.4	54%	15%	53	21	26	30%	84%	13%	0	11			33	1.28	9.2	123	146	$
16 TAM	3	4	0	41	43	3.70	3.59	1.19	597	483	705	3.2	2.8	9.4	3.3	63%	13%	47	23	30	32%	68%	6%	0	13			0	1.30	2.5	117	139	$
17 TAM	1	1	0	3	0	12.00	14.12	3.67	1550	1222	1922	2.3	12.0	0.0	0.0	62%	3%	56	25	19	32%	88%	####	0	8			0	2.31	-2.8	-290	-348	-$
1st Half	1	1	0	2	0	3.86	16.34	3.43	1170	1000	1356	2.3	15.4	0.0	0.0	56%	2%	55	36	9	31%	100%	100%	0	8			0	2.87	0.1	-384	-460	-$
2nd Half	0	0	0	1	0	40.50	10.49	4.50	2400	1667	3500	2.5	0.0	0.0	0.0	80%	7%	60	0	40	35%	0%	100%	0	8			0	0.35	-3.0	38	46	-$
18 Proj	**4**	**2**	**0**	**44**	**44**	**3.10**	**3.63**	**1.18**	**602**	**483**	**729**	**3.4**	**3.0**	**9.1**	**3.1**	**59%**	**14%**	**50**	**22**	**28**	**30%**	**75%**	**9%**	**0**						**6.7**	**111**	**134**	**$**

Chacin,Jhoulys

Chacin,Jhoulys				Health	D	LIMA Plan	C
Age: 30	Th: R	Role	SP	PT/Exp	B	Rand Var	0
Ht: 6' 3"	Wt: 215	Type	Pwr	Consist	A	MM	1103

Journeyman appeared to take a sizable step forward in 2017, but xERA and BPV/BPX were actually a carbon-copy of 2016. The only real change is that he was much more consistent in 2017 (DOM/DIS%). While disaster avoidance is nice, this is a run-of-the-mill skill set that comes with some implicit peril.

Yr Tm	W	L	Sv	IP	K	ERA	xERA	WHIP	oOPS	vL	vR	BF/G	Ctl	Dom	Cmd	FpK	SwK	G	L	F	H%	S%	hr/f	GS	APC	DOM%	DIS%	Sv%	LI	RAR	BPV	BPX	R$
13 COL	14	10	0	197	126	3.47	4.02	1.26	685	722	650	26.3	2.8	5.7	2.1	61%	8%	47	25	29	29%	73%	6%	31	96	29%	29%			9.7	53	69	$1
14 COL	1	7	0	63	42	5.40	4.56	1.44	790	751	821	24.7	4.0	6.0	1.5	63%	9%	43	22	35	29%	64%	12%	11	93	9%	73%			-13.0	21	25	-$
15 ARI *	9	7	0	155	89	3.39	3.82	1.35	729	982	497	25.9	3.1	5.2	1.7	55%	10%	47	19	33	30%	76%	15%	4	85	50%	50%	0	0.84	11.0	51	61	$
16 2 TM	6	8	0	144	119	4.81	4.36	1.44	745	762	728	18.6	3.4	7.4	2.2	61%	8%	48	23	29	33%	68%	11%	22	70	18%	59%	0	0.68	-11.1	67	80	-$
17 SD	13	10	0	180	153	3.89	4.38	1.27	693	789	602	23.9	3.6	7.6	2.1	59%	8%	49	19	32	28%	72%	11%	32	92	22%	28%			10.4	67	81	$1
1st Half	6	7	0	91	76	4.76	4.19	1.32	750	935	591	24.0	3.0	7.5	2.5	58%	9%	53	17	31	30%	67%	16%	16	88	25%	31%			-4.5	86	103	$
2nd Half	7	3	0	90	77	3.01	4.58	1.22	633	651	614	23.8	4.2	7.7	1.8	59%	8%	45	21	34	26%	77%	7%	16	95	19%	25%			14.9	48	58	$1
18 Proj	**9**	**10**	**0**	**174**	**136**	**4.01**	**4.58**	**1.33**	**711**	**751**	**672**	**22.0**	**3.5**	**7.0**	**2.0**	**60%**	**8%**	**47**	**21**	**32**	**29%**	**71%**	**10%**	**33**						**7.5**	**57**	**69**	**$**

GREG PYRON

Chafin,Andrew

Age: 28	Th: L	Role RP	Health	D	LIMA Plan	C
Ht: 6' 2"	Wt: 225	Type Pwr xGB	PT/Exp	D	Rand Var	+3
			Consist	A	MM	2200

2016 skills confirmed bullpen was a good place for him; results finally concurred in 2017. Fastball/slider blend generates oodles of GBs and Ks. Highly effective vL, but struggles vR and FpK/Ctl likely confine him to setup role. Still, 2nd half LI shows him ascending the pecking order.

Yr Tm	W	L	Sv	IP	K	ERA	xERA	WHIP	oOPS	vL	vR	BF/G	Ctl	Dom	Cmd	FpK	SwK	G	L	F	H%	S%	hr/f	GS	APC	DOM%	DIS%	Sv%	LI	RAR	BPV	BPX	R$
13 aa	10	7	0	126	73	3.87	4.34	1.48				25.9	3.1	5.2	1.7						33%	73%								-0.1	50	66	-$1
14 ARI *	9	8	0	162	105	4.50	5.21	1.58	685	641	701	24.5	3.5	5.8	1.6	58%	7%	54	18	28	33%	73%	0%	3	86	0%	0%			-15.1	38	45	-$10
15 ARI	5	1	2	75	58	2.76	3.70	1.15	587	524	631	4.6	3.6	7.0	1.9	54%	9%	58	19	23	26%	76%	6%	0	18			100	1.29	11.1	64	76	$6
16 ARI	0	1	0	23	28	6.75	3.40	1.46	703	569	824	3.1	4.4	11.1	2.5	60%	15%	51	24	25	37%	50%	7%	0	11			0	0.94	-7.2	111	132	-$6
17 ARI	1	0	0	51	61	3.51	3.31	1.34	699	565	792	3.1	3.7	10.7	2.9	52%	12%	56	21	22	34%	77%	17%	0	12			0	1.02	5.4	127	153	-$1
1st Half	1	0	0	28	38	1.93	2.37	1.07	542	477	585	3.1	2.6	12.2	4.8	53%	12%	61	22	16	34%	83%	9%	0	12			0	0.89	8.4	190	227	$4
2nd Half	0	0	0	23	23	5.40	4.59	1.67	876	658	1030	3.1	5.0	8.9	1.8	52%	11%	51	21	28	34%	71%	21%	0	12			0	1.16	-3.0	54	64	-$7
18 Proj	**2**	**1**	**0**	**44**	**40**	**3.76**	**3.97**	**1.39**	**726**	**601**	**813**	**4.4**	**3.8**	**8.2**	**2.2**	**53%**	**10%**	**57**	**20**	**23**	**32%**	**75%**	**13%**	**0**						**3.2**	**82**	**98**	**-$2**

Chapman,Aroldis

Age: 30	Th: L	Role RP	Health	D	LIMA Plan	B+
Ht: 6' 4"	Wt: 215	Type Pwr	PT/Exp	B	Rand Var	0
			Consist	B	MM	5530

Still waiting for 40 saves. Missed five weeks in 1st half (rotator cuff inflammation), then endured mid-season slump (9.2 Dom, 5.6 Ctl in 18 IP) before returning to the elite in Sept following tweak to fastball grip (12.8 Dom, 24% SwK, 1.5 Ctl in 12 IP). FpK says Ctl dip not a concern; strong finish re-confirms top-tier status.

Yr Tm	W	L	Sv	IP	K	ERA	xERA	WHIP	oOPS	vL	vR	BF/G	Ctl	Dom	Cmd	FpK	SwK	G	L	F	H%	S%	hr/f	GS	APC	DOM%	DIS%	Sv%	LI	RAR	BPV	BPX	R$
13 CIN	4	5	38	64	112	2.54	2.30	1.04	544	379	592	3.8	4.1	15.8	3.9	59%	17%	34	24	42	31%	81%	15%	0	16			88	1.38	10.4	186	243	$23
14 CIN	0	3	36	54	106	2.00	1.52	0.83	406	372	415	3.7	4.0	17.7	4.4	58%	21%	43	22	35	30%	75%	4%	0	17			95	1.44	11.6	231	275	$21
15 CIN	4	4	33	66	116	1.63	2.55	1.15	527	451	554	4.3	4.5	15.7	3.5	56%	20%	37	22	41	36%	88%	6%	0	18			92	1.24	19.1	177	211	$23
16 2 TM	4	1	36	58	90	1.55	2.24	0.86	452	462	448	3.8	2.8	14.0	5.0	57%	19%	46	25	29	29%	83%	6%	0	17			92	1.39	18.9	200	238	$25
17 NYY	4	3	22	50	69	3.22	3.15	1.13	584	577	588	4.0	3.6	12.3	3.5	62%	14%	49	16	35	32%	72%	7%	0	17			85	1.14	7.1	153	183	$13
1st Half	1	0	8	18	29	3.06	2.39	1.25	602	567	609	3.9	3.1	14.8	4.8	64%	14%	48	30	23	43%	73%	0%	0	17			80	1.15	2.8	209	250	$6
2nd Half	3	3	14	33	40	3.31	3.59	1.07	575	578	572	4.2	3.9	11.0	2.9	61%	14%	49	9	42	26%	72%	9%	0	17			88	1.13	4.2	122	146	$17
18 Proj	**4**	**3**	**41**	**58**	**89**	**2.62**	**2.72**	**1.05**	**535**	**522**	**539**	**3.8**	**3.5**	**13.8**	**3.9**	**60%**	**17%**	**45**	**20**	**34**	**32%**	**76%**	**7%**	**0**						**12.5**	**176**	**212**	**$24**

Chatwood,Tyler

Age: 28	Th: R	Role RP	Health	F	LIMA Plan	D+
Ht: 6' 0"	Wt: 185	Type Pwr xGB	PT/Exp	B	Rand Var	+4
			Consist	A	MM	1103

Disappointing follow-up to 2016 is actually just an expected correction, per xERA. SwK/FpK suggest Cmd could become slightly less hideous, and GB% is a foundation skill, just not enough on its own. Took an August vacation in bullpen, didn't come back with any new tricks. Hope he got a T-shirt.

Yr Tm	W	L	Sv	IP	K	ERA	xERA	WHIP	oOPS	vL	vR	BF/G	Ctl	Dom	Cmd	FpK	SwK	G	L	F	H%	S%	hr/f	GS	APC	DOM%	DIS%	Sv%	LI	RAR	BPV	BPX	R$
13 COL *	10	6	0	145	91	3.13	3.90	1.42	711	729	697	23.7	2.9	5.7	1.9	55%	7%	59	21	21	32%	77%	7%	20	89	15%	45%			13.1	64	84	$4
14 COL	1	0	0	24	20	4.50	3.56	1.21	711	472	1015	25.3	3.0	7.5	2.5	50%	10%	46	29	26	26%	68%	22%	4	89	25%	50%			-2.2	78	93	-$3
15																																	
16 COL	12	9	0	158	117	3.87	4.31	1.37	723	751	693	24.8	4.0	6.7	1.7	54%	8%	57	17	26	29%	74%	12%	27	94	22%	37%			6.2	47	56	$5
17 COL	8	15	1	148	120	4.69	4.39	1.44	788	837	736	19.1	4.7	7.3	1.6	53%	10%	58	20	22	28%	70%	22%	25	75	16%	52%	100	0.72	-6.1	41	49	-$1
1st Half	6	9	0	100	83	4.41	4.35	1.38	769	757	781	24.7	4.8	7.5	1.6	54%	10%	57	21	23	26%	72%	23%	17	98	24%	47%			-0.6	40	48	$4
2nd Half	2	6	1	48	37	5.29	4.48	1.57	827	1002	649	13.2	4.5	7.0	1.5	53%	11%	61	19	20	32%	68%	21%	8	50	0%	63%	100	0.68	-5.5	42	50	-$10
18 Proj	**8**	**11**	**0**	**131**	**103**	**4.44**	**4.38**	**1.44**	**762**	**826**	**697**	**19.3**	**4.2**	**7.1**	**1.7**	**54%**	**9%**	**58**	**19**	**23**	**30%**	**71%**	**15%**	**27**						**-1.2**	**52**	**63**	**-$1**

Chavez,Jesse

Age: 34	Th: R	Role RP	Health	B	LIMA Plan	C
Ht: 6' 2"	Wt: 175	Type Pwr	PT/Exp	B	Rand Var	+4
			Consist	A	MM	1201

Began 2017 as SP, but worked out of the bullpen Aug-Sept (25 IP). Dom, xERA and BPX indicate he was much more effective as RP. However, HR issues plagued him throughout and he lacks closer-worthy stuff, so it's tough to see a path to fantasy relevance no matter the role.

Yr Tm	W	L	Sv	IP	K	ERA	xERA	WHIP	oOPS	vL	vR	BF/G	Ctl	Dom	Cmd	FpK	SwK	G	L	F	H%	S%	hr/f	GS	APC	DOM%	DIS%	Sv%	LI	RAR	BPV	BPX	R$
13 OAK *	4	6	1	87	74	3.64	3.71	1.35	620	630	605	9.1	2.6	7.6	2.9	61%	10%	43	17	39	34%	72%	5%	0	27			50	0.93	2.4	95	124	$0
14 OAK	8	8	0	146	136	3.45	3.72	1.31	692	663	729	19.4	3.0	8.4	2.8	63%	9%	42	23	35	31%	78%	11%	21	75	29%	24%	0	0.66	5.2	89	106	$5
15 OAK	7	15	1	157	136	4.18	4.04	1.35	730	825	616	22.4	2.8	7.8	2.8	61%	9%	43	23	34	32%	72%	11%	26	86	23%	38%	100	0.74	-4.3	87	104	$1
16 2 TM	2	2	0	67	63	4.43	4.05	1.33	779	836	740	4.5	2.4	8.5	3.5	64%	10%	43	18	39	32%	73%	15%	0	18			0	0.90	-2.0	108	128	-$2
17 LAA	7	11	0	138	119	5.35	4.51	1.40	826	779	867	15.4	2.9	7.8	2.6	62%	8%	41	22	37	31%	67%	18%	21	61	10%	43%	0	0.74	-16.8	79	95	-$3
1st Half	5	8	0	91	69	5.04	4.79	1.35	813	711	892	22.6	3.0	6.8	2.3	63%	8%	41	21	38	28%	69%	18%	16	87	13%	44%	0	0.87	-7.7	62	74	-$1
2nd Half	2	3	0	47	50	5.94	3.99	1.49	852	887	813	9.6	2.9	9.6	3.3	61%	9%	41	25	34	36%	64%	20%	5	40	0%	40%	0	0.63	-9.1	114	137	-$9
18 Proj	**5**	**8**	**0**	**116**	**107**	**4.88**	**4.33**	**1.38**	**792**	**811**	**774**	**9.0**	**2.8**	**8.3**	**3.0**	**62%**	**9%**	**42**	**22**	**36**	**32%**	**69%**	**16%**	**0**						**-7.4**	**96**	**115**	**-$2**

Chen,Wei-Yin

Age: 32	Th: L	Role SP	Health	F	LIMA Plan	C
Ht: 6' 0"	Wt: 200	Type	PT/Exp	B	Rand Var	-2
			Consist	A	MM	1100

Tried to pitch through a partially torn UCL, but wound up missing most of 2017. He has had multiple platelet-rich plasma injections since the injury was first discovered in the summer 2016. At this point, TJS seems almost inevitable. If healthy, track record says he can be useful, but that's a huge "if."

Yr Tm	W	L	Sv	IP	K	ERA	xERA	WHIP	oOPS	vL	vR	BF/G	Ctl	Dom	Cmd	FpK	SwK	G	L	F	H%	S%	hr/f	GS	APC	DOM%	DIS%	Sv%	LI	RAR	BPV	BPX	R$
13 BAL	7	7	0	137	104	4.07	4.19	1.32	761	689	783	24.9	2.6	6.8	2.7	59%	8%	34	25	41	31%	73%	10%	23	95	13%	17%			-3.5	66	86	$1
14 BAL	16	6	0	186	136	3.54	3.86	1.23	727	670	746	24.9	1.7	6.6	3.9	61%	8%	41	22	38	30%	76%	10%	31	96	23%	29%			4.6	92	109	$10
15 BAL	11	8	0	191	153	3.34	4.01	1.22	758	576	815	25.5	1.9	7.2	3.7	68%	9%	40	20	39	30%	79%	12%	31	97	26%	19%			14.7	95	114	$13
16 MIA	5	5	0	123	100	4.96	4.23	1.28	789	778	791	23.6	1.8	7.3	4.2	64%	10%	40	21	38	31%	66%	15%	22	87	27%	27%			-11.8	102	121	-$1
17 MIA	2	1	0	33	25	3.82	4.56	1.03	612	523	646	14.7	2.5	6.8	2.8	63%	10%	37	19	44	24%	65%	7%	5	55	0%	40%	0	0.52	2.2	71	86	-$1
1st Half	2	1	0	27	20	4.33	4.85	1.19	657	517	710	22.4	3.0	6.7	2.2	63%	9%	37	21	42	26%	66%	9%	5	84	0%	40%			0.1	54	65	$0
2nd Half	0	0	0	6	5	1.50	3.37	0.33	363	567	286	5.0	0.0	7.5	0.0	60%	11%	33	13	53	14%	50%	0%	0	18			0	0.13	2.1	146	175	-$2
18 Proj	**4**	**2**	**0**	**58**	**45**	**4.07**	**4.55**	**1.23**	**730**	**611**	**767**	**23.3**	**2.2**	**6.9**	**3.1**	**64%**	**9%**	**39**	**21**	**40**	**29%**	**71%**	**11%**	**10**						**2.1**	**81**	**98**	**$0**

Cingrani,Tony

Age: 28	Th: L	Role RP	Health	D	LIMA Plan	C+
Ht: 6' 4"	Wt: 214	Type Pwr FB	PT/Exp	D	Rand Var	+4
			Consist	B	MM	2400

Don't let the ERA fool you, he took a significant step forward in 2017. PRO: Cmd growth backed by SwK/FpK; career-best BPV; 2nd half Dom. CON: Uptick in FB%; gopheritis became a huge problem. His hr/f is ripe for some regression, so if the Cmd gains stick, there's a solid Holds source lurking here.

Yr Tm	W	L	Sv	IP	K	ERA	xERA	WHIP	oOPS	vL	vR	BF/G	Ctl	Dom	Cmd	FpK	SwK	G	L	F	H%	S%	hr/f	GS	APC	DOM%	DIS%	Sv%	LI	RAR	BPV	BPX	R$
13 CIN *	10	4	0	136	162	2.60	2.46	1.06	649	533	693	18.2	3.6	10.7	3.0	57%	11%	34	21	45	25%	81%	13%	18	79	33%	28%	0	0.93	21.2	113	147	$18
14 CIN	2	8	0	63	61	4.55	4.51	1.53	811	613	862	21.5	5.0	8.7	1.7	54%	9%	35	22	44	30%	76%	15%	11	86	9%	64%	0	0.85	-6.3	35	41	-$5
15 CIN *	0	4	0	58	66	4.33	4.67	1.62	811	915	751	5.9	5.8	10.2	1.8	50%	12%	38	27	35	34%	75%	10%	1	19	0%	100%	0	1.24	-2.6	75	89	-$7
16 CIN	2	5	17	63	49	4.14	5.11	1.44	719	674	743	4.2	5.3	7.0	1.3	55%	9%	47	16	38	28%	72%	7%	0	17			74	1.16	0.4	8	10	$4
17 2 NL	0	0	0	43	52	4.22	3.57	1.22	791	838	750	3.7	2.5	11.0	4.3	62%	14%	41	16	43	31%	76%	21%	0	15			0	0.67	0.7	148	178	-$2
1st Half	0	0	0	15	15	2.35	3.79	0.98	724	865	621	3.8	1.8	8.8	5.0	61%	13%	45	10	45	22%	100%	21%	0	15			0	0.96	3.8	134	161	-$1
2nd Half	0	0	0	27	37	5.27	3.45	1.35	826	825	824	3.7	3.0	12.2	4.1	62%	14%	39	19	42	35%	68%	21%	0	16			0	0.53	-3.1	156	187	-$2
18 Proj	**2**	**3**	**0**	**51**	**57**	**3.74**	**4.07**	**1.30**	**764**	**797**	**742**	**4.4**	**3.5**	**10.0**	**2.8**	**57%**	**12%**	**42**	**18**	**41**	**30%**	**78%**	**16%**	**0**						**3.9**	**105**	**126**	**-$1**

Cishek,Steve

Age: 32	Th: R	Role RP	Health	B	LIMA Plan	B+
Ht: 6' 6"	Wt: 215	Type Pwr	PT/Exp	C	Rand Var	-5
			Consist	B	MM	2310

Missed first six weeks due to off-season left hip surgery (torn labrum), then seemingly turned back the clock to 2013 with GB tilt and success vL. But xERA casts doubt; performance vL was fluky (lousy 1.8 Cmd), and unchanged pitch mix questions GB% jump. BPX shows this skill set more pedestrian than it was in 2013.

Yr Tm	W	L	Sv	IP	K	ERA	xERA	WHIP	oOPS	vL	vR	BF/G	Ctl	Dom	Cmd	FpK	SwK	G	L	F	H%	S%	hr/f	GS	APC	DOM%	DIS%	Sv%	LI	RAR	BPV	BPX	R$
13 MIA	4	6	34	70	74	2.33	2.96	1.08	568	664	459	4.1	2.8	9.6	3.4	63%	10%	53	18	29	29%	79%	6%	0	16			94	1.23	13.2	126	165	$20
14 MIA	4	5	39	65	84	3.17	2.84	1.21	643	586	713	4.1	2.9	11.6	4.0	67%	10%	43	26	31	35%	74%	6%	0	17			91	1.61	4.6	151	180	$18
15 2 NL	2	6	4	55	48	3.58	4.42	1.48	720	754	696	4.1	4.4	7.8	1.8	64%	10%	46	22	32	32%	77%	8%	0	16			44	0.91	2.6	46	55	-$1
16 SEA	4	6	25	64	76	2.81	3.35	1.02	600	728	498	4.2	3.0	10.7	3.6	61%	12%	44	17	39	26%	79%	13%	0	17			78	1.52	10.9	135	160	$17
17 2 AL	3	2	1	45	41	2.01	3.42	0.90	491	663	413	3.6	2.8	8.3	2.9	64%	11%	56	18	26	21%	81%	10%	0	15			25	1.16	12.9	107	128	$6
1st Half	1	1	1	12	12	4.38	3.80	1.14	625	1027	463	3.6	2.9	8.8	3.0	48%	8%	57	16	27	26%	67%	20%	0	16			50	0.81	0.0	114	136	-$5
2nd Half	2	1	0	32	29	1.11	3.27	0.80	430	514	389	3.5	2.8	8.1	2.9	71%	12%	56	18	26	19%	88%	5%	0	14			0	1.31	12.9	104	125	$10
18 Proj	**3**	**4**	**5**	**58**	**59**	**3.59**	**3.74**	**1.17**	**654**	**722**	**604**	**3.9**	**3.2**	**9.2**	**2.8**	**66%**	**11%**	**49**	**20**	**31**	**28%**	**72%**	**12%**	**0**						**5.5**	**105**	**126**	**$4**

GREG PYRON

Claudio,Alexander

Age: 26	Th: L	Role RP	Health F	LIMA Plan B
Ht: 6' 3"	Wt: 180	Type Con xGB	PT/Exp D	Rand Var -1
			Consist C	MM 3010

Side-armer was unexpected 2nd half Sv source. Does he have staying power? PRO: Superb Ctl; elite GB% (only three qualified RP had higher GB% in 2017); dominance vL. CON: Puny Dom; low velocity (87 mph), ordinary vR. These aren't typical closer skills; handedness only increases odds of return to setup role.

Yr Tm	W	L	Sv	IP	K	ERA	xERA	WHIP	oOPS	vL	vR	BF/G	Ctl	Dom	Cmd	FpK	SwK	G	L	F	H%	S%	hr/f	GS	APC	DOM%	DIS%	Sv%	LI	RAR	BPV	BPX
13 aa	1	5	0	32	25	3.77	4.21	1.42				6.4	3.3	7.0	2.1						32%	75%								0.4	65	85
14 TEX *	2	3	0	55	38	2.63	2.82	1.13	693	465	855	8.7	1.3	6.2	4.8	46%	12%	58	25	17	31%	75%	0%	0	14			0	0.41	7.5	137	163
15 TEX *	4	2	0	56	42	3.38	4.48	1.35	762	716	813	4.9	2.2	6.8	3.1	65%	11%	51	16	33	33%	79%	27%	0	14			0	1.16	4.0	75	89
16 TEX *	4	1	1	68	40	2.28	2.78	1.14	662	449	752	6.0	1.9	5.4	2.8	65%	11%	63	17	20	29%	80%	6%	0	20			100	0.72	16.0	89	106
17 TEX	4	2	11	83	56	2.50	3.31	1.04	591	368	694	4.6	1.6	6.1	3.7	63%	10%	67	17	17	27%	78%	12%	1	16	0%	100%	73	1.18	18.9	111	133
1st Half	1	0	1	42	27	2.76	3.43	1.16	663	452	760	4.5	2.1	5.7	2.7	62%	10%	70	16	14	27%	80%	22%	1	15	0%	100%	33	1.05	8.3	94	112
2nd Half	3	2	10	40	29	2.23	3.19	0.92	514	276	622	4.7	1.1	6.5	5.8	65%	10%	63	17	20	27%	75%	4%	0	17			83	1.32	10.6	128	153
18 Proj	**4**	**2**	**7**	**65**	**44**	**2.89**	**3.52**	**1.12**	**616**	**394**	**714**	**5.1**	**1.8**	**6.1**	**3.4**	**64%**	**10%**	**65**	**17**	**19**	**29%**	**75%**	**10%**	**0**						**11.9**	**104**	**126**

Clevinger,Michael

Age: 27	Th: R	Role RP	Health A	LIMA Plan B
Ht: 6' 4"	Wt: 210	Type Pwr	PT/Exp D	Rand Var -1
			Consist C	MM 1303

12-6, 3.11 ERA in 122 IP at CLE. Vastly improved slider and curve gave him three pitches with 18%+ SwK, fueling Dom spike that made him an instant asset. However, Ctl and vL warts remain and cast doubt on a repeat. Expect lots of Ks, but holding this level requires more refinement along lines of 2nd half FpK gains.

Yr Tm	W	L	Sv	IP	K	ERA	xERA	WHIP	oOPS	vL	vR	BF/G	Ctl	Dom	Cmd	FpK	SwK	G	L	F	H%	S%	hr/f	GS	APC	DOM%	DIS%	Sv%	LI	RAR	BPV	BPX
13																																
14																																
15 aa	9	8	0	158	114	3.95	3.82	1.31				24.2	2.5	6.5	2.6						32%	70%								0.3	76	91
16 CLE *	14	4	0	146	119	4.73	4.91	1.53	768	505	976	18.7	4.3	7.4	1.7	61%	10%	38	22	40	31%	72%	13%	10	57	0%	60%	0	0.84	-9.8	45	54
17 CLE *	15	8	0	156	164	3.27	3.64	1.32	667	819	570	19.0	4.4	9.5	2.1	63%	13%	39	24	36	29%	79%	12%	21	78	33%	24%	0	0.71	20.8	81	98
1st Half	6	5	0	82	82	3.69	4.00	1.35	677	783	602	20.1	4.5	9.0	2.0	60%	15%	39	22	40	28%	77%	16%	9	83	22%	22%	0	0.69	6.8	68	81
2nd Half	9	3	0	74	82	2.81	4.11	1.29	661	844	551	18.2	4.4	10.0	2.3	65%	12%	40	26	35	30%	81%	9%	12	75	42%	25%	0	0.72	14.1	79	95
18 Proj	**14**	**9**	**0**	**174**	**170**	**3.84**	**4.56**	**1.39**	**738**	**708**	**759**	**19.3**	**4.1**	**8.8**	**2.1**	**62%**	**12%**	**40**	**23**	**37**	**31%**	**75%**	**10%**	**35**						**11.1**	**65**	**78**

Clippard,Tyler

Age: 33	Th: R	Role RP	Health A	LIMA Plan B+
Ht: 6' 3"	Wt: 200	Type Pwr xFB	PT/Exp C	Rand Var +1
			Consist B	MM 1410

Picked up a few saves in 2H, but his days of closing out games are long gone. FpK gives hope for sub-4.0 Ctl, but that's still an ugly number. Extreme FB% has always made him susceptible to HR, that's an even bigger risk now than in his 20s (see hr/f). Last three years: 6 teams, 4.50ish xERA are the tale of the tape here.

Yr Tm	W	L	Sv	IP	K	ERA	xERA	WHIP	oOPS	vL	vR	BF/G	Ctl	Dom	Cmd	FpK	SwK	G	L	F	H%	S%	hr/f	GS	APC	DOM%	DIS%	Sv%	LI	RAR	BPV	BPX
13 WAS	6	3	0	71	73	2.41	3.68	0.86	517	507	527	3.8	3.0	9.3	3.0	59%	15%	28	16	56	18%	81%	9%	0	16			0	1.10	12.8	90	118
14 WAS	7	4	1	70	82	2.18	3.26	1.00	541	642	423	3.7	2.9	10.5	3.6	63%	15%	37	14	49	27%	82%	6%	0	15			14	1.34	13.6	124	148
15 2 TM	5	4	19	71	64	2.92	4.96	1.13	599	468	745	4.4	3.9	8.1	2.1	56%	12%	21	18	61	23%	79%	7%	0	18			76	1.25	9.2	39	46
16 2 TM	4	6	3	63	72	3.57	4.15	1.27	716	753	679	3.8	3.7	10.3	2.8	57%	13%	31	19	50	29%	79%	13%	0	15			50	1.05	4.8	94	112
17 3 AL	2	8	5	60	72	4.77	4.60	1.29	711	677	735	3.9	4.6	10.7	2.3	59%	14%	32	17	51	27%	68%	13%	0	17			45	1.11	-3.1	78	94
1st Half	1	4	1	32	40	4.55	4.43	1.26	727	631	790	3.8	4.5	11.4	2.5	59%	16%	29	18	53	27%	71%	15%	0	16			20	1.24	-0.7	88	106
2nd Half	1	4	4	29	32	5.02	4.79	1.33	693	721	671	4.1	4.7	10.0	2.1	58%	13%	36	16	48	28%	65%	11%	0	17			67	0.96	-2.4	68	82
18 Proj	**3**	**6**	**1**	**58**	**65**	**4.29**	**4.50**	**1.23**	**676**	**656**	**694**	**3.8**	**4.1**	**10.1**	**2.4**	**58%**	**14%**	**31**	**17**	**52**	**27%**	**70%**	**11%**	**0**						**0.5**	**78**	**94**

Cobb,Alex

Age: 30	Th: R	Role SP	Health F	LIMA Plan C+
Ht: 6' 3"	Wt: 205	Type GB	PT/Exp C	Rand Var 0
			Consist F	MM 1105

Logged career-high IP in first full season post-May 2015 TJS. Velocity has returned, but ability to miss bats hasn't, as his splitter has been far less effective (2014: 18% SwK, 38% usage; 2017: 11% SwK, 14% usage). GB% and Ctl are assets, but without Dom resurgence, he's just got two legs of a tripod.

Yr Tm	W	L	Sv	IP	K	ERA	xERA	WHIP	oOPS	vL	vR	BF/G	Ctl	Dom	Cmd	FpK	SwK	G	L	F	H%	S%	hr/f	GS	APC	DOM%	DIS%	Sv%	LI	RAR	BPV	BPX
13 TAM	11	3	0	143	134	2.76	3.04	1.15	644	677	592	26.3	2.8	8.4	3.0	59%	10%	56	22	23	28%	80%	15%	22	101	36%	14%			19.5	109	142
14 TAM	10	9	0	166	149	2.87	3.16	1.14	619	590	646	25.2	2.5	8.1	3.2	59%	11%	56	16	27	29%	76%	9%	27	97	44%	22%			17.9	110	132
15																																
16 TAM *	1	3	0	37	24	9.18	9.27	2.12	968	1206	737	20.3	3.2	5.8	1.8	65%	8%	53	19	29	41%	59%	22%	5	77	20%	60%			-22.8	-15	-18
17 TAM	12	10	0	179	128	3.66	4.29	1.22	709	678	731	25.6	2.2	6.4	2.9	59%	7%	48	22	30	29%	74%	13%	29	98	38%	17%			15.4	82	98
1st Half	6	5	0	101	70	3.73	4.60	1.31	741	702	773	26.7	2.5	6.2	2.5	63%	8%	45	22	33	31%	74%	10%	16	101	38%	19%			7.8	68	81
2nd Half	6	5	0	78	58	3.58	3.90	1.10	666	639	681	24.2	1.8	6.7	3.6	52%	7%	52	21	27	26%	74%	19%	13	95	38%	15%			7.5	100	120
18 Proj	**11**	**11**	**0**	**189**	**142**	**3.98**	**4.13**	**1.30**	**757**	**728**	**782**	**22.6**	**2.3**	**6.8**	**3.0**	**60%**	**9%**	**52**	**20**	**28**	**31%**	**73%**	**15%**	**34**						**8.9**	**91**	**110**

Cole,A.J.

Age: 26	Th: R	Role SP	Health A	LIMA Plan D+
Ht: 6' 5"	Wt: 215	Type Pwr FB	PT/Exp D	Rand Var +4
			Consist C	MM 0101

3-5, 3.81 ERA in 52 IP at WAS. Two straight years of ERA starting with "6", but reasons for optimism? Yes, really! FpK trending nicely, just hasn't shown in Ctl yet. Can't get lefties out or keep ball in park, but upgraded slider (20% SwK) and velocity gains (+2 mph on FB) give some deep league hope... maybe in pen?

Yr Tm	W	L	Sv	IP	K	ERA	xERA	WHIP	oOPS	vL	vR	BF/G	Ctl	Dom	Cmd	FpK	SwK	G	L	F	H%	S%	hr/f	GS	APC	DOM%	DIS%	Sv%	LI	RAR	BPV	BPX
13 aa	4	2	0	45	41	2.57	2.21	0.97				24.6	1.9	8.2	4.4						27%	76%								7.3	135	176
14 a/a	13	3	0	134	93	3.39	4.49	1.41				22.7	2.0	6.2	3.1						35%	77%								5.8	80	96
15 WAS *	5	6	1	115	72	4.25	4.35	1.40	812	935	571	20.2	2.9	5.6	1.9	43%	10%	36	27	36	31%	71%	8%	1	52	0%	100%	100	0.48	-4.1	49	58
16 WAS *	9	10	0	163	129	6.02	5.97	1.59	779	783	773	24.0	3.0	7.1	2.4	58%	11%	32	13	55	35%	65%	11%	8	84	13%	38%			-36.8	41	48
17 WAS *	7	10	0	145	109	6.28	6.65	1.87	802	980	601	23.5	4.1	6.7	1.7	62%	10%	44	17	39	39%	67%	14%	8	85	0%	50%	0	0.67	-34.5	34	40
1st Half	5	2	0	69	40	6.56	6.39	1.91	717	701	733	25.2	4.3	5.2	1.2	42%	6%	50	22	28	38%	64%	0%	1	109	0%	100%			-18.8	27	32
2nd Half	2	8	0	76	69	6.04	6.89	1.84	812	1013	587	22.2	3.9	8.1	2.1	64%	11%	43	16	41	40%	69%	15%	7	83	0%	43%	0	0.66	-15.7	41	49
18 Proj	**6**	**7**	**0**	**109**	**87**	**4.74**	**5.08**	**1.52**	**827**	**952**	**684**	**22.3**	**3.4**	**7.2**	**2.1**	**62%**	**11%**	**43**	**17**	**40**	**34%**	**71%**	**9%**	**21**						**-5.2**	**58**	**70**

Cole,Gerrit

Age: 27	Th: R	Role SP	Health D	LIMA Plan B
Ht: 6' 4"	Wt: 225	Type Pwr	PT/Exp A	Rand Var +2
			Consist B	MM 2205

Put injury-plagued 2016 behind him by regaining 200 IP level. And that's not all he regained: BPV/BPX nestled right in line with 2013-15 peak. Heck, 2nd half skills were as good as he's ever been. Thanks to that hr/f number, you shouldn't have to pay full price for these nearly ace-level skills. UP: see 2015.

Yr Tm	W	L	Sv	IP	K	ERA	xERA	WHIP	oOPS	vL	vR	BF/G	Ctl	Dom	Cmd	FpK	SwK	G	L	F	H%	S%	hr/f	GS	APC	DOM%	DIS%	Sv%	LI	RAR	BPV	BPX
13 PIT *	15	10	0	185	138	3.27	2.80	1.15	638	614	658	23.7	2.7	6.7	2.5	63%	10%	49	25	26	28%	72%	8%	19	91	32%	16%			13.7	86	112
14 PIT *	14	6	0	160	151	3.44	3.33	1.21	693	729	659	24.9	2.5	8.5	3.4	62%	10%	49	19	32	31%	73%	9%	22	100	45%	14%			6.0	107	128
15 PIT	19	8	0	208	202	2.60	3.16	1.09	623	597	648	26.0	1.9	8.7	4.6	62%	11%	48	22	30	31%	77%	7%	32	101	59%	13%			35.0	132	157
16 PIT	7	10	0	116	98	3.88	4.17	1.44	754	870	652	24.1	2.8	7.6	2.7	60%	9%	46	25	29	35%	73%	7%	21	92	24%	29%			4.4	85	102
17 PIT	12	12	0	203	196	4.26	3.91	1.25	739	794	689	25.7	2.4	8.7	3.6	63%	10%	46	21	34	31%	71%	16%	33	100	24%	18%			2.6	115	138
1st Half	6	7	0	102	86	4.51	4.18	1.30	781	905	654	25.3	2.3	7.6	3.3	64%	9%	46	21	33	30%	71%	18%	17	97	18%	24%			-2.0	99	119
2nd Half	6	5	0	101	110	4.00	3.65	1.20	696	667	721	26.2	2.6	9.8	3.8	63%	11%	45	20	35	31%	71%	14%	16	103	31%	13%			4.5	129	155
18 Proj	**13**	**11**	**0**	**189**	**176**	**3.56**	**3.85**	**1.20**	**682**	**726**	**642**	**24.3**	**2.5**	**8.4**	**3.4**	**62%**	**10%**	**46**	**22**	**32**	**30%**	**73%**	**12%**	**31**						**18.6**	**109**	**131**

Colome,Alexander

Age: 29	Th: R	Role RP	Health D	LIMA Plan C
Ht: 6' 1"	Wt: 220	Type Pwr	PT/Exp A	Rand Var -2
			Consist C	MM 2230

Sequel to 2016 breakout didn't live up to billing. Too much of a good thing: increased usage of cutter reduced its effectiveness (2016: 24% SwK, 47% usage; 2017: 16% SwK, 67% usage). Waning FpK/Ctl never good for closer job security; 2016 xERA now looks like outlier. Heed that column.

Yr Tm	W	L	Sv	IP	K	ERA	xERA	WHIP	oOPS	vL	vR	BF/G	Ctl	Dom	Cmd	FpK	SwK	G	L	F	H%	S%	hr/f	GS	APC	DOM%	DIS%	Sv%	LI	RAR	BPV	BPX
13 TAM *	5	7	0	86	73	3.33	4.08	1.43	715	685	739	21.6	3.9	7.6	1.9	61%	12%	43	22	35	32%	79%	12%	3	88	33%	67%			5.7	67	87
14 TAM *	9	6	0	110	73	4.36	4.12	1.49	590	566	612	23.6	3.5	6.0	1.7	67%	9%	38	22	41	33%	69%	3%	3	77	67%	0%	0	0.68	-8.4	64	76
15 TAM	8	5	0	110	88	3.94	4.06	1.30	698	736	658	10.6	2.5	7.2	2.8	62%	11%	40	25	35	32%	71%	8%	13	40	8%	38%	0	1.06	0.3	79	94
16 TAM	2	4	37	57	71	1.91	2.85	1.02	572	479	638	4.0	2.4	11.3	4.7	63%	16%	47	23	30	29%	88%	15%	0	15			93	1.23	16.0	164	194
17 TAM	2	3	47	67	58	3.24	4.26	1.20	636	677	596	4.3	3.1	7.8	2.5	60%	12%	49	18	34	29%	74%	6%	0	15			89	1.41	9.2	84	101
1st Half	2	3	21	36	34	3.72	4.58	1.27	682	637	722	4.6	3.5	8.4	2.4	61%	13%	40	18	42	30%	72%	7%	0	16			84	1.56	2.9	76	91
2nd Half	0	0	26	30	24	2.67	3.86	1.12	581	721	440	4.0	2.7	7.1	2.7	60%	11%	58	18	24	28%	76%	5%	0	15			93	1.24	6.3	92	111
18 Proj	**2**	**3**	**33**	**65**	**61**	**3.41**	**3.89**	**1.19**	**642**	**658**	**627**	**4.9**	**2.8**	**8.4**	**3.0**	**62%**	**13%**	**48**	**21**	**31**	**29%**	**73%**	**10%**	**0**						**7.6**	**101**	**121**

GREG PYRON

Colon,Bartolo

Age: 45	Th: R	Role: SP	Health: D	LIMA Plan: C
Ht: 5' 11"	Wt: 285	Type: Con	PT/Exp: A	Rand Var: +5
			Consist: B	MM: 0003

Age finally caught up with him? It's a fair question we usually ask of guys a decade younger. Approach has long been a case of threading a needle: pinpoint Ctl + tiny Dom yield more FBs than you want to see. FpK, H%, S% point to some rebound, but too much risk for too little reward, especially in this era. Heed DIS%.

Yr Tm	W	L	Sv	IP	K	ERA	xERA	WHIP	oOPS	vL	vR	BF/G	Ctl	Dom	Cmd	FpK	SwK	G	L	F	H%	S%	hr/f	GS	APC	DOM%	DIS%	Sv%	LI	RAR	BPV	BPX	R$
13 OAK	18	6	0	190	117	2.65	4.00	1.17	659	681	636	25.6	1.4	5.5	4.0	65%	7%	42	21	38	30%	80%	6%	30	93	30%	33%			28.6	83	108	$21
14 NYM	15	13	0	202	151	4.09	3.82	1.23	716	681	755	27.3	1.3	6.7	5.0	66%	6%	39	22	39	32%	69%	9%	31	97	52%	39%			-8.8	102	121	$6
15 NYM	14	13	0	195	136	4.16	4.05	1.24	741	735	748	24.7	1.1	6.3	5.7	66%	7%	42	21	37	32%	70%	11%	31	82	29%	35%	0	0.76	-4.8	103	123	$7
16 NYM	15	8	0	192	128	3.43	4.26	1.21	729	795	664	23.3	1.5	6.0	4.0	63%	6%	43	23	34	30%	76%	11%	33	84	24%	30%	0	0.78	18.0	89	105	$15
17 2 TM	7	14	0	143	89	6.48	5.37	1.59	909	910	908	23.1	2.2	5.6	2.5	65%	6%	42	19	39	34%	62%	14%	28	82	11%	61%			-37.5	61	74	-$15
1st Half	2	8	0	63	42	8.14	5.42	1.78	946	879	1011	23.0	2.9	6.0	2.1	64%	5%	46	21	34	37%	54%	14%	13	84	8%	69%			-29.4	54	65	-$27
2nd Half	5	6	0	80	47	5.18	5.32	1.44	878	937	825	23.3	1.7	5.3	3.1	66%	6%	39	18	43	32%	70%	14%	15	79	13%	53%			-8.1	66	80	-$6
18 Proj	**8**	**10**	**0**	**131**	**85**	**5.00**	**4.83**	**1.39**	**819**	**834**	**805**	**23.1**	**1.8**	**5.8**	**3.3**	**65%**	**6%**	**42**	**21**	**38**	**32%**	**68%**	**13%**	**24**						**-10.3**	**78**	**94**	**-$3**

Conley,Adam

Age: 28	Th: L	Role: SP	Health: C	LIMA Plan: D+
Ht: 6' 3"	Wt: 200	Type: Pwr FB	PT/Exp: C	Rand Var: +4
			Consist: C	MM: 0103

8-8, 6.14 ERA in 103 IP at MIA. While 2016 xERA foretold this combustion, it was the disappearance of 2016 Dom gains that turned this into a true dumpster fire. Loss of 2.5 mph worth of velocity just added accelerant, leaving nothing but charred embers. Don't hang around sifting through them.

Yr Tm	W	L	Sv	IP	K	ERA	xERA	WHIP	oOPS	vL	vR	BF/G	Ctl	Dom	Cmd	FpK	SwK	G	L	F	H%	S%	hr/f	GS	APC	DOM%	DIS%	Sv%	LI	RAR	BPV	BPX	R$
13 aa	11	7	0	139	108	4.11	3.76	1.35				22.2	2.5	7.0	2.8						33%	69%								-4.2	87	114	$2
14 aaa	3	5	0	60	39	6.12	4.57	1.57				21.9	3.7	5.9	1.6						34%	58%								-17.6	55	65	-$9
15 MIA *	13	4	0	174	123	3.51	3.72	1.35	723	767	714	21.3	3.3	6.4	1.9	58%	11%	41	19	41	30%	75%	9%	11	73	18%	36%	0	0.72	9.6	65	77	$7
16 MIA	8	6	0	133	124	3.85	4.67	1.40	738	759	731	23.4	4.2	8.4	2.0	64%	10%	38	21	41	31%	75%	8%	25	91	24%	32%			5.6	54	64	$3
17 MIA *	11	11	0	165	105	6.46	5.90	1.63	852	822	861	21.6	3.8	5.7	1.5	58%	10%	40	19	42	32%	62%	14%	20	78	15%	55%	0	0.83	-42.8	18	21	-$16
1st Half	4	6	0	80	48	7.69	6.04	1.75	825	833	821	21.6	4.6	5.4	1.2	55%	11%	38	19	43	33%	55%	10%	6	75	0%	33%	0	0.96	-33.0	15	19	-$27
2nd Half	7	5	0	85	57	5.30	5.78	1.51	862	817	876	21.6	3.0	6.1	2.0	59%	9%	40	18	41	32%	70%	15%	14	80	21%	64%	0	0.77	-9.8	24	28	-$5
18 Proj	**10**	**8**	**0**	**145**	**106**	**4.83**	**5.36**	**1.50**	**810**	**819**	**807**	**26.4**	**3.7**	**6.6**	**1.8**	**60%**	**10%**	**39**	**19**	**42**	**32%**	**70%**	**9%**	**24**						**-8.5**	**36**	**44**	**-$4**

Corbin,Patrick

Age: 28	Th: L	Role: SP	Health: F	LIMA Plan: B
Ht: 6' 3"	Wt: 210	Type: Pwr GB	PT/Exp: B	Rand Var: +3
			Consist: A	MM: 1205

Posted third straight odd-numbered year with eerily similar skills. This one was driven by health: Velocity added a couple of ticks, and relied heavily on slider to fuel SwK/GB combo. 2nd half Dom hints at another level, though health risk cautions against projecting that line "times 2." Worth speculating, though.

Yr Tm	W	L	Sv	IP	K	ERA	xERA	WHIP	oOPS	vL	vR	BF/G	Ctl	Dom	Cmd	FpK	SwK	G	L	F	H%	S%	hr/f	GS	APC	DOM%	DIS%	Sv%	LI	RAR	BPV	BPX	R$
13 ARI	14	8	0	208	178	3.41	3.48	1.17	671	560	703	26.9	2.3	7.7	3.3	70%	11%	47	22	31	29%	73%	10%	32	96	34%	28%			11.6	100	131	$16
14																																	
15 ARI *	7	5	0	101	87	3.63	4.07	1.28	743	574	788	21.9	2.0	7.7	3.9	61%	11%	47	23	30	33%	74%	12%	16	78	25%	19%			4.2	100	119	$3
16 ARI	5	13	1	156	131	5.15	4.39	1.56	825	743	851	19.5	3.8	7.6	2.0	57%	10%	54	19	27	33%	70%	18%	24	71	21%	42%	100	0.89	-18.4	65	78	-$9
17 ARI	14	13	0	190	178	4.03	4.08	1.42	792	651	830	25.0	2.9	8.4	2.9	62%	11%	50	20	30	34%	76%	15%	32	93	31%	28%	0	0.76	7.6	102	122	$8
1st Half	6	7	0	91	78	4.76	4.35	1.51	832	693	866	25.4	2.6	7.7	3.0	65%	10%	52	18	30	35%	73%	17%	16	93	19%	38%			-4.5	99	119	-$1
2nd Half	8	6	0	99	100	3.36	3.85	1.33	751	616	793	24.6	3.2	9.1	2.9	60%	12%	49	22	29	32%	79%	14%	16	94	44%	19%	0	0.76	12.1	105	126	$16
18 Proj	**11**	**12**	**0**	**181**	**163**	**3.99**	**4.12**	**1.40**	**777**	**652**	**813**	**25.4**	**3.0**	**8.1**	**2.7**	**61%**	**11%**	**50**	**21**	**29**	**33%**	**75%**	**15%**	**30**						**8.3**	**94**	**114**	**$6**

Cotton,Jharel

Age: 26	Th: R	Role: SP	Health: B	LIMA Plan: B+
Ht: 5' 11"	Wt: 195	Type: Pwr xFB	PT/Exp: D	Rand Var: +2
			Consist: B	MM: 0203

9-10, 5.58 ERA in 129 IP at OAK. Finger injury cost him most of July. First half was merely bad, then second half came along and said "Hold my beer." Too many BBs plus too many FBs have ruined many a young pitcher. Watch from a distance, at least til 2016 (small MLB sample) FpK comes back.

Yr Tm	W	L	Sv	IP	K	ERA	xERA	WHIP	oOPS	vL	vR	BF/G	Ctl	Dom	Cmd	FpK	SwK	G	L	F	H%	S%	hr/f	GS	APC	DOM%	DIS%	Sv%	LI	RAR	BPV	BPX	R$
13																																	
14																																	
15 a/a	5	2	0	70	68	2.99	3.30	1.24				17.8	2.7	8.8	3.3						32%	77%								8.4	109	130	$4
16 OAK *	13	6	0	165	146	4.71	3.65	1.15	538	441	617	19.8	2.4	8.0	3.4	66%	13%	38	14	48	28%	62%	10%	5	88	20%	20%			-10.5	87	103	$8
17 OAK *	12	10	0	150	127	5.29	5.09	1.38	833	828	837	22.6	3.4	7.6	2.2	59%	10%	37	17	46	29%	67%	15%	24	91	13%	42%			-17.3	39	47	$0
1st Half	7	7	0	84	72	4.69	4.57	1.32	790	765	808	23.1	3.3	7.8	2.3	61%	10%	38	15	47	28%	70%	13%	13	92	15%	23%			-3.4	52	62	$4
2nd Half	5	3	0	67	55	6.05	5.74	1.46	885	898	873	21.9	3.5	7.4	2.1	57%	11%	36	18	45	29%	64%	18%	11	88	9%	64%			-13.9	24	29	-$6
18 Proj	**9**	**7**	**0**	**131**	**114**	**4.72**	**4.72**	**1.29**	**742**	**734**	**748**	**20.7**	**2.9**	**7.9**	**2.7**	**59%**	**10%**	**37**	**17**	**46**	**29%**	**68%**	**12%**	**26**						**-5.8**	**77**	**93**	**$2**

Coulombe,Daniel

Age: 28	Th: L	Role: RP	Health: A	LIMA Plan: C
Ht: 5' 10"	Wt: 190	Type: Pwr xGB	PT/Exp: B	Rand Var: -1
			Consist: C	MM: 2200

Career oOPS: .588 vL, .788 vR. So, he has seemingly mastered Job #1: get the lefties out. That will keep him sitting in big league bullpens for years to come. But the problems vR will keep him sitting, irrelevant, in your league's free agent pool.

Yr Tm	W	L	Sv	IP	K	ERA	xERA	WHIP	oOPS	vL	vR	BF/G	Ctl	Dom	Cmd	FpK	SwK	G	L	F	H%	S%	hr/f	GS	APC	DOM%	DIS%	Sv%	LI	RAR	BPV	BPX	R$
13																																	
14 LA *	0	0	1	25	30	2.87	3.90	1.40	768	819	731	4.6	3.9	10.5	2.7	64%	14%	44	31	25	35%	82%	25%	0	16			25	0.54	2.7	103	123	-$2
15 2 TM *	3	1	1	57	44	4.28	3.93	1.55	742	548	921	4.8	4.9	6.9	1.4	56%	8%	56	21	23	32%	70%	0%	0	19			25	0.59	-2.3	68	81	-$4
16 OAK *	3	1	0	73	80	3.46	2.89	1.14	634	557	692	5.2	2.9	9.9	3.4	61%	14%	62	17	21	30%	72%	24%	0	21			0	0.47	6.6	119	141	$4
17 OAK	2	2	0	52	39	3.48	4.41	1.32	714	596	851	3.0	3.8	6.8	1.8	52%	10%	56	17	27	28%	75%	10%	0	13			0	0.86	5.6	53	63	-$1
1st Half	1	1	0	27	21	1.98	4.10	1.06	625	605	644	3.5	3.0	6.9	2.3	56%	10%	53	16	31	24%	85%	8%	0	14			0	0.71	8.0	76	91	$3
2nd Half	1	1	0	24	18	5.18	4.77	1.60	807	588	1129	2.7	4.8	6.7	1.4	48%	9%	59	18	22	32%	68%	12%	0	11			0	0.98	-2.5	27	33	-$5
18 Proj	**2**	**1**	**0**	**51**	**44**	**3.80**	**3.99**	**1.32**	**693**	**593**	**795**	**3.7**	**3.8**	**7.9**	**2.1**	**55%**	**11%**	**59**	**17**	**24**	**30%**	**72%**	**10%**	**0**						**3.5**	**77**	**93**	**-$1**

Covey,Dylan

Age: 26	Th: R	Role: RP	Health: D	LIMA Plan: D
Ht: 6' 2"	Wt: 195	Type:	PT/Exp: D	Rand Var: +5
			Consist: D	MM: 0000

Rule 5 pick started season in rotation, got smoked in 8 starts, then spent 3 months on DL recovering from whiplash. (OK, it was an oblique, but whiplash would have been believable.) Came back in August, results were no better. Will return to minors for more seasoning, but age and skills say we might never see him again.

Yr Tm	W	L	Sv	IP	K	ERA	xERA	WHIP	oOPS	vL	vR	BF/G	Ctl	Dom	Cmd	FpK	SwK	G	L	F	H%	S%	hr/f	GS	APC	DOM%	DIS%	Sv%	LI	RAR	BPV	BPX	R$
13																																	
14																																	
15																																	
16 aa	2	1	0	29	20	2.33	3.76	1.46				20.9	5.4	6.2	1.2						27%	86%								6.7	51	60	-$2
17 CHW	0	7	0	70	41	7.71	5.67	1.67	979	894	1055	17.2	4.4	5.3	1.2	56%	7%	48	16	35	29%	59%	25%	12	64	0%	58%	0	0.66	-29.0	3	3	-$16
1st Half	0	4	0	38	22	8.12	5.89	1.81	1046	871	1206	21.9	3.8	5.3	1.4	56%	7%	45	19	36	32%	62%	27%	8	84	0%	63%			-17.5	15	17	-$19
2nd Half	0	3	0	32	19	7.24	5.39	1.52	887	922	856	13.4	5.0	5.3	1.1	55%	7%	53	14	33	25%	55%	22%	4	49	0%	50%	0	0.59	-11.5	-9	-11	-$12
18 Proj	**0**	**3**	**0**	**29**	**17**	**6.04**	**5.76**	**1.63**	**902**	**847**	**952**	**16.5**	**4.5**	**5.3**	**1.2**	**56%**	**7%**	**50**	**16**	**35**	**29%**	**67%**	**17%**	**5**						**-6.0**	**0**	**1**	**-$8**

Cueto,Johnny

Age: 32	Th: R	Role: SP	Health: D	LIMA Plan: B+
Ht: 5' 11"	Wt: 220	Type: Pwr	PT/Exp: A	Rand Var: +2
			Consist: B	MM: 1203

On surface, no smoking gun for collapse of this formerly rock-solid performer. A few more BBs, but FpK right in historical range. 2nd half depressed by three injury-marred starts. More LDs and FBs, with a lot more landing on the wrong side of the fence in 1st half. One counter-adjustment away from being a nice profit center.

Yr Tm	W	L	Sv	IP	K	ERA	xERA	WHIP	oOPS	vL	vR	BF/G	Ctl	Dom	Cmd	FpK	SwK	G	L	F	H%	S%	hr/f	GS	APC	DOM%	DIS%	Sv%	LI	RAR	BPV	BPX	R$
13 CIN	5	2	0	61	51	2.82	3.27	1.05	607	561	644	22.0	2.7	7.6	2.8	61%	11%	51	25	24	25%	79%	17%	11	87	18%	27%			7.8	93	121	$5
14 CIN	20	9	0	244	242	2.25	3.07	0.96	574	561	585	28.3	2.4	8.9	3.7	63%	10%	46	19	35	25%	82%	10%	34	108	56%	6%			44.7	120	144	$38
15 2 TM	11	13	0	212	176	3.44	3.76	1.13	675	598	743	27.1	2.0	7.5	3.8	63%	10%	43	22	36	29%	73%	9%	32	102	34%	28%			13.7	103	122	$17
16 SF	18	5	0	220	198	2.79	3.43	1.09	633	670	601	27.5	1.8	8.1	4.4	68%	10%	50	21	29	30%	76%	8%	32	103	53%	16%			38.0	124	148	$30
17 SF	8	8	0	147	136	4.52	4.53	1.45	814	833	793	25.9	3.2	8.3	2.6	64%	11%	39	25	36	33%	73%	14%	25	101	20%	40%			-2.9	79	95	$0
1st Half	6	7	0	106	96	4.26	4.30	1.33	774	770	778	26.6	2.7	8.2	3.0	65%	11%	40	26	34	31%	74%	17%	17	104	24%	35%			1.3	92	110	$6
2nd Half	2	1	0	42	40	5.18	5.15	1.73	911	1016	822	24.4	4.5	8.6	1.9	64%	10%	37	23	40	38%	71%	8%	8	96	13%	50%			-4.2	48	58	-$13
18 Proj	**11**	**7**	**0**	**174**	**159**	**3.87**	**4.18**	**1.28**	**735**	**760**	**712**	**24.9**	**2.8**	**8.2**	**3.0**	**65%**	**11%**	**43**	**23**	**34**	**31%**	**72%**	**11%**	**29**						**10.4**	**94**	**113**	**$10**

AY MURPHY

Darvish,Yu

Darvish,Yu					Health	F	LIMA Plan	C+
Age: 31	Th: R	Role	SP		PT/Exp	C	Rand Var	+1
Ht: 6' 5"	Wt: 220	Type	Pwr		Consist	A	MM	3503

Ah, the merits of component skills analysis and league context: ERA trending the wrong way; xERA is following in lockstep... but so is league ERA. Over to BPX, where we find relative stability and strength. Not found in box: free-agent status and post-season meltdown, both of which cloud the outlook.

Yr Tm	W	L	Sv	IP	K	ERA	xERA	WHIP	oOPS	vL	vR	BF/G	Ctl	Dom	Cmd	FpK	SwK	G	L	F	H%	S%	hr/f	GS	APC	DOM%	DIS%	Sv%	LI	RAR	BPV	BPX	R$
13 TEX	13	9	0	210	277	2.83	2.86	1.07	611	655	543	26.3	3.4	11.9	3.5	57%	13%	41	21	38	27%	80%	14%	32	108	56%	9%			26.7	140	183	$2
14 TEX	10	7	0	144	182	3.06	3.18	1.26	679	721	605	27.5	3.1	11.3	3.7	62%	11%	36	23	41	35%	79%	9%	22	105	50%	9%			12.2	136	162	$1
15																																	
16 TEX *	8	7	0	127	154	3.42	3.21	1.16	636	607	662	21.1	3.1	10.9	3.6	58%	13%	40	20	40	30%	75%	12%	17	93	47%	12%			12.0	119	141	$1
17 2 TM	10	12	0	187	209	3.86	3.68	1.16	689	778	600	24.7	2.8	10.1	3.6	59%	13%	41	22	37	29%	72%	15%	31	99	35%	26%			11.5	125	150	$1
1st Half	6	6	0	107	115	3.11	3.71	1.08	631	655	609	25.4	3.1	9.7	3.1	58%	12%	42	23	36	26%	77%	13%	17	103	29%	18%			16.4	110	131	$2
2nd Half	4	6	0	80	94	4.86	3.63	1.27	762	917	586	23.9	2.4	10.6	4.5	60%	14%	40	22	38	34%	67%	17%	14	93	43%	36%			-4.9	145	174	$
18 Proj	**12**	**8**	**0**	**174**	**208**	**3.67**	**3.61**	**1.18**	**680**	**740**	**613**	**23.6**	**2.9**	**10.7**	**3.7**	**59%**	**13%**	**40**	**22**	**39**	**31%**	**74%**	**14%**	**30**						**14.8**	**133**	**160**	**$1**

Davies,Zachary

Davies,Zachary					Health	A	LIMA Plan	C+
Age: 25	Th: R	Role	SP		PT/Exp	B	Rand Var	0
Ht: 6' 0"	Wt: 155	Type			Consist	A	MM	1103

Wins add shine to this package, but kind of like a street vendor's fake Rolex, he stripped out the guts: Ctl crept up, Dom crashed; that combo wrecked Cmd. FpK and SwK offer no consolation. There's a reason 17 Wins returned only $10. When those Wins go away, that's when your wrist turns green.

Yr Tm	W	L	Sv	IP	K	ERA	xERA	WHIP	oOPS	vL	vR	BF/G	Ctl	Dom	Cmd	FpK	SwK	G	L	F	H%	S%	hr/f	GS	APC	DOM%	DIS%	Sv%	LI	RAR	BPV	BPX	R$
13																																	
14 aa	10	7	0	110	94	3.70	3.98	1.32				21.7	2.5	7.7	3.1						33%	73%								0.6	90	107	$
15 MIL *	9	10	0	162	112	3.53	3.71	1.36	614	434	740	22.6	3.2	6.2	1.9	60%	11%	58	21	21	31%	74%	10%	6	90	33%	50%			8.7	67	80	$
16 MIL	11	7	0	163	135	3.97	3.98	1.25	728	768	691	24.4	2.1	7.4	3.6	62%	9%	45	22	33	31%	72%	12%	28	92	25%	29%			4.5	100	119	$
17 MIL	17	9	0	191	124	3.90	4.54	1.35	755	787	724	24.8	2.6	5.8	2.3	57%	8%	50	23	27	31%	74%	12%	33	94	12%	48%			10.7	63	76	$1
1st Half	9	4	0	91	60	5.03	4.81	1.50	841	886	799	23.8	3.0	5.9	2.0	57%	8%	50	22	28	32%	70%	16%	17	94	6%	65%			-7.5	55	65	$
2nd Half	8	5	0	100	64	2.88	4.29	1.22	671	695	647	25.8	2.3	5.8	2.6	57%	8%	50	24	26	29%	78%	7%	16	93	19%	31%			18.2	71	85	$2
18 Proj	**12**	**10**	**0**	**174**	**125**	**4.07**	**4.34**	**1.32**	**742**	**752**	**733**	**24.5**	**2.5**	**6.5**	**2.6**	**59%**	**9%**	**50**	**22**	**28**	**31%**	**71%**	**12%**	**29**						**6.1**	**76**	**91**	**$**

Davis,Wade

Davis,Wade					Health	D	LIMA Plan	C
Age: 32	Th: R	Role	RP		PT/Exp	B	Rand Var	-4
Ht: 6' 5"	Wt: 225	Type	Pwr		Consist	A	MM	3530

Fourth straight year of ERA besting xERA by at least a full run. This version abandoned 2016's (relative) focus on balls on the ground and in the park, in favor of blowing it past everyone... which he did pretty effectively, for a half. 2nd half xERA would be a warning sign, if xERA mattered here.

Yr Tm	W	L	Sv	IP	K	ERA	xERA	WHIP	oOPS	vL	vR	BF/G	Ctl	Dom	Cmd	FpK	SwK	G	L	F	H%	S%	hr/f	GS	APC	DOM%	DIS%	Sv%	LI	RAR	BPV	BPX	R$
13 KC	8	11	0	135	114	5.32	4.38	1.68	822	910	721	19.9	3.9	7.6	2.0	59%	8%	41	27	32	37%	69%	11%	24	80	21%	50%	0	0.85	-24.3	51	67	-$1
14 KC	9	2	3	72	109	1.00	2.08	0.85	408	513	298	3.9	2.9	13.6	4.7	61%	15%	48	22	30	29%	87%	0%	0	17			50	1.23	24.3	194	231	$1
15 KC	8	1	17	67	78	0.94	3.04	0.79	451	453	449	3.6	2.7	10.4	3.9	61%	12%	38	21	41	21%	92%	5%	0	15			94	1.22	25.1	131	157	$2
16 KC	2	1	27	43	47	1.87	3.47	1.13	537	489	586	3.9	3.3	9.8	2.9	53%	13%	49	18	33	30%	82%	0%	0	16			90	1.00	12.4	113	134	$1
17 CHC	4	2	32	59	79	2.30	3.49	1.14	600	493	690	4.1	4.3	12.1	2.8	59%	15%	40	21	38	28%	85%	12%	0	18			97	1.15	14.9	120	144	$2
1st Half	2	0	16	28	42	1.93	2.83	0.96	502	366	648	3.9	3.2	13.5	4.2	55%	14%	38	26	36	30%	81%	5%	0	17			100	1.11	8.4	172	206	$2
2nd Half	2	2	16	31	37	2.64	4.17	1.30	687	635	721	4.3	5.3	10.9	2.1	62%	17%	42	18	40	26%	89%	17%	0	19			94	1.18	6.5	73	88	$1
18 Proj	**4**	**2**	**35**	**58**	**71**	**2.57**	**3.55**	**1.11**	**574**	**522**	**623**	**4.0**	**3.8**	**11.0**	**2.9**	**58%**	**14%**	**43**	**21**	**37**	**28%**	**79%**	**8%**	**0**						**12.8**	**117**	**140**	**$2**

De Leon,Jose

De Leon,Jose					Health	C	LIMA Plan	C+
Age: 25	Th: R	Role	SP		PT/Exp	D	Rand Var	+5
Ht: 6' 1"	Wt: 220	Type	Pwr		Consist	F	MM	2400

Entered the season primed for an early callup, but back, forearm, elbow injuries wiped out the season. All were non-surgical and don't really change his long-term outlook, but first he needs to get—and stay—healthy.

Yr Tm	W	L	Sv	IP	K	ERA	xERA	WHIP	oOPS	vL	vR	BF/G	Ctl	Dom	Cmd	FpK	SwK	G	L	F	H%	S%	hr/f	GS	APC	DOM%	DIS%	Sv%	LI	RAR	BPV	BPX	R$
13																																	
14																																	
15 aa	2	6	0	77	90	4.59	4.35	1.30				19.7	3.2	10.5	3.3						32%	70%								-5.9	91	108	-$
16 LA *	9	1	0	103	109	3.85	3.45	1.11	937	658	1220	20.3	2.2	9.5	4.3	60%	11%	40	18	42	29%	71%	24%	4	76	0%	75%			4.3	117	139	$
17 TAM	1	0	0	3	2	10.13	8.30	2.63	1133	1833	333	15.0	10.1	6.8	0.7	60%	9%	60	10	30	35%	67%	33%	0	69			0	0.94	-1.9	-114	-137	-$
1st Half	1	0	0	3	2	10.13	8.30	2.63	1133	1833	333	15.0	10.1	6.8	0.7	60%	9%	60	10	30	35%	67%	33%	0	69			0	0.94	-1.9	-114	-137	-$
2nd Half																																	
18 Proj	**1**	**1**	**0**	**15**	**16**	**4.13**	**3.83**	**1.18**				**20.1**	**2.6**	**9.9**	**3.8**	**0%**	**0%**				**30%**	**70%**		**3**						**0.4**	**104**	**125**	**-$**

deGrom,Jacob

deGrom,Jacob					Health	A	LIMA Plan	C
Age: 30	Th: R	Role	SP		PT/Exp	A	Rand Var	+2
Ht: 6' 4"	Wt: 180	Type	Pwr		Consist	A	MM	3405

Re-established durability while getting in on the league-wide strikeout party, with full SwK validation. Then in 2nd half, he found the sub-2.0 Ctl he had misplaced since 2015, well-backed by FpK. When Cmd starts with a 5, something's going very right. If hr/f gets back down to league average... UP: Cy Young talk

Yr Tm	W	L	Sv	IP	K	ERA	xERA	WHIP	oOPS	vL	vR	BF/G	Ctl	Dom	Cmd	FpK	SwK	G	L	F	H%	S%	hr/f	GS	APC	DOM%	DIS%	Sv%	LI	RAR	BPV	BPX	R$
13 a/a	6	7	0	136	90	4.52	4.76	1.51				24.5	2.7	6.0	2.2						35%	70%								-10.9	59	77	-$
14 NYM *	13	6	0	179	168	2.59	2.83	1.16	613	639	594	24.5	2.6	8.4	3.2	63%	12%	45	23	31	30%	79%	6%	22	102	50%	18%			25.4	113	135	$1
15 NYM	14	8	0	191	205	2.54	3.04	0.98	574	663	475	25.0	1.8	9.7	5.4	68%	13%	44	21	35	29%	78%	9%	30	99	63%	13%			33.4	148	176	$3
16 NYM	7	8	0	148	143	3.04	3.57	1.20	685	624	749	25.2	2.2	8.7	4.0	64%	11%	46	23	32	32%	79%	12%	24	98	38%	13%			21.0	121	144	$1
17 NYM	15	10	0	201	239	3.53	3.39	1.19	682	693	671	26.7	2.6	10.7	4.1	64%	14%	45	21	34	32%	76%	16%	31	102	48%	23%			20.5	144	173	$2
1st Half	8	3	0	104	125	3.55	3.47	1.22	677	714	642	26.9	3.3	10.8	3.3	62%	15%	46	22	32	31%	76%	17%	16	103	50%	19%			10.4	130	156	$2
2nd Half	7	7	0	97	114	3.51	3.30	1.15	687	672	702	26.4	1.9	10.5	5.4	66%	13%	44	20	35	32%	76%	16%	15	101	47%	27%			10.1	160	192	$2
18 Proj	**15**	**8**	**0**	**189**	**208**	**3.26**	**3.46**	**1.16**	**670**	**673**	**667**	**25.2**	**2.2**	**9.9**	**4.4**	**65%**	**13%**	**45**	**22**	**33**	**32%**	**76%**	**13%**	**30**						**25.5**	**141**	**170**	**$2**

Delgado,Randall

Delgado,Randall					Health	F	LIMA Plan	B+
Age: 28	Th: R	Role	RP		PT/Exp	C	Rand Var	0
Ht: 6' 4"	Wt: 220	Type	Pwr		Consist	B	MM	1300

Really weird usage pattern—two months of RP, then two as a true swingman (5 GS, 5 RP)—came amid a skills resurgence, but apparently was too much for his elbow as soreness shelved him for rest of season. No structural damage or surgery, but wait and see if these skills hold before buying back in.

Yr Tm	W	L	Sv	IP	K	ERA	xERA	WHIP	oOPS	vL	vR	BF/G	Ctl	Dom	Cmd	FpK	SwK	G	L	F	H%	S%	hr/f	GS	APC	DOM%	DIS%	Sv%	LI	RAR	BPV	BPX	R$
13 ARI *	7	12	0	180	127	4.73	4.73	1.33	793	765	819	22.7	2.7	6.3	2.4	60%	9%	42	20	38	29%	70%	17%	19	91	16%	37%	0	0.75	-19.1	41	53	-$
14 ARI	4	4	0	78	86	4.87	3.89	1.36	701	690	710	7.2	4.1	10.0	2.5	56%	14%	35	21	44	33%	64%	7%	4	31	0%	75%	0	0.82	-10.8	83	99	-$
15 ARI	8	4	1	72	73	3.25	4.13	1.33	679	688	671	4.8	4.1	9.1	2.2	63%	13%	41	18	41	30%	79%	9%	1	20	0%	100%	33	1.07	6.3	72	86	$
16 ARI	5	2	0	75	68	4.44	4.85	1.51	777	867	715	4.3	4.3	8.2	1.9	63%	10%	41	21	38	32%	72%	9%	0	17			0	0.88	-2.3	49	59	-$
17 ARI	1	2	1	63	60	3.59	3.75	1.18	696	640	739	10.0	2.0	8.6	4.3	68%	12%	46	23	31	32%	72%	11%	5	40	20%	20%	50	0.62	5.9	125	150	$
1st Half	1	1	1	58	55	3.28	3.73	1.20	714	686	736	10.4	1.9	8.6	4.6	68%	12%	46	23	31	32%	76%	12%	5	41	20%	20%	100	0.61	7.7	128	153	$
2nd Half	0	1	0	5	5	7.20	4.03	1.00	472	200	775	6.7	3.6	9.0	2.5	75%	16%	46	15	38	25%	20%	0%	0	33			0	0.65	-1.8	89	107	-$
18 Proj	**3**	**2**	**0**	**58**	**56**	**3.89**	**4.18**	**1.30**	**720**	**728**	**714**	**6.2**	**3.0**	**8.6**	**2.8**	**63%**	**12%**	**43**	**22**	**35**	**31%**	**73%**	**11%**	**0**						**3.4**	**94**	**114**	**$**

DeSclafani,Anthony

DeSclafani,Anthony					Health	F	LIMA Plan	B+
Age: 28	Th: R	Role	SP		PT/Exp	C	Rand Var	0
Ht: 6' 1"	Wt: 195	Type			Consist	A	MM	1103

Missed full season with elbow problems, though never went under the knife and supposedly will be ready for spring. Last year we described him here as "still evolving." A year without throwing a pitch in anger doesn't move that process forward, so best to give him some space to re-construct his career.

Yr Tm	W	L	Sv	IP	K	ERA	xERA	WHIP	oOPS	vL	vR	BF/G	Ctl	Dom	Cmd	FpK	SwK	G	L	F	H%	S%	hr/f	GS	APC	DOM%	DIS%	Sv%	LI	RAR	BPV	BPX	R$
13 aa	5	4	0	75	52	4.25	4.42	1.36				24.1	1.8	6.2	3.5						34%	70%								-3.6	84	109	-$
14 MIA *	8	9	0	135	104	4.63	3.86	1.31	801	893	710	16.9	2.3	6.9	3.0	66%	9%	36	24	40	32%	64%	9%	5	42	20%	60%	0	0.40	-14.8	87	103	-$
15 CIN	9	13	0	185	151	4.05	4.04	1.35	742	783	697	25.3	2.7	7.4	2.7	63%	10%	45	21	34	32%	72%	9%	31	94	29%	23%			-1.9	83	99	$
16 CIN *	9	6	0	140	118	3.93	4.43	1.23	723	837	585	23.7	2.0	7.6	3.8	58%	10%	42	23	35	30%	75%	13%	20	98	25%	30%			4.6	80	95	$
17																																	
1st Half																																	
2nd Half																																	
18 Proj	**8**	**8**	**0**	**131**	**103**	**4.24**	**4.48**	**1.30**	**742**	**824**	**653**	**21.0**	**2.2**	**7.1**	**3.2**	**63%**	**10%**	**40**	**23**	**37**	**32%**	**70%**	**10%**	**26**						**1.9**	**86**	**104**	**$**

RAY MURPHY

Despaigne,Odrisamer

Age: 31	Th: R	Role RP	Health	B	LIMA Plan	D
Ht: 6' 0"	Wt: 200	Type	PT/Exp	C	Rand Var	-2
			Consist	D	MM	0001

2-3, 4.01 ERA in 58 IP at MIA. Rode the AAA shuttle for much of 1st half, finished strong after Aug rotation move. Several reasons not to trust ERA gains: soft-tossing Dom took Cmd to new depths; rising FB% an issue once hr/f corrects; posted 5.14 MLB xERA in 2nd half. Still the same guy, still unrosterable.

Yr Tm	W	L	Sv	IP	K	ERA	xERA	WHIP	oOPS	vL	vR	BF/G	Ctl	Dom	Cmd	FpK	SwK	G	L	F	H%	S%	hr/f	GS	APC	DOM%	DIS%	Sv%	LI	RAR	BPV	BPX	R$
13																																	
14 SD *	5	10	0	128	98	4.05	3.99	1.40	638	713	558	23.4	3.5	6.9	2.0	60%	8%	52	19	29	31%	71%	7%	16	97	38%	50%			-4.8	66	79	-$2
15 SD	5	9	0	126	69	5.80	4.39	1.38	803	789	815	16.1	2.3	4.9	2.2	58%	6%	50	22	27	30%	59%	15%	18	61	22%	50%	0	0.53	-28.5	55	66	-$11
16 2 TM *	1	11	0	119	71	6.18	6.28	1.84	884	858	908	14.9	4.0	5.4	1.4	53%	8%	40	26	35	37%	66%	9%	0	28			0	0.53	-29.1	26	31	-$20
17 MIA *	4	7	3	128	68	4.10	4.46	1.48	688	806	546	14.5	3.6	4.8	1.3	62%	8%	38	24	39	30%	73%	4%	8	54	13%	50%	100	0.66	4.1	35	42	-$1
1st Half	0	5	2	55	32	5.24	6.21	1.84	833	905	621	15.1	4.9	5.2	1.1	65%	4%	38	19	43	35%	73%	0%	1	69	0%	100%	100	0.40	-6.0	18	21	-$15
2nd Half	4	2	1	73	36	3.24	3.15	1.21	667	787	534	14.1	2.7	4.4	1.7	62%	9%	38	24	38	27%	74%	5%	7	52	14%	43%	100	0.69	10.1	52	63	$9
18 Proj	**2**	**5**	**0**	**80**	**46**	**4.81**	**5.61**	**1.54**	**834**	**869**	**801**	**15.3**	**3.5**	**5.2**	**1.5**	**58%**	**8%**	**40**	**24**	**36**	**31%**	**71%**	**10%**	**12**						**-4.5**	**17**	**20**	**-$7**

Devenski,Christopher

Age: 27	Th: R	Role RP	Health	A	LIMA Plan	B
Ht: 6' 3"	Wt: 210	Type Pwr FB	PT/Exp	C	Rand Var	-3
			Consist	B	MM	3511

Middle relief game-changer turned mortal down the stretch. Second half xERA hints it could've been worse, as wildness, FB% tilt, and gopheritis crept in. Still should be fine given stratospheric SwK, and he's shown better Ctl, FpK in the past. May not repeat Win total, but unique usage gives him platform to thrive.

Yr Tm	W	L	Sv	IP	K	ERA	xERA	WHIP	oOPS	vL	vR	BF/G	Ctl	Dom	Cmd	FpK	SwK	G	L	F	H%	S%	hr/f	GS	APC	DOM%	DIS%	Sv%	LI	RAR	BPV	BPX	R$
13																																	
14 aa	5	3	0	41	32	4.50	4.56	1.34				17.2	3.9	6.9	1.7						26%	73%								-3.9	34	41	-$2
15 aa	7	4	2	120	87	3.54	4.76	1.42				21.1	2.5	6.5	2.6						33%	79%								6.2	60	71	$2
16 HOU	4	4	1	108	104	2.16	3.48	0.91	551	639	465	8.5	1.7	8.6	5.2	64%	14%	33	26	41	27%	77%	4%	5	33	40%	40%	100	0.91	27.1	122	145	$17
17 HOU	8	5	4	81	100	2.68	3.39	0.94	588	414	762	5.1	2.9	11.2	3.8	65%	17%	40	15	45	23%	80%	14%	0	20			40	1.51	16.7	141	169	$15
1st Half	4	3	3	48	66	2.23	2.70	0.81	498	446	544	5.8	2.2	12.3	5.5	69%	19%	45	17	38	25%	77%	11%	0	23			60	1.44	12.7	184	220	$20
2nd Half	4	2	1	32	34	3.34	4.50	1.14	719	375	1131	4.4	3.9	9.5	2.4	59%	16%	33	14	53	22%	83%	16%	0	18			20	1.58	4.1	76	92	$6
18 Proj	**7**	**4**	**5**	**78**	**91**	**2.98**	**3.67**	**1.08**	**663**	**544**	**784**	**6.8**	**2.8**	**10.5**	**3.8**	**63%**	**16%**	**37**	**19**	**43**	**28%**	**79%**	**12%**	**0**						**13.2**	**129**	**155**	**$11**

Diaz,Edwin

Age: 24	Th: R	Role RP	Health	A	LIMA Plan	C+
Ht: 6' 3"	Wt: 165	Type Pwr FB	PT/Exp	C	Rand Var	-1
			Consist	B	MM	3530

Briefly booted from closer gig in mid-May, recovered just fine. Ups and downs are part of the package: SwK locks in top-notch Dom; Ctl slide more in line with subpar FpK, suggests BBs here to stay; 2nd half hr/f suppressed ERA, but FB% bump hints at HR risk. An effective stopper, but too many holes to join elite.

Yr Tm	W	L	Sv	IP	K	ERA	xERA	WHIP	oOPS	vL	vR	BF/G	Ctl	Dom	Cmd	FpK	SwK	G	L	F	H%	S%	hr/f	GS	APC	DOM%	DIS%	Sv%	LI	RAR	BPV	BPX	R$
13																																	
14																																	
15 aa	5	10	0	104	93	4.88	3.76	1.36				21.8	2.9	8.1	2.8						34%	62%								-11.8	96	114	-$4
16 SEA *	3	7	19	92	137	2.73	3.03	1.12	627	604	643	5.6	2.1	13.3	6.2	58%	19%	47	23	31	37%	79%	15%	0	17			86	1.34	16.7	194	230	$18
17 SEA	4	6	34	66	89	3.27	3.78	1.15	619	655	590	4.2	4.4	12.1	2.8	56%	17%	39	15	46	26%	79%	14%	0	17			87	1.64	8.8	118	141	$20
1st Half	2	3	12	31	41	3.77	4.05	1.29	727	773	692	4.4	4.4	11.9	2.7	57%	16%	40	13	47	27%	84%	22%	0	18			80	1.32	2.2	115	138	$14
2nd Half	2	3	22	35	48	2.83	3.55	1.03	514	540	493	4.1	4.4	12.3	2.8	54%	18%	38	16	46	25%	74%	6%	0	16			92	1.94	6.6	120	144	$25
18 Proj	**3**	**6**	**33**	**65**	**87**	**3.02**	**3.39**	**1.16**	**620**	**628**	**615**	**5.1**	**3.4**	**12.0**	**3.5**	**57%**	**18%**	**42**	**18**	**40**	**31%**	**78%**	**12%**	**0**						**10.8**	**144**	**174**	**$18**

Dickey,R.A.

Age: 43	Th: R	Role SP	Health	B	LIMA Plan	B
Ht: 6' 3"	Wt: 215	Type	PT/Exp	A	Rand Var	0
			Consist	A	MM	0103

Continued to tread water, but another year of "meh" skills says he's pitching on borrowed time. Recent xERA baseline your first sign to steer clear. Add in stagnant Cmd/BPV, spike in DIS%. At 43, this might be the end. We'll remember that magical Cy Young in 2012 and always wonder what was in the water that year.

Yr Tm	W	L	Sv	IP	K	ERA	xERA	WHIP	oOPS	vL	vR	BF/G	Ctl	Dom	Cmd	FpK	SwK	G	L	F	H%	S%	hr/f	GS	APC	DOM%	DIS%	Sv%	LI	RAR	BPV	BPX	R$
13 TOR	14	13	0	225	177	4.21	4.11	1.24	728	777	672	27.7	2.8	7.1	2.5	61%	10%	40	19	40	27%	71%	13%	34	103	29%	32%			-9.4	69	90	$7
14 TOR	14	13	0	216	173	3.71	4.01	1.23	705	659	740	26.9	3.1	7.2	2.3	63%	11%	42	20	38	27%	74%	11%	34	103	29%	24%			0.7	67	79	$9
15 TOR	11	11	0	214	126	3.91	4.54	1.19	708	664	747	26.8	2.6	5.3	2.1	59%	9%	42	21	37	26%	71%	10%	33	99	21%	30%			1.5	46	55	$9
16 TOR	10	15	0	170	126	4.46	4.75	1.37	788	790	787	24.3	3.3	6.7	2.0	62%	11%	42	22	36	29%	73%	15%	29	91	14%	28%	0	0.83	-5.6	50	60	$1
17 ATL	10	10	0	190	136	4.26	4.76	1.37	785	720	837	26.3	3.2	6.4	2.0	64%	9%	47	20	33	29%	73%	13%	31	94	19%	42%			2.2	55	66	$5
1st Half	6	5	0	97	62	4.44	5.11	1.40	795	762	821	26.4	3.6	5.7	1.6	63%	9%	49	17	34	28%	73%	14%	16	93	19%	56%			-1.0	33	40	$3
2nd Half	4	5	0	93	74	4.08	4.41	1.34	774	674	854	26.1	2.7	7.2	2.6	66%	10%	44	23	33	31%	73%	12%	15	96	20%	27%			3.2	78	94	$6
18 Proj	**7**	**8**	**0**	**131**	**94**	**4.55**	**4.76**	**1.33**	**766**	**724**	**801**	**25.2**	**3.1**	**6.5**	**2.1**	**63%**	**10%**	**44**	**21**	**35**	**29%**	**69%**	**13%**	**21**						**-3.1**	**56**	**68**	**$0**

Diekman,Jake

Age: 31	Th: L	Role RP	Health	D	LIMA Plan	C+
Ht: 6' 4"	Wt: 200	Type Pwr GB	PT/Exp	D	Rand Var	-5
			Consist	A	MM	2510

Debuted in September after three-surgery bout with colitis; a major victory just to return. Tough to draw much from 11 IP sample, but fortunate H%/S% quickly refutes that surface ERA. Skills paint a familiar RP picture, as high Dom/GB% a rock-solid asset, but Ctl/FpK combo relegates him to the middle innings.

Yr Tm	W	L	Sv	IP	K	ERA	xERA	WHIP	oOPS	vL	vR	BF/G	Ctl	Dom	Cmd	FpK	SwK	G	L	F	H%	S%	hr/f	GS	APC	DOM%	DIS%	Sv%	LI	RAR	BPV	BPX	R$
13 PHI *	2	4	11	68	71	4.53	4.30	1.65	598	368	765	4.1	5.5	9.3	1.7	59%	14%	51	29	20	36%	71%	5%	0	14			79	0.92	-5.6	84	110	-$2
14 PHI	5	5	0	71	100	3.80	2.99	1.42	692	577	748	4.3	4.4	12.7	2.9	55%	14%	43	26	30	38%	73%	8%	0	18			0	1.14	-0.5	129	154	$0
15 2 TM	2	1	0	58	69	4.01	3.54	1.44	689	729	660	3.9	4.8	10.6	2.2	59%	12%	56	15	28	33%	73%	11%	0	16			0	0.86	-0.4	96	115	-$3
16 TEX	4	2	4	53	59	3.40	3.76	1.17	594	625	578	3.3	4.4	10.0	2.3	53%	11%	48	20	32	26%	72%	9%	0	14			80	1.08	5.2	87	104	$4
17 TEX	0	0	1	11	13	2.53	4.49	1.31	523	466	560	4.1	8.4	11.0	1.3	53%	12%	59	14	27	15%	85%	17%	0	17			100	1.10	2.4	7	8	-$3
1st Half																																	
2nd Half	0	0	1	11	13	2.53	4.49	1.31	523	466	560	4.1	8.4	11.0	1.3	53%	12%	59	14	27	15%	85%	17%	0	17			100	1.10	2.4	7	8	-$3
18 Proj	**3**	**2**	**5**	**51**	**62**	**3.82**	**3.73**	**1.38**	**665**	**605**	**699**	**3.7**	**4.6**	**11.0**	**2.4**	**56%**	**13%**	**51**	**21**	**29**	**33%**	**73%**	**9%**	**0**						**3.3**	**101**	**121**	**$1**

Doolittle,Sean

Age: 31	Th: L	Role RP	Health	F	LIMA Plan	B
Ht: 6' 2"	Wt: 210	Type Pwr xFB	PT/Exp	C	Rand Var	-2
			Consist	A	MM	3530

Cleared injury hurdle and thrived in closer role after switching coasts in July. Top-notch FpK/SwK combo solidifies elite BPV, and he's death to lefties (1st half vL not a typo), but FB% tilt, 1st/2nd half ERA splits highlight his reliance on a favorable hr/f. Health still a concern, but should flirt with another 3.00 ERA.

Yr Tm	W	L	Sv	IP	K	ERA	xERA	WHIP	oOPS	vL	vR	BF/G	Ctl	Dom	Cmd	FpK	SwK	G	L	F	H%	S%	hr/f	GS	APC	DOM%	DIS%	Sv%	LI	RAR	BPV	BPX	R$
13 OAK	5	5	2	69	60	3.13	3.55	0.96	573	516	603	3.8	1.7	7.8	4.6	65%	12%	33	20	47	27%	68%	5%	0	15			29	1.21	6.3	106	138	$7
14 OAK	2	4	22	63	89	2.73	2.61	0.73	459	276	550	3.9	1.1	12.8	11.1	72%	17%	23	18	59	27%	66%	6%	0	15			85	1.29	7.8	200	238	$17
15 OAK	1	0	4	14	15	3.95	3.99	1.24	651	1065	531	4.8	3.3	9.9	3.0	65%	10%	32	19	49	32%	69%	6%	0	21			80	0.75	0.0	99	118	-$2
16 OAK	2	3	4	39	45	3.23	3.65	1.05	705	584	798	3.5	1.8	10.4	5.6	70%	16%	29	16	55	29%	77%	12%	0	14			67	1.18	4.6	144	171	$3
17 2 TM	2	0	24	51	62	2.81	3.42	0.86	517	371	559	3.7	1.8	10.9	6.2	71%	16%	31	19	50	26%	72%	8%	0	15			92	1.26	9.8	157	189	$16
1st Half	0	0	3	16	23	3.31	2.66	0.73	482	0	711	3.4	1.1	12.7	11.5	65%	17%	39	17	44	26%	60%	13%	0	14			75	1.36	2.1	215	258	$2
2nd Half	2	0	21	35	39	2.57	3.79	0.91	533	678	500	3.9	2.1	10.0	4.9	73%	16%	28	19	52	26%	76%	7%	0	15			95	1.21	7.7	131	157	$22
18 Proj	**3**	**3**	**35**	**58**	**70**	**3.27**	**3.63**	**1.01**	**613**	**468**	**678**	**3.6**	**2.0**	**10.8**	**5.6**	**70%**	**16%**	**30**	**18**	**52**	**30%**	**72%**	**9%**	**0**						**7.8**	**151**	**182**	**$19**

Drake,Oliver

Age: 31	Th: R	Role RP	Health	A	LIMA Plan	C
Ht: 6' 4"	Wt: 215	Type Pwr	PT/Exp	D	Rand Var	+5
			Consist	C	MM	2400

43rd round pick from nine years ago finally hung in majors all year, but H% gods ruined the story. While xERA confirms he deserved a better fate, shaky Ctl, 2nd half slide leave little room for optimism. Generates enough whiffs and grounders to stick around, but odds of minor league Sv totals carrying over are slim.

Yr Tm	W	L	Sv	IP	K	ERA	xERA	WHIP	oOPS	vL	vR	BF/G	Ctl	Dom	Cmd	FpK	SwK	G	L	F	H%	S%	hr/f	GS	APC	DOM%	DIS%	Sv%	LI	RAR	BPV	BPX	R$
13 aa	3	0	8	31	30	2.16	2.41	1.18				6.5	4.0	8.7	2.2						27%	83%								6.5	100	131	$4
14 aa	2	4	31	53	55	3.80	3.34	1.30				4.3	3.1	9.3	3.0						34%	70%								-0.4	111	132	$11
15 BAL *	1	2	23	60	66	1.78	3.03	1.31	708	609	774	4.5	4.4	10.0	2.3	56%	14%	48	15	37	31%	88%	6%	0	23			100	0.48	16.0	105	125	$12
16 BAL *	2	4	10	74	82	4.30	4.73	1.54	595	598	589	5.3	4.9	9.9	2.0	62%	15%	49	14	37	33%	75%	13%	0	21			77	0.72	-1.0	71	84	$1
17 2 TM	3	5	1	56	62	4.66	4.01	1.57	808	693	1030	3.9	4.0	10.0	2.5	63%	12%	49	25	26	37%	72%	14%	0	16			25	0.75	-2.1	98	118	-$4
1st Half	3	2	1	34	39	4.76	3.54	1.47	780	629	1030	4.0	3.7	10.3	2.8	69%	12%	53	24	23	36%	70%	19%	0	16			50	0.78	-1.7	117	140	-$2
2nd Half	0	3	0	22	23	4.50	4.75	1.73	847	773	1029	3.9	4.5	9.4	2.1	54%	13%	43	26	30	39%	75%	10%	0	16			0	0.71	-0.4	69	83	-$7
18 Proj	**2**	**4**	**0**	**58**	**63**	**4.23**	**3.95**	**1.35**	**679**	**594**	**858**	**4.1**	**4.3**	**9.8**	**2.2**	**60%**	**12%**	**47**	**25**	**27**	**31%**	**70%**	**13%**	**0**						**0.9**	**84**	**101**	**-$2**

RYAN BLOOMFIELD

Duffey,Tyler

Age: 27	Th: R	Role: RP	Health: A	LIMA Plan: C+
Ht: 6' 3"	Wt: 220	Type:	PT/Exp: C	Rand Var: +4
			Consist: F	MM: 2211

Lost out on fifth starter gig in camp, and while production out of 'pen was modest, there's more here. xERA suggests he deserved better; Cmd surge was backed by stout FpK/SwK combo; plus GB% sealed triple-digit BPV. If H%/S% ever straighten out, there's deep-league profit potential.

Yr Tm	W	L	Sv	IP	K	ERA	xERA	WHIP	oOPS	vL	vR	BF/G	Ctl	Dom	Cmd	FpK	SwK	G	L	F	H%	S%	hr/f	GS	APC	DOM%	DIS%	Sv%	LI	RAR	BPV	BPX	R$
13																																	
14 a/a	10	3	0	127	80	4.84	4.79	1.33				25.1	1.8	5.7	3.1						31%	67%								-17.2	58	69	-$
15 MIN *	12	9	0	196	148	3.20	3.33	1.28	702	664	738	25.1	2.3	6.8	2.9	64%	10%	50	19	31	33%	74%	8%	10	91	50%	20%			18.3	97	115	$
16 MIN *	10	13	0	164	133	6.06	5.74	1.49	876	714	1038	22.8	2.5	7.3	2.9	64%	9%	48	23	29	34%	63%	20%	26	88	23%	42%			-37.7	50	59	-$
17 MIN	2	3	1	71	67	4.94	4.02	1.37	721	744	708	5.5	2.3	8.5	3.7	64%	11%	50	19	31	34%	66%	13%	0	20			33	1.00	-5.1	119	143	-$
1st Half	0	2	0	40	41	4.28	3.66	1.18	628	656	609	5.8	2.3	9.2	4.1	62%	12%	51	16	33	31%	65%	11%	0	20			0	1.10	0.4	135	161	-$
2nd Half	2	1	1	31	26	5.81	4.50	1.61	832	864	815	5.2	2.3	7.5	3.3	67%	11%	48	22	30	38%	67%	16%	0	20			50	0.90	-5.5	99	118	-$
18 Proj	**4**	**4**	**5**	**87**	**76**	**4.04**	**4.01**	**1.30**	**720**	**669**	**758**	**8.3**	**2.3**	**7.8**	**3.4**	**64%**	**10%**	**49**	**21**	**30**	**32%**	**73%**	**15%**	**0**						**3.4**	**105**	**127**	**$**

Duffy,Danny

Age: 29	Th: L	Role: SP	Health: F	LIMA Plan: B
Ht: 6' 3"	Wt: 205	Type: Pwr FB	PT/Exp: A	Rand Var: -1
			Consist: B	MM: 1203

Injuries (June oblique, Sept elbow) derailed hopes for a 2016 repeat; fortunate hr/f kept it from being worse. 2nd half Ctl fell more in line with FpK and Cmd says he has mid-rotation skills, but there's just one sub-4.00 xERA and 150+ IP season in this box. Sept surgery, albeit minor, further tempers expectations.

Yr Tm	W	L	Sv	IP	K	ERA	xERA	WHIP	oOPS	vL	vR	BF/G	Ctl	Dom	Cmd	FpK	SwK	G	L	F	H%	S%	hr/f	GS	APC	DOM%	DIS%	Sv%	LI	RAR	BPV	BPX	R$
13 KC *	5	2	0	93	90	4.26	4.48	1.54	608	692	571	19.4	4.4	8.7	2.0	54%	11%	32	27	41	34%	73%	0%	5	94	20%	20%			-4.5	72	94	-$
14 KC	9	12	0	149	113	2.53	4.24	1.11	605	386	670	19.5	3.2	6.8	2.1	59%	8%	36	18	46	25%	81%	6%	25	78	32%	24%	0	0.87	22.3	50	60	$1
15 KC	7	8	1	137	102	4.08	4.56	1.39	746	593	785	19.6	3.5	6.7	1.9	57%	9%	39	25	36	30%	73%	10%	24	79	8%	29%	100	0.75	-2.0	44	52	$
16 KC	12	3	0	180	188	3.51	3.72	1.14	710	449	760	17.4	2.1	9.4	4.5	62%	13%	36	21	43	30%	76%	13%	26	64	38%	15%	0	0.72	15.1	127	151	$1
17 KC	9	10	0	146	130	3.81	4.34	1.26	709	451	766	25.4	2.5	8.0	3.2	65%	12%	39	20	41	32%	71%	8%	24	95	38%	25%			9.8	93	111	$
1st Half	4	4	0	69	54	3.54	4.74	1.37	727	667	741	26.2	3.3	7.1	2.2	64%	12%	40	21	40	32%	74%	5%	11	99	36%	36%			6.9	57	68	$
2nd Half	5	6	0	78	76	4.06	4.01	1.16	693	255	787	24.7	1.9	8.8	4.8	66%	12%	39	19	42	31%	68%	10%	13	91	38%	15%			2.9	125	150	$1
18 Proj	**10**	**9**	**0**	**167**	**152**	**3.75**	**4.36**	**1.25**	**712**	**459**	**769**	**20.8**	**2.6**	**8.2**	**3.1**	**62%**	**11%**	**38**	**21**	**41**	**31%**	**73%**	**9%**	**33**						**12.5**	**92**	**111**	**$1**

Dull,Ryan

Age: 28	Th: R	Role: RP	Health: D	LIMA Plan: C+
Ht: 5' 9"	Wt: 175	Type: Pwr xFB	PT/Exp: D	Rand Var: +4
			Consist: B	MM: 1310

A big step back from early-career dominance. Knee injury in May didn't help, nor did S% freefall. Several signs he can recover: continued to miss bats with ease, post-injury Ctl returned to normal, chipped away at FB%. 2016-17 xERAs ultimately suggest a late-inning gig is wishful thinking.

Yr Tm	W	L	Sv	IP	K	ERA	xERA	WHIP	oOPS	vL	vR	BF/G	Ctl	Dom	Cmd	FpK	SwK	G	L	F	H%	S%	hr/f	GS	APC	DOM%	DIS%	Sv%	LI	RAR	BPV	BPX	R$
13																																	
14 aa	5	5	6	56	49	3.34	4.28	1.34				5.9	2.5	7.8	3.1						33%	78%								2.8	84	100	$
15 OAK *	4	4	13	78	72	1.62	2.41	1.04	713	875	594	5.0	2.6	8.3	3.2	50%	11%	41	14	45	26%	89%	20%	0	20			93	1.13	22.6	109	130	$1
16 OAK	5	5	3	74	73	2.42	3.89	0.87	577	687	517	4.1	1.8	8.8	4.9	64%	13%	33	16	51	23%	82%	10%	0	17			50	1.13	16.2	121	144	$1
17 OAK	2	2	0	42	45	5.14	4.16	1.26	724	897	639	3.6	3.4	9.6	2.8	67%	13%	39	19	42	29%	63%	15%	0	15			0	1.06	-4.1	98	118	-$
1st Half	2	2	0	16	18	6.32	4.58	1.47	688	823	614	3.9	5.2	10.3	2.0	66%	14%	41	20	39	31%	57%	13%	0	17			0	1.31	-3.8	66	79	-$
2nd Half	0	0	0	26	27	4.44	3.91	1.14	745	945	653	3.4	2.4	9.2	3.9	67%	12%	37	19	44	28%	68%	16%	0	14			0	0.92	-0.3	117	140	-$
18 Proj	**3**	**3**	**2**	**58**	**58**	**3.94**	**4.14**	**1.13**	**667**	**815**	**591**	**3.9**	**2.7**	**9.1**	**3.4**	**66%**	**13%**	**37**	**18**	**46**	**28%**	**70%**	**11%**	**0**						**3.0**	**105**	**126**	**$**

Dyson,Sam

Age: 30	Th: R	Role: RP	Health: A	LIMA Plan: D+
Ht: 6' 1"	Wt: 205	Type: Pwr xGB	PT/Exp: B	Rand Var: +5
			Consist: C	MM: 1010

So much for a fourth straight sub-3.00 ERA. Blew first three saves of season and skills fell apart just as fast. SwK continued its plunge, Ctl unraveled, and 2nd half xERA questions "strong" finish. No injuries to explain this, so while leading indicators say he'll improve, he can get a lot better and still be pretty bad.

Yr Tm	W	L	Sv	IP	K	ERA	xERA	WHIP	oOPS	vL	vR	BF/G	Ctl	Dom	Cmd	FpK	SwK	G	L	F	H%	S%	hr/f	GS	APC	DOM%	DIS%	Sv%	LI	RAR	BPV	BPX	R$
13 MIA *	4	12	0	117	51	3.97	4.16	1.50	959	1014	919	19.5	3.3	3.9	1.2	48%	6%	69	5	26	32%	72%	18%	1	35	0%	100%	0	0.79	-1.5	39	51	-$
14 MIA *	5	2	1	67	49	2.33	3.20	1.33	653	781	553	6.3	3.3	6.5	2.0	60%	11%	63	19	18	31%	81%	4%	0	22			33	0.68	11.7	80	96	$
15 2 TM	5	4	2	75	71	2.63	2.74	1.14	603	557	633	4.1	2.5	8.5	3.4	60%	13%	69	17	14	30%	78%	13%	0	15			50	1.02	12.4	132	157	$
16 TEX	3	2	38	70	55	2.43	3.38	1.22	658	740	593	3.9	2.9	7.0	2.4	61%	9%	65	19	16	29%	83%	16%	0	14			88	1.32	15.3	90	107	$2
17 2 TM	4	10	14	55	34	6.09	5.28	1.77	860	924	811	4.7	4.9	5.6	1.1	53%	8%	63	17	20	33%	67%	21%	0	17			67	1.32	-11.7	8	10	-$
1st Half	1	7	1	25	18	8.64	5.68	2.16	1015	1331	831	4.9	5.4	6.5	1.2	53%	8%	61	16	23	39%	63%	29%	0	18			20	1.26	-13.2	10	12	-$1
2nd Half	3	3	13	30	16	3.94	4.93	1.45	708	625	786	4.6	4.6	4.9	1.1	53%	8%	65	18	18	28%	73%	12%	0	16			81	1.38	1.5	7	9	$
18 Proj	**3**	**4**	**5**	**58**	**41**	**4.23**	**4.30**	**1.48**	**750**	**801**	**711**	**4.5**	**3.9**	**6.3**	**1.6**	**56%**	**9%**	**65**	**18**	**18**	**31%**	**73%**	**17%**	**0**						**0.9**	**51**	**62**	**-$**

Edwards,Carl

Age: 26	Th: R	Role: RP	Health: A	LIMA Plan: B
Ht: 6' 3"	Wt: 170	Type: Pwr	PT/Exp: D	Rand Var: -3
			Consist: B	MM: 3520

Dominant sophomore campaign despite some 2nd half slippage. BPV backed it up, with mid-90s heat and 12-6 curve (19% SwK) nearly netting triple-digit Ks. But BBs remain a giant hurdle, and stagnant FpK, 2nd half Ctl doubt he'll clear it anytime soon. Ceiling is worth chasing late but forget another sub-3.00 ERA.

Yr Tm	W	L	Sv	IP	K	ERA	xERA	WHIP	oOPS	vL	vR	BF/G	Ctl	Dom	Cmd	FpK	SwK	G	L	F	H%	S%	hr/f	GS	APC	DOM%	DIS%	Sv%	LI	RAR	BPV	BPX	R$
13																																	
14 aa	1	2	0	48	40	2.72	2.04	1.13				19.0	3.9	7.4	1.9						25%	75%								6.0	94	112	$
15 CHC *	5	3	6	60	67	3.30	2.02	1.30	566	929	350	6.0	6.8	10.1	1.5	63%	10%	58	25	17	24%	73%	0%	0	14			67	0.19	4.9	109	130	$
16 CHC *	1	2	3	61	81	4.15	1.97	1.07	456	425	475	4.0	4.6	11.9	2.6	56%	18%	50	21	29	24%	61%	19%	0	17			75	0.95	0.3	126	149	$
17 CHC	5	4	0	66	94	2.98	3.22	1.01	506	437	574	3.6	5.2	12.8	2.5	57%	15%	44	19	36	20%	74%	13%	0	15			0	1.13	11.2	112	135	$
1st Half	2	1	0	33	45	2.48	2.92	0.92	493	348	642	3.6	4.4	12.4	2.8	57%	14%	48	21	31	18%	81%	21%	0	16			0	1.13	7.6	131	156	$
2nd Half	3	3	0	34	49	3.48	3.52	1.10	518	524	506	3.6	5.9	13.1	2.2	57%	16%	40	18	42	22%	69%	8%	0	15			0	1.13	3.7	95	114	$
18 Proj	**4**	**3**	**12**	**65**	**84**	**3.34**	**3.65**	**1.18**	**582**	**543**	**614**	**4.3**	**5.2**	**11.6**	**2.2**	**57%**	**16%**	**46**	**20**	**34**	**25%**	**74%**	**11%**	**0**						**8.2**	**94**	**113**	**$**

Eflin,Zach

Age: 24	Th: R	Role: SP	Health: F	LIMA Plan: C
Ht: 6' 6"	Wt: 215	Type: Con FB	PT/Exp: D	Rand Var: +5
			Consist: D	MM: 0001

1-5, 6.16 ERA in 64 IP at PHI. Second verse as bad as the first. Sure, we can point to unjust trifecta of H%-S%-hr/f. But we can also point to a minuscule whiff rate that locks in subpar Cmd, and an xERA that's right in line with surface stats, combined to create an MM score on life support. Still young, but pass anyway.

Yr Tm	W	L	Sv	IP	K	ERA	xERA	WHIP	oOPS	vL	vR	BF/G	Ctl	Dom	Cmd	FpK	SwK	G	L	F	H%	S%	hr/f	GS	APC	DOM%	DIS%	Sv%	LI	RAR	BPV	BPX	R$
13																																	
14																																	
15 aa	8	6	0	132	62	4.09	4.31	1.29				23.5	1.5	4.2	2.8						30%	70%								-2.0	54	64	$
16 PHI *	8	7	0	132	80	4.67	3.62	1.17	828	939	723	23.9	2.0	5.5	2.8	62%	6%	36	24	40	28%	62%	13%	11	90	18%	64%			-7.9	66	79	$
17 PHI *	2	9	0	108	68	6.02	5.96	1.52	896	926	856	24.6	2.3	5.7	2.5	64%	7%	44	18	38	33%	64%	19%	11	93	0%	36%			-22.0	30	36	-$1
1st Half	1	4	0	56	30	5.96	6.28	1.54	894	901	885	24.4	2.1	4.9	2.3	61%	7%	45	18	37	33%	65%	19%	8	94	0%	38%			-11.1	16	19	-$1
2nd Half	1	5	0	52	38	6.08	5.60	1.49	902	978	739	24.7	2.5	6.6	2.7	70%	8%	41	16	43	33%	62%	19%	3	89	0%	33%			-10.9	45	54	-$1
18 Proj	**4**	**7**	**0**	**102**	**62**	**4.99**	**5.05**	**1.35**	**806**	**866**	**728**	**24.2**	**2.1**	**5.5**	**2.7**	**65%**	**7%**	**40**	**20**	**40**	**30%**	**67%**	**12%**	**18**						**-8.0**	**61**	**74**	**-$**

Eickhoff,Jerad

Age: 27	Th: R	Role: SP	Health: D	LIMA Plan: C
Ht: 6' 4"	Wt: 245	Type: Pwr FB	PT/Exp: B	Rand Var: +1
			Consist: A	MM: 0203

Nothing went right, from a June DL stint (back), to a career-worst MLB ERA, to a hand injury that ended it all in late Aug. Too many walks; SwK slide, 90 mph FB say not to trust Dom gains; xERA confirms this wasn't luck-driven. Still owns 2016 BPV, so perhaps injuries caused this, but don't pay much to find out.

Yr Tm	W	L	Sv	IP	K	ERA	xERA	WHIP	oOPS	vL	vR	BF/G	Ctl	Dom	Cmd	FpK	SwK	G	L	F	H%	S%	hr/f	GS	APC	DOM%	DIS%	Sv%	LI	RAR	BPV	BPX	R$
13 aa	1	1	0	29	11	10.19	8.29	1.97				23.1	4.8	3.3	0.7						32%	50%								-22.6	-53	-70	-$1
14 aa	10	9	0	154	118	5.11	4.30	1.34				23.8	3.2	6.9	2.2						30%	64%								-26.1	55	66	-$
15 PHI *	15	8	0	184	155	4.14	4.08	1.27	621	830	458	24.3	2.6	7.6	2.9	65%	11%	38	22	40	30%	71%	9%	8	92	50%	13%			-4.1	75	89	$
16 PHI	11	14	0	197	167	3.65	4.06	1.16	740	822	645	24.6	1.9	7.6	4.0	61%	10%	40	20	39	29%	75%	13%	33	92	24%	24%			13.2	103	123	$1
17 PHI	4	8	0	128	118	4.71	4.94	1.52	794	900	670	24.0	3.7	8.3	2.2	57%	9%	38	22	40	34%	72%	10%	24	89	17%	38%			-5.6	65	78	-$
1st Half	0	7	0	77	65	4.93	5.02	1.53	788	911	646	24.6	3.5	7.6	2.2	54%	8%	41	21	38	34%	69%	10%	14	91	14%	29%			-5.4	61	74	-$
2nd Half	4	1	0	51	53	4.38	4.83	1.52	803	883	705	23.1	4.0	9.3	2.3	61%	10%	32	25	43	34%	75%	11%	10	86	20%	50%			-0.2	68	82	-$
18 Proj	**8**	**8**	**0**	**145**	**130**	**4.35**	**4.65**	**1.38**	**775**	**886**	**652**	**23.4**	**3.1**	**8.0**	**2.6**	**60%**	**10%**	**38**	**22**	**40**	**32%**	**72%**	**11%**	**26**						**0.2**	**76**	**92**	**$**

RYAN BLOOMFIELD

Eovaldi,Nathan

Age: 28	Th: R	Role SP	Health F	LIMA Plan C	
Ht: 6' 2"	Wt: 225	Type	PT/Exp C	Rand Var 0	
			Consist A	MM 1101	

Signed one-year, $2MM contract with TAM to recover from TJS. Must be nice. Made Sept rehab outings; should be ready for Opening Day. Pre-surgery velo never translated to Ks, and despite GB% tilt, xERA pegs this as a pretty vanilla skill set. Mix in health risk, likely IP limit, and there's little reason to speculate.

Yr Tm	W	L	Sv	IP	K	ERA	xERA	WHIP	oOPS	vL	vR	BF/G	Ctl	Dom	Cmd	FpK	SwK	G	L	F	H%	S%	hr/f	GS	APC	DOM%	DIS%	Sv%	LI	RAR	BPV	BPX	R$
13 MIA	4	6	0	106	78	3.39	4.21	1.32	681	665	691	25.1	3.4	6.6	2.0	59%	8%	44	22	34	30%	75%	6%	18	94	22%	17%			6.3	49	64	$2
14 MIA	6	14	0	200	142	4.37	3.90	1.33	732	768	688	25.9	1.9	6.4	3.3	63%	9%	45	22	33	33%	67%	7%	33	97	33%	30%			-15.5	86	102	-$3
15 NYY	14	3	0	154	121	4.20	3.98	1.45	716	781	656	24.9	2.9	7.1	2.5	60%	9%	52	22	26	34%	71%	8%	27	98	19%	30%			-4.5	80	95	$1
16 NYY	9	8	0	125	97	4.76	4.27	1.31	778	871	705	21.9	2.9	7.0	2.4	65%	10%	50	18	32	28%	69%	19%	21	86	19%	38%	0	0.70	-8.8	76	90	$1
17																																	
1st Half																																	
2nd Half																																	
18 Proj	6	6	0	102	76	4.31	4.46	1.35	735	785	687	23.7	2.6	6.7	2.6	62%	9%	48	21	31	31%	70%	10%	18						0.6	76	92	$0

Estrada,Marco

Age: 34	Th: R	Role SP	Health C	LIMA Plan B+	
Ht: 6' 0"	Wt: 180	Type Pwr xFB	PT/Exp A	Rand Var 0	
			Consist A	MM 0205	

Poster boy for inducing infield FBs and outpitching his peripherals suddenly... didn't. Skills-wise, this was a near mirror image of 2016, as major shifts in H%/S%, subtle hr/f rise made the difference. Gravity says he'll rebound, but ugly xERA baseline, 2nd half BPV, age all agree: might not see another sub-4.00 ERA.

Yr Tm	W	L	Sv	IP	K	ERA	xERA	WHIP	oOPS	vL	vR	BF/G	Ctl	Dom	Cmd	FpK	SwK	G	L	F	H%	S%	hr/f	GS	APC	DOM%	DIS%	Sv%	LI	RAR	BPV	BPX	R$
13 MIL	7	4	0	128	118	3.87	3.60	1.08	670	651	687	24.4	2.0	8.3	4.1	60%	11%	38	18	44	27%	70%	12%	21	95	43%	29%			0.0	110	144	$8
14 MIL	7	6	0	151	127	4.36	4.15	1.20	752	719	781	16.0	2.6	7.6	2.9	61%	11%	33	18	50	27%	71%	13%	18	65	11%	50%	0	0.63	-11.5	77	91	$2
15 TOR	13	8	0	181	131	3.13	4.61	1.04	633	638	626	21.3	2.7	6.5	2.4	57%	10%	32	16	52	22%	76%	9%	28	86	21%	29%	0	0.76	18.5	53	64	$20
16 TOR	9	9	0	176	165	3.48	4.46	1.12	639	602	680	24.9	3.3	8.4	2.5	59%	11%	33	18	48	25%	74%	10%	29	98	34%	17%			15.5	73	87	$16
17 TOR	10	9	0	186	176	4.98	5.01	1.38	785	686	864	24.4	3.4	8.5	2.5	59%	11%	30	19	50	31%	68%	11%	33	98	21%	30%			-14.4	69	82	$1
1st Half	4	6	0	96	105	4.86	4.49	1.41	799	750	837	24.6	3.3	9.8	3.0	60%	12%	32	21	47	34%	69%	12%	17	99	24%	24%			-5.9	99	118	$1
2nd Half	6	3	0	90	71	5.12	5.58	1.35	769	618	893	24.2	3.6	7.1	2.0	57%	10%	28	18	54	28%	67%	11%	16	98	19%	38%			-8.4	37	44	$1
18 Proj	11	9	0	189	167	4.26	4.84	1.24	718	648	784	22.6	3.2	8.0	2.5	59%	11%	32	18	50	27%	71%	11%	34						2.3	67	80	$9

Familia,Jeurys

Age: 28	Th: R	Role RP	Health F	LIMA Plan C+	
Ht: 6' 3"	Wt: 240	Type Pwr xGB	PT/Exp A	Rand Var 0	
			Consist B	MM 4331	

Blood clot in shoulder cost him three months, though surgery reportedly spared the dreaded thoracic outlet. Walks blew everything up, but take these numbers with small-sample grain of salt. Pre-injury profile featured plenty of whiffs, GBs, and impressive xERA. With rest, could quickly get back to... UP: 40 Sv

Yr Tm	W	L	Sv	IP	K	ERA	xERA	WHIP	oOPS	vL	vR	BF/G	Ctl	Dom	Cmd	FpK	SwK	G	L	F	H%	S%	hr/f	GS	APC	DOM%	DIS%	Sv%	LI	RAR	BPV	BPX	R$
13 NYM	0	0	1	11	8	4.22	5.79	1.97	908	889	918	5.8	7.6	6.8	0.9	52%	7%	52	15	33	31%	84%	18%	0	22			100	0.69	-0.5	-54	-70	-$5
14 NYM	2	5	5	77	73	2.21	3.36	1.18	587	821	377	4.2	3.7	8.5	2.3	53%	13%	57	15	28	28%	82%	5%	0	16			50	1.18	14.6	87	104	$7
15 NYM	2	2	43	78	86	1.85	2.62	1.00	569	616	531	4.1	2.2	9.9	4.5	61%	16%	58	20	22	28%	86%	14%	0	15			90	1.29	20.4	155	185	$27
16 NYM	3	4	51	78	84	2.55	3.08	1.21	574	629	526	4.1	3.6	9.7	2.7	57%	15%	63	18	19	31%	77%	3%	0	16			91	1.22	15.7	119	142	$27
17 NYM	2	2	6	25	25	4.38	4.17	1.46	636	760	542	4.3	5.5	9.1	1.7	44%	10%	60	21	19	31%	69%	8%	0	16			86	1.08	-0.1	54	65	-$1
1st Half	1	1	3	9	10	3.86	5.17	1.61	584	754	450	3.9	7.7	9.6	1.3	35%	11%	56	16	28	30%	73%	0%	0	15			75	1.34	0.6	-1	-1	-$2
2nd Half	1	1	3	15	15	4.70	3.63	1.37	667	761	597	4.5	4.1	8.8	2.1	49%	10%	63	23	14	32%	65%	17%	0	16			100	0.89	-0.6	88	106	$0
18 Proj	3	4	25	73	75	3.27	3.34	1.23	622	714	547	4.1	3.5	9.3	2.6	55%	14%	61	20	20	31%	74%	11%	0						9.7	111	134	$14

Faria,Jake

Age: 24	Th: R	Role SP	Health B	LIMA Plan B	
Ht: 6' 4"	Wt: 235	Type Pwr	PT/Exp D	Rand Var 0	
			Consist B	MM 1303	

5-4, 3.43 ERA in 87 IP at TAM. Led International League in Ks upon June call-up and came as advertised. Slider (14% SwK) and change-up (23%) were behind stellar Dom, though shaky Ctl drove 4.23 MLB xERA. Expect some growing pains, and he's yet to clear 160 IP in a season, but keeper track is pointing north.

Yr Tm	W	L	Sv	IP	K	ERA	xERA	WHIP	oOPS	vL	vR	BF/G	Ctl	Dom	Cmd	FpK	SwK	G	L	F	H%	S%	hr/f	GS	APC	DOM%	DIS%	Sv%	LI	RAR	BPV	BPX	R$
13																																	
14																																	
15 aa	7	3	0	75	85	2.80	2.58	1.14				22.9	3.4	10.2	3.0						29%	77%								10.8	118	141	$7
16 a/a	5	10	0	151	138	5.07	3.56	1.34				23.2	4.3	8.2	1.9						29%	62%								-16.3	74	88	-$3
17 TAM *	11	5	0	145	156	3.73	3.72	1.24	677	559	729	21.9	3.4	9.7	2.8	54%	13%	38	22	40	30%	75%	12%	14	90	36%	29%	0	0.76	11.3	90	108	$12
1st Half	9	1	0	91	107	3.48	3.48	1.18	557	491	579	22.8	2.9	10.6	3.7	60%	13%	40	21	38	31%	75%	9%	5	104	80%	0%			9.8	115	138	$20
2nd Half	2	4	0	54	49	4.14	4.84	1.34	747	583	832	20.9	4.3	8.1	1.9	52%	12%	37	22	41	27%	74%	13%	9	84	11%	44%	0	0.75	1.5	45	54	-$2
18 Proj	7	7	0	131	130	4.05	4.43	1.28	687	587	730	22.2	3.9	9.0	2.3	55%	13%	38	22	40	29%	71%	10%	24						4.9	73	88	$5

Farmer,Buck

Age: 27	Th: R	Role SP	Health A	LIMA Plan D+	
Ht: 6' 4"	Wt: 225	Type FB	PT/Exp D	Rand Var +5	
			Consist A	MM 0103	

5-5, 6.75 ERA in 48 IP at DET. Fourth straight 5.00+ ERA - is it deserved? H%/S% consistently derail support metrics that are already pedestrian. However, 2017 FpK/SwK show something there. It's not enough. xERA baseline offers little hope. FB% tilt just adds more risk, making his path to relevance rocky.

Yr Tm	W	L	Sv	IP	K	ERA	xERA	WHIP	oOPS	vL	vR	BF/G	Ctl	Dom	Cmd	FpK	SwK	G	L	F	H%	S%	hr/f	GS	APC	DOM%	DIS%	Sv%	LI	RAR	BPV	BPX	R$
13																																	
14 DET *	2	2	0	29	21	8.12	6.03	1.70	1054	1189	880	16.2	4.1	6.7	1.6	70%	11%	33	15	52	35%	51%	14%	2	49	0%	100%	0	0.42	-15.5	30	35	-$8
15 DET *	7	7	0	127	84	5.70	5.29	1.53	986	1067	920	18.4	3.0	5.9	2.0	60%	8%	45	15	40	33%	64%	18%	5	50	0%	80%	0	0.58	-27.2	38	45	-$12
16 DET *	5	7	0	129	100	5.11	5.57	1.60	771	903	604	16.8	3.5	7.0	2.0	60%	11%	52	11	37	34%	71%	13%	1	36	0%	100%	0	0.28	-14.7	42	49	-$9
17 DET *	11	9	0	172	137	6.07	6.02	1.67	843	875	803	24.1	2.9	7.2	2.4	64%	11%	32	21	47	38%	64%	13%	11	82	18%	64%			-36.3	52	62	-$15
1st Half	4	4	0	89	76	6.10	6.24	1.62	848	689	982	24.7	2.1	7.7	3.7	63%	15%	36	23	40	39%	64%	26%	4	80	50%	50%			-19.1	74	89	-$15
2nd Half	7	5	0	83	61	6.04	5.78	1.72	838	956	674	23.4	3.9	6.6	1.7	64%	9%	31	19	50	36%	65%	8%	7	83	0%	71%			-17.2	42	50	-$14
18 Proj	5	7	0	131	99	5.40	5.34	1.55	833	873	792	22.7	3.3	6.9	2.1	62%	10%	38	18	44	34%	68%	11%	23						-16.7	51	61	-$9

Fedde,Erick

Age: 25	Th: R	Role RP	Health B	LIMA Plan C	
Ht: 6' 4"	Wt: 180	Type xGB	PT/Exp F	Rand Var +5	
			Consist A	MM 1101	

0-1, 9.39 ERA in 15 IP at WAS. Former first-round pick stumbled in trio of MLB starts, then Sept DL stint (forearm) ended season. Prospect pedigree makes for rosy keeper outlook thanks to plus fastball with late life, hard slider, ability to induce GBs. MLEs say it'll take time, so monitor from a distance in 2018.

Yr Tm	W	L	Sv	IP	K	ERA	xERA	WHIP	oOPS	vL	vR	BF/G	Ctl	Dom	Cmd	FpK	SwK	G	L	F	H%	S%	hr/f	GS	APC	DOM%	DIS%	Sv%	LI	RAR	BPV	BPX	R$
13																																	
14																																	
15																																	
16 aa	2	1	0	29	24	5.30	5.47	1.72				26.7	3.3	7.3	2.2						40%	67%								-4.0	69	83	-$6
17 WAS *	4	6	0	106	80	5.38	5.04	1.47	1106	836	1445	14.2	2.8	6.9	2.5	71%	6%	62	17	21	34%	65%	50%	3	99	0%	100%			-13.3	57	69	-$6
1st Half	4	3	0	66	51	4.01	4.11	1.33				11.8	2.8	6.9	2.5						31%	72%	0%	0						2.8	69	83	$1
2nd Half	0	3	0	40	30	7.61	6.55	1.71	1106	836	1445	20.1	2.8	6.7	2.4	71%	6%	62	17	21	38%	55%	50%	3	99	0%	100%			-16.1	39	47	-$18
18 Proj	2	6	0	102	77	4.41	4.52	1.45	659	497	865	15.5	2.7	6.8	2.5	63%	8%	51	21	29	33%	72%	12%	15						-0.6	79	95	-$4

Feldman,Scott

Age: 35	Th: R	Role RP	Health F	LIMA Plan C	
Ht: 6' 6"	Wt: 225	Type	PT/Exp C	Rand Var +4	
			Consist A	MM 1001	

Return to rotation led to all-too-familiar xERA before knee surgery ended season in August. Yeah, we could pin poor ERA on hr/f spike, but he doesn't miss bats, saw spike in liners, and Cmd remained ho-hum. With injury risk magnified at 35, best case scenario is limited number of league-average IP.

Yr Tm	W	L	Sv	IP	K	ERA	xERA	WHIP	oOPS	vL	vR	BF/G	Ctl	Dom	Cmd	FpK	SwK	G	L	F	H%	S%	hr/f	GS	APC	DOM%	DIS%	Sv%	LI	RAR	BPV	BPX	R$
13 2TM	12	12	0	182	132	3.86	3.85	1.18	671	672	670	25.3	2.8	6.5	2.4	56%	8%	50	19	32	27%	70%	11%	30	100	30%	40%			0.0	71	92	$9
14 HOU	8	12	0	180	107	3.74	4.13	1.30	725	715	737	26.4	2.5	5.3	2.1	61%	7%	47	22	31	30%	73%	9%	29	102	10%	34%			0.0	54	64	$2
15 HOU	5	5	0	108	61	3.90	4.26	1.31	739	664	824	25.1	2.2	5.1	2.3	61%	7%	49	24	28	29%	74%	13%	18	98	28%	44%			0.8	58	69	$0
16 2AL	7	4	0	77	56	3.97	4.32	1.38	782	891	707	8.5	2.2	6.5	2.9	60%	8%	50	20	30	32%	75%	13%	5	33	0%	60%	0	0.71	2.0	86	102	$1
17 CIN	7	7	0	111	93	4.77	4.26	1.36	820	872	773	22.5	2.8	7.5	2.7	61%	9%	43	27	30	30%	71%	21%	21	91	19%	33%			-5.6	80	96	$0
1st Half	7	5	0	98	80	3.78	4.13	1.27	732	779	691	23.8	2.9	7.4	2.5	60%	8%	45	27	28	29%	73%	14%	17	97	24%	29%			7.0	76	92	$4
2nd Half	0	2	0	14	13	11.85	5.17	1.98	1350	1356	1342	16.8	2.0	8.6	4.3	61%	11%	29	29	43	35%	53%	48%	4	64	0%	50%			-12.6	107	129	-$26
18 Proj	5	6	0	116	80	4.47	4.49	1.34	779	785	773	17.5	2.5	6.2	2.5	60%	8%	48	23	29	30%	70%	15%	21						-1.6	69	84	-$1

RYAN BLOOMFIELD

Feliz,Michael

Age:	25	Th:	R	Role	RP	Health	C	LIMA Plan	C+
Ht:	6' 4"	Wt:	230	Type	Pwr FB	PT/Exp	D	Rand Var	+5
						Consist	B	MM	3500

Summer swoon led to six-week DL stint for shoulder in Aug. Brutal H%/S% combo torpedoed his ERA, but it's all good under the hood: misses enough bats to hold elite Dom, FpK spike bodes well for Ctl, pre-injury BPV was closer-worthy. Comes with injury risk now, but if that checks out... UP: sub-3.50 ERA

Yr	Tm	W	L	Sv	IP	K	ERA	xERA	WHIP	oOPS	vL	vR	BF/G	Ctl	Dom	Cmd	FpK	SwK	G	L	F	H%	S%	hr/f	GS	APC	DOM%	DIS%	Sv%	LI	RAR	BPV	BPX
13																																	
14																																	
15	HOU *	6	3	1	87	69	2.91	2.50	1.03	884	868	898	16.7	2.4	7.2	3.0	66%	13%	38	31	31	25%	75%	25%	0	35			100	0.05	11.2	95	114
16	HOU	8	1	0	65	95	4.43	2.94	1.18	659	705	619	5.7	3.0	13.2	4.3	51%	14%	42	21	37	34%	67%	18%	0	24			0	0.99	-1.9	175	207
17	HOU	4	2	0	48	70	5.63	3.89	1.56	854	879	839	4.7	4.1	13.1	3.2	63%	15%	31	27	42	41%	67%	15%	0	20			0	0.67	-7.5	134	161
1st Half		4	2	0	37	52	3.89	3.56	1.19	675	789	598	4.7	3.4	12.6	3.7	64%	16%	28	28	44	33%	70%	10%	0	19			0	0.84	2.1	142	170
2nd Half		0	0	0	11	18	11.45	4.98	2.82	1307	1139	1398	4.8	6.5	14.7	2.3	62%	12%	38	24	38	59%	63%	29%	0	21			0	0.22	-9.6	104	125
18	Proj	6	2	0	65	77	3.63	3.70	1.12	635	719	572	6.7	2.9	10.6	3.6	59%	15%	34	25	41	30%	71%	11%	0						5.8	124	149

Feliz,Neftali

Age:	30	Th:	R	Role	RP	Health	D	LIMA Plan	D+
Ht:	6' 3"	Wt:	235	Type	Pwr FB	PT/Exp	C	Rand Var	0
						Consist	C	MM	0200

More disappointment from one-time can't-miss prospect. Released twice, most recently after bout with numbness in finger. Health a major reason to steer clear; others include xERA in lockstep with ERA, inability to hold 2016 SwK/Dom gains, lack of GB%. LIMA grade out of 'pen confirms: stay away.

Yr	Tm	W	L	Sv	IP	K	ERA	xERA	WHIP	oOPS	vL	vR	BF/G	Ctl	Dom	Cmd	FpK	SwK	G	L	F	H%	S%	hr/f	GS	APC	DOM%	DIS%	Sv%	LI	RAR	BPV	BPX
13	TEX	0	0	0	5	4	0.00	4.72	1.50	659	629	665	3.5	3.9	7.7	2.0	38%	9%	21	29	50	35%	100%	0%	0	18			0	0.75	2.2	34	44
14	TEX *	3	2	20	60	45	2.69	3.11	1.00	586	513	663	4.3	2.8	6.8	2.4	66%	10%	27	22	51	20%	86%	11%	0	16			87	1.44	7.8	57	68
15	2 AL	3	4	10	48	39	6.38	4.58	1.56	821	768	876	4.4	3.4	7.3	2.2	57%	10%	38	26	37	35%	59%	9%	0	17			59	1.23	-14.3	57	67
16	PIT	4	2	2	54	61	3.52	3.71	1.14	696	641	742	3.5	3.5	10.2	2.9	59%	15%	38	23	39	25%	78%	19%	0	15			50	1.19	4.4	105	125
17	2 TM	2	5	8	46	37	5.48	5.39	1.37	794	834	764	4.0	4.5	7.2	1.6	62%	12%	33	22	45	25%	65%	15%	0	17			89	1.04	-6.4	20	24
1st Half		1	5	8	32	25	5.34	5.54	1.34	806	717	872	4.0	4.8	7.0	1.5	61%	11%	31	22	47	22%	69%	19%	0	18			89	1.21	-3.9	7	8
2nd Half		1	0	0	14	12	5.79	5.06	1.43	770	1096	531	4.1	3.9	7.7	2.0	64%	15%	36	21	43	32%	58%	6%	0	17			0	0.66	-2.5	48	58
18	Proj	3	4	0	51	44	4.94	4.92	1.33	767	699	828	4.0	3.7	7.7	2.1	60%	11%	34	23	42	27%	68%	14%	0						-3.7	50	60

Fields,Joshua

Age:	32	Th:	R	Role	RP	Health	A	LIMA Plan	B+
Ht:	6' 0"	Wt:	195	Type	Pwr xFB	PT/Exp	D	Rand Var	-5
						Consist	A	MM	2400

Amazing what shift in H% and S% can do, leading to a career year. Core skills remain rock-steady: Ctl got plenty of support from FpK, primo SwK hints at more Ks to come. But it's not all roses—xERA reflects HR risk, and we can't expect luck factor repeat. He's good; just not enough for late-inning role.

Yr	Tm	W	L	Sv	IP	K	ERA	xERA	WHIP	oOPS	vL	vR	BF/G	Ctl	Dom	Cmd	FpK	SwK	G	L	F	H%	S%	hr/f	GS	APC	DOM%	DIS%	Sv%	LI	RAR	BPV	BPX
13	HOU	1	3	5	38	40	4.97	4.11	1.29	783	884	706	3.9	4.3	9.5	2.2	51%	10%	37	11	52	26%	68%	16%	0	16			83	1.11	-5.2	70	92
14	HOU	4	6	4	55	70	4.45	3.30	1.23	637	665	613	4.3	2.8	11.5	4.1	59%	13%	31	21	48	36%	62%	3%	0	18			50	1.05	-4.7	141	168
15	HOU	4	1	0	51	67	3.55	3.37	1.14	602	705	530	3.9	3.4	11.9	3.5	60%	13%	34	18	48	33%	68%	4%	0	16			0	0.76	2.6	135	161
16	2 TM *	2	1	1	64	67	3.79	4.12	1.39	838	788	869	4.4	2.6	9.4	3.7	59%	14%	36	16	49	37%	73%	8%	0	16			100	0.49	3.2	116	138
17	LA	5	0	2	57	60	2.84	3.94	0.96	630	780	530	3.9	2.4	9.5	4.0	67%	14%	30	21	49	23%	82%	14%	0	16			40	0.88	10.7	115	138
1st Half		3	0	1	27	32	3.00	3.74	1.04	687	732	654	3.9	2.7	10.7	4.0	67%	14%	28	23	49	24%	86%	19%	0	17			25	1.01	4.5	126	151
2nd Half		2	0	1	30	28	2.70	4.12	0.90	579	819	417	3.9	2.1	8.4	4.0	68%	14%	31	20	49	22%	78%	10%	0	14			100	0.77	6.1	104	124
18	Proj	3	2	0	58	63	3.36	4.04	1.12	659	742	603	3.9	2.7	9.8	3.7	63%	14%	32	19	49	29%	75%	10%	0						7.2	116	140

Fiers,Mike

Age:	33	Th:	R	Role	SP	Health	A	LIMA Plan	C
Ht:	6' 2"	Wt:	200	Type	Pwr	PT/Exp	A	Rand Var	+4
						Consist	A	MM	1203

Rollercoaster year, as mid-season run (2.59 ERA in June/July) was bookended by months of ineptitude. Through it all, BPV continued steady descent thanks to 2nd half wildness, and he posted third straight 4.00+ xERA. DOM% a testament to lack of upside.

Yr	Tm	W	L	Sv	IP	K	ERA	xERA	WHIP	oOPS	vL	vR	BF/G	Ctl	Dom	Cmd	FpK	SwK	G	L	F	H%	S%	hr/f	GS	APC	DOM%	DIS%	Sv%	LI	RAR	BPV	BPX
13	MIL *	2	6	0	51	38	4.68	5.82	1.50	972	999	930	13.8	3.4	6.8	2.0	60%	9%	35	26	39	30%	77%	26%	3	37	0%	67%	0	1.02	-5.1	19	25
14	MIL *	14	10	0	174	174	2.90	3.07	1.08	531	517	542	21.9	1.9	9.0	4.7	58%	10%	33	20	47	29%	78%	8%	10	80	60%	0%	0	0.74	18.0	131	156
15	2 TM	7	10	0	180	180	3.69	4.00	1.25	713	664	756	24.5	3.2	9.0	2.8	60%	10%	38	20	42	30%	75%	11%	30	98	20%	20%	0	0.78	6.0	91	109
16	HOU	11	8	0	169	134	4.48	4.25	1.36	801	749	843	23.4	2.2	7.2	3.2	63%	9%	42	26	32	32%	71%	15%	30	89	30%	40%	0	0.76	-6.1	88	105
17	HOU	8	10	0	153	146	5.22	4.48	1.43	827	809	844	23.1	3.6	8.6	2.4	60%	10%	43	20	37	30%	70%	20%	28	91	18%	36%	0	0.75	-16.4	77	92
1st Half		5	3	0	84	74	3.98	4.24	1.30	783	713	863	23.8	3.1	8.0	2.6	61%	10%	49	17	34	28%	79%	22%	15	93	13%	33%			3.9	86	103
2nd Half		3	7	0	70	72	6.72	4.76	1.58	878	946	825	22.4	4.3	9.3	2.2	60%	9%	35	23	42	34%	60%	17%	13	88	23%	38%	0	0.74	-20.3	65	78
18	Proj	8	11	0	160	147	4.58	4.49	1.36	772	754	789	21.7	3.2	8.3	2.6	61%	10%	40	22	38	31%	71%	14%	31						-4.3	81	97

Finnegan,Brandon

Age:	25	Th:	L	Role	RP	Health	D	LIMA Plan	D+
Ht:	5' 11"	Wt:	212	Type	Pwr	PT/Exp	C	Rand Var	0
						Consist	A	MM	0200

Piqued interest of opening week FAABers with 9-K debut, but shoulder strain shelved him in April, again in June, then had surgery on OTHER shoulder in July. Even with a healthy return—and that's a leap—BBs remain a major issue, while once-promising GB% vanished in 2016. Let someone else take the risk.

Yr	Tm	W	L	Sv	IP	K	ERA	xERA	WHIP	oOPS	vL	vR	BF/G	Ctl	Dom	Cmd	FpK	SwK	G	L	F	H%	S%	hr/f	GS	APC	DOM%	DIS%	Sv%	LI	RAR	BPV	BPX
13																																	
14	KC	0	1	0	7	10	1.29	1.90	1.00	546	778	433	4.0	1.3	12.9	10.0	64%	14%	59	18	24	38%	86%	0%	0	17			0	0.67	2.1	234	278
15	2 TM *	5	8	1	105	102	5.51	4.88	1.55	713	765	695	11.8	5.0	8.7	1.7	58%	10%	54	17	29	32%	66%	22%	4	38	25%	50%	50	0.85	-20.2	54	65
16	CIN	10	11	0	172	145	3.98	4.87	1.36	748	633	781	23.7	4.4	7.6	1.7	54%	10%	38	23	39	26%	77%	15%	31	93	13%	39%			4.5	34	40
17	CIN	1	1	0	13	16	4.15	5.10	1.69	677	542	698	14.8	9.0	11.1	1.2	48%	12%	53	20	27	28%	76%	13%	4	60	25%	75%			0.3	-13	-15
1st Half		1	1	0	13	16	4.15	5.10	1.69	677	542	698	14.8	9.0	11.1	1.2	48%	12%	53	20	27	28%	76%	13%	4	60	25%	75%			0.3	-12	-15
2nd Half																																	
18	Proj	3	4	0	58	52	4.61	4.85	1.44	778	732	792	16.6	4.7	8.0	1.7	56%	10%	45	20	35	28%	72%	15%	10						-1.8	42	50

Fister,Doug

Age:	34	Th:	R	Role	SP	Health	D	LIMA Plan	C
Ht:	6' 8"	Wt:	210	Type		PT/Exp	B	Rand Var	+2
						Consist	B	MM	0103

5-9, 4.88 ERA in 90 IP at BOS. Released in June, started ALDS Game 3, but the redemption story isn't all that sweet. Used to rely on staunch GB%/Ctl combo to get by, the latter of which has been M.I.A. for two years. SwK still subpar, says not to trust Dom spike. Age, xERA baseline confirm the tank is running low.

Yr	Tm	W	L	Sv	IP	K	ERA	xERA	WHIP	oOPS	vL	vR	BF/G	Ctl	Dom	Cmd	FpK	SwK	G	L	F	H%	S%	hr/f	GS	APC	DOM%	DIS%	Sv%	LI	RAR	BPV	BPX
13	DET	14	9	0	209	159	3.67	3.38	1.31	710	687	738	26.7	1.9	6.9	3.6	59%	8%	54	21	24	33%	73%	9%	32	102	31%	22%	0	0.80	5.1	104	136
14	WAS	16	6	0	164	98	2.41	3.75	1.08	654	690	618	26.5	1.3	5.4	4.1	65%	6%	49	17	34	27%	84%	10%	25	99	36%	36%			26.8	88	105
15	WAS	5	7	1	103	63	4.19	4.49	1.40	796	738	860	18.0	2.1	5.5	2.6	62%	6%	45	21	34	32%	74%	12%	15	66	20%	47%	100	0.86	-3.0	65	78
16	HOU	12	13	0	180	115	4.64	4.89	1.43	788	946	606	24.3	3.1	5.7	1.9	60%	6%	45	20	34	30%	70%	12%	32	94	22%	47%			-10.1	43	51
17	BOS *	6	9	0	106	91	4.83	4.12	1.41	726	862	589	21.3	3.7	7.7	2.1	60%	8%	51	21	29	32%	66%	12%	15	85	33%	33%	0	1.06	-6.1	70	84
1st Half		1	1	0	27	19	4.68	4.42	1.55	783	1008	554	23.3	3.8	6.3	1.7	69%	9%	41	21	38	34%	68%	9%	2	103	0%	0%			-1.1	61	73
2nd Half		5	8	0	79	72	4.88	4.23	1.36	718	842	593	21.5	3.6	8.2	2.3	59%	8%	52	21	28	31%	65%	12%	13	83	38%	38%	0	1.10	-5.1	79	94
18	Proj	8	10	0	145	106	4.50	4.65	1.40	747	803	686	23.4	3.1	6.6	2.1	61%	7%	49	20	31	31%	69%	10%	26						-2.6	62	75

Flaherty,Jack

Age:	22	Th:	R	Role	SP	Health	A	LIMA Plan	B
Ht:	6' 4"	Wt:	205	Type		PT/Exp	D	Rand Var	+2
						Consist	F	MM	1201

0-2, 6.33 ERA in 21 IP at STL. MLB cup of coffee didn't taste good, but three-level ascent was impressive. Four-pitch mix lacks a truly plus offering, but his ability to limit BBs raises his floor. PCL performance (3.5 Cmd in 85 IP), xERA confirm this was a step forward. He could realize mid-rotation upside quickly.

Yr	Tm	W	L	Sv	IP	K	ERA	xERA	WHIP	oOPS	vL	vR	BF/G	Ctl	Dom	Cmd	FpK	SwK	G	L	F	H%	S%	hr/f	GS	APC	DOM%	DIS%	Sv%	LI	RAR	BPV	BPX
13																																	
14																																	
15																																	
16																																	
17	STL *	14	6	0	170	142	3.12	3.58	1.21	843	1096	588	22.1	2.4	7.5	3.2	63%	14%	48	22	30	30%	78%	21%	5	60	0%	80%	0	0.65	25.9	90	108
1st Half		8	3	0	90	77	2.80	3.24	1.13				23.8	2.1	7.7	3.7						29%	79%	0%	0						17.4	105	125
2nd Half		6	3	0	80	65	3.49	3.98	1.29	843	1096	588	20.5	2.7	7.3	2.7	63%	14%	48	22	30	31%	76%	21%	5	60	0%	80%	0	0.65	8.5	76	91
18	Proj	7	5	0	116	96	3.68	4.34	1.23	634	796	469	22.7	2.5	7.5	3.0	63%	14%	43	22	35	30%	73%	10%	21						9.7	89	107

RYAN BLOOMFIELD

Foltynewicz,Mike

Age: 26	Th: R	Role SP	Health B	LIMA Plan C	
Ht: 6' 4"	Wt: 220	Type Pwr	PT/Exp C	Rand Var +2	
			Consist C	MM 1203	

What was expected to be growth year didn't go quite as hoped as BPV/BPX were virtually identical to 2016. Swing-and-miss stuff compromised by Cmd drop, and he continues to be undermined by control issues—with walks, and occasionally with composure. Arm is still lapping his skills, so draft accordingly.

Yr	Tm	W	L	Sv	IP	K	ERA	xERA	WHIP	oOPS	vL	vR	BF/G	Ctl	Dom	Cmd	FpK	SwK	G	L	F	H%	S%	hr/f	GS	APC	DOM%	DIS%	Sv%	LI	RAR	BPV	BPX	R$
13	aa	5	3	3	103	85	3.22	3.19	1.29				18.4	4.4	7.4	1.7						26%	77%								8.3	68	89	$5
14	HOU *	7	8	0	121	103	5.36	4.77	1.53	864	1062	659	14.3	4.2	7.6	1.8	52%	10%	29	21	51	33%	66%	9%	0	20			0	0.38	-24.2	55	66	-$9
15	ATL *	5	12	0	143	132	5.26	5.96	1.62	896	950	843	22.7	3.6	8.3	2.3	63%	10%	33	23	44	36%	72%	14%	15	82	13%	40%	0	0.99	-22.9	46	55	-$13
16	ATL *	10	7	0	150	132	3.93	3.89	1.28	761	775	750	22.8	3.0	7.9	2.6	63%	10%	41	21	37	30%	73%	13%	22	96	23%	32%			4.8	75	89	$7
17	ATL	10	13	0	154	143	4.79	4.68	1.48	795	879	716	23.9	3.4	8.4	2.4	62%	10%	39	24	36	34%	70%	12%	28	96	11%	36%	0	0.76	-8.2	74	89	-$1
1st Half		6	5	0	87	76	3.83	4.62	1.34	753	849	660	23.5	3.1	7.9	2.5	63%	9%	38	24	38	30%	78%	14%	15	91	13%	47%	0	0.74	5.7	74	89	$7
2nd Half		4	8	0	67	67	6.04	4.74	1.66	846	916	782	24.3	3.9	9.0	2.3	62%	11%	41	25	34	38%	63%	8%	13	101	8%	23%			-13.9	75	90	-$11
18	Proj	10	13	0	174	159	4.27	4.56	1.43	778	832	730	23.1	3.2	8.2	2.6	63%	10%	39	23	37	33%	73%	11%	32						1.9	80	97	$2

Freeland,Kyle

Age: 25	Th: L	Role SP	Health A	LIMA Plan B	
Ht: 6' 3"	Wt: 170	Type GB	PT/Exp C	Rand Var 0	
			Consist C	MM 0003	

Rookie would have led team in starts and IP had he not moved to pen in final weeks. Mixed in a few more whiffs in 2nd half to mixed results, so he's still tinkering. Bigger issue is low FpK and poor Ctl. Most likely path to success is though GB% and mitigating HR damage; not exactly fantasy catnip.

Yr	Tm	W	L	Sv	IP	K	ERA	xERA	WHIP	oOPS	vL	vR	BF/G	Ctl	Dom	Cmd	FpK	SwK	G	L	F	H%	S%	hr/f	GS	APC	DOM%	DIS%	Sv%	LI	RAR	BPV	BPX	R$
13																																		
14																																		
15																																		
16	a/a	11	10	0	162	84	5.76	5.94	1.60				27.6	2.7	4.7	1.7						33%	66%								-31.4	16	19	-$14
17	COL	11	11	0	156	107	4.10	4.80	1.49	792	755	803	20.8	3.6	6.2	1.7	55%	8%	54	19	28	31%	75%	13%	28	78	14%	68%	0	0.69	5.0	45	54	$2
1st Half		8	6	0	94	55	3.84	4.86	1.45	776	771	777	25.6	3.5	5.3	1.5	55%	7%	56	17	26	30%	77%	14%	16	93	19%	69%			5.9	36	43	$5
2nd Half		3	5	0	62	52	4.48	4.71	1.54	817	733	843	16.4	3.9	7.5	1.9	55%	9%	50	21	30	34%	72%	11%	12	64	8%	67%	0	0.60	-0.9	58	69	-$4
18	Proj	10	11	0	160	113	4.27	4.70	1.48	818	766	834	21.3	3.3	6.4	1.9	55%	8%	52	19	28	32%	74%	13%	32						1.7	56	67	$0

Fulmer,Carson

Age: 24	Th: R	Role RP	Health A	LIMA Plan D	
Ht: 6' 0"	Wt: 195	Type Pwr xFB	PT/Exp D	Rand Var +2	
			Consist B	MM 0100	

2-3, 3.86 in 23 IP at CHW. College product has struggled with mechanics in both minors and bigs, with long-term role still under debate. Power arm hasn't translated to whiffs, which he'll need to divert attention from subpar FpK, shoddy Ctl, and HR proclivity—at least so far. More AAA time is likely; Reserve List stash.

Yr	Tm	W	L	Sv	IP	K	ERA	xERA	WHIP	oOPS	vL	vR	BF/G	Ctl	Dom	Cmd	FpK	SwK	G	L	F	H%	S%	hr/f	GS	APC	DOM%	DIS%	Sv%	LI	RAR	BPV	BPX	R$
13																																		
14																																		
15																																		
16	CHW *	6	12	0	115	102	5.76	4.92	1.64	873	828	924	17.6	5.2	8.0	1.5	51%	10%	44	26	29	33%	65%	20%	0	27			0	0.43	-22.2	54	64	-$11
17	CHW *	10	10	0	149	102	6.43	5.88	1.69	639	664	606	21.0	5.0	6.1	1.2	51%	9%	29	17	55	31%	64%	11%	5	61	20%	20%	0	0.98	-38.1	16	19	-$16
1st Half		6	5	0	80	52	6.33	6.12	1.71				22.5	4.8	5.8	1.2						32%	65%	0%	0						-19.4	10	12	-$17
2nd Half		4	5	0	70	50	6.53	5.61	1.67	639	664	606	19.5	5.3	6.5	1.2	51%	9%	29	17	55	30%	62%	11%	5	61	20%	20%	0	0.98	-18.7	22	26	-$16
18	Proj	3	4	0	44	36	5.14	6.04	1.67	787	785	790	19.4	5.1	7.3	1.4	51%	9%	34	20	45	31%	74%	12%	9						-4.2	6	7	-$6

Fulmer,Michael

Age: 25	Th: R	Role SP	Health A	LIMA Plan C+	
Ht: 6' 3"	Wt: 210	Type	PT/Exp C	Rand Var 0	
			Consist A	MM 2103	

In his young career, has been able to negotiate risk of low K totals by throwing strikes and keeping ball in the yard. Was clicking again until elbow injury compromised 2nd half Dom and blew up ERA/xERA before season-ending surgery in Sept. If healthy, 2018 should approximate 2017 1st half, minus the hr/f help. Solid.

Yr	Tm	W	L	Sv	IP	K	ERA	xERA	WHIP	oOPS	vL	vR	BF/G	Ctl	Dom	Cmd	FpK	SwK	G	L	F	H%	S%	hr/f	GS	APC	DOM%	DIS%	Sv%	LI	RAR	BPV	BPX	R$
13																																		
14																																		
15	aa	10	3	0	118	95	2.53	3.32	1.22				22.6	2.3	7.3	3.1						31%	81%								20.8	96	115	$11
16	DET *	12	8	0	174	148	3.26	3.40	1.16	652	621	684	23.9	2.4	7.7	3.1	61%	11%	49	19	32	28%	76%	11%	26	95	35%	31%			20.0	89	105	$17
17	DET	10	12	0	165	114	3.83	4.22	1.15	644	677	616	27.0	2.2	6.2	2.9	61%	10%	49	22	29	28%	68%	9%	25	99	36%	32%			10.8	80	96	$12
1st Half		7	6	0	102	78	3.19	3.97	1.13	610	599	620	27.5	2.1	6.9	3.3	63%	11%	50	21	29	29%	71%	5%	15	101	40%	20%			14.7	95	114	$20
2nd Half		3	6	0	63	36	4.86	4.65	1.19	699	811	610	26.3	2.3	5.1	2.3	58%	9%	48	23	29	26%	62%	15%	10	97	30%	50%			-3.9	56	68	$0
18	Proj	11	10	0	174	134	3.61	4.08	1.17	670	690	651	24.6	2.3	6.9	3.0	61%	10%	49	21	30	28%	72%	11%	28						16.0	89	108	$14

Gallardo,Yovani

Age: 32	Th: R	Role SP	Health D	LIMA Plan D+	
Ht: 6' 2"	Wt: 205	Type Pwr	PT/Exp A	Rand Var +2	
			Consist A	MM 0001	

You'd be hard-pressed to find less attractive back-to-back seasons in these pages. Ctl and Cmd paid no mind to increased velocity, and xERA is further threatened by 2nd half FB%. He did respond positively to bullpen outings, but those DOM/DIS chasms cannot be ignored. Don't be around when it gets uglier.

Yr	Tm	W	L	Sv	IP	K	ERA	xERA	WHIP	oOPS	vL	vR	BF/G	Ctl	Dom	Cmd	FpK	SwK	G	L	F	H%	S%	hr/f	GS	APC	DOM%	DIS%	Sv%	LI	RAR	BPV	BPX	R$
13	MIL	12	10	0	181	144	4.18	3.85	1.36	720	729	713	24.9	3.3	7.2	2.2	56%	7%	49	23	28	31%	71%	12%	31	98	26%	35%			-7.1	67	88	$2
14	MIL	8	11	0	192	146	3.51	3.72	1.29	698	637	742	25.5	2.5	6.8	2.7	57%	7%	51	20	29	31%	76%	12%	32	101	28%	28%			5.5	84	100	$5
15	TEX	13	11	0	184	121	3.42	4.46	1.42	729	765	694	24.0	3.3	5.9	1.8	59%	7%	49	22	29	31%	78%	9%	33	98	6%	42%			12.4	44	52	$5
16	BAL	6	8	0	118	85	5.42	5.36	1.58	813	808	815	22.9	4.7	6.5	1.4	54%	7%	43	20	37	31%	68%	12%	23	92	9%	52%			-17.8	12	14	-$9
17	SEA	5	10	1	131	94	5.72	5.34	1.52	820	787	852	20.6	4.1	6.5	1.6	58%	9%	44	19	37	29%	66%	16%	22	82	9%	59%	100	0.73	-21.9	27	32	-$9
1st Half		3	7	1	79	58	6.06	5.06	1.55	809	691	932	23.3	3.8	6.6	1.8	59%	8%	46	23	32	32%	62%	14%	14	92	14%	50%	100	0.75	-16.5	41	50	-$11
2nd Half		2	3	0	52	36	5.19	5.77	1.46	837	951	738	17.5	4.7	6.2	1.3	57%	9%	41	14	44	25%	73%	18%	8	71	0%	75%	0	0.71	-5.3	5	6	-$6
18	Proj	6	8	0	123	88	5.02	5.27	1.49	796	806	788	21.0	4.1	6.4	1.6	57%	8%	45	19	36	29%	70%	14%	25						-10.1	27	33	-$6

Gant,John

Age: 25	Th: R	Role RP	Health F	LIMA Plan C	
Ht: 6' 3"	Wt: 200	Type Pwr	PT/Exp D	Rand Var +5	
			Consist B	MM 0100	

0-1, 4.67 ERA in 17 IP at STL. After season was delayed by groin strain, spent most of year in AAA tightening Ctl and Cmd. With STL, pitched out of the pen (8/0 K/BB but 3 HR in 9 IP) before being trounced in two starts. Not toolsy, but could have limited value in either role... just probably not in 2018.

Yr	Tm	W	L	Sv	IP	K	ERA	xERA	WHIP	oOPS	vL	vR	BF/G	Ctl	Dom	Cmd	FpK	SwK	G	L	F	H%	S%	hr/f	GS	APC	DOM%	DIS%	Sv%	LI	RAR	BPV	BPX	R$
13																																		
14																																		
15	aa	8	5	0	100	76	4.28	4.28	1.53				24.2	3.8	6.9	1.8						34%	71%								-3.9	69	82	-$4
16	ATL *	4	7	0	106	99	5.17	5.30	1.60	831	765	909	14.6	3.9	8.4	2.2	60%	10%	42	24	34	36%	69%	14%	7	47	14%	29%	0	0.46	-12.8	60	72	-$8
17	STL *	6	6	0	121	88	4.81	5.38	1.53	884	987	808	21.0	2.7	6.6	2.4	61%	10%	54	13	33	35%	71%	22%	2	41	0%	100%	0	0.38	-6.7	52	62	-$4
1st Half		1	4	0	45	33	4.44	5.48	1.47	1026	1762	393	21.4	2.5	6.5	2.6	53%	11%	30	10	60	33%	75%	33%	0	61			0	0.21	-0.4	45	54	-$6
2nd Half		5	2	0	76	56	5.03	5.31	1.56	848	766	905	20.7	2.8	6.6	2.3	62%	10%	59	14	27	36%	69%	17%	2	38	0%	100%	0	0.40	-6.3	56	67	-$4
18	Proj	2	2	0	36	29	4.84	4.94	1.55	789	725	864	18.5	3.2	7.3	2.2	60%	10%	42	24	34	35%	70%	9%	7						-2.2	64	77	-$5

Garcia,Jaime

Age: 31	Th: L	Role SP	Health F	LIMA Plan B+	
Ht: 6' 2"	Wt: 215	Type Pwr xGB	PT/Exp A	Rand Var +1	
			Consist B	MM 2203	

In 2010, he won 13 games with 2.70 ERA. That year, he had nearly same IP, WHIP, Ctl, H%, Cmd, Dom, G/L/F, FpK, SwK as in 2017. This time around, S% was lower, hr/f was higher, but bigger difference is that 7.4 Dom, 2.0 Cmd used to be league average. No longer, though. As Ferris says, life moves pretty fast.

Yr	Tm	W	L	Sv	IP	K	ERA	xERA	WHIP	oOPS	vL	vR	BF/G	Ctl	Dom	Cmd	FpK	SwK	G	L	F	H%	S%	hr/f	GS	APC	DOM%	DIS%	Sv%	LI	RAR	BPV	BPX	R$
13	STL	5	2	0	55	43	3.58	3.35	1.30	725	905	666	26.0	2.4	7.0	2.9	68%	12%	63	14	23	31%	76%	15%	9	92	22%	22%			2.0	101	132	$0
14	STL	3	1	0	44	39	4.12	2.89	1.05	696	881	631	25.3	1.4	8.0	5.6	60%	13%	55	20	25	28%	65%	19%	7	90	43%	14%			-2.1	139	165	$0
15	STL	10	6	0	130	97	2.43	3.25	1.05	574	630	557	25.5	2.1	6.7	3.2	59%	9%	61	16	22	27%	78%	7%	20	93	50%	10%			24.5	104	124	$17
16	STL	10	13	0	172	150	4.67	3.83	1.37	779	702	798	23.2	3.0	7.9	2.6	60%	10%	57	18	25	31%	70%	20%	30	81	17%	40%	0	0.74	-10.1	96	114	$1
17	3 TM	5	10	0	157	129	4.41	4.34	1.41	759	683	781	24.9	3.7	7.4	2.0	56%	11%	55	19	27	31%	71%	14%	27	90	22%	44%			-1.1	67	81	$0
1st Half		2	6	0	93	69	4.35	4.46	1.33	742	690	757	26.1	3.6	6.7	1.9	57%	12%	55	18	28	28%	71%	16%	15	92	27%	40%			0.0	57	68	$2
2nd Half		3	4	0	64	60	4.50	4.17	1.52	783	673	814	23.4	3.8	8.4	2.2	56%	11%	54	20	25	35%	71%	12%	12	88	17%	50%			-1.1	82	98	-$2
18	Proj	8	9	0	145	122	4.14	4.05	1.35	740	704	750	23.9	3.2	7.6	2.3	58%	11%	57	18	25	31%	72%	15%	25						4.0	84	101	$3

ROB CARROLL

Garcia,Jarlin

Age: 25	Th: L	Role RP	Health C	LIMA Plan D+
Ht: 6' 3"	Wt: 215	Type FB	PT/Exp D	Rand Var +1
			Consist A	MM 0100

Three-pitch repertoire and Dom played better as RP in 1H than as SP in minors. FpK says that 2H Ctl regression was inevitable; more troubling was flare-up of old bicep issue that really burned him (16.71 ERA in Sept). There's talk of return to starting role, but health and ceiling are concerns. A wait-and-see guy.

Yr Tm	W	L	Sv	IP	K	ERA	xERA	WHIP	oOPS	vL	vR	BF/G	Ctl	Dom	Cmd	FpK	SwK	G	L	F	H%	S%	hr/f	GS	APC	DOM%	DIS%	Sv%	LI	RAR	BPV	BPX	R$
13																																	
14																																	
15 aa	1	3	0	37	30	5.84	5.28	1.64				23.4	4.2	7.3	1.7						35%	64%								-8.5	49	59	-$8
16 aa	1	3	0	40	24	5.54	4.53	1.39				18.6	2.6	5.3	2.1						31%	60%								-6.6	46	55	-$5
17 MIA	1	2	0	53	42	4.73	4.71	1.20	695	603	783	3.3	2.9	7.1	2.5	55%	12%	39	20	41	27%	62%	9%	0	13			0	0.96	-2.4	67	81	-$2
1st Half	0	1	0	26	24	3.08	4.05	0.87	583	564	602	3.0	1.7	8.2	4.8	57%	14%	33	19	47	23%	70%	9%	0	12			0	0.92	4.2	113	135	$2
2nd Half	1	1	0	27	18	6.33	5.43	1.52	792	639	931	3.6	4.0	6.0	1.5	54%	11%	44	21	36	31%	58%	10%	0	14			0	1.00	-6.6	22	26	-$6
18 Proj	1	3	0	58	42	4.68	5.03	1.36	763	651	869	5.6	3.0	6.5	2.1	55%	12%	40	20	40	30%	67%	9%	0						-2.3	52	62	-$4

Garcia,Luis

Age: 31	Th: R	Role RP	Health A	LIMA Plan B+
Ht: 6' 3"	Wt: 230	Type Pwr xGB	PT/Exp D	Rand Var -4
			Consist B	MM 2210

From a skills perspective, his career year.. though that is not saying much. H%/S% fortune drove his sub-3.00 ERA, as was his "ability" to keep the ball in the park in this particular year. So many signs of 2018 regression - too many to count. Best to just scan the xERA column - that's your baseline, range, reality.

Yr Tm	W	L	Sv	IP	K	ERA	xERA	WHIP	oOPS	vL	vR	BF/G	Ctl	Dom	Cmd	FpK	SwK	G	L	F	H%	S%	hr/f	GS	APC	DOM%	DIS%	Sv%	LI	RAR	BPV	BPX	R$
13 PHI *	3	2	4	53	40	3.00	3.58	1.41	764	746	775	5.2	5.1	6.8	1.3	47%	11%	56	17	27	27%	81%	13%	0	23			80	0.71	5.7	56	73	$1
14 PHI *	3	1	22	61	54	2.39	3.51	1.43	815	628	1042	5.0	4.5	8.0	1.8	49%	12%	70	12	19	32%	83%	25%	0	22			88	0.42	10.1	82	98	$9
15 PHI	4	6	2	67	63	3.51	3.80	1.64	748	878	660	4.2	5.0	8.5	1.7	52%	12%	63	22	15	35%	79%	13%	0	16			50	1.03	3.7	59	71	-$3
16 PHI *	7	4	13	70	55	4.01	4.79	1.59	895	1009	751	4.8	4.8	7.1	1.5	55%	12%	55	15	30	32%	77%	13%	0	17			81	0.90	1.5	48	57	$3
17 PHI	2	5	2	71	60	2.65	3.99	1.22	593	729	472	4.5	3.3	7.6	2.3	58%	13%	56	18	26	29%	79%	6%	0	15			29	0.85	15.0	82	98	$5
1st Half	1	1	0	30	24	3.00	4.25	1.13	620	811	448	4.6	2.7	7.2	2.7	58%	13%	44	21	35	28%	75%	7%	0	16			0	0.87	5.0	79	95	$2
2nd Half	1	4	2	41	36	2.40	3.77	1.28	574	670	489	4.4	3.7	7.8	2.1	58%	13%	65	16	19	30%	81%	4%	0	15			33	0.84	10.0	84	101	$7
18 Proj	3	3	2	51	43	3.64	4.03	1.35	685	795	601	4.4	3.7	7.6	2.0	54%	12%	59	19	22	30%	74%	12%	0						4.5	73	88	$0

Garrett,Amir

Age: 26	Th: L	Role SP	Health A	LIMA Plan D+
Ht: 6' 5"	Wt: 228	Type Pwr FB	PT/Exp D	Rand Var +5
			Consist F	MM 0101

3-8, 7.39 ERA in 71 IP at CIN. Final ERA was nearly identical to his PPG as freshman hoopster at St. Johns five years ago. While athleticism isn't an issue, season quickly went south as he struggled with release point on FB. Older but still a baseball newbie, he's going to need more reps. Still a long 3-pointer away.

Yr Tm	W	L	Sv	IP	K	ERA	xERA	WHIP	oOPS	vL	vR	BF/G	Ctl	Dom	Cmd	FpK	SwK	G	L	F	H%	S%	hr/f	GS	APC	DOM%	DIS%	Sv%	LI	RAR	BPV	BPX	R$
13																																	
14																																	
15																																	
16 a/a	7	8	0	145	114	3.60	3.30	1.33				24.0	4.2	7.1	1.7						28%	73%								10.4	70	84	$6
17 CIN *	5	12	0	138	115	7.42	6.79	1.71	937	954	933	20.9	4.3	7.4	1.7	56%	9%	43	18	38	33%	60%	28%	14	77	14%	50%	0	0.77	-52.3	12	15	-$22
1st Half	4	6	0	66	57	6.90	6.24	1.50	939	928	940	20.4	4.6	7.8	1.7	59%	9%	42	19	38	26%	62%	28%	12	85	17%	50%			-20.7	3	3	-$14
2nd Half	1	6	0	72	57	7.90	7.28	1.91	925	952	896	21.4	4.1	7.1	1.7	44%	11%	50	13	38	39%	59%	33%	2	54	0%	50%	0	0.78	-31.6	22	26	-$29
18 Proj	3	5	0	73	59	4.93	5.37	1.57	761	713	772	22.0	4.2	7.3	1.7	59%	9%	42	19	38	32%	72%	12%	14						-5.1	37	44	-$6

Garza,Matt

Age: 34	Th: R	Role SP	Health F	LIMA Plan D+
Ht: 6' 4"	Wt: 220	Type	PT/Exp B	Rand Var 0
			Consist A	MM 0001

There is a staggering amount of downward thrust in this profile. Virtually every skill has been eroding for at least four years, and with 115 DL days the past two seasons, his body is following suit. There's always a chance of him eking out a passable month or so, but be skeptical. At last look, gravity is undefeated.

Yr Tm	W	L	Sv	IP	K	ERA	xERA	WHIP	oOPS	vL	vR	BF/G	Ctl	Dom	Cmd	FpK	SwK	G	L	F	H%	S%	hr/f	GS	APC	DOM%	DIS%	Sv%	LI	RAR	BPV	BPX	R$
13 2 TM *	11	7	0	171	144	3.63	3.76	1.23	712	733	687	24.7	2.5	7.6	3.1	64%	10%	39	23	38	30%	74%	12%	24	101	38%	21%			5.0	83	108	$9
14 MIL	8	8	0	163	126	3.64	3.90	1.18	644	634	652	25.2	2.8	6.9	2.5	64%	9%	43	21	36	28%	70%	7%	27	94	33%	26%			2.1	72	85	$7
15 MIL	6	14	0	149	104	5.63	4.73	1.57	832	862	804	25.6	3.5	6.3	1.8	61%	8%	45	22	33	33%	67%	14%	25	92	8%	52%	0	0.83	-30.6	43	51	-$15
16 MIL	6	8	0	102	70	4.51	4.67	1.50	774	825	727	24.3	3.2	6.2	1.9	59%	8%	55	17	28	33%	72%	11%	19	90	5%	42%			-4.1	58	70	-$4
17 MIL	6	9	0	115	79	4.94	5.32	1.45	794	831	758	21.0	3.5	6.2	1.8	59%	8%	40	22	38	30%	69%	12%	22	80	5%	55%	0	0.75	-8.3	34	41	-$4
1st Half	3	4	0	66	47	4.36	4.51	1.29	749	771	729	23.0	2.3	6.4	2.8	60%	9%	46	20	34	30%	69%	12%	12	87	8%	50%			0.0	77	92	$1
2nd Half	3	5	0	49	32	5.73	6.50	1.66	850	905	796	19.0	5.2	5.9	1.1	58%	7%	32	25	43	29%	69%	13%	10	72	0%	60%	0	0.70	-8.3	-23	-28	-$9
18 Proj	6	9	0	116	81	4.93	5.17	1.49	791	831	754	21.6	3.6	6.3	1.7	60%	8%	43	21	35	31%	70%	12%	23						-8.2	37	45	-$5

Gausman,Kevin

Age: 27	Th: R	Role SP	Health C	LIMA Plan C
Ht: 6' 3"	Wt: 190	Type Pwr	PT/Exp B	Rand Var +3
			Consist B	MM 1303

As in seasons past, it took him until mid-year to hone in. Added more sliders and splitters and got soft contact and whiffs, just what the xERA ordered, and while the specter of regression looms, it looks like he's figuring things out. If he can ditch the false start, we'll reprise last year's UP: 3.50 ERA, 200 K

Yr Tm	W	L	Sv	IP	K	ERA	xERA	WHIP	oOPS	vL	vR	BF/G	Ctl	Dom	Cmd	FpK	SwK	G	L	F	H%	S%	hr/f	GS	APC	DOM%	DIS%	Sv%	LI	RAR	BPV	BPX	R$
13 BAL *	6	11	0	130	119	4.71	4.11	1.30	792	811	772	14.8	1.9	8.3	4.4	61%	10%	42	25	33	34%	65%	19%	5	40	0%	40%	0	0.80	-13.4	115	150	-$2
14 BAL *	8	10	0	157	125	3.60	3.92	1.35	685	700	662	21.1	3.2	7.2	2.2	57%	9%	41	23	35	31%	75%	6%	20	98	35%	25%			2.8	71	85	$2
15 BAL *	4	9	0	130	118	4.28	4.42	1.25	739	643	843	18.2	2.5	8.2	3.3	55%	12%	44	17	38	30%	72%	13%	17	75	35%	24%	0	0.72	-5.2	74	88	$0
16 BAL	9	12	0	180	174	3.61	3.84	1.28	742	659	812	25.2	2.4	8.7	3.7	57%	11%	44	21	35	32%	78%	15%	30	104	30%	20%			12.9	115	137	$11
17 BAL	11	12	0	187	179	4.68	4.44	1.49	808	807	808	24.0	3.4	8.6	2.5	60%	11%	43	22	35	34%	73%	15%	34	99	29%	35%			-7.3	84	101	$0
1st Half	4	7	0	86	67	6.07	5.54	1.84	897	810	952	23.7	4.3	7.0	1.6	58%	9%	41	24	35	37%	69%	14%	17	97	6%	53%			-18.2	29	35	-$21
2nd Half	7	5	0	101	112	3.49	3.59	1.20	722	803	656	24.3	2.7	10.0	3.7	62%	14%	45	20	35	31%	77%	16%	17	101	53%	18%			10.8	131	157	$18
18 Proj	10	11	0	174	166	3.97	4.23	1.37	772	739	800	22.1	2.9	8.6	3.0	59%	11%	43	21	35	32%	76%	15%	33						8.4	98	118	$6

Gaviglio,Sam

Age: 28	Th: R	Role SP	Health A	LIMA Plan C
Ht: 6' 2"	Wt: 195	Type	PT/Exp D	Rand Var +3
			Consist A	MM 0000

4-5, 4.36 ERA in 74 IP at SEA/KC. Older rookie pitched to low expectations with predictable results. Showed nice curveball, but lack of swing-and-miss stuff underscored mundane arsenal that batters abused in 2nd half until he was optioned, then traded. As the adage goes, there's really no there, there.

Yr Tm	W	L	Sv	IP	K	ERA	xERA	WHIP	oOPS	vL	vR	BF/G	Ctl	Dom	Cmd	FpK	SwK	G	L	F	H%	S%	hr/f	GS	APC	DOM%	DIS%	Sv%	LI	RAR	BPV	BPX	R$
13																																	
14 aa	5	12	0	137	102	4.93	5.12	1.60				24.2	3.0	6.7	2.3						37%	68%								-20.0	65	78	-$12
15 aaa	8	7	0	102	67	4.82	4.47	1.35				20.2	2.8	5.9	2.1						30%	67%								-10.8	45	54	-$3
16 a/a	8	7	0	165	102	4.99	4.80	1.43				25.0	2.1	5.5	2.7						33%	66%								-16.2	58	69	-$5
17 2 AL *	7	11	0	146	95	4.59	4.95	1.38	849	838	859	21.2	2.4	5.8	2.5	61%	8%	49	18	32	31%	71%	21%	13	73	0%	54%	0	0.64	-4.1	45	53	-$1
1st Half	5	6	0	84	44	3.73	4.28	1.22	775	678	846	22.7	2.0	4.7	2.3	62%	7%	52	17	31	27%	76%	22%	9	76	0%	44%	0	0.72	6.6	36	44	$7
2nd Half	2	5	0	62	51	5.76	5.85	1.61	998	1075	894	19.6	2.8	7.4	2.6	59%	10%	43	22	35	37%	66%	19%	4	68	0%	75%	0	0.50	-10.7	55	66	-$11
18 Proj	2	3	0	44	30	4.94	4.80	1.45	832	885	775	21.9	2.5	6.1	2.4	60%	9%	47	20	34	33%	68%	11%	8						-3.1	67	81	-$5

Gearrin,Cory

Age: 32	Th: R	Role RP	Health F	LIMA Plan B
Ht: 6' 3"	Wt: 200	Type Pwr GB	PT/Exp D	Rand Var -5
			Consist B	MM 1200

Late bloomer continues to pitch his way into relevance. Career-high IP yielded .163 oppBA when given a day's rest between appearances, and 2nd half says he could tap into more. Wildness, health grade, and ERA/xERA gulf warn of a potential washout at any time, but until that happens, let it ride.

Yr Tm	W	L	Sv	IP	K	ERA	xERA	WHIP	oOPS	vL	vR	BF/G	Ctl	Dom	Cmd	FpK	SwK	G	L	F	H%	S%	hr/f	GS	APC	DOM%	DIS%	Sv%	LI	RAR	BPV	BPX	R$
13 ATL	2	1	1	31	23	3.77	4.09	1.48	754	629	826	3.6	4.6	6.7	1.4	54%	10%	51	25	24	30%	75%	10%	0	13			33	0.71	0.3	24	31	-$3
14																																	
15 SF *	2	2	0	47	40	3.35	3.94	1.36	237	0	282	4.9	3.1	7.7	2.5	62%	18%	86	14	0	32%	77%	0%	0	7			0	0.98	3.5	79	94	-$2
16 SF	3	2	3	48	45	4.28	3.51	1.16	654	655	654	3.5	2.6	8.4	3.2	58%	12%	56	15	28	29%	63%	10%	0	13			43	1.40	-0.6	114	136	$1
17 SF	4	3	0	68	64	1.99	4.35	1.25	645	711	607	4.2	4.6	8.5	1.8	60%	11%	48	19	33	26%	86%	7%	0	16			0	0.82	19.9	53	64	$6
1st Half	2	2	0	37	29	2.17	4.80	1.37	691	539	768	5.0	4.8	7.0	1.5	57%	10%	50	20	30	28%	84%	3%	0	18			0	0.64	10.1	24	29	$4
2nd Half	2	1	0	31	35	1.76	3.84	1.11	586	918	395	3.4	4.4	10.3	2.3	64%	13%	44	18	38	24%	90%	11%	0	13			0	0.98	9.8	88	106	$8
18 Proj	3	2	0	58	54	3.21	4.12	1.25	665	720	639	3.8	3.9	8.4	2.2	59%	12%	51	19	31	28%	76%	9%	0						8.2	76	91	$2

ROB CARROLL

Gibson,Kyle

Age: 30	Th: R	Role SP	Health	C	LIMA Plan	B+
Ht: 6' 6"	Wt: 215	Type Pwr GB	PT/Exp	B	Rand Var	+2
			Consist	B	MM	1103

12-10, 5.07 ERA in 158 IP at MIN. Has teased us with stretches of growth before, only to disappoint later, but over last 11 GS (after yet another AAA stint): 3.55 ERA, 8.4 Dom, 3.9 Cmd, 3.44 xERA. Then again, 2nd half Ctl gain wasn't supported by FpK, and there's still 18 other lousy starts. Fool us twice...

Yr Tm	W	L	Sv	IP	K	ERA	xERA	WHIP	oOPS	vL	vR	BF/G	Ctl	Dom	Cmd	FpK	SwK	G	L	F	H%	S%	hr/f	GS	APC	DOM%	DIS%	Sv%	LI	RAR	BPV	BPX	R$
13 MIN *	9	9	0	153	97	4.50	4.44	1.46	874	875	869	24.2	3.2	5.7	1.8	52%	8%	50	21	28	32%	70%	13%	10	90	0%	70%			-12.0	49	64	-$5
14 MIN	13	12	0	179	107	4.47	4.01	1.31	679	705	650	24.4	2.9	5.4	1.9	57%	9%	54	19	27	29%	65%	8%	31	90	19%	35%			-16.0	51	61	-$1
15 MIN	11	11	0	195	145	3.84	3.94	1.29	698	702	693	25.7	3.0	6.7	2.2	61%	10%	53	20	27	29%	72%	11%	32	101	31%	31%			3.0	71	84	$7
16 MIN	6	11	0	147	104	5.07	4.70	1.56	820	886	760	26.1	3.4	6.4	1.9	59%	10%	49	23	29	33%	70%	14%	25	99	16%	56%			-16.0	51	60	-$9
17 MIN *	13	12	0	175	137	4.93	5.34	1.53	826	832	821	23.8	3.4	7.0	2.1	59%	10%	51	23	26	33%	71%	18%	29	90	17%	45%			-12.3	43	52	-$3
1st Half	4	8	0	83	59	5.96	6.79	1.81	933	931	934	24.0	4.4	6.3	1.5	57%	9%	50	21	28	35%	70%	19%	14	86	0%	79%			-16.4	12	15	-$19
2nd Half	9	4	0	92	78	4.00	4.04	1.27	733	738	728	23.6	2.5	7.7	3.0	61%	11%	51	25	24	31%	72%	18%	15	94	33%	13%			4.1	80	96	$12
18 Proj	**10**	**10**	**0**	**160**	**124**	**4.46**	**4.43**	**1.43**	**766**	**786**	**746**	**24.3**	**3.2**	**7.0**	**2.2**	**59%**	**10%**	**51**	**22**	**27**	**32%**	**72%**	**15%**	**28**						**-1.9**	**68**	**82**	**$0**

Giles,Ken

Age: 27	Th: R	Role RP	Health	A	LIMA Plan	C+
Ht: 6' 2"	Wt: 205	Type Pwr	PT/Exp	B	Rand Var	-3
			Consist	A	MM	4530

Post-season struggles may scare some off, but shrug off recency bias and take the long view. He's posted consistently elite skills for four full seasons, led by eye-popping SwK and solid FpK. Consider this a test of faith in sample sizes, and, if enough people shy away, a buying opportunity.

Yr Tm	W	L	Sv	IP	K	ERA	xERA	WHIP	oOPS	vL	vR	BF/G	Ctl	Dom	Cmd	FpK	SwK	G	L	F	H%	S%	hr/f	GS	APC	DOM%	DIS%	Sv%	LI	RAR	BPV	BPX	R$
13																																	
14 PHI *	5	1	13	74	97	1.56	1.22	0.94	450	436	461	4.1	2.9	11.7	4.0	63%	16%	44	15	41	28%	83%	3%	0	16			93	1.15	20.0	170	203	$17
15 PHI	6	3	15	70	87	1.80	3.24	1.20	569	574	565	4.3	3.2	11.2	3.5	60%	15%	45	22	33	34%	85%	3%	0	17			75	1.15	18.7	138	164	$14
16 HOU	2	5	15	66	102	4.11	2.96	1.29	709	590	823	4.1	3.4	14.0	4.1	64%	20%	40	25	36	38%	71%	15%	0	16			75	1.25	0.6	177	210	$7
17 HOU	1	3	34	63	83	2.30	3.11	1.04	566	583	551	3.9	3.0	11.9	4.0	62%	17%	44	18	38	30%	80%	7%	0	15			89	1.11	15.9	155	186	$21
1st Half	1	2	19	31	39	3.45	3.49	1.12	588	579	596	3.9	3.4	11.2	3.3	60%	15%	45	17	38	30%	70%	7%	0	15			90	0.87	3.5	131	157	$21
2nd Half	0	1	15	31	44	1.15	2.75	0.96	541	588	501	4.0	2.6	12.6	4.9	64%	18%	43	18	38	30%	93%	8%	0	15			88	1.37	12.4	179	214	$22
18 Proj	**2**	**3**	**36**	**65**	**90**	**2.49**	**3.10**	**1.11**	**595**	**575**	**613**	**3.9**	**3.1**	**12.4**	**4.0**	**63%**	**17%**	**43**	**20**	**37**	**32%**	**80%**	**8%**	**0**						**15.0**	**160**	**193**	**$21**

Giolito,Lucas

Age: 23	Th: R	Role SP	Health	A	LIMA Plan	B+
Ht: 6' 6"	Wt: 255	Type Pwr	PT/Exp	D	Rand Var	+2
			Consist	A	MM	0203

3-3, 2.38 ERA in 45 IP at CHW. Low MLB ERA was all about H%, S%; xERA was 4.15. Lower velocity dimmed his prospect star a bit, as was his lack of Cmd, though FpK, 2nd half Ctl offer some hope. But most glaring issue remains absence of even above average Dom; at 23, still has time—do you still have patience?

Yr Tm	W	L	Sv	IP	K	ERA	xERA	WHIP	oOPS	vL	vR	BF/G	Ctl	Dom	Cmd	FpK	SwK	G	L	F	H%	S%	hr/f	GS	APC	DOM%	DIS%	Sv%	LI	RAR	BPV	BPX	R$
13																																	
14																																	
15 aa	4	2	0	47	38	4.63	4.44	1.52				25.7	3.3	7.3	2.2						36%	68%								-3.9	76	90	-$4
16 WAS *	6	6	0	130	108	4.31	4.93	1.57	988	881	1112	21.1	4.1	7.5	1.8	55%	6%	41	27	32	34%	74%	29%	4	66	0%	75%	0	0.68	-1.9	55	65	-$4
17 CHW *	9	13	0	174	152	4.49	4.63	1.40	645	638	650	23.7	3.9	7.9	2.0	62%	11%	45	20	35	30%	72%	18%	7	101	29%	14%			-2.8	52	62	$2
1st Half	2	8	0	83	77	6.31	6.16	1.65				23.3	4.5	8.3	1.8						33%	66%	0%	0						-20.1	31	37	-$16
2nd Half	7	5	0	91	75	2.82	3.23	1.17	645	638	650	24.1	3.3	7.5	2.3	62%	11%	45	20	35	26%	81%	18%	7	101	29%	14%			17.3	73	87	$19
18 Proj	**10**	**10**	**0**	**174**	**147**	**4.28**	**4.71**	**1.41**	**736**	**719**	**751**	**22.7**	**3.4**	**7.6**	**2.3**	**62%**	**11%**	**45**	**20**	**35**	**32%**	**72%**	**10%**	**32**						**1.7**	**69**	**83**	**$2**

Givens,Mychal

Age: 28	Th: R	Role RP	Health	A	LIMA Plan	B
Ht: 6' 0"	Wt: 210	Type Pwr	PT/Exp	C	Rand Var	-3
			Consist	B	MM	3501

Before you get too excited about ERA/WHIP combo, note big assist from H%/S%, and that FpK did not support Ctl gain. Dom/SwK keep flashing upside, and LI confirms he's on verge of saves, but FB%, walks are sizable obstacles. And contrary to 2016-17 stats, vulturing eight wins a year is not a repeatable skill.

Yr Tm	W	L	Sv	IP	K	ERA	xERA	WHIP	oOPS	vL	vR	BF/G	Ctl	Dom	Cmd	FpK	SwK	G	L	F	H%	S%	hr/f	GS	APC	DOM%	DIS%	Sv%	LI	RAR	BPV	BPX	R$
13																																	
14 aa	0	0	0	25	23	4.53	3.92	1.77				6.5	8.2	8.2	1.0						31%	72%								-2.5	78	93	-$6
15 BAL *	6	2	15	87	101	2.19	2.07	1.05	538	555	527	5.9	2.4	10.4	4.3	63%	13%	39	30	31	31%	79%	5%	0	21			88	0.79	19.0	157	187	$18
16 BAL	8	2	0	75	96	3.13	3.64	1.27	664	1025	504	4.7	4.3	11.6	2.7	59%	15%	35	25	39	32%	78%	9%	0	20			0	1.10	9.7	104	124	$6
17 BAL	8	1	0	79	88	2.75	3.61	1.04	617	619	615	4.6	2.9	10.1	3.5	57%	13%	43	17	40	26%	81%	13%	0	19			0	1.13	15.6	125	150	$11
1st Half	6	0	0	40	39	2.25	3.86	1.05	622	546	657	4.7	2.7	8.8	3.3	60%	10%	43	20	37	25%	86%	13%	0	20			0	1.20	10.4	106	127	$13
2nd Half	2	1	0	39	49	3.26	3.38	1.03	611	685	567	4.4	3.0	11.4	3.8	55%	15%	42	14	43	27%	74%	13%	0	19			0	1.07	5.2	144	172	$9
18 Proj	**5**	**2**	**0**	**73**	**87**	**2.85**	**3.70**	**1.15**	**636**	**763**	**570**	**4.7**	**3.6**	**10.8**	**3.0**	**58%**	**14%**	**40**	**22**	**39**	**29%**	**79%**	**10%**	**0**						**13.5**	**115**	**138**	**$7**

Glasnow,Tyler

Age: 24	Th: R	Role SP	Health	B	LIMA Plan	B+
Ht: 6' 8"	Wt: 220	Type Pwr	PT/Exp	D	Rand Var	+2
			Consist	C	MM	1301

2-7, 7.69 ERA in 62 IP at PIT. No way to sugarcoat it: MLB work was terrible, with 1.3 Cmd, 6.03 xERA, and -5 BPV. MLEs—in particular 2nd half—offer better outlook, though even there, Ctl remains the central problem. Long-term potential is still that of future ace, but there's no denying doubt is starting to creep in.

Yr Tm	W	L	Sv	IP	K	ERA	xERA	WHIP	oOPS	vL	vR	BF/G	Ctl	Dom	Cmd	FpK	SwK	G	L	F	H%	S%	hr/f	GS	APC	DOM%	DIS%	Sv%	LI	RAR	BPV	BPX	R$
13																																	
14																																	
15 a/a	7	4	0	104	108	2.78	2.52	1.19				20.8	3.4	9.3	2.7						30%	76%								15.2	116	138	$9
16 PIT *	8	5	0	140	141	2.82	3.03	1.36	774	810	744	20.2	5.5	9.1	1.7	61%	12%	48	21	32	28%	80%	10%	4	63	0%	50%	0	0.55	23.6	87	104	$10
17 PIT *	11	9	0	155	167	4.64	4.59	1.48	997	1047	943	22.3	4.6	9.7	2.1	56%	8%	43	21	36	33%	71%	18%	13	81	8%	54%	0	0.81	-5.4	72	86	$1
1st Half	4	6	0	78	83	5.97	6.23	1.70	1000	1038	960	22.1	5.0	9.6	1.9	56%	8%	43	21	36	35%	69%	18%	12	87	8%	50%			-15.5	42	50	-$12
2nd Half	7	3	0	77	84	3.29	2.93	1.26	914	1071	750	22.5	4.2	9.8	2.4	58%	9%	44	17	39	30%	74%	14%	1	59	0%	100%	0	0.91	10.2	103	124	$15
18 Proj	**8**	**5**	**0**	**116**	**121**	**4.05**	**4.55**	**1.40**	**643**	**680**	**603**	**21.4**	**4.7**	**9.4**	**2.0**	**56%**	**9%**	**43**	**21**	**36**	**30%**	**73%**	**10%**	**23**						**4.4**	**64**	**77**	**$3**

Glover,Koda

Age: 25	Th: R	Role RP	Health	F	LIMA Plan	C
Ht: 6' 5"	Wt: 225	Type Pwr	PT/Exp	D	Rand Var	+5
			Consist	B	MM	1200

Since Sept 2016: torn labrum in hip, hip impingement, back stiffness, inflammation in rotator cuff. Last two ended 2017 season early, right as he was getting a shot at closing. Pinpoint Ctl at odds with FpK, but overall, a solid skill set for arm in growth mode, albeit one that's not entirely saves-worthy just yet.

Yr Tm	W	L	Sv	IP	K	ERA	xERA	WHIP	oOPS	vL	vR	BF/G	Ctl	Dom	Cmd	FpK	SwK	G	L	F	H%	S%	hr/f	GS	APC	DOM%	DIS%	Sv%	LI	RAR	BPV	BPX	R$
13																																	
14																																	
15																																	
16 WAS *	5	1	6	66	59	4.14	3.35	1.17	664	635	687	5.1	2.4	8.1	3.3	66%	11%	42	17	41	29%	66%	13%	0	16			75	0.86	0.4	97	116	$4
17 WAS	0	1	8	19	17	5.12	4.02	1.24	647	709	595	3.5	1.9	7.9	4.3	56%	11%	44	22	34	34%	57%	5%	0	14			80	1.58	-1.8	114	137	-$1
1st Half	0	1	8	19	17	5.12	4.02	1.24	647	709	595	3.5	1.9	7.9	4.3	56%	11%	44	22	34	34%	57%	5%	0	14			80	1.58	-1.8	114	137	-$1
2nd Half																																	
18 Proj	**2**	**2**	**0**	**58**	**51**	**3.93**	**4.24**	**1.26**	**607**	**700**	**530**	**4.0**	**2.6**	**8.0**	**3.1**	**59%**	**11%**	**44**	**22**	**34**	**31%**	**70%**	**8%**	**0**						**3.0**	**96**	**116**	**-$1**

Godley,Zachary

Age: 28	Th: R	Role RP	Health	A	LIMA Plan	B+
Ht: 6' 3"	Wt: 240	Type Pwr GB	PT/Exp	D	Rand Var	+2
			Consist	F	MM	2303

8-9, 3.37 ERA in 155 IP at ARI. Boosted Dom, SwK by throwing more curves, his best strikeout pitch (22% whiff rate), while maintaining elite GB%. Last missing piece is fewer walks, and he's shown glimpses of that, too: 2.6 Ctl, 64% FpK in May/June. Past skills suggest caution; that said... UP: 15 W, 3.00 ERA

Yr Tm	W	L	Sv	IP	K	ERA	xERA	WHIP	oOPS	vL	vR	BF/G	Ctl	Dom	Cmd	FpK	SwK	G	L	F	H%	S%	hr/f	GS	APC	DOM%	DIS%	Sv%	LI	RAR	BPV	BPX	R$
13																																	
14																																	
15 ARI *	7	2	0	61	44	4.10	3.90	1.36	688	528	809	15.9	4.1	6.5	1.6	58%	12%	46	22	32	27%	72%	13%	6	64	50%	33%	0	0.74	-1.0	50	59	-$1
16 ARI *	9	10	0	157	115	5.64	5.63	1.58	844	891	804	16.4	3.1	6.6	2.1	55%	12%	54	18	28	34%	66%	19%	9	43	0%	56%	0	0.85	-28.0	41	48	-$12
17 ARI *	10	10	0	183	188	3.30	2.79	1.15	657	648	664	23.4	3.4	9.2	2.7	61%	14%	55	19	26	28%	73%	15%	25	94	40%	8%	0	0.77	24.0	102	122	$20
1st Half	5	3	0	92	82	2.74	1.83	1.04	548	617	501	23.7	3.6	8.0	2.2	63%	15%	59	17	24	23%	74%	11%	10	92	50%	10%			18.3	101	121	$25
2nd Half	5	7	0	91	106	3.86	3.36	1.26	727	664	794	23.8	3.3	10.5	3.2	59%	13%	53	20	27	32%	73%	17%	15	95	33%	7%	0	0.78	5.6	131	157	$15
18 Proj	**10**	**9**	**0**	**160**	**160**	**3.73**	**3.74**	**1.30**	**729**	**722**	**735**	**18.9**	**3.2**	**9.1**	**2.8**	**60%**	**14%**	**53**	**19**	**28**	**32%**	**74%**	**14%**	**31**						**12.3**	**108**	**130**	**$9**

BRANDON KRUSE

Gohara,Luiz

Gohara,Luiz	Health A	LIMA Plan B+
Age: 21 Th: L Role SP	PT/Exp F	Rand Var 0
Ht: 6' 3" Wt: 210 Type Pwr xFB	Consist F	MM 1401

1-3, 4.91 ERA in 29 IP at ATL. Moved through three levels of minors and made Sept debut all in one season, thanks to deceptive delivery and elite Dom. Poor results vR caused by small sample and bad luck (42% H%/60% S%). 3.9 Cmd, 118 BPV in 5 MLB starts makes him worth speculating on as end-gamer.

Yr Tm	W	L	Sv	IP	K	ERA	xERA	WHIP	oOPS	vL	vR	BF/G	Ctl	Dom	Cmd	FpK	SwK	G	L	F	H%	S%	hr/f	GS	APC	DOM%	DIS%	Sv%	LI	RAR	BPV	BPX	R$
13																																	
14																																	
15																																	
16																																	
17 ATL *	5	6	0	117	130	4.04	3.99	1.40	800	348	892	20.5	3.5	10.0	2.9	62%	14%	35	21	44	35%	72%	6%	5	86	20%	20%			4.5	103	124	$
1st Half	1	1	0	30	32	4.22	3.03	1.24				15.1	3.1	9.7	3.2						33%	64%	0%	0						0.5	121	145	-$
2nd Half	4	5	0	87	98	4.08	4.39	1.46	800	348	892	23.3	3.6	10.1	2.8	62%	14%	35	21	44	36%	73%	6%	5	86	20%	20%			3.0	97	116	$
18 Proj	**4**	**5**	**0**	**109**	**115**	**4.12**	**4.50**	**1.35**	**743**	**330**	**828**	**21.9**	**3.4**	**9.6**	**2.8**	**62%**	**14%**	**35**	**21**	**44**	**32%**	**73%**	**10%**	**21**						**3.2**	**94**	**113**	**$**

Gonzales,Marco

Gonzales,Marco	Health C	LIMA Plan C
Age: 26 Th: L Role SP	PT/Exp D	Rand Var +2
Ht: 6' 1" Wt: 195 Type	Consist D	MM 0101

1-1, 6.08 ERA in 40 IP at STL/SEA. Former first-round pick gained some velocity after return from 2016 TJS, but fringe Dom, xERA illustrate bumpy ride ahead. Change-up (14% SwK) is only plus pitch, and RHB have been crushing him. DIS% history further highlights downside; he's simply too risky to roster.

Yr Tm	W	L	Sv	IP	K	ERA	xERA	WHIP	oOPS	vL	vR	BF/G	Ctl	Dom	Cmd	FpK	SwK	G	L	F	H%	S%	hr/f	GS	APC	DOM%	DIS%	Sv%	LI	RAR	BPV	BPX	R$
13																																	
14 STL *	11	5	0	119	103	3.36	3.78	1.27	737	397	827	19.5	2.9	7.8	2.7	61%	10%	36	23	41	30%	77%	10%	5	62	0%	40%	0	1.07	5.6	80	95	$
15 STL *	1	5	0	79	52	5.67	6.53	1.75	1286	500	1286	21.1	2.8	5.9	2.1	75%	3%	36	36	29	38%	69%	25%	1	66	0%	100%			-16.5	32	38	-$1
16																																	
17 2 TM *	9	5	0	120	88	4.52	4.60	1.37	924	835	954	21.0	2.5	6.6	2.6	60%	10%	45	23	32	32%	70%	18%	8	64	0%	75%	0	0.59	-2.3	61	73	$1
1st Half	4	3	0	54	37	3.84	4.43	1.27	1500	2500	1357	24.4	2.4	6.3	2.6	44%	14%	50	7	43	28%	76%	50%	1	58	0%	100%			3.5	52	63	$
2nd Half	5	2	0	67	50	5.06	4.73	1.45	865	754	905	19.0	2.6	6.8	2.6	62%	9%	45	24	31	34%	65%	13%	7	64	0%	71%	0	0.57	-5.8	68	81	$0
18 Proj	**4**	**4**	**0**	**80**	**58**	**4.77**	**4.88**	**1.49**	**774**	**603**	**829**	**20.7**	**2.6**	**6.5**	**2.5**	**61%**	**10%**	**41**	**24**	**35**	**34%**	**70%**	**10%**	**17**						**-4.1**	**66**	**79**	**-$4**

Gonzalez,Gio

Gonzalez,Gio	Health B	LIMA Plan D+
Age: 32 Th: L Role SP	PT/Exp A	Rand Var -3
Ht: 6' 0" Wt: 205 Type Pwr	Consist A	MM 2305

Lady Luck paid him back, as H%/S% swing drove down ERA, offset backslide in Ctl, FB%, as well as ongoing xERA decline. Second year with velo drop sent SwK, Dom falling to lowest levels since 2010, BPV to six-year low. Gap between 2017's ace surface stats, mid-rotation skills means someone's gonna overpay.

Yr Tm	W	L	Sv	IP	K	ERA	xERA	WHIP	oOPS	vL	vR	BF/G	Ctl	Dom	Cmd	FpK	SwK	G	L	F	H%	S%	hr/f	GS	APC	DOM%	DIS%	Sv%	LI	RAR	BPV	BPX	R$
13 WAS	11	8	0	196	192	3.36	3.60	1.25	668	568	696	25.6	3.5	8.8	2.5	61%	10%	44	23	33	30%	75%	10%	32	104	41%	28%			12.3	87	113	$12
14 WAS	10	10	0	159	162	3.57	3.41	1.20	647	628	653	24.2	3.2	9.2	2.9	58%	11%	45	19	37	30%	71%	7%	27	97	41%	26%			3.3	103	122	$9
15 WAS	11	8	0	176	169	3.79	3.66	1.42	711	641	732	24.5	3.5	8.7	2.4	60%	10%	54	20	27	35%	73%	6%	31	95	23%	29%			3.7	92	110	$4
16 WAS	11	11	0	177	171	4.57	3.87	1.34	730	633	756	23.9	3.0	8.7	2.9	57%	10%	48	23	30	33%	68%	13%	32	97	28%	31%			-8.3	101	120	$3
17 WAS	15	9	0	201	188	2.96	4.17	1.18	642	507	681	25.8	3.5	8.4	2.4	55%	9%	46	19	35	27%	79%	11%	32	105	38%	16%			34.8	80	96	$25
1st Half	7	3	0	107	104	2.77	4.25	1.21	665	465	722	26.0	3.9	8.7	2.2	53%	10%	43	20	37	26%	83%	13%	17	106	35%	12%			21.1	72	86	$26
2nd Half	8	6	0	94	84	3.17	4.07	1.14	617	556	634	25.7	3.1	8.1	2.6	58%	8%	48	18	33	27%	75%	9%	15	104	40%	20%			13.7	89	106	$23
18 Proj	**12**	**10**	**0**	**181**	**172**	**3.56**	**4.06**	**1.26**	**674**	**575**	**702**	**24.3**	**3.3**	**8.5**	**2.6**	**57%**	**10%**	**48**	**20**	**32**	**30%**	**74%**	**10%**	**30**						**17.8**	**90**	**108**	**$13**

Gonzalez,Miguel

Gonzalez,Miguel	Health D	LIMA Plan D+
Age: 34 Th: R Role SP	PT/Exp B	Rand Var -1
Ht: 6' 1" Wt: 170 Type FB	Consist B	MM 0003

One quick glance at zeroes in his MM score tells us to steer clear of fruitless IP. Career-low SwK, Dom show that he's not fooling many hitters, and giving up more fly balls only adds to ERA risk. He may throw first strike, but xERA suggests that batters will be getting the last word in 2018.

Yr Tm	W	L	Sv	IP	K	ERA	xERA	WHIP	oOPS	vL	vR	BF/G	Ctl	Dom	Cmd	FpK	SwK	G	L	F	H%	S%	hr/f	GS	APC	DOM%	DIS%	Sv%	LI	RAR	BPV	BPX	R$
13 BAL	11	8	0	171	120	3.78	4.28	1.23	713	689	736	23.7	2.8	6.3	2.3	59%	9%	39	21	40	27%	74%	11%	28	90	18%	36%	0	0.75	1.8	55	72	$7
14 BAL	10	9	0	159	111	3.23	4.36	1.30	751	772	724	24.9	2.9	6.3	2.2	61%	9%	37	21	42	28%	82%	12%	26	95	19%	38%	0	0.75	10.1	50	60	$6
15 BAL	9	12	0	145	109	4.91	4.45	1.40	795	831	761	23.9	3.2	6.8	2.1	62%	9%	40	24	36	30%	69%	15%	26	94	27%	50%			-17.0	54	65	-$4
16 CHW *	6	9	0	156	114	4.10	4.33	1.33	686	675	697	22.4	2.3	6.6	2.9	61%	8%	40	22	38	31%	72%	7%	23	88	26%	30%	0	0.77	1.8	69	82	$2
17 2 AL	8	13	0	156	100	4.62	5.58	1.42	792	857	730	25.3	3.2	5.8	1.8	67%	7%	36	20	44	30%	71%	10%	27	94	19%	44%			-4.9	32	39	-$1
1st Half	4	8	0	79	45	5.15	5.73	1.50	833	849	818	26.9	3.0	5.1	1.7	65%	7%	37	22	41	31%	70%	12%	13	97	31%	62%			-7.7	28	33	-$6
2nd Half	4	5	0	77	55	4.07	5.43	1.34	748	866	634	23.9	3.4	6.4	1.9	68%	7%	35	17	48	29%	73%	8%	14	90	7%	29%			2.7	37	45	$4
18 Proj	**7**	**10**	**0**	**145**	**100**	**4.55**	**5.13**	**1.37**	**774**	**814**	**735**	**23.6**	**2.9**	**6.2**	**2.1**	**64%**	**8%**	**38**	**21**	**42**	**30%**	**70%**	**10%**	**26**						**-3.4**	**49**	**59**	**-$1**

Goody,Nicholas

Goody,Nicholas	Health A	LIMA Plan A
Age: 26 Th: R Role RP	PT/Exp D	Rand Var -2
Ht: 5' 11" Wt: 195 Type Pwr xFB	Consist C	MM 2510

LIMA target for strikeouts, as nasty slider (25% SwK) drove Dom growth, and while LI is unimpressive, triple-digit BPV, 2nd half Cmd surge say he could handle higher-leverage work. Fortunate S% and extreme FB% add reason for concern, but $1 bid could return profit. If opportunity knocks... UP: 15 Sv

Yr Tm	W	L	Sv	IP	K	ERA	xERA	WHIP	oOPS	vL	vR	BF/G	Ctl	Dom	Cmd	FpK	SwK	G	L	F	H%	S%	hr/f	GS	APC	DOM%	DIS%	Sv%	LI	RAR	BPV	BPX	R$
13																																	
14 aa	0	3	0	16	16	7.95	8.08	2.06				5.2	5.7	9.2	1.6						40%	64%								-8.3	16	19	-$7
15 NYY *	2	2	8	68	74	2.39	2.98	1.26	794	833	729	5.5	3.4	9.8	2.8	69%	11%	47	21	32	32%	82%	0%	0	17			73	0.66	13.2	115	137	$7
16 NYY *	0	1	5	52	63	3.82	4.55	1.18	878	1097	758	4.7	2.8	10.8	3.8	59%	15%	23	21	56	28%	81%	16%	0	20			100	0.45	2.4	85	101	$2
17 CLE	1	2	0	55	72	2.80	3.60	1.08	632	590	651	3.9	3.3	11.9	3.6	58%	17%	28	23	48	28%	81%	12%	0	16			0	0.55	10.5	130	157	$4
1st Half	1	0	0	31	34	1.17	3.87	0.98	558	390	625	4.2	3.5	10.0	2.8	54%	14%	33	20	47	22%	96%	9%	0	17			0	0.60	12.0	95	114	$7
2nd Half	0	2	0	24	38	4.88	3.27	1.21	717	765	683	3.7	3.0	14.3	4.8	62%	20%	22	28	50	36%	64%	15%	0	15			0	0.50	-1.5	176	211	-$1
18 Proj	**3**	**4**	**2**	**58**	**74**	**3.38**	**3.78**	**1.15**	**701**	**704**	**698**	**4.2**	**3.1**	**11.5**	**3.7**	**59%**	**18%**	**26**	**25**	**49**	**30%**	**79%**	**14%**	**0**						**7.0**	**129**	**155**	**$4**

Gossett,Daniel

Gossett,Daniel	Health A	LIMA Plan C
Age: 25 Th: R Role SP	PT/Exp D	Rand Var +4
Ht: 6' 2" Wt: 185 Type	Consist F	MM 1103

4-11, 6.11 ERA in 91 IP at OAK. Definitely not a pretty debut. Below average FpK predicted 2nd half Ctl slide, and while some of ERA damage stemmed from ugly H% and hr/f, that should regress. Mediocre Dom limits upside to league average ceiling. 2016 offers hope; 2017 suggests patience.

Yr Tm	W	L	Sv	IP	K	ERA	xERA	WHIP	oOPS	vL	vR	BF/G	Ctl	Dom	Cmd	FpK	SwK	G	L	F	H%	S%	hr/f	GS	APC	DOM%	DIS%	Sv%	LI	RAR	BPV	BPX	R$
13																																	
14																																	
15																																	
16 a/a	6	5	0	108	78	2.98	3.01	1.20				24.1	2.4	6.5	2.8						30%	75%								16.1	92	109	$8
17 OAK *	8	15	0	168	127	5.32	5.52	1.51	906	898	911	22.7	3.0	6.8	2.3	57%	9%	43	25	32	33%	68%	21%	18	88	22%	50%			-19.9	42	51	-$7
1st Half	4	6	0	82	55	4.47	4.28	1.33	816	727	871	22.6	2.4	6.1	2.5	55%	10%	48	23	29	31%	68%	23%	4	89	50%	50%			-1.1	60	72	$1
2nd Half	4	9	0	86	72	6.13	6.69	1.69	932	939	925	22.8	3.5	7.6	2.2	57%	9%	42	25	33	36%	68%	21%	14	88	14%	50%			-18.8	27	32	-$14
18 Proj	**7**	**10**	**0**	**131**	**98**	**4.49**	**4.60**	**1.40**	**735**	**750**	**725**	**23.2**	**2.8**	**6.8**	**2.5**	**56%**	**10%**	**44**	**24**	**32**	**32%**	**70%**	**12%**	**24**						**-2.2**	**70**	**84**	**-$1**

Graveman,Kendall

Graveman,Kendall	Health F	LIMA Plan B+
Age: 27 Th: R Role SP	PT/Exp B	Rand Var 0
Ht: 6' 2" Wt: 200 Type Con GB	Consist A	MM 1003

BPV highlights his consistecny, which is not a good thing at this level. Shoulder problems cut into 2017 innings. FpK dip puts Ctl at risk, and combined with low SwK, creates thin margin for error. xERA neighborhood and health say he's no more than a late-round dart throw.

Yr Tm	W	L	Sv	IP	K	ERA	xERA	WHIP	oOPS	vL	vR	BF/G	Ctl	Dom	Cmd	FpK	SwK	G	L	F	H%	S%	hr/f	GS	APC	DOM%	DIS%	Sv%	LI	RAR	BPV	BPX	R$
13																																	
14 TOR *	4	2	0	49	26	2.51	3.58	1.26	556	625	500	16.7	1.3	4.9	3.6	78%	13%	64	29	7	32%	80%	0%	0	12			0	0.36	7.5	96	115	$1
15 OAK *	8	10	0	140	88	3.75	4.56	1.41	761	724	794	23.7	3.1	5.7	1.9	59%	7%	50	22	29	30%	77%	14%	21	90	19%	43%			3.7	42	50	$1
16 OAK	10	11	0	186	108	4.11	4.42	1.31	734	751	714	25.4	2.3	5.2	2.3	65%	8%	52	20	27	29%	71%	13%	31	91	16%	26%			1.8	63	74	$5
17 OAK	6	4	0	105	70	4.19	4.55	1.39	780	691	854	23.4	2.7	6.0	2.2	56%	7%	51	19	30	31%	72%	12%	19	88	16%	47%			2.2	63	75	$0
1st Half	2	2	0	47	32	3.83	4.44	1.28	747	769	731	24.3	2.7	6.1	2.3	55%	8%	51	18	31	28%	74%	13%	8	93	13%	38%			3.1	67	80	$1
2nd Half	4	2	0	58	38	4.47	4.65	1.47	806	640	963	22.7	2.8	5.9	2.1	57%	6%	52	19	29	33%	71%	11%	11	85	18%	55%			-0.8	60	72	$0
18 Proj	**8**	**7**	**0**	**131**	**81**	**4.16**	**4.61**	**1.36**	**754**	**708**	**797**	**22.8**	**2.5**	**5.6**	**2.2**	**60%**	**7%**	**51**	**20**	**29**	**31%**	**72%**	**11%**	**24**						**3.2**	**62**	**75**	**$1**

BRANT CHESSER

Gray,Jonathan

Age: 26	Th: R	Role SP		Health	F	LIMA Plan	B+
Ht: 6' 4"	Wt: 235	Type Pwr		PT/Exp	B	Rand Var	+2
				Consist	C	MM	2303

Growth, or plateau? PRO: Met 2017 UP: sub-4 ERA prediction with xERA, BPV support; rising GB% plays well in thin air; increased velocity for second year. CON: xERA, BPV largely unchanged from 2016; FpK says 2nd half Ctl surge won't last; falling SwK caps Dom. Even if healthy, might tread water for another year.

Yr	Tm	W	L	Sv	IP	K	ERA	xERA	WHIP	oOPS	vL	vR	BF/G	Ctl	Dom	Cmd	FpK	SwK	G	L	F	H%	S%	hr/f	GS	APC	DOM%	DIS%	Sv%	LI	RAR	BPV	BPX	R$
13																																		
14	aa	10	5	0	124	92	5.58	4.70	1.44				22.1	3.2	6.6	2.1						32%	62%								-28.2	51	60	-$8
15	COL *	6	8	0	155	123	5.35	5.68	1.67	856	755	949	23.2	3.2	7.1	2.2	58%	10%	42	25	33	37%	68%	10%	9	76	22%	33%			-26.5	55	65	-$16
16	COL	10	10	0	168	185	4.61	3.60	1.26	703	694	712	24.6	3.2	9.9	3.1	62%	12%	44	24	32	32%	65%	13%	29	96	41%	34%			-8.7	115	137	$6
17	COL	10	4	0	110	112	3.67	3.63	1.30	716	695	744	23.1	2.4	9.1	3.7	61%	9%	49	23	29	34%	74%	11%	20	92	35%	20%			9.4	125	151	$8
1st Half		1	0	0	18	19	3.93	3.96	1.42	752	815	646	20.0	3.9	9.3	2.4	60%	10%	52	23	25	33%	75%	15%	4	76	0%	25%			1.0	92	110	-$13
2nd Half		9	4	0	92	93	3.62	3.57	1.27	709	669	762	23.8	2.2	9.1	4.2	61%	9%	48	22	29	34%	73%	10%	16	96	44%	19%			8.4	132	158	$12
18	Proj	11	8	0	160	160	3.70	3.83	1.32	731	715	751	25.5	2.8	9.0	3.2	61%	11%	47	23	30	33%	75%	12%	26						12.9	112	135	$9

Gray,Sonny

Age: 28	Th: R	Role SP		Health	D	LIMA Plan	C+
Ht: 5' 10"	Wt: 190	Type Pwr GB		PT/Exp	A	Rand Var	+1
				Consist	B	MM	2203

Overcame April oblique issue to boost Dom/SwK, and Top 10 spin rates for CB/SL support new levels. Steady GB% continues to provide safe floor, but don't look to 2nd half for upside, as xERA shows that H%/S% hid skill regression. 2016 crash was injury-based anomaly; still, health history makes 200 IP a risky bet.

Yr	Tm	W	L	Sv	IP	K	ERA	xERA	WHIP	oOPS	vL	vR	BF/G	Ctl	Dom	Cmd	FpK	SwK	G	L	F	H%	S%	hr/f	GS	APC	DOM%	DIS%	Sv%	LI	RAR	BPV	BPX	R$
13	OAK *	15	10	0	182	165	3.20	3.29	1.28	570	622	499	23.4	2.8	8.1	2.9	60%	10%	53	20	28	32%	75%	8%	10	83	40%	20%	0	0.66	15.1	101	132	$13
14	OAK	14	10	0	219	183	3.08	3.36	1.19	627	639	614	27.2	3.0	7.5	2.5	58%	9%	56	18	26	28%	76%	9%	33	100	36%	21%			17.8	87	104	$16
15	OAK	14	7	0	208	169	2.73	3.62	1.08	590	579	601	26.8	2.6	7.3	2.9	59%	10%	53	17	31	26%	78%	9%	31	99	42%	23%			31.7	94	112	$26
16	OAK	5	11	0	117	94	5.69	4.30	1.50	818	757	880	23.5	3.2	7.2	2.2	61%	8%	54	19	27	33%	64%	17%	22	89	9%	45%			-21.7	75	89	-$9
17	2 AL	10	12	0	162	153	3.55	3.85	1.21	668	645	687	25.1	3.2	8.5	2.7	62%	12%	53	20	28	28%	75%	15%	27	99	37%	30%			16.2	98	118	$14
1st Half		3	4	0	73	69	4.09	3.57	1.24	685	655	713	25.2	2.8	8.5	3.0	63%	12%	56	22	23	31%	69%	15%	12	99	33%	33%			2.4	111	133	$6
2nd Half		7	8	0	90	84	3.11	4.09	1.18	654	636	668	25.1	3.4	8.4	2.5	60%	13%	50	18	32	26%	80%	15%	15	99	40%	27%			13.8	88	106	$20
18	Proj	10	12	0	174	154	3.90	3.98	1.28	701	675	725	24.3	3.1	8.0	2.6	61%	11%	53	19	28	30%	73%	14%	29						9.9	92	110	$9

Green,Chad

Age: 27	Th: R	Role RP		Health	B	LIMA Plan	B+
Ht: 6' 3"	Wt: 210	Type Pwr FB		PT/Exp	D	Rand Var	+1
				Consist	C	MM	3501

5-0, 1.83 ERA in 69 IP at NYY. Three-step transition to elite multi-inning RP: 1) Throw FB with increased velocity that misses bats; 2) Consistently fire strike one to improve control; 3) Find an out pitch to solve platoon splits (8.8 Cmd vL). Jump in FB% is a concern, but otherwise, he's a LIMA gem.

Yr	Tm	W	L	Sv	IP	K	ERA	xERA	WHIP	oOPS	vL	vR	BF/G	Ctl	Dom	Cmd	FpK	SwK	G	L	F	H%	S%	hr/f	GS	APC	DOM%	DIS%	Sv%	LI	RAR	BPV	BPX	R$
13																																		
14																																		
15	aa	5	14	0	149	108	4.84	5.48	1.65				24.6	2.8	6.5	2.4						38%	70%								-16.2	61	73	-$13
16	NYY *	9	10	1	140	135	3.01	3.88	1.25	852	1014	704	20.4	2.5	8.6	3.5	60%	13%	41	21	38	31%	81%	25%	8	70	25%	38%	100	0.68	20.4	97	115	$12
17	NYY *	7	1	0	96	130	3.20	2.48	1.10	454	411	476	8.3	2.8	12.2	4.4	66%	16%	26	27	47	33%	71%	7%	1	29	0%	0%	0	0.95	13.7	161	194	$11
1st Half		2	1	0	56	63	4.21	3.79	1.36	474	479	472	11.6	3.3	10.1	3.1	62%	15%	29	24	47	36%	69%	7%	1	30	0%	0%	0	0.86	1.0	111	133	$5
2nd Half		5	0	0	40	67	1.80	2.27	0.73	439	372	480	5.9	2.0	15.1	7.4	69%	16%	24	30	46	28%	78%	6%	0	27			0	1.01	12.6	219	262	$21
18	Proj	6	4	0	87	105	3.16	3.68	1.17	698	778	641	11.2	2.5	10.9	4.3	63%	15%	32	25	43	32%	78%	11%	4						12.8	137	165	$8

Greene,Shane

Age: 29	Th: R	Role RP		Health	B	LIMA Plan	B
Ht: 6' 4"	Wt: 210	Type Pwr		PT/Exp	C	Rand Var	-4
				Consist	B	MM	1321

Saves source? Maybe, but a sub-2 ERA elite closer, he's not. Rode 2nd half S%, GB% combination to success, but SwK drop at odds with Dom gain, and xERA, Cmd, and BPV histories all far from what you'd like to see. While Rolaids Relief Man Award no longer exists, he might win award for driving up sales of Rolaids.

Yr	Tm	W	L	Sv	IP	K	ERA	xERA	WHIP	oOPS	vL	vR	BF/G	Ctl	Dom	Cmd	FpK	SwK	G	L	F	H%	S%	hr/f	GS	APC	DOM%	DIS%	Sv%	LI	RAR	BPV	BPX	R$
13	aa	8	4	0	79	55	4.25	6.14	1.72				25.7	2.5	6.3	2.5						39%	77%								-3.8	50	65	-$6
14	NYY *	10	6	0	145	127	4.53	5.05	1.59	715	765	661	21.3	3.5	7.9	2.3	59%	11%	50	22	28	37%	72%	13%	14	90	36%	36%	0	0.70	-14.1	69	82	-$7
15	DET *	5	9	0	119	66	6.29	5.60	1.58	897	1017	757	20.9	3.0	5.0	1.7	62%	7%	44	23	33	33%	61%	14%	16	74	25%	56%	0	0.70	-34.1	24	28	-$17
16	DET	5	4	2	60	59	5.82	3.88	1.33	680	788	586	5.1	3.3	8.8	2.7	58%	13%	48	20	32	33%	53%	6%	3	20	0%	33%	67	1.26	-12.1	96	114	-$3
17	DET	4	3	9	68	73	2.66	4.07	1.24	631	758	542	4.0	4.5	9.7	2.1	59%	10%	47	18	35	27%	82%	10%	0	15			69	1.18	14.2	78	93	$9
1st Half		2	2	0	36	38	3.53	4.35	1.26	621	705	572	4.0	4.8	9.6	2.0	56%	9%	46	16	38	27%	74%	9%	0	15			0	1.17	3.6	67	81	$4
2nd Half		2	1	9	32	35	1.69	3.75	1.22	641	807	501	3.9	4.2	9.8	2.3	64%	10%	49	21	31	28%	92%	13%	0	15			90	1.19	10.5	90	108	$14
18	Proj	5	4	20	73	73	3.80	4.14	1.31	682	805	577	5.3	3.9	9.0	2.3	60%	10%	47	20	33	30%	73%	10%	0						5.0	82	99	$10

Gregerson,Luke

Age: 34	Th: R	Role RP		Health	B	LIMA Plan	C+
Ht: 6' 3"	Wt: 205	Type Pwr GB		PT/Exp	C	Rand Var	+5
				Consist	A	MM	4410

Use the sinker, Luke. Even with struggles, skills show he didn't deserve ERA dark side. Yes, he traded GB% for FB%/LD%, but consistent strike one, punchouts vouch for better days ahead. Better H% vR should aid cause, but big 2nd half problem was preventing HR—with some hr/f help, he's a decent holds source.

Yr	Tm	W	L	Sv	IP	K	ERA	xERA	WHIP	oOPS	vL	vR	BF/G	Ctl	Dom	Cmd	FpK	SwK	G	L	F	H%	S%	hr/f	GS	APC	DOM%	DIS%	Sv%	LI	RAR	BPV	BPX	R$
13	SD	6	8	4	66	64	2.71	3.27	1.01	572	624	521	3.7	2.4	8.7	3.6	60%	14%	45	20	35	27%	73%	5%	0	13			44	1.26	9.4	113	148	$8
14	OAK	5	5	3	72	59	2.12	3.24	1.01	604	526	663	3.9	1.9	7.3	3.9	60%	14%	52	15	33	26%	84%	9%	0	14			27	1.31	14.5	112	133	$9
15	HOU	7	3	31	61	59	3.10	2.71	0.95	573	606	537	3.7	1.5	8.7	5.9	67%	16%	60	16	23	28%	70%	13%	0	14			86	1.23	6.5	155	184	$19
16	HOU	4	3	15	58	67	3.28	2.84	0.97	589	746	439	3.9	2.8	10.5	3.7	63%	20%	60	14	26	26%	69%	14%	0	14			71	1.23	6.5	150	179	$11
17	HOU	2	3	1	61	70	4.57	3.66	1.34	790	802	782	4.0	3.0	10.3	3.5	64%	16%	50	18	32	32%	74%	24%	0	15			25	0.69	-1.6	134	161	-$1
1st Half		2	2	0	33	39	4.09	3.78	1.33	746	896	638	3.9	3.3	10.6	3.3	63%	17%	46	19	36	32%	76%	19%	0	15			0	0.74	1.1	127	152	$0
2nd Half		0	1	1	28	31	5.14	3.50	1.36	841	679	935	4.2	2.6	10.0	3.9	66%	15%	55	17	28	32%	71%	30%	0	15			50	0.63	-2.7	143	171	-$3
18	Proj	4	3	2	65	72	3.47	3.27	1.16	662	683	645	3.8	2.6	10.0	3.9	64%	17%	55	17	29	31%	73%	14%	0						7.1	143	172	$4

Greinke,Zack

Age: 34	Th: R	Role SP		Health	B	LIMA Plan	C
Ht: 6' 2"	Wt: 200	Type Pwr		PT/Exp	A	Rand Var	0
				Consist	B	MM	3305

Welcome back, Zack! Returned from one-year skill hiatus with increased SwK from slider, change-up to elevate Dom, regain 200-K status. Even though FpK slipped, career Ctl bodes well for limiting free passes, and second-highest BPV of career shows he's back on track. Has enough left in tank to be low-level ace.

Yr	Tm	W	L	Sv	IP	K	ERA	xERA	WHIP	oOPS	vL	vR	BF/G	Ctl	Dom	Cmd	FpK	SwK	G	L	F	H%	S%	hr/f	GS	APC	DOM%	DIS%	Sv%	LI	RAR	BPV	BPX	R$
13	LA	15	4	0	178	148	2.63	3.43	1.11	647	733	568	25.6	2.3	7.5	3.2	58%	11%	46	24	31	28%	79%	9%	28	101	39%	21%			27.0	96	125	$21
14	LA	17	8	0	202	207	2.71	2.93	1.15	660	627	689	25.7	1.9	9.2	4.8	63%	12%	49	23	29	32%	80%	12%	32	100	41%	13%			25.6	141	168	$21
15	LA	19	3	0	223	200	1.66	3.14	0.84	507	535	482	26.3	1.6	8.1	5.0	64%	13%	48	19	33	24%	84%	7%	32	101	56%	3%			63.3	128	152	$49
16	ARI	13	7	0	159	134	4.37	4.10	1.27	750	745	756	25.7	2.3	7.6	3.3	68%	11%	46	20	35	31%	70%	14%	26	96	31%	35%			-3.5	98	116	$6
17	ARI	17	7	0	202	215	3.20	3.41	1.07	659	657	662	25.0	2.0	9.6	4.8	62%	13%	47	18	35	29%	76%	13%	32	99	50%	22%			28.8	143	172	$29
1st Half		10	4	0	109	124	3.05	3.22	1.02	632	606	656	25.4	1.8	10.2	5.6	63%	14%	47	17	35	29%	77%	15%	17	100	47%	18%			17.7	160	192	$36
2nd Half		7	3	0	93	91	3.39	3.65	1.14	692	711	670	24.6	2.2	8.8	4.0	61%	12%	46	19	35	30%	74%	11%	15	98	53%	27%			11.1	123	147	$21
18	Proj	16	8	0	203	200	3.23	3.62	1.10	665	676	653	24.9	2.1	8.9	4.3	64%	12%	47	19	34	29%	75%	12%	32						28.2	128	155	$25

Griffin,A.J.

Age: 30	Th: R	Role RP		Health	F	LIMA Plan	D+
Ht: 6' 5"	Wt: 230	Type Pwr xFB		PT/Exp	C	Rand Var	+1
				Consist	B	MM	0201

Missed time with ankle, oblique injuries that hindered recovery from 2016 shoulder stiffness, which hindered recovery from 2015 shoulder strain, which hindered recovery from 2014 TJS. Even before injuries, Dom wasn't anything special, and FB% adds plenty of ERA risk. Might spend more time on DL than your roster.

Yr	Tm	W	L	Sv	IP	K	ERA	xERA	WHIP	oOPS	vL	vR	BF/G	Ctl	Dom	Cmd	FpK	SwK	G	L	F	H%	S%	hr/f	GS	APC	DOM%	DIS%	Sv%	LI	RAR	BPV	BPX	R$
13	OAK	14	10	0	200	171	3.83	4.10	1.13	688	666	713	25.7	2.4	7.7	3.2	60%	9%	32	18	49	26%	74%	13%	32	100	38%	19%			1.0	83	108	$14
14																																		
15																																		
16	TEX	7	4	0	119	107	5.07	4.80	1.36	833	978	697	22.1	3.5	8.1	2.3	57%	9%	29	23	48	28%	71%	17%	23	90	17%	52%			-12.9	59	70	-$2
17	TEX	6	6	0	77	61	5.94	5.62	1.34	852	810	880	18.8	3.3	7.1	2.2	62%	8%	29	13	58	26%	63%	14%	15	73	20%	60%	0	0.66	-15.0	47	56	-$4
1st Half		4	2	0	39	35	5.77	5.15	1.28	838	865	821	20.9	2.8	8.1	2.9	67%	9%	29	13	58	26%	66%	17%	8	81	25%	50%			-6.8	78	94	-$2
2nd Half		2	4	0	38	26	6.10	6.13	1.41	865	753	943	17.1	3.8	6.1	1.6	57%	8%	28	14	59	27%	61%	11%	7	67	14%	71%	0	0.58	-8.3	14	17	-$6
18	Proj	7	6	0	102	84	5.33	5.24	1.32	823	842	807	19.6	3.3	7.4	2.3	59%	9%	29	17	53	27%	67%	15%	21						-12.2	53	64	-$2

BRANT CHESSER

Grimm,Justin

Age: 29	Th: R	Role RP	Health B	LIMA Plan C
Ht: 6' 3"	Wt: 210	Type Pwr	PT/Exp D	Rand Var +5
			Consist B	MM 2400

Is his outlook the same as his last name? Hr/f, S% regression might help ERA, xERA is going the wrong way, thanks to ongoing issues with FpK/Ctl. Corresponding drops in LI, holds since 2015 say employer has noticed. Maybe things aren't as bad as 2nd half suggests, but as R$ shows, Ks aren't enough to offset bad ratios.

Yr	Tm	W	L	Sv	IP	K	ERA	xERA	WHIP	oOPS	vL	vR	BF/G	Ctl	Dom	Cmd	FpK	SwK	G	L	F	H%	S%	hr/f	GS	APC	DOM%	DIS%	Sv%	LI	RAR	BPV	BPX	R
13	2 TM *	10	12	0	146	113	5.78	5.37	1.61	846	860	830	17.9	3.4	6.9	2.1	58%	8%	43	21	36	35%	64%	13%	17	61	12%	59%	0	0.80	-34.4	49	64	-$1
14	CHC	5	2	0	69	70	3.78	3.49	1.25	632	528	684	4.0	3.5	9.1	2.6	61%	11%	49	16	35	31%	70%	6%	0	16			0	0.87	-0.4	96	115	$
15	CHC	3	5	3	50	67	1.99	3.09	1.15	575	507	608	3.3	4.7	12.1	2.6	59%	14%	45	25	30	27%	87%	12%	0	14			50	1.04	12.1	114	136	$
16	CHC	2	1	0	53	65	4.10	3.67	1.33	679	732	639	3.3	3.9	11.1	2.8	57%	13%	41	23	36	33%	71%	10%	0	13			0	0.67	0.6	113	134	-$
17	CHC	1	2	1	55	59	5.53	4.26	1.34	760	774	750	4.6	4.4	9.6	2.2	57%	12%	43	19	38	27%	65%	22%	0	19			33	0.70	-8.0	75	90	-$
1st Half		1	0	0	29	33	4.08	3.82	1.05	690	717	668	4.2	3.5	10.4	3.0	61%	13%	35	19	46	20%	74%	23%	0	18			0	0.74	1.0	107	128	$
2nd Half		0	2	1	27	26	7.09	4.77	1.65	828	851	816	5.2	5.4	8.8	1.6	54%	12%	50	20	30	32%	59%	22%	0	21			50	0.64	-9.0	40	48	-$
18	Proj	**2**	**2**	**0**	**51**	**57**	**4.75**	**4.11**	**1.35**	**717**	**732**	**708**	**4.1**	**4.3**	**10.1**	**2.3**	**57%**	**12%**	**44**	**21**	**35**	**30%**	**69%**	**17%**	**0**						**-2.4**	**86**	**104**	-$

Gsellman,Robert

Age: 24	Th: R	Role SP	Health D	LIMA Plan D+
Ht: 6' 4"	Wt: 205	Type	PT/Exp D	Rand Var +2
			Consist B	MM 0001

8-7, 5.19 ERA in 120 IP at NYM. Ugly 1st half line, as hr/f didn't do ERA any favors. Slider lost effectiveness, leading to fewer GBs, lower SwK, but rising FpK argues that Ctl deserved better. Then again, given history of pedestrian Cmd, fewer walks isn't exactly going to be a cure-all.

Yr	Tm	W	L	Sv	IP	K	ERA	xERA	WHIP	oOPS	vL	vR	BF/G	Ctl	Dom	Cmd	FpK	SwK	G	L	F	H%	S%	hr/f	GS	APC	DOM%	DIS%	Sv%	LI	RAR	BPV	BPX	R
13																																		
14																																		
15	aa	7	7	0	92	43	4.01	3.82	1.35				24.0	2.5	4.2	1.7						30%	69%								-0.5	48	58	-$
16	NYM *	8	11	0	160	121	3.75	3.85	1.33	639	589	682	23.6	2.7	6.8	2.6	61%	10%	54	23	23	32%	72%	4%	7	89	29%	14%	0	1.01	8.7	77	91	$
17	NYM *	9	7	0	138	93	5.23	5.56	1.58	807	813	803	20.3	3.3	6.0	1.8	64%	8%	49	22	29	33%	69%	14%	22	82	14%	45%	0	0.78	-14.8	33	40	-$
1st Half		5	5	0	76	57	6.16	4.77	1.62	878	881	876	20.9	3.1	6.8	2.2	62%	8%	53	20	27	35%	65%	18%	14	79	7%	43%	0	0.79	-16.9	69	83	-$1
2nd Half		4	2	0	62	36	4.09	4.85	1.54	677	716	628	20.8	3.6	5.2	1.4	68%	7%	42	25	33	32%	75%	9%	8	89	25%	50%			2.0	36	43	-$
18	Proj	**5**	**5**	**0**	**87**	**57**	**4.56**	**4.75**	**1.46**	**767**	**758**	**775**	**21.9**	**3.0**	**5.9**	**2.0**	**64%**	**8%**	**50**	**23**	**28**	**32%**	**69%**	**10%**	**17**						**-2.2**	**53**	**64**	-$

Guerra,Junior

Age: 33	Th: R	Role RP	Health F	LIMA Plan D+
Ht: 6' 0"	Wt: 205	Type Pwr FB	PT/Exp D	Rand Var +1
			Consist F	MM 0200

1-4, 5.12 ERA in 70 IP at MIL. We knew ERA would rise based on 2016's 4.18 MLB xERA; skills show it was worse than expected. Falling FpK/Ctl damaged WHIP, jump in FB% added to ERA risk, and calf/shin injuries killed Health grade. Sept bullpen IP bumped up 2nd half Dom/SwK, but still not enough to save him.

Yr	Tm	W	L	Sv	IP	K	ERA	xERA	WHIP	oOPS	vL	vR	BF/G	Ctl	Dom	Cmd	FpK	SwK	G	L	F	H%	S%	hr/f	GS	APC	DOM%	DIS%	Sv%	LI	RAR	BPV	BPX	R
13																																		
14																																		
15	CHW *	4	7	7	87	83	4.63	4.59	1.49	1033	1000	1044	11.1	4.4	8.6	1.9	63%	11%	57	21	21	32%	71%	33%	0	22			88	0.22	-7.2	62	74	-$
16	MIL *	9	5	0	148	119	3.20	2.88	1.16	633	618	645	23.6	3.3	7.2	2.2	58%	11%	45	19	36	26%	75%	8%	20	93	30%	20%			18.1	77	92	$1
17	MIL *	3	7	0	105	85	4.52	5.53	1.58	817	812	820	16.5	5.2	7.3	1.4	54%	11%	34	23	44	28%	78%	21%	14	59	0%	57%	0	0.58	-2.0	22	26	-$
1st Half		1	4	0	53	36	4.78	6.79	1.71	853	799	900	24.0	5.2	6.2	1.2	55%	10%	35	21	44	29%	82%	20%	8	89	0%	63%			-2.7	-12	-14	-$1
2nd Half		2	3	0	52	48	4.25	4.26	1.44	765	832	714	12.4	5.1	8.3	1.6	52%	13%	31	25	44	28%	74%	23%	6	40	0%	50%	0	0.47	0.7	56	67	-$
18	Proj	**3**	**3**	**0**	**58**	**48**	**4.06**	**5.15**	**1.41**	**745**	**750**	**740**	**19.4**	**4.4**	**7.5**	**1.7**	**55%**	**12%**	**38**	**22**	**41**	**28%**	**76%**	**12%**	**14**						**2.1**	**31**	**38**	-$

Hader,Joshua

Age: 24	Th: L	Role RP	Health A	LIMA Plan A
Ht: 6' 3"	Wt: 185	Type Pwr xFB	PT/Exp D	Rand Var -2
			Consist B	MM 1511

2-3, 2.08 ERA in 48 IP at MIL. Cut through bats in debut with stellar SwK, Dom, and while 2nd half BPV says he has future as closer, return to SP hasn't been ruled out. FB%, career Ctl still leave holes to fill before deeming elite, but at very least, Ks drive foundation for LIMA value, and perhaps... UP: 10 wins or 15 saves

Yr	Tm	W	L	Sv	IP	K	ERA	xERA	WHIP	oOPS	vL	vR	BF/G	Ctl	Dom	Cmd	FpK	SwK	G	L	F	H%	S%	hr/f	GS	APC	DOM%	DIS%	Sv%	LI	RAR	BPV	BPX	R
13																																		
14	aa	1	1	0	20	22	6.74	4.30	1.60				17.7	6.7	9.9	1.5						30%	57%								-7.4	71	85	-$
15	aa	4	7	1	104	104	4.07	4.06	1.36				18.1	3.2	9.0	2.8						33%	72%								-1.4	89	106	$
16	a/a	3	8	0	126	142	4.01	3.52	1.36				21.1	3.9	10.1	2.6						34%	70%								2.7	104	124	$
17	MIL *	5	7	0	100	112	3.90	4.12	1.29	554	454	608	8.7	4.6	10.1	2.2	59%	18%	34	14	51	26%	78%	9%	0	22			0	1.14	5.6	66	80	$
1st Half		3	4	0	61	50	4.73	5.43	1.49	404	424	390	13.9	5.4	7.3	1.4	55%	13%	27	9	64	24%	78%	0%	0	22			0	0.62	-2.8	12	15	$
2nd Half		2	3	0	38	62	2.58	2.67	0.97	585	460	651	5.4	3.3	14.6	4.4	59%	19%	37	16	47	29%	79%	13%	0	22			0	1.27	8.4	188	225	$1
18	Proj	**3**	**6**	**3**	**87**	**104**	**3.72**	**4.26**	**1.26**	**676**	**539**	**748**	**10.6**	**3.9**	**10.7**	**2.7**	**59%**	**19%**	**37**	**16**	**47**	**30%**	**74%**	**9%**	**2**						**6.8**	**102**	**123**	$

Hahn,Jesse

Age: 28	Th: R	Role SP	Health D	LIMA Plan D
Ht: 6' 4"	Wt: 215	Type	PT/Exp D	Rand Var +1
			Consist D	MM 0001

3-6, 5.30 ERA in 70 IP at OAK. Nightmare low-skill, high risk profile sums up bleak outlook. Injuries continue to pile up, xERA increased each month in 1st half, and shaky Ctl didn't help. Even though velocity increase held and GB% history is a plus, expecting anything beyond MLB roster filler is wishful thinking.

Yr	Tm	W	L	Sv	IP	K	ERA	xERA	WHIP	oOPS	vL	vR	BF/G	Ctl	Dom	Cmd	FpK	SwK	G	L	F	H%	S%	hr/f	GS	APC	DOM%	DIS%	Sv%	LI	RAR	BPV	BPX	R
13																																		
14	SD *	9	5	0	116	102	2.76	2.88	1.24	623	656	583	17.4	3.7	7.9	2.1	60%	11%	50	22	27	29%	78%	8%	12	84	33%	25%	0	0.89	14.0	90	108	$
15	OAK	6	6	0	97	64	3.35	3.83	1.17	623	735	502	25.4	2.3	6.0	2.6	61%	8%	53	25	23	28%	71%	7%	16	96	25%	19%			7.3	75	90	$
16	OAK *	3	11	0	113	57	5.78	6.09	1.79	860	1069	685	21.7	4.4	4.6	1.0	66%	6%	49	23	28	34%	68%	18%	9	79	11%	67%			-22.2	12	14	-$1
17	OAK *	5	6	0	95	68	5.36	4.97	1.64	748	821	689	21.1	4.0	6.5	1.6	58%	8%	46	25	29	35%	66%	6%	13	86	8%	46%	0	0.71	-11.7	54	65	-$
1st Half		3	6	0	70	55	5.30	4.83	1.51	748	821	689	22.6	3.5	7.1	2.0	58%	8%	46	25	29	34%	63%	6%		86	8%	46%			-8.1	57	69	-$
2nd Half		2	0	0	25	13	5.53	6.38	2.00				20.1	5.4	4.7	0.9						37%	71%	0%							-3.6	24	29	-$1
18	Proj	**4**	**4**	**0**	**73**	**45**	**4.91**	**5.30**	**1.65**	**797**	**900**	**700**	**20.9**	**4.1**	**5.6**	**1.4**	**61%**	**8%**	**50**	**24**	**26**	**34%**	**70%**	**7%**	**15**						**-4.9**	**18**	**21**	-$

Hamels,Cole

Age: 34	Th: L	Role SP	Health D	LIMA Plan B
Ht: 6' 4"	Wt: 205	Type Pwr	PT/Exp A	Rand Var -1
			Consist B	MM 1203

Strained oblique cost him two months and tanked 1st half Dom. But even if we focus solely on 2nd half skills, ongoing declines in Cmd and BPV, rising xERA make it unlikely he'll fully rebound. DOM/DIS trends further highlight the erosion. Stop paying premium price for what is now a mid-rotation arm.

Yr	Tm	W	L	Sv	IP	K	ERA	xERA	WHIP	oOPS	vL	vR	BF/G	Ctl	Dom	Cmd	FpK	SwK	G	L	F	H%	S%	hr/f	GS	APC	DOM%	DIS%	Sv%	LI	RAR	BPV	BPX	R
13	PHI	8	14	0	220	202	3.60	3.46	1.16	699	712	695	27.4	2.0	8.3	4.0	63%	13%	43	21	37	31%	71%	9%	33	104	45%	15%			7.2	115	149	$1
14	PHI	9	9	0	205	198	2.46	3.20	1.15	641	636	641	27.6	2.6	8.7	3.4	61%	13%	46	22	31	30%	81%	8%	30	105	57%	10%			32.3	111	132	$2
15	2 TM	13	8	0	212	215	3.65	3.39	1.19	669	646	675	27.5	2.6	9.1	3.5	61%	14%	48	21	31	30%	72%	12%	32	104	44%	19%			8.3	119	142	$1
16	TEX	15	5	0	201	200	3.32	3.83	1.31	699	605	722	26.5	3.5	9.0	2.6	57%	13%	50	20	31	31%	79%	14%	32	102	34%	25%			21.5	96	114	$1
17	TEX	11	6	0	148	105	4.20	4.61	1.20	693	483	749	25.6	3.2	6.4	2.0	56%	10%	48	19	34	26%	68%	12%	24	96	25%	33%			3.0	54	65	$
1st Half		3	0	0	44	22	4.12	4.97	1.17	670	437	720	25.6	3.3	4.5	1.4	55%	7%	50	19	32	23%	67%	12%	7	97	14%	43%			1.3	20	24	-$
2nd Half		8	6	0	104	83	4.23	4.46	1.22	702	497	762	25.6	3.2	7.2	2.2	57%	11%	47	19	35	27%	68%	12%	17	96	29%	29%			1.7	67	81	$1
18	Proj	**11**	**8**	**0**	**174**	**145**	**3.88**	**4.24**	**1.22**	**687**	**556**	**721**	**25.5**	**3.1**	**7.5**	**2.4**	**58%**	**11%**	**48**	**20**	**33**	**28%**	**71%**	**12%**	**28**						**10.4**	**77**	**93**	$1

Hammel,Jason

Age: 35	Th: R	Role SP	Health B	LIMA Plan C
Ht: 6' 6"	Wt: 225	Type	PT/Exp A	Rand Var +2
			Consist B	MM 1203

What happened to consistent R$? 1) Shift in H%/S% luck hurt WHIP; 2) Allowing more FB% offset decrease in hr/f; 3) Lost SwK on slider as hitters made 88% ct% in zone; 4) Wins faded with rising ERA. BPV says some rebound is possible, but rising xERA tells us R$ won't return to double digits.

Yr	Tm	W	L	Sv	IP	K	ERA	xERA	WHIP	oOPS	vL	vR	BF/G	Ctl	Dom	Cmd	FpK	SwK	G	L	F	H%	S%	hr/f	GS	APC	DOM%	DIS%	Sv%	LI	RAR	BPV	BPX	R
13	BAL	7	8	1	139	96	4.97	4.52	1.46	813	881	716	23.5	3.1	6.2	2.0	56%	8%	40	22	38	31%	70%	13%	23	89	9%	57%	100	0.77	-19.0	46	60	-$
14	2 TM	10	11	0	176	158	3.47	3.53	1.12	680	691	670	23.8	2.2	8.1	3.6	57%	10%	40	22	38	28%	74%	12%	29	93	48%	21%	0	0.75	5.9	103	122	$1
15	CHC	10	7	0	171	172	3.74	3.57	1.16	714	696	728	22.9	2.1	9.1	4.3	61%	11%	38	25	37	30%	73%	13%	31	89	32%	23%			4.6	122	146	$1
16	CHC	15	10	0	167	144	3.83	4.20	1.21	729	797	679	23.1	2.9	7.8	2.7	60%	11%	42	20	38	27%	74%	14%	30	87	33%	30%			7.3	83	98	$1
17	KC	8	13	0	180	145	5.29	4.92	1.43	773	775	771	25.1	2.4	7.2	3.0	62%	10%	38	21	41	33%	65%	11%	32	95	13%	28%			-20.7	82	98	-$
1st Half		4	7	0	89	70	5.08	5.24	1.48	777	763	794	25.1	2.9	7.1	2.4	62%	9%	35	22	43	33%	68%	10%	16	94	13%	38%			-7.8	62	74	-$
2nd Half		4	6	0	92	75	5.50	4.62	1.37	769	787	750	25.1	1.9	7.4	3.9	63%	10%	41	20	40	34%	63%	12%	16	95	13%	19%			-12.9	101	121	-$
18	Proj	**9**	**10**	**0**	**160**	**136**	**4.61**	**4.48**	**1.31**	**761**	**782**	**741**	**23.1**	**2.4**	**7.6**	**3.1**	**61%**	**10%**	**40**	**21**	**39**	**31%**	**69%**	**13%**	**28**						**-4.9**	**89**	**107**	$

BRANT CHESSER

Hand,Brad

Age: 28	Th: L	Role RP	Health B	LIMA Plan C
Ht: 6' 3"	Wt: 228	Type Pwr	PT/Exp B	Rand Var -2
			Consist B	MM 4531

As Cmd, BPV trends show, keeps establishing new level of performance and then beating it, culminating in utterly elite 2nd half. That'll be tough to top, or repeat, as FpK doesn't back Ctl growth, and xERA calls for mild regression. But that's nitpicking; 6.4 Cmd vs. RHB in 2017 says he's ready to lock down 9th.

Yr Tm	W	L	Sv	IP	K	ERA	xERA	WHIP	oOPS	vL	vR	BF/G	Ctl	Dom	Cmd	FpK	SwK	G	L	F	H%	S%	hr/f	GS	APC	DOM%	DIS%	Sv%	LI	RAR	BPV	BPX	R$
13 MIA *	4	6	0	102	83	4.03	3.96	1.46	553	530	564	19.9	4.9	7.3	1.5	52%	9%	42	20	37	29%	74%	9%	2	43	0%	50%	0	0.73	-2.1	58	76	-$3
14 MIA *	5	8	1	133	85	4.21	4.00	1.34	732	594	789	15.4	3.2	5.7	1.8	59%	7%	50	18	32	29%	70%	9%	16	56	13%	31%	100	0.58	-7.6	50	60	-$2
15 MIA	4	7	0	93	67	5.30	4.39	1.49	784	512	887	10.7	3.1	6.5	2.1	52%	9%	46	23	30	33%	65%	10%	12	41	8%	50%	0	0.60	-15.4	57	68	-$8
16 SD	4	4	1	89	111	2.92	3.34	1.11	589	421	689	4.4	3.6	11.2	3.1	59%	13%	47	17	36	28%	77%	10%	0	18			14	1.30	14.0	128	153	$9
17 SD	3	4	21	79	104	2.16	2.79	0.93	580	590	577	4.3	2.3	11.8	5.2	58%	14%	46	20	34	27%	85%	15%	0	17			81	1.35	21.6	175	210	$21
1st Half	1	4	2	43	51	2.53	2.98	0.98	588	666	550	4.5	2.5	10.8	4.3	57%	14%	51	19	30	27%	79%	13%	0	17			50	1.31	9.6	154	185	$15
2nd Half	2	0	19	37	53	1.72	2.58	0.87	571	467	604	4.1	2.0	13.0	6.6	59%	14%	40	21	39	27%	93%	17%	0	16			86	1.41	11.9	199	239	$29
18 Proj	3	3	36	73	90	2.96	3.23	1.10	629	515	678	5.1	2.9	11.2	3.9	57%	13%	46	20	34	30%	78%	13%	0						12.5	148	179	$21

Happ,J.A.

Age: 35	Th: L	Role SP	Health D	LIMA Plan C+
Ht: 6' 5"	Wt: 205	Type Pwr	PT/Exp A	Rand Var 0
			Consist A	MM 1203

Poised for another big year? PRO: BPV says this was his best season; owned similar Dom rate in 2012; in 11 GS after 8/1: 2.81 ERA, 9.6 Dom, 3.1 Cmd, 3.60 xERA, 118 BPV. CON: xERA not impressed; Ctl fell apart in 2nd half; injuries keep limiting IP. Much of 2016 R$ was H%, run support, so $20 is a longshot now.

Yr Tm	W	L	Sv	IP	K	ERA	xERA	WHIP	oOPS	vL	vR	BF/G	Ctl	Dom	Cmd	FpK	SwK	G	L	F	H%	S%	hr/f	GS	APC	DOM%	DIS%	Sv%	LI	RAR	BPV	BPX	R$
13 TOR	5	7	0	93	77	4.56	4.83	1.47	734	802	708	23.1	4.4	7.5	1.7	60%	8%	36	18	46	31%	71%	8%	18	96	28%	44%			-8.0	31	40	-$5
14 TOR	11	11	0	158	133	4.22	4.03	1.34	770	874	743	22.4	2.9	7.6	2.6	62%	8%	41	20	40	31%	72%	12%	26	90	23%	31%	0	0.82	-9.2	77	92	$1
15 2 TM	11	8	0	172	151	3.61	3.83	1.27	698	680	705	22.4	2.4	7.9	3.4	60%	9%	42	24	34	32%	74%	9%	31	89	23%	26%	0	0.78	7.5	99	117	$9
16 TOR	20	4	0	195	163	3.18	4.13	1.17	665	651	669	24.9	2.8	7.5	2.7	60%	10%	42	22	36	27%	77%	11%	32	95	31%	25%			24.2	81	96	$22
17 TOR	10	11	0	145	142	3.53	4.12	1.31	700	553	735	25.0	2.8	8.8	3.1	62%	10%	47	19	34	32%	77%	12%	25	99	24%	28%			14.9	106	128	$10
1st Half	2	5	0	51	51	3.71	3.77	1.18	708	824	685	24.0	1.6	9.0	5.7	64%	11%	45	22	34	32%	75%	15%	9	93	33%	22%			4.1	142	170	$2
2nd Half	8	6	0	94	91	3.43	4.33	1.39	695	435	763	25.6	3.5	8.7	2.5	61%	10%	48	18	34	32%	79%	11%	16	103	19%	31%			10.7	87	104	$14
18 Proj	13	10	0	174	159	3.65	4.18	1.27	697	641	712	23.5	2.8	8.2	3.0	61%	10%	44	21	35	31%	75%	12%	30						15.2	95	114	$12

Harris,Will

Age: 33	Th: R	Role RP	Health D	LIMA Plan A
Ht: 6' 4"	Wt: 250	Type Pwr	PT/Exp C	Rand Var +1
			Consist A	MM 4410

Follow trends in Dom, Cmd, and BPV, and witness his rocket ride to relief relevancy. Recurring shoulder issue cost him most of July/Aug, but metrics showed no ill effects other than loss of managerial confidence (see 2nd half LI). Don't make the same mistake—these are closer-worthy skills. UP: 25 Sv

Yr Tm	W	L	Sv	IP	K	ERA	xERA	WHIP	oOPS	vL	vR	BF/G	Ctl	Dom	Cmd	FpK	SwK	G	L	F	H%	S%	hr/f	GS	APC	DOM%	DIS%	Sv%	LI	RAR	BPV	BPX	R$
13 ARI	4	1	0	53	53	2.91	3.18	1.23	661	509	759	3.6	2.6	9.1	3.5	58%	11%	47	23	29	33%	77%	7%	0	14			0	1.01	6.2	119	155	$2
14 ARI *	3	5	1	75	67	2.37	3.58	1.30	740	721	757	4.3	3.6	8.1	2.3	55%	11%	35	25	40	30%	85%	10%	0	17			33	0.76	12.6	80	95	$3
15 HOU	5	5	2	71	68	1.90	3.25	0.90	525	455	586	4.1	2.8	8.6	3.1	60%	9%	51	20	30	20%	88%	15%	0	17			33	1.28	18.0	109	130	$12
16 HOU	1	2	12	64	69	2.25	2.91	1.05	560	513	603	3.9	2.1	9.7	4.6	64%	14%	58	17	25	31%	80%	7%	0	16			80	1.17	15.3	154	183	$11
17 HOU	3	2	2	45	52	2.98	3.05	0.97	613	606	619	3.8	1.4	10.3	7.4	60%	14%	48	16	35	28%	78%	17%	0	15			50	1.33	7.7	174	209	$4
1st Half	2	2	2	34	39	2.94	3.13	0.92	599	591	605	3.9	1.3	10.4	7.8	61%	13%	45	14	40	27%	77%	15%	0	15			50	1.56	5.9	175	210	$7
2nd Half	1	0	0	12	13	3.09	2.84	1.11	654	667	650	3.6	1.5	10.0	6.5	56%	16%	56	22	22	31%	82%	29%	0	14			0	0.75	1.8	173	208	-$3
18 Proj	3	3	2	58	65	2.46	3.20	1.03	593	532	644	3.9	2.3	10.1	4.4	61%	13%	50	18	32	28%	81%	13%	0						13.6	147	178	$7

Harvey,Matt

Age: 29	Th: R	Role SP	Health F	LIMA Plan D+
Ht: 6' 4"	Wt: 215	Type Pwr	PT/Exp B	Rand Var +5
			Consist C	MM 0101

Velocity, Dom, FpK, and SwK all in meltdown, imploding Ctl, more shoulder problems... seems safe to say that return from thoracic outlet syndrome did not go well. At a time when his career should be at its peak, his future is now an open question. Best to stay away until skills have been reestablished.

Yr Tm	W	L	Sv	IP	K	ERA	xERA	WHIP	oOPS	vL	vR	BF/G	Ctl	Dom	Cmd	FpK	SwK	G	L	F	H%	S%	hr/f	GS	APC	DOM%	DIS%	Sv%	LI	RAR	BPV	BPX	R$
13 NYM	9	5	0	178	191	2.27	2.73	0.93	530	456	603	26.5	1.6	9.6	6.2	64%	13%	48	20	33	29%	76%	5%	26	104	65%	4%			35.1	157	205	$28
14																																	
15 NYM	13	8	0	189	188	2.71	3.25	1.02	609	676	544	26.0	1.8	8.9	5.1	68%	12%	46	18	36	29%	78%	10%	29	96	55%	14%			29.2	137	164	$26
16 NYM	4	10	0	93	76	4.86	4.36	1.47	797	864	724	23.6	2.4	7.4	3.0	66%	11%	41	25	34	36%	67%	8%	17	89	18%	41%			-7.6	86	103	-$5
17 NYM	5	7	0	93	67	6.70	5.59	1.69	890	1025	774	22.7	4.6	6.5	1.4	58%	8%	43	23	34	31%	65%	21%	18	89	0%	61%	0	0.79	-26.8	15	18	-$13
1st Half	4	3	0	70	54	5.25	5.15	1.45	801	904	708	23.8	4.5	6.9	1.5	61%	9%	45	21	34	26%	71%	22%	13	94	0%	46%			-7.7	27	32	-$9
2nd Half	1	4	0	22	13	11.28	7.05	2.46	1125	1365	934	20.2	4.8	5.2	1.1	51%	6%	38	28	34	43%	54%	17%	5	77	0%	100%	0	0.79	-19.1	-21	-25	-$27
18 Proj	6	11	0	109	86	5.29	4.99	1.60	841	944	745	22.0	3.4	7.1	2.1	60%	9%	42	24	34	34%	70%	14%	22						-12.5	57	69	-$8

Hatcher,Chris

Age: 33	Th: R	Role RP	Health F	LIMA Plan C
Ht: 6' 1"	Wt: 200	Type Pwr FB	PT/Exp D	Rand Var 0
			Consist B	MM 1300

Oblique injury, inflated hr/f ruined his 2016, and while he picked up where he left off Cmd-wise, rise in FB% did him no favors. 2nd half skill decline likely caused by shoulder inflammation that lingered from June into Aug. Had great skills in 2014-15, but we're two seasons and two injuries removed from that upside.

Yr Tm	W	L	Sv	IP	K	ERA	xERA	WHIP	oOPS	vL	vR	BF/G	Ctl	Dom	Cmd	FpK	SwK	G	L	F	H%	S%	hr/f	GS	APC	DOM%	DIS%	Sv%	LI	RAR	BPV	BPX	R$
13 MIA *	4	4	33	76	56	5.88	6.43	1.84	961	1130	876	5.3	4.3	6.6	1.5	66%	7%	35	29	35	37%	69%	9%	0	26			92	0.62	-18.9	28	36	$0
14 MIA *	1	5	5	78	78	3.07	3.27	1.18	666	641	687	4.7	2.1	9.0	4.3	66%	11%	47	20	33	32%	76%	8%	0	18			50	0.99	6.5	129	153	$4
15 LA	3	5	4	39	45	3.69	3.47	1.23	685	688	682	3.4	3.0	10.4	3.5	60%	13%	43	18	39	32%	73%	10%	0	13			67	1.18	1.3	127	151	$1
16 LA	5	4	0	41	43	5.53	4.47	1.50	819	482	1028	4.9	4.6	9.5	2.0	60%	10%	44	17	38	31%	68%	18%	0	21			0	0.97	-6.7	68	81	-$4
17 2 TM	1	2	1	60	63	4.22	4.50	1.32	737	706	756	5.2	3.2	9.5	3.0	63%	13%	33	21	46	31%	74%	13%	0	21			20	0.80	1.0	97	116	-$1
1st Half	0	1	0	37	43	4.66	4.35	1.34	769	695	819	6.1	2.9	10.6	3.6	66%	14%	27	22	51	33%	71%	13%	0	25			0	0.42	-1.4	115	138	-$2
2nd Half	1	1	1	23	20	3.52	4.73	1.30	685	725	664	4.3	3.5	7.8	2.2	58%	12%	41	21	38	29%	78%	12%	0	16			25	1.21	2.4	65	78	$0
18 Proj	3	3	0	44	44	4.38	4.41	1.37	747	655	804	4.4	3.6	9.2	2.6	61%	12%	40	19	41	31%	73%	14%	0						-0.1	86	104	-$2

Heaney,Andrew

Age: 27	Th: L	Role SP	Health F	LIMA Plan B+
Ht: 6' 2"	Wt: 195	Type FB	PT/Exp D	Rand Var +5
			Consist F	MM 0201

1-2, 7.06 ERA in 22 IP at LAA. Recovery from TJS kept him out until July, shoulder impingement ended season in early Sept, but in between, made 5 MLB starts with 11.2 Dom. Has yet to throw more than 106 IP in an MLB season and his career xERA is 4.40. Speculate if you must, but just keep it to the end game.

Yr Tm	W	L	Sv	IP	K	ERA	xERA	WHIP	oOPS	vL	vR	BF/G	Ctl	Dom	Cmd	FpK	SwK	G	L	F	H%	S%	hr/f	GS	APC	DOM%	DIS%	Sv%	LI	RAR	BPV	BPX	R$
13 aa	4	1	0	34	20	3.65	3.83	1.34				23.3	2.5	5.3	2.1						31%	73%								0.9	61	79	-$2
14 MIA *	9	9	0	167	139	3.89	3.59	1.22	847	611	944	21.7	2.2	7.5	3.4	60%	10%	45	19	35	31%	70%	18%	5	68	0%	60%	0	0.66	-3.1	95	113	$5
15 LAA *	12	6	0	184	141	3.94	3.92	1.35	679	568	723	24.0	2.5	6.9	2.8	62%	9%	38	22	40	33%	71%	7%	18	91	22%	28%			0.5	84	100	$4
16 LAA	0	1	0	6	7	6.00	3.11	1.17	840	833	842	25.0	0.0	10.5	0.0	60%	14%	44	17	39	34%	60%	29%	1	87	0%	0%			-1.3	211	251	-$4
17 LAA *	2	3	0	39	39	5.36	7.11	1.50	1108	780	1184	21.1	3.0	8.9	3.0	61%	14%	30	22	48	31%	79%	40%	5	83	0%	60%			-4.8	17	21	-$5
1st Half																																	
2nd Half	2	3	0	39	39	5.36	7.11	1.50	1108	780	1184	21.1	3.0	8.9	3.0	61%	14%	30	22	48	31%	79%	40%	5	83	0%	60%			-4.8	17	21	-$5
18 Proj	8	6	0	116	97	4.31	4.80	1.35	755	639	789	22.2	2.5	7.5	3.0	61%	12%	33	22	44	31%	73%	12%	22						0.7	78	94	$1

Hellickson,Jeremy

Age: 31	Th: R	Role SP	Health D	LIMA Plan C
Ht: 6' 1"	Wt: 190	Type FB	PT/Exp A	Rand Var +1
			Consist B	MM 0103

When skill decline happens this suddenly and sharply, you start looking for explanations. No DL time, but suffered forearm cramp in April, back tightness in May, calf tightness in July, back issue again in Sept. So give him a pass on lousy season while keeping in mind that he wasn't exactly Kershaw prior to 2017.

Yr Tm	W	L	Sv	IP	K	ERA	xERA	WHIP	oOPS	vL	vR	BF/G	Ctl	Dom	Cmd	FpK	SwK	G	L	F	H%	S%	hr/f	GS	APC	DOM%	DIS%	Sv%	LI	RAR	BPV	BPX	R$
13 TAM	12	10	0	174	135	5.17	4.16	1.35	775	785	763	23.0	2.6	7.0	2.7	60%	10%	40	20	40	31%	64%	11%	31	90	16%	42%	0	1.04	-28.0	74	96	-$4
14 TAM *	2	9	0	88	75	5.36	6.12	1.71	759	585	966	21.1	2.7	7.7	2.8	63%	10%	36	23	41	40%	69%	10%	13	91	8%	46%			-17.6	67	79	-$12
15 ARI	9	12	0	146	121	4.62	4.22	1.33	781	790	774	23.6	2.7	7.5	2.8	63%	11%	42	21	36	31%	69%	13%	27	92	11%	37%			-11.9	83	98	-$1
16 PHI	12	10	0	189	154	3.71	4.02	1.15	709	751	672	24.1	2.1	7.3	3.4	61%	11%	41	25	34	28%	72%	13%	32	91	34%	31%			11.1	93	111	$15
17 2 TM	8	11	0	164	96	5.43	5.36	1.26	808	819	800	23.2	2.6	5.3	2.0	59%	9%	35	21	44	25%	63%	15%	30	87	10%	50%			-21.7	38	46	-$2
1st Half	5	5	0	96	49	4.48	5.48	1.27	812	796	825	23.9	2.5	4.6	1.8	58%	8%	36	20	44	26%	71%	13%	17	90	12%	59%			-1.5	29	34	-$3
2nd Half	3	6	0	68	47	6.78	5.19	1.26	803	845	761	22.2	2.7	6.3	2.4	61%	9%	33	23	44	25%	50%	18%	13	84	8%	38%			-20.2	52	62	-$8
18 Proj	9	11	0	160	118	4.86	4.79	1.30	796	808	786	22.5	2.5	6.6	2.7	61%	10%	37	22	40	29%	68%	14%	29						-9.8	68	81	$0

BRANDON KRUSE

Hembree,Heath

Age: 29	Th: R	Role RP	Health B	LIMA Plan C
Ht: 6' 4"	Wt: 210	Type Pwr	PT/Exp D	Rand Var +1
			Consist A	MM 1300

Dom, SwK have risen with shift to fewer FB, more sliders, and that has led to higher-leverage IP. Also made 2017 gains vL (4.2 Cmd) that were buried by 50% hit rate. But 2nd half loss of control, though offset by high S%, continued to leave xERA out to dry. Odds are this is as good as it gets, and it ain't enough.

Yr Tm	W	L	Sv	IP	K	ERA	xERA	WHIP	oOPS	vL	vR	BF/G	Ctl	Dom	Cmd	FpK	SwK	G	L	F	H%	S%	hr/f	GS	APC	DOM%	DIS%	Sv%	LI	RAR	BPV	BPX	R
13 SF *	1	4	31	63	64	3.40	3.40	1.21	392	375	396	4.0	2.4	9.2	3.9	55%	17%	53	13	33	32%	74%	0%	0	15			86	0.37	3.6	119	155	$1
14 BOS *	1	4	20	56	50	4.80	5.40	1.62	846	962	799	4.6	3.9	8.1	2.0	75%	10%	28	22	50	36%	72%	6%	0	29			83	0.81	-7.3	56	66	$
15 BOS *	2	5	8	57	40	3.47	4.06	1.33	795	862	741	4.6	3.3	6.4	2.0	63%	9%	27	25	48	29%	77%	13%	0	18			73	0.45	3.5	54	64	$
16 BOS	4	1	0	51	47	2.65	4.53	1.33	695	890	591	5.9	3.0	8.3	2.8	59%	10%	36	24	40	32%	85%	10%	0	23			0	0.93	9.7	82	98	$
17 BOS	2	3	0	62	70	3.63	4.05	1.45	803	803	803	4.4	2.6	10.2	3.9	61%	15%	39	21	41	37%	81%	14%	0	18			0	1.18	5.6	129	155	-$
1st Half	0	2	0	37	38	3.65	4.10	1.41	796	869	776	4.4	1.7	9.2	5.4	64%	14%	42	17	42	37%	80%	13%	0	18			0	1.29	3.2	140	168	-$
2nd Half	2	1	0	25	32	3.60	4.00	1.52	813	742	852	4.4	4.0	11.5	2.9	57%	16%	34	28	38	37%	82%	16%	0	18			0	1.00	2.3	112	135	$
18 Proj	**3**	**3**	**0**	**58**	**59**	**3.72**	**4.33**	**1.38**	**734**	**801**	**702**	**4.6**	**3.1**	**9.2**	**3.0**	**60%**	**13%**	**37**	**23**	**40**	**33%**	**78%**	**12%**	**0**						**4.6**	**97**	**117**	**-$**

Hendricks,Kyle

Age: 28	Th: R	Role SP	Health D	LIMA Plan B
Ht: 6' 3"	Wt: 190	Type Pwr	PT/Exp A	Rand Var -1
			Consist A	MM 2205

xERA shows this was another season with soft skills aided by a high strand rate. Hand tendinitis cost him six weeks and some 1st half skills, but even when healthy, can't seem to get over Dom/SwK hump that puts cap on growth. Last two ERAs create risk that someone will overpay and get burnt; don't let it be you.

Yr Tm	W	L	Sv	IP	K	ERA	xERA	WHIP	oOPS	vL	vR	BF/G	Ctl	Dom	Cmd	FpK	SwK	G	L	F	H%	S%	hr/f	GS	APC	DOM%	DIS%	Sv%	LI	RAR	BPV	BPX	R
13 a/a	13	4	0	166	106	2.46	3.17	1.22				24.9	1.9	5.7	2.9						31%	80%								28.9	90	117	$1
14 CHC *	17	7	0	183	127	3.45	3.42	1.23	610	584	633	24.7	1.9	6.3	3.3	64%	8%	48	19	33	31%	72%	5%	13	89	31%	23%			6.5	94	112	$1
15 CHC	8	7	0	180	167	3.95	3.28	1.16	677	797	580	23.1	2.2	8.4	3.9	63%	9%	51	22	27	30%	68%	13%	32	87	31%	22%			0.3	121	144	$
16 CHC	16	8	0	190	170	2.13	3.48	0.98	581	616	555	24.0	2.1	8.1	3.9	68%	10%	48	20	31	26%	82%	9%	30	93	33%	7%	0	0.76	48.2	115	136	$3
17 CHC	7	5	0	140	123	3.03	3.85	1.19	670	706	639	23.8	2.6	7.9	3.1	63%	9%	50	21	29	29%	80%	15%	24	95	21%	17%			22.9	101	121	$1
1st Half	4	3	0	62	51	4.09	4.08	1.20	686	681	690	23.0	3.1	7.4	2.4	62%	8%	51	20	29	26%	71%	18%	11	93	18%	36%			2.1	80	96	$
2nd Half	3	2	0	78	72	2.19	3.68	1.18	658	722	592	24.4	2.2	8.3	3.8	64%	10%	49	22	29	31%	87%	13%	13	97	23%	0%			20.8	118	141	$1
18 Proj	**12**	**8**	**0**	**189**	**167**	**3.13**	**3.75**	**1.14**	**649**	**693**	**611**	**23.3**	**2.3**	**8.0**	**3.5**	**65%**	**9%**	**50**	**21**	**30**	**29%**	**76%**	**12%**	**32**						**28.5**	**109**	**131**	**$2**

Hendriks,Liam

Age: 29	Th: R	Role RP	Health C	LIMA Plan A
Ht: 6' 0"	Wt: 200	Type Pwr	PT/Exp C	Rand Var 0
			Consist A	MM 2400

ERA/xERA keep rising as walks multiply thanks to fewer FpK, and 2nd half xERA shows how it could get worse. Probably won't sink that low, as skill trends rarely continue in a neat line, but it likely means 2015 was his peak. Grade "A" LIMA status could be ending soon.

Yr Tm	W	L	Sv	IP	K	ERA	xERA	WHIP	oOPS	vL	vR	BF/G	Ctl	Dom	Cmd	FpK	SwK	G	L	F	H%	S%	hr/f	GS	APC	DOM%	DIS%	Sv%	LI	RAR	BPV	BPX	R
13 MIN *	5	11	0	146	84	5.83	5.73	1.55	907	929	879	24.5	1.8	5.2	2.9	59%	9%	37	22	42	35%	63%	14%	8	89	0%	63%	0	0.64	-35.3	49	63	-$1
14 2AL *	13	4	0	176	121	3.18	3.21	1.13	786	814	762	21.7	1.0	6.2	6.2	70%	8%	39	25	37	31%	72%	8%	6	61	17%	50%	0	0.75	12.2	153	183	$1
15 TOR	5	0	0	65	71	2.92	2.95	1.08	605	746	499	4.5	1.5	9.9	6.5	69%	12%	46	23	31	33%	73%	5%	0	18			0	0.91	8.3	161	191	$
16 OAK	0	4	0	65	71	3.76	3.67	1.28	704	608	766	5.2	1.9	9.9	5.1	65%	12%	40	21	39	36%	73%	8%	0	20			0	0.95	3.4	143	170	$
17 OAK	4	2	1	64	78	4.22	3.80	1.25	663	634	680	3.9	3.2	11.0	3.4	60%	13%	42	19	39	33%	68%	10%	0	17			25	1.03	1.1	130	156	$
1st Half	3	1	0	34	45	4.81	3.32	1.34	686	764	625	4.4	2.9	12.0	4.1	59%	14%	51	16	33	38%	66%	13%	0	18			0	0.98	-1.9	166	199	$
2nd Half	1	1	1	30	33	3.56	4.31	1.15	634	427	735	3.5	3.6	9.8	2.8	62%	12%	31	23	46	28%	72%	8%	0	15			50	1.07	3.0	89	107	$
18 Proj	**3**	**2**	**0**	**65**	**72**	**3.86**	**3.89**	**1.26**	**675**	**654**	**690**	**4.5**	**2.8**	**9.9**	**3.5**	**61%**	**12%**	**40**	**21**	**39**	**33%**	**71%**	**9%**	**0**						**4.0**	**120**	**145**	**$**

Hernandez,David

Age: 33	Th: R	Role RP	Health F	LIMA Plan B+
Ht: 6' 3"	Wt: 245	Type Pwr FB	PT/Exp D	Rand Var -1
			Consist A	MM 1300

Lowest ERA, highest BPV since 2012, best Cmd of career—is he all the way back from TJS? Not so fast: FpK doesn't support pinpoint Ctl, hr/f helped supress ERA, and 2nd half Dom loss with no known injury adds a perplexing wrinkle. He's skilled enough to keep getting work, not skilled enough to offer any upside.

Yr Tm	W	L	Sv	IP	K	ERA	xERA	WHIP	oOPS	vL	vR	BF/G	Ctl	Dom	Cmd	FpK	SwK	G	L	F	H%	S%	hr/f	GS	APC	DOM%	DIS%	Sv%	LI	RAR	BPV	BPX	R
13 ARI	5	6	2	62	66	4.48	3.85	1.19	702	847	578	4.2	3.5	9.5	2.8	63%	13%	32	21	47	27%	67%	13%	0	17			25	1.14	-4.7	88	115	$
14																																	
15 ARI	1	5	0	34	33	4.28	3.94	1.31	778	739	803	3.6	2.9	8.8	3.0	55%	11%	39	19	41	30%	74%	15%	0	15			0	0.86	-1.3	96	115	-$
16 PHI	3	4	1	73	80	3.84	4.24	1.50	785	852	730	4.6	4.0	9.9	2.5	58%	12%	37	25	38	35%	80%	14%	0	18			33	0.85	3.1	86	103	-$
17 2 TM	3	1	2	55	52	3.11	3.66	1.04	611	618	605	3.3	1.5	8.5	5.8	59%	13%	43	17	40	30%	72%	7%	0	12			50	0.89	8.5	134	161	$
1st Half	0	0	1	26	29	2.10	3.17	0.94	516	539	496	3.5	1.8	10.2	5.8	61%	15%	46	11	43	30%	75%	0%	0	13			50	0.70	7.1	160	191	$
2nd Half	3	1	1	29	23	3.99	4.11	1.13	688	680	694	3.3	1.2	7.1	5.8	58%	12%	41	20	39	30%	69%	11%	0	12			50	1.04	1.3	113	135	$
18 Proj	**3**	**3**	**0**	**58**	**57**	**3.67**	**4.23**	**1.27**	**706**	**741**	**679**	**3.7**	**3.0**	**8.9**	**3.0**	**59%**	**12%**	**40**	**20**	**41**	**31%**	**75%**	**11%**	**0**						**4.9**	**98**	**118**	**$**

Hernandez,Felix

Age: 32	Th: R	Role SP	Health F	LIMA Plan B+
Ht: 6' 3"	Wt: 225	Type Pwr	PT/Exp A	Rand Var +4
			Consist B	MM 2203

Has been shell of former self for a while now, but after posting zero RAR, might be downgraded to ghost. With April groin tightness and two bouts of shoulder bursitis, it's possible he didn't pitch a single healthy inning all year. BPV, Cmd rebounds suggest there's still life in his skills, just not enough for a full recovery.

Yr Tm	W	L	Sv	IP	K	ERA	xERA	WHIP	oOPS	vL	vR	BF/G	Ctl	Dom	Cmd	FpK	SwK	G	L	F	H%	S%	hr/f	GS	APC	DOM%	DIS%	Sv%	LI	RAR	BPV	BPX	R
13 SEA	12	10	0	204	216	3.04	2.83	1.13	643	671	610	26.5	2.0	9.5	4.7	62%	11%	51	21	27	32%	75%	10%	31	102	61%	13%			20.8	146	190	$2
14 SEA	15	6	0	236	248	2.14	2.54	0.92	546	519	584	26.8	1.8	9.5	5.4	65%	13%	56	18	26	27%	80%	10%	34	101	65%	9%			46.7	157	187	$3
15 SEA	18	9	0	202	191	3.53	3.25	1.18	682	699	665	26.6	2.6	8.5	3.3	63%	11%	56	17	27	29%	74%	15%	31	98	61%	16%			10.8	118	140	$1
16 SEA	11	8	0	153	122	3.82	4.35	1.32	718	739	702	26.2	3.8	7.2	1.9	59%	10%	50	21	29	28%	75%	15%	25	98	16%	40%			7.1	54	64	$
17 SEA	6	5	0	87	78	4.36	4.02	1.29	791	854	743	23.0	2.7	8.1	3.0	61%	10%	47	23	30	29%	74%	22%	16	86	13%	31%			0.0	98	118	$
1st Half	3	2	0	39	33	4.66	3.90	1.53	916	770	1044	24.0	1.6	7.7	4.7	64%	9%	48	25	27	36%	78%	27%	7	85	14%	14%			-1.4	120	144	-$
2nd Half	3	3	0	48	45	4.13	4.13	1.10	681	940	506	22.2	3.6	8.4	2.4	59%	11%	46	21	33	22%	69%	19%	9	87	11%	44%			1.4	79	95	$
18 Proj	**11**	**8**	**0**	**160**	**143**	**3.91**	**3.97**	**1.25**	**732**	**774**	**698**	**23.8**	**2.9**	**8.1**	**2.8**	**61%**	**10%**	**50**	**21**	**29**	**29%**	**74%**	**18%**	**27**						**8.8**	**94**	**114**	**$1**

Herrera,Kelvin

Age: 28	Th: R	Role RP	Health A	LIMA Plan B
Ht: 5' 10"	Wt: 200	Type Pwr	PT/Exp C	Rand Var +1
			Consist C	MM 2320

Left game with forearm tightness on 8/22, but judging by stark difference between 1st/2nd half Ctl, sure looks like issue began in July. Note that this particular injury is often a precursor to TJS. Note also that he posted a pedestrian 5.6 Dom in Sept. Maybe he's fine; maybe you can also find less risky saves.

Yr Tm	W	L	Sv	IP	K	ERA	xERA	WHIP	oOPS	vL	vR	BF/G	Ctl	Dom	Cmd	FpK	SwK	G	L	F	H%	S%	hr/f	GS	APC	DOM%	DIS%	Sv%	LI	RAR	BPV	BPX	R
13 KC *	5	8	4	76	96	3.23	2.90	1.09	701	738	661	4.2	3.2	11.3	3.5	56%	15%	48	18	34	28%	76%	18%	0	17			67	1.19	6.0	121	157	$
14 KC	4	3	0	70	59	1.41	3.43	1.14	561	617	508	4.1	3.3	7.6	2.3	55%	13%	49	27	24	28%	86%	0%	0	16			0	1.14	20.1	73	87	$
15 KC	4	3	0	70	64	2.71	3.79	1.12	578	470	677	4.0	3.4	8.3	2.5	61%	14%	45	23	33	26%	78%	8%	0	15			0	1.17	10.7	81	97	$
16 KC	2	6	12	72	86	2.75	2.86	0.96	590	557	625	3.9	1.5	10.8	7.2	65%	16%	44	23	33	30%	75%	10%	0	15			80	1.22	12.8	175	208	$1
17 KC	3	3	26	59	56	4.25	4.30	1.35	784	840	720	4.0	3.0	8.5	2.8	60%	12%	48	18	34	31%	73%	15%	0	16			84	1.09	0.8	97	116	$1
1st Half	1	2	18	32	31	4.78	3.92	1.28	829	841	814	4.1	1.7	8.7	5.2	63%	13%	43	22	34	32%	71%	21%	0	15			90	1.10	-1.7	133	159	$1
2nd Half	2	1	8	27	25	3.62	4.78	1.43	728	835	603	4.0	4.6	8.2	1.8	57%	11%	52	13	34	31%	76%	7%	0	16			73	1.08	2.5	54	65	$
18 Proj	**3**	**3**	**22**	**58**	**57**	**3.37**	**3.89**	**1.20**	**684**	**705**	**661**	**3.8**	**2.9**	**8.8**	**3.0**	**60%**	**13%**	**47**	**20**	**33**	**30%**	**75%**	**11%**	**0**						**7.1**	**104**	**125**	**$1**

Hildenberger,Trevor

Age: 27	Th: R	Role RP	Health A	LIMA Plan A
Ht: 6' 2"	Wt: 211	Type Pwr xGB	PT/Exp F	Rand Var +2
			Consist F	MM 4210

1 Sv, 3.21 ERA in 42 IP at MIN. Never a big prospect due to low-90s FB, but deceptive sidearm delivery adds intriguing wrinkle, and Ctl/Dom output had FpK/SwK support. Add in GB%, and as 2nd half xERA, BPV show, he can be electric. While 42 MLB IP isn't a definitive sample, it's enough to speculate... UP: 30 Sv

Yr Tm	W	L	Sv	IP	K	ERA	xERA	WHIP	oOPS	vL	vR	BF/G	Ctl	Dom	Cmd	FpK	SwK	G	L	F	H%	S%	hr/f	GS	APC	DOM%	DIS%	Sv%	LI	RAR	BPV	BPX	R
13																																	
14																																	
15																																	
16 aa	2	3	16	39	34	0.98	1.73	0.86				4.5	1.5	7.9	5.2						25%	95%								15.3	155	184	$1
17 MIN *	5	4	7	73	70	3.28	3.76	1.26	664	637	680	5.1	1.9	8.7	4.5	65%	12%	59	18	24	34%	76%	15%	0	17			70	1.06	9.6	127	152	$
1st Half	2	1	6	34	29	3.07	4.57	1.53	580	500	629	6.4	3.1	7.7	2.5	46%	10%	88	13	0	37%	80%	0%	0	29			86	0.14	5.3	83	99	$
2nd Half	3	3	1	39	41	3.46	2.83	1.03	670	651	681	4.5	0.9	9.5	10.3	66%	12%	57	18	25	32%	69%	15%	0	16			33	1.12	4.3	180	216	$
18 Proj	**3**	**3**	**4**	**51**	**47**	**2.92**	**3.36**	**1.10**	**602**	**598**	**604**	**4.8**	**1.8**	**8.4**	**4.7**	**66%**	**12%**	**57**	**18**	**25**	**30%**	**76%**	**10%**	**0**						**9.0**	**138**	**166**	**$**

BRANDON KRUSE

Hill,Rich

Age: 38	Th: L	Role	RP	Health	F	LIMA Plan	C+
Ht: 6' 5"	Wt: 220	Type	Pwr FB	PT/Exp	C	Rand Var	0
				Consist	A	MM	2503

First half was marred by stubborn blister issue, but there's little in 2nd half line that isn't repeatable within established skill set. So only things standing between him and another productive season are luck, health, and vagaries of age. (A statement that's true for all of us, really.) If planets align... UP: 15 wins, 3.00 ERA

Yr Tm	W	L	Sv	IP	K	ERA	xERA	WHIP	oOPS	vL	vR	BF/G	Ctl	Dom	Cmd	FpK	SwK	G	L	F	H%	S%	hr/f	GS	APC	DOM%	DIS%	Sv%	LI	RAR	BPV	BPX	R$
13 CLE	1	2	0	39	51	6.28	4.13	1.73	719	696	749	2.9	6.8	11.9	1.8	48%	10%	42	20	38	38%	63%	8%	0	12			0	1.28	-11.5	51	67	-$8
14 2AL *	3	3	2	48	50	3.69	3.51	1.51	801	679	1125	4.6	4.9	9.3	1.9	41%	14%	38	31	31	35%	73%	0%	0	7			67	1.07	0.3	100	119	-$2
15 BOS *	7	5	0	83	81	3.53	3.57	1.36	410	358	423	10.2	4.6	8.8	1.9	61%	12%	48	16	35	29%	76%	9%	4	109	50%	0%			4.4	77	92	$2
16 2 TM	12	5	0	110	129	2.12	3.18	1.00	530	522	532	22.0	2.7	10.5	3.9	60%	11%	45	19	36	29%	79%	4%	20	91	40%	10%			28.2	140	166	$20
17 LA	12	8	0	136	166	3.32	3.67	1.09	639	845	583	22.1	3.3	11.0	3.4	62%	12%	37	17	46	27%	75%	13%	25	89	28%	24%			17.4	125	151	$18
1st Half	5	4	0	54	61	4.00	4.54	1.35	690	843	656	21.1	4.8	10.2	2.1	59%	11%	38	13	49	29%	73%	9%	11	88	18%	27%			2.4	68	82	$3
2nd Half	7	4	0	82	105	2.87	3.14	0.92	602	846	525	22.9	2.2	11.6	5.3	64%	13%	36	20	43	26%	78%	15%	14	90	36%	21%			15.0	163	195	$28
18 Proj	11	7	0	131	152	3.57	3.76	1.14	622	713	587	12.1	3.4	10.5	3.1	60%	11%	41	18	41	29%	71%	10%	9						12.7	117	141	$13

Hoffman,Jeff

Age: 25	Th: R	Role	SP	Health	A	LIMA Plan	D+
Ht: 6' 5"	Wt: 225	Type	Pwr	PT/Exp	D	Rand Var	+5
				Consist	D	MM	0101

6-5, 5.89 ERA in 99 IP at COL. MLB success was short-lived: 2.33 ERA, 11.3 Dom, 11.3 Cmd, 13% SwK in first 27 IP; 7.22 ERA, 6.0 Dom, 1.3 Cmd, 8% SwK after. Has power arm with upside to dream on, but it can be a long road from prospect to star, and skills say he hasn't even found the on-ramp yet in the tough terrain.

Yr Tm	W	L	Sv	IP	K	ERA	xERA	WHIP	oOPS	vL	vR	BF/G	Ctl	Dom	Cmd	FpK	SwK	G	L	F	H%	S%	hr/f	GS	APC	DOM%	DIS%	Sv%	LI	RAR	BPV	BPX	R$
13																																	
14																																	
15 aa	2	2	0	48	29	4.02	3.44	1.20				21.4	2.4	5.5	2.3						28%	68%								-0.3	61	73	-$2
16 COL *	6	13	0	150	119	5.45	5.81	1.64	881	858	906	22.3	3.9	7.1	1.8	58%	7%	50	22	28	34%	69%	23%	6	70	17%	83%	0	0.61	-23.4	36	42	-$13
17 COL *	9	8	0	149	118	6.03	4.87	1.48	833	711	952	19.4	3.6	7.1	2.0	60%	9%	41	18	41	32%	60%	12%	16	70	31%	44%	0	0.59	-30.7	49	59	-$8
1st Half	7	3	0	86	73	4.50	3.50	1.28	638	466	826	22.1	2.9	7.6	2.6	66%	10%	38	19	43	31%	64%	6%	7	82	57%	29%	0	0.69	-1.5	87	104	$4
2nd Half	2	5	0	63	45	8.15	6.76	1.76	970	900	1031	16.9	4.6	6.4	1.4	57%	7%	43	17	40	33%	55%	16%	9	64	11%	56%	0	0.53	-29.3	4	5	-$26
18 Proj	3	5	0	73	57	5.36	5.05	1.54	824	748	900	20.1	3.7	7.0	1.9	59%	9%	45	19	36	33%	67%	12%	16						-8.9	49	59	-$7

Holder,Jonathan

Age: 25	Th: R	Role	RP	Health	A	LIMA Plan	C+
Ht: 6' 2"	Wt: 235	Type	Pwr FB	PT/Exp	F	Rand Var	0
				Consist	F	MM	2400

1-1, 3.89 ERA in 39 IP at NYY. Followed up 2016's cup of coffee with even more impressive FpK, SwK, which supported 5.0 MLB Cmd. Projected ceiling is setup role; early skills are strong but xERA urges some caution. Highish FB% really the only thing holder-ing him back. (Thank you, good night!)

Yr Tm	W	L	Sv	IP	K	ERA	xERA	WHIP	oOPS	vL	vR	BF/G	Ctl	Dom	Cmd	FpK	SwK	G	L	F	H%	S%	hr/f	GS	APC	DOM%	DIS%	Sv%	LI	RAR	BPV	BPX	R$
13																																	
14																																	
15																																	
16 NYY *	5	1	16	70	86	2.80	1.92	0.88	753	411	851	5.4	1.5	11.1	7.4	64%	11%	33	7	59	29%	71%	6%	0	18			94	0.88	12.0	216	257	$16
17 NYY *	1	1	1	55	58	3.43	4.89	1.45	770	967	709	4.8	2.7	9.4	3.5	67%	13%	42	18	40	37%	80%	11%	0	18			25	0.71	6.3	95	114	-$1
1st Half	1	1	0	33	33	3.78	4.14	1.38	776	1133	669	4.5	2.2	8.9	4.1	65%	13%	44	17	40	35%	78%	13%	0	17			0	0.67	2.4	124	148	-$1
2nd Half	0	0	1	22	25	2.91	4.77	1.56	733	143	926	5.7	3.6	10.1	2.8	81%	14%	33	28	39	39%	83%	0%	0	21			50	0.92	3.9	99	119	-$2
18 Proj	2	1	0	44	50	3.70	3.77	1.21	615	886	533	5.1	2.4	10.3	4.2	65%	13%	44	17	40	33%	74%	11%	0						3.5	140	169	-$1

Holland,Derek

Age: 31	Th: L	Role	SP	Health	F	LIMA Plan	D
Ht: 6' 2"	Wt: 215	Type	Pwr	PT/Exp	B	Rand Var	+3
				Consist	B	MM	0001

Injuries that have been steadily ruining career since 2014 struck what may be the final blow, demolishing Ctl, Cmd en route to one of the least valuable performances of 2017. His 2nd half R$ canceled out the value from Kenley Jansen's entire season. If that actually happened to you, we apologize. Too soon, right?

Yr Tm	W	L	Sv	IP	K	ERA	xERA	WHIP	oOPS	vL	vR	BF/G	Ctl	Dom	Cmd	FpK	SwK	G	L	F	H%	S%	hr/f	GS	APC	DOM%	DIS%	Sv%	LI	RAR	BPV	BPX	R$
13 TEX	10	9	0	213	189	3.42	3.78	1.29	711	671	722	27.1	2.7	8.0	3.0	63%	10%	41	23	36	32%	76%	9%	33	99	39%	21%			11.6	90	117	$10
14 TEX *	4	1	0	57	45	2.90	4.38	1.37	601	618	596	20.0	2.5	7.1	2.8	66%	10%	41	17	41	33%	82%	0%	5	95	80%	0%	0	0.66	5.9	74	89	$1
15 TEX	4	3	0	59	41	4.91	4.25	1.30	828	740	848	24.5	2.6	6.3	2.4	63%	7%	42	23	35	28%	68%	17%	10	91	20%	50%			-6.9	63	75	-$3
16 TEX	7	9	0	107	67	4.95	5.15	1.41	770	578	812	21.0	2.9	5.6	1.9	62%	8%	38	22	40	30%	68%	11%	20	83	15%	50%	0	0.74	-10.0	38	45	-$3
17 CHW	7	14	0	135	104	6.20	5.86	1.71	918	719	974	21.6	5.0	6.9	1.4	63%	7%	38	22	40	31%	69%	18%	26	85	15%	54%	0	0.69	-30.7	6	7	-$15
1st Half	5	8	0	88	76	4.52	4.89	1.47	834	533	902	24.1	3.7	7.8	2.1	64%	9%	39	22	39	31%	76%	16%	16	96	25%	38%			-1.7	58	69	-$5
2nd Half	2	6	0	47	28	9.32	7.94	2.15	1060	927	1111	18.5	7.4	5.3	0.7	62%	6%	35	22	42	32%	60%	19%	10	71	0%	80%	0	0.60	-29.0	-91	-109	-$34
18 Proj	6	9	0	102	71	5.98	5.74	1.62	883	748	921	20.8	4.3	6.3	1.4	63%	7%	38	22	40	31%	67%	15%	22						-20.4	12	14	-$11

Holland,Greg

Age: 32	Th: R	Role	RP	Health	B	LIMA Plan	C
Ht: 5' 10"	Wt: 205	Type	Pwr	PT/Exp	C	Rand Var	-1
				Consist	A	MM	3530

Disappointing 2nd half, but all the damage came in Aug (13.50 ERA, 7.7 Dom, 6.70 xERA), same month he had cut finger. Big leap in FB% made worse by Ctl that refused to fall in line with FpK, and while Dom, SwK remain strong, BPV confirms he's not lights-out closer he used to be. Adjust expectations accordingly.

Yr Tm	W	L	Sv	IP	K	ERA	xERA	WHIP	oOPS	vL	vR	BF/G	Ctl	Dom	Cmd	FpK	SwK	G	L	F	H%	S%	hr/f	GS	APC	DOM%	DIS%	Sv%	LI	RAR	BPV	BPX	R$
13 KC	2	1	47	67	103	1.21	2.10	0.87	479	512	439	3.8	2.4	13.8	5.7	58%	17%	39	27	33	30%	89%	7%	0	16			94	1.34	22.0	201	262	$31
14 KC	1	3	46	62	90	1.44	2.29	0.91	472	494	444	3.7	2.9	13.0	4.5	57%	15%	48	17	35	28%	87%	7%	0	15			96	1.21	17.7	182	217	$26
15 KC	3	2	32	45	49	3.83	3.88	1.46	692	777	615	4.0	5.2	9.9	1.9	63%	15%	49	22	29	32%	73%	6%	0	15			86	1.23	0.7	63	75	$11
16																																	
17 COL	3	6	41	57	70	3.61	3.90	1.15	623	533	721	3.9	4.1	11.0	2.7	61%	16%	42	13	45	26%	73%	11%	0	14			91	1.33	5.3	108	129	$20
1st Half	1	0	26	30	40	1.48	3.50	0.99	492	425	569	3.7	4.2	11.9	2.9	62%	17%	40	13	48	25%	86%	3%	0	13			96	1.36	10.8	119	143	$30
2nd Half	2	6	15	27	30	6.00	4.37	1.33	752	646	860	4.1	4.0	10.0	2.5	60%	15%	43	14	43	28%	60%	19%	0	16			83	1.30	-5.5	93	112	$10
18 Proj	3	5	36	58	72	3.39	3.56	1.15	616	589	645	3.7	3.7	11.2	3.0	61%	15%	44	17	38	29%	73%	11%	0						6.9	123	149	$18

Holmberg,David

Age: 26	Th: L	Role	RP	Health	A	LIMA Plan	D
Ht: 6' 3"	Wt: 245	Type	FB	PT/Exp	D	Rand Var	-1
				Consist	D	MM	0000

2-4, 4.68 ERA in 58 IP at CHW. Looking for an arm that consistently delivers negative value? There's one right here! Not a single viable skill in sight! You get more walks than Ks in 120 MLB IP, with a 6.36 xERA! No risk of a DOMinant start, ever. Call now, and we'll throw in Grade-A Health for FREE! Hurry, while supplies last!

Yr Tm	W	L	Sv	IP	K	ERA	xERA	WHIP	oOPS	vL	vR	BF/G	Ctl	Dom	Cmd	FpK	SwK	G	L	F	H%	S%	hr/f	GS	APC	DOM%	DIS%	Sv%	LI	RAR	BPV	BPX	R$
13 ARI *	5	8	0	161	99	3.74	4.29	1.40	950	1100	900	25.2	3.0	5.5	1.8	55%	5%	25	25	50	31%	75%	0%	1	80	0%	100%			2.5	47	61	-$1
14 CIN *	4	8	0	123	68	4.84	5.59	1.65	849	958	817	21.9	3.5	5.0	1.4	55%	9%	38	17	45	34%	72%	19%	5	74	0%	100%	0	0.62	-16.6	25	30	-$12
15 CIN *	8	11	0	149	77	6.11	7.18	1.82	1025	574	1173	25.5	3.7	4.7	1.3	53%	5%	40	18	42	35%	70%	24%	6	89	0%	67%			-39.4	-10	-11	-$24
16 a/a	8	9	0	169	90	4.72	4.60	1.42				25.6	2.5	4.8	1.9						32%	67%								-11.0	42	50	-$4
17 CHW *	5	5	0	90	53	4.24	5.44	1.53	890	861	904	8.3	4.3	5.3	1.2	57%	7%	43	17	40	28%	79%	15%	7	29	0%	57%	0	0.66	1.3	8	10	-$3
1st Half	4	2	0	54	33	2.79	3.13	1.16	647	495	700	9.3	3.6	5.5	1.5	58%	6%	44	16	41	23%	81%	10%	6	37	0%	50%	0	0.42	10.5	46	55	$6
2nd Half	1	3	0	36	20	6.43	8.92	2.08	1264	1192	1320	7.3	5.3	5.0	0.9	54%	8%	42	19	39	34%	76%	23%	1	22	0%	100%	0	0.86	-9.2	-43	-52	-$17
18 Proj	3	4	0	58	32	5.04	6.03	1.63	892	943	867	11.9	3.8	5.0	1.3	55%	8%	41	18	42	31%	74%	12%	4						-4.9	6	7	-$7

Honeywell,Brent

Age: 23	Th: R	Role	SP	Health	A	LIMA Plan	B+
Ht: 6' 2"	Wt: 180	Type	Pwr FB	PT/Exp	F	Rand Var	+3
				Consist	C	MM	2301

Top 50 prospect has been tearing through minors with elite Cmd of five-pitch repertoire, including highly-rated screwball. 1st half performance was undermined by H%, S%, but 2nd half BPV should have your attention. May not break camp in bigs, but seems likely to get the call in 2018.

Yr Tm	W	L	Sv	IP	K	ERA	xERA	WHIP	oOPS	vL	vR	BF/G	Ctl	Dom	Cmd	FpK	SwK	G	L	F	H%	S%	hr/f	GS	APC	DOM%	DIS%	Sv%	LI	RAR	BPV	BPX	R$
13																																	
14																																	
15																																	
16 aa	3	2	0	59	48	2.67	3.33	1.20				23.8	2.1	7.3	3.4						31%	80%								11.1	101	120	$3
17 a/a	13	9	0	137	154	4.40	4.59	1.41				22.2	2.4	10.2	4.2						38%	70%								-0.7	121	146	$5
1st Half	8	8	0	86	99	5.65	5.31	1.56				23.6	2.7	10.3	3.8						41%	64%								-13.8	107	129	$1
2nd Half	5	1	0	50	56	2.25	3.34	1.16				20.0	1.9	10.0	5.3						33%	85%								13.1	153	183	$13
18 Proj	7	4	0	87	87	3.52	4.10	1.24				22.1	2.2	9.0	4.2	60%	9%	35	23	42	33%	74%	8%	16						9.0	117	141	$5

BRANDON KRUSE

Hoyt,James

Age: 31	Th: R	Role RP	Health A	LIMA Plan C+
Ht: 6' 6"	Wt: 230	Type Pwr	PT/Exp D	Rand Var +5
			Consist C	MM 2410

Rode heavy use of slider to elite Dom, Cmd, then scaled back as it flattened out and he began tipping pitches. That might explain huge 2nd half shift in Cmd despite FpK, SwK stability. Snakebitten 1st half H%-S%-hr/f hid how good he was, so there's sleeper potential here, but skill uncertainty means end-game flyer only.

Yr Tm	W	L	Sv	IP	K	ERA	xERA	WHIP	oOPS	vL	vR	BF/G	Ctl	Dom	Cmd	FpK	SwK	G	L	F	H%	S%	hr/f	GS	APC	DOM%	DIS%	Sv%	LI	RAR	BPV	BPX	R$
13 aa	0	1	1	33	26	3.44	2.08	1.13				5.9	4.1	7.3	1.8						24%	68%								1.7	87	114	-$2
14 a/a	3	3	7	60	61	3.95	5.18	1.62				5.1	3.9	9.3	2.4						38%	77%								-1.5	76	91	-$1
15 aaa	0	1	9	49	50	4.06	4.07	1.42				4.4	2.1	9.3	4.3						39%	69%								-0.6	136	162	-$1
16 HOU *	5	4	29	77	100	2.84	2.53	1.09	707	702	709	4.2	3.5	11.7	3.3	62%	15%	54	17	29	28%	78%	33%	0	17			88	0.63	12.8	129	153	$20
17 HOU	1	0	0	49	66	4.38	3.30	1.32	748	796	703	4.9	2.6	12.0	4.7	63%	18%	41	23	36	38%	71%	15%	0	20			0	0.63	-0.1	167	200	-$2
1st Half	1	0	0	29	49	5.59	2.55	1.28	815	1012	643	5.2	1.9	15.2	8.2	61%	18%	40	19	40	43%	61%	22%	0	22			0	0.86	-4.4	242	290	-$2
2nd Half	0	0	0	20	17	2.66	4.62	1.38	651	518	792	4.6	3.5	7.5	2.1	64%	17%	41	28	31	32%	81%	5%	0	18			0	0.34	4.3	59	71	-$2
18 Proj	**1**	**1**	**2**	**58**	**67**	**3.60**	**3.73**	**1.29**	**671**	**660**	**682**	**4.6**	**3.0**	**10.4**	**3.4**	**63%**	**17%**	**41**	**24**	**35**	**34%**	**74%**	**10%**	**0**						**5.4**	**124**	**149**	**$1**

Hudson,Daniel

Age: 31	Th: R	Role RP	Health F	LIMA Plan C
Ht: 6' 3"	Wt: 225	Type Pwr	PT/Exp C	Rand Var 0
			Consist A	MM 1401

Cmd, xERA, BPV keep moving backwards as walks start to devour everything in their path. 2nd half Dom spike looks awfully fishy with no change in SwK, though pairing more Ks with GB% increase would be winning combo... again, if not for Ctl. If PIT pitching coach Ray Searage can't fix you, maybe you can't be fixed.

Yr Tm	W	L	Sv	IP	K	ERA	xERA	WHIP	oOPS	vL	vR	BF/G	Ctl	Dom	Cmd	FpK	SwK	G	L	F	H%	S%	hr/f	GS	APC	DOM%	DIS%	Sv%	LI	RAR	BPV	BPX	R$
13																																	
14 ARI	0	1	0	3	2	13.50	4.22	1.50	769	500	1200	4.3	0.0	6.8	0.0	54%	8%	45	18	36	42%	0%	0%	0	16			0	0.68	-3.2	145	172	-$4
15 ARI	4	3	4	68	71	3.86	3.78	1.32	691	624	743	4.5	3.3	9.4	2.8	57%	13%	43	22	35	32%	73%	10%	1	18	0%	0%	67	1.11	0.9	101	121	$1
16 ARI	3	2	5	60	58	5.22	4.23	1.44	753	791	719	3.8	3.3	8.7	2.6	56%	12%	40	28	32	34%	64%	10%	0	16			71	1.16	-7.7	85	101	-$2
17 PIT	2	7	0	62	66	4.38	4.46	1.46	761	799	727	3.8	4.8	9.6	2.0	56%	12%	43	21	36	32%	72%	12%	0	16			0	0.90	-0.2	64	77	-$3
1st Half	1	4	0	35	32	4.67	4.84	1.44	790	804	777	3.8	4.2	8.3	2.0	55%	13%	38	22	39	30%	73%	15%	0	15			0	0.85	-1.3	54	64	-$4
2nd Half	1	3	0	27	34	4.00	3.93	1.48	720	789	669	3.9	5.7	11.3	2.0	58%	12%	51	18	31	34%	72%	5%	0	16			0	0.97	1.2	80	96	-$2
18 Proj	**3**	**5**	**0**	**73**	**77**	**4.54**	**4.29**	**1.43**	**742**	**770**	**719**	**3.8**	**4.2**	**9.5**	**2.3**	**57%**	**12%**	**44**	**23**	**34**	**33%**	**69%**	**10%**	**0**						**-1.6**	**80**	**96**	**-$3**

Hughes,Jared

Age: 32	Th: R	Role RP	Health C	LIMA Plan B+
Ht: 6' 7"	Wt: 240	Type xGB	PT/Exp C	Rand Var 0
			Consist B	MM 1000

One-trick GB% pony managed to add more Ks, yet still didn't even raise Dom to league average level. Five years of S% fortune has allowed him to continually outperform xERA and earn some high leverage work, but things are gonna get ugly fast if that ever changes. Is this really the best use of your $1 bid?

Yr Tm	W	L	Sv	IP	K	ERA	xERA	WHIP	oOPS	vL	vR	BF/G	Ctl	Dom	Cmd	FpK	SwK	G	L	F	H%	S%	hr/f	GS	APC	DOM%	DIS%	Sv%	LI	RAR	BPV	BPX	R$
13 PIT *	3	3	2	55	39	2.99	4.11	1.51	786	967	664	5.0	3.8	6.4	1.7	58%	12%	56	20	23	33%	80%	8%	0	18			100	0.70	5.9	63	82	-$1
14 PIT	7	5	0	64	36	1.96	3.34	1.09	609	592	622	4.1	2.7	5.0	1.9	60%	11%	65	19	17	24%	85%	13%	0	14			0	1.09	14.1	62	74	$7
15 PIT	3	1	0	67	36	2.28	3.86	1.33	720	684	741	3.7	2.6	4.8	1.9	61%	10%	64	18	19	30%	84%	8%	0	13			0	1.14	13.9	60	72	$2
16 PIT	1	1	1	59	34	3.03	4.62	1.42	794	849	751	3.8	3.3	5.2	1.5	60%	10%	58	16	26	30%	82%	12%	0	14			33	0.72	8.5	39	46	-$1
17 MIL	5	3	1	60	48	3.02	3.73	1.22	723	912	628	3.6	3.6	7.2	2.0	57%	12%	62	19	19	27%	77%	13%	0	14			25	0.92	9.9	73	87	$4
1st Half	3	1	1	32	23	3.38	3.99	1.28	736	898	637	3.9	3.7	6.5	1.8	56%	11%	64	17	19	28%	74%	11%	0	15			25	0.75	3.9	60	71	$3
2nd Half	2	2	0	28	25	2.60	3.44	1.16	706	935	617	3.4	3.6	8.1	2.3	59%	13%	60	21	19	26%	80%	15%	0	13			0	1.09	6.0	88	105	$5
18 Proj	**4**	**3**	**0**	**65**	**46**	**3.08**	**4.19**	**1.35**	**777**	**896**	**709**	**3.7**	**3.3**	**6.3**	**1.9**	**59%**	**11%**	**61**	**18**	**21**	**30%**	**80%**	**13%**	**0**						**10.3**	**62**	**75**	**$1**

Hunter,Tommy

Age: 31	Th: R	Role RP	Health D	LIMA Plan B+
Ht: 6' 3"	Wt: 250	Type Pwr	PT/Exp D	Rand Var -2
			Consist B	MM 3300

Underwent two hernia surgeries prior to 2016, then fractured a vertebrae in back. Clean bill of health brought velocity back to upper 90s, mixing in more cutters and curves aided Dom. Got an assist from S%, so xERA says he's not a sub-3.00 ERA pitcher, but skills are reborn enough to be a usable bullpen piece.

Yr Tm	W	L	Sv	IP	K	ERA	xERA	WHIP	oOPS	vL	vR	BF/G	Ctl	Dom	Cmd	FpK	SwK	G	L	F	H%	S%	hr/f	GS	APC	DOM%	DIS%	Sv%	LI	RAR	BPV	BPX	R$
13 BAL	6	5	4	86	68	2.81	3.55	0.98	617	857	344	4.9	1.5	7.1	4.9	64%	11%	39	21	40	25%	78%	11%	0	19			67	1.09	11.2	105	137	$10
14 BAL	3	2	11	61	45	2.97	3.27	1.10	643	639	647	4.0	1.8	6.7	3.8	65%	8%	51	24	25	29%	75%	9%	0	14			65	1.16	5.8	101	120	$7
15 2 TM	4	2	1	60	47	4.18	3.93	1.24	711	754	674	4.3	2.1	7.0	3.4	66%	11%	45	21	35	30%	69%	11%	0	15			50	0.82	-1.6	93	111	-$1
16 2 AL *	4	3	1	49	30	3.67	4.23	1.34	678	715	656	4.3	1.9	5.4	2.8	65%	10%	50	25	26	32%	74%	4%	0	15			33	0.77	3.1	67	80	$0
17 TAM	3	5	1	59	64	2.61	3.31	0.97	588	501	649	3.7	2.1	9.8	4.6	65%	12%	44	21	35	27%	78%	12%	0	14			100	1.21	12.7	141	169	$7
1st Half	0	2	1	23	25	2.35	3.47	1.13	644	505	748	3.6	2.7	9.8	3.6	69%	11%	43	31	26	30%	83%	13%	0	15			100	1.05	5.7	123	147	$1
2nd Half	3	3	0	36	39	2.78	3.20	0.87	548	497	583	3.8	1.8	9.8	5.6	63%	14%	45	14	41	25%	74%	11%	0	14			0	1.34	7.0	153	183	$10
18 Proj	**4**	**4**	**0**	**58**	**58**	**3.14**	**3.57**	**1.11**	**657**	**641**	**668**	**4.0**	**2.1**	**9.0**	**4.4**	**65%**	**12%**	**46**	**22**	**32**	**30%**	**75%**	**11%**	**0**						**8.7**	**129**	**156**	**$3**

Iglesias,Raisel

Age: 28	Th: R	Role RP	Health D	LIMA Plan C
Ht: 6' 2"	Wt: 188	Type Pwr	PT/Exp C	Rand Var -3
			Consist A	MM 3431

Move to pen continues to suit him, with only fluky 2nd half LD, H% preventing more valuable season. Dom, SwK have risen in step with velocity, and big leap in FpK could lead to better Ctl, possibly elite Cmd. Last piece of puzzle is solving LHB; 2.7 Cmd vL in 2nd half is a good start. At peak age, he's poised to shine.

Yr Tm	W	L	Sv	IP	K	ERA	xERA	WHIP	oOPS	vL	vR	BF/G	Ctl	Dom	Cmd	FpK	SwK	G	L	F	H%	S%	hr/f	GS	APC	DOM%	DIS%	Sv%	LI	RAR	BPV	BPX	R$
13																																	
14																																	
15 CIN *	4	10	0	124	122	4.26	3.75	1.21	682	753	618	20.9	2.7	8.8	3.3	62%	13%	47	21	32	30%	68%	14%	16	87	38%	25%	0	0.72	-4.6	93	110	$2
16 CIN	3	2	6	78	83	2.53	3.77	1.14	623	777	483	8.8	3.0	9.5	3.2	54%	12%	41	21	38	29%	82%	9%	5	34	20%	20%	75	1.01	16.1	110	131	$9
17 CIN	3	3	28	76	92	2.49	3.38	1.11	576	709	452	4.9	3.2	10.9	3.4	65%	15%	42	25	32	30%	80%	8%	0	20			93	0.99	17.5	130	156	$20
1st Half	2	2	15	40	46	1.59	3.33	0.93	467	669	310	4.4	3.6	10.4	2.9	64%	13%	47	19	34	22%	86%	7%	0	18			94	0.99	13.6	115	138	$26
2nd Half	1	1	13	36	46	3.47	3.41	1.29	681	741	612	5.3	2.7	11.4	4.2	66%	16%	38	31	31	37%	75%	10%	0	21			93	1.00	4.0	147	176	$14
18 Proj	**3**	**3**	**38**	**80**	**91**	**2.88**	**3.50**	**1.13**	**624**	**747**	**510**	**6.5**	**2.8**	**10.3**	**3.7**	**62%**	**14%**	**42**	**24**	**34**	**30%**	**78%**	**10%**	**0**						**14.5**	**130**	**157**	**$22**

Iwakuma,Hisashi

Age: 37	Th: R	Role SP	Health F	LIMA Plan C
Ht: 6' 3"	Wt: 210	Type	PT/Exp B	Rand Var -2
			Consist C	MM 1001

Shoulder problems that were speculated on prior to start of season became reality, sidelining him after five starts, ending with arthroscopic surgery in late Sept. Expected to resume throwing by spring training. Age, steady erosion of skills and value even before injury make him a dicey pick, no matter how late.

Yr Tm	W	L	Sv	IP	K	ERA	xERA	WHIP	oOPS	vL	vR	BF/G	Ctl	Dom	Cmd	FpK	SwK	G	L	F	H%	S%	hr/f	GS	APC	DOM%	DIS%	Sv%	LI	RAR	BPV	BPX	R$
13 SEA	14	6	0	220	185	2.66	3.29	1.01	630	599	667	26.2	1.7	7.6	4.4	63%	11%	49	18	34	26%	80%	12%	33	94	48%	21%			32.6	117	152	$29
14 SEA	15	9	0	179	154	3.52	3.00	1.05	642	702	573	25.3	1.1	7.7	7.3	66%	10%	50	21	29	30%	70%	13%	28	91	43%	14%			4.9	139	165	$16
15 SEA	9	5	0	130	111	3.54	3.34	1.06	674	703	645	25.8	1.5	7.7	5.3	68%	11%	50	18	31	28%	73%	15%	20	93	40%	25%			6.7	127	152	$11
16 SEA	16	12	0	199	147	4.12	4.43	1.33	776	766	785	25.3	2.1	6.6	3.2	64%	8%	41	21	38	31%	73%	12%	33	90	24%	30%			1.8	82	98	$8
17 SEA	0	2	0	31	16	4.35	5.55	1.26	803	1111	563	21.3	3.5	4.6	1.3	61%	8%	41	16	43	22%	75%	17%	6	79	0%	83%			0.0	9	10	-$4
1st Half	0	2	0	31	16	4.35	5.55	1.26	803	1111	563	21.3	3.5	4.6	1.3	61%	8%	41	16	43	22%	75%	17%	6	79	0%	83%			0.0	8	10	-$4
2nd Half																																	
18 Proj	**5**	**4**	**0**	**87**	**60**	**4.12**	**4.61**	**1.26**	**760**	**853**	**672**	**24.2**	**2.5**	**6.3**	**2.5**	**64%**	**9%**	**45**	**19**	**36**	**28%**	**73%**	**14%**	**15**						**2.6**	**69**	**84**	**$1**

Jackson,Edwin

Age: 34	Th: R	Role RP	Health D	LIMA Plan D+
Ht: 6' 2"	Wt: 215	Type Pwr	PT/Exp C	Rand Var 0
			Consist B	MM 0101

5-6, 5.21 ERA in 76 IP at BAL/WAS. How do two different teams look at that 2016 line and think, "Yes, gimme some of THAT!"?? And 2017 was more of the same, just with a better strand rate. Which probably means that THREE teams will pursue him in 2018. Please don't make the same mistake.

Yr Tm	W	L	Sv	IP	K	ERA	xERA	WHIP	oOPS	vL	vR	BF/G	Ctl	Dom	Cmd	FpK	SwK	G	L	F	H%	S%	hr/f	GS	APC	DOM%	DIS%	Sv%	LI	RAR	BPV	BPX	R$
13 CHC	8	18	0	175	135	4.98	3.98	1.46	775	816	741	25.1	3.0	6.9	2.3	56%	9%	51	20	28	33%	66%	10%	31	95	16%	35%			-24.1	72	94	-$9
14 CHC	6	15	0	141	123	6.33	4.32	1.64	869	930	816	22.6	4.0	7.9	2.0	55%	11%	39	26	35	35%	62%	12%	27	89	11%	56%	0	0.77	-45.0	50	59	-$19
15 2 NL	4	3	1	56	40	3.07	4.41	1.17	622	565	657	4.9	3.4	6.5	1.9	54%	11%	41	22	37	25%	75%	7%	0	19			50	0.77	6.1	44	52	$2
16 2 NL	5	7	0	84	61	5.89	5.36	1.58	857	786	914	17.8	4.4	6.5	1.5	53%	10%	40	21	39	31%	66%	14%	13	67	15%	54%	0	0.78	-17.6	17	20	-$9
17 2 TM *	7	6	2	117	89	4.28	5.46	1.53	891	792	983	15.4	4.1	6.8	1.7	55%	10%	37	16	47	30%	78%	18%	13	81	15%	46%	67	0.70	1.1	27	32	-$1
1st Half	1	0	2	38	23	3.37	4.89	1.69	1411	1583	1286	9.4	6.1	5.4	0.9	55%	8%	27	27	45	29%	82%	20%	0	36			67	0.32	4.6	30	36	-$7
2nd Half	6	6	0	79	66	4.72	5.73	1.45	845	732	953	22.5	3.1	7.5	2.4	55%	11%	38	15	47	31%	76%	17%	13	92	15%	46%			-3.5	33	40	$2
18 Proj	**4**	**5**	**0**	**73**	**54**	**4.94**	**5.34**	**1.50**	**802**	**764**	**832**	**12.0**	**4.1**	**6.7**	**1.6**	**55%**	**10%**	**41**	**20**	**39**	**30%**	**70%**	**12%**	**5**						**-5.2**	**28**	**34**	**-$5**

BRANDON KRUSE

Jansen,Kenley

			Health: B	LIMA Plan: C
Age: 30	Th: R	Role: RP	PT/Exp: A	Rand Var: -5
Ht: 6' 5"	Wt: 275	Type: Pwr FB	Consist: A	MM: 5530

Improbably, answered "Can he get better?" affirmatively. Ridiculous 1st half Cmd "regressed" in 2nd half... and he still led MLB in Cmd by wide margin. With elite Dom and SwK, doesn't need 2nd half GB% to stick—but if it does, opening query may get same answer next year.

Yr	Tm	W	L	Sv	IP	K	ERA	xERA	WHIP	oOPS	vL	vR	BF/G	Ctl	Dom	Cmd	FpK	SwK	G	L	F	H%	S%	hr/f	GS	APC	DOM%	DIS%	Sv%	LI	RAR	BPV	BPX	R$
13	LA	4	3	28	77	111	1.88	2.29	0.86	509	531	494	3.9	2.1	13.0	6.2	64%	16%	37	24	39	29%	83%	10%	0	17			88	1.33	18.8	192	251	$24
14	LA	2	3	44	65	101	2.76	2.43	1.13	610	710	521	3.9	2.6	13.9	5.3	67%	17%	35	28	37	38%	78%	9%	0	16			90	1.27	7.9	193	230	$21
15	LA	2	1	36	52	80	2.41	2.46	0.78	513	566	459	3.7	1.4	13.8	10.0	70%	18%	35	11	54	29%	77%	10%	0	15			95	1.22	10.0	223	266	$22
16	LA	3	2	47	69	104	1.83	2.48	0.67	446	542	352	3.5	1.4	13.6	9.5	68%	18%	30	15	55	26%	76%	6%	0	14			89	1.21	19.9	214	255	$33
17	LA	5	0	41	68	109	1.32	2.17	0.75	476	640	315	4.0	0.9	14.4	15.6	73%	19%	38	21	41	32%	89%	9%	0	16			98	1.30	25.6	250	300	$34
1st Half		4	0	18	34	53	0.79	2.25	0.53	356	474	250	3.8	0.3	14.0	53.0	78%	18%	31	16	52	27%	88%	3%	0	15			100	1.36	14.9	255	305	$37
2nd Half		1	0	23	34	56	1.83	2.08	0.96	588	778	382	4.1	1.6	14.7	9.3	68%	19%	45	25	30	36%	90%	19%	0	16			96	1.24	10.7	245	293	$30
18	**Proj**	**3**	**1**	**41**	**65**	**102**	**2.04**	**2.37**	**0.78**	**495**	**619**	**374**	**3.6**	**1.3**	**14.0**	**10.6**	**70%**	**18%**	**36**	**19**	**45**	**30%**	**79%**	**9%**	**0**						**18.7**	**231**	**278**	**$29**

Jeffress,Jeremy

			Health: A	LIMA Plan: C
Age: 30	Th: R	Role: RP	PT/Exp: C	Rand Var: +3
Ht: 6' 0"	Wt: 205	Type: Pwr xGB	Consist: B	MM: 1100

As it turned out, faltering Ctl in 2nd half of 2016 portended doom. FpK confirms how much he lost the plate, and RHB solved him, leaving sinker-induced GB% as only plus skill. His hr/f is bound to improve, but xERA says this wasn't just misfortune. Flicker of hope in 2nd half Dom, SwK, but save opps may be gone for good.

Yr	Tm	W	L	Sv	IP	K	ERA	xERA	WHIP	oOPS	vL	vR	BF/G	Ctl	Dom	Cmd	FpK	SwK	G	L	F	H%	S%	hr/f	GS	APC	DOM%	DIS%	Sv%	LI	RAR	BPV	BPX	R$
13	TOR *	2	0	7	38	35	1.78	3.43	1.43	592	284	829	4.6	4.5	8.3	1.8	60%	12%	69	23	8	32%	88%	50%	0	19			88	0.67	9.7	86	113	$3
14	2 TM *	5	2	5	74	65	2.33	3.68	1.44	709	967	509	5.1	3.7	7.9	2.1	60%	7%	59	26	16	34%	83%	7%	0	16			63	0.85	12.9	90	107	$4
15	MIL	5	0	0	68	67	2.65	3.08	1.26	666	752	617	4.0	2.9	8.9	3.0	56%	12%	58	24	18	32%	81%	15%	0	15			0	1.15	11.0	117	139	$4
16	2 TM	3	2	27	58	42	2.33	3.64	1.26	656	906	475	4.1	2.8	6.5	2.3	61%	10%	60	24	16	30%	82%	7%	0	15			96	1.08	13.3	80	95	$14
17	2 TM	5	2	0	65	51	4.68	4.74	1.64	830	871	810	4.8	4.7	7.0	1.5	53%	10%	59	17	24	32%	75%	21%	1	19	0%	100%	0	0.85	-2.6	37	44	-$5
1st Half		1	2	0	30	17	5.46	5.16	1.69	867	924	842	4.3	4.2	5.2	1.2	57%	8%	57	21	22	32%	70%	18%	0	16			0	0.84	-4.0	13	15	-$10
2nd Half		4	0	0	36	34	4.04	4.39	1.60	799	829	783	5.4	5.0	8.6	1.7	50%	12%	62	13	25	32%	80%	23%	1	21	0%	100%	0	0.86	1.4	58	69	$0
18	**Proj**	**4**	**3**	**0**	**65**	**54**	**3.90**	**4.18**	**1.46**	**746**	**869**	**679**	**4.4**	**3.9**	**7.4**	**1.9**	**56%**	**10%**	**59**	**20**	**20**	**32%**	**76%**	**16%**	**0**						**3.7**	**65**	**78**	**-$2**

Jimenez,Joe

			Health: B	LIMA Plan: C
Age: 23	Th: R	Role: RP	PT/Exp: F	Rand Var: +5
Ht: 6' 3"	Wt: 220	Type: Pwr FB	Consist: F	MM: 1410

0-2, 12.32 ERA in 19 IP at DET. "Future closer" tag proved to be albatross, at least in first go-round, as he lost a month to back injury and battled lost velocity in late-season MLB work. FpK hints that Ctl can be reined in, and SwK suggests raw material to succeed in 9th. There's time, but also work to be done.

Yr	Tm	W	L	Sv	IP	K	ERA	xERA	WHIP	oOPS	vL	vR	BF/G	Ctl	Dom	Cmd	FpK	SwK	G	L	F	H%	S%	hr/f	GS	APC	DOM%	DIS%	Sv%	LI	RAR	BPV	BPX	R$
13																																		
14																																		
15																																		
16	a/a	3	3	20	36	42	2.63	1.57	0.98				3.6	3.0	10.5	3.6						27%	72%								7.0	147	175	$11
17	DET *	1	3	4	44	47	6.43	5.80	1.72	999	635	1234	4.0	4.5	9.6	2.2	62%	13%	34	23	43	39%	63%	13%	0	17			67	0.55	-11.2	65	79	-$7
1st Half		1	1	3	16	22	6.30	6.67	1.84	961	875	1017	4.0	5.8	12.0	2.1	60%	14%	31	23	46	40%	69%	33%	0	17			60	0.75	-3.9	57	68	-$6
2nd Half		0	2	1	28	25	6.51	5.29	1.65	1008	560	1286	4.0	3.7	8.3	2.3	62%	12%	35	23	42	38%	59%	8%	0	17			100	0.49	-7.3	71	85	-$8
18	**Proj**	**2**	**4**	**2**	**51**	**57**	**4.35**	**4.38**	**1.42**				**3.9**	**3.8**	**10.0**	**2.7**	**60%**	**12%**	**35**	**21**	**44**	**35%**	**70%**	**7%**	**0**						**0.0**	**92**	**111**	**-$2**

Jimenez,Ubaldo

			Health: B	LIMA Plan: C
Age: 34	Th: R	Role: SP	PT/Exp: A	Rand Var: +5
Ht: 6' 5"	Wt: 210	Type: Pwr	Consist: A	MM: 1303

Misfortune with hr/f, S%, 2nd half H% accelerated dumpster fire that was waning days of bad contract, while FpK screamed strike zone estrangement, and GB tilt eroded. Next deal may be tough get, unless team talks itself into 2nd half Dom, which SwK doesn't support. If someone does give him a look, don't follow suit.

Yr	Tm	W	L	Sv	IP	K	ERA	xERA	WHIP	oOPS	vL	vR	BF/G	Ctl	Dom	Cmd	FpK	SwK	G	L	F	H%	S%	hr/f	GS	APC	DOM%	DIS%	Sv%	LI	RAR	BPV	BPX	R$
13	CLE	13	9	0	183	194	3.30	3.66	1.33	684	661	708	24.3	3.9	9.6	2.4	58%	9%	44	20	36	31%	78%	9%	32	99	28%	25%			12.7	88	114	$11
14	BAL	6	9	0	125	116	4.81	4.47	1.52	737	779	683	22.1	5.5	8.3	1.5	55%	7%	41	22	37	29%	70%	11%	22	92	14%	50%	0	0.74	-16.5	20	23	-$7
15	BAL	12	10	0	184	168	4.11	3.81	1.36	728	702	756	24.7	3.3	8.2	2.5	60%	8%	49	22	29	32%	72%	13%	32	96	22%	25%			-3.3	85	101	$4
16	BAL	8	12	1	142	125	5.44	4.73	1.56	772	885	690	22.0	4.6	7.9	1.7	58%	9%	49	18	33	33%	66%	11%	25	86	12%	48%	100	0.73	-21.9	46	55	-$8
17	BAL	6	11	0	143	139	6.81	4.66	1.59	902	972	840	20.9	3.7	8.8	2.4	53%	9%	43	21	36	34%	61%	21%	25	83	12%	52%	0	0.67	-43.2	80	96	-$15
1st Half		3	3	0	74	62	6.48	4.99	1.48	837	989	724	20.4	4.3	7.6	1.8	55%	8%	46	19	35	28%	60%	20%	11	82	18%	55%	0	0.62	-19.2	45	54	-$13
2nd Half		3	8	0	69	77	7.17	4.32	1.71	965	957	973	21.4	3.0	10.0	3.3	52%	9%	40	23	37	40%	62%	21%	14	85	7%	50%	0	0.73	-24.0	118	142	-$18
18	**Proj**	**7**	**11**	**0**	**145**	**139**	**5.21**	**4.54**	**1.50**	**814**	**862**	**772**	**21.2**	**3.9**	**8.6**	**2.2**	**56%**	**9%**	**45**	**21**	**34**	**33%**	**69%**	**17%**	**30**						**-15.2**	**74**	**89**	**-$6**

Johnson,Jim

			Health: B	LIMA Plan: B
Age: 35	Th: R	Role: RP	PT/Exp: B	Rand Var: +5
Ht: 6' 6"	Wt: 250	Type: Pwr GB	Consist: B	MM: 1310

Surprisingly boosted 2016 Dom in 1st half, this time with some SwK support, but then things unraveled. Last save came 7/20 as 2nd half became toxic stew of lost Ctl, fewer GB, and trifecta of misfortune (H%, S%, hr/f), with Achilles issue thrown in. Might be able to shake it off, but age adds risk.

Yr	Tm	W	L	Sv	IP	K	ERA	xERA	WHIP	oOPS	vL	vR	BF/G	Ctl	Dom	Cmd	FpK	SwK	G	L	F	H%	S%	hr/f	GS	APC	DOM%	DIS%	Sv%	LI	RAR	BPV	BPX	R$
13	BAL	3	8	50	70	56	2.94	3.17	1.28	699	740	653	3.9	2.3	7.2	3.1	61%	9%	58	20	21	32%	79%	11%	0	15			85	1.39	8.0	103	134	$22
14	2 AL	5	2	2	53	42	7.09	4.66	1.95	861	941	776	4.9	5.9	7.1	1.2	63%	8%	58	20	22	37%	63%	14%	0	18			67	0.60	-22.0	4	5	-$12
15	2 NL	2	6	10	67	50	4.46	3.67	1.46	743	675	793	4.0	2.7	6.8	2.5	61%	8%	62	17	21	34%	70%	11%	0	15			59	1.41	-4.1	89	106	-$1
16	ATL	2	6	20	65	68	3.06	3.17	1.19	631	590	671	4.1	2.8	9.5	3.4	57%	8%	55	22	23	32%	74%	8%	0	16			87	1.29	9.0	128	152	$11
17	ATL	6	3	22	57	61	5.56	4.22	1.48	737	813	669	4.2	4.0	9.7	2.4	60%	10%	49	21	31	34%	64%	16%	0	16			71	1.03	-8.4	94	113	$6
1st Half		5	1	18	36	44	3.53	2.93	1.04	553	518	590	4.1	2.3	11.1	4.9	63%	11%	53	19	28	31%	66%	8%	0	16			78	1.21	3.6	169	203	$18
2nd Half		1	2	4	21	17	9.00	6.90	2.24	993	1300	761	4.3	6.9	7.3	1.1	56%	9%	44	23	33	37%	63%	23%	0	16			50	0.79	-12.0	-32	-39	-$15
18	**Proj**	**4**	**5**	**9**	**58**	**55**	**3.95**	**4.16**	**1.50**	**763**	**828**	**706**	**4.0**	**3.6**	**8.5**	**2.4**	**59%**	**9%**	**52**	**21**	**27**	**34%**	**77%**	**16%**	**0**						**3.0**	**87**	**105**	**$2**

Jones,Nate

			Health: F	LIMA Plan: C+
Age: 32	Th: R	Role: RP	PT/Exp: D	Rand Var: -3
Ht: 6' 5"	Wt: 220	Type: Pwr	Consist: A	MM: 4410

Elbow nerve issue, which required season-ending surgery in July, derailed him from possible fast track to saves and likely caused atypical Ctl struggles in limited IP. He's expected to be okay by spring training, but health issues have become chronic; if he returns to form, could thrive in high-leverage role... UP: 25 Sv

Yr	Tm	W	L	Sv	IP	K	ERA	xERA	WHIP	oOPS	vL	vR	BF/G	Ctl	Dom	Cmd	FpK	SwK	G	L	F	H%	S%	hr/f	GS	APC	DOM%	DIS%	Sv%	LI	RAR	BPV	BPX	R$
13	CHW	4	5	0	78	89	4.15	2.87	1.22	659	710	621	4.5	3.0	10.3	3.4	61%	14%	51	21	28	33%	66%	9%	0	18			0	1.36	-2.8	133	173	$1
14	CHW	0	0	0	0	0	0.00	0.00	0.00		3000	2000	2.5	0.0	0.0	0.0						0%	20%	0%	0	15			0	1.50	0.0	-22	-26	-$5
15	CHW	2	2	0	19	27	3.32	2.51	0.95	695	567	770	3.8	2.8	12.8	4.5	59%	16%	46	14	41	21%	85%	33%	0	15			0	1.17	1.5	177	211	-$1
16	CHW	5	3	3	71	80	2.29	2.97	0.89	552	667	477	3.9	1.9	10.2	5.3	64%	15%	46	21	33	26%	80%	12%	0	14			25	1.53	16.5	156	185	$12
17	CHW	1	0	0	12	15	2.31	3.30	1.29	675	514	881	4.5	4.6	11.6	2.5	59%	12%	54	19	27	31%	86%	14%	0	18			0	1.12	2.9	115	138	-$3
1st Half		1	0	0	12	15	2.31	3.30	1.29	675	514	881	4.5	4.6	11.6	2.5	59%	12%	54	19	27	31%	86%	14%	0	18			0	1.12	2.9	115	138	-$3
2nd Half																																		
18	**Proj**	**4**	**3**	**4**	**58**	**66**	**2.88**	**3.18**	**1.02**	**596**	**686**	**533**	**4.0**	**2.3**	**10.2**	**4.4**	**62%**	**14%**	**48**	**21**	**31**	**29%**	**75%**	**11%**	**0**						**10.6**	**146**	**176**	**$7**

Junis,Jakob

			Health: A	LIMA Plan: B+
Age: 25	Th: R	Role: SP	PT/Exp: D	Rand Var: 0
Ht: 6' 2"	Wt: 225	Type: FB	Consist: B	MM: 1203

9-3, 4.30 ERA in 98 IP at KC. After yo-yoing between AAA/MLB, raised eyebrow with 13.5 Cmd in Aug, though still didn't deliver on promise overall. SwK suggests dominance not there, but if he can keep 2nd half Ctl gains—and FpK says he's got a shot—upside may be 2nd half xERA over full season.

Yr	Tm	W	L	Sv	IP	K	ERA	xERA	WHIP	oOPS	vL	vR	BF/G	Ctl	Dom	Cmd	FpK	SwK	G	L	F	H%	S%	hr/f	GS	APC	DOM%	DIS%	Sv%	LI	RAR	BPV	BPX	R$
13																																		
14																																		
15																																		
16	a/a	10	10	0	149	115	5.37	5.22	1.46				23.6	2.2	6.9	3.2						35%	65%								-21.7	68	81	-$6
17	KC *	12	8	0	169	148	4.09	4.24	1.28	762	783	740	21.7	2.2	7.9	3.6	62%	9%	40	20	40	32%	72%	12%	16	76	19%	31%	0	0.88	5.6	90	108	$10
1st Half		4	4	0	77	73	4.23	4.77	1.37	914	835	975	21.6	2.8	8.5	3.0	61%	10%	40	16	44	32%	74%	18%	6	73	17%	50%	0	0.88	1.2	72	86	$4
2nd Half		8	4	0	92	75	3.97	3.79	1.20	673	760	567	21.8	1.6	7.3	4.6	62%	9%	40	22	38	32%	69%	8%	10	78	20%	20%	0	0.88	4.4	115	138	$15
18	**Proj**	**7**	**7**	**0**	**131**	**108**	**4.12**	**4.46**	**1.30**	**754**	**770**	**739**	**22.2**	**2.1**	**7.5**	**3.5**	**62%**	**9%**	**40**	**20**	**40**	**32%**	**72%**	**10%**	**24**						**3.9**	**95**	**115**	**$4**

KRISTOPHER OLSON

Kahnle,Thomas

Age: 28	Th: R	Role RP	Health A	LIMA Plan B+
Ht: 6' 1"	Wt: 235	Type Pwr	PT/Exp D	Rand Var +1
			Consist B	MM 4510

Simplified delivery (lower leg kick, straighter path to home) to harness Ctl, still managed to up velocity to 98 mph and, voila! breakout. If Ctl gains hold, and FpK says they mostly will, old adage "buy skills, not roles" applies. And even if it isn't clear from whence opps will come... UP: 25 saves

Yr Tm	W	L	Sv	IP	K	ERA	xERA	WHIP	oOPS	vL	vR	BF/G	Ctl	Dom	Cmd	FpK	SwK	G	L	F	H%	S%	hr/f	GS	APC	DOM%	DIS%	Sv%	LI	RAR	BPV	BPX	R$
13 aa	1	3	15	60	61	3.73	3.89	1.58				5.7	7.3	9.2	1.3						27%	78%								1.0	70	91	$2
14 COL	2	1	0	69	63	4.19	3.82	1.19	628	570	683	5.3	4.1	8.3	2.0	50%	11%	47	17	36	25%	67%	10%	0	20			0	0.83	-3.8	64	76	-$1
15 COL *	1	4	8	60	59	5.35	4.46	1.57	778	829	744	4.7	6.1	8.8	1.5	51%	14%	55	24	21	30%	67%	17%	0	18			67	0.83	-10.3	60	71	-$5
16 CHW *	1	2	8	54	54	3.27	3.06	1.40	678	575	735	4.4	5.6	9.0	1.6	54%	11%	49	23	28	29%	76%	10%	0	17			67	0.83	6.2	89	106	$2
17 2 AL	2	4	0	63	96	2.59	2.74	1.12	606	730	525	3.7	2.4	13.8	5.6	62%	18%	41	21	38	38%	79%	8%	0	15			0	1.06	13.7	201	242	$6
1st Half	0	2	0	31	53	2.30	2.17	0.96	527	651	441	3.8	2.0	15.2	7.6	63%	18%	40	26	34	37%	79%	10%	0	15			0	1.08	8.0	238	285	$7
2nd Half	2	2	0	31	43	2.87	3.34	1.28	680	806	601	3.6	2.9	12.4	4.3	61%	17%	41	18	41	38%	79%	6%	0	14			0	1.05	5.7	164	196	$5
18 Proj	**2**	**3**	**4**	**58**	**72**	**2.73**	**3.30**	**1.16**	**612**	**679**	**566**	**3.9**	**3.2**	**11.2**	**3.5**	**56%**	**15%**	**47**	**21**	**32**	**32%**	**78%**	**9%**	**0**						**11.6**	**139**	**167**	**$5**

Karns,Nathan

Age: 30	Th: R	Role SP	Health F	LIMA Plan C
Ht: 6' 3"	Wt: 225	Type Pwr	PT/Exp C	Rand Var +4
			Consist B	MM 1301

First he broke out (2.01 ERA, 12.9 Dom, 8.0 Cmd, 15% SwK in May), then he broke down, shockingly. Future now clouded by recovery from mid-July thoracic outlet surgery. Was especially lethal vR, with 30/1 K/BB, held back only by 47% H%, 22% hr/f. Watch health in spring, as GB-Dom combo very intriguing.

Yr Tm	W	L	Sv	IP	K	ERA	xERA	WHIP	oOPS	vL	vR	BF/G	Ctl	Dom	Cmd	FpK	SwK	G	L	F	H%	S%	hr/f	GS	APC	DOM%	DIS%	Sv%	LI	RAR	BPV	BPX	R$
13 WAS *	10	7	0	145	130	4.48	4.73	1.43	1060	1266	845	23.6	3.5	8.1	2.3	64%	10%	36	31	33	32%	73%	36%	3	82	0%	67%			-10.9	59	77	-$2
14 TAM *	10	10	0	157	134	6.62	5.65	1.65	661	384	859	24.3	4.2	7.7	1.8	49%	10%	43	13	43	35%	60%	23%	2	103	50%	50%			-55.9	44	53	-$21
15 TAM	7	5	0	147	145	3.67	3.89	1.28	699	690	708	23.0	3.4	8.9	2.6	58%	10%	42	22	37	30%	76%	13%	26	90	15%	27%	0	0.80	5.2	87	104	$6
16 SEA	6	2	1	94	101	5.15	4.32	1.48	760	628	875	19.0	4.3	9.6	2.2	57%	11%	40	23	37	34%	67%	11%	15	76	40%	27%	100	0.62	-11.2	76	90	-$4
17 KC	2	2	0	45	51	4.17	3.58	1.19	743	804	698	20.9	2.6	10.1	3.9	58%	13%	50	12	38	29%	73%	20%	8	83	25%	38%	0	0.72	1.1	141	169	-$1
1st Half	2	2	0	45	51	4.17	3.58	1.19	743	804	698	20.9	2.6	10.1	3.9	58%	13%	50	12	38	29%	73%	20%	8	83	25%	38%	0	0.72	1.1	140	168	-$1
2nd Half																																	
18 Proj	**5**	**4**	**0**	**87**	**88**	**4.64**	**4.24**	**1.36**	**758**	**736**	**775**	**21.2**	**3.5**	**9.1**	**2.6**	**58%**	**11%**	**44**	**19**	**37**	**32%**	**70%**	**15%**	**17**						**-3.1**	**93**	**112**	**-$1**

Kela,Keone

Age: 25	Th: R	Role RP	Health F	LIMA Plan A
Ht: 6' 1"	Wt: 215	Type Pwr FB	PT/Exp D	Rand Var -5
			Consist A	MM 2510

If he ever cinches closer role, he'll have taken circuitous route. Opened season in AAA due to his effect on "clubhouse culture," then July shoulder issue required two DL stints. There are reasons - old (Ctl, FpK) and new (FB spike) - to doubt reliability. Could get a 9th inning shot but is no lock to succeed.

Yr Tm	W	L	Sv	IP	K	ERA	xERA	WHIP	oOPS	vL	vR	BF/G	Ctl	Dom	Cmd	FpK	SwK	G	L	F	H%	S%	hr/f	GS	APC	DOM%	DIS%	Sv%	LI	RAR	BPV	BPX	R$
13																																	
14 aa	2	1	5	39	47	2.22	2.45	1.34				4.5	6.3	11.1	1.8						28%	83%								7.3	114	135	$
15 TEX	7	5	1	60	68	2.39	3.01	1.16	615	739	527	3.6	2.7	10.1	3.8	58%	14%	51	21	29	32%	82%	9%	0	15			25	1.21	11.7	139	166	$
16 TEX	5	1	0	34	45	6.09	3.57	1.38	779	577	872	4.3	4.5	11.9	2.6	55%	12%	44	22	34	32%	59%	21%	0	18			0	0.84	-8.0	115	137	-$
17 TEX	4	1	2	39	51	2.79	3.77	0.91	479	644	370	3.9	4.0	11.9	3.0	57%	11%	30	12	57	19%	74%	9%	0	16			67	0.90	7.5	115	138	$
1st Half	4	1	1	31	42	2.64	3.60	0.88	473	640	375	4.0	3.8	12.3	3.2	56%	11%	32	10	59	20%	75%	8%	0	16			50	0.94	6.5	129	154	$
2nd Half	0	0	1	8	9	3.38	4.46	1.00	500	651	343	3.6	4.5	10.1	2.3	59%	11%	26	21	53	18%	71%	10%	0	15			100	0.76	1.0	65	78	-$
18 Proj	**6**	**2**	**7**	**51**	**64**	**3.55**	**3.74**	**1.23**	**642**	**705**	**604**	**3.9**	**3.9**	**11.3**	**2.9**	**56%**	**13%**	**42**	**17**	**41**	**31%**	**73%**	**10%**	**0**						**5.1**	**117**	**141**	**$**

Kelly,Joe

Age: 30	Th: R	Role RP	Health D	LIMA Plan B+
Ht: 6' 1"	Wt: 190	Type Pwr	PT/Exp D	Rand Var -4
			Consist B	MM 1300

Theory that failed starter with 99 mph FB would thrive in pen seems validated on surface, but H%, S% did much of work. SwK verfies that elite Dom may never arrive. Still, some positives: spike in FpK hints at better Ctl to come, and induces plenty of GB. Upside, though, seems to be safe LIMA arm, not closer.

Yr Tm	W	L	Sv	IP	K	ERA	xERA	WHIP	oOPS	vL	vR	BF/G	Ctl	Dom	Cmd	FpK	SwK	G	L	F	H%	S%	hr/f	GS	APC	DOM%	DIS%	Sv%	LI	RAR	BPV	BPX	R$
13 STL	10	5	0	124	79	2.69	4.17	1.35	694	691	696	14.4	3.2	5.7	1.8	55%	8%	51	21	28	30%	83%	9%	15	53	0%	47%	0	0.87	18.1	46	60	$
14 2 TM	6	4	0	96	66	4.20	4.00	1.35	693	689	695	24.4	3.9	6.2	1.6	57%	7%	55	21	24	28%	70%	11%	17	93	18%	35%			-5.5	38	45	-$
15 BOS *	11	7	0	153	124	4.76	4.53	1.44	768	702	836	22.5	3.3	7.3	2.2	62%	8%	46	25	29	32%	68%	12%	25	95	8%	40%			-15.2	61	73	-$
16 BOS *	5	1	2	75	82	4.02	4.92	1.58	828	899	791	8.9	3.8	9.8	2.6	52%	11%	47	28	25	38%	76%	18%	6	37	17%	67%	67	1.11	1.5	87	103	-$
17 BOS	4	1	0	58	52	2.79	4.14	1.19	573	671	509	4.4	4.2	8.1	1.9	64%	11%	51	23	26	26%	77%	7%	0	19			0	1.09	11.2	61	73	$
1st Half	3	0	0	34	24	1.07	4.09	1.10	507	703	405	4.2	4.0	6.4	1.6	61%	10%	57	24	18	24%	89%	0%	0	19			0	0.98	13.7	43	51	$
2nd Half	1	1	0	24	28	5.18	4.21	1.32	659	639	665	4.8	4.4	10.4	2.3	68%	13%	41	22	38	30%	62%	13%	0	19			0	1.25	-2.5	85	102	-$
18 Proj	**4**	**2**	**0**	**58**	**55**	**3.84**	**4.20**	**1.36**	**689**	**717**	**668**	**6.6**	**3.9**	**8.5**	**2.2**	**60%**	**10%**	**48**	**24**	**28**	**31%**	**73%**	**11%**	**0**						**3.7**	**73**	**88**	**$**

Kennedy,Ian

Age: 33	Th: R	Role SP	Health C	LIMA Plan C
Ht: 6' 0"	Wt: 200	Type Pwr xFB	PT/Exp A	Rand Var +1
			Consist B	MM 0203

Wowed with 2.30 ERA in five April starts, but things soon fell apart in big way. After two years, extreme FB tilt here to stay, leaving him at mercy of hr/f. Dom took second straight dip, and Ctl headed in wrong direction, too, which FpK suggests was legit. In most leagues, he'll do more harm than good.

Yr Tm	W	L	Sv	IP	K	ERA	xERA	WHIP	oOPS	vL	vR	BF/G	Ctl	Dom	Cmd	FpK	SwK	G	L	F	H%	S%	hr/f	GS	APC	DOM%	DIS%	Sv%	LI	RAR	BPV	BPX	R$
13 2 NL	7	10	0	181	163	4.91	4.14	1.40	781	828	736	25.6	3.6	8.1	2.2	62%	10%	38	23	39	31%	68%	13%	31	100	26%	35%			-23.4	64	83	-$
14 SD	13	13	0	201	207	3.63	3.56	1.29	698	689	706	25.6	3.1	9.3	3.0	64%	11%	40	23	38	32%	73%	8%	33	103	33%	15%			2.8	100	119	$
15 SD	9	15	0	168	174	4.28	3.74	1.30	815	842	788	23.8	2.8	9.3	3.3	61%	11%	38	23	39	31%	74%	17%	30	97	13%	27%			-6.5	108	129	$
16 KC	11	11	0	196	184	3.68	4.40	1.22	722	709	735	24.8	3.0	8.5	2.8	62%	10%	33	20	47	28%	77%	13%	33	102	30%	27%			12.3	81	97	$1
17 KC	5	13	0	154	131	5.38	5.04	1.32	804	818	791	21.8	3.6	7.7	2.1	58%	10%	36	16	48	26%	66%	16%	30	88	13%	57%			-19.3	56	67	-$
1st Half	2	6	0	74	62	4.72	5.09	1.18	714	754	677	21.9	4.0	7.5	1.9	55%	9%	38	11	51	21%	68%	15%	14	91	14%	57%			-3.3	43	52	$
2nd Half	3	7	0	80	69	5.99	4.99	1.46	882	875	889	21.8	3.2	7.8	2.5	60%	10%	35	20	45	31%	64%	16%	16	85	13%	56%			-16.0	67	81	-$
18 Proj	**7**	**12**	**0**	**160**	**146**	**4.73**	**4.70**	**1.31**	**786**	**793**	**780**	**22.5**	**3.3**	**8.2**	**2.5**	**60%**	**10%**	**36**	**19**	**45**	**28%**	**70%**	**15%**	**29**						**-7.3**	**74**	**89**	**$**

Kershaw,Clayton

Age: 30	Th: L	Role SP	Health F	LIMA Plan C
Ht: 6' 4"	Wt: 228	Type Pwr	PT/Exp A	Rand Var -2
			Consist A	MM 5505

For second year, returned first-round value despite being sidelined for extended period. 148 BPV, 3.32 xERA in Sept eases fears to a point, but "F" health grade remains. Thrived despite worst hr/f luck of career. Given acquisition cost, this is all about risk tolerance—he's great, but fits best if you have depth.

Yr Tm	W	L	Sv	IP	K	ERA	xERA	WHIP	oOPS	vL	vR	BF/G	Ctl	Dom	Cmd	FpK	SwK	G	L	F	H%	S%	hr/f	GS	APC	DOM%	DIS%	Sv%	LI	RAR	BPV	BPX	R$
13 LA	16	9	0	236	232	1.83	2.93	0.92	521	477	532	27.5	2.0	8.8	4.5	65%	12%	46	23	31	26%	82%	6%	33	104	67%	3%			59.2	130	169	$4
14 LA	21	3	0	198	239	1.77	2.27	0.86	521	477	531	27.7	1.4	10.8	7.7	69%	15%	52	19	29	29%	81%	7%	27	101	81%	4%			48.2	187	223	$4
15 LA	16	7	0	233	301	2.13	2.31	0.88	521	554	511	27.0	1.6	11.6	7.2	68%	16%	50	22	28	29%	79%	10%	33	103	76%	3%			52.6	194	231	$4
16 LA	12	4	0	149	172	1.69	2.43	0.72	472	309	529	25.9	0.7	10.4	15.6	70%	16%	49	20	30	26%	80%	8%	21	98	76%	5%			45.9	196	233	$3
17 LA	18	4	0	175	202	2.31	2.98	0.95	604	734	570	25.1	1.5	10.4	6.7	69%	15%	48	19	33	28%	85%	16%	27	93	56%	7%			44.1	171	206	$3
1st Half	12	2	0	116	135	2.32	3.00	0.91	602	815	549	26.4	1.5	10.4	6.8	69%	14%	46	20	34	26%	85%	17%	17	99	65%	0%			29.2	170	204	$4
2nd Half	6	2	0	59	67	2.30	2.95	1.02	606	585	611	23.1	1.5	10.3	6.7	70%	17%	52	17	31	31%	83%	13%	10	83	40%	20%			14.9	174	208	$1
18 Proj	**16**	**5**	**0**	**181**	**211**	**2.42**	**2.78**	**0.89**	**551**	**535**	**556**	**24.6**	**1.3**	**10.5**	**7.8**	**69%**	**15%**	**50**	**20**	**31**	**28%**	**77%**	**12%**	**27**						**43.2**	**180**	**217**	**$3**

Keuchel,Dallas

Age: 30	Th: L	Role SP	Health D	LIMA Plan C+
Ht: 6' 3"	Wt: 205	Type Pwr xGB	PT/Exp A	Rand Var 0
			Consist B	MM 3203

Missed nearly two months with neck issue and wasn't quite right upon return, though faltering Ctl hurt less than hr/f misfortune. Elite GB% remains intact, and SwK says don't sweat Dom dip in 2nd half. On the other hand, H% may tick up a bit. But if you bid to xERA, not 2015 Cy Young, he's unlikely to disappoint.

Yr Tm	W	L	Sv	IP	K	ERA	xERA	WHIP	oOPS	vL	vR	BF/G	Ctl	Dom	Cmd	FpK	SwK	G	L	F	H%	S%	hr/f	GS	APC	DOM%	DIS%	Sv%	LI	RAR	BPV	BPX	R$
13 HOU	6	10	0	154	123	5.15	3.72	1.54	812	750	832	22.0	3.0	7.2	2.4	63%	9%	56	21	23	35%	69%	17%	22	81	18%	36%	0	0.90	-24.4	81	106	-$1
14 HOU	12	9	0	200	146	2.93	3.07	1.18	655	595	674	27.9	2.2	6.6	3.0	65%	9%	64	17	19	30%	76%	10%	29	104	41%	17%			20.1	102	121	$1
15 HOU	20	8	0	232	216	2.48	2.80	1.02	575	461	606	27.6	2.0	8.4	4.2	61%	11%	62	19	20	28%	79%	14%	33	106	42%	6%			42.3	137	164	$3
16 HOU	9	12	0	168	144	4.55	3.65	1.29	736	603	772	27.0	2.6	7.7	3.0	63%	10%	57	19	24	31%	67%	16%	26	103	35%	19%			-7.5	104	124	$
17 HOU	14	5	0	146	125	2.90	3.32	1.12	619	435	666	25.4	2.9	7.7	2.7	60%	11%	67	15	18	26%	78%	21%	23	95	30%	22%			26.1	106	127	$1
1st Half	9	0	0	76	69	1.67	2.81	0.87	513	278	567	25.7	2.1	8.2	3.8	61%	11%	67	14	18	23%	87%	17%	11	94	55%	0%			25.1	135	162	$3
2nd Half	5	5	0	70	56	4.24	3.90	1.39	720	563	765	25.1	3.7	7.2	1.9	59%	12%	66	17	17	29%	73%	25%	12	96	8%	42%			1.0	73	88	$
18 Proj	**14**	**8**	**0**	**174**	**148**	**3.21**	**3.50**	**1.20**	**667**	**526**	**705**	**25.5**	**2.7**	**7.7**	**2.8**	**61%**	**11%**	**63**	**17**	**20**	**29%**	**77%**	**18%**	**27**						**24.6**	**105**	**126**	**$1**

KRISTOPHER OLSON

Kimbrel,Craig

Age: 30	Th: R	Role RP	Health	B	LIMA Plan	C		
Ht: 6' 0"	Wt: 210	Type Pwr FB	PT/Exp	A	Rand Var	-3		
			Consist	C	MM	5530		

Elite Cmd led to season for the ages. SwK says Ks a bit more legit than pinpoint Ctl, but lest you think it unrepeatable, consider how much 2017 looks like 2012 (16.7 Dom, 2.0 Ctl), aside from that year's 70% FpK. Even if Ctl slips back to "mere mortal" level, his stuff is plenty good enough to get job done.

Yr Tm	W	L	Sv	IP	K	ERA	xERA	WHIP	oOPS	vL	vR	BF/G	Ctl	Dom	Cmd	FpK	SwK	G	L	F	H%	S%	hr/f	GS	APC	DOM%	DIS%	Sv%	LI	RAR	BPV	BPX	R$
13 ATL	4	3	50	67	98	1.21	2.12	0.88	487	574	393	3.8	2.7	13.2	4.9	56%	14%	47	24	29	28%	91%	10%	0	15			93	1.30	22.0	189	247	$32
14 ATL	0	3	47	62	95	1.61	2.36	0.91	430	425	436	3.9	3.8	13.9	3.7	58%	17%	41	23	35	26%	83%	5%	0	17			92	1.44	16.2	166	198	$26
15 SD	4	2	39	59	87	2.58	2.61	1.04	569	629	508	3.9	3.3	13.2	4.0	61%	16%	46	20	34	30%	80%	14%	0	17			91	1.49	10.1	171	204	$22
16 BOS	2	6	31	53	83	3.23	3.33	1.09	539	514	559	3.9	5.1	14.1	2.8	68%	15%	29	23	48	27%	72%	8%	0	16			94	1.50	6.3	123	146	$16
17 BOS	5	0	35	69	126	1.43	1.83	0.68	444	572	335	3.8	1.8	16.4	9.0	63%	20%	37	19	44	28%	88%	13%	0	17			90	1.34	24.9	262	314	$32
1st Half	2	0	23	36	64	1.01	1.66	0.48	293	501	129	3.7	1.3	16.1	12.8	70%	20%	42	16	42	23%	81%	4%	0	17			96	1.38	14.7	276	331	$40
2nd Half	3	0	12	33	62	1.89	2.02	0.90	599	638	562	3.9	2.4	16.7	6.9	56%	20%	32	23	45	33%	92%	21%	0	17			80	1.28	10.1	246	295	$24
18 Proj	**4**	**2**	**38**	**65**	**110**	**2.10**	**2.43**	**0.89**	**508**	**567**	**454**	**3.7**	**3.1**	**15.1**	**4.9**	**63%**	**18%**	**37**	**21**	**42**	**28%**	**82%**	**13%**	**0**						**18.2**	**203**	**245**	**$27**

Kintzler,Brandon

Age: 33	Th: R	Role RP	Health	D	LIMA Plan	C		
Ht: 6' 0"	Wt: 190	Type Con xGB	PT/Exp	D	Rand Var	-2		
			Consist	C	MM	1011		

Resumed racking up saves despite non-traditional closer skill set... until trade deadline. Never one to miss many bats, his Dom, SwK hit all-time low in 2nd half, and needed H% help to rescue ERA. Given 2nd half return of strong GB tilt, might be able to hold another job, but in the ninth again? Let's not get crazy.

Yr Tm	W	L	Sv	IP	K	ERA	xERA	WHIP	oOPS	vL	vR	BF/G	Ctl	Dom	Cmd	FpK	SwK	G	L	F	H%	S%	hr/f	GS	APC	DOM%	DIS%	Sv%	LI	RAR	BPV	BPX	R$
13 MIL	3	3	0	77	58	2.69	3.03	1.06	567	540	586	4.3	1.9	6.8	3.6	60%	9%	57	24	18	29%	74%	5%	0	15			0	1.05	11.2	107	139	$5
14 MIL	3	3	0	58	31	3.24	3.87	1.34	781	648	859	3.7	2.5	4.8	1.9	60%	7%	57	18	25	29%	81%	17%	0	14			0	1.04	3.6	54	65	-$1
15 MIL *	1	2	0	26	17	6.46	6.58	1.94	1021	1017	1000	5.4	3.3	6.0	1.8	56%	9%	63	29	8	42%	64%	50%	0	21			0	0.59	-8.0	47	56	-$9
16 MIN *	4	3	17	70	43	3.73	4.21	1.33	705	673	730	4.5	1.5	5.5	3.7	65%	7%	62	18	20	33%	73%	14%	0	15			81	1.01	4.0	87	104	$7
17 2 TM	4	3	29	71	39	3.03	4.31	1.15	638	535	734	4.0	2.0	4.9	2.4	62%	6%	55	19	27	27%	75%	8%	0	15			83	1.17	11.7	67	81	$17
1st Half	2	1	21	35	24	2.55	3.88	1.05	613	566	655	3.9	1.8	6.1	3.4	62%	7%	49	24	27	26%	79%	11%	0	16			88	1.28	7.9	89	107	$24
2nd Half	2	2	8	36	15	3.50	4.75	1.25	661	508	810	4.1	2.3	3.8	1.7	63%	5%	60	14	26	28%	72%	6%	0	15			73	1.07	3.8	45	53	$9
18 Proj	**4**	**3**	**2**	**73**	**41**	**3.87**	**4.25**	**1.27**	**711**	**613**	**790**	**4.1**	**2.0**	**5.1**	**2.6**	**62%**	**6%**	**58**	**19**	**24**	**30%**	**71%**	**11%**	**0**						**4.4**	**75**	**90**	**$1**

Kluber,Corey

Age: 32	Th: R	Role SP	Health	C	LIMA Plan	C		
Ht: 6' 4"	Wt: 215	Type Pwr	PT/Exp	A	Rand Var	-1		
			Consist	B	MM	5505		

Already one of MLB's best, authored masterpiece despite missing month with back pain, from which he returned with a vengeance. Hard to find a discouraging sign. Dom rise backed by SwK? Check. Ctl validated by FpK? Check. Maybe a wee bit of H%, S% luck. But he's pretty much all smoke, no mirrors.

Yr Tm	W	L	Sv	IP	K	ERA	xERA	WHIP	oOPS	vL	vR	BF/G	Ctl	Dom	Cmd	FpK	SwK	G	L	F	H%	S%	hr/f	GS	APC	DOM%	DIS%	Sv%	LI	RAR	BPV	BPX	R$
13 CLE	11	5	0	147	136	3.85	3.25	1.26	729	751	704	23.4	2.0	8.3	4.1	60%	11%	46	26	29	33%	72%	12%	24	88	33%	25%	0	0.73	0.3	119	155	$6
14 CLE	18	9	0	236	269	2.44	2.74	1.09	624	687	553	28.0	1.9	10.3	5.3	64%	12%	48	21	31	33%	80%	7%	34	103	62%	12%			37.7	158	189	$30
15 CLE	9	16	0	222	245	3.49	3.07	1.05	650	740	549	27.7	1.8	9.9	5.4	63%	13%	42	22	36	30%	70%	11%	32	102	47%	13%			13.0	150	178	$22
16 CLE	18	9	0	215	227	3.14	3.45	1.06	631	648	615	26.9	2.4	9.5	4.0	62%	13%	44	19	36	28%	74%	11%	32	100	59%	16%			27.8	129	153	$29
17 CLE	18	4	0	204	265	2.25	2.67	0.87	556	575	539	26.8	1.6	11.7	7.4	64%	16%	45	22	33	28%	81%	13%	29	102	66%	14%			52.9	191	229	$45
1st Half	7	2	0	80	105	3.02	2.81	1.00	597	679	527	26.2	2.2	11.8	5.3	65%	15%	49	18	33	30%	74%	13%	12	99	50%	25%			13.2	178	214	$24
2nd Half	11	2	0	123	160	1.75	2.57	0.79	529	508	547	27.2	1.2	11.7	10.0	64%	16%	42	25	34	27%	87%	14%	17	104	76%	6%			39.7	198	238	$59
18 Proj	**17**	**8**	**0**	**218**	**257**	**2.96**	**3.06**	**0.98**	**602**	**637**	**568**	**26.0**	**1.9**	**10.6**	**5.7**	**63%**	**14%**	**44**	**21**	**34**	**29%**	**74%**	**12%**	**32**						**37.5**	**164**	**197**	**$36**

Knebel,Corey

Age: 26	Th: R	Role RP	Health	D	LIMA Plan	C		
Ht: 6' 4"	Wt: 220	Type Pwr FB	PT/Exp	C	Rand Var	-5		
			Consist	B	MM	3531		

Health, altered approach, uptick in velocity, gains vR helped launch him into stratosphere. Last blemish is Ctl, which FpK verifies needs work. Also unlikely to see such a high S% again. Still, SwK says strikeouts are legit, and xERA, BPV concur that, even with walks, he's elite enough to keep saves coming.

Yr Tm	W	L	Sv	IP	K	ERA	xERA	WHIP	oOPS	vL	vR	BF/G	Ctl	Dom	Cmd	FpK	SwK	G	L	F	H%	S%	hr/f	GS	APC	DOM%	DIS%	Sv%	LI	RAR	BPV	BPX	R$
13																																	
14 DET *	5	1	3	54	64	3.06	2.28	1.13	776	733	826	5.1	4.1	10.6	2.6	59%	9%	48	16	36	27%	74%	0%	0	21			50	0.37	4.6	119	142	$4
15 MIL *	1	2	6	66	76	3.67	3.92	1.27	744	764	728	4.2	3.3	10.4	3.2	58%	10%	49	20	31	32%	76%	20%	0	17			75	0.49	2.3	99	118	$2
16 MIL	1	4	2	33	38	4.68	4.13	1.47	708	510	909	4.1	4.4	10.5	2.4	61%	8%	42	21	37	35%	69%	9%	0	17			50	1.00	-2.0	89	106	-$3
17 MIL	1	4	39	76	126	1.78	2.99	1.16	568	510	629	4.1	4.7	14.9	3.2	51%	15%	38	17	45	32%	89%	10%	0	18			87	1.49	24.2	157	188	$27
1st Half	0	1	13	40	68	1.13	2.78	1.08	512	473	558	4.0	5.0	15.4	3.1	49%	14%	40	19	41	30%	93%	7%	0	18			81	1.53	15.8	161	193	$26
2nd Half	1	3	26	36	58	2.48	3.22	1.24	627	553	694	4.2	4.5	14.4	3.2	54%	16%	37	15	48	34%	85%	11%	0	18			90	1.45	8.4	153	184	$27
18 Proj	**2**	**5**	**41**	**73**	**102**	**2.87**	**3.52**	**1.26**	**636**	**536**	**733**	**4.1**	**4.3**	**12.6**	**2.9**	**56%**	**12%**	**41**	**19**	**40**	**33%**	**81%**	**10%**	**0**						**13.3**	**129**	**156**	**$21**

Kontos,George

Age: 33	Th: R	Role RP	Health	D	LIMA Plan	B+		
Ht: 6' 3"	Wt: 215	Type Pwr	PT/Exp	C	Rand Var	0		
			Consist	B	MM	1200		

Dumped by SF after rough H%/S% luck in July; PIT saw skills, took him in, but only got 15 IP before groin injury. Odd for 33-year-old with 91 mph FB to hit new Dom peak, but SwK shows more support than in previous 9+ Dom season (2012). He's not a sub-3 ERA arm, as xERA attests. You can probably do better.

Yr Tm	W	L	Sv	IP	K	ERA	xERA	WHIP	oOPS	vL	vR	BF/G	Ctl	Dom	Cmd	FpK	SwK	G	L	F	H%	S%	hr/f	GS	APC	DOM%	DIS%	Sv%	LI	RAR	BPV	BPX	R$
13 SF *	5	4	4	79	67	4.38	4.14	1.30	788	1024	689	4.6	2.4	7.6	3.2	65%	11%	38	25	37	32%	69%	11%	0	17			67	1.01	-5.0	82	106	$1
14 SF *	7	3	4	80	71	2.85	2.87	1.16	587	498	635	5.9	2.5	7.9	3.2	56%	10%	39	18	43	30%	76%	3%	0	20			67	0.56	8.8	108	128	$8
15 SF	4	4	0	73	44	2.33	3.98	0.94	595	684	544	3.9	1.5	5.4	3.7	58%	10%	43	22	35	23%	83%	11%	0	14			0	1.00	14.7	78	93	$8
16 SF	3	2	0	53	35	2.53	4.56	1.16	605	660	569	3.8	3.4	5.9	1.8	61%	11%	44	23	32	25%	80%	6%	0	14			0	0.93	10.9	37	44	$3
17 2 NL	1	6	1	66	70	3.39	3.76	1.22	709	773	672	4.3	2.7	9.5	3.5	63%	17%	47	20	34	31%	78%	15%	0	16			14	1.14	7.9	123	147	$2
1st Half	0	2	0	40	44	2.72	3.59	1.21	675	861	559	4.5	2.9	10.0	3.4	64%	17%	49	22	30	31%	84%	16%	0	17			0	1.07	8.0	127	152	$4
2nd Half	1	4	1	27	26	4.39	4.01	1.24	761	618	827	4.0	2.4	8.8	3.7	62%	17%	44	17	39	31%	69%	14%	0	15			25	1.22	-0.1	116	139	$0
18 Proj	**2**	**3**	**0**	**44**	**37**	**3.82**	**4.28**	**1.28**	**735**	**763**	**718**	**4.1**	**2.6**	**7.7**	**3.0**	**62%**	**14%**	**44**	**21**	**35**	**31%**	**73%**	**11%**	**0**						**2.9**	**90**	**109**	**-$2**

Kopech,Michael

Age: 22	Th: R	Role SP	Health	A	LIMA Plan	B		
Ht: 6' 3"	Wt: 205	Type Pwr	PT/Exp	F	Rand Var	0		
			Consist	F	MM	2401		

21-year-old with triple-digit FB earned Aug promotion to AAA after torrid five-start stretch in AA (0.51 ERA, 49/5 K/BB in 35 IP). Ctl/Cmd improvement largely stuck in three AAA starts (17/5 K/BB in 15 IP). Not on CHW 40-man roster, so may return to minors to start year, but it won't be long now. Get in line.

Yr Tm	W	L	Sv	IP	K	ERA	xERA	WHIP	oOPS	vL	vR	BF/G	Ctl	Dom	Cmd	FpK	SwK	G	L	F	H%	S%	hr/f	GS	APC	DOM%	DIS%	Sv%	LI	RAR	BPV	BPX	R$
13																																	
14																																	
15																																	
16																																	
17 a/a	9	8	0	134	156	3.57	2.99	1.31				22.2	4.7	10.5	2.2						31%	73%								13.1	107	128	$10
1st Half	4	5	0	75	88	5.07	4.01	1.56				21.9	6.6	10.6	1.6						31%	68%								-6.6	83	100	$2
2nd Half	5	3	0	59	68	2.25	2.16	1.09				23.2	2.6	10.3	3.9						32%	78%								15.4	150	180	$20
18 Proj	**5**	**4**	**0**	**73**	**84**	**3.88**	**4.00**	**1.24**				**22.4**	**3.9**	**10.4**	**2.6**	**59%**	**12%**	**40**	**20**	**40**	**30%**	**71%**	**10%**	**13**						**4.3**	**99**	**119**	**$3**

Kuhl,Chad

Age: 25	Th: R	Role SP	Health	A	LIMA Plan	B+		
Ht: 6' 3"	Wt: 216	Type Pwr	PT/Exp	C	Rand Var	0		
			Consist	B	MM	0103		

Growth, if any, coming at a glacial pace. Step back in Ctl was predictable, given ongoing FpK issues, and while Dom rose with increased velocity, SwK remained a bit dubious. And GB tilt hasn't materialized, despite heavy use of sinker. Young enough to still make a leap, but little sign of it yet.

Yr Tm	W	L	Sv	IP	K	ERA	xERA	WHIP	oOPS	vL	vR	BF/G	Ctl	Dom	Cmd	FpK	SwK	G	L	F	H%	S%	hr/f	GS	APC	DOM%	DIS%	Sv%	LI	RAR	BPV	BPX	R$
13																																	
14																																	
15 aa	11	5	0	153	82	2.87	3.52	1.25				23.9	2.3	4.8	2.1						29%	78%								20.6	58	69	$11
16 PIT *	11	7	0	154	106	3.79	4.72	1.39	757	854	676	21.7	2.2	6.2	2.8	57%	9%	44	20	36	32%	76%	9%	14	82	21%	36%			7.6	61	72	$5
17 PIT	8	11	0	157	142	4.35	4.68	1.47	793	893	698	21.9	4.1	8.1	2.0	58%	10%	42	23	35	32%	72%	11%	31	87	16%	23%			0.2	55	66	$1
1st Half	2	6	0	75	62	5.26	4.88	1.49	836	1018	667	20.7	3.5	7.4	2.1	58%	12%	41	21	37	33%	66%	10%	16	81	6%	25%			-8.3	59	71	-$7
2nd Half	6	5	0	82	80	3.51	4.50	1.45	750	772	728	23.3	4.7	8.8	1.9	58%	9%	43	25	32	31%	78%	11%	15	93	27%	20%			8.6	51	61	$8
18 Proj	**9**	**10**	**0**	**174**	**135**	**4.12**	**4.77**	**1.41**	**786**	**881**	**702**	**24.3**	**3.2**	**7.0**	**2.2**	**58%**	**10%**	**43**	**22**	**35**	**32%**	**73%**	**10%**	**30**						**5.0**	**60**	**72**	**$3**

KRISTOPHER OLSON

Lackey,John

Age: 39	Th: R	Role SP	Health D	LIMA Plan B
Ht: 6' 6"	Wt: 235	Type Pwr	PT/Exp A	Rand Var +2
			Consist A	MM 1203

There are worse skill sets, but he's managed to use this profile to good effect thus far. Still, there are also signs of age-related decline, most notably xERA, Cmd, inversion of DOM/DIS. If he was 10 years younger, we'd write off 2017 as a blip and project a rebound. But if he doesn't retire, 2017 becomes the new baseline.

Yr Tm	W	L	Sv	IP	K	ERA	xERA	WHIP	oOPS	vL	vR	BF/G	Ctl	Dom	Cmd	FpK	SwK	G	L	F	H%	S%	hr/f	GS	APC	DOM%	DIS%	Sv%	LI	RAR	BPV	BPX	R$
13 BOS	10	13	0	189	161	3.52	3.50	1.16	703	657	760	26.8	1.9	7.7	4.0	64%	10%	47	18	35	29%	75%	13%	29	99	38%	14%			8.1	111	145	$12
14 2 TM	14	10	0	198	164	3.82	3.67	1.28	730	719	742	26.9	2.1	7.5	3.5	68%	10%	44	22	34	32%	74%	12%	31	99	35%	23%			-1.9	99	117	$6
15 STL	13	10	0	218	175	2.77	3.81	1.21	679	749	620	27.2	2.2	7.2	3.3	71%	10%	46	21	33	30%	81%	10%	33	95	33%	18%			32.2	95	113	$21
16 CHC	11	8	0	188	180	3.35	3.68	1.06	645	694	609	25.8	2.5	8.6	3.4	68%	12%	41	23	36	26%	73%	13%	29	98	41%	17%			19.6	105	125	$21
17 CHC	12	12	0	171	149	4.59	4.48	1.28	785	865	711	23.6	2.8	7.9	2.8	65%	11%	41	20	39	28%	72%	18%	30	89	13%	43%	0	0.77	-4.8	85	102	$7
1st Half	5	9	0	93	83	5.24	4.51	1.35	849	903	803	25.3	2.9	8.1	2.8	68%	10%	43	19	38	28%	70%	22%	16	97	13%	50%			-10.1	87	105	$2
2nd Half	7	3	0	78	66	3.81	4.44	1.19	707	823	586	21.7	2.7	7.6	2.9	63%	11%	39	21	40	27%	74%	13%	14	82	14%	36%	0	0.77	5.3	82	99	$13
18 Proj	**11**	**9**	**0**	**160**	**140**	**4.20**	**4.20**	**1.20**	**719**	**786**	**659**	**23.8**	**2.5**	**7.9**	**3.1**	**66%**	**11%**	**42**	**21**	**37**	**28%**	**70%**	**15%**	**27**						**3.0**	**93**	**112**	**$9**

Lamet,Dinelson

Age: 25	Th: R	Role SP	Health A	LIMA Plan B
Ht: 6' 4"	Wt: 187	Type Pwr FB	PT/Exp D	Rand Var +2
			Consist D	MM 1403

7-8, 4.57 ERA in 114 IP at SD. Teased with elite skills through first seven GS, but FpK warned that Ctl was headed north. Still, he dominates RHB, and SwK, Dom already where they need to be. Now, just needs to rein in Ctl, solve LHB; 2nd half vL went in right direction at least. A work in progress worth watching.

Yr Tm	W	L	Sv	IP	K	ERA	xERA	WHIP	oOPS	vL	vR	BF/G	Ctl	Dom	Cmd	FpK	SwK	G	L	F	H%	S%	hr/f	GS	APC	DOM%	DIS%	Sv%	LI	RAR	BPV	BPX	R$
13																																	
14																																	
15																																	
16 a/a	5	9	0	85	85	4.11	3.47	1.35				22.1	3.6	8.9	2.5						33%	69%								0.8	97	116	$1
17 SD *	10	10	0	153	179	4.26	3.60	1.28	707	867	537	21.7	4.3	10.5	2.5	56%	13%	37	20	43	29%	70%	15%	21	92	24%	19%			1.9	91	109	$9
1st Half	6	4	0	76	90	4.33	3.66	1.24	737	1026	438	20.6	3.5	10.6	3.0	55%	15%	37	13	51	31%	68%	17%	7	88	29%	14%			0.3	101	121	$10
2nd Half	4	6	0	77	89	4.19	4.33	1.31	690	784	588	23.5	5.0	10.4	2.1	56%	11%	37	23	39	27%	71%	13%	14	95	21%	21%			1.6	67	80	$
18 Proj	**9**	**12**	**0**	**160**	**175**	**4.21**	**4.37**	**1.31**	**696**	**874**	**509**	**23.5**	**4.1**	**9.9**	**2.4**	**56%**	**13%**	**37**	**19**	**44**	**31%**	**69%**	**9%**	**28**						**2.8**	**83**	**100**	**$6**

Law,Derek

Age: 27	Th: R	Role RP	Health A	LIMA Plan B+
Ht: 6' 2"	Wt: 210	Type Pwr	PT/Exp D	Rand Var +1
			Consist F	MM 1210

4 Sv, 5.06 ERA in 37 IP at SF. Got shot as fill-in closer that skills said he deserved. But after four May saves, June was cruel (10 ER in 7 IP), and he was off to AAA, not to be seen again until Sept. Biggest changes: lack of FpK/Ctl, GB%; struggles vL. Still owns 2016 line, though, so don't lose sight of him altogether.

Yr Tm	W	L	Sv	IP	K	ERA	xERA	WHIP	oOPS	vL	vR	BF/G	Ctl	Dom	Cmd	FpK	SwK	G	L	F	H%	S%	hr/f	GS	APC	DOM%	DIS%	Sv%	LI	RAR	BPV	BPX	R$
13																																	
14 aa	2	0	13	28	24	2.90	2.66	1.27				4.2	4.6	7.8	1.7						27%	76%								2.9	87	103	$
15 aa	0	1	13	26	27	6.32	6.28	1.87				4.3	3.2	9.6	3.0						46%	64%								-7.5	95	113	-$
16 SF	4	2	1	55	50	2.13	3.24	0.96	570	523	598	3.5	1.5	8.2	5.6	63%	11%	50	22	28	28%	80%	7%	0	13			50	0.90	14.0	136	161	$
17 SF *	5	2	14	70	55	4.18	5.17	1.60	840	967	747	4.7	3.5	7.1	2.0	56%	10%	38	23	39	36%	75%	11%	0	16			74	0.85	1.5	57	69	$
1st Half	3	2	6	37	32	5.93	6.57	1.80	895	1056	763	4.6	3.8	7.7	2.1	59%	10%	37	24	39	39%	69%	13%	0	17			75	0.97	-7.2	42	51	-$
2nd Half	2	0	8	33	24	2.21	3.60	1.37	584	300	684	4.8	3.2	6.5	2.0	38%	12%	44	17	39	32%	84%	0%	0	12			73	0.49	8.7	75	90	$
18 Proj	**4**	**2**	**5**	**58**	**50**	**3.38**	**4.30**	**1.31**	**682**	**746**	**634**	**4.1**	**2.6**	**7.8**	**3.0**	**60%**	**10%**	**42**	**23**	**35**	**33%**	**75%**	**6%**	**0**						**7.0**	**90**	**108**	**$**

Leake,Mike

Age: 30	Th: R	Role SP	Health B	LIMA Plan B
Ht: 5' 10"	Wt: 170	Type Con GB	PT/Exp A	Rand Var +1
			Consist A	MM 2005

Rough stretch left him on the outs in STL, but in 2nd half, much can be laid at feet of lady luck. Fortunes stabilized in SEA, and he closed on high note (3.27 xERA, 149 BPV in Sept), even with minor lat strain. In final analysis, he's still the same GB-heavy, low-Dom IP eater he's always been. Bid accordingly.

Yr Tm	W	L	Sv	IP	K	ERA	xERA	WHIP	oOPS	vL	vR	BF/G	Ctl	Dom	Cmd	FpK	SwK	G	L	F	H%	S%	hr/f	GS	APC	DOM%	DIS%	Sv%	LI	RAR	BPV	BPX	R$
13 CIN	14	7	0	192	122	3.37	3.93	1.25	719	717	721	25.8	2.2	5.7	2.5	59%	7%	49	21	30	29%	77%	12%	31	94	29%	35%			11.8	69	90	$1
14 CIN	11	13	0	214	164	3.70	3.45	1.25	730	801	674	27.3	2.1	6.9	3.3	60%	8%	53	20	26	31%	73%	13%	33	97	30%	27%			1.2	98	117	$
15 2 NL	11	10	0	192	119	3.70	3.95	1.16	686	727	635	25.9	2.3	5.6	2.4	61%	7%	52	22	27	26%	72%	14%	30	92	27%	33%			6.1	68	81	$1
16 STL	9	12	0	177	125	4.69	3.93	1.32	756	761	752	25.2	1.5	6.4	4.2	62%	7%	54	21	25	33%	66%	14%	30	89	23%	33%			-10.8	105	125	$
17 2 TM	10	13	0	186	130	3.92	4.03	1.28	742	785	700	25.2	1.8	6.3	3.5	63%	9%	54	22	25	31%	72%	14%	31	90	29%	26%			10.1	97	116	$
1st Half	6	6	0	106	72	2.97	3.81	1.08	654	684	625	26.4	2.0	6.1	3.1	61%	9%	57	20	23	27%	75%	12%	16	96	31%	13%			18.1	92	110	$2
2nd Half	4	7	0	80	58	5.18	4.31	1.54	844	909	784	24.0	1.6	6.5	4.1	65%	9%	50	24	26	37%	69%	15%	15	83	27%	40%			-8.1	103	124	-$
18 Proj	**10**	**13**	**0**	**189**	**133**	**3.94**	**4.08**	**1.31**	**752**	**787**	**719**	**24.6**	**1.8**	**6.3**	**3.5**	**63%**	**8%**	**53**	**22**	**26**	**32%**	**73%**	**14%**	**32**						**9.7**	**96**	**116**	**$**

LeBlanc,Wade

Age: 33	Th: L	Role RP	Health B	LIMA Plan B+
Ht: 6' 3"	Wt: 205	Type	PT/Exp D	Rand Var +2
			Consist B	MM 0100

Career-best GB% helped him see some early success as low-leverage reliever, but then came 25 ER in 27.2 IP from June to mid-Aug, and DL stint (quad). Waived in late Aug, and no one volunteered to pay short money owed to LHP who can't get out LHB. (Go figure.) Next stop: involuntary retirement.

Yr Tm	W	L	Sv	IP	K	ERA	xERA	WHIP	oOPS	vL	vR	BF/G	Ctl	Dom	Cmd	FpK	SwK	G	L	F	H%	S%	hr/f	GS	APC	DOM%	DIS%	Sv%	LI	RAR	BPV	BPX	R$
13 2 TM *	4	6	1	105	69	5.69	6.09	1.71	855	1003	780	13.2	3.3	5.9	1.8	64%	9%	39	22	39	36%	68%	9%	7	57	0%	71%	100	0.67	-23.5	30	39	-$1
14 2 AL *	11	5	0	158	110	4.14	4.52	1.45	625	627	623	20.4	2.6	6.3	2.4	59%	9%	40	24	36	34%	72%	6%	3	41	0%	33%	0	0.53	-7.7	67	80	-$
15																																	
16 2 TM *	11	2	2	152	114	3.25	5.07	1.45	776	680	801	19.6	2.2	6.8	3.0	63%	10%	34	21	45	34%	82%	17%	8	50	0%	38%	100	0.62	17.6	66	78	$
17 PIT	5	2	1	68	54	4.50	4.20	1.19	717	833	658	5.7	2.3	7.1	3.2	60%	10%	46	23	31	28%	66%	15%	0	21			33	0.71	-1.2	92	110	$
1st Half	3	2	1	44	34	4.47	4.06	1.22	703	887	602	5.9	1.8	6.9	3.8	58%	10%	49	22	29	31%	65%	13%	0	23			33	0.89	-0.6	102	122	$
2nd Half	2	0	0	24	20	4.56	4.47	1.14	744	706	760	5.2	3.0	7.6	2.5	63%	9%	40	24	36	23%	68%	20%	0	19			0	0.41	-0.6	73	87	$
18 Proj	**3**	**1**	**0**	**44**	**33**	**4.88**	**4.70**	**1.34**	**793**	**840**	**775**	**8.3**	**2.6**	**6.9**	**2.7**	**62%**	**10%**	**40**	**22**	**38**	**30%**	**68%**	**14%**	**0**						**-2.8**	**73**	**87**	**-$**

Leclerc,Jose

Age: 24	Th: R	Role RP	Health B	LIMA Plan D+
Ht: 6' 0"	Wt: 190	Type Pwr xFB	PT/Exp D	Rand Var -4
			Consist D	MM 0410

Hung around periphery of saves picture in injury-plagued pen, but hasn't displayed Ctl that says that's where he belongs. Even miniscule H% couldn't save him in 2nd half; who needs hits when everyone gets a free pass? SwK says there's raw material for effective late-inning reliever here, with emphasis on "raw."

Yr Tm	W	L	Sv	IP	K	ERA	xERA	WHIP	oOPS	vL	vR	BF/G	Ctl	Dom	Cmd	FpK	SwK	G	L	F	H%	S%	hr/f	GS	APC	DOM%	DIS%	Sv%	LI	RAR	BPV	BPX	R$
13																																	
14																																	
15 aa	6	8	0	103	83	6.59	5.07	1.76				18.2	6.4	7.2	1.1						32%	61%								-33.4	46	55	-$1
16 TEX *	2	7	2	81	79	3.50	3.07	1.39	710	1068	507	6.7	5.9	8.8	1.5	58%	12%	29	26	45	27%	75%	0%	0	22			29	0.26	6.9	82	97	$
17 TEX	2	3	2	46	60	3.94	4.97	1.38	585	688	513	4.3	7.9	11.8	1.5	55%	16%	40	10	50	22%	73%	8%	0	18			67	0.90	2.3	18	22	-$
1st Half	1	1	1	23	37	2.74	3.37	1.09	515	661	418	4.4	5.1	14.5	2.8	59%	20%	39	9	52	26%	78%	9%	0	19			100	0.91	4.6	140	168	$
2nd Half	1	2	1	23	23	5.16	7.14	1.68	651	714	605	4.2	10.7	9.1	0.9	51%	12%	40	12	48	18%	69%	8%	0	18			50	0.89	-2.2	-107	-128	-$
18 Proj	**2**	**4**	**2**	**51**	**55**	**4.28**	**5.12**	**1.39**	**658**	**808**	**556**	**5.4**	**6.2**	**9.8**	**1.6**	**54%**	**15%**	**40**	**11**	**50**	**27%**	**70%**	**6%**	**0**						**0.5**	**26**	**31**	**-$**

Leiter,Mark

Age: 27	Th: R	Role RP	Health A	LIMA Plan B+
Ht: 6' 0"	Wt: 195	Type Pwr	PT/Exp D	Rand Var +4
			Consist C	MM 1201

3-6, 4.96 ERA in 91 IP at PHI. Fringy prospect with subpar fastball bounced between bullpen, rotation, so it's hard to buy into strong Aug/Sept skills (BPV 136/143). Home runs hurt bottom line; he generates enough GB to not be so volatile. Rosterable if late-season work was light bulb going on, but ceiling likely low.

Yr Tm	W	L	Sv	IP	K	ERA	xERA	WHIP	oOPS	vL	vR	BF/G	Ctl	Dom	Cmd	FpK	SwK	G	L	F	H%	S%	hr/f	GS	APC	DOM%	DIS%	Sv%	LI	RAR	BPV	BPX	R$
13																																	
14																																	
15 aa	2	6	0	47	33	5.57	5.48	1.60				26.0	2.1	6.3	2.9						38%	64%								-9.3	69	82	-$
16 aa	6	3	1	104	79	3.74	3.80	1.27				18.4	2.6	6.9	2.7						30%	73%								5.8	75	90	$
17 PHI *	5	7	0	121	115	5.14	5.03	1.34	785	816	757	14.8	2.8	8.6	3.1	60%	9%	49	20	31	31%	68%	22%	11	56	27%	27%	0	0.59	-11.7	62	75	-$
1st Half	2	0	0	49	45	5.06	4.87	1.43	692	607	772	11.0	3.6	8.3	2.3	59%	7%	49	17	34	32%	68%	17%	2	37	50%	0%	0	0.42	-4.2	58	70	-
2nd Half	3	7	0	72	70	5.20	5.13	1.28	829	921	751	19.6	2.3	8.8	3.8	61%	10%	49	22	29	30%	67%	25%	9	76	22%	33%	0	0.78	-7.5	71	86	$
18 Proj	**5**	**7**	**0**	**116**	**100**	**4.40**	**4.23**	**1.35**	**776**	**792**	**762**	**20.0**	**2.6**	**7.8**	**3.0**	**60%**	**9%**	**48**	**19**	**33**	**32%**	**72%**	**15%**	**20**						**-0.6**	**96**	**116**	**$**

KRISTOPHER OLSON

Leone,Dominic

Age: 26	Th: R	Role	RP	Health	A	LIMA Plan	B+
Ht: 5' 11"	Wt: 210	Type	Pwr	PT/Exp	D	Rand Var	-3
				Consist	D	MM	3410

A snapshot tutorial on bullpen volatility. 2014 rookie stud loses it all; rediscovers effectiveness again 2½ years and two teams later. Found his old dominance in 1st half; Ctl and GB% reappeared afterward. But heed the ERA/xERA disconnect. Now a flyer again in deep strikeout leagues, with UP: Save opps.

Yr Tm	W	L	Sv	IP	K	ERA	xERA	WHIP	oOPS	vL	vR	BF/G	Ctl	Dom	Cmd	FpK	SwK	G	L	F	H%	S%	hr/f	GS	APC	DOM%	DIS%	Sv%	LI	RAR	BPV	BPX	R$
13 aa	1	2	4	18	15	3.33	3.04	1.08				4.4	2.5	7.6	3.0						25%	74%								1.2	85	110	-$1
14 SEA	8	2	0	66	70	2.17	2.98	1.16	624	800	511	4.8	3.4	9.5	2.8	56%	14%	55	21	25	29%	84%	10%	0	19			0	0.98	12.8	112	134	$7
15 2 TM *	2	8	1	52	39	6.33	4.56	1.55	884	668	1083	5.7	4.4	6.7	1.5	62%	10%	45	22	33	32%	58%	11%	0	22			25	1.26	-15.2	52	61	-$9
16 ARI *	5	3	1	62	52	5.02	5.90	1.57	1095	1170	1044	4.7	3.4	7.6	2.3	61%	12%	47	17	36	34%	73%	21%	0	19			33	0.49	-6.4	38	45	-$4
17 TOR	3	0	1	70	81	2.56	3.64	1.05	625	627	624	4.3	2.9	10.4	3.5	57%	15%	40	18	42	28%	79%	8%	0	17			20	1.12	15.6	125	150	$8
1st Half	1	0	0	38	42	3.11	4.22	1.12	652	740	605	4.9	3.6	10.0	2.8	53%	16%	32	19	49	26%	76%	9%	0	19			0	1.02	5.8	93	112	$6
2nd Half	2	0	1	33	39	1.93	2.98	0.98	593	470	646	3.7	2.2	10.7	4.9	62%	14%	51	16	33	29%	83%	8%	0	15			25	1.22	9.8	163	195	$11
18 Proj	**4**	**2**	**2**	**65**	**69**	**3.37**	**3.66**	**1.17**	**686**	**764**	**644**	**4.4**	**2.8**	**9.5**	**3.4**	**57%**	**14%**	**47**	**19**	**34**	**30%**	**74%**	**10%**	**0**						**7.9**	**120**	**145**	**$4**

Lester,Jon

Age: 34	Th: L	Role	SP	Health	B	LIMA Plan	B+
Ht: 6' 4"	Wt: 240	Type	Pwr	PT/Exp	A	Rand Var	+2
				Consist	A	MM	2305

Less-than-vintage Ctl took root as hr/f continued to trend poorly and then some. 2nd half H%, LD upticks piled on, crushing his ERA and WHIP. Perfect recent health ends with August DL stint (lat/back). Dom remains solid, suggesting a rebound. But another birthday hints at 1st half as your future benchmark.

Yr Tm	W	L	Sv	IP	K	ERA	xERA	WHIP	oOPS	vL	vR	BF/G	Ctl	Dom	Cmd	FpK	SwK	G	L	F	H%	S%	hr/f	GS	APC	DOM%	DIS%	Sv%	LI	RAR	BPV	BPX	R$
13 BOS	15	8	0	213	177	3.75	3.88	1.29	702	670	711	27.4	2.8	7.5	2.6	61%	9%	45	20	35	31%	73%	8%	33	108	45%	21%			2.9	81	106	$9
14 2 AL	16	11	0	220	220	2.46	3.19	1.10	635	697	617	27.7	2.0	9.0	4.6	61%	10%	42	21	37	31%	81%	7%	32	109	59%	9%			34.8	129	154	$26
15 CHC	11	12	0	205	207	3.34	3.13	1.12	661	658	662	25.9	2.1	9.1	4.4	61%	11%	49	22	29	31%	72%	10%	32	100	44%	16%			15.8	135	161	$19
16 CHC	19	5	0	203	197	2.44	3.42	1.02	602	540	620	24.9	2.3	8.7	3.8	63%	11%	47	20	33	26%	82%	12%	32	99	50%	16%			43.7	120	143	$34
17 CHC	13	8	0	181	180	4.33	3.96	1.32	750	554	808	23.8	3.0	9.0	3.0	58%	11%	46	21	32	32%	71%	16%	32	98	25%	34%			0.5	105	126	$9
1st Half	5	4	0	102	104	3.69	3.72	1.23	708	523	765	24.6	2.9	9.1	3.2	61%	11%	49	19	32	30%	74%	14%	17	102	24%	29%			8.4	113	135	$14
2nd Half	8	4	0	78	76	5.17	4.27	1.44	802	595	860	22.9	3.1	8.7	2.8	54%	11%	43	24	33	33%	69%	18%	15	93	27%	40%			-7.8	95	113	$1
18 Proj	**13**	**9**	**0**	**196**	**192**	**3.71**	**3.83**	**1.22**	**702**	**585**	**736**	**24.0**	**2.6**	**8.8**	**3.3**	**59%**	**11%**	**46**	**21**	**32**	**30%**	**74%**	**14%**	**33**						**15.6**	**112**	**135**	**$16**

Liriano,Francisco

Age: 34	Th: L	Role	RP	Health	D	LIMA Plan	D+
Ht: 6' 2"	Wt: 225	Type	Pwr	PT/Exp	A	Rand Var	+2
				Consist	B	MM	1303

Reversed 2016 HR issues even with FB increase, but FpK continued to erode and take Ctl with it. Dom deteriorated badly in The Season Of The Strikeout, as trend vR now looks ominous. Demoted to bullpen role over final two months; demand says he'll get more SP opportunities. Difficult to see how this ends well.

Yr Tm	W	L	Sv	IP	K	ERA	xERA	WHIP	oOPS	vL	vR	BF/G	Ctl	Dom	Cmd	FpK	SwK	G	L	F	H%	S%	hr/f	GS	APC	DOM%	DIS%	Sv%	LI	RAR	BPV	BPX	R$
13 PIT *	18	9	0	180	182	3.36	3.15	1.26	611	321	689	24.4	3.4	9.1	2.7	58%	14%	50	24	25	31%	74%	8%	26	96	38%	27%			11.1	102	133	$15
14 PIT	7	10	0	162	175	3.38	3.33	1.30	644	735	622	23.8	4.5	9.7	2.2	56%	14%	54	19	27	29%	76%	12%	29	94	28%	28%			7.2	85	102	$6
15 PIT	12	7	0	187	205	3.38	3.21	1.21	631	592	641	24.9	3.4	9.9	2.9	57%	15%	51	22	26	30%	74%	12%	31	96	45%	13%			13.5	116	138	$15
16 2 TM	8	13	0	163	168	4.69	4.21	1.48	773	739	783	23.6	4.7	9.3	2.0	56%	12%	52	18	30	31%	73%	19%	29	90	24%	45%	0	0.74	-10.1	70	83	-$2
17 2 AL	6	7	0	97	85	5.66	5.15	1.63	824	655	878	11.6	4.9	7.9	1.6	54%	10%	45	20	35	33%	66%	11%	18	46	17%	50%	0	0.86	-15.6	32	39	-$8
1st Half	4	4	0	62	58	5.66	5.12	1.61	834	683	870	21.8	4.9	8.4	1.7	55%	11%	43	20	37	33%	66%	12%	13	85	23%	46%			-10.0	39	47	-$8
2nd Half	2	3	0	35	27	5.66	5.20	1.66	807	622	895	6.2	4.9	6.9	1.4	53%	9%	48	20	31	33%	65%	9%	5	25	0%	60%	0	0.91	-5.6	19	23	-$9
18 Proj	**7**	**9**	**0**	**145**	**137**	**4.85**	**4.56**	**1.50**	**763**	**649**	**800**	**13.8**	**4.5**	**8.5**	**1.9**	**55%**	**11%**	**49**	**20**	**31**	**32%**	**69%**	**12%**	**11**						**-8.7**	**58**	**70**	**-$4**

Lively,Ben

Age: 26	Th: R	Role	SP	Health	A	LIMA Plan	B+
Ht: 6' 4"	Wt: 190	Type	FB	PT/Exp	D	Rand Var	0
				Consist	F	MM	0001

4-7, 4.26 ERA in 89 IP at PHI. Contact-heavy profile was aided early by pinpoint control and HR avoidance. Survived first 6 MLB starts (3.72 over 39 IP). Wasn't as fortunate in 2nd half, as Ctl, h% ticked upward, and HR began to hurt. History of poor Dom and GB% cap his ceiling; DOM%/DIS% screams a warning.

Yr Tm	W	L	Sv	IP	K	ERA	xERA	WHIP	oOPS	vL	vR	BF/G	Ctl	Dom	Cmd	FpK	SwK	G	L	F	H%	S%	hr/f	GS	APC	DOM%	DIS%	Sv%	LI	RAR	BPV	BPX	R$
13																																	
14 aa	3	6	0	72	69	4.32	4.16	1.40				23.4	4.4	8.6	2.0						30%	72%								-5.2	66	79	-$3
15 aa	8	7	0	144	98	4.72	5.39	1.56				25.2	2.8	6.1	2.2						35%	72%								-13.4	46	54	-$8
16 a/a	18	5	0	171	120	3.27	2.65	1.06				23.7	2.3	6.3	2.8						26%	71%								19.3	86	102	$21
17 PHI *	11	12	0	186	121	4.22	4.27	1.35	813	872	753	25.0	2.3	5.9	2.5	59%	8%	38	18	44	32%	70%	10%	15	94	7%	40%			3.2	63	76	$6
1st Half	7	4	0	95	51	3.40	3.53	1.23	806	813	798	25.7	1.9	4.8	2.6	62%	7%	40	17	42	30%	73%	7%	6	99	0%	33%			11.2	70	84	$13
2nd Half	4	8	0	91	70	5.08	5.04	1.46	819	911	716	24.3	2.8	7.0	2.5	56%	9%	36	18	46	33%	67%	13%	9	91	11%	44%			-8.1	57	68	-$2
18 Proj	**7**	**9**	**0**	**116**	**83**	**4.32**	**5.04**	**1.32**	**801**	**858**	**742**	**24.4**	**2.6**	**6.4**	**2.4**	**59%**	**8%**	**38**	**18**	**44**	**30%**	**70%**	**8%**	**20**						**0.6**	**60**	**72**	**$1**

Lopez,Reynaldo

Age: 24	Th: R	Role	SP	Health	A	LIMA Plan	B+
Ht: 6' 0"	Wt: 185	Type	Pwr FB	PT/Exp	D	Rand Var	0
				Consist	A	MM	0203

3-3, 4.91 ERA in 48 IP at CHW. It clicked after poor Triple-A 1st half, as next 8 starts (47 IP, 63/15 K/BB, 2.68 ERA) fueled mid-August promotion. Slowed by nagging back injury as Dom, SwK vanished in Sept; GB% decline didn't help. High-octane stuff gives legit prospect a future; command may determine where.

Yr Tm	W	L	Sv	IP	K	ERA	xERA	WHIP	oOPS	vL	vR	BF/G	Ctl	Dom	Cmd	FpK	SwK	G	L	F	H%	S%	hr/f	GS	APC	DOM%	DIS%	Sv%	LI	RAR	BPV	BPX	R$
13																																	
14																																	
15																																	
16 WAS *	10	10	0	153	151	4.51	4.46	1.40	772	666	885	21.6	3.5	8.9	2.5	56%	10%	41	23	35	33%	71%	9%	6	73	17%	50%	0	0.62	-6.1	74	88	$1
17 CHW *	9	10	0	169	145	4.51	4.45	1.36	741	808	676	23.5	3.5	7.8	2.2	61%	9%	30	22	48	30%	71%	9%	8	96	0%	50%			-3.3	57	68	$3
1st Half	6	4	0	81	70	4.93	5.01	1.50				23.3	4.1	7.7	1.9						31%	71%	0%	0						-5.8	46	55	-$1
2nd Half	3	6	0	88	76	4.13	3.94	1.24	741	808	676	23.7	3.0	7.8	2.6	61%	9%	30	22	48	28%	71%	9%	8	96	0%	50%			2.5	69	83	$7
18 Proj	**8**	**9**	**0**	**145**	**132**	**4.47**	**4.77**	**1.37**	**737**	**746**	**730**	**22.7**	**3.5**	**8.2**	**2.4**	**59%**	**10%**	**35**	**22**	**43**	**31%**	**71%**	**11%**	**27**						**-2.0**	**67**	**81**	**$2**

Lorenzen,Michael

Age: 26	Th: R	Role	RP	Health	D	LIMA Plan	B+
Ht: 6' 3"	Wt: 215	Type	Pwr xGB	PT/Exp	C	Rand Var	+2
				Consist	D	MM	2201

Held onto velocity, Dom gains derived from 2016 move to the pen—but the good news ends here. Ctl reverted to sub-par rotation-form all season. Decent 1st half became 2nd half nightmare, as HR-prone ways returned and H% luck turned bad. Bat-missing, multi-inning xGBer is watchable, but inconsistency keeps us leery.

Yr Tm	W	L	Sv	IP	K	ERA	xERA	WHIP	oOPS	vL	vR	BF/G	Ctl	Dom	Cmd	FpK	SwK	G	L	F	H%	S%	hr/f	GS	APC	DOM%	DIS%	Sv%	LI	RAR	BPV	BPX	R$
13																																	
14 aa	4	6	0	121	76	3.50	4.16	1.38				21.1	3.2	5.7	1.8						30%	77%								3.6	48	58	-$1
15 CIN *	8	11	0	156	100	4.59	5.12	1.52	882	1007	784	20.5	3.8	5.8	1.5	57%	9%	41	28	31	31%	73%	16%	21	74	0%	57%	0	0.69	-12.1	28	33	-$8
16 CIN	2	1	0	50	48	2.88	2.87	1.08	630	548	708	5.8	2.3	8.6	3.7	63%	10%	63	21	16	28%	78%	23%	0	22			0	0.84	8.1	133	158	$3
17 CIN	8	4	2	83	80	4.45	3.97	1.35	695	770	635	5.2	3.7	8.7	2.4	52%	11%	55	20	25	31%	69%	15%	0	20			29	1.00	-0.9	90	108	$2
1st Half	4	2	1	43	38	3.16	4.14	1.27	657	709	617	5.4	3.8	8.0	2.1	51%	11%	55	18	28	28%	78%	12%	0	20			33	0.86	6.3	75	90	$6
2nd Half	4	2	1	40	42	5.80	3.80	1.44	733	830	653	4.9	3.6	9.4	2.6	52%	11%	54	23	23	34%	60%	19%	0	20			25	1.14	-7.2	105	125	-$1
18 Proj	**5**	**3**	**0**	**73**	**64**	**4.01**	**3.88**	**1.32**	**710**	**735**	**688**	**6.3**	**3.3**	**8.0**	**2.4**	**56%**	**10%**	**55**	**22**	**23**	**30%**	**72%**	**17%**	**0**						**3.1**	**88**	**106**	**$1**

Lugo,Seth

Age: 28	Th: R	Role	SP	Health	D	LIMA Plan	C
Ht: 6' 4"	Wt: 225	Type		PT/Exp	C	Rand Var	+2
				Consist	B	MM	0101

Mild UCL tear delayed season until June. Despite velocity loss upon his return, posted intriguing 2nd half Dom, Ctl gains reflected in BPV. But these come minus SwK and FpK support, while lofty H% history is doing him no favors. Broad repertoire offers hope, but DOM% and bottom line to date still point to limited upside.

Yr Tm	W	L	Sv	IP	K	ERA	xERA	WHIP	oOPS	vL	vR	BF/G	Ctl	Dom	Cmd	FpK	SwK	G	L	F	H%	S%	hr/f	GS	APC	DOM%	DIS%	Sv%	LI	RAR	BPV	BPX	R$
13																																	
14																																	
15 a/a	8	7	0	136	103	4.27	4.41	1.39				23.9	2.3	6.8	2.9						34%	70%								-5.3	77	92	-$1
16 NYM *	8	6	0	137	96	4.80	5.14	1.50	666	672	661	15.6	2.8	6.3	2.3	64%	10%	43	19	38	33%	70%	10%	8	57	13%	38%	0	0.65	-10.3	48	57	-$5
17 NYM	7	5	0	101	85	4.71	4.36	1.37	770	772	768	22.9	2.2	7.5	3.4	59%	9%	42	24	34	33%	68%	12%	18	86	17%	33%	0	0.79	-4.4	96	115	$0
1st Half	3	1	0	25	17	3.55	4.83	1.34	741	719	764	26.8	2.8	6.0	2.1	63%	7%	41	25	34	30%	77%	11%	4	94	25%	50%			2.5	51	61	-$3
2nd Half	4	4	0	76	68	5.09	4.21	1.38	779	788	769	21.9	2.0	8.1	4.0	58%	10%	43	23	34	35%	65%	12%	14	84	14%	29%	0	0.76	-6.9	111	133	$1
18 Proj	**6**	**5**	**0**	**109**	**83**	**4.56**	**4.68**	**1.41**	**811**	**814**	**808**	**21.6**	**2.5**	**6.8**	**2.8**	**61%**	**9%**	**42**	**22**	**36**	**33%**	**70%**	**10%**	**21**						**-2.7**	**77**	**92**	**-$2**

JOCK THOMPSON

Lyles,Jordan

Age: 27	Th: R	Role RP	Health F	LIMA Plan D+	
Ht: 6' 4"	Wt: 230	Type	PT/Exp D	Rand Var +5	
			Consist C	MM 0000	

1-5, 7.75 ERA in 70 IP at COL/SD. Failed-SP-turned-RP with career mop-up profile avoided DL, turned in abysmal effort that earned late-July DFA. Resurfaced in Sept, slaughtered in his only starts of year. Only reason he's in this book is so other struggling arms can say, "At least I'm not Jordan Lyles."

Yr Tm	W	L	Sv	IP	K	ERA	xERA	WHIP	oOPS	vL	vR	BF/G	Ctl	Dom	Cmd	FpK	SwK	G	L	F	H%	S%	hr/f	GS	APC	DOM%	DIS%	Sv%	LI	RAR	BPV	BPX	R$
13 HOU *	9	11	1	165	103	5.64	5.11	1.53	801	751	859	21.8	3.0	5.6	1.9	56%	7%	48	21	30	33%	64%	12%	25	91	8%	40%	50	1.01	-36.2	39	50	-$14
14 COL	7	4	0	127	90	4.33	3.90	1.37	750	844	654	24.8	3.3	6.4	2.0	57%	8%	52	23	26	30%	70%	12%	22	95	5%	32%			-9.3	57	68	-$2
15 COL	2	5	0	49	30	5.14	4.45	1.49	751	797	697	21.2	3.5	5.5	1.6	58%	8%	50	26	25	32%	63%	5%	10	77	0%	30%			-7.1	33	39	-$6
16 COL *	8	7	1	103	53	6.80	6.56	1.87	790	902	713	10.1	4.2	4.6	1.1	60%	7%	51	24	25	36%	63%	8%	5	24	20%	80%	25	0.98	-33.3	10	11	-$18
17 2 NL *	2	6	0	90	70	7.11	6.52	1.66	948	1030	879	9.3	3.0	7.0	2.4	55%	10%	49	19	32	36%	59%	21%	5	33	0%	40%	0	0.44	-30.5	32	38	-$15
1st Half	0	2	0	35	25	6.88	4.52	1.50	901	1077	765	6.0	2.3	6.4	2.8	50%	9%	52	19	29	33%	58%	23%	0	23			0	0.37	-11.0	82	99	-$13
2nd Half	2	4	0	54	45	7.27	6.71	1.76	993	989	997	14.6	3.4	7.5	2.2	61%	10%	47	19	34	38%	60%	20%	5	54	0%	40%	0	0.60	-19.5	36	43	-$16
18 Proj	**2**	**3**	**0**	**44**	**29**	**6.53**	**5.07**	**1.67**	**870**	**936**	**812**	**11.0**	**3.4**	**6.1**	**1.8**	**58%**	**9%**	**50**	**21**	**29**	**35%**	**62%**	**14%**	**2**						**-11.7**	**45**	**55**	**-$9**

Lynn,Lance

Age: 31	Th: R	Role SP	Health F	LIMA Plan C	
Ht: 6' 5"	Wt: 280	Type Pwr	PT/Exp B	Rand Var -3	
			Consist B	MM 1205	

Impressive return from TJS, though with plenty of reasons for concern. Fortunate H% and 2nd half HR avoidance kept runs off the board despite Dom plunge and mediocre control. Can't ignore HR-suffocating sinker and ERA/xERA history. But if Dom, Ctl are trends... DN: 4.00+ ERA.

Yr Tm	W	L	Sv	IP	K	ERA	xERA	WHIP	oOPS	vL	vR	BF/G	Ctl	Dom	Cmd	FpK	SwK	G	L	F	H%	S%	hr/f	GS	APC	DOM%	DIS%	Sv%	LI	RAR	BPV	BPX	R$
13 STL	15	10	0	202	198	3.97	3.63	1.31	701	765	652	25.9	3.4	8.8	2.6	63%	10%	43	23	34	32%	70%	7%	33	102	52%	27%			-2.6	88	115	$8
14 STL	15	10	0	204	181	2.74	3.81	1.26	662	697	635	26.2	3.2	8.0	2.5	60%	9%	44	20	36	30%	80%	6%	33	105	30%	18%			25.2	80	95	$16
15 STL	12	11	0	175	167	3.03	3.95	1.37	708	809	623	24.2	3.5	8.6	2.5	56%	9%	44	22	34	33%	80%	8%	31	98	32%	29%			20.2	82	98	$11
16																																	
17 STL	11	8	0	186	153	3.43	4.61	1.23	707	818	601	23.5	3.8	7.4	2.0	55%	9%	44	20	36	25%	78%	14%	33	95	15%	42%			21.3	53	64	$16
1st Half	6	5	0	90	86	3.90	4.31	1.17	724	814	638	23.6	3.6	8.6	2.4	53%	10%	43	18	39	23%	77%	20%	16	97	25%	44%			5.1	79	95	$16
2nd Half	5	3	0	96	67	2.99	4.90	1.29	690	821	566	23.5	3.9	6.3	1.6	56%	9%	45	21	34	27%	79%	8%	17	94	6%	41%			16.3	29	35	$16
18 Proj	**12**	**9**	**0**	**181**	**158**	**3.74**	**4.53**	**1.33**	**721**	**817**	**636**	**23.9**	**3.6**	**7.8**	**2.2**	**57%**	**9%**	**44**	**21**	**35**	**30%**	**74%**	**10%**	**31**						**13.8**	**66**	**80**	**$10**

Lyons,Tyler

Age: 30	Th: L	Role RP	Health F	LIMA Plan B+	
Ht: 6' 4"	Wt: 210	Type Pwr	PT/Exp D	Rand Var 0	
			Consist C	MM 2311	

4-1, 3 Sv, 2.83 ERA in 54 IP at STL. Rehab from knee surgery, intercostal strain limited him until late May. Converted SP then rode slider to dominance, HR containment and high-leverage RP role. Handedness, velocity say full-time saves aren't likely despite gains vR—nor is a 2nd half repeat. Deep-league end-gamer.

Yr Tm	W	L	Sv	IP	K	ERA	xERA	WHIP	oOPS	vL	vR	BF/G	Ctl	Dom	Cmd	FpK	SwK	G	L	F	H%	S%	hr/f	GS	APC	DOM%	DIS%	Sv%	LI	RAR	BPV	BPX	R$
13 STL *	9	6	0	153	112	4.08	3.21	1.18	725	630	762	21.1	2.1	6.6	3.2	59%	9%	47	19	33	30%	65%	10%	8	66	25%	25%	0	0.97	-4.0	93	121	$6
14 STL *	8	6	0	120	97	4.87	4.99	1.45	682	280	806	19.7	2.2	7.3	3.3	62%	11%	43	16	40	35%	68%	10%	4	49	0%	25%	0	0.54	-16.7	79	95	-$6
15 STL *	12	6	0	155	138	3.75	5.12	1.37	751	746	752	19.7	1.7	8.1	4.8	60%	10%	39	25	36	35%	79%	19%	8	56	13%	25%	0	0.61	4.1	102	121	$5
16 STL	2	0	0	48	46	3.38	3.68	1.02	667	464	788	6.2	2.6	8.6	3.3	72%	11%	40	24	36	23%	78%	20%	0	23			0	0.59	4.8	102	122	$2
17 STL *	5	1	3	77	82	3.16	3.11	1.16	608	573	630	5.6	2.8	9.7	3.5	61%	11%	42	21	37	31%	75%	7%	0	18			75	0.95	11.3	116	140	$7
1st Half	1	0	1	46	38	3.90	4.36	1.31	695	692	694	9.0	2.2	7.5	3.3	56%	10%	47	18	35	32%	74%	9%	0	23			50	0.86	2.6	82	98	$3
2nd Half	4	1	2	31	44	2.05	2.88	0.95	533	485	568	3.5	3.5	12.9	3.7	64%	11%	36	24	40	27%	79%	4%	0	16			100	0.99	8.7	152	182	$14
18 Proj	**5**	**2**	**2**	**73**	**76**	**3.37**	**3.79**	**1.15**	**693**	**582**	**751**	**6.3**	**2.6**	**9.4**	**3.6**	**63%**	**11%**	**41**	**22**	**37**	**30%**	**75%**	**12%**	**0**						**8.8**	**118**	**142**	**$6**

Madson,Ryan

Age: 37	Th: R	Role RP	Health D	LIMA Plan B	
Ht: 6' 6"	Wt: 225	Type Pwr GB	PT/Exp C	Rand Var -3	
			Consist C	MM 4310	

Another lesson in reliever volatility. Stunning late-career effort follows poor, dead-armed 2016 2nd half (4.40 ERA, 5.9 Dom) in which age seemed to be showing. Dom and velocity soared all season; rock-solid Ctl and GB% have never looked better. Even with regression, still owns closer experience. UP: 20 Saves

Yr Tm	W	L	Sv	IP	K	ERA	xERA	WHIP	oOPS	vL	vR	BF/G	Ctl	Dom	Cmd	FpK	SwK	G	L	F	H%	S%	hr/f	GS	APC	DOM%	DIS%	Sv%	LI	RAR	BPV	BPX	R$
13																																	
14																																	
15 KC	1	2	3	63	58	2.13	3.17	0.96	573	547	597	3.6	2.0	8.2	4.1	66%	14%	55	13	32	26%	82%	9%	0	13			60	1.12	14.3	128	152	$7
16 OAK	6	7	30	65	49	3.62	4.24	1.28	701	695	706	4.3	2.8	6.8	2.5	56%	12%	46	23	31	30%	75%	12%	0	16			81	1.38	4.6	72	85	$14
17 2 TM	5	4	2	59	67	1.83	2.43	0.80	491	506	478	3.7	1.4	10.2	7.4	59%	14%	55	24	21	27%	78%	7%	0	14			40	1.11	18.4	180	216	$12
1st Half	1	4	1	32	31	2.53	2.95	0.94	552	604	519	3.7	1.7	8.7	5.2	52%	11%	54	26	20	27%	75%	12%	0	15			25	1.12	7.2	143	171	$8
2nd Half	4	0	1	27	36	1.00	1.86	0.63	413	422	400	3.6	1.0	12.0	12.0	68%	16%	57	21	23	26%	82%	0%	0	14			100	1.09	11.2	224	268	$16
18 Proj	**6**	**4**	**7**	**65**	**65**	**3.08**	**3.29**	**1.06**	**611**	**606**	**616**	**3.9**	**2.2**	**9.0**	**4.1**	**60%**	**13%**	**52**	**21**	**26**	**29%**	**72%**	**9%**	**0**						**10.3**	**133**	**160**	**$9**

Maeda,Kenta

Age: 30	Th: R	Role SP	Health A	LIMA Plan B	
Ht: 6' 1"	Wt: 175	Type Pwr	PT/Exp A	Rand Var +2	
			Consist B	MM 2303	

Disappointing encore to fine rookie year. Despite improved Cmd, fell victim to HR boom as GB% dropped and hr/f climbed all year long. Exceeded 5 innings just 7 times, as occasional bullpen stints, LA's rotating depth depressed IP. Even with a repeat of reduced rotation role, FpK and SwK point to valuable upside.

Yr Tm	W	L	Sv	IP	K	ERA	xERA	WHIP	oOPS	vL	vR	BF/G	Ctl	Dom	Cmd	FpK	SwK	G	L	F	H%	S%	hr/f	GS	APC	DOM%	DIS%	Sv%	LI	RAR	BPV	BPX	R$
13																																	
14																																	
15 for	15	8	0	176	170	4.32	4.37	1.27				24.8	3.2	8.7	2.7						28%	73%								-7.7	65	77	$7
16 LA	16	11	0	176	179	3.48	3.63	1.14	649	730	580	22.4	2.6	9.2	3.6	61%	12%	44	20	36	29%	73%	12%	32	92	25%	19%			15.3	118	140	$19
17 LA	13	6	1	134	140	4.22	3.89	1.15	714	781	647	19.2	2.3	9.4	4.1	64%	13%	38	22	40	29%	69%	15%	25	75	24%	36%	100	0.73	2.3	123	148	$12
1st Half	6	3	1	69	71	4.15	3.91	1.13	685	760	614	20.4	2.3	9.2	3.9	65%	15%	38	21	41	29%	68%	13%	12	79	33%	25%	100	0.71	1.7	119	142	$1
2nd Half	7	3	0	65	69	4.29	3.87	1.18	743	801	683	18.1	2.2	9.6	4.3	63%	11%	38	23	39	30%	71%	17%	13	72	15%	46%	0	0.75	0.5	129	154	$12
18 Proj	**13**	**8**	**0**	**160**	**163**	**3.76**	**3.87**	**1.17**	**701**	**774**	**632**	**20.1**	**2.5**	**9.2**	**3.7**	**63%**	**12%**	**40**	**21**	**38**	**29%**	**74%**	**15%**	**32**						**11.8**	**117**	**141**	**$14**

Mahle,Tyler

Age: 23	Th: R	Role SP	Health A	LIMA Plan B+	
Ht: 6' 3"	Wt: 210	Type xGB	PT/Exp D	Rand Var -4	
			Consist F	MM 1103	

1-2, 2.70 ERA in 20 IP at CIN. Prospect with xGB tilt posted 138/30 K/BB, 2.06 ERA in 144 IP between AA/AAA before holding his own in 4 MLB starts. Stuff says #4-5 SP; command and consistency (allowed 3+ runs twice in 28 starts across 3 levels) point to more. Rookie flyer... UP: 12 wins, 3.75 ERA.

Yr Tm	W	L	Sv	IP	K	ERA	xERA	WHIP	oOPS	vL	vR	BF/G	Ctl	Dom	Cmd	FpK	SwK	G	L	F	H%	S%	hr/f	GS	APC	DOM%	DIS%	Sv%	LI	RAR	BPV	BPX	R$
13																																	
14																																	
15																																	
16 aa	6	3	0	71	58	6.70	6.90	1.65				22.8	2.8	7.4	2.6						36%	64%								-22.0	26	31	-$1
17 CIN *	11	9	0	164	135	2.88	3.41	1.21	684	893	598	23.7	2.4	7.4	3.0	61%	7%	52	15	33	30%	79%	0%	4	92	0%	25%			30.0	92	111	$1
1st Half	7	5	0	98	90	2.33	3.00	1.09				24.0	2.0	8.2	4.2						29%	83%	0%	0						24.5	122	146	$2
2nd Half	4	4	0	66	46	3.68	4.01	1.39	684	893	598	23.3	3.2	6.2	2.0	61%	7%	52	15	33	31%	74%	0%	4	92	0%	25%			5.5	62	75	$
18 Proj	**8**	**7**	**0**	**131**	**104**	**4.19**	**4.42**	**1.34**	**739**	**986**	**642**	**22.8**	**2.7**	**7.2**	**2.7**	**61%**	**7%**	**52**	**15**	**33**	**31%**	**72%**	**12%**	**24**						**2.8**	**87**	**105**	**$**

Manaea,Sean

Age: 26	Th: L	Role SP	Health B	LIMA Plan B+	
Ht: 6' 5"	Wt: 245	Type Pwr	PT/Exp C	Rand Var 0	
			Consist A	MM 1203	

Instead of a step up, stepped back in roller-coaster year. Despite early Ctl woes, Dom, SwK and GB% prevailed through June. But all that disappeared, as LHB and RHB alike tore into his 2nd half. Sept finish (3.54 ERA), age, 1st half skills point to a rebound. But volatility, reduced velocity lower our expectations.

Yr Tm	W	L	Sv	IP	K	ERA	xERA	WHIP	oOPS	vL	vR	BF/G	Ctl	Dom	Cmd	FpK	SwK	G	L	F	H%	S%	hr/f	GS	APC	DOM%	DIS%	Sv%	LI	RAR	BPV	BPX	R$
13																																	
14																																	
15 aa	6	1	0	50	51	2.49	3.59	1.33				22.9	3.6	9.2	2.6						32%	84%								9.0	95	114	$
16 OAK *	9	9	0	163	141	3.63	3.78	1.20	713	526	754	23.3	2.3	7.8	3.4	65%	12%	44	21	35	29%	74%	14%	24	87	33%	29%	0	0.78	11.2	89	105	$1
17 OAK	12	10	0	159	140	4.37	4.49	1.40	763	593	809	23.9	3.1	7.9	2.5	60%	12%	44	21	35	33%	71%	11%	29	93	17%	38%			-0.2	81	97	$
1st Half	7	4	0	79	84	3.87	3.83	1.22	653	408	710	23.6	3.5	9.6	2.7	61%	15%	48	19	33	29%	70%	10%	14	93	14%	21%			4.7	103	123	$1
2nd Half	5	6	0	80	56	4.86	5.16	1.58	862	728	903	24.1	2.7	6.3	2.3	59%	9%	41	22	37	35%	72%	11%	15	93	20%	53%			-4.9	60	72	-$
18 Proj	**11**	**11**	**0**	**174**	**153**	**3.89**	**4.34**	**1.34**	**745**	**580**	**787**	**23.2**	**2.9**	**7.9**	**2.8**	**62%**	**12%**	**44**	**21**	**35**	**32%**	**74%**	**11%**	**31**						**10.0**	**88**	**106**	**$**

JOCK THOMPSON

Marquez,German

Age: 23	Th: R	Role: SP	Health: A	LIMA Plan: B+
Ht: 6' 1"	Wt: 185	Type:	PT/Exp: C	Rand Var: +2
			Consist: B	MM: 1203

Looked gassed in Sept (5.28 ERA, 6.5 Dom, 23% hr/f), but check out near across-the-board 2nd half skills bump. HR the only issue for rookie with GB tilt and 13 starts in Coors. Plus velocity never wavered; broad repertoire a plus. Seeds of a workhorse here. With 2H hr/f reversal, SwK bump... UP: 4.00 ERA, 15 W.

Yr Tm	W	L	Sv	IP	K	ERA	xERA	WHIP	oOPS	vL	vR	BF/G	Ctl	Dom	Cmd	FpK	SwK	G	L	F	H%	S%	hr/f	GS	APC	DOM%	DIS%	Sv%	LI	RAR	BPV	BPX	R$
13																																	
14																																	
15																																	
16 COL *	12	7	0	187	139	4.58	4.88	1.43	932	933	931	24.9	2.3	6.7	2.9	63%	10%	55	30	15	34%	70%	18%	3	59	0%	33%	0	0.51	-9.1	65	77	$0
17 COL	11	7	0	162	147	4.39	4.23	1.38	806	757	853	24.2	2.7	8.2	3.0	60%	10%	45	22	33	32%	73%	15%	29	92	10%	34%			-0.6	97	116	$5
1st Half	5	4	0	64	56	4.38	4.71	1.41	782	826	736	23.5	3.3	7.9	2.4	59%	9%	40	22	38	33%	70%	8%	12	91	8%	25%			-0.2	73	87	$0
2nd Half	6	3	0	98	91	4.39	3.93	1.35	821	710	925	24.6	2.4	8.3	3.5	60%	10%	49	21	30	32%	75%	22%	17	92	12%	41%			-0.4	112	135	$8
18 Proj	**12**	**7**	**0**	**174**	**146**	**4.30**	**4.37**	**1.40**	**809**	**768**	**849**	**24.0**	**2.6**	**7.6**	**2.9**	**60%**	**10%**	**45**	**22**	**33**	**33%**	**73%**	**13%**	**31**						**1.2**	**90**	**108**	**$3**

Martes,Francis

Age: 22	Th: R	Role: RP	Health: A	LIMA Plan: C
Ht: 6' 1"	Wt: 225	Type: Pwr	PT/Exp: D	Rand Var: +4
			Consist: F	MM: 1401

5-2, 5.80 ERA in 54 IP at HOU. Elite-but-unpolished SP prospect struggling with Triple-A control rushed to the next level after just 32 IP—with predictable results. Mid-90s velocity played up out of the pen as Dom spiked; H%, HR woes say command is an issue. SwK offers optimism, but likely needs more experience.

Yr Tm	W	L	Sv	IP	K	ERA	xERA	WHIP	oOPS	vL	vR	BF/G	Ctl	Dom	Cmd	FpK	SwK	G	L	F	H%	S%	hr/f	GS	APC	DOM%	DIS%	Sv%	LI	RAR	BPV	BPX	R$
13																																	
14																																	
15																																	
16 aa	9	6	0	125	120	3.92	3.19	1.30				20.6	3.3	8.6	2.6						33%	68%								4.2	103	122	$6
17 HOU *	5	4	0	87	103	5.41	5.25	1.67	765	761	769	9.7	5.7	10.7	1.9	59%	13%	43	22	35	36%	69%	14%	4	32	50%	50%	0	0.64	-11.2	71	85	-$7
1st Half	2	2	0	54	57	4.87	5.46	1.75	777	535	1022	18.9	6.0	9.6	1.6	56%	12%	43	25	32	36%	74%	11%	4	79	50%	50%	0	0.62	-3.4	60	72	-$8
2nd Half	3	2	0	33	46	6.27	4.03	1.55	758	918	638	5.7	5.2	12.5	2.4	61%	13%	42	20	38	36%	61%	16%	0	23			0	0.64	-7.8	106	127	-$5
18 Proj	**5**	**4**	**0**	**73**	**82**	**4.74**	**4.33**	**1.50**	**752**	**747**	**756**	**10.1**	**4.6**	**10.2**	**2.2**	**59%**	**13%**	**43**	**22**	**35**	**35%**	**69%**	**10%**	**8**						**-3.4**	**80**	**96**	**-$3**

Martinez,Carlos

Age: 26	Th: R	Role: SP	Health: A	LIMA Plan: C+
Ht: 6' 0"	Wt: 190	Type: Pwr GB	PT/Exp: A	Rand Var: +2
			Consist: A	MM: 2305

Almost ace-caliber 1st half, with only problems being fringy Ctl and team support. But 2nd half Dom plunge, HR spike, H% reversal fueled ERA regression and then some, aborting that next step up. ERA/xERA split says final three months weren't as bad as they looked. Floor offers consistent value as we wait for his best.

Yr Tm	W	L	Sv	IP	K	ERA	xERA	WHIP	oOPS	vL	vR	BF/G	Ctl	Dom	Cmd	FpK	SwK	G	L	F	H%	S%	hr/f	GS	APC	DOM%	DIS%	Sv%	LI	RAR	BPV	BPX	R$
13 STL *	8	4	1	108	86	3.24	3.09	1.25	704	764	661	11.9	2.9	7.1	2.4	62%	10%	52	19	29	30%	74%	4%	1	23	0%	100%	100	0.75	8.3	88	115	$6
14 STL	2	4	1	89	84	4.03	3.54	1.41	713	849	609	6.8	3.6	8.5	2.3	58%	14%	51	22	27	34%	70%	6%	7	24	14%	14%	17	1.34	-3.2	83	99	-$3
15 STL	14	7	0	180	184	3.01	3.28	1.29	687	756	623	24.4	3.2	9.2	2.9	63%	11%	54	20	25	32%	78%	11%	29	92	41%	21%	0	0.82	21.2	113	134	$15
16 STL	16	9	0	195	174	3.04	3.69	1.22	643	730	540	26.1	3.2	8.0	2.5	62%	10%	56	18	26	29%	77%	11%	31	98	32%	23%			27.7	91	108	$20
17 STL	12	11	0	205	217	3.64	3.64	1.22	694	783	608	26.8	3.1	9.5	3.1	59%	11%	51	19	30	30%	75%	16%	32	98	41%	19%			18.1	116	140	$18
1st Half	6	6	0	106	121	2.88	3.43	1.07	600	698	516	26.6	3.2	10.2	3.2	60%	11%	50	17	33	27%	77%	11%	16	99	50%	13%			19.4	125	150	$29
2nd Half	6	5	0	99	96	4.47	3.89	1.38	786	856	710	27.0	3.0	8.8	2.9	58%	11%	53	20	27	32%	73%	22%	16	97	31%	25%			-1.4	107	128	$7
18 Proj	**13**	**9**	**0**	**196**	**192**	**3.35**	**3.75**	**1.26**	**690**	**777**	**604**	**21.1**	**3.2**	**8.8**	**2.8**	**60%**	**11%**	**53**	**19**	**28**	**30%**	**77%**	**14%**	**38**						**24.3**	**105**	**127**	**$17**

Martinez,Nick

Age: 27	Th: R	Role: SP	Health: A	LIMA Plan: D+
Ht: 6' 1"	Wt: 200	Type: Con	PT/Exp: D	Rand Var: +2
			Consist: B	MM: 0001

3-8, 5.59 ERA in 111 IP at TEX. Teased briefly in April (13 IP, 10/1 K/BB, 47% GB%) and noise out of TEX hinted that he might be figuring something out. Ultimately became one of the HR onslaught's big casualties. Second half oOPS suggests a mercy-killing was in order. A DIS% history to believe in.

Yr Tm	W	L	Sv	IP	K	ERA	xERA	WHIP	oOPS	vL	vR	BF/G	Ctl	Dom	Cmd	FpK	SwK	G	L	F	H%	S%	hr/f	GS	APC	DOM%	DIS%	Sv%	LI	RAR	BPV	BPX	R$
13 aa	2	0	0	32	19	1.54	0.32	0.66				22.3	2.2	5.4	2.5						15%	79%								9.2	102	133	$4
14 TEX	5	12	0	140	77	4.55	5.24	1.46	795	832	746	21.0	3.5	4.9	1.4	53%	7%	33	20	47	29%	72%	8%	24	83	4%	58%	0	0.84	-14.1	5	6	-$8
15 TEX *	8	8	0	156	91	3.91	4.76	1.46	799	676	904	22.2	3.1	5.3	1.7	60%	8%	42	24	34	31%	76%	11%	21	88	5%	43%	0	0.69	1.0	36	43	-$2
16 TEX *	9	9	0	144	73	5.39	5.76	1.59	908	1022	810	20.4	2.5	4.6	1.9	51%	6%	50	16	34	34%	68%	17%	5	54	0%	100%	0	0.81	-21.3	24	28	-$11
17 TEX *	7	8	0	149	84	4.94	5.00	1.30	838	853	826	20.5	2.2	5.1	2.4	60%	7%	42	21	37	28%	68%	19%	18	79	11%	61%	0	0.70	-10.7	27	32	-$1
1st Half	4	3	0	76	41	4.66	4.76	1.23	764	799	739	20.6	2.3	4.8	2.1	62%	7%	42	20	38	25%	70%	16%	11	83	9%	64%	0	0.73	-2.9	19	23	$2
2nd Half	3	5	0	73	43	5.23	5.25	1.37	942	917	965	20.3	2.0	5.4	2.6	56%	7%	41	23	36	30%	66%	22%	7	73	14%	57%	0	0.66	-7.8	36	43	-$3
18 Proj	**4**	**7**	**0**	**94**	**52**	**5.02**	**5.15**	**1.38**	**791**	**802**	**781**	**20.8**	**2.4**	**5.0**	**2.1**	**56%**	**7%**	**43**	**20**	**37**	**30%**	**67%**	**12%**	**19**						**-7.7**	**46**	**55**	**-$5**

Maton,Phil

Age: 25	Th: R	Role: RP	Health: A	LIMA Plan: A
Ht: 6' 3"	Wt: 220	Type: Pwr GB	PT/Exp: F	Rand Var: +4
			Consist: F	MM: 2310

3-2, 4.19 ERA in 43 IP at SD. Triple-A closer with June promotion after just 31 impressive IP—43/10 K/BB, 14 saves, 2.59 ERA—in the high minors. Flashed the goods in small sample debut, as SwK, FpK, GB% all point to upside. Has time to fix 2.3 hr/9, and if he does quickly... UP: 3.25 ERA, 20 saves.

Yr Tm	W	L	Sv	IP	K	ERA	xERA	WHIP	oOPS	vL	vR	BF/G	Ctl	Dom	Cmd	FpK	SwK	G	L	F	H%	S%	hr/f	GS	APC	DOM%	DIS%	Sv%	LI	RAR	BPV	BPX	R$
13																																	
14																																	
15																																	
16																																	
17 SD *	4	3	14	68	71	3.71	4.20	1.26	778	912	679	4.0	2.8	9.4	3.3	61%	14%	45	22	32	31%	77%	26%	0	16			100	0.99	5.5	88	106	$8
1st Half	2	1	14	34	36	2.18	2.31	1.06	360	444	325	4.0	1.9	9.7	5.0	52%	17%	42	26	32	32%	79%	0%	0	13			100	0.90	9.0	164	197	$18
2nd Half	2	2	0	35	35	5.19	4.19	1.44	869	980	778	4.1	3.6	9.1	2.5	63%	13%	46	21	33	29%	75%	31%	0	17			0	1.01	-3.6	89	107	-$1
18 Proj	**3**	**3**	**5**	**58**	**60**	**3.97**	**3.95**	**1.29**	**680**	**770**	**607**	**4.1**	**2.9**	**9.3**	**3.2**	**63%**	**13%**	**46**	**21**	**33**	**30%**	**77%**	**19%**	**0**						**2.8**	**112**	**135**	**$2**

Matz,Steven

Age: 27	Th: L	Role: SP	Health: F	LIMA Plan: C
Ht: 6' 2"	Wt: 200	Type:	PT/Exp: C	Rand Var: +5
			Consist: C	MM: 1103

Was supposedly ready following Oct '16 bone spur removal. DL'd in Mar, resurfaced in June. Dom was M.I.A. before he was shut down for good in Aug. Projected fit again after more elbow surgery (compressed nerve correction). Considerable skills are not yet a distant memory, but multiple surgeries may be chipping away.

Yr Tm	W	L	Sv	IP	K	ERA	xERA	WHIP	oOPS	vL	vR	BF/G	Ctl	Dom	Cmd	FpK	SwK	G	L	F	H%	S%	hr/f	GS	APC	DOM%	DIS%	Sv%	LI	RAR	BPV	BPX	R$
13																																	
14 aa	6	5	0	71	60	2.25	2.97	1.15				23.6	1.6	7.6	4.7						32%	81%								13.1	137	164	$6
15 NYM *	12	4	0	137	122	2.13	2.75	1.12	650	650	644	23.5	2.7	8.0	2.9	62%	9%	46	21	34	28%	84%	12%	6	96	17%	17%			31.1	100	119	$19
16 NYM	9	8	0	132	129	3.40	3.39	1.21	689	698	686	24.9	2.1	8.8	4.2	65%	10%	51	21	28	32%	75%	14%	22	98	36%	23%			12.9	130	154	$10
17 NYM	2	7	0	67	48	6.08	4.76	1.53	860	763	887	22.9	2.6	6.5	2.5	59%	7%	47	22	31	34%	63%	17%	13	90	8%	38%			-14.1	72	87	-$8
1st Half	2	1	0	27	18	2.67	4.37	1.07	681	526	738	27.0	2.3	6.0	2.6	52%	5%	51	15	34	23%	88%	18%	4	104	25%	0%			5.6	74	89	$3
2nd Half	0	6	0	40	30	8.39	5.01	1.84	962	946	965	21.1	2.7	6.8	2.5	63%	9%	45	26	30	40%	55%	17%	9	84	0%	56%			-19.8	72	86	-$16
18 Proj	**8**	**8**	**0**	**131**	**107**	**3.96**	**4.18**	**1.33**	**729**	**701**	**737**	**22.9**	**2.4**	**7.4**	**3.1**	**61%**	**8%**	**48**	**21**	**31**	**32%**	**73%**	**12%**	**24**						**6.4**	**95**	**114**	**$4**

Maurer,Brandon

Age: 27	Th: R	Role: RP	Health: C	LIMA Plan: B+
Ht: 6' 5"	Wt: 230	Type: Pwr	PT/Exp: C	Rand Var: +5
			Consist: A	MM: 1300

Mid-90s stuff, plenty of swing-and-miss, good control—and results that don't reflect any of this. Lofty H%s and inability to consistently induce GBs are only part of it. S% points to inability to pitch with men on base—.950+ OPS over the past two years. Profile has upside, but we're staying away until we see a fix.

Yr Tm	W	L	Sv	IP	K	ERA	xERA	WHIP	oOPS	vL	vR	BF/G	Ctl	Dom	Cmd	FpK	SwK	G	L	F	H%	S%	hr/f	GS	APC	DOM%	DIS%	Sv%	LI	RAR	BPV	BPX	R$
13 SEA *	8	12	0	137	111	5.95	5.38	1.57	883	919	835	18.8	3.3	7.3	2.2	59%	10%	44	19	37	35%	63%	15%	14	70	21%	43%	0	0.74	-35.2	50	65	-$14
14 SEA *	2	4	3	89	75	4.23	4.06	1.34	705	631	759	7.4	2.6	7.6	2.9	63%	10%	39	18	43	33%	69%	6%	7	30	0%	43%	75	0.72	-5.4	84	100	-$2
15 SD	7	4	0	51	39	3.00	3.83	1.06	568	427	711	3.9	2.6	6.9	2.6	61%	13%	48	22	30	26%	73%	7%	0	15			0	1.15	6.1	78	93	$4
16 SD	0	5	13	70	72	4.52	4.16	1.26	686	648	722	4.2	3.0	9.3	3.1	60%	12%	38	20	42	32%	65%	8%	0	17			68	1.02	-2.9	103	123	$3
17 2 TM	3	6	22	59	59	6.52	4.45	1.55	838	757	902	3.9	2.9	8.9	3.1	67%	11%	39	26	35	38%	58%	12%	0	15			85	1.06	-15.8	100	120	$2
1st Half	0	4	15	31	31	6.32	3.79	1.24	721	655	762	3.8	2.0	8.9	4.4	72%	12%	42	23	34	34%	47%	10%	0	15			88	1.22	-7.6	126	151	$6
2nd Half	3	2	7	28	28	6.75	5.21	1.89	951	837	1057	4.0	3.9	9.0	2.3	64%	9%	35	29	36	41%	67%	14%	0	15			78	0.90	-8.3	71	85	-$3
18 Proj	**3**	**5**	**0**	**58**	**55**	**4.60**	**4.42**	**1.44**	**772**	**694**	**843**	**4.1**	**3.0**	**8.6**	**2.9**	**64%**	**11%**	**40**	**24**	**37**	**35%**	**70%**	**11%**	**0**						**-1.7**	**91**	**110**	**-$3**

OCK THOMPSON

McAllister,Zach

Age: 30	Th: R	Role RP	Health C	LIMA Plan B+	
Ht: 6' 6"	Wt: 240	Type Pwr FB	PT/Exp C	Rand Var -4	
			Consist B	MM 1300	

Ditched the slider and found dominance vR. The giveback vL was essentially 3 Aug HR, but it prevented a career year. Heed xERA as it warns that career best in S% may regress, especially as a flyballer with an elevated hr/f. Passable deep league filler, but lacks the gaudy Dom for widespread fantasy appeal.

Yr Tm	W	L	Sv	IP	K	ERA	xERA	WHIP	oOPS	vL	vR	BF/G	Ctl	Dom	Cmd	FpK	SwK	G	L	F	H%	S%	hr/f	GS	APC	DOM%	DIS%	Sv%	LI	RAR	BPV	BPX
13 CLE	9	9	0	134	101	3.75	4.46	1.36	739	737	741	24.1	3.3	6.8	2.1	61%	7%	37	22	41	30%	75%	8%	24	96	21%	42%			1.9	48	63
14 CLE *	11	8	0	155	121	4.04	3.95	1.34	750	789	715	19.5	2.5	7.0	2.9	62%	8%	42	21	37	33%	70%	7%	15	66	13%	47%	0	0.91	-5.6	84	100
15 CLE	4	4	1	69	84	3.00	3.37	1.35	702	632	764	4.9	3.0	11.0	3.7	57%	11%	43	21	36	36%	81%	10%	1	20	0%	0%	50	0.87	8.2	137	163
16 CLE	3	2	0	52	54	3.44	4.59	1.45	742	692	788	4.4	4.0	9.3	2.3	60%	10%	36	22	43	33%	80%	9%	2	18	0%	50%	0	0.96	4.8	74	88
17 CLE	2	2	0	62	66	2.61	3.97	1.19	670	843	535	5.0	3.0	9.6	3.1	64%	10%	36	21	43	29%	85%	12%	0	20			0	0.51	13.3	104	125
1st Half	1	0	0	36	43	2.52	3.80	1.15	625	696	575	5.3	3.5	10.9	3.1	62%	11%	35	20	45	29%	84%	11%	0	22			0	0.40	8.1	113	136
2nd Half	1	2	0	26	23	2.73	4.22	1.25	730	1006	473	4.6	2.4	7.9	3.3	68%	9%	36	23	41	30%	86%	13%	0	16			0	0.63	5.3	91	110
18 Proj	3	3	0	58	59	3.18	4.29	1.31	708	783	642	5.0	3.1	9.2	2.9	62%	10%	37	22	41	32%	80%	11%	0						8.4	96	115

McCarthy,Brandon

Age: 34	Th: R	Role RP	Health F	LIMA Plan B+	
Ht: 6' 7"	Wt: 235	Type Pwr	PT/Exp D	Rand Var -1	
			Consist B	MM 1201	

Is there a Health Grade LOWER than an F? Three more DL stints (shoulder, knee, blisters) run the career total to 14. 1st half work was solid, but not worth the headache of holding him during the injury downtime. His 2014 is a distant unicorn as age, sinking Dom, and role uncertainty push him to fantasy periphery.

Yr Tm	W	L	Sv	IP	K	ERA	xERA	WHIP	oOPS	vL	vR	BF/G	Ctl	Dom	Cmd	FpK	SwK	G	L	F	H%	S%	hr/f	GS	APC	DOM%	DIS%	Sv%	LI	RAR	BPV	BPX
13 ARI	5	11	0	135	76	4.53	3.95	1.35	759	716	807	26.2	1.4	5.1	3.6	68%	6%	48	25	27	33%	67%	10%	22	91	18%	36%			-11.1	79	103
14 2 TM	10	15	0	200	175	4.05	3.11	1.28	746	751	741	26.1	1.5	7.9	5.3	67%	9%	53	23	25	34%	72%	16%	32	95	28%	25%			-7.6	133	158
15 LA	3	0	0	23	29	5.87	2.99	1.22	898	691	1124	23.5	1.6	11.3	7.3	66%	12%	38	22	40	29%	68%	38%	4	92	50%	25%			-5.4	178	212
16 LA	2	3	0	40	44	4.95	4.53	1.38	642	720	587	17.1	5.9	9.9	1.7	60%	8%	35	27	38	28%	62%	6%	9	70	33%	22%	0	0.83	-3.8	33	40
17 LA	6	4	0	93	72	3.98	4.39	1.25	668	639	701	20.2	2.6	7.0	2.7	65%	9%	42	25	33	31%	68%	5%	16	76	19%	25%	0	0.72	4.3	75	90
1st Half	6	3	0	72	57	3.25	4.16	1.11	591	573	612	22.3	2.5	7.1	2.9	64%	9%	44	23	33	28%	71%	6%	13	86	23%	15%			9.8	83	100
2nd Half	0	1	0	21	15	6.53	5.22	1.74	904	856	952	15.7	3.0	6.5	2.1	68%	8%	35	30	35	39%	60%	4%	3	55	0%	67%	0	0.63	-5.5	48	58
18 Proj	4	6	0	94	79	4.72	4.60	1.41	745	740	751	18.7	3.2	7.5	2.3	65%	8%	41	26	33	33%	66%	7%	19						-4.2	67	81

McCullers,Lance

Age: 24	Th: R	Role SP	Health F	LIMA Plan A	
Ht: 6' 1"	Wt: 205	Type Pwr xGB	PT/Exp C	Rand Var +4	
			Consist A	MM 3403	

His 1st half looked like start of career year, but a back injury limited 2nd half IP and tanked results (Cmd, H%, S% all melted down). Quality post-season renews hope, but health concerns linger and 1st half alone can't erase long-term FpK, Ctl concerns. Every draft will have one believer keeping his price up; be careful.

Yr Tm	W	L	Sv	IP	K	ERA	xERA	WHIP	oOPS	vL	vR	BF/G	Ctl	Dom	Cmd	FpK	SwK	G	L	F	H%	S%	hr/f	GS	APC	DOM%	DIS%	Sv%	LI	RAR	BPV	BPX
13																																
14																																
15 HOU *	9	8	1	158	172	2.70	2.69	1.14	659	590	729	21.5	3.2	9.8	3.0	57%	10%	46	22	32	29%	79%	9%	22	96	36%	18%			24.6	115	137
16 HOU	6	5	0	81	106	3.22	3.24	1.54	736	751	722	25.1	5.0	11.8	2.4	57%	13%	57	22	21	38%	80%	12%	14	96	21%	14%			9.7	112	133
17 HOU	7	4	0	119	132	4.25	3.15	1.30	696	605	764	23.3	3.0	10.0	3.3	55%	12%	61	19	20	34%	67%	13%	22	92	32%	18%			1.6	137	165
1st Half	7	1	0	87	103	2.69	2.70	1.07	602	569	633	23.6	2.6	10.7	4.1	56%	13%	64	16	20	30%	77%	14%	15	94	47%	0%			17.9	164	196
2nd Half	0	3	0	32	29	8.53	4.51	1.93	909	721	1006	22.6	4.3	8.2	1.9	54%	10%	56	25	19	42%	53%	10%	7	86	0%	57%			-16.3	67	81
18 Proj	8	7	0	145	164	3.88	3.38	1.33	681	610	737	22.0	3.7	10.2	2.7	56%	12%	57	22	22	34%	71%	11%	27						8.5	118	142

McGee,Jake

Age: 31	Th: L	Role RP	Health D	LIMA Plan A	
Ht: 6' 3"	Wt: 230	Type Pwr FB	PT/Exp C	Rand Var -1	
			Consist C	MM 2310	

Tale of two halves: 1st half flashbacked to TAM days as Cmd, H%, and hr/f all returned, making him a force. Three dud outings (9 ER, 11 baserunners in 1.3 IP) explain 2nd half flop. Late-July back issue may have lingered, but mostly just RP volatility. Still has closer skills, needs opportunity.

Yr Tm	W	L	Sv	IP	K	ERA	xERA	WHIP	oOPS	vL	vR	BF/G	Ctl	Dom	Cmd	FpK	SwK	G	L	F	H%	S%	hr/f	GS	APC	DOM%	DIS%	Sv%	LI	RAR	BPV	BPX
13 TAM	5	3	1	63	75	4.02	3.20	1.18	659	678	648	3.7	3.2	10.8	3.4	63%	12%	43	19	39	30%	70%	13%	0	16			20	1.16	-1.2	130	169
14 TAM	5	2	19	71	90	1.89	2.68	0.90	486	572	452	3.8	2.0	11.4	5.6	65%	14%	38	19	43	29%	79%	3%	0	16			83	1.38	16.3	166	198
15 TAM	1	2	6	37	48	2.41	2.95	0.94	544	607	513	3.8	1.9	11.6	6.0	62%	13%	39	16	46	30%	78%	7%	0	16			60	1.30	7.1	173	206
16 COL	2	3	15	46	38	4.73	4.76	1.58	887	821	922	3.6	3.2	7.5	2.4	66%	9%	40	22	38	34%	76%	16%	0	15			79	0.78	-3.0	68	80
17 COL	0	2	3	57	58	3.61	3.86	1.10	624	690	585	3.7	2.5	9.1	3.6	62%	10%	41	19	41	29%	68%	6%	0	15			50	1.09	5.3	115	138
1st Half	0	0	1	34	41	2.91	3.56	1.03	584	645	540	3.9	2.4	10.9	4.6	65%	11%	36	22	43	30%	75%	8%	0	17			25	1.11	6.1	145	173
2nd Half	0	2	2	23	17	4.63	4.34	1.20	685	782	643	3.4	2.7	6.6	2.4	59%	9%	47	15	38	29%	59%	4%	0	13			100	1.07	-0.8	70	84
18 Proj	1	3	5	58	58	3.66	4.04	1.20	689	723	671	3.6	2.6	9.0	3.4	63%	10%	41	19	40	31%	72%	9%	0						5.0	110	133

McHugh,Collin

Age: 31	Th: R	Role SP	Health F	LIMA Plan B	
Ht: 6' 2"	Wt: 190	Type Pwr	PT/Exp A	Rand Var 0	
			Consist A	MM 1203	

5-2, 3.55 ERA in 63 IP at HOU. Elbow injury cost him the 1st half of the season. He was back to himself by 2nd half results, but G/L/F profile says he took a different route. New slider was part of FB jump, while boosting SwK and Dom (8.8 in MLB). If elbow holds, he's a usable 185 IP in the bank.

Yr Tm	W	L	Sv	IP	K	ERA	xERA	WHIP	oOPS	vL	vR	BF/G	Ctl	Dom	Cmd	FpK	SwK	G	L	F	H%	S%	hr/f	GS	APC	DOM%	DIS%	Sv%	LI	RAR	BPV	BPX
13 2 NL *	6	9	0	139	85	5.41	5.62	1.60	1053	1252	914	22.8	2.2	5.5	2.5	54%	9%	40	28	32	36%	67%	18%	5	62	0%	80%	0	0.56	-26.5	49	64
14 HOU *	11	9	0	174	167	2.91	2.49	1.05	588	609	556	22.4	2.4	8.7	3.5	58%	11%	42	24	34	27%	74%	9%	25	99	40%	12%			17.8	118	141
15 HOU	19	7	0	204	171	3.89	3.90	1.28	705	648	755	26.8	2.3	7.6	3.2	62%	11%	45	20	35	32%	71%	9%	32	101	41%	25%			1.8	96	114
16 HOU	13	10	0	185	177	4.34	4.15	1.41	790	804	777	24.1	2.6	8.6	3.3	67%	11%	41	21	38	34%	73%	12%	33	96	27%	27%			-3.4	103	123
17 HOU *	5	2	0	79	71	4.07	4.61	1.43	747	809	694	19.8	2.9	8.1	2.8	63%	13%	33	22	45	34%	74%	9%	12	90	25%	33%			2.8	79	94
1st Half	0	0	0	2	1	38.16	32.29	7.26				10.1	9.6	3.5	0.4						72%	42%	0%	0						-8.3	-54	-65
2nd Half	5	2	0	77	70	3.19	3.89	1.28	747	809	694	21.1	2.7	8.2	3.0	63%	13%	33	22	45	31%	79%	9%	12	90	25%	33%			11.1	88	106
18 Proj	11	7	0	160	144	3.76	4.31	1.30	734	735	734	23.1	2.5	8.1	3.3	63%	12%	40	21	38	32%	74%	9%	28						11.7	97	117

Mejia,Adalberto

Age: 25	Th: L	Role SP	Health B	LIMA Plan C	
Ht: 6' 3"	Wt: 195	Type Pwr	PT/Exp D	Rand Var 0	
			Consist C	MM 0101	

4-7, 4.50 ERA in 98 IP at MIN. Definition of "5th starter" with a deep, mediocre repertoire and fringe skills (Cmd, SwK) good enough for 5 IP/start. Added velocity to all 4 pitches. xERA hints at his downside, though 2nd half H% was egregious given Cmd, FpK, SwK, S%, AND hr/f improvements. Could be a little more here.

Yr Tm	W	L	Sv	IP	K	ERA	xERA	WHIP	oOPS	vL	vR	BF/G	Ctl	Dom	Cmd	FpK	SwK	G	L	F	H%	S%	hr/f	GS	APC	DOM%	DIS%	Sv%	LI	RAR	BPV	BPX
13																																
14 aa	7	9	0	108	72	5.00	4.58	1.46				21.0	2.5	6.0	2.4						34%	65%								-16.8	65	77
15 aa	5	2	0	51	33	3.20	2.99	1.25				17.4	3.3	5.9	1.8						28%	74%								4.8	69	82
16 MIN *	9	5	0	134	101	4.16	4.48	1.35	1098	2500	808	24.4	2.2	6.8	3.1	62%	5%	33	25	42	33%	72%	0%	0	42			0	0.05	0.5	75	90
17 MIN *	5	8	0	127	102	4.47	5.07	1.54	822	812	824	20.4	3.6	7.3	2.0	57%	11%	39	23	38	34%	73%	11%	21	83	5%	38%			-1.7	53	63
1st Half	3	4	0	72	56	4.67	4.82	1.46	808	864	795	20.5	3.9	7.0	1.8	55%	9%	44	17	39	30%	72%	15%	11	84	0%	36%			-2.7	42	50
2nd Half	2	4	0	55	47	4.20	5.40	1.64	837	752	854	20.3	3.2	7.7	2.4	59%	13%	34	28	37	38%	75%	7%	10	82	10%	40%			1.0	69	83
18 Proj	7	7	0	116	96	4.22	4.81	1.46	771	725	780	20.8	3.0	7.4	2.5	57%	11%	38	24	38	34%	72%	8%	24						2.0	69	83

Melancon,Mark

Age: 33	Th: R	Role RP	Health D	LIMA Plan A	
Ht: 6' 2"	Wt: 210	Type xGB	PT/Exp A	Rand Var +5	
			Consist A	MM 4230	

Forearm issues ate the bulk of his season and resulted in September surgery. The injury likely played a role in the H% and hr/f explosions and FpK tumble. Still had his base skills (Cmd, GB rate). Should have health and role to start '18, too, making him a worthy bounceback bet.

Yr Tm	W	L	Sv	IP	K	ERA	xERA	WHIP	oOPS	vL	vR	BF/G	Ctl	Dom	Cmd	FpK	SwK	G	L	F	H%	S%	hr/f	GS	APC	DOM%	DIS%	Sv%	LI	RAR	BPV	BPX
13 PIT	3	2	16	71	70	1.39	2.33	0.96	511	357	638	3.9	1.0	8.9	8.8	65%	12%	60	24	16	31%	85%	3%	0	14			76	1.31	21.6	170	222
14 PIT	3	5	33	71	71	1.90	2.50	0.87	473	415	524	3.8	1.4	9.0	6.5	69%	14%	57	20	23	27%	78%	5%	0	14			89	1.37	16.1	159	190
15 PIT	3	2	51	77	62	2.23	3.00	0.93	541	380	673	3.8	1.6	7.3	4.4	62%	12%	58	20	23	26%	78%	8%	0	14			96	1.35	16.4	123	146
16 2 NL	2	2	47	71	65	1.64	3.01	0.90	511	560	471	3.6	1.5	8.2	5.4	66%	11%	54	21	25	26%	84%	6%	0	14			92	1.04	22.4	139	165
17 SF	1	2	11	30	29	4.50	3.61	1.43	794	715	883	4.1	1.8	8.7	4.8	56%	10%	53	22	26	38%	70%	13%	0	16			69	1.12	-0.5	139	167
1st Half	1	2	11	21	19	4.35	3.66	1.35	774	663	900	4.0	1.3	8.3	6.3	59%	11%	51	20	29	36%	72%	16%	0	16			73	1.23	0.0	142	171
2nd Half	0	0	0	9	10	4.82	3.47	1.61	834	824	844	4.3	2.9	9.6	3.3	51%	9%	57	25	18	42%	67%	0%	0	16			0	0.88	-0.5	131	157
18 Proj	2	3	30	58	53	2.93	3.18	1.01	580	502	651	3.7	1.4	8.2	5.8	63%	12%	55	20	24	29%	73%	10%	0						10.2	142	171

PAUL SPORER

Mendez,Yohander

Age: 23	Th: L	Role	RP	PT/Exp	D	Rand Var	+2
Ht: 6' 5"	Wt: 200	Type		Consist	F	MM	1101
				Health	A	LIMA Plan	D+

0-0, 5.11 ERA in 12 IP at TEX. Spent season at AA to hone fastball command before a cup of coffee. The scouting report entices: size, deep arsenal (four pitches), elite changeup—a prospect rarity—and velocity. His 8.4 Dom and 3.0 Cmd as a minor leaguer lay the foundation for mid-rotation upside.

Yr Tm	W	L	Sv	IP	K	ERA	xERA	WHIP	oOPS	vL	vR	BF/G	Ctl	Dom	Cmd	FpK	SwK	G	L	F	H%	S%	hr/f	GS	APC	DOM%	DIS%	Sv%	LI	RAR	BPV	BPX	R$
13																																	
14																																	
15																																	
16 TEX *	8	2	0	81	58	3.18	2.54	1.20	878	1300	664	17.1	3.7	6.4	1.7	41%	11%	33	20	47	27%	72%	0%	0	37			0	0.29	10.1	78	93	$6
17 TEX *	7	9	0	150	111	5.16	5.07	1.34	869	528	1040	20.1	3.0	6.7	2.2	52%	9%	34	20	46	28%	68%	16%	0	27			0	0.75	-14.9	32	38	-$2
1st Half	5	5	0	93	65	4.88	4.82	1.30				25.5	3.6	6.3	1.8						24%	71%	0%	0						-6.0	20	24	$2
2nd Half	2	4	0	57	46	5.63	5.48	1.41	869	528	1040	15.1	2.0	7.2	3.6	52%	9%	34	20	46	33%	64%	16%	0	27			0	0.75	-8.9	64	77	-$8
18 Proj	**5**	**4**	**0**	**80**	**59**	**4.49**	**4.17**	**1.30**				**19.7**	**3.1**	**6.7**	**2.2**	**0%**	**0%**				**28%**	**69%**		**18**						**-1.3**	**54**	**65**	**-$1**

Middleton,Keynan

Age: 24	Th: R	Role	RP	PT/Exp	D	Rand Var	0
Ht: 6' 2"	Wt: 185	Type	Pwr FB	Consist	B	MM	2410
				Health	A	LIMA Plan	A

Hit a wall in July (7 ER in 8 IP), rebounded for a solid finish (3.08 ERA, 6.4 Cmd in last 26 IP). Elite SwK says more Dom coming, though be wary of Ctl after 2nd half FpK fade. Fastball command is source of HR issues, though raw total should drop if 2nd half GB tilt is real. Not closing yet, but keep a star by his name.

Yr Tm	W	L	Sv	IP	K	ERA	xERA	WHIP	oOPS	vL	vR	BF/G	Ctl	Dom	Cmd	FpK	SwK	G	L	F	H%	S%	hr/f	GS	APC	DOM%	DIS%	Sv%	LI	RAR	BPV	BPX	R$
13																																	
14																																	
15																																	
16 a/a	0	1	8	30	28	3.59	3.39	1.23				5.7	2.4	8.5	3.6						32%	72%								2.2	112	133	$1
17 LAA	6	1	3	58	63	3.86	4.09	1.34	791	733	834	3.8	2.8	9.7	3.5	57%	17%	38	21	41	33%	79%	16%	0	15			60	0.96	3.6	116	139	$3
1st Half	2	0	0	24	25	3.38	4.48	1.13	643	515	716	3.6	3.8	9.4	2.5	62%	17%	29	21	50	25%	75%	10%	0	14			0	0.73	2.9	75	89	$1
2nd Half	4	1	3	34	38	4.19	3.83	1.49	881	837	920	4.0	2.1	10.0	4.8	54%	17%	43	21	36	37%	81%	22%	0	16			60	1.12	0.7	143	172	$4
18 Proj	**4**	**3**	**9**	**58**	**65**	**3.87**	**4.05**	**1.34**	**793**	**736**	**836**	**3.8**	**2.8**	**10.0**	**3.6**	**57%**	**17%**	**37**	**21**	**42**	**33%**	**79%**	**17%**	**0**						**3.5**	**121**	**146**	**$4**

Miley,Wade

Age: 31	Th: L	Role	SP	PT/Exp	A	Rand Var	+5
Ht: 6' 0"	Wt: 220	Type	Pwr	Consist	A	MM	0203
				Health	B	LIMA Plan	D+

Fell apart completely as his consistently high H% was finally paired with a terrible Ctl (including MLB-high 93 BB) for the ultimate disaster. Strand rate saved him in 1st half, but buckled under the pressure of nearly 2 runners per IP in 2nd half. Even a drop in walks wouldn't return much value. Hard pass.

Yr Tm	W	L	Sv	IP	K	ERA	xERA	WHIP	oOPS	vL	vR	BF/G	Ctl	Dom	Cmd	FpK	SwK	G	L	F	H%	S%	hr/f	GS	APC	DOM%	DIS%	Sv%	LI	RAR	BPV	BPX	R$
13 ARI	10	10	0	203	147	3.55	3.79	1.32	727	704	732	25.7	2.9	6.5	2.2	59%	8%	52	21	27	30%	76%	13%	33	98	30%	30%			7.8	68	89	$7
14 ARI	8	12	0	201	183	4.34	3.59	1.40	746	727	752	26.2	3.4	8.2	2.4	63%	10%	51	21	28	32%	71%	14%	33	97	24%	24%			-14.8	86	102	-$3
15 BOS	11	11	0	194	147	4.46	4.16	1.37	740	674	760	26.0	3.0	6.8	2.3	61%	9%	49	21	30	32%	68%	9%	32	100	34%	28%			-11.9	70	83	-$1
16 2 AL	9	13	0	166	137	5.37	4.13	1.42	808	671	842	23.7	2.7	7.4	2.8	60%	9%	47	23	30	33%	65%	16%	30	91	13%	37%			-24.1	87	103	-$6
17 BAL	8	15	0	157	142	5.61	4.99	1.73	841	663	875	22.8	5.3	8.1	1.5	54%	8%	50	23	27	34%	70%	19%	32	95	16%	63%			-24.2	31	37	-$13
1st Half	3	6	0	81	74	4.54	4.78	1.66	797	560	832	23.2	5.1	8.2	1.6	54%	8%	53	21	26	33%	76%	19%	16	98	19%	56%			-1.8	41	49	-$8
2nd Half	5	9	0	76	68	6.75	5.23	1.80	888	733	926	22.3	5.6	8.1	1.4	54%	9%	47	25	28	34%	65%	20%	16	93	13%	69%			-22.4	20	24	-$18
18 Proj	**9**	**13**	**0**	**160**	**136**	**5.11**	**4.70**	**1.57**	**814**	**682**	**845**	**23.2**	**4.1**	**7.7**	**1.9**	**57%**	**9%**	**49**	**22**	**28**	**33%**	**70%**	**16%**	**30**						**-14.8**	**54**	**65**	**-$8**

Miller,Andrew

Age: 33	Th: L	Role	RP	PT/Exp	B	Rand Var	-5
Ht: 6' 7"	Wt: 205	Type	Pwr	Consist	B	MM	5510
				Health	D	LIMA Plan	B+

Right knee limited his 2nd half with two DL stints. A 4th straight drop in H% covered some skill regression (Dom, Ctl, and GB% all dropped), but FpK and SwK keep his foundation sturdy. Looked great in post-season. Remains a force, even without guaranteed save opportunities.

Yr Tm	W	L	Sv	IP	K	ERA	xERA	WHIP	oOPS	vL	vR	BF/G	Ctl	Dom	Cmd	FpK	SwK	G	L	F	H%	S%	hr/f	GS	APC	DOM%	DIS%	Sv%	LI	RAR	BPV	BPX	R$
13 BOS	1	2	0	31	48	2.64	2.47	1.37	624	725	526	3.6	5.0	14.1	2.8	59%	14%	56	21	23	36%	85%	20%	0	15			0	0.81	4.6	153	199	-$1
14 2 AL	5	5	1	62	103	2.02	1.80	0.80	456	467	446	3.3	2.5	14.9	6.1	59%	15%	47	22	31	29%	77%	9%	0	14			50	1.54	13.2	226	270	$11
15 NYY	3	2	36	62	100	2.04	2.14	0.86	475	602	444	4.1	2.9	14.6	5.0	66%	18%	48	18	33	27%	81%	13%	0	16			95	1.22	14.6	210	250	$24
16 2 AL	10	1	12	74	123	1.45	1.63	0.69	487	523	474	3.9	1.1	14.9	13.7	62%	17%	54	17	29	28%	91%	20%	0	16			86	1.23	25.1	271	322	$25
17 CLE	4	3	2	63	95	1.44	2.59	0.83	440	481	424	4.3	3.0	13.6	4.5	63%	17%	40	24	36	26%	86%	7%	0	17			50	1.29	22.6	181	218	$13
1st Half	3	2	2	42	65	1.49	2.42	0.71	408	525	363	4.4	2.1	13.8	6.5	63%	17%	35	24	41	25%	82%	6%	0	18			100	1.27	15.0	205	245	$19
2nd Half	1	1	0	20	30	1.33	2.97	1.08	503	392	551	4.0	4.9	13.3	2.7	62%	16%	48	25	28	27%	90%	9%	0	16			0	1.33	7.6	133	159	$2
18 Proj	**5**	**3**	**5**	**65**	**102**	**2.01**	**2.35**	**0.92**	**507**	**536**	**495**	**3.8**	**3.0**	**14.1**	**4.8**	**63%**	**17%**	**47**	**22**	**31**	**29%**	**82%**	**12%**	**0**						**18.9**	**199**	**240**	**$13**

Miller,Shelby

Age: 27	Th: R	Role	SP	PT/Exp	C	Rand Var	-3
Ht: 6' 3"	Wt: 225	Type	Pwr	Consist	C	MM	0200
				Health	F	LIMA Plan	D+

TJS ended season early and four starts aren't much to go on. Velo, SwK, and Dom spikes carried over from spring and severe mechanical issues from '16 improved. Recovery will limit '18 output. Already-suspect command will hold him back as it's usually last to return after this injury.

Yr Tm	W	L	Sv	IP	K	ERA	xERA	WHIP	oOPS	vL	vR	BF/G	Ctl	Dom	Cmd	FpK	SwK	G	L	F	H%	S%	hr/f	GS	APC	DOM%	DIS%	Sv%	LI	RAR	BPV	BPX	R$
13 STL	15	9	0	173	169	3.06	3.73	1.21	670	761	588	23.3	3.0	8.8	3.0	62%	10%	38	20	41	29%	79%	10%	31	96	23%	35%			17.2	94	123	$16
14 STL	10	9	0	183	127	3.74	4.44	1.27	697	707	690	23.9	3.6	6.2	1.7	60%	7%	40	19	41	26%	74%	10%	31	89	23%	42%	0	0.75	0.1	33	40	$5
15 ATL	6	17	0	205	171	3.02	4.02	1.25	663	732	594	26.1	3.2	7.5	2.3	61%	10%	48	18	34	29%	77%	6%	33	98	30%	24%			23.7	75	89	$13
16 ARI *	8	13	0	152	114	5.69	5.68	1.62	867	943	767	24.0	3.1	6.7	2.2	59%	8%	42	23	35	36%	66%	12%	20	87	5%	50%			-28.2	46	54	-$13
17 ARI	2	2	0	22	20	4.09	5.09	1.45	668	840	421	24.8	4.9	8.2	1.7	55%	10%	44	21	35	31%	71%	4%	4	97	25%	25%			0.7	37	44	-$4
1st Half	2	2	0	22	20	4.09	5.09	1.45	668	840	421	24.8	4.9	8.2	1.7	55%	10%	44	21	35	31%	71%	4%	4	97	25%	25%			0.7	37	44	-$4
2nd Half																																	
18 Proj	**4**	**5**	**0**	**58**	**48**	**4.46**	**4.76**	**1.38**	**710**	**813**	**594**	**23.9**	**3.7**	**7.5**	**2.0**	**59%**	**9%**	**43**	**20**	**36**	**31%**	**68%**	**8%**	**10**						**-0.7**	**56**	**67**	**-$2**

Minor,Mike

Age: 30	Th: L	Role	RP	PT/Exp	D	Rand Var	-2
Ht: 6' 4"	Wt: 210	Type	Pwr FB	Consist	F	MM	2311
				Health	F	LIMA Plan	B

Transition to pen couldn't have gone better after missing two years. Amped velocity (+4 to 94 MPH) and slider usage (+11 to 36%) en route to a brilliant effort. Dom, Cmd, FpK, SwK, GB, and hr/f were all career bests, improving beyond normal SP-to-RP gains. These skills are ready for the 9th. UP: 20 Sv

Yr Tm	W	L	Sv	IP	K	ERA	xERA	WHIP	oOPS	vL	vR	BF/G	Ctl	Dom	Cmd	FpK	SwK	G	L	F	H%	S%	hr/f	GS	APC	DOM%	DIS%	Sv%	LI	RAR	BPV	BPX	R$
13 ATL	13	9	0	205	181	3.21	3.68	1.09	657	583	680	25.6	2.0	8.0	3.9	64%	10%	35	22	43	28%	75%	9%	32	98	41%	16%			16.6	102	132	$20
14 ATL *	8	14	0	163	132	5.00	5.34	1.45	798	887	774	23.9	2.6	7.3	2.8	61%	8%	41	23	36	33%	70%	13%	25	97	24%	28%			-25.3	54	64	-$8
15																																	
16 a/a	0	4	0	42	32	8.51	7.67	1.96				20.2	5.5	6.9	1.3						35%	59%								-22.5	-4	-5	-$14
17 KC	6	6	6	78	88	2.55	3.53	1.02	585	423	664	4.7	2.5	10.2	4.0	65%	13%	42	16	41	28%	77%	6%	0	18			67	1.20	17.3	135	162	$13
1st Half	4	1	0	40	42	2.01	3.58	0.99	547	374	633	4.9	2.5	9.4	3.8	63%	12%	44	18	38	28%	79%	3%	0	19			0	1.00	11.7	125	149	$13
2nd Half	2	5	6	37	46	3.13	3.48	1.04	625	477	698	4.5	2.7	11.1	4.2	68%	14%	40	14	46	29%	74%	10%	0	18			67	1.39	5.6	146	175	$13
18 Proj	**4**	**3**	**6**	**73**	**76**	**3.17**	**3.85**	**1.12**	**636**	**553**	**667**	**5.5**	**2.6**	**9.4**	**3.6**	**64%**	**11%**	**40**	**19**	**40**	**29%**	**75%**	**9%**	**0**						**10.6**	**117**	**140**	**$8**

Minter,A.J.

Age: 24	Th: L	Role	RP	PT/Exp	F	Rand Var	+2
Ht: 6' 0"	Wt: 205	Type	Pwr FB	Consist	C	MM	4510
				Health	A	LIMA Plan	A

0-1, 3.00 ERA in 15 IP at ATL. Was a double espresso in his cup of coffee as newly found control led to a blistering 26 K (with elite SwK) and just 2 BB. Fanning nearly half your batters helps outrun a massive H%. Experience and left-handedness could keep him from the 9th for now, but skills may force the issue.

Yr Tm	W	L	Sv	IP	K	ERA	xERA	WHIP	oOPS	vL	vR	BF/G	Ctl	Dom	Cmd	FpK	SwK	G	L	F	H%	S%	hr/f	GS	APC	DOM%	DIS%	Sv%	LI	RAR	BPV	BPX	R$
13																																	
14																																	
15																																	
16 aa	1	0	0	19	28	3.53	2.62	1.26				4.2	3.4	13.3	3.9						40%	69%								1.5	170	202	-$2
17 ATL *	1	3	0	33	43	4.30	3.98	1.46	595	418	696	4.0	4.2	11.7	2.8	63%	19%	38	22	41	38%	70%	8%	0	16			0	0.87	0.2	114	137	-$4
1st Half	0	0	0	3	3	0.00	1.36	1.21				4.0	7.1	7.8	1.1						18%	100%	0%	0						1.6	99	119	-$7
2nd Half	1	3	0	30	41	4.73	4.26	1.48	595	418	696	4.0	4.0	12.1	3.0	63%	19%	38	22	41	40%	68%	8%	0	16			0	0.87	-1.4	119	142	-$3
18 Proj	**3**	**4**	**5**	**58**	**86**	**3.52**	**3.18**	**1.13**	**540**	**393**	**623**	**3.3**	**3.5**	**13.4**	**3.9**	**63%**	**19%**	**37**	**22**	**41**	**34%**	**70%**	**8%**	**0**						**6.0**	**163**	**196**	**$6**

PAUL SPORER

Miranda,Ariel

Age: 29	Th: L	Role SP	Health A	LIMA Plan B	
Ht: 6' 2"	Wt: 190	Type Pwr xFB	PT/Exp C	Rand Var 0	
			Consist A	MM 0203	

If he could keep the ball in the yard at a passable clip, there are skills to be an MLB 5th starter, but his hr/f and FB rate have yielded a 2.0 HR/9 in 2016-17, besting only Jered Weaver. There is some H%-aided home success, but that xERA sets your scary baseline. Pass.

Yr Tm	W	L	Sv	IP	K	ERA	xERA	WHIP	oOPS	vL	vR	BF/G	Ctl	Dom	Cmd	FpK	SwK	G	L	F	H%	S%	hr/f	GS	APC	DOM%	DIS%	Sv%	LI	RAR	BPV	BPX
13 for	5	4	0	78	76	3.87	4.22	1.35				25.0	3.9	8.8	2.3						30%	77%								0.0	66	86
14																																
15 aa	5	2	0	45	32	5.11	4.52	1.59				24.8	4.0	6.4	1.6						35%	66%								-6.4	60	72
16 2 AL *	9	9	0	159	114	5.28	5.33	1.48	738	859	707	22.0	3.3	6.5	2.0	60%	8%	31	18	51	31%	68%	14%	10	76	10%	30%	0	0.86	-21.3	32	38
17 SEA	8	7	0	160	137	5.12	5.15	1.27	781	735	792	21.9	3.5	7.7	2.2	61%	12%	32	16	52	25%	67%	15%	29	86	14%	28%	0	0.73	-15.0	53	64
1st Half	7	4	0	99	74	3.82	5.05	1.14	687	569	713	23.8	3.2	6.7	2.1	65%	10%	35	15	49	23%	75%	13%	17	90	24%	35%			6.6	48	58
2nd Half	1	3	0	61	63	7.23	5.31	1.48	924	942	919	19.6	4.1	9.3	2.3	55%	13%	26	17	57	28%	58%	19%	12	81	0%	17%	0	0.68	-21.6	60	71
18 Proj	**8**	**7**	**0**	**145**	**122**	**5.42**	**5.39**	**1.42**	**851**	**901**	**838**	**21.7**	**3.7**	**7.6**	**2.1**	**59%**	**11%**	**30**	**17**	**53**	**28%**	**68%**	**14%**	**28**						**-19.1**	**45**	**55**

Montas,Frankie

Age: 25	Th: R	Role RP	Health F	LIMA Plan C	
Ht: 6' 2"	Wt: 255	Type Pwr xFB	PT/Exp D	Rand Var +5	
			Consist C	MM 0300	

1-1, 7.03 ERA in 32 IP at OAK. Exhibit 5,927,014 that velocity doesn't guarantee success. His 98 mph fastball just doesn't faze the opposition. LHBs destroy him and could push him into a "ROOGY" role if changeup doesn't develop. Can miss bats which keeps a glimmer of hope, but still a long way to go.

Yr Tm	W	L	Sv	IP	K	ERA	xERA	WHIP	oOPS	vL	vR	BF/G	Ctl	Dom	Cmd	FpK	SwK	G	L	F	H%	S%	hr/f	GS	APC	DOM%	DIS%	Sv%	LI	RAR	BPV	BPX
13																																
14																																
15 CHW *	5	7	0	127	117	3.85	3.47	1.41	699	921	560	17.9	4.3	8.3	1.9	53%	13%	38	16	46	32%	71%	6%	2	41	0%	50%	0	0.31	1.8	86	102
16 a/a	0	0	0	16	19	2.59	3.23	1.15				9.1	1.5	10.7	7.0						36%	80%								3.2	196	233
17 OAK *	1	3	0	61	65	6.59	5.92	1.54	974	1267	751	8.4	3.9	9.6	2.4	63%	12%	35	24	41	33%	62%	26%	0	27			0	0.43	-16.9	46	56
1st Half	1	2	0	38	44	7.43	6.92	1.75	964	1255	773	6.9	4.5	10.3	2.3	63%	12%	34	23	43	38%	61%	24%	0	26			0	0.44	-14.4	40	48
2nd Half	0	1	0	23	22	5.23	4.29	1.21	1054	1316	250	13.4	3.1	8.5	2.8	59%	11%	50	33	17	26%	63%	100%	0	37			0	0.41	-2.5	60	72
18 Proj	**1**	**3**	**0**	**51**	**50**	**5.26**	**4.85**	**1.41**	**647**	**813**	**538**	**11.6**	**3.9**	**8.9**	**2.3**	**63%**	**12%**	**34**	**23**	**43**	**31%**	**66%**	**11%**	**3**						**-5.6**	**66**	**80**

Montero,Rafael

Age: 27	Th: R	Role RP	Health F	LIMA Plan D+	
Ht: 6' 0"	Wt: 185	Type Pwr	PT/Exp D	Rand Var +2	
			Consist F	MM 0201	

5-11, 5.52 ERA in 119 IP at NYM. Issues excused by earlier small samples turned out to be real as Ctl and H% soared in career-high IP. Strong FpK should be helping walks, but he loses his stuff later in counts. Dom, SwK, and GB lean keep a flicker of hope alive, especially if his 2.6 minor league Ctl comes to the majors.

Yr Tm	W	L	Sv	IP	K	ERA	xERA	WHIP	oOPS	vL	vR	BF/G	Ctl	Dom	Cmd	FpK	SwK	G	L	F	H%	S%	hr/f	GS	APC	DOM%	DIS%	Sv%	LI	RAR	BPV	BPX
13 a/a	12	7	0	155	132	2.60	2.52	1.09				22.5	1.8	7.6	4.3						30%	76%								24.3	133	173
14 NYM *	7	7	0	124	110	3.35	3.57	1.30	825	923	711	19.7	3.7	8.0	2.1	60%	9%	34	22	44	29%	77%	15%	8	84	13%	50%	0	0.60	6.1	76	90
15 NYM	0	1	0	10	13	4.50	3.62	1.40	661	1457	471	9.2	4.5	11.7	2.6	50%	10%	48	19	33	37%	64%	0%	1	38	100%	0%	0	1.31	-0.7	115	137
16 NYM *	8	10	0	148	111	6.29	6.51	1.85	965	1131	840	20.3	5.0	6.7	1.4	60%	9%	36	32	32	36%	67%	22%	3	43	0%	67%	0	0.54	-38.4	22	26
17 NYM *	5	13	0	148	144	4.99	5.10	1.64	832	808	856	16.9	4.9	8.8	1.8	63%	11%	48	19	32	35%	71%	11%	18	65	17%	28%	0	0.71	-11.5	62	74
1st Half	1	6	0	61	65	4.28	4.59	1.58	815	813	816	12.8	5.1	9.7	1.9	62%	11%	46	19	34	35%	74%	6%	3	40	33%	67%	0	0.74	0.6	77	92
2nd Half	4	7	0	87	79	5.48	4.86	1.68	838	805	877	21.9	4.8	8.2	1.7	64%	11%	49	19	32	35%	68%	12%	15	87	13%	20%	0	0.69	-12.1	45	54
18 Proj	**5**	**9**	**0**	**116**	**103**	**4.83**	**5.07**	**1.59**	**788**	**817**	**758**	**18.6**	**4.4**	**8.0**	**1.8**	**62%**	**10%**	**42**	**20**	**37**	**34%**	**71%**	**9%**	**24**						**-6.7**	**45**	**54**

Montgomery,Jordan

Age: 25	Th: L	Role SP	Health A	LIMA Plan C+	
Ht: 6' 6"	Wt: 225	Type Pwr FB	PT/Exp C	Rand Var 0	
			Consist A	MM 1203	

The unheralded southpaw had an impressive debut as a 4-pitch arsenal gave him weapons vL and vR with a healthy Dom and SwK combo. S% wavered and inflated his 2nd half ERA, but part of it was a tighter leash (see: APC drop). FB% presents HR concern, but everything else points to mid-rotation potential.

Yr Tm	W	L	Sv	IP	K	ERA	xERA	WHIP	oOPS	vL	vR	BF/G	Ctl	Dom	Cmd	FpK	SwK	G	L	F	H%	S%	hr/f	GS	APC	DOM%	DIS%	Sv%	LI	RAR	BPV	BPX
13																																
14																																
15																																
16 a/a	14	5	0	139	113	3.02	4.24	1.46				23.9	3.2	7.3	2.3						34%	80%								20.2	76	90
17 NYY	9	7	0	155	144	3.88	4.42	1.23	684	662	687	22.4	3.0	8.3	2.8	60%	12%	41	18	42	29%	73%	11%	29	87	17%	28%			9.1	89	107
1st Half	6	4	0	87	83	3.62	4.32	1.21	688	676	690	24.1	2.9	8.6	3.0	63%	14%	41	16	43	29%	75%	11%	15	93	20%	13%			7.9	96	115
2nd Half	3	3	0	68	61	4.21	4.54	1.26	678	651	684	20.5	3.0	8.0	2.7	56%	11%	40	20	40	29%	70%	11%	14	81	14%	43%			1.2	81	97
18 Proj	**12**	**8**	**0**	**174**	**155**	**3.90**	**4.54**	**1.32**	**697**	**656**	**705**	**22.2**	**3.0**	**8.0**	**2.7**	**59%**	**12%**	**40**	**18**	**41**	**31%**	**73%**	**9%**	**32**						**9.7**	**83**	**100**

Montgomery,Michael

Age: 29	Th: L	Role RP	Health A	LIMA Plan C+	
Ht: 6' 5"	Wt: 215	Type Pwr xGB	PT/Exp B	Rand Var -2	
			Consist B	MM 1103	

Split season between SP and RP, doing his best work in the former with a 2.7 Cmd despite a higher ERA (4.15). Top-flight GB% helped mitigate HR, but Dom and Ctl losses give xERA credence. Platoon-free throughout career. A full-time SP role would be intriguing as the former top prospect still has upside.

Yr Tm	W	L	Sv	IP	K	ERA	xERA	WHIP	oOPS	vL	vR	BF/G	Ctl	Dom	Cmd	FpK	SwK	G	L	F	H%	S%	hr/f	GS	APC	DOM%	DIS%	Sv%	LI	RAR	BPV	BPX
13 aaa	7	8	0	109	65	5.50	5.00	1.61				24.1	3.9	5.4	1.4						33%	65%								-21.9	35	45
14 aaa	10	5	0	126	81	5.49	4.72	1.53				21.9	3.7	5.8	1.6						33%	63%								-27.2	45	54
15 SEA *	8	9	0	155	112	4.33	3.95	1.34	754	841	725	24.0	3.1	6.5	2.1	63%	9%	51	20	29	30%	69%	13%	16	91	19%	50%			-7.1	62	73
16 2 TM	4	5	0	100	92	2.52	3.42	1.17	652	570	691	8.4	3.4	8.3	2.4	56%	12%	58	23	19	27%	82%	16%	7	31	0%	14%	0	0.75	20.6	93	110
17 CHC	7	8	3	131	100	3.38	4.20	1.21	632	631	632	12.3	3.8	6.9	1.8	60%	9%	58	17	25	26%	74%	11%	14	47	7%	29%	100	0.93	15.8	58	69
1st Half	1	5	2	64	52	2.80	4.04	1.27	623	530	667	11.5	4.2	7.3	1.7	59%	9%	61	18	22	27%	78%	8%	5	44	20%	0%	100	0.95	12.4	56	68
2nd Half	6	3	1	66	48	3.93	4.35	1.15	640	759	601	13.1	3.4	6.5	1.9	61%	9%	55	16	29	24%	68%	13%	9	50	0%	44%	100	0.91	3.5	59	70
18 Proj	**8**	**8**	**0**	**145**	**113**	**3.57**	**4.13**	**1.25**	**671**	**659**	**676**	**12.2**	**3.6**	**7.0**	**2.0**	**59%**	**10%**	**57**	**19**	**24**	**27%**	**73%**	**12%**	**11**						**14.1**	**65**	**78**

Moore,Andrew

Age: 24	Th: R	Role SP	Health A	LIMA Plan C	
Ht: 6' 0"	Wt: 185	Type Con xFB	PT/Exp D	Rand Var +1	
			Consist A	MM 0000	

1-5, 5.34 ERA in 59 IP at SEA. Ask him about the juiced ball! The high hr/f has a role in his 2.1 HR/9, but when half of your batted balls are in the air, trouble ensues. It's exacerbated by a minuscule 4.7 MLB Dom, though 1.2 Ctl is a building block. A quality MiLB record says cutting HR opens a path to success.

Yr Tm	W	L	Sv	IP	K	ERA	xERA	WHIP	oOPS	vL	vR	BF/G	Ctl	Dom	Cmd	FpK	SwK	G	L	F	H%	S%	hr/f	GS	APC	DOM%	DIS%	Sv%	LI	RAR	BPV	BPX
13																																
14																																
15																																
16 aa	9	3	0	108	77	3.78	4.46	1.34				23.7	1.5	6.4	4.4						34%	74%								5.4	101	120
17 SEA *	5	11	0	169	118	4.19	4.27	1.18	784	839	740	21.1	1.6	6.3	4.0	65%	8%	29	22	49	28%	71%	14%	9	84	0%	56%	0	0.76	3.5	79	94
1st Half	5	3	0	95	75	3.19	3.29	1.08	654	0	850	23.1	1.6	7.2	4.5	69%	7%	27	14	59	28%	75%	8%	1	100	0%	0%			13.6	113	135
2nd Half	0	8	0	74	43	5.46	5.51	1.30	800	891	720	19.1	1.6	5.2	3.3	64%	9%	29	23	48	29%	65%	15%	8	82	0%	63%	0	0.76	-10.1	35	42
18 Proj	**3**	**3**	**0**	**58**	**40**	**4.25**	**5.12**	**1.27**	**689**	**751**	**635**	**21.7**	**1.6**	**6.2**	**4.0**	**64%**	**9%**	**29**	**23**	**48**	**31%**	**71%**	**9%**	**11**						**0.8**	**76**	**92**

Moore,Matt

Age: 29	Th: L	Role SP	Health F	LIMA Plan C	
Ht: 6' 3"	Wt: 210	Type Pwr FB	PT/Exp B	Rand Var +2	
			Consist B	MM 0203	

His 2016/17 disparity highlights the volatility of pitching. Outside of the H%/S% swing, only minor differences in his base skills (Cmd, FpK, SwK all a bit lower) yet ERA was nearly 1.5 runs worse. His xERA string, though, says we shoulda known this all along. Should be dirt cheap, but he's not for the risk-averse.

Yr Tm	W	L	Sv	IP	K	ERA	xERA	WHIP	oOPS	vL	vR	BF/G	Ctl	Dom	Cmd	FpK	SwK	G	L	F	H%	S%	hr/f	GS	APC	DOM%	DIS%	Sv%	LI	RAR	BPV	BPX
13 TAM	17	4	0	150	143	3.29	4.23	1.30	655	617	672	23.8	4.5	8.6	1.9	51%	10%	39	18	42	27%	77%	8%	27	97	26%	22%			10.6	48	63
14 TAM	0	2	0	10	6	2.70	4.75	1.50	777	1010	703	22.0	4.5	5.4	1.2	44%	7%	45	27	27	29%	86%	11%	2	92	0%	50%			1.3	-1	-2
15 TAM *	5	7	0	103	93	5.12	5.22	1.48	839	785	866	23.4	3.1	8.1	2.6	60%	10%	39	22	39	34%	69%	11%	12	88	17%	67%			-14.7	59	71
16 2 TM	13	12	0	198	178	4.08	4.48	1.29	694	654	706	25.4	3.3	8.1	2.5	62%	11%	38	20	42	29%	72%	10%	33	100	36%	33%			2.6	73	87
17 SF	6	15	0	174	148	5.52	5.16	1.53	835	1047	767	24.7	3.5	7.6	2.2	61%	9%	38	20	42	33%	67%	12%	31	90	16%	42%	0	0.75	-25.1	60	72
1st Half	3	8	0	95	81	5.78	5.38	1.62	875	1143	784	25.7	3.9	7.7	2.0	61%	10%	37	21	42	35%	66%	11%	17	93	18%	47%			-16.6	48	58
2nd Half	3	7	0	79	67	5.22	4.89	1.42	787	922	746	23.5	2.9	7.6	2.6	62%	9%	38	20	41	32%	67%	13%	14	86	14%	36%	0	0.71	-8.4	74	88
18 Proj	**9**	**12**	**0**	**174**	**153**	**4.64**	**4.84**	**1.43**	**776**	**847**	**752**	**24.6**	**3.4**	**7.9**	**2.3**	**60%**	**10%**	**38**	**20**	**41**	**32%**	**71%**	**12%**	**30**						**-6.0**	**67**	**80**

PAUL SPORER

Morgan,Adam

Age: 28	Th: L	Role RP	Health A	LIMA Plan A
			PT/Exp D	Rand Var +4
Ht: 6' 1"	Wt: 200	Type Pwr	Consist A	MM 2401

3-3, 4.12 ERA in 54.2 IP at PHI. Former soft-tossing SP's skills began to flourish in first year from the 'pen. Added velocity to FB and SL became deadly (29% SwK), boosting SwK to Devenski-esque levels with a sharp GB spike. Dom isn't elite yet, but if that 2nd half BPX is any indication, a bigger role awaits.

Yr Tm	W	L	Sv	IP	K	ERA	xERA	WHIP	oOPS	vL	vR	BF/G	Ctl	Dom	Cmd	FpK	SwK	G	L	F	H%	S%	hr/f	GS	APC	DOM%	DIS%	Sv%	LI	RAR	BPV	BPX	R$
13 aaa	2	7	0	71	42	4.66	6.24	1.69				20.1	3.3	5.3	1.6						34%	76%								-7.0	15	20	-$9
14																																	
15 PHI *	5	13	0	153	77	5.16	5.53	1.51	775	617	820	23.6	2.7	4.5	1.7	66%	10%	31	20	49	31%	69%	10%	15	83	0%	33%			-22.5	17	20	-$13
16 PHI *	8	12	0	164	137	5.54	5.51	1.45	878	726	927	22.6	2.2	7.5	3.4	60%	11%	37	25	38	34%	66%	16%	21	85	14%	38%	0	0.72	-27.2	64	76	-$8
17 PHI *	3	4	0	72	74	4.68	4.77	1.38	737	597	837	6.2	3.0	9.3	3.1	62%	17%	46	20	34	33%	70%	20%	0	24			0	0.72	-2.9	80	96	-$2
1st Half	0	2	0	36	33	6.61	7.11	1.70	1023	710	1246	7.4	2.9	8.3	2.9	64%	16%	40	25	35	38%	66%	35%	0	34			0	0.41	-10.0	37	44	-$12
2nd Half	3	2	0	36	41	2.75	3.41	1.06	567	529	593	5.3	3.0	10.3	3.4	60%	18%	49	18	33	28%	77%	10%	0	21			0	0.83	7.1	130	156	$8
18 Proj	**3**	**5**	**0**	**73**	**77**	**3.51**	**3.92**	**1.25**	**681**	**552**	**743**	**6.2**	**2.8**	**9.6**	**3.4**	**62%**	**15%**	**40**	**22**	**38**	**32%**	**75%**	**11%**	**0**						**7.6**	**115**	**139**	**$2**

Morrow,Brandon

Age: 33	Th: R	Role RP	Health F	LIMA Plan A
			PT/Exp D	Rand Var 0
Ht: 6' 3"	Wt: 205	Type Pwr	Consist F	MM 2310

6-0, 2.06 ERA in 43.2 IP at LA. Best velo, SwK, FpK of career from the bullpen resulted in sizeable Dom/Ctl gains, as he morphed into a productive late-inning arm. Trouble is he can't seem to stay healthy, and that wildly fluctuating BPX from year to year brings with it a lot of red flags. Look elsewhere for Ks.

Yr Tm	W	L	Sv	IP	K	ERA	xERA	WHIP	oOPS	vL	vR	BF/G	Ctl	Dom	Cmd	FpK	SwK	G	L	F	H%	S%	hr/f	GS	APC	DOM%	DIS%	Sv%	LI	RAR	BPV	BPX	R$
13 TOR	2	3	0	54	42	5.63	4.58	1.49	880	1014	706	24.2	3.0	7.0	2.3	52%	9%	37	20	43	31%	68%	16%	10	91	10%	50%			-11.8	60	78	-$7
14 TOR	1	3	0	33	30	5.67	4.15	1.65	832	948	708	11.4	4.9	8.1	1.7	52%	9%	51	19	30	35%	64%	7%	6	48	0%	33%	0	0.68	-7.9	44	52	-$6
15 SD	2	0	0	33	23	2.73	3.65	1.09	681	613	761	25.2	1.9	6.3	3.3	53%	11%	47	21	32	27%	79%	10%	5	97	20%	20%			5.0	86	103	$0
16 SD *	2	1	2	47	26	6.63	8.26	2.06	769	966	660	7.2	3.3	4.9	1.5	53%	10%	44	26	30	40%	70%	13%	0	13			50	0.69	-14.3	-3	-3	-$12
17 LA *	6	5	8	64	66	4.33	3.66	1.21	454	308	532	3.9	2.0	9.4	4.7	69%	17%	45	24	31	33%	65%	0%	0	14			73	0.85	0.2	132	159	$5
1st Half	2	5	6	32	30	5.87	5.19	1.33	293	0	481	4.4	1.7	8.7	5.0	64%	17%	42	19	38	34%	60%	0%	0	15			75	0.40	-5.9	102	122	$1
2nd Half	4	0	2	32	36	2.81	3.23	1.09	507	425	548	3.7	2.3	10.1	4.5	71%	17%	46	25	29	33%	71%	0%	0	13			67	0.98	6.1	145	174	$10
18 Proj	**4**	**3**	**2**	**58**	**54**	**3.90**	**3.99**	**1.32**	**731**	**793**	**676**	**5.6**	**2.5**	**8.4**	**3.4**	**58%**	**12%**	**46**	**22**	**32**	**34%**	**71%**	**8%**	**0**						**3.3**	**109**	**131**	**$1**

Morton,Charlie

Age: 34	Th: R	Role SP	Health F	LIMA Plan C+
			PT/Exp C	Rand Var +1
Ht: 6' 5"	Wt: 235	Type Pwr GB	Consist B	MM 2203

Missed all of June with a lat strain, but still easily managed the best BPV of his career. PRO: Dom gains supported by strong SwK, climbing velocity; steady FpK says solid Ctl should stick; GB% skills remain. CON: Has never reached 180 IP, and he isn't getting any younger. Late career spikes hardly ever repeat.

Yr Tm	W	L	Sv	IP	K	ERA	xERA	WHIP	oOPS	vL	vR	BF/G	Ctl	Dom	Cmd	FpK	SwK	G	L	F	H%	S%	hr/f	GS	APC	DOM%	DIS%	Sv%	LI	RAR	BPV	BPX	R$
13 PIT *	8	6	0	154	101	3.46	3.47	1.30	683	844	552	22.6	3.1	5.9	1.9	59%	9%	63	18	19	29%	74%	9%	20	86	30%	25%			7.7	63	83	$5
14 PIT	6	12	0	157	126	3.72	3.45	1.27	682	664	698	25.6	3.3	7.2	2.2	61%	8%	56	21	23	30%	71%	9%	26	96	31%	19%			0.4	76	90	$3
15 PIT *	11	10	0	149	112	4.41	4.16	1.37	769	894	633	24.1	2.9	6.7	2.3	62%	8%	57	21	21	32%	69%	15%	23	87	22%	26%			-8.3	66	79	$0
16 PHI	1	1	0	17	19	4.15	3.10	1.33	651	743	559	17.8	4.2	9.9	2.4	62%	13%	63	21	16	32%	68%	14%	4	69	50%	25%			0.1	106	126	-$3
17 HOU	14	7	0	147	163	3.62	3.46	1.19	692	561	805	24.7	3.1	10.0	3.3	61%	11%	52	19	29	31%	72%	13%	25	95	40%	16%			13.3	127	153	$15
1st Half	5	3	0	58	65	4.06	3.56	1.37	764	675	838	25.2	3.6	10.1	2.8	57%	11%	51	24	24	33%	74%	18%	10	95	30%	30%			2.1	115	138	$3
2nd Half	9	4	0	89	98	3.34	3.39	1.08	644	479	782	24.3	2.7	9.9	3.6	64%	12%	52	16	32	29%	71%	9%	15	96	47%	7%			11.2	135	162	$24
18 Proj	**10**	**7**	**0**	**131**	**121**	**3.88**	**3.75**	**1.26**	**707**	**693**	**718**	**23.8**	**3.1**	**8.4**	**2.7**	**61%**	**10%**	**55**	**20**	**25**	**31%**	**70%**	**12%**	**22**						**7.6**	**101**	**121**	**$7**

Musgrove,Joe

Age: 25	Th: R	Role RP	Health A	LIMA Plan A
			PT/Exp C	Rand Var +3
Ht: 6' 5"	Wt: 265	Type	Consist A	MM 2201

Jury's still out on his long-term role, but these skills blossomed from the bullpen in 2nd half. Pairs strong Ctl with solid ground game, and with two pitches (cutter/change-up) yielding above-average SwK, Dom looks to be a future skill, as well. Still just 25, could be a sneaky LIMA option moving forward.

Yr Tm	W	L	Sv	IP	K	ERA	xERA	WHIP	oOPS	vL	vR	BF/G	Ctl	Dom	Cmd	FpK	SwK	G	L	F	H%	S%	hr/f	GS	APC	DOM%	DIS%	Sv%	LI	RAR	BPV	BPX	R$
13																																	
14																																	
15 aa	4	0	1	45	29	2.49	3.47	1.00				21.5	1.2	5.8	4.9						24%	88%								8.2	99	118	$4
16 HOU *	11	8	0	147	131	3.63	4.01	1.20	758	822	710	21.9	1.6	8.0	5.0	62%	10%	43	21	36	32%	74%	14%	10	89	30%	30%	0	0.78	10.1	120	143	$11
17 HOU	7	8	2	109	98	4.77	4.09	1.33	798	763	829	12.2	2.3	8.1	3.5	64%	12%	45	21	34	32%	69%	16%	15	46	13%	53%	50	0.89	-5.6	106	127	$2
1st Half	4	7	0	67	56	6.01	4.71	1.53	895	844	934	22.8	2.8	7.5	2.7	62%	11%	42	21	38	34%	65%	18%	13	88	15%	54%			-13.8	78	94	-$5
2nd Half	3	1	2	42	42	2.79	3.13	1.00	632	640	624	6.6	1.5	9.0	6.0	66%	14%	51	22	27	29%	76%	13%	2	24	0%	50%	50	0.95	8.1	151	181	$12
18 Proj	**5**	**3**	**0**	**73**	**63**	**3.66**	**3.86**	**1.18**	**745**	**753**	**738**	**13.0**	**1.7**	**7.9**	**4.5**	**63%**	**12%**	**46**	**21**	**33**	**30%**	**74%**	**15%**	**7**						**6.2**	**118**	**142**	**$3**

Nelson,Jimmy

Age: 29	Th: R	Role SP	Health B	LIMA Plan C+
			PT/Exp A	Rand Var +3
Ht: 6' 6"	Wt: 250	Type Pwr GB	Consist C	MM 2301

Marvelous breakout was soured by Sept shoulder injury; expected to miss large chunk of 2018. Coupled top-10 Dom, quality GB tilt with Ctl gains, though FpK perhaps a bit shaky to maintain it. This is a talented arm, no doubt, but until we see more consistency (and full health), proceed with caution.

Yr Tm	W	L	Sv	IP	K	ERA	xERA	WHIP	oOPS	vL	vR	BF/G	Ctl	Dom	Cmd	FpK	SwK	G	L	F	H%	S%	hr/f	GS	APC	DOM%	DIS%	Sv%	LI	RAR	BPV	BPX	R$
13 MIL *	10	10	0	162	147	3.67	3.79	1.43	286	473	63	22.3	4.0	8.2	2.0	49%	11%	42	33	25	33%	74%	0%	1	36	0%	0%	0	0.28	4.0	81	105	$3
14 MIL *	12	11	0	180	151	3.01	3.14	1.21	793	804	782	23.5	2.7	7.6	2.8	63%	10%	48	20	32	30%	76%	8%	12	79	25%	42%	0	0.83	16.3	96	114	$13
15 MIL	11	13	0	177	148	4.11	3.90	1.29	704	876	568	25.1	3.3	7.5	2.3	60%	10%	51	20	29	29%	70%	12%	30	93	43%	30%			-3.3	75	89	$5
16 MIL	8	16	0	179	140	4.62	4.80	1.52	791	779	802	25.2	4.3	7.0	1.6	58%	8%	49	19	31	31%	73%	15%	32	93	9%	50%			-9.5	37	44	-$5
17 MIL	12	6	0	175	199	3.49	3.25	1.25	689	710	670	25.1	2.5	10.2	4.1	61%	12%	50	22	27	34%	74%	13%	29	95	48%	24%			18.8	145	175	$16
1st Half	6	4	0	97	104	3.43	3.44	1.25	714	704	724	25.3	2.3	9.6	4.2	63%	12%	50	20	30	34%	76%	13%	16	94	38%	31%			11.1	139	166	$18
2nd Half	6	2	0	78	95	3.56	3.02	1.25	658	718	607	24.9	2.6	10.9	4.1	58%	12%	51	25	24	35%	73%	13%	13	96	62%	15%			7.7	154	185	$15
18 Proj	**5**	**5**	**0**	**87**	**86**	**3.86**	**3.89**	**1.33**	**712**	**750**	**678**	**24.3**	**3.2**	**8.9**	**2.8**	**60%**	**11%**	**50**	**21**	**29**	**32%**	**73%**	**12%**	**15**						**5.4**	**102**	**123**	**$2**

Neris,Hector

Age: 29	Th: R	Role RP	Health A	LIMA Plan C+
			PT/Exp C	Rand Var -3
Ht: 6' 2"	Wt: 215	Type Pwr FB	Consist C	MM 2431

First season as closer witnessed hefty FpK gains, as he shored up what had been a shaky Ctl/Cmd resume. Dom is in good shape as he continues to miss bats with an even filthier splitter (25% SwK). Risk comes with all those fly balls and if that Ctl is sustainable. Still, this is a solid second-tier closer.

Yr Tm	W	L	Sv	IP	K	ERA	xERA	WHIP	oOPS	vL	vR	BF/G	Ctl	Dom	Cmd	FpK	SwK	G	L	F	H%	S%	hr/f	GS	APC	DOM%	DIS%	Sv%	LI	RAR	BPV	BPX	R$
13 aa	6	4	0	97	79	5.12	4.80	1.43				9.0	3.6	7.3	2.0						30%	68%								-15.0	45	59	-$6
14 PHI *	7	3	2	78	60	4.16	3.92	1.30	0	0	0	6.6	3.4	6.9	2.0	100%	22%	50	0	50	28%	71%	0%	0	9			40	1.97	-4.0	57	68	$1
15 PHI *	3	5	1	78	70	4.21	5.00	1.56	772	770	772	5.8	4.2	8.1	1.9	52%	14%	39	15	46	34%	76%	15%	0	21			33	0.69	-2.4	56	67	-$5
16 PHI	4	4	2	80	102	2.58	3.22	1.11	620	632	607	4.2	3.4	11.4	3.4	52%	16%	42	25	34	29%	83%	14%	0	17			33	1.11	16.0	135	160	$9
17 PHI	4	5	26	75	86	3.01	4.08	1.26	689	716	660	4.3	3.1	10.4	3.3	59%	17%	33	23	44	32%	81%	10%	0	17			90	1.10	12.4	113	136	$16
1st Half	2	2	7	34	39	3.41	3.86	1.19	680	640	714	4.0	2.9	10.2	3.5	60%	16%	33	23	44	30%	78%	13%	0	16			70	1.04	4.0	117	141	$11
2nd Half	2	3	19	40	47	2.68	4.25	1.31	696	767	605	4.6	3.3	10.5	3.1	59%	17%	32	23	45	34%	84%	8%	0	17			100	1.15	8.4	109	130	$21
18 Proj	**4**	**4**	**37**	**73**	**80**	**3.22**	**4.02**	**1.25**	**696**	**718**	**673**	**4.5**	**3.2**	**10.0**	**3.2**	**58%**	**16%**	**37**	**22**	**41**	**31%**	**79%**	**11%**	**0**						**10.2**	**109**	**132**	**$19**

Newcomb,Sean

Age: 25	Th: L	Role SP	Health A	LIMA Plan D+
			PT/Exp D	Rand Var +1
Ht: 6' 5"	Wt: 255	Type Pwr	Consist B	MM 0303

4-9, 4.32 ERA with 108 K in 100 IP at ATL. Rookie LH's first cup of coffee yielded a mixed bag. SwK, Dom both in good shape for Ks now, but ugly Ctl/FpK combo won't help that WHIP. A decent arm to invest in long-term, but with all those baserunners, anticipate some growing pains.

Yr Tm	W	L	Sv	IP	K	ERA	xERA	WHIP	oOPS	vL	vR	BF/G	Ctl	Dom	Cmd	FpK	SwK	G	L	F	H%	S%	hr/f	GS	APC	DOM%	DIS%	Sv%	LI	RAR	BPV	BPX	R$
13																																	
14																																	
15 aa	2	2	0	36	35	3.40	2.98	1.37				21.6	6.0	8.7	1.4						26%	76%								2.5	82	97	-$2
16 aa	8	7	0	140	135	5.64	4.25	1.62				23.0	5.3	8.7	1.6						35%	63%								-25.1	79	93	-$10
17 ATL *	7	12	0	158	172	4.13	4.44	1.57	780	753	790	23.1	5.3	9.8	1.8	59%	12%	44	23	33	34%	75%	11%	19	96	11%	26%			4.4	79	94	$0
1st Half	4	5	0	82	85	3.12	3.52	1.42	557	991	378	23.2	4.9	9.4	1.9	66%	11%	49	21	31	32%	78%	5%	4	96	25%	25%			12.6	90	108	$8
2nd Half	3	7	0	76	87	5.23	4.83	1.73	844	681	909	23.9	5.8	10.3	1.8	56%	12%	42	24	34	37%	71%	13%	15	96	7%	27%			-8.2	49	59	-$9
18 Proj	**8**	**10**	**0**	**160**	**165**	**4.41**	**4.72**	**1.52**	**716**	**781**	**690**	**22.5**	**5.5**	**9.3**	**1.7**	**60%**	**12%**	**45**	**22**	**33**	**32%**	**71%**	**7%**	**31**						**-1.0**	**43**	**51**	**-$1**

ALEC DOPP

Nicasio,Juan

Age: 31	Th: R	Role RP	Health A	LIMA Plan B	
Ht: 6' 4"	Wt: 252	Type Pwr	PT/Exp C	Rand Var -2	
			Consist A	MM 2310	

After years of futility, found home as late-inning RP. Threw harder than ever before and maintained quality Dom, consistent SwK. Difference this time around was that beautiful Ctl, a product of his top-10 FpK. Proceed carefully given that xERA/ERA gap, but these skill gains bode well for future Sv chances.

Yr Tm	W	L	Sv	IP	K	ERA	xERA	WHIP	oOPS	vL	vR	BF/G	Ctl	Dom	Cmd	FpK	SwK	G	L	F	H%	S%	hr/f	GS	APC	DOM%	DIS%	Sv%	LI	RAR	BPV	BPX
13 COL	9	9	0	158	119	5.14	4.41	1.47	785	737	827	22.7	3.7	6.8	1.9	57%	8%	45	21	34	32%	66%	10%	31	92	16%	65%			-24.7	47	61
14 COL *	9	8	1	129	89	5.50	6.06	1.59	860	900	827	13.3	3.3	6.2	1.9	59%	8%	46	20	34	33%	70%	18%	14	49	7%	50%	100	0.76	-28.0	21	25
15 LA	1	3	1	58	65	3.86	4.04	1.56	742	969	634	4.9	4.9	10.0	2.0	62%	12%	43	25	32	37%	73%	2%	1	20	0%	100%	33	1.05	0.8	68	81
16 PIT	10	7	0	118	138	4.50	3.70	1.37	774	934	638	9.9	3.4	10.5	3.1	63%	11%	44	22	35	34%	70%	14%	12	42	25%	50%	0	0.89	-4.5	119	141
17 3 NL	5	5	6	72	72	2.61	3.64	1.08	610	544	664	3.8	2.5	9.0	3.6	67%	12%	46	22	33	29%	78%	8%	0	16			60	1.18	15.6	118	142
1st Half	1	4	0	35	37	2.80	3.89	1.22	599	541	645	3.8	3.6	9.4	2.6	64%	12%	46	22	33	32%	74%	0%	0	16			0	1.21	6.8	97	116
2nd Half	4	1	6	37	35	2.43	3.40	0.95	619	546	679	3.9	1.5	8.5	5.8	70%	12%	46	22	33	26%	83%	15%	0	16			86	1.14	8.8	137	165
18 Proj	**4**	**3**	**9**	**58**	**59**	**3.53**	**3.90**	**1.26**	**697**	**732**	**671**	**5.1**	**3.1**	**9.2**	**3.0**	**65%**	**11%**	**45**	**22**	**33**	**31%**	**74%**	**10%**	**0**						**6.0**	**105**	**127**

Nicolino,Justin

Age: 26	Th: L	Role RP	Health B	LIMA Plan D+	
Ht: 6' 3"	Wt: 195	Type Con	PT/Exp C	Rand Var 0	
			Consist A	MM 0001	

2-3, 5.06 ERA in 48 IP at MIA. Spent bulk of the year rehabbing from injury. It's nice to be able to show some consistent Dom growth, but when the end point still leaves him shy of 5 K/9, there's not much hope for usable skills. FpK has eroded, too, and if he can't keep runners off base, that high WHIP won't change. Pass.

Yr Tm	W	L	Sv	IP	K	ERA	xERA	WHIP	oOPS	vL	vR	BF/G	Ctl	Dom	Cmd	FpK	SwK	G	L	F	H%	S%	hr/f	GS	APC	DOM%	DIS%	Sv%	LI	RAR	BPV	BPX
13 aa	3	2	0	45	27	6.16	6.49	1.88				23.7	2.5	5.3	2.1						41%	65%								-12.8	48	62
14 aa	14	4	0	170	67	3.29	3.48	1.18				24.4	1.0	3.5	3.4						30%	72%								9.4	80	95
15 MIA *	12	11	0	189	74	4.36	5.16	1.51	758	722	768	25.6	2.4	3.5	1.5	65%	5%	44	18	38	32%	73%	9%	12	87	0%	50%			-9.4	18	22
16 MIA *	10	12	0	164	78	5.07	4.97	1.42	798	687	837	21.8	1.8	4.3	2.3	63%	5%	46	22	32	32%	66%	9%	13	67	0%	69%	0	0.93	-17.9	38	46
17 MIA *	7	8	0	127	68	4.39	5.77	1.59	905	986	873	16.5	3.2	4.8	1.5	60%	7%	47	27	26	32%	76%	17%	8	42	0%	63%	0	0.66	-0.5	15	18
1st Half	1	4	0	59	34	5.48	7.41	1.81	971	1154	894	20.9	3.9	5.2	1.3	60%	8%	49	25	26	34%	76%	26%	5	57	0%	40%	0	0.67	-8.1	-13	-16
2nd Half	6	4	0	68	34	3.45	4.35	1.41	856	849	859	13.8	2.7	4.5	1.7	60%	6%	45	28	26	31%	77%	11%	3	36	0%	100%	0	0.65	7.6	40	48
18 Proj	**5**	**5**	**0**	**87**	**43**	**4.53**	**5.28**	**1.52**	**815**	**826**	**811**	**19.0**	**2.6**	**4.4**	**1.7**	**61%**	**6%**	**46**	**24**	**30**	**32%**	**72%**	**11%**	**18**						**-1.9**	**34**	**41**

Nola,Aaron

Age: 25	Th: R	Role SP	Health D	LIMA Plan C+	
Ht: 6' 2"	Wt: 195	Type Pwr GB	PT/Exp B	Rand Var 0	
			Consist A	MM 3405	

Lower back strain shelved him early on, but he recovered in time for a dynamic 2nd half. Possesses two skills you look for in a future ace: Dom and GB% (both products of elite CB/CH combo), and he even bolstered a previously so-so FpK. Reaching 200+ IP is next big step, but DOM%/DIS% trend looks mighty fine.

Yr Tm	W	L	Sv	IP	K	ERA	xERA	WHIP	oOPS	vL	vR	BF/G	Ctl	Dom	Cmd	FpK	SwK	G	L	F	H%	S%	hr/f	GS	APC	DOM%	DIS%	Sv%	LI	RAR	BPV	BPX
13																																
14 aa	2	0	0	24	14	2.86	5.09	1.32				19.9	1.8	5.1	2.8						29%	88%								2.6	38	46
15 PHI *	16	6	0	187	151	3.10	3.58	1.17	703	834	618	24.1	1.8	7.2	4.1	64%	9%	48	20	32	30%	77%	15%	13	86	31%	23%			19.9	105	126
16 PHI	6	9	0	111	121	4.78	3.25	1.31	712	703	720	24.2	2.4	9.8	4.2	61%	10%	55	20	25	36%	64%	13%	20	90	35%	15%			-8.1	146	174
17 PHI	12	11	0	168	184	3.54	3.49	1.21	679	741	624	25.7	2.6	9.9	3.8	64%	11%	50	19	31	32%	74%	13%	27	99	44%	15%			17.0	135	162
1st Half	5	5	0	65	64	4.13	3.86	1.29	689	785	603	24.7	3.0	8.8	2.9	63%	10%	49	20	30	31%	71%	14%	11	95	27%	27%			1.8	104	125
2nd Half	7	6	0	103	120	3.16	3.27	1.16	674	712	638	26.3	2.4	10.5	4.4	65%	13%	50	18	32	33%	76%	12%	16	101	56%	6%			15.2	153	184
18 Proj	**12**	**12**	**0**	**181**	**196**	**3.36**	**3.39**	**1.20**	**674**	**718**	**637**	**25.6**	**2.4**	**9.7**	**4.0**	**63%**	**11%**	**51**	**20**	**29**	**33%**	**75%**	**13%**	**29**						**22.2**	**140**	**168**

Nolasco,Ricky

Age: 35	Th: R	Role SP	Health F	LIMA Plan C	
Ht: 6' 2"	Wt: 235	Type	PT/Exp B	Rand Var +1	
			Consist A	MM 0103	

Second season post-elbow injury was just about unrosterable. Dom/SwK improved a tick, but he looked gassed in 2nd half as Cmd/Ctl bottomed out, FB lost some muscle and struggled to keep the ball on the ground. Now entering his age-35 campaign, any amount of investment here is asking for trouble.

Yr Tm	W	L	Sv	IP	K	ERA	xERA	WHIP	oOPS	vL	vR	BF/G	Ctl	Dom	Cmd	FpK	SwK	G	L	F	H%	S%	hr/f	GS	APC	DOM%	DIS%	Sv%	LI	RAR	BPV	BPX
13 2 NL	13	11	0	199	165	3.70	3.62	1.21	693	721	660	24.5	2.1	7.4	3.6	60%	11%	43	24	33	31%	71%	9%	33	94	33%	24%	0	0.75	4.0	99	129
14 MIN	6	12	0	159	115	5.38	4.13	1.52	861	906	816	25.7	2.2	6.5	3.0	58%	9%	42	22	36	35%	67%	12%	27	98	19%	37%			-32.1	79	94
15 MIN	5	2	0	37	35	6.75	4.34	1.71	856	758	942	19.2	3.4	8.4	2.5	52%	10%	41	28	32	40%	59%	8%	8	74	13%	50%	0	0.71	-12.8	80	95
16 2 AL	8	14	0	198	144	4.42	4.35	1.24	744	711	770	25.5	2.0	6.6	3.3	61%	9%	43	19	38	30%	68%	11%	32	98	28%	34%			-5.5	85	101
17 LAA	6	15	0	181	143	4.92	4.87	1.45	849	790	908	23.8	2.9	7.1	2.5	60%	11%	40	21	39	32%	72%	16%	33	94	12%	48%			-12.6	68	82
1st Half	4	9	0	100	83	4.42	4.52	1.33	837	773	899	24.9	2.4	7.5	3.1	63%	11%	41	18	40	30%	76%	19%	17	94	18%	41%			-0.8	89	106
2nd Half	2	6	0	81	60	5.53	5.32	1.60	864	809	918	22.8	3.4	6.6	1.9	56%	11%	39	23	38	34%	68%	12%	16	93	6%	56%			-11.8	44	52
18 Proj	**9**	**13**	**0**	**174**	**137**	**5.12**	**4.78**	**1.45**	**820**	**772**	**865**	**22.9**	**2.7**	**7.1**	**2.6**	**58%**	**11%**	**41**	**22**	**37**	**33%**	**68%**	**12%**	**33**						**-16.3**	**73**	**88**

Norris,Bud

Age: 33	Th: R	Role RP	Health D	LIMA Plan B	
Ht: 6' 0"	Wt: 215	Type Pwr	PT/Exp B	Rand Var +2	
			Consist A	MM 1310	

First full year from the bullpen was a roller-coaster thanks to eye-popping H%-S%-hr/f fluctuation. PRO: Dom gains backed by career-best SwK; continues to keep the ball out of the air. CON: FpK/Ctl attrition doesn't help his cause for Save opportunities. If a Dom boost is all you need, there are safer sources.

Yr Tm	W	L	Sv	IP	K	ERA	xERA	WHIP	oOPS	vL	vR	BF/G	Ctl	Dom	Cmd	FpK	SwK	G	L	F	H%	S%	hr/f	GS	APC	DOM%	DIS%	Sv%	LI	RAR	BPV	BPX
13 2AL	10	12	0	177	147	4.18	4.27	1.49	779	889	629	24.2	3.4	7.5	2.2	61%	10%	40	21	38	34%	74%	8%	30	94	23%	30%	0	0.88	-6.8	61	79
14 BAL	15	8	0	165	139	3.65	3.77	1.22	710	753	659	24.5	2.8	7.6	2.7	60%	8%	42	21	37	28%	74%	11%	28	98	29%	25%			1.9	80	95
15 2 TM	3	11	0	83	71	6.72	4.42	1.58	895	899	890	9.9	3.4	7.7	2.3	58%	10%	43	23	34	34%	59%	17%	11	39	9%	64%	0	0.82	-28.3	69	82
16 2 NL	6	10	0	113	102	5.10	4.36	1.46	763	915	646	14.1	3.9	8.1	2.1	62%	10%	48	22	31	32%	67%	14%	19	57	26%	37%	0	0.75	-12.7	67	79
17 LAA	2	6	19	62	74	4.21	3.74	1.34	693	540	798	4.5	3.9	10.7	2.7	53%	13%	45	25	31	32%	72%	16%	3	18	0%	0%	83	1.14	1.1	111	133
1st Half	1	2	11	33	42	2.43	3.36	1.11	580	422	710	4.0	3.5	11.3	3.2	53%	14%	45	21	34	29%	82%	11%	0	18			85	1.18	7.9	132	159
2nd Half	1	4	8	29	32	6.28	4.22	1.60	814	689	878	5.0	4.4	10.0	2.3	53%	13%	45	28	28	36%	63%	22%	3	19	0%	0%	80	1.09	-6.8	85	102
18 Proj	**2**	**6**	**9**	**58**	**59**	**4.58**	**4.22**	**1.44**	**763**	**752**	**770**	**6.7**	**3.8**	**9.2**	**2.4**	**57%**	**11%**	**45**	**23**	**32**	**33%**	**72%**	**16%**	**0**						**-1.6**	**86**	**104**

Norris,Daniel

Age: 25	Th: L	Role RP	Health F	LIMA Plan D+	
Ht: 6' 2"	Wt: 195	Type Pwr	PT/Exp C	Rand Var +2	
			Consist A	MM 0203	

Former 2nd-round pick missed significant time on DL; results weren't pretty when he did pitch. He would be so easy to write off if not for 2016's FpK/SwK and occasional bursts of Dom. There is some latent skill aching to emerge, but until there are more consistent signs, you'll need to watch from afar.

Yr Tm	W	L	Sv	IP	K	ERA	xERA	WHIP	oOPS	vL	vR	BF/G	Ctl	Dom	Cmd	FpK	SwK	G	L	F	H%	S%	hr/f	GS	APC	DOM%	DIS%	Sv%	LI	RAR	BPV	BPX
13																																
14 TOR *	6	2	0	65	83	4.98	4.14	1.35	667	594	719	15.0	4.1	11.5	2.8	43%	7%	35	20	45	32%	66%	11%	1	28	0%	0%	0	0.85	-10.0	95	113
15 2AL *	6	12	0	151	114	5.03	4.96	1.55	732	880	680	22.7	3.7	6.8	1.8	53%	9%	39	17	43	33%	68%	11%	13	80	15%	46%			-19.9	49	58
16 DET *	10	9	0	149	140	4.50	4.81	1.51	762	648	800	22.3	3.2	8.4	2.6	64%	11%	38	23	39	36%	71%	12%	13	85	23%	31%	0	0.72	-5.7	76	91
17 DET	5	8	0	102	86	5.31	5.18	1.61	840	928	813	20.9	3.9	7.6	2.0	55%	9%	39	22	39	35%	68%	10%	18	83	6%	44%	0	0.65	-12.0	49	59
1st Half	4	6	0	81	77	5.00	4.88	1.62	847	984	807	24.5	3.9	8.6	2.2	55%	10%	40	21	39	36%	71%	10%	15	99	7%	40%			-6.4	67	80
2nd Half	1	2	0	21	9	6.53	6.45	1.60	813	733	839	13.3	3.9	3.9	1.0	56%	8%	35	26	39	31%	58%	7%	3	48	0%	67%	0	0.41	-5.5	-22	-27
18 Proj	**7**	**10**	**0**	**131**	**114**	**4.79**	**5.03**	**1.55**	**799**	**771**	**808**	**17.9**	**3.7**	**7.9**	**2.1**	**58%**	**10%**	**38**	**23**	**40**	**34%**	**71%**	**9%**	**25**						**-6.9**	**56**	**68**

Nova,Ivan

Age: 31	Th: R	Role SP	Health F	LIMA Plan B	
Ht: 6' 5"	Wt: 245	Type	PT/Exp A	Rand Var +1	
			Consist B	MM 1103	

A tale of two halves results-wise (see: $R, H%/S% splits). Mid-season bout with knee inflammation never landed him on the DL, but his results from that point on seem to indicate lingering issues. There are some bankable skills here - pinpoint control, GB lean - but health and inconsistency are holding him back.

Yr Tm	W	L	Sv	IP	K	ERA	xERA	WHIP	oOPS	vL	vR	BF/G	Ctl	Dom	Cmd	FpK	SwK	G	L	F	H%	S%	hr/f	GS	APC	DOM%	DIS%	Sv%	LI	RAR	BPV	BPX
13 NYY *	11	6	0	157	130	3.08	3.57	1.29	678	676	680	24.8	2.8	7.4	2.7	54%	10%	54	20	26	31%	78%	8%	20	91	40%	25%	0	0.77	15.2	86	112
14 NYY	2	2	0	21	12	8.27	4.53	1.84	1033	764	1444	24.0	2.6	5.2	2.0	64%	5%	49	20	31	36%	59%	26%	4	82	0%	75%			-11.6	51	60
15 NYY	6	11	0	94	63	5.07	4.50	1.40	793	899	682	24.3	3.2	6.0	1.9	55%	8%	49	19	32	30%	66%	13%	17	90	18%	53%			-12.9	50	60
16 2 TM	12	8	1	162	127	4.17	3.74	1.25	778	857	716	21.4	1.6	7.1	4.5	62%	10%	54	19	28	32%	71%	16%	26	72	31%	42%	100	0.74	0.5	117	139
17 PIT	11	14	0	187	131	4.14	4.30	1.28	781	858	713	25.3	1.7	6.3	3.6	64%	9%	46	23	31	31%	73%	16%	31	86	19%	29%			5.1	91	109
1st Half	8	5	0	108	60	3.08	4.18	1.11	695	742	649	27.1	1.1	5.0	4.6	64%	8%	48	24	28	28%	76%	11%	16	90	25%	25%			17.0	87	104
2nd Half	3	9	0	79	71	5.58	4.45	1.51	891	1023	787	23.4	2.6	8.1	3.1	65%	10%	42	23	35	34%	69%	21%	15	82	13%	33%			-11.9	95	114
18 Proj	**11**	**13**	**0**	**174**	**132**	**3.89**	**4.17**	**1.30**	**785**	**865**	**715**	**22.9**	**1.9**	**6.8**	**3.6**	**63%**	**9%**	**48**	**21**	**30**	**31%**	**76%**	**16%**	**31**						**10.1**	**99**	**119**

ALEC DOPP

O'Day,Darren			Health F	LIMA Plan A
Age: 35	Th: R	Role RP	PT/Exp C	Rand Var 0
Ht: 6' 4"	Wt: 220	Type Pwr FB	Consist B	MM 3510

More shoulder woes took a two-week chunk out of the season, though surface stats indicated this was 2016 repeat. But among the concerns: 1) Swinging strikes down all year; 2) No FpK support for his 2nd half Ctl improvement; 3) Second half H%/S% suppressed ERA. There are younger and healthier RP options.

Yr	Tm	W	L	Sv	IP	K	ERA	xERA	WHIP	oOPS	vL	vR	BF/G	Ctl	Dom	Cmd	FpK	SwK	G	L	F	H%	S%	hr/f	GS	APC	DOM%	DIS%	Sv%	LI	RAR	BPV	BPX	R$
13	BAL	5	3	2	62	59	2.18	3.38	1.00	617	922	443	3.6	2.2	8.6	3.9	63%	12%	37	22	41	26%	85%	10%	0	14			33	1.22	12.9	110	144	$8
14	BAL	5	2	4	69	73	1.70	2.99	0.89	550	633	497	4.0	2.5	9.6	3.8	59%	14%	45	17	38	23%	87%	10%	0	16			50	1.33	17.3	128	152	$12
15	BAL	6	2	6	65	82	1.52	2.95	0.93	540	627	493	3.8	1.9	11.3	5.9	66%	15%	35	20	45	29%	89%	7%	0	16			55	1.21	19.7	164	196	$14
16	BAL	3	1	3	31	38	3.77	3.89	1.23	717	862	648	3.9	3.8	11.0	2.9	68%	15%	34	22	44	28%	78%	17%	0	16			60	1.09	1.6	109	129	$1
17	BAL	2	3	2	60	76	3.43	3.29	1.08	609	677	565	3.8	3.6	11.3	3.2	65%	11%	48	15	38	26%	74%	16%	0	16			50	0.96	6.9	133	160	$4
1st Half		1	2	2	27	32	4.28	3.86	1.21	573	479	627	4.0	4.6	10.5	2.3	69%	11%	48	15	36	27%	65%	8%	0	16			67	1.21	0.3	92	110	$1
2nd Half		1	1	0	33	44	2.73	2.86	0.97	639	826	510	3.6	2.7	12.0	4.4	61%	12%	47	14	39	25%	85%	22%	0	15			0	0.77	6.6	168	201	$7
18	Proj	**4**	**2**	**2**	**58**	**71**	**3.82**	**3.65**	**1.16**	**659**	**768**	**597**	**3.7**	**3.5**	**11.1**	**3.1**	**65%**	**13%**	**42**	**18**	**41**	**28%**	**72%**	**15%**	**0**						**3.9**	**124**	**149**	**$3**

Odorizzi,Jake			Health D	LIMA Plan B
Age: 28	Th: R	Role SP	PT/Exp A	Rand Var -1
Ht: 6' 2"	Wt: 190	Type Pwr xFB	Consist B	MM 0203

Missed two stints with hamstring and back problems, which seemed to take a bite out of his skills (BPX history). While Dom and SwK are steady, FpK trend is ominous. With additional baserunners, significant FB% lean becomes potentially explosive. Should bounce back some, but limited signs of upside, even at 28.

Yr	Tm	W	L	Sv	IP	K	ERA	xERA	WHIP	oOPS	vL	vR	BF/G	Ctl	Dom	Cmd	FpK	SwK	G	L	F	H%	S%	hr/f	GS	APC	DOM%	DIS%	Sv%	LI	RAR	BPV	BPX	R$
13	TAM *	9	7	1	154	129	3.83	3.46	1.22	744	846	627	21.5	2.7	7.5	2.8	57%	8%	32	26	42	29%	71%	8%	4	76	0%	50%	100	0.80	0.7	83	108	$7
14	TAM	11	13	0	168	174	4.13	3.96	1.28	692	663	726	23.2	3.2	9.3	2.9	61%	10%	30	21	49	31%	71%	9%	31	98	35%	32%			-8.0	90	108	$4
15	TAM	9	9	0	169	150	3.35	3.99	1.15	680	630	745	25.0	2.4	8.0	3.3	60%	11%	37	22	41	29%	75%	9%	28	98	25%	11%			12.8	92	110	$13
16	TAM	10	6	0	188	166	3.69	4.32	1.19	715	578	814	23.4	2.6	8.0	3.1	58%	10%	37	19	44	28%	75%	12%	33	100	21%	42%			11.5	88	105	$13
17	TAM	10	8	0	143	127	4.14	5.01	1.24	736	686	773	21.6	3.8	8.0	2.1	54%	12%	31	22	47	24%	76%	16%	28	94	11%	50%			3.8	49	59	$8
1st Half		5	3	0	79	67	4.08	4.80	1.25	768	801	746	22.3	3.1	7.6	2.5	54%	11%	33	24	43	26%	78%	18%	15	96	7%	47%			2.7	65	78	$9
2nd Half		5	5	0	64	60	4.22	5.30	1.23	695	549	809	20.8	4.8	8.4	1.8	53%	12%	28	19	53	22%	73%	13%	13	91	15%	54%			1.1	29	34	$8
18	Proj	**10**	**8**	**0**	**160**	**143**	**3.90**	**4.74**	**1.23**	**720**	**637**	**790**	**21.8**	**3.4**	**8.1**	**2.4**	**57%**	**11%**	**33**	**21**	**47**	**27%**	**75%**	**13%**	**30**						**8.9**	**65**	**79**	**$10**

Oh,Seung-Hwan			Health A	LIMA Plan B+
Age: 35	Th: R	Role RP	PT/Exp B	Rand Var 0
Ht: 5' 10"	Wt: 205	Type Pwr xFB	Consist D	MM 1320

How not to endear yourself to "traditional closer" manager in one easy step: Give up seven home runs in 9th inning work. FpK and SwK backed up some from 2016 debut, but remain strong, and along with H%, point to at least a minor rebound. But it's not a good era for serving up all those fly balls. Shaky saves source.

Yr	Tm	W	L	Sv	IP	K	ERA	xERA	WHIP	oOPS	vL	vR	BF/G	Ctl	Dom	Cmd	FpK	SwK	G	L	F	H%	S%	hr/f	GS	APC	DOM%	DIS%	Sv%	LI	RAR	BPV	BPX	R$
13	for	4	1	28	52	51	2.16	2.36	0.93				4.0	2.2	8.9	4.1						23%	86%								10.9	121	158	$17
14	for	2	4	39	67	77	2.18	2.22	0.90				3.9	2.2	10.4	4.8						24%	85%								12.9	146	174	$23
15	for	2	3	41	69	63	3.39	4.23	1.28				4.5	2.6	8.1	3.2						31%	79%								4.9	79	94	$17
16	STL	6	3	19	80	103	1.92	2.96	0.92	510	455	555	4.1	2.0	11.6	5.7	67%	18%	40	19	41	29%	82%	7%	0	17			83	1.30	22.3	173	205	$22
17	STL	1	6	20	59	54	4.10	4.94	1.40	794	1006	642	4.3	2.3	8.2	3.6	63%	14%	29	22	49	34%	77%	11%	0	17			83	1.35	1.9	93	112	$6
1st Half		1	4	16	37	34	3.68	4.87	1.36	767	1036	523	4.8	2.5	8.3	3.4	60%	13%	29	21	50	33%	80%	11%	0	19			84	1.67	3.1	91	109	$12
2nd Half		0	2	4	23	20	4.76	5.04	1.46	837	934	790	3.6	2.0	7.9	4.0	68%	15%	28	23	49	35%	72%	11%	0	14			80	0.96	-1.1	95	114	-$3
18	Proj	**2**	**4**	**20**	**65**	**66**	**3.78**	**4.18**	**1.22**	**702**	**776**	**651**	**3.9**	**2.2**	**9.2**	**4.2**	**65%**	**16%**	**33**	**21**	**46**	**32%**	**74%**	**11%**	**0**						**4.7**	**117**	**140**	**$9**

Osuna,Roberto			Health A	LIMA Plan C+
Age: 23	Th: R	Role RP	PT/Exp A	Rand Var +2
Ht: 6' 2"	Wt: 215	Type Pwr	Consist A	MM 5530

The More Than Meets the Eye Dept.: Walks continue to plummet, pointing to another sub-1.00 WHIP; more SwK than ever means Dom is legit; GB/FB has flipped in right direction; S% correction will be boon for ERA. Still just a pup and owns pristine Reliability grades. If your leaguemates see "just another closer," pounce.

Yr	Tm	W	L	Sv	IP	K	ERA	xERA	WHIP	oOPS	vL	vR	BF/G	Ctl	Dom	Cmd	FpK	SwK	G	L	F	H%	S%	hr/f	GS	APC	DOM%	DIS%	Sv%	LI	RAR	BPV	BPX	R$
13																																		
14																																		
15	TOR	1	6	20	70	75	2.58	3.41	0.92	591	638	537	4.0	2.1	9.7	4.7	63%	15%	34	20	46	25%	77%	9%	0	16			87	1.36	11.8	131	156	$15
16	TOR	4	3	36	74	82	2.68	3.45	0.93	603	729	480	4.0	1.7	10.0	5.9	70%	16%	33	20	47	27%	78%	10%	0	16			86	1.39	13.8	145	172	$24
17	TOR	3	4	39	64	83	3.38	2.65	0.86	507	505	509	3.8	1.3	11.7	9.2	64%	17%	48	18	34	31%	60%	6%	0	15			80	1.36	7.8	202	242	$24
1st Half		2	0	19	32	44	2.25	2.58	0.75	484	523	458	3.5	0.8	12.4	14.7	70%	20%	38	20	42	29%	73%	7%	0	13			86	1.14	8.3	216	259	$28
2nd Half		1	4	20	32	39	4.50	2.72	0.97	528	490	564	4.1	1.7	11.0	6.5	58%	15%	57	16	27	32%	50%	5%	0	16			74	1.60	-0.6	187	224	$20
18	Proj	**2**	**4**	**41**	**58**	**69**	**3.12**	**2.96**	**0.90**	**555**	**606**	**509**	**3.7**	**1.6**	**10.7**	**6.8**	**65%**	**16%**	**45**	**19**	**36**	**28%**	**68%**	**9%**	**0**						**8.8**	**173**	**209**	**$23**

Otero,Dan			Health A	LIMA Plan A
Age: 33	Th: R	Role RP	PT/Exp D	Rand Var +2
Ht: 6' 3"	Wt: 205	Type Con xGB	Consist C	MM 3000

Love to see "6"s leading both the FpK and G columns, but are those skills enough to be fantasy relevant in today's game? With 2016's Dom, the answer is yes ... but his uninspiring SwK history calls that season's whiffs into question. Knocks RHH out, but this is only deep-league injury replacement material.

Yr	Tm	W	L	Sv	IP	K	ERA	xERA	WHIP	oOPS	vL	vR	BF/G	Ctl	Dom	Cmd	FpK	SwK	G	L	F	H%	S%	hr/f	GS	APC	DOM%	DIS%	Sv%	LI	RAR	BPV	BPX	R$
13	OAK *	3	0	15	66	44	1.27	1.97	0.99	613	613	613	4.5	1.0	5.9	6.2	63%	6%	56	20	24	29%	86%	0%	0	18			94	0.75	21.3	173	226	$15
14	OAK	8	2	1	87	45	2.28	3.50	1.10	607	698	539	4.8	1.6	4.7	3.0	69%	7%	56	24	20	28%	80%	7%	0	17			25	1.26	15.6	76	91	$9
15	OAK *	4	4	0	74	42	5.25	5.08	1.42	886	884	887	5.6	1.3	5.0	3.9	73%	7%	49	23	28	34%	64%	15%	0	18			0	0.77	-11.8	75	89	-$7
16	CLE	5	1	1	71	57	1.53	2.95	0.91	526	522	529	4.3	1.3	7.3	5.7	67%	8%	62	18	20	27%	84%	5%	0	16			50	0.79	23.2	136	162	$12
17	CLE	3	0	0	60	38	2.85	3.41	1.20	693	872	581	4.7	1.4	5.7	4.2	68%	8%	64	24	12	30%	80%	26%	0	16			0	0.54	11.2	108	130	$2
1st Half		1	0	0	31	22	3.48	3.66	1.26	716	669	752	4.8	1.7	6.4	3.7	66%	6%	61	25	14	30%	79%	36%	0	17			0	0.42	3.3	107	128	$0
2nd Half		2	0	0	29	16	2.17	3.12	1.14	665	1211	411	4.5	0.9	5.0	5.3	69%	9%	67	23	10	31%	81%	11%	0	16			0	0.67	7.8	109	131	$5
18	Proj	**3**	**1**	**0**	**58**	**38**	**3.15**	**3.50**	**1.14**	**656**	**759**	**588**	**4.7**	**1.3**	**5.9**	**4.6**	**68%**	**8%**	**61**	**22**	**17**	**30%**	**74%**	**13%**	**0**						**8.6**	**110**	**133**	**$2**

Ottavino,Adam			Health F	LIMA Plan C
Age: 32	Th: R	Role RP	PT/Exp D	Rand Var +1
Ht: 6' 5"	Wt: 220	Type Pwr	Consist D	MM 1400

Life can be rugged in mountain country. Shoulder woes kept his health risk elevated. His first pitch was a dart-throw all year long, his xGB ways evaporated, and come the second half, his manager's confidence in him was shot (LI). Health, skills, trust—they all seek rebuilding.

Yr	Tm	W	L	Sv	IP	K	ERA	xERA	WHIP	oOPS	vL	vR	BF/G	Ctl	Dom	Cmd	FpK	SwK	G	L	F	H%	S%	hr/f	GS	APC	DOM%	DIS%	Sv%	LI	RAR	BPV	BPX	R$
13	COL	1	3	0	78	78	2.64	3.62	1.33	672	853	544	6.6	3.6	9.0	2.5	61%	12%	46	22	33	32%	82%	7%	0	25			0	1.01	11.8	89	116	$2
14	COL	1	4	1	65	70	3.60	3.09	1.28	735	943	645	3.6	2.2	9.7	4.4	61%	12%	47	19	34	35%	74%	10%	0	14			17	1.31	1.1	140	166	$0
15	COL	1	0	3	10	13	0.00	1.89	0.48	265	321	217	3.5	1.7	11.3	6.5	51%	13%	63	5	32	16%	100%	0%	0	14			100	1.05	5.0	198	236	$1
16	COL	1	3	7	27	35	2.67	2.32	0.93	528	780	350	3.1	2.3	11.7	5.0	52%	11%	62	17	21	27%	77%	23%	0	13			58	1.28	5.1	187	222	$4
17	COL	2	3	0	53	63	5.06	5.03	1.63	786	898	727	3.9	6.6	10.6	1.6	47%	10%	37	22	41	31%	72%	14%	0	17			0	0.89	-4.6	29	34	-$6
1st Half		1	2	0	29	38	5.02	4.46	1.50	703	819	643	4.0	6.6	11.9	1.8	46%	11%	34	30	36	30%	69%	17%	0	18			0	1.30	-2.4	49	59	-$5
2nd Half		1	1	0	25	25	5.11	5.72	1.78	879	984	823	3.7	6.6	9.1	1.4	47%	8%	40	14	46	33%	75%	13%	0	16			0	0.47	-2.3	5	6	-$7
18	Proj	**2**	**3**	**0**	**58**	**64**	**4.19**	**4.47**	**1.48**	**764**	**915**	**688**	**3.9**	**4.6**	**9.9**	**2.1**	**54%**	**10%**	**42**	**20**	**38**	**33%**	**75%**	**12%**	**0**						**1.2**	**73**	**88**	**-$3**

Pagan,Emilio			Health A	LIMA Plan A
Age: 27	Th: R	Role RP	PT/Exp F	Rand Var +1
Ht: 6' 3"	Wt: 210	Type Pwr xFB	Consist D	MM 1400

2-3, 3.22 in 50 IP at SEA. Showed some glimmers in four separate stints with the club. Hard FB/SL combination yielded excellent 10.0 Dom and 7.0 Cmd in MLB, and 2nd half improvement in FpK and SwK points to its legitimacy. A weapon against LHH and reducing his FB are his most pressing tasks. Watchable.

Yr	Tm	W	L	Sv	IP	K	ERA	xERA	WHIP	oOPS	vL	vR	BF/G	Ctl	Dom	Cmd	FpK	SwK	G	L	F	H%	S%	hr/f	GS	APC	DOM%	DIS%	Sv%	LI	RAR	BPV	BPX	R$
13																																		
14																																		
15																																		
16	a/a	5	3	10	65	71	3.05	3.78	1.32				6.6	4.1	9.8	2.4						30%	82%								9.1	84	100	$7
17	SEA *	4	4	5	82	86	3.18	2.28	0.95	610	825	502	5.4	1.8	9.4	5.3	63%	14%	22	21	57	27%	69%	9%	0	21			83	1.09	11.9	157	188	$11
1st Half		2	2	5	42	41	3.39	1.36	0.90	413	896	129	5.8	2.2	8.7	4.0	59%	13%	12	16	72	25%	60%	6%	0	35			83	2.54	5.0	146	175	$13
2nd Half		2	2	0	40	45	2.95	3.79	1.01	657	805	585	5.3	1.4	10.2	7.5	63%	15%	25	22	53	30%	79%	11%	0	19			0	0.90	6.9	150	180	$10
18	Proj	**3**	**3**	**0**	**58**	**62**	**3.10**	**4.13**	**1.05**	**566**	**687**	**506**	**5.7**	**2.2**	**9.7**	**4.4**	**63%**	**15%**	**27**	**22**	**51**	**29%**	**75%**	**8%**	**0**						**9.0**	**120**	**145**	**$4**

BRENT HERSHEY

Parker,Blake

Age: 33	**Th:** R	**Role** RP	**Health**	A	**LIMA Plan**	B
Ht: 6' 3"	**Wt:** 225	**Type** Pwr FB	**PT/Exp**	D	**Rand Var**	-1
			Consist	B	**MM**	3420

Journeyman grabs opportunity, works a fastball/splitter combo into double-digit value and some late season saves. SwK believes in Dom improvement more than FpK does for Ctl. GB lean should help mitigate inevitable ERA/WHIP pullback due to H% correction. Relievers are volatile beasts, but skills here for repeat.

Yr	Tm	W	L	Sv	IP	K	ERA	xERA	WHIP	oOPS	vL	vR	BF/G	Ctl	Dom	Cmd	FpK	SwK	G	L	F	H%	S%	hr/f	GS	APC	DOM%	DIS%	Sv%	LI	RAR	BPV	BPX
13	CHC *	1	3	8	64	75	2.72	2.82	1.18	626	572	661	3.9	3.7	10.5	2.8	61%	12%	29	22	49	29%	80%	7%	0	17			89	0.70	9.1	112	146
14	CHC *	1	2	25	57	63	3.33	4.41	1.38	784	575	921	4.5	3.0	10.1	3.4	56%	12%	32	22	46	36%	80%	10%	0	20			93	0.50	2.8	101	120
15																																	
16	2 AL *	2	2	20	57	58	3.89	3.31	1.21	707	701	712	4.2	3.4	9.1	2.7	60%	11%	48	13	38	29%	70%	5%	0	20			91	1.26	2.1	93	110
17	LAA	3	3	8	67	86	2.54	2.78	0.83	527	483	568	3.6	2.1	11.5	5.4	60%	14%	47	18	35	24%	76%	13%	0	15			73	1.20	15.1	174	209
1st Half		3	2	1	35	51	2.04	2.44	0.93	493	446	527	3.6	2.3	13.0	5.7	60%	15%	53	19	28	32%	78%	5%	0	15			33	1.18	10.1	202	243
2nd Half		0	1	7	32	35	3.09	3.13	0.72	570	516	640	3.6	2.0	9.8	5.0	59%	13%	41	17	42	15%	71%	20%	0	15			88	1.23	5.0	143	171
18	**Proj**	**2**	**3**	**18**	**65**	**75**	**3.09**	**3.57**	**1.03**	**611**	**558**	**656**	**3.8**	**2.7**	**10.4**	**3.8**	**60%**	**13%**	**39**	**20**	**42**	**27%**	**75%**	**11%**	**0**						**10.2**	**131**	**158**

Paulino,David

Age: 24	**Th:** R	**Role** SP	**Health**	C	**LIMA Plan**	C+
Ht: 6' 7"	**Wt:** 215	**Type** Pwr xFB	**PT/Exp**	D	**Rand Var**	+5
			Consist	C	**MM**	2403

Year started late (bone bruise, elbow) and ended early (PED suspension). The surface-statters will pass, but he racks up Ks, shows good control, and that small sample ERA/WHIP lies at the feet of H%, S%, and hr/f. Fly balls need to be tamed and health is far from pristine, but worth a spot on your late-game flyer list.

Yr	Tm	W	L	Sv	IP	K	ERA	xERA	WHIP	oOPS	vL	vR	BF/G	Ctl	Dom	Cmd	FpK	SwK	G	L	F	H%	S%	hr/f	GS	APC	DOM%	DIS%	Sv%	LI	RAR	BPV	BPX
13																																	
14																																	
15																																	
16	HOU *	5	5	1	85	85	2.76	2.81	1.13	665	770	393	16.8	2.0	9.0	4.4	59%	6%	43	13	43	32%	76%	0%	1	42	0%	100%	100	0.36	15.0	140	167
17	HOU	2	0	0	29	34	6.52	4.17	1.48	914	843	984	21.3	2.2	10.6	4.9	59%	11%	30	19	51	37%	63%	19%	6	88	0%	33%			-7.7	139	167
1st Half		2	0	0	29	34	6.52	4.17	1.48	914	843	984	21.3	2.2	10.6	4.9	59%	11%	30	19	51	37%	63%	19%	6	88	0%	33%			-7.7	139	167
2nd Half																																	
18	**Proj**	**8**	**5**	**0**	**131**	**144**	**4.32**	**3.97**	**1.24**	**673**	**633**	**713**	**20.0**	**2.2**	**9.9**	**4.4**	**59%**	**11%**	**37**	**21**	**42**	**32%**	**72%**	**15%**	**24**						**0.6**	**134**	**161**

Paxton,James

Age: 29	**Th:** L	**Role** SP	**Health**	F	**LIMA Plan**	C+
Ht: 6' 4"	**Wt:** 235	**Type** Pwr	**PT/Exp**	C	**Rand Var**	-1
			Consist	B	**MM**	3403

2016's second-half gains hinted this was coming, but additional bumps in FpK and SwK carried Cmd and run prevention to new levels. BPV trend tells one story, but IP history tells another (pectoral, foream were 2017's culprits). Both are valid, which should keep his draft day price in check. Avoid the bidding war.

Yr	Tm	W	L	Sv	IP	K	ERA	xERA	WHIP	oOPS	vL	vR	BF/G	Ctl	Dom	Cmd	FpK	SwK	G	L	F	H%	S%	hr/f	GS	APC	DOM%	DIS%	Sv%	LI	RAR	BPV	BPX
13	SEA *	11	11	0	170	131	4.25	4.35	1.48	533	790	475	22.8	3.2	6.9	2.1	54%	10%	59	17	24	34%	71%	13%	4	96	25%	25%			-8.1	67	88
14	SEA	6	4	0	74	59	3.04	3.50	1.20	612	527	629	23.3	3.5	7.2	2.0	54%	8%	55	23	23	28%	74%	6%	13	91	23%	8%			6.4	67	80
15	SEA	3	4	0	67	56	3.90	4.47	1.43	704	1054	606	22.8	3.9	7.5	1.9	53%	7%	48	17	34	31%	76%	11%	13	85	15%	38%			0.5	56	67
16	SEA *	10	10	0	172	159	4.06	4.19	1.33	717	733	714	23.0	2.1	8.3	4.0	62%	12%	48	22	30	35%	71%	8%	20	98	30%	15%			2.7	107	127
17	SEA	12	5	0	136	156	2.98	3.36	1.10	602	463	630	23.0	2.4	10.3	4.2	65%	13%	45	22	33	31%	74%	8%	24	95	54%	21%			23.2	143	171
1st Half		5	3	0	68	79	3.44	3.74	1.28	664	487	692	23.9	3.3	10.5	3.2	65%	13%	42	25	33	34%	74%	8%	12	98	50%	25%			7.7	119	142
2nd Half		7	2	0	68	77	2.51	3.00	0.93	536	445	559	22.1	1.6	10.2	6.4	64%	13%	48	20	32	29%	75%	7%	12	92	58%	17%			15.5	167	200
18	**Proj**	**11**	**7**	**0**	**145**	**153**	**3.21**	**3.54**	**1.19**	**651**	**651**	**650**	**22.2**	**2.4**	**9.5**	**4.0**	**61%**	**11%**	**48**	**21**	**31**	**32%**	**75%**	**9%**	**26**						**20.5**	**132**	**159**

Pazos,James

Age: 27	**Th:** L	**Role** RP	**Health**	A	**LIMA Plan**	C+
Ht: 6' 2"	**Wt:** 235	**Type** Pwr	**PT/Exp**	D	**Rand Var**	+4
			Consist	F	**MM**	3400

Four confidence-building pluses: 1) Lively mid-90s FB; 2) FpK jump foretells a drop in Ctl; 3) Small sample LD%, H% and hr/f ballooned his 2nd half stats; 4) Strong GB% history. RPs are fickle, and he still needs to solve RHH, but his manager got to trust him more as the year went on. Maybe you should, too.

Yr	Tm	W	L	Sv	IP	K	ERA	xERA	WHIP	oOPS	vL	vR	BF/G	Ctl	Dom	Cmd	FpK	SwK	G	L	F	H%	S%	hr/f	GS	APC	DOM%	DIS%	Sv%	LI	RAR	BPV	BPX
13																																	
14	aa	0	1	6	42	36	1.77	2.26	1.22				6.1	4.1	7.8	1.9						28%	84%								10.2	99	117
15	NYY *	3	1	3	48	44	1.55	2.67	1.23	476	606	250	5.1	3.7	8.4	2.3	43%	6%	43	14	43	29%	88%	0%	0	8			75	0.44	14.2	100	119
16	NYY *	3	2	1	31	37	4.84	5.25	1.75	1408	1250	1569	4.7	6.6	10.8	1.7	53%	12%	46	23	31	36%	74%	50%	0	8			50	0.46	-2.5	70	84
17	SEA	4	5	0	54	65	3.86	3.65	1.40	723	561	821	4.1	4.0	10.9	2.7	63%	13%	51	22	27	34%	76%	18%	0	16			0	1.11	3.3	117	140
1st Half		2	1	0	33	41	3.00	3.08	1.15	620	524	670	4.3	3.8	11.2	2.9	61%	12%	59	17	23	29%	77%	16%	0	18			0	0.98	5.5	135	162
2nd Half		2	4	0	21	24	5.23	4.54	1.79	867	604	1064	3.7	4.4	10.5	2.4	67%	14%	41	28	31	40%	76%	20%	0	13			0	1.27	-2.2	89	107
18	**Proj**	**4**	**5**	**0**	**58**	**65**	**3.43**	**3.59**	**1.24**	**630**	**471**	**734**	**4.0**	**3.5**	**10.1**	**2.9**	**65%**	**13%**	**48**	**24**	**28**	**30%**	**76%**	**16%**	**0**						**6.6**	**112**	**135**

Peacock,Brad

Age: 30	**Th:** R	**Role** SP	**Health**	F	**LIMA Plan**	C
Ht: 6' 1"	**Wt:** 210	**Type** Pwr FB	**PT/Exp**	C	**Rand Var**	-1
			Consist	B	**MM**	1303

Adding a 2-seamer and increasing slider usage allowed him to strut his stuff, especially in the second half, when the throwing strikes/throwing hard duo found its balance. With a minor GB lean and even some Cmd upside, he should remain in the rotation, though asking for a stats repeat is a stretch. A solid SP3.

Yr	Tm	W	L	Sv	IP	K	ERA	xERA	WHIP	oOPS	vL	vR	BF/G	Ctl	Dom	Cmd	FpK	SwK	G	L	F	H%	S%	hr/f	GS	APC	DOM%	DIS%	Sv%	LI	RAR	BPV	BPX
13	HOU *	11	8	0	162	141	4.21	4.23	1.31	779	919	594	21.0	3.3	7.8	2.4	56%	8%	37	19	45	29%	73%	14%	14	83	21%	29%	0	0.79	-7.0	60	78
14	HOU	4	9	0	132	119	4.72	4.59	1.56	801	793	811	21.0	4.8	8.1	1.7	57%	9%	37	21	42	31%	74%	12%	24	85	13%	46%	0	0.81	-15.8	32	38
15	HOU	0	1	0	5	3	5.40	5.05	1.40	808	1167	422	22.0	3.6	5.4	1.5	68%	6%	31	31	38	31%	57%	0%	1	85	0%	100%			-0.9	9	11
16	HOU *	5	7	0	149	123	5.13	5.27	1.55	700	718	686	20.3	3.5	7.4	2.2	58%	9%	41	9	49	34%	69%	14%	5	49	20%	60%	0	0.40	-17.3	52	62
17	HOU	13	2	0	132	161	3.00	3.70	1.19	615	759	501	16.1	3.9	11.0	2.8	63%	12%	44	19	38	30%	77%	8%	21	66	24%	14%	0	0.68	22.1	115	138
1st Half		5	1	0	50	73	2.72	3.45	1.23	547	619	484	10.9	5.4	13.2	2.4	59%	15%	43	21	36	31%	77%	3%	7	47	43%	14%	0	0.61	10.0	112	134
2nd Half		8	1	0	82	88	3.17	3.86	1.17	654	848	509	22.5	3.0	9.6	3.3	65%	11%	44	17	39	29%	77%	11%	14	91	14%	14%	0	0.76	12.1	116	139
18	**Proj**	**11**	**6**	**0**	**160**	**166**	**3.51**	**4.28**	**1.31**	**721**	**821**	**628**	**22.1**	**3.5**	**9.4**	**2.7**	**60%**	**11%**	**41**	**17**	**42**	**31%**	**76%**	**9%**	**25**						**16.6**	**94**	**113**

Pelfrey,Mike

Age: 34	**Th:** R	**Role** SP	**Health**	F	**LIMA Plan**	D
Ht: 6' 7"	**Wt:** 240	**Type** GB	**PT/Exp**	B	**Rand Var**	+3
			Consist	B	**MM**	0001

Wayback Machine: In his first Forecaster box in 2007, we commented that he "looked overmatched" and referenced his "1.1 Cmd." Not uncommon for a pitcher's first 21 MLB innings, but in the years since (min. 5 GS), Cmd never broke the 1.9 barrier. And given that recent R$ string, he still looks … well, you know.

Yr	Tm	W	L	Sv	IP	K	ERA	xERA	WHIP	oOPS	vL	vR	BF/G	Ctl	Dom	Cmd	FpK	SwK	G	L	F	H%	S%	hr/f	GS	APC	DOM%	DIS%	Sv%	LI	RAR	BPV	BPX
13	MIN	5	13	0	153	101	5.19	4.59	1.55	789	762	821	23.4	3.1	6.0	1.9	55%	6%	43	21	36	34%	67%	7%	29	94	14%	48%			-24.9	44	57
14	MIN	0	3	0	24	10	7.99	6.83	1.99	924	648	1315	23.8	6.8	3.8	0.6	50%	5%	44	18	38	30%	62%	15%	5	91	0%	100%			-12.4	-94	-112
15	MIN	6	11	0	165	86	4.26	4.45	1.48	772	834	716	23.8	2.5	4.7	1.9	58%	6%	51	23	26	33%	71%	7%	30	89	20%	40%			-6.1	47	56
16	DET	4	10	0	119	56	5.07	5.31	1.73	877	923	828	22.5	3.5	4.2	1.2	58%	7%	52	22	26	34%	73%	14%	22	86	0%	73%	0	0.72	-12.9	12	15
17	CHW	3	12	0	120	79	5.93	5.56	1.58	853	903	809	16.1	4.7	5.9	1.3	59%	7%	50	16	34	28%	67%	19%	21	67	5%	71%	0	0.65	-23.2	9	11
1st Half		3	6	0	65	41	4.13	5.20	1.36	726	795	661	20.2	3.9	5.6	1.5	58%	7%	49	17	34	27%	74%	13%	13	84	8%	62%	0	0.72	1.8	24	29
2nd Half		0	6	0	55	38	8.07	6.00	1.83	994	1030	963	13.2	5.6	6.3	1.1	61%	7%	52	14	34	30%	61%	25%	8	56	0%	88%	0	0.60	-25.0	-8	-10
18	**Proj**	**3**	**9**	**0**	**102**	**61**	**5.67**	**5.47**	**1.63**	**860**	**899**	**823**	**22.2**	**4.0**	**5.4**	**1.3**	**59%**	**7%**	**50**	**19**	**31**	**31%**	**68%**	**16%**	**15**						**-16.4**	**17**	**20**

Peralta,Wandy

Age: 26	**Th:** L	**Role** RP	**Health**	A	**LIMA Plan**	B+
Ht: 6' 0"	**Wt:** 220	**Type** Pwr GB	**PT/Exp**	D	**Rand Var**	0
			Consist	C	**MM**	1211

Recent history with pitchers named Wandy or Peralta are not favorable, but: 1) swing-and-miss portends Dom upside; 2) the GB% looks like it will stick; and 3) there's very little platoon split. A deep-league buying opportunity on name alone? That's probably a stretch. But no harm in watching from afar for now.

Yr	Tm	W	L	Sv	IP	K	ERA	xERA	WHIP	oOPS	vL	vR	BF/G	Ctl	Dom	Cmd	FpK	SwK	G	L	F	H%	S%	hr/f	GS	APC	DOM%	DIS%	Sv%	LI	RAR	BPV	BPX
13																																	
14																																	
15	aa	7	7	0	117	70	6.67	6.24	1.90				19.0	5.1	5.4	1.1						36%	64%								-38.9	24	28
16	CIN *	4	2	3	83	54	4.05	4.44	1.53	1036	773	1178	6.0	4.0	5.9	1.5	46%	12%	46	23	31	32%	74%	13%	0	13			43	0.49	1.5	48	57
17	CIN	3	4	0	65	57	3.76	3.96	1.19	681	639	711	3.8	3.3	7.9	2.4	56%	16%	54	16	30	26%	72%	15%	0	15			0	0.81	4.8	85	102
1st Half		3	1	0	36	34	3.47	3.55	1.02	640	630	645	3.9	2.7	8.4	3.1	60%	16%	54	16	30	23%	72%	17%	0	15			0	0.84	4.0	110	132
2nd Half		0	3	0	28	23	4.13	4.54	1.41	730	651	791	3.7	4.1	7.3	1.8	52%	15%	54	17	29	30%	73%	13%	0	14			0	0.79	0.8	52	63
18	**Proj**	**3**	**4**	**2**	**73**	**60**	**4.08**	**4.42**	**1.42**	**752**	**710**	**784**	**5.1**	**3.7**	**7.5**	**2.0**	**55%**	**16%**	**54**	**16**	**29**	**31%**	**73%**	**10%**	**0**						**2.5**	**67**	**81**

BRENT HERSHEY

Perdomo,Luis

Age: 25	Th: R	Role SP		Health	A		LIMA Plan	C	
Ht: 6' 2"	Wt: 185	Type xGB		PT/Exp	B		Rand Var	+2	
				Consist	A		MM	1003	

Hit DL with shoulder injury after one start; went on to post 4.40+ ERA in each month. Age, fact he skipped AA/AAA entirely, and flashes of better skills (like 1st half xERA) could merit speculation for deep leaguers, but upside is scant. Failed to throw a single PQS-DOM in 29 tries—that's hard to do. So is drafting him.

Yr Tm	W	L	Sv	IP	K	ERA	xERA	WHIP	oOPS	vL	vR	BF/G	Ctl	Dom	Cmd	FpK	SwK	G	L	F	H%	S%	hr/f	GS	APC	DOM%	DIS%	Sv%	LI	RAR	BPV	BPX	R$
13																																	
14																																	
15																																	
16 SD	9	10	0	147	105	5.71	4.20	1.59	847	861	834	18.9	2.8	6.4	2.3	59%	9%	59	20	21	35%	67%	22%	20	68	10%	40%	0	0.65	-27.5	77	91	-$12
17 SD	8	11	0	164	118	4.67	4.32	1.51	784	807	763	24.7	3.6	6.5	1.8	61%	9%	62	17	21	32%	70%	16%	29	88	0%	48%			-6.4	60	72	-$3
1st Half	3	4	0	78	65	4.71	3.80	1.44	776	892	689	24.1	3.4	7.5	2.2	65%	10%	65	15	19	32%	69%	20%	14	88	0%	36%			-3.4	85	102	-$3
2nd Half	5	7	0	85	53	4.64	4.81	1.57	791	744	842	25.3	3.7	5.6	1.5	58%	8%	59	19	23	33%	71%	13%	15	88	0%	60%			-3.0	38	45	-$4
18 Proj	**9**	**11**	**0**	**160**	**113**	**4.80**	**4.34**	**1.51**	**781**	**794**	**769**	**21.5**	**3.3**	**6.4**	**1.9**	**60%**	**9%**	**61**	**18**	**21**	**33%**	**70%**	**15%**	**32**						**-8.7**	**65**	**78**	**-$5**

Perez,Martin

Age: 27	Th: L	Role SP		Health	C		LIMA Plan	D+	
Ht: 6' 0"	Wt: 200	Type GB		PT/Exp	A		Rand Var	0	
				Consist	A		MM	0003	

Stayed healthy save for a brief DL stint (hand) in July, but the good news ends there. Career-low FpK, SwK helped cement third straight 4.50+ xERA, while once-elite GB% took another tumble. Four years removed from positive R$, BPX history confirms he's nowhere near average. Safe to scratch off your lists.

Yr Tm	W	L	Sv	IP	K	ERA	xERA	WHIP	oOPS	vL	vR	BF/G	Ctl	Dom	Cmd	FpK	SwK	G	L	F	H%	S%	hr/f	GS	APC	DOM%	DIS%	Sv%	LI	RAR	BPV	BPX	R$
13 TEX *	15	8	0	168	109	3.77	4.27	1.35	728	759	718	25.0	2.5	5.9	2.3	61%	10%	48	21	31	31%	75%	12%	20	93	35%	45%			2.0	56	72	$5
14 TEX	4	3	0	51	35	4.38	3.73	1.34	743	707	753	25.9	3.3	6.1	1.8	60%	8%	53	23	25	30%	67%	8%	8	97	13%	38%			-4.1	52	61	-$2
15 TEX *	3	7	0	104	68	4.73	4.69	1.49	729	537	777	22.5	2.3	5.9	2.5	65%	8%	60	18	22	35%	67%	5%	14	87	21%	50%			-9.9	66	79	-$8
16 TEX	10	11	0	199	103	4.39	4.92	1.41	741	537	786	25.9	3.4	4.7	1.4	64%	8%	53	20	26	29%	70%	10%	33	93	12%	48%			-5.0	22	26	-$1
17 TEX	13	12	0	185	115	4.82	4.96	1.54	812	666	849	25.3	3.1	5.6	1.8	59%	7%	47	25	28	33%	71%	13%	32	97	9%	66%			-10.5	43	52	-$4
1st Half	4	6	0	82	61	4.70	4.95	1.65	842	860	838	24.5	3.5	6.7	1.9	59%	8%	44	27	29	36%	73%	12%	15	96	7%	53%			-3.5	48	57	-$9
2nd Half	9	6	0	103	54	4.91	4.96	1.44	788	503	858	26.1	2.7	4.7	1.7	59%	7%	50	23	27	30%	69%	15%	17	98	12%	76%			-7.0	40	47	$0
18 Proj	**9**	**13**	**0**	**174**	**104**	**4.63**	**4.86**	**1.47**	**783**	**624**	**822**	**24.9**	**3.0**	**5.4**	**1.8**	**61%**	**8%**	**51**	**22**	**27**	**32%**	**70%**	**11%**	**30**						**-5.8**	**45**	**54**	**-$4**

Petit,Yusmeiro

Age: 33	Th: R	Role RP		Health	A		LIMA Plan	B	
Ht: 6' 1"	Wt: 255	Type Pwr xFB		PT/Exp	C		Rand Var	-1	
				Consist	B		MM	2301	

Career year with plenty of volume out of middle relief, and while BPV nods in approval, repeat odds seem slim: SwK spike still isn't enough to support elite Dom; FB% says he rolled sevens with hr/f and won; repeat of W/Sv combo is unlikely. Good enough to be effective, just use xERA as your baseline.

Yr Tm	W	L	Sv	IP	K	ERA	xERA	WHIP	oOPS	vL	vR	BF/G	Ctl	Dom	Cmd	FpK	SwK	G	L	F	H%	S%	hr/f	GS	APC	DOM%	DIS%	Sv%	LI	RAR	BPV	BPX	R$
13 SF *	9	7	0	136	115	4.36	4.47	1.30	660	562	717	24.3	1.6	7.6	4.7	69%	13%	30	26	44	33%	70%	7%	7	91	29%	29%	0	0.73	-8.3	108	141	$1
14 SF	5	5	0	117	133	3.69	3.03	1.02	635	777	510	11.8	1.7	10.2	6.0	69%	13%	36	21	43	30%	66%	9%	12	43	17%	17%	0	0.52	0.7	152	182	$8
15 SF	1	1	1	76	59	3.67	4.34	1.18	743	828	680	7.5	1.8	7.0	3.9	62%	10%	33	21	46	29%	75%	10%	1	27	0%	100%	100	0.84	2.7	89	106	$1
16 WAS	3	5	1	62	49	4.50	4.51	1.32	793	925	698	7.4	2.2	7.1	3.3	65%	9%	42	17	41	30%	73%	15%	1	27	0%	0%	50	0.82	-2.4	89	106	-$2
17 LAA	5	2	4	91	101	2.76	3.64	0.95	571	645	514	5.9	1.8	10.0	5.6	64%	11%	33	18	49	28%	76%	8%	1	22	100%	0%	80	0.92	18.0	142	171	$14
1st Half	2	0	1	48	52	2.61	3.77	0.95	571	682	492	6.1	2.0	9.7	4.7	62%	11%	35	16	49	26%	78%	8%	0	23			50	0.86	10.4	132	158	$14
2nd Half	3	2	3	43	49	2.93	3.49	0.95	571	607	542	5.7	1.5	10.3	7.0	66%	11%	31	20	49	29%	73%	8%	1	22	100%	0%	100	0.99	7.6	154	184	$15
18 Proj	**4**	**3**	**0**	**73**	**70**	**3.48**	**4.05**	**1.10**	**669**	**751**	**608**	**6.7**	**1.8**	**8.7**	**4.8**	**65%**	**11%**	**35**	**19**	**46**	**29%**	**74%**	**10%**	**0**						**7.9**	**121**	**145**	**$4**

Petricka,Jacob

Age: 30	Th: R	Role RP		Health	F		LIMA Plan	D+	
Ht: 6' 5"	Wt: 220	Type Pwr xGB		PT/Exp	D		Rand Var	+5	
				Consist	D		MM	1100	

Battled elbow issues all year, eventually lost with surgery in October. Ignore that small-sample BPV; it was driven by fluky Dom spike, and he missed even fewer bats. Ditto for Ctl that's out of touch with his personal baseline. Lucky to even make this book—odds are decent he won't get ink in the 2019 edition.

Yr Tm	W	L	Sv	IP	K	ERA	xERA	WHIP	oOPS	vL	vR	BF/G	Ctl	Dom	Cmd	FpK	SwK	G	L	F	H%	S%	hr/f	GS	APC	DOM%	DIS%	Sv%	LI	RAR	BPV	BPX	R$
13 CHW *	6	1	1	74	58	2.63	3.92	1.56	688	775	644	6.9	4.8	7.1	1.5	51%	9%	63	21	16	33%	82%	0%	0	20			50	0.94	11.3	70	92	$1
14 CHW	1	6	14	73	55	2.96	3.57	1.37	671	830	549	4.6	4.1	6.8	1.7	61%	8%	63	17	19	30%	78%	7%	0	18			78	1.52	7.0	53	63	$5
15 CHW	4	3	2	52	33	3.63	3.77	1.42	716	851	666	3.5	3.1	5.7	1.8	65%	9%	65	18	17	32%	74%	7%	0	13			67	1.16	2.1	62	73	-$1
16 CHW	0	0	0	8	7	4.50	5.73	2.00	854	650	886	4.3	9.0	7.9	0.9	54%	8%	70	9	22	31%	80%	20%	0	17			0	1.04	-0.3	-53	-63	-$5
17 CHW	1	1	0	26	26	7.01	4.11	1.75	947	928	959	4.5	2.1	9.1	4.3	62%	7%	47	26	27	42%	64%	25%	0	18			0	0.94	-8.4	132	159	-$8
1st Half	1	0	0	11	13	9.28	3.76	1.88	1017	1238	848	5.7	2.5	11.0	4.3	71%	8%	46	29	26	45%	53%	33%	0	22			0	0.54	-6.5	153	183	-$10
2nd Half	0	1	0	15	13	5.40	4.37	1.67	897	651	1029	3.9	1.8	7.8	4.3	56%	7%	48	24	28	39%	73%	20%	0	16			0	1.15	-1.9	118	141	-$6
18 Proj	**2**	**2**	**0**	**44**	**31**	**4.12**	**4.52**	**1.47**	**707**	**709**	**706**	**4.8**	**4.1**	**6.5**	**1.6**	**60%**	**8%**	**59**	**20**	**22**	**31%**	**73%**	**11%**	**0**						**1.3**	**44**	**53**	**-$4**

Phelps,David

Age: 31	Th: R	Role RP		Health	F		LIMA Plan	B+	
Ht: 6' 2"	Wt: 200	Type Pwr		PT/Exp	C		Rand Var	0	
				Consist	C		MM	2400	

Tried to return from elbow impingement in Aug, ultimately had surgery in Sept. Held 2016's velocity gains and most of its Dom, but xERA and Cmd say it wasn't enough to hide growing wildness. With DL stints now in five straight seasons, there's less risk—and better skills—out there in the middle innings.

Yr Tm	W	L	Sv	IP	K	ERA	xERA	WHIP	oOPS	vL	vR	BF/G	Ctl	Dom	Cmd	FpK	SwK	G	L	F	H%	S%	hr/f	GS	APC	DOM%	DIS%	Sv%	LI	RAR	BPV	BPX	R$
13 NYY	6	5	0	87	79	4.98	3.97	1.42	749	756	738	17.1	3.6	8.2	2.3	59%	7%	42	22	36	33%	65%	9%	12	68	17%	25%	0	0.92	-12.0	70	91	-$4
14 NYY	5	5	1	113	92	4.38	4.21	1.42	751	699	805	15.5	3.7	7.3	2.0	62%	6%	41	24	35	31%	72%	11%	17	60	18%	35%	100	0.86	-8.9	52	62	-$4
15 MIA	4	8	0	112	77	4.50	4.48	1.36	729	758	705	21.0	2.7	6.2	2.3	65%	5%	42	23	35	31%	68%	9%	19	81	16%	47%	0	0.72	-7.4	60	71	-$4
16 MIA	7	6	4	87	114	2.28	3.17	1.14	582	725	465	5.5	3.9	11.8	3.0	56%	10%	46	21	33	30%	83%	9%	5	23	20%	0%	40	1.18	20.4	131	155	$13
17 2 TM	4	5	0	56	62	3.40	3.95	1.38	693	777	602	4.4	4.2	10.0	2.4	61%	10%	45	25	29	33%	78%	12%	0	18			0	1.11	6.6	90	108	$1
1st Half	2	4	0	39	41	3.92	3.93	1.33	719	738	693	4.5	3.7	9.5	2.6	61%	10%	46	23	31	31%	74%	16%	0	19			0	1.00	2.1	94	113	$1
2nd Half	2	1	0	17	21	2.16	3.99	1.50	632	895	451	4.2	5.4	11.3	2.1	60%	9%	44	30	26	37%	84%	0%	0	17			0	1.34	4.5	81	97	$0
18 Proj	**5**	**5**	**0**	**65**	**72**	**3.56**	**3.98**	**1.35**	**690**	**816**	**578**	**5.6**	**4.1**	**10.0**	**2.4**	**60%**	**9%**	**44**	**25**	**31**	**32%**	**76%**	**12%**	**0**						**6.4**	**91**	**109**	**$2**

Pineda,Michael

Age: 29	Th: R	Role SP		Health	F		LIMA Plan	A	
Ht: 6' 7"	Wt: 260	Type Pwr		PT/Exp	A		Rand Var	+5	
				Consist	A		MM	3300	

Fell victim to TJS in July. Before then, it was a familiar dose of elite skills that came with worsening hr/f, which torpedoed ERA. Uncanny BPV baseline should keep him on your radar, but surgery timeline offers little chance at meaningful production in 2018. Best bet: Check back in 2019 and hope the gopheritis subsides.

Yr Tm	W	L	Sv	IP	K	ERA	xERA	WHIP	oOPS	vL	vR	BF/G	Ctl	Dom	Cmd	FpK	SwK	G	L	F	H%	S%	hr/f	GS	APC	DOM%	DIS%	Sv%	LI	RAR	BPV	BPX	R$
13 a/a	2	1	0	32	28	5.23	4.30	1.32				16.7	3.7	7.8	2.1						28%	64%								-5.5	52	68	-$4
14 NYY	5	5	0	76	59	1.89	3.39	0.83	526	533	518	22.3	0.8	7.0	8.4	67%	12%	39	19	42	25%	81%	5%	13	88	38%	23%			17.5	120	143	$11
15 NYY	12	10	0	161	156	4.37	3.21	1.23	752	741	762	24.7	1.2	8.7	7.4	64%	12%	48	22	30	34%	68%	15%	27	94	30%	37%			-8.1	152	180	$6
16 NYY	6	12	0	176	207	4.82	3.45	1.35	784	801	770	23.6	2.7	10.6	3.9	67%	15%	46	22	33	35%	68%	17%	32	94	9%	25%			-13.6	142	168	$1
17 NYY	8	4	0	96	92	4.39	3.77	1.29	769	760	777	24.1	2.0	8.6	4.4	65%	13%	51	19	31	32%	74%	22%	17	91	35%	29%			-0.4	131	157	$3
1st Half	8	4	0	93	91	4.05	3.63	1.22	730	710	746	24.5	1.9	8.8	4.6	66%	13%	52	18	30	31%	74%	20%	16	93	38%	25%			3.5	136	162	$4
2nd Half	0	0	0	3	1	15.00	8.48	3.33	1614	1750	1489	18.0	3.0	3.0	1.0	44%	6%	38	25	38	45%	71%	50%	1	65	0%	100%			-3.9	-12	-14	-$23
18 Proj	**3**	**2**	**0**	**44**	**44**	**4.29**	**3.56**	**1.20**	**717**	**709**	**724**	**22.3**	**1.9**	**9.2**	**4.8**	**65%**	**13%**	**47**	**20**	**32**	**32%**	**68%**	**16%**	**8**						**0.4**	**139**	**168**	**-$1**

Pivetta,Nick

Age: 25	Th: R	Role SP		Health	A		LIMA Plan	B+	
Ht: 6' 5"	Wt: 220	Type Pwr		PT/Exp	D		Rand Var	+4	
				Consist	F		MM	1203	

8-10, 6.02 ERA in 133 IP at PHI. Rude awakening in rookie season, though trifecta of misfortune (H%, S%, hr/f) and 4.33 MLB xERA all hint it should've gone better. SwK says he's unlikely to repeat that Dom, so while breakout odds are virtually nil in the short term, 2nd half BPV suggests he can be usable in deeper leagues.

Yr Tm	W	L	Sv	IP	K	ERA	xERA	WHIP	oOPS	vL	vR	BF/G	Ctl	Dom	Cmd	FpK	SwK	G	L	F	H%	S%	hr/f	GS	APC	DOM%	DIS%	Sv%	LI	RAR	BPV	BPX	R$
13																																	
14																																	
15 aa	2	4	0	43	28	8.13	7.25	1.92				20.5	5.6	5.8	1.0						33%	60%								-22.3	-9	-10	-$14
16 a/a	12	8	0	149	121	3.90	3.94	1.33				22.9	3.1	7.4	2.4						31%	73%								5.4	72	85	$7
17 PHI *	13	10	0	165	172	5.21	4.90	1.41	846	701	983	22.5	3.2	9.4	2.9	59%	9%	44	20	36	34%	67%	18%	26	94	12%	31%			-17.3	75	90	$1
1st Half	6	4	0	77	81	3.91	4.51	1.39	890	809	955	23.2	3.1	9.5	3.1	50%	9%	39	24	36	35%	75%	17%	9	96	11%	33%			4.2	90	108	$7
2nd Half	7	6	0	88	91	6.34	4.17	1.43	823	650	999	22.5	3.4	9.3	2.8	64%	10%	46	18	36	33%	59%	19%	17	92	12%	29%			-21.5	100	120	-$4
18 Proj	**9**	**9**	**0**	**145**	**131**	**4.31**	**4.55**	**1.39**	**762**	**648**	**868**	**24.5**	**3.5**	**8.1**	**2.3**	**59%**	**9%**	**43**	**20**	**36**	**31%**	**73%**	**13%**	**25**						**0.8**	**72**	**87**	**$2**

RYAN BLOOMFIELD

Pomeranz,Drew

Age: 29	Th: L	Role: SP	Health: C	LIMA Plan: C
Ht: 6' 6"	Wt: 240	Type: Pwr	PT/Exp: A	Rand Var: -2
			Consist: A	MM: 1303

Don't be fooled by ERA, R$—BPX points to skill erosion (esp. 2H). Lifted FpK to manageable levels, but Ctl remained an issue as ball% was subpar. Lost some SwK/Dom swagger, too, as power curve didn't miss as many bats as 2016. There are Ks to be had here, but they'll come with some risk.

Yr Tm	W	L	Sv	IP	K	ERA	xERA	WHIP	oOPS	vL	vR	BF/G	Ctl	Dom	Cmd	FpK	SwK	G	L	F	H%	S%	hr/f	GS	APC	DOM%	DIS%	Sv%	LI	RAR	BPV	BPX	R
13 COL *	8	6	0	113	95	5.86	5.64	1.69	951	405	1150	21.2	4.3	7.6	1.8	54%	8%	51	17	32	35%	66%	19%	4	52	0%	100%	0	0.78	-27.7	43	57	-$1
14 OAK *	8	5	0	115	106	2.90	3.48	1.24	586	664	563	16.7	3.3	8.3	2.5	52%	9%	46	18	36	29%	81%	10%	10	57	50%	20%	0	0.75	12.0	82	97	$
15 OAK	5	6	3	86	82	3.66	3.84	1.19	651	438	749	6.7	3.2	8.6	2.6	58%	12%	43	21	36	28%	71%	9%	9	27	22%	33%	50	1.27	3.2	88	105	$
16 2 TM	11	12	0	171	186	3.32	3.71	1.18	658	643	663	22.7	3.4	9.8	2.9	56%	12%	46	17	37	28%	77%	14%	30	92	30%	27%	0	0.83	18.3	108	128	$1
17 BOS	17	6	0	174	174	3.32	4.22	1.35	711	778	692	23.1	3.6	9.0	2.5	60%	10%	43	22	35	32%	79%	11%	32	96	19%	22%			22.3	87	104	$1
1st Half	7	4	0	78	89	3.81	3.77	1.33	731	951	673	22.2	2.9	10.3	3.6	61%	11%	43	23	34	34%	76%	15%	15	94	33%	27%			5.3	128	153	$1
2nd Half	10	2	0	96	85	2.92	4.62	1.37	694	644	709	23.9	4.1	8.0	1.9	60%	9%	43	21	35	30%	81%	8%	17	98	6%	18%			17.0	54	64	$2
18 Proj	**13**	**8**	**0**	**160**	**159**	**3.68**	**4.25**	**1.35**	**719**	**706**	**723**	**23.5**	**3.5**	**9.0**	**2.5**	**59%**	**11%**	**44**	**20**	**36**	**32%**	**76%**	**11%**	**28**						**13.4**	**88**	**106**	**$1**

Porcello,Rick

Age: 29	Th: R	Role: SP	Health: A	LIMA Plan: A
Ht: 6' 5"	Wt: 205	Type:	PT/Exp: A	Rand Var: +3
			Consist: A	MM: 1205

What a difference a year can make. PRO: Sharp H% spike likely due for some correction; elite FpK bolstered an already strong Ctl; career-best Dom/SwK. CON: Once a GB% artist, he's now a fly-ball machine, which won't help his 1.7 HR/9 from 2017. A solid No. 4-5 SP; just don't expect a return to 2016.

Yr Tm	W	L	Sv	IP	K	ERA	xERA	WHIP	oOPS	vL	vR	BF/G	Ctl	Dom	Cmd	FpK	SwK	G	L	F	H%	S%	hr/f	GS	APC	DOM%	DIS%	Sv%	LI	RAR	BPV	BPX	R
13 DET	13	8	0	177	142	4.32	3.32	1.28	709	808	602	23.0	2.1	7.2	3.4	60%	9%	55	21	24	32%	68%	14%	29	89	31%	31%	0	0.84	-10.0	105	137	$
14 DET	15	13	0	205	129	3.43	3.74	1.23	712	732	686	26.3	1.8	5.7	3.1	64%	8%	49	22	29	30%	74%	9%	31	95	32%	32%	0	0.83	7.9	80	96	$1
15 BOS	9	15	0	172	149	4.92	3.77	1.36	787	815	751	26.3	2.0	7.8	3.9	60%	9%	46	22	33	34%	67%	14%	28	98	43%	32%			-20.3	111	132	-$
16 BOS	22	4	0	223	189	3.15	3.72	1.01	635	600	672	27.0	1.3	7.6	5.9	64%	9%	43	19	38	28%	73%	9%	33	103	55%	9%			28.6	123	147	$3
17 BOS	11	17	0	203	181	4.65	4.49	1.40	826	856	798	26.8	2.1	8.0	3.8	67%	10%	39	21	40	34%	73%	15%	33	103	30%	24%			-7.3	104	125	$
1st Half	4	10	0	105	99	5.06	4.48	1.51	859	830	888	27.5	1.8	8.5	4.7	68%	10%	37	22	41	38%	70%	12%	17	106	24%	18%			-9.1	120	143	-$
2nd Half	7	7	0	98	82	4.21	4.50	1.27	788	889	703	26.1	2.5	7.5	3.0	66%	9%	41	20	39	28%	76%	18%	16	99	38%	31%			1.8	88	105	$1
18 Proj	**14**	**13**	**0**	**203**	**173**	**3.97**	**4.20**	**1.27**	**759**	**780**	**737**	**25.6**	**1.9**	**7.7**	**4.0**	**65%**	**9%**	**43**	**21**	**37**	**31%**	**74%**	**14%**	**32**						**9.8**	**107**	**129**	**$1**

Pressly,Ryan

Age: 29	Th: R	Role: RP	Health: D	LIMA Plan: C
Ht: 6' 3"	Wt: 210	Type: Pwr	PT/Exp: D	Rand Var: +5
			Consist: A	MM: 2310

Massive S%, hr/f fluctuation threw things out of whack, but this was best season of career skill-wise, as Dom and SwK continued their annual ascent and he added more GBs. Throws hard (95.8 vel), but rickety FpK and Ctl aren't closer caliber yet. Combine that with health risk and xERA history, best to stay away.

Yr Tm	W	L	Sv	IP	K	ERA	xERA	WHIP	oOPS	vL	vR	BF/G	Ctl	Dom	Cmd	FpK	SwK	G	L	F	H%	S%	hr/f	GS	APC	DOM%	DIS%	Sv%	LI	RAR	BPV	BPX	R
13 MIN	3	3	0	77	49	3.87	4.29	1.28	677	746	614	6.4	3.2	5.8	1.8	46%	8%	44	21	35	28%	70%	6%	0	24			0	0.70	-0.1	40	52	-$
14 MIN *	3	4	6	89	63	3.65	4.26	1.47	779	887	715	6.3	3.1	6.3	2.0	59%	9%	47	27	26	34%	75%	12%	0	15			75	0.81	1.0	66	79	-$
15 MIN	3	2	0	28	22	2.93	4.39	1.41	645	678	626	4.4	3.9	7.2	1.8	59%	9%	47	20	33	33%	77%	0%	0	16			0	0.93	3.5	48	58	-$
16 MIN	6	7	1	75	67	3.70	4.36	1.35	725	659	767	4.6	2.7	8.0	2.9	57%	12%	39	24	36	33%	76%	10%	0	17			17	1.19	4.5	87	103	$
17 MIN	2	3	0	61	61	4.70	3.71	1.16	697	816	618	4.4	2.8	9.0	3.2	58%	13%	51	17	33	27%	64%	19%	0	16			0	0.94	-2.6	115	138	-$
1st Half	1	2	0	24	27	8.25	3.89	1.46	889	1167	712	4.2	3.0	10.1	3.4	57%	14%	46	19	35	34%	45%	25%	0	15			0	0.96	-11.5	125	150	-$1
2nd Half	1	1	0	37	34	2.41	3.59	0.96	558	573	548	4.6	2.7	8.2	3.1	59%	12%	54	15	31	23%	81%	13%	0	16			0	0.92	9.0	108	129	$
18 Proj	**3**	**3**	**7**	**58**	**55**	**4.08**	**4.07**	**1.27**	**709**	**756**	**674**	**4.7**	**2.9**	**8.5**	**3.0**	**56%**	**12%**	**46**	**20**	**34**	**31%**	**71%**	**13%**	**0**						**2.0**	**99**	**119**	**$**

Price,David

Age: 32	Th: L	Role: SP	Health: F	LIMA Plan: B+
Ht: 6' 5"	Wt: 215	Type: Pwr	PT/Exp: A	Rand Var: -1
			Consist: A	MM: 2303

Between two DL trips and a late-year move to the 'pen, it was an odd 2017. PRO: SwK, Dom, FpK, velocity all vintage. CON: Ball% bottomed out, which explains Ctl spike; health risk. BPX says the ingredients are still here for a No. 2-3 SP, but with elbow woes, command issues...be cautious.

Yr Tm	W	L	Sv	IP	K	ERA	xERA	WHIP	oOPS	vL	vR	BF/G	Ctl	Dom	Cmd	FpK	SwK	G	L	F	H%	S%	hr/f	GS	APC	DOM%	DIS%	Sv%	LI	RAR	BPV	BPX	R
13 TAM	10	8	0	187	151	3.33	3.34	1.10	661	489	712	27.4	1.3	7.3	5.6	68%	8%	45	22	33	30%	72%	9%	27	100	56%	11%			12.4	119	155	$1
14 2 AL	15	12	0	248	271	3.26	3.00	1.08	647	657	644	29.7	1.4	9.8	7.1	70%	11%	41	21	38	32%	73%	10%	34	110	59%	3%			14.7	159	189	$2
15 2 AL	18	5	0	220	225	2.45	3.36	1.08	621	658	609	27.8	1.9	9.2	4.8	67%	12%	40	23	36	30%	80%	8%	32	106	63%	9%			41.1	132	157	$3
16 BOS	17	9	0	230	228	3.99	3.60	1.20	721	749	712	27.2	2.0	8.9	4.6	65%	12%	44	22	34	32%	71%	14%	35	103	40%	23%			5.6	130	154	$1
17 BOS	6	3	0	75	76	3.38	4.14	1.19	652	494	697	19.8	2.9	9.2	3.2	67%	13%	40	22	39	30%	75%	10%	11	78	27%	36%	0	0.85	9.1	105	126	$
1st Half	3	2	0	41	36	4.61	4.72	1.27	735	609	763	25.3	3.3	7.9	2.4	64%	13%	40	19	41	27%	69%	14%	7	102	29%	43%			-1.3	71	85	$
2nd Half	3	1	0	34	40	1.87	3.47	1.10	551	393	607	15.6	2.4	10.7	4.4	71%	13%	40	26	34	33%	83%	3%	4	60	25%	25%	0	0.88	10.3	146	174	$1
18 Proj	**13**	**7**	**0**	**174**	**179**	**3.44**	**3.85**	**1.20**	**665**	**590**	**688**	**23.5**	**2.5**	**9.3**	**3.6**	**67%**	**12%**	**41**	**23**	**36**	**31%**	**74%**	**10%**	**30**						**19.8**	**117**	**141**	**$1**

Pruitt,Austin

Age: 28	Th: R	Role: RP	Health: A	LIMA Plan: C
Ht: 5' 10"	Wt: 180	Type:	PT/Exp: D	Rand Var: +3
			Consist: D	MM: 1101

7-5, 5.31 ERA in 83 IP at TAM. Spent MLB debut mostly from the 'pen, during which he flaunted a quality FpK/Ctl tandem with solid GB% baseline. Lacks premium velocity nor one signature putaway pitch for high-leverage role, so expect Dom, SwK to hover around average as he looks to find a permanent home.

Yr Tm	W	L	Sv	IP	K	ERA	xERA	WHIP	oOPS	vL	vR	BF/G	Ctl	Dom	Cmd	FpK	SwK	G	L	F	H%	S%	hr/f	GS	APC	DOM%	DIS%	Sv%	LI	RAR	BPV	BPX	R
13																																	
14																																	
15 aa	10	7	0	160	100	3.76	4.16	1.44				26.2	2.2	5.6	2.5						35%	72%								4.1	77	91	$
16 aaa	8	11	0	163	120	5.47	6.04	1.54				25.3	1.8	6.7	3.8						36%	68%								-25.6	65	78	-$1
17 TAM *	7	6	2	108	92	4.96	4.90	1.40	827	704	925	11.6	2.0	7.7	3.8	66%	10%	48	21	32	35%	67%	13%	8	44	25%	13%	67	0.61	-8.0	88	105	$
1st Half	5	1	2	43	40	5.19	4.70	1.48	843	740	906	7.8	1.9	8.2	4.3	64%	10%	46	30	25	39%	63%	7%	1	30	0%	0%	67	0.52	-4.4	120	144	-$
2nd Half	2	5	0	64	52	4.82	5.03	1.34	815	685	940	17.8	2.1	7.3	3.4	67%	10%	49	14	37	31%	69%	15%	7	67	29%	14%	0	0.75	-3.6	67	80	$
18 Proj	**6**	**6**	**0**	**102**	**79**	**4.95**	**4.38**	**1.45**	**811**	**691**	**906**	**16.1**	**2.0**	**7.0**	**3.6**	**66%**	**10%**	**48**	**20**	**32**	**35%**	**68%**	**12%**	**16**						**-7.4**	**99**	**119**	**-$**

Quintana,Jose

Age: 29	Th: L	Role: SP	Health: A	LIMA Plan: B
Ht: 6' 1"	Wt: 220	Type: Pwr	PT/Exp: A	Rand Var: +1
			Consist: A	MM: 2305

ERA jumped nearly a full run (blame S%, hr/f for some of it), but BPX also got a boost as Dom soared to elite levels in 2nd half and he re-padded his FpK and GB%. Lack of SwK increase says to temper expectations for Ks moving forward, but by now, we know what to expect: 200 IP, mid-3s ERA. Not bad, but not elite.

Yr Tm	W	L	Sv	IP	K	ERA	xERA	WHIP	oOPS	vL	vR	BF/G	Ctl	Dom	Cmd	FpK	SwK	G	L	F	H%	S%	hr/f	GS	APC	DOM%	DIS%	Sv%	LI	RAR	BPV	BPX	R
13 CHW	9	7	0	200	164	3.51	3.85	1.22	695	717	687	25.2	2.5	7.4	2.9	66%	9%	43	20	37	29%	75%	10%	33	101	36%	21%			8.8	86	112	$1
14 CHW	9	11	0	200	178	3.32	3.51	1.24	662	686	653	25.9	2.3	8.0	3.4	66%	9%	45	22	33	33%	73%	5%	32	105	25%	19%			10.3	104	124	$
15 CHW	9	10	0	206	177	3.36	3.60	1.27	722	663	740	26.9	1.9	7.7	4.0	69%	9%	47	23	30	33%	75%	9%	32	105	38%	16%			15.4	112	134	$1
16 CHW	13	12	0	208	181	3.20	3.98	1.16	687	650	698	26.2	2.2	7.8	3.6	65%	8%	40	21	39	30%	76%	10%	32	103	47%	19%			25.3	101	119	$2
17 2 TM	11	11	0	189	207	4.15	3.71	1.22	701	584	732	24.7	2.9	9.9	3.4	67%	9%	45	21	34	31%	69%	13%	32	99	31%	22%			4.8	122	147	$1
1st Half	4	8	0	95	94	4.37	4.23	1.30	729	635	757	24.9	3.4	8.9	2.6	69%	9%	42	20	37	30%	69%	12%	16	99	38%	25%			-0.2	89	106	$
2nd Half	7	3	0	94	113	3.93	3.22	1.15	673	528	709	24.5	2.4	10.8	4.5	65%	9%	47	21	31	32%	69%	14%	16	100	25%	19%			5.0	155	186	$1
18 Proj	**13**	**10**	**0**	**203**	**201**	**3.70**	**3.85**	**1.21**	**696**	**622**	**717**	**24.7**	**2.5**	**8.9**	**3.6**	**67%**	**9%**	**44**	**21**	**35**	**31%**	**72%**	**11%**	**33**						**16.5**	**116**	**140**	**$1**

Ramirez,Erasmo

Age: 28	Th: R	Role: RP	Health: A	LIMA Plan: B
Ht: 5' 10"	Wt: 215	Type:	PT/Exp: B	Rand Var: +1
			Consist: A	MM: 1101

Re-established starter role with SEA in Aug/Sept; sported a 3.92 ERA and 7.8 Dom in that span. FpK, SwK, GB% all point to mostly average peripheral skills here, and it doesn't help that LHB are still mashing against him. That, along with consistently high xERA, means the upside here isn't much.

Yr Tm	W	L	Sv	IP	K	ERA	xERA	WHIP	oOPS	vL	vR	BF/G	Ctl	Dom	Cmd	FpK	SwK	G	L	F	H%	S%	hr/f	GS	APC	DOM%	DIS%	Sv%	LI	RAR	BPV	BPX	R
13 SEA *	8	6	0	121	96	4.36	4.71	1.42	772	791	742	23.3	3.1	7.2	2.3	59%	9%	42	21	36	32%	73%	14%	13	91	0%	38%	0	0.74	-7.3	56	73	-$
14 SEA *	7	11	0	162	117	4.34	4.66	1.38	815	790	848	21.2	2.5	6.5	2.6	61%	11%	38	19	43	32%	72%	13%	14	76	14%	50%	0	0.63	-12.0	59	70	-$
15 TAM	11	6	0	163	126	3.75	3.76	1.13	655	567	753	19.6	2.2	6.9	3.2	65%	11%	48	21	32	28%	69%	10%	27	71	19%	33%	0	0.70	4.3	91	109	$1
16 TAM	7	11	2	91	63	3.77	4.26	1.28	766	905	685	5.9	2.6	6.3	2.4	63%	9%	53	15	32	28%	76%	16%	1	21	0%	0%	33	1.43	4.7	74	88	$
17 2 AL	5	6	1	131	109	4.39	4.25	1.17	733	829	670	14.6	2.1	7.5	3.5	62%	11%	43	19	38	28%	68%	15%	19	54	11%	26%	50	1.00	-0.4	98	118	$
1st Half	4	2	1	63	50	4.69	4.08	1.22	738	771	716	11.8	2.0	7.1	3.6	65%	11%	49	17	33	30%	65%	14%	8	43	0%	38%	100	1.11	-2.6	102	122	$
2nd Half	1	4	0	68	59	4.10	4.40	1.13	729	883	627	18.7	2.3	7.8	3.5	59%	11%	37	20	43	26%	72%	15%	11	71	18%	18%	0	0.83	2.1	95	114	$
18 Proj	**6**	**8**	**0**	**116**	**91**	**4.11**	**4.33**	**1.21**	**731**	**791**	**686**	**12.6**	**2.3**	**7.1**	**3.0**	**62%**	**10%**	**45**	**18**	**36**	**28%**	**71%**	**14%**	**10**						**3.5**	**87**	**105**	**$**

ALEC DOPP

Ramirez,J.C.

Age: 29	Th: R	Role RP		Health C		LIMA Plan C+	
Ht: 6' 4"	Wt: 250	Type GB		PT/Exp C		Rand Var +1	
				Consist A		MM 0001	

First year in rotation led to positive R$ with good GB tilt. Mediocre skill set hit a wall in the 2nd half, despite acceptable surface stats, capped by a season-ending elbow injury (which might have been an issue for longer than reported). Lots of risk, little skills upside.

Yr Tm	W	L	Sv	IP	K	ERA	xERA	WHIP	oOPS	vL	vR	BF/G	Ctl	Dom	Cmd	FpK	SwK	G	L	F	H%	S%	hr/f	GS	APC	DOM%	DIS%	Sv%	LI	RAR	BPV	BPX	R$
13 PHI *	5	3	3	73	52	5.66	5.24	1.67	975	1019	944	6.3	5.0	6.5	1.3	53%	10%	39	22	40	32%	67%	18%	0	23			75	0.57	-16.1	34	44	-$9
14 a/a	2	3	3	44	24	3.67	4.84	1.45				5.4	3.9	4.8	1.2						28%	80%								0.4	16	19	-$2
15 2 TM *	2	4	1	67	45	3.61	4.02	1.41	764	571	901	4.9	3.6	6.1	1.7	59%	10%	44	17	39	30%	75%	10%	0	21			17	1.22	2.9	55	66	-$2
16 2 TM	3	4	2	79	59	4.35	4.07	1.26	713	659	763	4.8	2.5	6.8	2.7	61%	10%	55	17	28	29%	70%	17%	0	18			33	0.97	-1.5	87	103	$0
17 LAA	11	10	0	147	105	4.15	4.49	1.34	761	891	640	23.0	3.0	6.4	2.1	60%	9%	51	18	30	29%	73%	15%	24	85	8%	33%	0	0.77	3.7	64	76	$5
1st Half	7	6	0	92	75	4.60	4.16	1.29	788	958	641	21.4	2.3	7.3	3.3	61%	10%	47	21	32	30%	71%	19%	15	80	13%	33%	0	0.75	-2.7	96	115	$7
2nd Half	4	4	0	55	30	3.42	5.09	1.43	712	784	637	26.1	4.2	4.9	1.2	58%	7%	59	14	28	28%	77%	8%	9	96	0%	33%			6.4	10	12	$1
18 Proj	**6**	**6**	**0**	**102**	**69**	**4.31**	**4.72**	**1.43**	**779**	**825**	**735**	**8.3**	**3.3**	**6.1**	**1.8**	**60%**	**9%**	**54**	**17**	**29**	**30%**	**74%**	**15%**	**0**						**0.6**	**52**	**62**	**-$2**

Ramirez,Jose

Age: 28	Th: R	Role RP		Health A		LIMA Plan B	
Ht: 6' 1"	Wt: 215	Type Pwr FB		PT/Exp D		Rand Var -5	
				Consist B		MM 0201	

One step forward (GB spike), and one step back (more HR). A favorable LD and H% led to shiny ERA, but continued Ctl issues and lack of FpK point to more baserunners and higher xERA. S% only thing keeping him relevant; it's not something you can count on continuing.

Yr Tm	W	L	Sv	IP	K	ERA	xERA	WHIP	oOPS	vL	vR	BF/G	Ctl	Dom	Cmd	FpK	SwK	G	L	F	H%	S%	hr/f	GS	APC	DOM%	DIS%	Sv%	LI	RAR	BPV	BPX	R$
13 a/a	2	6	1	74	66	4.82	4.80	1.46				18.5	4.7	8.1	1.7						28%	72%								-8.7	40	53	-$5
14 NYY	0	2	0	10	10	5.40	5.53	1.80	908	375	1267	6.1	6.3	9.0	1.4	49%	11%	20	23	57	33%	75%	12%	0	26			0	0.50	-2.0	-10	-12	-$5
15 2 AL *	5	1	10	70	61	4.89	4.46	1.56	1154	1209	1108	6.3	4.7	7.8	1.7	62%	8%	41	15	44	33%	68%	0%	0	27			91	0.21	-8.1	64	76	-$2
16 ATL *	5	4	6	74	71	3.23	3.92	1.46	700	733	677	4.6	4.7	8.6	1.8	57%	12%	33	24	43	31%	79%	5%	0	17			60	0.99	8.7	75	89	$4
17 ATL	2	3	0	62	56	3.19	4.59	1.19	678	647	699	3.8	4.2	8.1	1.9	58%	12%	46	12	42	23%	80%	13%	0	15			0	1.08	8.9	57	68	$2
1st Half	2	2	0	33	27	3.00	4.46	1.09	614	511	688	3.6	4.1	7.4	1.8	59%	13%	48	12	40	21%	76%	9%	0	14			0	1.14	5.5	48	57	$4
2nd Half	0	1	0	29	29	3.41	4.73	1.31	745	799	710	4.0	4.3	9.0	2.1	57%	11%	44	11	44	25%	84%	17%	0	16			0	1.02	3.4	67	80	$0
18 Proj	**3**	**3**	**0**	**73**	**67**	**4.27**	**4.97**	**1.42**	**805**	**812**	**800**	**4.7**	**4.5**	**8.3**	**1.9**	**58%**	**12%**	**41**	**17**	**43**	**29%**	**75%**	**13%**	**0**						**0.8**	**48**	**57**	**-$2**

Ramos,A.J.

Age: 31	Th: R	Role RP		Health B		LIMA Plan C+	
Ht: 5' 10"	Wt: 200	Type Pwr		PT/Exp A		Rand Var 0	
				Consist B		MM 1520	

Post-closer blues. While Dom was still good after 2nd half trade to NYM, Ctl continued to be the bugaboo. More first-pitch strikes would go a long way in maintaining a high-leverage role, which will largely determine his value moving forward. Still a save speculation play, but walks and trend vR are worrisome.

Yr Tm	W	L	Sv	IP	K	ERA	xERA	WHIP	oOPS	vL	vR	BF/G	Ctl	Dom	Cmd	FpK	SwK	G	L	F	H%	S%	hr/f	GS	APC	DOM%	DIS%	Sv%	LI	RAR	BPV	BPX	R$
13 MIA	3	4	0	80	86	3.15	3.97	1.26	603	740	484	5.0	4.8	9.7	2.0	61%	12%	39	19	43	28%	75%	5%	0	20			0	0.98	7.1	61	79	$3
14 MIA	7	0	0	64	73	2.11	3.89	1.23	543	522	555	4.0	6.0	10.3	1.7	57%	14%	42	19	39	25%	82%	2%	0	16			0	1.36	12.9	42	49	$6
15 MIA	2	4	32	70	87	2.30	3.10	1.01	562	602	529	3.9	3.3	11.1	3.3	59%	17%	43	16	40	26%	82%	9%	0	15			84	1.27	14.4	132	157	$21
16 MIA	1	4	40	64	73	2.81	4.24	1.36	600	578	627	4.1	4.9	10.3	2.1	60%	12%	36	26	38	32%	78%	2%	0	17			93	1.15	10.9	66	78	$18
17 2 NL	2	4	27	59	72	3.99	4.33	1.41	694	656	738	4.2	5.2	11.0	2.1	52%	12%	40	20	39	31%	75%	12%	0	18			90	1.07	2.7	76	91	$10
1st Half	2	3	13	28	37	3.49	4.04	1.27	647	738	561	4.2	4.8	11.8	2.5	49%	13%	35	18	46	30%	76%	10%	0	17			93	1.03	3.0	96	115	$14
2nd Half	0	1	14	30	35	4.45	4.62	1.55	736	595	927	4.3	5.6	10.4	1.8	54%	11%	44	22	34	32%	74%	14%	0	19			88	1.11	-0.3	57	68	$7
18 Proj	**2**	**3**	**12**	**58**	**69**	**3.66**	**4.21**	**1.34**	**645**	**622**	**669**	**4.0**	**4.9**	**10.7**	**2.2**	**56%**	**13%**	**40**	**21**	**39**	**30%**	**74%**	**9%**	**0**						**5.0**	**78**	**94**	**$5**

Ramos,Edubray

Age: 25	Th: R	Role RP		Health A		LIMA Plan C+	
Ht: 6' 0"	Wt: 160	Type Pwr		PT/Exp D		Rand Var +2	
				Consist C		MM 2500	

Hard-throwing RHP put himself on the radar with electric FB/SL combo after finding semblance of Ctl in 2nd half (27 IP). Too early to know whether it's for real, but even incremental gains in FpK and SwK will determine if he can carve out higher-leverage role. Either way, his Dom will make him an intriguing end-gamer.

Yr Tm	W	L	Sv	IP	K	ERA	xERA	WHIP	oOPS	vL	vR	BF/G	Ctl	Dom	Cmd	FpK	SwK	G	L	F	H%	S%	hr/f	GS	APC	DOM%	DIS%	Sv%	LI	RAR	BPV	BPX	R$
13																																	
14																																	
15 aa	1	2	0	20	16	4.04	3.25	1.42				4.8	4.4	7.0	1.6						31%	68%								-0.2	81	96	-$4
16 PHI *	3	4	10	79	75	2.64	2.52	1.01	687	794	572	4.4	1.7	8.6	5.0	59%	11%	37	25	38	28%	77%	12%	0	15			71	1.09	15.0	145	173	$12
17 PHI	2	7	0	58	75	4.21	3.98	1.47	699	856	580	4.3	4.4	11.7	2.7	61%	12%	37	27	36	38%	72%	7%	0	17			0	0.93	1.0	108	129	-$2
1st Half	0	7	0	31	38	5.52	5.01	1.81	784	840	730	4.2	6.4	11.0	1.7	60%	11%	40	24	36	39%	70%	10%	0	17			0	0.93	-4.4	44	52	-$9
2nd Half	2	0	0	27	37	2.70	2.97	1.09	588	879	429	4.5	2.0	12.5	6.2	61%	13%	34	30	36	37%	75%	4%	0	17			0	0.93	5.5	182	219	$5
18 Proj	**3**	**5**	**0**	**65**	**77**	**3.65**	**3.93**	**1.31**	**655**	**788**	**543**	**4.4**	**3.7**	**10.6**	**2.9**	**60%**	**12%**	**37**	**26**	**37**	**34%**	**73%**	**7%**	**0**						**5.7**	**105**	**127**	**$1**

Ray,Robbie

Age: 26	Th: L	Role SP		Health B		LIMA Plan C	
Ht: 6' 2"	Wt: 195	Type Pwr		PT/Exp B		Rand Var -1	
				Consist A		MM 2503	

Ace up your sleeve? Three-year gains in Dom and SwK punctuated breakout campaign but needs to improve Ctl and FpK to reach elite status. Increasing FB rate and normal regression in H% and S% could hinder a repeat performance. Be careful going all-in with this card, as the price may not justify the production.

Yr Tm	W	L	Sv	IP	K	ERA	xERA	WHIP	oOPS	vL	vR	BF/G	Ctl	Dom	Cmd	FpK	SwK	G	L	F	H%	S%	hr/f	GS	APC	DOM%	DIS%	Sv%	LI	RAR	BPV	BPX	R$
13 aa	5	2	0	58	50	4.42	4.27	1.44				22.4	3.1	7.8	2.5						34%	69%								-4.0	79	103	-$3
14 DET *	8	10	0	129	79	5.85	5.78	1.73	993	889	1038	20.2	4.0	5.5	1.4	54%	6%	35	24	41	35%	66%	12%	6	61	17%	50%	0	0.65	-33.5	30	36	-$17
15 ARI *	7	15	0	169	166	3.55	3.86	1.42	731	723	733	22.5	3.9	8.8	2.3	61%	9%	44	22	35	34%	75%	7%	23	98	22%	26%			8.6	88	104	$3
16 ARI	8	15	0	174	218	4.90	3.62	1.47	770	684	797	24.3	3.7	11.3	3.1	56%	12%	46	22	33	37%	69%	15%	32	99	22%	19%			-15.4	128	152	-$2
17 ARI	15	5	0	162	218	2.89	3.47	1.15	646	622	651	23.8	3.9	12.1	3.1	60%	15%	40	19	40	28%	82%	16%	28	97	43%	25%			29.4	130	156	$24
1st Half	8	4	0	100	128	3.06	3.77	1.20	645	634	647	25.8	4.3	11.5	2.7	60%	14%	39	19	42	28%	80%	14%	16	105	50%	19%			16.0	107	129	$27
2nd Half	7	1	0	62	90	2.61	2.99	1.08	647	606	658	21.0	3.3	13.1	3.9	60%	16%	43	20	37	29%	86%	20%	12	87	33%	33%			13.3	166	199	$20
18 Proj	**13**	**8**	**0**	**174**	**213**	**3.67**	**3.73**	**1.30**	**709**	**667**	**721**	**23.8**	**3.7**	**11.0**	**3.0**	**58%**	**13%**	**43**	**21**	**36**	**32%**	**76%**	**14%**	**30**						**14.7**	**119**	**143**	**$13**

Reed,Addison

Age: 29	Th: R	Role RP		Health A		LIMA Plan B	
Ht: 6' 4"	Wt: 230	Type Pwr		PT/Exp C		Rand Var -2	
				Consist B		MM 3311	

Consistent performer with good Cmd, Dom, FpK, SwK, and health. Proven track record as double-digit earner in 4 of past 5 seasons. Big question is where he lands, as he's got the skills and track record to be an effective closer. If role uncertainty makes him slip on draft day, he's a high-floor gamble worth taking.

Yr Tm	W	L	Sv	IP	K	ERA	xERA	WHIP	oOPS	vL	vR	BF/G	Ctl	Dom	Cmd	FpK	SwK	G	L	F	H%	S%	hr/f	GS	APC	DOM%	DIS%	Sv%	LI	RAR	BPV	BPX	R$
13 CHW	5	4	40	71	72	3.79	3.75	1.11	603	608	597	4.3	2.9	9.1	3.1	65%	12%	33	22	45	28%	67%	7%	0	17			83	1.19	0.7	96	125	$19
14 ARI	1	7	32	59	69	4.25	3.51	1.21	740	610	863	4.1	2.3	10.5	4.6	66%	14%	29	23	48	32%	72%	14%	0	16			84	1.25	-3.7	134	160	$11
15 2 NL	3	3	4	56	51	3.38	4.15	1.38	714	699	726	4.4	3.1	8.2	2.7	57%	9%	43	18	39	34%	76%	5%	0	17			50	1.18	4.1	86	103	$1
16 NYM	4	2	1	78	91	1.97	3.08	0.94	536	532	538	3.8	1.5	10.5	7.0	70%	12%	39	23	38	30%	81%	5%	0	15			20	1.23	21.3	166	197	$12
17 2 TM	2	3	19	76	76	2.84	3.81	1.05	656	662	651	4.0	1.8	9.0	5.1	67%	14%	41	18	41	28%	81%	13%	0	15			90	1.30	14.2	133	160	$15
1st Half	0	2	14	42	42	2.59	3.86	1.10	676	655	691	4.3	1.1	9.1	8.4	69%	14%	38	17	45	32%	83%	9%	0	16			88	1.39	9.1	150	180	$18
2nd Half	2	1	5	34	34	3.15	3.74	0.99	630	672	603	3.7	2.6	8.9	3.4	65%	14%	44	19	37	22%	79%	18%	0	15			100	1.19	5.1	112	134	$11
18 Proj	**3**	**3**	**10**	**73**	**75**	**2.86**	**3.71**	**1.08**	**635**	**632**	**636**	**3.8**	**2.1**	**9.3**	**4.5**	**66%**	**13%**	**40**	**20**	**40**	**29%**	**79%**	**11%**	**0**						**13.4**	**130**	**156**	**$10**

Reyes,Alex

Age: 23	Th: R	Role SP		Health F		LIMA Plan B	
Ht: 6' 3"	Wt: 175	Type Pwr FB		PT/Exp F		Rand Var 0	
				Consist D		MM 1403	

Return imminent but question marks remain. Should return from TJS early in 2018, but Ctl and FpK are still concerns, and IP limits will be in play. Though pedigree is there, needs reps and health to to take next step forward. High risk and still a keeper gem but not necessarily high reward on THIS draft day.

Yr Tm	W	L	Sv	IP	K	ERA	xERA	WHIP	oOPS	vL	vR	BF/G	Ctl	Dom	Cmd	FpK	SwK	G	L	F	H%	S%	hr/f	GS	APC	DOM%	DIS%	Sv%	LI	RAR	BPV	BPX	R$
13																																	
14																																	
15 aa	3	2	0	35	48	3.24	1.87	1.13				17.1	4.4	12.4	2.8						30%	70%								3.1	144	172	$1
16 STL *	6	4	1	111	129	3.84	3.57	1.39	578	672	509	18.0	4.3	10.4	2.4	56%	12%	43	15	41	34%	72%	2%	5	66	20%	0%	100	0.95	4.8	103	123	$4
17																																	
1st Half																																	
2nd Half																																	
18 Proj	**9**	**6**	**0**	**131**	**143**	**3.87**	**4.36**	**1.29**	**623**	**671**	**588**	**21.1**	**4.3**	**9.9**	**2.3**	**56%**	**12%**	**41**	**20**	**40**	**29%**	**71%**	**8%**	**25**						**7.8**	**79**	**95**	**$7**

JOSEPH PYTLESKI

Richard,Clayton

Age: 34	Th: L	Role RP	Health	D	LIMA Plan	C
Ht: 6' 5"	Wt: 240	Type xGB	PT/Exp	B	Rand Var	+5
			Consist	B	MM	1005

PRO: Rock-solid GB%; Dom upgrade; FpK history suggests Ctl rebound could stick. CON: Tattooed all year vR (3.2 hr/9); Dom trend looks maxed out. With health, he'll eat innings again. But positive R$ will depend on RHB containment, improved defensive support and similar Cmd. It seems like a lot to ask of a 34 year-old.

Yr Tm	W	L	Sv	IP	K	ERA	xERA	WHIP	oOPS	vL	vR	BF/G	Ctl	Dom	Cmd	FpK	SwK	G	L	F	H%	S%	hr/f	GS	APC	DOM%	DIS%	Sv%	LI	RAR	BPV	BPX	R$
13 SD	2	5	0	53	24	7.01	4.94	1.63	947	639	1050	19.9	3.6	4.1	1.1	54%	6%	52	21	27	29%	62%	25%	11	71	0%	82%	0	0.89	-20.4	7	9	-$12
14 a/a	1	2	0	21	6	7.45	9.82	2.27				27.1	2.3	2.5	1.1						42%	69%								-9.8	-37	-44	-$9
15 CHC *	9	4	0	105	44	2.99	4.13	1.34	714	534	820	13.3	1.9	3.7	2.0	61%	7%	59	26	15	31%	79%	14%	3	27	0%	33%	0	0.90	12.7	45	53	$4
16 2 NL	3	4	1	68	41	3.33	4.60	1.66	761	654	799	8.5	4.1	5.5	1.3	63%	9%	65	17	18	34%	81%	10%	9	30	11%	33%	100	0.64	7.2	30	35	-$3
17 SD	8	15	0	197	151	4.79	3.99	1.52	842	676	899	26.8	2.7	6.9	2.6	62%	9%	59	21	20	35%	71%	19%	32	95	25%	38%			-10.5	88	106	-$4
1st Half	5	8	0	104	73	4.85	4.13	1.51	845	683	897	26.3	2.7	6.3	2.4	63%	9%	58	22	20	34%	70%	19%	17	94	24%	29%			-6.3	77	92	-$4
2nd Half	3	7	0	93	78	4.73	3.83	1.52	839	668	901	27.4	2.7	7.5	2.8	62%	10%	61	20	19	36%	71%	19%	15	96	27%	47%			-4.2	101	121	-$5
18 Proj	**9**	**13**	**0**	**189**	**123**	**4.61**	**4.39**	**1.54**	**815**	**640**	**881**	**15.4**	**3.0**	**5.9**	**1.9**	**61%**	**9%**	**60**	**21**	**19**	**33%**	**72%**	**17%**	**29**						**-5.8**	**62**	**75**	**-$6**

Richards,Garrett

Age: 30	Th: R	Role SP	Health	F	LIMA Plan	B+
Ht: 6' 3"	Wt: 210	Type Pwr GB	PT/Exp	C	Rand Var	-4
			Consist	A	MM	2203

Stem cell treatment for torn UCL did the trick. But injury magnet only lasted 5 IP in Apr before being shelved by an irritated biceps nerve. Sept return yielded 5 promising starts, as top-shelf skills and velocity looked vintage in small sample. High-risk, high-reward flyer. With health... UP: 14 W, 165 K.

Yr Tm	W	L	Sv	IP	K	ERA	xERA	WHIP	oOPS	vL	vR	BF/G	Ctl	Dom	Cmd	FpK	SwK	G	L	F	H%	S%	hr/f	GS	APC	DOM%	DIS%	Sv%	LI	RAR	BPV	BPX	R$
13 LAA	7	8	1	145	101	4.16	3.70	1.34	699	751	626	13.2	2.7	6.3	2.3	54%	9%	58	19	23	31%	70%	11%	17	50	18%	24%	50	0.78	-5.2	75	98	$0
14 LAA	13	4	0	169	164	2.61	3.08	1.04	529	519	542	26.1	2.7	8.8	3.2	55%	11%	51	21	28	28%	74%	4%	26	101	58%	8%			23.4	113	135	$21
15 LAA	15	12	0	207	176	3.65	3.75	1.24	664	628	707	27.0	3.3	7.6	2.3	60%	12%	55	17	28	28%	73%	12%	32	102	34%	31%			8.1	81	97	$13
16 LAA	1	3	0	35	34	2.34	4.03	1.33	683	483	858	24.7	3.9	8.8	2.3	57%	11%	46	25	29	31%	84%	7%	6	103	33%	0%			7.9	78	92	$0
17 LAA	0	2	0	28	27	2.28	3.35	0.90	494	517	470	18.0	2.3	8.8	3.9	61%	13%	54	17	29	25%	75%	5%	6	71	17%	17%			7.1	129	154	$0
1st Half	0	0	0	5	4	0.00	2.41	0.86	399	500	311	18.0	1.9	7.7	4.0	63%	8%	83	8	8	25%	100%	0%	1	76	0%	0%			2.5	148	178	-$6
2nd Half	0	2	0	23	23	2.74	3.51	0.91	513	520	503	18.0	2.3	9.0	3.8	60%	14%	48	18	33	25%	70%	5%	5	70	20%	20%			4.6	125	150	$1
18 Proj	**9**	**7**	**0**	**145**	**134**	**3.32**	**3.82**	**1.16**	**624**	**586**	**664**	**23.9**	**3.0**	**8.3**	**2.8**	**58%**	**12%**	**51**	**20**	**29**	**29%**	**72%**	**9%**	**24**						**18.6**	**98**	**118**	**$13**

Rivero,Felipe

Age: 26	Th: L	Role RP	Health	B	LIMA Plan	C
Ht: 6' 2"	Wt: 210	Type Pwr	PT/Exp	C	Rand Var	-5
			Consist	A	MM	4431

Fast start at the right place, grabbed closer role in June and never let go. Dom, SwK look entrenched, GB% ticked up again, even volatile Ctl cooperated. Change-up produced all kinds of swing-and-miss, as fastball velocity jumped into the upper-90s. Even with regression, continued dominance vR suggests staying power.

Yr Tm	W	L	Sv	IP	K	ERA	xERA	WHIP	oOPS	vL	vR	BF/G	Ctl	Dom	Cmd	FpK	SwK	G	L	F	H%	S%	hr/f	GS	APC	DOM%	DIS%	Sv%	LI	RAR	BPV	BPX	R$
13																																	
14 aa	2	7	0	44	31	4.34	4.60	1.49				18.8	3.5	6.4	1.9						33%	72%								-3.2	54	65	-$4
15 WAS	2	1	2	48	43	2.79	3.41	0.95	544	486	600	3.9	2.0	8.0	3.9	62%	12%	45	21	33	26%	70%	5%	0	16			67	1.10	7.0	112	133	$4
16 2 NL	1	6	1	77	92	4.09	3.45	1.29	671	765	626	4.4	3.9	10.8	2.8	57%	15%	48	22	30	32%	70%	12%	0	17			25	1.04	0.9	115	137	$0
17 PIT	5	3	21	75	88	1.67	3.00	0.89	473	255	571	4.1	2.4	10.5	4.4	58%	16%	53	19	28	26%	84%	8%	0	16			91	1.21	25.0	156	187	$23
1st Half	3	2	3	44	49	0.82	2.73	0.68	390	276	454	4.0	2.0	10.0	4.9	54%	16%	58	15	27	19%	93%	7%	0	16			100	1.46	19.2	161	194	$25
2nd Half	2	1	18	31	39	2.87	3.35	1.18	576	218	692	4.2	2.9	11.2	3.9	63%	16%	46	24	30	34%	77%	8%	0	17			90	0.90	5.7	149	178	$20
18 Proj	**3**	**4**	**39**	**73**	**84**	**2.90**	**3.20**	**1.08**	**578**	**482**	**624**	**4.3**	**2.6**	**10.4**	**3.9**	**60%**	**15%**	**49**	**21**	**30**	**30%**	**75%**	**9%**	**0**						**13.0**	**143**	**172**	**$23**

Roark,Tanner

Age: 31	Th: R	Role SP	Health	A	LIMA Plan	B
Ht: 6' 2"	Wt: 235	Type Pwr	PT/Exp	A	Rand Var	+1
			Consist	A	MM	1205

Odd-year blues as newly-minted "power pitcher" struggled vL again. Dom continued ascent to league-average levels, stable GB% helped, but once-elite Ctl is no longer cooperating. Sub-par Cmd, hr/f volatility and H% swings—both in-season and year-to-year—make him a moving target that H2Hers should avoid.

Yr Tm	W	L	Sv	IP	K	ERA	xERA	WHIP	oOPS	vL	vR	BF/G	Ctl	Dom	Cmd	FpK	SwK	G	L	F	H%	S%	hr/f	GS	APC	DOM%	DIS%	Sv%	LI	RAR	BPV	BPX	R$
13 WAS *	16	4	2	159	103	3.04	2.60	1.08	476	634	358	13.2	1.8	5.8	3.3	71%	7%	50	24	26	28%	72%	3%	5	54	40%	0%	100	0.95	16.3	99	129	$18
14 WAS	15	10	0	199	138	2.85	3.80	1.09	632	672	591	25.7	1.8	6.3	3.5	65%	9%	41	21	38	28%	77%	7%	31	97	29%	26%			21.7	84	100	$19
15 WAS	4	7	1	111	70	4.38	4.17	1.31	784	866	709	11.7	2.1	5.7	2.7	60%	8%	48	22	31	30%	71%	15%	12	45	17%	50%	50	0.90	-5.7	71	85	-$2
16 WAS	16	10	0	210	172	2.83	4.00	1.17	634	617	648	25.1	3.1	7.4	2.4	58%	9%	49	20	31	27%	79%	9%	33	99	36%	18%	0	0.81	35.3	75	89	$24
17 WAS	13	11	0	181	166	4.67	4.21	1.33	729	836	618	24.3	3.2	8.2	2.6	59%	10%	48	20	32	31%	68%	14%	30	101	23%	30%	0	0.76	-6.9	89	106	$6
1st Half	6	6	0	96	78	5.27	4.64	1.48	764	879	650	24.8	3.4	7.3	2.2	59%	10%	46	23	31	33%	66%	13%	17	103	24%	35%			-10.7	65	78	-$2
2nd Half	7	5	0	86	88	3.99	3.76	1.17	688	788	577	23.7	2.9	9.2	3.1	58%	11%	51	16	33	28%	70%	14%	13	98	23%	23%	0	0.74	3.9	116	139	$15
18 Proj	**13**	**10**	**0**	**181**	**152**	**4.11**	**4.25**	**1.28**	**709**	**785**	**635**	**23.1**	**3.0**	**7.5**	**2.5**	**59%**	**10%**	**48**	**20**	**32**	**30%**	**70%**	**12%**	**32**						**5.6**	**82**	**98**	**$9**

Robertson,David

Age: 33	Th: R	Role RP	Health	A	LIMA Plan	C+
Ht: 5' 11"	Wt: 195	Type Pwr	PT/Exp	B	Rand Var	-5
			Consist	C	MM	4510

9th inning gig ended with late-July trade to NYY. Made up for lost saves with stunning 2nd half ERA/WHIP, fueled by rediscovery of GB tilt, H% luck, hr/f plunge. Just volatile enough to keep us antsy. But elite SwK/Dom along with Ctl rebound say he's plenty good enough to close—and still offers value even if he doesn't.

Yr Tm	W	L	Sv	IP	K	ERA	xERA	WHIP	oOPS	vL	vR	BF/G	Ctl	Dom	Cmd	FpK	SwK	G	L	F	H%	S%	hr/f	GS	APC	DOM%	DIS%	Sv%	LI	RAR	BPV	BPX	R$
13 NYY	5	1	3	66	77	2.04	2.66	1.04	584	484	695	3.7	2.4	10.4	4.3	59%	10%	51	20	29	29%	84%	11%	0	15			60	1.19	15.0	151	197	$9
14 NYY	4	5	39	64	96	3.08	2.38	1.06	588	437	765	4.1	3.2	13.4	4.2	61%	13%	44	23	33	31%	75%	16%	0	17			89	1.67	5.3	177	211	$20
15 CHW	6	5	34	63	86	3.41	2.60	0.93	573	462	651	4.2	1.8	12.2	6.6	68%	14%	36	30	34	30%	67%	14%	0	16			83	1.35	4.3	184	219	$21
16 CHW	5	3	37	62	75	3.47	3.94	1.36	684	610	756	4.3	4.6	10.8	2.3	61%	13%	45	14	40	32%	77%	10%	0	17			84	1.44	5.6	93	111	$17
17 2 AL	9	2	14	68	98	1.84	2.71	0.85	488	441	527	4.3	3.0	12.9	4.3	59%	17%	47	16	37	23%	85%	12%	0	17			88	1.19	21.2	176	211	$21
1st Half	3	2	12	28	42	3.18	3.04	0.95	574	447	691	4.3	2.9	13.3	4.7	63%	18%	34	16	50	27%	74%	14%	0	17			92	1.33	4.1	175	210	$17
2nd Half	6	0	2	40	56	0.90	2.44	0.78	425	435	415	4.3	3.2	12.6	4.0	56%	17%	56	16	28	21%	93%	9%	0	17			67	1.07	17.1	176	211	$24
18 Proj	**7**	**3**	**2**	**65**	**88**	**2.95**	**3.11**	**1.09**	**602**	**532**	**664**	**4.2**	**3.2**	**12.2**	**3.8**	**61%**	**15%**	**45**	**18**	**37**	**30%**	**76%**	**12%**	**0**						**11.3**	**155**	**187**	**$9**

Robles,Hansel

Age: 27	Th: R	Role RP	Health	A	LIMA Plan	C
Ht: 5' 11"	Wt: 185	Type Pwr FB	PT/Exp	D	Rand Var	+1
			Consist	B	MM	0300

7-5, 4.92 ERA in 57 IP at NYM. Promising April (1.84 ERA, 17 Ks through 15 IP) gave way to BB-and-HR-plagued May, AAA demotion. Just marginal improvement (4.11 ERA, 4.1 Ctl) followed 2nd half return. Walks were a year-long issue, Dom promise is fading, GB% is stagnant. Young enough, but skills are in reverse.

Yr Tm	W	L	Sv	IP	K	ERA	xERA	WHIP	oOPS	vL	vR	BF/G	Ctl	Dom	Cmd	FpK	SwK	G	L	F	H%	S%	hr/f	GS	APC	DOM%	DIS%	Sv%	LI	RAR	BPV	BPX	R$
13																																	
14 aa	7	6	0	111	91	4.36	4.18	1.39				15.5	3.3	7.4	2.3						32%	70%								-8.4	69	83	-$3
15 NYM	4	3	0	54	61	3.67	3.64	1.02	655	560	717	3.8	3.0	10.2	3.4	60%	13%	33	18	49	24%	70%	12%	0	16			0	1.02	2.0	113	135	$3
16 NYM	6	4	1	78	85	3.48	4.31	1.35	703	586	784	4.9	4.2	9.8	2.4	59%	12%	30	29	41	32%	77%	8%	0	20			33	1.07	6.8	73	86	$3
17 NYM *	7	6	4	80	78	5.39	5.31	1.54	750	712	771	5.4	5.0	8.8	1.7	54%	9%	34	22	44	30%	70%	15%	0	21			50	1.11	-10.2	41	49	-$3
1st Half	4	2	3	39	36	7.30	8.05	2.03	921	678	1008	5.5	6.6	8.3	1.3	52%	10%	42	20	37	35%	69%	23%	0	18			50	1.18	-14.3	-4	-4	-$12
2nd Half	3	4	1	41	42	3.54	2.65	1.06	640	724	580	5.4	3.5	9.3	2.6	56%	9%	29	23	48	23%	71%	11%	0	23			50	1.05	4.1	94	113	$7
18 Proj	**4**	**5**	**0**	**65**	**66**	**4.38**	**4.70**	**1.35**	**750**	**664**	**803**	**5.2**	**4.2**	**9.2**	**2.2**	**57%**	**11%**	**33**	**24**	**44**	**29%**	**71%**	**12%**	**0**						**-0.2**	**62**	**75**	**-$1**

Rodney,Fernando

Age: 41	Th: R	Role RP	Health	B	LIMA Plan	C
Ht: 5' 11"	Wt: 230	Type Pwr GB	PT/Exp	B	Rand Var	+1
			Consist	A	MM	2420

As after 2015, he looked done in April (7 BB, 2 HR, 12 ER in 10 IP). Saved 35 games, coughed up 1 HR afterward. Again racked up Ks via that change-up, GBs with his sinking fastball. Typically spotty Ctl minimized by best hr/f in 3 years. Age says this MO is walking the edge; maybe 2018 is the year. Maybe...

Yr Tm	W	L	Sv	IP	K	ERA	xERA	WHIP	oOPS	vL	vR	BF/G	Ctl	Dom	Cmd	FpK	SwK	G	L	F	H%	S%	hr/f	GS	APC	DOM%	DIS%	Sv%	LI	RAR	BPV	BPX	R$
13 TAM	5	4	37	67	82	3.38	3.24	1.34	634	716	538	4.3	4.9	11.1	2.3	56%	13%	51	25	25	32%	74%	7%	0	18			82	1.34	4.0	97	126	$17
14 SEA	1	6	48	66	76	2.85	3.19	1.34	646	726	530	4.1	3.8	10.3	2.7	60%	11%	49	24	27	34%	79%	6%	0	16			94	1.36	7.3	110	131	$1
15 2 TM	7	5	16	63	58	4.74	4.05	1.40	776	845	721	4.1	4.2	8.3	2.0	59%	10%	51	18	31	30%	70%	16%	0	16			70	1.22	-6.0	66	79	$4
16 2 NL	2	4	25	65	74	3.44	3.66	1.39	668	726	611	4.2	5.1	10.2	2.0	57%	13%	55	22	23	31%	77%	14%	0	17			89	1.13	6.0	79	94	$1
17 ARI	5	4	39	55	65	4.23	3.63	1.19	582	662	497	3.8	4.2	10.6	2.5	59%	13%	52	16	32	29%	63%	7%	0	16			87	1.28	0.9	106	127	$1
1st Half	2	2	21	29	34	4.30	3.73	1.09	569	633	506	3.8	4.3	10.4	2.4	61%	13%	46	16	37	25%	60%	8%	0	16			88	1.50	0.2	96	115	$2
2nd Half	3	2	18	26	31	4.15	3.51	1.31	595	690	487	3.8	4.2	10.7	2.6	56%	13%	58	15	27	33%	67%	6%	0	16			86	1.04	0.7	117	141	$1
18 Proj	**4**	**4**	**25**	**58**	**66**	**4.14**	**3.76**	**1.30**	**655**	**731**	**578**	**3.8**	**4.4**	**10.2**	**2.3**	**58%**	**12%**	**53**	**18**	**29**	**30%**	**69%**	**12%**	**0**						**1.5**	**94**	**114**	**$1**

JOCK THOMPSON

Rodon,Carlos

Rodon,Carlos				Health	F	LIMA Plan	C
Age: 25	Th: L	Role	SP	PT/Exp	B	Rand Var	+3
Ht: 6' 3"	Wt: 235	Type	Pwr	Consist	A	MM	1401

Biceps bursitis shelved him until late June. Flashed big Dom, improving Ctl along with five straight 2-runs-or-less starts through late Aug until shoulder bursitis ended season in early Sept. Resulting surgery now has him out again until mid-2018. The skills promise remains evident, but some extended health is required.

Yr Tm	W	L	Sv	IP	K	ERA	xERA	WHIP	oOPS	vL	vR	BF/G	Ctl	Dom	Cmd	FpK	SwK	G	L	F	H%	S%	hr/f	GS	APC	DOM%	DIS%	Sv%	LI	RAR	BPV	BPX	R$
13																																	
14																																	
15 CHW	9	6	0	139	139	3.75	4.00	1.44	725	524	799	23.3	4.6	9.0	2.0	53%	11%	47	23	30	32%	75%	10%	23	94	26%	26%	0	0.87	3.7	63	75	$2
16 CHW	9	10	0	165	168	4.04	3.96	1.39	763	609	799	25.5	2.9	9.2	3.1	54%	11%	44	21	35	34%	75%	14%	28	100	18%	25%			3.1	107	128	$4
17 CHW	2	5	0	69	76	4.15	4.07	1.37	770	746	777	24.8	4.0	9.9	2.5	56%	11%	44	22	34	30%	76%	19%	12	98	33%	25%			1.7	91	109	-$1
1st Half	0	1	0	5	2	0.00	8.40	1.60	489	125	722	22.0	10.8	3.6	0.3	41%	3%	50	29	21	14%	100%	0%	1	94	0%	0%			2.7	-199	-238	-$11
2nd Half	2	4	0	64	74	4.48	3.84	1.35	788	825	777	25.0	3.5	10.4	3.0	57%	12%	44	22	35	32%	73%	20%	11	99	36%	27%			-0.9	114	136	$0
18 Proj	4	5	0	87	92	4.28	4.13	1.40	757	644	791	23.8	3.8	9.5	2.5	55%	11%	45	22	33	32%	73%	15%	15						0.8	92	110	-$1

Rodriguez,Eduardo

Rodriguez,Eduardo				Health	F	LIMA Plan	B
Age: 25	Th: L	Role	SP	PT/Exp	C	Rand Var	0
Ht: 6' 2"	Wt: 220	Type	Pwr FB	Consist	A	MM	1303

Fine start (2.77 ERA through end of May) derailed by chronic kneecap issue that DL'd him for 6+ weeks and plagued him going forward. Off-season surgery will now shelve him until May or June. Dom jumped as SwK ticked upward, FpK showed promise and still checks RHBs. With better luck, health... UP: 3.50 ERA.

Yr Tm	W	L	Sv	IP	K	ERA	xERA	WHIP	oOPS	vL	vR	BF/G	Ctl	Dom	Cmd	FpK	SwK	G	L	F	H%	S%	hr/f	GS	APC	DOM%	DIS%	Sv%	LI	RAR	BPV	BPX	R$
13 aa	4	3	0	60	52	4.68	3.83	1.34				22.5	3.4	7.8	2.3						31%	66%								-6.0	74	97	-$3
14 aa	6	8	0	120	93	4.42	4.35	1.46				23.3	2.8	7.0	2.5						35%	69%								-10.0	77	92	-$5
15 BOS *	14	9	0	170	136	3.92	3.95	1.30	701	820	662	24.1	2.4	7.2	3.1	57%	9%	43	24	33	32%	71%	10%	21	96	33%	33%			0.9	84	100	$7
16 BOS *	3	11	0	145	120	4.75	4.51	1.31	726	711	730	22.2	3.0	7.4	2.5	59%	11%	31	23	46	29%	69%	11%	20	93	30%	35%			-10.0	55	65	-$2
17 BOS	6	7	0	137	150	4.19	4.21	1.28	736	808	718	23.3	3.3	9.8	3.0	61%	12%	35	22	43	31%	71%	12%	24	98	17%	21%	0	0.77	2.8	101	122	$6
1st Half	4	2	0	61	65	3.54	4.06	1.15	709	825	682	22.5	3.1	9.6	3.1	58%	12%	35	21	44	27%	75%	13%	10	93	20%	10%	0	0.74	6.1	102	122	$10
2nd Half	2	5	0	76	85	4.72	4.34	1.39	756	796	746	23.9	3.4	10.0	2.9	63%	12%	35	23	42	34%	69%	11%	14	103	14%	29%			-3.4	101	121	$2
18 Proj	6	8	0	131	130	4.07	4.30	1.25	716	764	703	22.4	2.9	9.0	3.1	60%	11%	35	23	43	30%	71%	11%	24						4.7	95	115	$5

Rodriguez,Francisco

Rodriguez,Francisco				Health	A	LIMA Plan	C
Age: 36	Th: R	Role	RP	PT/Exp	B	Rand Var	+5
Ht: 6' 0"	Wt: 195	Type	Pwr	Consist	C	MM	1200

2016 GB% hike mitigated Ctl plunge, but no 2017 magic as both fell apart. H% bit hard in April; ongoing HR onslaught, BB woes cost him closer role in early May—and roster spot in June. Aging change-up-centric soft-tosser has pulled out a rabbit before, but if he's done, it was quite a run: 4th all-time in Saves.

Yr Tm	W	L	Sv	IP	K	ERA	xERA	WHIP	oOPS	vL	vR	BF/G	Ctl	Dom	Cmd	FpK	SwK	G	L	F	H%	S%	hr/f	GS	APC	DOM%	DIS%	Sv%	LI	RAR	BPV	BPX	R$
13 2 TM	3	2	10	47	54	2.70	3.22	1.20	734	513	1003	4.0	2.7	10.4	3.9	60%	11%	36	25	39	31%	86%	15%	0	16			100	0.91	6.7	129	168	$6
14 MIL	5	5	44	68	73	3.04	2.99	0.99	648	526	772	3.9	2.4	9.7	4.1	59%	12%	44	21	35	23%	83%	23%	0	15			90	1.19	5.8	132	157	$23
15 MIL	1	3	38	57	62	2.21	2.76	0.86	547	538	558	3.6	1.7	9.8	5.6	63%	14%	46	24	30	24%	81%	14%	0	14			95	1.01	12.3	153	183	$22
16 DET	3	4	44	58	52	3.24	3.74	1.13	642	648	634	3.9	3.2	8.0	2.5	61%	12%	55	16	29	26%	75%	13%	0	15			90	1.46	6.8	90	107	$20
17 DET	2	5	7	25	23	7.82	5.65	1.66	1006	1178	835	4.2	3.9	8.2	2.1	54%	10%	30	19	51	31%	61%	21%	0	15			54	1.04	-10.8	50	60	-$5
1st Half	2	5	7	25	23	7.82	5.65	1.66	1006	1178	835	4.2	3.9	8.2	2.1	54%	10%	30	19	51	31%	61%	21%	0	15			54	1.04	-10.8	50	60	-$5
2nd Half																																	
18 Proj	2	3	0	29	27	4.89	4.59	1.38	804	812	793	4.0	3.8	8.4	2.2	59%	12%	42	21	38	29%	71%	19%	0						-1.9	68	81	-$4

Rogers,Taylor

Rogers,Taylor				Health	A	LIMA Plan	B+
Age: 27	Th: L	Role	RP	PT/Exp	D	Rand Var	-2
Ht: 6' 3"	Wt: 170	Type	Pwr	Consist	B	MM	1210

Exhibit A on why bullpens are like a box of chocolates. Good 1st half fueled by plus Ctl and GB% repeats, despite Dom, H%, S% warning signs. Strikeouts then rebounded in 2nd half as everything else abruptly fell apart. A LOOGY at best, and mediocre SwK, FpK remain instructive. You have better RP options.

Yr Tm	W	L	Sv	IP	K	ERA	xERA	WHIP	oOPS	vL	vR	BF/G	Ctl	Dom	Cmd	FpK	SwK	G	L	F	H%	S%	hr/f	GS	APC	DOM%	DIS%	Sv%	LI	RAR	BPV	BPX	R$
13																																	
14 aa	11	6	0	145	91	4.09	4.45	1.48				26.0	2.4	5.6	2.4						35%	71%								-6.3	71	84	-$3
15 aaa	11	12	0	174	98	5.56	5.58	1.65				27.8	2.4	5.1	2.1						37%	65%								-34.3	46	55	-$18
16 MIN *	3	2	0	79	75	4.61	4.97	1.48	719	547	811	5.3	2.6	8.5	3.3	56%	8%	51	20	28	37%	71%	14%	0	18			0	0.84	-4.1	88	104	-$4
17 MIN	7	3	0	56	49	3.07	4.31	1.31	693	560	766	3.4	3.4	7.9	2.3	58%	9%	45	24	31	30%	81%	12%	0	13			0	1.23	8.8	74	89	$3
1st Half	4	1	0	30	22	2.08	4.09	1.09	597	731	528	3.4	2.1	6.5	3.1	56%	8%	51	18	31	27%	84%	7%	0	12			0	1.22	8.5	91	109	$6
2nd Half	3	2	0	25	27	4.26	4.57	1.58	802	384	1049	3.4	5.0	9.6	1.9	60%	10%	37	33	30	33%	78%	19%	0	13			0	1.23	0.3	54	64	-$1
18 Proj	5	3	9	58	49	4.18	4.44	1.46	765	556	879	4.9	3.2	7.6	2.4	58%	9%	46	24	30	34%	73%	11%	0						1.3	76	92	$2

Romano,Sal

Romano,Sal				Health	A	LIMA Plan	C
Age: 24	Th: R	Role	SP	PT/Exp	D	Rand Var	0
Ht: 6' 5"	Wt: 270	Type	xGB	Consist	F	MM	0103

5-8, 4.45 ERA in 87 IP at CIN. Big GBer with mid-90s fastball posted 2.8 Ctl from August on. Sept finish (3.49 ERA, 7.6 Dom) a plus. But sub-par SwK, historically lofty H% say it won't be enough. Fastball/slider combo needs third pitch; future may be in the pen. Has foundation, but little here suggests a big step up.

Yr Tm	W	L	Sv	IP	K	ERA	xERA	WHIP	oOPS	vL	vR	BF/G	Ctl	Dom	Cmd	FpK	SwK	G	L	F	H%	S%	hr/f	GS	APC	DOM%	DIS%	Sv%	LI	RAR	BPV	BPX	R$
13																																	
14																																	
15 aa	0	4	0	23	8	13.77	9.68	2.32				16.9	4.9	3.2	0.7						39%	38%								-27.8	-49	-59	-$17
16 aa	6	11	0	156	127	5.01	5.09	1.51				25.0	2.2	7.3	3.3						37%	67%								-15.9	82	97	-$7
17 CIN *	6	12	0	136	101	4.44	4.55	1.50	799	793	805	22.7	3.7	6.6	1.8	55%	9%	50	20	30	33%	71%	12%	16	94	6%	31%			-1.4	57	68	-$3
1st Half	1	4	0	50	26	4.04	4.89	1.57	1304	1042	1556	21.9	3.4	4.7	1.4	28%	4%	20	10	70	33%	75%	29%	1	82	0%	100%			2.0	35	42	-$8
2nd Half	5	8	0	86	74	4.67	4.36	1.47	779	783	776	23.1	3.8	7.8	2.1	56%	9%	52	20	28	33%	68%	10%	15	94	7%	27%			-3.4	69	82	$1
18 Proj	6	12	0	145	110	4.64	4.63	1.50	763	766	760	23.5	3.0	6.8	2.2	56%	9%	52	20	28	34%	69%	8%	27						-5.0	70	84	-$5

Romero,Enny

Romero,Enny				Health	C	LIMA Plan	B+
Age: 27	Th: L	Role	RP	PT/Exp	D	Rand Var	0
Ht: 6' 3"	Wt: 215	Type	Pwr FB	Consist	B	MM	1400

Rising Dom, SwK trend and history vR are reasons to watch gas-throwing lefty with power fastball/slider arsenal. But chronically spotty control, inability to generate GBs and consistently elevated H% keep us peering from a distance. Has both stuff and time to be somebody, but we aren't betting on it.

Yr Tm	W	L	Sv	IP	K	ERA	xERA	WHIP	oOPS	vL	vR	BF/G	Ctl	Dom	Cmd	FpK	SwK	G	L	F	H%	S%	hr/f	GS	APC	DOM%	DIS%	Sv%	LI	RAR	BPV	BPX	R$
13 TAM *	11	7	0	153	99	2.80	3.12	1.31	349	500	298	21.8	4.4	5.8	1.3	42%	6%	64	7	29	26%	80%	0%	1	70	0%	0%			20.0	57	74	$10
14 aaa	5	11	0	126	101	5.53	5.29	1.61				22.3	3.8	7.2	1.9						35%	66%								-27.8	50	60	-$13
15 TAM *	1	3	1	76	69	5.67	5.40	1.66	798	975	695	8.5	3.6	8.2	2.3	51%	11%	47	21	32	38%	65%	3%	0	26			33	0.62	-16.1	67	80	-$11
16 TAM	2	0	1	46	50	5.91	4.79	1.53	738	824	685	3.9	5.5	9.9	1.8	56%	13%	37	22	40	31%	63%	14%	0	16			50	0.75	-9.7	43	52	-$6
17 WAS	2	4	2	56	65	3.56	4.23	1.40	736	832	682	4.6	3.7	10.5	2.8	52%	13%	39	19	42	34%	79%	11%	0	19			50	0.89	5.5	106	127	$0
1st Half	2	3	2	38	41	3.35	4.25	1.35	734	918	619	4.7	3.6	9.8	2.7	54%	12%	39	19	41	32%	80%	12%	0	20			50	1.12	4.7	97	116	$3
2nd Half	0	1	0	18	24	4.00	4.16	1.50	740	624	793	4.6	4.0	12.0	3.0	49%	15%	38	18	44	39%	76%	9%	0	19			0	0.44	0.8	124	149	-$5
18 Proj	1	2	0	36	41	4.12	4.26	1.33	668	722	637	4.8	4.3	10.1	2.4	53%	13%	39	20	40	30%	72%	12%	0						1.1	85	102	-$3

Romo,Sergio

Romo,Sergio				Health	D	LIMA Plan	A
Age: 35	Th: R	Role	RP	PT/Exp	D	Rand Var	-1
Ht: 5' 11"	Wt: 185	Type	Pwr FB	Consist	B	MM	2400

Uncharacteristic BB woes and HR struggles crushed him early in LA; March back woes and June DL stint (ankle) didn't help. Rebounded with TAM in Aug despite sub-vintage FpK. Age, FB tilt and 86 mph won't incite a bidding war, but 2nd half says there's something left. "Proven closer experience" could mean... UP: 10 Sv

Yr Tm	W	L	Sv	IP	K	ERA	xERA	WHIP	oOPS	vL	vR	BF/G	Ctl	Dom	Cmd	FpK	SwK	G	L	F	H%	S%	hr/f	GS	APC	DOM%	DIS%	Sv%	LI	RAR	BPV	BPX	R$
13 SF	5	8	38	60	58	2.54	3.39	1.08	614	745	511	3.8	1.8	8.7	4.8	69%	14%	41	24	36	30%	80%	8%	0	15			88	1.58	9.9	126	165	$21
14 SF	6	4	23	58	59	3.72	3.27	0.95	622	777	528	3.6	1.9	9.2	4.9	69%	15%	37	18	45	25%	67%	13%	0	14			82	1.26	0.1	130	154	$13
15 SF	0	5	2	57	71	2.98	2.70	1.06	622	929	467	3.3	1.6	11.1	7.1	70%	17%	45	23	32	35%	72%	7%	0	13			50	1.26	6.9	181	216	$3
16 SF	1	0	4	31	33	2.64	3.50	1.08	709	790	674	2.9	2.1	9.7	4.7	65%	15%	38	14	47	28%	86%	14%	0	12			100	1.27	5.9	135	160	$2
17 2 TM	3	1	0	56	59	3.56	3.99	1.10	661	733	633	4.1	3.1	9.5	3.1	59%	15%	37	20	43	25%	75%	15%	0	17			0	0.88	5.5	104	125	$3
1st Half	1	1	0	25	30	6.20	4.22	1.42	853	985	815	3.7	4.4	10.9	2.5	60%	15%	35	25	40	29%	64%	27%	0	16			0	0.73	-5.6	92	111	-$6
2nd Half	2	0	0	31	29	1.45	3.80	0.84	490	590	440	4.5	2.0	8.4	4.1	58%	15%	39	16	45	23%	88%	6%	0	18			0	1.04	11.1	113	136	$9
18 Proj	2	2	0	51	55	3.45	3.81	1.12	686	813	629	3.6	2.4	9.7	4.0	63%	15%	39	19	42	29%	75%	12%	0						5.7	126	152	$2

JOCK THOMPSON

Rondon,Bruce

Rondon,Bruce						Health	F	LIMA Plan	D+
Age: 27	Th:	R	Role	RP		PT/Exp	D	Rand Var	+3
Ht: 6' 3"	Wt:	275	Type	Pwr	FB	Consist	C	MM	0410

1-3, 10.91 ERA in 16 IP at DET. Even with velocity downtick, fastball/slider combo still generates plenty of swing-and-miss. But already-poor Ctl disintegrated, inability to generate GB kept lofty H% chronic, and LHBs walloped him. Once a legit closer-in-waiting, now a struggling flame-thrower to watch from afar.

Yr Tm	W	L	Sv	IP	K	ERA	xERA	WHIP	oOPS	vL	vR	BF/G	Ctl	Dom	Cmd	FpK	SwK	G	L	F	H%	S%	hr/f	GS	APC	DOM%	DIS%	Sv%	LI	RAR	BPV	BPX	R$
13 DET *	2	3	15	58	63	2.68	2.58	1.18	720	873	608	3.9	3.8	9.6	2.6	47%	15%	47	24	29	29%	78%	9%	0	15			79	0.93	8.5	110	143	$9
14																																	
15 DET	1	0	5	31	36	5.81	4.31	1.61	770	865	696	4.1	5.5	10.5	1.9	54%	12%	41	25	34	35%	64%	10%	0	17			56	1.14	-7.1	58	69	-$5
16 DET *	7	4	9	58	68	3.80	4.03	1.42	583	416	781	4.2	4.7	10.6	2.3	59%	16%	32	17	51	33%	76%	12%	0	15			64	1.08	2.8	88	105	$5
17 DET *	3	4	2	52	54	6.12	6.32	2.03	890	1219	584	4.3	6.8	9.4	1.4	47%	13%	40	30	30	40%	69%	8%	0	16			50	0.85	-11.4	58	70	-$10
1st Half	1	2	0	31	30	5.69	7.40	2.32	843	1029	697	4.7	7.4	8.7	1.2	36%	10%	31	31	38	44%	74%	0%	0	18			0	1.09	-5.1	50	61	-$14
2nd Half	2	2	2	21	25	6.76	4.75	1.63	907	1275	530	3.8	6.0	10.4	1.7	52%	14%	43	30	27	34%	58%	13%	0	15			67	0.76	-6.3	72	87	-$5
18 Proj	4	3	2	51	57	5.25	5.10	1.65	783	721	844	4.1	5.6	10.1	1.8	57%	15%	36	20	44	36%	68%	7%	0						-5.6	44	54	-$5

Rondon,Hector

Rondon,Hector						Health	A	LIMA Plan	A
Age: 30	Th:	R	Role	RP		PT/Exp	C	Rand Var	+4
Ht: 6' 3"	Wt:	230	Type	Pwr		Consist	A	MM	3400

Repeat of HR woes and disappearance of elite Ctl crushed ERA. Sept MRI revealed bone chips in his elbow, suggesting imminent surgery. But Dom trend and SwK look terrific, FpK says Ctl will rebound, GB% remains solid. With health and overdue hr/f correction, a prime end-gamer. UP: Sub-3 ERA, 20 saves

Yr Tm	W	L	Sv	IP	K	ERA	xERA	WHIP	oOPS	vL	vR	BF/G	Ctl	Dom	Cmd	FpK	SwK	G	L	F	H%	S%	hr/f	GS	APC	DOM%	DIS%	Sv%	LI	RAR	BPV	BPX	R$
13 CHC	2	1	0	55	44	4.77	4.39	1.41	737	546	908	5.4	4.1	7.2	1.8	54%	11%	43	22	35	29%	68%	10%	0	21			0	0.65	-6.1	40	52	-$5
14 CHC	4	4	29	63	63	2.42	2.99	1.06	526	616	454	4.0	2.1	9.0	4.2	65%	12%	49	23	28	30%	77%	4%	0	16			88	1.16	10.4	131	156	$17
15 CHC	6	4	30	70	69	1.67	3.04	1.00	568	640	503	3.9	1.9	8.9	4.6	63%	11%	52	20	27	28%	86%	8%	0	15			88	1.51	19.8	138	164	$23
16 CHC	2	3	18	51	58	3.53	2.95	0.98	641	743	569	3.7	1.4	10.2	7.3	72%	11%	46	20	34	28%	71%	18%	0	15			78	1.09	4.2	170	202	$10
17 CHC	4	1	0	57	69	4.24	3.46	1.22	724	810	677	3.9	3.1	10.8	3.5	64%	12%	48	17	35	30%	72%	20%	0	16			0	0.72	0.8	136	164	$1
1st Half	2	1	0	31	37	4.40	3.62	1.24	713	769	679	3.9	3.5	10.9	3.1	61%	11%	46	18	36	30%	70%	18%	0	17			0	0.78	-0.2	125	149	$0
2nd Half	2	0	0	27	32	4.05	3.29	1.20	736	865	675	3.9	2.7	10.8	4.0	67%	14%	51	15	34	31%	74%	22%	0	15			0	0.65	1.0	150	180	$2
18 Proj	4	2	0	58	65	3.59	3.38	1.13	673	741	629	3.8	2.5	10.1	4.1	66%	12%	48	18	33	29%	74%	17%	0						5.5	142	171	$3

Ross,Joe

Ross,Joe						Health	F	LIMA Plan	C
Age: 25	Th:	R	Role	SP		PT/Exp	C	Rand Var	+3
Ht: 6' 4"	Wt:	225	Type			Consist	C	MM	1200

5-3, 5.01 ERA in 74 IP at WAS. Following lost 2016 2nd half (shoulder inflammation), WAS schedule, uneven performance kept him on Triple-A shuttle until late May. Retained Cmd, but both GB%, velocity declined as HR spiked. Season ended with TJS in late July. History makes him worth a revisit in 2019.

Yr Tm	W	L	Sv	IP	K	ERA	xERA	WHIP	oOPS	vL	vR	BF/G	Ctl	Dom	Cmd	FpK	SwK	G	L	F	H%	S%	hr/f	GS	APC	DOM%	DIS%	Sv%	LI	RAR	BPV	BPX	R$
13																																	
14 aa	2	0	0	20	17	3.89	4.51	1.28				20.5	0.4	7.7	17.8						37%	72%								-0.4	388	462	-$2
15 WAS *	10	8	0	153	127	3.45	3.09	1.15	628	809	461	20.2	2.4	7.5	3.1	59%	12%	50	16	34	29%	72%	10%	13	72	38%	15%	0	0.71	9.6	96	115	$11
16 WAS	7	5	0	105	93	3.43	3.96	1.30	713	824	611	23.5	2.5	8.0	3.2	56%	11%	43	27	30	33%	76%	10%	19	90	26%	32%			9.9	97	116	$5
17 WAS *	7	5	0	101	86	5.34	6.05	1.54	867	923	806	24.5	2.5	7.7	3.0	64%	10%	38	25	38	35%	70%	19%	13	93	31%	46%			-12.3	51	62	-$5
1st Half	6	5	0	91	77	5.45	6.01	1.54	865	923	807	24.8	2.3	7.6	3.3	63%	11%	38	25	37	36%	69%	18%	11	93	36%	45%			-12.3	59	71	-$5
2nd Half	1	0	0	10	9	4.35	5.22	1.55	881	922	795	23.0	4.4	7.8	1.8	70%	9%	34	24	41	28%	85%	25%	2	89	0%	50%			0.0	36	43	-$8
18 Proj	1	1	0	15	12	4.15	4.28	1.33	746	867	632	22.4	2.4	7.7	3.2	60%	11%	44	22	34	32%	71%	11%	3						0.4	95	115	-$4

Ross,Tyson

Ross,Tyson						Health	F	LIMA Plan	D+
Age: 31	Th:	R	Role	SP		PT/Exp	C	Rand Var	+5
Ht: 6' 6"	Wt:	245	Type	Pwr	xGB	Consist	D	MM	0201

3-3, 7.71 ERA in 49 IP at TEX. Rehab from thoracic outlet syndrome surgery delayed season until June. Began to reclaim elite GB% in 2nd half but with zero hint of any Dom or Ctl. July blister issues piled on; banished to pen for mop-up work in late Sept. History points to ceiling; getting there is another matter.

Yr Tm	W	L	Sv	IP	K	ERA	xERA	WHIP	oOPS	vL	vR	BF/G	Ctl	Dom	Cmd	FpK	SwK	G	L	F	H%	S%	hr/f	GS	APC	DOM%	DIS%	Sv%	LI	RAR	BPV	BPX	R$
13 SD	3	8	0	125	119	3.17	3.20	1.15	627	709	548	14.4	3.2	8.6	2.7	54%	12%	55	15	30	28%	74%	8%	16	57	44%	13%	0	1.09	10.8	102	133	$7
14 SD	13	14	0	196	195	2.81	3.02	1.21	634	635	632	26.2	3.3	9.0	2.7	58%	13%	57	21	22	30%	79%	11%	31	101	48%	23%			22.6	107	127	$16
15 SD	10	12	0	196	212	3.26	3.07	1.31	652	721	584	24.9	3.9	9.7	2.5	58%	13%	62	19	20	32%	75%	9%	33	98	33%	18%			17.0	111	132	$12
16 SD	0	1	0	5	5	11.81	3.68	1.88	986	1033	873	27.0	1.7	8.4	5.0	70%	15%	47	37	16	47%	30%	0%	1	94	0%	0%			-5.0	131	156	-$6
17 TEX *	6	5	0	79	51	7.97	6.69	1.95	856	759	952	21.0	6.3	5.8	0.9	46%	7%	47	19	35	34%	59%	13%	10	81	0%	60%	0	0.65	-35.3	10	11	-$19
1st Half	3	2	0	33	20	8.68	6.35	1.82	598	507	729	22.1	5.1	5.4	1.0	48%	7%	38	24	38	33%	51%	6%	3	89	0%	33%			-17.8	9	10	-$18
2nd Half	3	3	0	46	31	7.13	6.73	2.02	950	876	1014	20.2	7.0	6.1	0.9	46%	7%	50	17	33	34%	65%	16%	7	78	0%	71%	0	0.61	-15.7	13	16	-$19
18 Proj	5	6	0	87	73	5.39	4.78	1.59	788	784	791	21.2	4.9	7.5	1.5	53%	11%	55	18	26	32%	66%	12%	18						-11.1	36	44	-$7

Rusin,Chris

Rusin,Chris						Health	D	LIMA Plan	B
Age: 31	Th:	L	Role	RP		PT/Exp	C	Rand Var	-1
Ht: 6' 2"	Wt:	195	Type		xGB	Consist	D	MM	2101

Soft-tosser delivered real value in first full season out of the pen—in Coors no less. PRO: 2nd half Dom, Ctl gains came with legit SwK, FpK support; worm-killing sinker remains entrenched; velocity ticked up. CON: 1st half a H% creation, early success vR looks unrepeatable, xERA is a tell. Manage your expectations.

Yr Tm	W	L	Sv	IP	K	ERA	xERA	WHIP	oOPS	vL	vR	BF/G	Ctl	Dom	Cmd	FpK	SwK	G	L	F	H%	S%	hr/f	GS	APC	DOM%	DIS%	Sv%	LI	RAR	BPV	BPX	R$
13 CHC *	10	13	0	187	90	4.21	4.41	1.40	750	521	819	24.7	2.6	4.3	1.6	58%	8%	48	23	29	30%	71%	13%	13	79	0%	54%			-8.0	34	44	-$3
14 CHC *	8	13	0	159	83	5.54	6.05	1.67	830	458	1128	26.4	2.7	4.7	1.8	59%	8%	48	18	34	35%	68%	7%	0	49			0	0.32	-35.3	24	28	-$19
15 COL *	9	12	0	166	98	6.00	6.61	1.72	867	867	867	24.3	2.9	5.3	1.8	67%	9%	52	21	27	36%	68%	15%	22	90	18%	50%	0	0.77	-41.8	15	18	-$23
16 COL	3	5	0	84	69	3.74	3.52	1.25	706	716	701	12.1	2.5	7.4	3.0	58%	10%	58	21	21	31%	70%	10%	7	44	0%	43%	0	0.75	4.7	102	122	$2
17 COL	5	1	2	85	71	2.65	3.48	1.11	645	703	607	5.7	2.0	7.5	3.7	59%	13%	59	17	24	28%	81%	15%	0	20			67	1.14	17.9	118	142	$9
1st Half	3	0	1	45	33	2.40	3.73	0.96	540	689	429	5.8	2.4	6.6	2.8	57%	12%	55	20	24	23%	78%	10%	0	21			50	1.06	10.9	87	104	$12
2nd Half	2	1	1	40	38	2.93	3.20	1.28	755	722	772	5.5	1.6	8.6	5.4	62%	14%	62	13	25	34%	84%	21%	0	19			100	1.21	7.1	152	182	$6
18 Proj	4	3	0	73	56	3.68	3.90	1.29	740	735	743	8.4	2.3	7.0	3.1	60%	11%	57	19	24	31%	75%	14%	0						6.0	99	120	$1

Ryu,Hyun-Jin

Ryu,Hyun-Jin						Health	F	LIMA Plan	B+
Age: 31	Th:	L	Role	SP		PT/Exp	D	Rand Var	0
Ht: 6' 3"	Wt:	250	Type	Pwr		Consist	C	MM	2203

1st half HR barrage hurt as he struggled vL early on, and formerly fine Ctl was MIA all season. But an effective comeback after losing two years to labrum, elbow surgeries. GB% looks salvageable, FpK, SwK look vintage, velocity inched up throughout, and he still owns deception vR. With health, there's upside.

Yr Tm	W	L	Sv	IP	K	ERA	xERA	WHIP	oOPS	vL	vR	BF/G	Ctl	Dom	Cmd	FpK	SwK	G	L	F	H%	S%	hr/f	GS	APC	DOM%	DIS%	Sv%	LI	RAR	BPV	BPX	R$
13 LA	14	8	0	192	154	3.00	3.51	1.20	660	738	633	26.1	2.3	7.2	3.1	59%	9%	51	19	31	30%	77%	9%	30	102	33%	20%			20.5	97	126	$16
14 LA	14	7	0	152	139	3.38	3.23	1.19	658	665	656	24.3	1.7	8.2	4.8	62%	9%	47	22	30	33%	72%	6%	26	94	42%	27%			6.9	127	151	$11
15																																	
16 LA	0	1	0	5	4	11.57	5.53	2.14	1144	800	1238	24.0	3.9	7.7	2.0	54%	11%	41	24	35	43%	44%	17%	1	89	0%	100%			-4.2	54	64	-$6
17 LA	5	9	1	127	116	3.77	4.25	1.37	792	962	730	21.6	3.2	8.2	2.6	60%	11%	45	23	32	31%	79%	19%	24	85	13%	33%	100	0.76	9.3	85	102	$4
1st Half	3	6	1	73	69	4.21	4.08	1.40	850	1094	757	22.5	2.7	8.5	3.1	58%	12%	47	21	32	32%	78%	22%	13	85	8%	31%	100	0.76	1.3	105	126	$4
2nd Half	2	3	0	54	47	3.17	4.49	1.31	708	753	693	20.5	3.8	7.8	2.0	63%	10%	43	25	32	28%	81%	14%	11	85	18%	36%			7.9	58	70	$5
18 Proj	8	7	0	131	116	3.56	4.05	1.27	713	800	684	22.4	2.6	8.0	3.0	61%	10%	46	22	31	31%	75%	12%	24						12.8	97	117	$8

Sabathia,CC

Sabathia,CC						Health	F	LIMA Plan	C+
Age: 37	Th:	L	Role	SP		PT/Exp	A	Rand Var	+1
Ht: 6' 6"	Wt:	300	Type	Pwr		Consist	A	MM	1203

Terrific pen helped cut workload, offense boosted win total. Held up physically despite 4+ weeks of DL time (hamstring, knee). Back-end skills earned best R$ in 5 years, and look rock solid—but age begs to differ. As good as it gets; risk still trumps reward. End-gamer with... DN: 5.00 ERA, less than 100 IP.

Yr Tm	W	L	Sv	IP	K	ERA	xERA	WHIP	oOPS	vL	vR	BF/G	Ctl	Dom	Cmd	FpK	SwK	G	L	F	H%	S%	hr/f	GS	APC	DOM%	DIS%	Sv%	LI	RAR	BPV	BPX	R$
13 NYY	14	13	0	211	175	4.78	3.89	1.37	770	662	804	28.4	2.8	7.5	2.7	65%	10%	45	22	33	32%	68%	13%	32	104	28%	22%			-23.7	83	108	-$2
14 NYY	3	4	0	46	48	5.28	3.29	1.48	875	570	921	26.1	2.0	9.4	4.8	70%	11%	48	22	30	37%	71%	23%	8	100	13%	25%			-8.7	142	169	-$5
15 NYY	6	10	0	167	137	4.73	4.08	1.42	797	516	864	25.0	2.7	7.4	2.7	62%	9%	46	22	32	32%	71%	17%	29	93	17%	41%			-15.9	84	100	-$6
16 NYY	9	12	0	180	152	3.91	4.22	1.32	713	662	725	25.6	3.3	7.6	2.3	61%	10%	50	17	33	30%	74%	13%	30	97	23%	33%			6.3	77	92	$7
17 NYY	14	5	0	149	120	3.69	4.20	1.27	715	683	722	23.1	3.0	7.3	2.4	61%	9%	50	22	28	28%	76%	17%	27	87	22%	37%			12.2	77	93	$12
1st Half	7	2	0	75	62	3.46	4.18	1.25	689	609	702	24.2	2.9	7.4	2.6	60%	9%	50	20	30	29%	76%	13%	13	89	31%	31%			8.3	84	100	$13
2nd Half	7	3	0	73	58	3.93	4.23	1.30	743	735	744	22.0	3.2	7.1	2.2	62%	9%	50	25	25	28%	76%	22%	14	85	14%	43%			3.9	70	84	$10
18 Proj	9	7	0	131	108	4.06	4.26	1.32	741	652	762	23.6	3.0	7.5	2.5	62%	10%	49	21	30	30%	74%	16%	23						4.8	81	97	$4

JOCK THOMPSON

Salazar,Danny

Age: 28	Th: R	Role: SP	Health: D	LIMA Plan: A	
			PT/Exp: A	Rand Var: +5	
Ht: 6' 0"	Wt: 195	Type: Pwr	Consist: A	MM: 3503	

Shoulder and elbow injuries—the latter a repeat from '16—cut his season short again. Ctl issues carried over, but Dom surge offset the impact. Career-long HR issues were exposed by juiced ball. 2nd half xERA shows the potential, and the base skills can't be ignored, even as health and volatile IP cloud future.

Yr Tm	W	L	Sv	IP	K	ERA	xERA	WHIP	oOPS	vL	vR	BF/G	Ctl	Dom	Cmd	FpK	SwK	G	L	F	H%	S%	hr/f	GS	APC	DOM%	DIS%	Sv%	LI	RAR	BPV	BPX	R$
13 CLE *	8	8	1	145	176	3.08	2.86	1.11	655	588	733	18.4	2.4	10.9	4.6	67%	15%	34	26	40	32%	75%	14%	10	82	20%	0%			14.0	150	195	$14
14 CLE *	10	14	0	171	184	4.25	4.63	1.43	751	696	786	23.4	3.3	9.7	3.0	59%	12%	34	23	42	35%	73%	10%	20	93	30%	25%			-10.7	89	106	-$2
15 CLE	14	10	0	185	195	3.45	3.44	1.13	673	724	628	25.2	2.6	9.5	3.7	59%	12%	44	19	37	29%	74%	12%	30	102	33%	17%			11.6	123	147	$18
16 CLE	11	6	0	137	161	3.87	3.75	1.34	697	628	755	23.4	4.1	10.6	2.6	54%	12%	48	17	35	32%	74%	13%	25	96	36%	28%			5.5	104	124	$8
17 CLE	5	6	0	103	145	4.28	3.38	1.34	721	780	671	19.1	3.8	12.7	3.3	60%	17%	39	25	36	35%	72%	16%	19	79	26%	16%	0	0.67	1.0	141	170	$3
1st Half	3	5	0	55	77	5.40	3.82	1.58	843	976	728	20.8	4.6	12.6	2.8	58%	16%	37	28	35	38%	71%	22%	10	86	10%	20%	0	0.67	-7.1	118	142	-$3
2nd Half	2	1	0	48	68	3.00	2.91	1.06	569	536	596	17.3	3.0	12.8	4.3	63%	18%	42	22	36	32%	73%	8%	9	71	44%	11%	0	0.68	8.0	168	202	$10
18 Proj	9	7	0	145	184	3.71	3.53	1.24	673	675	671	20.1	3.5	11.4	3.3	59%	15%	42	22	36	32%	74%	13%	29						11.6	131	158	$11

Sale,Chris

Age: 29	Th: L	Role: SP	Health: B	LIMA Plan: C	
			PT/Exp: A	Rand Var: 0	
Ht: 6' 6"	Wt: 180	Type: Pwr	Consist: B	MM: 5505	

A year after trading Ks for efficiency, he put up only the 2nd 300-K season since '02 with the same APC. Almost a lock for 200 IP at this point. His excellence comes from pairing such a brilliant Ctl with his insane Dom totals, and DOM% keeps volatility in check. With Kershaw's health, perhaps he's now the #1 SP?

Yr Tm	W	L	Sv	IP	K	ERA	xERA	WHIP	oOPS	vL	vR	BF/G	Ctl	Dom	Cmd	FpK	SwK	G	L	F	H%	S%	hr/f	GS	APC	DOM%	DIS%	Sv%	LI	RAR	BPV	BPX	R$
13 CHW	11	14	0	214	226	3.07	2.94	1.07	636	360	699	28.9	1.9	9.5	4.9	63%	11%	47	21	32	30%	76%	13%	30	108	70%	10%			21.2	144	187	$23
14 CHW	12	4	0	174	208	2.17	2.81	0.97	567	393	608	26.3	2.0	10.8	5.3	67%	14%	41	18	41	29%	81%	8%	26	106	58%	4%			33.7	158	188	$27
15 CHW	13	11	0	209	274	3.41	2.74	1.09	649	610	657	27.5	1.8	11.8	6.5	67%	15%	43	22	35	34%	73%	13%	31	107	65%	10%			14.3	185	220	$23
16 CHW	17	10	0	227	233	3.34	3.43	1.04	651	585	663	28.3	1.8	9.3	5.2	62%	12%	41	21	38	29%	73%	12%	32	107	66%	13%			23.9	137	163	$29
17 BOS	17	8	0	214	308	2.90	2.79	0.97	603	531	617	26.6	1.8	12.9	7.2	67%	15%	39	20	41	32%	76%	12%	32	107	69%	3%			38.6	201	241	$40
1st Half	11	3	0	121	166	2.61	2.82	0.90	548	571	544	27.5	1.6	12.4	7.5	67%	17%	37	22	41	31%	74%	8%	17	109	88%	0%			26.0	193	232	$50
2nd Half	6	5	0	94	142	3.27	2.75	1.07	671	495	711	25.5	2.0	13.6	6.8	67%	14%	41	18	41	34%	78%	17%	15	105	47%	7%			12.6	210	252	$26
18 Proj	17	10	0	222	288	3.11	3.04	1.02	632	532	651	25.9	1.8	11.7	6.3	65%	14%	41	20	39	31%	75%	13%	33						34.2	179	215	$34

Samardzija,Jeff

Age: 33	Th: R	Role: SP	Health: A	LIMA Plan: B	
			PT/Exp: A	Rand Var: +3	
Ht: 6' 5"	Wt: 225	Type:	Consist: A	MM: 2205	

Great example of how HR can sink a SP: 1.5 HR/9 overshadowed an insane 9.2 Cmd in first 20 starts for a 5.05 ERA. What he'd give for a consistent +70% strand rate. Stable IP, FpK, and SwK fuel 200+ IP a year with an elite reliability profile. Has developed into a true workhorse and that, along with xERA, says keep investing.

Yr Tm	W	L	Sv	IP	K	ERA	xERA	WHIP	oOPS	vL	vR	BF/G	Ctl	Dom	Cmd	FpK	SwK	G	L	F	H%	S%	hr/f	GS	APC	DOM%	DIS%	Sv%	LI	RAR	BPV	BPX	R$
13 CHC	8	13	0	214	214	4.34	3.49	1.35	736	783	695	27.7	3.3	9.0	2.7	60%	11%	48	20	31	32%	70%	13%	33	105	33%	18%			-12.5	100	130	$1
14 2TM	7	13	0	220	202	2.99	3.05	1.07	646	662	631	26.6	1.8	8.3	4.7	65%	12%	50	19	31	29%	75%	11%	33	101	58%	9%			20.3	129	154	$19
15 CHW	11	13	0	214	163	4.96	4.25	1.29	765	839	689	28.4	2.1	6.9	3.3	62%	10%	39	21	40	31%	64%	11%	32	104	28%	28%			-26.4	85	101	-$2
16 SF	12	11	0	203	167	3.81	4.00	1.20	710	780	639	25.9	2.4	7.4	3.1	63%	10%	46	20	34	29%	72%	12%	32	100	28%	34%			9.6	93	110	$14
17 SF	9	15	0	208	205	4.42	3.67	1.14	734	771	692	26.5	1.4	8.9	6.4	65%	11%	41	22	36	31%	65%	14%	32	102	41%	16%			-1.6	141	170	$14
1st Half	3	9	0	105	117	4.63	3.18	1.14	749	789	706	26.9	1.1	10.0	9.0	63%	12%	43	25	31	34%	63%	18%	16	103	56%	13%			-3.5	172	206	$12
2nd Half	6	6	0	103	88	4.21	4.18	1.13	718	754	676	26.1	1.7	7.7	4.6	67%	10%	40	19	42	29%	67%	11%	16	101	25%	19%			1.9	111	134	$15
18 Proj	10	13	0	203	182	4.25	3.97	1.18	727	778	674	25.9	1.9	8.1	4.3	64%	10%	43	21	36	30%	68%	13%	31						2.7	115	139	$11

Sanchez,Aaron

Age: 26	Th: R	Role: SP	Health: F	LIMA Plan: C	
			PT/Exp: B	Rand Var: -1	
Ht: 6' 4"	Wt: 220	Type: Pwr GB	Consist: C	MM: 1103	

Juiced ball fueled a rash of blister issues and he "led" the league with three blister-related DL trips, tanking his season. Raw stuff is great (95 mph heat, hammer curve), but hasn't fully translated (weak SwK, modest FpK). Cost will sink, but use 2016 xERA as a guide and heed health risk when buying.

Yr Tm	W	L	Sv	IP	K	ERA	xERA	WHIP	oOPS	vL	vR	BF/G	Ctl	Dom	Cmd	FpK	SwK	G	L	F	H%	S%	hr/f	GS	APC	DOM%	DIS%	Sv%	LI	RAR	BPV	BPX	R$
13																																	
14 TOR *	5	9	3	133	102	3.96	3.47	1.37	367	469	306	12.1	4.5	6.9	1.5	53%	7%	66	15	20	28%	71%	6%	0	19			100	1.17	-3.6	65	77	$0
15 TOR	7	6	0	92	61	3.22	4.08	1.28	666	878	435	9.3	4.3	5.9	1.4	53%	7%	61	18	22	25%	78%	16%	11	35	0%	45%	0	1.08	8.5	30	36	$4
16 TOR	15	2	0	192	161	3.00	3.77	1.17	625	657	592	26.3	3.0	7.5	2.6	61%	9%	54	20	25	28%	77%	11%	30	97	43%	17%			28.2	88	105	$21
17 TOR	1	3	0	36	24	4.25	5.70	1.72	836	654	955	20.9	5.0	6.0	1.2	59%	6%	48	24	29	32%	80%	17%	8	77	13%	75%			0.5	-1	-1	-$6
1st Half	0	1	0	24	18	3.33	4.91	1.27	719	661	753	20.6	3.3	6.7	2.0	62%	8%	40	23	37	26%	81%	14%	5	76	20%	60%			3.1	48	57	-$4
2nd Half	1	2	0	12	6	6.17	7.72	2.66	1032	640	1338	21.3	8.5	4.6	0.5	55%	3%	60	26	15	40%	79%	29%	3	78	0%	100%			-2.6	-108	-130	-$10
18 Proj	8	8	0	174	136	3.37	4.21	1.23	672	767	594	23.5	3.4	7.0	2.0	59%	9%	54	19	27	27%	76%	14%	27						21.1	65	79	$12

Sanchez,Anibal

Age: 34	Th: R	Role: RP	Health: D	LIMA Plan: C	
			PT/Exp: B	Rand Var: +5	
Ht: 6' 0"	Wt: 205	Type: Pwr	Consist: C	MM: 1301	

3-7, 6.41 ERA in 105 IP at DET. After leading MLB in HR/9 from 2013-14 (0.4), he has an MLB-worst 1.8 since then. Cmd got worse and FB rate went up, but hr/f shows why the jump was so stark. Solid FpK and SwK losing out to horrid H% and S% as stuff wanes. Add in failing health and a rebound is unlikely.

Yr Tm	W	L	Sv	IP	K	ERA	xERA	WHIP	oOPS	vL	vR	BF/G	Ctl	Dom	Cmd	FpK	SwK	G	L	F	H%	S%	hr/f	GS	APC	DOM%	DIS%	Sv%	LI	RAR	BPV	BPX	R$
13 DET	14	8	0	182	202	2.57	3.08	1.15	616	673	548	25.7	2.7	10.0	3.7	62%	13%	45	22	33	32%	79%	6%	29	103	55%	14%			29.1	131	170	$22
14 DET	8	5	0	126	102	3.43	3.58	1.10	597	562	648	23.4	2.1	7.3	3.4	60%	10%	46	19	35	29%	67%	3%	21	95	33%	10%	0	0.75	4.9	97	116	$8
15 DET	10	10	0	157	138	4.99	4.11	1.28	768	681	866	26.4	2.8	7.9	2.8	65%	10%	40	21	39	29%	66%	16%	25	101	40%	24%			-19.9	85	101	-$1
16 DET	7	13	0	153	135	5.87	4.59	1.46	828	771	888	19.1	3.1	7.9	2.5	67%	10%	40	19	41	32%	64%	16%	26	74	12%	38%	0	0.84	-31.8	77	91	-$10
17 DET *	3	9	0	121	118	6.53	7.05	1.64	906	822	989	16.9	2.6	8.8	3.3	61%	10%	36	25	40	37%	66%	19%	17	66	12%	35%	0	0.58	-32.4	46	55	-$15
1st Half	0	2	0	54	50	6.63	7.00	1.64	898	749	1049	13.4	3.2	8.4	2.6	64%	9%	34	19	47	35%	66%	18%	3	47	33%	33%	0	0.39	-15.1	26	31	-$17
2nd Half	3	7	0	67	68	6.45	4.36	1.64	910	862	958	21.9	2.1	9.1	4.3	59%	11%	36	28	36	39%	66%	20%	14	85	7%	36%			-17.3	121	145	-$13
18 Proj	4	7	0	102	95	5.78	4.57	1.49	849	775	928	19.0	2.7	8.4	3.1	63%	10%	38	22	40	34%	66%	17%	21						-17.8	95	114	-$8

Santana,Ervin

Age: 35	Th: R	Role: SP	Health: B	LIMA Plan: D+	
			PT/Exp: A	Rand Var: -3	
Ht: 6' 2"	Wt: 175	Type:	Consist: A	MM: 1105	

One of those workhorses who never really gets his due. Perhaps xERA and early career volatility have kept interest at bay and age will likely do the same going forward. Hit rate no doubt aided his 2017, but a top-25 BA-against since 2013 shows his skill. Cost will offset potential regression. Buy for the high floor.

Yr Tm	W	L	Sv	IP	K	ERA	xERA	WHIP	oOPS	vL	vR	BF/G	Ctl	Dom	Cmd	FpK	SwK	G	L	F	H%	S%	hr/f	GS	APC	DOM%	DIS%	Sv%	LI	RAR	BPV	BPX	R$
13 KC	9	10	0	211	161	3.24	3.66	1.14	668	675	659	26.8	2.2	6.9	3.2	66%	10%	46	21	33	27%	77%	12%	32	100	44%	16%			16.2	89	116	$15
14 ATL	14	10	0	196	179	3.95	3.57	1.31	724	763	676	26.4	2.9	8.2	2.8	63%	12%	43	25	33	32%	71%	9%	31	96	32%	29%			-5.0	91	108	$5
15 MIN *	10	5	0	129	90	3.79	4.09	1.31	729	804	651	26.6	2.9	6.3	2.2	61%	10%	41	22	38	29%	74%	10%	17	99	47%	35%			2.7	56	67	$4
16 MIN	7	11	0	181	149	3.38	4.20	1.22	682	667	697	24.9	2.6	7.4	2.8	59%	10%	43	22	36	29%	76%	10%	30	98	27%	27%			18.2	83	99	$12
17 MIN	16	8	0	211	167	3.28	4.54	1.13	678	646	705	26.2	2.6	7.1	2.7	64%	11%	41	16	42	25%	78%	12%	33	98	27%	27%			28.1	77	92	$25
1st Half	10	5	0	111	86	3.07	4.61	1.09	649	592	701	26.5	3.1	7.0	2.3	61%	9%	43	15	42	22%	80%	13%	17	100	29%	18%			17.7	63	76	$30
2nd Half	6	3	0	100	81	3.51	4.47	1.17	710	712	709	25.8	2.1	7.3	3.5	67%	12%	39	18	43	28%	76%	11%	16	96	25%	38%			10.5	93	111	$19
18 Proj	12	8	0	189	149	3.68	4.47	1.19	695	695	695	25.3	2.6	7.1	2.8	63%	11%	42	19	39	28%	74%	11%	30						15.9	78	94	$14

Santiago,Hector

Age: 30	Th: L	Role: RP	Health: F	LIMA Plan: D	
			PT/Exp: B	Rand Var: +2	
Ht: 6' 0"	Wt: 215	Type: Pwr xFB	Consist: B	MM: 0101	

4-8, 5.63 ERA in 70 IP at MIN. Shoulder and back injuries limited IP while his severe flyball lean was exploited by the HR explosion. SwK always warned that Dom was unsturdy while FpK hinted that below average Ctl could be even worse and the bill finally came due. Just nothing here to feel good about.

Yr Tm	W	L	Sv	IP	K	ERA	xERA	WHIP	oOPS	vL	vR	BF/G	Ctl	Dom	Cmd	FpK	SwK	G	L	F	H%	S%	hr/f	GS	APC	DOM%	DIS%	Sv%	LI	RAR	BPV	BPX	R$
13 CHW	4	9	0	149	137	3.56	4.38	1.40	739	686	762	19.3	4.3	8.3	1.9	57%	9%	36	20	44	30%	78%	9%	23	79	26%	35%	0	0.88	5.5	46	59	$1
14 LAA	6	9	0	127	108	3.75	4.53	1.36	698	606	732	18.1	3.7	7.6	2.0	56%	8%	31	19	50	29%	76%	8%	24	76	8%	50%	0	0.80	-0.1	45	54	$0
15 LAA	9	9	0	181	162	3.59	4.74	1.26	723	633	752	23.5	3.5	8.1	2.3	57%	9%	30	16	54	27%	78%	10%	32	96	19%	31%	0	0.74	8.4	58	69	$9
16 2AL	13	10	0	182	144	4.70	5.26	1.36	774	750	780	23.8	3.9	7.1	1.8	55%	9%	34	16	50	27%	71%	12%	33	96	18%	48%			-11.4	35	41	$2
17 MIN *	5	10	0	94	68	6.54	6.12	1.63	782	1521	627	19.0	5.0	6.6	1.3	56%	8%	30	18	51	29%	64%	13%	14	82	14%	50%	0	0.84	-25.4	5	6	-$12
1st Half	4	7	0	70	50	5.14	5.08	1.41	781	1537	629	19.7	4.2	6.5	1.5	55%	8%	31	18	51	26%	70%	14%	13	84	15%	46%	0	0.84	-6.8	18	22	-$7
2nd Half	1	3	0	24	18	10.63	9.15	2.30	804	1350	573	17.5	7.5	6.8	0.9	63%	9%	17	25	58	37%	55%	0%	1	58	0%	100%			-18.6	-24	-29	-$24
18 Proj	6	10	0	116	91	5.87	6.09	1.64	862	993	824	19.7	5.0	7.1	1.4	56%	8%	32	18	51	30%	68%	13%	25						-21.6	2	3	-$12

PAUL SPORER

Saupold,Warwick		Health	C	LIMA Plan	D
Age: 28	Th: R Role RP	PT/Exp	D	Rand Var	0
Ht: 6' 1"	Wt: 195 Type	Consist	A	MM	0000

3-2, 4.88 ERA in 63 IP at DET. It's almost as if the skills from his 10 MLB IP in '16 weren't indicative of his true talent. Instead, he's the definition of "mop-up reliever": poor Ctl and SwK, mediocre FpK, neutral GB/FB lean, and his MiLB HR suppression didn't show up (0.7 MiLB, 1.3 MLB). No real upside, either.

Yr Tm	W	L	Sv	IP	K	ERA	xERA	WHIP	oOPS	vL	vR	BF/G	Ctl	Dom	Cmd	FpK	SwK	G	L	F	H%	S%	hr/f	GS	APC	DOM%	DIS%	Sv%	LI	RAR	BPV	BPX	R$
13 aa	7	6	0	129	67	3.98	4.76	1.51				25.4	3.6	4.6	1.3						30%	76%								-1.8	26	34	-$4
14 aa	8	11	0	140	98	5.58	5.21	1.59				22.9	4.2	6.3	1.5						32%	66%								-31.8	36	43	-$14
15 a/a	6	8	1	124	72	5.02	4.34	1.48				18.3	3.3	5.3	1.6						32%	65%								-16.2	49	59	-$8
16 DET *	8	3	0	84	49	3.68	4.49	1.51	940	686	1099	15.1	3.0	5.2	1.7	55%	12%	54	26	20	33%	75%	0%	0	26			0	0.41	5.2	52	62	$0
17 DET *	5	2	0	103	69	4.69	5.23	1.61	779	827	752	8.8	4.5	6.0	1.3	59%	8%	43	20	37	32%	73%	13%	0	24			0	0.68	-4.2	32	38	-$6
1st Half	3	1	0	68	43	3.53	4.43	1.46	634	871	526	12.7	3.6	5.7	1.6	64%	11%	48	15	37	31%	78%	10%	0	25			0	0.61	7.0	45	54	-$1
2nd Half	2	1	0	35	26	6.94	6.48	1.91	874	803	919	5.9	6.2	6.7	1.1	55%	7%	40	24	36	34%	66%	14%	0	24			0	0.72	-11.2	-28	-34	-$16
18 Proj	4	2	0	58	37	4.94	5.68	1.62	801	841	779	10.1	4.2	5.8	1.4	58%	8%	43	20	37	33%	70%	8%	0						-4.2	12	15	-$6

Scherzer,Max		Health	B	LIMA Plan	C
Age: 33	Th: R Role SP	PT/Exp	A	Rand Var	-3
Ht: 6' 3"	Wt: 210 Type Pwr xFB	Consist	A	MM	4505

His first DL stint since '09 didn't prevent a 9th straight 30-start season and his insane 1st half curbed any effects of the 2nd half dip in Cmd. HRs remain the fly in the ointment, though most are solos (68% since '15). Age is creeping, but skills are ironclad. Brilliant BPV and stable IP keep him atop SP lists.

Yr Tm	W	L	Sv	IP	K	ERA	xERA	WHIP	oOPS	vL	vR	BF/G	Ctl	Dom	Cmd	FpK	SwK	G	L	F	H%	S%	hr/f	GS	APC	DOM%	DIS%	Sv%	LI	RAR	BPV	BPX	R$
13 DET	21	3	0	214	240	2.90	3.16	0.97	583	645	494	26.1	2.4	10.1	4.3	64%	13%	36	19	45	27%	73%	8%	32	106	63%	3%			25.6	132	172	$33
14 DET	18	5	0	220	252	3.15	3.24	1.18	663	685	629	27.4	2.6	10.3	4.0	63%	12%	37	22	42	33%	76%	8%	33	110	39%	6%			16.2	131	156	$20
15 WAS	14	12	0	229	276	2.79	3.00	0.92	600	657	538	27.2	1.3	10.9	8.1	71%	16%	36	19	46	29%	76%	11%	33	102	58%	9%			32.9	173	207	$37
16 WAS	20	7	0	228	284	2.96	3.33	0.97	619	757	477	26.5	2.2	11.2	5.1	65%	16%	33	19	48	27%	77%	12%	34	105	65%	12%			34.7	153	182	$38
17 WAS	16	6	0	201	268	2.51	3.13	0.90	565	690	425	25.2	2.5	12.0	4.9	65%	16%	37	17	47	26%	79%	11%	31	100	65%	3%			45.7	165	198	$41
1st Half	9	5	0	114	151	2.06	2.96	0.78	520	632	394	27.0	1.9	12.0	6.3	65%	17%	37	15	48	24%	82%	10%	16	107	81%	0%			32.2	179	214	$53
2nd Half	7	1	0	87	117	3.10	3.35	1.06	623	761	463	23.2	3.2	12.1	3.8	65%	16%	36	20	44	28%	76%	12%	15	93	47%	7%			13.5	145	174	$26
18 Proj	16	7	0	203	259	2.98	3.37	0.99	604	715	478	24.8	2.6	11.5	4.5	66%	16%	35	18	46	27%	75%	11%	31						34.5	151	182	$33

Senzatela,Antonio		Health	A	LIMA Plan	B+
Age: 23	Th: R Role RP	PT/Exp	D	Rand Var	+2
Ht: 6' 1"	Wt: 180 Type GB	Consist	B	MM	1101

A solid debut given that he pitches in Coors and skipped AAA, but as with so many COL SPs, only the road starts were usable (5.15/4.02 home/road ERA). Decent GB lean can't mask subpar Dom and Cmd while SwK offers no hope for more. Showed mettle, but until that's a fantasy category, it's a pass.

Yr Tm	W	L	Sv	IP	K	ERA	xERA	WHIP	oOPS	vL	vR	BF/G	Ctl	Dom	Cmd	FpK	SwK	G	L	F	H%	S%	hr/f	GS	APC	DOM%	DIS%	Sv%	LI	RAR	BPV	BPX	R$
13																																	
14																																	
15																																	
16 aa	4	1	0	35	22	2.79	3.45	1.29				20.3	2.6	5.6	2.1						30%	79%								6.0	70	83	$0
17 COL	10	5	0	135	102	4.68	4.36	1.30	756	745	767	15.7	3.1	6.8	2.2	62%	7%	50	22	28	28%	67%	16%	20	62	10%	50%	0	0.64	-5.3	66	79	$3
1st Half	9	3	0	90	65	4.68	4.36	1.25	762	801	720	23.4	2.8	6.5	2.3	64%	7%	49	22	29	27%	67%	19%	15	91	13%	33%	0	0.72	-3.6	68	81	$8
2nd Half	1	2	0	44	37	4.67	4.37	1.40	744	607	842	9.5	3.9	7.5	1.9	58%	7%	53	21	26	31%	66%	9%	5	38	0%	100%	0	0.57	-1.7	62	74	-$6
18 Proj	8	4	0	102	74	4.12	4.41	1.32	740	680	791	14.6	3.1	6.5	2.1	60%	7%	51	22	27	30%	70%	11%	13						2.9	64	77	$2

Severino,Luis		Health	A	LIMA Plan	C
Age: 24	Th: R Role SP	PT/Exp	B	Rand Var	+1
Ht: 6' 2"	Wt: 215 Type Pwr	Consist	D	MM	4405

Prospect growth isn't linear! A posterboy for the mantra, this fantasy afterthought last spring blossomed into an ace by refining base skills. Results not only dominated throughout '17, but left top 10 FpK, SwK, and GB rate to bet on for '18. xERA agrees. Postseason rebound showed maturity. Pay the extra dollar.

Yr Tm	W	L	Sv	IP	K	ERA	xERA	WHIP	oOPS	vL	vR	BF/G	Ctl	Dom	Cmd	FpK	SwK	G	L	F	H%	S%	hr/f	GS	APC	DOM%	DIS%	Sv%	LI	RAR	BPV	BPX	R$
13																																	
14 aa	2	2	0	25	26	2.82	2.61	1.10				16.3	2.1	9.5	4.5						32%	75%								2.8	148	176	$0
15 NYY *	14	5	0	162	143	3.07	2.97	1.16	705	705	702	21.5	2.8	8.0	2.9	63%	10%	50	20	30	29%	75%	17%	11	93	9%	27%			17.7	97	115	$17
16 NYY *	11	9	0	148	135	5.25	4.75	1.43	812	747	872	18.0	2.7	8.2	3.1	59%	9%	46	24	31	35%	64%	17%	11	58	9%	64%	0	0.70	-19.4	80	95	-$4
17 NYY	14	6	0	193	230	2.98	3.11	1.04	603	667	550	25.3	2.4	10.7	4.5	65%	13%	51	19	31	29%	76%	14%	31	99	65%	13%			32.9	158	189	$30
1st Half	5	3	0	94	107	3.15	3.04	1.07	615	671	575	25.3	2.3	10.2	4.5	63%	13%	56	17	27	30%	75%	15%	15	100	60%	20%			14.1	156	187	$25
2nd Half	9	3	0	99	123	2.82	3.18	1.01	592	665	522	25.3	2.5	11.2	4.6	67%	14%	45	21	34	28%	78%	13%	16	99	69%	6%			18.8	158	190	$35
18 Proj	15	9	0	189	210	3.30	3.35	1.14	650	659	641	24.9	2.5	10.0	4.0	63%	11%	48	21	31	31%	75%	13%	30						24.5	139	168	$23

Sewald,Paul		Health	A	LIMA Plan	C
Age: 28	Th: R Role RP	PT/Exp	D	Rand Var	+1
Ht: 6' 3"	Wt: 205 Type Pwr xFB	Consist	B	MM	1300

A perfectly cromulent middle reliever with too many flaws to close (vL issues, below average velocity, too many HRs), but enough skills to get another shot (vR dominance, strong SwK, solid Cmd) at 50-60 IP. Could be pivotal in your 15-team NL East-only league, I guess.

Yr Tm	W	L	Sv	IP	K	ERA	xERA	WHIP	oOPS	vL	vR	BF/G	Ctl	Dom	Cmd	FpK	SwK	G	L	F	H%	S%	hr/f	GS	APC	DOM%	DIS%	Sv%	LI	RAR	BPV	BPX	R$
13																																	
14																																	
15 aa	3	0	24	51	46	2.13	2.27	0.99				4.4	1.8	8.1	4.4						27%	81%								11.6	136	162	$15
16 aaa	5	3	19	66	67	3.29	4.06	1.29				4.8	3.0	9.2	3.1						31%	80%								7.3	89	105	$10
17 NYM	0	6	0	65	69	4.55	4.25	1.21	706	826	627	4.8	2.9	9.5	3.3	61%	12%	32	22	46	30%	65%	10%	0	20			0	0.89	-1.5	103	124	-$1
1st Half	0	2	0	33	41	4.32	3.70	1.35	759	928	631	5.3	2.4	11.1	4.6	64%	12%	31	28	40	38%	69%	8%	0	22			0	0.60	0.2	143	172	-$2
2nd Half	0	4	0	32	28	4.78	4.85	1.06	646	683	624	4.4	3.4	7.9	2.3	58%	12%	33	16	51	21%	59%	11%	0	18			0	1.16	-1.7	62	74	-$1
18 Proj	2	4	0	58	58	3.92	4.33	1.19	699	806	631	4.6	2.8	9.0	3.2	60%	12%	32	21	47	29%	71%	10%	0						3.1	96	116	$0

Shaw,Bryan		Health	A	LIMA Plan	A
Age: 30	Th: R Role RP	PT/Exp	C	Rand Var	0
Ht: 6' 1"	Wt: 220 Type Pwr GB	Consist	A	MM	3300

Added velocity to his cutter for 2nd straight season (94 mph) while 2016 Ctl issues regressed back to career levels thanks to a 1.5 bb/9 in final 50 appearances (supported by 2nd half FpK gains). If it sticks, he becomes a high-volume (MLB-high 359 relief IP since '13) middle RP force with strong Dom, SwK, and GB rate.

Yr Tm	W	L	Sv	IP	K	ERA	xERA	WHIP	oOPS	vL	vR	BF/G	Ctl	Dom	Cmd	FpK	SwK	G	L	F	H%	S%	hr/f	GS	APC	DOM%	DIS%	Sv%	LI	RAR	BPV	BPX	R$
13 CLE	7	3	1	75	73	3.24	3.58	1.17	586	678	506	4.5	3.4	8.8	2.6	57%	11%	43	25	33	29%	73%	6%	0	18			20	0.99	5.8	88	115	$5
14 CLE	5	5	2	76	64	2.59	3.62	1.09	602	776	493	3.9	2.6	7.5	2.9	59%	11%	46	18	36	27%	79%	8%	0	16			22	1.37	10.8	90	107	$7
15 CLE	3	3	2	64	54	2.95	3.81	1.22	693	673	704	3.6	2.7	7.6	2.8	62%	11%	46	24	31	29%	81%	14%	0	14			33	1.21	8.0	89	105	$3
16 CLE	2	5	1	67	69	3.24	3.58	1.26	686	756	637	3.7	3.8	9.3	2.5	53%	12%	54	19	27	29%	79%	17%	0	15			25	1.13	7.8	98	116	$2
17 CLE	4	6	3	77	73	3.52	3.43	1.21	653	586	693	3.9	2.6	8.6	3.3	58%	13%	56	22	22	32%	72%	11%	0	15			50	1.07	7.9	119	142	$5
1st Half	2	3	2	40	35	2.95	3.86	1.29	657	575	698	4.0	4.1	7.9	1.9	54%	12%	58	20	22	29%	76%	4%	0	16			67	0.77	6.9	68	82	$5
2nd Half	2	3	1	37	38	4.14	3.01	1.14	648	595	682	3.9	1.0	9.2	9.5	61%	13%	54	24	22	34%	66%	17%	0	15			33	1.38	1.0	172	206	$5
18 Proj	3	4	0	58	58	3.06	3.50	1.17	630	632	628	3.7	2.8	9.0	3.3	58%	12%	52	22	26	30%	76%	11%	0						9.3	117	141	$3

Sherfy,Jimmie		Health	A	LIMA Plan	A
Age: 26	Th: R Role RP	PT/Exp	F	Rand Var	-3
Ht: 6' 0"	Wt: 175 Type Pwr	Consist	C	MM	2310

2-0, 0.00 ERA in 11 IP at ARI. Strong Dom and poor Ctl underscored his MiLB career prior to '17 before mechanical adjustments yielded major Ctl gains (including just 2 BB in his 11 MLB IP). High-effort delivery and limited arsenal make him a ROOGY with upside if Ctl gains stick and his 11.7 MiLB Dom shows up.

Yr Tm	W	L	Sv	IP	K	ERA	xERA	WHIP	oOPS	vL	vR	BF/G	Ctl	Dom	Cmd	FpK	SwK	G	L	F	H%	S%	hr/f	GS	APC	DOM%	DIS%	Sv%	LI	RAR	BPV	BPX	R$
13																																	
14 aa	3	1	1	38	38	6.16	4.85	1.52				4.5	4.3	9.0	2.1						34%	60%								-11.3	65	78	-$5
15 aa	1	6	2	50	41	8.58	5.63	1.82				5.2	5.3	7.5	1.4						37%	50%								-28.3	49	59	-$15
16 a/a	3	4	22	43	47	4.76	3.65	1.20				4.3	4.0	9.9	2.4						25%	66%								-3.0	76	90	$8
17 ARI *	4	1	21	60	57	2.83	2.65	0.99	418	258	492	4.1	1.8	8.7	4.8	63%	8%	54	4	42	27%	76%	0%	0	14			88	0.75	11.2	137	164	$15
1st Half	2	0	10	30	30	1.64	2.46	0.85				4.1	0.9	9.0	10.2						25%	94%	0%	0						10.2	244	292	$18
2nd Half	2	1	11	29	27	4.07	2.84	1.13	418	258	492	4.1	2.7	8.4	3.1	63%	8%	54	4	42	29%	64%	0%	0	14			85	0.75	1.1	105	126	$12
18 Proj	4	3	8	58	58	3.72	3.87	1.16				4.3	2.6	9.0	3.5	61%	9%	41	22	37	29%	72%	12%	0						4.6	111	134	$5

PAUL SPORER

Shields,James

Age: 36	Th: R	Role SP	Health D	LIMA Plan D+
Ht: 6' 3"	Wt: 215	Type Pwr FB	PT/Exp A	Rand Var +2
			Consist B	MM 0203

Ace, then innings-eater, now further devolved into... what, exactly? Strained lat cost most of 1st half, then shelved late due to bad knees. In between, skills were little better than the year before. Still owed a tidy $21 million in 2018, so he'll be around. Just don't let him anywhere near YOUR roster. DN: DFA

Yr Tm	W	L	Sv	IP	K	ERA	xERA	WHIP	oOPS	vL	vR	BF/G	Ctl	Dom	Cmd	FpK	SwK	G	L	F	H%	S%	hr/f	GS	APC	DOM%	DIS%	Sv%	LI	RAR	BPV	BPX	R$
13 KC	13	9	0	229	196	3.15	3.72	1.24	678	614	753	27.8	2.7	7.7	2.9	58%	10%	42	23	35	30%	77%	9%	34	108	32%	18%			20.2	87	113	$16
14 KC	14	8	0	227	180	3.21	3.56	1.18	702	698	706	27.6	1.7	7.1	4.1	63%	10%	45	21	34	30%	76%	10%	34	107	38%	21%			14.8	104	124	$15
15 SD	13	7	0	202	216	3.91	3.67	1.33	776	890	660	26.1	3.6	9.6	2.7	60%	13%	45	21	34	31%	77%	18%	33	101	30%	18%			1.2	99	117	$8
16 2 TM	6	19	0	182	135	5.85	5.26	1.60	891	866	915	24.9	4.1	6.7	1.6	54%	9%	40	21	38	31%	69%	18%	33	95	9%	42%			-37.1	29	34	-$17
17 CHW	5	7	0	117	103	5.23	5.15	1.44	824	929	724	24.6	4.1	7.9	1.9	58%	10%	38	18	44	28%	71%	17%	21	96	5%	33%			-12.6	49	58	-$4
1st Half	2	1	0	32	26	3.98	5.75	1.42	795	959	647	23.5	4.8	7.4	1.5	55%	9%	33	17	51	25%	82%	15%	6	91	0%	33%			1.5	13	16	-$4
2nd Half	3	6	0	85	77	5.70	4.94	1.45	835	918	753	25.0	3.8	8.1	2.1	59%	11%	40	19	41	29%	67%	19%	15	98	7%	33%			-14.1	62	74	-$5
18 Proj	**7**	**9**	**0**	**145**	**125**	**4.87**	**4.96**	**1.44**	**819**	**881**	**758**	**24.3**	**3.9**	**7.8**	**2.0**	**57%**	**10%**	**40**	**20**	**41**	**29%**	**73%**	**17%**	**25**						**-9.2**	**53**	**64**	**-$3**

Shoemaker,Matthew

Age: 31	Th: R	Role SP	Health F	LIMA Plan B+
Ht: 6' 2"	Wt: 225	Type FB	PT/Exp B	Rand Var +1
			Consist B	MM 1201

Another major injury. Expected to be ready for spring after surgery to release radial nerve in forearm. Before that, a mixed bag: kept solid K rate, and FpK points to Ctl rebound. But gopheritis return more than canceled out the good. The skill to watch: G/F ratio. When less than 1, he's had problems. (Now, note projection.)

Yr Tm	W	L	Sv	IP	K	ERA	xERA	WHIP	oOPS	vL	vR	BF/G	Ctl	Dom	Cmd	FpK	SwK	G	L	F	H%	S%	hr/f	GS	APC	DOM%	DIS%	Sv%	LI	RAR	BPV	BPX	R$
13 LAA *	11	13	0	189	131	4.25	4.70	1.35	328	490	0	26.3	1.3	6.2	4.6	53%	10%	42	25	33	34%	71%	0%	1	93	0%	0%			-9.1	99	128	$0
14 LAA *	17	4	0	162	144	3.47	3.54	1.17	658	702	610	20.2	1.8	8.0	4.5	63%	11%	41	20	39	31%	73%	9%	20	78	35%	20%	0	0.81	5.3	121	144	$12
15 LAA	7	10	0	135	116	4.46	4.12	1.26	758	727	791	22.8	2.3	7.7	3.3	60%	10%	39	18	42	29%	71%	14%	24	84	38%	42%	0	0.76	-8.2	93	111	$1
16 LAA	9	13	0	160	143	3.88	3.90	1.23	723	705	745	24.7	1.7	8.0	4.8	68%	13%	40	24	36	32%	71%	10%	27	92	26%	30%			6.1	117	139	$9
17 LAA	6	3	0	78	69	4.52	4.69	1.30	788	791	783	23.3	3.2	8.0	2.5	64%	12%	38	15	47	28%	72%	15%	14	90	21%	36%			-1.5	72	87	$1
1st Half	6	3	0	78	69	4.52	4.69	1.30	788	791	783	23.3	3.2	8.0	2.5	64%	12%	38	15	47	28%	72%	15%	14	90	21%	36%			-1.5	73	87	$1
2nd Half																																	
18 Proj	**6**	**5**	**0**	**94**	**81**	**4.19**	**4.43**	**1.26**	**755**	**747**	**763**	**22.7**	**2.3**	**7.8**	**3.4**	**63%**	**11%**	**39**	**19**	**42**	**30%**	**72%**	**12%**	**17**						**2.0**	**95**	**115**	**$2**

Shreve,Chasen

Age: 27	Th: L	Role RP	Health B	LIMA Plan B+
Ht: 6' 4"	Wt: 195	Type Pwr FB	PT/Exp D	Rand Var 0
			Consist B	MM 1400

Dominated LHB like never before. But faced twice as many righties, and most of his wildness and long-ball problems came against them. It's a path toward LOOGY-dom that many of his ilk have traveled before. It can be a long and lucrative journey, and these days, some marginally valuable fantasy roster filler..

Yr Tm	W	L	Sv	IP	K	ERA	xERA	WHIP	oOPS	vL	vR	BF/G	Ctl	Dom	Cmd	FpK	SwK	G	L	F	H%	S%	hr/f	GS	APC	DOM%	DIS%	Sv%	LI	RAR	BPV	BPX	R$
13 aa	3	1	0	43	24	5.65	4.91	1.73				5.4	4.9	5.1	1.1						34%	65%								-9.4	41	54	-$8
14 ATL *	5	3	9	76	91	2.68	2.68	1.08	526	652	408	4.9	1.8	10.7	6.1	65%	12%	48	16	35	34%	76%	0%	0	14			90	0.47	10.0	185	220	$10
15 NYY	6	2	0	58	64	3.09	4.13	1.41	738	755	727	4.3	5.1	9.9	1.9	53%	12%	46	13	41	28%	86%	16%	0	19			0	1.05	6.3	64	77	$1
16 NYY *	2	1	1	50	49	4.24	3.42	1.11	823	1058	711	3.9	3.8	8.9	2.3	62%	14%	45	15	40	21%	70%	22%	0	15			100	0.69	-0.3	66	79	$1
17 NYY	4	1	0	45	58	3.77	4.33	1.32	712	498	829	4.5	5.0	11.5	2.3	59%	15%	37	17	45	28%	79%	15%	0	19			0	0.93	3.3	88	106	$0
1st Half	2	1	0	22	25	2.91	4.24	1.20	590	604	584	4.2	5.0	10.4	2.1	60%	15%	45	16	38	25%	79%	10%	0	18			0	1.29	3.9	76	91	$1
2nd Half	2	0	0	24	33	4.56	4.39	1.44	815	416	1049	4.8	4.9	12.5	2.5	58%	16%	30	18	52	31%	79%	19%	0	21			0	0.56	-0.6	100	120	$0
18 Proj	**3**	**1**	**0**	**44**	**50**	**3.88**	**4.28**	**1.30**	**724**	**679**	**748**	**4.3**	**4.5**	**10.3**	**2.3**	**59%**	**14%**	**41**	**16**	**43**	**27%**	**77%**	**16%**	**0**						**2.6**	**82**	**99**	**-$1**

Simmons,Shae

Age: 27	Th: R	Role RP	Health F	LIMA Plan C+
Ht: 5' 11"	Wt: 190	Type Pwr	PT/Exp F	Rand Var +5
			Consist C	MM 5510

A flexor strain pretty much ruined 2017 after TJS cost him most of the two prior seasons. So yes, that "F" in Health has been well-earned. But heavy mid-90s sinker was still there in late-season return. We'll go with the same finish here as last year: Has to prove he can stay healthy, but keep him on your radar.

Yr Tm	W	L	Sv	IP	K	ERA	xERA	WHIP	oOPS	vL	vR	BF/G	Ctl	Dom	Cmd	FpK	SwK	G	L	F	H%	S%	hr/f	GS	APC	DOM%	DIS%	Sv%	LI	RAR	BPV	BPX	R$
13																																	
14 ATL *	1	3	15	46	50	2.73	2.39	1.19	598	489	730	3.8	3.7	9.9	2.6	63%	12%	53	25	23	30%	76%	8%	0	14			100	1.36	5.7	121	144	$7
15																																	
16 ATL	0	0	0	7	3	1.35	3.20	0.90	560	286	909	3.6	0.0	4.1	0.0	52%	7%	62	24	14	28%	83%	0%	0	15			0	0.48	2.3	113	134	-$3
17 SEA	0	2	0	8	8	7.04	4.35	1.04	600	286	783	3.3	4.7	9.4	2.0	57%	11%	44	6	50	18%	29%	11%	0	13			0	0.67	-2.5	64	77	-$5
1st Half																																	
2nd Half	0	2	0	8	8	7.04	4.35	1.04	600	286	783	3.3	4.7	9.4	2.0	57%	11%	44	6	50	18%	29%	11%	0	13			0	0.67	-2.5	65	78	-$5
18 Proj	**1**	**3**	**2**	**36**	**44**	**3.04**	**2.87**	**1.30**				**3.6**	**4.1**	**10.8**	**2.6**	**0%**	**0%**				**34%**	**75%**		**0**						**5.9**	**123**	**148**	**$0**

Sims,Lucas

Age: 24	Th: R	Role SP	Health A	LIMA Plan D+
Ht: 6' 2"	Wt: 220	Type Pwr FB	PT/Exp D	Rand Var +1
			Consist D	MM 0300

3-6, 5.62 ERA in 58 IP at ATL. Notable shift for hard-throwing rookie: he didn't throw as hard. It appeared to be an effort to rein in poor control, and it helped. But it also took a bite out of Dom and SwK rates, and the overall result wasn't pretty. Plenty of room to grow, but there's little sign he'll be ready to help in 2018.

Yr Tm	W	L	Sv	IP	K	ERA	xERA	WHIP	oOPS	vL	vR	BF/G	Ctl	Dom	Cmd	FpK	SwK	G	L	F	H%	S%	hr/f	GS	APC	DOM%	DIS%	Sv%	LI	RAR	BPV	BPX	R$
13																																	
14																																	
15 aa	4	2	0	48	51	3.89	2.47	1.31				21.9	5.6	9.7	1.7						28%	68%								0.4	104	124	-$1
16 a/a	7	11	0	141	144	5.88	5.27	1.74				23.0	6.5	9.2	1.4						33%	67%								-29.5	55	65	-$15
17 ATL *	10	10	0	173	161	5.01	4.78	1.37	869	918	827	21.3	3.2	8.4	2.6	66%	9%	38	23	39	31%	68%	13%	10	70	10%	60%	0	0.74	-14.0	62	74	$1
1st Half	6	3	0	90	85	5.03	5.00	1.37				23.6	3.2	8.5	2.6						30%	69%	0%	0						-7.5	55	66	$2
2nd Half	4	7	0	83	76	4.99	4.53	1.38	869	918	827	19.4	3.2	8.2	2.6	66%	9%	38	23	39	32%	66%	13%	10	70	10%	60%	0	0.74	-6.5	69	83	$0
18 Proj	**4**	**4**	**0**	**65**	**64**	**4.87**	**5.00**	**1.49**	**736**	**801**	**681**	**21.7**	**4.7**	**8.8**	**1.9**	**66%**	**9%**	**38**	**23**	**39**	**32%**	**70%**	**10%**	**13**						**-4.1**	**49**	**59**	**-$4**

Skaggs,Tyler

Age: 26	Th: L	Role SP	Health F	LIMA Plan C
Ht: 6' 4"	Wt: 215	Type Pwr	PT/Exp D	Rand Var +1
			Consist C	MM 1201

Off to a pretty good start, and then—stop me if you've heard this one—left his last April outing with strained oblique that sidelined him until August, then struggled to the finish. STILL only in mid-20s, STILL owns the skills that made him a Grade 9C prospect a few years back. But hasn't been fully healthy in FIVE years.

Yr Tm	W	L	Sv	IP	K	ERA	xERA	WHIP	oOPS	vL	vR	BF/G	Ctl	Dom	Cmd	FpK	SwK	G	L	F	H%	S%	hr/f	GS	APC	DOM%	DIS%	Sv%	LI	RAR	BPV	BPX	R$
13 ARI *	8	13	0	143	127	4.48	4.16	1.40	780	710	799	23.2	3.1	8.0	2.6	62%	9%	45	20	35	34%	68%	17%	7	94	29%	43%			-10.9	82	107	-$2
14 LAA	5	5	0	113	86	4.30	3.59	1.21	674	742	655	25.8	2.4	6.8	2.9	64%	9%	50	19	31	30%	65%	9%	18	95	44%	22%			-7.8	87	103	$0
15																																	
16 LAA *	6	6	0	82	88	3.24	3.36	1.26	750	804	734	19.7	3.4	9.7	2.9	60%	9%	43	23	34	31%	76%	10%	10	88	30%	30%			9.6	103	122	$5
17 LAA	2	6	0	85	76	4.55	4.41	1.39	790	734	806	22.8	3.0	8.0	2.7	62%	8%	42	22	37	32%	71%	14%	16	87	25%	38%			-2.0	85	102	-$2
1st Half	1	1	0	29	29	3.99	4.02	1.26	690	569	723	24.2	2.8	8.9	3.2	64%	10%	40	23	37	32%	71%	10%	5	89	40%	20%			1.3	103	124	-$2
2nd Half	1	5	0	56	47	4.85	4.62	1.46	839	808	848	22.2	3.1	7.6	2.5	61%	7%	43	21	36	32%	72%	16%	11	86	18%	45%			-3.4	75	90	-$3
18 Proj	**5**	**8**	**0**	**116**	**107**	**4.17**	**4.26**	**1.32**	**728**	**721**	**731**	**22.1**	**3.0**	**8.3**	**2.8**	**62%**	**9%**	**44**	**22**	**35**	**32%**	**71%**	**11%**	**22**						**2.7**	**90**	**109**	**$2**

Smith,Carson

Age: 28	Th: R	Role RP	Health F	LIMA Plan B
Ht: 6' 6"	Wt: 215	Type Pwr xGB	PT/Exp D	Rand Var -5
			Consist C	MM 5510

Got a September cup of coffee in return from May 2016 TJS—and looked great. Before the surgery, skills were about as good as any reliever's. Don't expect him to assume a significant late-innings role again right out of the chute. But if he's healthy and pitches like he has most of his career... UP: 15 saves

Yr Tm	W	L	Sv	IP	K	ERA	xERA	WHIP	oOPS	vL	vR	BF/G	Ctl	Dom	Cmd	FpK	SwK	G	L	F	H%	S%	hr/f	GS	APC	DOM%	DIS%	Sv%	LI	RAR	BPV	BPX	R$
13 aa	1	3	15	50	61	2.50	2.48	1.18				4.6	3.2	10.9	3.4						33%	78%								8.4	140	182	$8
14 SEA *	2	3	10	51	48	2.44	2.98	1.24	249	83	369	4.3	2.6	8.4	3.2	64%	10%	81	6	13	33%	79%	0%	0	13			77	0.62	8.3	118	140	$5
15 SEA	2	5	13	70	92	2.31	2.20	1.01	542	593	502	4.1	2.8	11.8	4.2	59%	13%	65	17	18	31%	77%	7%	0	15			72	1.40	14.2	180	214	$13
16 BOS	0	0	0	3	2	0.00	3.69	1.13	473	250	571	3.7	3.4	6.8	2.0	36%	4%	75	0	25	27%	100%	0%	0	16			0	0.47	1.4	83	99	-$4
17 BOS	0	0	1	7	7	1.35	2.72	1.35	613	333	697	3.4	2.7	9.5	3.5	71%	10%	61	33	6	37%	89%	0%	0	14			100	0.66	2.5	136	164	-$4
1st Half																																	
2nd Half	0	0	1	7	7	1.35	2.72	1.35	613	333	697	3.4	2.7	9.5	3.5	71%	10%	61	33	6	37%	89%	0%	0	14			100	0.66	2.5	136	163	-$4
18 Proj	**1**	**3**	**2**	**51**	**60**	**2.61**	**2.77**	**1.14**	**565**	**610**	**529**	**4.2**	**2.9**	**10.6**	**3.6**	**59%**	**13%**	**65**	**17**	**18**	**32%**	**77%**	**9%**	**0**						**10.9**	**155**	**186**	**$4**

ROD TRUESDELL

Smith,Joe

Age: 34	Th: R	Role	RP	Health	D	LIMA Plan	A
Ht: 6' 2"	Wt: 205	Type	Pwr GB	PT/Exp	C	Rand Var	+3
				Consist	B	MM	4310

Missed a month with shoulder inflammation; otherwise, this was not just a great rebound season, these were the best skills of his career. First-ever double-digit Dom rate, and he didn't walk a single batter after July! A top LIMA option primarily, but he also returns to usual spot on list of dark-horse save candidates.

Yr Tm	W	L	Sv	IP	K	ERA	xERA	WHIP	oOPS	vL	vR	BF/G	Ctl	Dom	Cmd	FpK	SwK	G	L	F	H%	S%	hr/f	GS	APC	DOM%	DIS%	Sv%	LI	RAR	BPV	BPX	R$
13 CLE	6	2	3	63	54	2.29	3.59	1.22	643	698	592	3.7	3.3	7.7	2.3	59%	9%	49	21	30	28%	85%	10%	0	14			38	1.37	12.3	77	101	$6
14 LAA	7	2	15	75	68	1.81	2.67	0.80	491	584	385	3.8	1.8	8.2	4.5	66%	8%	59	15	26	22%	80%	8%	0	15			79	1.25	17.8	136	162	$18
15 LAA	5	5	5	65	57	3.58	3.49	1.27	684	786	587	3.9	2.6	7.9	3.0	63%	8%	52	23	25	32%	72%	9%	0	14			56	1.29	3.1	101	120	$3
16 2 TM	2	5	6	52	40	3.46	4.05	1.25	716	726	708	4.0	3.1	6.9	2.2	66%	9%	50	23	27	27%	79%	20%	0	15			67	0.90	4.7	69	81	$2
17 2 AL	3	0	1	54	71	3.33	2.65	1.04	601	701	546	3.6	1.7	11.8	7.1	67%	12%	50	21	29	34%	69%	11%	0	14			50	1.22	6.8	196	235	$4
1st Half	3	0	0	32	47	3.41	2.49	1.14	642	751	556	3.8	2.3	13.4	5.9	69%	14%	46	25	28	37%	73%	15%	0	14			0	1.15	3.7	204	244	$0
2nd Half	0	0	1	22	24	3.22	2.87	0.90	542	566	535	3.4	0.8	9.7	12.0	65%	9%	53	17	30	30%	63%	6%	0	13			100	1.30	3.1	184	220	$2
18 Proj	**3**	**2**	**4**	**58**	**60**	**3.26**	**3.31**	**1.10**	**631**	**704**	**584**	**3.6**	**2.1**	**9.3**	**4.4**	**65%**	**10%**	**51**	**21**	**28**	**30%**	**73%**	**12%**	**0**						**7.9**	**139**	**167**	**$5**

Smoker,Josh

Age: 29	Th: L	Role	RP	Health	C	LIMA Plan	C+
Ht: 6' 2"	Wt: 250	Type	Pwr	PT/Exp	D	Rand Var	+5
				Consist	D	MM	1500

Continued to fan lots of hitters, regardless of handedness, with mid-90s heat and a split. But gave away 2016 control gains and then some, and allowed an opponent SLG of .485—essentially turning every hitter he faced into Andrew McCutchen. That's not going to earn anybody a significant late-inning role.

Yr Tm	W	L	Sv	IP	K	ERA	xERA	WHIP	oOPS	vL	vR	BF/G	Ctl	Dom	Cmd	FpK	SwK	G	L	F	H%	S%	hr/f	GS	APC	DOM%	DIS%	Sv%	LI	RAR	BPV	BPX	R$
13																																	
14																																	
15 aa	1	0	0	21	21	3.81	3.46	1.51				4.3	5.1	8.8	1.7						34%	72%								0.4	94	112	-$4
16 NYM *	6	2	3	72	90	4.38	5.51	1.58	790	1048	594	4.4	2.9	11.2	3.8	75%	16%	29	26	44	42%	75%	27%	0	13			60	1.11	-1.7	107	127	-$1
17 NYM	1	2	0	56	68	5.11	4.55	1.70	858	849	867	4.9	5.1	10.9	2.1	57%	13%	43	22	35	37%	74%	18%	0	20			0	0.87	-5.2	79	94	-$7
1st Half	1	2	0	29	36	7.45	4.61	1.86	924	974	892	6.5	5.3	11.2	2.1	62%	14%	47	18	34	40%	64%	23%	0	25			0	0.81	-11.1	84	100	-$12
2nd Half	0	0	0	27	32	2.63	4.48	1.54	780	757	813	3.9	4.9	10.5	2.1	51%	13%	38	27	35	35%	87%	12%	0	16			0	0.91	5.8	72	86	-$2
18 Proj	**2**	**1**	**0**	**44**	**53**	**4.53**	**4.20**	**1.64**	**849**	**837**	**861**	**4.5**	**4.2**	**11.0**	**2.6**	**56%**	**13%**	**42**	**24**	**35**	**39%**	**76%**	**15%**	**0**						**-0.9**	**102**	**123**	**-$5**

Snell,Blake

Age: 25	Th: L	Role	SP	Health	A	LIMA Plan	B
Ht: 6' 4"	Wt: 180	Type	Pwr	PT/Exp	D	Rand Var	0
				Consist	C	MM	1403

5-7, 4.04 ERA in 129 IP at TAM. PRO: General skills step-up in 2nd half, led by improving GB rate and drop in walks; SwK spike supported by velo several mph above 1st half. CON: FpK didn't support the Ctl gains; low H% drove some of ERA dip. Encouraging progress overall, but walks will be an issue without more strike ones.

Yr Tm	W	L	Sv	IP	K	ERA	xERA	WHIP	oOPS	vL	vR	BF/G	Ctl	Dom	Cmd	FpK	SwK	G	L	F	H%	S%	hr/f	GS	APC	DOM%	DIS%	Sv%	LI	RAR	BPV	BPX	R$
13																																	
14																																	
15 a/a	12	4	0	113	119	1.97	2.49	1.12				21.2	3.3	9.4	2.8						28%	85%								27.8	112	133	$18
16 TAM *	9	13	0	152	176	3.77	4.57	1.61	728	656	747	21.7	4.9	10.4	2.1	57%	12%	37	27	36	38%	77%	6%	19	90	26%	37%			7.9	90	107	$1
17 TAM *	10	7	0	173	171	3.95	4.31	1.40	707	494	741	23.6	3.9	8.9	2.2	54%	11%	44	18	38	31%	75%	11%	24	95	17%	29%			8.7	71	86	$7
1st Half	5	5	0	91	92	4.56	5.47	1.63	796	584	839	25.3	4.6	9.0	2.0	54%	9%	41	22	38	35%	76%	13%	9	99	0%	44%			-2.2	55	66	-$1
2nd Half	5	2	0	82	79	3.28	4.06	1.15	653	415	684	22.3	3.2	8.6	2.7	54%	12%	46	16	38	27%	75%	10%	15	93	27%	20%			11.0	94	112	$16
18 Proj	**9**	**7**	**0**	**131**	**137**	**3.66**	**4.37**	**1.40**	**708**	**572**	**735**	**24.3**	**4.1**	**9.5**	**2.3**	**55%**	**11%**	**41**	**22**	**37**	**33%**	**76%**	**9%**	**23**						**11.3**	**79**	**96**	**$5**

Soria,Joakim

Age: 34	Th: R	Role	RP	Health	D	LIMA Plan	A
Ht: 6' 3"	Wt: 200	Type	Pwr	PT/Exp	C	Rand Var	0
				Consist	B	MM	3310

Lost a month to oblique strain in Aug/Sept, and 2nd half fade suggests it was bothering him for a while. Before that, was flashing some of his best skills in a while, even spurring some "closer" talk. But healthy 2015-16 appear the exceptions. Even if spring role looks promising, no better than a Plan B saves option.

Yr Tm	W	L	Sv	IP	K	ERA	xERA	WHIP	oOPS	vL	vR	BF/G	Ctl	Dom	Cmd	FpK	SwK	G	L	F	H%	S%	hr/f	GS	APC	DOM%	DIS%	Sv%	LI	RAR	BPV	BPX	R$
13 TEX	1	0	0	24	28	3.80	3.43	1.35	624	316	943	3.9	5.3	10.6	2.0	56%	10%	52	18	30	29%	73%	12%	0	17			0	1.04	0.2	78	102	-$3
14 2 AL	2	4	18	44	48	3.25	2.93	0.99	605	675	503	3.8	1.2	9.7	8.0	63%	10%	43	22	35	32%	67%	5%	0	14			90	1.12	2.7	164	195	$9
15 2 TM	3	1	24	68	64	2.53	3.54	1.09	628	722	536	3.8	2.5	8.5	3.4	61%	10%	42	23	35	27%	83%	13%	0	16			80	1.35	12.0	105	125	$15
16 KC	5	8	1	67	68	4.05	3.95	1.46	800	669	931	4.2	3.6	9.2	2.5	63%	12%	50	20	30	33%	77%	18%	0	17			13	1.25	1.1	95	113	$0
17 KC	4	3	1	56	64	3.70	3.24	1.23	592	679	524	3.9	3.2	10.3	3.2	58%	13%	55	22	23	34%	68%	3%	0	17			13	1.14	4.6	131	158	$2
1st Half	4	2	0	33	44	3.55	2.94	1.39	602	682	527	4.1	3.5	12.0	3.4	56%	13%	59	21	20	40%	72%	0%	0	18			0	1.10	3.3	158	189	$3
2nd Half	0	1	1	23	20	3.91	3.63	1.00	577	672	521	3.7	2.7	7.8	2.9	61%	14%	48	23	28	25%	59%	6%	0	16			25	1.19	1.3	93	112	$0
18 Proj	**3**	**4**	**9**	**58**	**60**	**3.60**	**3.62**	**1.21**	**651**	**682**	**623**	**3.8**	**2.9**	**9.3**	**3.2**	**61%**	**12%**	**50**	**22**	**29**	**31%**	**71%**	**9%**	**0**						**5.4**	**115**	**139**	**$5**

Stammen,Craig

Age: 34	Th: R	Role	RP	Health	F	LIMA Plan	B+
Ht: 6' 4"	Wt: 230	Type	Pwr GB	PT/Exp	D	Rand Var	-1
				Consist	F	MM	2201

Fully healthy for first time since 2015, and pitched pretty well, although 2nd half ERA was a hit- and strand-rate aberration. Sept skills dip (4.45 xERA, 48 BPV) could be workload related; coming off extensive elbow problems, that's at least mildly concerning. A decent LIMA option if healthy—but that's no given.

Yr Tm	W	L	Sv	IP	K	ERA	xERA	WHIP	oOPS	vL	vR	BF/G	Ctl	Dom	Cmd	FpK	SwK	G	L	F	H%	S%	hr/f	GS	APC	DOM%	DIS%	Sv%	LI	RAR	BPV	BPX	R$
13 WAS	7	6	0	82	79	2.76	3.07	1.29	684	761	634	6.2	3.0	8.7	2.9	61%	13%	60	16	24	33%	79%	7%	0	23			0	0.95	11.2	114	149	$5
14 WAS	4	5	0	73	56	3.84	3.49	1.27	708	767	660	6.2	1.7	6.9	4.0	61%	11%	48	23	29	33%	70%	8%	0	23			0	1.05	-0.9	104	124	$0
15 WAS	0	0	0	4	3	0.00	5.18	1.25	525	500	536	3.4	6.8	6.8	1.0	71%	12%	55	9	36	19%	100%	0%	0	13			0	1.63	2.0	-28	-33	-$4
16 a/a	0	4	0	24	13	5.19	6.88	1.71				5.5	2.3	4.9	2.1						36%	74%								-3.0	11	13	-$6
17 SD	2	3	0	80	74	3.14	3.92	1.20	684	803	592	5.5	3.1	8.3	2.6	65%	12%	52	17	31	27%	81%	17%	0	21			0	1.18	12.1	95	114	$4
1st Half	0	1	0	46	45	4.53	3.92	1.27	754	942	601	7.2	3.0	8.9	3.0	66%	12%	52	17	31	28%	73%	24%	0	28			0	0.72	-1.0	109	131	$0
2nd Half	2	2	0	35	29	1.30	3.93	1.10	579	575	580	4.1	3.4	7.5	2.2	65%	12%	52	17	31	25%	92%	7%	0	16			0	1.55	13.1	74	89	$9
18 Proj	**4**	**4**	**0**	**73**	**63**	**3.43**	**3.94**	**1.22**	**689**	**770**	**628**	**5.5**	**2.7**	**7.8**	**2.9**	**63%**	**12%**	**52**	**19**	**29**	**29%**	**75%**	**13%**	**0**						**8.3**	**98**	**118**	**$3**

Steckenrider,Drew

Age: 27	Th: R	Role	RP	Health	A	LIMA Plan	B
Ht: 6' 5"	Wt: 215	Type	Pwr FB	PT/Exp	F	Rand Var	-4
				Consist	C	MM	3520

1-1, 2.34 ERA with 1 Sv in 35 IP at MIA. Left to languish for half the year in Triple-A, but dominant stint after late-July recall should end that nonsense. With conversion to relief complete, the question now becomes whether he gets a shot at the ninth. The old adage applies here—draft skills, not roles. UP: 30 Sv

Yr Tm	W	L	Sv	IP	K	ERA	xERA	WHIP	oOPS	vL	vR	BF/G	Ctl	Dom	Cmd	FpK	SwK	G	L	F	H%	S%	hr/f	GS	APC	DOM%	DIS%	Sv%	LI	RAR	BPV	BPX	R$
13																																	
14																																	
15																																	
16 a/a	1	1	13	42	45	3.24	1.84	1.09				4.8	3.9	9.7	2.5						27%	69%								4.9	121	144	$6
17 MIA *	1	2	6	68	90	2.18	2.96	1.15	674	693	661	4.3	3.5	11.9	3.4	68%	14%	42	20	38	30%	87%	13%	0	19			86	1.27	18.3	127	152	$9
1st Half	0	2	5	35	38	2.46	2.96	1.13	944	1100	895	4.9	2.7	9.7	3.6	70%	12%	57	21	21	30%	82%	0%	0	22			83	0.66	8.1	118	142	$9
2nd Half	1	0	1	33	52	1.89	2.95	1.18	632	656	614	3.8	4.3	14.2	3.3	68%	15%	38	20	42	32%	91%	15%	0	18			100	1.34	10.1	137	164	$9
18 Proj	**3**	**3**	**12**	**65**	**83**	**2.81**	**3.60**	**1.17**	**596**	**635**	**569**	**4.5**	**3.4**	**11.5**	**3.4**	**68%**	**15%**	**40**	**20**	**40**	**30%**	**82%**	**12%**	**0**						**12.5**	**135**	**163**	**$10**

Stephens,Jackson

Age: 24	Th: R	Role	SP	Health	A	LIMA Plan	D+
Ht: 6' 2"	Wt: 220	Type	xFB	PT/Exp	D	Rand Var	+5
				Consist	C	MM	0101

2-1, 4.68 ERA in 25 IP at CIN. But that was a 6.50 ERA in all outings of more than 3 innings, and a 0.00 ERA in all outings of 3 innings or less. Regardless, these are all small sample sizes and this weak-skilled flyballer profiles as no more than a #5 starter/long reliever.

Yr Tm	W	L	Sv	IP	K	ERA	xERA	WHIP	oOPS	vL	vR	BF/G	Ctl	Dom	Cmd	FpK	SwK	G	L	F	H%	S%	hr/f	GS	APC	DOM%	DIS%	Sv%	LI	RAR	BPV	BPX	R$
13																																	
14																																	
15																																	
16 aa	8	11	0	151	118	4.65	4.69	1.50				24.2	2.7	7.0	2.6						36%	69%								-8.6	74	88	-$4
17 CIN *	9	11	0	164	118	5.93	5.92	1.62	727	867	623	22.0	3.5	6.5	1.9	57%	9%	36	17	46	34%	66%	19%	4	59	0%	75%	0	0.55	-31.8	29	35	-$13
1st Half	5	4	0	81	61	6.17	6.57	1.76	983	1556	583	23.2	4.0	6.8	1.7	62%	16%	17	33	50	36%	67%	33%	1	91	0%	0%			-18.1	23	28	-$17
2nd Half	4	7	0	83	57	5.69	5.28	1.47	655	686	633	21.0	2.9	6.2	2.1	56%	7%	40	14	46	32%	64%	15%	3	54	0%	100%	0	0.52	-13.7	37	44	-$9
18 Proj	**4**	**6**	**0**	**87**	**64**	**5.42**	**5.53**	**1.56**	**877**	**879**	**875**	**24.2**	**3.1**	**6.7**	**2.2**	**56%**	**7%**	**40**	**14**	**46**	**32%**	**71%**	**13%**	**16**						**-11.4**	**55**	**66**	**-$8**

ROD TRUESDELL

Stephenson,Robert

Age: 25 | Th: R | Role: RP | Ht: 6' 2" | Wt: 200 | Type: Pwr FB
Health: A | PT/Exp: D | Consist: C | LIMA Plan: D+ | Rand Var: 0 | MM: 0203

5-6, 4.68 ERA in 85 IP at CIN. Power-armed prospect still battling control demons. Slight 2nd half improvements in both K and BB rates found matching SwK and FpK support. So... there's hope. Hasn't reached Treasure Island yet, but if this projection is his Mr. Hyde, the Dr. Jekyll side is... UP: 4.00 ERA.

Yr	Tm	W	L	Sv	IP	K	ERA	xERA	WHIP	oOPS	vL	vR	BF/G	Ctl	Dom	Cmd	FpK	SwK	G	L	F	H%	S%	hr/f	GS	APC	DOM%	DIS%	Sv%	LI	RAR	BPV	BPX	R$
13	aa	0	2	0	17	16	6.27	6.60	1.98				20.0	7.1	8.9	1.2						36%	71%								-5.0	32	41	-$7
14	aa	7	10	0	137	128	5.24	4.56	1.43				21.5	4.7	8.4	1.8						28%	67%								-25.3	51	61	-$7
15	a/a	8	11	0	134	128	4.84	4.05	1.46				22.9	5.0	8.6	1.7						30%	68%								-14.5	68	82	-$4
16	CIN *	10	12	0	174	137	5.97	5.53	1.60	893	958	824	24.0	5.0	7.1	1.4	53%	10%	34	24	41	30%	66%	19%	8	90	0%	63%			-38.1	23	28	-$14
17	CIN *	6	8	1	125	125	4.73	4.74	1.44	805	785	818	16.1	4.8	9.0	1.9	54%	13%	38	22	41	29%	73%	13%	11	59	0%	36%	100	0.63	-5.7	51	62	-$1
1st Half		1	3	1	51	50	5.68	5.45	1.50	1020	1094	980	12.2	5.1	8.9	1.7	52%	12%	36	21	43	27%	69%	21%	0	35			100	0.56	-8.3	31	37	-$9
2nd Half		5	5	0	74	75	4.07	4.25	1.41	702	674	724	20.8	4.6	9.1	2.0	55%	14%	38	22	40	29%	75%	8%	11	84	0%	36%	0	0.71	2.6	65	78	$5
18	Proj	**8**	**10**	**0**	**145**	**135**	**4.45**	**5.13**	**1.48**	**777**	**799**	**759**	**19.1**	**4.9**	**8.4**	**1.7**	**54%**	**12%**	**36**	**23**	**41**	**29%**	**75%**	**14%**	**30**						**-1.7**	**34**	**41**	**-$1**

Stewart,Brock

Age: 26 | Th: R | Role: RP | Ht: 6' 3" | Wt: 210 | Type: Pwr xFB
Health: D | PT/Exp: D | Consist: C | LIMA Plan: B+ | Rand Var: -2 | MM: 1301

0-0, 3.41 ERA in 34 IP at LA. Former 3B set back early by shoulder tendinitis, then built up frequent flyer miles with five round trips between AAA Oklahoma City and LA. Odd 7.9 Ctl in MLB starts not his norm; showed his usual fine command otherwise. Still gaining experience, but there's palpable upside here.

Yr	Tm	W	L	Sv	IP	K	ERA	xERA	WHIP	oOPS	vL	vR	BF/G	Ctl	Dom	Cmd	FpK	SwK	G	L	F	H%	S%	hr/f	GS	APC	DOM%	DIS%	Sv%	LI	RAR	BPV	BPX	R$
13																																		
14																																		
15																																		
16	LA *	9	6	0	138	124	2.97	3.22	1.14	856	743	924	21.0	1.8	8.1	4.4	60%	11%	42	13	45	31%	77%	18%	5	69	20%	40%	0	0.69	20.7	123	147	$14
17	LA *	0	1	1	52	49	3.51	4.33	1.40	678	700	653	9.9	3.8	8.6	2.3	61%	11%	41	19	40	31%	79%	11%	4	34	0%	75%	100	0.43	5.4	70	84	-$2
1st Half		0	0	1	15	18	2.10	2.48	0.82	178	125	205	9.3	0.6	10.3	17.5	70%	15%	43	29	29	27%	87%	0%	0	30			100	0.12	4.3	403	483	$1
2nd Half		0	1	0	36	32	4.11	5.11	1.64	777	780	766	10.1	5.2	7.9	1.5	60%	10%	41	17	42	33%	77%	12%	4	35	0%	75%	0	0.50	1.1	49	59	-$3
18	Proj	**3**	**3**	**0**	**116**	**111**	**3.49**	**4.30**	**1.24**	**610**	**608**	**610**	**19.6**	**2.6**	**8.7**	**3.3**	**60%**	**10%**	**42**	**17**	**41**	**31%**	**75%**	**8%**	**23**						**12.4**	**105**	**126**	**$5**

Strahm,Matt

Age: 26 | Th: L | Role: RP | Ht: 6' 3" | Wt: 185 | Type: Pwr xFB
Health: F | PT/Exp: D | Consist: A | LIMA Plan: D+ | Rand Var: +2 | MM: 0301

Torn patellar tendon ended high-ceiling lefty's disappointing season in July, then came a trade to SD. With KC, shuttled in and out of rotation in minors and spent 2016 mostly in 'pen, so change of scenery can only help. But that's injury time missed in four of the last five years. End-game speculation at best.

Yr	Tm	W	L	Sv	IP	K	ERA	xERA	WHIP	oOPS	vL	vR	BF/G	Ctl	Dom	Cmd	FpK	SwK	G	L	F	H%	S%	hr/f	GS	APC	DOM%	DIS%	Sv%	LI	RAR	BPV	BPX	R$
13																																		
14																																		
15																																		
16	KC *	5	10	0	124	114	4.49	5.24	1.48	484	641	411	12.4	2.7	8.3	3.1	53%	13%	47	24	29	35%	73%	0%	0	21			0	1.66	-4.6	72	86	-$3
17	KC	2	5	0	35	37	5.45	5.01	1.50	779	728	794	6.4	5.7	9.6	1.7	59%	11%	37	19	44	28%	67%	15%	3	27	0%	33%	0	0.81	-4.7	34	40	-$5
1st Half		2	5	0	35	37	5.45	5.01	1.50	779	728	794	6.4	5.7	9.6	1.7	59%	11%	37	19	44	28%	67%	15%	3	27	0%	33%	0	0.81	-4.7	34	40	-$5
2nd Half																																		
18	Proj	**4**	**9**	**0**	**73**	**73**	**5.07**	**5.04**	**1.49**	**747**	**696**	**762**	**7.8**	**4.5**	**9.1**	**2.0**	**59%**	**11%**	**37**	**19**	**44**	**31%**	**70%**	**12%**	**0**						**-6.3**	**57**	**68**	**-$5**

Straily,Dan

Age: 29 | Th: R | Role: SP | Ht: 6' 2" | Wt: 220 | Type: Pwr xFB
Health: A | PT/Exp: A | Consist: B | LIMA Plan: B | Rand Var: 0 | MM: 0205

Five teams in five years; good enough to own but not good enough to keep. Extreme flyballer has given up 31 HR in each of the last two years. Built on prior control gains and even missed more bats. So, he's improving. But big flies will continue without big K and/or GB spikes—and there's no sign of either of those happening.

Yr	Tm	W	L	Sv	IP	K	ERA	xERA	WHIP	oOPS	vL	vR	BF/G	Ctl	Dom	Cmd	FpK	SwK	G	L	F	H%	S%	hr/f	GS	APC	DOM%	DIS%	Sv%	LI	RAR	BPV	BPX	R$
13	OAK *	13	9	0	184	151	3.48	3.26	1.22	666	711	617	23.2	3.2	7.4	2.3	60%	12%	36	20	44	28%	74%	8%	27	91	22%	33%			8.7	76	99	$12
14	2 TM *	8	11	0	170	147	5.75	5.34	1.53	832	765	906	21.8	3.9	7.8	2.0	47%	12%	35	16	49	32%	65%	13%	8	63	13%	25%	0	0.60	-42.2	44	52	-$15
15	HOU *	10	10	0	139	113	5.31	5.66	1.57	747	796	681	23.5	2.1	7.3	3.4	47%	10%	42	21	38	38%	67%	10%	3	73	0%	67%	0	0.64	-23.2	75	89	-$10
16	CIN	14	8	0	191	162	3.76	4.72	1.19	712	645	763	23.3	3.4	7.6	2.2	61%	11%	32	20	48	25%	75%	12%	31	90	16%	16%	0	0.77	10.1	54	65	$15
17	MIA	10	9	0	182	170	4.26	4.61	1.30	783	761	807	23.3	3.0	8.4	2.8	62%	13%	34	20	46	30%	73%	13%	33	93	18%	33%			2.2	83	100	$8
1st Half		5	4	0	89	90	3.44	4.05	1.10	673	570	771	22.5	2.8	9.1	3.2	62%	12%	39	17	44	27%	74%	11%	16	92	31%	19%			10.1	104	125	$18
2nd Half		5	5	0	93	80	5.05	5.16	1.49	884	918	842	24.1	3.1	7.8	2.5	62%	13%	30	22	47	32%	73%	15%	17	95	6%	47%			-7.9	64	77	-$1
18	Proj	**11**	**9**	**0**	**181**	**159**	**4.40**	**4.84**	**1.34**	**788**	**763**	**814**	**22.8**	**3.0**	**7.9**	**2.6**	**59%**	**12%**	**34**	**19**	**47**	**30%**	**72%**	**12%**	**33**						**-0.9**	**72**	**87**	**$5**

Strasburg,Stephen

Age: 29 | Th: R | Role: SP | Ht: 6' 4" | Wt: 235 | Type: Pwr
Health: D | PT/Exp: A | Consist: A | LIMA Plan: C | Rand Var: -2 | MM: 4505

Let's flip things around... CON: Another year, another injury, this time an elbow impingement that cost him almost a month. PRO: Literally, everything else. Look, BPX doesn't lie: when he's out there, he's consistently brilliant. But R$ and RAR tell you all you need to know about both the potential and the risk.

Yr	Tm	W	L	Sv	IP	K	ERA	xERA	WHIP	oOPS	vL	vR	BF/G	Ctl	Dom	Cmd	FpK	SwK	G	L	F	H%	S%	hr/f	GS	APC	DOM%	DIS%	Sv%	LI	RAR	BPV	BPX	R$
13	WAS	8	9	0	183	191	3.00	2.98	1.05	587	629	550	24.4	2.8	9.4	3.4	59%	11%	52	17	31	27%	74%	11%	30	95	43%	10%			19.5	125	163	$19
14	WAS	14	11	0	215	242	3.14	2.78	1.12	672	653	687	25.5	1.8	10.1	5.6	65%	12%	46	23	31	32%	76%	13%	34	97	47%	9%			16.0	158	188	$20
15	WAS	11	7	0	127	155	3.46	2.94	1.11	653	572	737	22.7	1.8	11.0	6.0	66%	12%	42	23	34	33%	72%	12%	23	89	39%	22%			7.8	168	200	$13
16	WAS	15	4	0	148	183	3.60	3.30	1.10	637	615	658	24.9	2.7	11.2	4.2	65%	12%	40	21	39	31%	70%	11%	24	99	58%	13%			10.8	146	174	$17
17	WAS	15	4	0	175	204	2.52	3.25	1.02	581	573	589	25.0	2.4	10.5	4.3	63%	13%	47	19	34	29%	78%	9%	28	98	46%	11%			39.9	148	178	$31
1st Half		9	2	0	103	122	3.51	3.36	1.10	649	636	663	26.4	2.5	10.7	4.4	61%	13%	45	21	34	31%	72%	12%	16	103	44%	13%			10.8	149	179	$30
2nd Half		6	2	0	73	82	1.11	3.09	0.89	479	470	486	23.2	2.4	10.2	4.3	67%	14%	50	16	34	26%	89%	3%	12	91	50%	8%			29.1	147	176	$33
18	Proj	**16**	**6**	**0**	**181**	**213**	**2.76**	**3.25**	**1.04**	**596**	**575**	**616**	**23.5**	**2.4**	**10.6**	**4.5**	**65%**	**13%**	**45**	**20**	**35**	**30%**	**76%**	**10%**	**30**						**35.7**	**150**	**180**	**$29**

Stratton,Chris

Age: 27 | Th: R | Role: SP | Ht: 6' 3" | Wt: 190 | Type:
Health: A | PT/Exp: D | Consist: B | LIMA Plan: D+ | Rand Var: +2 | MM: 0103

4-4, 3.68 ERA in 59 IP at SF. A few signs of life from the former first rounder, as he notched a couple of big strikeout games, and threw more strike-ones. But still gives up lots of hard contact, SwK rate doesn't support further Dom upside, and 2nd half ERA was strand-rate driven. Is "very mediocre" an oxymoron?

Yr	Tm	W	L	Sv	IP	K	ERA	xERA	WHIP	oOPS	vL	vR	BF/G	Ctl	Dom	Cmd	FpK	SwK	G	L	F	H%	S%	hr/f	GS	APC	DOM%	DIS%	Sv%	LI	RAR	BPV	BPX	R$
13																																		
14	aa	1	1	0	23	15	3.97	6.53	1.95				21.9	4.8	5.9	1.2						38%	80%								-0.6	29	35	-$5
15	a/a	5	10	0	148	92	4.80	4.06	1.46				24.4	4.0	5.6	1.4						30%	66%								-15.3	50	59	-$8
16	SF *	13	6	0	136	89	4.63	4.35	1.48	767	687	850	20.8	3.1	5.9	1.9	42%	8%	41	16	44	33%	67%	7%	0	24			0	0.31	-7.4	60	71	-$1
17	SF *	8	9	1	138	107	5.32	5.65	1.65	738	811	670	22.0	3.4	7.0	2.0	59%	9%	43	28	29	36%	69%	10%	10	80	20%	30%	50	0.68	-16.3	49	59	-$9
1st Half		3	6	0	69	49	7.49	6.92	1.83	732	929	583	21.4	2.9	6.3	2.2	44%	13%	55	18	27	40%	59%	0%	0	32			0	0.53	-26.6	36	43	-$23
2nd Half		5	3	1	69	58	3.15	4.37	1.47	739	804	676	22.8	4.0	7.6	1.9	60%	9%	42	29	29	32%	81%	11%	10	89	20%	30%	100	0.71	10.3	64	77	$6
18	Proj	**10**	**8**	**0**	**145**	**104**	**4.52**	**5.05**	**1.54**	**735**	**802**	**671**	**22.0**	**3.4**	**6.5**	**1.9**	**60%**	**9%**	**42**	**29**	**29**	**34%**	**71%**	**8%**	**29**						**-3.0**	**43**	**52**	**-$3**

Street,Huston

Age: 34 | Th: R | Role: RP | Ht: 6' 0" | Wt: 205 | Type: Pwr FB
Health: F | PT/Exp: C | Consist: F | LIMA Plan: D+ | Rand Var: -5 | MM: 0100

PRO: Wow, a 0.00 ERA! CON: In 4 IP. Second straight injury-riddled season—what he didn't strain (lat, triceps, groin, rotator cuff), he impinged (shoulder). Skills were slipping even before all that. Sure, there's a chance he regains 2014 form. There's also a chance you win the lottery. Which is the better use of a buck?

Yr	Tm	W	L	Sv	IP	K	ERA	xERA	WHIP	oOPS	vL	vR	BF/G	Ctl	Dom	Cmd	FpK	SwK	G	L	F	H%	S%	hr/f	GS	APC	DOM%	DIS%	Sv%	LI	RAR	BPV	BPX	R$
13	SD	2	5	33	57	46	2.70	3.93	1.02	691	689	693	3.8	2.2	7.3	3.3	64%	12%	30	22	48	22%	89%	16%	0	15			94	1.22	8.1	79	104	$17
14	2 TM	2	2	41	59	57	1.37	3.36	0.94	521	482	561	3.8	2.1	8.6	4.1	64%	13%	36	20	43	26%	90%	6%	0	15			93	1.45	17.4	112	134	$23
15	LAA	3	3	40	62	57	3.18	4.13	1.16	641	758	522	4.1	2.9	8.2	2.9	56%	13%	34	20	45	27%	77%	9%	0	17			89	1.56	6.0	82	98	$19
16	LAA	3	2	9	22	14	6.45	6.28	1.93	975	675	1240	4.0	4.8	5.6	1.2	61%	9%	36	22	42	35%	71%	15%	0	15			75	1.02	-6.2	-15	-18	-$3
17	LAA	0	0	0	4	3	0.00	4.11	0.75	414	0	633	3.8	2.3	6.8	3.0	60%	11%	36	27	36	19%	100%	0%	0	14			0	0.11	2.2	75	90	-$4
1st Half		0	0	0	3	3	0.00	2.42	0.33	300	0	429	3.3	0.0	9.0	0.0	70%	11%	43	29	29	15%	0%	0%	0	12			0	0.08	1.6	183	219	-$4
2nd Half		0	0	0	1	0	0.00	11.32	2.00	650	0	1167	5.0	9.0	0.0	0.0	40%	10%	25	25	50	26%	100%	0%	0	20			0	0.20	0.5	-240	-288	-$4
18	Proj	**1**	**1**	**0**	**15**	**12**	**4.40**	**5.02**	**1.33**	**785**	**823**	**745**	**4.1**	**3.7**	**7.3**	**2.0**	**60%**	**11%**	**36**	**21**	**43**	**26%**	**75%**	**16%**	**0**						**-0.1**	**47**	**57**	**-$4**

ROD TRUESDELL

Strickland,Hunter

Age: 29	Th: R	Role RP	Health A	LIMA Plan B+	
Ht: 6' 4"	Wt: 220	Type Pwr	PT/Exp D	Rand Var -5	
			Consist D	MM 1300	

PRO: Another sparkling ERA; tough on RHB; FpK belies jump in walks, which should regress (and did in 2nd half). CON: BPX reveals an ominous slide; sharp FB% spike; SwK slowly dropping along with fastball velocity; troubles vL increasing. Rocketing xERA presages an ERA spike. DN: Overvalued at $1

Yr Tm	W	L	Sv	IP	K	ERA	xERA	WHIP	oOPS	vL	vR	BF/G	Ctl	Dom	Cmd	FpK	SwK	G	L	F	H%	S%	hr/f	GS	APC	DOM%	DIS%	Sv%	LI	RAR	BPV	BPX	R$
13																																	
14 SF *	2	1	12	43	48	1.98	2.10	0.90	440	500	400	3.4	0.9	10.0	11.2	84%	13%	56	25	19	30%	81%	0%	0	11			100	0.45	9.2	289	345	$9
15 SF *	4	4	5	73	70	2.28	1.63	0.87	543	509	562	3.8	1.6	8.6	5.3	65%	15%	40	20	40	25%	76%	8%	0	13			71	1.28	15.1	164	196	$12
16 SF	3	3	3	61	57	3.10	3.72	1.13	589	741	515	3.5	2.8	8.4	3.0	57%	12%	47	22	30	29%	74%	8%	0	14			38	1.29	8.2	101	120	$5
17 SF	4	3	1	61	58	2.64	4.97	1.43	702	876	587	3.9	4.3	8.5	2.0	62%	11%	39	17	44	32%	83%	5%	0	14			33	1.37	13.0	55	66	$2
1st Half	1	2	1	29	31	2.15	4.95	1.47	640	928	445	3.8	5.5	9.5	1.7	61%	12%	39	19	42	32%	86%	3%	0	13			100	1.44	8.0	39	47	$1
2nd Half	3	1	0	32	27	3.09	5.00	1.41	756	826	709	4.1	3.1	7.6	2.5	63%	11%	38	15	46	33%	81%	7%	0	15			0	1.29	5.0	70	83	$3
18 Proj	**3**	**3**	**0**	**58**	**55**	**3.29**	**4.20**	**1.22**	**640**	**774**	**561**	**3.7**	**3.1**	**8.6**	**2.8**	**61%**	**12%**	**42**	**19**	**39**	**30%**	**74%**	**6%**	**0**						**7.6**	**92**	**111**	**$2**

Stripling,Ross

Age: 28	Th: R	Role RP	Health A	LIMA Plan A	
Ht: 6' 3"	Wt: 210	Type Pwr GB	PT/Exp D	Rand Var +2	
			Consist B	MM 3301	

Took well to full-time 'pen work, with spike in whiffs well supported by fastball speed and SwK increases. Best of all, did that while maintaining pinpoint control and groundball tilt. That hr/f rate should regress as well, and 2nd half xERA shows the upside. Seems destined for low-LI roles, but with opportunity... UP: 15 saves

Yr Tm	W	L	Sv	IP	K	ERA	xERA	WHIP	oOPS	vL	vR	BF/G	Ctl	Dom	Cmd	FpK	SwK	G	L	F	H%	S%	hr/f	GS	APC	DOM%	DIS%	Sv%	LI	RAR	BPV	BPX	R$
13 aa	6	4	1	94	70	3.51	4.03	1.36				18.7	1.8	6.7	3.6						35%	74%								4.2	100	130	$1
14																																	
15 aa	3	6	0	67	44	5.20	4.91	1.42				22.0	2.6	5.9	2.3						32%	65%								-10.3	45	54	-$6
16 LA *	5	11	0	117	87	4.06	4.09	1.30	709	656	752	17.8	2.5	6.7	2.7	64%	8%	51	20	29	31%	71%	11%	14	72	14%	50%	0	0.99	1.9	71	84	$2
17 LA	3	5	2	74	74	3.75	3.57	1.18	691	554	796	6.2	2.3	9.0	3.9	65%	12%	49	22	29	30%	73%	17%	2	24	50%	0%	40	0.86	5.5	126	152	$4
1st Half	0	3	1	38	40	4.03	3.80	1.42	753	732	768	7.4	2.4	9.5	4.0	66%	11%	43	25	32	38%	73%	9%	0	30			50	0.81	1.6	127	153	-$1
2nd Half	3	2	1	36	34	3.47	3.31	0.94	623	362	826	5.3	2.2	8.4	3.8	63%	13%	57	18	26	21%	74%	28%	2	19	50%	0%	33	0.91	4.0	126	151	$9
18 Proj	**4**	**5**	**0**	**73**	**70**	**3.51**	**3.66**	**1.24**	**721**	**600**	**816**	**9.1**	**2.3**	**8.6**	**3.7**	**64%**	**12%**	**51**	**21**	**29**	**32%**	**76%**	**15%**	**0**						**7.6**	**122**	**147**	**$2**

Stroman,Marcus

Age: 27	Th: R	Role SP	Health F	LIMA Plan C+	
Ht: 5' 8"	Wt: 180	Type Pwr xGB	PT/Exp A	Rand Var 0	
			Consist A	MM 3205	

Basically the same season as 2016, skills-wise, with S% fortune the only real difference. That's why we say "Buy skills, not stats." By skills, he's a mid-3s ERA pitcher. Which ain't bad! But with his pedestrian Dom rates, the ceiling will be low. Buy, but don't be looking for further upside or big profit.

Yr Tm	W	L	Sv	IP	K	ERA	xERA	WHIP	oOPS	vL	vR	BF/G	Ctl	Dom	Cmd	FpK	SwK	G	L	F	H%	S%	hr/f	GS	APC	DOM%	DIS%	Sv%	LI	RAR	BPV	BPX	R$
13 aa	9	5	0	112	114	3.70	3.81	1.20				22.5	2.1	9.2	4.4						32%	74%								2.3	117	153	$6
14 TOR *	13	10	1	166	151	3.70	3.23	1.20	633	646	620	20.3	2.0	8.1	4.0	58%	9%	54	18	28	33%	69%	6%	20	80	45%	35%	100	0.84	0.8	124	147	$9
15 TOR	4	0	0	27	18	1.67	3.13	0.96	554	514	646	25.8	2.0	6.0	3.0	66%	8%	64	18	18	24%	88%	14%	4	93	75%	25%			7.6	96	114	$2
16 TOR	9	10	0	204	166	4.37	3.55	1.29	720	741	698	26.7	2.4	7.3	3.1	61%	10%	60	20	20	31%	68%	17%	32	97	34%	31%			-4.5	106	125	$5
17 TOR	13	9	0	201	164	3.09	3.66	1.31	715	650	769	25.3	2.8	7.3	2.6	59%	10%	62	18	20	31%	80%	18%	33	95	39%	27%			31.5	97	117	$17
1st Half	8	4	0	100	84	3.41	3.49	1.26	719	610	805	25.6	2.2	7.5	3.5	60%	10%	61	17	22	31%	78%	20%	16	96	38%	19%			11.8	116	139	$19
2nd Half	5	5	0	101	80	2.77	3.82	1.36	711	686	732	25.0	3.4	7.2	2.1	57%	10%	63	19	17	31%	82%	15%	17	95	41%	35%			19.7	78	94	$16
18 Proj	**13**	**10**	**0**	**203**	**172**	**3.53**	**3.62**	**1.28**	**704**	**686**	**721**	**24.9**	**2.6**	**7.6**	**3.0**	**59%**	**10%**	**60**	**19**	**21**	**31%**	**75%**	**15%**	**33**						**20.8**	**107**	**128**	**$14**

Strop,Pedro

Age: 33	Th: R	Role RP	Health D	LIMA Plan A	
Ht: 6' 1"	Wt: 220	Type Pwr xGB	PT/Exp C	Rand Var -2	
			Consist B	MM 4400	

Wild April (8 BB in 8 IP) aside, not much difference from past few seasons. Crazy 1st half vR eventually turned around, and was offset anyway by gains vL. Don't be concerned by Dom drop; SwK as good as ever. FpK rebounded in 2nd half; GB climb a plus. Still a prime LIMA reliever who turns $1 into profit every year.

Yr Tm	W	L	Sv	IP	K	ERA	xERA	WHIP	oOPS	vL	vR	BF/G	Ctl	Dom	Cmd	FpK	SwK	G	L	F	H%	S%	hr/f	GS	APC	DOM%	DIS%	Sv%	LI	RAR	BPV	BPX	R$
13 2 TM	2	5	1	57	66	4.55	3.24	1.24	663	653	671	3.8	4.1	10.4	2.5	55%	13%	49	26	26	29%	64%	14%	0	15			25	1.25	-4.9	103	135	-$2
14 CHC	2	4	2	61	71	2.21	2.65	1.07	535	621	478	3.8	3.7	10.5	2.8	56%	16%	55	24	21	27%	79%	7%	0	14			33	1.12	11.5	122	145	$6
15 CHC	2	6	3	68	81	2.91	2.98	1.00	538	641	475	3.6	3.8	10.7	2.8	58%	17%	51	20	29	23%	73%	11%	0	14			60	1.30	8.8	118	141	$7
16 CHC	2	2	0	47	60	2.85	2.58	0.89	517	608	470	3.5	2.9	11.4	4.0	53%	16%	58	16	25	24%	71%	15%	0	14			0	0.98	7.8	164	195	$4
17 CHC	5	4	0	60	65	2.83	3.58	1.18	619	498	705	3.6	3.9	9.7	2.5	54%	16%	59	11	30	28%	78%	9%	0	15			0	1.09	11.3	107	128	$5
1st Half	2	2	0	30	34	3.34	3.36	1.25	693	444	873	3.6	3.9	10.3	2.6	52%	14%	66	7	28	30%	76%	14%	0	15			0	1.15	3.7	123	147	$2
2nd Half	3	2	0	31	31	2.35	3.78	1.11	543	556	533	3.7	3.8	9.1	2.4	56%	17%	53	14	33	26%	79%	4%	0	15			0	1.02	7.6	91	110	$7
18 Proj	**4**	**4**	**0**	**58**	**66**	**2.86**	**3.26**	**1.07**	**574**	**563**	**580**	**3.4**	**3.6**	**10.3**	**2.9**	**55%**	**16%**	**56**	**15**	**28**	**26%**	**75%**	**10%**	**0**						**10.7**	**122**	**147**	**$5**

Suter,Brent

Age: 28	Th: L	Role RP	Health B	LIMA Plan B+	
Ht: 6' 5"	Wt: 195	Type	PT/Exp D	Rand Var 0	
			Consist B	MM 0003	

3-2, 3.42 ERA in 82 IP at MIL. Rode the AAA shuttle for 1st half, then stayed up for good in June. The classic "crafty lefty;" skills profile shows a guy living on the edge with fringy stuff, pinpoint control. Dom is key: he can survive at 2017 levels, but not much lower. If previous sub-tipping-point Dom returns... DN: 5.00 ERA

Yr Tm	W	L	Sv	IP	K	ERA	xERA	WHIP	oOPS	vL	vR	BF/G	Ctl	Dom	Cmd	FpK	SwK	G	L	F	H%	S%	hr/f	GS	APC	DOM%	DIS%	Sv%	LI	RAR	BPV	BPX	R$
13																																	
14 aa	10	10	0	152	98	4.98	5.11	1.52				23.6	3.4	5.8	1.7						32%	69%								-23.3	34	40	-$9
15 a/a	8	4	0	118	66	3.04	4.32	1.46				19.5	3.3	5.0	1.5						32%	80%								13.4	45	53	$2
16 MIL *	8	8	2	132	74	3.94	5.07	1.49	773	1051	592	14.2	1.3	5.1	3.8	68%	9%	43	19	37	36%	74%	12%	2	25	0%	100%	100	0.75	4.1	83	98	$0
17 MIL *	6	3	0	118	93	3.94	4.68	1.38	702	541	755	15.5	2.3	7.1	3.1	67%	9%	45	24	31	33%	75%	10%	14	58	21%	43%	0	0.67	6.1	73	88	$2
1st Half	3	2	0	52	41	4.85	5.69	1.56	755	499	895	12.6	2.5	7.2	2.9	70%	8%	47	19	34	36%	72%	6%	1	35	0%	100%	0	0.57	-3.1	60	72	-$5
2nd Half	3	1	0	67	52	3.24	4.16	1.25	689	556	728	19.6	2.2	7.0	3.3	67%	10%	45	25	30	31%	78%	11%	13	72	23%	38%	0	0.74	9.2	91	109	$8
18 Proj	**8**	**6**	**0**	**145**	**99**	**3.89**	**4.67**	**1.42**	**784**	**571**	**865**	**16.4**	**2.3**	**6.1**	**2.7**	**68%**	**9%**	**46**	**23**	**32**	**33%**	**75%**	**9%**	**24**						**8.4**	**72**	**87**	**$2**

Swarzak,Anthony

Age: 32	Th: R	Role RP	Health B	LIMA Plan B	
Ht: 6' 4"	Wt: 215	Type Pwr FB	PT/Exp D	Rand Var -3	
			Consist F	MM 2410	

Actually a trade-deadline target—who'd've thunk? And hey, that distinction was well earned in clearly the best season of career. Took to shorter outings (see BF/G) with aplomb, as velocity and whiffs spiked. Now, can he repeat? Shiny new skills say "why not?" But xERA says ERA is likely to bump up a bit.

Yr Tm	W	L	Sv	IP	K	ERA	xERA	WHIP	oOPS	vL	vR	BF/G	Ctl	Dom	Cmd	FpK	SwK	G	L	F	H%	S%	hr/f	GS	APC	DOM%	DIS%	Sv%	LI	RAR	BPV	BPX	R$
13 MIN	3	2	0	96	69	2.91	3.79	1.16	649	772	540	8.1	2.1	6.5	3.1	61%	8%	45	19	36	29%	77%	7%	0	31			0	0.78	11.4	84	109	$5
14 MIN	3	2	0	86	47	4.60	4.74	1.49	752	733	768	7.6	2.9	4.9	1.7	60%	7%	45	20	36	33%	68%	5%	4	28	0%	75%	0	0.82	-9.2	32	39	-$7
15 CLE	0	0	0	13	13	3.38	3.85	1.65	799	636	886	6.1	2.7	8.8	3.3	74%	11%	43	32	25	41%	81%	9%	0	20			0	0.29	1.0	106	126	-$5
16 NYY *	2	6	7	78	63	5.88	5.87	1.44	847	858	839	8.1	2.0	7.3	3.7	68%	10%	46	11	43	33%	64%	28%	0	19			88	0.67	-16.2	58	69	-$5
17 2 TM	6	4	2	77	91	2.33	3.37	1.03	595	575	605	4.3	2.6	10.6	4.1	65%	15%	44	16	41	29%	81%	8%	0	18			40	1.37	19.4	144	172	$12
1st Half	4	2	0	36	36	2.72	3.65	1.05	565	480	605	4.3	2.5	8.9	3.6	72%	16%	44	17	39	29%	73%	3%	0	17			0	1.00	7.3	116	139	$9
2nd Half	2	2	2	41	55	1.98	3.12	1.02	621	645	606	4.3	2.6	12.1	4.6	60%	13%	44	14	43	29%	89%	13%	0	18			50	1.69	12.0	168	201	$14
18 Proj	**3**	**3**	**5**	**65**	**70**	**3.32**	**3.76**	**1.19**	**696**	**710**	**686**	**5.5**	**2.4**	**9.7**	**4.0**	**64%**	**13%**	**45**	**15**	**40**	**32%**	**76%**	**11%**	**0**						**8.4**	**132**	**159**	**$5**

Syndergaard,Noah

Age: 25	Th: R	Role SP	Health F	LIMA Plan B	
Ht: 6' 6"	Wt: 240	Type Pwr GB	PT/Exp C	Rand Var 0	
			Consist A	MM 5403	

Partially torn lat in right shoulder wrecked season. Came back with a few IP late just to show he could (and hit 100 mph). Add in history of elbow issues, and even risk takers swallow hard before drafting. But make no mistake: when healthy, as skilled as ANYONE. UP: Cy Young Award DN: Chris Young durability

Yr Tm	W	L	Sv	IP	K	ERA	xERA	WHIP	oOPS	vL	vR	BF/G	Ctl	Dom	Cmd	FpK	SwK	G	L	F	H%	S%	hr/f	GS	APC	DOM%	DIS%	Sv%	LI	RAR	BPV	BPX	R$
13 aa	6	1	0	54	63	3.04	3.42	1.09				19.2	1.8	10.4	5.7						31%	79%								5.5	151	197	$4
14 aaa	9	7	0	133	129	3.62	3.88	1.33				21.2	2.3	8.7	3.7						35%	73%								2.0	114	136	$3
15 NYM *	12	7	0	180	195	2.99	2.87	1.03	645	691	601	23.8	1.9	9.8	5.1	64%	13%	46	20	34	29%	76%	14%	24	99	42%	17%			21.5	145	173	$23
16 NYM	14	9	0	184	218	2.60	2.90	1.15	639	713	581	24.0	2.1	10.7	5.1	64%	15%	51	22	27	34%	79%	9%	30	95	50%	10%	0	0.78	36.1	164	195	$25
17 NYM	1	2	0	30	34	2.97	2.75	1.05	573	493	656	17.7	0.9	10.1	11.3	56%	14%	58	19	24	36%	69%	0%	7	66	43%	29%			5.2	194	232	$0
1st Half	1	2	0	27	32	3.29	2.71	1.10	595	538	655	22.8	0.7	10.5	16.0	56%	14%	58	18	24	38%	67%	0%	5	86	60%	20%			3.6	208	249	$0
2nd Half	0	0	0	3	2	0.00	3.24	0.67	311	0	650	5.0	3.0	6.0	2.0	60%	13%	57	29	14	13%	100%	0%	2	16	0%	50%			1.6	62	74	-$5
18 Proj	**10**	**7**	**0**	**160**	**179**	**3.11**	**3.07**	**1.12**	**637**	**651**	**625**	**24.7**	**1.6**	**10.1**	**6.2**	**61%**	**14%**	**52**	**20**	**29**	**34%**	**74%**	**9%**	**25**						**24.6**	**167**	**201**	**$19**

ROD TRUESDELL

Taillon,Jameson

Age: 26	Th: R	Role: SP	Health: D	LIMA Plan: C+
Ht: 6' 5"	Wt: 225	Type: Pwr	PT/Exp: C	Rand Var: +2
			Consist: B	MM: 2203

After long return from TJ surgery, slammed with testicular cancer this go-round. PRO: 2016 reflects ceiling; fluky hit rate; better vL in past. CON: Two years of sub-par SwK, ugly DOM/DIS%, poor health. Still has ace ceiling and right age for breakout, but underlying warts suggest he might be one year away.

Yr	Tm	W	L	Sv	IP	K	ERA	xERA	WHIP	oOPS	vL	vR	BF/G	Ctl	Dom	Cmd	FpK	SwK	G	L	F	H%	S%	hr/f	GS	APC	DOM%	DIS%	Sv%	LI	RAR	BPV	BPX	R$
13	a/a	5	10	0	147	117	4.16	3.94	1.39				23.9	3.0	7.2	2.4						33%	70%								-5.3	79	103	-$2
14																																		
15																																		
16	PIT *	9	6	0	166	133	3.25	3.21	1.09	702	731	671	23.1	1.3	7.2	5.5	62%	9%	52	20	27	30%	73%	15%	18	86	11%	28%			19.3	139	165	$16
17	PIT	8	7	0	134	125	4.44	4.15	1.48	789	833	751	23.5	3.1	8.4	2.7	62%	9%	47	25	28	36%	71%	10%	25	93	16%	32%			-1.4	93	112	$0
1st Half		4	2	0	58	50	2.97	3.93	1.35	738	670	792	24.4	3.1	7.8	2.5	63%	9%	53	23	23	32%	81%	13%	10	92	10%	20%			9.9	87	105	$6
2nd Half		4	5	0	76	75	5.57	4.31	1.58	825	939	721	22.9	3.1	8.9	2.9	62%	9%	43	26	31	39%	64%	8%	15	93	20%	40%			-11.3	98	117	-$5
18	**Proj**	**9**	**9**	**0**	**174**	**151**	**3.77**	**3.91**	**1.28**	**713**	**750**	**680**	**22.8**	**2.4**	**7.8**	**3.2**	**62%**	**9%**	**49**	**23**	**27**	**32%**	**72%**	**10%**	**31**						**12.7**	**102**	**123**	**$9**

Tanaka,Masahiro

Age: 29	Th: R	Role: SP	Health: D	LIMA Plan: B+
Ht: 6' 3"	Wt: 215	Type: Pwr	PT/Exp: A	Rand Var: +5
			Consist: A	MM: 3303

On surface, a huge step back from past. Blame early extreme hr/f bug. As that settled down late, surface stats followed. With upper-tier FpK/SwK combo, GB tilt, and 4.5+ Cmd vL/R, his warts aren't skill-related; history of nagging injuries is what to be wary of. A premium buy-low target—just don't expect 200 innings.

Yr	Tm	W	L	Sv	IP	K	ERA	xERA	WHIP	oOPS	vL	vR	BF/G	Ctl	Dom	Cmd	FpK	SwK	G	L	F	H%	S%	hr/f	GS	APC	DOM%	DIS%	Sv%	LI	RAR	BPV	BPX	R$
13	for	22	0	1	199	164	1.52	2.41	1.03				29.5	1.7	7.4	4.4						29%	88%								57.7	132	173	$38
14	NYY	13	5	0	136	141	2.77	2.76	1.06	657	632	687	27.1	1.4	9.3	6.7	62%	14%	47	24	29	31%	79%	14%	20	100	50%	5%			16.3	155	185	$16
15	NYY	12	7	0	154	139	3.51	3.34	0.99	674	697	654	25.4	1.6	8.1	5.1	63%	12%	47	19	34	25%	73%	17%	24	95	50%	21%			8.6	129	153	$17
16	NYY	14	4	0	200	165	3.07	3.68	1.08	645	655	635	26.0	1.6	7.4	4.6	64%	11%	48	21	31	28%	76%	12%	31	95	35%	16%			27.7	116	138	$24
17	NYY	13	12	0	178	194	4.74	3.51	1.24	771	746	790	25.1	2.1	9.8	4.7	64%	15%	49	18	33	32%	68%	21%	30	94	30%	23%			-8.5	147	177	$9
1st Half		6	7	0	91	90	5.56	3.96	1.40	852	821	875	24.8	2.5	8.9	3.6	63%	15%	49	18	32	33%	67%	24%	16	90	31%	31%			-13.4	121	145	$0
2nd Half		7	5	0	88	104	3.90	3.07	1.07	682	661	697	25.4	1.6	10.7	6.5	66%	16%	49	18	33	31%	70%	18%	14	98	29%	14%			4.9	175	210	$19
18	**Proj**	**13**	**8**	**0**	**174**	**172**	**3.58**	**3.50**	**1.12**	**702**	**690**	**712**	**24.8**	**1.8**	**8.9**	**5.0**	**64%**	**14%**	**48**	**20**	**32**	**30%**	**75%**	**17%**	**28**						**16.6**	**138**	**167**	**$18**

Teheran,Julio

Age: 27	Th: R	Role: SP	Health: A	LIMA Plan: B+
Ht: 6' 2"	Wt: 205	Type: Pwr	PT/Exp: A	Rand Var: 0
			Consist: B	MM: 1205

Worst season of career in both stats and skills. Late rebound wasn't good enough to point to 2018 bounce-back, especially given long history of mediocre pre-2017 xERAs. Three straight seasons of sub-2 Cmd vs. LH continues to hold back skills from matching top prospect pedigree.

Yr	Tm	W	L	Sv	IP	K	ERA	xERA	WHIP	oOPS	vL	vR	BF/G	Ctl	Dom	Cmd	FpK	SwK	G	L	F	H%	S%	hr/f	GS	APC	DOM%	DIS%	Sv%	LI	RAR	BPV	BPX	R$
13	ATL	14	8	0	186	170	3.20	3.67	1.17	700	823	580	25.8	2.2	8.2	3.8	65%	11%	38	21	41	30%	78%	10%	30	96	27%	23%			15.3	105	137	$16
14	ATL	14	13	0	221	186	2.89	3.73	1.08	639	687	587	26.8	2.1	7.6	3.6	60%	11%	35	21	44	28%	77%	8%	33	99	55%	21%			23.2	93	111	$22
15	ATL	11	8	0	201	171	4.04	4.15	1.31	737	893	583	25.5	3.3	7.7	2.3	57%	11%	40	24	36	29%	73%	13%	33	99	36%	27%			-1.9	68	81	$6
16	ATL	7	10	0	188	167	3.21	3.95	1.05	650	756	564	25.3	2.0	8.0	4.1	62%	11%	39	19	42	27%	74%	10%	30	99	43%	23%			22.8	108	128	$20
17	ATL	11	13	0	188	151	4.49	4.93	1.37	772	787	753	25.4	3.4	7.2	2.1	64%	10%	40	20	40	29%	72%	14%	32	96	19%	34%			-3.1	55	66	$4
1st Half		6	6	0	90	62	5.30	5.36	1.44	826	878	765	24.6	3.4	6.2	1.8	67%	9%	38	20	41	29%	69%	16%	16	93	13%	44%			-10.5	36	43	-$4
2nd Half		5	7	0	98	89	3.75	4.53	1.30	721	703	742	26.1	3.5	8.1	2.3	61%	10%	42	20	38	29%	75%	11%	16	100	25%	25%			7.3	72	87	$11
18	**Proj**	**10**	**11**	**0**	**181**	**154**	**4.05**	**4.62**	**1.30**	**739**	**803**	**674**	**25.0**	**3.1**	**7.6**	**2.5**	**62%**	**10%**	**40**	**21**	**40**	**29%**	**73%**	**12%**	**30**						**7.0**	**72**	**87**	**$7**

Tepera,Ryan

Age: 30	Th: R	Role: RP	Health: A	LIMA Plan: B
Ht: 6' 2"	Wt: 195	Type: Pwr	PT/Exp: D	Rand Var: -2
			Consist: B	MM: 1211

Middleman worked way into higher leverage work as season went along. Triple-digit BPV in two of final three months confirms value. Late-game potential limited by 1.8 Cmd vL and lack of consistent GB pitch—that 2016 GB% was in a tiny 18 IP sample. View as a staff-filling LIMA arm more than as a saves speculation.

Yr	Tm	W	L	Sv	IP	K	ERA	xERA	WHIP	oOPS	vL	vR	BF/G	Ctl	Dom	Cmd	FpK	SwK	G	L	F	H%	S%	hr/f	GS	APC	DOM%	DIS%	Sv%	LI	RAR	BPV	BPX	R$
13	aa	10	8	1	116	85	5.48	5.15	1.62				15.6	4.5	6.6	1.5						33%	67%								-23.1	38	50	-$10
14	aaa	7	3	2	64	54	5.11	5.90	1.76				5.7	3.8	7.6	2.0						39%	71%								-10.8	55	66	-$6
15	TOR *	3	3	4	67	51	2.45	2.69	1.00	670	568	746	4.8	2.9	6.8	2.3	64%	10%	45	16	38	21%	85%	22%	0	15			80	0.50	12.5	68	81	$8
16	TOR *	1	3	18	64	54	3.92	4.32	1.46	635	679	598	4.8	4.0	7.6	1.9	45%	14%	58	15	26	32%	75%	7%	0	15			95	0.67	2.1	63	75	$4
17	TOR	7	1	2	78	81	3.59	4.03	1.13	633	715	581	4.4	3.6	9.4	2.6	62%	13%	42	18	41	27%	70%	9%	0	17			50	1.00	7.3	92	110	$7
1st Half		4	1	1	42	43	3.02	3.90	1.01	539	613	492	4.7	3.7	9.3	2.5	59%	14%	40	18	42	24%	68%	2%	0	19			50	0.95	6.9	86	103	$10
2nd Half		3	0	1	36	38	4.25	4.18	1.28	729	820	673	4.1	3.5	9.5	2.7	65%	13%	43	17	39	29%	73%	15%	0	16			50	1.05	0.5	98	117	$4
18	**Proj**	**5**	**2**	**2**	**73**	**67**	**4.01**	**4.45**	**1.27**	**701**	**696**	**702**	**4.6**	**3.6**	**8.4**	**2.3**	**63%**	**12%**	**43**	**17**	**40**	**28%**	**71%**	**10%**	**0**						**3.1**	**74**	**89**	**$2**

Thompson,Jake

Age: 24	Th: R	Role: SP	Health: A	LIMA Plan: D+
Ht: 6' 4"	Wt: 225	Type:	PT/Exp: D	Rand Var: +3
			Consist: C	MM: 0001

3-2, 3.88 ERA in 46 IP at PHI. That decent MLB ERA will pull in some speculators. Here's why you shouldn't follow suit: 1) Base skills keep on eroding; 2) Doesn't miss bats or get strike one; 3) DIS% says he's terrible in half of his starts. Still young enough to fulfill prior upside, but odds are it won't happen anytime soon.

Yr	Tm	W	L	Sv	IP	K	ERA	xERA	WHIP	oOPS	vL	vR	BF/G	Ctl	Dom	Cmd	FpK	SwK	G	L	F	H%	S%	hr/f	GS	APC	DOM%	DIS%	Sv%	LI	RAR	BPV	BPX	R$
13																																		
14	aa	4	1	0	47	45	3.60	3.58	1.36				21.7	4.1	8.7	2.1						31%	74%								0.8	84	100	-$1
15	aa	11	7	0	133	102	4.13	4.05	1.34				23.0	2.7	6.9	2.5						32%	70%								-2.7	72	86	$2
16	PHI *	14	11	0	183	110	4.03	4.23	1.34	852	902	798	24.6	3.3	5.4	1.6	49%	7%	46	17	37	28%	74%	16%	10	92	10%	60%			3.6	37	43	$6
17	PHI *	8	16	0	165	114	5.89	6.17	1.71	858	666	965	22.6	3.9	6.2	1.6	55%	8%	46	16	38	35%	67%	16%	8	73	13%	50%	0	0.74	-31.0	25	30	-$16
1st Half		3	9	0	80	58	7.68	6.98	1.93	979	1044	946	21.2	3.8	6.5	1.7	60%	11%	33	17	50	40%	59%	11%	0	29			0	0.71	-32.9	31	37	-$31
2nd Half		5	7	0	84	57	4.18	5.40	1.50	844	629	967	24.3	3.9	6.0	1.5	55%	8%	48	16	36	29%	79%	17%	8	89	13%	50%			1.9	19	23	-$2
18	**Proj**	**7**	**7**	**0**	**102**	**72**	**5.14**	**5.15**	**1.51**	**822**	**746**	**877**	**23.2**	**3.6**	**6.4**	**1.8**	**52%**	**7%**	**47**	**16**	**37**	**32%**	**68%**	**10%**	**19**						**-9.8**	**43**	**52**	**-$6**

Thornburg,Tyler

Age: 29	Th: R	Role: RP	Health: F	LIMA Plan: C
Ht: 5' 11"	Wt: 190	Type: Pwr FB	PT/Exp: D	Rand Var: 0
			Consist: F	MM: 1300

Thoracic outlet syndrome led to mid-season shoulder surgery. The healthy 2016 version pointed to an emerging bullpen arm with late-game potential, so if healthy in the spring, he certainly can get back into that mix. But history of elbow and shoulder problems make him dart throw at best.

Yr	Tm	W	L	Sv	IP	K	ERA	xERA	WHIP	oOPS	vL	vR	BF/G	Ctl	Dom	Cmd	FpK	SwK	G	L	F	H%	S%	hr/f	GS	APC	DOM%	DIS%	Sv%	LI	RAR	BPV	BPX	R$
13	MIL *	3	10	0	141	121	4.43	4.64	1.50	575	479	684	18.5	3.6	7.7	2.2	60%	7%	36	24	39	34%	72%	1%	7	59	29%	29%	0	0.52	-9.8	64	84	-$7
14	MIL	3	1	0	30	28	4.25	4.91	1.52	670	458	808	4.9	6.4	8.5	1.3	54%	11%	36	19	45	29%	70%	3%	0	19			0	0.94	-1.9	-5	-6	-$3
15	MIL *	2	9	0	123	78	5.49	6.49	1.68	723	741	709	13.5	3.7	5.7	1.6	61%	10%	35	24	41	33%	72%	17%	0	27			0	0.73	-23.2	7	8	-$17
16	MIL	8	5	13	67	90	2.15	3.24	0.94	541	413	635	3.9	3.4	12.1	3.6	56%	13%	32	23	45	24%	82%	9%	0	17			62	1.51	16.9	137	163	$17
17																																		
1st Half																																		
2nd Half																																		
18	**Proj**	**2**	**2**	**0**	**29**	**28**	**3.91**	**4.58**	**1.35**	**745**	**643**	**834**	**7.9**	**3.5**	**8.7**	**2.5**	**59%**	**10%**	**35**	**24**	**42**	**31%**	**74%**	**10%**	**0**						**1.6**	**75**	**90**	**-$3**

Tillman,Chris

Age: 30	Th: R	Role: RP	Health: D	LIMA Plan: D+
Ht: 6' 5"	Wt: 200	Type: Pwr	PT/Exp: A	Rand Var: +5
			Consist: B	MM: 0103

A lost season, partly due to early shoulder soreness that likely lingered. Problem is, even healthy, pre-2017 version wasn't very appealing. Stagnantly poor FpK, SwK give him little upside. Those prior mid-3s ERAs always came with H%/S% help. Hoping for that again would be fool's gold. Speculate elsewhere.

Yr	Tm	W	L	Sv	IP	K	ERA	xERA	WHIP	oOPS	vL	vR	BF/G	Ctl	Dom	Cmd	FpK	SwK	G	L	F	H%	S%	hr/f	GS	APC	DOM%	DIS%	Sv%	LI	RAR	BPV	BPX	R$
13	BAL	16	7	0	206	179	3.71	3.87	1.22	730	744	711	25.6	3.0	7.8	2.6	57%	9%	39	22	40	27%	76%	14%	33	105	24%	18%			4.0	77	101	$13
14	BAL	13	6	0	207	150	3.34	4.21	1.23	671	670	672	25.6	2.9	6.5	2.3	58%	8%	41	20	39	28%	76%	8%	34	100	29%	26%			10.2	59	70	$11
15	BAL	11	11	0	173	120	4.99	4.58	1.39	763	698	828	23.9	3.3	6.2	1.9	58%	8%	43	21	35	30%	65%	10%	31	95	16%	32%			-22.0	43	52	-$5
16	BAL	16	6	0	172	140	3.77	4.45	1.28	732	728	735	23.8	3.5	7.3	2.1	57%	9%	41	22	36	28%	74%	10%	30	98	30%	33%			9.0	58	68	$11
17	BAL	1	7	0	93	63	7.84	6.20	1.89	981	1001	962	18.5	4.9	6.1	1.2	48%	8%	40	23	37	34%	63%	20%	19	75	0%	68%	0	0.62	-39.9	-6	-7	-$22
1st Half		1	5	0	49	36	7.90	6.25	2.14	1003	1020	983	22.5	4.8	6.6	1.4	50%	8%	40	26	34	40%	66%	17%	11	89	0%	73%			-21.4	8	10	-$26
2nd Half		0	2	0	44	27	7.77	6.14	1.61	955	976	934	15.2	5.1	5.5	1.1	45%	7%	39	21	40	25%	57%	23%	8	62	0%	63%	0	0.51	-18.5	-22	-26	-$18
18	**Proj**	**6**	**8**	**0**	**145**	**104**	**4.96**	**5.27**	**1.47**	**813**	**808**	**816**	**19.5**	**3.9**	**6.5**	**1.7**	**52%**	**8%**	**40**	**22**	**37**	**29%**	**71%**	**15%**	**30**						**-10.8**	**30**	**36**	**-$5**

STEPHEN NICKRAND

Tomlin,Josh

Age: 33	Th: R	Role SP	Health F	LIMA Plan A	
Ht: 6' 1"	Wt: 190	Type Con	PT/Exp B	Rand Var +4	
			Consist A	MM 1103	

Seasonal xERA consistency is his baseline, but it doesn't feel that way to owners, as he keeps going through ruts (see 1st half). As a brittle soft-tosser who lives in the strike zone, in-season inconsistency is embedded in his profile. But steady triple-digit BPVs, pinpoint control keep him a viable LIMA stash.

Yr Tm	W	L	Sv	IP	K	ERA	xERA	WHIP	oOPS	vL	vR	BF/G	Ctl	Dom	Cmd	FpK	SwK	G	L	F	H%	S%	hr/f	GS	APC	DOM%	DIS%	Sv%	LI	RAR	BPV	BPX	R$
13 CLE *	2	0	0	23	11	2.52	1.91	0.92	500	0	667	14.3	0.0	4.4	0.0	67%	8%	38	0	63	28%	69%	0%	0	36			0	0.23	3.8	0	0	$0
14 CLE *	8	10	0	144	119	4.24	4.54	1.24	781	718	848	18.8	1.6	7.4	4.8	68%	10%	37	27	36	31%	71%	15%	16	69	13%	38%	0	0.94	-8.9	100	119	$2
15 CLE *	8	4	0	90	71	3.79	4.11	1.08	642	448	838	23.3	1.0	7.1	6.8	66%	10%	38	16	46	28%	74%	15%	10	95	50%	10%			1.9	136	162	$6
16 CLE	13	9	0	174	118	4.40	4.22	1.19	778	685	845	24.2	1.0	6.1	5.9	68%	8%	44	21	35	29%	71%	18%	29	87	17%	28%	0	0.74	-4.4	104	123	$8
17 CLE	10	9	0	141	109	4.98	4.18	1.28	807	826	794	22.5	0.9	7.0	7.8	69%	9%	40	23	37	33%	65%	14%	26	80	23%	31%			-10.8	119	143	$2
1st Half	4	9	0	86	64	6.17	4.52	1.49	893	837	940	23.5	1.2	6.7	5.8	68%	8%	40	25	36	36%	62%	16%	16	83	19%	38%			-19.3	107	128	-$7
2nd Half	6	0	0	55	45	3.11	3.67	0.95	656	800	566	20.9	0.5	7.4	15.0	69%	10%	40	21	40	28%	72%	10%	10	77	30%	20%			8.5	137	164	$17
18 Proj	**12**	**8**	**0**	**160**	**122**	**4.26**	**4.15**	**1.16**	**763**	**727**	**791**	**22.0**	**0.9**	**6.9**	**7.3**	**68%**	**9%**	**40**	**22**	**38**	**30%**	**69%**	**14%**	**29**						**1.9**	**117**	**141**	**$9**

Torres,Carlos

Age: 35	Th: R	Role RP	Health A	LIMA Plan D+	
Ht: 6' 1"	Wt: 180	Type Pwr	PT/Exp C	Rand Var 0	
			Consist B	MM 0200	

Prior reliability went up in flames in this debacle. Steadily worsening FpK makes it unlikely his control will return to level of acceptability, something he needs to succeed given marginal ability to miss bats. Leverage Index, horrible second half makes mop-up man role his upside now, which won't have any value to you.

Yr Tm	W	L	Sv	IP	K	ERA	xERA	WHIP	oOPS	vL	vR	BF/G	Ctl	Dom	Cmd	FpK	SwK	G	L	F	H%	S%	hr/f	GS	APC	DOM%	DIS%	Sv%	LI	RAR	BPV	BPX	R$
13 NYM *	10	9	0	158	126	3.60	4.02	1.22	701	678	716	14.2	2.0	7.2	3.6	67%	11%	44	20	37	30%	76%	16%	9	40	11%	22%	0	1.04	5.3	84	109	$8
14 NYM	8	6	2	97	96	3.06	3.57	1.31	715	680	734	5.5	3.5	8.9	2.5	61%	12%	47	17	36	31%	81%	12%	1	22	100%	0%	40	1.07	8.1	90	107	$5
15 NYM	5	6	0	58	48	4.68	3.88	1.37	743	750	739	4.1	2.8	7.5	2.7	61%	10%	48	23	29	33%	66%	10%	0	16			0	1.09	-5.1	85	101	-$3
16 MIL	3	3	2	82	78	2.73	3.94	1.15	655	632	673	4.7	3.3	8.5	2.6	60%	12%	45	21	35	27%	80%	10%	0	18			40	1.05	14.8	88	104	$7
17 MIL	4	4	1	73	56	4.21	5.06	1.53	785	785	784	4.8	4.1	6.9	1.7	57%	10%	46	20	34	31%	76%	13%	0	19			25	0.83	1.3	38	46	-$3
1st Half	4	4	1	42	34	4.25	4.91	1.51	805	780	830	4.8	3.4	7.2	2.1	58%	10%	45	18	36	32%	77%	15%	0	18			25	0.98	0.6	62	74	-$1
2nd Half	0	0	0	30	22	4.15	5.28	1.55	754	792	715	4.9	5.0	6.5	1.3	55%	9%	46	23	31	30%	75%	11%	0	19			0	0.61	0.8	5	7	-$5
18 Proj	**3**	**3**	**0**	**65**	**54**	**4.37**	**4.64**	**1.39**	**736**	**738**	**734**	**4.8**	**3.7**	**7.5**	**2.0**	**58%**	**11%**	**46**	**21**	**33**	**30%**	**71%**	**11%**	**0**						**-0.1**	**58**	**70**	**-$2**

Torres,Jose

Age: 24	Th: L	Role RP	Health A	LIMA Plan B+	
Ht: 6' 2"	Wt: 175	Type Pwr xFB	PT/Exp D	Rand Var +1	
			Consist F	MM 0200	

Low-leverage lefties with 4+ ERAs typically aren't good investments. Three reasons why this one might be... 1) Elite skills in 1st half; 2) 3.9+ Cmd vL/R; 3) Age is on his side. But you'll want to temper expectations for a flyballer with strike one struggles. Monitor from a distance in all but deep or dynasty formats.

Yr Tm	W	L	Sv	IP	K	ERA	xERA	WHIP	oOPS	vL	vR	BF/G	Ctl	Dom	Cmd	FpK	SwK	G	L	F	H%	S%	hr/f	GS	APC	DOM%	DIS%	Sv%	LI	RAR	BPV	BPX	R$
13																																	
14																																	
15																																	
16 SD *	1	2	2	42	35	1.48	1.93	1.06	774	1069	200	5.1	3.1	7.4	2.4	57%	7%	22	22	56	26%	86%	0%	0	15			100	1.48	14.0	103	122	$4
17 SD	7	4	1	68	63	4.21	4.32	1.16	753	714	776	4.6	2.1	8.3	3.9	57%	12%	35	18	46	28%	71%	14%	0	17			50	0.71	1.2	105	127	$4
1st Half	4	2	1	36	39	4.21	3.79	1.10	729	688	759	4.4	2.0	9.7	4.9	57%	14%	37	18	45	28%	70%	16%	0	16			50	0.67	0.7	135	162	$5
2nd Half	3	2	0	32	24	4.22	4.95	1.22	779	750	792	4.8	2.3	6.8	3.0	57%	10%	34	19	47	27%	73%	13%	0	18			0	0.76	0.6	73	87	$2
18 Proj	**5**	**4**	**0**	**65**	**56**	**3.96**	**4.63**	**1.21**	**729**	**698**	**746**	**4.8**	**2.8**	**7.8**	**2.8**	**57%**	**11%**	**35**	**19**	**46**	**28%**	**73%**	**12%**	**0**						**3.2**	**79**	**95**	**$1**

Treinen,Blake

Age: 30	Th: R	Role RP	Health A	LIMA Plan B	
Ht: 6' 5"	Wt: 225	Type Pwr xGB	PT/Exp C	Rand Var +3	
			Consist A	MM 3230	

Started and ended season as closer of two different teams. In aggregate, rising skills in roles of higher leverage put him in position to nail down stopper role, as he did in second half. That late surge came with full support too, including tons of first-pitch and swinging Ks and continued xGB tilt. UP: 40 Sv

Yr Tm	W	L	Sv	IP	K	ERA	xERA	WHIP	oOPS	vL	vR	BF/G	Ctl	Dom	Cmd	FpK	SwK	G	L	F	H%	S%	hr/f	GS	APC	DOM%	DIS%	Sv%	LI	RAR	BPV	BPX	R$
13 aa	6	7	0	119	68	4.60	5.14	1.55				24.7	2.5	5.1	2.0						34%	71%								-10.7	43	56	-$8
14 WAS *	10	5	0	131	79	3.46	4.10	1.40	678	798	564	17.9	2.3	5.4	2.4	57%	8%	59	22	19	33%	75%	3%	7	49	0%	43%	0	0.56	4.5	69	82	$1
15 WAS	2	5	0	68	65	3.86	3.25	1.39	692	934	493	4.7	4.3	8.6	2.0	59%	11%	62	23	15	32%	72%	15%	0	17			0	0.93	0.9	81	96	-$2
16 WAS	4	1	1	67	63	2.28	3.32	1.22	648	737	600	3.6	4.2	8.5	2.0	57%	11%	66	14	20	27%	84%	15%	0	14			33	1.23	15.8	84	100	$6
17 2 TM	3	6	16	76	74	3.93	3.58	1.39	736	875	622	4.5	3.0	8.8	3.0	59%	13%	58	19	23	35%	73%	12%	0	17			76	1.30	4.0	114	137	$7
1st Half	0	2	3	35	30	6.11	4.25	1.70	857	970	780	4.8	3.3	7.6	2.3	52%	12%	60	16	25	39%	63%	11%	0	17			60	0.94	-7.6	86	103	-$8
2nd Half	3	4	13	40	44	2.01	3.03	1.12	617	798	443	4.3	2.7	9.8	3.7	66%	15%	57	22	21	30%	86%	14%	0	16			81	1.63	11.7	140	167	$19
18 Proj	**3**	**4**	**34**	**65**	**61**	**3.38**	**3.64**	**1.34**	**702**	**855**	**587**	**4.6**	**3.4**	**8.4**	**2.5**	**59%**	**12%**	**61**	**19**	**20**	**32%**	**76%**	**13%**	**0**						**7.9**	**99**	**119**	**$15**

Triggs,Andrew

Age: 29	Th: R	Role RP	Health F	LIMA Plan C	
Ht: 6' 4"	Wt: 220	Type GB	PT/Exp D	Rand Var 0	
			Consist C	MM 1101	

After dealing with calf, back issues in debut, hip surgery cut season in half. Prospect of sustained impact dims given flunking health and emerging Ctl concerns fueled by subpar FpK. Extreme prospectors can tuck away history of triple-digit BPV as reason for dart throw, but only in deepest of leagues.

Yr Tm	W	L	Sv	IP	K	ERA	xERA	WHIP	oOPS	vL	vR	BF/G	Ctl	Dom	Cmd	FpK	SwK	G	L	F	H%	S%	hr/f	GS	APC	DOM%	DIS%	Sv%	LI	RAR	BPV	BPX	R$
13																																	
14 a/a	4	3	20	62	30	3.42	3.77	1.29				5.8	2.3	4.3	1.8						29%	74%								2.4	48	57	$7
15 aa	0	2	17	61	55	1.47	2.26	1.09				5.5	1.8	8.0	4.4						32%	85%								18.8	148	177	$12
16 OAK *	3	2	2	75	71	4.20	3.61	1.26	699	759	648	7.6	2.2	8.5	3.9	54%	10%	51	24	25	34%	67%	12%	6	39	17%	33%	67	0.46	-0.1	116	138	$1
17 OAK	5	6	0	65	50	4.27	4.48	1.33	733	648	795	23.6	2.6	6.9	2.6	58%	10%	50	18	33	31%	72%	13%	12	90	17%	50%			0.7	81	98	$0
1st Half	5	6	0	65	50	4.27	4.48	1.33	733	648	795	23.6	2.6	6.9	2.6	58%	10%	50	18	33	31%	72%	13%	12	90	17%	50%			0.7	81	97	$0
2nd Half																																	
18 Proj	**5**	**6**	**0**	**116**	**94**	**4.02**	**4.14**	**1.29**	**703**	**679**	**722**	**8.0**	**2.5**	**7.3**	**2.9**	**56%**	**10%**	**50**	**20**	**30**	**31%**	**71%**	**11%**	**0**						**4.9**	**92**	**110**	**$2**

Tropeano,Nicholas

Age: 27	Th: R	Role SP	Health F	LIMA Plan B+	
Ht: 6' 4"	Wt: 200	Type Pwr xFB	PT/Exp D	Rand Var 0	
			Consist A	MM 0203	

Another arm felled by elbow surgery. Will be 18 months post-TJS by the time spring comes around. Should it matter? Plus off-speed stuff pushed SwK to impact levels pre-injury, and FpK says Ctl should've been better. Just heed risk—both in terms of health and xFB approach—and relegate him to your end game.

Yr Tm	W	L	Sv	IP	K	ERA	xERA	WHIP	oOPS	vL	vR	BF/G	Ctl	Dom	Cmd	FpK	SwK	G	L	F	H%	S%	hr/f	GS	APC	DOM%	DIS%	Sv%	LI	RAR	BPV	BPX	R$
13 aa	7	10	5	134	113	4.69	4.95	1.46				20.4	2.6	7.6	2.9						35%	70%								-13.6	71	92	-$4
14 HOU *	10	8	0	146	115	3.46	2.72	1.09	626	648	576	21.2	2.5	7.1	2.8	54%	9%	40	13	46	26%	70%	0%	4	92	0%	25%			5.1	91	109	$10
15 LAA *	6	8	0	126	118	4.46	4.57	1.48	700	712	686	22.5	3.1	8.5	2.7	64%	12%	39	21	40	36%	70%	5%	7	81	29%	0%	0	0.68	-7.7	85	102	-$4
16 LAA	3	2	0	68	68	3.56	4.75	1.48	843	885	798	22.8	4.1	9.0	2.2	60%	13%	33	17	49	31%	85%	15%	13	93	8%	31%			5.3	62	74	-$1
17																																	
1st Half																																	
2nd Half																																	
18 Proj	**7**	**7**	**0**	**131**	**121**	**4.21**	**4.70**	**1.34**	**752**	**781**	**720**	**21.7**	**3.1**	**8.3**	**2.7**	**62%**	**13%**	**35**	**19**	**46**	**31%**	**72%**	**10%**	**25**						**2.4**	**79**	**96**	**$3**

Tuivailala,Sam

Age: 25	Th: R	Role RP	Health A	LIMA Plan B+	
Ht: 6' 3"	Wt: 225	Type Pwr	PT/Exp D	Rand Var -4	
			Consist F	MM 1210	

3-3, 2.55 ERA in 42 IP at STL. Electric spring helped him carve out bullpen role, and he acquitted himself well. But friendly H%/S% helped him hold onto it and won't repeat, he wasn't used in close games (see LI), and he doesn't miss enough bats to warrant a late-game look. A LIMA RP in deep leagues, nothing more.

Yr Tm	W	L	Sv	IP	K	ERA	xERA	WHIP	oOPS	vL	vR	BF/G	Ctl	Dom	Cmd	FpK	SwK	G	L	F	H%	S%	hr/f	GS	APC	DOM%	DIS%	Sv%	LI	RAR	BPV	BPX	R$
13																																	
14 STL *	2	1	2	23	29	3.98	4.59	1.52	2075	2333	1914	4.8	3.9	11.2	2.8	60%	14%	0	29	71	39%	75%	40%	0	21			50	1.06	-0.7	103	122	-$2
15 STL *	3	2	17	60	58	2.08	2.92	1.30	744	699	775	4.3	5.1	8.8	1.7	60%	12%	49	19	32	27%	87%	17%	0	19			100	1.05	13.9	85	101	$10
16 STL *	3	2	17	56	64	5.96	4.91	1.67	759	741	774	4.6	4.5	10.4	2.3	57%	6%	44	25	31	40%	62%	0%	0	18			74	0.10	-12.1	93	111	-$1
17 STL *	4	3	6	64	50	2.23	2.69	1.02	626	693	589	4.4	2.0	7.1	3.6	64%	10%	49	20	32	26%	84%	10%	0	17			100	0.43	16.7	102	123	$10
1st Half	3	1	5	34	29	2.30	2.78	1.02	650	824	577	4.5	2.4	7.7	3.2	60%	10%	49	18	33	24%	85%	12%	0	19			100	0.51	8.7	93	112	$12
2nd Half	1	2	1	29	21	2.15	2.58	1.02	608	618	601	4.3	1.5	6.5	4.2	68%	10%	49	21	31	27%	82%	9%	0	16			100	0.37	8.0	117	141	$7
18 Proj	**2**	**2**	**2**	**44**	**39**	**3.53**	**4.21**	**1.29**	**679**	**746**	**639**	**4.5**	**3.3**	**8.0**	**2.4**	**65%**	**10%**	**49**	**20**	**32**	**31%**	**74%**	**8%**	**0**						**4.5**	**82**	**98**	**$0**

STEPHEN NICKRAND

Urena,Jose

Age: 26 | Th: R | Role: RP | Ht: 6' 2" | Wt: 200 | Type:
Health: B | PT/Exp: C | Consist: A | LIMA Plan: C | Rand Var: -2 | MM: 0005

After this mini-breakout, he'll be viewed as a mid-rotation target. Don't follow suit. Underneath his sub-4 ERA were unrosterable skills. Neither FpK nor SwK give any hope they'll get better soon. Extreme hit and strand rates were his saving grace; see ugly 2015/2016 stats when they normalize. Beware of the fall.

Yr Tm	W	L	Sv	IP	K	ERA	xERA	WHIP	oOPS	vL	vR	BF/G	Ctl	Dom	Cmd	FpK	SwK	G	L	F	H%	S%	hr/f	GS	APC	DOM%	DIS%	Sv%	LI	RAR	BPV	BPX	R$
13																																	
14 aa	13	8	0	162	100	3.78	3.82	1.24				25.3	1.6	5.6	3.5						31%	71%								-0.7	87	104	$5
15 MIA *	7	6	0	129	61	4.32	4.75	1.52	818	871	777	18.1	3.2	4.3	1.4	58%	9%	48	20	32	32%	72%	7%	9	50	0%	56%	0	0.59	-5.7	31	37	-$6
16 MIA *	7	12	1	132	92	5.33	4.62	1.45	800	864	725	14.1	3.5	6.3	1.8	56%	9%	48	22	30	31%	64%	13%	12	51	8%	50%	33	0.90	-18.6	45	53	-$6
17 MIA	14	7	0	170	113	3.82	5.07	1.27	735	752	719	21.3	3.4	6.0	1.8	59%	9%	43	19	38	26%	76%	13%	28	85	7%	46%	0	0.73	11.3	37	45	$11
1st Half	6	3	0	76	48	3.42	5.22	1.23	711	589	812	19.1	3.2	5.7	1.8	62%	9%	40	19	41	26%	76%	9%	11	74	0%	36%	0	0.69	8.8	34	41	$11
2nd Half	8	4	0	93	65	4.15	4.95	1.31	756	869	633	23.5	3.6	6.3	1.8	56%	8%	46	18	36	26%	75%	17%	17	95	12%	53%			2.4	40	48	$12
18 Proj	10	13	0	181	116	4.58	5.05	1.40	780	825	735	18.6	3.2	5.8	1.8	57%	9%	46	20	34	30%	70%	11%	35						-5.0	41	49	-$1

Urias,Julio

Age: 21 | Th: L | Role: RP | Ht: 6' 0" | Wt: 215 | Type: Pwr
Health: A | PT/Exp: D | Consist: A | LIMA Plan: C | Rand Var: 0 | MM: 1200

0-2, 5.40 ERA in 23 IP at LA. Top pitching prospect's shoulder went under knife mid-season, shelving him for at least 12 months. Excellent debut at age 19 a season earlier hints at anchor upside once healthy. But given age, expect club to take time with his recovery. Don't expect ROI until 2019 at earliest.

Yr Tm	W	L	Sv	IP	K	ERA	xERA	WHIP	oOPS	vL	vR	BF/G	Ctl	Dom	Cmd	FpK	SwK	G	L	F	H%	S%	hr/f	GS	APC	DOM%	DIS%	Sv%	LI	RAR	BPV	BPX	R$
13																																	
14																																	
15 a/a	3	5	0	73	72	4.04	3.14	1.19				19.4	2.2	9.0	4.0						33%	65%								-0.7	128	153	$0
16 LA *	10	3	0	122	128	2.69	3.24	1.24	728	740	725	17.1	2.8	9.5	3.4	63%	11%	44	27	30	33%	80%	8%	15	79	13%	33%	0	0.73	22.5	118	140	$13
17 LA *	3	2	0	55	39	3.91	2.97	1.31	768	1343	570	20.5	4.4	6.5	1.5	52%	9%	40	28	32	27%	69%	4%	5	82	20%	40%			3.0	70	84	-$1
1st Half	3	2	0	55	39	3.91	2.97	1.31	768	1343	570	20.5	4.4	6.5	1.5	52%	9%	40	28	32	27%	69%	4%	5	82	20%	40%			3.0	70	84	-$1
2nd Half																																	
18 Proj	2	1	0	29	26	3.70	4.16	1.25	667	1006	561	19.2	3.1	8.2	2.6	56%	10%	42	27	31	31%	70%	6%	6						2.4	82	99	-$2

Vargas,Jason

Age: 35 | Th: L | Role: SP | Ht: 6' 0" | Wt: 215 | Type:
Health: F | PT/Exp: C | Consist: D | LIMA Plan: C | Rand Var: 0 | MM: 0005

Second-best season of career at age 34 fueled entirely by 1st half deluge of run support and luck. Early xERA told us it wouldn't last—sure enough, he imploded in 2nd half. Steadily mediocre skills last three healthy years confirm he's still the back-end rotation guy we've come to expect. Profit only as an end-gamer.

Yr Tm	W	L	Sv	IP	K	ERA	xERA	WHIP	oOPS	vL	vR	BF/G	Ctl	Dom	Cmd	FpK	SwK	G	L	F	H%	S%	hr/f	GS	APC	DOM%	DIS%	Sv%	LI	RAR	BPV	BPX	R$
13 LAA	9	8	0	150	109	4.02	4.30	1.39	758	789	747	26.8	2.8	6.5	2.4	61%	9%	40	21	38	32%	74%	9%	24	99	33%	42%			-2.9	61	80	$0
14 KC	11	10	0	187	128	3.71	4.13	1.27	713	661	731	26.3	2.0	6.2	3.1	63%	9%	38	23	39	31%	74%	8%	30	100	27%	30%			0.8	74	88	$5
15 KC	5	2	0	43	27	3.98	4.71	1.35	740	809	712	20.3	2.5	5.7	2.3	65%	8%	41	19	40	30%	74%	9%	9	76	0%	22%			-0.1	53	63	-$2
16 KC *	0	2	0	28	25	5.78	6.29	1.42	552	1333	430	17.0	1.3	7.9	5.9	64%	11%	36	15	48	34%	67%	6%	3	70	33%	0%			-5.5	94	112	-$6
17 KC	18	11	0	180	134	4.16	4.86	1.33	766	843	747	23.6	2.9	6.7	2.3	66%	10%	40	19	40	29%	74%	12%	32	91	22%	41%			4.4	60	73	$10
1st Half	12	3	0	101	74	2.22	4.56	1.12	632	760	596	25.3	2.1	6.6	3.1	66%	10%	38	19	43	28%	84%	6%	16	96	38%	25%			26.7	76	92	$29
2nd Half	6	8	0	78	60	6.66	5.25	1.61	926	975	916	21.9	3.9	6.9	1.8	66%	10%	43	19	37	31%	64%	20%	16	87	6%	56%			-22.3	40	48	-$14
18 Proj	12	10	0	189	133	4.40	4.97	1.37	774	810	764	24.8	2.8	6.4	2.3	65%	9%	41	20	40	30%	72%	12%	32						-0.9	58	69	$3

Velasquez,Vincent

Age: 26 | Th: R | Role: SP | Ht: 6' 3" | Wt: 205 | Type: Pwr
Health: F | PT/Exp: C | Consist: B | LIMA Plan: C | Rand Var: +4 | MM: 1303

2-7, 5.13 ERA in 72 IP at PHI. Early elbow pains sabotaged 1st half results, then finger issue requiring surgery shelved him for good. Health risk supports move to pen as only way he can stay upright. History of spotty control, high rate of hard contact, and ominous xERA trend further evidence of his downside as a SP.

Yr Tm	W	L	Sv	IP	K	ERA	xERA	WHIP	oOPS	vL	vR	BF/G	Ctl	Dom	Cmd	FpK	SwK	G	L	F	H%	S%	hr/f	GS	APC	DOM%	DIS%	Sv%	LI	RAR	BPV	BPX	R$
13																																	
14																																	
15 HOU *	5	1	0	89	97	3.54	3.01	1.20	720	644	808	12.7	3.4	9.9	2.9	61%	11%	31	22	47	30%	72%	7%	7	51	14%	0%	0	0.64	4.6	108	129	$4
16 PHI	8	6	0	131	152	4.12	3.81	1.33	765	780	750	23.0	3.1	10.4	3.4	60%	12%	35	24	41	33%	75%	15%	24	92	17%	13%			1.1	117	140	$5
17 PHI	2	7	0	72	68	5.13	4.65	1.50	851	879	824	21.0	4.3	8.5	2.0	63%	10%	43	23	35	30%	72%	21%	15	85	7%	40%			-6.8	59	71	-$5
1st Half	2	5	0	50	53	5.58	4.32	1.46	843	878	813	22.0	3.8	9.5	2.5	65%	11%	41	23	36	32%	68%	22%	10	89	0%	40%			-7.5	89	107	-$5
2nd Half	0	2	0	22	15	4.09	5.48	1.59	871	879	857	19.0	5.3	6.1	1.2	59%	7%	45	22	33	28%	81%	19%	5	76	20%	40%			0.7	-10	-12	-$7
18 Proj	5	8	0	131	129	4.32	4.58	1.41	798	800	795	21.5	4.0	8.9	2.2	61%	10%	39	23	38	31%	75%	15%	26						0.6	70	84	$0

Verlander,Justin

Age: 35 | Th: R | Role: SP | Ht: 6' 5" | Wt: 225 | Type: Pwr FB
Health: D | PT/Exp: A | Consist: A | LIMA Plan: C | Rand Var: 0 | MM: 2305

Post-season stud looked like anchor again after trade. Friendly H%/S% in 2nd half drove ace-like stats. But skills during that period nearly identical to year prior, with xERA showing his true baseline -- an ERA between 3.50 and low 4.00s. In-season inconsistency part of aging profile now, but still owns a firm $20 floor.

Yr Tm	W	L	Sv	IP	K	ERA	xERA	WHIP	oOPS	vL	vR	BF/G	Ctl	Dom	Cmd	FpK	SwK	G	L	F	H%	S%	hr/f	GS	APC	DOM%	DIS%	Sv%	LI	RAR	BPV	BPX	R$
13 DET	13	12	0	218	217	3.46	3.75	1.31	691	658	739	27.2	3.1	8.9	2.9	65%	11%	38	23	39	33%	76%	8%	34	109	38%	21%			10.9	94	122	$11
14 DET	15	12	0	206	159	4.54	4.27	1.40	756	686	849	27.9	2.8	6.9	2.4	62%	9%	40	20	41	33%	68%	7%	32	107	31%	31%			-20.4	66	79	-$3
15 DET	5	8	0	133	113	3.38	4.03	1.09	634	620	650	26.8	2.2	7.6	3.5	64%	10%	35	20	46	28%	72%	7%	20	108	40%	30%			9.7	92	110	$9
16 DET	16	9	0	228	254	3.04	3.63	1.00	630	603	657	26.6	2.3	10.0	4.5	64%	13%	34	19	48	27%	76%	11%	34	108	62%	9%			32.2	132	157	$33
17 2AL	15	8	0	206	219	3.36	4.15	1.17	660	712	614	25.7	3.1	9.6	3.0	62%	11%	33	24	43	28%	77%	11%	33	107	55%	15%			25.3	98	118	$24
1st Half	5	4	0	95	92	4.47	4.93	1.45	725	700	750	25.9	4.2	8.7	2.1	61%	10%	34	23	43	32%	71%	8%	16	106	50%	25%			-1.3	57	68	$3
2nd Half	10	4	0	111	127	2.43	3.53	0.94	599	725	499	25.5	2.3	10.3	4.5	62%	12%	33	24	43	24%	85%	15%	17	108	59%	6%			26.5	135	161	$41
18 Proj	16	9	0	203	209	3.51	4.06	1.12	652	667	637	25.4	2.7	9.3	3.4	63%	11%	34	22	44	28%	73%	11%	31						21.2	106	128	$23

Vincent,Nick

Age: 31 | Th: R | Role: RP | Ht: 6' 0" | Wt: 185 | Type: Pwr xFB
Health: D | PT/Exp: D | Consist: B | LIMA Plan: A | Rand Var: -3 | MM: 1200

Extreme FBer keeps delivering results worthy of an end-staff LIMA stash. Pinpoint control now backed by two-year stretch of top-tier FpK, so it can stick. Surging LI hints at another chance for saves. Problem is, history of good-not-great SwK for a reliever, three seasons of mediocre xERA suggest otherwise. He is who he is.

Yr Tm	W	L	Sv	IP	K	ERA	xERA	WHIP	oOPS	vL	vR	BF/G	Ctl	Dom	Cmd	FpK	SwK	G	L	F	H%	S%	hr/f	GS	APC	DOM%	DIS%	Sv%	LI	RAR	BPV	BPX	R$
13 SD *	10	6	1	72	69	2.61	2.88	1.17	525	781	313	4.1	2.8	8.6	3.1	56%	12%	43	23	34	30%	80%	3%	0	16			50	1.08	11.1	107	140	$8
14 SD	1	2	0	55	62	3.60	3.00	1.00	626	825	507	3.4	1.8	10.1	5.6	61%	12%	33	22	45	30%	66%	8%	0	14			0	1.07	1.0	145	173	$2
15 SD *	5	4	1	73	75	2.98	4.31	1.45	698	756	649	4.7	3.1	9.1	2.9	63%	10%	32	28	40	36%	81%	0%	0	16			20	0.55	8.9	97	115	$2
16 SEA	4	4	3	60	65	3.73	3.90	1.13	700	658	723	4.1	2.2	9.7	4.3	69%	14%	32	20	48	29%	75%	14%	0	16			33	1.26	3.4	124	147	$4
17 SEA	3	3	0	65	50	3.20	4.65	1.16	643	672	627	3.8	1.8	7.0	3.8	67%	11%	31	21	48	31%	72%	3%	0	14			0	1.34	9.2	85	103	$3
1st Half	2	1	0	32	23	1.71	4.52	0.98	558	443	625	3.8	1.7	6.5	3.8	67%	10%	34	18	48	27%	83%	2%	0	14			0	1.06	10.4	83	100	$7
2nd Half	1	2	0	33	27	4.64	4.77	1.33	720	877	629	3.8	1.9	7.4	3.9	67%	11%	29	23	48	35%	64%	4%	0	13			0	1.58	-1.1	88	105	-$1
18 Proj	3	3	0	58	53	3.42	4.38	1.20	687	762	642	3.9	2.2	8.3	3.8	66%	12%	33	21	46	31%	74%	7%	0						6.7	101	122	$2

Vizcaino,Arodys

Age: 27 | Th: R | Role: RP | Ht: 6' 0" | Wt: 230 | Type: Pwr
Health: F | PT/Exp: C | Consist: A | LIMA Plan: B | Rand Var: -4 | MM: 2430

Early strong skills helped land him closer gig in 2nd half. Shiny ERA will lead some to view him as an emerging stopper, but pump the brakes: H%/S% help was only reason ERA had "2" in front. Still, now-elite SwK confirms he has stuff to stick, and ability to handle role validated by 2nd half LI/Sv% combo. UP: 40 Sv

Yr Tm	W	L	Sv	IP	K	ERA	xERA	WHIP	oOPS	vL	vR	BF/G	Ctl	Dom	Cmd	FpK	SwK	G	L	F	H%	S%	hr/f	GS	APC	DOM%	DIS%	Sv%	LI	RAR	BPV	BPX	R$
13																																	
14 CHC *	1	1	1	37	31	4.91	4.85	1.58	837	200	1318	4.5	4.2	7.6	1.8	59%	7%	40	20	40	34%	69%	17%	0	19			50	0.02	-5.3	59	70	-$5
15 ATL	3	1	9	34	37	1.60	3.66	1.19	615	583	641	3.9	3.5	9.9	2.8	58%	12%	35	28	37	31%	87%	3%	0	15			90	1.12	9.8	97	116	$6
16 ATL	1	4	10	39	50	4.42	4.09	1.63	681	607	748	4.2	6.1	11.6	1.9	56%	14%	54	16	30	37%	73%	10%	0	17			71	1.15	-1.1	78	93	$0
17 ATL	5	3	14	57	64	2.83	4.02	1.10	627	749	527	3.8	3.3	10.0	3.0	60%	15%	39	16	45	26%	80%	10%	0	14			82	1.28	10.8	109	131	$11
1st Half	3	2	1	33	37	2.45	3.81	1.06	635	732	558	3.8	3.0	10.1	3.4	61%	15%	41	16	42	25%	87%	14%	0	14			33	1.10	7.7	120	144	$10
2nd Half	2	1	13	24	27	3.33	4.31	1.15	617	772	481	3.8	3.7	10.0	2.7	59%	16%	35	16	49	28%	73%	6%	0	14			93	1.53	3.1	93	111	$13
18 Proj	4	3	28	58	65	3.48	3.96	1.25	642	667	619	3.8	3.7	10.2	2.8	58%	15%	43	18	39	31%	74%	9%	0						6.3	104	125	$14

STEPHEN NICKRAND

Wacha,Michael

Age: 27	Th: R	Role SP	Health	D	LIMA Plan	B
Ht: 6' 6"	Wt: 215	Type Pwr	PT/Exp	A	Rand Var	+2
			Consist	A	MM	1203

Solid rebound season after shoulder woes, eroding xERA had pointed towards pen as likely destination. Surge in FpK without SwK dip say he can do it again. The question is durability—has only averaged 160 IP over the last three seasons, and chronic shoulder issues don't tend to go away.

Yr Tm	W	L	Sv	IP	K	ERA	xERA	WHIP	oOPS	vL	vR	BF/G	Ctl	Dom	Cmd	FpK	SwK	G	L	F	H%	S%	hr/f	GS	APC	DOM%	DIS%	Sv%	LI	RAR	BPV	BPX	R$
13 STL *	9	4	0	150	127	2.79	2.68	1.06	603	493	710	19.3	2.2	7.7	3.5	58%	12%	44	17	39	27%	77%	7%	9	69	22%	33%	0	0.66	19.9	105	137	$16
14 STL	5	6	0	107	94	3.20	3.70	1.20	636	581	687	23.5	2.8	7.9	2.8	64%	11%	42	22	36	30%	74%	5%	19	89	26%	21%			7.2	87	104	$5
15 STL	17	7	0	181	153	3.38	3.91	1.21	672	617	716	25.4	2.9	7.6	2.6	63%	10%	46	22	32	29%	76%	11%	30	98	23%	23%			13.1	83	99	$16
16 STL	7	7	0	138	114	5.09	4.33	1.48	800	733	849	22.4	2.9	7.4	2.5	59%	9%	47	24	30	34%	67%	12%	24	86	25%	33%	0	0.72	-15.3	80	95	-$6
17 STL	12	9	0	166	158	4.13	4.01	1.36	735	724	745	23.4	3.0	8.6	2.9	66%	10%	48	21	31	33%	72%	12%	30	90	27%	30%			4.7	100	120	$8
1st Half	5	3	0	80	77	4.16	4.10	1.43	765	803	733	22.7	3.3	8.7	2.7	63%	10%	47	22	31	34%	73%	11%	15	88	33%	27%			1.9	93	111	$4
2nd Half	7	6	0	86	81	4.10	3.93	1.30	708	648	755	24.1	2.7	8.5	3.1	68%	10%	49	20	31	32%	71%	12%	15	92	20%	33%			2.8	106	128	$11
18 Proj	**11**	**8**	**0**	**152**	**133**	**4.14**	**4.22**	**1.34**	**729**	**685**	**765**	**22.8**	**2.9**	**7.9**	**2.7**	**63%**	**10%**	**47**	**22**	**31**	**32%**	**71%**	**11%**	**28**						**4.1**	**89**	**107**	**$5**

Wainwright,Adam

Age: 36	Th: R	Role SP	Health	F	LIMA Plan	C
Ht: 6' 7"	Wt: 235	Type	PT/Exp	B	Rand Var	+3
			Consist	B	MM	1101

Remember when he was a 200-IP lock? Neither do we. Back, elbow ailments muddy outlook further. Even healthy version hasn't missed bats in years, leaving pinpoint control as only path to success. Sadly, another path he could be taking is the Steve Carlton path to retirement. Let's give him one final mulligan year.

Yr Tm	W	L	Sv	IP	K	ERA	xERA	WHIP	oOPS	vL	vR	BF/G	Ctl	Dom	Cmd	FpK	SwK	G	L	F	H%	S%	hr/f	GS	APC	DOM%	DIS%	Sv%	LI	RAR	BPV	BPX	R$
13 STL	19	9	0	242	219	2.94	2.94	1.07	636	631	639	28.1	1.3	8.2	6.3	65%	10%	49	23	28	31%	74%	8%	34	104	59%	9%			27.5	139	181	$29
14 STL	20	9	0	227	179	2.38	3.31	1.03	580	625	542	28.1	2.0	7.1	3.6	61%	9%	46	24	30	27%	78%	5%	32	102	56%	22%			38.1	98	117	$30
15 STL	2	1	0	28	20	1.61	3.35	1.04	590	661	540	15.9	1.3	6.4	5.0	54%	8%	51	26	23	30%	83%	0%	4	55	25%	0%	0	0.51	8.1	110	131	$1
16 STL	13	9	0	199	161	4.62	4.23	1.40	785	841	739	25.7	2.7	7.3	2.7	61%	9%	44	25	31	33%	69%	12%	33	97	27%	33%			-10.6	81	96	$1
17 STL	12	5	0	123	96	5.11	4.64	1.50	794	821	768	22.8	3.3	7.0	2.1	60%	8%	47	25	28	33%	67%	13%	23	90	30%	39%	0	0.74	-11.4	62	75	-$2
1st Half	8	5	0	85	74	5.17	4.43	1.54	807	793	818	23.8	3.4	7.8	2.3	57%	8%	48	24	27	35%	67%	12%	16	95	31%	38%			-8.5	76	91	-$1
2nd Half	4	0	0	38	22	4.97	5.10	1.42	765	872	622	20.6	3.1	5.2	1.7	66%	7%	45	26	29	30%	67%	14%	7	80	29%	43%	0	0.68	-2.9	34	40	-$4
18 Proj	**6**	**4**	**0**	**87**	**68**	**4.33**	**4.42**	**1.37**	**744**	**798**	**691**	**23.6**	**2.9**	**7.0**	**2.4**	**62%**	**8%**	**46**	**25**	**29**	**32%**	**70%**	**11%**	**15**						**0.3**	**72**	**87**	**-$1**

Walker,Taijuan

Age: 25	Th: R	Role SP	Health	D	LIMA Plan	B
Ht: 6' 4"	Wt: 235	Type Pwr	PT/Exp	B	Rand Var	-1
			Consist	A	MM	1203

Doubled value, but will it stick? PRO: 125+ BPV in two months; steep GB tilt now. CON: Sub-20 BPV in two others; still much more disastrous than dominant. Age, skill flashes, prior upside still give reason to hope for more. But shaky health, spotty growth are stronger reasons to believe he needs more time.

Yr Tm	W	L	Sv	IP	K	ERA	xERA	WHIP	oOPS	vL	vR	BF/G	Ctl	Dom	Cmd	FpK	SwK	G	L	F	H%	S%	hr/f	GS	APC	DOM%	DIS%	Sv%	LI	RAR	BPV	BPX	R$
13 SEA *	10	10	0	156	156	3.33	3.04	1.22	546	536	563	22.6	3.3	9.0	2.7	57%	10%	38	21	40	30%	74%	0%	3	78	0%	0%			10.3	101	132	$11
14 SEA *	9	7	0	116	109	3.85	3.70	1.25	642	729	501	20.5	3.2	8.4	2.7	61%	10%	47	27	26	29%	73%	7%	5	78	20%	0%	0	0.57	-1.5	82	97	$4
15 SEA	11	8	0	170	157	4.56	3.78	1.20	716	714	719	24.3	2.1	8.3	3.9	63%	11%	39	22	39	30%	66%	13%	29	91	34%	34%			-12.6	110	131	$5
16 SEA *	9	11	0	149	124	4.21	4.46	1.26	767	721	809	21.7	2.7	7.5	2.8	64%	10%	44	18	38	28%	74%	18%	25	92	28%	40%			-0.5	57	67	$5
17 ARI	9	9	0	157	146	3.49	4.30	1.33	732	727	736	24.4	3.5	8.4	2.4	59%	9%	49	18	33	31%	77%	11%	28	98	18%	32%			16.9	83	100	$10
1st Half	6	3	0	69	60	3.50	4.54	1.37	718	749	693	25.3	3.6	7.8	2.1	57%	10%	49	19	32	31%	76%	7%	12	98	17%	33%			7.3	69	83	$8
2nd Half	3	6	0	88	86	3.48	4.12	1.30	743	712	776	23.8	3.4	8.8	2.6	60%	9%	49	18	33	30%	78%	14%	16	98	19%	31%			9.6	94	112	$11
18 Proj	**10**	**11**	**0**	**174**	**158**	**3.95**	**4.21**	**1.28**	**733**	**727**	**740**	**22.7**	**3.1**	**8.2**	**2.7**	**61%**	**10%**	**46**	**20**	**34**	**30%**	**73%**	**14%**	**31**						**8.8**	**89**	**107**	**$9**

Warren,Adam

Age: 30	Th: R	Role RP	Health	D	LIMA Plan	B
Ht: 6' 1"	Wt: 225	Type Pwr	PT/Exp	C	Rand Var	-5
			Consist	B	MM	1200

Former middling long-reliever found home in shorter stints, posting best stats and skills of career. Here's why it won't happen again: 1) Dom jump not supported by SwK; 2) Absurd hit rate drove ERA down; 3) Subpar FpK dove further as season went along, so BB are going up. Heed Rand Var and expect regression.

Yr Tm	W	L	Sv	IP	K	ERA	xERA	WHIP	oOPS	vL	vR	BF/G	Ctl	Dom	Cmd	FpK	SwK	G	L	F	H%	S%	hr/f	GS	APC	DOM%	DIS%	Sv%	LI	RAR	BPV	BPX	R$
13 NYY	3	2	1	77	64	3.39	4.02	1.43	766	896	625	9.7	3.5	7.5	2.1	56%	11%	45	22	32	31%	81%	13%	2	38	0%	50%	100	0.58	4.5	63	82	-$1
14 NYY	3	6	3	79	76	2.97	3.31	1.11	615	525	690	4.7	2.7	8.7	3.2	58%	12%	45	24	31	29%	73%	6%	0	19			50	1.26	7.4	105	126	$6
15 NYY	7	7	1	131	104	3.29	3.84	1.16	648	603	680	12.4	2.7	7.1	2.7	60%	9%	45	23	32	28%	73%	8%	17	50	18%	12%	100	1.01	10.9	79	94	$9
16 2 TM	7	4	0	65	52	4.68	4.80	1.35	742	635	800	4.8	4.0	7.2	1.8	60%	10%	44	17	40	27%	70%	14%	1	20	0%	0%	0	1.05	-4.0	43	51	-$1
17 NYY	3	2	1	57	54	2.35	3.80	0.87	491	548	457	4.8	2.4	8.5	3.6	52%	10%	44	17	39	22%	76%	7%	0	20			25	1.11	14.2	111	133	$8
1st Half	2	1	1	32	30	2.23	3.76	0.80	429	551	358	5.3	2.5	8.4	3.3	56%	11%	48	14	38	21%	72%	3%	0	22			25	0.90	8.5	109	131	$10
2nd Half	1	1	0	25	24	2.52	3.83	0.96	570	542	588	4.4	2.2	8.6	4.0	48%	9%	38	21	41	24%	81%	11%	0	19			0	1.34	5.7	113	136	$5
18 Proj	**4**	**3**	**0**	**58**	**51**	**3.65**	**4.32**	**1.24**	**693**	**679**	**702**	**5.4**	**2.9**	**7.9**	**2.8**	**55%**	**10%**	**43**	**19**	**38**	**30%**	**74%**	**10%**	**0**						**5.1**	**87**	**105**	**$1**

Watson,Tony

Age: 33	Th: L	Role RP	Health	A	LIMA Plan	B
Ht: 6' 4"	Wt: 225	Type	PT/Exp	C	Rand Var	-1
			Consist	A	MM	2210

Perennial sneaky saves speculation got stopper taste again in 1st half but couldn't hold onto it, as skills simply weren't closer-worthy. Worrisome BPV and xERA trends, increasing struggles vR, age also put into question whether days of setup work are numbered. Best to allocate your speculative bullpen dollars elsewhere.

Yr Tm	W	L	Sv	IP	K	ERA	xERA	WHIP	oOPS	vL	vR	BF/G	Ctl	Dom	Cmd	FpK	SwK	G	L	F	H%	S%	hr/f	GS	APC	DOM%	DIS%	Sv%	LI	RAR	BPV	BPX	R$
13 PIT	3	1	2	72	54	2.39	3.44	0.88	544	483	582	4.2	1.5	6.8	4.5	63%	12%	44	19	37	24%	76%	7%	0	16			50	1.14	13.1	103	135	$9
14 PIT	10	2	2	77	81	1.63	2.76	1.02	613	531	646	3.9	1.7	9.4	5.4	65%	14%	48	21	32	30%	88%	8%	0	15			22	1.34	20.1	149	177	$13
15 PIT	4	1	1	75	62	1.91	3.42	0.96	525	493	536	3.8	2.0	7.4	3.6	66%	12%	48	21	32	26%	81%	5%	0	14			33	1.38	19.1	104	124	$10
16 PIT	2	5	15	68	58	3.06	4.01	1.06	672	577	711	3.9	2.7	7.7	2.9	64%	13%	44	18	38	24%	79%	14%	0	15			75	1.07	9.4	89	106	$10
17 2 NL	7	4	10	67	53	3.38	4.36	1.38	764	691	808	4.1	2.7	7.2	2.7	66%	13%	48	23	30	32%	81%	15%	0	14			56	1.27	8.1	82	98	$7
1st Half	4	1	10	37	29	3.89	4.75	1.49	838	703	909	4.6	2.2	7.1	3.2	66%	14%	38	25	37	34%	81%	16%	0	16			63	1.33	2.1	84	101	$8
2nd Half	3	3	0	30	24	2.73	3.80	1.25	659	677	642	3.6	3.3	7.3	2.2	66%	12%	61	19	19	29%	80%	13%	0	13			0	1.20	6.0	80	96	$4
18 Proj	**5**	**4**	**2**	**65**	**54**	**3.54**	**4.07**	**1.21**	**691**	**641**	**716**	**3.8**	**2.6**	**7.4**	**2.9**	**65%**	**13%**	**49**	**20**	**31**	**29%**	**74%**	**12%**	**0**						**6.6**	**91**	**110**	**$3**

Weaver,Luke

Age: 24	Th: R	Role SP	Health	A	LIMA Plan	C+
Ht: 6' 2"	Wt: 170	Type Pwr	PT/Exp	D	Rand Var	+2
			Consist	A	MM	3305

7-2, 3.88 ERA in 60 IP at STL. Former first-rounder got even better in second taste of majors (152 BPV). That near-4 ERA in bigs was result of H% and hr/f misfortune. Late-season dominance came with zero skill cracks, putting him in line for a full-season breakout in 2018. With opportunity... UP: 3.00 ERA, 200 K

Yr Tm	W	L	Sv	IP	K	ERA	xERA	WHIP	oOPS	vL	vR	BF/G	Ctl	Dom	Cmd	FpK	SwK	G	L	F	H%	S%	hr/f	GS	APC	DOM%	DIS%	Sv%	LI	RAR	BPV	BPX	R$
13																																	
14																																	
15																																	
16 STL *	8	7	0	119	120	2.80	3.60	1.20	870	1025	761	21.8	1.8	9.0	5.0	56%	10%	31	37	33	33%	80%	21%	8	76	13%	38%	0	0.71	20.4	137	163	$12
17 STL *	17	4	0	138	132	3.47	3.47	1.23	699	575	793	20.0	2.4	8.6	3.6	59%	10%	49	24	27	32%	73%	16%	10	80	40%	30%	0	0.64	15.2	112	135	$15
1st Half	7	1	0	56	48	2.38	2.73	1.10				20.0	2.1	7.7	3.6						29%	80%	0%	0						13.7	114	137	$15
2nd Half	10	3	0	82	85	4.21	3.97	1.32	699	575	793	20.0	2.5	9.3	3.7	59%	10%	49	24	27	35%	69%	16%	10	80	40%	30%	0	0.64	1.5	111	133	$15
18 Proj	**14**	**8**	**0**	**181**	**178**	**3.33**	**3.66**	**1.19**	**641**	**636**	**645**	**23.9**	**2.1**	**8.8**	**4.1**	**58%**	**10%**	**42**	**29**	**29**	**32%**	**74%**	**10%**	**30**						**23.0**	**121**	**146**	**$18**

Wheeler,Zack

Age: 28	Th: R	Role SP	Health	F	LIMA Plan	C
Ht: 6' 4"	Wt: 195	Type Pwr	PT/Exp	D	Rand Var	+5
			Consist	F	MM	1301

Slow return from 2015 TJS continues as elbow soreness lingers, but even a healthy outlook is worrisome. Control often is last to come back post-surgery, put further at risk by his pre-injury wildness. Now three years since going under knife, that 2014 breakout is a distant memory. He's a high-risk dart throw now.

Yr Tm	W	L	Sv	IP	K	ERA	xERA	WHIP	oOPS	vL	vR	BF/G	Ctl	Dom	Cmd	FpK	SwK	G	L	F	H%	S%	hr/f	GS	APC	DOM%	DIS%	Sv%	LI	RAR	BPV	BPX	R$
13 NYM *	11	7	0	169	148	3.38	3.58	1.29	696	766	639	23.1	3.7	7.9	2.2	52%	9%	43	23	33	29%	77%	10%	17	102	29%	35%			10.2	72	94	$9
14 NYM	11	11	0	185	187	3.54	3.37	1.33	678	745	615	24.8	3.8	9.1	2.4	54%	10%	54	19	27	31%	75%	10%	32	103	31%	22%			4.5	92	109	$6
15																																	
16																																	
17 NYM	3	7	0	86	81	5.21	4.55	1.59	828	858	804	22.7	4.2	8.4	2.0	61%	10%	47	23	30	34%	71%	19%	17	92	18%	47%			-9.1	64	77	-$7
1st Half	3	5	0	70	65	5.01	4.47	1.51	786	857	727	22.1	4.0	8.4	2.1	59%	9%	47	23	30	33%	71%	18%	14	90	21%	43%			-5.7	68	81	-$5
2nd Half	0	2	0	16	16	6.06	4.88	1.90	1000	859	1083	25.7	5.0	8.8	1.8	69%	11%	50	20	30	37%	74%	27%	3	99	0%	67%			-3.4	53	63	-$12
18 Proj	**4**	**8**	**0**	**102**	**98**	**4.39**	**4.36**	**1.48**	**778**	**777**	**779**	**23.6**	**4.2**	**8.7**	**2.1**	**60%**	**10%**	**50**	**21**	**30**	**32%**	**74%**	**17%**	**18**						**-0.4**	**71**	**86**	**-$3**

STEPHEN NICKRAND

Williams,Trevor

Age: 26	Th: R	Role	SP	Health	A	LIMA Plan	C+
Ht: 6' 3"	Wt: 230	Type		PT/Exp	C	Rand Var	0
				Consist	A	MM	0003

Former 2nd rounder got first full MLB stint. The takeaway? Blah. Nothing here to suggest prior upside is lurking, as skills were average across the board. Even sub-indicators showing few glimmers of hope. Consistent 1st/2nd half xERA says 4.50 ERA is your baseline. Of course, simply ignoring him also works.

Yr Tm	W	L	Sv	IP	K	ERA	xERA	WHIP	oOPS	vL	vR	BF/G	Ctl	Dom	Cmd	FpK	SwK	G	L	F	H%	S%	hr/f	GS	APC	DOM%	DIS%	Sv%	LI	RAR	BPV	BPX	R$
13																																	
14 aa	0	1	0	15	12	6.66	6.48	1.99				24.0	3.4	7.1	2.1						44%	63%								-5.4	68	81	-$6
15 a/a	7	10	0	131	84	4.79	5.13	1.60				23.2	3.1	5.8	1.9						35%	70%								-13.4	49	59	-$10
16 PIT *	10	7	0	123	70	4.10	5.03	1.54	1054	1359	885	19.9	2.8	5.1	1.8	56%	10%	45	25	30	34%	74%	31%	1	32	0%	100%	0	0.70	1.3	40	48	-$2
17 PIT	7	9	0	150	117	4.07	4.47	1.31	715	742	688	20.7	3.1	7.0	2.3	61%	9%	48	21	31	30%	70%	10%	25	78	16%	24%	0	0.75	5.3	68	82	$5
1st Half	3	3	0	65	48	4.82	4.52	1.27	728	715	741	17.4	2.3	6.6	2.8	61%	10%	44	22	34	30%	63%	10%	10	63	10%	20%	0	0.73	-3.7	78	93	$0
2nd Half	4	6	0	85	69	3.49	4.42	1.34	704	763	647	24.3	3.7	7.3	2.0	61%	8%	51	20	29	30%	76%	10%	15	94	20%	27%			9.1	61	73	$9
18 Proj	10	11	0	174	119	4.27	4.79	1.44	775	816	735	23.8	3.0	6.2	2.0	61%	9%	48	21	31	32%	71%	8%	31						1.9	56	67	$1

Wilson,Justin

Age: 30	Th: L	Role	RP	Health	A	LIMA Plan	B
Ht: 6' 2"	Wt: 205	Type	Pwr	PT/Exp	C	Rand Var	-1
				Consist	A	MM	2500

Top-tier closer gets traded, loses job, and promptly falls apart. Surging pre-2017 skills along with electric 1st half give hope for turnaround, with one huge caveat: Subpar FpK masked control warts early, then sabotaged him late. He's been better, so side with rebound. Without saves, value is minimal. But Sv+Holds leagues...

Yr Tm	W	L	Sv	IP	K	ERA	xERA	WHIP	oOPS	vL	vR	BF/G	Ctl	Dom	Cmd	FpK	SwK	G	L	F	H%	S%	hr/f	GS	APC	DOM%	DIS%	Sv%	LI	RAR	BPV	BPX	R$
13 PIT	6	1	0	74	59	2.08	3.59	1.06	543	501	563	5.1	3.4	7.2	2.1	59%	10%	53	17	30	24%	82%	7%	0	21			0	1.11	16.3	68	89	$8
14 PIT	3	4	0	60	61	4.20	3.68	1.32	643	681	622	3.7	4.5	9.2	2.0	61%	10%	51	14	34	29%	68%	7%	0	15			0	1.05	-3.4	72	86	-$2
15 NYY	5	0	0	61	66	3.10	3.17	1.13	602	629	588	3.3	3.0	9.7	3.3	60%	13%	44	27	29	30%	73%	7%	0	14			0	1.26	6.5	118	140	$4
16 DET	4	5	1	59	65	4.14	3.37	1.33	708	772	667	3.8	2.6	10.0	3.8	59%	13%	55	15	30	35%	71%	12%	0	15			17	1.25	0.3	142	169	$0
17 2 TM	4	4	13	58	80	3.41	4.02	1.29	631	701	599	3.8	5.4	12.4	2.3	53%	13%	37	18	44	30%	76%	9%	0	17			81	1.21	6.8	92	110	$8
1st Half	3	3	8	31	46	2.64	3.15	0.98	587	703	544	3.7	3.5	13.5	3.8	50%	15%	35	16	49	26%	81%	13%	0	17			89	1.35	6.5	161	193	$15
2nd Half	1	1	5	27	34	4.28	5.21	1.65	671	696	658	4.0	7.6	11.2	1.5	57%	11%	40	21	40	33%	73%	4%	0	18			71	1.06	0.3	15	18	$1
18 Proj	4	3	0	58	70	3.63	3.94	1.31	651	704	623	3.7	4.5	10.8	2.4	57%	12%	44	19	37	31%	74%	8%	0						5.2	97	117	$1

Wittgren,Nick

Age: 27	Th: R	Role	RP	Health	D	LIMA Plan	C+
Ht: 6' 2"	Wt: 210	Type	FB	PT/Exp	D	Rand Var	+2
				Consist	A	MM	1200

On surface, a middling reliever who won't be drafted in most leagues. But near-5 ERA was hit-rate driven. Second straight 100+ BPV season came with good SwK/FpK support this time, so it can stick. And K/BB actually was better vL, which could help expand role. If bone spur cleanup works, an intriguing $1 target.

Yr Tm	W	L	Sv	IP	K	ERA	xERA	WHIP	oOPS	vL	vR	BF/G	Ctl	Dom	Cmd	FpK	SwK	G	L	F	H%	S%	hr/f	GS	APC	DOM%	DIS%	Sv%	LI	RAR	BPV	BPX	R$
13																																	
14 aa	5	5	20	66	46	4.02	4.79	1.44				5.4	1.9	6.3	3.4						35%	73%								-2.2	82	98	$5
15 a/a	1	6	20	64	54	3.75	3.89	1.21				4.9	1.2	7.7	6.4						33%	71%								1.7	156	185	$7
16 MIA	4	3	0	52	42	3.14	4.16	1.16	671	618	717	4.4	1.7	7.3	4.2	62%	7%	39	21	40	30%	78%	10%	0	18			0	1.01	6.7	102	121	$2
17 MIA	3	1	0	42	43	4.68	4.43	1.39	800	915	720	4.8	2.8	9.1	3.3	65%	12%	33	24	43	35%	69%	9%	0	20			0	0.74	-1.7	101	121	-$3
1st Half	1	1	0	33	34	3.51	3.96	1.20	739	815	688	4.7	1.6	9.2	5.7	68%	11%	33	23	44	33%	75%	10%	0	20			0	0.75	3.5	133	159	-$1
2nd Half	2	0	0	9	9	9.00	6.51	2.11	992	1206	822	5.1	7.0	9.0	1.3	57%	13%	33	27	40	40%	56%	8%	0	21			0	0.69	-5.2	-16	-19	-$9
18 Proj	2	4	0	58	50	3.60	4.27	1.23	730	755	712	4.7	1.5	7.8	5.2	66%	10%	36	22	42	33%	74%	8%	0						5.4	114	137	$0

Wojciechowski,Asher

Age: 29	Th: R	Role	RP	Health	C	LIMA Plan	D+
Ht: 6' 4"	Wt: 235	Type	Pwr xFB	PT/Exp	D	Rand Var	+3
				Consist	D	MM	0100

4-3, 6.50 ERA in 62 IP at CIN. Somehow managed to stay MLB-employed in spite of horrible stats. Before you identify elevated H% as reason to fish, its history says to expect more of same. And as an extreme FB pitcher, we can't expect hr/f to be on his side either. Tuck away 2nd half BPV... then keep it tucked.

Yr Tm	W	L	Sv	IP	K	ERA	xERA	WHIP	oOPS	vL	vR	BF/G	Ctl	Dom	Cmd	FpK	SwK	G	L	F	H%	S%	hr/f	GS	APC	DOM%	DIS%	Sv%	LI	RAR	BPV	BPX	R$
13 a/a	11	8	1	160	110	3.91	3.62	1.29				23.5	2.9	6.2	2.1						29%	71%								-0.9	64	83	$4
14 aaa	4	4	0	76	48	5.33	6.08	1.63				22.5	2.5	5.7	2.3						36%	70%								-14.9	34	41	-$9
15 HOU *	8	5	0	132	86	5.68	5.92	1.67	965	1125	694	23.7	3.3	5.9	1.8	53%	6%	20	31	49	35%	67%	7%	3	62	0%	67%	0	0.52	-27.8	31	37	-$15
16 a/a	5	5	0	86	49	6.64	7.38	1.99				20.6	4.5	5.2	1.1						37%	68%								-25.9	2	2	-$18
17 CIN *	6	3	0	93	91	5.32	5.24	1.42	899	978	819	11.9	2.8	8.8	3.2	66%	11%	29	20	51	33%	67%	15%	8	44	13%	38%	0	0.60	-11.0	69	83	-$3
1st Half	3	1	0	52	45	4.50	5.09	1.38	995	1041	956	15.6	2.4	7.8	3.3	71%	10%	27	17	56	33%	73%	16%	4	60	0%	50%	0	0.61	-0.9	68	82	-$1
2nd Half	3	2	0	41	46	6.37	4.57	1.46	849	950	738	9.8	3.3	10.1	3.1	63%	11%	30	22	48	35%	60%	14%	4	39	25%	25%	0	0.60	-10.2	101	121	-$5
18 Proj	4	3	0	58	47	5.78	5.63	1.61	906	987	826	14.8	3.4	7.3	2.2	66%	11%	29	20	51	35%	67%	9%	8						-10.2	48	58	-$7

Wood,Alex

Age: 27	Th: L	Role	SP	Health	F	LIMA Plan	C
Ht: 6' 4"	Wt: 215	Type	Pwr GB	PT/Exp	B	Rand Var	0
				Consist	A	MM	3303

Career year fueled by taking Cmd to next level. As FpK inches higher each year, pinpoint control can stick. And great BPV in four of last five seasons underscores consistency. Just don't expect another sub-3 ERA, as this one had both H% and S% help. And health risk serves as reminder to use 150 IP as baseline.

Yr Tm	W	L	Sv	IP	K	ERA	xERA	WHIP	oOPS	vL	vR	BF/G	Ctl	Dom	Cmd	FpK	SwK	G	L	F	H%	S%	hr/f	GS	APC	DOM%	DIS%	Sv%	LI	RAR	BPV	BPX	R$
13 ATL *	8	5	0	140	132	2.43	2.83	1.22	670	622	690	13.4	2.8	8.5	3.0	62%	10%	49	24	27	32%	80%	5%	11	42	27%	36%	0	0.60	24.7	113	147	$13
14 ATL	11	11	0	172	170	2.78	3.20	1.14	651	667	645	19.8	2.4	8.9	3.8	62%	10%	46	19	35	30%	79%	10%	24	77	42%	13%	0	0.91	20.4	121	144	$16
15 2 NL	12	12	0	190	139	3.84	4.01	1.36	724	517	788	25.0	2.8	6.6	2.4	63%	8%	49	23	28	32%	73%	9%	32	91	28%	22%			2.8	70	84	$5
16 LA	1	4	0	60	66	3.73	3.32	1.26	660	774	620	18.2	3.0	9.8	3.3	64%	10%	53	20	27	33%	72%	12%	10	70	30%	20%	0	0.60	3.4	128	152	$0
17 LA	16	3	0	152	151	2.72	3.36	1.06	620	607	625	22.7	2.2	8.9	4.0	67%	12%	53	20	27	28%	79%	14%	25	84	44%	24%	0	0.78	30.8	131	157	$25
1st Half	9	0	0	74	87	1.83	2.52	0.91	485	479	488	20.6	2.4	10.6	4.4	66%	14%	66	15	19	27%	80%	6%	12	79	58%	0%	0	0.80	22.9	169	202	$33
2nd Half	7	3	0	79	64	3.55	4.14	1.19	739	755	733	25.1	2.1	7.3	3.6	68%	11%	44	24	33	29%	78%	17%	13	88	31%	46%			7.9	98	117	$17
18 Proj	12	6	0	156	150	3.20	3.60	1.18	658	650	661	20.4	2.5	8.6	3.4	65%	11%	52	21	28	30%	76%	12%	31						22.3	117	141	$16

Wood,Blake

Age: 32	Th: R	Role	RP	Health	B	LIMA Plan	C
Ht: 6' 5"	Wt: 233	Type	Pwr GB	PT/Exp	D	Rand Var	+5
				Consist	B	MM	2400

Middlemen whose clubs don't trust them don't warrant your faith either. Still, some seeds of hope for the very brave: 1) High K rate has SwK backing; 2) Big growth in 2nd half obscured by crazy-bad luck; 3) 46% hit rate vL drove wide L/R splits and won't repeat; 4) Keeps ball on ground. There are worse dart throws.

Yr Tm	W	L	Sv	IP	K	ERA	xERA	WHIP	oOPS	vL	vR	BF/G	Ctl	Dom	Cmd	FpK	SwK	G	L	F	H%	S%	hr/f	GS	APC	DOM%	DIS%	Sv%	LI	RAR	BPV	BPX	R$
13 CLE *	2	0	0	24	23	3.31	4.41	1.82	700	500	833	4.1	7.1	8.8	1.2	50%	12%	50	25	25	36%	80%	0%	0	21			0	0.15	1.7	80	105	-$4
14 CLE *	0	2	0	39	36	7.04	6.97	2.26	673	625	729	5.5	8.9	8.3	0.9	67%	6%	40	20	40	38%	68%	0%	0	18			0	0.20	-16.0	39	47	-$13
15 aaa	2	5	29	59	49	5.19	5.05	1.71				4.7	4.5	7.6	1.7						37%	68%								-8.9	64	77	$3
16 CIN	6	5	1	77	81	3.99	3.86	1.43	752	722	775	4.7	4.5	9.5	2.1	56%	11%	53	19	28	32%	75%	16%	0	19			17	1.05	1.9	82	97	$1
17 2 TM	3	4	0	74	84	5.45	3.84	1.57	777	953	649	4.6	4.0	10.2	2.5	58%	12%	52	23	25	38%	66%	15%	0	18			0	0.66	-10.0	105	126	-$6
1st Half	0	4	0	37	37	4.42	3.91	1.50	732	970	595	4.7	4.4	9.1	2.1	58%	12%	58	22	20	35%	70%	10%	0	18			0	0.58	-0.3	80	96	-$6
2nd Half	3	0	0	38	47	6.45	3.76	1.65	818	941	708	4.5	3.6	11.2	3.1	58%	12%	47	24	29	41%	63%	19%	0	17			0	0.73	-9.7	130	156	-$7
18 Proj	3	4	0	65	69	4.21	3.91	1.37	683	761	624	4.4	4.2	9.5	2.3	57%	12%	52	22	26	31%	71%	14%	0						1.2	87	105	-$1

Wood,Travis

Age: 31	Th: L	Role	RP	Health	A	LIMA Plan	D+
Ht: 5' 11"	Wt: 175	Type	Pwr FB	PT/Exp	C	Rand Var	+5
				Consist	C	MM	0101

By far the most underwhelming of the Wood trifecta. While others show reason for hope as you peel back the onion, this one hasn't missed bats in years, still allows too many balls in the sky, and is getting torched by RHers more and more. This is one case where even regression is not enough to save him.

Yr Tm	W	L	Sv	IP	K	ERA	xERA	WHIP	oOPS	vL	vR	BF/G	Ctl	Dom	Cmd	FpK	SwK	G	L	F	H%	S%	hr/f	GS	APC	DOM%	DIS%	Sv%	LI	RAR	BPV	BPX	R$
13 CHC	9	12	0	200	144	3.11	4.34	1.15	643	599	656	25.7	3.0	6.5	2.2	61%	8%	33	22	44	26%	76%	7%	32	97	34%	22%			18.8	47	62	$15
14 CHC	8	13	0	174	146	5.03	4.59	1.53	782	619	837	25.2	3.9	7.6	1.9	57%	7%	34	23	42	33%	69%	9%	31	98	19%	42%			-27.5	42	50	-$11
15 CHC	5	4	4	101	118	3.84	3.67	1.24	663	597	698	7.8	3.5	10.5	3.0	62%	11%	35	23	43	31%	72%	10%	9	32	22%	22%	100	0.79	1.5	108	128	$5
16 CHC	4	0	0	61	47	2.95	4.75	1.13	664	447	865	3.3	3.5	6.9	2.0	66%	8%	37	22	41	23%	80%	11%	0	13			0	1.02	9.3	44	53	$4
17 2 TM	4	7	0	94	65	6.80	6.05	1.73	911	820	935	11.2	4.3	6.2	1.4	62%	6%	36	21	43	33%	64%	14%	14	44	0%	71%	0	0.90	-28.3	10	12	-$15
1st Half	1	2	0	29	21	6.28	6.26	1.81	851	866	845	5.4	5.7	6.6	1.2	62%	7%	38	21	40	34%	65%	8%	0	21			0	0.98	-6.8	-18	-21	-$13
2nd Half	3	5	0	65	44	7.03	5.96	1.70	936	786	967	21.6	3.7	6.1	1.6	62%	6%	35	22	44	33%	63%	16%	14	84	0%	71%			-21.5	21	25	-$16
18 Proj	4	4	0	87	69	4.88	5.30	1.48	793	630	865	6.6	4.0	7.2	1.8	63%	8%	36	22	42	30%	71%	12%	8						-5.6	35	42	-$5

STEPHEN NICKRAND

Woodruff,Brandon

Age: 25	Th: R	Role SP	Health C	LIMA Plan B+
Ht: 6' 4"	Wt: 215	Type Pwr GB	PT/Exp D	Rand Var 0
			Consist C	MM 1203

2-3, 4.81 ERA in 43 IP at MIL. Underrated SP prospect strained hammy after mid-season recall and never found footing. Topped minors in Ks in 2016 with mid-90s sinking stuff. Next step is refining change-up, which will help struggles vL and enable him to tap into upside. With health, adjustment... UP: 200 K

Yr Tm	W	L	Sv	IP	K	ERA	xERA	WHIP	oOPS	vL	vR	BF/G	Ctl	Dom	Cmd	FpK	SwK	G	L	F	H%	S%	hr/f	GS	APC	DOM%	DIS%	Sv%	LI	RAR	BPV	BPX	R$
13																																	
14																																	
15																																	
16 aa	10	8	0	114	107	4.52	3.53	1.29				23.4	2.7	8.5	3.2						33%	64%								-4.6	105	125	$
17 MIL *	8	8	0	118	91	4.66	4.62	1.40	719	872	566	20.8	2.9	6.9	2.4	62%	9%	47	19	34	32%	69%	11%	8	90	38%	63%			-4.3	60	72	$
1st Half	6	4	0	63	51	4.37	4.32	1.32				21.9	2.6	7.2	2.8						31%	70%	0%	0						-0.1	70	84	$
2nd Half	2	4	0	55	40	4.98	4.96	1.50	719	872	566	19.8	3.2	6.6	2.0	62%	9%	47	19	34	33%	68%	11%	8	90	38%	63%			-4.2	50	60	-$
18 Proj	**10**	**9**	**0**	**160**	**133**	**4.23**	**4.48**	**1.35**	**655**	**802**	**506**	**22.9**	**2.9**	**7.5**	**2.6**	**62%**	**9%**	**47**	**19**	**34**	**32%**	**70%**	**8%**	**29**						**2.5**	**83**	**100**	**$**

Wright,Steven

Age: 33	Th: R	Role SP	Health F	LIMA Plan D+
Ht: 6' 2"	Wt: 215	Type	PT/Exp C	Rand Var +5
			Consist B	MM 0001

Early knee surgery wiped out season before it began. It was karma for those hoping for 2016 stats again, as they were result of knuckleball magic rather than sturdy foundation. Long history of subpar FpK, so-so SwK, age all confirm what the aberration is in this five-year box. Flunking health seals fate. Pass.

Yr Tm	W	L	Sv	IP	K	ERA	xERA	WHIP	oOPS	vL	vR	BF/G	Ctl	Dom	Cmd	FpK	SwK	G	L	F	H%	S%	hr/f	GS	APC	DOM%	DIS%	Sv%	LI	RAR	BPV	BPX	R$
13 BOS *	10	7	0	149	83	4.86	5.62	1.79	659	760	350	24.5	5.0	5.0	1.0	46%	9%	38	26	36	34%	73%	0%	1	61	0%	100%	0	0.57	-18.2	23	30	-$1
14 BOS *	6	6	0	121	74	4.55	5.06	1.46	632	667	603	23.5	2.4	5.5	2.4	56%	10%	59	21	21	33%	71%	17%	1	58	0%	0%	0	0.26	-12.1	46	55	-$
15 BOS *	7	9	0	125	83	4.95	5.17	1.54	722	671	770	22.6	3.3	6.0	1.8	55%	9%	43	14	43	33%	70%	12%	9	74	22%	56%	0	0.76	-15.3	38	46	-$
16 BOS	13	6	0	157	127	3.33	4.42	1.24	653	608	686	27.3	3.3	7.3	2.2	55%	11%	44	19	37	29%	75%	7%	24	104	46%	25%			16.6	65	77	$1
17 BOS	1	3	0	24	13	8.25	5.59	1.88	1148	1039	1210	22.8	1.9	4.9	2.6	59%	7%	41	23	35	36%	64%	27%	5	77	0%	60%			-11.5	56	67	-$1
1st Half	1	3	0	24	13	8.25	5.59	1.88	1148	1039	1210	22.8	1.9	4.9	2.6	59%	7%	41	23	35	36%	64%	27%	5	77	0%	60%			-11.5	57	68	-$1
2nd Half																																	
18 Proj	**6**	**8**	**0**	**102**	**65**	**4.93**	**5.41**	**1.60**	**893**	**800**	**962**	**23.6**	**2.9**	**5.7**	**2.0**	**57%**	**9%**	**43**	**19**	**39**	**33%**	**74%**	**14%**	**19**						**-7.2**	**46**	**55**	**-$**

Yates,Kirby

Age: 31	Th: R	Role RP	Health C	LIMA Plan A
Ht: 5' 10"	Wt: 210	Type Pwr xFB	PT/Exp D	Rand Var +3
			Consist F	MM 2510

After years of bouncing around, he looked the part of future closer in this one. While ERA eroded late—it was inflated by S% and hr/f—skills remained elite. Credit addition of splitter as a third pitch for elite SwK. FB% adds peril, but held up well when used in tight games late. At minimum, LIMA gem.... UP: 30 Sv

Yr Tm	W	L	Sv	IP	K	ERA	xERA	WHIP	oOPS	vL	vR	BF/G	Ctl	Dom	Cmd	FpK	SwK	G	L	F	H%	S%	hr/f	GS	APC	DOM%	DIS%	Sv%	LI	RAR	BPV	BPX	R$
13 aaa	3	2	20	62	75	2.31	2.17	1.12				4.8	3.5	11.0	3.2						31%	80%								11.9	137	178	$1
14 TAM *	1	2	17	61	70	2.41	2.61	1.16	699	844	644	4.2	3.7	10.3	2.8	60%	9%	32	23	45	29%	82%	9%	0	19			94	0.66	10.0	115	138	$1
15 TAM *	2	2	6	46	48	7.56	7.83	1.72	1004	1254	840	4.8	4.0	9.4	2.3	65%	10%	25	22	52	34%	64%	30%	0	20			86	0.43	-20.3	3	4	-$
16 NYY *	2	2	4	58	64	4.46	4.18	1.45	746	584	829	4.5	4.1	10.0	2.4	64%	12%	44	23	34	35%	70%	14%	0	20			57	0.61	-1.9	91	108	-$
17 2 TM	4	5	1	57	88	3.97	3.24	1.11	698	839	594	3.7	3.0	14.0	4.6	63%	18%	29	15	56	31%	75%	18%	0	16			25	0.85	2.7	177	213	$
1st Half	2	1	0	27	42	2.70	3.13	1.20	706	987	532	4.1	2.7	14.2	5.3	64%	19%	31	20	49	36%	89%	17%	0	16			0	0.58	5.5	191	229	$
2nd Half	2	4	1	30	46	5.10	3.34	1.03	690	722	663	3.4	3.3	13.8	4.2	61%	17%	27	10	63	25%	58%	18%	0	15			33	1.06	-2.7	164	197	$
18 Proj	**3**	**4**	**2**	**58**	**77**	**3.47**	**3.75**	**1.23**	**720**	**756**	**699**	**4.0**	**3.5**	**11.9**	**3.4**	**62%**	**14%**	**34**	**18**	**47**	**31%**	**81%**	**17%**	**0**						**6.4**	**132**	**159**	**$**

Ynoa,Gabriel

Age: 25	Th: R	Role SP	Health B	LIMA Plan D+
Ht: 6' 2"	Wt: 205	Type Con xFB	PT/Exp D	Rand Var +5
			Consist B	MM 0000

2-3, 4.15 ERA in 35 IP at BAL. Guys like this who miss bats with a low K rate often are good targets, as those whiffs usually convert into Ks. Problem is, he missed fewer bats as season wore on, which puts into question how good his stuff really is. And that nifty 2nd half Ctl was a total fluke—see terrible FpK. Nothing here.

Yr Tm	W	L	Sv	IP	K	ERA	xERA	WHIP	oOPS	vL	vR	BF/G	Ctl	Dom	Cmd	FpK	SwK	G	L	F	H%	S%	hr/f	GS	APC	DOM%	DIS%	Sv%	LI	RAR	BPV	BPX	R$
13																																	
14 aa	3	2	0	66	38	4.04	4.52	1.29				24.8	1.4	5.1	3.5						31%	72%								-2.5	69	83	-$
15 aa	9	9	0	152	72	4.46	4.45	1.34				25.4	1.8	4.3	2.4						31%	68%								-9.3	47	55	-$
16 NYM *	13	5	0	173	87	4.01	4.50	1.42	745	749	742	20.9	2.4	4.5	1.9	59%	11%	49	26	25	32%	73%	0%	3	32	33%	67%	0	0.60	3.9	43	51	$
17 BAL *	8	12	0	141	88	6.39	6.06	1.66	810	969	653	21.1	2.3	5.6	2.4	58%	10%	38	14	48	37%	61%	9%	4	60	0%	50%	0	0.66	-35.4	45	54	-$1
1st Half	2	7	0	61	32	8.54	8.10	2.09	924	1280	668	19.8	3.1	4.7	1.5	64%	12%	33	12	55	42%	58%	13%	0	57			0	0.64	-31.3	9	11	-$3
2nd Half	6	5	0	80	56	4.77	4.51	1.34	737	817	639	22.3	1.7	6.3	3.7	54%	9%	41	15	44	33%	65%	7%	4	63	0%	50%	0	0.67	-4.1	84	101	-$
18 Proj	**4**	**4**	**0**	**58**	**33**	**4.93**	**5.62**	**1.50**	**805**	**889**	**703**	**21.9**	**2.1**	**5.1**	**2.4**	**54%**	**9%**	**41**	**15**	**44**	**34%**	**68%**	**6%**	**11**						**-4.1**	**53**	**64**	**-$**

Ziegler,Brad

Age: 38	Th: R	Role RP	Health D	LIMA Plan C
Ht: 6' 4"	Wt: 220	Type xGB	PT/Exp B	Rand Var 0
			Consist B	MM 2010

The perennial veteran closer you can draft late (434 ADP in 2017) who will give you double-digit saves. Three reasons those days are coming to an end: 1) Always-iffy Cmd fell off cliff; 2) Marginal command sub-indicators give no hope it will improve; 3) Almost 40 now, so nagging injuries more likely to linger.

Yr Tm	W	L	Sv	IP	K	ERA	xERA	WHIP	oOPS	vL	vR	BF/G	Ctl	Dom	Cmd	FpK	SwK	G	L	F	H%	S%	hr/f	GS	APC	DOM%	DIS%	Sv%	LI	RAR	BPV	BPX	R$
13 ARI	8	1	13	73	44	2.22	3.16	1.14	594	647	550	3.8	2.7	5.4	2.0	63%	10%	70	19	11	26%	81%	13%	0	13			87	1.50	14.8	72	94	$1
14 ARI	5	3	1	67	54	3.49	3.23	1.25	681	596	734	4.1	3.2	7.3	2.3	59%	11%	64	17	19	29%	73%	14%	0	14			11	1.39	2.1	86	102	$
15 ARI	0	3	30	68	36	1.85	3.24	0.96	524	621	430	4.0	2.3	4.8	2.1	59%	9%	73	14	14	22%	82%	11%	0	14			94	1.37	17.7	76	91	$1
16 2 TM	4	7	22	68	58	2.25	3.59	1.37	669	723	630	4.2	3.4	7.7	2.2	56%	12%	63	19	18	33%	84%	6%	0	15			79	1.48	16.3	86	102	$1
17 MIA	1	4	10	47	26	4.79	4.43	1.55	756	663	836	4.0	3.1	5.0	1.6	61%	9%	64	20	16	34%	67%	4%	0	13			67	1.11	-2.5	49	59	-$
1st Half	1	2	0	29	17	6.52	4.76	1.83	848	743	931	4.1	4.0	5.3	1.3	57%	9%	65	21	14	38%	62%	7%	0	13			0	0.92	-7.7	29	34	-$
2nd Half	0	2	10	18	9	2.00	3.91	1.11	592	535	648	3.8	1.5	4.5	3.0	68%	9%	63	18	18	29%	80%	0%	0	13			77	1.45	5.2	82	98	$
18 Proj	**2**	**5**	**8**	**65**	**41**	**3.86**	**3.94**	**1.30**	**662**	**643**	**678**	**3.9**	**2.8**	**5.7**	**2.1**	**61%**	**10%**	**65**	**18**	**16**	**31%**	**69%**	**5%**	**0**						**4.0**	**71**	**86**	**$**

Zimmermann,Jordan

Age: 32	Th: R	Role SP	Health D	LIMA Plan C
Ht: 6' 2"	Wt: 225	Type Con	PT/Exp B	Rand Var +4
			Consist B	MM 0003

Free-fall continued. Sure, H%, S%, hr/f rates all did harm. But the only thing he does well now is get strike one. As RH thump him more and more each season, it's an indication that he has run out of tricks. This is what happens when you live in strike zone but can't miss bats. Without a new pitch, that won't change.

Yr Tm	W	L	Sv	IP	K	ERA	xERA	WHIP	oOPS	vL	vR	BF/G	Ctl	Dom	Cmd	FpK	SwK	G	L	F	H%	S%	hr/f	GS	APC	DOM%	DIS%	Sv%	LI	RAR	BPV	BPX	R$
13 WAS	19	9	0	213	161	3.25	3.50	1.09	654	702	601	27.0	1.7	6.8	4.0	67%	9%	48	21	31	28%	73%	10%	32	96	47%	16%			16.2	103	134	$2
14 WAS	14	5	0	200	182	2.66	3.22	1.07	631	655	606	25.0	1.3	8.2	6.3	71%	11%	40	24	36	31%	77%	6%	32	91	50%	13%			26.6	130	155	$2
15 WAS	13	10	0	202	164	3.66	3.82	1.20	699	776	617	25.2	1.7	7.3	4.2	67%	9%	42	22	36	31%	74%	11%	33	94	27%	18%			7.5	105	125	$1
16 DET *	9	8	0	126	74	4.41	4.88	1.39	804	738	862	22.1	2.2	5.3	2.4	65%	8%	43	18	39	31%	72%	10%	18	90	17%	39%	0	0.73	-3.3	43	51	-$
17 DET	8	13	0	160	103	6.08	5.46	1.55	888	903	872	24.6	2.5	5.8	2.3	67%	8%	33	25	42	33%	64%	13%	29	91	10%	48%			-33.9	48	58	-$1
1st Half	5	6	0	92	65	5.58	5.25	1.47	879	876	882	24.9	2.8	6.4	2.2	64%	9%	33	24	43	30%	68%	16%	16	94	6%	50%			-13.8	49	58	-$
2nd Half	3	7	0	68	38	6.75	5.74	1.66	898	933	857	24.2	2.0	5.0	2.5	71%	8%	33	26	40	37%	59%	8%	13	88	15%	46%			-20.1	48	58	-$1
18 Proj	**9**	**12**	**0**	**160**	**106**	**4.98**	**5.03**	**1.43**	**822**	**834**	**810**	**23.6**	**2.1**	**6.0**	**2.8**	**68%**	**8%**	**38**	**23**	**39**	**33%**	**68%**	**11%**	**29**						**-12.3**	**66**	**79**	**-$**

Zych,Tony

Age: 27	Th: R	Role RP	Health F	LIMA Plan B+
Ht: 6' 3"	Wt: 190	Type Pwr	PT/Exp D	Rand Var -5
			Consist B	MM 1200

Former closer speculation can't stay on field, and when he does, he can't find home plate. Tiny rate of first-pitch strikes won't change that, and as hitters get familiar with him, he's avoiding their bats less and less often. Only a friendly H%, S%, and hr/f kept ERA below 4. Save your late-round dart for a better target.

Yr Tm	W	L	Sv	IP	K	ERA	xERA	WHIP	oOPS	vL	vR	BF/G	Ctl	Dom	Cmd	FpK	SwK	G	L	F	H%	S%	hr/f	GS	APC	DOM%	DIS%	Sv%	LI	RAR	BPV	BPX	R$
13 aa	5	5	3	56	34	3.69	3.90	1.44				5.1	3.5	5.4	1.6						31%	74%								1.2	55	72	-$
14 aa	4	5	2	58	30	5.80	6.00	1.77				5.9	2.8	4.6	1.6						38%	66%								-14.8	34	40	-$
15 SEA *	1	2	9	67	70	2.91	3.06	1.16	628	588	642	5.0	1.5	9.5	6.2	74%	15%	50	13	37	35%	75%	6%	1	21	0%	0%	82	1.22	8.7	179	214	$
16 SEA	1	0	0	14	21	3.29	3.48	1.46	642	630	652	5.0	6.6	13.8	2.1	48%	11%	50	14	36	36%	75%	0%	0	21			0	0.44	1.5	99	118	-$
17 SEA	6	3	1	41	35	2.66	4.51	1.25	617	746	557	3.8	4.6	7.7	1.7	54%	10%	50	21	30	26%	80%	6%	0	14			50	1.18	8.5	42	50	$
1st Half	3	2	1	24	18	2.66	4.88	1.31	685	909	555	3.7	4.6	6.8	1.5	56%	11%	49	16	34	26%	83%	9%	0	14			50	1.03	5.0	27	33	$
2nd Half	3	1	0	17	17	2.65	4.00	1.18	522	411	559	4.0	4.8	9.0	1.9	50%	9%	50	27	23	26%	75%	0%	0	15			0	1.40	3.6	61	74	$
18 Proj	**4**	**3**	**0**	**44**	**37**	**3.94**	**4.27**	**1.36**	**728**	**862**	**671**	**4.4**	**3.5**	**7.7**	**2.2**	**53%**	**10%**	**50**	**23**	**27**	**32%**	**71%**	**8%**	**0**						**2.3**	**72**	**86**	**-$**

STEPHEN NICKRAND

HE NEXT TIER
Pitchers

The preceding section provided player boxes and analysis for 406 pitchers. As we know, far more than 406 pitchers will play in the major leagues in 2018. Many of those additional pitchers are covered in the minor league section, but that still leaves a gap: established major leaguers who don't play enough, or well enough, to merit a player box.

This section looks to fill that gap. Here, you will find "The Next Tier" of pitchers who are mostly past their growth years, but who are likely to see some playing time in 2018. We are including their 2016-17 MLB stats here for reference for you to do your own analysis. This way, if Jacob Turner is rumored to be pushing for rotation spot at some point in 2018, a quick check here would confirm that his past skills do not indicate long-term success as a starter. Or if Austin Brice sneaks into a more promient bullpen role in 2018, this chart shows that a strong SwK and improved FpK in 2017 indicate some latent skills that his ERA doesn't account for.

Pitcher	T	Yr	Age	W	Sv	IP	K	ERA	xERA	WHIP	vL	vR	CTL	DOM	CMD	SwK	FpK	G/L/F	H%	S%	BPV
Abad, Fernando	L	16	30	1	1	46	41	3.70	4.61	1.34	459	789	4.3	8.0	1.9	8	61	43/19/38	28	26	49
		17	31	2	1	43	37	3.33	4.35	1.25	636	696	2.9	7.7	2.6	7	57	45/19/36	29	24	82
Albers, Matt	R	16	33	2	0	51	30	6.34	5.32	1.68	979	924	3.3	5.3	1.6	7	60	49/17/34	34	34	32
		17	34	7	2	61	63	1.62	3.19	0.85	583	484	2.5	9.3	3.7	9	62	51/19/30	20	11	129
Avilan, Luis	L	16	26	3	0	19	28	3.28	2.89	1.15	519	451	4.7	13.1	2.8	18	60	51/21/28	31	32	136
		17	27	2	0	46	52	2.93	3.54	1.39	571	826	4.3	10.2	2.4	15	54	54/25/21	34	21	99
Beck, Chris	R	16	25	2	0	25	20	6.45	5.61	1.91	1115	686	6.1	7.2	1.2	11	49	46/26/28	36	33	-11
		17	26	2	0	64	42	6.45	5.94	1.67	930	922	4.8	5.9	1.2	8	56	40/21/38	29	33	-5
Benoit, Joaquin	R	16	38	3	1	48	52	2.81	4.24	1.27	701	559	4.5	9.8	2.2	15	58	39/22/39	27	18	71
		17	39	1	2	50	46	4.67	5.01	1.30	745	686	4.0	8.3	2.1	14	64	33/17/50	26	33	53
Bergman, Christian	R	16	27	1	0	24	22	8.55	4.92	1.86	1125	972	2.2	8.2	3.7	10	70	37/24/39	39	42	100
		17	28	4	0	54	33	5.00	5.17	1.41	802	892	2.5	5.5	2.2	8	67	38/22/41	29	28	48
Blanton, Joe	R	16	35	7	0	80	80	2.48	3.97	1.01	546	587	2.9	9.0	3.1	15	65	33/22/46	24	20	94
		17	36	2	0	44	39	5.71	4.90	1.50	989	820	2.7	8.0	3.0	13	62	33/22/45	33	32	82
Brice, Austin	R	16	23	0	0	14	14	7.07	3.63	1.00	620	566	3.2	9.0	2.8	13	56	53/16/32	19	75	106
		17	24	0	0	32	26	5.03	4.04	1.24	718	780	2.0	7.3	3.7	11	63	51/17/32	28	35	106
Brothers, Rex	L	17	29	4	0	23	33	7.37	3.74	1.51	644	848	4.7	12.8	2.8	15	62	39/25/36	36	50	120
Broxton, Jonathan	R	16	31	4	0	60	57	4.34	3.97	1.26	708	650	3.6	8.5	2.4	10	59	48/24/28	27	32	82
		17	32	0	0	15	16	7.11	5.54	2.24	1330	782	6.5	9.5	1.5	13	58	43/28/30	43	31	16
Buchholz, Clay	R	16	31	8	0	139	93	4.79	5.11	1.33	788	695	3.6	6.0	1.7	10	62	41/16/43	27	32	31
		17	32	0	0	7	5	12.68	7.31	2.68	1195	1122	3.8	6.3	1.7	7	71	28/25/47	48	50	17
Capps, Carter	R	17	26	0	0	12	7	6.69	4.25	1.16	1109	377	1.5	5.2	3.5	8	73	53/18/30	26	58	84
Cosart, Jarred	R	16	25	0	0	57	38	6.00	5.32	1.75	683	818	6.2	6.0	1.0	7	54	61/21/18	32	35	-19
		17	26	0	0	24	15	4.88	6.52	1.88	889	676	7.1	5.6	0.8	7	52	51/21/29	33	29	-62
de la Rosa, Jorge	L	16	34	8	0	134	108	5.51	4.90	1.64	849	865	4.2	7.3	1.7	11	55	47/21/32	33	30	41
		17	35	3	0	51	45	4.23	4.59	1.31	545	821	3.7	7.9	2.1	15	55	45/16/38	27	28	66
Duensing, Brian	L	16	33	1	0	13	10	4.12	4.66	1.22	619	772	2.1	6.9	3.3	10	65	24/33/43	28	29	69
		17	34	1	0	62	61	2.75	3.80	1.22	682	667	2.6	8.8	3.4	11	58	49/18/34	31	19	115
Duke, Zach	L	16	32	2	2	61	68	2.36	3.38	1.26	580	635	4.3	10.0	2.3	11	59	59/18/24	30	19	102
		17	33	1	0	18	12	3.98	4.35	1.05	661	628	3.0	6.0	2.0	12	64	51/19/30	20	31	56
Dunn, Mike	L	16	30	6	0	42	38	3.42	4.26	1.28	702	766	2.4	8.1	3.5	13	59	28/30/43	32	22	88
		17	31	5	0	50	57	4.49	4.79	1.42	771	692	5.0	10.2	2.0	11	52	33/22/46	28	27	59
Farquhar, Danny	R	16	29	1	0	35	46	3.08	3.57	1.37	774	792	3.8	11.8	3.1	14	54	38/29/33	30	10	124
		17	30	4	0	49	45	4.22	5.13	1.36	539	734	5.1	8.2	1.6	13	58	42/14/45	27	31	30
Freeman, Sam	L	16	28	0	0	7	8	13.75	8.02	3.06	883	1279	11.3	10.0	0.9	10	59	37/30/33	44	45	-101
		17	29	2	0	60	59	2.55	3.86	1.25	507	652	4.1	8.9	2.2	12	57	59/15/26	28	19	87
Gee, Dillon	R	16	29	8	0	125	89	4.68	4.85	1.46	835	795	2.7	6.4	2.4	8	61	41/21/38	32	26	62
		17	30	3	1	49	44	3.48	4.59	1.41	942	727	2.7	7.5	2.7	11	64	41/19/40	32	18	80
Gomez, Jeanmar	R	16	28	3	37	68	47	4.88	4.40	1.47	837	706	2.9	6.2	2.1	8	56	52/22/26	33	33	63
		17	29	3	2	22	21	7.33	3.97	1.72	1259	790	2.9	8.6	3.0	11	53	51/24/25	38	35	105
Grace, Matt	L	16	27	0	0	3	4	0.00	1.68	0.33	333	0	0.0	12.0	0.0	18	40	67/0/33	17	0	261
		17	28	1	2	50	31	4.32	4.38	1.36	550	817	3.2	5.6	1.7	8	61	61/18/20	29	32	52
Grilli, Jason	R	16	39	7	4	59	81	4.12	3.95	1.29	877	613	4.9	12.4	2.5	14	57	30/20/50	27	26	99
		17	40	2	1	40	48	6.30	4.72	1.60	931	927	4.1	10.8	2.7	12	57	27/27/47	32	31	90
Guerra, Javy	R	16	30	0	0	6	4	5.90	7.44	1.97	571	865	10.3	5.9	0.6	7	47	56/6/39	24	27	-132
		17	31	1	0	21	12	3.00	4.76	1.43	771	745	3.0	5.1	1.7	6	67	54/18/28	31	18	44
Hardy, Blaine	L	16	29	1	0	25	20	3.57	4.85	1.47	643	743	4.3	7.1	1.7	9	64	48/18/34	30	23	39
		17	30	1	0	33	28	5.98	5.60	1.78	843	970	3.5	7.6	2.2	10	57	33/23/44	36	29	52
Hughes, Phil	R	16	29	1	0	59	34	5.95	5.24	1.51	956	797	2.0	5.2	2.6	7	70	35/24/41	33	36	53
		17	30	4	0	53	38	5.92	5.52	1.60	1107	766	2.2	6.4	2.9	7	68	30/24/46	33	32	64
Infante, Gregory	R	17	29	2	0	54	49	3.15	4.54	1.20	640	650	3.3	8.1	2.5	11	50	36/23/41	27	25	70

THE NEXT TIER

Pitcher	T	Yr	Age	W	Sv	IP	K	ERA	xERA	WHIP	vL	vR	CTL	DOM	CMD	SwK	FpK	G/L/F	H%	S%	BPV
Jennings, Dan	L	16	28	4	1	60	46	2.09	4.31	1.41	654	694	4.2	6.9	1.6	9	53	54/24/22	31	15	43
		17	29	3	0	62	51	3.47	4.26	1.35	628	701	4.5	7.4	1.6	8	60	60/19/21	26	21	50
Kelley, Shawn	R	16	31	3	7	58	80	2.64	2.92	0.90	792	539	1.7	12.4	7.3	16	66	36/14/49	26	19	191
		17	32	3	4	26	25	7.27	5.77	1.54	780	1098	3.8	8.7	2.3	14	72	26/14/60	24	32	57
Koehler, Tom	R	16	29	9	0	176	147	4.34	4.79	1.47	772	755	4.2	7.5	1.8	10	59	42/23/34	30	27	41
		17	30	1	0	72	62	6.73	5.23	1.63	989	804	4.4	7.7	1.8	9	54	40/22/38	31	37	39
Krol, Ian	L	16	24	2	0	51	56	3.18	3.09	1.31	721	686	2.3	9.9	4.3	11	60	56/21/23	36	22	150
		17	25	2	0	49	44	5.33	4.68	1.45	822	788	3.9	8.1	2.1	12	61	41/22/36	31	33	60
Latos, Mat	R	16	28	7	0	70	42	4.89	5.46	1.49	767	828	3.9	5.4	1.4	7	57	43/19/38	29	29	14
		17	29	0	0	15	10	6.60	6.08	1.80	1335	920	4.8	6.0	1.3	11	57	44/14/42	30	27	0
Locke, Jeff	L	16	28	9	0	127	73	5.45	5.09	1.53	752	876	3.1	5.2	1.7	9	61	47/20/32	33	34	34
		17	29	0	0	32	26	8.16	5.38	1.78	941	840	4.2	7.3	1.7	8	61	47/20/33	36	47	43
Logan, Boone	L	16	31	2	1	46	57	3.71	3.25	1.02	477	759	3.9	11.1	-	17	65	50/17/33	23	35	122
		17	32	1	0	21	28	4.71	3.26	1.38	711	638	3.9	12.0	3.1	18	56	50/23/27	35	33	140
Loup, Aaron	L	16	28	0	0	14	15	5.11	3.50	1.35	821	882	2.6	9.6	3.8	8	59	40/33/28	34	35	120
		17	29	2	0	57	64	3.78	4.04	1.54	721	721	4.6	10.1	2.2	10	61	53/20/26	34	24	89
McFarland, T.J.	L	16	26	2	0	24	7	7.07	5.53	1.78	916	942	3.7	2.6	0.7	6	58	60/18/22	33	40	-15
		17	27	4	0	54	29	5.33	4.46	1.52	548	860	2.8	4.8	1.7	7	53	67/15/18	32	36	56
McGowan, Dustin	R	16	34	1	1	67	63	2.82	4.00	1.22	918	468	4.4	8.5	1.9	15	59	54/17/28	24	19	65
		17	35	8	0	77	64	4.78	4.30	1.35	759	800	3.1	7.5	2.4	12	59	51/19/30	29	31	78
Meyer, Alex	R	16	26	1	0	25	29	5.74	5.04	1.67	1023	705	6.1	10.4	1.7	9	45	38/18/44	32	33	38
		17	27	4	0	67	75	3.76	4.35	1.34	738	553	5.6	10.1	1.8	11	53	46/22/31	25	26	53
Milone, Tommy	L	16	29	3	0	69	49	5.73	4.73	1.53	851	859	2.9	6.4	2.2	9	65	46/24/30	32	32	61
		17	30	1	1	48	38	7.67	5.22	1.64	664	1073	2.6	7.1	2.7	8	66	36/24/40	32	41	71
Motte, Jason	R	16	33	0	0	23	24	5.04	4.37	1.55	903	970	3.1	9.3	3.0	9	67	43/19/39	32	23	103
		17	34	1	0	40	27	3.58	5.16	1.19	655	708	4.5	6.0	1.4	8	65	45/15/40	20	24	11
Moylan, Peter	R	16	37	2	0	44	34	3.46	3.91	1.31	973	542	3.3	6.9	2.1	10	57	61/17/21	29	24	75
		17	38	0	0	59	46	3.50	3.99	1.10	986	479	3.8	7.0	1.8	12	62	61/16/23	22	31	62
Oberg, Scott	R	16	26	1	1	26	20	5.19	4.57	1.42	993	549	3.8	6.9	1.8	10	55	56/11/33	29	35	56
		17	27	0	0	58	55	4.96	4.15	1.62	816	790	3.7	8.5	2.3	13	69	57/19/24	37	31	88
Peralta, Wily	R	16	26	7	0	127	93	4.88	4.40	1.53	880	832	3.0	6.6	2.2	9	56	50/23/27	35	28	64
		17	27	5	0	57	52	7.88	5.28	1.84	1030	874	5.0	8.2	1.6	9	64	45/22/34	36	42	34
Perez, Oliver	L	16	34	2	0	40	46	4.95	4.19	1.45	720	790	4.5	10.4	2.3	10	54	39/23/38	34	33	82
		17	35	0	1	33	39	4.64	4.18	1.33	665	888	3.3	10.6	3.3	11	64	33/18/49	33	33	114
Ramirez, Noe	R	16	26	0	0	13	15	6.23	4.77	1.85	862	1109	5.5	10.4	1.9	12	61	36/22/42	38	25	51
		17	27	0	0	13	14	2.77	3.51	0.85	1178	351	3.5	9.7	2.8	15	53	47/17/37	14	22	106
Rzepczynski, Marc	L	16	30	1	0	47	46	2.67	3.99	1.59	674	716	5.5	8.8	1.6	12	50	67/12/20	34	18	53
		17	31	2	1	31	25	4.05	4.32	1.58	650	794	5.8	7.2	1.3	12	50	70/16/14	31	26	22
Salas, Fernando	R	16	30	3	6	73	64	3.93	4.12	1.12	682	714	2.3	7.9	3.4	11	66	39/17/44	26	29	95
		17	31	2	0	58	56	5.26	4.53	1.53	728	817	3.4	8.7	2.5	14	60	47/16/36	34	33	89
Siegrist, Kevin	L	16	26	6	3	61	66	2.79	4.09	1.11	690	631	3.8	9.7	2.5	11	59	34/20/46	22	16	83
		17	27	1	1	39	43	4.83	4.67	1.56	828	792	5.1	9.9	2.0	11	56	36/25/39	34	29	55
Sipp, Tony	L	16	32	1	1	43	40	5.00	4.96	1.62	894	1012	3.8	8.3	2.2	13	55	36/18/46	32	21	62
		17	33	0	0	37	39	5.82	4.33	1.40	852	807	3.9	9.5	2.4	13	53	49/13/38	28	36	92
Smith, Chris	R	16	34	0	0	24	29	2.98	3.67	1.12	512	554	4.8	10.8	2.2	15	63	46/21/33	22	24	86
		17	35	0	0	55	31	6.85	6.06	1.49	754	977	3.6	5.1	1.4	8	54	37/20/43	24	39	9
Tazawa, Junichi	R	16	29	3	0	49	54	4.21	3.81	1.24	628	807	2.6	9.9	3.9	13	62	40/19/41	29	27	126
		17	30	3	0	55	38	5.72	5.33	1.40	719	812	3.6	6.2	1.7	9	62	36/25/40	28	39	29
Tepesch, Nick	R	16	27	0	0	4	3	11.25	5.05	1.75	1000	1000	0.0	6.8	0.0	5	84	25/31/44	40	67	125
		17	28	1	0	15	9	5.33	7.12	2.04	915	1306	5.3	5.3	1.0	6	56	37/18/46	30	12	-32
Turner, Jacob	R	16	24	1	0	24	18	6.69	5.59	2.02	705	1203	6.0	6.7	1.1	8	59	51/27/22	35	30	-10
		17	25	2	0	39	23	5.08	5.49	1.49	749	950	3.5	5.3	1.5	6	56	43/19/38	28	28	23
Uehara, Koji	R	16	40	2	7	47	63	3.45	3.31	0.96	478	812	2.1	12.1	5.7	16	65	21/20/58	27	27	159
		17	41	3	2	43	50	3.98	4.07	1.16	761	614	2.5	10.5	4.2	17	72	25/25/50	28	28	124
Volquez, Edinson	R	16	32	10	0	189	139	5.38	4.73	1.55	799	788	3.6	6.6	1.8	9	56	51/20/29	32	33	50
		17	33	4	0	92	81	4.20	4.86	1.42	810	613	5.2	7.9	1.5	9	56	46/22/33	28	28	27
Whitley, Chase	R	16	26	0	0	14	15	2.55	3.81	1.13	353	1000	1.9	9.6	5.0	13	67	42/19/40	27	14	139
		17	27	2	2	57	43	4.10	4.83	1.12	655	612	2.5	6.8	2.7	14	65	33/24/44	26	37	65
Wilson, Alex	R	16	29	4	0	73	49	2.96	4.50	1.22	728	665	2.6	6.0	2.3	9	58	44/19/37	29	23	61
		17	30	2	2	60	42	4.50	4.78	1.37	687	829	2.3	6.3	2.8	9	55	42/23/36	31	31	73
Worley, Vance	R	16	28	2	1	86	56	3.55	4.81	1.38	763	731	3.7	5.8	1.6	5	55	48/18/34	28	21	33
		17	29	2	1	71	50	6.95	5.17	1.81	885	1004	3.8	6.3	1.7	6	58	49/23/28	38	38	38

5-Year Injury Log

The following chart details the disabled list stints for all players during the past five years. Use this as a supplement to our health grades in the player profile boxes as well as the "Risk Management" charts that start on page 258. It's also where to turn when in May you want to check whether, say, Joe Panik's concussion should be concerning (answer: Yes, very).

For each injury, the number of days the player missed during the season is listed. A few DL stints are for fewer than 15 days (or fewer than 10 days in 2017); these are cases when a player was placed on the DL prior to Opening Day (only in-season time lost is listed).

Abbreviations:
Lt, L = left
Rt, R = right
fx = fractured
R/C = rotator cuff
str = strained
surg = surgery
TJS = Tommy John surgery (ulnar collateral ligament reconstruction)
x 2 = two occurrences of the same injury
x 3 = three occurrences of the same injury

Throughout the spring and all season long, BaseballHQ.com has comprehensive injury coverage.

FIVE-YEAR INJURY LOG —Hitters

Batter	Yr	Days	Injury
Abreu,Jose	14	15	L ankle tendinitis
Ackley,Dustin	15	28	R lumbar strain
	16	126	Dislocated R should
Adams,Matt	13	15	R oblique strain
	14	14	Tightness in L calf
	15	105	Strained R quad
	16	22	L should inflammation
Adduci,James	17	54	Strained R oblique muscle
Adrianza,Ehire	14	82	Strained R hamstring x 2
	16	109	Fractured L foot
	17	48	R oblique muscle; ab muscle
Ahmed,Nick	16	72	R hip impingement
	17	95	Fractured R hand
Alberto,Hanser	17	182	Tightness in R shoulder
Alford,Anthony	17	62	Fractured L wrist
Almonte,Abraham	17	66	Strained R biceps; L hammy
Alonso,Yonder	13	41	R hand contusion
	14	55	Strained R forearm/R wrist tend
	15	46	Low back strain; bruised R shoulder
Altherr,Aaron	16	117	Repair torn tendon L wrist
	17	43	Strained R hamstring x 2
Amarista,Alexi	16	56	Strnd R hamstring x 2
Aoki,Norichika	14	20	Strained L groin
	15	40	Concussion; fx fibula
Arcia,Oswaldo	14	35	Strained R wrist
	15	30	R hip flexor strain
	16	21	Strained R elbow
Arenado,Nolan	14	40	Fractured L middle finger
Asche,Cody	14	26	Strained L hamstring
	16	61	Strained R oblique muscle
Austin,Tyler	17	107	Fx L ankle; strained R ham
Avila,Alex	13	31	L forearm bruise; Concussion
	14	5	Concussion
	15	55	Loose bodies in L knee
	16	66	Strained R hamstring x 2
Aybar,Erick	13	20	Bruised L heel
	16	15	Bruised R foot
	17	41	Bruised L foot
Baez,Javier	16	12	Bruised L thumb
Bandy,Jett	17	30	Fractured rib

FIVE-YEAR INJURY LOG —Hitters

Batter	Yr	Days	Injury
Bautista,Jose	13	40	L hip bone bruise
	16	53	Sprnd L knee; L big toe
Beckham,Gordon	13	54	Fractured hamate bone, L wrist
	14	25	Strained L oblique
	16	56	Strained L hamstring x2
Beckham,Tim	14	133	Rec. from surgery R Knee- torn ACL
	15	25	R hamstring strain
	17	10	Sprained L ankle
Bellinger,Cody	17	10	Sprained R ankle
Belt,Brandon	14	81	Concussion x 2/Fx L thumb
	17	57	Concussion
Beltran,Carlos	14	29	Concussion; hyper ext. Rt elbow
	15	16	Strained L oblique
Beltre,Adrian	14	12	Strained L quadriceps
	15	21	Sprained L thumb
	17	68	Tight R calf; L hammy
Benintendi,Andrew	16	20	Sprnd L knee
Bethancourt,Christian	16	33	Strnd L intercostal
Betts,Mookie	15	13	Concussion
Bird,Gregory	16	183	Rec fr surg.-torn labrum R should
	17	116	Bruised R ankle
Blackmon,Charlie	16	15	Turf toe on L foot
Blanco,Andres	16	39	Fractured L index finger
Blanco,Gregor	15	9	Concussion
	16	24	R should impingement
Blash,Jabari	16	42	Sprnd L middle finger
Bogaerts,Xander	14	7	Concussion
Bogusevic,Brian	13	77	L hamstring strain
Bonifacio,Emilio	14	39	Strained R ribcage
	15	16	Strained L oblique
Bour,Justin	16	62	Sprnd R ankle
	17	55	BruisedL ankle; strained R oblique
Bourjos,Peter	13	100	Fx Rt wrist; Strained Lt hammy
	16	15	Sprnd R should
	17	10	Elbow injury
Bradley,Jackie	17	20	Sprained R knee; L thumb
Brantley,Michael	16	164	R should fatigue; rec fr R should surg.
	17	61	Sprained R ankle x2
Brantly,Rob	15	45	Avulsion fracture, L thumb

FIVE-YEAR INJURY LOG —Hitters

Batter	Yr	Days	Injury
Braun,Ryan	13	28	R thumb contusion
	14	10	strained R oblique muscle
	17	42	Strained L calf x 2
Brignac,Reid	14	31	Sprained L ankle
Brito,Socrates	16	42	Fractured toe R foot
	17	74	Dislocated L ring finger
Brown,Trevor	17	19	Sprained R ankle
Bruce,Jay	14	16	Rec from meniscus repair on L knee
Butler,Billy	16	7	Concussion
Buxton,Byron	15	45	Sprained L thumb
	17	17	Strained L groin
Cabrera,Asdrubal	13	22	R quadriceps strain
	15	16	Strained R hamstring
	16	17	Strained patella tendon L knee
	17	21	Sprained L thumb x 2
Cabrera,Melky	13	82	Strained L knee; Tendinitis
	14	21	Fractured R pinky finger
Cabrera,Miguel	15	41	L calf strain
	17	10	Strained R groin
Cain,Lorenzo	13	26	Strained L oblique
	14	18	Strained L groin
	16	30	Strained L hamstring
Calhoun,Kole	14	35	Sprained R ankle
Camargo,Johan	17	27	Bruised R knee
Canha,Mark	16	146	Strained back
Cano,Robinson	17	12	Strained R quadriceps
Carpenter,Matt	16	29	Strained R oblique muscle
Carrera,Ezequiel	16	15	Strained L Achilles tendon
	17	13	Fractured R foot
Casali,Curtis	14	5	Concussion
	15	40	Strained L hamstring
Castellanos,Nick	16	51	Fractured L hand
Castillo,Welington	13	5	Surgery - R knee
	14	19	L ribcage inflammation
	17	24	Tendinitis R should; testicular injury
Castro,Jason	13	13	Cyst on R knee
	15	19	Strained R quad
	17	11	Concussion
Castro,Starlin	17	52	Strained R ham x2
Ceciliani,Darrell	15	27	Strained L hamstring
	17	135	L shoulder subluxation
Cervelli,Francisco	13	156	Fractured R hand
	14	64	Hamstring injury
	16	38	Fractured L hand
	17	59	Concussion x 2; L wrist inflam; L quad
Cespedes,Yoenis	13	15	Strained muscle, L hand
	16	15	Strained R quadriceps
	17	79	Strained L ham; strained R ham
Chapman,Matt	17	11	L knee cellulitis
Chirinos,Robinson	15	37	L shoulder strain
	16	60	Fractured R forearm
Chisenhall,Lonnie	16	17	R forearm injury
	17	73	Sprnd R shoulder; concussion; R calf
Choo,Shin-Soo	14	35	Bone spur in L elbow
	16	124	Strnd R calf/L ham/back; FX L 4arm
Clevenger,Steve	13	169	L oblique strain
	16	95	Fractured R hand

FIVE-YEAR INJURY LOG —Hitters

Batter	Yr	Days	Injury
Coghlan,Chris	13	84	R calf irritation
	16	41	Sore/strained R ribcage
	17	57	Bruised L wrist
Colon,Christian	14	12	fractured right middle finger
Conforto,Michael	17	48	Bruised L hand; Disloc L shoulder
Contreras,Willson	17	32	Strained R hamstring
Cooper,Garrett	17	46	L hamstring tendinitis
Corporan,Carlos	13	20	Concussion
	15	46	Sprained L thumb
Correa,Carlos	17	47	Torn ligament in L thumb
Cozart,Zack	15	116	R knee surgery
	16	7	Sore R knee
	17	21	Strained R quad; L quad
Crawford,Brandon	17	12	Strained R groin
Cron,C.J.	16	42	Fractured L hand
	17	15	Bruised L foot
Culberson,Charlie	15	67	Lumbar disc inflammation
Cuthbert,Cheslor	17	41	Sprained L wrist
d Arnaud,Travis	14	14	Concussion
	15	88	Hyperextended L elbow; fx R hand
	16	56	Strained R rotator cuff
	17	19	Bone bruise in R wrist
Dahl,David	17	108	Stress reaction in ribcage
d'Arnaud,Chase	13	61	L thumb surgery
Davidson,Matthew	16	94	Fractured R foot
	17	18	Bruised R wrist
Davis,Chris	14	14	Strained L oblique
	17	29	Strained R oblique
Davis,Khristopher	15	37	Torn meniscus, R knee
Davis,Rajai	13	24	Strained oblique
	17	10	Strained L hamstring
Decker,Jaff	15	13	L calf strain
Delmonico,Nick	17	11	Sprained R wrist
Descalso,Daniel	16	40	Fractured L hand
DeShields Jr.,Delino	15	20	Strained L hamstring
Desmond,Ian	17	72	Fx L hand; strained R calf x 2
Diaz,Aledmys	16	40	Fractured R thumb
Diaz,Elias	16	128	Disc R elbow, cellulitis L knee
Dickerson,Alex	17	182	Herniated disc
Dickerson,Corey	15	98	Non-displaced rib fx; fasciitis L ft x2
Dietrich,Derek	14	53	Strained R wrist
	16	11	Bruised R knee
Donaldson,Josh	17	42	Strained R calf
Dozier,Hunter	17	60	Strained L oblique
Drew,Stephen	13	31	R Hamstring tight; Concussion
	16	42	Vertigo
	17	112	Strained R hamstring
Duda,Lucas	13	46	Strained L intercostal
	15	16	Lower back strain
	16	117	Stress fracture lower back
	17	21	Hyperextended L elbow
Duffy,Matt	16	78	Recovering from surg. on L Achilles
	17	182	Recovery surgery L Achilles
Dyson,Jarrod	13	37	R ankle sprain
	16	16	Strained R oblique muscle
	17	13	Strained R groin

FIVE-YEAR INJURY LOG —Hitters

Batter	Yr	Days	Injury
Eaton,Adam	13	100	L elbow strain
	14	31	Rt oblique muscle; Rt hamstring
	17	155	Torn ACL in L knee
Eibner,Brett	16	15	Sprnd L ankle
Ellis,A.J.	13	15	L oblique strain
	14	54	Sprained R ankle/L knee surgery
	15	15	R knee inflammation
Ellsbury,Jacoby	15	49	R knee sprain
	17	33	Concussion
Encarnacion,Edwin	13	13	Surgery (cart) - L wrist
	14	39	Strained R quadriceps
Escobar,Alcides	14	16	Sore R shoulder
	15	7	Concussion & L cheek contusion
Escobar,Yunel	16	13	Concussion
	17	72	Strained L ham; R oblique
Espinosa,Danny	13	15	Broken bone in R wrist
Ethier,Andre	16	160	Fractured tibia R leg
	17	152	Herniated lumbar disc
Featherston,Taylor	15	16	Uppen back strain
Federowicz,Tim	15	128	Torn meniscus, R knee
Fields,Josh	17	10	Strained lower back
Flaherty,Ryan	15	30	Strained R groin x2
	17	88	Strained R shoulder
Flores,Wilmer	16	17	Strained L hamstring
	17	12	Infection in R knee
Florimon Jr.,Pedro	17	26	Dislocated/sprained R ankle
Flowers,Tyler	13	28	R shoulder surgery
	16	33	Fractured L hand
	17	10	Bruised L wrist
Forsythe,Logan	13	71	Plantar fasciitis, R foot
	16	27	Fractured L scapula
	17	34	Fractured R big toe
Fowler,Dexter	13	15	R wrist soreness
	14	43	Strained R intercostal
	16	32	Strained R hamstring
	17	25	Spur R heel; L forearm
Fowler,Dustin	17	93	Ruptured patella tendon in R knee
Franco,Maikel	15	48	Fractured L wrist
Franklin,Nick	15	42	Strained L oblique
	16	7	Concussion
Frazier,Adam	17	29	Strained L ham x 2
Frazier,Clint	17	33	Strained L oblique
Freeman,Freddie	13	15	Strained R oblique
	15	47	Strained R oblique; bruised R wrist
	17	47	Fractured L wrist
Freese,David	13	8	Strained lower back
	14	17	Fractured R middle finger
	15	40	Fractured R index finger
	17	13	Strained R hamstring
Fuentes,Rey	17	35	Bruised L thumb
Fuld,Sam	14	36	Concussion
	16	183	Strained L should
Gallo,Joey	17	7	Concussion
Galvis,Freddy	14	15	Staph infection in L knee
Garcia,Adonis	17	106	L Ach tendints; torn ligmnt L ring fing

FIVE-YEAR INJURY LOG —Hitters

Batter	Yr	Days	Injury
Garcia,Avisail	13	30	Bruised R heel
	14	128	Surgery on L shoulder torn labrum
	16	14	Sprnd R knee
	17	13	Sprained R thumb
Garcia,Leury	17	70	Sprained L finger; R thumb
Garcia,Willy	17	46	Concussion
Gattis,Evan	13	26	Oblique strain
	14	21	Bulging thoracic disc in back
	16	11	Rec fr surg. to repair sports hernia
	17	30	Concussion; R wrist
Gennett,Scooter	15	14	L hand laceration
	16	14	Strained R oblique muscle
Gentry,Craig	13	27	Fractured L hand
	14	39	Fx R hand; lower back strain
	16	90	Strained R lumbar spine
	17	10	Fractured R finger
Giavotella,Johnny	15	41	Personal medical condition
Gillaspie,Conor	14	11	Sore/bruised L hand
	17	53	Back spasms x 2
Gillespie,Cole	14	25	Strained oblique muscle
Goldschmidt,Paul	14	58	Fractured L hand
Gomes,Yan	14	7	Concussion
	15	42	R knee sprain
	16	77	Separated R should
Gomez,Carlos	15	15	R hamstring strain
	16	15	Bruised L rib cage
	17	42	Strained R ham; cyst R shoulder
Gomez,Miguel	17	50	R knee inflammation
Gonzalez,Adrian	17	79	Sore R elbow; hern disk low back
Gonzalez,Carlos	13	29	Sprained R middle finger
	14	51	L knee tendinitis/L finger inflam
	17	11	Strained R shoulder
Goodwin,Brian	17	46	Strained L groin
Gordon,Alex	15	54	Strained L groin
	16	33	Fractured R wrist
Gordon,Dee	15	11	Dislocated L thumb
Gosewisch,Tuffy	15	129	Torn L ACL
Gosselin,Phil	15	105	Avulsion fracture, L thumb
Grandal,Yasmani	13	85	R knee sprain
	15	7	Concussion
	16	9	Sore R forearm
Granderson,Curtis	13	113	Fx finger Lt hand; Fx Lt finger
Green,Grant	14	39	Lumbar strain
Gregorius,Didi	13	23	Concussion; R elbow strain
	17	26	Strained R shoulder
Grichuk,Randal	15	47	R elbow strain
	17	11	Strained lower back
Grossman,Robert	17	18	Fractured L thumb
Gutierrez,Franklin	13	123	Strained R hamstring x 2
	17	118	Strained L ham; aRhritis in spine
Guyer,Brandon	13	60	Fractured R middle finger
	14	24	Fractured L thumb
	16	23	Strained L hamstring
	17	43	L wrist injury
Gyorko,Jedd	13	32	Strained R groin
	14	52	Plantar fasciitis in L foot
	17	16	Strained R hamstring

FIVE-YEAR INJURY LOG —Hitters

Batter	Yr	Days	Injury
Hamilton,Billy	16	25	Strained L oblique; concussion
	17	12	Fractured L thumb
Hamilton,Josh	14	55	Surgery on L thumb torn UCL
	15	38	Jammed & sprianed R Shoulder;
	15	89	L knee infl; L hammy; rec R shld surg
	16	142	Recovering from surg. on L knee
Hanigan,Ryan	13	50	Sprained L wrist; L oblique
	14	54	Strained L oblique; Rt hamstring
	15	61	Fractured knuckle, R hand
	16	58	L ankle tendinitis; neck strain
	17	16	Strained L groin
Haniger,Mitch	17	66	Strained R oblique; facial laceration
Hardy,J.J.	15	47	Groin strain; L shoulder strain
	16	46	Fractured L foot
	17	81	Fractured R wrist
Harper,Bryce	13	35	L knee bursitis
	14	64	Surgery on L thumb
	17	44	Hyperextended L knee
Harrison,Josh	15	46	Torn L thumb ligaments
	16	7	Strained R groin
	17	28	Fractured metacarpal in L hand
Headley,Chase	13	17	Broken L thumb
	14	15	Strained R calf
Heathcott,Zachary	15	62	Strained R quad
Hechavarria,Adeiny	13	15	Bruised L elbow
	14	11	Strained R triceps
	17	59	Strained IL oblique; L ham
Hedges,Austin	17	12	Concussion
Heisey,Chris	13	58	Strained R hamstring
	17	54	Ruptured R biceps; strained L groin
Hernandez,Cesar	15	21	Dislocated L thumb
	15	35	L hamstring strain
	17	36	Strained L oblique
Hernandez,Enrique	16	32	L ribcage inflammation
Hernandez,Gorkys	15	11	L shoulder discomfort
Hernandez,Marco	17	150	L shoulder subluxation
Hernandez,Oscar	15	91	Fractured L hand
Hernandez,Teoscar	17	18	Bruised L knee
Herrera,Dilson	15	26	Fractured R middle finger
Herrera,Odubel	17	17	Strained L hamstring
Herrmann,Chris	16	51	Strained R hamstring; fx L wrist
Heyward,Jason	13	55	Fx R jaw; appendectomy
	17	24	Sprained R finger; lacerated R hand
Hicks,Aaron	13	22	L hamstring strain
	14	22	Strained R shoulder;concussion
	15	34	Strained L ham; R forearm
	16	15	Strained R hamstring
	17	68	Strained R oblique; L oblique
Hill,Aaron	13	71	Broken L hand
	17	32	Strained R forearm
Holliday,Matt	13	15	Strained R hamstring
	15	85	Strained R quad x 2
	16	52	Fractured L thumb
	17	42	Viral infection
Holt,Brock	14	23	Concussion
	16	42	Concussion
	17	86	Vertigo
Hosmer,Eric	14	31	Stress fracture in R hand

FIVE-YEAR INJURY LOG —Hitters

Batter	Yr	Days	Injury
Howard,Ryan	13	86	L knee inflammation
Hundley,Nick	15	24	Cervical strain
	16	37	Strained L oblique; concussion
Iannetta,Chris	17	7	Concussion
Iglesias,Jose	14	184	Stress fracture in both shins
	16	15	Strained L hamstring
	17	7	Concussion
Inciarte,Ender	14	7	Concussion
	15	31	Strained R hamstring
	16	26	Strained L hamstring
Infante,Omar	13	39	Sprained L ankle
	14	15	Disc irritation in lower back
Jackson,Austin	13	33	Strained R hamstring
	15	22	Sprained R ankle
	16	115	Torn meniscus L knee
	17	52	Hyperextended L big toe; L quad
Janish,Paul	13	40	Recovery from L shoulder surgery
Jankowski,Travis	17	102	Bone bruise in R foot
Jaso,John	13	67	Concussion
	14	15	Concussion
	15	88	L wrist contusion; L knee bursitis
Jay,Jon	15	79	Bone bruise, L wrist + tendon
	16	70	Fractured R forearm
Jennings,Desmond	13	39	Fractured L middle finger
	14	30	Bruised L Knee
	15	142	L knee bursitis
	16	48	Bruised L knee; strained L hamstring
Johnson,Chris	15	40	Infection, L hand, Fx L hand
Johnson,Kelly	15	26	R oblique strain
Johnson,Micah	17	99	Fractured L wrist
Johnson,Reed	13	43	L knee tendinitis
	15	159	Strained L calf
Jones,JaCoby	17	15	Lacerated lip
Jones,Ryder	17	10	Bruised R hand/wrist
Joseph,Caleb	16	30	Testicular injury
Joyce,Matt	15	35	Concussion
Judge,Aaron	16	19	Strained R oblique
Kang,Jung-Ho	15	14	Torn L meniscus, fx L tibia
	16	49	Sore L should; recov L knee surg.
Kelly,Don	15	175	Fractured R ring finger
Kemp,Matt	13	97	Str R ham; Sore A/c joint, L ankle
	14	16	Recovering from surgery on L ankle
	17	31	Strained R hamstring x 2
Kendrick,Howie	13	35	Sprained L knee
	15	56	Strained L hamstring
	16	9	Strained L calf
	17	62	Strained R Ab; L ham
Kiermaier,Kevin	16	54	Fractured L hand
	17	70	Fractured R hip
Kim,Hyun-soo	16	15	Strained R hamstring
Kinsler,Ian	13	28	R intercostal strain
	17	10	Strained L hamstring
Kipnis,Jason	14	26	Strained R oblique
	15	15	R shoulder inflammation
	17	72	R shoulder inflam; R ham x2
Knapp,Andrew	17	37	Fractured R hand
Kratz,Erik	13	35	L knee surgery
	15	36	Plantar fasciitis, L foot

FIVE-YEAR INJURY LOG —Hitters

Batter	Yr	Days	Injury
La Stella, Tommy	15	119	Strained R oblique
	16	27	Strained R hamstring
Lagares, Juan	14	39	Strnd R intercostal/str R hamstring
	16	66	Torn lig L thumb; sprnd L thumb
	17	66	Strained L oblique; L thumb
Laird, Gerald	13	16	Kidney stone
	15	130	Lower back spasms
Lamb, Jacob	15	46	Stress reaction, L foot
LaRoche, Adam	14	13	Strained R quadriceps
Lavarnway, Ryan	14	76	Strained L wrist
Lawrie, Brett	13	61	Sprained L ankle; L ribcage
	14	95	Strained L oblique; fx Rt finger
	16	68	Strained L hamstring
Lind, Adam	14	52	Fx R foot; lower back tightness
Liriano, Rymer	16	183	Facial bone fractures
Lobaton, Jose	16	22	L elbow tendinitis
Loney, James	15	55	Broken finger; R oblique
Lough, David	15	8	Strained L hamstring
Lowrie, Jed	14	18	Fractured R index finger
	15	93	Torn ligament, R thumb
	16	74	Bunion on L foot; bruised R shin
Lucroy, Jonathan	15	41	Broken L toe
Machado, Manny	13	5	Torn ligament - L knee
	14	79	Surgery L knee 10/13; R knee surg
Mahtook, Mikie	16	46	Fractured L hand
Maile, Luke	17	59	Inflam in R knee
Margot, Manuel	17	31	Strained R calf
Marisnick, Jake	15	16	Strained L hamstring
	17	7	Concussion
Marmolejos, Jose	17	98	L forearm strain
Marte, Jefry	17	23	Fractured L foot
Marte, Ketel	16	32	Sprnd L thumb; mono
Marte, Starling	13	19	R hand contusion
	14	13	Concussion
Martin, Leonys	16	14	Strained L hamstring
Martin, Russell	14	26	Strained L hamstring
	17	45	Nerve irritation L shoulder; L oblique
Martinez, J.D.	13	65	Sprnd R knee; Sprained L wrist
	16	48	Fractured R elbow
	17	42	Sprained ligament in R foot
Martinez, Jose	17	22	Strained L groin
Martinez, Victor	15	31	L knee inflammation
	17	47	Irregular heartbeat x2
Mastroianni, Darin	16	40	Strained L oblique
Mathis, Jeff	13	44	Broken R collarbone
	15	53	Fractured R ring finger
	17	38	Fractured R hand
Mauer, Joe	13	41	Concussion
	14	40	Strained R oblique muscle
	17	10	strained lower back
Maybin, Cameron	13	163	Strained L knee; Sore R wrist
	14	29	Ruptured L biceps tendon
	16	60	Sprnd L thumb; fractured L wrist
	17	27	Strained L oblique; MCL R knee
McCann, Brian	13	36	Recovery from R shoulder surgery
	14	8	Concussion
	17	17	Concussion; sore R knee

FIVE-YEAR INJURY LOG —Hitters

Batter	Yr	Days	Injury
McCann, James	16	21	Sprnd R ankle
	17	14	Laceration on L hand
McCutchen, Andrew	14	15	Fractured L rib
Mercer, Jordy	15	34	Lower leg contusion
Mesoraco, Devin	14	20	strnd L hamstring/strnd L oblique
	15	133	L hip strain
	16	154	Torn labrum L should
	17	86	Rec surg R hip; sprnd L Shld; Fx R foot
Middlebrooks, Will	13	17	Low back strain
	14	94	Fx Rt index finger; strained Rt calf
	16	36	Strained R lower leg
Miller, Bradley	17	44	Strained L ab; L groin
Molina, Yadier	13	15	Sprained R knee
	14	50	Torn ligament in R thumb
Moncada, Yoan	17	11	Bone bruise in R shin
Montero, Miguel	13	28	Lower back strain
	15	21	Sprained L thumb
	16	16	Stiffness lower back
	17	12	Strained groin
Moore, Tyler	15	13	L ankle sprain
Moran, Colin	17	56	Facial fractures
Moreland, Mitch	13	15	Strained R hamstring
	15	14	L elbow surgery
Morrison, Logan	13	70	Recovery from R knee surgery
	14	56	Strained R hamstring
	16	34	Strained R forearm, strained L wrist
Morse, Michael	13	38	Strained R quad
	15	40	R ring finger strain
	17	124	Concussion
Moss, Brandon	16	28	Sprnd L ankle
Moustakas, Mike	16	146	Torn ACL R knee; fractured L thumb
Murphy, Daniel	14	11	Strained R calf
	15	25	Strained L quad
Murphy, Tom	17	74	Fractured R forearm
Myers, Wil	14	80	Sprained R wrist
	15	104	Bone spurs, L wrist + tend
Napoli, Mike	14	14	Sprained L ring finger
	17	10	strained lower back
Nava, Daniel	15	54	Strained L thumb
	16	51	Strained L groin; tend. L kneecap
	17	57	Strained L Ham x 2; lower back x 2
Navarro, Dioner	15	40	Strained L hamstring
Nicholas, Brett	17	26	Surg L knee to repair torn meniscus
Nieuwenhuis, Kirk	15	30	Pinched nerve in back
Nimmo, Brandon	17	64	Strained R ham; collapsed lung
Norris, Derek	13	15	Fractured big toe, L foot
Nunez, Eduardo	13	61	L ribcage strain
	14	16	Strained R hamstring
	15	12	L oblique strain
	17	21	Strained hamstring
Orlando, Paulo	17	82	Fractured shin
Owings, Chris	14	65	Strained L shoulder
	16	42	Plantar fasciitis L foot
	17	62	Fractured R middle finger
Ozuna, Marcell	13	69	Torn L thumb ligament
Pacheco, Jordan	14	33	R shoulder tendinitis
	16	122	R should tendinitis

FIVE-YEAR INJURY LOG —Hitters

Batter	Yr	Days	Injury
Pagan,Angel	13	125	Strained R hamstring
	14	43	Strained back
	15	21	R patella tendinitis
	16	21	Strained L hamstring
Panik,Joe	15	54	Lower back discomfort + inflam
	16	29	Concussion
	17	10	Concussion
Parker,Jarrett	17	109	Fractured R collarbone
Parra,Gerardo	16	53	Sprnd L ankle
	17	30	Strained R quadriceps
Pearce,Steve	13	61	L wrist tendinitis x2
	15	33	L oblique strain
	16	43	Strnd R ham, strnd flexor R elbow
	17	32	Strained R calf
Pederson,Joc	16	18	Sprnd AC joint R should
	17	32	Strained R groin; concussion
Pedroia,Dustin	14	29	L thumb/wrist surgery
	15	67	R hamstring strain x2
	17	45	Sprained L wrist; L knee inflam
Pena,Brayan	16	147	L knee inflammation + surg.
Pena,Ramiro	13	105	R shoulder impingement
Pence,Hunter	15	112	L oblique; Fx L forearm; sore L wrist
	16	58	Strained R hamstring
	17	20	Strained L hamstring
Pennington,Cliff	14	64	Sprained ligament in L thumb
	16	77	Strained L hamstring x 2
Peralta,David	16	118	R wrist inflam; lower back strain
Peralta,Jhonny	16	80	Strained + torn ligament L thumb
	17	29	Upper respiratory ailment
Perez,Eury	14	70	Fractured L toe
Perez,Juan	15	12	Left oblique strain
Perez,Roberto	16	78	Fractured R thumb
Perez,Salvador	13	7	Concussion
	17	16	Strained R intercostal
Petit,Gregorio	15	37	R hand contusion
Pham,Thomas	15	63	L quadriceps strain
	16	43	Strained L oblique
Phegley,Joshua	17	44	Concussion; L oblique
Phillips,Brandon	14	38	Surg torn ligament on L thumb
Pierzynski,A.J.	13	15	Strained R oblique
	16	37	Strained L hamstring x2
Pillar,Kevin	16	15	Sprnd L thumb
Pinder,Chad	17	37	Strained L hamstring
Pirela,Jose	15	32	Concussion
Piscotty,Stephen	17	32	Strained R ham; R groin
Plouffe,Trevor	13	23	Concussion; Strained L calf
	14	15	Strained L oblique
	16	73	Fract L rib; strnd L oblique
Polanco,Gregory	17	45	Strained L ham x 3
Pollock,A.J.	14	93	Fractured R hand
	16	146	Fractured R elbow; strained L groin
	17	50	Strained R groin
Pompey,Dalton	17	182	Concussion
Posey,Buster	17	7	Concussion
Prado,Martin	14	14	Appendectomy
	15	29	R shoulder sprain
	17	136	Strained R ham x 2; R knee

FIVE-YEAR INJURY LOG —Hitters

Batter	Yr	Days	Injury
Presley,Alex	14	56	Strained R oblique muscle
	17	26	Concussion; strained R hip
Profar,Jurickson	14	183	Torn muscle in R shoulder
	15	183	Recovery from shoulder surgery
Puig,Yasiel	15	79	Strained R hamstring
	16	18	Strained L hamstring
Pujols,Albert	13	65	Plantar fasciitis
Raburn,Ryan	13	15	Strained L Achilles
	14	14	Sore R wrist
	17	67	Strained L trapezius muscle
Ramirez,Hanley	13	60	Str L hamMY; R thumb ligament
	14	14	Strained R oblique
	15	30	R shoulder inflammation
Ramos,Wilson	13	64	Strained L hamstring x 2
	14	50	Strained R hamstring/Fx L hand
	17	85	Surgery on R knee to repair torn ACL
Rasmus,Colby	13	41	L oblique str; contusion - L eye
	14	33	Tightness in R hamstring
	16	23	Ear infection
	17	51	Recov surgery on hip; hip tend
Reddick,Josh	13	39	Sprained R wrist x 2
	14	44	Strained R knee;hyper Rt knee
	15	8	Strained R oblique
	16	39	Fractured L thumb
	17	7	Concussion
Reimold,Nolan	13	129	Str Rt hammy; Nerve inflam neck
	14	108	Strnd L calf; cervical spine fusion
Rendon,Anthony	15	89	Strained L quad; Sprain L knee
Renfroe,Hunter	17	10	Strained neck
Revere,Ben	13	78	Broken R foot
	16	30	Strained R oblique muscle
Reyes,Jose	13	74	Sprained L ankle
	14	19	Tightness in L hamstring
	15	27	Cracked L rib
	16	14	Strained L intercostal
	17	10	Strained L oblique
Reynolds,Mark	16	19	Recovering from L wrist surg.
Rickard,Joey	16	73	R thumb ligament injury
	17	19	Sprnd L pinky finger & middle finger
Riddle,J.T.	17	68	L biceps tendinitis
Rivera,T.J.	17	65	Partially torn UCL in R elbow
Robertson,Daniel	17	35	Neck spasms
Robinson,Shane	13	15	Strained R shoulder
	14	34	Surgery on L shoulder
	16	48	Strained R hip flexor; R ankle
Rodriguez,Sean	17	106	Recovery from L shoulder surgery
Rodriguez,Yorman	13	127	L hip surgery
	16	183	Strained L hamstring
Rojas,Miguel	17	70	Fractured R thumb
Rosales,Adam	13	25	Strained L intercostal
Rosario,Eddie	16	1	Fractured L thumb
Rua,Ryan	15	69	Sprained R ankle
Ruf,Darin	14	49	Strained L oblique
Ruggiano,Justin	14	65	Surgery L ankle/strnd L hamstring
	16	53	L should strain; L hamstring strain
Ruiz,Carlos	13	29	Strained R hamstring
	14	26	Concussion
Russell,Addison	17	44	Strained R foot

FIVE-YEAR INJURY LOG —Hitters

Batter	Yr	Days	Injury
Rutledge,Josh	14	11	Viral infection
	16	108	Patellar tendinitis L knee
	17	127	Strained L ham: concussion
Saladino,Tyler	17	48	Back spasms
Saltalamacchia,Jarrod	14	17	Concussion
	15	10	Strained neck
Sanchez,Gary	17	27	Strained R biceps
Sanchez,Hector	13	15	Strained R shoulder
	14	37	Concussion
	15	27	Strained L hamstring
	17	57	Concussion; bruised R foot
Sandoval,Pablo	13	15	Strained L foot
	16	173	Strained L should
	17	59	Sprained R knee; ear infection
Sano,Miguel	16	30	Strained L hamstring
	17	39	Stress reaction in L shin
Santana,Carlos	14	10	Concussion
	14	21	Bone bruise in L knee
Santana,Daniel	16	69	Sprnd AC joint L should; strain ham.
	17	54	Bacterial infection; strained L quad
Santana,Domingo	16	85	Sore R elbow; sore R should
Santander,Anthony	17	136	R elbow inflammation
Saunders,Michael	13	18	Sprained R shoulder
	14	74	Strained Lt oblique; A/C joint inflam
	15	168	L knee inflam; rec L knee surg
Schafer,Logan	14	13	Strained R hamstring
Schebler,Scott	17	17	Strained L shoulder
Schoop,Jonathan	15	78	R knee sprain
Schwarber,Kyle	16	178	Torn ligaments L knee
Segedin,Robert	17	118	Strained R big toe
Segura,Jean	15	15	Fractured R pinky finger
	17	33	Strained R ham; high R ankle sprain
Semien,Marcus	17	81	Bruised R wrist
Shuck,J.B.	15	15	Strained L hamstring
Simmons,Andrelton	16	36	Torn ligament L thumb
Skipworth,Kyle	16	67	Recovering from surg. on L ankle
Slater,Austin	17	59	Strained R groin
Smith,Kevan	16	26	Back injury (sacroiliac joint dysfunct)
Smith,Mallex	16	87	Fractured L thumb
	17	13	Strained R hamstring
Smoak,Justin	13	19	R oblique strain
	14	23	Strained L quadriceps
Smolinski,Jacob	14	53	Bone bruise in L foot
	17	153	Recovery surgery R shoulder
Sogard,Eric	16	183	Cervical strain
	17	16	Strained L ankle
Solano,Donovan	13	34	Strained L intercostal muscle
Solarte,Yangervis	16	41	Strained R hamstring
	17	37	Strained L oblique muscle
Soler,Jorge	15	56	L oblique; Sprain L ankle
	16	59	Strained L hamstring
	17	34	Strained L oblique
Soto,Geovany	14	126	Strained R groin; surg. Rt knee
	16	121	L knee infl; R knee inf.; torn meniscus
	17	154	R elbow inflam
Souza,Steven	14	22	Bruised L shoulder
	15	54	Fractured L hand; cut finger
	16	28	Brsd/strnd L hip, rec from surg. L hip

FIVE-YEAR INJURY LOG —Hitters

Batter	Yr	Days	Injury
Span,Denard	14	7	Concussion
	15	98	Core muscle surg; back; torn labr.
	17	15	Sprained R shoulder
Spangenberg,Cory	15	45	L knee contusion
	16	166	Strained L quadriceps
Springer,George	14	68	L quadriceps injury
	15	70	Fx R wrist; concussion
	17	12	L quadriceps injury
Stanton,Giancarlo	13	41	Strained R hamstring
	15	100	L wrist hamate fracture
	16	23	Strained L groin
Starling,Bubba	17	36	Strained R oblique
Stassi,Max	13	32	Concussion
	16	37	Surg. to repair fractured L wrist
	17	10	L hand inflammation
Stewart,Chris	14	21	Surgery on R knee
	15	12	Strained R hamstring
	16	80	L knee injury
	17	19	Strained L hamstring
Story,Trevor	16	62	Torn ligament L thumb
	17	12	Strained L shoulder
Stubbs,Drew	16	79	Sprnd L little toe
Sucre,Jesus	13	72	L wrist sprain
	16	127	Fractured fibula leg
Susac,Andrew	15	58	Sprained R wrist
	17	28	strained trap x 2
Swihart,Blake	15	17	Sprained L foot
	16	120	Sprnd L ankle
Szczur,Matthew	16	18	Strained R hamstring
Taylor,Chris	15	14	Fractured R wrist
Taylor,Michael	17	37	Strained R oblique muscle
Teagarden,Taylor	13	37	Dislocated L thumb
	14	37	Strained L hamstring
Tejada,Ruben	13	37	R quad strain
	16	16	strnd L quadriceps
Thompson,Trayce	16	79	Lower back injury
Tilson,Charlie	16	61	Torn L hamstring
	17	182	Stress reaction in R foot
Toles,Andrew	17	144	Torn ACL in R knee
Tomas,Yasmany	17	117	R groin tendinitis
Tomlinson,Kelby	16	31	Sprnd L thumb
Travis,Devon	15	101	L shoulder strain; inflam
	16	52	Recovering from surg. on L should
	17	117	Bone bruise in R knee
Trout,Mike	17	46	Torn ligament in L thumb
Trumbo,Mark	14	78	Stress fracture in L foot
	17	10	Strained ribcage
Tucker,Preston	16	52	Strained R should
Tulowitzki,Troy	13	27	Fractured rib, R ribcage
	14	69	Strained L hip flexor
	16	21	Strained R quadriceps
	17	98	Strained R ham; sprained R ankle
Turner,Justin	13	35	Intercostal strain
	14	19	Strained L hamstring
	15	13	R thigh skin infection
	17	21	Strained R hamstring
Turner,Stuart	17	29	Strained R hamstring
Turner,Trea	17	71	Strained R ham; fractured R wrist

FIVE-YEAR INJURY LOG —Hitters

Batter	Yr	Days	Injury
Upton,Melvin	13	21	R adductor strain
	15	66	Sesamoiditis, L foot
Utley,Chase	13	31	Strained R oblique
	15	44	R ankle inflammation
Valbuena,Luis	13	29	R oblique strain
	16	66	Strained R hamstring
	17	31	Strained R hamstring
Valencia,Danny	14	21	Sprained L hand
	16	14	Strained L hamstring
Van Slyke,Scott	13	17	L shoulder bursitis
	15	15	L mid-back inflammation
	16	107	R wrist injury; lower back strain
Vazquez,Christian	15	189	R elbow sprain
	16	12	Recovering from TJS
Villanueva,Christian	16	183	Fractured fibula R leg
Villar,Jonathan	17	17	Strained lower back
Vogt,Stephen	17	31	Sprained L knee
Votto,Joey	14	103	Strained L quadriceps x 2
Walker,Neil	13	32	Strained R oblique; R finger cut
	14	15	Appendectomy
	16	27	Herniated disk lower back
	17	44	Strained L hamstring
Weeks,Jemile	16	148	Strained R hamstring
Weeks,Rickie	13	53	L hamstring surgery
	17	45	Impingement in R shoulder
Wendle,Joe	17	28	Strained R shoulder
Werth,Jayson	13	32	Strained R hamstring
	15	78	Rec. R shldr surg.; L wrist cont.
	17	84	Bruised L foot
Wieters,Matt	14	94	Strained R Elbow; TJS
	15	61	Recovery from R elbow surgery
Williams,Mason	15	106	R shoulder inflammation
	16	106	Recovering from surg. on R should
Williamson,Mac	16	36	Strnd L should; strained R quadricep
	17	22	Strained L quadriceps
Winker,Jesse	17	19	Strained L hip flexor
Wolters,Tony	16	12	Concussion
	17	13	Concussion
Wong,Kolten	14	15	Sore L shoulder
	17	37	Strained L elbow; R triceps
Wright,David	13	48	Strained R hamstring
	15	131	Strained R hamstring
	16	122	Herniated disc neck
	17	182	Herniated cervical disc
Yelich,Christian	14	13	Strained lower back
	15	33	Rt knee contusion; low back strain
Young Jr.,Eric	14	21	Strained R hamstring
Young,Chris	14	15	Strained R quadriceps
	16	76	Strained R hamstring; R forearm
Zimmerman,Ryan	13	15	Strained L hamstring
	14	110	Fx R thumb/strained R hamstring
	15	47	Plantar fasciitis, L foot
	16	33	Bruised L wrist; strained L ribcage
Zobrist,Ben	14	15	Dislocated L thumb
	15	30	Medial meniscus tear, L knee
	17	15	L wrist inflammation
Zunino,Mike	13	38	Fractured L hamate bone

FIVE-YEAR INJURY LOG — Pitchers

Pitchers	Yr	Days	Injury
Adleman,Timothy	16	74	Strnd L oblique
Albers,Matt	14	157	R shoulder tendinitis
	15	84	Broken finger,R hand
Alexander,Scott	17	29	Strained R hamstring
Almonte,Miguel	17	40	R rotator cuff inflam
Alvarez,Dario	17	10	Strained L elbow
Alvarez,Henderson	13	95	Mild R shoulder inflammation
	14	14	R shoulder inflammation
	15	169	R shoulder inflammation x2
	16	184	Rec fr surg. on R should
Alvarez,R.J.	16	71	Rec fr surg.R elbow remv bone chips
Anderson,Brett	13	119	R foot stress fracture
	14	144	Strained lower back/fx L finger
	16	163	Rec fr back surg. - bulging disc
	17	80	Strained lower back
Anderson,Chase	15	19	R triceps inflammation
	17	52	Strained L oblique muscle
Anderson,Cody	15	18	L oblique strain
	17	182	Surgery on R elbow
Anderson,Tyler	16	36	Strnd R oblique muscle
	17	99	L knee inflammation x2
Andriese,Matt	17	87	Strained groin; stress reaction R hip
Arrieta,Jake	14	34	Tightness in R shoulder
Arroyo,Bronson	17	104	Strained R shoulder
Avilan,Luis	17	15	L triceps soreness
Axford,John	17	45	Strained R shoulder
Baez,Pedro	15	43	R pectoral strain
	17	12	Bruised R wrist
Bailey,Andrew	13	100	Rt biceps soreness; Rt shoulder str
	16	14	Strnd L hamstring
	17	163	R shoulder inflam x2
Bailey,Homer	14	16	Strained flexor tendon in R elbow
	15	174	Torn UCL,R elbow; TJS surgery
	16	116	Rec fr TJS
	17	86	Bone spurs R elbow
Banuelos,Manuel	15	35	L elbow inflammation
	16	51	Rec fr surg. L elbow spur
Barnes,Daniel	17	10	R shoulder impingement
Barnes,Jacob	16	37	Sore R elbow
Barnes,Matt	17	10	Strained lower back
Barnette,Tony	17	16	Sprained R ring finger
Barraclough,Kyle	17	20	R shoulder impingement
Barrett,Aaron	15	86	R elbow sprain; R biceps
	16	183	Rec fr TJS
Barrett,Jake	17	41	Stiffness in R shoulder
Barrios,Yhonathan	16	184	Strnd R should
Bass,Anthony	14	49	Chest injury/strained R intercostal
Bassitt,Chris	16	157	Torn ligament R elbow
	17	115	Recovery from TJS
Bastardo,Antonio	17	63	Strained L quadriceps
Baumann,Buddy	16	89	Strnd lower back
	17	112	Strained L shoulder
Beato,Pedro	17	18	Strained L hamstring
Bedrosian,Cam	16	55	Flexor tendinitis R finger
	17	56	Strained R groin
Beeler,Dallas	15	43	R shoulder inflammation
	16	183	R should inflammation

FIVE-YEAR INJURY LOG — Pitchers

Pitchers	Yr	Days	Injury
Belisle, Matt	15	74	R elbow inflammation
	16	48	Strnd R calf
Beliveau, Jeff	15	171	L shoulder fatigue
Benoit, Joaquin	16	22	R should inflammation
	17	20	Sprained FT knee; L knee Inflam
Bergman, Christian	14	60	Fractured L hand/thumb
	15	32	R shoulder fatigue
	16	50	Strnd L oblique
Betancourt, Rafael	13	98	Strained R groin; R elbow; Appx
	15	18	Sinus infection & vertigo symptoms
Bettis, Chad	15	36	R elbow inflammation
	17	131	Testicular cancer
Biddle, Jesse	16	183	Rec fr TJS
Black, Ray	16	30	Bone spur R elbow
Blackburn, Paul	17	37	Bruised R forearm
Blair, Aaron	16	15	Strnd L knee
Blanton, Joe	17	25	R shoulder inflammation
Blazek, Michael	15	52	Fractured R hand
	16	36	Strnd R forearm; R elbow imping
Blevins, Jerry	15	167	Fractured L forearm
Bolsinger, Michael	16	44	Strnd L oblique muscle
	17	10	L knee inflammation
Bonilla, Lisalverto	17	22	R elbow inflammation
Boshers, Jeffrey	16	22	L elbow inflammation
Boxberger, Brad	16	116	Strnd L oblique; recov. core surg.
	17	89	Strained R flexor
Boyer, Blaine	15	12	R elbow inflammation
	17	26	Strained R elbow; strained neck
Bradley, Archie	15	98	R shoulder tend; facial bruise
Breslow, Craig	13	36	L shoulder tendinitis
	14	13	Strained L shoulder
	17	20	Sore L thoracic rib cage
Brice, Austin	17	59	Ulnar neuritis in R elbow; R lat strain
Britton, Zach	17	76	Strained L forearm x2
Brooks, Aaron	16	183	Bruised hip
Brown, Brooks	15	74	R shoulder inflammation x2
Broxton, Jonathan	13	108	R flexor strain x 2
	14	9	Rec from surgery R elbow/forearm
Buchholz, Clay	13	93	Neck strain
	14	28	Hyperextended L knee
	15	86	R flexor strain
	17	166	Torn flexor in R forearm
Bumgarner, Madison	17	85	Bruised ribs, sprained L shoulder
Bundy, Dylan	15	11	Strained right shoulder
Burgos, Enrique	15	27	Sore R shoulder
Bush, Matt	17	21	Sprained MCL in R knee
Butler, Eddie	14	40	R rotator cuff inflammation
Cabrera, Mauricio	17	35	Strained R elbow
Cahill, Trevor	13	47	R hip contusion
	16	32	Patellar tendinitis R knee
	17	85	Strnd back; R should; R Shld impinge
Caminero, Arquimedes	16	17	Strnd L quadriceps
Campos, Leonel	17	42	Strained groin
Campos, Vicente	17	23	Recovery surgery ulnar nerve R elbow
Capps, Carter	14	97	Sprained R elbow
	15	63	R elbow strain
	16	183	Rec fr TJS
	17	92	Recovery from TJS; blood clots

FIVE-YEAR INJURY LOG — Pitchers

Pitchers	Yr	Days	Injury
Capuano, Chris	13	39	L lat strain; Strained L calf
	15	43	Strained R quadriceps
	16	130	Sore L elbow
Carpenter, David	14	15	Strained R biceps
	15	80	R shoulder inflammation
Carrasco, Carlos	15	13	R shoulder inflammation
	16	38	Strnd L hamstring
Cashner, Andrew	14	82	Sore R elbow/sore R shoulder
	16	37	Strnd R hamstring; str neck
	17	25	Tendinitis in R biceps; L oblique
Casilla, Santiago	13	53	Cyst on R knee
	14	24	Strained R hamstring
Castro, Miguel	16	26	R should inflammation
Cecil, Brett	13	13	L elbow soreness
	14	16	Strained L groin
	16	46	Strnd L triceps
Cedeno, Xavier	17	153	Tightness in L forearm
Cessa, Luis	17	47	Ribcage injury
Chacin, Jhoulys	13	15	L lower back strain
	14	128	R shoulder inflammation/strain
Chafin, Andrew	16	62	L should tendinitis
Chapman, Aroldis	14	41	Facial fractures, concussion
	17	35	L rotator cuff injury
Chargois, J.T.	17	26	R elbow surgery
Chatwood, Tyler	13	31	R elbow inflammation
	14	168	Strnd R elbow/strnd L hamstring
	16	33	Tightness upper back x 2
	17	10	Strained R calf
Chavez, Jesse	15	19	Fractured rib
Chen, Wei-Yin	13	58	Strained R oblique
	16	57	Sprnd L elbow
	17	122	L arm fatigue
Cingrani, Tony	13	15	Strained lower back
	14	17	L shoulder tendinitis
	15	37	Strained L shoulder
	17	47	Strained R oblique
Cishek, Steve	16	15	Torn labrum L hip
Claudio, Alexander	16	148	R should stiffness
Cobb, Alex	13	60	Concussion
	14	38	Strained L oblique muscle
	15	183	R forearm tendinitis; TJS
	16	149	Rec fr TJS
	17	15	Turf toe in R big toe
Cole, Gerrit	14	63	Tightness R lat/R shoulder fatigue
	16	66	R elbow inflam; R triceps strain
Cole, Taylor	17	10	Fractured R toe
Coleman, Louis	14	14	Bone bruised/sprained R mid finger
	16	29	R should fatigue
Collins, Tim	14	27	Strained flexor in L elbow
	15	183	L elbow surgery
	16	183	Rec fr TJS
Collmenter, Josh	16	55	Tightness R should
Colome, Alex	13	94	Strained R elbow
	15	34	Pneumonia
	16	16	R biceps tendinitis
Colon, Bartolo	13	15	L groin strain
	17	22	Strained L oblique
Conley, Adam	16	43	L middle finger tendinitis

FIVE-YEAR INJURY LOG — Pitchers

Pitchers	Yr	Days	Injury
Cook,Ryan	14	39	Strned R forearm; Rt shoulder inflam
	16	183	Strnd back muscle
Corbin,Patrick	14	184	Recovering from TJS
	15	91	Recovery from L elbow surgery
Cosart,Jarred	15	37	Vertigo
	17	142	Strained R ham; bruised foot
Cotham,Caleb	16	125	R should inflammation
Cotton,Jharel	17	24	Blister on R thumb
Covey,Dylan	17	80	Strained L oblique
Cravy,Tyler	15	17	R elbow impingement
Crichton,Stefan	17	17	Strained R shoulder
Crow,Aaron	15	183	R elbow surgery
Cueto,Johnny	13	130	Strained R lat x 2; R shoulder
	17	48	Blisters on R hand
Cumpton,Brandon	15	106	R elbow surgery
Cunniff,Brandon	15	101	Strained R groin
Darnell,Logan	15	15	Pneumonia
Darvish,Yu	13	15	Upper back strain
	14	61	Rt elbow inflam; stiff neck
	15	183	R elbow surgery
	16	88	Rec fr TJS; R should strain
	17	10	Lower back tightness
Davis,Erik	14	183	Sprained R elbow
	15	43	Recovery from R elbow surgery
Davis,Rookie	17	14	Bruised R forearm
Davis,Wade	16	48	Strnd flexor R forearm
Dayton,Grant	17	90	Strained L intercostal; stiff neck x 2
De La Rosa,Jorge	15	15	Strained L groin
	16	27	Strnd L groin
De La Rosa,Rubby	16	105	R elbow inflammation
	17	20	R shoulder inflammation
Deduno,Samuel	13	31	R shoulder soreness
	15	91	Lower back strain
deGrom,Jacob	14	12	Tendinitis in R rotator cuff
Delabar,Steve	13	29	R shoulder inflammation
Delgado,Randall	15	68	Sprained R ankle
	17	77	R elbow inflammation
DeSclafani,Anthony	16	68	Strnd oblique muscle
	17	182	Sprained UCL in R elbow
Despaigne,Odrisamer	17	10	Strained L oblique muscle
Detwiler,Ross	13	116	Back strain; x 2
	15	18	L shoulder inflammation
Diaz,Jairo	16	183	Rec fr TJS
	17	48	Recovery surgery R elbow
Diaz,Jose	17	17	R arm fatigue
Diaz,Miguel	17	67	Strained R forearm
Diekman,Jake	16	16	Lacerated L index finger
	17	156	Colitis
Dominguez,Jose	13	69	L quad strain
Doolittle,Sean	14	36	Strained R intercostal muscle
	15	136	L shoulder strain; torn rotator cuff
	16	64	Strnd L should
	17	38	Strained L shoulder
Doubront,Felix	14	59	Strained L calf/strained L shoulder
	16	182	Sprnd L elbow
Duensing,Brian	15	15	R intercostal strain
	16	75	Surg. on L elbow
	17	12	Lower back spasms

FIVE-YEAR INJURY LOG — Pitchers

Pitchers	Yr	Days	Injury
Duffy,Danny	13	99	Recov Rt elbow surg; Rt flexor strain
	15	30	L biceps tendinitis
	17	57	Strained L oblique; L elbow imping
Duke,Zach	17	114	Surgery on L elbow
Dull,Ryan	17	68	Strained R knee
Dunn,Mike	16	58	Strnd L forearm
	17	10	Back spasms
Dyson,Sam	17	11	Bruised R hand
Eaton,Adam	17	155	Torn ACL in L knee
Edgin,Josh	16	37	Rec fr TJS
Edwards,Jonathan	16	183	Strnd flexor tendon R elbow
Eflin,Zach	16	55	Patellar tendinopathy both knees
	17	50	Rec surg pat tend both knees; R shldr
Eickhoff,Jerad	17	50	Strnd upper back; nerve irrit R hand
Elias,Roenis	14	7	Strained flexor muscle in R elbow
	17	138	R intercostal injury
Enns,Dietrich	17	19	Strained L shoulder
Eovaldi,Nathan	13	79	Mild R shoulder inflammation
	16	52	R elbow tendon injury
	17	183	Rec. Tommy John surgery
Erlin,Robbie	17	182	TJS L elbow
Erlin,Robert	14	88	Sore L elbow
	16	165	Strnd L elbow
Escobar,Eduardo	16	16	Strnd L groin
Estrada,Marco	13	64	Strained L hamstring
	16	24	Back strain
Familia,Jeurys	13	128	R elbow surgery
	17	106	Blood clot in R shoulder
Faria,Jake	17	26	Strained L abdominal
Fedde,Erick	17	27	Strained flexor in R forearm
Feldman,Scott	14	18	R biceps tendinitis
	15	83	R shoulder sprain; R knee surg
	17	69	R knee inflammation x 2
Feliz,Michael	17	38	R shoulder injury
Feliz,Neftali	13	155	Recovery from R elbow surgery
	15	38	Axillary abscess on R side
	17	13	Ulnar nerve palsy in R arm
Ferrell,Jeff	16	23	R should impingement
Fields,Josh	14	19	Sore R forearm
Fien,Casey	15	29	R shoulder strain
	16	27	R elbow tendinitis
	17	70	R shoulder impingement
Fife,Stephen	13	66	R shoulder bursitis x 2
	14	14	Recovery from TJS
Figaro,Alfredo	13	30	Strained R oblique
Finnegan,Brandon	17	168	Strained L trapezius; torn R labrum
Fister,Doug	14	41	Strained R lat
	15	34	R forearm tightness
Flores,Kendry	15	41	R shoulder tendinitis
Flynn,Brian	17	123	Strained L groin
Foltynewicz,Mike	15	13	Costochondritis
	16	26	Sore R elbow
Frasor,Jason	15	22	R shoulder strain
Freeland,Kyle	17	10	Strained L groin
Frias,Carlos	15	61	R lower back tightness
	16	24	Strnd R oblique
Friedrich,Christian	13	53	Lower back inflammation
	17	182	Strained L lat muscle

FIVE-YEAR INJURY LOG — Pitchers

Pitchers	Yr	Days	Injury
Fulmer,Michael	17	11	Ulnar neuritis in R elbow
Furbush,Charlie	15	88	L biceps tendinitis
	16	183	L biceps tendinitis
Gadea,Kevin	17	182	R elbow tendinitis
Gallardo,Yovani	13	17	Strained L hamstring
	16	56	R biceps tendinitis
Gant,John	16	54	Strnd L oblique
	17	47	Strained R groin
Garcia,Jaime	13	135	L shoulder strain
	14	69	L shoulder inflammation x 2
	15	75	L groin strain; recov L shldr surg
Garcia,Jarlin	17	10	Strained L biceps
Garcia,Jason Emilio	15	85	R shoulder tendinitis
Garcia,Luis	14	13	Strained R forearm
Garcia,Yimi	16	163	Sore R biceps
Garrett,Amir	17	10	R hip inflammation
Garza,Matt	13	51	Strained L lat
	14	27	Strained L oblique
	15	15	R shoulder tendinitis
	16	70	Strnd R lat
	17	45	Strained R groin; bruised chest;R leg
Gausman,Kevin	15	43	R shoulder tendinitis
	16	22	R should tendinitis
Gearrin,Cory	14	184	Sprained R elbow
	16	43	Strnd R should
Gee,Dillon	14	55	Tightness in R lat
	15	25	Groin strain
Germen,Gonzalez	14	29	Illness/Flu
Gibson,Kyle	16	45	Sore/strnd R should
Gimenez,Chris	16	30	Infection lower L leg
Glasnow,Tyler	16	35	Sore R should
Glover,Koda	17	128	L hip imping; lower back strain
Goeddel,Erik	15	81	Strained R elbow
Goins,Ryan	16	30	Tightness R forearm
Gomez,Jeanmar	13	23	R forearm tightness
	17	16	R elbow impingement
Gonzalez,Chi Chi	17	182	TJS July 2017
Gonzalez,Gio	14	30	L shoulder inflammation
Gonzalez,Miguel	13	17	R thumb blister
	14	11	Strained R oblique
	15	45	R shoulder tend; R groin strain
	16	25	Strnd R groin
	17	26	A/C joint inflammation in R shoulder
Graham,J.R.	15	16	R shoulder inflammation
Graveman,Kendall	15	100	Strained L oblique
	17	76	Strained R shoulder x2
Gray,Jonathan	16	20	Strnd abdominal muscle
	17	77	Stress fracture in L foot
Gray,Sonny	16	55	Strnd R forearm; R trap.
	17	30	Strained lat muscle R shoulder
Green,Chad	16	26	Strnd tendon R forearm
Greene,Shane	16	37	Blister on R middle finger
Gregerson,Luke	16	17	Strnd L oblique
Greinke,Zack	13	33	Broken L collarbone
	16	37	Strnd L oblique

FIVE-YEAR INJURY LOG — Pitchers

Pitchers	Yr	Days	Injury
Griffin,A.J.	14	184	Strained flexor muscle in R elbow
	15	172	R shoulder strain
	16	48	R should stiffness
	17	81	Gout L ankle; L intercoastal
Grilli,Jason	13	42	Strained R forearm
	14	28	Strained L oblique
	15	80	Torn L Achilles tendon
Grimm,Justin	15	26	R forearm inflammation
	17	14	Infection in R index finger
Grosser,Alec	16	58	Back strain
Gsellman,Robert	17	48	Strained L hamstring
Guerra,Deolis	15	59	R knee inflammation
Guerra,Javy	15	16	R shoulder inflammation
Guerra,Junior	16	25	R elbow inflammation
	17	63	Strained R calf; bruised R shin
Guerrieri,Taylor	17	26	Strained R elbow
Gustave,Jandel	17	164	Tightness in R forearm
Hahn,Jesse	15	86	R forearm strain
	16	27	Strnd R should
	17	10	Strained R triceps
Hale,David	15	61	Groin strain
Haley,Justin	17	71	R biceps tendinitis; R shoulder
Hamels,Cole	14	27	L biceps tendinitis
	17	54	Strained R oblique
Hammel,Jason	13	38	R forearm tenderness
Hand,Brad	14	40	Sprained R ankle
Happ,J.A.	13	89	Head contusion
	14	18	Strained back
	17	42	L elbow inflammation
Hardy,Blaine	16	16	L should impingement
Harrell,Lucas	16	47	Strnd R groin
Harris,Mitch	15	16	Groin strain
	16	183	Strnd R elbow
Harris,Will	17	41	R shoulder inflam x2
Harrison,Matt	13	177	Inflamed nerve in lower back
	14	55	Lower back inflam; back surg recov
	15	156	Lower back inflam; back surg
	16	183	Lower back inflammation
Harvey,Matt	13	34	Torn R UCL
	14	183	Recovering from TJS
	16	90	Thoracic outlet synd, R should
	17	79	Stress fracture R scapula
Hatcher,Chris	15	58	L oblique strain
	16	75	Strnd L oblique
	17	51	R shoulder inflammation
Hathaway,Steve	17	182	Bursitis in L shoulder
Heaney,Andrew	16	180	Strnd L flexor
	17	130	Recovery surgery UCL L elbow
Hellickson,Jeremy	14	99	Recovering from surgery on R elbow
	15	22	Strained L hamstring
Hembree,Heath	15	37	R shoulder soreness
Henderson,Jim	13	15	Strained R hamstring
	14	150	R shoulder inflammation
	15	39	Recovery from R shoulder surgery
	16	60	R biceps tendinitis
Hendricks,Kyle	17	46	R hand tendinitis
Hendriks,Liam	16	40	Strnd R triceps

FIVE-YEAR INJURY LOG — Pitchers

Pitchers	Yr	Days	Injury
Hernandez,David	14	184	Surgery on R elbow torn ligament
	15	64	Recovery from R elbow surgery
Hernandez,Felix	16	49	Strnd R calf
	17	98	R shoulder bursitis; R biceps tend
Heston,Chris	16	96	Strnd oblique muscle
Hill,Rich	16	58	Blister L finger; L groin
	17	39	Blister L middle finger x 2
Hinojosa,Dalier	16	64	Bruised R hand
Hochevar,Luke	14	184	TJS
	15	32	Recovery from R elbow surgery
	16	67	Thoracic outlet syndrome
Holaday,Bryan	16	26	Bruised L thumb
Holland,Derek	14	164	Recovering from surgery on L knee
	15	130	Subscapular strain in R shoulder
	16	62	L should inflammation
Holland,Greg	15	18	R pectoral strain
Hollands,Mario	14	24	Strained flexor in L elbow
	15	183	Strained flexor tendon,L forearm
	16	61	Rec fr TJS
Hoover,J.J.	17	23	R shoulder inflammation
House,T.J.	15	20	L shoulder inflammation
Howell,J.P.	17	72	Strained L shoulder x2
Hudson,Daniel	13	183	Recovery from R elbow surgery
	14	155	Recovering from TJS
Huff,David	14	20	Strained L quadriceps
Hughes,Jared	13	57	R shoulder inflammation
	16	27	Strnd L lat back
Hughes,Phil	13	6	R upper back thoracic injury
	15	32	Lower back inflammation
	16	115	L knee injury
	17	112	R biceps tendon inflam; TOS surgery
Hunter,Tommy	14	17	Strained L groin
	16	39	Back strain; core muscle surg.
	17	32	Strained R calf
Hutchison,Drew	13	131	Recovery from R elbow surgery
Iglesias,Raisel	15	36	Strained L oblique
	16	51	R should impingement
Iwakuma,Hisashi	14	35	Torn tendon in R middle finger
	15	73	R lat strain
	17	144	R shoulder inflam
Jackson,Edwin	14	29	Strained R lat
	16	31	Strnd R triceps
Jackson,Luke	16	10	Stress reaction lower back
	17	13	Strained R shoulder
Jansen,Kenley	15	40	L foot surgery
Jeffress,Jeremy	17	12	strained lower back
Jenkins,Chad	14	24	Fractured R hand
Jennings,Dan	14	24	Concussion
	15	24	Neck inflammation
Jepsen,Kevin	13	82	Rt tricep tightness; Appendectomy
Jimenez,Ubaldo	14	29	Sprained R ankle
Johnson,Brian	17	21	L shoulder impingement
Johnson,Erik	16	94	Sprnd R elbow
Johnson,Jim	16	24	Strnd R groin
Johnson,Steve	13	86	Strained Rt oblique; Strained Rt lat
Jones,Nate	14	184	Strained L hip;TJS
	15	131	Recovery from R elbow surgery
	17	150	R elbow neuritis

FIVE-YEAR INJURY LOG — Pitchers

Pitchers	Yr	Days	Injury
Jones,Zach	16	80	Sore R should
Kahnle,Thomas	14	17	R shoulder inflammation
Karns,Nathan	16	65	Strnd lower back
	17	130	Nerve irritation in R elbow
Kazmir,Scott	13	18	Strained R rib cage
	16	31	Inflammation cervical spine
	17	182	Strained L hip
Kela,Keone	16	85	R elbow impingement
	17	60	Sore R shoulder x2
Kelley,Shawn	14	29	Strained lumbar spine
	15	14	Strained L calf
	17	72	Str low back;R Trap;bone chips R elb
Kelly,Casey	13	183	R elbow surgery
	14	184	Recovering from TJS
Kelly,Joe	14	85	Strained L hamstring
	15	8	R biceps tightness
	16	32	R should impingement
	17	21	Strained L hamstring
Kendrick,Kyle	13	8	Inflammation - R shoulder
	15	31	R shoulder inflammation
Kennedy,Ian	15	15	Strained L hamstring
	17	16	Strained R hamstring
Kershaw,Clayton	14	38	Back muscle inflam/strnd L shoulder
	16	47	Herniated disc lower back
	17	39	Strained lower back
Keuchel,Dallas	17	61	Pinched nerve in neck; strained neck
Kimbrel,Craig	16	23	Torn meniscus L knee
Kintzler,Brandon	14	15	Strained R rotator cuff
	15	75	L knee tendinitis
Kluber,Corey	13	32	Sprained finger,R hand
	17	29	strained lower back
Knebel,Corey	16	67	Strnd L oblique
Koehler,Tom	17	28	R shoulder bursitis
Kontos,George	16	28	Strnd flexor R elbow
	17	16	Strained R groin
Krol,Ian	14	15	L shoulder inflammation
	17	28	Strained L oblique muscle
Lackey,John	13	176	R biceps strain
	16	16	Strnd R should
	17	12	Plantar fasciitis in R foot
Ladendorf,Tyler	16	47	Sprnd L wrist
Lamb,John	16	30	Rec fr back surg.
Latos,Mat	14	76	Recovering from surgery on L knee
	15	21	L knee inflammation
Law,Derek	16	17	Strnd R elbow
Lazo,Raudel	16	18	Strnd L should
Leake,Mike	15	15	Strained L hamstring
	16	9	Shingles
LeBlanc,Wade	17	14	Strained L quadriceps
Leclerc,Jose	17	25	Bruised R index finger
Lee,Chris	16	18	Strnd L should
Lester,Jon	17	15	L shoulder fatigue
Liberatore,Adam	16	16	L elbow inflammation
	17	137	Strained L groin; L forearm tightness
Lindblom,Josh	17	35	L side injury
Lindgren,Jacob	15	28	L elbow surgery

FIVE-YEAR INJURY LOG — Pitchers

Pitchers	Yr	Days	Injury
Liriano,Francisco	13	41	Fractured R forearm
	14	32	Strained L oblique
	17	22	L shoulder inflammation
Lobstein,Kyle	15	102	L shoulder soreness
Locke,Jeff	14	12	Strained R oblique
	17	60	L biceps tendinitis
Logan,Boone	14	86	Diverticulitis/L elbow inflam x 3
	15	18	L elbow inflammation
	16	19	L should inflammation
	17	72	Strained lat muscle
Lopez,Reynaldo	17	13	Strained back
Lorenzen,Michael	16	80	Sprnd UCL R elbow
Loup,Aaron	16	55	Sore L elbow
Lowe,Mark	13	16	Neck stiffness
Lugo,Seth	17	82	Part torn UCL R elb; R shldr imping
Lyles,Jordan	14	62	Fractured L hand
	15	126	Sprained L big toe
Lynn,Lance	15	13	Strained R forearm
	16	183	Rec fr TJS
Lyons,Tyler	14	36	Strained L shoulder
	16	62	Stress reaction R knee
	17	42	Rec surg R knee; R intercostal
Machi,Jean	15	18	Strained L groin
Madson,Ryan	13	127	Recovery from R elbow surgery
	17	15	Sprained R finger
Maeda,Kenta	17	14	Hamstring tightness
Manaea,Sean	16	15	Strnd pronator L forearm
	17	15	Strained L shoulder
Maness,Seth	16	85	Strnd R elbow/inflammation
Manship,Jeff	14	37	Strained R quadriceps
	16	16	R wrist tendinitis
Mariot,Michael	14	32	Strained R hamstring
	16	46	Sprnd R ankle
Marksberry,Matt	16	64	L rotator cuff inflammation
Marshall,Evan	15	27	Fractured skull
	17	88	Strained R hamstring
Martin,Chris	15	22	R elbow tendinitis
Martin,Ethan	14	51	Strained R shoulder
Martinez,Carlos	15	9	Right shoulder strain
Masset,Nick	13	183	Recovery from R shoulder surgery
	14	15	Strained patellar tendon in L knee
Mateo,Marcos	15	24	Strained neck
Mattheus,Ryan	13	67	Fractured R hand
Matusz,Brian	16	20	Strnd L intercostal
Matz,Steven	15	53	Partially torn L lat muscle
	16	42	Tightness L should
	17	109	L elbow inflam; Ulnar nerve irritation
Matzek,Tyler	16	46	Anxiety disorder
Maurer,Brandon	15	55	R shoulder inflammation
May,Trevor	16	75	Strnd lower back x 2
	17	182	TJS R elbow
McAllister,Zach	13	50	Sprained R middle finger
	14	27	Strained lower back
	16	22	R hip injury
McCarthy,Brandon	13	65	R shoulder inflammation
	15	161	Torn UCL,R elbow
	16	173	Rec fr TJS
	17	79	Sore L shldr; R knee tend; blist R hand

FIVE-YEAR INJURY LOG — Pitchers

Pitchers	Yr	Days	Injury
McCullers,Lance	16	103	Sore R elbow; R should
	17	49	Sore lower back x2
McFarland,T.J.	16	57	L knee inflammation
	17	11	Bruised L ankle
McGee,Jake	15	86	Torn L knee menisc rec R elbow surg
	16	21	L knee inflammation
	17	10	Strained mid-back
McGowan,Dustin	13	101	Strnd Rt oblique; Sore Rt shoulder
McHugh,Collin	14	15	R middle finger injury
	17	114	Hypertrophy in R arm
McKirahan,Andrew	16	183	Rec fr TJS
Medlen,Kris	14	184	Recovering from TJS
	15	112	Recovery from R elbow surgery
	16	144	R rotator cuff inflammation
Mejia,Adalberto	17	36	Brachialis strain in L arm
Melancon,Mark	17	56	R elbow tendinitis x 2
Mengden,Daniel	17	48	Fractured R foot
Meyer,Alex	17	77	Back spasms; R shoulder inflam
Miley,Wade	16	12	Inflammation L should
	17	10	Medical
Miller,Andrew	13	85	L foot surgery
	15	27	L flexor forearm muscle strain
	17	39	Patella tendinitis in R knee x2
Miller,Justin	13	62	Recovery from R elbow surgery
	16	59	Strnd L oblique
Miller,Shelby	16	24	Sprnd R index finger
	17	160	R elbow inflammation
Milone,Tommy	14	23	Neck inflammation
	15	13	Strained L elbow
	16	28	L biceps tendinitis
	17	87	Sprained L knee
Minaya,Juan	17	24	Strained R Ab
Minor,Mike	14	37	L shoulder tendinitis
	15	185	L rotator cuff inflammation
	16	183	Rec fr surg. on L should
Mitchell,Bryan	15	10	Concussion,nasal fracture
	16	143	Surg. to repair fractured L big toe
Montas,Frankie	16	113	Rec fr rib re-section surg.
Montero,Rafael	15	158	R rotator cuff inflammation
Moore,Matt	13	36	L elbow soreness
	14	174	L elbow injury
	15	88	Recovery from L elbow surgery
Moran,Brian	14	184	L elbow inflammation
Moreland,Mitch	14	111	Surgery on L ankle impingement
Moreno,Diego	15	64	R elbow inflammation
	17	63	R shoulder bursitis
Morin,Michael	14	15	Lacerated L foot
	15	38	L oblique strain
	17	36	Stiff neck
Morris,AJ	16	76	Strnd R should
Morris,Bryan	15	22	Lower back strain
	16	130	Herniated lumbar disc
Morrow,Brandon	13	121	R forearm strain
	14	122	Torn tendon sheath in R hand
	15	153	R shoulder inflammation

FIVE-YEAR INJURY LOG — Pitchers

Pitchers	Yr	Days	Injury
Morton,Charlie	13	74	Recovery from R elbow surgery
	14	35	R hip inflammation
	15	51	Hip injury
	16	162	Strnd L hamstring
	17	40	Strained R lat muscle
Moscot,Jon	15	111	L shoulder surgery
	16	38	Strnd R intercostal; L should inflam
Motte,Jason	13	183	R elbow surgery
	14	77	Recovery TJS/strained lower back
	15	42	R shoulder strain
	16	96	Strnd R rotator cuff
	17	35	Strained back; R oblique
Mujica,Edward	15	28	Fractured R thumb
Mullee,Conor	16	93	Numbness R hand
Musgrove,Joe	17	13	R shoulder injury
Nathan,Joe	15	179	R elbow flexor strain
	16	68	Rec fr TJS
Nelson,Jimmy	15	13	Head contusion
	17	17	strained rotator cuff R shoulder
Nesbitt,Angel	16	36	Sprnd R ankle
Nicasio,Juan	15	11	L abdominal strain
Nicolino,Justin	17	18	Bruised L index finger
Nola,Aaron	16	61	Strnd R elbow
	17	27	Strained lower back
Nolasco,Ricky	14	38	Strained R elbow
	15	144	R ankle impinge.; R elbow inflam
Nolin,Sean	15	41	Recovery fr. bi-lateral core surgery
	16	183	Strnd L elbow
Norris,Bud	14	11	Strained R groin
	15	20	Bronchitis
	16	15	Strnd mid-back
	17	21	R knee inflam x2
Norris,Daniel	15	27	R oblique strain
	16	52	Strnd R oblique muscle; lower back
	17	57	Strained L groin
Nova,Ivan	13	27	R triceps inflammation
	14	162	Torn UCL R elbow
	15	81	Recovery from R elbow surgery
Nuno,Vidal	13	23	Strained L groin
O Day,Darren	16	87	Strnd R rotator cuff; R hamstring
	17	14	Strained R shoulder
O Flaherty,Eric	13	135	L elbow surgery
	14	95	Recovering from TJS
	15	31	L shoulder strain
	16	78	L elbow neuritis; strnd R knee
	17	53	Strnd low back; L rotatr cuff tend
O Grady,Chris	17	42	Strained R oblique
O Rourke,Ryan	17	182	Strained L elbow/forearm
Oberg,Scott	16	42	Axillary artery thrombosis R arm
Oberholtzer,Brett	15	60	Blisters on pitching hand x2
Odorizzi,Jake	15	32	Strained L oblique
	17	30	Strained L ham; lower back
Ogando,Nefi	16	47	Fractured R rib
	17	146	Strained R hand
Oliver,Darren	13	22	L shoulder strain
Olmos,Edgar	15	47	L shoulder impingement
Olson,Tyler	15	24	R knee contusion
Osich,Josh	16	35	Strnd L forearm

FIVE-YEAR INJURY LOG — Pitchers

Pitchers	Yr	Days	Injury
Osuna,Roberto	17	10	Cervical spasms
Ottavino,Adam	15	161	R triceps inflammation
	16	138	Rec fr TJS
	17	10	R shoulder inflammation
Outman,Josh	15	120	L shoulder soreness
Parker,Jarrod	14	184	Recovering from TJS
	15	184	Recovery from R elbow surgery
	16	183	Fractured R elbow
Parra,Manny	13	30	Strained L pectoral muscle
	15	53	L Bicep tend.,elbow strain; str. neck
Paulino,David	17	44	R arm inflam; bone spurs R elbow
Paxton,James	14	115	Strained L lat in back
	15	107	Strained tendon in L middle finger
	16	16	Bruised L elbow
	17	61	Strained L forearm; L pec muscle
Peacock,Brad	15	184	L intercostal strain; rec R hip surg
Pelfrey,Mike	13	15	Back strain
	14	149	Strained L groin
	16	34	Strnd lower back
Peralta,Wily	15	63	Strained L oblique
	17	32	Strained R calf
Perdomo,Luis	17	12	R shoulder inflammation
Perez,Martin	13	43	Cracked ulna bone,L forearm
	14	141	L elbow inflammation
	15	109	Recovery from L elbow surgery
	17	10	Fractured R thumb
Perez,Williams	15	34	L foot contusion
	16	86	Strnd R rotator cuff
Perkins,Glen	14	10	Strained L Forearm
	16	173	Strnd L should
	17	137	Surgery on L shoulder
Petricka,Jacob	15	15	Strained R forearm
	16	151	R hip impingement
	17	115	Strained R lat; R elbow x2
Phegley,Joshua	16	109	Strnd R knee + inflammation
Phelps,David	13	71	R forearm strain
	14	56	R elbow inflammation/tendinitis
	15	49	Stress fracture,R forearm
	16	33	Strnd L oblique
	17	54	R elbow imping x2
Pinder,Branden	16	164	Strnd R elbow
Pineda,Michael	13	98	Recovery from R shoulder surgery
	14	99	Strained muscle in R shoulder
	15	27	Strained R forearm
	17	79	Torn UCL in R elbow
Pomeranz,Drew	13	45	L bicep tendinitis
	14	26	Fractured R hand
	15	14	Sprained L AC joint
	17	12	Strained flexor in L forearm
Porcello,Rick	15	24	Strained R triceps
Pressly,Ryan	15	91	R lat strain
Price,David	13	47	L triceps strain
	17	106	Strained L elbow; L elbow inflam
Putnam,Zach	13	110	R elbow soreness
	14	15	R shoulder inflammation
	15	15	R groin strain
	16	104	Ulnar neuritis R elbow
	17	159	R elbow inflam

FIVE-YEAR INJURY LOG — Pitchers

Pitchers	Yr	Days	Injury
Qualls,Chad	15	14	Pinched nerve
	16	27	Illness
	17	32	R elbow tightness; back spasms
Ramirez,J.C.	17	41	Strained R forearm
Ramirez,Neil	14	12	Sore R triceps
	15	113	L ab soreness; R shoulder inflam
Ramos,A.J.	14	17	R shoulder inflammation
	16	16	Fractured R middle finger
Ravin,Josh	15	34	L hernia
	16	140	Fractured L forearm; R triceps strain
Ravin,Joshua	17	47	Strained R groin
Ray,Robbie	17	26	Concussion
Rea,Colin	16	63	R elbow injury
Reed,Cody	16	18	Back spasms
Reyes,Alex	17	182	Surgery on R elbow
Reynolds,Matt	13	112	Strained L elbow
	14	184	Recovering from TJS
Richard,Clayton	13	122	L shoulder surgery; stomach virus
	16	24	Blister on L middle finger
Richards,Garrett	14	39	Torn patellar tendon in L knee
	15	15	Recovery from L knee surgery
	16	150	Torn UCL R elbow
	17	151	Strained R biceps
Rienzo,Andre	15	20	L knee laceration
Rivero,Armando	17	182	Strained R shoulder
Rivero,Felipe	15	29	Gastrointestinal bleeding
Robertson,David	14	14	Strained L groin
Rodgers,Brady	17	29	TJS
Rodon,Carlos	16	22	Sprnd L wrist
	17	95	Bursitis in L biceps; L shoulder inflam
Rodriguez,Eduardo	16	59	Dislocated R kneecap
	17	45	R knee subluxation
Rodriguez,Fernando	13	183	R elbow surgery
	14	31	Recovering from TJS
	16	91	Strnd R should
Rodriguez,Paco	14	55	Strained L shoulder
	15	127	Strained L elbow
	16	183	Rec fr TJS
Roe,Chaz	15	22	R shoulder injury
	17	85	Strained R lat muscle
Romero,Enny	16	15	Strnd back
	17	28	Strained L forearm
Romo,Sergio	16	81	Strnd flexor tendon R elbow
	17	10	Sprained L ankle
Rondon,Bruce	14	184	Surgery on R elbow
	15	71	R biceps tendinitis
Rondon,Hector	16	18	Strnd R triceps
Rosenthal,Trevor	16	51	R rotator cuff inflammation
	17	56	Strained R lat; R elbow irritation
Ross,Joe	16	77	R should inflammation
	17	79	TJS
Ross,Robbie	17	132	Flu; L elbow inflam
Ross,Tyson	13	17	L shoulder subluxation
	16	178	R should inflammation
	17	94	Rec surg TOS; blister index finger
Rosscup,Zachary	14	31	Sore L shoulder
	15	58	L shoulder inflammation
	16	183	L should inflammation

FIVE-YEAR INJURY LOG — Pitchers

Pitchers	Yr	Days	Injury
Rumbelow,Nick	16	31	Rec fr TJS
Rusin,Chris	16	43	Strnd L should
	17	10	Strained R oblique muscle
Ryu,Hyun-Jin	14	35	Strained R hip/L shoulder inflam
	15	183	L shoulder inflammation
	16	171	L elbow tendinitis; L should surg.
	17	30	Bruised L hip; bruised L foot
Sabathia,CC	13	5	Strained L hamstring
	14	141	Fluid in R knee
	15	16	R knee inflammation
	16	15	Strnd L groin
	17	29	Strained L ham; R knee inflam
Sadler,Casey	15	34	R elbow discomfort
Salas,Fernando	13	36	R shoulder irritation
	14	21	R shoulder inflammation
Salazar,Danny	16	15	R elbow inflammation
	17	60	Sore R shoulder; R elbow inflam
Sale,Chris	14	30	Strained flexor muscle in R elbow
	15	7	Fractured R foot
Sampson,Adrian	16	101	Strnd R flexor mass
Sanchez,Aaron	15	40	R lat strain
	17	146	Laceration/blister R middle finger x2
Sanchez,Anibal	13	20	Strained R shoulder
	14	66	Strnd R pectoral muscle;cut Rt finger
	15	46	R rotator cuff inflammation
	17	14	Strained L hamstring
Santana,Ervin	16	16	Strnd lower back
Santiago,Hector	17	107	Strained L shoulder
Santos,Sergio	13	109	R triceps strain
	14	34	Strained R elbow/forearm
	15	108	R elbow surgery
Saupold,Warwick	16	46	Strnd R groin
Scahill,Rob	15	67	R forearm tightness
Scheppers,Tanner	14	158	R elbow inflammation x2
	15	29	L knee inflam; R ankle sprain
	16	159	Torn cartilage L knee
	17	13	Sore L abdominal muscle
Scherzer,Max	17	10	Neck inflammation
Schugel,Andrew	14	111	R hamstring injury
	16	10	R should injury
Schultz,Bo	16	48	Rec fr surg. on L hip
	17	182	Torn UCL in R elbow
Scribner,Evan	16	151	Strnd lat R should
	17	129	Strained R flexor
Severino,Luis	16	16	Strnd R triceps
Shields,James	17	58	Strained R lat muscle
Shoemaker,Matthew	14	13	Strained Lt oblique
	16	28	Fractured skull,hematoma
	17	106	Strained R forearm
Shreve,Chasen	16	24	Sprnd AC joint L should
Siegrist,Kevin	14	60	Strained L forearm
	16	14	Mononucleosis
	17	43	Sprnd cervical spine; L forearm tend.
Simmons,Shae	14	62	Strained R shoulder
	16	128	Rec fr TJS
	17	154	Strained flexor in R forearm
Sipp,Tony	17	32	Sore L calf

FIVE-YEAR INJURY LOG — Pitchers

Pitchers	Yr	Days	Injury
Skaggs,Tyler	14	81	Strained L forearm; Rt hammy
	15	184	Recovery from L elbow surgery
	17	98	Strained R oblique muscle
Smith,Burch	15	180	R elbow surgery
Smith,Caleb	17	15	Viral infection
Smith,Carson	16	167	Tommy John surg.
	17	157	Recovery from TJS
Smith,Joe	16	39	Strnd L hamstring
	17	33	R shoulder inflammation
Smith,Will	16	60	Torn LCL R knee
	17	182	Surgery on L elbow
Smoker,Josh	17	36	Strained L shoulder
Smyly,Drew	15	118	L shoulder soreness x2
	17	182	Strained flexor in L arm
Solis,Sammy	15	20	L shoulder inflammation
	16	59	L should inflam; sore R knee
	17	73	L elbow inflammation
Soria,Joakim	13	99	Recovery from R elbow surgery
	14	50	Strained L oblique
	17	29	Strained L oblique
Sparkman,Glenn	17	88	Fractured R thumb
Stammen,Craig	15	173	Torn R flexor tendon
Stephenson,Robert	17	10	Bruised R shoulder
Stewart,Brock	17	66	R shoulder tendinitis
Stites,Matthew	15	58	R elbow pain
Storen,Drew	16	16	R should inflammation
	17	22	Sprained R elbow
Strahm,Matt	17	92	Torn patellar tendon in L knee
Strasburg,Stephen	13	15	Strained R latissimus dorsi
	15	58	L oblique; neck strain
	16	33	Sore R elbow; strnd upper back
	17	23	R elbow nerve impingement
Stratton,Chris	17	10	Dislocated/sprained R ankle
Street,Huston	13	15	Strained L calf
	16	94	R knee inflammation; strnd L oblique
	17	170	Strained R lat; R groin
Stroman,Marcus	15	159	Torn ACL,L knee
Strop,Pedro	13	15	Lower back strain
	14	23	Strained L groin
	16	43	Torn meniscus L knee
Surkamp,Eric	13	88	Recovery from L elbow surgery
	15	6	Strained upper back
Suter,Brent	17	19	strained L rotator cuff
Swarzak,Anthony	13	7	Fractured ribs
	16	26	Strnd R rotator cuff
Syndergaard,Noah	17	145	Torn R lat muscle
Taillon,Jameson	16	15	R should fatigue
	17	37	Ttesticular cancer
Tanaka,Masahiro	14	74	R elbow inflammation
	15	35	Strained R forearm
	17	10	R shoulder inflam
Taylor,Ben	17	35	Strained L intercostal muscle
Tazawa,Junichi	16	18	R should impingement
	17	36	Rib cage inflammation
Teheran,Julio	16	17	Strnd R lat muscle
Thatcher,Joe	14	57	Sprained L ankle
Therrien,Jesen	17	20	strained R elbow

FIVE-YEAR INJURY LOG — Pitchers

Pitchers	Yr	Days	Injury
Thornburg,Tyler	14	114	Sore R elbow
	17	182	R shoulder impingement
Thornton,Matt	13	20	Strained R oblique
	16	50	Tendinitis L Achilles
Tillman,Chris	13	5	Strained L abdominal
	16	18	Bursitis R should
	17	35	Bursitis in R shoulder
Tolleson,Shawn	13	170	Strained lower back
	16	41	Sprnd lower back
	17	182	Strained flexor in R arm
Tomlin,Josh	13	146	Recovery from R elbow surgery
	15	117	R shoulder surgery
	17	32	Strained L hamstring
Travieso,Nick	17	182	R shoulder inflammation
Triggs,Andrew	16	14	Bruised L shin
	17	113	Strained L hip
Tropeano,Nicholas	16	96	Torn lig R elbow; strnd R should
	17	182	Surgery on R elbow to repair UCL
Tsao,Chin-Hui	16	133	Strnd R triceps
Turner,Jacob	14	24	Strained R shoulder
	15	183	Strained flexor tendon,R elbow
Uehara,Koji	15	66	Fx R wrist; Strain L ham
	16	47	Strnd R pectoral muscle
	17	11	Strained neck
Urena,Jose	15	28	L knee contusion
Valdez,Cesar	17	54	R shoulder impingement
Vargas,Cesar	16	127	Sore R elbow
Vargas,Jason	13	56	Blood clot,L arm
	14	23	Appendectomy
	15	131	Torn lig.,L elbow; L flexor strain x2
	16	166	Rec fr surg. on L elbow
Varvaro,Anthony	15	133	Torn flexor tendon in R elbow
Velasquez,Vincent	16	17	Strnd R biceps
	17	99	Strnd flexor R elbow; R index fing str
Venditte,Patrick	15	51	Strained R shoulder
Ventura,Yordano	15	20	Ulnar neuritis
VerHagen,Drew	14	28	Stress reaction in spine
	16	108	Thoracic outlet syndrome R should
Verlander,Justin	15	66	Strained R triceps
Vincent,Nick	14	34	R shoulder fatigue
	16	39	Strnd mid-back
Vizcaino,Arodys	13	183	Recovery from R elbow surgery
	16	67	R should inflam; strnd R oblique
	17	14	Strained R index finger
Volquez,Edinson	17	96	Blister R thumb; L knee tendinitis
Wacha,Michael	14	74	Stress reaction in R shoulder
	16	36	R should inflammation
Wahl,Bobby	17	130	Strained R shoulder
Wainwright,Adam	15	162	Torn L Achilles
	17	44	Tightness mid-back; R elbow imping
Walden,Jordan	13	17	R shoulder inflammation
	14	30	Strained L hamstring
	15	155	R biceps inflammation
	16	183	Strnd R should
Walker,Taijuan	14	73	R shoulder impingement
	16	31	R foot tendinitis
	17	24	Blister on R index finger

FIVE-YEAR INJURY LOG — Pitchers

Pitchers	Yr	Days	Injury
Warren,Adam	17	46	Strnd trapezius; lower back strain x2
Weaver,Jered	13	51	Fractured L elbow
	15	49	L hip inflammation
	17	88	L hip inflammation
Webb,Daniel	15	24	Mid R back strain
	16	157	Strnd flexor R elbow
Webb,Ryan	16	27	Strnd R pectoral muscle
Weber,Ryan	17	122	Strained R biceps
Whalen,Rob	16	40	R should fatigue
	17	27	Strained calf
Wheeler,Zack	15	183	Torn ligament,R elbow
	16	183	Rec fr TJS
	17	83	R biceps tend; stress reaction R arm
Whitley,Chase	15	143	Sprained R elbow
	16	162	Rec fr TJS
Wilhelmsen,Tom	15	25	Hyperextended R elbow
	16	15	Lower back spasms
Wilson,Alex	13	83	Sprained R thumb
	16	14	Sore R should
Wilson,C.J.	14	23	Sprained R ankle
	15	66	L elbow inflammation
	16	183	L should tendinitis
Winkler,Daniel	15	158	Recovery from R elbow surgery
	16	175	Fractured R elbow
	17	141	Recovery surgery fractured R elbow
Withrow,Chris	14	127	TJS
	16	24	R elbow inflammation

FIVE-YEAR INJURY LOG — Pitchers

Pitchers	Yr	Days	Injury
Wittgren,Nick	17	65	Strained R elbow
Wojciechowski,Asher	14	87	Strained R lat muscle
Wood,Alex	16	112	Sore L tricep/elbow; Debride L elbow
	17	24	SC joint inflam L shoulder x 2
Wood,Blake	13	103	Recovery from R elbow surgery
Woodruff,Brandon	17	41	Strained R hamstring
Workman,Brandon	15	175	R elbow soreness
	16	183	Rec fr TJS
Worley,Vance	16	16	Strnd R groin
Wright,Mike	15	34	Strained L calf
	17	36	Bursitis in R shoulder
Wright,Steven	14	70	Recov surgery sports hernia
	15	51	Concussion
	16	15	Bursitis R should
	17	153	Surgery on L knee
Wright,Wesley	15	95	L shoulder inflammation
Yates,Kirby	15	41	R pectoral strain
Ynoa,Gabriel	17	16	Strained R hamstring
Ynoa,Michael	17	12	Strained flexor in R hip
Young,Chris	13	18	Strained L quad
	16	18	R forearm strain
Ziegler,Brad	17	37	Strained R back
Zimmermann,Jordan	16	60	Strnd R lat; neck
Zych,Tony	16	112	R/C tendinitis R should
	17	54	Rec surg R biceps; flexor mass R elb

PROSPECTS

Top 75 Impact Prospects for 2018

by Rob Gordon and Jeremy Deloney

Looking for a rookie infusion in 2018? Here's the place to start. As in past years, in the following pages you'll find skills and narrative profiles of the 75 rookie-eligible prospects most likely to contribute and have an impact in the 2018 season.

This year, we've arranged and ranked this rookie class a bit differently than in the past. The changes better reflect the current fantasy prospect landscape. We've ranked the Top 40 prospects in terms of projected 2018 rotisserie value from our figures elsewhere in this book. Beyond those 40 players, we provide 35 more, presented in alphabetical order, who could see time in the majors in 2018, but whose raw skill might be less polished or a step below the others in terms of potential 2018 impact. Keep in mind that this list is but one snapshot in time; players develop at different paces and making that one adjustment or catching a playing-time break along the way can make all the difference. The ranking chart also projects 2018 Mayberry scores to get a quick snapshot of a player.

Starting below, each of the 75 players is listed in alphabetical order with his own narrative capsule. Consider it a primer on his strengths and weaknesses that attempt to balance raw skill, readiness for the majors and likelihood of 2018 playing time.

For additional information, including profiles of over 1000 minor leaguers, statistics, and our overall HQ100 top prospect list, see our sister publication, the *2018 Minor League Baseball Analyst*—as well as the weekly scouting reports and minor league information on BaseballHQ.com. Happy prospecting!

Ronald Acuna (OF, ATL) had arguably the best season of any player in the minors, slashing .325/.374/.522 with 31 doubles, 21 home runs, and 44 SB across three levels. A more aggressive approach at the plate (43 BB/144 K) fueled the breakout, but raised some concerns about his readiness to hit major league pitching. The sky is the limit with Acuna.

Willy Adames (SS, TAM) has advanced one level per year in the minors and is poised to make his major league debut in 2018. He should challenge for the starting shortstop job after hitting .277/.360/.415 with 10 HR and 11 SB in Triple-A. He plays above his average tools and has a chance to be an above average defensive shortstop for years to come.

Chance Adams (RHP, NYY) was a little-known 5th round pick in 2015, but has vastly exceeded expectations and has already thrived in Triple-A. He has succeeded with two plus pitches in his mid-90s fastball and hard slider. His control and command still could use a slight upgrade, but he can be very tough to hit (.193 oppBA in 2017).

Sandy Alcantara (RHP, STL) has some of the best velocity in the minors with a fastball that sits at 94-97 and tops out at 100 mph. He mixes in a solid changeup, but his curve and control are below average. He pitched exclusively in relief with a brief stint

with the Cardinals in September 2017, and has the power stuff to carve out a role at the back-end of the Cardinals pen in 2018.

Jorge Alfaro (C, PHI) is an offensive-minded backstop who put up impressive numbers in his brief MLB debut, slashing .318/.360/.514 in 107 AB. His ultra-aggressive approach (3 BB/33 K) raises a huge red flag, but he has a quick bat and plus raw power. The athletic backstop has tools to stick behind the dish, but needs to be more consistent.

Anthony Alford (OF, TOR) made his big league debut in May, but that ended quickly after he suffered a left hamate fracture. He had a breakout 2015 campaign before a mediocre 2016 season, but exhibited all five tools again while in Double-A in 2017. If he reaches his ceiling, he'll be a top-of-the-order hitter who steals a lot of bases. He could be the Opening Day CF in Toronto.

Kolby Allard (LHP, ATL) has seen his fastball take a step back since being drafted, but still has good velocity and plus late life. His curve might be his best offering, which often results in swings and misses, and it's backed up by an above-average change-up.

Greg Allen (OF, CLE) may not be in line to win a starting job in spring training, but he has the tools and skills to be a useful reserve outfielder for the Indians. With his plus speed and on base skills, he has made a steady climb throughout the minors and can be counted on to provide stolen bases. There is very little power in his repertoire, however.

Brian Anderson (3B, MIA) has solid across-the-board tools, but none stand out as plus, though he does have a strong arm. Anderson put up his best pro season in 2017 hitting .275 with a career-best 22 home runs and then hit .262 in 84 AB with the Marlins. He heads into 2018 as the likely backup to veteran 3B Martin Prado who has battled injuries in recent years. Nothing flashy here, but you could do worse in NL-only leagues.

Miguel Andujar (3B, NYY) had his best season as a pro in 2017 by hitting .315/.352/.498 between Double-A and Triple-A that culminated with a trip to the majors at age 22. He set a career-high with 16 HR and has plus ability to put the bat to the ball. He is also a legitimate 3B with a very strong arm and nimble footwork.

Christian Arroyo (3B/SS, SF) was limited to just 25 games at Triple-A after he missed time with a broken wrist. Arroyo re-injured the wrist in winter ball, but should be ready to take over as the Giants everyday 3B in 2018. Power and speed aren't a big part of his game, but he does have a career .300 average.

Harrison Bader (OF, STL) continues to exceed expectations, showing solid across-the-board tools. An aggressive approach at the plate mixed with bat speed results in average to above-average power. In 2017, he slashed .283/.347/.469 with 20 HR and 15 SB at Triple-A, but scuffled once he reached the majors. The cost-conscious Cardinals will give him plenty of AB in 2018.

Franklin Barreto (SS, OAK) wasn't particularly strong in his 68 AB with Oakland in 2017 (.191 with 31 strikeouts), but the future is very bright for the multi-tooled infielder. He set a

Top 75 Impact Prospects for 2018

Mayberry scores are explained in the Encyclopedia, and here reflect 2018 only, not a player's long-term impact. Batters are dark shaded; pitchers are lighter shaded.

RANK/BATTER/POS, TM	POWER	SPEED	BATAVG
RANK/PITCHER/POS, TM	ERA	DOM	SAVES
1 Ronald Acuna (OF, ATL)	2	3	4
2 Dustin Fowler (OF, NYY)	1	2	3
3 Willie Calhoun (2B, TEX)	3	1	1
4 Victor Robles (OF, WAS)	2	3	4
5 Nick Senzel (3B, CIN)	2	2	4
6 J.P. Crawford (SS, PHI)	1	1	1
7 Brian Anderson (3B, MIA)	1	0	2
8 Christian Arroyo (3B/SS, SF)	1	1	3
9 Jeimer Candelario (3B, DET)	2	1	4
10 Ryan McMahon (1B/2B, COL)	3	1	4
11 Brett Phillips (OF, MIL)	2	2	2
12 Alex Verdugo (OF, LA)	2	1	3
13 Lewis Brinson (OF, MIL)	2	2	2
14 Greg Allen (OF, CLE)	0	2	3
15 Franklin Barreto (SS/2B, OAK)	1	2	4
16 Alex Reyes (RHP, STL)	3	5	0
17 Jorge Alfaro (C, PHI)	2	0	1
18 Anthony Alford (OF, TOR)	1	2	3
19 Harrison Bader (OF, STL)	2	1	1
20 Jake Bauers (OF/1B, TAM)	1	1	3
21 Jack Flaherty (RHP, STL)	3	2	0
22 Scott Kingery (2B, PHI)	2	3	2
23 Francisco Mejia (C, CLE)	1	0	4
24 Brent Honeywell (RHP, TAM)	2	2	0
25 Austin Meadows (OF, PIT)	3	1	3
26 Tyler O'Neill (OF, STL)	3	2	1
27 Fernando Tatis Jr. (SS, SD)	3	3	1
28 Willy Adames (INF, TAM)	1	1	4
29 Jordan Luplow (OF, PIT)	2	0	1
30 Tom Murphy (C, COL)	3	0	2
31 Gleyber Torres (INF, NYY)	1	1	3
32 Brandon Woodruff (RHP, MIL)	1	2	0
33 Austin Hays (OF, BAL)	2	2	4
34 Michael Kopech (RHP, CHW)	1	4	0
35 Tyler Mahle (RHP, CIN)	3	1	0
36 Colin Moran (3B, HOU)	2	1	3
37 Brendan Rodgers (SS, COL)	3	1	4
38 Chance Sisco (C, BAL)	1	0	4
39 Luiz Gohara (LHP, ATL)	1	3	0
40 Carson Kelly (C, STL)	1	0	2

THE NEXT 35

BATTER/POS, TM	POWER	SPEED	BATAVG
PITCHER/POS, TM	ERA	DOM	SAVES
Chance Adams (RHP, NYY)	3	3	0
Sandy Alcantara (RHP, STL)	1	3	1
Kolby Allard (LHP, ATL)	2	2	0
Miguel Andujar (3B, NYY)	1	1	3
Bobby Bradley (OF, CLE)	2	0	0
Walker Buehler (RHP, LA)	3	4	1
Beau Burrows (RHP, DET)	1	3	0
Michael Chavis (3B, BOS)	2	1	2
Zack Collins (C, CHW)	2	0	2
Jose De Leon (RHP, TAM)	2	3	0
Mauricio Dubon (SS, MIL)	1	3	1
Hunter Dozier (3B, KC)	2	1	3
Lucas Erceg (3B, MIL)	2	0	1
Erick Fedde (RHP, WAS)	1	1	0
Stephen Gonsalves (LHP, MIN)	2	2	0
Nick Gordon (SS, MIN)	1	2	3
Eloy Jimenez (OF, CHW)	2	1	3
Mitch Keller (RHP, PIT)	3	2	0
Jorge Mateo (SS, OAK)	1	3	3
Yohander Mendez (LHP, TEX)	2	2	0
Ryan Mountcastle (3B, BAL)	1	1	2
Sheldon Neuse (3B, OAK)	2	1	3
Kevin Newman (SS, PIT)	0	1	2
A.J. Puk (LHP, OAK)	3	4	0
Cal Quantrill (RHP, SD)	2	1	0
Edwin Rios (3B/OF/1B, LAD)	3	1	2
Chris Shaw (OF/1B, SF)	3	0	2
Justus Sheffield (LHP, NYY)	1	2	0
Magneuris Sierra (OF, STL)	0	2	2
Mike Soroka (RHP, ATL)	3	2	0
D.J. Stewart (OF, BAL)	2	1	2
Christin Stewart (OF, DET)	3	1	1
Rowdy Tellez (1B, TOR)	2	0	1
Kyle Tucker (OF, HOU)	3	3	2
Luis Urias (SS/2B, SD)	1	1	4

career-high in HR (15) while continuing to exhibit plus bat speed and natural hitting tendencies. His SB output declined, but he has above average speed.

Jake Bauers (OF/1B, TAM) doesn't wow with any one particular talent, but he is an on-base machine with average power potential. He routinely works counts and draws an inordinate number of walks while smashing doubles to all fields. He also surprisingly set a career-high in SB (20) and logged equal time at 1B and at the outfield corners.

Bobby Bradley (1B, CLE) is known for two things: his prodigious power and high strikeout totals. He's hit at least 23 HR in each full season as a pro, but it has also come at the expense of his BA and strikeout rate, though the latter improved at Double-A in 2017. He'll be given a chance to continue to work on his swing in order to curb his pull-conscious ways, but the power is legitimate double-plus by major league standards.

Lewis Brinson (OF, MIL) had a great season at Triple-A, hitting .331/.400/.562 with 13 HR and 11 SB in 299 AB. Brinson looked overmatched when called up, striking out in 17 of 47 AB and hitting just .106 before a hamstring injury ended his season early. His power and speed mix has plenty of appeal and solid plate discipline should allow him to hit for average once he finds a way to consistent playing time.

Walker Buehler (RHP, LA) has rocketed up the prospect charts since he put to rest concerns about his health and durability. The Dodgers continue to monitor his use as he recovers from Tommy John surgery, but when on the mound he was dominant, striking out 12.8 per nine innings with a mid-90s fastball, plus curve, slider, and change. Buehler should get a long look at a rotation spot in 2018.

Beau Burrows (RHP, DET) was dominant in High-A through 11 starts before his promotion to Double-A in June. Despite some struggles at the higher level, he impressed with his consistent and lively fastball that reaches the mid-90s. His breaking balls need polish, but his four-pitch repertoire and power arm could see the majors by mid-season with a rebuilding Tigers rotation.

Willie Calhoun (OF/2B, TEX) has been a revelation the last few years with his surprising power production. He upped his HR total in 2017 from 27 to 31, good enough for 5th in the minors. The short but strong left-handed hitter will compete for a starting role in spring training and could be a candidate for Rookie of the Year.

Jeimer Candelario (3B, DET) was the gem of the deadline trade with the Cubs. He was outstanding in his 94 AB with the Tigers at the end of the season (.330/.406/.468) and likely cemented his status as the Opening Day starter at 3B for 2018. If his power continues to develop, he could enter the top echelon of third basemen in the American League.

Michael Chavis (3B, BOS) doesn't have an opening on the BOS depth chart at 3B, so he got some action at 1B in the Arizona Fall League. He had a breakout campaign between High-A and Double-A after hitting 31 HR—a career best by far. He also

improved as a hitter, exhibiting better barrel control and pitch recognition.

Zack Collins (C, CHW) had an inconsistent season in his first full year as a pro, but there is a lot to be excited about. He reached Double-A at age 22 and will likely begin 2018 at that same level. However, if he continues to improve his glove work behind the plate and maintains his advanced approach, he could reach the majors quickly. Plus raw power is the calling card here.

J.P. Crawford (SS, PHI) muddled his way to yet another pedestrian season, hitting .243/.351/.405, but did blast a career-best 15 HR and was much better in the second half. Defensive chops and plus arm will keep him in the Phillies lineup once there's more clarity on the team's 2018 middle infield plans. His quick bat, contact ability, and strike zone judgment (79 BB/97 K) should allow him to hit for average eventually.

Jose De Leon (RHP, TAM) was on the disabled list for most of the season due to a variety of ailments—lat, shoulder, elbow. However, he has high strikeout potential and can add pep to his mid-to-high 90s fastball. His slider may be his best offering, but he needs to prove his health. De Leon is 25, and 2018 will be a key season for his future.

Hunter Dozier (3B/OF, KC) missed the majority of the season due to oblique and wrist injuries, but brings valuable offensive attributes and defensive versatility. The Royals may have plentiful job opportunities and he could be a logical replacement at 3B or the outfield. At his peak, he could hit for an above average BA with at least average pop.

Mauricio Dubon (SS, MIL) uses a quick bat and plus bat-on-ball skills to make consistent contact and take advantage of his plus speed. He split time between 2B and SS, and Dubon could get a chance to compete for the 2B job in 2018. Swiped a career best 38 bases while slashing .274/.330/.712 between Double and Triple-A in 2017.

Lucas Erceg (3B, MIL) failed to duplicate his breakout of 2016, but remains the Brewers 3B of the future. Erceg has an aggressive approach at the plate and plus raw power (33 doubles and 15 home runs in 2017). He moves well at 3B with a cannon for arm, but remains a bit of a long-shot for 2018 value.

Erick Fedde (RHP, WAS), a polished 24-year-old righty, had his MLB debut cut short with a forearm flexor sprain, but should be ready to go by spring. His best offerings are a 91-94 mph fastball and a plus swing-and-miss slider, which he will throw in any count. Advanced command allows his stuff to play up, but change-up needs improvement for him to have sustained success in the majors, where he posted a 9.39 ERA in 3 starts in 2017.

Jack Flaherty (RHP, STL) doesn't blow hitters away with high octane stuff, but has an advanced idea of how to set hitters up. Does have a good 89-93 mph fastball, slider, curve, and plus change-up and now owns a minor league career ERA of 2.77. Struggled in five late-season starts with the Cardinals, but should see plenty of action in 2018 and profiles as a solid mid-rotation strike-thrower.

Dustin Fowler (OF, OAK) will be given a chance to win the starting CF job in spring training after suffering a torn knee tendon in his major league debut in late June. He can expand the strike zone at times with his swing-happy approach, but he has the power and speed to evolve into a 20 HR/20 SB player.

Luiz Gohara (LHP, ATL) came over to the Braves in a trade with Seattle and has a big time arm, featuring a 70-grade heater that tops out at 99 mph. A hard slider gives Gohara a second plus offering, but the lack of a quality third pitch could push him to the bullpen down the road. Held his own in five big league starts and he should compete for a rotation spot in 2018.

Stephen Gonsalves (LHP, MIN) may not have the highest upside, but he has the command and advanced secondary offerings to be a rotation stalwart for several years to come. He works with a low-90s fastball and mixes in a variety of offerings, particularly an above average change-up to keep hitters at bay.

Nick Gordon (SS, MIN) is progressing nicely with his instincts and hitting approach. He set an easy career-high in HR (9) while also becoming more disciplined at the plate. Though he increased his strikeout rate, he makes acceptable contact and hits hard line drives to all fields. He has the defensive tools to play both middle infield spots.

Austin Hays (OF, BAL) enjoyed the biggest breakout campaign of any prospect in 2017 by hitting .329/.365/.593 with 32 HR between High-A and Double-A. He ended up earning a September callup to the big leagues. Not only did he showcase his impressive offensive talents, but he proved to be a very sound defender in CF. He could have a starting role in 2018.

Brent Honeywell (RHP, TAM) spent the majority of the season at Triple-A where he posted a 3.64 ERA, 2.3 Ctl, and 11.1 Dom. Though the ERA was a bit inflated, those numbers are in line with his career norms. He repeats his smooth and athletic delivery which positively impacts his command. With a deep mix of pitches, including a screwball, he keeps hitters guessing.

Eloy Jimenez (OF, CHW) has quickly proven to be one of the top prospects in the game. He was acquired from the Cubs in a major July trade and found success at both High-A and Double-A in 2017. For the year, the tall slugger batted .312/.379/.568 with 19 HR. He has the tools and work ethic to potentially become a perennial All-Star.

Mitch Keller (RHP, PIT) dominated in 2017 despite dealing with several nagging injuries, going 8-5 with a 3.03 ERA and a miniscule .202 BAA in 116 IP. Keller's best offering is his plus mid-90s sinking fastball that he locates well to both sides of the plate. Mixes in an above-average curve and a usable change-up. Keller could compete for a rotation spot by mid-2018 if not sooner.

Carson Kelly (C, STL) is known more for his defense than his bat, but the 23-year-old backstop has good bat-on-ball skills and popped a career high 10 HR. He looked over-matched when filling in for Yadier Molina in St. Louis, but with the future Hall of Famer inked to a deal through 2020, Kelly and his fantasy owners will have to bide their time. Still, he remains worth a roster spot in two-catcher formats.

Scott Kingery (2B, PHI) doesn't look like a blue-chip prospect, but has surprising pop for his 5-10, 180 frame. Kingery had a breakout season posting career bests across the board, hitting .304/.359/.530 with 26 HR and 29 SB between Double- and Triple-A. His previous career high in home runs was 5 in 2016 so he will need to prove he can repeat at this level, but the speed is legit and he is nearly ready to see plenty of action in Philadelphia.

Michael Kopech (RHP, CHW) is one of the main reasons why the White Sox farm system is the best in baseball. Between Double-A (22 starts) and Triple-A (3 starts), he held hitters to a .193 oppBA while posting an 11.5 Dom. He regularly sits in the mid-to-high 90s with his fastball and can wipe out hitters with his nasty, hard slider.

Jordan Luplow (OF, PIT) isn't the flashiest prospect on this list, but his production in 2017 is hard to ignore—.302/.381/.527 with 22 doubles and 23 HR between Double and Triple-A. Luplow scuffled when he reached the majors—hitting just .205—but he did blast 3 HR in 78 MLB AB. He should open 2018 as the Pirates 4th OF and could see plenty of action.

Tyler Mahle (RHP, CIN) has quietly developed into one of the better pitching prospects in the NL. The 23-year-old has a low-90s fastball that plays up due to his ability to add and subtract and locate. His other offerings—slider, curve, and change—are average at best, but give him the ability to keep hitters off-balance. Mahle posted a 2.06 ERA in 144.1 minor league innings and then went 1-2 with a 2.70 ERA in 4 starts with the Reds.

Jorge Mateo (SS, OAK) was acquired from the Yankees at the trade deadline and he immediately became one of the organization's top prospects. Between High-A and Double-A, the right-handed hitter batted .267/.322/.459 with 12 HR and 52 SB. His strikeouts increased dramatically, but he impacts the game with his speed and exciting flair.

Ryan McMahon (1B/2B, COL) had a bounce-back season, hitting .355 with 39 doubles, 20 HR, and 11 SB between Double and Triple-A and getting into 17 games with the Rockies. Now being groomed as super-utility type, he split time at 2B, 3B, and 1B. He lacks a clear role for 2018, but the bat will play and is worth owning.

Austin Meadows (OF, PIT) had his worst professional season, hitting .250 with just 4 HR in 294 Triple-A AB. Hamstring and oblique injuries hampered his production and and have dogged him for several years. Plus offensive tools remain intact, but he hasn't been healthy and productive since 2015. Too much talent to give up on just yet, but needs a 500-AB season.

Francisco Mejia (C, CLE) earned brief time in the majors in 2016 and also saw action at 3B in the Arizona Fall League. He established a career-high in HR (14) while maintaining his high BA (career .293). He likely isn't ready to be the Indians full-time backstop due to his defensive shortcomings, but his bat will be an asset in that lineup soon.

Yohander Mendez (LHP, TEX) returned to Double-A in 2017 and set a career-high in IP before appearing in seven games out of the bullpen with the Rangers. His two main pitches at present are a 90-95 mph fastball and plus change-up. If he can continue to improve his slider, he has a high upside and #2-3 starter potential.

Colin Moran (3B, HOU) often gets overlooked based upon a scouting report (all contact, no power) that is no longer accurate. In a repeat season at Triple-A, he drastically upped his BA and HR outputs while significantly reducing his strikeout rate. With size and strength, he has become one of the top prospects in the deep Astros system. He can play the infield corners and LF.

Ryan Mountcastle (3B/SS, BAL) is a significant part of the Orioles prospect resurgence. He switched from SS to 3B upon his promotion to Double-A, but Manny Machado blocks him there. Regardless of his defensive home, he has the bat to play anywhere. He hit .287/.312/.489 with 18 HR between High-A and Double-A as a 20-year-old.

Tom Murphy (C, COL) was sidelined for most of the season with a fractured wrist. When he finally returned he struggled, hitting just .255 at Triple-A and then .042 with the Rockies. When healthy, Murphy has above-average power and stroked 20+ HR in every year since 2013. At 26, he is one of the oldest players on this list, but with Jonathan Lucroy hitting free agency Murphy could get another shot in 2018.

Sheldon Neuse (3B/SS, OAK) was an under-the-radar acquisition from Washington in a mid-July trade and he brings solid but unspectacular skills to Oakland. He performed on three levels in 2016, ending the year in Double-A. He's advancing quickly based upon his hitting ability. He offers plus raw power and a mature approach at the plate.

Kevin Newman (SS, PIT) uses a contact-oriented approach to spray line drives to all fields and rarely strikes out. Newman moves well in the field with an average arm and should be able to stick at short. Below-average power and average speed limit his fantasy appeal, but the Pirates will likely need infield help in 2018 so he could see plenty of action.

Brett Phillips (OF, MIL) isn't an elite-level prospect, but he does have an interesting power/speed mix that fantasy owners crave. The 23-year-old hit .305 with 19 HR and 9 SB at Triple-A and then .276 in 87 AB with the Brewers. Assuming he makes the MLB club, he should put together some decent counting stats even if his BA falters.

A.J. Puk (LHP, OAK) finished 3rd in the minors in strikeouts in his first full season of pro ball. He was dominant, particularly late in the season, finishing with 184 strikeouts in only 125 innings. With his tall frame and fastball that reaches the high-90s, he has top-of-the-rotation stuff. Though his delivery became cleaner, he still struggles to repeat it, negatively impacting his command.

Cal Quantrill (RHP, SD) was the 8th overall pick in the 2016 draft, but doesn't have the overpowering stuff you would expect from such an early pick. Does compete well with a three-pitch mix highlighted by a 92-94 mph fastball and a plus change-up. He's a solid #3 or #4 starter who should be in the majors by mid-to-late 2018.

Alex Reyes (RHP, STL) missed all of the 2017 season with Tommy John surgery and 50 games in 2016 due to a suspension for marijuana use. When he is on the mound Reyes has electric stuff, highlighted by a 100 mph heater and a nasty, late breaking slider. Reyes should be ready to return to action at some point during spring training. Fully healthy, he has the stuff to be a Top 20 fantasy starter.

Edwin Rios (3B/OF/1B, LA) put together another impressive offensive season, hitting .309/.362/.533 with 34 doubles and 24 home runs between Double and Triple-A. Rios is a below average runner and defender and must continue to hit to have value. His best position is at the plate where his LH power bat plays well.

Victor Robles (OF, WAS) is the best athlete on this list and is fresh off a season that saw him slash .300/.382/.458 with 10 HR and 27 SB between High-A and Double-A and then hit .250 in 24 MLB AB. The Nats will need to find a place for him to play, but once they do he has the speed and developing power to be a fantasy stud.

Brendan Rodgers (SS, COL) started the season on fire, hitting .387/.407/.671 with 36 extra base hits in 222 High-A. He slowed down when moved up to Double-A, but on the year still hit .336 with 18 HR despite missing most of August with a quad injury. Rodgers has exciting offensive upside and has the bat speed and size to hit for average and power, despite an aggressive approach at the plate (just 14 BB in 2017). Rodgers will have to wait for an opening but the bat could be worth it.

Chris Shaw (OF/1B, SF) has the best power in a relatively thin system, but poor speed and a below average glove likely limit him to 1B in the majors. He can be overly aggressive as he hunts pitches he can drive out of the park. He did blast a career-best 24 home runs while hitting .292, and looks ready to make his MLB debut.

Justus Sheffield (LHP, NYY) is on the verge of the majors and could be an option for the bullpen in the near-term should the need arise. He missed two months with an oblique injury, but was good when healthy. Though his strikeout rate decreased in his first season above High-A, he has the fastball/slider combo to be a menace to hitters from both sides of the plate.

Nick Senzel (3B, CIN) was the best pure hitter in the 2016 draft and the Reds scooped him up with the second pick. Senzel has a good understanding of the strike zone, a quick bat, and above-average power, though for now he is more of a gap hitter. He's an above-average defender at 3B with a plus arm.

Magneuris Sierra (OF, STL) has some of the best speed in a suddenly thin Cardinals system and held his own in his MLB debut, hitting .317 in 60 AB. He moves well in CF with a strong arm, but poor power and low walk totals limits his fantasy appeal. He profiles more as a 4th OF, but his glove and speed should get him plenty of chances in 2018.

Chance Sisco (C, BAL) has never been one to dazzle with the glove, but he has a feel for hitting and penchant for improving at facets of the game. He set a career-high in HR (9), but power isn't necessarily his thing. He projects as a high BA backstop who puts the ball in play with hard line drives. He has a good chance of making the major league roster during spring training.

Mike Soroka (RHP, ATL) is a tall, durable starter with a good three-pitch mix, highlighted by a good low-90s sinking fastball. Shows a nice ability to spin a breaking ball and has good feel for his change-up. He more than held his own as a 20-year-old at Double-A, going 11-8 with a 2.75 ERA. Doesn't rack up tons of punch outs, but pounds the zone and keeps the ball on the ground.

Christin Stewart (OF, DET) led the Double-A Eastern League in both HR and strikeouts and should be able to work his way to the majors by mid-season. After smashing 30 HR in 2016, he added 28 HR in 2017. Despite his propensity to swing and miss, he will work deep counts and find pitches to drive. The rest of his game is limited, but the power is mammoth.

D.J. Stewart (OF, BAL) doesn't look the part of a solid prospect, but he certainly hits like one. He was a first round pick in 2015 and disappointed with a less-than-stellar 2016 campaign. He was elevated to Double-A in 2017 and produced 21 HR with 20 SB. The power output easily eclipsed his 10 HR from 2016 and he now is prominently in the Orioles' plans for the near future.

Fernando Tatis Jr. (SS, SD) has developed more quickly than anticipated. The 18-year-old hit .281 with 21 home runs and 29 SB as one of the youngest players in the Midwest League, and was then skipped up to Double-A to finish the season. Plus defender at SS with a strong arm gives him added value and could facilitate an early MLB debut. Tatis embodies the new age player combining power (22 HR), plate discipline (77 BB), and an aggressive approach (141 K) at the plate.

Rowdy Tellez (1B, TOR) is behind Justin Smoak on the depth chart and he didn't have a productive season as a 22-year-old in Triple-A. However, the left-handed hitter tweaked his swing to focus on more contact and use of the entire field. This left his HR output down (23 HR in 2016 to 6 in 2017), but he has the hitting skills to force his way to the majors in 2018.

Gleyber Torres (SS, NYY) underwent Tommy John surgery in late June and is poised to return quickly in 2018. This has not hampered his prospect status as he played all season at age 20 and reached Triple-A. He has 20+ HR potential and should be a high BA hitter due to his barrel control and pitch recognition. Though a natural shortstop, he has seen action at 2B and 3B which increases his versatility and chances at reaching the big leagues.

Kyle Tucker (OF, HOU) is blessed with natural hitting skills and advanced pitch recognition. Now that he is starting to realize his plus power potential quicker than anticipated, he is among the top position player prospects in baseball. He hit 25 HR while stealing 21 bases in a 2017 campaign between High-A and Double-A. Currently a CF, he is likely to move to a corner.

Luis Urias (SS/2B, SD) uses a quick bat and an advanced approach at the plate to get the most of his abilities. Just 5-9, 160, Urias has below average power and speed, but makes consistent contact and is willing to draw walks (68 BB/65 K). He split time at 2B and SS in 2017 and could push the Padres for playing time in 2018.

Alex Verdugo (OF, LA) has developed into a solid fantasy prospect. Advanced approach at the plate results in 90% ct% rate and a .300 average. Power development will determine his long-term value, but don't be fooled by his career .438 Slg%, as there is more in the tank if he opts to trade some of his selectivity for more juice.

Brandon Woodruff (RHP, MIL) comes after hitters with a plus 93-95 mph sinking fastball and backs it up with an above-average slider and a fringe change-up. He pounds the strike zone, inducing weak contact and keeping the ball on the ground. Woodruff isn't going to be a fantasy stud, but should settle in a solid mid-rotation starter in NL-only formats.

Top International Players for 2018 and Beyond

Since the 2008 edition, the *Baseball Forecaster* has profiled a handful of Japanese prospects who may make the jump to Major League Baseball in the coming years. This provides owners in deep keeper leagues to get the jump on talent before they arrive in the states. For example, that first column in 2008 included names like Koji Uehara (who made his MLB debut in 2009), Norichika Aoki (2012), and even a "hugely talented young pitcher" named Yu Darvish (also 2012).

As more MLB teams now draw regularly from the international player pool, we've expanded our coverage to include both Korean players as well as top Carribean talent—both high-upside teenagers of the past international signing period and Cuban players that could draw the interest of mutliple MLB teams. With each, we list a "possible" MLB ETA—but for most of these, you'll need to be patient.

Japanese and Korean Players *(by Tom Mulhall)*

Last season was not a banner year for new players from Japan or Korea. But that looks to change in 2018 as at press time, it seems likely that Shohei Ohtani will sign with an MLB club in 2018. But the question remains if he will be strictly a pitcher, or will he get enough AB to be a worthy selection as a hitter. For more on Ohtani, and his interesting quandry for fantasy leaguers, see page 227.

Here's the rest of the Far East landscape, non-Ohtani division:

Shogo Akiyama (OF, Seibu Lions) is just the sixth player with a 200-hit season and is the only player to do that in a season since the "deader" ball was introduced in 2011. He followed 2015 with two solid five-category seasons and seems to be increasing his power. While he still has two years left on his contract, he has accumulated enough time for domestic free agency, which is usually a good time to be posted. Akiyama is a solid defender and durable player who can play in the majors.
Probable ETA: 2019

Yoshihisa Hirano (RHP, ORIX Buffaloes) has been solid for the last eight seasons, other than a disappointing 2015. Both his fastball and forkball are above average and the premier closer in Japan has excellent command of his pitches. The Red Sox and Cards are interested and depending on where he lands he could be valuable, even as a middle reliever.
Probable ETA: 2018

Takayuki Kajitani (OF, Yokohama DeNA Baystars) is similar to Aoki and could provide double-digit SB for an MLB team with a decent BA. The former Central League stolen base champion could be a productive 4th OF in MLB.
Possible ETA: 2018

Ryusuke Kikuchi (2B, Hiroshima Toyo Carp) is a plus defender with decent batting skills. He's another player who does nothing great but everything well. The question is whether his adequate hitting skills can make the transition to MLB. If so, Kikuchi could be a solid utility man, as he has shown he can handle 2B, SS and 3B.
Possible ETA: 2018.

Yusei Kikuchi (LHP, Seibu Lions) drew interest from as many as 11 MLB teams when it looked like he might pass up the Japanese draft to sign in 2009. Kikuchi has a career ERA of 2.80 and had an elite 2017 season with a 1.97 ERA, 217 strikeouts and just 49 walks in 187.2 IP. His 98 mph fastball is complemented by a highly effective hard slider. He apparently has a handshake deal that he will be posted after the 2018 season if he has two double-digit win seasons in a row. If he can stay healthy, Kikuchi could be the best Japanese free agent pitcher to join MLB not named Ohtani.
Probable ETA: 2019

Takayuki Kishi (RHP, Tohoku Rakuten Golden Eagles) has an unusual overhand delivery and throws a four-seam fastball around 90 mph. He has the typical assortment of complementary pitches, including a change-up, slider and a solid curveball, and could be a decent middle or end-of-the-rotation SP. The drawback is his history of injuries, although he had no major issues in 2017. He is interested in playing MLB ball, and his losing record despite a 2.76 ERA may lead his team to let him go.
Possible ETA: 2018.

Yoshihiro Maru (OF, Hiroshima Toyo Carp) comes from a financially strapped team that sometimes posts their players early for financial reasons, as they did with Kenta Maeda. The durable Maru is a superior defender and winner of multiple Golden Gloves who can handle CF in the majors. With 15/15 potential, there are a lot of MLB teams with worse 4th outfielders.
Possible ETA: 2018

Sho Nakata (1B/OF, Nippon-Ham Fighters) has shown power, but that rarely translates to the majors. Nakata has contact issues and struggles with breaking pitches. He does not do much other than hit HR and even those were down in 2017. He is also limited defensively so a full time job does not seem probable.
Possible ETA: 2018.

Takahiro Norimoto (RHP, Rakuten Golden Eagles) was drafted the same year as Ohtani and has somewhat pitched in his shadow, even though he won Rookie of the Year over Ohtani. Just 5'10" and 178 pounds, he nevertheless possesses an excellent fastball that sits in the low to mid 90s, coupled with several solid out pitches. He is signed through 2019 after which he is almost certain to be posted. And his team does have a history of posting their stars early, like Tanaka and Iwakuma. If you miss out on Ohtani, Norimoto could be a nice consolation prize.
Possible ETA: 2019

Ah-Seop Son (OF, Lotte Giants) is one of the better hitters in the Korean League. The diminutive lefty has a good eye and a ton of speed, routinely stealing 30-40 bases. A multiple Gold Glove winner, he could play any of the outfield spots and could make a solid 4th OF in the majors. In 2015 he was posted too early by his team who received no acceptable offers, but his time may be coming soon.
Possible ETA: 2019

Tomoyuki Sugano (RH SP, Yomiuri Giants) is possibly the second best pitcher in Japan behind Ohtani, consistently leading the league in ERA, WHIP, and strikeouts. The former Central League MVP has a career ERA of 2.25 and supposedly has

What Shohei Ohtani Means for your Fantasy League

Ohtani, Shohei – Pitcher — Health A — LIMA Plan C

Age: 23 | Th: R | Role SP — PT/Exp B — Rand Var -1
Ht: 6'3" | Wt: 189 | Type Pwr — Consist D — MM 2303

Yr	Tm	W	L	Sv	IP	K	ERA	xERA	WHIP	oOPS	vL	vR	BF/G	Ctl	Dom	Cmd	FpK	SwK	G	L	F	H%	S%	hr/f	GS	APC	DOM%	DIS%	Sv%	LI	RAR	BPV	BPX	R$
13	for	3	0	0	62	44	5.25	4.84	1.66				21.2	6.0	6.4	1.1						29%	69%								-10.6	35	45	-$8
14	for	11	4	0	155	170	3.24	3.41	1.32				26.8	4.1	9.8	2.4						31%	77%								9.6	97	116	$8
15	for	15	5	0	161	186	2.78	2.10	1.02				28.1	3.2	10.4	3.3						26%	75%								23.4	128	153	$24
16	for	10	4	0	140	165	2.32	2.07	1.08				26.0	3.6	10.6	3.0						28%	80%								32.4	129	153	$21
17	for	2	2	0	16	18	6.17	5.34	1.79				18.8	9.6	10.0	1.0						23%	70%								-3.6	41	49	-$6
1st Half																																		
2nd Half													24.7	3.7	9.3	2.6	61%	10%	44	20	36	29%	75%	11%	26						16.6	91	110	$13
18	Proj	11	6	0	160	165	3.52	4.05	1.23																									

Ohtani, Shohei – Batter — Health A — LIMA Plan D+

Age: 23 | Bats: L | Pos: DH — PT/Exp F — Rand Var 0
Ht: 6'3" | Wt: 189 | Consist F — MM 4323

Yr	Tm	AB	R	HR	RBI	SB	BA	xBA	OBP	SLG	OPS	vL	vR	bb%	ct%	Eye	G	L	F	h%	HctX	PX	xPX	hr/f	Spd	SBO	SB%	#Wk	DOM	DIS	RC/G	RAR	BPV	BPX	R$
13	for	189	14	2	20	4	222		260	345	605			5	68	0.16				32	114				96	14%	76%				2.94	0.0	4	10	$0
14	for	212	31	6	30	1	255		310	434	744			7	79	0.37				30	136				95	2%	100%				4.63	0.0	68	184	$5
15	for	109	15	3	17	1	188		233	307	541			6	63	0.16				27	97				90	4%	100%				2.29	0.0	-30	-81	-$1
16	for	323	63	13	65	6	300		383	488	871			12	71	0.47				39	123				93	8%	74%				6.78	0.0	37	106	$16
17	for	191	22	5	30	0	312		371	482	852			8	70	0.31				42	116				96	2%	0%				6.47	0.0	22	67	$6
1st Half																																			
2nd Half																																			
18	Proj	258	38	10	40	3	255	250	315	447	761	761	761	8	70	0.29	44	20	36	33	123			15%	113	6%	82%				4.82	-5.1	26	78	$6

Remember Daisuke Matsuzaka and his "gyroball"? That level of hype might seem quaint compared to the impending arrival of 23-year-old Shohei Ohtani, whose two-way skills have led headline writers to the easy moniker "The Babe Ruth of Japan."

There is certainly some substance behind it: Ohtani is already one of the top players in Japan. In Baseball Forecaster style, we attempt to set his MLB expectations, as well as examine the fantasy league ramifications of a two-way player.

Shohei Ohtani, pitcher:

Ohtani's pitching workload was limited in the 2017 Japanese season due to an ankle injury, which originally occurred in October 2016 and eventually required surgery in October 2017. Looking back at his most recent healthy seasons (2015-16), Ohtani's Dom and BPV are quite comparable to the final Japanese seasons of Yu Darvish and Masahiro Tanaka. However, Darvish and Tanaka both exhibited pinpoint (sub-2.0) Ctl in Japan, while Ohtani's Ctl has been more pedestrian.

How Ohtani's control will translate to MLB is a key question, especially given the significant difference in the balls between Japan and MLB. Tanaka's control remained exceptional, but he's less of a stylistic comp: his velocity is lower and he relies on his split-finger pitch more heavily. Darvish's stuff is the better comp to Ohtani, and Darvish's Ctl spiked to 4.2 in his first season in TEX, before gradually improving in subsequent years.

Besides control, the other potential limit on Ohtani as a pitcher is his workload. After pitching only minimally in 2017, and never exceeding 160 IP in a Japanese season, it's unclear how many starts he could reasonably be expected to make in MLB in 2018.

Bottom line: Buy the skills enthusiastically, but don't over-project his IP.

Shohei Ohtani, batter:

Ohtani is also a capable batter who really enjoys hitting, to the point where his U.S. destination may be influenced by which team can offer him more consistent opportunities to hit. While the batting stats in this box are, well, fine, the value proposition of "Ohtani: The Batter" certainly falls short of the pitching side.

As for the shape of that value: Ohtani's shaky contact rate in Japan could be exacerbated into a full-blown weakness in MLB's high-strikeout environment. But his power is clearly above-average, and will be the skill that provides the thrust to this skill set. Then again, it's not like power is in short supply on major league rosters these days.

Ohtani's batting opportunities figure to be woven around his pitching responsibilities, making him unlikely to get enough AB to be a serious mixed-league contributor. For instance, he likely won't be used as a hitter on the day before or after his starts, which will cap his AB total. We noted above that his innings total is likely to be monitored, but it's impossible to predict whether he will stay active as a batter while he is skipping a few turns in the rotation.

Bottom line: AL or NL-only leagues, and/or leagues with daily lineup moves, will be the environments where owners are best able to realize value from him as a batter.

—*Ray Murphy*

Shohei Ohtani: A Commissioner's Primer

by Brian Walton, CreativeSports.com

Shohei Ohtani's unique set of skills as a potential two-way player create some headaches for commissioners. How do you handle his eligibility, at the draft table and in lineups?

Before you decide what you will do regarding Ohtani's scoring in 2018, you must understand what will be possible. Will your fantasy league scoring system be able to accommodate a true two-way player and exactly what options will your stats providers make available to you?

Among the options: 1) Hitter only; 2) Pitcher only; 3) Two completely distinct Ohtanis (both hitter/pitcher can accrue stats in the league; a team could own one Ohtani or both); 4) Both hitter/pitcher are separate players, but they are tied together (drafted as one and only one team, but can be activated separately, but would go on the DL together, traded together or cut together).

For reference, here are the plans of a few major game operators/stat services:

- The NFBC ruled that Ohtani will be a pitcher only in 2018 (option #2).
- OnRoto will allow each individual league on their site to choose any of options 1-4 above. (The only option onRoto is NOT planning to allow is for an owner to accrue Ohtani's stats as both a hitter and a pitcher from just one active roster slot.)
- Fantrax will default him to one position when he signs, then if he gains additional eligibility by your league's rules, they will add that eligibility. But if he is active as a pitcher, his batting stats won't count, and vice-versa. (Essentially #4 above, once he gains the necessary eligibility.)

As you work toward identifying the best approach for your league, we have a three-step recommendation for commissioners:

1) Contact your stats provider; understand what is possible.
2) Make an early decision and communicate it to the entire league.
3) Write a "Two-Way Player" section to reflect the ruling and include it in the league constitution as soon as possible prior to the 2018 season.

With Ohtani's arrival imminent, you can take action now. Do not wait until spring.

command of seven pitches. Although he is nearing free agency, he has evidenced little desire to leave the Giants, the most popular team in Japan. Sugano even stayed in college an extra year to make sure they would draft him. The odds of him coming to MLB are remote.
Possible ETA: 2020

Yoshitomo Tsutsugo (OF, Yokohama DeNA BayStar) is a multiple All-Star who had a good showing in the World Baseball Classic. Tsutsugo is one of the premier power hitters in Japan, having hit 44 HR in 2016. But he tailed off to 28 HR in 2017 and defense is something of a challenge. While he has a desire to play in MLB, he would be a risky selection.
Possible ETA: 2019

Tetsuto Yamada (2B/SS, Tokyo Yakult Swallows) became only the ninth player in Japanese baseball history to hit for the "Triple 3" with a .329 BA, 38 HR and 34 SB in 2015, leading his league in all three categories and earning the MVP award. He followed that with .304/38/30 in 2016 before being overworked and tailing off to .247/24/14 in 2017. Possibly the best all-round offensive player in Japan, Yamada is just 26. It is possible that his team could post him early like they did Kaz Ishii and Nori Aoki. He is capable of going 15/15 in MLB and maybe even 20/20, which isn't bad for a middle infielder.
Possible ETA: 2019

Caveat about pitching stats in Japan: Japan instituted a new "deader" ball in 2011. A more hitter-friendly ball was introduced in 2013 and HRs increased to pre-2011 levels, but the slightly smaller and lighter ball still favors pitchers. Continue to be somewhat skeptical when analyzing pitching stats.

Caveat about hitting stats in Korea: Korean ball parks are notoriously hitter friendly. Jung-ho Kang hit 40 HR in Korea the year before he joined the Pirates.

Carribean Players *(by Jeremy Deloney)*

Wander Franco (SS, TAM) led a deep 2017 international class and no prospect got more consistent, positive reviews than the switch-hitter who signed for $3.8 million. Franco, who turns 17 years old in March 2018, is considered an advanced, polished player with both the bat and glove. He makes easy contact from both sides and has the above average bat speed and natural strength that projects to future power. Blessed with athleticism and solid foot speed, he also can steal bases and cover lots of ground in the middle infield. There are no obvious shortcomings in his present tool set.
Possible ETA: 2022

Raimfer Salinas (OF, Venezuela) is still unsigned, but the toolsy outfielder has the potential to hit in the middle of a big league lineup one day. His athleticism oozes from his lean 6'0" 170 pound frame and has the projection to grow significantly over the coming years. As a hitter, he focuses on line drives with hard contact to the gaps. Though Salinas doesn't have much present pop, his bat speed and swing path should lead to future power. There is some swing-and-miss to his game, however. With plus speed and advanced instincts, he should be able to stick in CF over the long haul.
Possible ETA: 2024

Julio Rodriguez (OF, SEA) is a large-framed 16-year-old who had among the best raw power in the international signing class and signed for $1.75 million. His current game is as impressive, thanks to his above average tools. Rodriguez swings a quick bat and has the ability to hit for both BA and power. Though presently has above average speed, he is likely to slow down as he continues to grow. There are some concerns about his swing, but there is plenty of time to master a smoother stroke. This is a prospect who could be a run producer in the middle of the lineup, but the development time will be long.
Possible ETA: 2023

Ronny Mauricio (SS, NYM) signed with the Mets at 16 years old for a $2.1 million bonus. The team projects him to be a potential All-Star shortstop. Mauricio is very lean and offers outstanding agility and body control for his age. He will be given time to develop, as his long and thin frame needs to add good weight for him to realize his offensive upside. He has a high baseball IQ and a a switch-hitter, makes good contact from both sides of the plate. He hits a lot of doubles now and those should turn into HR has he grows. As a defender, he ranges well to both sides and has the plus arm to make throws from deep in the hole.
Possible ETA: 2024

Everson Pereira (OF, NYY) is another 16-year-old who has a terrific array of talents on both sides of the ball. Signed for a $1.5 million bonus, the right-handed hitter has excellent bat speed, advanced pitch recognition with a patient approach, and the ability to put bat to ball with relative ease. He's more of a gap hitter with merely average power potential, but he uses the entire field and makes loud contact. Defensively, he is a solid CF with polished instincts and above average range. Pereira runs well and could be an ideal top-of-the-order hitter.
Possible ETA: 2024

Luis Garcia (SS, PHI) was one of the more fundamentally-sound signees from this international class. The Phillies signed the 17-year-old to a $2.5 million bonus, based mostly on his potential plus defensive skills. He is a smooth defender with the range, footwork, and arm to be a signficant contributor. Garcia makes both spectacular and routine plays look easy. As a hitter, he'll likely never be much of a power threat, but he makes consistent contact from both sides of the plate and can use the entire field with his approach. His plate patience is also admirable and could lead to a potentially high OBP.
Possible ETA: 2023

Jelfry Marte (SS, Dominican Republic) signed with the Twins as a 16-year-old in July 2017 for a $3M bonus, but the team voided his contact in November due to an issue with his physical. At press time he was a free agent. Though some see him as a light-hitting shortstop, others envision a switch-hitter who could grow into average power. His short, lean frame needs significant muscle to realize any long ball power, but his bat control and plate coverage are advanced for his age. Marte is a true shortstop with well above average range and sufficient arm strength. All of his tools play up due to his innate feel for the game.
Possible ETA: 2024

MAJOR LEAGUE EQUIVALENTS

In his 1985 *Baseball Abstract*, Bill James introduced the concept of major league equivalencies. His assertion was that, with the proper adjustments, a minor leaguer's statistics could be converted to an equivalent major league level performance with a great deal of accuracy.

Because of wide variations in the level of play among different minor leagues, it is difficult to get a true reading on a player's potential. For instance, a .300 batting average achieved in the high-offense Pacific Coast League is not nearly as much of an accomplishment as a similar level in the Eastern League. MLEs normalize these types of variances, for all statistical categories.

The actual MLEs are not projections. They represent how a player's previous performance might look at the major league level. However, the MLE stat line can be used in forecasting future performance in just the same way as a major league stat line would.

The model we use contains a few variations to James' version and updates all of the minor league and ballpark factors. In addition, we designed a module to convert pitching statistics, which is something James did not originally do.

Players are listed if they spent at least part of 2016 or 2017 in Triple-A or Double-A and had at least 100 AB or 30 IP within those two levels (players who split a season at both levels are indicated as a/a). Major league and Single-A (and lower) stats are excluded. Each player is listed in the organization with which they finished the season. Some players over age 30 with major-league experience have been omitted for space.

These charts also provide the unique perspective of looking at two years' worth of data. These are only short-term trends, for sure. But even here we can find small indications of players improving their skills, or struggling, as they rise through more difficult levels of competition. Since players—especially those with any modicum of talent —are promoted rapidly through major league systems, a two-year scan is often all we get to spot any trends. Five-year trends do appear in the *Minor League Baseball Analyst.*

Used correctly, MLEs are excellent indicators of potential. But, just like we cannot take traditional major league statistics at face value, the same goes for MLEs. The underlying measures of base skill—contact rates, pitching command ratios, BPV, etc.—are far more accurate in evaluating future talent than raw home runs, batting averages or ERAs. This chart format focuses more on those underlying gauges.

Here are some things to look for as you scan these charts:

Target players who...
- had a full season's worth of playing time in AA and then another full year in AAA
- had consistent playing time from one year to the next
- improved their base skills as they were promoted

Raise the warning flag for players who...
- were stuck at the same level both years, or regressed
- displayed marked changes in playing time from one year to the next
- showed large drops in BPIs from one year to the next

BATTER	yr	b	age	pos	lvl	org	ab	hr	sb	ba	bb%	ct%	px	sx	bpv
Abreu,Osvaldo	17	R	23	SS	aa	WAS	431	4	1	220	5	73	49	51	-43
Acuna,Ronald	17	R	20	CF	a/a	ATL	442	16	29	306	8	73	94	113	19
Adames,Cristhian	17	B	26	2B	aaa	COL	323	8	2	231	6	77	91	86	22
Adames,Willy	16	R	21	SS	aa	TAM	486	9	11	247	11	72	92	114	21
	17	R	22	SS	aaa	TAM	506	9	10	258	11	71	84	100	4
Adams,Caleb	16	R	23	LF	aa	LAA	246	3	8	211	6	63	57	123	-53
Adams,David	16	R	29	2B	aaa	TOR	206	2	2	203	10	72	80	49	-13
Adams,Lane	16	R	27	RF	a/a	CHC	428	7	31	215	7	66	72	123	-28
	17	R	28	CF	aaa	ATL	178	5	12	197	6	55	98	128	-47
Aguilar,Jesus	16	R	26	1B	aaa	CLE	515	25	0	217	8	76	117	15	19
Aguilera,Eric	16	L	26	1B	aa	LAA	459	11	0	235	5	66	99	52	-30
	17	L	27	1B	aa	TEX	387	12	1	189	10	64	92	33	-37
Alberto,Hanser	16	R	24	SS	aaa	TEX	265	5	2	238	2	88	62	58	25
Albies,Ozhaino	16	B	19	2B	a/a	ATL	552	6	29	287	9	81	77	142	48
	17	B	20	2B	aaa	ATL	411	8	19	254	6	75	66	157	15
Alcantara,Arismendy	16	B	25	2B	aaa	OAK	398	9	28	250	6	67	106	165	18
Alfaro,Jorge	16	R	23	C	aa	PHI	404	14	2	253	4	70	106	75	-3
	17	R	24	C	aaa	PHI	324	6	1	212	4	59	79	65	-70
Alford,Anthony	17	R	23	CF	a/a	TOR	257	5	16	297	11	80	73	93	31
Allday,Forrestt	16	L	25	CF	a/a	LAA	133	0	4	221	8	82	41	63	-1
	17	L	26	RF	a/a	LAA	302	1	8	244	12	82	24	52	-11
Allemand,Blake	17	B	25	2B	aa	MIL	336	7	2	240	7	78	79	70	13
Allen,Brandon	16	L	30	1B	aaa	CIN	231	4	0	144	10	70	56	17	-47
Allen,Greg	17	B	24	CF	a/a	CLE	258	2	17	241	7	79	60	117	13
Allen,Greg	16	B	23	CF	aa	CLE	145	3	6	270	10	80	79	121	42
Allie,Stetson	16	R	25	RF	aa	PIT	365	12	1	209	8	67	108	60	-11
Almanzar,Michael	16	R	26	3B	aaa	BAL	410	10	1	214	6	71	88	47	-19
	17	R	27	3B	aaa	WAS	366	7	0	209	3	70	67	34	-49
Almora,Albert	16	R	22	CF	aaa	CHC	320	3	8	272	2	85	60	106	24
Alvarez,Dariel	16	R	28	RF	aaa	BAL	524	4	6	244	4	82	59	59	3
Alvarez,Eddy	16	B	26	SS	a/a	CHW	430	5	8	217	9	76	53	84	-9
	17	B	27	SS	a/a	CHW	429	3	6	196	12	70	45	72	-38
Alvarez,Eliezer	17	B	23	2B	aa	STL	186	3	7	227	7	68	84	112	-10
Alvarez,Pedro	17	L	30	1B	aaa	BAL	547	20	1	177	6	66	88	36	-39
Amaral,Beau	16	L	25	CF	a/a	CIN	256	4	4	221	8	76	61	93	-3
	17	L	26	CF	aaa	CIN	168	0	2	184	8	71	35	86	-45
Anderson,Brian	16	R	23	3B	aa	MIA	301	6	0	222	10	79	57	43	-4
	17	R	24	3B	a/a	MIA	429	18	1	243	9	73	108	64	20
Anderson,Lars	16	L	29	1B	a/a	LA	286	6	2	211	10	75	84	58	4
Anderson,Tim	16	R	23	SS	aaa	CHW	247	3	9	267	3	73	60	118	-19
Andreoli,John	16	R	26	CF	aaa	CHC	507	9	31	211	12	61	82	139	-22
	17	R	27	CF	aaa	CHC	430	10	18	194	10	60	103	143	-12
Andujar,Miguel	16	R	21	3B	aa	NYY	282	2	2	262	7	84	59	67	19
	17	R	22	3B	a/a	NYY	481	18	5	302	5	84	103	63	49
Anna,Dean	16	L	30	2B	aaa	STL	334	1	3	196	8	78	39	61	-23
Aplin,Andrew	16	L	25	CF	aaa	HOU	399	4	15	182	7	71	53	123	-23
	17	L	26	RF	aaa	SEA	232	5	4	201	12	72	72	87	-3
Aquino,Aristides	17	R	23	RF	aa	CIN	459	19	9	215	8	65	125	114	12
Arakawa,Tim	16	L	23	LF	a/a	LAA	149	0	6	151	8	76	30	95	-23
	17	L	24	2B	a/a	LAA	240	3	6	208	11	64	39	73	-67
Arcia,Francisco	16	L	27	C	a/a	MIA	311	1	0	194	7	72	38	29	-57
	17	L	28	C	a/a	LAA	132	0	1	170	6	74	20	70	-54
Arcia,Orlando	16	R	22	SS	aaa	MIL	404	6	11	236	5	79	66	113	15
Arcia,Oswaldo	17	L	26	RF	aaa	ARI	341	16	0	263	8	69	139	76	29
Ard,Taylor	17	R	27	1B	aa	MIA	368	10	3	182	7	62	100	49	-42
Arencibia,J.P.	16	R	30	C	aaa	TAM	357	12	1	187	2	62	100	37	-56
Arnold,Jeff	16	R	28	C	aa	SF	164	2	1	183	6	61	83	73	-54
Arozarena,Randy	17	R	22	LF	aa	STL	163	3	7	236	13	78	73	115	34
Arroyo,Christian	16	R	21	SS	aa	SF	474	2	1	263	6	84	68	55	18
Arteaga,Humberto	16	R	22	SS	aa	KC	207	0	1	193	2	78	33	84	-29
	17	R	23	SS	aa	KC	453	1	4	243	5	85	27	73	-6
Asche,Cody	16	L	26	LF	a/a	PHI	127	6	1	226	8	69	138	54	22
	17	L	27	DH	aaa	CHW	291	11	3	238	12	67	104	57	-4
Asencio,Yeison	16	R	27	RF	a/a	SD	191	1	2	212	2	83	31	73	-13
Astudillo,Williams	16	R	25	C	aa	ATL	322	4	1	241	1	96	31	33	23
Asuaje,Carlos	16	L	25	2B	aaa	SD	535	6	7	257	6	81	67	100	21
	17	L	26	2B	aaa	SD	228	2	1	194	10	83	44	85	14
Austin,Tyler	16	R	25	1B	a/a	NYY	378	18	5	270	13	68	161	72	51
	17	R	26	1B	a/a	NYY	185	10	0	254	9	65	169	74	38
Avelino,Abiatal	16	R	21	2B	aa	NYY	127	0	1	239	7	84	67	57	23
	17	R	22	2B	a/a	NYY	291	3	7	245	6	84	55	121	29
Avery,Xavier	16	L	26	CF	aaa	BAL	303	6	16	220	9	54	97	109	-53
	17	L	27	CF	aaa	ATL	371	10	17	197	12	45	125	141	-54
Bader,Harrison	16	R	22	CF	a/a	STL	465	15	10	235	6	68	98	98	-8
	17	R	23	CF	aaa	STL	431	16	12	254	6	71	93	89	-2
Baez,Jeffrey	17	R	24	RF	aa	CHC	276	9	6	196	8	76	88	89	18
Balaguert ,Yasiel	17	R	24	1B	aa	CHC	477	13	0	231	6	75	84	23	-10
Ballou,Isaac	16	L	26	RF	a/a	WAS	400	5	6	225	9	76	61	103	3
	17	L	27	LF	aa	WAS	124	1	2	157	8	58	62	93	-74
Barfield,Jeremy	17	R	29	RF	a/a	BOS	355	20	1	245	7	70	141	42	19
Barnes,Austin	16	R	27	C	aaa	LA	336	5	14	239	8	81	74	123	37
Barnes,Barrett	16	R	25	LF	aa	PIT	405	7	8	263	7	71	95	110	10
Barnes,Brandon	16	R	30	RF	aaa	COL	238	4	7	228	4	72	72	100	-14
Barnum,Keon	16	L	23	1B	aa	CHW	283	3	1	167	7	63	60	38	-73
	17	L	24	1B	aa	CHW	333	16	0	196	10	57	138	35	-30
Baron,Steven	16	R	26	C	a/a	SEA	232	2	2	236	10	71	43	72	-36
	17	R	27	C	a/a	SEA	215	2	0	195	8	68	42	15	-70

BATTER	yr	b	age	pos	lvl	org	ab	hr	sb	ba	bb%	ct%	px	sx	bpv
Barreto,Franklin	17	R	21	SS	aaa	OAK	469	11	12	264	4	69	86	116	-11
Basto,Nick	16	R	22	LF	aa	CHW	80	0	0	163	7	84	34	23	-12
	17	R	23	1B	aa	CHW	477	14	0	234	9	69	96	21	-24
Bauers,Jake	16	L	21	RF	aa	TAM	493	12	8	246	11	80	78	69	27
	17	L	22	LF	aaa	TAM	486	12	19	245	13	74	87	102	25
Bautista,Rafael	16	R	23	CF	aa	WAS	543	3	49	263	7	81	29	129	3
	17	R	24	CF	aaa	WAS	176	0	6	220	4	83	37	101	3
Beaty,Matt	17	L	24	1B	aa	LA	438	13	2	288	6	86	87	45	39
Beck,Preston	16	L	26	RF	a/a	TEX	357	6	5	232	7	79	83	109	29
	17	L	27	RF	aaa	TEX	229	1	1	198	7	77	39	72	-22
Bednar,Brandon	16	R	24	2B	aa	SF	224	2	4	262	3	80	53	95	-2
	17	R	25	3B	aa	SF	411	1	2	252	5	82	45	61	-4
Bell,Josh	16	B	24	1B	aaa	PIT	421	12	3	268	11	81	87	59	35
Bellinger,Cody	16	L	21	1B	a/a	LA	410	24	7	253	11	75	129	70	48
Belza,Thomas	16	L	27	3B	aa	MIL	181	1	3	202	7	69	64	80	-33
Bemboom,Anthony	16	L	26	C	a/a	LAA	239	1	4	181	7	76	45	92	-19
	17	L	27	C	aaa	COL	133	3	0	238	11	75	86	59	11
Benintendi,Andrew	16	L	22	CF	aa	BOS	237	6	7	285	8	86	112	117	88
Benjamin,Michael	16	R	24	2B	aa	COL	285	4	4	203	5	72	64	60	-33
Beresford,James	16	L	27	3B	aaa	MIN	465	0	2	233	7	81	26	72	-18
Bernard,Wynton	16	R	26	LF	a/a	DET	376	5	18	242	7	80	57	135	21
	17	R	27	CF	aaa	SF	193	1	10	210	5	74	47	141	-12
Berset,Chris	16	B	28	C	aaa	CIN	289	2	1	209	7	75	28	45	-50
Berti,Jon	16	R	26	2B	a/a	TOR	292	3	26	218	10	76	63	158	23
	17	R	27	2B	aaa	TOR	215	3	20	186	8	71	67	169	5
Betancourt,Javier	16	R	21	2B	aa	MIL	343	5	3	219	8	81	55	64	3
	17	R	22	2B	aa	MIL	338	7	3	242	6	84	73	84	34
Bianchi,Jeff	16	R	30	2B	aaa	COL	216	1	1	199	6	74	28	49	-52
Bichette,Dante	16	R	24	1B	aa	NYY	367	10	4	229	12	75	85	63	14
	17	R	25	3B	aa	NYY	244	4	0	239	12	77	51	32	-17
Biondi,Patrick	17	L	26	CF	aa	NYM	264	2	24	204	12	72	24	122	-29
Blandino,Alex	16	R	24	2B	aa	CIN	401	9	13	219	12	67	80	79	-19
	17	R	25	2B	a/a	CIN	393	12	4	239	13	74	116	53	33
Blash,Jabari	16	R	27	LF	aaa	SD	177	7	1	198	13	52	159	30	-27
	17	R	28	RF	aaa	SD	235	12	2	211	11	53	168	64	-9
Bolasky,Devyn	17	L	24	RF	a/a	NYY	158	1	1	195	6	76	48	99	-13
Bolinger,Royce	17	R	27	RF	aa	TEX	325	7	0	199	4	64	88	46	-51
Bonifacio,Jorge	16	R	23	RF	aaa	KC	495	13	5	243	7	72	93	98	6
Borbon,Julio	16	L	30	LF	aa	BAL	424	5	21	214	6	83	36	111	5
Borenstein,Zachary	16	L	26	LF	aaa	ARI	357	6	10	222	6	61	105	135	-17
	17	L	27	LF	aaa	ARI	384	15	1	220	7	60	148	98	2
Bortnick,Tyler	16	R	29	2B	a/a	DET	167	4	3	214	8	76	74	104	13
Bostick,Christopher	16	R	23	2B	a/a	WAS	484	7	10	232	7	72	74	107	-3
	17	R	24	LF	aaa	PIT	486	6	7	269	8	79	72	80	13
Bote,David	16	R	23	3B	a/a	CHC	47	1	0	244	6	73	28	18	-64
	17	R	24	2B	aa	CHC	470	12	4	247	9	75	92	82	20
Bousfield,Auston	16	R	23	CF	a/a	SD	367	3	8	153	8	66	55	89	-45
	17	R	24	CF	aa	SD	297	3	13	210	8	81	45	96	7
Boyd,B.J.	16	L	23	RF	aaa	OAK	30	0	0	248	6	89	0	15	-25
	17	L	24	CF	aa	OAK	533	4	13	283	5	85	52	109	25
Boyd,Jayce	16	R	26	LF	aa	NYM	270	2	2	212	8	77	49	37	-23
	17	R	27	LF	aaa	NYM	246	8	2	223	7	75	94	61	8
Bradley,Bobby	17	L	21	1B	aa	CLE	467	20	3	241	9	75	114	58	29
Brady,Patrick	16	R	28	3B	aa	SEA	251	2	5	190	11	63	70	115	-35
Brantly,Rob	16	L	27	C	aaa	SEA	303	10	0	192	2	78	79	41	-8
	17	L	28	C	aaa	CHW	287	8	2	233	5	82	62	53	7
Bregman,Alex	16	R	22	SS	a/a	HOU	314	17	5	274	10	86	125	88	94
Brentz,Bryce	16	R	28	LF	a/a	BOS	244	4	2	212	5	68	104	65	-15
Brignac,Reid	16	L	30	2B	aaa	ATL	363	6	4	204	10	66	75	70	-32
Brinson,Lewis	16	R	22	CF	a/a	MIL	393	13	12	249	4	77	106	131	40
	17	R	23	CF	aaa	MIL	299	11	8	284	7	76	112	107	41
Brito,Socrates	16	L	24	RF	aaa	ARI	303	4	5	253	3	77	68	114	6
	17	L	25	RF	aaa	ARI	292	3	4	243	4	74	74	110	0
Britton,Buck	16	L	30	LF	aaa	MIN	253	2	0	158	5	78	53	59	-18
Brockmeyer,Cael	16	R	25	1B	a/a	CHC	133	2	0	216	4	65	96	42	-40
	17	R	26	C	a/a	CHC	204	5	0	159	5	65	76	46	-51
Brown,Aaron	16	L	24	CF	aa	PHI	228	3	2	193	7	68	85	115	-11
	17	L	25	RF	aa	PHI	90	2	0	188	1	55	71	29	-112
Brown,Domonic	16	L	29	RF	aaa	TOR	464	6	4	199	6	73	64	41	-31
Brown,Trevor	17	R	26	C	aaa	SF	196	1	2	135	3	74	19	46	-66
Broxton,Keon	16	R	26	CF	aaa	MIL	178	6	12	234	7	60	146	146	16
Brugman,Jaycob	16	L	24	CF	a/a	OAK	543	9	6	255	7	76	86	95	17
	17	L	25	CF	aaa	OAK	153	1	2	233	9	80	33	69	-15
Bruno,Stephen	16	R	26	2B	a/a	CHC	73	1	1	204	4	62	67	101	-58
	17	R	27	3B	aaa	CHC	219	6	5	209	2	76	73	78	-9
Bueno,Ronald	16	B	24	2B	aa	CIN	33	0	0	227	13	57	0	64	-123
	17	B	25	3B	a/a	CHW	216	6	1	191	10	74	84	57	4
Burg,Alex	16	R	29	DH	a/a	TEX	270	5	1	166	6	69	83	35	-32
Burks,Charcer	17	R	22	LF	aa	CHC	456	9	15	255	13	74	73	93	11
Burns,Andrew	16	R	26	2B	aaa	TOR	418	7	11	205	6	77	79	83	9
Burns,Billy	16	B	27	CF	aaa	KC	46	0	3	227	3	59	21	96	-111
	17	B	28	CF	aaa	KC	354	0	17	233	8	80	21	109	-13
Buss,Nicholas	16	L	30	RF	aaa	LAA	331	4	5	210	5	73	75	102	-5
Butler,Joey	16	R	30	LF	aaa	CLE	413	6	3	194	7	69	59	73	-39
Buxton,Byron	16	R	23	CF	aaa	MIN	190	10	6	288	6	68	155	156	57
Cabrera,Ramon	16	B	27	C	aaa	CIN	54	0	0	222	2	86	13	15	-36
	17	B	28	C	aaa	MIA	198	4	1	171	5	78	62	55	-9

BATTER	yr	b	age	pos	lvl	org	ab	hr	sb	ba	bb%	ct%	px	sx	bpv
Caldwell,Bruce	17	L	26	3B	a/a	STL	339	11	2	205	11	60	94	58	-41
Calhoun,Willie	16	L	22	2B	aa	LA	503	26	0	241	7	86	110	36	59
	17	L	23	2B	aaa	TEX	486	24	3	267	6	86	107	81	70
Calixte,Orlando	16	R	24	RF	a/a	KC	471	8	15	243	6	77	79	122	21
	17	R	25	SS	aaa	SF	378	9	15	208	4	74	76	139	11
Camargo,Johan	16	B	23	2B	aa	ATL	446	4	1	252	5	79	69	74	6
Campana,Tony	16	L	30	LF	aaa	CHW	203	0	7	163	5	81	9	76	-33
Campbell,Eric	16	R	29	1B	aaa	NYM	302	4	4	214	8	76	61	94	-4
Candelario,Jeimer	16	B	23	3B	a/a	CHC	474	11	0	250	10	76	104	51	26
	17	B	24	3B	aaa	DET	407	14	1	244	9	72	130	77	38
Canelo,Malquin	17	R	23	SS	aa	PHI	389	5	10	199	8	67	73	98	-27
Canha,Mark	17	R	28	RF	aaa	OAK	272	8	3	224	8	73	116	101	32
Cantwell,Patrick	16	R	26	C	aaa	TEX	183	0	3	217	6	69	35	48	-68
Caratini,Victor	16	B	23	C	aa	CHC	412	5	2	259	10	78	68	56	4
	17	B	24	C	aaa	CHC	292	8	1	293	7	81	105	72	44
Carbonell,Daniel	17	R	26	LF	aa	SF	191	3	4	210	5	75	69	97	-3
Cardona,Jose	17	R	23	CF	a/a	TEX	446	6	13	249	4	88	48	88	26
Cardullo,Stephen	16	R	29	LF	aaa	COL	406	12	4	253	6	84	93	90	50
Carhart,Ben	16	R	26	1B	a/a	CHC	210	5	1	208	3	79	76	49	1
Carrillo,Xorge	16	R	27	C	a/a	NYM	290	3	0	209	6	79	47	20	-27
	17	R	28	C	aaa	NYM	252	6	0	197	5	67	73	11	-60
Carrizales,Omar	16	L	21	CF	aa	COL	80	0	4	250	4	80	21	108	-21
	17	L	22	CF	aa	COL	432	5	10	251	9	79	63	93	12
Casali,Curtis	16	R	28	C	aaa	TAM	63	2	0	205	16	76	49	3	-23
	17	R	29	C	aaa	TAM	300	4	0	211	9	72	43	25	-51
Casteel,Ryan	16	R	25	1B	a/a	SEA	337	5	2	202	6	65	74	80	-42
	17	R	26	1B	a/a	SEA	389	10	1	228	6	73	84	37	-14
Castellanos,Alex	16	R	30	3B	aaa	COL	164	4	1	241	5	59	114	69	-42
Castillo,Ali	16	R	27	2B	a/a	SF	380	0	8	264	4	86	35	99	11
	17	R	28	2B	a/a	SF	345	1	4	221	4	89	31	66	8
Castillo,Erick	17	R	24	C	aa	CHC	204	1	0	221	8	76	43	19	-38
Castillo,Ivan	16	B	21	SS	a/a	CLE	244	2	9	189	3	83	49	136	19
	17	B	22	3B	aa	CLE	69	1	1	193	11	82	51	59	10
Castillo,Rusney	16	R	29	CF	aaa	BOS	395	2	8	234	5	79	57	119	10
Castro,Daniel	16	R	24	SS	aaa	ATL	214	2	0	224	3	86	47	49	5
	17	R	25	SS	aaa	COL	395	2	1	272	4	89	50	33	14
Castro,Harold	16	L	23	2B	aa	DET	392	3	5	220	2	83	43	67	-7
	17	L	24	CF	aa	DET	414	1	17	258	4	86	35	114	15
Cave,Jake	16	L	24	LF	a/a	NYY	426	8	6	249	7	72	99	111	17
	17	L	25	CF	a/a	NYY	406	21	2	278	6	67	144	78	21
Cecchini,Garin	16	L	25	1B	aaa	MIL	424	4	9	225	5	82	51	92	10
	17	L	26	3B	aaa	KC	290	3	2	228	3	77	73	78	-3
Cecchini,Gavin	16	R	23	SS	aaa	NYM	446	6	3	264	7	85	59	61	23
	17	R	24	2B	aaa	NYM	453	4	4	211	6	83	51	70	10
Ceciliani,Darrell	16	L	26	LF	aaa	TOR	304	9	9	239	7	80	97	100	42
	17	L	27	CF	aaa	TOR	77	0	1	139	3	68	12	57	-94
Centeno,Juan	16	L	27	C	aaa	MIN	49	1	1	211	6	91	34	48	19
	17	L	28	C	aaa	HOU	235	1	0	226	4	79	36	34	-37
Chang,Yu-Cheng	17	R	22	SS	aa	CLE	439	21	9	210	9	71	131	106	40
Chapman,Matt	16	R	23	3B	a/a	OAK	514	28	6	212	10	64	160	102	37
	17	R	24	3B	aaa	OAK	175	11	4	218	10	61	161	98	22
Chavis,Michael	17	R	22	3B	aa	BOS	248	11	1	239	6	77	128	46	37
Choi,Ji-Man	16	L	25	1B	aaa	LAA	188	3	3	279	10	78	96	63	29
	17	L	26	1B	aaa	NYY	288	15	3	253	10	65	161	53	25
Choice,Michael	16	R	27	DH	aaa	CLE	252	12	0	212	4	63	127	32	-26
	17	R	28	RF	a/a	MIL	199	8	1	197	8	64	123	37	-18
Ciriaco,Juan	16	R	26	SS	a/a	COL	240	2	7	231	2	87	40	93	14
	17	R	27	2B	a/a	COL	110	2	4	182	2	81	32	49	-29
Ciuffo,Nick	17	L	22	C	aa	TAM	371	6	2	221	9	71	89	56	-7
Coats,Jason	16	R	26	RF	aaa	CHW	297	8	1	273	6	71	106	53	0
Cole,Hunter	16	R	24	RF	aa	SF	469	10	2	247	6	72	88	71	-6
	17	R	25	RF	aa	SF	281	5	2	226	9	74	99	90	22
Coleman,Dusty	16	R	29	SS	aaa	KC	188	3	4	184	4	62	90	113	-35
Collier,Zach	16	L	26	RF	a/a	WAS	362	3	6	217	7	63	71	111	-41
	17	L	27	CF	a/a	WAS	205	5	4	221	7	65	101	95	-13
Collins,Tyler	16	L	26	LF	aaa	DET	257	6	3	186	6	70	60	63	-37
	17	L	27	RF	aaa	DET	260	8	9	249	9	68	98	104	1
Conger,Hank	16	B	28	C	aaa	TAM	109	2	0	132	3	72	67	42	-37
	17	B	29	C	aaa	ARI	180	4	0	176	6	68	68	35	-49
Contreras,Willson	16	R	24	C	aaa	CHC	204	7	3	307	10	82	116	87	66
Cooper,Garrett	16	R	26	1B	a/a	MIL	428	7	2	248	5	79	70	39	-3
	17	R	27	1B	a/a	NYY	306	18	0	314	9	78	148	37	62
Coppola,Zachary	17	L	23	CF	aa	PHI	325	0	24	222	9	78	21	112	-16
Corcino,Edgar	16	B	24	RF	aa	MIN	183	2	1	254	5	79	64	100	11
	17	B	25	RF	aa	MIN	459	5	4	269	7	81	50	63	0
Cordell,Ryan	16	R	24	CF	aa	TEX	405	16	10	234	6	74	114	123	37
	17	R	25	RF	aaa	MIL	261	8	6	232	6	70	108	116	16
Cordero,Franchy	16	L	22	CF	a/a	SD	258	5	9	262	6	68	81	121	-11
	17	L	23	CF	aaa	SD	390	11	10	273	4	66	119	129	7
Coulter,Clint	16	R	23	RF	aa	MIL	95	2	1	321	4	82	61	60	3
	17	R	24	RF	aa	MIL	385	16	2	225	8	73	109	50	11
Court,Ryan	16	R	28	3B	a/a	BOS	364	3	3	242	9	72	68	82	-12
Cowart,Kaleb	16	B	24	3B	aaa	LAA	414	6	13	228	6	71	94	114	8
	17	B	25	3B	aaa	LAA	367	8	13	245	7	75	78	87	6
Cowgill,Collin	16	R	30	CF	aaa	CLE	359	3	5	190	7	71	54	82	-32
Cox,Zack	17	L	28	DH	aa	DET	274	2	1	226	8	69	47	35	-57
Coyle,Sean	16	R	24	2B	a/a	LAA	375	6	7	153	7	56	78	88	-70
	17	R	25	DH	aa	BAL	134	1	2	134	9	67	56	83	-42

BATTER	yr	b	age	pos	lvl	org	ab	hr	sb	ba	bb%	ct%	px	sx	bpv
Coyle,Tommy	16	L	26	2B	aa	TAM	181	1	8	145	7	67	61	144	-24
Cozens,Dylan	16	L	22	RF	aa	PHI	521	37	17	254	9	60	217	126	70
	17	L	23	RF	aaa	PHI	476	25	7	192	10	54	141	89	-25
Crawford,J.P.	16	L	21	SS	a/a	PHI	472	7	11	235	12	81	55	70	16
	17	L	22	SS	aaa	PHI	474	14	4	224	13	77	83	88	29
Crawford,Rashad	17	L	24	CF	aa	NYY	376	5	15	194	6	72	56	143	-8
Cron,Kevin	16	R	23	1B	aa	ARI	465	23	3	209	6	69	130	68	13
	17	R	24	1B	aa	ARI	515	21	1	259	8	71	122	35	10
Cronenworth,Jake	17	L	23	SS	aa	TAM	158	1	1	255	10	86	31	31	0
Cruz,Luis	16	R	23	C	a/a	STL	175	2	1	217	5	64	59	77	-63
Cruz,Tony	16	R	30	C	aaa	KC	318	4	1	200	8	71	65	31	-38
Cruzado,Victor	16	B	24	LF	aa	NYM	364	7	5	223	10	74	61	63	-16
	17	B	25	CF	aaa	NYM	301	5	2	204	9	69	59	47	-44
Cuevas,Noel	16	R	25	CF	a/a	COL	331	3	6	274	3	83	66	111	26
	17	R	26	RF	aaa	COL	493	11	11	275	3	78	74	124	16
Culberson,Charlie	16	R	27	SS	aaa	LA	265	3	5	210	5	72	74	85	-17
	17	R	28	SS	aaa	LA	384	3	5	195	4	78	38	76	-26
Culver,Cito	16	R	24	SS	a/a	NYY	398	4	2	236	8	66	71	72	-39
	17	R	25	SS	aaa	NYY	349	12	1	199	7	63	112	62	-22
Cunningham,Todd	16	B	27	RF	aaa	LAA	349	4	15	212	9	80	48	111	9
	17	B	28	RF	aaa	LA	292	3	5	224	9	78	65	96	14
Curcio,Keith	17	L	25	RF	aa	ATL	401	3	9	188	9	80	37	106	2
Curley,Chris	16	R	29	1B	aa	MIA	282	5	1	197	7	65	70	46	-54
Curtis,Jermaine	16	R	29	3B	aaa	CIN	285	8	5	241	11	80	75	56	21
Dahl,David	16	L	22	CF	a/a	COL	350	16	14	307	9	73	152	122	73
	17	L	23	LF	aaa	COL	70	2	1	229	3	76	77	118	8
Daniel,Andrew	16	R	23	3B	a/a	LAA	448	4	8	247	7	74	58	84	-14
	17	R	24	2B	aa	ATL	190	2	8	178	11	69	51	105	-29
Davidson,Matthew	16	R	25	3B	aaa	CHW	284	8	0	224	9	63	115	20	-29
Davis,Dylan	17	R	24	LF	aa	SF	327	7	0	194	7	68	81	24	-39
Davis,Glynn	16	R	25	CF	aa	BAL	247	4	5	214	6	73	70	81	-16
	17	R	26	CF	aa	BAL	98	1	1	183	3	69	43	78	-56
Davis,Ike	16	L	29	1B	aaa	NYY	234	8	0	208	10	63	114	24	-27
Davis,J.D.	16	R	23	3B	aa	HOU	485	20	1	236	7	66	135	34	-2
	17	R	24	3B	a/a	HOU	412	19	4	234	7	68	119	46	-3
Davis,Johnny	16	B	26	LF	aa	MIL	218	1	14	234	5	67	38	158	-43
	17	B	27	CF	aa	MIL	505	5	47	236	6	72	44	149	-19
Davis,Jonathan	17	R	25	CF	aa	TOR	446	9	16	223	11	72	74	108	3
Davis,Taylor	16	R	27	C	a/a	CHC	279	2	1	217	8	85	48	62	15
	17	R	28	C	aaa	CHC	357	4	0	230	7	84	61	30	9
De La Cruz,Maikis	16	R	26	RF	aa	NYM	330	3	5	185	6	73	53	59	-36
De La Guerra,Chad	17	L	25	SS	aa	BOS	196	3	2	246	8	73	90	57	0
De Leon,Michael	17	B	20	SS	aa	TEX	394	2	3	218	4	88	36	53	6
Dean,Austin	16	R	23	LF	aa	MIA	480	8	1	220	8	75	77	74	4
	17	R	24	LF	aa	MIA	234	4	3	257	5	77	80	103	17
Dean,Matt	16	R	24	3B	aa	TOR	233	5	1	195	8	59	78	44	-72
	17	R	25	1B	aa	TOR	97	3	0	174	9	54	107	7	-76
Decker,Cody	16	R	29	1B	a/a	BOS	304	14	1	194	5	56	166	71	-10
Decker,Jaff	16	L	26	CF	aaa	TAM	349	10	15	215	12	73	88	102	18
	17	L	27	CF	aaa	OAK	351	4	11	221	7	69	49	79	-44
Deglan,Kellin	16	L	24	C	aa	TEX	268	7	1	170	5	56	92	53	-74
DeJong,Paul	16	R	23	3B	aa	STL	496	17	2	228	6	66	117	58	-10
	17	R	24	SS	aaa	STL	177	10	0	263	4	72	128	31	8
Delfino,Mitch	16	R	25	3B	aaa	SF	186	2	0	201	6	75	33	31	-49
Delmonico,Nick	16	L	24	1B	a/a	CHW	402	14	2	239	8	68	125	65	11
	17	L	25	3B	aaa	CHW	378	10	3	222	9	77	76	75	10
Demeritte,Travis	17	R	23	2B	aa	ATL	458	13	5	203	10	66	86	96	-17
DeMichele,Joey	16	L	25	2B	aa	CHW	468	9	2	194	7	68	77	96	-20
DeMuth,Dustin	16	L	25	1B	aa	MIL	115	0	0	246	5	69	45	81	-53
	17	L	26	1B	aa	MIL	377	10	6	224	9	64	96	71	-24
Den Dekker,Matthew	16	L	29	LF	aaa	WAS	372	6	16	172	8	64	65	94	-45
DePew,Jake	16	R	24	C	aa	TAM	284	7	2	182	7	70	72	55	-28
	17	R	25	C	aa	BOS	101	1	1	191	6	78	21	45	-44
Deshields Jr.,Delino	16	R	24	CF	aaa	TEX	207	2	17	225	12	68	60	101	-24
Devers,Rafael	17	L	21	3B	a/a	BOS	322	17	0	307	9	80	134	54	63
Dewees,Donnie	17	L	24	CF	aa	KC	464	7	17	252	8	81	71	124	36
Diaz,Aledmys	17	R	27	SS	aaa	STL	170	3	2	208	4	80	62	69	-1
Diaz,Argenis	16	R	29	2B	aaa	DET	323	2	1	197	5	79	38	36	-32
Diaz,Chris	16	R	26	SS	aa	PIT	226	1	4	188	10	79	46	68	-7
	17	R	27	SS	aa	MIA	188	0	2	195	9	74	40	76	-30
Diaz,Elias	16	R	26	C	a/a	PIT	101	0	1	229	3	80	21	26	-47
	17	R	27	C	aaa	PIT	218	2	2	227	4	81	40	52	-19
Diaz,Francisco	16	B	26	C	a/a	NYY	90	0	0	218	12	86	21	56	1
	17	B	27	C	a/a	NYY	171	0	0	194	5	81	26	32	-34
Diaz,Yandy	16	R	25	3B	a/a	CLE	444	8	9	285	12	79	72	90	24
	17	R	26	3B	aaa	CLE	309	4	1	309	14	81	61	42	14
Dickerson,Alex	16	L	26	LF	aaa	SD	217	7	0	304	4	84	99	64	44
Dickson,O Koyea	17	R	27	LF	aaa	LA	403	18	3	199	7	70	114	68	9
Dickson,OKoyea	16	R	26	LF	aaa	LA	329	15	1	275	7	77	137	59	50
Difo,Wilmer	16	R	24	SS	a/a	WAS	415	5	25	237	7	84	47	116	24
	17	R	25	SS	aaa	WAS	40	0	0	150	9	83	33	40	-10
Dini,Nick	17	R	24	C	aa	KC	216	2	7	286	6	87	40	65	14
Dixon,Brandon	16	R	24	2B	aa	CIN	419	17	14	248	7	62	135	100	1
	17	R	25	3B	aaa	CIN	440	14	14	228	6	66	116	95	0
Dominguez,Chris	16	R	30	1B	aaa	BOS	278	10	6	208	3	69	109	104	3
Dominguez,Matt	16	R	27	3B	aaa	TOR	475	16	1	235	5	82	78	27	10
	17	R	28	3B	aaa	BOS	424	12	2	233	4	81	77	42	9

BATTER	yr	b	age	pos	lvl	org	ab	hr	sb	ba	bb%	ct%	px	sx	bpv
Dosch,Drew	17	L	25	3B	a/a	BAL	463	7	3	218	7	68	71	81	-30
Dowdy,Jeremy	16	R	26	C	aa	CHW	183	3	0	201	10	81	61	30	3
Dozier,Hunter	16	R	25	3B	a/a	KC	486	17	5	256	8	72	135	76	35
	17	R	26	3B	a/a	KC	100	3	1	200	9	49	160	98	-26
Drake,Blake	16	R	23	CF	aa	STL	193	4	2	223	8	68	75	77	-28
	17	R	24	RF	aa	STL	41	2	1	196	9	82	71	43	17
Dubon,Mauricio	16	R	22	SS	aa	BOS	251	5	5	327	4	85	109	130	74
	17	R	23	SS	a/a	MIL	492	8	31	247	6	83	61	100	23
Duenez,Samir	17	L	21	1B	aa	KC	523	14	9	243	6	77	79	86	12
Duffy,Matthew	16	R	27	3B	aaa	TEX	401	10	1	185	5	63	86	63	-46
Dugan,Kelly	16	L	26	LF	aa	CHC	274	10	1	222	7	72	108	40	4
	17	L	27	RF	aa	ARI	313	10	3	221	7	69	111	81	6
Duggar,Steven	16	L	23	CF	aa	SF	243	1	8	306	10	77	77	120	26
	17	L	24	CF	aaa	SF	46	1	2	224	13	70	63	69	-22
Eaves,Kody	16	L	23	3B	aa	DET	325	9	5	199	9	66	126	105	17
	17	L	24	3B	a/a	DET	332	11	6	245	8	74	102	103	26
Edman,Tommy	17	S	22	SS	aa	STL	219	2	4	232	6	84	55	84	19
Eibner,Brett	16	R	28	CF	aaa	OAK	197	9	4	241	13	67	124	94	25
	17	R	29	RF	aaa	LA	117	3	0	176	5	63	76	73	-56
Elizalde,Sebastian	16	L	25	RF	aa	CIN	408	5	5	274	4	82	53	91	8
	17	L	26	RF	aaa	CIN	506	7	3	234	5	83	43	57	-4
Elmore,Jake	16	R	29	2B	aaa	MIL	150	1	8	245	10	84	24	77	0
Ely,Andrew	17	L	24	SS	aa	CHC	282	3	1	234	12	76	57	61	-5
Engel,Adam	16	R	25	CF	a/a	CHW	455	6	30	209	8	68	80	160	3
	17	R	26	CF	aaa	CHW	165	6	3	182	8	62	139	94	7
Ervin,Phillip	16	R	24	LF	aa	CIN	419	14	34	227	13	76	100	130	49
	17	R	25	LF	aaa	CIN	363	6	18	221	8	73	70	103	-5
Escalera,Alfredo	16	R	21	CF	aa	KC	202	2	4	266	3	74	77	79	-12
	17	R	22	LF	aa	KC	456	6	13	250	4	74	55	100	-20
Escobar,Elvis	16	L	22	CF	aa	PIT	112	2	2	220	7	76	48	124	-5
	17	L	23	CF	aa	PIT	383	3	4	260	6	81	42	82	-4
Espinal,Edwin	16	R	22	1B	aa	PIT	394	6	0	264	4	82	69	28	2
	17	R	23	1B	a/a	PIT	497	13	1	273	4	85	77	31	21
Estrada,Thairo	17	R	21	SS	aa	NYY	495	7	8	294	6	88	48	80	28
Evans,Phillip	16	R	24	SS	aa	NYM	361	7	1	289	4	80	88	39	14
	17	R	25	3B	aaa	NYM	466	8	1	217	6	79	62	46	-8
Evans,Zane	16	R	25	C	a/a	KC	246	4	0	195	3	73	54	38	-46
	17	R	26	C	aa	KC	122	3	2	177	1	71	45	60	-56
Farmer,Kyle	16	R	26	C	aa	LA	266	4	2	221	7	80	79	72	23
	17	R	27	C	a/a	LA	347	8	1	259	6	82	75	40	15
Featherston,Taylor	16	R	27	3B	aaa	PHI	402	13	5	223	5	70	109	101	10
	17	R	28	3B	aaa	TAM	257	6	7	194	8	54	91	83	-66
Federowicz,Tim	16	R	29	C	aaa	CHC	229	6	2	225	5	71	79	42	-28
Feliz,Anderson	16	B	24	SS	aa	PIT	347	3	6	224	8	72	73	98	-5
	17	B	25	LF	a/a	PIT	309	4	10	205	9	69	71	106	-14
Ferguson,Andrew	16	R	24	LF	aa	HOU	52	3	2	288	8	71	159	138	69
	17	R	25	CF	a/a	HOU	415	7	13	223	9	71	69	78	-19
Fernandez,Jose Migı	17	L	29	2B	a/a	LA	343	12	0	239	5	87	74	25	26
Ficociello,Dominic	16	B	24	1B	aa	DET	423	4	4	218	9	72	62	73	-20
	17	B	25	1B	a/a	DET	445	8	10	253	9	70	78	94	-8
Field,Johnny	16	R	24	CF	a/a	TAM	450	10	13	237	5	72	103	116	19
	17	R	25	CF	aaa	TAM	445	10	11	227	5	74	94	92	10
Field,Tommy	16	R	29	2B	aaa	MIN	318	8	2	186	7	73	80	64	-7
Fields,Daniel	16	L	25	RF	a/a	LA	159	1	5	182	10	50	46	117	-108
Fields,Roemon	16	L	26	CF	aa	TOR	497	4	36	197	7	76	38	133	-9
	17	L	27	CF	a/a	TOR	406	0	42	248	7	78	35	152	2
Figueroa,Cole	16	L	29	2B	aaa	MIA	229	1	4	214	7	86	46	102	25
Fisher,Derek	16	L	23	CF	a/a	HOU	478	17	21	223	12	63	115	110	2
	17	L	24	CF	aaa	HOU	343	14	11	254	6	73	116	78	23
Fleming,Billy	16	R	24	2B	aa	NYY	128	1	0	227	9	80	59	42	0
	17	R	25	2B	a/a	NYY	315	10	4	232	5	85	78	85	40
Fletcher,David	17	R	23	2B	a/a	LAA	448	2	16	230	5	86	37	102	14
Flores,Jorge	16	R	25	SS	aa	TOR	252	2	3	165	6	82	35	58	-10
	17	R	26	2B	a/a	ARI	76	0	0	207	3	66	43	28	-85
Flores,Ramon	16	L	24	RF	aaa	MIL	28	1	0	211	5	71	71	17	-40
	17	L	25	RF	aaa	LAA	413	7	8	247	10	79	60	91	13
Flores,Rudy	16	L	26	LF	aa	ARI	160	4	1	270	6	62	127	98	-5
	17	L	27	LF	a/a	ARI	356	8	1	224	4	64	107	58	-32
Florimon Jr.,Pedro	16	B	30	LF	aaa	PIT	298	4	11	206	8	65	66	117	-35
Fontana,Nolan	16	L	25	SS	a/a	HOU	395	2	4	165	7	66	51	52	-64
	17	L	26	SS	aaa	LAA	361	6	9	208	12	66	90	114	-4
Ford,Mike	16	L	24	1B	aa	NYY	143	5	0	264	18	80	108	18	52
	17	L	25	1B	a/a	NYY	429	21	1	246	16	81	105	44	54
Fowler,Dustin	16	L	22	CF	aa	NYY	541	13	25	275	4	83	96	145	61
	17	L	23	CF	aaa	NYY	297	14	12	273	4	76	129	143	62
France,Ty	17	R	23	3B	aa	SD	363	4	1	259	5	80	60	53	-4
Franco,Angel	16	B	26	2B	aaa	KC	209	1	0	183	4	83	47	72	0
	17	B	27	2B	a/a	ARI	96	0	1	228	4	78	28	49	-39
Franco,Carlos	16	L	25	3B	a/a	ATL	424	4	3	231	11	62	54	58	-67
	17	L	26	1B	a/a	ATL	461	17	1	204	9	62	87	33	-55
Franklin,Nick	16	B	25	2B	aaa	TAM	240	4	8	218	8	72	83	94	2
Frazier,Adam	16	L	25	LF	aaa	PIT	261	0	15	300	9	89	51	110	48
Frazier,Clint	16	R	22	LF	a/a	NYY	463	18	13	258	9	71	122	117	39
	17	R	23	LF	aaa	NYY	273	13	8	239	11	72	129	100	44
Freeman,Michael	16	L	29	2B	aaa	SEA	446	3	8	238	7	72	54	110	-21
Freeman,Ronnie	16	R	25	C	a/a	ARI	219	2	0	216	5	74	61	29	-33
	17	R	26	C	aaa	ARI	222	2	0	203	5	73	58	55	-33
Freiman,Nathan	16	R	30	1B	a/a	BOS	337	8	0	224	9	71	92	48	-7

BATTER	yr	b	age	pos	lvl	org	ab	hr	sb	ba	bb%	ct%	px	sx	bpv
Freitas,David	16	R	27	C	a/a	CHC	332	5	2	239	6	75	83	62	-2
	17	R	28	C	aaa	ATL	236	2	0	197	8	80	35	28	-24
Fuenmayor,Balbino	16	R	27	1B	aaa	KC	358	4	0	234	3	75	66	11	-37
Fuentes,Josh	17	R	24	3B	aa	COL	414	13	6	299	4	78	115	97	43
Fuentes,Reymond	16	L	25	CF	aaa	KC	240	0	12	215	6	71	41	128	-30
	17	L	26	CF	aaa	ARI	175	0	8	278	4	79	54	134	10
Gale,Rocky	16	R	28	C	a/a	SD	354	4	1	188	6	79	35	39	-29
	17	R	29	C	aaa	SD	342	1	0	203	4	80	42	38	-27
Gallagher,Cameron	16	R	24	C	aa	KC	301	3	2	236	9	81	60	42	6
	17	R	25	C	aaa	KC	260	4	0	254	5	86	52	21	3
Gallo,Joey	16	L	23	3B	aaa	TEX	359	20	2	212	14	55	186	103	28
Galloway,Isaac	16	R	27	CF	aaa	MIA	441	7	25	214	6	70	66	124	-15
	17	R	28	CF	a/a	MIA	117	5	8	264	8	68	108	79	2
Gamache,Dan	16	L	26	DH	aaa	PIT	176	2	0	213	11	68	54	35	-49
	17	L	27	1B	aa	WAS	385	4	0	205	7	71	61	42	-37
Gamel,Benjamin	16	L	24	CF	aaa	NYY	483	6	17	286	8	78	68	115	18
	17	L	25	RF	aaa	SEA	60	1	1	253	14	78	39	66	-9
Garcia,Alejandro	16	R	25	LF	a/a	HOU	253	2	7	249	3	84	42	76	1
	17	R	26	LF	a/a	HOU	323	3	4	187	2	83	50	90	3
Garcia,Anthony	16	R	24	RF	a/a	STL	340	8	2	200	7	76	76	46	-6
	17	R	25	LF	a/a	STL	386	12	7	246	8	78	85	81	21
Garcia,Carlos	16	B	24	LF	aa	KC	279	2	8	233	7	80	53	110	13
	17	B	25	2B	aa	SF	132	1	5	218	2	83	42	120	6
Garcia,Edwin	16	R	25	1B	a/a	TEX	215	0	4	182	4	83	25	59	-21
Garcia,Jose Adolis	17	R	24	RF	a/a	STL	445	12	12	258	6	74	103	88	17
Garcia,Leury	16	B	25	LF	aaa	CHW	310	5	14	265	6	75	55	111	-9
Garcia,Rene	16	R	26	C	a/a	MIL	182	0	1	209	3	87	25	38	-12
	17	R	27	C	a/a	MIL	166	4	1	281	4	86	57	25	5
Garcia,Willy	16	R	24	RF	aaa	PIT	462	5	5	222	6	70	82	79	-19
Garlick,Kyle	16	R	24	RF	aa	LA	292	7	1	258	5	68	141	72	17
	17	R	25	LF	aa	LA	268	14	1	205	8	66	117	48	-11
Garneau,Dustin	16	R	29	C	aaa	COL	185	11	1	237	5	74	138	42	29
Garver,Mitch	16	R	25	C	a/a	MIN	434	9	1	237	8	73	92	25	-9
	17	R	26	C	aaa	MIN	320	15	2	263	12	71	148	51	44
Gelalich,Jeff	16	L	25	CF	aa	CIN	237	2	9	230	6	53	100	150	-49
	17	L	26	CF	a/a	CHW	89	1	3	220	7	66	35	72	-71
Gerber,Mike	16	L	24	CF	a/a	DET	153	3	5	233	10	71	94	116	17
	17	L	25	CF	a/a	DET	367	12	8	262	9	72	104	99	21
Gibbons,Zach	17	R	24	LF	aa	LAA	301	3	6	214	7	82	54	68	7
Gibson,Derrik	16	R	27	3B	aa	NYM	392	2	11	225	8	78	45	112	-1
	17	R	28	3B	aaa	COL	376	4	6	206	5	74	67	124	1
Gillaspie,Casey	16	B	23	1B	a/a	TAM	472	15	4	253	13	72	114	70	25
	17	B	24	1B	aaa	CHW	458	12	1	192	8	74	76	53	-7
Gindl,Caleb	17	L	29	CF	aa	SF	169	5	0	241	6	74	100	90	19
Glaesmann,Todd	16	R	26	CF	a/a	ARI	357	10	4	232	4	75	99	104	19
	17	R	27	CF	aaa	CHC	63	1	1	136	3	51	39	59	-137
Glenn,Alex	16	L	25	RF	aa	MIA	214	6	0	242	6	75	85	54	0
	17	L	26	LF	aa	MIA	201	3	2	155	7	59	70	90	-64
Goebbert,Jake	16	L	29	LF	aaa	TAM	321	7	0	171	8	65	79	42	-48
Goeddel,Tyler	17	R	25	LF	a/a	CIN	405	6	14	234	10	75	70	99	11
Goetzman,Granden	16	R	24	LF	aa	TAM	313	4	19	208	4	74	63	155	2
	17	R	25	LF	a/a	TAM	159	3	9	229	5	71	83	156	7
Gomez,Hector	17	R	29	3B	aaa	PHI	212	6	0	186	2	73	94	69	-5
Gomez,Miguel	17	B	25	2B	aa	SF	308	6	0	273	3	87	70	60	29
Gonzalez,Alfredo	16	R	24	C	a/a	CHW	284	0	2	187	7	73	32	59	-49
	17	R	25	C	aa	CHW	216	4	4	189	11	78	50	63	-5
Gonzalez,Benji	16	B	26	SS	aa	SEA	502	4	17	237	9	80	67	116	28
	17	B	27	SS	aaa	WAS	291	0	2	195	7	82	25	55	-20
Gonzalez,Erik	16	R	25	SS	aaa	CLE	429	9	10	267	4	77	95	78	18
	17	R	26	SS	aaa	CLE	160	5	4	224	3	65	86	113	-27
Gonzalez,Miguel	16	R	26	C	aaa	DET	214	2	0	212	7	76	55	17	-30
	17	R	27	C	a/a	DET	164	3	2	184	5	75	38	45	-45
Goodrum,Niko	16	B	24	3B	aa	MIN	182	5	6	243	9	68	100	108	5
	17	B	25	RF	aaa	MIN	461	12	10	246	5	72	92	117	11
Goodwin,Brian	16	L	26	CF	aaa	WAS	436	11	13	248	9	72	92	79	6
	17	L	27	RF	aaa	WAS	90	1	2	210	8	61	68	46	-69
Gordon,Nick	17	L	22	SS	aa	MIN	519	8	12	262	8	74	83	123	18
Gore,Terrance	16	R	25	CF	aa	KC	253	0	37	207	8	75	10	144	-33
	17	R	26	LF	a/a	KC	225	1	17	216	6	74	29	161	-17
Goris,Diego	16	R	26	3B	a/a	SD	342	7	1	204	3	78	58	46	-18
	17	R	27	SS	aaa	SD	439	7	3	217	4	75	58	55	-30
Gose,Anthony	16	L	26	CF	a/a	DET	340	5	13	174	7	58	74	118	-57
Gosselin,Phil	17	R	29	2B	aaa	TEX	273	1	2	202	4	75	34	68	-42
Gotta,Cade	16	R	25	RF	aa	TAM	291	4	17	218	6	81	75	135	38
	17	R	26	RF	a/a	TAM	431	4	33	236	9	77	54	121	6
Graeter,Steven	16	R	27	2B	aa	COL	250	5	4	247	7	77	72	64	1
	17	R	28	2B	aa	COL	348	8	5	219	5	78	72	67	1
Granite,Zach	16	L	24	CF	aa	MIN	525	3	44	263	6	91	39	149	55
	17	L	25	CF	aaa	MIN	284	5	14	315	7	87	68	122	56
Graterol,Juan	16	R	27	C	aaa	LAA	227	1	1	230	3	85	34	41	-14
Grayson,Casey	17	L	26	1B	aa	STL	195	2	0	212	9	64	48	20	-80
Green,Austin	16	R	26	C	aa	DET	186	3	0	192	2	81	56	24	-16
Green,Dean	16	L	27	DH	a/a	DET	476	18	2	247	6	79	96	34	19
Green,Grant	16	R	29	3B	aaa	SF	348	4	1	249	2	78	62	83	-6
Gregor,Conrad	16	L	24	1B	aa	HOU	370	7	0	181	9	80	70	46	9
Greiner,Grayson	16	R	24	C	a/a	DET	212	6	1	256	4	71	94	76	-7
	17	R	25	C	a/a	DET	342	12	0	207	9	76	97	28	9

BATTER	yr	b	age	pos	lvl	org	ab	hr	sb	ba	bb%	ct%	px	sx	bpv
Guerrero,Emilio	17	R	25	1B	aa	TOR	266	3	2	236	5	75	67	72	-11
Guerrero,Gabriel	16	R	23	RF	a/a	ARI	418	7	5	214	5	74	88	105	8
	17	R	24	CF	aa	CIN	501	8	3	265	7	77	66	69	-5
Guillorme,Luis	17	L	23	2B	aa	NYM	481	1	4	262	14	87	31	52	17
Guillotte,Andrew	17	R	24	LF	a/a	TOR	236	3	7	233	8	75	45	103	-13
Gurriel,Lourdes	17	R	24	2B	aa	TOR	170	4	2	220	5	80	74	56	8
Guzman,Ronald	16	L	22	1B	a/a	TEX	463	13	2	251	7	76	91	79	16
	17	L	23	1B	aaa	TEX	470	9	3	264	7	80	64	76	12
Haase,Eric	16	R	24	C	aa	CLE	226	10	0	190	6	64	149	50	5
	17	R	25	C	a/a	CLE	339	22	3	232	10	64	169	90	41
Hager,Jake	16	R	23	2B	a/a	TAM	451	3	6	205	4	76	62	85	-11
	17	R	24	2B	aaa	TAM	271	3	3	205	4	82	47	87	0
Haniger,Mitch	16	R	26	CF	a/a	ARI	458	19	9	273	10	74	133	97	55
	17	R	27	RF	aaa	SEA	39	2	0	207	12	84	109	15	53
Hankins,Todd	16	R	26	2B	a/a	CLE	484	8	17	198	5	68	70	137	-18
	17	R	27	CF	a/a	CLE	314	2	13	191	6	68	44	99	-50
Hannemann,Jacob	16	L	25	CF	aa	CHC	291	8	20	211	6	78	85	132	33
	17	L	26	CF	a/a	CHC	409	5	23	199	7	67	85	127	-11
Hanson,Alen	16	B	24	2B	aaa	PIT	432	7	33	243	6	81	59	146	28
Happ,Ian	16	B	22	2B	aa	CHC	248	7	5	237	6	73	91	69	0
Harrell,Connor	16	R	25	CF	aa	DET	366	8	5	231	5	68	75	73	-36
Harrison,Travis	16	R	24	LF	aa	MIN	434	5	12	203	10	69	69	87	-23
	17	R	25	LF	aa	MIN	276	3	3	161	12	62	88	78	-33
Hassan,Alexander	16	R	28	1B	aaa	LA	254	1	1	182	9	71	27	46	-62
Hawkins,Courtney	16	R	23	LF	aa	CHW	418	10	0	175	5	63	100	18	-52
	17	R	24	LF	aa	CHW	295	10	0	176	7	59	92	51	-60
Hayes,Danny	16	L	26	1B	aaa	CHW	184	8	0	206	12	66	134	41	9
	17	L	27	1B	aaa	CHW	439	15	0	185	11	59	110	25	-43
Hays,Austin	17	R	22	CF	aa	BAL	261	14	1	286	4	80	107	57	33
Healy,Ryon	16	R	24	1B	a/a	OAK	337	11	1	292	7	76	127	80	44
Heathcott,Zachary	16	L	26	CF	aaa	CHW	180	2	2	200	11	58	62	103	-63
	17	L	27	CF	a/a	SF	416	9	9	222	9	68	85	95	-13
Hebert,Brock	16	R	25	3B	aa	SEA	170	1	3	194	18	59	78	116	-28
	17	R	26	2B	aa	SEA	70	2	1	143	4	65	51	55	-71
Hedges,Austin	16	R	24	C	aaa	SD	313	15	1	268	3	80	116	48	35
Heidt,Gunnar	17	R	25	3B	aa	TOR	432	11	9	205	8	63	91	84	-31
Heineman,Scott	17	R	25	LF	aa	TEX	468	8	10	257	8	71	81	117	4
Heineman,Tyler	16	B	25	C	aaa	HOU	239	2	1	213	7	78	47	58	-18
	17	B	26	C	aaa	MIL	199	2	1	222	6	79	72	44	1
Henry,Jabari	16	R	26	DH	aa	LAA	352	12	2	184	8	63	96	48	-40
Heredia,Guillermo	16	R	25	CF	a/a	SEA	343	3	4	258	10	83	44	84	17
Hermosillo,Michael	17	R	22	CF	a/a	LAA	393	7	25	229	9	71	71	117	-6
Hernandez,Gorkys	16	R	29	CF	aaa	SF	437	5	14	234	8	77	57	101	2
Hernandez,Marco	16	L	24	SS	aaa	BOS	223	4	4	303	5	75	77	108	6
Hernandez,Oscar	16	R	23	C	aa	ARI	144	6	3	183	3	80	99	56	23
	17	R	24	C	aa	ARI	233	7	0	180	6	72	83	21	-25
Hernandez,Teoscar	16	R	24	RF	a/a	HOU	423	8	25	263	7	78	83	118	29
	17	R	25	RF	aaa	TOR	400	17	15	252	10	71	136	125	53
Herrera,Dilson	16	R	22	2B	aaa	CIN	423	16	6	264	8	77	110	90	40
	17	R	23	2B	aaa	CIN	239	6	2	238	5	71	75	60	-27
Herrera,Juan	16	R	23	SS	aa	STL	150	0	2	145	3	73	26	73	-58
Herrera,Rosell	16	B	24	LF	aa	COL	425	5	30	280	10	81	51	119	24
	17	B	25	LF	aaa	COL	320	2	14	248	7	77	65	126	15
Herum,Marty	17	R	26	3B	aa	ARI	162	2	1	253	3	81	68	66	8
Hicks,D.J.	16	L	26	1B	aa	MIN	420	4	2	223	8	71	70	40	-31
Hicks,John	16	R	27	C	a/a	DET	323	8	3	260	5	74	94	72	6
	17	R	28	C	aaa	DET	208	6	4	227	2	69	85	82	-25
Higashioka,Kyle	16	R	26	C	a/a	NYY	370	21	0	250	8	77	136	25	43
Hinojosa,C.J.	16	R	22	SS	aa	SF	226	2	1	238	8	79	51	83	1
	17	R	23	SS	aa	SF	373	3	5	247	7	88	39	58	15
Hinshaw,Chad	16	R	26	CF	aa	LAA	205	4	12	164	8	60	72	126	-48
	17	R	27	CF	aaa	MIA	258	3	5	185	7	64	71	84	-46
Hobson,K.C.	16	L	26	DH	aa	TOR	141	3	0	143	8	72	66	43	-27
	17	L	27	1B	aa	SF	203	8	1	207	7	67	87	67	-26
Hoenecke,Paul	16	L	26	C	aa	LA	139	6	0	250	2	82	96	36	23
	17	L	27	C	aa	LA	173	6	1	180	3	69	101	27	-28
Hoes,LJ	16	R	26	CF	aaa	BAL	396	6	7	216	8	83	46	70	10
Hood,Destin	16	R	26	LF	aaa	MIA	476	11	9	230	6	73	92	93	7
	17	R	27	LF	aaa	MIA	219	10	4	209	10	62	118	79	-10
Horan,Tyler	16	L	26	LF	aa	SF	287	9	4	233	9	67	107	110	8
	17	L	27	LF	aa	SF	79	1	0	187	7	67	58	78	-47
Hoskins,Rhys	16	R	23	1B	aa	PHI	498	34	6	253	10	71	159	65	54
	17	R	24	1B	aaa	PHI	401	27	3	255	12	78	143	83	78
Houchins,Zach	17	R	25	3B	a/a	LAA	488	11	5	214	6	79	77	74	14
Hoying,Jared	16	L	27	CF	aaa	TEX	390	12	13	219	7	76	92	129	33
	17	L	28	CF	aaa	TEX	366	7	11	207	6	74	76	101	-1
Hudson,Joe	16	R	25	C	aa	CIN	207	2	0	187	13	66	73	23	-44
	17	R	26	C	aa	CIN	217	1	0	158	12	73	63	16	-29
Hunter,Cedric	16	L	28	RF	aaa	PHI	330	10	5	252	4	79	79	52	3
	17	L	29	DH	aaa	CIN	40	1	0	237	2	74	98	28	-13
Hyams,Levi	16	L	27	1B	a/a	ATL	242	4	0	190	4	65	75	54	-53
	17	L	28	1B	aa	ATL	90	0	0	156	4	69	5	15	-106
Hyde,Mott	16	R	24	SS	aa	HOU	280	2	2	187	7	65	55	76	-59
	17	R	25	2B	aa	HOU	82	2	4	177	11	53	55	84	-96
Ibanez,Andy	16	R	23	2B	aa	TEX	307	5	4	235	7	83	69	83	29
	17	R	24	2B	aa	TEX	310	7	5	242	7	83	65	83	25
Ijames,Stewart	16	L	28	LF	aa	ARI	244	8	1	206	9	65	131	37	-5
	17	L	29	LF	a/a	ARI	148	4	1	174	8	55	111	84	-49
Jackson,Joe	16	L	24	LF	aa	TEX	413	4	2	238	6	76	63	58	-13
Jackson,Ryan	16	R	28	SS	aaa	LAA	290	0	3	185	9	68	28	38	-72
	17	R	29	SS	aaa	WAS	106	0	0	178	9	73	13	20	-72
Jagielo,Eric	16	L	24	3B	aa	CIN	365	7	0	194	11	59	87	21	-65
	17	L	25	1B	a/a	CIN	309	5	0	184	11	68	58	19	-49
James,Jared	17	L	23	LF	aa	ATL	340	5	1	248	9	79	58	81	7
James,Mac	17	R	24	DH	aa	TAM	154	1	0	209	7	77	30	30	-43
Jamieson,Sean	16	R	27	2B	aaa	ARI	172	1	0	194	6	60	56	64	-81
Jansen,Danny	17	R	22	C	a/a	TOR	246	5	1	295	11	89	88	60	67
Jennings,Desmond	17	R	31	CF	aaa	NYM	207	5	2	166	6	71	62	86	-25
Jensen,Kyle	16	R	28	1B	aaa	ARI	498	19	1	224	5	57	148	50	-24
Jhang,Jin-De	16	L	23	C	a/a	PIT	208	1	1	263	5	93	49	43	35
	17	L	24	C	aa	PIT	273	2	1	211	5	91	37	66	24
Jimenez,A.J.	16	R	26	C	aaa	TOR	228	4	1	217	5	83	84	59	27
	17	R	27	C	aaa	TEX	196	5	1	197	2	73	70	31	-36
Joe,Connor	17	R	25	RF	aa	ATL	294	4	2	187	12	76	50	72	-8
Johnson,Kyle	16	R	27	CF	a/a	NYM	249	2	3	161	6	66	59	59	-56
Johnson,Micah	16	L	26	2B	aaa	LA	464	4	20	215	6	73	57	114	-15
	17	L	27	CF	aaa	ATL	135	1	5	228	10	64	48	119	-49
Johnson,Sherman	16	L	26	2B	a/a	LAA	459	9	14	201	11	74	70	109	8
	17	L	27	1B	a/a	LAA	395	4	10	205	10	72	55	96	-17
Jones,Corey	16	L	29	2B	a/a	DET	420	6	6	220	7	83	60	73	19
Jones,Hunter	16	R	25	CF	aa	CHW	133	2	2	187	6	74	63	81	-16
	17	R	26	CF	aa	CHW	410	7	10	198	8	75	74	102	6
Jones,JaCoby	16	R	24	CF	a/a	DET	369	6	11	234	7	66	97	124	-6
	17	R	25	CF	aaa	DET	351	8	11	220	8	67	88	119	-7
Jones,James	16	L	28	LF	aaa	TEX	276	2	9	184	6	62	57	115	-58
Jones,Ryder	16	L	22	3B	aa	SF	474	12	1	231	5	82	80	35	14
	17	L	23	3B	aaa	SF	237	9	6	277	9	75	125	115	54
Joseph,Corban	16	L	28	2B	a/a	BAL	371	7	4	261	6	87	59	68	29
	17	L	29	2B	a/a	WAS	309	5	1	217	6	84	54	29	4
Judge,Aaron	16	R	24	RF	aaa	NYY	352	20	5	254	11	69	142	80	36
Juengel,Matt	16	R	26	3B	a/a	MIA	466	8	1	231	6	80	79	80	21
	17	R	27	1B	aaa	MIA	200	4	1	202	5	78	76	68	6
Kaczmarski,Kevin	17	L	26	RF	aa	NYM	452	5	14	238	12	77	50	99	4
Kay,Grant	17	R	24	3B	a/a	TAM	431	6	12	233	9	75	91	117	27
Keller,Alec	17	L	25	RF	aa	WAS	288	2	5	227	5	76	48	93	-18
Kelly,Carson	16	R	22	C	a/a	STL	329	5	0	255	6	78	60	31	-18
	17	R	23	C	aaa	STL	244	8	0	254	10	83	81	28	25
Kelly,Dalton	17	L	23	1B	aa	TAM	192	6	5	269	12	65	136	94	23
Kelly,Tyler	16	B	28	LF	aaa	NYM	271	1	3	240	8	80	58	58	0
	17	B	29	3B	aaa	PHI	22	1	0	216	10	88	98	35	62
Kemmer,Jon	16	L	26	RF	aaa	HOU	407	13	6	215	6	61	123	81	-18
	17	L	27	LF	aaa	HOU	304	10	4	224	8	59	114	96	-27
Kemp,Anthony	16	L	25	2B	aaa	HOU	255	2	7	254	9	84	42	99	18
	17	L	26	2B	aaa	HOU	504	6	15	254	4	89	50	119	42
Kemp,Jeff	16	R	26	2B	aa	BAL	153	3	3	153	8	59	67	72	-71
	17	R	27	3B	aa	BAL	78	2	1	204	9	63	47	35	-82
Keyes,Kevin	16	R	27	DH	a/a	WAS	324	9	1	175	10	61	105	32	-39
Kieboom,Spencer	16	R	25	C	aa	WAS	309	4	0	205	11	78	47	15	-21
	17	R	26	C	a/a	WAS	220	4	0	210	8	77	69	19	-13
Kiner-Falefa,Isiah	16	R	21	3B	aa	TEX	402	0	5	239	8	87	18	75	3
	17	R	22	3B	aa	TEX	513	5	15	275	7	85	58	92	31
Kingery,Scott	16	R	22	2B	aa	PHI	156	2	3	224	3	74	56	67	-32
	17	R	23	2B	a/a	PHI	543	24	25	275	6	77	112	142	54
Kirkland,Wade	16	R	27	2B	aa	OAK	256	1	1	173	3	62	48	83	-80
Kivlehan,Patrick	16	R	27	3B	aaa	SD	370	8	3	192	4	63	85	68	-51
Knapp,Andrew	16	B	25	C	aaa	PHI	403	8	2	242	8	69	90	59	-18
Knizner,Andrew	17	R	22	C	aa	STL	182	3	0	305	6	85	76	35	24
Kozma,Pete	16	R	28	SS	aaa	NYY	445	2	9	177	6	75	38	82	-33
	17	R	29	SS	aaa	TEX	40	0	1	231	3	75	64	80	-15
Kramer,Kevin	17	L	24	2B	aa	PIT	202	5	6	273	7	73	116	124	40
Krauss,Marc	16	L	29	1B	aaa	NYM	229	8	1	150	9	55	112	53	-56
Krieger,Tyler	17	B	23	2B	aa	CLE	418	5	10	210	8	75	71	89	1
Krizan,Jason	16	L	27	LF	a/a	DET	456	8	2	249	9	90	74	65	58
	17	L	28	DH	a/a	DET	427	6	5	233	8	84	63	74	29
Kubitza,Kyle	16	L	26	LF	aaa	ATL	396	5	10	177	11	62	72	125	-34
	17	L	27	RF	aaa	ATL	286	4	4	193	10	60	45	107	-68
Lake,Junior	16	R	26	RF	aaa	TOR	281	6	8	206	9	67	81	97	-16
	17	R	27	LF	aaa	BOS	61	0	2	224	5	65	47	107	-59
LaMarre,Ryan	16	R	28	CF	aaa	BOS	317	8	15	271	7	70	88	83	-8
	17	R	29	CF	aaa	OAK	170	0	6	193	6	59	29	117	-92
Lambo,Andrew	16	L	28	DH	aaa	OAK	216	3	1	215	7	77	67	89	3
	17	L	29	LF	aaa	OAK	45	0	0	101	1	55	40	39	-132
Landry,Leon	16	L	27	LF	aa	SEA	465	5	4	197	6	80	49	93	2
	17	L	28	LF	aa	CIN	106	0	2	175	4	72	35	127	-37
Lara,Jordy	16	R	25	RF	aa	ATL	155	4	0	203	5	76	71	38	-15
Latimore,Quincy	16	R	27	LF	aa	BAL	392	11	2	171	8	66	85	65	-28
	17	R	28	RF	aa	LA	155	2	2	211	2	72	52	80	-39
Laureano,Ramon	16	R	22	CF	aa	HOU	124	4	8	294	11	70	136	129	52
	17	R	23	RF	aa	HOU	463	9	20	206	7	73	78	144	12
LaValley,Gavin	17	R	23	1B	aa	CIN	247	3	0	248	8	70	80	25	-32
Lavarnway,Ryan	16	R	29	C	a/a	TOR	331	5	1	220	9	75	75	33	-11
Law,Adam	16	R	26	3B	aa	SEA	238	3	12	270	9	78	57	98	8
	17	R	27	2B	aa	SEA	63	0	0	180	1	56	43	47	-122
Leblebijian,Jason	16	R	25	3B	aa	TOR	270	6	4	263	8	65	116	77	-7
	17	R	26	3B	aaa	TOR	427	10	3	238	7	66	97	87	-15

BATTER	yr	b	age	pos	lvl	org	ab	hr	sb	ba	bb%	ct%	px	sx	bpv
Lee,Braxton	17	L	24	CF	aa	MIA	476	3	19	282	12	75	49	101	-6
Lee,Hak-Ju	16	L	26	SS	aaa	SF	162	2	3	219	8	63	67	86	-50
Lemon,Marcus	16	L	28	SS	a/a	CHW	278	1	1	171	7	70	34	69	-55
Leonard,Patrick	16	R	24	3B	a/a	TAM	407	7	7	223	6	61	103	88	-33
	17	R	25	3B	aaa	TAM	503	10	13	235	7	69	84	99	-12
Leyba,Domingo	16	B	21	SS	aa	ARI	156	4	4	295	9	85	75	84	46
	17	B	22	SS	aa	ARI	58	2	0	263	7	89	87	44	54
Lien,Connor	16	R	22	CF	aa	ATL	223	6	12	226	9	57	121	142	-10
	17	R	23	CF	aa	ATL	374	9	17	158	6	50	97	135	-67
Lin,Tzu-Wei	16	L	22	SS	aa	BOS	372	2	8	213	7	84	38	100	14
	17	L	23	SS	a/a	BOS	300	6	8	257	8	81	75	105	33
Lindsey,Taylor	16	L	25	1B	a/a	SD	392	8	3	183	7	72	72	68	-18
Lino,Gabriel	16	R	23	C	aa	PHI	63	3	0	284	8	76	104	33	16
	17	R	24	C	a/a	STL	263	4	0	230	7	67	93	32	-30
Lipka,Matthew	16	R	24	CF	a/a	ATL	378	3	14	219	7	70	66	142	-9
	17	R	25	LF	a/a	TEX	98	0	4	142	2	63	44	180	-53
Liriano,Rymer	17	R	26	RF	aaa	CHW	449	14	5	213	7	64	86	83	-36
Littlewood,Marcus	16	B	24	C	a/a	SEA	214	0	2	245	12	74	79	52	-1
	17	B	25	C	aa	SEA	281	8	1	207	4	71	71	40	-36
Locastro,Tim	16	R	24	SS	aa	LA	191	1	8	249	3	90	38	112	35
	17	R	25	CF	a/a	LA	471	8	27	262	4	83	72	135	40
Lockhart,Daniel	16	L	24	2B	aa	CHC	155	1	2	183	5	74	44	46	-43
	17	L	25	2B	aa	ARI	78	1	2	183	10	84	67	90	39
Lollis,Ryan	16	L	30	RF	aaa	SF	372	2	4	193	7	80	31	87	-11
Lombardozzi,Steve	16	B	28	2B	aaa	WAS	225	0	2	217	5	86	23	72	-4
Longhi,Nick	17	R	22	1B	aa	CIN	256	8	0	269	6	81	93	28	21
Lopes,Christian	16	R	24	2B	aa	TOR	404	3	8	270	6	80	76	85	20
	17	R	25	3B	aaa	TOR	333	6	17	247	11	82	86	113	55
Lopes,Tim	16	R	22	2B	aa	SEA	510	1	25	271	9	81	45	126	17
	17	R	23	2B	aa	TOR	469	6	16	253	8	80	70	92	21
Lopez,Deiner	17	B	23	SS	aa	BOS	231	2	4	229	5	70	40	100	-47
Lopez,Jack	16	R	24	SS	aa	KC	267	5	8	169	4	76	53	96	-15
	17	R	25	2B	a/a	KC	425	4	16	231	4	73	44	98	-33
Lopez,Nicky	17	L	22	SS	aa	KC	232	0	6	248	6	87	23	85	6
Lopez,Rafael	16	L	29	C	aaa	CIN	155	1	1	174	5	67	64	42	-57
Lough,David	16	L	30	CF	aaa	MIA	156	1	2	206	6	83	49	80	7
Loveless,Derrick	16	L	23	RF	aa	TOR	169	7	3	195	11	63	138	96	16
	17	L	24	LF	aa	TOR	190	1	2	230	14	67	55	71	-34
Lucas,Jeremy	16	R	25	C	a/a	CLE	357	10	1	227	9	76	98	41	14
	17	R	26	DH	aaa	CLE	43	0	0	121	5	69	0	38	-102
Lugo,Dawel	16	R	22	3B	aa	ARI	173	4	1	299	2	91	77	92	58
	17	R	22	3B	aa	DET	516	11	3	256	5	85	71	79	34
Lukes,Nathan	17	L	23	LF	aa	TAM	359	2	5	241	7	77	49	90	-9
Luplow,Jordan	17	R	24	LF	a/a	PIT	414	19	4	274	9	79	106	67	40
Lutz,Donald	16	L	27	1B	a/a	CIN	211	2	1	173	5	53	51	55	-120
Machado,Dixon	16	R	24	SS	aaa	DET	492	3	15	244	10	84	55	92	28
Macias,Brandon	16	R	28	3B	a/a	MIL	170	3	0	160	5	78	58	35	-17
Maggi,Drew	16	R	27	SS	a/a	LA	336	3	13	238	6	76	57	99	-6
	17	R	28	3B	aaa	LA	255	4	5	213	8	69	71	68	-29
Maile,Luke	16	R	25	C	aaa	TAM	194	2	0	207	6	78	61	19	-19
	17	R	26	C	aaa	TOR	54	0	0	151	6	74	0	38	-77
Mancini,Trey	16	R	24	1B	a/a	BAL	546	19	2	255	8	72	100	63	4
Margot,Manuel	16	R	22	CF	aaa	SD	517	4	21	258	5	86	51	138	36
	17	R	23	CF	aaa	SD	20	0	1	122	9	78	23	110	-16
Marin,Adrian	16	R	22	SS	aa	BAL	406	4	9	210	5	79	39	86	-16
	17	R	23	2B	aa	BAL	433	2	7	223	5	76	34	101	-28
Marincov,Tyler	16	R	25	RF	aa	OAK	374	7	5	226	8	73	69	82	-13
	17	R	26	RF	aa	OAK	286	6	4	220	7	62	105	83	-26
Mariscal,Chris	17	R	24	SS	aa	SEA	155	1	0	214	7	77	29	60	-34
Marjama,Mike	16	R	27	C	aa	TAM	278	4	2	230	5	79	84	65	15
	17	R	28	C	aaa	SEA	341	9	2	195	6	74	79	54	-10
Marlette,Tyler	16	R	23	C	aa	SEA	50	1	1	281	5	75	63	39	-26
	17	R	24	C	aa	SEA	368	10	0	213	7	72	89	48	-13
Marmolejos,Jose	17	L	24	LF	aa	WAS	400	11	0	252	8	78	77	59	8
Maron,Camden	16	L	25	C	aa	MIA	162	1	1	268	11	84	43	33	5
	17	L	26	C	aa	MIA	233	4	0	235	12	77	61	32	-8
Marrero,Chris	16	R	28	1B	aaa	BOS	490	19	0	254	8	79	111	37	35
Marrero,Christian	16	L	30	LF	aa	PHI	195	6	0	218	14	74	90	29	7
Marrero,Deven	16	R	26	SS	aaa	BOS	363	1	9	188	5	72	36	88	-45
	17	R	27	SS	aaa	BOS	183	2	1	221	3	68	89	43	-37
Mars,Danny	17	B	23	LF	aa	BOS	477	5	10	286	5	79	57	82	-2
Marte,Jefry	16	R	25	1B	aaa	LAA	162	2	2	211	8	74	76	66	-6
	17	R	26	1B	aaa	LAA	185	6	4	202	6	78	78	66	8
Marte,Ketel	16	B	23	SS	aaa	SEA	28	0	2	182	5	96	43	116	65
	17	B	24	SS	aaa	ARI	311	4	5	287	5	87	77	118	58
Marte,Luis	16	R	23	SS	aa	TEX	265	4	5	238	2	76	71	84	-8
	17	R	24	3B	a/a	TEX	360	6	7	218	1	83	53	90	6
Martin,Jason	17	L	22	LF	aa	HOU	300	10	6	253	5	69	130	98	21
Martin,Kyle	17	L	25	1B	aa	PHI	436	19	2	164	8	63	106	57	-26
Martin,Richie	17	R	23	SS	aa	OAK	286	2	10	198	6	79	46	128	5
Martin,Trey	16	R	24	CF	aa	CHC	215	2	11	161	5	71	27	116	-49
	17	R	25	CF	aa	CHC	317	4	5	235	3	67	73	79	-40
Martinez,Alberth	16	R	25	LF	aa	SD	32	0	0	135	3	78	47	51	-29
	17	R	26	LF	aa	SD	395	8	5	212	5	76	78	81	4
Martinez,Harold	16	R	26	3B	aa	PHI	255	8	0	229	5	71	95	32	-16
	17	R	27	1B	a/a	PHI	128	1	0	171	6	68	51	83	-49
Martinez,Jose	16	R	28	1B	aaa	STL	442	7	7	212	6	78	67	73	1
Martinez,Osvaldo	16	R	28	SS	aaa	BAL	343	4	6	201	4	81	36	74	-14

BATTER	yr	b	age	pos	lvl	org	ab	hr	sb	ba	bb%	ct%	px	sx	bpv
Martini,Nick	16	L	26	RF	a/a	STL	401	4	7	210	9	79	46	97	4
	17	L	27	LF	a/a	STL	459	6	5	247	10	77	64	92	7
Martinson,Jason	16	R	28	3B	aaa	WAS	455	9	9	183	6	53	104	109	-57
	17	R	29	2B	aaa	TEX	183	5	0	159	6	49	95	48	-98
Marzilli,Evan	16	L	25	CF	a/a	ARI	409	1	11	199	11	67	57	120	-26
	17	L	26	CF	a/a	ARI	402	5	11	217	10	72	62	121	-5
Mateo,Jorge	17	R	22	SS	aa	OAK	257	6	20	272	7	74	108	162	45
Mathisen,Wyatt	17	R	24	3B	aa	PIT	375	4	3	249	9	79	51	62	-5
Maxwell III,Bruce	16	L	26	C	aaa	OAK	193	8	1	280	10	78	111	35	31
	17	L	27	C	aaa	OAK	84	1	0	231	6	81	92	26	18
May,Jacob	16	B	24	CF	aaa	CHW	301	1	15	226	4	72	58	118	-22
	17	B	25	CF	aaa	CHW	415	3	24	210	6	68	41	135	-43
Mayfield,Jack	16	R	26	2B	a/a	HOU	250	8	3	175	5	74	88	59	-5
	17	R	27	2B	a/a	HOU	424	14	7	221	4	74	97	89	9
Mazzilli,L.J.	16	R	26	2B	a/a	NYM	414	4	6	187	8	78	51	89	-1
	17	R	27	RF	a/a	NYM	370	4	7	200	10	77	57	74	-3
McBroom,Ryan	16	R	24	1B	aa	TOR	29	1	0	124	8	76	48	29	-29
	17	R	25	1B	aa	NYY	486	17	1	226	7	73	90	28	-9
McCarthy,Joe	17	L	23	1B	aa	TAM	454	6	17	254	15	76	80	122	37
McDonald,Chase	16	R	24	DH	aa	HOU	392	14	0	195	7	64	92	13	-50
McElroy,Casey	16	L	27	3B	aaa	SD	222	1	0	215	6	80	58	49	-7
McFarland,Chris	16	R	24	2B	aa	MIL	227	2	4	171	3	73	35	66	-52
McGee,Stephen	16	R	25	C	a/a	MIA	124	2	1	147	9	65	69	38	-53
	17	R	26	C	aa	SD	230	6	0	222	15	66	98	25	-17
McGuire,Reese	16	L	21	C	aa	TOR	319	1	5	243	9	88	53	73	38
	17	L	22	C	aa	TOR	115	6	2	266	11	82	105	82	61
McKinney,Billy	16	L	22	RF	aa	NYY	426	4	4	241	12	75	61	70	-3
	17	L	23	RF	a/a	NYY	441	17	2	260	8	76	115	83	39
McMahon,Ryan	16	L	22	3B	aa	COL	466	11	9	243	9	67	112	101	8
	17	L	23	1B	a/a	COL	470	17	8	340	6	80	120	88	59
McVaney,Jeff	16	R	26	RF	a/a	DET	368	5	10	253	11	85	83	127	68
	17	R	27	RF	a/a	DET	187	2	2	186	7	77	57	89	-6
Meadows,Austin	16	L	21	CF	a/a	PIT	293	10	15	252	9	77	143	155	88
	17	L	22	CF	aaa	PIT	284	3	10	236	7	82	66	101	27
Medina,Yhoxian	16	R	26	2B	a/a	CLE	255	3	4	220	3	84	62	95	21
	17	R	27	3B	aa	CLE	33	1	0	153	7	77	34	84	-23
Medrano,Kevin	16	L	26	3B	a/a	ARI	269	0	4	224	5	86	39	89	12
	17	L	27	2B	a/a	ARI	338	2	1	266	6	81	66	70	11
Mejia,Alex	16	R	25	SS	a/a	STL	269	1	1	196	5	83	43	59	-6
	17	R	26	SS	a/a	STL	433	5	2	249	5	83	66	37	7
Mejia,Erick	17	B	23	SS	a/a	LA	356	6	21	256	7	75	66	126	7
Mejia,Francisco	17	B	22	C	aa	CLE	347	12	6	283	6	85	94	80	53
Mejias-Brean,Seth	16	R	25	3B	aaa	CIN	435	6	4	204	6	75	56	62	-23
	17	R	26	3B	a/a	SEA	422	3	4	222	6	73	41	78	-39
Mendez,Luis	16	B	23	3B	a/a	TEX	242	1	5	191	8	75	24	68	-40
	17	B	24	2B	a/a	TEX	24	0	2	71	23	69	33	54	-35
Meneses,Heiker	16	R	25	SS	a/a	MIN	74	0	1	132	9	62	38	115	-68
	17	R	26	2B	a/a	BOS	307	1	9	251	3	69	49	103	-44
Meneses,Joey	16	R	24	RF	aa	ATL	222	2	0	217	6	79	54	54	-10
	17	R	25	1B	aa	ATL	360	8	0	253	9	73	51	25	-40
Mercado,Oscar	17	R	23	CF	aa	STL	477	11	33	265	5	75	72	127	9
Mercedes,Melvin	17	B	25	2B	a/a	OAK	201	0	4	207	11	80	27	98	-5
Merrifield,Whit	16	R	27	2B	aaa	KC	274	5	14	214	5	76	81	110	15
	17	R	28	2B	aaa	KC	34	2	1	338	2	86	154	58	90
Mesa,Melky	16	R	29	CF	a/a	TOR	253	4	4	200	5	63	90	88	-40
Michael,Levi	16	R	25	2B	aa	MIN	316	1	4	187	5	71	34	123	-39
	17	R	26	CF	a/a	MIN	336	6	7	236	8	69	69	86	-25
Michalczewski,Trey	16	B	21	3B	aa	CHW	487	10	3	202	9	65	88	90	-23
	17	B	22	3B	aa	CHW	368	9	8	226	10	62	87	93	-31
Michelena,Arturo	17	R	23	3B	aa	HOU	162	1	0	187	5	70	19	36	-82
Middlebrooks,Will	16	R	28	3B	a/a	MIL	252	7	1	231	3	71	121	76	9
	17	R	29	3B	aaa	TEX	306	16	0	199	6	65	121	29	-21
Mier,Jio	16	R	26	SS	aaa	TOR	224	3	2	195	7	77	64	57	-8
	17	R	27	3B	a/a	NYM	238	3	2	182	4	69	70	43	-47
Mieses,Johan	17	R	22	CF	aa	LA	294	14	0	145	7	57	117	27	-55
Miller,Anderson	17	L	23	RF	aa	KC	213	2	3	215	4	72	45	51	-51
Miller,Ian	16	L	24	CF	aa	SEA	430	0	46	232	9	85	23	169	30
	17	L	25	CF	a/a	SEA	512	3	35	261	5	76	45	143	-6
Miller,Michael	16	R	27	2B	a/a	BOS	335	1	11	202	7	86	40	97	19
	17	R	28	2B	aaa	BOS	280	2	3	231	8	79	46	66	-11
Miller,Ryan	16	R	24	C	aa	SD	198	6	3	208	5	65	126	103	2
Mitchell,Ronnie	16	L	25	RF	aa	MIA	184	4	1	233	8	78	87	49	15
Moncada,Yoan	16	B	21	2B	aa	BOS	177	9	8	264	12	61	149	137	31
	17	B	22	2B	aaa	CHW	309	10	14	255	12	63	95	114	-13
Moncrief,Carlos	16	L	28	LF	aa	SF	176	4	5	216	12	73	81	79	7
	17	L	29	RF	aaa	SF	171	1	3	223	7	66	86	50	-36
Mondesi,Raul	16	B	21	SS	a/a	KC	172	5	18	263	7	70	109	176	37
	17	B	22	SS	aaa	KC	321	10	17	286	4	72	122	152	41
Monell,Johnny	16	L	30	C	aaa	NYM	417	11	1	193	5	75	77	53	-9
Monge,Joseph	17	R	22	CF	aa	BOS	193	2	4	229	4	74	64	97	-14
Montero,Jesus	16	R	27	DH	aaa	TOR	489	10	1	276	4	80	70	32	-3
	17	R	28	DH	aaa	BAL	49	0	0	111	3	64	10	28	-120
Moon,Chan	16	B	25	2B	a/a	HOU	161	2	4	221	7	71	36	71	-51
Moon,Logan	16	R	24	RF	aa	KC	351	3	3	231	6	68	72	72	-34
	17	R	25	RF	a/a	KC	373	6	5	238	5	66	85	84	-32
Mooney,Peter	16	L	26	SS	a/a	MIA	406	3	2	224	8	87	39	53	13
	17	L	27	SS	aaa	MIA	403	3	2	172	8	81	45	76	0
Moore,Dylan	17	R	25	SS	aa	ATL	421	6	9	175	9	72	39	70	-37

BATTER	yr	b	age	pos	lvl	org	ab	hr	sb	ba	bb%	ct%	px	sx	bpv
Moore,Logan	16	L	26	C	a/a	PHI	177	5	0	190	7	63	89	31	-52
	17	L	27	C	aaa	PHI	210	5	0	193	9	57	81	50	-72
Mora,Angelo	16	B	23	SS	aa	PHI	367	4	2	221	6	75	65	80	-9
	17	B	24	2B	a/a	PHI	398	8	4	256	5	77	77	80	4
Moran,Colin	16	L	24	3B	aaa	HOU	459	8	2	216	7	68	63	46	-48
	17	L	25	3B	aaa	HOU	302	12	0	240	6	77	90	37	5
Moreno,Rando	16	B	24	SS	a/a	SF	324	1	4	226	4	82	41	96	-2
	17	B	25	SS	aa	SF	186	0	3	178	5	85	18	51	-19
Morin,Parker	16	L	25	C	aaa	KC	234	1	0	153	6	68	38	41	-70
	17	L	26	C	a/a	KC	128	1	0	147	2	69	35	28	-80
Moroff,Max	16	B	23	2B	aaa	PIT	421	7	8	213	16	68	74	89	-8
	17	B	24	SS	aaa	PIT	185	11	4	228	16	66	145	56	30
Motter,Taylor	16	R	27	SS	aaa	TAM	350	10	16	187	7	77	78	95	15
	17	R	28	SS	aaa	SEA	100	5	4	279	9	84	110	103	77
Mountcastle,Ryan	17	R	20	3B	aa	BAL	153	3	0	181	2	74	68	49	-28
Moya,Steven	16	L	25	RF	a/a	DET	409	17	3	254	3	75	117	93	28
	17	L	26	RF	a/a	DET	375	15	4	185	6	62	106	86	-26
Mullins II,Cedric	17	B	23	CF	aa	BAL	309	11	7	220	7	78	80	88	18
Muncy,Max	16	L	26	LF	aaa	OAK	223	6	4	219	12	73	79	101	10
	17	L	27	3B	aaa	LA	320	9	2	251	10	67	99	55	-12
Mundell,Brian	17	R	23	1B	aa	COL	172	3	1	297	11	85	73	44	36
Muno,Daniel	16	B	27	3B	a/a	MIA	215	1	1	191	13	71	56	67	-25
	17	B	28	3B	aaa	SEA	293	6	9	214	12	60	96	76	-36
Munoz,Yairo	16	R	21	SS	aa	OAK	387	7	5	217	5	79	64	80	4
	17	R	22	SS	a/a	OAK	446	10	18	272	4	81	78	118	31
Murphy,Jack	16	B	28	C	aaa	LA	208	2	0	197	11	67	47	20	-66
	17	B	29	C	a/a	LA	163	0	0	108	7	66	33	17	-89
Murphy,John	16	R	25	C	aaa	MIN	263	2	0	212	6	79	56	23	-18
	17	R	26	C	aaa	ARI	261	4	0	186	6	80	42	15	-26
Murphy,Max	17	R	25	RF	aa	MIN	206	1	0	231	7	76	65	78	-7
Murphy,Sean	17	R	23	C	aa	OAK	191	3	0	183	8	81	47	34	-10
Murphy,Tom	16	R	25	C	aaa	COL	303	15	1	296	4	73	169	87	64
	17	R	26	C	aaa	COL	141	3	0	222	4	57	116	63	-49
Myles,Bryson	16	R	27	LF	a/a	CLE	208	6	8	198	8	71	92	104	8
Naquin,Tyler	16	L	25	CF	aaa	CLE	70	1	1	257	9	76	64	72	-3
	17	L	26	CF	aaa	CLE	295	8	4	262	8	75	86	80	9
Narvaez,Omar	16	B	24	C	a/a	CHW	188	2	0	203	6	84	41	24	-10
Nathans,Tucker	16	L	28	LF	aa	BAL	212	3	1	200	4	76	51	45	-30
	17	L	29	DH	a/a	BAL	89	2	1	216	2	63	61	51	-79
Navarro Jr,Efren	16	L	30	1B	aaa	STL	465	4	0	203	6	75	41	48	-38
Navarro,Reynaldo	16	B	27	SS	aaa	LAA	163	1	0	172	2	78	47	45	-30
	17	B	28	2B	aaa	LAA	492	4	4	204	6	79	45	52	-20
Naylor,Josh	17	L	20	1B	aa	SD	156	2	2	247	9	77	65	53	-6
Negron,Kristopher	16	R	30	SS	aaa	CHC	375	6	14	194	3	69	75	120	-21
Newman,Kevin	16	R	23	SS	aa	PIT	233	2	5	258	8	89	45	98	40
	17	R	24	SS	a/a	PIT	509	3	10	245	5	87	52	105	33
Ngoepe,Gift	16	R	26	SS	aaa	PIT	332	6	4	187	7	56	105	83	-49
	17	R	27	SS	aaa	PIT	264	5	2	188	8	61	99	98	-30
Nicholas,Brett	16	L	28	C	aaa	TEX	400	9	1	228	7	73	87	50	-7
Nido,Tomas	17	R	23	C	aa	NYM	367	8	0	215	8	80	70	39	6
Nieto,Adrian	16	B	27	C	aaa	MIA	113	1	1	163	10	61	46	37	-87
	17	B	28	C	a/a	CIN	217	3	0	194	5	67	52	50	-61
Nimmo,Brandon	16	L	23	CF	aaa	NYM	392	8	5	290	8	78	87	89	25
	17	L	24	CF	aaa	NYM	163	2	0	178	13	63	84	38	-40
Nogowski,John	16	R	23	1B	aa	OAK	23	1	0	111	9	86	73	-8	21
	17	R	24	1B	aa	STL	207	2	2	266	10	87	49	55	25
Nola,Austin	16	R	27	2B	aaa	MIA	372	4	3	220	5	82	62	60	9
	17	R	28	C	a/a	MIA	257	2	2	189	10	79	41	47	-13
Noonan,Nick	16	L	27	SS	aaa	SD	342	3	0	229	4	73	73	33	-28
	17	L	28	3B	aaa	MIL	268	2	3	197	5	74	50	90	-27
Norfork,Khayyan	16	R	27	2B	a/a	WAS	76	0	1	137	8	67	35	68	-67
	17	R	28	2B	aa	WAS	280	2	1	216	7	72	40	49	-51
Noriega,Gabriel	16	R	26	3B	aa	MIL	331	3	4	223	4	81	39	58	-17
	17	R	27	3B	a/a	MIL	210	2	0	196	2	72	37	28	-68
Norwood,John	17	R	25	RF	aa	MIA	473	16	4	254	11	67	96	76	-11
Nottingham,Jacob	16	R	21	C	aa	MIL	415	11	9	228	6	65	79	77	-39
	17	R	22	C	aa	MIL	325	10	7	210	10	71	112	93	25
Numata,Chace	17	B	25	C	aa	PHI	305	3	0	210	7	85	51	36	10
Nunez,Antonio	16	R	23	SS	aa	HOU	69	0	1	267	10	75	11	33	-59
	17	R	24	SS	aa	HOU	363	2	7	196	9	68	29	77	-63
Nunez,Dom	17	L	22	C	aa	COL	297	10	6	203	13	73	86	75	12
Nunez,Gustavo	16	B	28	SS	aa	DET	348	1	10	225	7	83	35	92	3
	17	B	29	SS	aa	NYM	259	1	8	213	6	80	36	92	-12
Nunez,Renato	16	R	22	3B	aaa	OAK	505	19	2	214	5	76	98	67	13
	17	R	23	LF	aaa	OAK	473	23	2	216	7	68	131	61	12
O Brien,Peter	16	R	26	LF	aaa	ARI	406	16	1	206	4	57	143	96	-20
	17	R	27	1B	a/a	LA	341	12	0	154	7	50	127	40	-71
O Conner,Justin	16	R	24	C	aa	TAM	25	1	0	135	0	58	62	29	-106
	17	R	25	C	a/a	TAM	309	7	3	194	6	64	91	69	-37
O Hearn,Ryan	17	L	24	1B	a/a	KC	479	16	1	227	8	68	110	49	-5
O Neill,Tyler	16	R	21	RF	aa	SEA	492	23	12	282	11	66	141	103	33
	17	R	22	LF	aaa	STL	495	25	12	224	8	68	131	101	27
Oberste,Matt	16	R	25	DH	aa	NYM	413	7	1	238	7	77	68	49	-7
	17	R	26	1B	aa	NYM	455	5	3	246	10	71	66	71	-19
OBrien,Chris	16	B	27	C	a/a	BAL	249	6	0	152	12	74	59	19	-25
O'Brien,Chris	17	B	28	DH	a/a	BAL	79	2	0	154	13	66	51	19	-61
O'Grady,Brian	17	L	25	CF	aa	CIN	169	8	7	160	17	60	118	120	5
Oh,Danny	16	L	27	LF	aa	OAK	276	0	9	189	5	78	29	89	-25
OHearn,Ryan	16	L	23	1B	aa	KC	414	12	3	240	9	66	116	55	-5
Ohlman,Mike	16	R	26	C	a/a	STL	251	5	1	233	7	64	83	73	-40
	17	R	27	C	aaa	TOR	282	11	4	196	13	52	150	54	-28
Olson,Matt	16	L	22	RF	aaa	OAK	464	14	1	222	12	70	123	54	23
	17	L	23	1B	aaa	OAK	294	17	2	236	11	70	138	73	34
Olt,Mike	16	R	28	1B	a/a	SD	166	4	1	196	11	55	98	39	-66
ONeill,Michael	16	R	24	RF	aa	NYY	176	1	4	218	6	69	60	114	-29
O'Neill,Michael	17	R	25	LF	aa	TEX	271	7	10	237	8	67	83	122	-13
Opitz,Shane	16	L	24	SS	a/a	TOR	240	2	6	199	7	80	53	84	2
	17	L	25	SS	aaa	TOR	246	1	6	237	6	83	55	70	12
Orf,Nate	16	R	26	2B	a/a	MIL	454	2	7	226	8	84	43	82	11
	17	R	27	2B	aaa	MIL	434	7	5	251	8	78	81	119	30
Oropesa,Ricky	16	L	27	1B	a/a	SF	252	6	0	173	8	64	71	16	-62
Ortega,Angel	16	R	23	SS	aa	MIL	247	3	4	222	1	82	47	49	-16
	17	R	24	SS	aa	MIL	471	10	14	238	5	79	56	81	-4
Ortega,Rafael	16	L	25	LF	aaa	LAA	322	3	10	255	3	85	57	116	29
	17	L	26	CF	aaa	SD	419	4	17	250	6	86	62	113	42
Ortiz,Danny	16	L	26	CF	aaa	PIT	436	13	5	204	5	77	87	71	9
	17	L	27	CF	aaa	PIT	411	12	4	229	4	78	93	65	14
Osborne,Zach	16	R	26	SS	aa	COL	206	0	1	217	4	89	23	45	-1
Osuna,Jose	16	R	24	1B	a/a	PIT	473	10	3	248	6	82	94	71	37
Palka,Daniel	16	L	25	RF	a/a	MIN	503	27	7	223	8	59	161	87	10
	17	L	26	RF	aaa	MIN	332	10	1	250	7	74	82	72	-3
Papi,Mike	16	L	24	LF	aa	CLE	259	7	3	208	12	70	107	79	14
	17	L	25	RF	a/a	CLE	415	10	5	231	12	79	67	56	12
Parker,Jarrett	16	L	27	RF	aaa	SF	194	10	1	216	9	58	157	106	8
	17	L	28	CF	aaa	SF	112	2	1	183	12	65	62	59	-44
Parmelee,Chris	16	L	28	1B	aaa	NYY	214	10	0	214	10	76	109	19	19
	17	L	29	1B	aaa	MIA	169	4	0	163	11	59	92	39	-52
Parmley,Ian	16	L	27	RF	aa	TOR	282	2	10	250	7	67	47	137	-36
	17	L	28	RF	aaa	TOR	246	1	10	228	5	71	47	100	-36
Patterson,Jordan	16	L	24	RF	aaa	COL	427	11	7	270	7	72	106	130	29
	17	L	25	1B	aaa	COL	484	20	2	253	5	72	126	80	25
Paulino,Carlos	17	R	28	C	a/a	MIN	165	2	1	230	8	74	47	60	-32
Paulino,Dorssys	17	R	23	LF	aa	CLE	315	5	5	239	10	76	59	68	-5
Paulsen,Benjamin	16	L	29	1B	aaa	COL	288	4	1	229	5	75	80	89	3
Payton,Mark	16	L	25	LF	a/a	NYY	345	7	8	252	8	83	71	120	44
	17	L	26	LF	a/a	NYY	324	6	3	225	6	75	69	85	-2
Paz,Andy	16	R	23	C	aa	OAK	150	1	2	283	9	84	58	55	18
	17	R	24	C	aa	OAK	179	0	2	217	6	78	16	49	-49
Pena,Francisco	16	R	27	C	aaa	BAL	191	4	0	213	6	85	68	39	20
	17	R	28	C	aaa	BAL	180	5	1	211	4	77	69	30	-17
Pena,Roberto	16	R	24	C	a/a	HOU	255	6	0	198	3	81	69	34	-4
	17	R	25	C	aaa	CHW	200	2	0	176	4	83	39	8	-25
Penalver,Carlos	16	R	22	SS	aa	CHC	407	0	2	187	5	80	41	52	-18
	17	R	23	SS	aa	CHC	382	3	1	235	4	80	38	81	-13
Peraza,Jose	16	R	22	SS	aaa	CIN	288	2	9	269	7	83	58	104	25
Perez,Audry	16	R	28	C	aaa	BAL	306	6	0	248	5	79	51	21	-23
Perez,Carlos	16	R	26	C	aaa	LAA	39	2	0	283	2	77	146	78	54
	17	R	27	C	aaa	LAA	261	3	3	269	7	81	63	69	11
Perez,Eury	16	R	26	LF	aaa	TAM	223	2	16	217	4	77	46	170	4
	17	R	27	CF	aaa	MIA	238	1	25	289	5	79	55	144	15
Perez,Fernando	17	L	24	1B	aa	SD	212	3	0	195	6	67	57	47	-57
Perez,Juan	16	L	25	2B	aaa	CIN	367	6	10	223	7	71	65	102	-17
	17	L	26	SS	aaa	CIN	80	3	5	256	11	72	119	88	35
Perez,Juan	16	R	30	RF	aaa	CHC	381	6	11	210	3	71	87	112	-5
Perez,Michael	16	L	24	C	aa	ARI	122	3	0	191	5	74	72	52	-20
	17	L	25	C	a/a	ARI	271	4	0	242	9	74	94	33	0
Perez,Stephen	16	B	26	2B	a/a	WAS	301	4	10	217	12	78	45	89	-2
	17	B	27	2B	a/a	WAS	266	3	7	169	9	65	45	81	-60
Perez,Yefri	16	B	25	CF	aa	MIA	328	1	33	231	9	78	28	143	-4
	17	B	26	CF	aa	MIA	248	0	9	147	12	73	35	139	-14
Perio,Noah	17	L	26	2B	aa	SD	430	3	6	249	5	84	39	84	6
Perkins,Cameron	16	R	26	CF	aaa	PHI	408	8	10	261	4	83	70	100	27
	17	R	27	CF	aaa	PHI	257	6	2	239	9	77	83	60	12
Peter,Jake	16	L	23	2B	a/a	CHW	481	5	7	246	8	77	58	60	-11
	17	L	24	2B	a/a	CHW	463	12	9	250	7	69	80	89	-18
Peterson,D.J.	16	R	25	1B	a/a	SEA	455	15	1	226	6	69	110	38	-12
	17	R	26	3B	aaa	CHW	468	13	5	209	7	75	72	66	-8
Peterson,Dustin	16	R	22	LF	aa	ATL	524	11	4	271	8	79	95	73	30
	17	R	23	LF	aaa	ATL	314	1	1	207	7	71	34	51	-59
Phillips,Anthony	16	R	26	SS	aa	LAA	347	1	8	227	8	73	35	87	-36
	17	R	27	SS	aa	COL	287	3	2	189	5	73	43	29	-54
Phillips,Brett	16	L	22	CF	aa	MIL	441	15	11	222	13	63	109	111	-1
	17	L	23	RF	aaa	MIL	383	16	6	263	8	61	144	125	14
Pina,Eudy	16	R	25	DH	aa	CHW	382	3	5	207	5	72	37	73	-50
Pina,Manny	16	R	29	C	aaa	MIL	237	3	1	251	5	79	85	64	13
Pinder,Chad	16	R	24	SS	aaa	OAK	426	11	4	236	5	73	97	110	13
	17	R	25	2B	aaa	OAK	64	1	2	226	7	60	62	79	-71
Pineda,Jeremias	16	B	26	CF	aa	MIA	203	0	14	158	8	57	27	130	-93
	17	B	27	CF	aa	MIA	170	0	8	196	9	60	52	140	-57
Pinto,Josmil	16	R	27	C	aaa	MIL	286	8	0	245	6	71	105	53	-1
Pirela,Jose	16	R	27	LF	aaa	SD	137	1	1	193	4	80	57	88	3
	17	R	28	1B	aaa	SD	181	8	5	249	5	82	97	103	48
Pizzano,Dario	16	L	25	LF	a/a	SEA	320	2	0	203	6	81	49	59	-5
	17	L	26	LF	a/a	SEA	412	11	2	226	7	86	64	59	30
Plaia,Colton	16	R	26	C	aa	NYM	216	1	0	192	6	69	40	25	-70
	17	R	27	C	aa	NYM	137	1	0	204	12	71	49	34	-39

BATTER	yr	b	age	pos	lvl	org	ab	hr	sb	ba	bb%	ct%	px	sx	bpv
Plawecki,Kevin	16	R	25	C	aaa	NYM	190	5	0	233	4	88	72	30	28
	17	R	26	C	aaa	NYM	247	7	0	253	5	80	80	35	5
Pleffner,Shawn	16	L	27	1B	aa	WAS	300	2	1	225	8	77	50	58	-15
Polanco,Jorge	16	B	23	2B	aaa	MIN	293	8	4	262	7	82	91	99	47
Pompey,Dalton	16	B	24	CF	aaa	TOR	337	4	16	250	10	76	57	97	-2
Powell,Boog	16	L	23	CF	aaa	SEA	248	2	8	232	6	80	44	103	2
	17	L	24	CF	aaa	OAK	222	4	9	290	9	84	62	108	39
Prime,Correlle	16	R	22	1B	aa	COL	324	2	3	233	6	69	69	45	-41
	17	R	23	1B	aa	COL	272	7	2	269	6	67	76	58	-38
Procyshen,Jordan	17	L	24	C	aa	BOS	215	3	0	183	9	66	65	31	-53
Profar,Juremi	17	R	21	3B	aa	TEX	415	9	1	253	4	86	54	46	10
Profar,Jurickson	16	B	23	SS	aaa	TEX	169	4	3	251	7	83	71	67	26
	17	B	24	SS	aaa	TEX	327	5	4	247	9	89	67	62	48
Puello,Cesar	16	R	25	RF	aaa	NYY	230	5	16	257	12	72	83	96	9
	17	R	26	RF	aaa	LAA	346	8	12	253	5	70	95	106	-2
Pullin,Andrew	16	L	23	LF	aa	PHI	188	9	0	311	5	78	114	26	22
	17	L	24	LF	a/a	PHI	504	18	4	238	6	78	114	75	40
Querecuto,Juniel	16	B	24	3B	a/a	TAM	340	2	2	209	6	75	60	80	-15
	17	B	25	SS	aaa	SF	293	1	5	197	7	75	34	56	-41
Quinn,Roman	16	B	23	CF	aa	PHI	286	5	25	255	8	72	85	168	26
	17	B	24	CF	aaa	PHI	175	2	9	242	8	67	67	129	-21
Quintana,Gabriel	16	R	24	3B	aa	SD	456	18	4	216	4	65	131	71	-6
	17	R	25	1B	aa	DET	434	18	1	229	4	68	127	74	5
Rademacher,Bijan	16	L	25	LF	a/a	CHC	326	8	0	260	9	77	87	27	5
	17	L	26	RF	aaa	CHC	289	5	2	239	9	73	70	61	-15
Ramirez,Harold	16	R	22	CF	aa	TOR	383	2	6	295	5	81	58	110	15
	17	R	23	RF	aa	TOR	444	5	4	247	6	84	51	63	9
Ramirez,Nick	16	L	27	1B	aa	MIL	282	12	0	178	12	65	116	32	-10
Ramirez,Tyler	17	L	22	LF	aa	OAK	208	3	2	279	10	73	68	65	-12
Ramos,Henry	16	B	24	RF	a/a	BOS	361	6	6	249	5	79	74	102	18
	17	B	25	RF	a/a	LA	194	7	2	301	6	83	90	65	36
Ramos,Mauricio	16	R	24	3B	aa	KC	483	7	4	262	3	79	71	53	-2
	17	R	25	3B	aa	KC	356	8	0	231	3	72	63	49	-37
Ramsay,James	16	L	24	LF	aa	HOU	338	3	3	167	8	77	57	79	-4
Ramsey,Caleb	16	L	28	RF	aaa	WAS	427	3	4	227	7	76	59	72	-10
Ramsey,James	16	L	27	RF	aaa	SEA	351	6	4	209	7	59	89	79	-53
Ravelo,Rangel	16	R	24	1B	aaa	OAK	367	6	1	239	8	81	77	65	24
	17	R	25	1B	aaa	STL	306	6	1	272	7	80	87	49	19
Read,Raudy	17	R	24	C	aa	WAS	411	13	2	232	5	78	91	43	11
Reed,A.J.	16	L	23	1B	aaa	HOU	261	12	0	251	8	70	148	37	29
	17	L	24	1B	aaa	HOU	476	22	0	205	9	62	123	27	-24
Reed,Michael	16	R	24	CF	aaa	MIL	411	6	14	209	12	66	70	93	-29
	17	R	25	LF	aa	MIL	168	8	5	198	16	60	101	58	-27
Refsnyder,Rob	16	R	25	3B	aaa	NYY	209	2	5	287	7	83	51	87	16
	17	R	26	2B	aaa	TOR	150	2	2	296	10	75	95	94	27
Reginatto,Leonardo	16	R	26	SS	a/a	MIN	483	2	7	229	5	80	38	75	-14
	17	R	27	3B	aaa	MIN	277	3	0	270	8	79	52	18	-18
Reinheimer,Jack	16	R	24	SS	aaa	ARI	500	1	14	246	6	79	57	107	7
	17	R	25	SS	aaa	ARI	482	3	8	225	6	79	37	82	-16
Renda,Tony	16	R	25	LF	a/a	CIN	366	3	15	284	6	88	71	117	58
	17	R	26	3B	aaa	ARI	208	1	2	198	4	87	32	56	1
Renfroe,Hunter	16	R	24	RF	aaa	SD	533	21	3	248	3	74	116	84	21
	17	R	25	RF	aaa	SD	55	3	1	426	7	84	153	93	104
Reyes,Franmil	17	R	22	RF	aa	SD	507	22	4	246	8	72	114	65	18
Reyes,Pablo	17	R	24	2B	aa	PIT	420	8	18	250	10	82	67	103	35
Reyes,Victor	17	B	23	RF	aa	ARI	479	3	15	276	4	82	65	109	23
Reynolds,Matt	16	R	26	3B	aaa	NYM	269	1	6	199	6	70	53	101	-32
	17	R	27	LF	aaa	NYM	128	3	1	242	8	69	84	59	-21
Rice,Ian	17	R	24	C	aa	CHC	331	15	0	207	14	69	103	31	-2
Riddle,J.T.	16	L	25	SS	a/a	MIA	445	3	5	249	6	80	52	95	3
Rijo,Wendell	16	R	21	2B	aa	MIL	177	1	2	181	7	73	64	62	-24
	17	R	22	2B	aa	MIL	81	0	2	182	8	71	33	118	-37
Riley,Austin	17	R	20	3B	aa	ATL	178	8	2	296	11	69	103	81	5
Rios,Edwin	16	L	22	3B	aa	LA	122	5	0	240	5	72	116	23	2
	17	L	23	1B	a/a	LA	475	20	1	276	5	73	122	31	13
Ritchie,Jamie	17	R	24	C	aa	HOU	242	3	3	226	13	78	42	61	-6
Rivera,T.J.	16	R	28	3B	aaa	NYM	405	7	2	260	3	82	73	48	11
	17	R	29	3B	aaa	NYM	21	1	0	205	3	80	70	25	-7
Rivera,Yadiel	16	R	24	SS	aaa	MIL	304	1	3	192	2	71	43	118	-40
	17	R	25	SS	aaa	MIL	376	4	3	175	5	67	52	78	-54
Rivero,Carlos	16	R	28	3B	aaa	ARI	415	12	1	214	4	75	95	44	-3
	17	R	29	3B	aaa	ARI	206	5	0	221	5	76	75	37	-14
Robbins,Mason	17	L	24	RF	aa	CHW	480	3	4	244	4	88	25	60	1
Roberson,Tim	16	R	27	DH	aa	BOS	223	3	0	213	5	68	85	21	-42
	17	R	28	C	aaa	BOS	69	0	0	194	2	67	42	11	-90
Roberts,James	16	R	25	2B	aa	MIA	181	0	1	185	9	78	22	43	-37
Robertson,Daniel	16	R	22	SS	aaa	TAM	436	4	2	237	11	74	60	66	-11
Robinson,Drew	16	L	24	RF	aaa	TEX	467	16	13	224	10	65	124	130	20
	17	L	25	2B	aaa	TEX	265	8	5	228	11	69	117	109	24
Robinson,Errol	17	R	23	SS	aa	LA	227	2	9	242	9	75	44	106	-13
Rodgers,Brendan	17	R	21	SS	aa	COL	150	6	0	263	4	77	83	33	-5
Rodriguez,Aderlin	17	R	26	1B	aa	BAL	484	17	0	221	7	74	78	25	-20
Rodriguez,Herlis	17	L	23	CF	a/a	PHI	172	4	3	202	2	71	70	65	-35
Rodriguez,Jonathan	16	R	27	1B	a/a	STL	437	10	3	202	8	61	86	53	-52
	17	R	28	1B	a/a	MIN	452	18	2	260	13	70	118	52	18
Rodriguez,Luigi	16	B	24	LF	aa	CLE	158	3	5	201	4	62	73	116	-47
	17	L	25	LF	aa	CLE	286	11	6	248	5	66	134	59	2

BATTER	yr	b	age	pos	lvl	org	ab	hr	sb	ba	bb%	ct%	px	sx	bpv
Rodriguez,Nellie	17	R	23	1B	aaa	CLE	377	15	0	159	11	53	125	13	-60
Rodriguez,Reynaldo	16	R	30	1B	aaa	MIN	173	3	2	178	8	69	62	61	-39
Rodriguez,Ronny	16	R	24	2B	aaa	CLE	450	9	3	237	4	79	80	82	14
	17	R	25	2B	aaa	CLE	447	14	12	261	4	79	78	82	13
Rogers,Jason	16	R	28	3B	aaa	PIT	372	5	1	220	9	75	58	49	-18
	17	R	29	1B	aaa	PIT	253	7	2	235	8	79	63	62	3
Rohlfing,Danny	16	R	27	C	a/a	ARI	154	4	0	225	4	66	100	33	-37
	17	R	28	C	aa	MIN	225	3	0	121	7	50	51	52	-126
Rojas Jr.,Mel	16	B	26	RF	a/a	ATL	379	10	10	218	8	71	97	110	14
	17	B	27	RF	aaa	ATL	212	4	2	197	7	69	63	51	-41
Rojas,Jose	17	L	24	3B	aa	LAA	172	4	0	205	3	76	73	56	-11
Roller,Kyle	16	L	28	DH	aaa	TAM	162	4	0	173	9	54	111	36	-65
Romanski,Jake	16	R	26	C	aa	BOS	334	3	0	272	3	84	64	21	1
	17	R	27	C	a/a	BOS	176	1	0	219	1	85	23	38	-25
Romero,Stefen	16	R	28	RF	aaa	SEA	418	15	1	235	6	79	96	71	27
Rondon,Cleuluis	17	B	23	SS	aa	MIA	162	0	1	189	5	70	38	37	-66
Rondon,Jose	16	R	22	SS	aa	SD	456	5	10	250	3	80	59	88	3
	17	R	23	SS	a/a	SD	300	4	2	256	5	78	72	76	7
Rosa,Angel	16	R	24	3B	a/a	LAA	308	4	6	162	5	64	59	114	-50
	17	R	25	3B	aa	LAA	49	0	1	163	11	59	19	45	-110
Rosa,Garabez	16	R	27	2B	a/a	BAL	529	8	2	248	2	72	58	36	-49
	17	R	28	RF	aa	BAL	523	11	1	239	3	75	51	46	-37
Rosa,Viosergy	16	L	26	1B	aa	OAK	459	6	1	210	11	65	86	23	-41
	17	L	27	1B	aa	OAK	517	12	0	206	7	69	80	33	-33
Rosario,Amed	16	R	21	SS	aa	NYM	214	2	5	311	7	73	86	127	17
	17	R	22	SS	aaa	NYM	393	6	14	274	5	79	59	116	11
Rosario,Eddie	16	L	25	CF	aaa	MIN	160	6	4	287	4	83	117	78	58
Rosario,Jose	16	R	25	2B	a/a	NYY	258	4	4	252	2	77	63	91	-10
	17	R	26	2B	a/a	BOS	53	0	0	135	3	73	17	46	-74
Rosario,Rainel	16	R	27	LF	a/a	BOS	330	2	2	222	6	84	47	70	7
Rua,Ryan	17	R	27	LF	a/a	TEX	177	6	2	216	4	64	97	103	-28
Ruf,Darin	16	R	30	1B	aaa	PHI	350	19	0	246	6	71	132	49	20
Ruiz,Rio	16	L	22	3B	aaa	ATL	465	8	1	246	10	71	78	43	-16
	17	L	23	3B	aaa	ATL	388	13	1	201	9	66	94	54	-24
Russell,Michael	17	R	24	3B	aa	TAM	386	5	17	214	6	74	69	128	4
Sabol,Stefan	16	R	24	RF	aa	NYM	218	4	2	195	9	54	103	61	-61
Saez,Jorge	16	R	26	C	aa	TOR	125	5	0	205	6	63	135	31	-17
	17	R	27	C	aa	NYY	201	9	1	220	12	62	114	42	-20
Salcedo,Erick	17	B	24	SS	aa	BAL	408	4	2	217	7	85	30	39	-7
Sanchez, Tony	16	R	28	C	aaa	SF	199	3	0	154	8	73	54	32	-37
Sanchez,Adrian	16	R	26	3B	a/a	WAS	350	0	6	220	4	84	41	82	3
	17	R	27	SS	a/a	WAS	274	4	3	201	5	78	58	82	-4
Sanchez,Carlos	16	B	24	2B	aaa	CHW	235	7	8	219	6	72	88	104	5
Sanchez,Gary	16	R	24	C	aaa	NYY	284	10	6	263	6	82	109	86	56
Sanchez,Hector	16	B	27	1B	aaa	SD	204	10	0	229	6	71	142	8	14
	17	B	28	C	aaa	SD	26	1	0	199	4	62	140	-8	-32
Sands,Jerry	16	R	29	1B	aaa	CHW	270	6	0	193	7	70	72	37	-37
Sardinas,Luis	16	B	23	SS	aaa	SD	182	0	6	207	4	85	22	75	-9
	17	B	24	2B	aaa	BAL	310	4	5	281	3	85	37	78	2
Sawyer,Wynston	17	R	26	C	aa	LA	184	3	1	233	5	72	88	45	-15
Scavuzzo,Jacob	16	R	22	LF	aa	LA	421	10	4	248	5	74	84	81	1
	17	R	23	LF	a/a	LA	278	14	2	210	3	66	119	50	-16
Schafer,Logan	16	L	30	RF	aaa	MIN	216	3	4	215	7	80	46	80	-1
Schebler,Scott	16	L	26	CF	aaa	CIN	289	12	2	277	5	75	135	97	49
Schimpf,Ryan	16	L	28	3B	aaa	SD	166	10	0	270	7	73	166	31	52
	17	L	29	3B	aaa	SD	242	11	0	143	8	46	139	48	-74
Schoop,Sharlon	16	R	29	2B	a/a	BAL	305	4	0	182	7	72	57	51	-38
Schrader,Jake	16	R	25	1B	aa	ATL	341	11	2	208	7	61	114	50	-35
Schrock,Max	16	L	22	2B	aa	OAK	23	0	0	357	0	100	28	51	40
	17	L	23	2B	aa	OAK	417	5	3	286	6	89	46	57	25
Schroder,Myles	16	B	29	CF	a/a	SF	395	2	6	202	3	77	48	99	-17
Schulz,Nick	16	R	25	RF	aa	SD	393	9	4	247	8	69	90	50	-17
	17	R	26	CF	a/a	SD	399	12	6	193	8	66	93	67	-22
Schwind,Jonathan	16	R	26	RF	a/a	PIT	168	2	2	198	9	73	58	74	-21
Schwindel,Frank	16	R	24	1B	aa	KC	455	16	1	244	3	79	87	39	7
	17	R	25	DH	a/a	KC	529	17	0	291	2	82	103	23	24
Scivicque,Kade	17	R	24	C	a/a	ATL	315	4	0	231	7	76	41	35	-39
Scruggs,Xavier	16	R	29	1B	aaa	MIA	317	14	3	231	13	65	146	63	22
Seferina,Darren	17	L	23	2B	aa	STL	173	4	9	255	9	74	67	112	6
Segedin,Robert	16	R	28	3B	aaa	LA	373	16	2	254	7	73	130	95	39
	17	R	29	3B	aaa	LA	97	3	0	248	3	78	90	36	4
Seitzer,Cameron	16	L	26	1B	aaa	TAM	135	0	0	148	5	67	18	17	-100
	17	L	27	DH	aa	CHW	227	5	2	191	7	68	83	48	-31
Selsky,Steve	16	R	27	1B	aaa	CIN	296	8	2	243	8	69	120	56	4
	17	R	28	RF	aaa	BOS	297	9	1	189	5	62	86	35	-61
Senzel,Nick	17	R	22	3B	aa	CIN	209	12	5	345	12	78	137	86	72
Serna,KC	16	R	27	SS	aa	PHI	336	3	4	239	8	78	53	60	-9
	17	R	28	2B	a/a	MIA	296	6	1	194	6	74	76	62	-10
Sever,Joe	16	R	26	3B	aa	CLE	419	3	2	219	4	70	57	48	-49
	17	R	27	3B	a/a	CLE	442	6	4	243	5	80	54	56	-8
Severino,Pedro	16	R	23	C	aaa	WAS	291	2	3	260	6	84	43	39	-5
	17	R	24	C	aaa	WAS	211	4	1	212	6	77	40	27	-39
Shaffer,Richie	16	R	25	3B	aaa	TAM	428	9	3	193	11	63	96	49	-33
	17	R	26	LF	aaa	CLE	463	24	3	199	10	58	142	60	-15
Shank,Zach	16	R	25	3B	a/a	SEA	414	2	1	249	6	74	51	65	-30
	17	R	26	RF	aaa	SEA	368	2	11	174	6	69	51	119	-34
Shaw,Chris	16	L	23	1B	aa	SF	232	4	0	233	8	74	105	78	20
	17	L	24	LF	a/a	SF	469	17	0	257	7	68	124	30	-6

BATTER	yr	b	age	pos	lvl	org	ab	hr	sb	ba	bb%	ct%	px	sx	bpv
Shoemaker,Brady	16	R	29	1B	a/a	CHW	329	7	0	169	9	69	70	27	-40
Shuck,J.B.	16	L	29	LF	aaa	CHW	154	2	3	230	5	89	52	87	35
Sierra,Magneuris	17	L	21	RF	aa	STL	326	1	15	257	5	82	51	108	11
Sierra,Moises	16	R	28	RF	aa	MIA	268	6	5	280	8	80	86	97	36
Simcox,A.J.	17	R	23	SS	aa	DET	436	7	10	226	5	82	64	117	28
Singleton,Jonathan	16	L	25	1B	aaa	HOU	410	15	0	165	12	64	102	22	-29
	17	L	26	1B	aa	HOU	385	15	2	172	18	58	120	42	-22
Sisco,Chance	16	L	21	C	aa	BAL	426	6	2	300	11	78	74	40	9
	17	L	22	C	aaa	BAL	344	6	2	232	8	67	68	49	-44
Skole,Matt	16	L	27	1B	aaa	WAS	499	19	2	212	10	72	99	49	6
	17	L	28	1B	aaa	WAS	212	8	0	177	8	65	124	42	-11
Slater,Austin	16	R	24	LF	a/a	SF	390	13	7	265	11	74	98	65	17
	17	R	25	RF	aaa	SF	184	3	3	274	6	75	74	59	-9
Smalling,Tim	16	R	29	3B	aaa	COL	232	2	0	190	4	82	28	49	-23
Smith,Bryson	16	R	28	CF	a/a	CIN	166	0	1	153	6	71	19	76	-62
Smith,Dominic	16	L	21	1B	aa	NYM	484	12	2	273	8	83	83	54	33
	17	L	22	1B	aaa	NYM	457	13	1	278	7	77	92	47	11
Smith,Dwight	16	L	24	LF	aa	TOR	471	14	10	243	7	78	95	90	31
	17	L	25	RF	aaa	TOR	395	8	7	257	10	80	72	69	19
Smith,Jordan	16	L	26	RF	a/a	CLE	403	7	14	229	8	75	90	107	23
	17	L	27	CF	a/a	CLE	307	2	6	181	6	74	39	71	-37
Smith,Kevan	16	R	28	C	aaa	CHW	183	6	0	171	6	75	86	13	-14
	17	R	29	C	aaa	CHW	53	0	0	295	8	77	75	35	-3
Smith,Mallex	16	L	23	CF	a/a	ATL	31	0	4	393	11	70	110	166	41
	17	L	24	CF	aaa	TAM	186	3	19	237	8	72	66	159	5
Smith,Tyler	16	R	25	SS	aaa	SEA	392	4	5	220	4	79	50	59	-18
	17	R	26	SS	aaa	TEX	333	4	3	190	8	74	51	41	-33
Snider,Travis	16	L	28	LF	aaa	KC	277	2	0	194	9	73	60	51	-27
Solano,Donovan	16	R	29	3B	aaa	NYY	511	7	2	265	4	80	66	60	2
Soler,Jorge	16	R	24	LF	a/a	CHC	37	0	0	137	18	51	0	18	-153
	17	R	25	RF	aaa	KC	273	17	1	226	12	66	133	35	8
Sosa,Ruben	17	B	27	2B	a/a	KC	268	3	13	205	8	73	68	152	11
Soto,Elliot	16	R	27	2B	aaa	MIA	158	1	2	204	13	73	33	86	-27
	17	R	28	SS	aaa	CHC	244	1	3	183	7	75	54	78	-19
Soto,Neftali	16	R	27	1B	a/a	WAS	456	8	2	237	5	76	74	54	-8
	17	R	28	1B	a/a	WAS	515	17	0	251	6	75	98	40	5
Sparks,Taylor	16	R	23	3B	aa	CIN	224	9	2	174	7	57	103	74	-50
	17	R	24	3B	aa	CIN	62	2	0	127	13	62	97	39	-36
Sportman,J.P.	16	R	24	LF	aa	OAK	483	4	14	232	4	81	62	117	20
	17	R	25	RF	aa	OAK	513	8	11	234	5	75	69	100	-1
Stallings,Jacob	16	R	27	C	aaa	PIT	257	5	0	181	3	71	83	34	-32
	17	R	28	C	aaa	PIT	216	3	1	251	6	84	66	50	17
Stamets,Eric	16	R	25	SS	a/a	CLE	317	6	7	212	6	67	90	128	-8
	17	R	26	SS	a/a	CLE	374	13	8	229	7	72	112	89	21
Starling,Bubba	16	R	24	CF	a/a	KC	399	5	9	161	4	61	86	110	-46
	17	R	25	RF	aaa	KC	278	5	4	215	5	74	69	74	-15
Stassi,Brock	16	L	27	1B	aaa	PHI	375	12	1	234	12	75	105	39	23
	17	L	28	1B	a/a	PHI	179	3	0	202	8	70	45	20	-61
Stassi,Max	16	R	25	C	aaa	HOU	243	5	1	188	5	68	80	42	-39
	17	R	26	C	a/a	HOU	250	10	1	216	10	65	115	56	-10
Staton,Allen	16	R	24	2B	aa	STL	180	2	2	240	7	77	60	83	-4
Stevens,River	16	L	24	3B	aa	SD	276	4	4	206	6	78	41	85	-18
	17	L	25	3B	a/a	SD	161	0	0	193	5	78	38	57	-27
Stevenson,Andrew	16	L	22	CF	aa	WAS	256	2	11	233	7	79	49	112	4
	17	L	23	CF	a/a	WAS	389	2	9	245	6	74	37	106	-28
Stewart,Christin	17	L	24	LF	aa	DET	485	23	2	225	9	69	130	76	22
Stewart,D.J.	17	L	24	LF	aa	BAL	457	17	16	229	11	77	82	101	28
Strausborger,Ryan	16	R	28	RF	aaa	SEA	274	4	11	179	5	65	56	93	-55
	17	R	29	CF	a/a	MIN	125	1	4	189	11	58	72	105	-55
Stuart,Champ	16	R	24	CF	aa	NYM	184	2	12	170	6	54	42	133	-96
	17	R	25	CF	aa	NYM	320	5	33	196	11	54	88	144	-47
Stubbs,Garrett	16	L	23	C	aa	HOU	120	3	4	289	8	89	93	105	82
	17	L	24	C	a/a	HOU	340	3	8	191	8	79	47	86	-1
Sturgeon,Cole	16	L	25	CF	a/a	BOS	436	5	5	249	4	84	60	66	14
	17	L	26	CF	aa	BOS	406	4	8	233	7	76	65	84	-3
Suchy,Michael	17	R	24	RF	aa	PIT	250	3	2	182	7	59	60	79	-75
Suiter,Jerrick	17	R	24	RF	aa	PIT	347	8	6	261	11	74	88	90	18
Susac,Andrew	16	R	26	C	aaa	MIL	249	6	0	201	7	71	79	31	-29
	17	R	27	C	aaa	MIL	171	6	0	159	9	62	107	17	-43
Swanson,Dansby	16	R	22	SS	aa	ATL	333	8	7	252	10	76	80	125	27
	17	R	23	SS	aaa	ATL	38	1	1	203	12	72	45	51	-33
Sweeney,Darnell	16	B	25	2B	aaa	PHI	400	6	11	212	8	71	72	107	-10
	17	B	26	CF	aaa	CIN	443	9	14	225	8	70	84	97	-7
Swihart,Blake	16	B	24	C	aaa	BOS	103	1	2	238	14	82	47	54	11
	17	B	25	C	aaa	BOS	195	3	1	179	6	70	61	73	-36
Taijeron,Travis	16	R	27	RF	aaa	NYM	459	12	1	204	8	54	150	68	-25
	17	R	28	RF	aaa	NYM	448	17	1	200	10	56	136	56	-28
Tanielu,Nick	16	R	24	2B	a/a	HOU	371	6	1	217	4	81	53	40	-11
Tapia,Raimel	16	L	22	CF	a/a	COL	528	7	19	322	4	89	68	130	59
	17	L	23	CF	aaa	COL	263	2	9	348	3	84	83	128	49
Tarsovich,Jordan	16	R	25	3B	aa	LA	169	4	5	194	11	78	74	77	19
	17	R	26	3B	aa	OAK	341	2	10	200	9	74	47	108	-14
Tauchman,Mike	16	L	26	CF	aaa	COL	475	1	16	252	6	83	49	121	20
	17	L	27	CF	aaa	COL	420	12	11	285	6	81	99	114	51
Tavarez,Aneury	16	L	24	RF	a/a	BOS	400	6	17	317	6	82	85	130	48
	17	L	25	RF	a/a	BOS	196	4	7	263	7	80	63	103	20
Taylor,Beau	16	L	26	C	aa	OAK	339	3	1	232	11	71	77	37	-21
	17	L	27	C	a/a	OAK	210	3	0	240	9	73	62	52	-24

BATTER	yr	b	age	pos	lvl	org	ab	hr	sb	ba	bb%	ct%	px	sx	bpv
Taylor,Chris	16	R	26	SS	aaa	LA	304	2	13	268	8	74	88	123	21
	17	R	27	SS	aaa	LA	43	1	1	184	7	86	70	140	57
Taylor,Chuck	16	B	23	LF	aa	ARI	84	1	1	225	6	81	74	61	14
	17	B	24	LF	aa	SEA	471	8	8	239	11	77	65	90	12
Taylor,Kevin	17	L	26	LF	aa	NYM	383	3	2	254	13	83	46	43	8
Taylor,Tyrone	16	R	22	RF	aa	MIL	465	9	8	225	7	83	52	75	14
	17	R	23	LF	aa	MIL	85	1	2	241	9	77	85	122	31
Tejada,Luis	16	R	24	LF	aa	SD	195	4	3	229	9	75	92	103	26
	17	R	25	1B	aa	LAA	171	3	2	176	7	74	40	71	-36
Tejada,Ruben	16	R	27	SS	a/a	SF	153	1	0	257	4	82	65	67	11
	17	R	28	SS	aaa	BAL	175	5	0	217	9	84	58	46	17
Telis,Tomas	16	B	25	C	aaa	MIA	336	4	3	276	6	86	59	86	32
	17	B	26	C	aaa	MIA	280	4	4	231	5	87	52	90	30
Tellez,Rowdy	16	L	21	1B	aa	TOR	438	22	4	288	11	77	141	59	63
	17	L	22	1B	aaa	TOR	445	6	6	223	9	78	78	73	15
Tendler,Luke	17	L	26	DH	aa	TEX	420	11	1	214	8	72	86	52	-10
Terdoslavich,Joseph	16	B	28	1B	a/a	BAL	451	12	1	192	11	78	77	39	8
	17	B	29	1B	aaa	PIT	346	5	2	226	9	80	62	42	0
Thaiss,Matt	17	L	22	1B	aa	LAA	178	1	4	277	17	69	77	60	-11
Thomas,Dillon	16	L	24	RF	aa	COL	374	4	11	274	6	74	103	79	16
	17	L	25	LF	a/a	COL	273	5	7	207	6	62	85	86	-46
Thompson,David	17	R	24	3B	aa	NYM	476	16	8	240	8	77	95	66	23
Thompson,Trayce	17	R	26	CF	aaa	LA	339	7	2	172	5	67	72	91	-35
Thon,Dickie	17	R	26	2B	aa	STL	169	3	1	204	5	63	83	68	-50
Tilson,Charlie	16	L	24	CF	aaa	STL	351	3	11	236	7	82	55	133	29
Tobias,Josh	17	B	25	2B	aa	BOS	332	2	3	242	4	76	58	43	-26
Tocci,Carlos	17	R	22	CF	a/a	PHI	484	3	4	268	5	82	44	83	0
Toles,Andrew	16	L	24	CF	a/a	LA	231	6	12	280	5	81	109	113	57
Tomlinson,Kelby	16	R	26	SS	aaa	SF	185	0	9	238	8	83	33	109	10
	17	R	27	2B	aaa	SF	108	0	7	244	9	86	33	90	18
Tomscha,Damek	17	R	26	3B	aa	PHI	159	3	1	263	5	86	47	43	7
Torres,Gleyber	17	R	21	SS	a/a	NYY	201	8	7	280	13	75	117	87	48
Torres,Nick	16	R	23	LF	a/a	SD	503	10	8	250	3	70	96	71	-15
	17	R	24	LF	aa	SD	437	9	3	255	5	73	64	58	-28
Torres,Ramon	16	B	23	SS	a/a	KC	461	2	17	237	5	82	39	100	0
	17	B	24	SS	aaa	KC	295	4	13	258	4	88	44	103	28
Toscano,Dian	16	L	27	RF	aa	LA	177	0	2	188	9	64	21	90	-81
Toups,Corey	16	R	23	2B	aa	KC	338	8	14	256	8	70	115	128	28
	17	R	24	2B	a/a	KC	387	6	11	223	8	65	82	123	-20
Tovar,Wilfredo	16	R	25	SS	aaa	MIN	450	1	25	226	6	86	47	123	31
	17	R	26	SS	aaa	STL	360	4	15	213	5	80	53	85	0
Towey,Cal	16	L	26	RF	a/a	LAA	450	9	11	217	11	61	95	109	-25
	17	L	27	1B	a/a	MIA	315	4	2	184	13	57	87	67	-55
Trahan,Blake	17	R	24	SS	aa	CIN	455	2	12	215	11	79	37	76	-6
Travis,Sam	16	R	23	1B	aaa	BOS	173	5	1	272	8	75	106	53	20
	17	R	24	1B	aaa	BOS	304	5	5	260	10	80	63	60	10
Trevino,Jose	17	R	25	C	aa	TEX	402	6	1	215	4	88	37	33	1
Trinkwon,Brandon	16	L	24	3B	aa	LA	270	3	4	202	9	83	44	80	10
Triunfel,Alberto	16	R	22	SS	a/a	TEX	293	1	3	168	4	77	36	62	-36
	17	R	23	SS	aa	LAA	301	3	3	225	5	76	45	68	-28
Triunfel,Carlos	16	R	26	2B	aaa	CIN	378	4	1	244	1	77	76	50	-12
Tromp,Jiandido	17	R	24	RF	a/a	PHI	465	16	8	250	5	71	112	84	11
Tucker,Cole	17	B	21	SS	aa	PIT	167	2	10	251	10	81	55	142	34
Tucker,Kyle	17	L	20	CF	aa	HOU	287	15	7	251	6	75	136	83	50
Tucker,Preston	16	L	26	LF	a/a	HOU	230	6	1	233	5	69	104	86	-3
	17	L	27	RF	aaa	HOU	492	15	1	186	7	73	80	73	-5
Tuiasosopo,Matt	16	R	30	1B	aaa	ATL	211	8	0	189	10	55	155	28	-26
Turner,Stuart	16	R	25	C	aa	MIN	322	4	4	206	8	75	75	57	-5
	17	R	26	C	aaa	CIN	59	0	0	199	4	71	0	18	-101
Turner,Trea	16	R	23	SS	aaa	WAS	331	5	23	285	10	77	94	164	52
Unroe,Riley	17	B	22	2B	aa	TAM	245	2	5	203	13	68	54	96	-27
Urena,Richard	16	B	20	SS	aa	TOR	124	0	0	262	3	84	69	96	26
	17	B	21	SS	aa	TOR	510	5	0	238	5	79	75	42	1
Urias,Luis	17	R	20	SS	aa	SD	442	3	7	294	13	85	48	89	32
Urrutia,Henry	16	L	29	RF	a/a	BAL	396	4	1	240	6	80	51	38	-12
Urshela,Giovanny	16	R	25	3B	aaa	CLE	468	7	0	246	3	86	59	36	10
	17	R	26	3B	aaa	CLE	297	5	0	234	5	84	52	34	1
Valaika,Pat	16	R	24	SS	a/a	COL	541	12	8	240	4	77	101	93	27
	17	R	25	SS	aaa	COL	45	1	0	240	6	74	76	73	-6
Valdespin,Jordany	16	L	29	2B	aaa	DET	293	2	8	196	5	76	45	100	-17
Valentin,Jesmuel	16	B	22	2B	a/a	PHI	446	9	4	252	9	80	71	90	24
	17	B	23	2B	aaa	PHI	96	1	0	205	5	81	35	26	-28
Valenzuela,Luis	17	L	24	2B	a/a	ATL	266	2	4	230	5	79	50	110	0
Valera,Breyvic	16	B	24	2B	a/a	STL	395	0	9	259	7	88	34	78	19
	17	B	25	2B	aaa	STL	424	6	9	273	7	91	57	92	53
Valle,Sebastian	16	R	26	C	aa	NYY	228	4	0	182	5	63	79	38	-62
Van Slyke,Scott	16	R	30	LF	aaa	LA	29	1	1	157	4	78	62	94	0
	17	R	31	1B	aaa	CIN	230	5	2	173	8	62	88	64	-44
VanMeter,Josh	16	L	21	3B	aa	SD	106	2	2	185	6	81	40	59	-12
	17	L	22	3B	aa	CIN	475	6	16	257	11	77	70	86	14
Vargas,Ildemaro	16	B	25	SS	a/a	ARI	521	5	16	264	6	92	50	108	53
	17	B	26	2B	aaa	ARI	487	6	5	250	4	90	63	88	46
Vargas,Kennys	16	B	26	1B	aaa	MIN	330	12	1	205	14	70	106	44	8
	17	B	27	1B	aaa	MIN	178	8	0	224	13	67	116	47	2
Varona,Dayron	16	R	28	RF	aaa	TAM	435	11	8	185	3	71	96	94	-1
	17	R	29	RF	aaa	TAM	71	2	2	216	5	65	99	136	-6
Vasquez,Danry	16	L	22	LF	aa	HOU	211	3	6	238	6	87	59	76	33
Vazquez,Christian	16	R	26	C	aaa	BOS	152	2	2	255	8	77	71	56	0

BATTER	yr	b	age	pos	lvl	org	ab	hr	sb	ba	bb%	ct%	px	sx	bpv
Vazquez,Jan	16	B	25	C	a/a	COL	205	1	5	207	8	78	55	81	0
	17	B	26	C	a/a	COL	206	6	2	262	8	74	79	71	-3
Velazquez,Andrew	17	B	23	SS	aa	TAM	374	7	15	209	7	66	80	119	-23
Verdugo,Alex	16	L	21	CF	aa	LA	433	5	8	285	8	87	63	87	44
Verdugo,Alex	16	L	20	CF	aa	LA	477	13	2	264	8	85	77	39	31
Vertigan,Brett	16	L	26	CF	aa	OAK	415	1	10	203	7	75	44	98	-20
	17	L	27	LF	aa	OAK	249	1	5	233	9	72	63	95	-11
Vidal,David	17	R	28	2B	a/a	MIA	461	9	1	218	8	76	72	46	-8
Vielma,Engelb	16	B	22	SS	aa	MIN	314	0	8	251	8	79	27	107	-10
	17	B	23	SS	a/a	MIN	415	0	3	220	9	79	35	67	-24
Villanueva,Christian	17	R	26	3B	aaa	SD	398	12	3	231	6	75	95	59	9
Vincej,Zach	16	R	25	SS	aa	CIN	399	3	7	259	6	75	68	86	-8
	17	R	26	SS	aaa	CIN	378	3	3	227	6	84	49	67	9
Vinicio,Jose	16	B	23	2B	a/a	BOS	228	2	6	249	3	80	37	106	-12
	17	B	24	2B	a/a	CHW	325	4	8	206	3	70	61	110	-32
Vogelbach,Daniel	16	L	24	1B	aaa	SEA	459	17	0	246	14	74	104	38	19
	17	L	25	1B	aaa	SEA	459	14	2	244	11	74	83	40	0
Voit,Luke	16	R	25	1B	aa	STL	482	14	1	252	8	79	85	25	24
	17	R	26	1B	aaa	STL	269	10	1	277	8	78	114	37	30
Vosler,Jason	16	L	23	3B	aa	CHC	92	1	0	220	7	68	82	27	-38
	17	L	24	3B	aa	CHC	452	19	1	218	10	70	102	63	1
Wade,LaMonte	17	L	23	LF	aa	MIN	424	6	8	278	14	83	63	98	40
Wade,Tyler	16	L	22	SS	aa	NYY	505	6	27	254	12	78	52	143	21
	17	L	23	SS	aaa	NYY	339	7	23	287	9	75	88	142	34
Walding,Mitch	16	L	24	3B	aa	PHI	70	3	1	186	11	62	99	67	-30
	17	L	25	3B	aa	PHI	351	22	1	204	9	57	168	71	3
Waldrop,Kyle	16	L	25	RF	aaa	CIN	325	5	3	227	5	79	72	59	2
	17	L	26	RF	aa	CIN	453	8	3	246	7	74	74	50	-15
Walker,Adam	16	R	25	LF	aaa	MIN	478	22	6	218	7	54	165	96	-7
	17	R	26	LF	a/a	CIN	294	14	3	170	5	54	153	76	-26
Walker,Christian	16	R	25	LF	aaa	BAL	504	18	1	240	6	70	110	46	-5
	17	R	26	1B	aaa	ARI	514	21	3	250	7	76	117	94	40
Walker,Keenyn	16	B	26	RF	aa	CHW	329	2	16	195	10	60	66	131	-46
Walker,Ryan	16	L	24	2B	aa	MIN	297	2	10	242	8	77	44	122	-4
	17	L	25	2B	a/a	MIN	379	3	11	215	10	76	49	122	3
Wallach,Chad	16	R	25	C	aa	CIN	200	8	0	224	15	73	110	23	17
	17	R	26	C	aaa	CIN	226	8	1	191	4	67	99	44	-30
Walsh,Colin	16	B	27	LF	aaa	OAK	201	3	0	222	14	64	89	49	-28
	17	B	28	2B	a/a	HOU	347	8	3	195	15	62	99	60	-24
Walters,Zachary	16	B	27	1B	aaa	LA	333	8	2	224	5	77	82	79	8
	17	B	28	1B	a/a	KC	136	1	1	164	3	70	44	60	-60
Ward,Drew	16	L	22	3B	aa	WAS	178	2	0	208	10	70	60	29	-41
	17	L	23	3B	aa	WAS	413	8	0	210	10	65	75	21	-52
Ward,Nelson	16	L	24	2B	aa	SD	453	5	26	196	10	68	53	111	-33
	17	L	25	2B	aa	SEA	264	1	7	226	7	66	44	81	-58
Washington,David	16	L	26	RF	a/a	STL	421	21	3	209	11	50	178	56	-19
	17	L	27	1B	aaa	BAL	368	15	6	206	6	53	126	78	-51
Wass,Wade	16	R	25	C	aa	LAA	127	1	4	168	12	55	38	95	-96
	17	R	26	DH	aa	LAA	191	9	8	223	10	56	143	114	-6
Watkins,Logan	16	L	27	2B	aaa	CHC	337	1	10	210	5	75	46	126	-11
	17	L	28	2B	a/a	DET	273	2	4	200	10	77	29	83	-21
Way,Bo	16	L	25	CF	aa	LAA	425	2	19	233	6	76	33	100	-26
	17	L	26	CF	a/a	LAA	364	1	16	205	5	78	25	103	-23
Weber,Garrett	16	R	27	2B	a/a	MIA	251	2	0	200	7	72	37	61	-47
Weeks,Drew	17	R	24	RF	aa	COL	471	15	11	236	7	76	90	83	15
Weiss,Erich	16	L	25	2B	aa	PIT	456	4	5	237	8	78	65	95	11
	17	L	26	2B	aaa	PIT	332	5	5	240	9	77	79	102	23
Wendle,Joe	16	L	26	2B	aaa	OAK	491	9	12	247	4	74	98	148	31
	17	L	27	2B	aaa	OAK	478	5	10	232	3	80	66	120	16
Westbrook,Jamie	16	R	21	2B	aa	ARI	435	5	9	256	5	85	56	81	23
	17	R	22	LF	aa	ARI	377	7	2	255	3	88	66	67	33
White,Max	17	L	24	LF	aa	COL	371	6	20	236	10	68	92	123	5
White,T.J.	16	R	24	3B	aa	MIN	197	0	7	194	6	74	39	152	-14
	17	R	25	3B	aa	MIN	366	12	2	251	8	75	112	67	29
White,Tyler	16	R	26	1B	aaa	HOU	174	10	1	196	6	79	102	61	29
	17	R	27	3B	aaa	HOU	436	15	4	224	6	69	93	67	-14
Wilkerson,Shannon	16	R	28	CF	aa	MIN	199	1	1	195	5	83	46	66	2
Wilkerson,Steve	17	B	25	3B	aa	BAL	245	5	4	239	7	73	54	61	-30
Wilkins,Andrew	16	L	28	RF	aaa	MIL	327	8	2	181	8	65	95	70	-24
Williams,Jackson	16	R	30	C	a/a	COL	236	1	0	164	6	79	37	37	-30
	17	R	31	C	a/a	PIT	189	1	0	162	7	72	23	22	-72
Williams,Justin	16	L	21	RF	aa	TAM	148	5	0	219	3	77	91	82	15
	17	L	22	RF	aa	TAM	366	12	5	274	8	79	93	85	33
Williams,Mason	16	L	25	CF	aaa	NYY	125	0	1	267	4	80	52	87	-1
	17	L	26	CF	aaa	NYY	399	2	16	228	6	80	27	105	-13
Williams,Matt	16	R	27	SS	aaa	STL	338	1	8	205	9	74	47	82	-19
	17	R	28	SS	aaa	PHI	274	5	8	195	6	82	58	90	17
Williams,Nick	16	L	23	LF	aaa	PHI	497	14	6	246	4	69	119	124	18
	17	L	24	RF	aaa	PHI	282	14	4	250	5	63	142	88	2
Williamson,Mac	16	R	26	LF	aaa	SF	208	7	2	217	4	69	112	67	-4
	17	R	27	RF	aaa	SF	351	9	3	196	5	65	90	70	-34
Wilson,Jacob	16	R	26	3B	a/a	STL	310	10	2	178	7	68	98	53	-18
	17	R	27	3B	aa	STL	431	13	2	209	8	74	80	51	-5
Wilson,Kenneth	16	R	26	CF	a/a	MIA	428	2	25	222	10	73	53	119	-9
	17	R	27	CF	a/a	OAK	296	2	11	194	6	68	37	107	-52
Winker,Jesse	16	L	23	RF	aaa	CIN	380	3	0	284	13	82	56	16	5
	17	L	24	RF	aaa	CIN	299	2	2	277	10	82	58	29	4
Wisdom,Patrick	17	R	26	3B	aaa	STL	456	23	2	203	6	63	137	52	-9
Witte,Jantzen	16	R	26	3B	a/a	BOS	396	3	4	246	8	82	76	63	25
	17	R	27	1B	aaa	BOS	244	2	2	220	11	76	52	64	-12
Wong,Joey	16	L	28	SS	aaa	COL	257	1	1	195	10	77	41	54	-20
Wong,Kean	16	L	21	2B	aa	TAM	446	4	8	249	6	82	50	74	3
	17	L	22	2B	a/a	TAM	422	4	15	240	7	77	54	77	-10
Wood,Eric	16	R	24	3B	a/a	PIT	402	12	4	216	9	76	92	88	26
	17	R	25	3B	aaa	PIT	416	13	6	212	9	67	112	111	11
Woodward,Trent	16	B	24	C	aa	HOU	48	1	0	213	7	71	96	12	-20
	17	B	25	3B	a/a	HOU	157	3	0	207	9	62	75	43	-58
Wren,Kyle	16	L	25	LF	aa	MIL	398	2	23	281	11	79	44	134	16
	17	L	26	LF	aaa	MIL	476	4	17	227	7	80	48	130	14
Wynns,Austin	16	R	26	C	a/a	BAL	91	1	1	216	6	82	74	66	22
	17	R	27	C	aa	BAL	370	8	1	219	10	78	52	48	-10
Yarbrough,Alex	16	B	25	2B	a/a	LAA	524	3	9	223	4	71	64	76	-33
	17	B	26	SS	aa	MIA	364	3	4	201	7	65	60	97	-44
Yastrzemski,Mike	16	L	26	RF	a/a	BAL	466	12	11	201	9	71	90	107	9
	17	L	27	RF	a/a	BAL	354	12	2	213	9	67	92	86	-12
Ynoa,Rafael	16	B	29	2B	aaa	COL	482	2	5	213	6	80	54	76	-2
Young,Chesny	16	R	24	2B	aa	CHC	491	3	12	265	8	85	48	65	16
	17	R	25	2B	aaa	CHC	421	5	1	211	6	80	33	60	-21
Zagunis,Mark	16	R	23	LF	a/a	CHC	358	8	4	255	10	75	100	93	31
	17	R	24	LF	aaa	CHC	330	10	3	225	14	67	102	57	-2
Zehner,Zack	17	R	25	LF	aa	NYY	431	12	7	237	12	67	96	89	-5
Zimmer,Bradley	16	L	24	CF	a/a	CLE	468	13	32	229	12	61	121	133	5
	17	L	25	CF	aaa	CLE	126	4	7	266	8	65	148	129	36
Zunino,Mike	16	R	25	C	aaa	SEA	280	13	0	236	8	70	117	30	1

PITCHER	yr	t	age	lvl	org	ip	era	whip	bf/g	ctl	dom	cmd	hr/9	h%	s%	bpv
Acevedo,Doming	17	R	23	a/a	NYY	92	3.68	1.33	23.8	2.7	7.6	2.9	1.2	32	77	72
Achter,A.J.	16	R	28	aaa	LAA	46	3.89	1.09	6.2	2.8	5.0	1.8	1.7	21	73	30
Adams,Austin	16	R	25	aa	LAA	41	4.26	1.53	5.6	5.7	11.1	1.9	0.5	34	72	99
Adams,Austin L	17	R	26	aaa	WAS	59	2.84	1.62	6.0	6.2	11.0	1.8	0.4	36	83	98
Adams,Chance	16	R	22	aa	NYY	70	3.01	1.01	20.5	3.4	8.1	2.4	1.0	21	75	87
	17	R	23	a/a	NYY	150	3.41	1.27	22.8	3.8	7.0	1.9	1.0	27	77	60
Adams,Spencer	16	R	20	aa	CHW	55	4.39	1.34	25.6	1.7	3.9	2.4	0.4	32	66	59
	17	R	21	aa	CHW	153	6.03	1.65	26.2	2.7	6.0	2.3	1.5	36	66	30
Additon,Nick	16	L	29	aaa	BAL	80	6.30	1.90	23.7	3.2	4.1	1.3	1.3	37	68	-4
	17	L	30	aa	COL	26	4.42	1.82	23.8	4.2	6.2	1.5	0.6	38	76	39
Adkins,Hunter	16	R	26	a/a	MIA	84	7.55	1.77	14.3	4.5	5.8	1.3	1.6	33	59	6
	17	R	27	a/a	TAM	67	6.58	1.88	12.1	5.3	4.6	0.9	1.5	33	67	-7
Adleman,Timothy	16	R	29	aaa	CIN	57	3.76	1.51	24.6	2.0	4.8	2.4	1.0	34	78	39
Alaniz,Ruben	16	R	25	a/a	DET	74	3.59	1.65	6.3	4.0	7.0	1.8	0.1	37	77	69
	17	R	26	a/a	DET	69	4.54	1.80	7.6	4.3	7.6	1.8	1.3	37	78	34
Alcantara,Raul	16	R	24	a/a	OAK	136	4.52	1.44	23.1	2.1	5.6	2.7	0.8	34	70	60
Alcantara,Sandy	17	R	22	aa	STL	125	5.43	1.60	22.1	3.9	6.3	1.6	1.0	33	67	38
Alcantara,Victor	16	R	23	aa	LAA	111	5.76	1.70	17.3	4.9	5.6	1.1	0.8	33	66	29
	17	R	24	a/a	DET	75	4.84	1.79	8.8	6.0	7.1	1.2	0.1	35	71	61
Alexander,Tyler	16	L	22	aa	DET	34	3.73	1.30	23.6	1.1	4.9	4.6	1.1	32	75	89
	17	L	23	aa	DET	138	6.32	1.68	23.0	1.5	6.4	4.1	1.5	39	64	67
Allard,Kolby	17	L	20	aa	ATL	150	4.34	1.49	24.0	3.0	7.2	2.4	0.8	35	72	68
Almonte,Miguel	16	R	23	a/a	KC	76	7.14	1.94	11.3	5.4	7.0	1.3	1.1	37	63	27
	17	R	24	a/a	KC	47	2.31	1.39	12.4	2.6	8.0	3.1	0.6	35	86	92
Almonte,Yency	16	R	22	aa	COL	30	4.58	1.53	26.1	5.3	5.2	1.0	1.8	25	77	2
	17	R	23	a/a	COL	111	4.15	1.63	22.5	4.6	5.9	1.3	1.3	31	78	22
Altavilla,Dan	16	R	24	aa	SEA	57	2.53	1.26	5.4	3.6	8.9	2.5	0.6	30	82	96
Alvarado,Carlos	16	R	27	aa	SF	19	4.05	0.89	4.5	0.0	8.9	0.0	1.0	30	57	0
	17	R	28	aa	SF	59	4.75	1.72	6.2	5.2	8.2	1.6	1.0	35	74	50
Alvarez,R.J.	16	R	25	a/a	CHC	25	8.69	2.10	5.9	4.5	9.8	2.2	0.8	47	57	62
	17	R	26	aaa	TEX	45	5.67	1.75	4.5	6.6	8.9	1.3	0.5	34	66	69
Ames,Jeff	16	R	25	aa	TAM	63	3.36	1.51	5.7	6.0	7.3	1.2	1.1	27	82	45
	17	R	26	aaa	TAM	63	5.65	1.74	6.3	5.7	9.2	1.6	1.1	35	69	56
Anderson,Drew	17	R	23	a/a	PHI	114	4.30	1.25	21.2	3.4	6.4	1.9	1.3	26	70	46
Anderson,Isaac	16	R	23	aa	LA	22	8.67	1.76	19.8	2.4	5.7	2.4	1.5	38	50	23
	17	R	24	aa	LA	45	10.43	2.03	18.3	3.5	5.4	1.5	1.8	39	47	-8
Anderson,John	16	L	28	a/a	TOR	115	8.17	2.28	19.5	4.0	5.8	1.4	1.5	43	65	-4
Anderson,Justin	17	R	25	aa	LAA	59	7.20	1.76	6.4	4.9	4.7	1.0	1.3	32	60	3
Anderson,Matt	16	R	25	aa	SEA	62	4.94	1.55	6.6	2.5	6.9	2.8	0.4	38	66	82
Anderson,Tanner	17	R	24	aa	PIT	133	4.62	1.52	19.3	2.4	5.2	2.1	0.5	35	69	56
Antolin,Dustin	16	R	27	aaa	TOR	53	3.04	1.65	5.2	5.6	8.3	1.5	0.8	33	84	60
	17	R	28	aaa	WAS	50	8.77	2.31	10.7	6.7	5.9	0.9	0.7	41	60	18
Appel,Mark	16	R	25	aaa	PHI	38	6.85	2.00	23.1	5.5	6.7	1.2	1.1	38	66	22
	17	R	26	aaa	PHI	82	7.13	2.11	23.8	6.4	5.4	0.8	1.3	36	67	0
Aquino,Jayson	16	L	24	a/a	BAL	128	5.07	1.67	23.1	2.7	5.1	1.9	0.7	36	69	39
	17	L	25	aaa	BAL	115	5.87	1.80	25.2	3.8	5.9	1.5	1.1	37	68	24
Archer,Tristan	16	R	26	aa	MIL	82	5.26	1.50	7.2	1.2	7.2	6.0	0.6	39	64	141
	17	R	27	a/a	MIL	71	6.12	1.79	6.7	2.9	6.5	2.2	1.1	39	66	40
Armenteros,Roge	16	R	22	aa	HOU	18	2.23	1.24	24.8	1.9	5.7	3.0	0.6	31	84	82
	17	R	23	a/a	HOU	124	2.14	1.07	20.1	2.6	9.4	3.7	0.6	29	83	129
Armstrong,Shawn	16	R	26	aaa	CLE	49	2.61	1.37	4.4	5.9	10.2	1.7	0.0	30	79	112
Aro,Jonathan	16	R	26	aaa	SEA	36	2.74	1.18	6.0	2.4	5.1	2.1	0.5	28	78	67
	17	R	27	aaa	SEA	43	3.94	1.16	6.8	2.5	8.2	3.3	1.2	28	71	89
Ascher,Steve	16	L	23	aa	TAM	46	5.11	1.48	7.6	3.5	6.1	1.7	1.0	31	67	42
Ash,Brett	16	R	25	aa	SEA	135	6.04	1.87	25.4	2.2	3.3	1.5	0.7	39	67	12
	17	R	26	a/a	SEA	81	9.50	2.17	19.2	3.3	4.2	1.3	1.7	41	56	-21
Asher,Alec	16	R	25	a/a	PHI	59	3.40	1.10	25.5	1.4	5.2	3.8	1.1	27	74	83
	17	R	26	aaa	BAL	50	6.58	1.95	24.0	3.3	5.3	1.6	1.4	39	68	7
Astin,Barrett	16	R	25	aa	CIN	103	3.52	1.25	11.4	2.6	7.2	2.7	1.1	29	76	72
	17	R	26	aaa	CIN	49	8.13	2.33	9.6	4.6	6.7	1.5	1.0	45	64	18
Avila,Andres	16	R	26	aa	OAK	73	4.39	1.42	7.7	2.7	7.4	2.7	1.1	33	72	65
Aviles,Robbie	16	R	25	aa	CLE	55	6.02	1.89	8.1	3.3	4.4	1.3	1.0	38	69	8
	17	R	26	a/a	CLE	61	4.98	1.42	6.3	2.6	3.9	1.5	0.8	30	65	29
Baker,Corey	16	R	27	a/a	STL	130	7.12	1.89	21.1	3.9	6.2	1.6	2.0	37	66	-1
	17	R	28	aa	STL	40	3.54	1.64	7.1	2.8	5.3	1.8	0.6	36	79	45
Baldonado,Albert	16	L	23	aa	NYM	40	5.86	1.90	5.6	5.1	9.1	1.8	1.2	40	71	47
	17	L	24	a/a	NYM	60	5.97	1.61	5.3	4.8	8.4	1.8	1.6	32	66	39
Ball,Trey	17	L	23	aa	BOS	125	6.87	2.03	24.2	4.4	6.1	1.4	1.4	39	68	8
Balog,Alex	16	R	24	aa	COL	55	7.58	2.11	24.5	4.0	3.9	1.0	2.3	37	68	-46
Banda,Anthony	16	L	23	a/a	ARI	150	3.49	1.47	24.7	3.3	7.7	2.3	0.7	34	77	74
	17	L	24	aaa	ARI	122	5.70	1.51	24.0	3.6	7.1	2.0	1.1	33	63	49
Banks,Tanner	17	L	26	aa	CHW	55	9.25	2.18	23.0	3.2	5.5	1.7	1.9	42	58	-11
Banuelos,Manuel	16	L	25	a/a	ATL	49	6.90	2.09	18.4	6.2	6.3	1.0	1.3	37	68	8
	17	L	26	aaa	LAA	95	5.11	1.73	11.1	4.4	6.7	1.5	0.3	37	69	55
Barbato,John	16	R	24	aaa	NYY	48	3.81	1.55	6.81	4.9	7.7	1.6	0.8	32	77	57
	17	R	25	aaa	PIT	39	4.43	1.42	6.18	3.3	7.3	2.2	2.4	28	81	18
Barbosa,Andrew	16	L	29	a/a	NYM	44	2.63	1.19	21.9	3.5	6.6	1.9	0.4	26	79	76
	17	L	30	aaa	MIL	66	6.34	1.63	8.2	4.0	6.6	1.7	1.5	33	63	24
Bard,Luke	17	R	27	a/a	MIN	65	4.40	1.77	7.31	3.9	10.1	2.6	1.0	42	77	76
Barker,Brandon	16	R	24	aa	BAL	145	4.93	1.50	23.3	2.9	5.4	1.9	1.3	32	71	28
	17	R	25	a/a	BAL	123	5.97	1.76	21.6	3.9	6.8	1.7	0.9	37	66	41
Barlow,Scott	16	R	24	aa	LA	124	5.30	1.64	23.1	3.7	6.2	1.7	0.8	35	68	42
	17	R	25	a/a	LA	140	3.92	1.22	21.7	3.6	8.5	2.3	1.1	27	71	78
Barnes,Daniel	16	R	27	a/a	TOR	61	1.07	0.61	5.13	1.0	9.0	8.9	0.6	19	91	247
Barnette,Tyler	16	R	24	a/a	CHW	84	7.26	1.87	10.6	4.3	5.5	1.3	0.9	37	60	22
Barria,Jaime	17	R	21	a/a	LAA	76	3.38	1.26	20.7	2.0	6.4	3.2	0.9	31	76	81
Bartsch,Kyle	16	L	25	aa	KC	46	5.17	1.80	8.51	3.4	5.1	1.5	1.1	37	73	15
Bawcom,Logan	17	R	29	aaa	OAK	71	4.33	1.68	6.8	4.3	5.7	1.3	0.7	34	75	37
Baxendale,D.J.	16	R	26	a/a	MIN	116	3.87	1.43	13.3	2.0	5.9	2.9	0.5	35	73	77
	17	R	27	a/a	MIN	76	3.99	1.65	9.7	2.7	5.0	1.9	0.3	37	75	50
Beal,Evan	16	R	23	a/a	KC	58	4.74	1.46	8.0	3.2	6.0	1.8	1.6	30	73	26
Beck,Chris	16	R	26	aaa	CHW	66	5.33	1.84	14.1	3.9	5.6	1.4	0.8	38	71	27
Beck,Landon	17	R	25	aa	STL	41	5.04	1.70	5.0	4.0	7.6	1.9	0.8	37	71	55
Beede,Tyler	16	R	23	aa	SF	147	3.82	1.51	26.6	3.5	7.1	2.0	0.6	34	75	67
	17	R	24	aaa	SF	109	5.74	1.66	25.7	3.3	5.7	1.7	1.0	35	66	31
Beeks,Jalen	16	L	23	aa	BOS	65	6.06	1.76	23.0	4.0	6.5	1.6	0.9	37	66	38
	17	L	24	a/a	BOS	145	4.69	1.48	24.0	3.8	7.7	2.0	1.0	33	70	60
Bell,Chadwick	16	L	27	aaa	DET	98	4.87	1.76	13.6	4.7	5.9	1.3	0.5	35	71	42
Bencomo,Omar	16	R	27	a/a	MIN	84	5.29	1.71	15.9	2.7	5.1	1.9	0.9	37	70	31
	17	R	28	a/a	MIA	93	6.91	1.78	19.4	2.7	7.0	2.6	1.7	39	64	31
Berg,Dave	16	R	23	aa	CHC	43	7.41	2.04	6.1	2.3	5.4	2.3	0.0	44	60	59
Bergjans,Tommy	17	R	25	a/a	PHI	56	8.58	1.79	19.8	2.9	5.9	2.0	2.9	35	57	-22
Bergman,Christia	16	R	28	aaa	COL	52	5.57	1.65	23.1	2.5	4.0	1.6	2.1	32	73	-16
	17	R	29	aaa	SEA	86	6.95	1.75	24.6	2.1	5.1	2.4	0.9	39	59	40
Bernardino,Brenn	17	L	25	aa	CIN	40	7.52	2.04	5.2	5.3	7.9	1.5	1.9	39	66	9
Berrios,Jose	16	R	22	aaa	MIN	111	3.39	1.13	25.9	3.0	8.4	2.8	0.8	28	72	97
	17	R	23	aaa	MIN	40	1.71	1.00	25.3	2.0	7.1	3.6	0.6	26	87	111
Berry,Timothy	16	L	25	aa	SD	69	9.96	2.53	19.4	6.1	5.4	0.9	1.5	43	60	-18
	17	L	26	a/a	BAL	49	4.48	2.15	6.8	8.7	8.7	1.0	0.2	38	78	63
Bethancourt,Chris	17	R	26	aaa	SD	42	8.73	2.09	6.0	6.8	3.9	0.6	1.6	33	59	-22
Biddle,Jesse	17	L	26	aa	ATL	50	4.43	1.69	8.3	3.6	8.0	2.2	0.7	39	74	66
Bieber,Shane	17	R	22	aa	CLE	54	2.99	1.31	25.0	0.9	6.3	7.2	0.4	36	77	171
Binford,Christian	16	R	24	a/a	KC	141	6.49	1.61	25.0	3.0	5.2	1.8	1.3	34	61	20
	17	R	25	a/a	KC	147	8.36	1.92	25.9	3.0	5.6	1.9	1.9	38	58	-2
Bird,Kyle	16	L	23	aa	TAM	49	3.49	1.40	6.5	3.1	6.1	1.9	0.8	31	77	55
	17	L	24	a/a	TAM	75	3.80	1.49	6.0	3.9	7.3	1.9	0.4	33	74	71
Blach,Ty	16	L	26	aaa	SF	163	4.13	1.32	25.9	2.2	5.1	2.3	0.5	31	68	64
Black,Corey	16	R	25	a/a	CHC	53	5.12	1.78	5.1	6.4	8.7	1.4	0.2	36	69	75
Blackburn,Clayto	16	R	23	aaa	SF	136	4.92	1.42	23.1	2.3	5.8	2.5	1.0	32	67	53
	17	R	24	aaa	TEX	96	6.09	1.57	21.1	2.6	6.0	2.3	0.5	36	59	61
Blackburn,Paul	16	R	23	aa	SEA	143	4.25	1.40	23.2	2.2	5.5	2.5	0.6	33	70	64
	17	R	24	aaa	OAK	80	3.58	1.32	22.0	2.9	5.0	1.7	0.7	29	74	50
Blackford,Alex	16	R	26	aa	LAA	111	4.38	1.36	21.2	4.4	6.9	1.6	1.3	26	72	44
	17	R	27	a/a	LAA	67	8.31	1.78	20.6	4.9	5.8	1.2	1.5	33	53	9
Blackmar,Mark	16	R	24	aa	WAS	57	7.29	1.60	28.0	3.7	3.2	0.9	1.3	30	54	-4
Blair,Aaron	16	R	24	aaa	ATL	72	5.84	1.75	25.2	4.3	7.8	1.8	0.5	38	65	61
	17	R	25	aaa	ATL	127	6.58	1.80	23.5	4.5	6.3	1.4	0.8	36	62	36
Blazek,Michael	17	R	28	aaa	MIL	85	4.29	1.62	14.5	3.6	5.4	1.5	0.6	34	74	39
Bleich,Jeremy	16	L	29	a/a	PHI	42	6.12	2.10	6.9	3.6	3.9	1.1	1.3	39	73	-13
	17	L	30	a/a	LA	62	4.98	1.53	7.1	2.1	5.7	2.7	0.7	36	67	60
Bleier,Richard	16	L	29	aaa	NYY	58	6.08	1.87	22.7	2.2	2.9	1.4	0.5	39	66	12
Bolsinger,Michael	16	R	28	aaa	TOR	54	7.07	2.00	13.8	4.2	7.9	1.9	1.5	41	66	27
	17	R	29	aaa	TOR	48	2.91	1.51	12.9	1.9	5.9	3.1	0.6	36	82	74
Bonilla,Lisalverto	16	R	26	a/a	LA	111	5.19	1.58	15.7	3.2	7.7	2.4	0.6	37	66	73
	17	R	27	aaa	CIN	63	4.89	1.67	15.6	3.8	6.8	1.8	1.2	35	73	37
Borucki,Ryan	17	L	23	a/a	TOR	52	2.42	1.07	25.4	1.7	7.1	4.2	0.5	29	79	124
Boscan,Wilfredo	16	R	27	aaa	ATL	93	5.58	1.82	21.6	2.3	4.6	2.0	0.7	39	69	33
	17	R	28	aaa	NYM	126	6.28	1.99	23.3	3.4	4.2	1.2	0.9	39	68	7
Bostick,Akeem	17	R	22	aa	HOU	80	5.54	1.62	19.8	2.2	5.9	2.7	0.9	37	66	55
Boyd,Matt	16	L	25	aaa	DET	64	3.19	1.38	24.4	2.9	6.2	2.1	0.9	31	80	56
	17	L	26	aaa	DET	51	4.17	1.20	25.6	2.7	7.2	2.7	1.7	26	73	57
Bracewell,Ben	16	R	26	aa	OAK	88	2.62	1.25	12.4	2.7	4.6	1.7	0.4	28	80	56
	17	R	27	a/a	OAK	113	6.73	1.84	18.7	3.8	4.4	1.1	0.7	36	62	19
Bradford,Chase	16	R	27	aaa	NYM	66	4.93	1.61	5.2	1.7	5.9	3.4	0.6	38	69	76
Bradley,Archie	16	R	24	aaa	ARI	41	2.18	1.14	23.0	3.8	8.6	2.3	0.0	28	79	114
Bradley,Jed	16	L	26	a/a	ATL	108	4.37	1.69	13.9	3.8	7.5	1.9	0.2	38	72	72
Brady,Michael	16	R	29	a/a	WAS	81	4.51	1.44	19.2	1.8	5.8	3.2	1.0	34	71	66
	17	R	30	aaa	OAK	53	4.25	1.22	12.7	1.1	6.1	5.4	0.9	32	67	121
Bragg,Sam	16	R	23	aa	OAK	65	4.93	1.32	7.5	2.6	7.7	3.0	1.2	32	65	75
	17	R	24	aa	OAK	68	3.59	1.40	6.4	2.1	5.9	2.8	0.5	34	75	76
Brasier,Ryan	16	R	29	aaa	OAK	61	5.44	1.52	5.7	3.4	7.5	2.2	1.1	34	66	54
Brault,Steven	16	L	24	aaa	PIT	71	5.40	1.68	20.0	4.7	8.1	1.7	0.9	36	68	56
	17	L	25	aaa	PIT	120	2.69	1.30	23.6	3.7	6.4	1.7	0.4	28	80	68
Bray,Tyler	17	R	26	a/a	STL	58	4.92	1.86	6.8	5.0	6.1	1.2	0.4	37	72	43
Brebbia,John	16	R	26	a/a	STL	68	6.17	1.75	7.2	2.7	7.5	2.8	1.3	40	66	53
Bremer,Tyler	16	R	27	a/a	MIA	73	4.97	1.64	8.0	4.4	5.5	1.2	0.8	32	70	32
Brennan,Brandon	16	R	25	aa	CHW	66	9.97	2.12	13.5	4.4	6.2	1.4	0.8	42	50	24
	17	R	26	a/a	CHW	60	6.36	1.91	6.7	5.2	6.9	1.3	0.2	39	64	54
Brewer,Colten	17	R	25	a/a	NYY	51	4.82	1.68	6.6	3.0	7.8	2.6	0.5	40	71	76
Brice,Austin	16	R	24	a/a	MIA	102	3.71	1.31	13.2	2.9	6.4	2.2	0.6	31	72	71
Bridwell,Parker	16	R	25	a/a	BAL	66	5.73	1.64	13.3	4.4	5.7	1.3	1.5	31	68	12
	17	R	26	a/a	LAA	40	6.21	1.58	16.1	2.3	6.8	3.0	1.7	36	64	45
Brinley,Ryan	17	R	24	aa	WAS	45	5.85	1.58	5.35	2.7	6.6	2.4	0.4	37	61	70
Britton,Drake	16	L	27	aaa	DET	41	6.76	1.99	5.38	5.5	2.7	0.5	0.9	34	65	-10
Brooks,Aaron	16	R	26	aaa	CHC	16	9.33	1.94	15.5	2.3	5.4	2.3	3.2	37	57	-35
	17	R	27	aaa	MIL	146	6.93	1.74	25.5	1.8	5.2	2.9	2.1	37	65	12
Brooks,Craig	17	R	25	aa	CHC	40	6.14	1.75	5.58	7.3	10.7	1.5	0.3	36	62	92
Broussard,Geoff	16	R	26	a/a	LAA	62	7.92	1.78	6.51	3.7	7.6	2.0	2.0	37	58	19
	17	R	27	a/a	CIN	52	5.28	1.67	5.22	3.2	6.0	1.9	1.6	35	73	19
Broussard,Joe	16	R	25	a/a	LA	44	2.62	1.23	5.09	2.4	9.1	3.8	0.5	33	80	123
	17	R	26	a/a	LA	63	3.98	1.38	5.54	2.7	8.4	3.1	1.1	33	75	81
Brown,Dennis	16	R	26	a/a	CLE	137	6.88	1.75	22.3	3.3	6.1	1.9	1.4	36	62	23
	17	R	27	a/a	CLE	77	6.73	1.67	11.2	2.9	5.3	1.8	1.4	35	61	18
Brown,Mitch	17	R	23	aa	CLE	48	8.33	1.90	6.91	7.9	5.7	0.7	0.7	30	53	30

PITCHER	yr	t	age	lvl	org	ip	era	whip	bf/g	ctl	dom	cmd	hr/9	h%	s%	bpv
Browning,Wil	17	R	29	aaa	TOR	58	11.24	2.61	8.02	7.2	6.7	0.9	1.3	44	55	-2
Broyles,Shane	16	R	25	aa	COL	51	9.16	1.97	6.78	6.9	9.0	1.3	1.1	37	52	42
	17	R	26	a/a	COL	55	2.75	1.22	4.6	3.1	9.4	3.0	1.8	28	89	75
Brubaker,Jonatha	17	R	24	aa	PIT	130	6.08	1.81	23.1	3.4	6.0	1.8	0.7	39	66	39
Buchanan,David	16	R	27	aaa	PHI	167	6.39	1.64	27.7	2.6	4.1	1.6	1.3	34	62	8
Buchanan,Jake	16	R	27	aaa	CHC	141	5.37	1.62	26.1	2.6	5.3	2.0	0.5	36	65	51
	17	R	28	aaa	ARI	106	5.21	1.57	22.1	2.5	4.6	1.8	0.7	34	67	36
Buehler,Walker	17	R	23	a/a	LA	72	4.41	1.24	12.8	2.9	10.5	3.6	0.8	33	65	121
Bundy,Bobby	16	R	26	a/a	BAL	50	4.87	1.64	6.03	3.8	6.4	1.7	1.0	34	72	38
Burdi,Zack	16	R	21	a/a	CHW	64	3.56	1.20	6.13	5.8	11.7	2.0	0.6	24	71	116
	17	R	22	aaa	CHW	33	4.64	1.53	5	4.8	12.4	2.6	0.6	39	69	113
Burgos,Hiram	16	R	29	aaa	MIL	143	5.63	1.82	24.6	3.9	5.4	1.4	0.9	37	69	23
	17	R	30	a/a	MIL	62	8.66	2.04	16.8	3.4	6.9	2.0	2.4	41	61	-6
Burnes,Corbin	17	R	23	aa	MIL	86	3.22	1.26	21.9	2.4	7.6	3.2	0.3	33	74	105
Burrows,Beau	17	R	21	aa	DET	76	5.70	1.61	22.5	3.9	7.5	1.9	0.6	36	64	62
Busenitz,Alan	16	R	26	a/a	MIN	61	4.91	1.54	5.91	2.4	6.2	2.6	0.5	36	67	68
Butler,Eddie	16	R	25	aaa	COL	89	6.34	1.66	26.6	2.9	2.6	0.9	1.3	32	63	-13
	17	R	26	aaa	CHC	46	2.53	1.53	24.8	2.5	4.8	1.9	0.2	35	83	56
Buttrey,Ty	16	R	23	aa	BOS	79	5.75	1.82	11.1	5.5	5.0	0.9	0.7	33	68	22
	17	R	24	a/a	BOS	64	6.85	1.77	7.31	5.2	8.4	1.6	0.5	38	59	64
Cabrera,Genesis	17	L	21	aa	TAM	65	4.36	1.74	24.6	3.8	6.4	1.7	0.9	37	76	39
Cabrera,Mauricio	16	R	23	aa	ATL	34	4.60	1.48	5.79	6.6	8.3	1.3	0.0	28	65	90
	17	R	24	a/a	ATL	40	9.54	2.28	5.37	11.0	6.9	0.6	0.3	33	54	47
Callahan,Jamie	17	R	23	a/a	NYM	52	3.58	1.43	5.39	3.3	10.2	3.1	0.8	37	77	103
Camarena,Daniel	16	L	24	a/a	NYY	136	5.63	1.48	21.6	1.7	6.2	3.5	1.3	35	64	64
	17	L	25	a/a	NYY	118	5.28	1.59	23.7	2.7	4.9	1.8	0.9	34	68	32
Campos,Leonel	16	R	29	aaa	SD	50	4.78	1.73	6.15	5.6	8.6	1.5	0.4	36	71	71
	17	R	30	aaa	TOR	33	2.87	1.46	5.38	5.0	8.0	1.6	0.9	29	84	60
Campos,Vicente	16	R	24	a/a	ARI	83	3.74	1.31	22.9	2.2	5.7	2.6	0.1	32	69	86
Caramo,Yender	16	R	25	a/a	KC	118	3.14	1.29	13.8	1.8	4.2	2.3	0.5	30	76	57
	17	R	26	aaa	KC	84	6.70	1.74	15.3	1.4	2.6	1.9	1.4	36	63	-3
Carasiti,Matt	16	R	25	a/a	COL	46	2.97	1.08	4.08	2.0	6.9	3.4	1.5	25	82	78
	17	R	26	aaa	CHC	50	3.81	1.64	4.82	4.4	10.0	2.3	0.4	39	76	93
Carle,Shane	16	R	25	aaa	COL	111	7.72	2.01	19.9	2.9	5.3	1.8	1.0	41	61	19
	17	R	26	aaa	COL	62	7.51	1.93	8.17	3.6	5.3	1.5	1.6	38	63	-1
Carpenter,Ryan	16	L	26	aaa	COL	69	10.87	2.35	13.7	3.7	6.4	1.7	3.0	43	57	-43
	17	L	27	aaa	COL	156	5.94	1.64	25.8	2.6	6.6	2.6	1.6	36	67	37
Carpenter,Tyler	16	R	24	aa	LAA	71	7.63	1.88	22.3	2.3	5.4	2.3	0.9	41	58	37
	17	R	25	aa	LAA	71	6.34	1.74	23	2.9	4.3	1.5	1.0	36	63	16
Carroll,Cody	17	R	25	aa	NYY	47	3.98	1.53	7.92	4.8	9.3	1.9	1.2	33	78	63
Carter,Will	16	R	23	aa	NYY	43	6.53	1.75	24.6	4.3	5.1	1.2	0.3	36	60	38
	17	R	24	aa	NYY	47	4.77	1.76	14.3	2.8	3.7	1.3	0.9	36	74	10
Case,Andrew	17	R	24	a/a	TOR	48	3.25	1.32	5.48	2.7	4.1	1.5	0.8	28	78	35
Cash,Ralston	16	R	25	a/a	LA	69	3.67	1.36	6.27	4.2	9.0	2.1	0.3	32	72	96
	17	R	26	a/a	SEA	49	6.39	1.84	6.34	3.9	9.9	2.5	0.9	43	65	74
Casilla,Jose	16	R	27	a/a	SF	53	4.77	1.80	6.95	3.5	4.7	1.4	0.9	36	75	19
Casimiro,Ranfi	17	R	25	aa	PHI	45	4.52	1.42	9.61	2.5	5.2	2.1	1.2	31	72	35
Castellani,Ryan	17	R	21	aa	COL	157	7.29	1.65	26.1	3.0	6.1	2.0	1.4	35	56	28
Castillo,Diego	17	R	23	a/a	TAM	72	3.55	1.26	5.73	2.7	9.9	3.7	0.4	35	71	129
Castillo,Fabio	16	R	27	a/a	SD	78	5.40	1.70	25.1	4.0	6.2	1.5	1.2	34	70	27
	17	R	28	a/a	LA	91	5.15	1.56	16	3.4	6.7	2.0	1.1	34	69	46
Castillo,Lendy	16	R	27	aa	CLE	51	8.13	1.92	5.71	5.4	7.0	1.3	0.9	37	56	32
Castillo,Luis	17	R	25	aa	CIN	80	4.34	1.38	24.1	1.8	7.7	4.2	0.9	35	70	102
Castro,Simon	16	R	28	aaa	COL	53	5.14	1.60	4.71	2.4	6.8	2.8	1.3	37	71	52
	17	R	29	aaa	OAK	38	4.34	1.42	4.88	5.5	10.6	1.9	0.8	31	70	92
Caughel,Lindsey	17	R	27	aa	SEA	158	4.89	1.44	24.9	2.4	5.4	2.3	1.3	32	69	38
Cessa,Luis	16	R	24	aaa	NYY	77	4.43	1.43	21.9	3.0	6.8	2.2	1.4	31	74	45
	17	R	25	aaa	NYY	78	4.83	1.58	24.6	3.3	6.4	1.9	1.2	34	72	37
Chacin,Alejandro	16	R	23	aa	CIN	61	2.65	1.57	5.12	4.5	10.0	2.2	0.5	37	84	93
	17	R	24	aaa	CIN	69	3.31	1.51	6.82	3.8	7.1	1.9	0.7	33	79	61
Chaffee,Ryan	16	R	28	a/a	MIA	47	5.99	2.00	7.26	5.3	6.0	1.1	0.4	39	68	35
Chapman,Jaye	16	R	29	a/a	TAM	54	5.64	1.36	4.23	2.9	8.2	2.8	1.0	33	59	78
	17	R	30	a/a	TEX	36	10.13	2.30	6.09	6.2	4.7	0.8	1.7	38	56	-26
Chapman,Kevin	16	L	28	aaa	HOU	61	5.85	1.82	5.55	4.2	8.8	2.1	0.9	40	68	60
Chargois,J.T.	16	R	26	a/a	MIN	47	1.87	1.26	4.88	2.7	8.1	3.0	0.5	32	87	101
Chirinos,Yonny	16	R	23	aa	TAM	67	5.28	1.45	20.3	1.6	5.1	3.1	0.7	34	63	68
	17	R	24	a/a	TAM	168	3.58	1.16	24.8	1.5	6.5	4.3	0.9	30	72	105
Cimber,Adam	16	R	26	a/a	SD	57	4.41	1.41	5.28	2.4	4.0	1.6	0.7	31	69	35
	17	R	27	a/a	SD	81	3.67	1.09	6.44	1.2	5.5	4.7	1.3	27	73	96
Claiborne,Prestor	16	R	28	aa	SF	45	3.53	1.24	5.41	3.1	7.5	2.4	0.9	29	74	76
	17	R	29	aaa	TEX	38	2.59	1.74	4.56	4.2	7.2	1.7	0.6	37	87	54
Clark,Brian	16	L	23	a/a	CHW	57	3.20	1.46	6.55	2.0	6.7	3.3	0.2	37	77	98
	17	L	24	aaa	CHW	49	4.79	1.67	6.15	2.6	6.9	2.7	0.8	39	72	62
Clarke,Taylor	16	R	23	aa	ARI	98	5.00	1.49	24.7	2.1	5.6	2.7	1.1	34	68	52
	17	R	24	a/a	ARI	145	4.03	1.35	22.4	3.3	7.1	2.2	1.1	30	73	60
Cleavinger,Garret	17	L	23	aa	PHI	54	7.28	1.82	6.59	5.4	8.7	1.6	1.0	37	59	50
Clemens,Paul	16	R	28	aaa	MIA	75	6.35	1.57	23.6	3.6	5.9	1.7	0.8	33	59	41
	17	R	29	aa	MIN	53	4.66	1.78	14.4	4.7	5.0	1.1	1.2	33	77	9
Clevinger,Michael	16	R	26	aaa	CLE	93	4.27	1.50	23.6	3.8	7.2	1.9	1.0	32	74	53
	17	R	27	aaa	CLE	34	3.87	1.58	21.4	4.4	7.0	1.6	1.1	32	79	42
Clifton,Trevor	17	R	22	aa	CHC	100	6.73	1.80	22.1	4.3	6.8	1.6	0.8	37	62	40
Cochran-Gill,Trey	16	R	24	aa	OAK	73	3.59	1.45	7.46	3.1	5.7	1.9	0.7	32	77	50
Cole,A.J.	16	R	24	aaa	WAS	125	6.15	1.66	25.4	2.9	6.4	2.2	1.4	36	65	34
	17	R	25	aaa	WAS	93	7.66	2.08	25.4	3.8	6.3	1.7	0.8	43	62	30
Cole,Taylor	16	R	27	aa	TOR	62	5.39	1.80	23.7	2.8	6.3	2.2	1.2	39	72	34
Coleman,Casey	16	R	29	aaa	TAM	53	3.71	1.40	5.88	3.4	7.0	2.1	0.7	32	74	67
	17	R	30	aaa	HOU	64	7.13	1.87	25	4.5	6.1	1.4	1.1	37	62	22
Coley,Austin	17	R	25	aa	PIT	144	4.20	1.51	21.5	2.2	5.6	2.6	0.7	35	73	58
Collier,Tommy	16	R	27	aa	DET	131	5.54	1.70	23.6	2.7	4.4	1.6	1.2	35	69	13
Comer,Kevin	17	R	25	a/a	HOU	67	3.84	1.60	6.54	3.6	9.1	2.5	0.7	38	77	82
Concepcion,Gera	16	L	24	a/a	CHC	60	6.06	1.68	6.39	4.3	6.6	1.5	1.0	34	64	36
Conley,Adam	17	L	27	aaa	MIA	62	7.00	1.81	24	3.9	4.7	1.2	1.1	35	61	11
Conlon,P.J.	17	L	24	aa	NYM	136	5.09	1.59	21.4	3.2	6.3	2.0	1.3	34	71	3
Coonrod,Sam	16	R	24	aa	SF	77	4.11	1.48	25.6	4.9	5.1	1.0	0.8	27	74	3
	17	R	25	aa	SF	104	6.47	1.62	19.2	4.1	6.7	1.6	0.6	35	58	5
Cooper,Matt	16	R	25	aa	CHW	41	3.79	1.20	8.67	2.9	8.7	3.0	0.8	30	70	9
	17	R	26	aa	CHW	72	7.11	1.90	24.3	4.0	8.0	2.0	0.2	43	59	7
Copeland,Scott	16	R	29	aaa	TOR	50	4.74	1.66	25.1	3.7	4.5	1.2	0.8	33	72	2
	17	R	30	aaa	MIA	138	6.71	1.95	25.2	4.0	5.8	1.5	1.5	38	67	
Copping,Corey	17	R	23	aa	LA	68	4.18	1.26	5.66	4.1	6.9	1.7	1.0	25	69	5
Cordero,Jimmy	17	R	26	aa	WAS	51	9.07	2.08	6.13	7.3	5.6	0.8	1.4	33	56	
Cortes,Nestor	17	L	23	a/a	NYY	100	2.86	1.26	14.1	3.0	7.9	2.6	0.4	31	77	9
Cosart,Jake	17	R	23	aa	BOS	49	4.05	1.56	5.69	7.9	7.8	1.0	1.0	22	77	5
Cosart,Jarred	16	R	26	aaa	MIA	51	5.77	1.96	24.2	5.1	4.1	0.8	1.6	34	74	-1
Coshow,Cale	16	R	24	aa	NYY	89	6.11	1.87	11.6	5.8	6.0	1.0	0.9	34	68	2
	17	R	25	a/a	NYY	60	5.43	1.98	6.39	4.1	9.4	2.3	0.9	45	73	6
Cotton,Chris	16	L	26	a/a	HOU	61	4.74	1.67	8.55	2.4	3.7	1.5	0.9	35	73	1
Cotton,Jharel	16	R	24	aaa	OAK	136	5.90	1.30	20	2.8	8.3	2.9	1.5	30	57	6
Couch,Keith	16	R	27	a/a	BOS	127	6.11	1.80	26.7	3.1	4.0	1.3	0.9	36	66	1
Cravy,Tyler	16	R	27	aaa	MIL	56	7.23	1.74	12.2	4.8	8.1	1.7	0.9	36	57	5
	17	R	28	aaa	MIL	53	7.23	1.83	5.91	4.2	5.0	1.2	1.8	34	63	-1
Crichton,Stefan	16	R	24	aa	BAL	72	4.71	1.57	6.62	3.3	6.2	1.8	0.6	35	70	5
	17	R	25	aaa	BAL	48	4.19	1.52	7.13	2.5	8.0	3.2	0.5	38	72	9
Crick,Kyle	16	R	24	aa	SF	109	6.84	1.92	22.5	6.1	6.0	1.0	0.7	35	63	3
	17	R	25	aaa	SF	29	3.38	1.44	5.2	4.2	9.8	2.3	0.3	35	76	10
Crockett,Kyle	16	L	25	aaa	CLE	30	5.43	1.62	4.59	3.6	6.1	1.7	0.8	35	66	4
	17	L	26	aaa	CLE	48	4.82	1.40	3.97	2.4	6.6	2.7	0.5	34	64	7
Crouse,Matt	16	L	26	a/a	DET	126	5.06	1.61	18	3.7	4.2	1.1	0.7	32	68	2
	17	L	27	a/a	DET	142	7.15	1.87	23	3.2	4.3	1.4	1.6	37	63	-
Crownover,Matthe	17	L	24	aa	WAS	84	5.72	1.71	22.4	3.8	4.0	1.0	1.3	32	69	-
Cuevas,William	16	R	26	aaa	BOS	131	7.00	1.85	24.5	3.8	4.6	1.2	1.7	35	65	-1
	17	R	27	aaa	MIA	104	6.18	1.62	19.2	4.1	5.6	1.4	1.0	32	62	2
Culver,Malcom	16	R	26	aaa	KC	68	4.69	1.66	6.89	3.7	6.2	1.7	0.5	36	71	4
	17	R	27	aaa	KC	37	5.57	1.93	5.54	5.0	6.2	1.2	0.3	39	69	4
Cunniff,Brandon	16	R	28	a/a	ATL	55	4.80	1.52	5.58	4.7	6.4	1.4	0.6	30	68	5
	17	R	29	aaa	MIA	55	5.93	1.72	6.9	5.3	6.8	1.3	1.3	32	67	2
Curtis,Zac	16	L	24	aa	ARI	20	4.55	1.43	4.4	3.0	11.4	3.8	1.8	36	75	9
	17	L	25	aa	SEA	51	4.42	1.39	5.28	3.5	8.9	2.6	0.6	34	68	9
Curtiss,John	17	R	24	a/a	MIN	49	1.91	1.10	4.95	4.4	9.8	2.2	0.0	26	81	12
Cyr,Tyler	17	R	24	aa	SF	49	2.96	1.69	4.74	4.0	8.7	2.2	0.6	39	84	7
Dahlstrand,Jacob	16	R	24	aa	BOS	19	7.99	1.89	22.8	4.0	3.1	0.8	1.6	34	58	-2
	17	R	25	aa	BOS	77	9.06	2.17	13.2	5.9	3.5	0.6	1.2	36	57	-1
Danish,Tyler	16	R	22	a/a	CHW	105	5.59	1.44	23.5	2.3	5.3	2.2	0.3	34	58	6
	17	R	23	aaa	CHW	138	6.39	1.80	24.6	3.2	4.1	1.3	1.3	35	66	-
Darnell,Logan	16	L	27	aaa	MIN	110	5.31	1.66	27.3	3.4	3.2	1.0	0.8	33	68	
	17	L	28	aaa	TAM	75	5.51	1.89	29.3	2.2	5.1	2.3	1.6	39	75	1
Davis,Austin	17	L	24	aa	PHI	47	3.56	1.57	6.45	4.0	7.6	1.9	0.7	35	79	6
Davis,Rookie	16	R	23	a/a	CIN	125	5.48	1.60	23	3.0	5.0	1.6	1.4	33	69	1
	17	R	24	a/a	CIN	74	6.83	1.67	23.7	2.6	6.8	2.6	2.1	36	63	2
Davis,Tyler	17	R	24	aa	TEX	81	3.30	1.07	26.4	1.1	4.1	3.6	1.2	26	75	7
Dawson,Shane	16	L	23	aa	TOR	134	5.50	1.76	23.6	5.1	5.5	1.1	0.9	33	69	2
	17	L	24	aa	TOR	111	8.29	2.07	20.1	4.2	4.2	1.0	2.1	37	63	-3
Dayton,Grant	16	L	29	a/a	LA	52	3.39	0.99	5.21	2.0	11.8	5.8	0.5	32	65	19
De Fratus,Justin	16	R	29	a/a	WAS	58	5.82	1.80	5.95	4.7	4.9	1.0	0.8	34	67	1
	17	R	30	a/a	SEA	98	6.77	1.76	26.5	1.5	3.7	2.5	1.8	37	65	
De Jong,Chase	16	R	23	a/a	LA	147	3.46	1.14	22.4	2.3	7.0	3.0	1.1	27	74	8
	17	R	24	a/a	SEA	113	7.19	1.68	25.4	3.0	5.4	1.8	1.9	34	60	
De La Cruz,Joel	16	R	27	aaa	ATL	58	6.28	1.83	12.8	4.2	5.6	1.3	0.9	36	66	2
De Leon,Jose	16	R	24	aaa	LA	86	3.45	1.04	20.8	1.9	9.7	5.0	1.1	29	71	14
De Los Santos,At	16	R	24	a/a	CIN	58	4.12	1.60	5.55	5.4	8.8	1.6	0.7	33	75	6
	17	R	25	a/a	LAA	38	3.40	1.24	5.89	3.1	8.5	2.7	0.7	30	75	9
De Los Santos,Er	17	R	22	aa	SD	150	5.16	1.39	24.3	3.0	7.0	2.4	0.8	32	63	6
De Paula,Rafael	16	R	25	a/a	SD	64	3.04	1.36	5.98	3.1	10.3	3.3	0.3	37	77	12
	17	R	26	a/a	CIN	50	5.14	1.60	7.12	4.1	7.3	1.8	1.6	32	72	3
Dean,Pat	16	L	27	aaa	MIN	87	8.37	1.99	26.2	2.2	3.8	1.7	1.4	40	58	
Deetz,Dean	17	R	24	a/a	HOU	85	4.56	1.50	14.6	5.0	8.9	1.8	0.8	32	71	7
Delgado,Casey	16	R	26	a/a	NYM	58	5.88	1.84	26.8	3.3	5.8	1.8	0.9	39	68	3
	17	R	27	aa	NYM	114	7.38	2.16	24.6	5.8	5.2	0.9	0.9	39	65	
DeLoach,Tyler	16	L	25	a/a	LAA	63	3.43	1.42	5.2	3.5	8.3	2.4	0.3	34	75	9
DeNato,Joey	17	L	25	a/a	PHI	51	3.43	1.74	7.05	6.0	4.9	0.8	0.7	31	82	2
Derby,Bubba	17	R	23	a/a	MIL	113	4.03	1.35	15.8	3.0	6.5	2.2	0.8	31	72	6
Dermody,Matt	16	L	26	a/a	TOR	36	2.49	1.44	4.95	2.0	5.5	2.8	0.4	35	83	7
	17	L	27	aaa	TOR	43	5.83	1.88	6.12	2.8	6.4	2.3	2.0	39	74	1
Despaigne,Odrisa	16	R	29	aaa	BAL	88	6.40	1.87	23	3.4	5.2	1.5	0.9	38	65	2
	17	R	30	aaa	MIA	70	4.17	1.56	15.3	3.6	4.8	1.3	0.9	32	75	2
Diaz,Dayan	16	R	27	aaa	CIN	56	4.61	1.59	6.18	3.1	6.1	2.0	0.5	36	70	5
	17	R	28	aaa	HOU	48	4.21	1.45	5.86	3.2	7.8	2.4	0.5	35	71	8
Diaz,Edwin	16	R	22	aa	SEA	41	2.82	1.09	9.95	1.5	10.7	7.0	0.7	34	77	1
Diaz,Luis	16	R	24	aa	SD	56	7.46	1.80	25.9	3.1	6.5	2.1	1.6	38	60	2
	17	R	25	a/a	LAA	111	5.46	1.66	18.5	3.8	7.4	1.9	1.1	36	68	
Dickson,Cody	16	L	24	aa	PIT	140	4.46	1.74	22.8	6.1	5.4	0.9	0.5	31	74	
	17	L	25	a/a	PIT	72	7.26	2.15	10	6.7	6.3	0.9	1.5	37	68	
Dimock,Michael	16	R	27	a/a	SD	46	6.04	1.35	6.23	3.3	9.0	2.7	1.6	31	58	
	17	R	28	a/a	LAA	37	6.83	1.83	5.69	3.7	7.4	2.0	1.1	39	63	
Dirks,Caleb	16	R	23	aa	ATL	61	1.69	1.22	5.02	3.0	8.8	2.9	0.6	31	89	1
	17	R	24	aaa	ATL	40	5.16	1.40	6.3	3.2	8.7	2.7	1.4	32	67	

ITCHER	yr	t	age	lvl	org	ip	era	whip	bf/g	ctl	dom	cmd	hr/9	h%	s%	bpv
)onatello,Sean	16	R	26	aa	MIA	50	4.82	1.50	4.73	2.4	3.6	1.5	0.2	33	65	41
	17	R	27	a/a	DET	60	6.18	1.75	6.13	3.3	6.1	1.9	1.4	37	67	24
)oolittle,Ryan	16	R	28	a/a	OAK	44	3.94	1.54	6.4	3.3	4.4	1.3	0.9	32	77	22
)orris,Jacob	17	R	24	a/a	HOU	72	3.22	1.28	6.87	3.3	8.2	2.5	1.0	30	79	77
)rabek,Kyle	16	R	29	aaa	ARI	69	8.18	2.16	22.8	4.6	4.0	0.9	0.6	40	60	6
)ragmire,Brady	16	R	23	aa	TOR	72	5.70	1.71	7.24	3.7	4.5	1.2	1.6	32	70	-4
	17	R	24	a/a	WAS	82	5.43	1.86	10.1	4.2	3.5	0.8	1.0	35	72	-1
)rake,Oliver	16	R	29	aaa	BAL	56	4.49	1.68	5.39	5.0	9.2	1.8	1.3	35	77	52
)uncan,Frank	16	R	24	a/a	PIT	139	3.05	1.40	21.7	2.4	6.0	2.5	0.3	34	77	77
	17	R	25	a/a	ARI	152	7.73	1.88	26.4	2.9	4.6	1.6	1.4	38	59	4
)unning,Jake	16	R	28	aaa	SF	59	6.10	1.82	5.62	4.9	5.1	1.0	0.6	35	65	27
	17	R	29	a/a	CHW	25	12.21	2.69	9.71	6.5	6.5	1.0	2.0	45	54	-28
)uRapau,Montan	16	R	24	aa	PIT	49	4.52	1.42	4.18	3.5	7.4	2.1	1.1	31	71	56
	17	R	25	a/a	PIT	53	2.83	1.26	5.14	3.8	8.2	2.2	0.4	29	78	92
)ykstra,James	16	R	26	aa	CHW	102	6.20	1.97	17.5	3.9	4.8	1.2	0.4	39	67	26
	17	R	27	a/a	TEX	98	8.22	2.13	16.8	3.5	4.8	1.4	0.7	42	59	15
)ykxhoorn,Brock	17	R	23	aa	HOU	99	5.69	1.68	17.9	3.6	6.8	1.9	0.9	36	66	45
)ziedzic,Jonathar	16	L	25	aaa	KC	140	4.82	1.57	23.6	4.1	5.4	1.3	0.8	32	70	36
	17	L	26	aaa	KC	46	6.29	1.58	22.3	3.2	5.8	1.8	1.7	32	64	15
:ades,Ryan	16	R	25	aa	MIN	113	5.91	1.60	19.3	3.6	5.6	1.6	0.4	35	60	51
	17	R	26	a/a	MIN	87	5.31	1.44	12.4	3.9	5.2	1.3	0.4	30	61	49
:chemendia,Pedr	16	R	25	a/a	STL	49	4.00	1.42	6.89	3.5	5.5	1.6	1.3	29	77	27
	17	R	26	a/a	STL	75	5.42	1.64	8.58	2.3	3.8	1.6	1.3	34	69	8
:dwards,Andrew	16	R	25	a/a	KC	61	5.08	1.71	6.61	5.0	8.6	1.7	1.1	35	72	51
	17	R	26	a/a	KC	36	9.36	2.18	7.26	4.4	6.9	1.6	0.9	44	55	29
:flin,Zach	16	R	22	aaa	PHI	68	4.18	1.07	24.2	1.6	6.5	4.1	0.4	29	59	120
	17	R	23	aaa	PHI	43	5.81	1.67	24.3	3.2	6.9	2.2	0.8	37	65	55
:ge,Cody	16	L	25	aaa	LAA	51	4.75	1.56	5.35	4.8	6.7	1.4	0.3	32	68	62
	17	L	26	aaa	LAA	39	5.70	1.57	6.64	3.0	7.6	2.5	0.2	38	61	86
:itel,Derek	16	R	29	aaa	SD	69	4.06	1.55	5.56	5.5	7.2	1.3	0.7	30	75	55
	17	R	30	aa	WAS	45	5.21	1.84	17.3	6.7	6.1	0.9	0.8	32	72	32
:lias,Roenis	16	L	28	aaa	BOS	125	6.28	1.93	28.3	5.3	6.2	1.2	1.1	37	68	21
	17	L	29	a/a	BOS	37	10.16	2.07	22.4	3.1	4.6	1.5	3.4	37	56	-64
:llis,Chris	16	R	24	a/a	ATL	146	6.07	1.68	23.5	5.9	6.7	1.1	0.4	32	62	53
	17	R	25	a/a	STL	131	6.87	1.68	19.7	3.4	6.7	2.0	1.1	36	59	41
:manuel,Kent	16	L	24	aa	HOU	83	6.19	1.60	21.5	2.2	5.4	2.5	1.0	36	61	43
	17	L	25	a/a	HOU	116	6.27	1.91	22	2.8	6.0	2.2	1.1	41	68	32
:nns,Dietrich	16	L	25	a/a	NYY	135	2.64	1.48	22.3	4.4	6.8	1.6	0.6	31	84	58
	17	L	26	aaa	MIN	51	3.69	1.48	21.9	2.9	6.1	2.1	0.8	33	77	55
:ppler,Tyler	16	R	23	aa	PIT	162	4.85	1.46	25.7	1.8	4.8	2.6	0.8	34	67	54
	17	R	24	aaa	PIT	136	6.61	1.71	22.9	2.4	5.0	2.1	1.8	35	64	8
:sch,Jacob	16	R	26	a/a	MIA	142	6.10	1.67	24.5	3.3	4.7	1.4	0.7	35	62	29
	17	R	27	a/a	SD	39	4.35	1.80	26	3.8	3.8	1.0	0.8	35	77	11
:scobar,Edwin	16	L	24	aaa	ARI	98	4.33	1.55	22.6	3.3	4.9	1.5	0.7	33	73	35
:shelman,Tom	16	R	22	aa	PHI	61	6.10	1.73	21.5	2.5	7.2	2.9	0.7	41	64	70
	17	R	23	a/a	PHI	150	2.98	1.12	25.7	1.1	5.4	4.9	1.0	28	78	107
:sparza,Matt	17	R	23	aa	CLE	95	6.51	1.56	24.4	3.7	5.2	1.4	1.9	29	62	1
:spinal,Yoel	17	R	25	a/a	TAM	44	9.95	2.08	7.92	10.5	9.4	0.9	1.0	31	49	52
:spino,Paolo	16	R	29	aaa	WAS	153	5.32	1.60	26	2.2	5.7	2.6	1.0	36	68	48
:stevez,Wirkin	17	R	25	aa	WAS	62	4.71	1.75	25.8	4.2	4.2	1.0	0.5	34	72	24
aria,Jake	16	R	23	a/a	TAM	151	4.91	1.31	23.1	4.1	8.2	2.0	0.8	28	62	76
	17	R	24	aaa	TAM	59	4.17	1.34	22.2	3.7	11.1	3.0	1.3	33	73	96
armer,Buck	16	R	25	aaa	DET	100	5.48	1.66	22.4	2.9	6.5	2.2	1.2	36	69	39
	17	R	26	aaa	DET	124	5.81	1.71	26.7	2.6	6.4	2.4	0.9	38	66	51
arrell,Luke	16	R	25	aaa	KC	91	4.47	1.53	20.8	4.0	6.1	1.5	1.2	31	74	32
	17	R	26	aaa	CIN	117	6.37	1.59	23.4	4.0	7.5	1.9	1.5	33	62	35
'arris,James	16	R	24	aa	CHC	36	3.31	1.16	5.51	2.6	8.0	3.1	0.6	30	72	104
	17	R	25	a/a	COL	58	5.34	1.49	5.18	3.0	8.0	2.7	2.1	32	71	38
'asola,John	16	R	25	a/a	TEX	40	4.42	1.47	5.96	2.5	8.2	3.3	0.5	37	69	97
aulkner,Andrew	16	L	24	aaa	TEX	45	4.99	1.50	4.78	4.3	6.3	1.5	0.7	31	66	50
	17	L	25	aaa	BAL	39	3.87	1.72	5.16	6.7	6.9	1.0	0.3	32	76	58
edde,Erick	16	R	23	aa	WAS	29	5.30	1.73	26.7	3.3	7.1	2.2	0.3	39	67	68
	17	R	24	a/a	WAS	90	4.70	1.36	13	2.4	6.5	2.7	0.8	32	66	72
ernandez,Jose	17	L	24	aa	TOR	46	7.32	1.98	5.43	5.4	7.8	1.4	1.0	39	63	36
'ernandez,Pedro	16	R	22	aa	KC	29	5.27	1.54	15.8	3.2	4.9	1.6	0.7	33	65	38
	17	R	23	a/a	KC	77	4.14	1.40	8.33	2.8	6.4	2.3	0.5	33	70	71
ernandez,Raul	16	R	26	aa	MIN	38	4.66	1.56	6.4	3.7	5.2	1.4	0.5	33	69	42
	17	R	27	a/a	MIN	48	6.59	2.03	8.31	5.3	6.8	1.3	2.2	37	72	-10
errell,Jeff	17	R	27	a/a	DET	56	3.20	1.31	4.65	2.8	7.3	2.7	0.4	32	75	90
errell,Riley	17	R	24	aa	HOU	52	4.78	1.44	6.15	2.5	8.3	3.4	0.4	37	65	105
eyereisen,J.P.	16	R	23	aa	NYY	58	2.52	1.34	5.77	4.5	10.4	2.3	0.7	31	84	98
	17	R	24	a/a	NYY	63	4.63	1.46	7.33	4.4	7.2	1.6	1.1	30	71	49
ierro,Edwin	17	R	24	a/a	TAM	89	4.76	1.53	11.8	2.5	5.8	2.3	0.6	35	68	60
illmyer,Heath	16	R	22	aa	OAK	39	2.85	1.07	19	1.8	5.6	3.1	0.6	27	76	88
	17	R	23	aa	OAK	150	4.04	1.52	22.4	3.0	5.6	1.9	1.1	33	77	36
ilomeno,Joe	16	L	23	aa	TEX	41	2.87	1.47	5.87	7.2	8.9	1.2	0.8	24	83	73
	17	L	24	aa	TEX	37	11.50	2.40	6.6	6.1	6.9	1.1	2.6	41	53	-33
innegan,Kyle	16	R	25	aa	OAK	42	2.56	1.35	5.84	4.4	6.9	1.6	0.6	28	83	63
	17	R	26	a/a	OAK	60	4.77	1.64	5.85	3.8	6.5	1.7	1.2	34	74	33
laherty,Jack	17	R	22	a/a	STL	149	2.66	1.16	23.7	2.1	7.4	3.5	0.8	30	80	100
leck,Kaleb	16	R	27	aaa	ARI	31	6.79	1.97	5.12	5.4	8.3	1.6	0.9	40	65	44
	17	R	28	aaa	ARI	54	6.12	1.79	5.7	3.9	6.9	1.8	1.3	37	67	31
lemer,Matt	16	R	26	a/a	COL	102	5.59	1.62	18.2	2.6	4.0	1.6	1.8	32	70	-5
	17	R	27	aaa	COL	127	8.23	1.95	23.2	2.8	4.1	1.4	2.7	36	63	-43
lexen,Chris	17	R	23	aa	NYM	49	2.46	0.91	25.9	1.6	8.3	5.2	1.1	25	80	142
lores,Jose	17	R	28	a/a	SF	112	4.45	1.53	15.7	3.6	6.8	1.9	0.3	35	69	68
lores,Kendry	16	R	25	a/a	MIA	97	6.04	1.88	24	4.0	5.8	1.4	0.8	38	67	28

PITCHER	yr	t	age	lvl	org	ip	era	whip	bf/g	ctl	dom	cmd	hr/9	h%	s%	bpv
Floro,Dylan	17	R	27	aaa	LA	60	5.12	1.63	8.09	1.6	4.5	2.8	1.5	36	73	27
Flynn,Brian	16	L	26	aaa	KC	24	3.70	1.63	11.7	4.7	8.2	1.8	0.4	36	77	73
	17	L	27	aaa	KC	50	7.35	2.00	11	2.4	6.8	2.9	2.0	42	67	19
Font,Wilmer	16	R	26	a/a	TOR	66	5.24	1.40	23.2	1.9	6.1	3.3	1.5	32	67	56
	17	R	27	aaa	LA	134	4.17	1.28	22	2.3	9.5	4.1	0.8	34	69	120
Franco,Mike	17	R	26	a/a	TAM	90	4.11	1.56	14.6	5.5	6.6	1.2	1.0	29	76	41
Frankoff,Seth	16	R	28	a/a	LA	68	5.61	1.75	12.4	2.3	6.3	2.7	0.5	40	66	65
	17	R	29	aaa	CHC	117	5.49	1.55	21.2	4.1	7.0	1.7	1.6	31	68	29
Freeland,Kyle	16	L	23	a/a	COL	162	5.66	1.59	27.5	2.7	4.6	1.7	1.3	33	66	18
Freeman,Michael	16	L	25	aa	HOU	56	8.70	2.31	7.81	5.9	3.9	0.7	1.0	39	61	-11
	17	L	26	aa	HOU	20	4.13	2.15	7.1	7.7	5.3	0.7	0.5	36	81	22
Freeman,Sam	16	L	29	aaa	MIL	55	6.66	2.02	8.92	5.2	5.6	1.1	0.8	38	66	20
French,Parker	17	R	24	aa	COL	129	10.16	2.08	26.3	4.3	3.7	0.9	2.5	36	53	-51
Frias,Carlos	16	R	27	a/a	LA	43	5.27	1.43	18.4	2.3	5.2	2.2	0.5	33	61	59
	17	R	28	aaa	CLE	38	12.03	2.34	6.54	6.4	3.4	0.5	2.7	35	49	-67
Frias,Edison	16	R	26	a/a	HOU	93	4.74	1.56	21.3	3.9	5.6	1.4	0.8	32	70	37
	17	R	27	a/a	COL	73	7.86	2.12	9.75	5.3	4.7	0.9	1.0	38	62	2
Fried,Max	17	L	23	a/a	ATL	93	7.42	1.71	20	4.9	7.9	1.6	0.9	35	55	51
Friedrichs,Kyle	17	R	25	aa	OAK	51	7.25	1.68	12.7	3.0	5.0	1.6	1.2	35	57	18
Fry,Jace	17	L	24	aa	CHW	45	3.99	1.64	6.12	5.7	8.9	1.6	0.3	35	74	81
Fry,Paul	16	L	24	aaa	SEA	55	2.95	1.48	4.92	4.7	9.2	2.0	0.2	34	79	96
	17	L	25	a/a	BAL	60	5.77	1.85	8.54	5.6	9.1	1.6	1.1	38	70	50
Fulmer,Carson	16	R	23	a/a	CHW	103	5.49	1.65	21.9	5.2	8.0	1.5	0.8	34	67	56
	17	R	24	aaa	CHW	126	6.90	1.77	23.1	5.0	5.9	1.2	1.5	33	62	11
Gabryszwski,Jere	16	R	23	aa	TOR	146	6.82	1.72	22.9	3.2	5.1	1.6	1.3	35	61	17
Gage,Matt	16	L	23	aa	SF	136	4.49	1.43	25.1	2.4	6.1	2.5	0.1	35	66	81
	17	L	24	a/a	SF	145	5.35	1.74	25.5	2.6	4.9	1.9	0.5	38	68	42
Gagnon,Drew	16	R	26	a/a	MIL	68	6.03	1.59	8.37	3.7	6.6	1.8	0.7	35	61	53
	17	R	27	aaa	LAA	86	6.64	1.68	12.5	3.9	7.0	1.8	0.6	37	58	56
Gallegos,Giovann	16	R	25	a/a	NYY	78	2.11	1.07	7.22	2.3	10.1	4.4	0.9	30	86	137
	17	R	26	aaa	NYY	43	2.97	1.12	6.1	2.6	11.6	4.5	1.3	31	81	135
Gallen,Zac	17	R	22	a/a	STL	92	4.54	1.44	23.1	2.4	5.3	2.2	1.0	32	71	42
Gant,John	16	R	24	aaa	ATL	56	5.25	1.65	20.8	3.8	8.0	2.1	0.9	37	69	60
	17	R	25	aaa	STL	103	4.83	1.52	24.9	2.3	6.7	3.0	1.0	36	70	67
Garces,Frank	16	L	26	aaa	SD	114	4.56	1.57	13.6	3.0	6.4	2.1	1.2	34	74	40
Garcia,Edgar	16	R	29	a/a	ARI	123	7.16	1.84	22.1	4.1	5.0	1.2	1.1	36	61	12
Garcia,Jason	16	R	24	aa	BAL	124	5.97	1.77	23.7	4.1	4.2	1.0	0.5	35	64	24
	17	R	25	aa	BAL	75	6.76	1.98	9.52	5.5	7.5	1.4	0.8	39	65	38
Garcia,Luis	16	R	29	aaa	PHI	55	3.59	1.57	5	5.1	6.7	1.3	0.8	31	79	45
Garcia,Onelki	17	L	28	a/a	KC	85	6.94	1.93	18.4	4.0	5.4	1.3	1.0	38	64	16
Garcia,Yeudy	17	R	25	aa	PIT	72	7.34	2.05	12.1	6.4	6.5	1.0	1.2	36	64	15
Garner,David	16	R	24	aa	CHC	54	5.05	1.85	5.83	6.1	7.9	1.3	0.4	37	71	60
	17	R	25	a/a	CHC	44	4.05	1.69	5.71	5.5	8.6	1.6	1.4	33	81	43
Garner,Perci	16	R	28	a/a	CLE	79	2.70	1.21	7.74	2.9	5.9	2.0	0.3	28	77	76
	17	R	29	a/a	CLE	16	10.43	2.05	5.87	12.1	7.7	0.6	0.0	26	43	74
Garrett,Amir	16	L	24	a/a	CIN	145	3.74	1.35	24.1	4.2	7.2	1.7	0.6	29	73	70
	17	L	25	aaa	CIN	68	7.46	1.82	22.4	3.5	6.8	1.9	1.2	39	59	33
Garrett,Reed	16	R	23	a/a	TEX	99	7.38	1.78	16.9	4.4	6.0	1.4	1.0	35	58	26
	17	R	24	aa	TEX	69	7.07	1.78	7.18	4.6	7.4	1.6	1.7	35	63	19
Garrido,Santiago	16	R	27	aa	DET	43	9.85	2.35	9.75	4.5	6.1	1.4	1.7	44	58	-10
Garton,Ryan	16	R	27	aaa	TAM	32	4.30	1.60	6.43	3.2	8.8	2.8	0.3	40	72	94
	17	R	28	aaa	SEA	45	3.56	1.38	6.1	5.2	9.6	1.9	0.5	30	74	93
Gaviglio,Sam	16	R	26	a/a	SEA	165	4.90	1.41	24.9	2.0	5.5	2.8	0.8	33	66	62
	17	R	27	aaa	SEA	72	4.82	1.40	23.4	1.6	5.8	3.6	0.7	34	65	83
German,Domingo	17	R	25	a/a	NYY	109	4.17	1.40	23.1	3.0	8.1	2.7	1.1	33	74	71
Gibaut,Ian	17	R	24	aa	TAM	53	2.82	1.27	5.02	4.7	9.3	2.0	1.1	26	84	76
Gibson,Daniel	16	L	25	a/a	ARI	44	4.43	1.82	4.5	4.7	5.7	1.2	1.0	35	78	23
	17	L	26	a/a	ARI	35	4.52	1.95	6.19	5.4	5.1	0.9	0.6	36	77	22
Gillies,Darin	17	R	25	aa	SEA	60	4.18	1.49	6.59	3.9	6.0	1.5	0.7	31	73	47
Gilmartin,Sean	16	L	26	aaa	NYM	107	4.76	1.49	24.4	2.5	6.4	2.6	0.9	35	69	60
	17	L	27	aaa	STL	50	8.83	2.05	15.1	3.2	5.3	1.7	1.7	40	57	-3
Giolito,Lucas	16	R	22	a/a	WAS	108	3.79	1.53	22.4	3.9	7.9	2.0	0.5	35	75	75
	17	R	23	aaa	CHW	129	5.23	1.56	23.5	4.4	8.3	1.9	1.3	33	69	49
Girodo,Chad	16	L	25	aaa	TOR	36	5.40	2.02	5.96	3.7	5.1	1.4	1.8	39	78	-12
	17	L	26	aaa	TOR	48	4.84	2.01	7.67	3.9	5.3	1.4	0.9	40	77	18
Glasnow,Tyler	16	R	23	a/a	PIT	117	2.47	1.30	21.8	5.3	9.0	1.7	0.4	27	82	92
	17	R	24	aaa	PIT	93	2.61	1.13	24.6	3.4	10.7	3.2	0.7	29	80	124
Glover,Koda	16	R	23	a/a	WAS	46	3.73	1.19	5.63	2.1	8.2	3.9	0.7	32	70	115
Godley,Zachary	16	R	26	a/a	ARI	82	4.68	1.61	24.2	3.0	6.0	2.0	0.9	35	72	43
	17	R	27	aaa	ARI	28	2.90	1.19	22.5	5.5	7.2	1.3	0.0	22	73	92
Goforth,David	16	R	28	aaa	MIL	51	6.14	2.10	6.02	6.8	5.1	0.7	0.6	36	70	18
	17	R	29	aaa	MIL	54	4.71	1.79	5.22	4.6	4.8	1.0	1.4	33	78	0
Gohara,Luiz	17	L	21	a/a	ATL	87	3.75	1.41	19.4	3.8	10.2	2.7	0.7	35	74	101
Goldberg,Brad	16	R	26	a/a	CHW	57	3.41	1.51	5.22	4.7	6.7	1.4	0.6	31	78	56
	17	R	27	aaa	CHW	40	4.26	1.86	6.29	5.7	8.5	1.5	0.5	38	77	60
Gomber,Austin	16	L	23	aa	STL	19	1.69	1.14	19.1	4.3	6.2	1.4	0.0	24	83	85
	17	L	24	aa	STL	143	4.38	1.36	23	3.4	7.0	2.1	1.2	29	71	52
Gomez,Roberto	17	R	28	aaa	SF	97	5.32	1.74	11.7	4.0	6.3	1.6	0.7	37	69	41
Gonsalves,Stephe	16	L	22	aa	MIN	74	2.19	1.14	22.7	4.3	8.9	2.1	0.1	26	80	110
	17	L	23	a/a	MIN	110	4.80	1.39	23.2	2.7	7.8	2.8	1.2	33	68	70
Gonzales,Marco	17	L	25	aaa	SEA	80	3.74	1.18	24.7	2.5	6.2	2.5	0.8	28	70	74
Gonzalez,Alex	16	R	24	aaa	TEX	138	5.90	1.67	24.8	3.1	4.8	1.6	0.6	36	63	35
Gonzalez,Carlos	16	R	26	aa	CIN	62	5.99	1.54	5.51	3.9	7.0	1.8	0.9	33	61	50
	17	R	27	aa	CIN	36	7.11	1.85	6.41	5.3	5.3	1.0	1.3	33	62	6
Gonzalez,Juan	16	R	26	aaa	STL	43	6.40	1.91	5.18	6.6	6.9	1.0	0.6	35	65	40
Gonzalez,Rayan	16	R	26	aa	COL	52	5.16	1.71	5.13	4.8	6.1	1.3	0.6	34	69	42
Gonzalez,Severin	16	R	24	a/a	PHI	46	3.98	1.42	9.3	1.7	5.9	3.5	0.8	35	74	78
	17	R	25	a/a	MIA	80	6.29	1.52	7.93	2.1	5.2	2.5	1.4	34	60	36

PITCHER	yr	t	age	lvl	org	ip	era	whip	bf/g	ctl	dom	cmd	hr/9	h%	s%	bpv
Gorski,Darin	16	L	29	aaa	NYM	69	6.17	1.66	20.5	3.8	5.3	1.4	1.0	33	63	24
Gossett,Daniel	16	R	24	a/a	OAK	108	3.06	1.22	24.2	2.4	6.6	2.7	0.4	30	75	90
	17	R	25	aaa	OAK	76	4.38	1.39	23	2.8	6.5	2.3	0.7	32	69	66
Goudeau,Ashton	16	R	24	aa	KC	93	7.27	1.73	21.1	2.4	5.3	2.2	1.4	37	59	22
	17	R	25	aa	KC	57	7.75	2.09	13.3	3.0	5.3	1.8	1.3	42	63	9
Grace,Matt	16	L	28	aaa	WAS	47	4.49	1.82	6.28	2.1	4.5	2.1	0.3	40	74	48
	17	L	29	aaa	WAS	20	5.21	1.91	7.15	4.3	7.1	1.7	1.1	39	75	31
Graham,J.R.	16	R	26	a/a	NYY	41	5.46	1.78	6.99	4.2	7.8	1.9	0.7	39	69	56
	17	R	27	a/a	NYY	30	6.88	2.11	6.36	4.3	7.7	1.8	1.5	43	69	21
Green,Chad	16	R	25	aaa	NYY	95	2.27	1.20	23.8	2.3	7.9	3.4	0.4	31	82	111
	17	R	26	aaa	NYY	27	6.76	2.02	25.8	4.2	9.0	2.1	0.5	45	65	68
Greene,Conner	16	R	21	aa	TOR	69	5.31	1.45	24.5	4.4	5.7	1.3	0.8	28	63	40
	17	R	22	aa	TOR	133	6.84	1.90	24.1	5.8	5.4	0.9	0.6	35	62	28
Greenwood,Nick	16	L	29	a/a	MIN	112	4.75	1.51	23.1	1.2	3.3	2.7	0.9	34	70	38
Gregorio,Joan	16	R	24	a/a	SF	134	5.85	1.50	22.3	3.5	8.6	2.5	0.9	35	61	75
	17	R	25	aaa	SF	74	3.72	1.51	24.6	4.5	6.1	1.4	1.0	29	78	37
Griffin,Foster	17	L	22	aa	KC	105	4.90	1.59	25.6	3.0	5.8	1.9	1.1	34	71	37
Grills,Evan	16	L	24	a/a	HOU	112	4.30	1.31	24.4	1.4	5.4	4.0	1.4	31	72	70
Grimes,Matthew	16	R	25	aa	BAL	58	6.04	1.69	23.6	3.8	4.6	1.2	1.0	33	65	15
	17	R	26	aa	BAL	85	7.09	1.90	23.6	4.0	4.6	1.2	2.2	35	67	-26
Griset,Ben	17	L	25	aa	NYM	49	3.68	1.47	6.01	5.2	5.7	1.1	0.5	28	75	48
Grover,Taylor	16	R	25	aa	BOS	45	6.74	1.85	10	3.5	6.8	2.0	1.1	39	64	35
	17	R	26	aa	BOS	75	7.17	1.81	12	4.5	7.6	1.7	1.6	36	62	25
Grullon,Juan	16	L	26	a/a	TEX	61	5.55	1.67	8.61	4.5	7.1	1.6	1.2	34	69	34
Gsellman,Robert	16	R	23	a/a	NYM	115	4.06	1.29	23.6	2.3	5.9	2.6	0.7	31	69	70
	17	R	24	a/a	NYM	18	5.49	2.11	18.1	4.5	5.2	1.2	0.6	41	73	20
Guduan,Reymin	16	L	24	a/a	HOU	56	4.77	1.67	5.84	5.9	8.6	1.5	0.5	34	71	69
	17	L	25	aaa	HOU	46	5.61	1.66	5.29	2.5	7.8	3.2	0.7	40	66	82
Guerra,Deolis	17	R	28	aaa	LAA	41	2.14	0.92	4.95	1.7	7.1	4.1	0.6	25	80	124
Guerrero,Jordan	16	L	22	aa	CHW	136	5.60	1.66	24.3	5.1	6.4	1.3	1.0	32	67	35
	17	L	23	aa	CHW	146	5.88	1.62	26	3.1	7.4	2.4	0.7	38	62	67
Guerrero,Tayron	16	R	25	a/a	MIA	50	6.02	1.59	4.97	4.4	7.4	1.7	0.8	33	61	55
	17	R	26	a/a	MIA	31	6.13	1.96	4.99	8.3	7.8	0.9	1.6	30	72	19
Guerrieri,Taylor	16	R	24	a/a	TAM	146	4.55	1.36	21.8	2.9	4.7	1.6	0.7	29	67	42
Guillon,Ismael	17	L	25	a/a	CIN	70	6.65	2.17	8.69	7.0	8.3	1.2	1.1	40	70	29
Guilmet,Preston	16	R	29	aaa	DET	68	4.28	1.67	4.72	2.0	7.6	3.8	0.7	41	75	92
Gunkel,Joe	16	R	25	a/a	BAL	161	5.60	1.57	25.3	1.3	4.8	3.8	1.3	36	66	58
	17	R	26	a/a	MIA	124	6.47	1.62	20.4	1.7	4.4	2.6	1.5	35	62	26
Gurka,Jason	16	L	28	aaa	COL	21	2.57	1.93	5.63	3.0	9.0	3.0	1.9	43	96	43
	17	L	29	aaa	LAA	51	3.55	1.52	5.11	2.3	7.7	3.3	0.9	37	79	83
Gustave,Jandel	16	R	24	aaa	HOU	57	4.17	1.29	4.99	3.5	7.4	2.1	0.2	31	65	90
Hader,Joshua	16	L	22	a/a	MIL	126	4.07	1.38	21.2	4.1	9.9	2.4	0.5	34	70	102
	17	L	23	aaa	MIL	52	5.58	1.57	19	5.0	7.6	1.5	2.6	27	74	1
Hahn,Jesse	16	R	27	aaa	OAK	67	6.30	2.02	21.5	5.3	4.7	0.9	0.7	37	68	15
	17	R	28	aaa	OAK	25	5.53	2.00	20.1	5.4	4.7	0.9	0.4	37	71	24
Hale,David	16	R	29	aaa	BAL	100	9.23	2.30	23.3	2.8	4.1	1.5	1.5	44	60	-17
	17	R	30	a/a	LA	82	5.38	1.76	25	1.6	5.0	3.1	1.0	39	70	49
Haley,Justin	16	R	25	a/a	BOS	147	4.44	1.41	23	3.1	6.3	2.0	0.7	32	69	59
	17	R	26	aaa	BOS	61	4.70	1.36	21.4	1.8	5.2	2.9	2.0	29	74	28
Haley,Trey	16	R	26	a/a	PIT	56	7.49	2.06	5.78	7.5	5.3	0.7	0.7	34	62	19
Hall,Brooks	16	R	26	a/a	MIL	98	5.79	1.51	12.9	2.6	5.1	2.0	1.3	33	63	29
	17	R	27	a/a	ARI	60	6.78	1.78	16.2	2.8	5.3	1.9	0.5	39	60	42
Hancock,Justin	17	R	27	a/a	CHC	51	6.40	2.06	5.82	5.1	7.1	1.4	0.4	41	67	45
Harper,Bryan	16	L	27	a/a	WAS	45	3.26	1.30	4.67	4.3	6.2	1.5	1.2	24	81	40
Harper,Ryne	16	R	27	aa	SEA	68	3.56	1.40	6.84	3.7	10.2	2.8	0.3	36	74	112
	17	R	28	aa	SEA	54	4.39	1.47	5.61	3.9	7.3	1.9	1.0	32	72	54
Harris,Greg	17	R	23	aa	TAM	97	6.09	1.57	14.7	4.1	7.6	1.9	1.5	32	64	37
Harris,Jon	17	R	24	aa	TOR	143	7.28	1.81	25.4	3.2	6.0	1.9	1.6	37	61	13
Harrison,Jordan	16	L	24	aa	TAM	24	3.13	1.42	4.13	7.2	5.4	0.7	0.0	22	75	67
	17	L	25	aa	TAM	58	4.25	1.72	4.94	7.3	6.5	0.9	0.4	29	74	53
Hart,Donnie	16	L	26	aa	BAL	46	3.58	1.26	4.73	1.5	7.6	5.2	0.3	35	70	145
	17	L	27	aaa	BAL	15	3.40	1.62	5.24	1.5	9.5	6.5	0.8	44	81	157
Hathaway,Steve	16	L	26	a/a	ARI	45	3.36	1.48	4.72	4.7	6.2	1.3	0.5	30	78	55
Hauschild,Mike	16	R	26	aaa	HOU	140	3.70	1.44	24.8	2.6	6.3	2.4	0.5	34	74	70
	17	R	27	aaa	HOU	90	4.57	1.58	22.1	5.0	6.4	1.3	0.7	31	71	45
Hayes,Drew	16	R	29	aaa	CIN	59	6.50	2.04	7.54	5.2	4.9	0.9	0.7	38	67	14
Haynes,Kyle	16	R	25	a/a	NYY	124	8.08	1.97	25.7	4.3	6.0	1.4	1.6	38	60	3
Head,Louis	16	R	26	aa	CLE	68	3.72	1.35	6.27	2.6	6.3	2.4	0.5	32	73	72
	17	R	27	aaa	CLE	61	4.71	1.62	5.45	4.9	6.7	1.4	0.4	33	70	56
Healy,Tucker	16	R	26	aaa	OAK	52	5.16	1.50	5.14	5.1	10.1	2.0	0.6	34	65	89
	17	R	27	aaa	OAK	43	5.80	1.86	5.71	4.9	5.4	1.1	0.7	36	68	27
Hedges,Zach	16	R	24	aa	CHC	47	2.98	1.30	24.4	1.8	5.1	2.9	0.4	32	78	77
	17	R	25	a/a	CHC	146	5.60	1.76	25.8	2.7	3.9	1.5	0.9	36	69	13
Heller,Ben	16	R	25	a/a	NYY	48	2.57	1.06	3.8	3.1	8.5	2.8	0.6	26	78	107
	17	R	26	aaa	NYY	56	4.11	1.20	5.53	3.8	10.6	2.8	1.5	27	72	90
Herb,Tyler	16	R	24	aa	SEA	55	6.69	1.76	23.1	4.6	5.8	1.3	0.8	35	61	31
	17	R	25	aa	SF	163	4.26	1.55	27.4	3.0	6.1	2.1	0.6	35	72	58
Heredia,Luis	17	R	23	aa	PIT	52	4.15	1.59	6.41	5.7	6.0	1.0	0.6	29	74	45
Herget,Jimmy	17	R	24	a/a	CIN	62	4.18	1.46	5.1	3.5	9.0	2.6	1.0	34	74	77
Herget,Kevin	16	R	25	a/a	STL	39	3.84	1.63	4.73	2.9	7.8	2.7	0.2	40	75	88
	17	R	26	a/a	STL	82	5.27	1.62	10.4	2.9	6.8	2.4	1.0	36	69	52
Hernandez,Ariel	17	R	25	aa	CIN	50	4.76	1.74	5.85	8.2	8.8	1.1	0.3	30	71	77
Hernandez,Carlos	16	L	29	a/a	COL	130	7.79	2.23	23.5	1.6	4.4	2.7	1.1	45	65	19
Hernandez,Jefri	16	R	25	a/a	TEX	32	4.05	1.76	6.17	6.2	7.1	1.1	0.3	34	76	57
	17	R	26	aa	BAL	49	4.55	1.81	7.62	3.6	5.6	1.5	2.2	35	83	-12
Herrera,Ronald	16	R	21	a/a	NYY	137	5.58	1.54	24.9	2.7	7.7	2.8	1.0	36	64	70
	17	R	22	a/a	NYY	66	2.21	0.97	22.9	2.2	5.7	2.7	0.8	23	82	80

PITCHER	yr	t	age	lvl	org	ip	era	whip	bf/g	ctl	dom	cmd	hr/9	h%	s%	bp
Hess,David	17	R	24	aa	BAL	154	4.85	1.44	24.4	3.5	6.2	1.8	1.1	30	68	4
Hessler,Keith	16	L	27	a/a	SD	42	3.84	1.49	5.17	3.4	8.1	2.4	0.2	36	73	9
	17	L	28	aaa	SD	45	5.08	1.84	5.15	4.5	5.3	1.2	1.3	35	75	
Heston,Chris	16	R	28	aaa	SF	81	5.70	1.69	24.4	3.9	4.5	1.2	0.8	33	66	2
	17	R	29	aaa	MIN	62	11.29	2.59	22.3	4.9	4.5	0.9	2.7	43	58	-6
Heyer,Kurt	16	R	25	a/a	STL	94	6.41	1.68	12.5	2.6	5.4	2.1	0.8	37	61	4
Higgins,Tyler	16	R	25	aa	MIA	73	4.79	1.41	7.02	2.6	4.4	1.7	0.8	31	67	3
	17	R	26	aa	MIA	60	4.92	1.66	7.94	2.9	5.7	2.0	1.3	35	73	2
Hill,Cameron	16	R	22	a/a	CLE	17	2.75	1.02	5.94	1.1	5.3	5.0	1.3	25	81	10
	17	R	23	a/a	CLE	64	4.09	1.36	6.25	2.6	5.3	2.1	1.2	30	74	3
Hill,Taylor	16	R	27	aaa	WAS	155	7.08	1.77	26.3	2.7	4.3	1.6	1.4	36	61	
	17	R	28	aaa	WAS	154	8.22	1.89	26.8	2.5	3.2	1.3	2.0	36	59	-3
Hill,Tim	16	L	26	aa	KC	45	4.29	1.61	6.38	3.8	7.5	2.0	1.4	34	78	3
	17	L	27	aa	KC	69	6.29	1.80	8.85	2.9	7.4	2.6	0.3	42	62	7
Hissong,Travis	16	R	25	aa	NYY	33	4.18	1.29	9.13	2.2	7.2	3.2	1.3	31	72	7
	17	R	26	aa	MIL	50	7.29	1.96	8.91	6.3	8.0	1.3	1.5	36	64	2
Hofacket,Adam	17	R	23	a/a	LAA	53	4.41	1.40	6.08	1.6	6.8	4.2	0.8	35	70	9
Hoffman,Jeff	16	R	23	aaa	COL	119	5.49	1.60	23.9	3.5	7.2	2.0	1.1	35	67	4
	17	R	24	aaa	COL	50	6.32	1.50	21.4	3.7	6.5	1.8	0.7	32	56	5
Holder,Jonathan	16	R	23	a/a	NYY	61	2.57	0.83	5.6	1.2	11.9	10.3	0.7	30	72	28
	17	R	24	aaa	NYY	16	2.31	1.71	6.04	4.9	10.0	2.0	0.8	39	90	7
Holmberg,David	16	L	25	a/a	CHW	169	4.75	1.43	25.6	2.5	4.8	1.9	0.8	32	67	4
Holmes,Brian	16	L	25	a/a	HOU	52	4.87	1.51	18.6	2.5	7.7	3.1	1.2	36	70	7
	17	L	26	aaa	HOU	53	8.90	1.96	13.4	4.5	6.5	1.4	1.7	38	55	
Holmes,Clay	16	R	23	aa	PIT	136	5.13	1.64	23.4	4.2	5.4	1.3	0.7	33	68	3
	17	R	24	aaa	PIT	113	4.54	1.62	20	5.1	6.3	1.2	0.4	32	71	5
Holmes,Grant	17	R	21	aa	OAK	148	5.05	1.49	22	3.5	7.6	2.2	0.8	34	66	6
Honeywell,Brent	16	R	21	aa	TAM	59	2.62	1.18	23.7	2.1	7.2	3.5	0.6	30	80	10
	17	R	22	a/a	TAM	137	4.40	1.41	22.2	2.4	10.2	4.2	0.9	38	70	12
House,Austin	16	R	25	a/a	COL	61	7.43	1.94	6.42	3.6	6.5	1.8	0.9	41	61	3
	17	R	26	aaa	COL	68	2.59	1.43	5.9	3.4	5.1	1.5	0.4	31	82	5
House,T.J.	16	L	27	aaa	CLE	72	5.79	2.30	11.2	6.1	4.7	0.8	1.0	40	76	-
	17	L	28	aaa	TOR	133	7.24	2.19	27.9	5.3	5.6	1.0	1.2	40	67	
Houser,Adrian	16	R	23	aa	MIL	70	7.59	1.72	24.5	3.2	6.1	1.9	0.9	37	54	4
Howard,Sam	16	L	23	aa	COL	90	6.20	1.99	27.1	3.2	5.1	1.6	1.7	39	72	-
	17	L	24	a/a	COL	127	4.84	1.51	23	3.4	5.6	1.6	1.1	31	70	3
Hu,Chih-Wei	16	R	23	a/a	TAM	147	3.46	1.33	24.5	2.4	6.1	2.6	0.5	32	74	7
	17	R	24	aaa	TAM	62	4.17	1.40	8.39	1.9	7.2	3.7	1.6	33	76	7
Hudson,Dakota	17	R	23	a/a	STL	153	3.75	1.45	26.1	2.9	4.6	1.6	0.4	32	74	4
Huffman,Chris	17	R	25	a/a	SD	102	3.86	1.48	24.3	2.1	6.1	2.8	1.1	34	77	5
Hunter,Kyle	16	L	27	a/a	SEA	76	5.63	1.72	12	3.9	4.4	1.1	0.8	34	67	1
	17	L	28	a/a	SEA	72	5.56	1.84	10.8	2.5	5.3	2.2	1.4	39	72	2
Hurlbut,David	16	L	27	a/a	MIN	162	5.20	1.79	26.7	1.8	4.3	2.4	0.8	39	71	3
	17	L	28	aaa	MIN	131	5.79	1.95	27.1	2.5	5.1	2.0	0.6	42	69	3
Hurlbutt,Dustin	17	R	25	a/a	OAK	49	5.12	1.52	21.1	5.0	4.9	1.0	1.1	27	68	2
Hursh,Jason	16	R	25	a/a	ATL	73	2.72	1.46	7.27	4.3	5.3	1.2	0.0	31	79	6
	17	R	26	a/a	ATL	52	6.14	1.94	6.56	3.5	7.3	2.1	0.6	43	67	5
Hutchison,Drew	16	R	26	aaa	PIT	138	5.17	1.49	23.8	3.6	6.9	1.9	1.2	31	68	4
	17	R	27	aaa	PIT	159	5.14	1.65	25.4	3.7	5.2	1.4	1.0	33	70	2
Infante,Gregory	16	R	29	a/a	PHI	62	7.74	2.17	7.89	6.2	7.3	1.2	1.6	39	66	
	17	R	30	aaa	CHW	15	2.43	1.26	5.1	5.9	8.2	1.4	0.0	24	79	9
Irvin,Cole	17	L	23	aa	PHI	84	4.92	1.27	26.6	2.6	6.2	2.4	1.5	28	66	4
Isaacs,Dusty	17	R	26	aa	TOR	62	5.33	1.49	6.48	4.6	8.9	1.9	1.4	31	67	5
Jackson,Luke	16	R	25	a/a	TEX	46	4.88	1.84	5.99	7.0	9.1	1.3	1.4	33	77	4
	17	R	26	aaa	ATL	24	8.42	2.10	13.3	6.8	7.1	1.0	0.8	38	58	3
James,Joshua	17	R	24	aa	HOU	76	5.51	1.66	16.2	3.9	7.4	1.9	0.1	38	64	7
Janas,Stephen	16	R	24	a/a	ATL	85	3.72	1.25	7.87	1.9	5.2	2.8	0.6	30	71	7
Jankowski,Jordan	16	R	27	aaa	HOU	72	4.42	1.34	5.85	4.0	10.4	2.6	0.9	32	68	9
	17	R	28	aaa	LA	43	6.99	1.81	4.9	5.8	8.9	1.5	1.0	37	61	5
Jannis,Mickey	16	R	29	a/a	NYM	121	7.25	1.88	24.7	5.5	4.0	0.7	0.8	33	60	
	17	R	30	aa	NYM	122	6.14	1.82	27	4.0	4.8	1.2	1.2	35	68	
Jaye,Myles	16	R	25	a/a	DET	162	5.27	1.48	24.9	2.5	5.8	2.3	0.9	34	65	5
	17	R	26	a/a	DET	132	5.54	1.83	24.5	3.6	6.1	1.7	1.0	38	71	3
Jemiola,Zach	16	R	22	aa	COL	162	6.69	1.79	27.6	2.8	4.0	1.4	1.3	36	63	
	17	R	23	aaa	COL	82	8.97	2.02	24.7	4.4	3.4	0.8	1.9	35	57	-3
Jenkins,Tyrell	16	R	24	aaa	ATL	84	3.11	1.67	22.1	4.0	5.2	1.3	0.4	34	81	4
	17	R	25	aaa	SD	82	8.08	2.06	23.6	5.3	4.9	0.9	1.6	36	62	-1
Jensen,Chris	16	R	26	a/a	OAK	147	6.03	1.52	23.7	3.0	4.8	1.6	1.3	31	62	2
	17	R	27	aaa	OAK	85	7.45	1.83	13.1	3.2	4.4	1.4	0.9	37	58	1
Jerez,Williams	16	L	24	aa	BOS	65	6.21	1.80	7.51	4.4	7.5	1.7	0.9	38	65	4
	17	L	25	aa	BOS	63	4.76	1.62	7.4	3.7	6.4	1.7	1.1	34	73	3
Jester,Jason	16	R	25	aa	SD	56	3.66	1.45	5.12	2.1	9.0	4.3	0.7	39	76	11
	17	R	26	aaa	SD	67	6.29	1.70	5.71	3.4	4.3	1.2	1.1	34	63	1
Jewell,Jake	17	R	24	aa	LAA	125	6.73	1.72	23.6	3.2	5.0	1.6	1.2	35	61	1
Jimenez,Dedgar	17	L	21	aa	BOS	46	3.69	1.53	25.2	3.6	4.1	1.1	0.9	30	78	2
Jiminian,Johendi	16	R	24	aa	COL	59	3.66	1.71	6.99	4.1	5.8	1.4	1.0	34	81	2
	17	R	25	aa	COL	63	8.04	2.25	8.91	6.7	4.4	0.7	2.1	35	67	-3
Johnson,Brian	16	L	26	aaa	BOS	77	6.83	1.92	24.3	5.2	5.0	1.0	1.5	34	66	
	17	L	27	aaa	BOS	90	5.05	1.65	23.8	3.5	5.3	1.5	1.4	33	73	1
Johnson,Chase	16	R	24	aa	SF	52	4.44	1.49	9.4	3.4	5.4	1.6	0.4	32	69	5
Johnson,Cole	16	R	28	a/a	ARI	52	5.80	1.54	19	1.7	5.1	3.0	0.9	36	62	5
Johnson,D.J.	16	R	27	aa	LAA	69	5.87	2.02	7.13	4.8	7.0	1.5	0.2	42	68	5
	17	R	28	aaa	COL	64	4.87	1.68	6.73	4.3	5.0	1.2	1.0	33	72	2
Johnson,Erik	16	R	27	aaa	CHW	49	3.80	1.52	26.6	3.6	5.2	1.4	1.6	30	82	1
Johnson,Jeff	16	R	26	aaa	CLE	53	4.08	1.59	4.9	4.5	7.4	1.7	0.7	34	75	5
	17	R	27	aaa	CLE	55	4.78	1.86	5.15	7.2	7.4	1.0	0.7	33	74	4
Johnson,Jordan	17	R	24	aa	SF	92	6.06	1.63	19.6	4.0	5.3	1.3	1.2	32	64	2

TCHER	yr	t	age	lvl	org	ip	era	whip	bf/g	ctl	dom	cmd	hr/9	h%	s%	bpv
hnson,Michael	17	L	26	aa	LA	61	3.47	1.43	6.51	3.4	8.4	2.5	1.5	32	83	57
hnson,Patrick	16	R	28	aa	MIA	128	4.99	1.57	18.2	2.8	5.9	2.1	1.2	34	71	37
hnson,Pierce	16	R	25	aaa	CHC	63	7.27	1.82	13.3	6.4	8.9	1.4	1.3	34	60	42
	17	R	26	aaa	CHC	54	5.03	1.64	5.64	4.7	9.9	2.1	0.5	38	68	86
hnson,Stephen	16	R	25	aaa	CIN	75	6.96	1.79	9.84	5.6	6.5	1.2	1.6	32	63	12
kisch,Eric	16	L	27	a/a	TEX	63	5.52	1.92	11.1	4.0	4.6	1.1	0.9	37	72	11
	17	L	28	a/a	ARI	141	5.38	1.64	21.6	3.0	4.7	1.6	1.0	34	68	22
nes,Chris	16	L	28	aaa	LAA	118	7.19	1.86	24.1	3.0	4.8	1.6	0.7	39	60	25
nes,Christian	16	L	25	aa	SF	63	5.52	1.57	5.8	4.5	5.5	1.2	0.3	32	62	50
	17	L	26	aa	SF	25	7.51	2.27	6.45	4.9	6.8	1.4	0.8	44	66	27
nes,Tyler	16	R	27	aa	NYY	46	3.51	1.67	6.21	2.7	10.5	3.9	0.3	45	78	125
	17	R	28	aaa	NYY	64	6.55	1.67	6.5	3.4	8.3	2.5	1.4	38	62	53
rge,Felix	16	R	22	aa	MIN	74	4.96	1.43	28.7	1.4	3.2	2.3	0.9	32	66	33
	17	R	23	a/a	MIN	149	5.40	1.66	26.7	2.6	5.2	2.0	1.1	36	69	30
ngmann,Taylor	16	R	27	a/a	MIL	106	6.41	1.87	23.7	6.8	6.9	1.0	0.9	33	65	35
	17	R	28	a/a	MIL	123	4.23	1.61	21	4.7	6.4	1.4	1.0	32	76	38
nis,Jakob	16	R	24	a/a	KC	149	5.08	1.42	23.4	2.1	6.9	3.3	1.1	34	66	73
	17	R	25	aaa	KC	71	3.80	1.27	24.2	2.0	8.6	4.3	0.8	34	72	118
rado,Ariel	16	R	20	aa	TEX	44	4.10	1.39	23	2.1	6.3	2.9	0.7	34	71	76
	17	R	21	aa	TEX	157	6.19	1.69	26.2	2.3	4.6	2.0	1.1	36	64	23
alish,Jake	17	L	26	a/a	KC	87	4.92	1.76	19	2.5	5.2	2.1	0.6	39	72	43
aminsky,Rob	16	L	22	aa	CLE	137	4.23	1.40	23.1	3.2	5.1	1.6	0.6	30	70	48
eller,Brad	17	R	22	aa	ARI	131	6.27	1.76	23	4.1	6.6	1.6	0.6	37	63	47
elly,Casey	16	R	27	aaa	ATL	74	4.73	1.52	21.4	3.9	4.7	1.2	0.8	30	70	27
	17	R	28	aaa	SF	101	5.82	1.87	24.9	3.8	5.6	1.5	1.4	37	71	10
elly,Michael	16	R	24	a/a	SD	99	4.37	1.44	22.3	3.6	7.0	2.0	0.7	32	70	64
	17	R	25	a/a	SD	127	5.08	1.51	19.6	4.0	7.2	1.8	0.9	33	67	55
ennedy,Brett	17	R	23	aa	SD	141	5.15	1.45	23.2	2.5	7.1	2.8	1.2	34	67	61
ent,Steve	16	L	27	a/a	ATL	57	5.66	1.92	6.47	3.9	7.8	2.0	1.0	41	71	46
eselica,Sean	17	L	24	aa	PIT	74	4.85	1.71	7.94	5.2	7.0	1.3	0.3	35	70	59
ckham,Mike	17	L	29	a/a	MIA	146	5.20	1.51	23.4	1.8	5.6	3.2	1.0	35	67	61
ekhefer,Dean	16	L	27	aaa	STL	35	2.48	1.35	4.99	2.2	4.2	1.9	0.5	31	83	48
	17	L	28	aaa	SEA	44	5.69	1.96	4.32	4.2	6.7	1.6	0.7	41	71	38
ngham,Nick	17	R	26	aaa	PIT	113	5.83	1.64	25.3	2.6	5.6	2.2	0.8	37	64	46
nley,Tyler	16	R	25	a/a	MIA	60	6.27	1.75	6.19	4.9	7.6	1.6	0.6	36	63	54
	17	R	26	aa	MIA	26	6.95	2.10	4.74	6.3	9.6	1.5	0.8	43	66	53
pper,Jordan	16	R	24	aa	LAA	153	4.58	1.48	26.3	2.6	4.3	1.7	0.7	32	69	36
	17	R	25	a/a	BAL	132	4.99	1.79	23.5	2.9	3.8	1.3	0.9	36	73	9
rsch,Chris	16	L	25	aa	TAM	145	3.98	1.55	25.4	3.7	5.9	1.6	0.5	33	74	50
ttredge,Andrew	16	R	26	a/a	SEA	72	4.31	1.54	8.48	2.4	8.7	3.6	0.7	39	72	100
	17	R	27	aaa	TAM	68	2.10	1.22	6.74	2.5	8.3	3.3	0.3	32	83	115
ein,Phil	16	R	27	aaa	PHI	78	3.15	1.31	14.7	2.5	8.2	3.2	1.1	32	81	84
onowski,Alex	16	R	24	aa	LAA	20	7.26	2.01	19.6	3.8	5.3	1.4	0.0	42	60	44
	17	R	25	a/a	LAA	129	5.19	1.43	22	2.1	5.3	2.5	1.3	32	66	41
napp,Ricky	16	R	24	a/a	NYM	58	3.85	1.26	26.4	2.5	6.7	2.7	0.3	31	68	90
	17	R	25	a/a	NYM	172	6.79	1.73	26.9	2.3	4.4	1.9	1.1	37	61	20
night,Dusten	17	R	27	aaa	SF	60	4.39	1.61	8.63	5.1	6.9	1.4	0.9	32	74	45
nudson,Guido	16	R	27	a/a	SEA	47	4.85	1.39	6.34	4.0	6.2	1.6	1.1	28	67	42
och,Matt	16	R	26	a/a	ARI	121	5.27	1.61	25.6	1.5	4.4	2.9	0.9	36	68	48
	17	R	27	aaa	ARI	45	9.49	2.09	22.1	3.0	3.9	1.3	2.3	39	57	-42
oerner,Brody	17	R	24	aa	NYY	71	5.97	1.84	27.5	2.9	4.8	1.7	1.4	38	70	7
ohlscheen,Stepl	16	R	28	aa	MIL	50	4.09	1.59	4.38	3.9	9.2	2.4	0.8	37	76	78
	17	R	29	aaa	MIL	41	7.34	2.04	7.06	3.8	6.5	1.7	2.5	39	69	-17
olarek,Adam	16	L	27	a/a	TAM	60	4.20	1.53	5.58	5.8	7.5	1.3	0.2	30	70	74
	17	L	28	aaa	TAM	44	2.45	1.58	4.69	4.0	7.5	1.9	0.0	37	83	82
opech,Michael	17	R	21	a/a	CHW	134	3.57	1.31	22.2	4.7	10.5	2.2	0.5	31	73	107
owalczyk,Karch	17	R	26	aa	LA	62	3.96	1.58	6.23	3.2	5.4	1.7	0.8	34	77	36
rehbiel,Joey	16	R	24	aa	ARI	56	3.91	1.41	4.52	4.1	8.8	2.2	0.8	32	74	78
	17	R	25	a/a	ARI	57	3.90	1.43	5.24	4.4	9.8	2.2	0.6	34	73	94
uchno,John	16	R	25	a/a	PIT	84	6.12	1.64	9.9	3.4	3.6	1.1	1.2	32	64	1
uhl,Chad	16	R	24	aaa	PIT	84	3.27	1.41	22.1	1.8	5.7	3.1	1.1	33	81	60
urcz,Aaron	16	R	26	a/a	OAK	68	3.99	1.22	6	2.4	5.6	2.3	0.6	29	67	69
	17	R	27	a/a	OAK	51	6.70	1.64	5.79	3.2	5.2	1.6	1.1	34	59	25
abourt,Jairo	17	L	23	a/a	DET	53	3.36	1.40	6.01	5.4	8.0	1.5	0.8	27	78	65
adwig,A.J.	17	R	25	a/a	DET	116	7.20	1.86	23.7	1.9	4.9	2.6	1.5	39	63	20
ail,Brady	16	R	23	a/a	NYY	124	6.88	1.71	24.4	3.4	4.7	1.4	1.4	34	61	5
	17	R	24	a/a	NYY	145	6.95	1.66	23.2	3.2	5.2	1.7	1.8	33	61	4
akind,Jared	16	L	24	aa	PIT	66	3.21	1.32	5.82	3.9	6.7	1.7	0.4	29	76	71
	17	L	25	aa	MIA	36	9.56	2.28	8.27	4.8	8.0	1.7	0.9	46	56	35
amb,John	16	L	26	aaa	CIN	29	7.70	1.93	23.2	3.3	6.7	2.1	0.5	42	57	53
	17	L	27	aaa	LAA	70	5.70	1.72	24.6	3.2	5.0	1.5	1.1	35	68	20
amb,Will	16	L	26	aaa	CHW	54	6.92	1.80	6.44	5.1	5.7	1.1	1.8	32	65	-2
	17	L	27	a/a	COL	67	8.18	2.21	9.32	6.5	7.0	1.1	3.2	36	70	-44
amet,Dinelson	16	R	24	a/a	SD	85	3.92	1.33	22.1	3.7	9.5	2.6	0.5	33	70	103
ara,Rainy	16	R	25	a/a	NYM	113	5.48	1.56	19.9	3.3	4.7	1.4	1.0	32	66	23
auer,Eric	17	L	22	aa	SD	55	5.36	1.46	23.6	2.9	6.6	2.3	1.2	33	65	51
awrence,Casey	16	R	29	a/a	TOR	162	6.34	1.80	26.7	2.5	4.6	1.8	1.1	38	65	18
azo,Raudel	16	L	27	a/a	MIA	42	3.10	1.50	5.33	2.7	5.7	2.1	0.2	35	78	66
	17	L	28	a/a	BAL	24	9.49	2.14	6.04	4.6	5.6	1.2	2.4	38	58	-32
eathersich,Jack	16	L	26	a/a	CHC	15	2.89	1.56	4.2	6.3	8.6	1.4	0.0	32	79	88
	17	L	27	aaa	CHC	44	3.39	1.36	4.52	6.1	11.6	1.9	0.7	28	76	106
eBlanc,Randy	17	R	25	aa	MIN	79	5.93	1.81	19.2	3.0	4.3	1.4	0.2	38	64	37
eclerc,Jose	16	R	23	a/a	TEX	66	3.80	1.34	7.03	5.6	8.8	1.6	0.6	26	72	82
edbetter,David	17	R	25	a/a	TEX	110	6.47	1.75	17.4	4.9	5.5	1.1	1.7	31	66	0
ee,Chris	16	L	24	aa	BAL	51	3.76	1.21	25.9	2.4	2.7	1.2	0.9	25	71	18
	17	L	25	aaa	BAL	116	7.08	2.11	21.3	5.0	5.4	1.1	1.1	39	67	7
ee,Nick	16	L	25	aa	WAS	50	5.99	2.03	5.39	8.5	7.9	0.9	1.0	33	71	35
ee,Thomas	16	R	27	aaa	STL	56	7.29	2.05	14.4	3.1	4.5	1.4	0.5	42	62	22

PITCHER	yr	t	age	lvl	org	ip	era	whip	bf/g	ctl	dom	cmd	hr/9	h%	s%	bpv
Lee,Zach	16	R	25	aaa	SEA	148	6.65	1.70	24.8	2.2	5.5	2.4	1.3	37	62	33
	17	R	26	aaa	SD	67	7.57	1.96	20	4.3	4.5	1.0	1.4	36	62	-6
Leibrandt,Brandoı	17	L	25	a/a	PHI	137	4.69	1.58	24.1	3.3	5.8	1.8	1.0	34	72	37
Leiter,Mark	16	R	25	aa	PHI	104	4.28	1.36	18.9	2.8	6.9	2.5	1.0	31	71	64
Lewicki,Artie	16	R	24	aa	DET	67	4.29	1.38	23.6	1.8	6.0	3.3	0.6	34	69	83
	17	R	25	a/a	DET	141	4.63	1.44	24	2.2	6.2	2.8	0.6	35	67	75
Leyer,Robinson	16	R	23	aa	CHW	33	6.84	2.05	6.63	5.9	8.0	1.4	0.3	41	64	56
	17	R	24	aa	CHW	58	5.09	1.74	7	6.1	8.2	1.4	0.4	35	69	65
Light,Pat	16	R	25	aaa	MIN	38	3.41	1.43	5.2	4.9	7.8	1.6	0.3	30	75	78
	17	R	26	aaa	SEA	55	5.58	1.75	5.98	5.8	4.6	0.8	0.6	31	67	26
Lillis-White,Connc	17	L	25	aa	LAA	45	5.73	1.53	7.47	7.1	9.2	1.3	1.0	26	63	66
Liranzo,Jesus	16	R	21	aa	BAL	19	4.05	1.12	6.68	5.7	8.2	1.5	1.8	13	72	53
	17	R	22	aa	BAL	65	5.86	1.66	9.4	6.4	9.3	1.5	1.8	29	69	36
Littell,Zack	17	R	22	aa	MIN	86	3.38	1.32	25.3	2.8	7.3	2.6	0.5	32	75	85
Littrell,Corey	16	L	24	a/a	STL	67	4.58	1.47	5.42	4.1	7.4	1.8	1.0	31	71	55
	17	L	25	aa	STL	35	5.57	1.62	5.5	5.6	5.3	0.9	0.6	29	65	36
Lively,Ben	16	R	24	a/a	PHI	171	3.65	1.12	24	2.4	6.3	2.6	0.8	27	69	77
	17	R	25	aaa	PHI	97	4.18	1.40	25.6	2.2	6.4	2.9	0.4	35	69	86
Lloyd,Kyle	16	R	26	aa	SD	130	4.46	1.52	18.8	2.9	5.6	1.9	0.8	34	72	46
	17	R	27	a/a	SD	147	6.34	1.67	24.5	3.3	6.7	2.1	0.7	37	61	55
Lobstein,Kyle	16	L	27	aaa	BAL	51	6.37	1.89	12.1	3.8	5.6	1.5	0.8	39	66	26
	17	L	28	a/a	MIA	43	2.94	1.73	6.47	5.4	5.1	1.0	0.7	32	85	26
Lockett,Walker	16	R	22	a/a	SD	53	3.13	1.09	22.9	0.7	5.8	9.0	0.7	30	74	204
	17	R	23	aaa	SD	55	4.39	1.48	23.8	1.9	4.5	2.4	1.3	33	74	31
Lollis,Matt	16	R	26	a/a	CHW	56	4.64	1.49	6.56	6.0	7.3	1.2	1.2	26	72	44
Long,Grayson	17	R	23	aa	DET	126	3.57	1.33	21.7	2.9	6.7	2.3	0.7	31	75	69
Long,Jaron	16	R	25	a/a	WAS	107	4.57	1.59	24.8	2.1	4.8	2.3	1.0	35	73	37
	17	R	26	a/a	WAS	164	4.80	1.48	26.2	1.9	5.0	2.6	1.3	33	71	38
Long,Lucas	17	R	25	aa	BAL	128	3.79	1.47	17.8	2.7	6.3	2.4	0.6	34	75	66
Lopez,Frank	16	L	22	aa	TEX	92	6.76	1.80	18.5	3.6	6.4	1.8	1.0	38	62	34
Lopez,Jorge	16	R	23	a/a	MIL	125	7.30	1.98	23.9	5.4	6.9	1.3	1.4	37	64	15
	17	R	24	aa	MIL	104	6.64	1.60	11.8	3.8	7.7	2.0	1.0	35	58	55
Lopez,Jose	17	R	24	aa	CIN	96	4.01	1.35	23.6	4.0	7.7	1.9	1.4	28	76	51
Lopez,Reynaldo	16	R	22	a/a	WAS	109	4.31	1.33	23.9	3.1	8.8	2.8	1.2	32	71	79
	17	R	23	aaa	CHW	121	4.43	1.38	23.1	3.9	8.6	2.2	1.3	30	72	63
Lopez,Yoan	16	R	23	aa	ARI	62	7.68	1.89	20.9	5.0	4.4	0.9	1.9	33	62	-20
Lovvorn,Zach	17	R	23	aa	KC	117	6.69	1.80	17.5	2.8	5.9	2.1	0.7	39	61	44
Lowry,Thaddius	16	R	22	aa	CHW	24	4.78	1.25	24.4	1.6	3.7	2.4	0.0	31	57	72
	17	R	23	aa	CHW	82	8.79	1.97	14	4.1	5.9	1.4	1.6	38	56	2
Lucas,Josh	16	R	26	a/a	STL	60	4.94	1.40	5.65	2.6	8.2	3.2	0.8	35	65	91
	17	R	27	aaa	STL	60	4.15	1.43	5.43	2.0	7.6	3.9	0.5	37	71	107
Lucchesi,Joey	17	L	24	aa	SD	60	2.54	1.21	24.3	2.2	6.4	2.9	0.5	30	81	86
Luetge,Lucas	16	L	29	aaa	LAA	56	5.52	1.73	5.28	4.4	7.2	1.6	0.6	37	67	53
	17	L	30	aaa	BAL	32	6.97	2.13	6.53	4.5	7.2	1.6	2.0	41	71	-2
Lugo,Luis	17	L	23	aa	CLE	134	5.73	1.70	23.3	4.0	4.7	1.2	1.6	32	70	-1
Lugo,Seth	16	R	27	aaa	NYM	73	6.50	1.80	16.1	2.4	6.0	2.5	1.1	40	64	40
Lujan,Matt	16	L	28	aaa	SF	49	5.08	1.84	19	4.7	6.4	1.4	1.4	36	76	16
	17	L	29	aa	SF	70	7.53	2.04	22.8	2.8	5.3	1.9	1.2	42	63	15
Lyles,Jordan	16	R	26	aaa	COL	45	7.92	2.12	27.6	4.1	4.2	1.0	1.5	39	63	-16
	17	R	27	aaa	SD	20	4.89	1.53	17.4	3.5	6.9	2.0	0.4	35	66	67
Maddox,Austin	16	R	25	a/a	BOS	43	5.52	1.44	7.1	4.0	6.7	1.7	1.0	30	62	48
	17	R	26	a/a	BOS	49	4.34	1.45	5.69	5.5	6.5	1.2	0.5	27	69	59
Mader,Michael	16	L	22	aa	ATL	30	3.37	1.33	24.9	2.0	7.1	3.6	0.0	35	72	116
	17	L	23	aa	ATL	65	5.99	1.84	8.61	6.6	7.0	1.1	0.8	33	67	38
Magill,Matthew	16	R	27	a/a	CIN	52	7.58	2.01	6.61	5.8	8.4	1.5	1.7	39	64	21
	17	R	28	aaa	SD	96	4.39	1.71	22.8	3.8	5.1	1.3	1.2	34	77	16
Magnifico,Damier	16	R	25	aaa	MIL	62	4.76	1.62	5.29	5.0	7.2	1.4	0.3	34	69	64
	17	R	26	a/a	LAA	53	7.56	2.18	5.67	6.6	8.1	1.2	0.4	42	63	51
Mahle,Greg	16	L	23	aaa	LAA	33	7.71	1.87	5.11	3.0	5.8	1.9	1.6	38	60	10
	17	L	24	a/a	LAA	72	5.54	1.47	6.15	3.1	5.6	1.8	0.8	32	62	47
Mahle,Tyler	16	R	22	aa	CIN	71	7.00	1.69	23	2.9	7.5	2.6	2.3	36	63	22
	17	R	23	a/a	CIN	144	2.90	1.17	24	2.1	7.6	3.6	0.8	30	78	102
Maness,Seth	17	R	29	aaa	KC	47	8.72	1.99	9.41	1.8	4.8	2.7	1.6	41	56	17
Mantiply,Joe	16	L	25	a/a	DET	59	3.64	1.29	4.35	2.0	8.1	4.0	0.4	35	71	121
	17	L	26	aaa	NYY	70	4.05	1.62	8.89	2.6	6.5	2.5	0.6	38	75	64
Mapes,Tyler	16	R	25	aa	WAS	155	4.43	1.54	27	2.5	3.6	1.4	0.7	33	72	23
Marin,Terance	16	R	27	aaa	CHW	110	6.04	1.70	19.1	3.2	3.9	1.2	1.3	33	66	0
Mariot,Michael	16	R	28	a/a	PHI	36	3.67	1.27	5.13	4.1	5.5	1.3	1.5	23	78	26
	17	R	29	aaa	PHI	57	6.40	1.76	5.8	3.9	7.7	2.0	1.1	38	64	45
Markel,Parker	16	R	26	a/a	TAM	71	3.64	1.63	7.38	3.6	6.0	1.7	0.1	36	76	61
Markey,Brad	16	R	24	aa	CHC	131	3.82	1.51	21.7	3.2	3.8	1.2	1.0	30	78	13
	17	R	25	a/a	CHC	79	3.56	1.34	8.22	1.7	6.9	4.0	1.2	33	78	88
Marks,Justin	16	L	28	aaa	TAM	140	5.49	1.62	24.8	3.9	6.4	1.6	1.1	33	68	34
	17	L	29	aaa	LA	76	6.53	1.76	8.65	4.4	6.4	1.5	0.7	36	61	41
Marksberry,Matt	16	L	26	a/a	ATL	43	3.27	1.57	5.51	4.1	6.9	1.7	0.5	34	80	59
Maronde,Nick	16	L	27	a/a	CLE	48	4.60	1.67	5.67	3.0	5.5	1.9	0.8	36	73	40
Marquez,German	16	R	21	a/a	COL	167	4.42	1.38	26.9	2.2	6.6	3.0	1.1	33	71	68
Marte,Kelvin	16	L	29	aaa	PIT	74	5.65	1.57	9.5	3.1	5.0	1.6	0.6	34	63	39
	17	L	30	aaa	MIA	86	6.08	1.87	12.6	5.1	5.5	1.1	1.1	35	68	15
Martes,Francis	16	R	21	aa	HOU	125	3.72	1.27	20.5	3.2	8.5	2.6	0.3	32	69	102
	17	R	22	aaa	HOU	32	4.75	1.95	19.3	6.6	9.6	1.5	1.1	38	78	48
Martin,Cody	16	R	27	aaa	SEA	114	4.10	1.36	19.1	2.6	7.3	2.8	0.5	34	69	88
	17	R	28	aaa	SEA	57	5.26	1.57	12.4	2.4	8.4	3.5	1.3	38	69	76
Martin,Josh	16	R	27	aaa	CLE	66	4.96	1.54	6.12	3.6	6.2	1.7	0.7	33	68	49
	17	R	28	aaa	CLE	36	4.85	1.62	5.33	2.4	6.5	2.7	0.7	38	70	64
Martin,Kyle	16	R	25	aaa	BOS	67	5.51	1.57	8.13	3.4	8.5	2.5	0.9	37	65	72
	17	R	26	aaa	BOS	54	6.98	2.02	7.86	5.3	6.5	1.2	1.6	37	68	3

PITCHER	yr	t	age	lvl	org	ip	era	whip	bf/g	ctl	dom	cmd	hr/9	h%	s%	bpv
Martinez,David	17	R	30	aaa	HOU	136	4.95	1.56	23.9	3.1	5.1	1.7	1.2	32	71	24
Martinez,Nicholas	16	R	26	a/a	TEX	105	5.21	1.55	24.2	1.8	4.9	2.8	0.8	36	67	53
	17	R	27	aaa	TEX	38	2.81	1.11	21.1	1.9	4.1	2.2	0.9	25	79	52
Mateo,Luis	16	R	26	a/a	NYM	67	2.91	1.44	5.6	2.7	5.7	2.1	0.4	33	80	64
	17	R	27	a/a	NYM	54	7.03	1.95	7.2	5.2	7.1	1.4	1.7	37	66	10
Mateo,Victor	16	R	27	a/a	ATL	51	9.67	2.58	12.5	5.8	4.5	0.8	1.5	43	62	-30
Mayers,Mike	16	R	25	a/a	STL	144	3.83	1.44	24.5	3.1	6.8	2.2	0.8	33	75	62
	17	R	26	aaa	STL	110	4.23	1.62	15.7	2.8	6.1	2.2	1.1	36	77	40
Mayza,Tim	17	L	25	a/a	TOR	53	4.76	1.66	5.89	4.3	8.1	1.9	1.2	35	74	49
Mazza,Chris	16	R	27	aa	MIA	80	6.03	1.69	19	3.7	4.4	1.2	1.0	33	65	13
	17	R	28	aa	MIA	147	4.51	1.60	23.2	2.9	4.5	1.5	0.5	34	71	35
McAvoy,Kevin	16	R	23	aa	BOS	116	7.50	1.75	24.2	4.2	5.2	1.2	0.8	35	55	24
	17	R	24	aa	BOS	118	5.70	1.64	23.8	3.8	6.0	1.6	0.7	35	64	42
McCain,Shane	17	L	26	aa	TEX	51	8.16	1.80	6.5	1.7	5.2	3.1	2.4	37	58	6
McCarthy,Kevin	16	R	24	a/a	KC	68	3.65	1.30	5.96	3.2	6.3	1.9	1.0	28	75	54
	17	R	25	aaa	KC	32	4.03	1.52	5.55	2.7	3.8	1.4	0.9	32	75	20
McCarthy,Mike	16	R	29	a/a	BOS	40	8.65	2.33	16	4.4	2.0	0.4	1.5	39	63	-48
McCoy,Patrick	16	L	28	aaa	COL	44	8.40	2.37	5.85	6.8	5.1	0.8	0.9	40	63	1
McCurry,Brendan	16	R	24	a/a	HOU	82	3.51	1.29	6.02	2.3	8.8	3.9	0.7	34	75	113
	17	R	25	aaa	HOU	45	4.24	1.44	5.43	2.2	8.9	4.1	1.1	37	73	104
McGough,Scott	16	R	27	a/a	BAL	76	7.78	2.02	8.51	3.5	5.3	1.5	1.4	40	62	3
	17	R	28	a/a	BAL	56	3.92	1.94	6.63	4.2	7.8	1.8	0.8	41	82	46
McGowan,Kevin	16	R	25	a/a	NYM	51	3.53	1.42	8.05	3.1	7.3	2.4	0.5	34	75	77
	17	R	26	aaa	NYM	65	4.58	1.52	6.01	3.8	6.6	1.8	1.2	32	73	40
McGowin,Kyle	16	R	25	a/a	LAA	142	6.96	1.76	24.1	3.5	6.9	1.9	1.3	37	61	33
	17	R	26	a/a	WAS	88	8.53	1.99	25	4.0	5.3	1.3	1.8	38	58	-9
McGrath,Kyle	16	L	24	a/a	SD	50	1.40	0.91	5.53	1.6	8.0	5.0	0.8	25	91	144
McGuire,Deck	16	R	27	a/a	STL	141	6.08	1.59	23	3.7	6.2	1.7	1.5	32	64	22
	17	R	28	aa	CIN	168	5.02	1.56	26.3	4.1	7.2	1.8	1.3	32	71	41
McKinney,Brett	16	R	26	aa	PIT	67	5.04	1.66	6.82	3.8	6.7	1.7	0.4	36	68	58
	17	R	27	aaa	PIT	62	5.00	1.71	7.06	4.4	6.0	1.4	1.2	34	73	22
McMyne,Kyle	16	R	27	aa	CIN	57	8.51	2.14	6.12	3.8	4.8	1.3	0.8	42	58	11
	17	R	28	aaa	CIN	63	9.40	2.34	7.88	6.8	4.8	0.7	1.2	39	59	-10
McRae,Alex	16	R	23	aa	PIT	88	5.82	1.77	25.4	2.5	5.5	2.2	0.7	39	67	44
	17	R	24	aa	PIT	150	4.94	1.67	24.9	2.4	4.3	1.8	0.6	36	70	33
Means,John	16	L	23	aa	BAL	96	5.80	1.64	23.8	2.4	4.0	1.7	0.8	35	64	24
	17	L	24	aa	BAL	142	5.17	1.60	24.2	2.6	6.8	2.6	1.2	37	70	52
Medina,Jhondanie	16	R	23	a/a	PIT	70	4.46	1.48	6.5	5.0	7.3	1.5	0.8	29	71	56
	17	R	24	aa	LAA	35	6.44	1.54	6.93	5.8	8.2	1.4	1.3	28	59	48
Meisinger,Ryan	17	R	23	aa	BAL	63	3.70	1.38	6.46	3.3	8.4	2.5	0.3	34	72	96
Meisner,Casey	17	R	22	aa	OAK	59	4.68	1.47	21.1	3.9	4.7	1.2	0.6	30	67	37
Mejia,Adalberto	16	L	23	a/a	MIN	132	3.90	1.30	24.7	2.1	7.0	3.4	0.9	32	72	84
	17	L	24	aaa	MIN	29	4.35	1.43	20.3	2.1	5.4	2.6	0.4	34	68	69
Mejia,Miguel	16	R	28	a/a	CHC	61	6.50	1.76	7.32	3.0	6.9	2.3	0.7	40	62	55
	17	R	29	aaa	CHC	22	8.18	1.99	7.55	5.1	3.4	0.7	1.8	33	61	-33
Mella,Keury	17	R	24	aa	CIN	134	7.09	1.77	22.8	3.5	6.3	1.8	1.6	36	61	18
Melotakis,Mason	16	L	25	aa	MIN	33	3.81	1.68	4.17	3.3	8.8	2.6	0.9	40	80	73
	17	L	26	a/a	MIN	50	5.03	1.47	5.15	4.3	7.3	1.7	0.8	31	66	59
Melville,Timothy	17	R	28	aaa	SD	76	3.28	1.27	24	3.9	6.3	1.6	0.6	27	75	64
Mendez,Roman	16	R	26	aaa	BOS	64	5.63	1.59	8.82	4.6	6.6	1.4	1.2	31	66	34
Mendez,Yohande	16	L	21	a/a	TEX	78	2.55	1.15	18.2	3.6	6.7	1.9	0.3	26	77	85
	17	L	22	aa	TEX	138	5.17	1.34	23.9	3.0	6.8	2.2	1.9	28	68	33
Mendoza,Francis	16	R	29	aaa	TEX	54	8.70	1.89	6.02	3.6	5.7	1.6	0.8	39	51	28
Mengden,Daniel	16	R	23	a/a	OAK	98	1.81	1.12	22.8	2.7	7.1	2.6	0.4	28	85	97
	17	R	24	aaa	OAK	41	4.89	1.55	19.9	3.9	7.0	1.8	1.1	33	70	46
Merritt,Ryan	16	L	24	aaa	CLE	143	5.05	1.52	25.9	1.5	4.6	3.0	1.2	35	69	46
	17	L	25	aaa	CLE	116	4.23	1.51	26.5	2.2	4.8	2.2	1.9	31	80	9
Merryweather,Juli	16	R	25	aa	CLE	74	5.33	1.52	24.7	2.2	5.8	2.6	0.9	35	65	55
	17	R	26	aa	CLE	129	7.52	1.74	23.5	2.8	6.4	2.3	1.5	37	57	29
Miller,Jared	16	L	23	a/a	ARI	33	5.01	1.27	5.57	4.1	9.1	2.2	0.9	28	61	83
	17	L	24	a/a	ARI	71	3.53	1.21	5.37	3.6	9.9	2.8	0.6	30	71	111
Miller,Shelby	16	R	26	aaa	ARI	51	4.47	1.46	27.1	1.8	7.8	4.4	0.7	37	70	109
Mills,Alec	16	R	25	a/a	KC	126	4.13	1.41	22.1	2.3	6.9	3.0	0.8	34	72	78
Milner,Hoby	16	L	25	a/a	PHI	65	3.45	1.36	5.55	2.3	8.9	3.8	1.0	35	78	103
Milone,Tommy	16	L	29	a/a	MIN	49	2.62	1.28	28.5	0.9	5.4	6.1	1.0	33	85	126
	17	L	30	aa	NYM	20	8.43	2.05	24.4	1.3	3.9	3.0	5.9	34	80	-116
Minaya,Juan	16	R	26	aaa	CHW	52	4.60	1.56	6.7	4.0	6.7	1.7	0.6	34	70	55
	17	R	27	aaa	CHW	19	1.81	1.41	6.18	2.7	5.7	2.1	0.0	34	86	77
Minor,Mike	16	L	29	a/a	KC	42	8.04	1.91	20	5.3	6.9	1.3	2.0	35	60	0
Miranda,Ariel	16	L	27	aaa	BAL	101	6.22	1.67	23.8	3.3	5.9	1.8	1.6	34	65	18
Misiewicz,Anthon	17	L	23	aa	TAM	70	4.98	1.35	24.2	2.2	6.4	2.9	1.0	32	64	69
Mitchell,Bryan	16	R	25	a/a	NYY	16	4.37	1.55	17.1	3.4	9.5	2.8	0.9	38	74	85
	17	R	26	aaa	NYY	64	4.65	1.43	19.3	2.1	7.6	3.6	0.2	37	65	110
Mitchell,Evan	16	R	24	aa	CIN	47	4.11	1.44	6.03	3.4	5.4	1.6	0.6	31	72	48
Mizenko,Tyler	16	R	26	aa	SF	54	6.10	1.98	5.11	4.8	5.5	1.2	1.3	37	71	7
Molina,Jose	16	L	25	aa	LAA	62	7.75	2.01	11.9	3.7	5.9	1.6	0.9	41	60	25
Molina,Marcos	17	R	22	aa	NYM	78	5.68	1.56	26.3	2.9	6.7	2.3	0.8	35	63	58
Moll,Sam	16	L	24	aaa	COL	47	6.90	1.89	5.31	3.9	5.6	1.4	1.3	37	64	11
	17	L	25	aaa	OAK	54	4.36	1.67	4.88	3.2	6.1	1.9	0.7	37	74	48
Montero,Rafael	16	R	26	a/a	NYM	129	5.75	1.73	23.5	4.1	6.1	1.5	1.1	35	68	27
	17	R	27	aaa	NYM	29	2.80	1.18	23.2	4.2	9.5	2.3	1.0	26	81	88
Montgomery,Jord	16	L	24	a/a	NYY	139	3.17	1.50	24.1	3.3	7.3	2.2	0.5	35	79	73
Montgomery,Mark	16	R	26	a/a	NYY	46	3.98	1.49	5.97	5.2	10.1	1.9	0.6	33	74	88
	17	R	27	aaa	STL	67	3.20	1.11	5.7	2.2	7.4	3.3	0.6	28	73	104
Moore,Andrew	16	R	22	aa	SEA	108	4.02	1.38	23.9	1.5	6.4	4.3	0.8	35	72	99
	17	R	23	a/a	SEA	110	3.57	1.19	21	1.8	7.2	4.0	1.2	30	75	95
Morales,Andrew	16	R	23	aa	STL	78	4.06	1.29	22.9	2.1	6.8	3.2	1.2	31	73	71
	17	R	24	a/a	STL	26	4.35	1.83	5.33	4.2	8.2	1.9	0.8	40	77	56

PITCHER	yr	t	age	lvl	org	ip	era	whip	bf/g	ctl	dom	cmd	hr/9	h%	s%
Morales,Osmer	17	R	25	a/a	LAA	127	4.97	1.50	21.9	3.6	7.3	2.0	1.4	32	71
Moreno,Diego	16	R	29	a/a	NYY	56	8.01	2.11	8.63	3.9	7.8	2.0	1.4	44	62
	17	R	30	aaa	CLE	29	1.46	1.05	5.55	2.0	5.6	2.8	0.5	26	89
Morgan,Adam	16	L	26	aaa	PHI	50	4.77	1.40	26.5	2.1	7.5	3.5	1.1	34	68
	17	L	27	aaa	PHI	17	6.47	1.74	6.58	2.9	5.9	2.0	0.7	38	61
Morimando,Shaw	16	L	24	a/a	CLE	152	4.40	1.54	24.6	3.6	5.7	1.6	0.7	33	72
	17	L	25	aaa	CLE	159	6.16	1.82	28.4	3.7	5.3	1.4	1.6	35	69
Morris,Akeel	16	R	24	aa	ATL	61	4.75	1.66	5.82	6.3	11.0	1.8	0.7	36	72
	17	R	25	a/a	ATL	54	3.70	1.47	6.47	4.8	8.8	1.8	0.6	32	75
Morrison,Preston	17	R	24	aa	CHC	119	7.41	1.68	19.2	3.2	5.5	1.7	1.3	35	56
Morrow,Bryce	16	R	28	aa	SD	50	8.36	2.14	27.5	4.6	4.0	0.9	1.5	38	61
Mortensen,Jared	16	R	28	aa	TAM	72	6.90	1.81	9.85	7.9	8.4	1.1	1.0	30	61
Moscot,Jon	16	R	25	aaa	CIN	50	7.59	1.88	25.9	3.4	4.8	1.4	2.4	35	64
Moss,Benton	17	R	24	aa	TAM	70	4.55	1.50	23.3	2.5	6.2	2.5	1.4	33	74
Moya,Gabriel	17	L	22	aa	MIN	58	1.08	0.90	4.62	2.4	11.0	4.6	0.4	27	91
Muhammad,ElHaj	16	R	25	a/a	CIN	51	6.08	1.87	7.03	4.8	5.6	1.2	1.1	36	68
Mujica,Jose	17	R	21	aa	TAM	154	3.66	1.23	25	2.6	4.5	1.7	1.1	26	74
Murray,Colton	16	R	26	aaa	PHI	37	4.62	1.64	6.05	4.4	7.3	1.7	0.8	35	73
	17	R	27	a/a	PHI	53	6.20	1.73	5.88	3.0	8.6	2.9	1.4	40	66
Musgrave,Harriso	16	L	24	a/a	COL	153	5.32	1.51	26.6	3.2	4.8	1.5	1.6	30	69
	17	L	25	aaa	COL	54	9.30	2.00	21.8	4.7	4.8	1.0	2.3	35	55
Musgrove,Joe	16	R	24	a/a	HOU	85	3.13	1.16	21.3	1.0	7.8	7.5	1.1	32	78
Naile,James	16	R	23	a/a	OAK	28	6.36	1.58	24.7	2.6	4.0	1.5	0.7	34	58
	17	R	24	aa	OAK	62	3.80	1.30	18.2	2.5	4.9	2.0	0.7	29	72
Nakaushiro,Yuhei	17	L	28	a/a	ARI	68	3.32	1.47	5.81	3.9	6.6	1.7	0.3	32	77
Nappo,Gregory	16	L	28	aaa	MIA	68	6.84	1.94	12.5	5.2	5.9	1.1	1.5	36	67
	17	L	29	a/a	MIA	23	5.10	1.66	6.34	3.8	6.7	1.8	1.4	34	73
Navas,Carlos	17	R	25	aa	OAK	53	3.93	1.38	6.71	2.6	6.4	2.5	0.7	33	72
Neal,Zachary	16	R	28	aaa	OAK	62	4.79	1.51	24.3	1.4	3.4	2.5	0.9	34	69
	17	R	29	aaa	OAK	99	6.31	1.60	20.8	1.0	2.8	2.8	0.9	36	60
Neiman,Troy	17	R	27	aa	COL	64	6.22	1.83	8.5	4.4	6.2	1.4	1.7	35	69
Nesbitt,Angel	16	R	26	a/a	DET	44	6.97	2.17	5.63	3.7	5.7	1.5	0.7	43	67
Neverauskas,Dov	16	R	23	a/a	PIT	58	3.97	1.37	5.17	3.5	7.1	2.0	0.2	32	69
	17	R	24	aaa	PIT	50	3.87	1.61	5.57	4.1	6.5	1.6	0.2	35	74
Newberry,Jake	17	R	23	a/a	KC	62	3.43	1.50	6.23	3.9	5.2	1.3	0.6	31	78
Newcomb,Sean	16	L	23	aa	ATL	140	5.53	1.58	22.8	5.1	8.7	1.7	0.3	35	63
	17	L	24	aaa	ATL	58	3.81	1.57	23	5.7	10.1	1.8	0.5	34	76
Nicolino,Justin	16	L	25	aaa	MIA	85	5.71	1.46	26	1.5	4.1	2.7	1.1	33	62
	17	L	26	aaa	MIA	79	3.98	1.47	24.2	2.9	4.8	1.6	1.2	31	77
Niebla,Luis	17	R	26	a/a	COL	51	8.91	2.28	16.1	6.0	4.5	0.8	1.4	39	61
Nielsen,Trey	16	R	25	a/a	STL	127	4.50	1.57	23.3	3.1	5.1	1.6	1.0	33	74
	17	R	26	a/a	STL	49	4.60	1.57	7.74	2.6	4.5	1.7	1.5	33	75
Norris,Daniel	16	L	23	a/a	DET	80	5.76	1.65	23.8	3.7	7.6	2.0	0.5	37	63
Northcraft,Aaron	16	R	26	a/a	SD	91	4.76	1.56	14.2	3.1	6.0	1.9	1.0	34	71
Nuding,Zach	16	R	26	a/a	LAA	106	6.33	1.80	18.1	3.6	4.8	1.3	1.2	36	66
Nunez,Miguel	16	R	24	aa	PHI	46	3.84	1.65	4.6	5.7	8.4	1.5	0.5	34	77
	17	R	25	aa	PHI	35	4.51	1.65	6.59	5.4	5.4	1.0	1.3	29	76
O Grady,Chris	16	L	26	a/a	LAA	96	4.01	1.55	11.3	2.1	5.7	2.7	0.6	36	74
	17	L	27	aaa	MIA	55	4.20	1.30	18.7	2.7	7.1	2.6	1.2	30	72
O Sullivan,Sean	16	R	29	aaa	BOS	105	7.17	1.93	26.3	3.0	5.4	1.8	0.9	40	62
	17	R	30	aaa	WAS	36	8.36	2.27	18.1	5.7	4.3	0.7	1.9	38	65
Oaks,Trevor	16	R	23	a/a	LA	126	3.16	1.24	25.6	1.2	5.3	4.4	0.7	32	76
	17	R	24	aaa	LA	84	4.16	1.37	23.5	1.8	6.5	3.7	0.6	35	69
Oberholtzer,Brett	17	L	28	aaa	TOR	131	6.91	2.14	27.1	3.8	4.3	1.1	0.8	41	67
Ogando,Emilio	17	L	24	a/a	KC	138	4.55	1.49	24.8	2.7	4.5	1.7	1.1	32	72
Okert,Steven	16	L	25	aaa	SF	47	4.48	1.52	5.01	2.2	9.4	4.4	0.3	41	69
	17	L	26	aaa	SF	25	4.00	1.06	4.09	3.1	6.0	1.9	1.3	21	68
Oliver,Andrew	16	L	29	aaa	BAL	87	5.67	1.93	14.7	4.7	6.3	1.4	1.0	38	72
	17	L	30	aaa	MIL	21	9.10	2.55	7.16	6.8	6.3	0.9	3.2	40	70
Olmos,Edgar	16	L	26	aaa	BAL	69	4.46	1.71	7.41	4.3	7.8	1.8	0.8	37	75
	17	L	27	aaa	BOS	87	4.38	1.54	13.1	4.2	6.0	1.4	0.9	31	73
Olson,Tyler	16	L	27	aaa	CLE	44	7.39	1.99	8.53	3.7	5.1	1.4	1.1	39	63
	17	L	28	aaa	CLE	42	4.80	1.28	5.06	3.4	7.9	2.3	2.1	26	71
Omahen,John	16	R	27	a/a	ARI	127	7.48	1.95	23.3	3.5	4.2	1.2	1.2	38	62
Ortega,Jorge	16	R	23	aa	MIL	97	7.22	1.63	24	1.6	4.2	2.7	1.2	36	55
Ortiz,Luis	16	R	21	aa	MIL	63	4.61	1.71	19	2.7	6.2	2.3	0.9	38	75
	17	R	22	aa	MIL	94	6.01	1.50	18.5	3.9	6.6	1.7	1.8	29	64
Oswalt,Corey	17	R	24	aa	NYM	134	3.43	1.52	24.3	3.4	7.0	2.1	0.9	34	80
Overton,Dillon	16	L	25	aaa	OAK	126	4.60	1.60	26.5	2.5	5.9	2.4	0.5	37	71
	17	L	26	aaa	SD	91	7.15	1.66	21.5	2.7	4.0	1.5	1.9	33	60
Owens,Henry	16	L	24	aaa	BOS	138	5.65	1.73	26.1	6.2	7.3	1.2	1.1	31	69
	17	L	25	a/a	BOS	126	6.14	2.04	23.5	9.4	6.8	0.7	0.7	31	69
Pagan,Emilio	16	R	25	a/a	SEA	65	3.00	1.30	6.52	4.0	9.8	2.5	1.0	30	81
Palmquist,Cody	17	R	23	a/a	TEX	53	5.25	1.25	6.34	2.3	5.2	2.2	1.6	26	62
Paniagua,Juan	16	R	26	aa	CHC	65	5.07	1.57	6.93	5.9	7.0	1.2	0.8	29	68
	17	R	27	aaa	CHC	29	6.75	2.26	13.2	6.1	5.0	0.8	0.7	40	69
Pannone,Thomas	17	L	23	aa	TOR	117	3.85	1.27	23.9	2.4	7.2	3.1	1.4	30	75
Paredes,Eduardo	16	R	21	aa	LAA	48	4.36	1.42	5.85	2.7	7.2	2.7	1.2	33	73
	17	R	22	a/a	LAA	50	2.83	1.24	5.93	3.6	9.0	2.5	0.5	30	78
Parsons,Wes	17	R	25	a/a	ATL	111	4.40	1.56	16.2	3.7	7.4	2.0	0.5	35	71
Partch,Curtis	16	R	29	aaa	PIT	60	3.45	1.54	6.26	5.3	6.4	1.2	0.2	30	76
Pasquale,Nick	16	R	26	a/a	CLE	77	5.44	1.75	25.2	4.5	5.0	1.1	0.6	34	68
	17	R	27	a/a	CLE	86	8.17	1.93	20.4	5.1	5.6	1.1	1.4	35	58
Paulino,David	16	R	22	a/a	HOU	78	2.40	1.09	17.9	1.9	9.4	5.1	0.5	32	79
Paxton,James	16	L	28	aaa	SEA	51	4.32	1.31	19	2.7	7.4	2.8	1.1	31	70
Payamps,Joel	17	R	23	a/a	ARI	104	5.39	1.50	23.7	2.0	4.8	2.4	1.2	33	66
Payano,Pedro	17	R	23	aa	TEX	84	5.05	1.67	22.3	5.0	6.7	1.4	0.5	34	69
Payano,Victor	16	L	24	a/a	TEX	128	5.66	1.68	23	4.6	6.6	1.4	1.3	33	68

TCHER	yr	t	age	lvl	org	ip	era	whip	bf/g	ctl	dom	cmd	hr/9	h%	s%	bpv
ayano,Victor	17	L	25	a/a	MIA	65	4.50	1.52	7.66	6.3	9.2	1.5	0.8	29	71	73
eacock,Brad	16	R	28	aaa	HOU	117	5.17	1.63	23.7	3.3	7.2	2.2	1.0	36	69	52
earce,Matt	16	R	22	a/a	STL	27	7.52	1.75	24.7	3.6	6.7	1.8	1.6	36	58	20
	17	R	23	a/a	STL	164	5.06	1.41	25.7	1.7	4.4	2.6	1.0	32	65	46
ena,Felix	16	R	26	aaa	CHC	63	4.13	1.25	7.16	3.5	9.3	2.7	0.7	31	67	101
	17	R	27	aaa	CHC	39	6.61	1.68	7.3	3.5	8.4	2.4	1.5	37	62	49
ena,Richelson	16	R	23	a/a	TEX	61	6.36	1.76	12.7	4.1	6.7	1.6	1.7	35	67	16
	17	R	24	aa	TEX	33	4.60	1.49	28.7	1.8	5.0	2.7	1.1	34	71	48
eoples,Michael	16	R	25	a/a	CLE	165	5.05	1.66	26.4	3.2	3.7	1.2	0.5	34	68	24
	17	R	26	a/a	CLE	89	8.87	2.17	26.1	3.8	3.5	0.9	1.5	39	59	-26
erakslis,Stepher	16	R	25	a/a	CHC	75	4.34	1.41	9.92	2.4	5.8	2.4	1.1	32	72	49
	17	R	26	a/a	CHC	73	4.07	1.43	9.17	3.1	7.7	2.5	0.4	34	71	84
eralta,Freddy	17	R	21	aa	MIL	64	3.36	1.29	20.1	4.8	11.4	2.4	0.4	31	74	118
eralta,Starling	16	R	26	a/a	CHC	71	5.03	1.58	8.41	3.8	3.7	1.0	0.6	31	68	21
eralta,Wandy	16	L	25	a/a	CIN	76	3.74	1.46	6.48	3.7	5.9	1.6	0.5	32	75	54
eralta,Wily	16	R	27	aaa	MIL	41	7.73	2.06	20.2	4.0	6.6	1.6	1.2	41	62	20
	17	R	28	aaa	MIL	16	3.91	1.62	5.46	5.9	4.4	0.7	0.0	29	73	46
erez,David	16	R	24	aa	TEX	54	6.45	1.86	9.03	5.8	6.9	1.2	1.0	35	65	31
erez,Tyson	17	R	28	aaa	HOU	44	5.59	1.68	6.43	2.1	4.4	2.0	1.1	36	68	22
erez,Williams	16	R	25	aaa	ATL	24	3.32	1.06	23.6	2.8	7.6	2.7	0.8	25	71	90
	17	R	26	aaa	CHC	120	5.85	1.63	23.3	4.0	6.2	1.5	0.6	34	63	46
errin,Jon	17	R	24	aa	MIL	105	4.54	1.53	19.9	2.1	6.6	3.2	1.3	36	74	60
erry,Blake	17	R	25	aa	SEA	62	7.14	1.84	7.22	5.0	8.2	1.6	0.9	38	60	51
erry,Chris	16	R	26	aa	STL	53	4.36	1.61	6.38	7.4	8.4	1.1	0.4	28	72	75
eters,Dillon	17	L	25	aa	MIA	46	2.77	1.19	20.3	2.4	6.6	2.7	0.2	30	76	95
eterson,David	16	R	26	a/a	ATL	52	8.06	2.16	6.17	4.8	6.2	1.3	0.6	42	61	27
	17	R	27	aaa	ATL	68	5.65	1.68	6.09	2.3	5.8	2.4	0.6	38	65	56
eterson,Eric	16	R	23	aa	HOU	54	4.28	1.26	8.11	1.5	8.0	5.4	0.8	34	67	137
eterson,Mark	16	R	26	a/a	KC	60	4.94	1.61	6.3	3.8	6.3	1.6	1.3	33	73	28
	17	R	27	a/a	KC	59	6.80	2.05	8.66	5.0	4.9	1.0	1.1	38	67	3
eterson,Stepher	16	L	29	a/a	MIL	62	4.60	1.75	4.89	5.1	5.7	1.1	0.0	35	71	54
eterson,Tim	16	R	25	aa	NYM	44	4.87	1.58	5.37	3.0	9.0	3.0	0.9	39	70	84
	17	R	26	a/a	NYM	58	2.41	1.05	5.22	2.2	7.2	3.3	0.4	27	78	110
'eifer,Philip	17	L	25	a/a	ATL	59	4.87	1.83	6.72	7.4	10.0	1.3	0.4	36	72	80
hillips,Evan	16	R	22	aa	ATL	34	6.26	1.70	7.05	4.6	10.2	2.2	0.6	40	62	85
	17	R	23	a/a	ATL	51	8.22	1.97	6.15	6.7	8.3	1.2	1.2	37	57	34
erpont,Matt	16	R	25	aa	COL	67	4.77	1.60	7.63	3.6	7.1	2.0	1.1	35	72	47
	17	R	26	aa	COL	62	3.37	1.11	8.74	2.3	5.8	2.5	1.2	25	75	60
ike,Tyler	17	L	23	aa	ATL	75	6.57	2.02	24.1	8.8	9.2	1.1	0.4	36	65	65
ll,Tyler	16	R	26	a/a	NYM	166	4.64	1.46	26.3	2.2	5.8	2.7	0.7	34	68	65
	17	R	27	a/a	NYM	91	4.08	1.61	26.8	2.8	4.3	1.6	1.0	34	77	20
mentel,Carlos	16	R	27	aaa	SD	145	5.97	1.77	23.8	3.8	6.1	1.6	1.1	36	67	29
ineyro,Ivan	16	R	25	a/a	MIA	25	10.33	2.11	15.6	5.5	4.0	0.7	0.8	37	47	2
	17	R	26	a/a	ARI	86	5.63	1.59	16.5	1.8	6.2	3.5	1.1	37	66	67
into,Ricardo	16	R	22	aa	PHI	156	4.86	1.42	24.5	2.9	5.2	1.8	1.4	29	69	26
	17	R	23	aaa	PHI	61	4.90	1.50	13.8	2.8	6.0	2.2	0.7	34	67	55
vetta,Nick	16	R	23	a/a	PHI	149	4.35	1.41	23.3	3.3	7.4	2.2	1.0	32	71	62
	17	R	24	aaa	PHI	32	1.82	1.01	24.5	0.6	9.0	15.1	0.4	33	83	365
lutko,Adam	16	R	25	a/a	CLE	162	5.15	1.48	24.8	2.8	5.7	2.1	0.9	33	66	46
	17	R	26	aaa	CLE	136	8.43	1.92	26.8	4.1	4.9	1.2	2.2	35	58	-23
oncedeleon,Dan	16	R	24	aa	STL	151	4.35	1.39	23.5	3.5	6.3	1.8	0.6	30	69	59
	17	R	25	aaa	STL	29	2.74	1.30	19.9	4.2	6.0	1.4	0.7	26	81	56
ounders,Brooks	16	R	26	aaa	KC	80	3.81	1.47	11.1	4.2	7.8	1.8	0.6	32	74	71
	17	R	27	aaa	LAA	51	2.79	1.21	5.44	2.5	6.9	2.7	1.0	28	82	75
ovse,Max	16	R	23	aa	ATL	71	4.20	1.27	26.3	1.7	5.4	3.2	0.6	31	67	80
	17	R	24	a/a	SEA	71	6.27	1.60	14.2	3.3	6.7	2.0	0.6	36	59	59
owers,Alex	17	R	25	aa	CIN	61	7.25	2.07	8.73	5.0	10.6	2.1	1.3	46	66	56
ries,Jordan	16	R	26	a/a	CHC	131	6.20	1.71	20.4	3.3	6.6	2.0	1.2	37	65	36
ruitt,Austin	16	R	27	aaa	TAM	163	5.23	1.50	25.1	1.7	6.6	3.9	1.4	36	69	70
runeda,Benino	16	R	28	a/a	KC	58	4.92	1.51	7.56	5.9	8.6	1.5	0.7	29	67	69
ugliese,James	17	R	25	aa	CHC	78	2.53	1.38	8.22	4.3	4.6	1.1	0.7	26	84	35
uk,A.J.	17	L	22	aa	OAK	64	4.95	1.48	21.2	3.3	10.0	3.0	0.3	39	64	114
urke,Matt	16	L	26	aaa	CHW	38	4.46	1.64	6.57	6.2	7.4	1.2	1.1	29	76	39
	17	L	27	aaa	CHW	66	4.88	1.64	6.1	4.4	8.9	2.0	0.7	37	70	72
uantrill,Cal	17	R	22	aa	SD	42	5.51	1.88	24.9	3.5	6.1	1.7	1.3	39	73	22
uiala,Yoanys	17	R	23	aa	HOU	50	3.52	1.72	19	2.0	5.2	2.7	0.6	39	80	55
amirez,Jose	16	R	26	aaa	ATL	41	2.86	1.50	4.96	4.3	8.2	1.9	0.7	33	83	68
amirez,Nick	17	L	28	a/a	MIL	79	1.88	1.26	6.61	3.1	4.9	1.6	0.7	27	89	49
amirez,Noe	16	R	27	aaa	BOS	44	3.17	1.59	6.42	2.8	8.7	3.0	0.9	39	83	82
	17	R	28	aaa	LAA	53	3.50	1.25	5.83	3.0	8.2	2.7	1.1	29	77	78
amirez,Yefrey	17	R	24	aa	BAL	124	4.37	1.45	22.1	4.0	7.3	1.8	1.3	30	74	47
amsey,Matthew	17	R	28	a/a	MIL	50	7.25	1.92	4.44	4.5	8.8	2.0	1.3	41	63	43
anaudo,Anthony	16	R	27	aaa	CHW	110	4.13	1.27	23.7	1.4	5.5	3.8	1.5	30	74	66
avenelle,Adam	16	R	24	aa	DET	30	6.00	1.76	5.04	5.2	5.5	1.1	1.3	32	68	11
	17	R	25	aa	DET	52	6.69	1.81	5.77	3.9	6.6	1.7	1.6	36	65	16
ay,Corey	17	R	25	aa	KC	143	7.81	1.99	23.7	4.1	4.6	1.1	1.5	37	61	-9
eed,Chris	16	L	26	a/a	MIA	81	5.17	1.49	14.6	4.0	5.6	1.4	1.1	30	67	31
eed,Cody	16	L	23	aaa	CIN	73	4.27	1.51	24.3	2.7	7.2	2.6	1.0	35	74	62
	17	L	24	aaa	CIN	106	4.54	1.80	23.4	5.6	7.4	1.3	0.8	36	76	46
eed,Jake	16	R	24	a/a	MIN	71	4.74	1.37	5.93	3.2	7.2	2.3	0.3	33	63	84
	17	R	25	a/a	MIN	38	3.26	1.48	6.05	4.5	6.0	1.3	0.3	30	77	58
egnault,Kyle	16	L	28	aa	NYM	21	5.53	1.85	6.44	1.4	6.1	4.2	0.5	43	69	90
	17	L	29	a/a	NYM	65	3.86	1.69	6.48	4.9	7.2	1.5	0.2	36	76	66
eid-Foley,Sean	17	R	22	aa	TOR	133	6.49	1.70	22.2	3.7	7.2	1.9	1.8	35	66	21
eyes,Alex	16	R	22	aaa	STL	65	5.33	1.51	20.2	4.2	11.6	2.7	0.8	38	64	105
eyes,Arturo	16	R	24	aaa	STL	101	4.67	1.43	22.7	3.2	6.0	1.9	1.0	31	69	44
	17	R	25	aaa	STL	63	5.56	1.48	12.4	2.5	4.5	1.8	0.8	32	62	37

PITCHER	yr	t	age	lvl	org	ip	era	whip	bf/g	ctl	dom	cmd	hr/9	h%	s%	bpv
Reyes,James	17	L	28	aaa	TEX	66	5.50	1.71	8.26	3.3	4.3	1.3	1.7	33	72	-7
Reyes,Jesus	17	R	24	aa	CIN	52	5.46	1.92	24.5	4.3	6.6	1.5	0.9	39	72	33
Reyes,Scarlyn	17	R	28	aa	NYM	40	6.61	1.74	8	4.0	4.9	1.2	1.4	33	64	4
Reynolds,Danny	16	R	25	aa	LAA	34	7.84	1.80	7.07	7.0	6.9	1.0	0.6	32	54	45
	17	R	26	a/a	ATL	61	4.42	1.73	6.76	5.6	6.6	1.2	0.0	35	72	64
Rhame,Jacob	16	R	23	aaa	LA	63	3.81	1.35	4.87	3.6	8.5	2.4	0.8	32	74	82
	17	R	24	aaa	NYM	54	4.23	1.28	4.92	1.7	9.7	5.5	1.0	36	70	143
Richards,Trevor	17	R	24	aa	MIA	75	3.94	1.37	22.5	2.4	7.9	3.3	0.6	35	71	99
Richy,John	16	R	24	aa	PHI	69	6.32	1.70	23.8	3.8	5.1	1.3	1.2	34	63	17
	17	R	25	a/a	PHI	38	8.81	2.21	16.1	2.8	4.6	1.7	0.9	44	58	10
Rienzo,Andre	16	R	28	a/a	MIA	33	4.79	1.77	5.47	5.8	7.0	1.2	0.6	34	73	47
	17	R	29	aaa	SD	41	3.22	1.73	8.96	6.0	6.2	1.0	0.6	32	83	40
Rios,Francisco	17	R	22	aa	TOR	86	5.54	1.70	16.9	4.2	5.8	1.4	1.3	33	70	19
Rios,Yacksel	17	R	24	aa	PHI	56	2.43	0.94	5.72	2.3	8.8	3.8	1.0	24	81	119
Rivero,Alexis	16	R	22	aa	PHI	33	4.81	1.71	6.57	3.8	7.8	2.1	1.3	37	75	43
	17	R	23	a/a	PHI	66	5.56	1.63	6.87	3.7	6.2	1.7	1.5	33	69	22
Rivero,Armando	16	R	28	aaa	CHC	68	2.69	1.33	6.53	5.2	10.8	2.1	0.5	30	81	107
Roach,Donn	16	R	27	aaa	DET	138	5.70	1.61	22.6	1.9	4.0	2.1	0.7	36	64	37
Roberts,Will	16	R	26	a/a	CLE	89	6.59	1.82	24.2	4.3	3.3	0.8	1.6	32	66	-22
Robinson,Andrew	16	R	28	aa	WAS	58	2.97	1.32	6.9	3.2	7.5	2.4	1.0	30	82	70
	17	R	29	aa	WAS	39	5.24	1.39	4.32	3.5	8.1	2.3	1.4	30	65	56
Rodgers,Brady	16	R	26	aaa	HOU	132	3.29	1.31	24.8	1.6	6.5	4.1	0.5	34	76	106
	17	R	27	aaa	HOU	16	1.10	0.99	20.8	0.5	4.9	9.6	0.0	29	88	236
Rodriguez,Bryan	16	R	25	a/a	SD	145	5.10	1.68	25.2	2.7	4.3	1.6	1.0	35	71	19
	17	R	26	a/a	SD	138	5.90	1.75	22.5	2.6	3.5	1.3	0.6	36	65	17
Rodriguez,Dereck	17	R	25	aa	MIN	75	5.86	1.68	22.6	3.6	5.7	1.6	1.4	34	68	17
Rodriguez,Joely	16	L	25	a/a	PHI	68	3.65	1.50	6.42	3.2	6.6	2.0	0.6	34	76	62
	17	L	26	aaa	TEX	27	8.10	2.13	6.08	6.6	5.4	0.8	2.4	34	66	-33
Rodriguez,Richar	16	R	26	aaa	BAL	82	3.92	1.43	7.23	3.2	7.0	2.2	0.9	32	75	61
	17	R	27	aaa	BAL	71	3.50	1.36	7.03	2.9	8.2	2.9	0.8	33	77	86
Rogers,Chad	16	R	27	aaa	ATL	62	6.39	1.63	8.16	4.1	6.5	1.6	1.5	33	63	23
Rogers,Tyler	16	R	26	a/a	SF	66	4.26	1.58	4.92	3.6	5.1	1.4	0.1	34	71	52
	17	R	27	aaa	SF	76	3.03	1.47	5.92	3.7	4.0	1.1	0.2	30	78	40
Rollins,David	16	L	27	aaa	SEA	45	4.27	1.13	4.84	1.2	5.1	4.4	0.8	29	63	101
	17	L	28	aaa	CHC	42	7.06	1.77	6.02	5.7	6.5	1.1	1.7	31	62	11
Romano,Sal	16	R	23	aa	CIN	156	5.25	1.54	25.2	2.3	7.5	3.3	0.9	37	66	80
	17	R	24	aaa	CIN	49	4.43	1.56	21.6	3.3	5.0	1.5	0.2	34	70	50
Romero,Fernandc	17	R	23	aa	MIN	125	5.03	1.63	23.2	3.4	6.9	2.0	0.4	37	67	67
Rondon,Jorge	16	R	28	aaa	PIT	57	4.02	1.55	5.83	4.4	4.2	1.0	0.4	30	73	34
Roney,Bradley	16	R	24	a/a	ATL	68	4.50	1.82	7.14	8.1	10.2	1.3	0.6	34	75	74
	17	R	25	aa	ATL	24	5.60	1.78	7.36	7.7	11.5	1.5	1.9	32	74	49
Rosario,Miguel	16	R	23	aa	PIT	34	2.27	1.04	5.64	3.4	6.3	1.8	0.3	23	78	85
	17	R	24	aa	PIT	45	2.46	1.84	7.77	7.7	6.8	0.9	0.2	32	86	56
Rosario,Randy	17	L	23	aa	MIN	57	5.82	1.67	8.05	3.8	5.7	1.5	0.8	35	65	35
Roseboom,David	16	L	24	aa	NYM	58	2.18	0.99	4.23	2.8	7.1	2.5	0.8	22	83	87
Ross,Austin	16	R	28	aaa	MIL	72	4.87	1.48	6.55	3.2	7.5	2.4	1.2	33	69	58
	17	R	29	a/a	CIN	127	3.99	1.67	24.8	3.4	4.4	1.3	0.8	34	78	22
Ross,Greg	16	R	27	aa	WAS	54	1.21	1.22	21.8	2.2	4.1	1.9	0.2	29	91	61
	17	R	28	a/a	WAS	135	8.64	2.00	25	3.9	3.8	1.0	1.6	37	57	-22
Rosscup,Zachary	17	L	29	aaa	COL	40	3.67	1.34	5.79	3.2	8.2	2.6	1.3	30	78	66
Roth,Michael	16	L	26	aaa	TEX	145	3.90	1.49	22.4	2.9	4.5	1.5	0.7	32	75	37
	17	L	27	aaa	TAM	112	7.02	1.95	21.3	2.8	5.1	1.9	1.7	39	67	-1
Routt,Nick	16	L	25	a/a	CIN	68	2.96	1.41	5.78	3.9	6.6	1.7	0.4	31	79	66
	17	L	26	aaa	CIN	36	10.08	2.37	8.81	4.3	4.8	1.1	1.7	43	57	-24
Rowen,Benjamin	16	R	28	aaa	MIL	58	2.91	1.48	5.55	2.4	5.3	2.2	0.2	35	79	68
	17	R	29	aaa	NYM	63	5.20	1.78	5.39	2.2	5.8	2.7	1.0	40	72	47
Rowley,Chris	17	R	27	aaa	TOR	116	3.43	1.35	16.7	2.4	5.8	2.4	0.7	32	76	65
Rucinski,Drew	16	R	28	aaa	CHC	155	7.49	1.81	25.6	2.8	5.2	1.9	1.1	38	58	23
	17	R	29	aaa	MIN	63	4.42	1.46	7.28	1.8	5.7	3.2	0.7	35	70	76
Rumbelow,Nick	17	R	26	a/a	NYY	40	1.65	1.00	6.16	2.8	8.1	2.9	0.0	26	82	125
Runion,Sam	16	R	28	a/a	WAS	49	9.47	1.84	6.96	3.6	4.3	1.2	0.2	38	43	32
Ruth,Eric	16	R	26	a/a	NYY	47	4.17	1.44	13.3	3.7	6.8	1.9	0.3	33	70	72
Ryan,Kyle	17	L	26	aaa	DET	45	7.33	2.29	4.83	6.2	6.0	1.0	1.3	40	69	-1
Sadler,Casey	17	R	27	a/a	PIT	67	6.66	1.70	15.1	1.6	5.2	3.3	0.8	39	60	61
Sadzeck,Connor	16	R	25	aa	TEX	141	5.67	1.55	24.6	3.8	6.8	1.8	1.4	32	66	34
	17	R	26	aa	TEX	94	9.26	1.95	11.8	4.4	8.2	1.9	1.7	40	52	24
Salas,Javier	16	R	24	aa	MIL	47	7.58	1.85	17	8.3	5.5	0.7	0.3	29	55	45
Sampson,Adrian	16	R	25	aaa	SEA	80	3.52	1.27	25.2	1.3	5.8	4.5	0.5	33	73	112
Sampson,Keyvius	16	R	25	aaa	CIN	62	2.71	1.18	13.8	3.5	7.7	2.2	0.6	27	79	84
	17	R	26	aaa	MIA	79	7.39	2.10	14.9	7.3	7.8	1.1	1.1	37	65	30
Sanburn,Nolan	16	R	25	aa	CHW	74	4.80	1.50	9.41	3.3	6.0	1.8	0.6	33	67	54
Sanchez,Angel	17	R	28	aaa	PIT	55	5.52	1.56	6.22	2.9	7.7	2.7	0.8	37	64	71
Sanchez,Jake	16	R	27	aa	OAK	67	3.88	1.37	6.35	2.6	7.3	2.8	0.3	34	70	94
	17	R	28	a/a	OAK	26	1.76	1.15	4.55	2.2	8.2	3.7	0.0	32	83	134
Sanchez,Mario	17	R	23	aa	PHI	56	3.49	1.30	12.2	2.1	4.5	2.1	1.3	28	79	32
Santana,Edgar	16	R	25	a/a	PIT	57	4.61	1.48	7.25	2.8	6.2	2.2	0.9	33	70	54
	17	R	26	aaa	PIT	58	3.94	1.61	5.84	2.1	6.4	3.0	0.7	38	77	69
Santos,Eduard	16	R	27	aaa	OAK	63	5.00	1.60	6.19	6.4	7.2	1.1	0.5	29	68	59
Santos,Luis	16	R	25	aa	TOR	82	5.82	1.62	21.4	2.6	6.9	2.6	1.2	37	65	52
	17	R	26	a/a	TOR	115	6.23	1.60	18.1	4.3	6.4	1.5	1.6	31	64	21
Sappington,Mark	16	R	26	a/a	TAM	52	7.48	2.11	6.1	8.3	6.8	0.8	0.4	36	62	42
Saupold,Warwick	16	R	26	aaa	DET	74	3.33	1.47	17.7	3.1	4.6	1.5	0.5	32	78	42
	17	R	27	aaa	DET	40	4.38	1.77	26.4	4.5	5.6	1.2	0.6	35	75	34
Sborz,Josh	16	R	23	aa	LA	17	4.93	1.57	7.32	3.1	7.8	2.5	1.3	36	72	54
	17	R	24	aa	LA	117	4.61	1.50	21	4.0	5.3	1.3	0.7	30	69	39
Schlosser,Gus	16	R	28	a/a	LA	43	7.50	1.85	7.67	2.2	6.8	3.1	1.4	41	60	47
Schreiber,Brad	16	R	25	a/a	TAM	37	7.49	1.98	5.92	3.4	6.1	1.8	1.4	40	63	16
	17	R	26	aa	COL	41	10.52	2.29	6.82	6.7	6.0	0.9	0.7	41	51	17

PITCHER	yr	t	age	lvl	org	ip	era	whip	bf/g	ctl	dom	cmd	hr/9	h%	s%	bpv
Schultz,Jaime	16	R	25	aaa	TAM	131	4.77	1.63	21.5	5.1	9.4	1.9	1.0	35	72	66
Schuster,Patrick	16	L	26	aaa	PHI	45	1.90	1.42	4.99	4.3	7.7	1.8	0.0	32	85	88
	17	L	27	aaa	OAK	52	7.53	1.97	5.7	3.4	6.9	2.0	1.2	41	62	30
Scioneaux,Tate	17	R	25	aa	PIT	83	3.33	1.22	7.14	1.8	5.7	3.1	0.5	31	73	86
Scott,Robby	16	L	27	aaa	BOS	78	4.33	1.27	9.97	2.0	6.5	3.2	1.5	30	71	63
Scott,Tanner	17	L	23	aa	BAL	69	2.73	1.49	12.4	6.6	10.0	1.5	0.3	30	81	95
Scott,Tayler	16	R	24	aa	MIL	27	6.48	1.62	4.93	5.4	5.9	1.1	1.4	28	61	19
	17	R	25	a/a	TEX	75	4.37	1.82	6.42	5.3	7.2	1.3	0.9	36	78	39
Scribner,Troy	16	R	25	a/a	LAA	132	4.07	1.30	22.7	3.9	6.7	1.7	0.8	27	70	59
	17	R	26	aaa	LAA	103	4.52	1.42	21.9	3.1	7.4	2.4	1.0	32	70	63
Secrest,Kelly	16	L	25	aa	NYM	16	6.55	1.63	6.06	5.7	9.1	1.6	0.6	34	58	73
	17	L	26	a/a	NYM	45	4.93	2.03	7.28	5.2	8.6	1.6	1.0	42	77	43
Seddon,Joel	16	R	24	aa	OAK	143	5.15	1.53	23.1	3.0	3.8	1.3	0.8	32	66	21
	17	R	25	a/a	OAK	98	5.88	1.70	13	3.2	5.4	1.7	0.7	36	65	37
Self,Derek	16	R	26	a/a	WAS	56	6.06	1.86	8.24	3.4	5.5	1.6	1.0	38	68	24
	17	R	27	a/a	WAS	62	5.16	1.63	7.41	3.3	4.2	1.3	1.2	32	71	9
Selman,Sam	17	L	27	a/a	KC	68	3.80	1.29	6.62	5.7	9.7	1.7	0.3	26	69	102
Severino,Luis	16	R	22	aaa	NYY	77	4.90	1.45	25.4	2.3	8.0	3.5	0.7	37	66	97
Sewald,Paul	16	R	26	aaa	NYM	66	3.22	1.25	4.77	2.7	8.9	3.3	1.1	31	79	93
Shaban,Ronnie	16	R	26	a/a	STL	58	3.59	1.44	5.53	2.6	5.4	2.0	1.1	32	79	38
Shackelford,Kevir	16	R	27	a/a	CIN	44	3.17	1.58	5.58	4.3	5.2	1.2	0.6	32	81	36
	17	R	28	aaa	CIN	47	2.13	1.37	5.62	4.1	9.2	2.3	0.5	32	86	93
Shafer,Justin	17	R	25	a/a	TOR	62	4.89	1.50	6.86	4.4	6.2	1.4	1.2	29	70	32
Sheffield,Justus	17	L	21	aa	NYY	93	4.43	1.61	24.3	3.4	7.0	2.1	2.0	33	81	20
Shepherd,Chandl	16	R	24	a/a	BOS	64	4.07	1.15	6.35	2.8	7.2	2.6	1.0	26	67	76
	17	R	25	aaa	BOS	60	6.38	1.68	7.9	3.2	8.1	2.5	1.0	39	62	61
Sherfy,Jimmie	16	R	25	a/a	ARI	43	4.50	1.16	4.28	3.9	9.9	2.5	1.5	25	66	82
	17	R	26	aaa	ARI	49	3.45	1.06	4.32	1.8	8.9	4.9	1.2	29	73	130
Sherriff,Ryan	16	L	26	aaa	STL	67	3.31	1.52	5.9	3.2	6.2	1.9	0.5	34	79	58
	17	L	27	aaa	STL	54	4.20	1.20	4.49	2.4	5.9	2.5	0.4	29	63	81
Shibuya,Tim	16	R	27	a/a	LA	79	5.35	1.49	17.8	1.4	3.9	2.8	1.2	34	66	37
	17	R	28	a/a	LA	63	4.19	1.30	13.7	1.2	4.1	3.6	0.5	32	67	80
Shipley,Braden	16	R	24	aaa	ARI	119	4.05	1.40	26.5	1.6	4.8	3.0	0.5	34	71	71
	17	R	25	aaa	ARI	105	6.12	1.75	25.3	3.5	4.8	1.4	1.6	34	68	0
Shirley,Tommy	16	L	28	a/a	DET	106	8.11	2.27	20	4.1	4.4	1.1	1.6	41	65	-23
Sides,Grant	16	R	27	aa	CLE	62	4.80	1.36	6.14	4.4	7.6	1.7	0.8	28	65	66
Sierra,Yaisel	17	R	26	a/a	LA	71	3.71	1.58	8.01	3.8	8.6	2.3	0.4	37	76	83
Simmons,Seth	16	R	28	a/a	SD	121	3.64	1.33	14.8	3.0	6.3	2.1	1.0	30	76	54
Simms,John	16	R	24	aa	WAS	93	4.48	1.29	13.1	3.0	6.2	2.1	0.9	29	67	59
	17	R	25	a/a	WAS	157	5.29	1.47	24.9	2.7	5.7	2.1	1.0	32	65	43
Sims,Lucas	16	R	22	a/a	ATL	141	5.72	1.70	22.7	6.2	9.2	1.5	1.1	33	67	56
	17	R	23	aaa	ATL	115	4.71	1.31	23.8	3.0	9.2	3.0	1.6	31	69	75
Sitton,Kraig	16	L	28	a/a	SEA	52	3.10	1.27	5.09	1.5	5.2	3.5	0.4	32	75	92
	17	L	29	aaa	SF	65	5.00	1.68	6.22	2.6	4.8	1.9	0.7	37	70	36
Skoglund,Eric	16	L	24	aa	KC	156	4.70	1.33	24	2.3	6.2	2.7	1.3	30	68	56
	17	L	25	a/a	KC	104	5.57	1.72	23.6	3.0	7.0	2.4	1.4	38	70	40
Skulina,Tyler	16	R	25	aa	CHC	129	6.35	1.84	22.2	5.3	5.3	1.0	1.3	33	67	7
Slack,Ryne	16	L	24	aa	TEX	49	5.18	1.67	5.61	5.8	6.2	1.1	1.1	30	71	28
	17	L	25	a/a	TEX	44	5.46	1.91	6.55	5.9	6.9	1.2	1.0	36	73	29
Slania,Dan	16	R	24	a/a	SF	96	2.93	1.23	13.4	2.6	7.4	2.9	0.5	31	77	93
	17	R	25	a/a	SF	141	7.02	1.83	26.3	4.1	5.8	1.4	1.2	36	62	19
Slegers,Aaron	16	R	24	aa	MIN	145	4.28	1.44	24.8	2.9	5.1	1.8	0.8	32	71	44
	17	R	25	aaa	MIN	148	5.35	1.62	27.4	2.0	5.6	2.8	0.9	37	68	52
Smith,Blake	16	R	29	aaa	CHW	71	4.79	1.58	8.05	3.7	7.3	2.0	1.0	35	71	52
Smith,Caleb	16	L	25	aa	NYY	64	6.13	1.75	10.8	3.3	8.2	2.5	0.9	40	65	63
	17	L	26	a/a	NYY	101	3.57	1.35	22.1	3.2	7.4	2.3	1.1	30	78	62
Smith,Chris	16	R	28	a/a	TOR	61	2.87	1.45	5.51	3.9	9.4	2.4	0.7	35	82	90
	17	R	29	aaa	TOR	34	7.64	1.76	5.42	2.0	4.7	2.3	2.6	35	62	-15
Smith,Josh	16	L	27	a/a	PIT	65	9.11	2.06	6.44	5.2	7.1	1.3	1.5	39	55	13
	17	L	28	a/a	BOS	72	4.69	1.82	9.51	5.7	7.2	1.3	0.8	35	75	40
Smith,Josh	16	R	29	aaa	CIN	45	6.00	1.74	22.8	3.3	6.0	1.8	1.6	36	69	15
	17	R	30	aaa	OAK	41	4.90	1.33	9.03	2.7	6.8	2.5	0.9	31	64	67
Smith,Kyle	16	R	24	aa	HOU	82	5.96	1.73	13.9	3.2	6.3	2.0	1.8	36	70	14
	17	R	25	a/a	HOU	76	4.65	1.46	17.2	2.0	6.0	3.0	0.5	35	67	78
Smith,Murphy	16	R	29	a/a	TOR	73	2.25	1.40	7.16	3.9	6.5	1.7	0.9	29	89	50
	17	R	30	a/a	TOR	86	5.96	1.68	9.89	2.5	4.4	1.7	1.5	35	67	7
Smith,Nate	16	L	25	aaa	LAA	150	4.80	1.48	24.9	2.5	6.1	2.4	1.0	34	69	54
Smoker,Josh	16	L	28	aaa	NYM	57	4.20	1.61	4.85	2.8	9.9	3.5	0.7	41	75	103
Sneed,Cy	16	R	24	aa	HOU	118	4.79	1.45	20.1	2.5	7.3	2.9	1.1	34	69	69
	17	R	25	a/a	HOU	115	6.53	1.72	20	3.0	6.4	2.1	1.3	37	63	33
Snell,Blake	16	L	24	aaa	TAM	63	3.91	1.55	22.9	4.2	11.0	2.6	0.7	39	76	100
	17	L	25	aaa	TAM	44	3.69	1.62	27.9	3.5	10.5	3.0	1.2	40	82	84
Snelten,D.J.	17	L	25	a/a	SF	74	2.85	1.28	5.93	3.1	7.1	2.3	0.5	31	79	82
Snodgrass,Jack	16	L	29	a/a	TEX	45	6.88	1.97	21.7	4.6	5.6	1.2	1.5	37	67	0
Snow,Forrest	16	R	28	a/a	SEA	54	3.64	1.30	7.94	2.7	8.0	3.0	0.6	33	72	97
	17	R	29	a/a	MIL	85	5.40	1.61	11.4	3.2	8.4	2.6	1.4	37	70	56
Somsen,Layne	16	R	27	aaa	LA	31	4.81	1.76	7.02	6.1	7.6	1.2	1.1	33	75	40
	17	R	28	a/a	LA	61	2.82	1.68	7.04	4.6	7.1	1.5	0.5	35	84	55
Sopko,Andrew	16	R	22	aa	LA	31	6.31	1.66	23.2	3.0	6.3	2.1	1.4	36	64	31
	17	R	23	aa	LA	105	4.83	1.52	19.8	3.5	5.5	1.6	1.0	31	70	32
Soroka,Michael	17	R	20	aa	ATL	154	3.75	1.28	24.2	2.2	6.8	3.1	0.7	32	72	88
Soto,Giovanni	16	L	25	aaa	CHC	49	6.09	1.87	6.97	5.9	8.4	1.4	0.6	38	66	56
	17	L	26	aaa	CHW	25	6.63	1.64	7.06	4.4	9.4	2.1	1.7	35	62	47
Speer,David	17	L	25	a/a	CLE	59	6.93	2.01	6.83	3.8	5.4	1.4	0.4	41	63	34
Speier, James	17	R	22	aa	ARI	69	5.76	1.88	9	4.2	5.6	1.3	0.7	38	69	30
Spitzbarth,Shea	17	R	23	aa	LA	54	3.51	1.36	7.05	2.7	7.2	2.6	0.6	33	75	82
Spomer,Kurt	16	R	27	a/a	DET	56	4.01	1.67	6.16	2.6	5.8	2.2	0.6	38	76	53
	17	R	28	a/a	DET	50	6.31	1.77	5.47	5.1	4.6	0.9	0.2	34	61	35

PITCHER	yr	t	age	lvl	org	ip	era	whip	bf/g	ctl	dom	cmd	hr/9	h%	s%
Spurlin,Tyler	16	R	25	aa	MIL	41	5.25	1.83	4.69	6.1	6.4	1.0	0.0	35	68
Stanek,Ryne	16	R	25	a/a	TAM	103	5.51	1.51	13.1	4.5	8.3	1.9	0.9	33	64
	17	R	26	aaa	TAM	45	1.72	1.16	4.81	3.7	10.0	2.7	0.0	31	84
Stankiewicz,Tedd	16	R	23	aa	BOS	136	6.09	1.55	23.7	2.7	5.5	2.0	1.2	34	61
	17	R	24	aa	BOS	140	6.69	1.76	25.6	2.5	5.5	2.2	1.0	38	61
Staumont,Josh	16	R	23	aa	KC	50	4.05	1.77	21	6.9	10.7	1.6	0.4	37	77
	17	R	24	a/a	KC	125	7.45	1.86	22.5	7.4	8.0	1.1	1.3	32	60
Steckenrider,Drev	16	R	25	a/a	MIA	42	3.56	1.14	4.89	4.1	9.2	2.3	0.2	27	67
Stephens,Jacksoi	16	R	22	aa	CIN	151	4.87	1.53	24.4	2.8	7.1	2.6	0.6	36	68
	17	R	23	aaa	CIN	139	6.15	1.70	24.2	3.5	6.3	1.8	1.3	36	65
Stephens,Jordan	17	R	25	aa	CHW	92	4.60	1.65	25.6	4.2	6.9	1.6	0.6	35	72
Stephenson,Robe	16	R	23	aaa	CIN	137	6.11	1.62	25.3	5.2	7.1	1.4	1.6	30	65
	17	R	24	aaa	CIN	40	4.84	1.15	20	3.1	8.7	2.8	2.3	23	68
Stewart,Brock	16	R	25	a/a	LA	110	2.41	1.05	22.4	1.4	8.0	5.9	0.4	31	78
	17	R	26	aaa	LA	17	3.72	1.46	14.8	1.5	10.5	7.1	1.2	41	79
Stewart,Kohl	16	R	22	aa	MIN	92	3.66	1.59	25.4	4.2	3.8	0.9	0.4	31	77
	17	R	23	a/a	MIN	82	6.28	1.83	22.4	5.4	5.0	0.9	0.7	34	65
Stilson,John	16	R	26	a/a	TOR	50	5.41	1.64	6.33	4.7	6.2	1.3	0.5	33	66
	17	R	27	a/a	TOR	54	4.88	1.62	6.27	4.4	6.7	1.5	1.5	32	74
Stites,Matthew	16	R	26	a/a	ARI	52	3.55	1.45	4.76	4.4	6.3	1.4	0.2	31	74
	17	R	27	aaa	ARI	27	6.69	2.64	6.49	7.3	4.1	0.6	0.7	43	74
Stock,Robert	17	R	28	aa	CIN	45	5.36	1.90	8.56	5.6	5.6	1.0	0.0	37	69
Stoffel,Jason	16	R	28	a/a	BAL	59	3.63	1.47	4.6	3.6	8.9	2.5	1.4	33	81
Stout,Eric	16	L	23	aa	KC	72	5.14	1.50	7.44	3.2	7.0	2.2	0.4	35	64
	17	L	24	aaa	KC	69	3.81	1.43	6.55	3.9	5.8	1.5	0.5	30	74
Strahm,Matt	16	L	25	aa	KC	102	4.77	1.50	20.1	2.2	7.4	3.4	1.4	36	72
Stratton,Chris	16	R	26	aaa	SF	126	4.65	1.46	25.6	3.0	6.0	2.0	0.4	34	67
	17	R	27	aaa	SF	79	6.53	1.77	24.3	2.8	6.3	2.3	1.1	39	63
Stull,Cody	17	L	25	aa	OAK	43	6.38	2.00	7.92	5.1	4.3	0.8	0.8	36	68
Suarez,Albert	16	R	27	aaa	SF	46	5.33	1.55	22.2	3.0	6.1	2.0	0.6	35	64
Suarez,Andrew	16	L	24	aa	SF	114	5.36	1.63	26.7	2.1	6.0	2.9	0.9	38	68
	17	L	25	a/a	SF	156	4.28	1.59	26.4	2.6	6.4	2.4	0.6	37	73
Suero,Wander	16	R	25	aa	WAS	55	3.38	1.64	6.32	3.8	6.2	1.6	0.6	35	80
	17	R	26	a/a	WAS	65	2.38	1.30	4.98	2.9	7.1	2.5	0.5	31	83
Sulbaran,Juan	16	R	27	a/a	STL	146	6.57	1.66	23.4	3.7	5.8	1.6	1.2	34	61
Sulser,Cole	16	R	26	a/a	CLE	45	6.26	1.67	6.69	2.9	7.0	2.4	0.3	39	60
	17	R	27	a/a	CLE	63	3.91	1.79	6.49	5.1	7.0	1.4	1.0	35	81
Suter,Brent	16	L	27	aaa	MIL	111	4.28	1.55	18.6	1.2	4.7	3.9	0.5	37	72
	17	L	28	aaa	MIL	37	5.12	1.59	16.2	2.0	7.2	3.5	1.5	37	72
Tago,Peter	16	R	24	aa	CHW	60	5.10	1.52	6.82	5.4	10.1	1.9	0.5	34	65
	17	R	25	aa	SEA	39	3.20	1.35	5.81	5.8	9.4	1.6	0.3	28	75
Taillon,Jameson	16	R	25	aaa	PIT	62	2.88	1.01	23.6	1.0	6.9	7.3	0.3	30	71
Tapia,Domingo	17	R	26	a/a	CIN	88	6.12	1.88	10.9	3.2	7.2	2.3	1.4	41	70
Taveras,Jose	17	R	24	a/a	PHI	52	2.40	1.14	23	2.9	7.1	2.5	1.5	24	90
Taylor,Corey	17	R	24	aa	NYM	62	5.44	1.72	6.74	2.5	6.0	2.4	0.6	39	68
Taylor,Cory	17	R	24	aa	SF	128	5.81	1.71	23.1	4.5	5.9	1.3	0.6	34	65
Taylor,Josh	16	L	23	aa	ARI	55	6.87	1.78	22.9	3.2	6.4	2.0	0.8	39	60
	17	L	24	aa	ARI	97	6.98	2.00	14.2	4.6	7.0	1.5	0.9	40	64
Taylor,Logan	16	R	25	aa	NYM	86	4.75	1.63	8.66	4.2	8.6	2.0	0.6	37	70
	17	R	26	a/a	NYM	47	6.46	1.84	7.82	5.0	5.5	1.1	1.7	33	68
Tenuta,Matt	17	L	24	aa	KC	53	8.11	2.09	15.4	3.1	5.2	1.7	1.8	41	63
Tepera,Ryan	16	R	29	aaa	TOR	45	4.03	1.45	5.23	3.9	7.3	1.9	0.9	31	74
Tepesch,Nicholas	16	R	28	aaa	KC	116	5.03	1.56	23.1	2.3	3.5	1.5	0.6	34	67
	17	R	29	aaa	TOR	47	7.22	1.83	21.9	2.5	5.9	2.4	2.2	38	65
Therrien,Jesen	17	R	24	a/a	PHI	57	1.79	0.98	5.58	1.5	8.8	6.0	0.6	29	85
Thome,Andrew	17	R	24	a/a	HOU	53	4.19	1.45	6.29	3.2	5.9	1.8	0.5	33	71
Thompson,Jake	16	R	22	aaa	PHI	130	3.61	1.33	25.6	2.8	5.4	1.9	1.0	29	76
	17	R	23	aaa	PHI	118	6.67	1.77	24.7	3.7	6.0	1.6	1.1	36	63
Thompson,Ryan	16	R	24	aa	HOU	40	2.13	1.18	6.95	2.3	4.4	1.9	0.0	28	80
	17	R	25	a/a	HOU	67	4.44	1.48	7.75	1.7	7.0	4.2	0.7	37	70
Thornton,Trent	16	R	23	aa	HOU	46	2.72	1.14	26	1.0	6.0	6.2	1.1	30	82
	17	R	24	a/a	HOU	131	5.59	1.52	22.8	1.5	6.0	4.1	0.9	37	64
Thurman,Andrew	16	R	25	aa	ATL	63	10.30	2.24	16.7	7.9	6.4	0.8	1.7	36	53
Tolliver,Ashur	16	L	28	a/a	LAA	40	3.13	1.52	5.83	3.6	7.3	2.0	1.0	33	83
	17	L	29	a/a	SEA	43	8.62	2.28	6.14	8.2	5.6	0.7	0.5	38	60
Tomshaw,Matt	16	L	28	a/a	MIA	89	4.94	1.45	16.5	2.2	7.6	3.5	0.9	36	67
	17	L	29	aa	MIA	163	5.34	1.72	27.4	2.4	4.8	2.0	1.1	37	70
Tonkin,Michael	17	R	28	aaa	MIN	42	2.90	1.45	5.74	3.4	9.5	2.8	0.3	37	80
Torrez,Daury	17	R	24	aa	CHC	77	1.88	1.11	7.07	1.7	5.5	3.3	0.9	27	89
Tracy,Matthew	16	L	28	aa	MIA	79	7.06	1.99	15.2	3.6	5.2	1.4	0.9	40	64
	17	L	29	a/a	MIN	80	8.08	2.05	22.9	4.1	5.4	1.3	1.7	39	62
Travieso,Nick	16	R	22	aa	CIN	117	5.60	1.68	22.9	4.6	6.4	1.4	1.3	33	69
Trivino,Lou	16	R	23	aa	OAK	18	2.82	1.23	6.19	3.4	4.8	1.4	0.5	26	78
	17	R	24	a/a	OAK	68	3.57	1.38	5.98	2.7	6.8	2.5	0.0	34	71
Tseng,Jen-Ho	16	R	22	aa	CHC	113	4.96	1.64	23	2.5	4.8	1.9	1.1	35	72
	17	R	23	a/a	CHC	145	3.04	1.27	24.8	2.4	6.5	2.7	0.8	30	79
Tuivailala,Sam	16	R	24	aaa	STL	47	5.83	1.60	4.91	4.2	12.1	2.8	0.6	42	62
	17	R	25	aaa	STL	21	1.60	0.88	4.38	1.3	6.9	5.2	0.9	23	90
Turley,Josh	16	L	26	a/a	DET	153	6.01	1.74	26.8	2.5	5.6	2.2	1.2	37	67
	17	L	27	a/a	DET	49	8.72	2.35	21	6.8	4.6	0.7	1.4	38	63
Turley,Nik	17	L	28	a/a	MIN	92	3.36	1.36	16.7	3.4	8.8	2.6	0.6	33	76
Turner,Colton	17	L	26	a/a	CHW	55	5.75	1.64	7.05	3.1	7.5	2.4	1.3	37	67
Turner,Jacob	16	R	25	aaa	CHW	107	5.84	1.70	26.8	2.7	6.0	2.2	1.0	37	66
	17	R	26	aaa	WAS	66	6.93	1.92	22.3	5.0	5.8	1.2	0.8	37	63
Uhen,Josh	17	R	25	aa	MIL	59	5.87	1.98	6.4	4.7	6.7	1.4	0.3	41	68
Underwood,Duan	16	R	22	aa	CHC	59	5.68	1.78	20.8	4.7	6.2	1.3	1.2	35	70
	17	R	23	aa	CHC	138	5.85	1.53	24	3.5	5.5	1.6	1.0	32	62

ITCHER	yr	t	age	lvl	org	ip	era	whip	bf/g	ctl	dom	cmd	hr/9	h%	s%	bpv
nsworth,Dylan	17	R	25	a/a	SEA	128	4.04	1.30	24.1	1.6	5.3	3.4	0.7	32	70	79
rena,Jose	16	R	25	aaa	MIA	48	4.38	1.55	17.6	4.4	6.1	1.4	0.8	31	73	42
rias,Julio	16	L	20	aaa	LA	45	1.54	0.89	15.2	1.4	8.8	6.4	0.4	27	85	187
	17	L	21	aaa	LA	31	2.81	1.10	20.5	3.7	8.2	2.2	0.3	26	74	102
aldespina,Jose	16	R	24	a/a	TEX	64	4.73	1.69	7.22	3.6	4.7	1.3	0.8	34	73	23
'aldez,Framber	17	L	24	aa	HOU	49	7.38	1.93	19.4	4.3	8.5	2.0	0.8	42	61	54
'aldez,Jose	16	R	26	a/a	LAA	46	2.88	1.39	5.05	4.7	7.1	1.5	0.8	28	82	58
	17	R	27	aaa	SD	41	5.78	1.62	5.47	3.4	7.6	2.2	0.4	38	62	74
'aldez,Phillips	16	R	25	aa	WAS	88	6.40	1.90	25.9	4.2	4.7	1.1	0.8	37	66	14
	17	R	26	a/a	WAS	67	5.53	1.54	8.36	2.7	5.7	2.1	0.3	36	62	63
an Steensel,Tod	17	R	26	aa	MIN	59	2.10	1.44	6.94	4.3	6.8	1.6	0.0	32	84	78
'argas,Cesar	17	R	26	a/a	SD	69	6.82	1.74	7.29	5.1	8.0	1.6	0.4	37	58	64
'asto,Jerry	16	L	24	aa	COL	30	4.82	1.85	4.47	5.3	7.8	1.5	1.0	37	75	42
	17	L	25	aaa	COL	54	9.41	2.03	6.35	4.4	7.8	1.8	1.8	41	54	12
'elazquez,Hector	17	R	29	aaa	BOS	102	3.78	1.43	22.8	2.7	5.0	1.8	0.9	31	76	39
'entura,Angel	16	R	23	aa	MIL	55	5.92	1.66	22.4	4.6	7.2	1.6	2.0	31	70	14
	17	R	24	a/a	MIL	129	4.84	1.44	22.1	3.6	5.2	1.4	1.2	29	69	26
'erHagen,Drew	17	R	27	aaa	DET	97	7.40	2.02	24.8	4.7	4.8	1.0	0.9	38	62	9
'errett,Logan	17	R	27	aaa	BAL	60	7.38	1.69	6.76	4.1	5.9	1.4	1.8	32	58	6
ieira,Thyago	17	R	24	a/a	SEA	54	4.80	1.44	5.61	3.7	6.6	1.8	0.4	32	65	67
illegas,Kender	17	R	24	aa	TOR	40	6.36	1.91	9.45	5.8	4.9	0.8	0.9	34	66	14
'iza,Tyler	16	R	22	aa	PHI	94	5.57	1.45	25.1	2.2	5.0	2.3	1.4	32	64	31
	17	R	23	aa	PHI	140	6.33	1.60	23.8	3.1	5.7	1.8	1.5	33	63	19
oelker,Paul	16	R	24	aa	DET	54	5.15	1.65	4.64	4.2	10.4	2.4	1.3	38	72	71
	17	R	25	a/a	DET	32	3.08	1.37	4.47	2.5	7.5	3.0	1.0	33	82	76
'oth,Austin	16	R	24	aaa	WAS	157	4.55	1.53	25.3	3.7	6.2	1.7	0.8	33	71	48
	17	R	25	a/a	WAS	121	7.57	1.92	24.9	3.8	5.2	1.4	1.7	37	62	-5
Vaddell,Brandon	16	L	22	aa	PIT	118	4.90	1.67	24.1	4.5	5.9	1.3	0.7	34	71	39
	17	L	23	aa	PIT	66	4.75	1.54	19.2	4.0	6.2	1.6	0.5	33	68	55
Vade,Konner	16	R	25	aa	COL	77	8.38	1.98	9.96	3.6	4.2	1.2	1.7	37	59	-18
	17	R	26	aa	COL	109	7.13	1.74	15.1	2.1	4.8	2.2	2.1	36	63	-1
Vagner,Michael	16	R	25	a/a	CHC	84	5.28	1.67	19.9	4.7	6.4	1.4	0.7	33	68	42
Vagner,Tyler	16	R	25	aaa	ARI	27	3.40	1.64	23.8	3.6	4.1	1.1	0.3	34	79	32
	17	R	26	aaa	TEX	125	7.99	1.94	20.6	4.4	4.9	1.1	1.7	36	60	-11
Vahl,Bobby	16	R	24	a/a	OAK	50	2.93	1.26	4.89	4.3	8.9	2.1	0.6	28	78	92
Valden,Marcus	16	R	28	a/a	MIN	56	3.47	1.36	5.61	2.9	4.7	1.6	0.2	31	73	57
	17	R	29	aaa	BOS	106	6.71	1.86	17	4.0	5.3	1.3	0.5	38	62	33
Valsh,Connor	17	R	25	a/a	CHW	56	4.46	1.56	6.32	6.1	8.5	1.4	0.2	31	69	82
Valter,Corey	16	R	24	aa	OAK	100	2.52	1.19	13.9	1.4	3.9	2.9	0.2	30	78	80
	17	R	25	a/a	OAK	117	5.00	1.73	17.2	2.7	4.6	1.7	0.3	38	69	41
Valter,Johnny	16	R	25	aa	STL	49	7.89	1.72	24.7	4.0	5.5	1.4	0.6	35	51	36
Valters,Blair	16	L	27	aa	CHW	101	5.85	1.89	22.6	5.6	6.1	1.1	0.7	36	68	33
Valters,Jeffrey	16	R	29	aaa	NYM	66	6.16	1.65	5.24	3.9	5.0	1.3	1.3	32	64	12
Vang,Wei-Chung	16	L	24	a/a	MIL	133	4.88	1.49	24	2.5	6.4	2.5	0.7	35	67	64
	17	L	25	aaa	MIL	57	2.23	1.32	5.02	1.8	6.3	3.4	1.1	32	89	75
Varmoth,Tyler	17	R	25	a/a	LAA	52	3.87	1.39	6.48	3.3	7.4	2.3	1.1	31	75	62
Vatson,Shane	17	R	24	aa	PHI	83	5.08	1.87	11.8	4.5	4.2	0.9	1.6	34	77	-13
Veaver,Luke	16	R	23	a/a	STL	83	1.50	1.01	24.5	1.3	8.9	6.8	0.4	31	88	190
	17	R	24	aaa	STL	78	3.15	1.21	20.8	2.2	7.0	3.1	0.4	31	74	101
Vebb,Tyler	16	L	26	aaa	NYY	73	5.48	1.61	8.94	3.4	8.2	2.4	1.0	37	67	65
	17	L	27	aaa	MIL	50	4.89	1.46	5.63	1.8	9.1	5.0	1.5	38	71	108
Veber,Ryan	16	R	26	aaa	ATL	62	3.62	1.55	10.4	2.3	5.0	2.2	0.2	36	75	63
	17	R	27	aaa	SEA	32	1.06	0.91	19.7	1.2	4.4	3.6	0.3	24	91	104
Vebster,Allen	17	R	27	aaa	TEX	58	8.88	2.04	23.6	3.4	5.1	1.5	2.6	38	60	-35
Veigel,Patrick	17	R	23	a/a	ATL	78	5.54	1.55	22.8	3.6	6.9	1.9	0.9	34	64	52
Veir,T.J.	16	R	25	aa	SD	49	7.93	1.76	14.1	3.8	6.9	1.8	1.4	37	55	29
	17	R	26	aa	SD	58	3.22	1.38	6.77	2.6	6.9	2.6	0.8	33	79	72
Veller,Blayne	16	R	26	a/a	LAA	72	8.23	1.78	20.7	3.9	7.3	1.9	2.3	35	57	3
Vendelken,Jeffre	16	R	23	aaa	OAK	46	5.51	1.87	5.53	5.4	10.4	1.9	1.1	41	72	63
Vest,Aaron	16	R	26	a/a	HOU	82	4.30	1.54	7.32	1.8	6.2	3.4	0.5	37	72	84
	17	R	27	a/a	SEA	68	4.91	2.06	7.91	1.8	5.2	2.8	0.3	45	75	57
Vest,Matthew	16	R	28	aaa	LA	46	3.01	1.12	4.69	1.6	5.7	3.6	0.2	30	72	107
Vhalen,Rob	16	R	22	a/a	ATL	120	3.12	1.36	23.9	3.5	7.6	2.2	0.3	32	77	85
	17	R	23	aaa	SEA	53	7.52	1.65	23.8	3.3	6.4	1.9	1.6	34	55	23
Vheeler,Beck	16	R	28	a/a	NYM	56	6.78	1.82	5.5	5.7	9.4	1.6	1.2	37	63	51
	17	R	29	aaa	NYM	58	9.65	2.37	7.39	6.3	6.2	1.0	2.1	40	61	-25
Vheeler,Jason	16	L	26	a/a	MIN	169	4.57	1.44	25.7	2.3	5.5	2.4	0.8	33	69	53
	17	L	27	a/a	BAL	95	6.09	1.66	17	2.7	5.6	2.1	1.3	36	65	27
Vhitehead,David	16	R	24	aa	PIT	46	9.70	2.37	21.7	9.3	3.7	0.4	1.0	34	57	-9
Vhitehouse,Matt	17	L	26	a/a	CLE	117	6.88	1.71	17.6	2.8	5.0	1.8	1.5	35	62	9
Vieland,Joe	16	R	26	aaa	SEA	124	6.01	1.71	21.7	2.7	7.1	2.6	1.1	39	66	53
Viles,Collin	17	R	23	aa	TEX	150	6.76	1.67	24	1.9	5.3	2.8	1.7	36	62	27
Vilk,Adam	16	L	29	aaa	TAM	87	5.25	1.49	25.1	1.6	5.9	3.7	1.2	35	67	69
	17	L	30	aaa	MIN	44	9.54	2.07	24.1	2.0	5.0	2.4	2.2	41	55	-10
Vilkerson,Aaron	16	R	27	a/a	MIL	147	5.14	1.51	22.7	2.9	7.6	2.6	0.9	35	67	68
	17	R	28	aa	MIL	142	5.39	1.51	25.7	2.9	7.0	2.4	1.4	34	67	48
Villiams,Austen	16	R	24	aa	WAS	51	7.71	2.09	24.9	4.3	4.3	1.0	1.0	39	62	-1
	17	R	25	aa	WAS	46	8.89	2.04	22.3	2.3	5.4	2.3	1.3	42	55	19
Villiams,Ryan	16	R	25	aaa	CHC	44	3.88	1.42	20.7	2.6	5.1	2.0	0.9	31	75	42
Villiams,Taylor	17	R	26	aa	MIL	47	5.03	1.79	9.78	4.9	8.9	1.8	0.7	39	72	66
Villiams,Trevor	16	R	24	aaa	PIT	110	3.49	1.45	23.6	2.6	4.8	1.8	0.5	33	76	50
Vilson,Tyler	16	R	27	aaa	BAL	24	7.21	1.66	17.7	1.4	5.8	4.3	0.6	40	54	91
	17	R	28	aaa	BAL	114	7.01	1.90	26.9	3.5	4.2	1.2	1.1	37	63	4
Vimmers,Alex	16	R	28	a/a	MIN	57	5.76	1.72	5.72	4.5	6.5	1.4	0.4	36	65	52
	17	R	29	aaa	MIN	47	5.56	1.31	5.75	2.6	6.4	2.5	1.5	29	61	48
Vindle,Tom	16	L	24	aa	PHI	32	7.03	1.91	5.99	4.1	8.1	2.0	1.8	39	66	23
	17	L	25	aa	PHI	51	5.35	1.31	5.85	3.9	6.6	1.7	0.9	27	59	56
Vingenter,Trey	17	R	23	aa	SD	48	3.42	1.28	3.98	3.8	10.0	2.7	1.4	29	80	84

PITCHER	yr	t	age	lvl	org	ip	era	whip	bf/g	ctl	dom	cmd	hr/9	h%	s%	bpv
Winkelman,Alex	17	L	23	aa	HOU	71	4.97	1.79	18.3	3.7	7.2	2.0	0.9	39	73	48
Winkler,Kyle	16	R	26	a/a	TAM	33	3.61	1.30	4.49	3.9	8.1	2.1	1.0	29	75	71
	17	R	27	a/a	TAM	53	5.44	1.87	5.1	5.7	7.1	1.3	1.0	36	72	32
Wisler,Matthew	16	R	24	aaa	ATL	27	4.67	1.40	28.1	1.8	6.5	3.6	1.1	34	69	77
	17	R	25	aaa	ATL	94	4.66	1.56	22.8	2.2	5.2	2.4	0.7	36	71	51
Withrow,Matt	17	R	24	aa	ATL	48	6.54	1.57	21.2	4.8	7.1	1.5	1.8	29	62	20
Wojciechowski,As	16	R	28	a/a	MIA	86	7.31	2.08	21	4.8	4.9	1.0	1.3	38	66	-5
	17	R	29	aaa	CIN	31	2.93	1.36	16	2.8	7.9	2.8	0.8	33	82	82
Wolff,Sam	16	R	25	aa	TEX	50	6.58	1.92	23.8	6.3	5.5	0.9	1.5	32	68	0
	17	R	26	a/a	TEX	43	4.02	1.59	4.74	4.5	9.5	2.1	1.3	35	79	61
Wood,Hunter	16	R	23	aa	TAM	49	3.89	1.24	20	3.6	7.8	2.1	1.0	27	71	72
	17	R	24	a/a	TAM	123	6.04	1.59	17.5	3.5	7.2	2.1	1.3	34	63	44
Woodruff,Brandor	16	R	23	aa	MIL	114	4.35	1.27	23.3	2.7	8.3	3.1	0.4	33	64	106
	17	R	24	aaa	MIL	75	4.57	1.45	20.1	2.9	7.1	2.5	1.1	33	71	60
Wotherspoon,Mat	16	R	25	a/a	NYY	90	3.80	1.41	10.6	4.0	7.3	1.8	0.6	31	74	67
	17	R	26	a/a	BAL	68	2.72	1.41	7.54	4.0	8.7	2.2	0.8	32	84	77
Wright,Austin	16	L	27	aa	ARI	44	6.56	1.79	7.45	5.5	6.2	1.1	1.4	32	65	14
Wright,Daniel	16	R	25	a/a	CIN	104	7.54	1.84	19.3	3.0	6.5	2.2	1.3	39	59	30
	17	R	26	aaa	LAA	93	7.26	1.69	22	3.2	4.9	1.5	1.5	34	58	7
Wright,Justin	16	L	27	a/a	STL	52	6.29	1.90	5.22	6.1	5.8	1.0	0.6	35	65	32
Wright,Mike	16	R	26	aaa	BAL	76	4.74	1.48	25.3	1.9	4.4	2.3	1.5	32	73	23
	17	R	27	aaa	BAL	83	5.34	1.68	23.3	3.5	6.2	1.8	0.9	36	69	41
Wynkoop,Jack	17	L	24	aa	COL	150	7.09	1.69	28.2	1.5	3.7	2.4	1.6	36	60	8
Yacabonis,Jimmy	16	R	24	aa	BAL	44	2.56	1.24	5.29	2.9	7.6	2.6	0.5	30	81	90
	17	R	25	aaa	BAL	61	1.83	1.16	5.96	4.9	5.9	1.2	0.0	22	82	80
Yarbrough,Ryan	16	L	25	aa	SEA	128	3.99	1.33	21.3	2.3	5.9	2.5	0.6	32	70	71
	17	L	26	aaa	TAM	157	4.87	1.47	25.9	2.6	7.5	2.9	1.4	34	71	60
Yardley,Eric	16	R	26	a/a	SD	71	3.43	1.49	6.22	2.1	4.9	2.3	0.7	34	79	51
	17	R	27	a/a	SD	70	2.59	1.23	5.81	1.7	5.8	3.4	0.6	31	81	90
Ynoa,Gabriel	16	R	23	aaa	NYM	154	3.64	1.34	25.7	2.1	3.9	1.9	0.7	30	74	40
	17	R	24	aaa	BAL	106	7.12	1.76	23.2	2.4	5.3	2.2	0.8	39	58	38
Young,Alex	17	L	24	aa	ARI	137	5.13	1.60	22.4	4.1	5.6	1.4	1.0	32	69	28
Younginer IV,Mac	16	R	26	a/a	ATL	56	5.67	1.64	5.43	4.2	8.0	1.9	0.4	37	63	73
	17	R	27	aaa	LA	62	5.81	1.74	7.11	3.7	8.0	2.2	1.3	38	69	45
Ysla,Luis	16	L	24	a/a	BOS	56	5.78	1.78	6.48	4.8	8.2	1.7	0.8	38	67	56
	17	L	25	aa	LA	58	6.43	1.86	7.55	5.8	6.7	1.2	0.5	36	64	43
Yuhl,Keegan	16	R	24	a/a	HOU	124	4.72	1.47	22.1	1.9	6.4	3.3	0.9	35	69	74
	17	R	25	aaa	HOU	20	14.87	2.71	15.5	6.2	5.1	0.8	1.6	45	42	-29
Zastryzny,Rob	16	L	24	a/a	CHC	136	5.10	1.38	23.7	3.5	6.7	1.9	1.0	30	64	54
	17	L	25	aaa	CHC	47	6.78	1.53	14.6	2.8	6.3	2.3	1.4	33	56	39
Zeid,Joshua	16	R	29	a/a	NYM	92	5.35	1.66	25.6	4.6	5.4	1.2	1.3	31	70	17

LEADERBOARDS

This section provides rankings of projected skills indicators for 2018. Rather than take shots in the dark predicting league leaders in the exact number of home runs, or stolen bases, or strikeouts, the Forecaster's Leaderboards focus on the component elements of each skill.

For batters, we've ranked the top players in terms of pure power, speed, and batting average skill, breaking each down in a number of different ways. For pitchers, we rank some of the key base skills, differentiating between starters and relievers, and provide a few interesting cuts that might uncover some late round sleepers. Plus, some potential gainers/faders lists in several categories.

These are clearly not exhaustive lists of sorts and filters—drop us a note if you see something we should consider for next year's book. Also, the database at BaseballHQ.com allows you to construct your own custom sorts and filters. Finally, remember that these are just tools. Some players will appear on multiple lists—even mutually exclusive lists—so you have to assess what makes most sense and make decisions for your specific application.

Power

Top PX, 400+ AB: Top power skills among projected full-time players.

Top PX, –300 AB: Top power skills among projected part-time players; possible end-game options are here.

Position Scarcity: See which positions have deepest power options.

Top PX, ct% over 80%: Top power skills among the top contact hitters. Best pure power options here.

Top PX, ct% under 70%: Top power skills among the worst contact hitters; free-swingers who might be prone to streakiness and lower BAs.

Top PX, FB% over 40%: Top power skills among the most extreme fly ball hitters. Most likely to convert their power into home runs.

Top PX, FB% under 35%: Top power skills among those with lesser fly ball tendencies. There may be more downside to their home run potential.

Speed

Top Spd, 400+ AB: Top speed skills among projected full-time players.

Top Spd, -300 AB: Top speed skills among projected part-time players; possible end-game options here.

Position Scarcity: See which positions have deepest speed options.

Top Spd, OB% .330 and above: Top speed skills among those who get on base most often. Best opportunities for stolen bases here.

Top Spd, OB% under .300: Top speed skills among those who have trouble getting on base; worth watching if they can improve OB%.

Top Spd, SBO% over 20%: Top speed skills among those who get the green light most often. Most likely to convert their speed into stolen bases.

Top Spd, SBO% under 15%: Top speed skills among those who are currently not running; sleeper SBs here if given more opportunities.

Batting Average

Top ct%, 400+ AB: Top contact skills among projected full-time players. Contact is strongly correlated to higher BAs.

Top ct%, -300 AB: Top contact skills among projected part-time players; possible end-gamers here.

Low ct%, 400+ AB: The poorest contact skills among projected full-time players. Potential BA killers.

Top ct%, bb% over 9%: Top contact skills among the most patient hitters. Best batting average upside here.

Top ct%, bb% under 6%: Top contact skills among the least patient hitters; free-swingers who might be prone to streakiness or lower BAs.

Top ct%, GB% over 50%: Top contact skills among the most extreme ground ball hitters. A ground ball has a higher chance of becoming a hit than a non-HR fly ball so there may be some batting average upside here.

Top ct%, GB% under 40%: Top contact skills from those with lesser ground ball tendencies. These players make contact but hit more fly balls, which tend to convert to hits at a lower rate than GB.

Potential Gainers and Faders

These charts look to identify upcoming changes in performance by highlighting 2017 results that were in conflict with their corresponding skill indicators. Additional details are provided on the page in which the charts appear.

Pitching Skills

Top Command: Leaders in projected K/BB rates.

Top Control: Leaders in fewest projected walks allowed.

Top Dominance: Leaders in projected strikeout rate.

Top Ground Ball Rate: GB pitchers tend to have lower ERAs (and higher WHIP) than fly ball pitchers.

Top Fly Ball Rate: FB pitchers tend to have higher ERAs (and lower WHIP) than ground ball pitchers.

High GB, Low Dom: GB pitchers tend to have lower K rates, but these are the most extreme examples.

High GB, High Dom: The best at dominating hitters and keeping the ball down. These are the pitchers who keep runners off the bases and batted balls in the park, a skills combination that is the most valuable a pitcher can own.

Lowest xERA: Leaders in projected skills-based ERA.

Top BPV: Two lists of top skilled pitchers. For starters, those projected to be rotation regulars (180+ IP) and fringe starters with skill (<150 IP). For relievers, those projected to be frontline closers (10+ saves) and high-skilled bullpen fillers (<9 saves).

PRO (Positive Relative Outcomes) Scores

These lists prioritize the pitcher vs. batter event in terms of total batters faced and total plate appearances, and categorize the outcomes of these events in terms of positive or negative. By providing a "common denominator," PRO allows for simpler comparision of all pitchers and all batters. See page 61 for a detailed explanation.

Best Net Scores: Ranked by Positive Outcome% – Negative Outcome%.

Worst Net Scores: Ranked by Negative Outcome% – Positive Outcome%.

Best Positive Scores: Ranked by Positive Outcome%.

Worst Negative Scores: Ranked by Negative Outcome%.

Risk Management

These lists include players who've accumulated the most days on the disabled list over the past five years (Grade "F" in Health) and whose performance was the most consistent over the past three years. Also listed are the most reliable batters and pitchers overall, with a focus on positional and skills reliability. As a reminder, reliability in this context is not tied to skill level; it is a gauge of which players manage to accumulate playing time and post consistent output from year to year, whether that output is good or bad.

Mayberry Portfolio3 Plan

Players are sorted and ranked based on how they fit into the three draft tiers of the Portfolio3 Plan used in conjunction with the Mayberry Method, as detailed on page 57.

Daily Fantasy Indicators

Players splits, teams and park factors designed to give you an edge in DFS.

BATTER SKILLS RANKING - Power

TOP PX, 400+ AB

NAME	POS	PX
Gallo,Joey	3 5	219
Judge,Aaron	9	195
Stanton,Giancarlo	9	187
Martinez,J.D.	9	177
Story,Trevor	6	171
Zunino,Mike	2	170
Thames,Eric	3 7	168
Schwarber,Kyle	7	166
Davis,Khristopher	0 7	165
Sano,Miguel	0 5	163
Trout,Mike	8	159
Olson,Matt	3	157
Davis,Chris	3	152
Upton,Justin	7	151
Freeman,Freddie	3	151
Renfroe,Hunter	9	151
Conforto,Michael	7 8	149
Donaldson,Josh	5	148
DeJong,Paul	4 6	147
Grichuk,Randal	7 9	147
Duda,Lucas	0 3	147
Bellinger,Cody	3 7	146
Belt,Brandon	3	145
Harper,Bryce	9	144
Sanchez,Gary	2	143
Arenado,Nolan	5	142
Goldschmidt,Paul	3	141
Cruz,Nelson	0	140
Bryant,Kris	5	139
Carpenter,Matt	3	138
Bird,Gregory	3	137
Schebler,Scott	9	137
Tomas,Yasmany	7	136
Hoskins,Rhys	3 7	136
Santana,Domingo	9	135
Duvall,Adam	7	135
Bruce,Jay	9	135
Davidson,Matt	0 5	134
Cespedes,Yoenis	7	133
Contreras,Willson	2	132

TOP PX, 300 or fewer AB

NAME	POS	PX
Schimpf,Ryan	5	193
Carter,Chris	3	152
Aguilar,Jesus	3	144
Murphy,Tom	2	143
Hernandez,Teoscar	7	143
Broxton,Keon	8	140
Valaika,Pat	6	140
Goodwin,Brian	7 8	136
Rupp,Cameron	2	133
Adams,Matt	3	129
Blash,Jabari	9	127
Vargas,Kennys	0 3	126
McMahon,Ryan	3	125
Marisnick,Jake	8	125
Phillips,Brett	8	124
Kivlehan,Patrick	9	123
Frazier,Clint	7	119
Garver,Mitch	2	118
O Neill,Tyler	O	117
Cordero,Franchy	8	115
Perez,Roberto	2	112
Rosales,Adam	6	112
Saunders,Michael	9	112

POSITIONAL SCARCITY

NAME	POS	PX
Davis,Khristopher	DH	165
Sano,Miguel	2	163
Duda,Lucas	3	147
Moss,Brandon	4	143
Napoli,Mike	5	142
Cruz,Nelson	6	140
Zunino,Mike	CA	170
Sanchez,Gary	2	143
Murphy,Tom	3	143
Rupp,Cameron	4	133
Contreras,Willson	5	132
Chirinos,Robinson	6	128
Grandal,Yasmani	7	128
Iannetta,Chris	8	124
Gallo,Joey	1B	219
Thames,Eric	2	168
Olson,Matt	3	157
Carter,Chris	4	152
Davis,Chris	5	152
Freeman,Freddie	6	151
Duda,Lucas	7	147
Bellinger,Cody	8	146
Belt,Brandon	9	145
Aguilar,Jesus	10	144
DeJong,Paul	2B	147
Dozier,Brian	2	129
Happ,Ian	3	124
Moncada,Yoan	4	114
Odor,Rougned	5	113
Baez,Javier	6	112
Kipnis,Jason	7	112
Schoop,Jonathan	8	112
Gallo,Joey	3B	219
Schimpf,Ryan	2	193
Sano,Miguel	3	163
Donaldson,Josh	4	148
Arenado,Nolan	5	142
Bryant,Kris	6	139
Davidson,Matt	7	134
Lamb,Jacob	8	130
Chapman,Matt	9	129
Valbuena,Luis	10	128
Story,Trevor	SS	171
DeJong,Paul	2	147
Valaika,Pat	3	140
Correa,Carlos	4	123
Bregman,Alex	5	120
Seager,Corey	6	120
Pinder,Chad	7	116
Russell,Addison	8	115
Judge,Aaron	OF	195
Stanton,Giancarlo	2	187
Martinez,J.D.	3	177
Thames,Eric	4	168
Schwarber,Kyle	5	166
Davis,Khristopher	6	165
Trout,Mike	7	159
Upton,Justin	8	151
Renfroe,Hunter	9	151
Conforto,Michael	10	149
Grichuk,Randal	11	147
Bellinger,Cody	12	146
Harper,Bryce	13	144
Hernandez,Teoscar	14	143
Broxton,Keon	15	140
Schebler,Scott	16	137

TOP PX, ct% over 75%

NAME	Ct%	PX
Trout,Mike	76	159
Freeman,Freddie	76	151
Donaldson,Josh	76	148
Harper,Bryce	76	144
Sanchez,Gary	76	143
Arenado,Nolan	83	142
Bryant,Kris	75	139
Carpenter,Matt	76	138
Cespedes,Yoenis	78	133
Contreras,Willson	77	132
Blackmon,Charlie	81	131
Encarnacion,Edwin	78	130
Dozier,Brian	77	129
Votto,Joey	82	128
Bour,Justin	77	127
Castellanos,Nick	76	127
Abreu,Jose	80	125
Rizzo,Anthony	82	125
Chisenhall,Lonnie	77	124
Rendon,Anthony	82	123
Correa,Carlos	77	123
Joseph,Tommy	76	122
Gattis,Evan	79	122
Braun,Ryan	79	122
Gonzalez,Carlos	75	121
Springer,George	76	121
Haniger,Mitch	76	120
Bregman,Alex	82	120
Seager,Corey	77	120
Rosario,Eddie	78	119
Zimmerman,Ryan	76	119
Devers,Rafael	77	117
Martinez,Jose	80	115
Turner,Justin	85	115
McCutchen,Andrew	78	114
Moustakas,Mike	85	114
Machado,Manny	82	113
Odor,Rougned	76	113
Kepler,Max	79	113
Ozuna,Marcell	77	112

TOP PX, ct% under 70%

NAME	Ct%	PX
Gallo,Joey	55	219
Judge,Aaron	63	195
Schimpf,Ryan	62	193
Stanton,Giancarlo	70	187
Story,Trevor	64	171
Zunino,Mike	63	170
Thames,Eric	68	168
Schwarber,Kyle	65	166
Davis,Khristopher	68	165
Sano,Miguel	60	163
Carter,Chris	59	152
Davis,Chris	60	152
Upton,Justin	69	151
Grichuk,Randal	69	147
Moss,Brandon	66	143
Murphy,Tom	64	143
Napoli,Mike	64	142
Broxton,Keon	60	140
Santana,Domingo	64	135
Davidson,Matt	62	134
Rupp,Cameron	66	133
Chapman,Matt	67	129
Souza,Steven	65	129

Top PX, FB% over 40%

NAME	FB%	PX
Gallo,Joey	46	219
Judge,Aaron	47	195
Schimpf,Ryan	64	193
Stanton,Giancarlo	41	187
Martinez,J.D.	41	177
Story,Trevor	47	171
Zunino,Mike	47	170
Schwarber,Kyle	45	166
Davis,Khristopher	41	165
Sano,Miguel	41	163
Trout,Mike	41	159
Olson,Matt	44	157
Carter,Chris	50	152
Davis,Chris	40	152
Upton,Justin	43	151
Renfroe,Hunter	45	151
Conforto,Michael	40	149
Donaldson,Josh	41	148
DeJong,Paul	42	147
Grichuk,Randal	43	147
Duda,Lucas	47	147
Bellinger,Cody	45	146
Belt,Brandon	47	145
Moss,Brandon	48	143
Hernandez,Teoscar	42	143
Napoli,Mike	48	142
Arenado,Nolan	44	142
Valaika,Pat	46	140
Bryant,Kris	43	139
Carpenter,Matt	48	138
Bird,Gregory	48	137
Hoskins,Rhys	42	136
Goodwin,Brian	43	136
Duvall,Adam	48	135
Bruce,Jay	44	135
Davidson,Matt	42	134
Cespedes,Yoenis	45	133
Smoak,Justin	42	132
Granderson,Curtis	45	131
Encarnacion,Edwin	42	130

Top PX, FB% under 35%

NAME	FB%	PX
Sanchez,Gary	35	143
Goldschmidt,Paul	33	141
Broxton,Keon	33	140
Tomas,Yasmany	32	136
Santana,Domingo	29	135
Contreras,Willson	29	132
Souza,Steven	35	129
Pham,Thomas	27	128
Bour,Justin	34	127
Vargas,Kennys	33	126
Abreu,Jose	35	125
Correa,Carlos	29	123
Braun,Ryan	30	122
Gonzalez,Carlos	33	121
Springer,George	33	121
Seager,Corey	32	120
Zimmerman,Ryan	35	119
Altherr,Aaron	32	118
Alfaro,Jorge	31	118
Martinez,Jose	31	115
Taylor,Michael	33	115
Cordero,Franchy	31	115
Beckham,Tim	32	113

BATTER SKILLS RANKING - Speed

TOP Spd, 400+ AB

NAME	POS	Spd
Gordon,Dee	4	204
Hamilton,Billy	8	188
Buxton,Byron	8	183
Hernandez,Cesar	4	179
Albies,Ozhaino	4	178
Turner,Trea	6	175
Rosario,Amed	6	168
Margot,Manuel	8	162
Anderson,Tim	6	161
Moncada,Yoan	4	157
DeShields Jr.,Delino	78	156
Fowler,Dexter	8	151
Arcia,Orlando	6	148
Eaton,Adam	8	147
Taylor,Chris	478	145
Beckham,Tim	6	144
Hechavarria,Adeiny	6	143
Mahtook,Mikie	89	143
Blackmon,Charlie	8	142
Inciarte,Ender	8	142
Spangenberg,Cory	57	140
Pollock,A.J.	8	137
Crawford,J.P.	5	136
Kiermaier,Kevin	8	135
Williams,Nick	9	135
Sanchez,Yolmer	45	133
Marte,Starling	78	132
Cain,Lorenzo	8	131
Mancini,Trey	37	131
LeMahieu,DJ	4	131
Merrifield,Whit	4	129
Segura,Jean	6	129
Gardner,Brett	78	129
Altuve,Jose	4	128
Escobar,Alcides	6	128
Swanson,Dansby	6	125
Rosario,Eddie	7	125
Gamel,Ben	79	124
Zimmer,Bradley	8	124
Pirela,Jose	7	124

TOP Spd, 300 or fewer AB

NAME	POS	Spd
Cordero,Franchy	8	175
Tapia,Raimel	9	168
Hanson,Alen	49	167
Dyson,Jarrod	8	166
Quinn,Roman	O	162
Tomlinson,Kelby	45	148
Jankowski,Travis	7	147
Marte,Ketel	6	146
Blanco,Gregor	78	145
Torreyes,Ronald	456	144
Phillips,Brett	8	143
Engel,Adam	8	143
Broxton,Keon	8	137
Fuentes,Reymond	8	136
Robles,Victor	9	135
Powell,Boog	8	133
Machado,Dixon	46	130
Duffy,Matt	0	130
Allen,Greg	8	129
Ahmed,Nick	6	129
Fisher,Derek	7	128
Davis,Rajai	78	128
Gonzalez,Erik	4	127

POSITIONAL SCARCITY

NAME	POS	Spd
Dahl,David	DH	154
Duffy,Matt	2	130
Dickerson,Corey	3	111
Escobar,Eduardo	4	105
Young,Chris	5	100
Realmuto,Jacob	CA	121
Herrmann,Chris	2	120
Barnes,Austin	3	115
Alfaro,Jorge	4	113
Knapp,Andrew	5	111
Cervelli,Francisco	6	111
Joseph,Caleb	7	108
Sisco,Chance	8	103
Mancini,Trey	1B	131
Guzman,Ronald	2	124
Bellinger,Cody	3	123
Myers,Wil	4	119
Moran,Colin	5	118
McMahon,Ryan	6	116
Desmond,Ian	7	113
Martinez,Jose	8	111
Rua,Ryan	9	108
Valencia,Danny	10	108
Gordon,Dee	2B	204
Hernandez,Cesar	2	179
Albies,Ozhaino	3	178
Mondesi,Raul	4	168
Hanson,Alen	5	167
Moncada,Yoan	6	157
Tomlinson,Kelby	7	148
Taylor,Chris	8	145
Peraza,Jose	9	139
Tomlinson,Kelby	3B	148
Torreyes,Ronald	2	144
Spangenberg,Cory	3	140
Crawford,J.P.	4	136
Sanchez,Yolmer	5	133
Reyes,Jose	6	129
Camargo,Johan	7	128
Bregman,Alex	8	123
Diaz,Yandy	9	122
Anderson,Brian	10	120
Turner,Trea	SS	175
Rosario,Amed	2	168
Anderson,Tim	3	161
Arcia,Orlando	4	148
Barreto,Franklin	5	148
Marte,Ketel	6	146
Torreyes,Ronald	7	144
Beckham,Tim	8	144
Hamilton,Billy	OF	188
Buxton,Byron	2	183
Cordero,Franchy	3	175
Tapia,Raimel	4	168
Smith,Mallex	5	167
Hanson,Alen	6	167
Dyson,Jarrod	7	166
Quinn,Roman	8	162
Margot,Manuel	9	162
DeShields Jr.,Delino	10	156
Fowler,Dexter	11	151
Eaton,Adam	12	147
Jankowski,Travis	13	147
Blanco,Gregor	14	145
Taylor,Chris	15	145
Phillips,Brett	16	143

TOP Spd, .330+ OBP

NAME	OBP	Spd
Hernandez,Cesar	367	179
Albies,Ozhaino	332	178
Turner,Trea	344	175
Moncada,Yoan	343	157
Fowler,Dexter	372	151
Tomlinson,Kelby	336	148
Eaton,Adam	363	147
Blanco,Gregor	334	145
Blackmon,Charlie	383	142
Inciarte,Ender	344	142
Pollock,A.J.	339	137
Crawford,J.P.	331	136
Marte,Starling	335	132
Cain,Lorenzo	353	131
LeMahieu,DJ	378	131
Segura,Jean	333	129
Gardner,Brett	348	129
Altuve,Jose	390	128
Calhoun,Willie	330	125
Ellsbury,Jacoby	339	124
Wong,Kolten	349	124
Bregman,Alex	352	123
Bellinger,Cody	349	123
Bogaerts,Xander	357	123
Panik,Joe	340	123
Peralta,David	334	123
Naquin,Tyler	336	122
Adames,Willy	336	122
Diaz,Yandy	369	122
Pence,Hunter	330	122
Herrera,Odubel	335	121
Aoki,Norichika	343	121
Trout,Mike	431	120
Jackson,Austin	347	120
Frazier,Adam	349	120
Myers,Wil	337	119
Andrus,Elvis	335	119
Benintendi,Andrew	351	118
Reddick,Josh	337	118
Bryant,Kris	395	118

TOP Spd, OBP under .300

NAME	OBP	Spd
Hamilton,Billy	300	188
Cordero,Franchy	273	175
Mondesi,Raul	284	168
Hanson,Alen	275	167
Anderson,Tim	283	161
Dahl,David	300	154
Barreto,Franklin	279	148
Engel,Adam	266	143
Hechavarria,Adeiny	293	143
Fuentes,Reymond	284	136
Fowler,Dustin	299	134
Lagares,Juan	294	134
Sanchez,Yolmer	294	133
Ahmed,Nick	281	129
Escobar,Alcides	285	128
Gonzalez,Erik	274	127
Jones,JaCoby	296	126
Diaz,Aledmys	293	125
Grichuk,Randal	287	122
Bader,Harrison	296	121
Adams,Lane	292	120
Herrmann,Chris	297	120
Galvis,Freddy	292	120

Top Spd, SBO% over 20%

NAME	SBO%	Spd
Gordon,Dee	40%	204
Hamilton,Billy	53%	188
Buxton,Byron	25%	183
Turner,Trea	42%	175
Mondesi,Raul	31%	168
Tapia,Raimel	21%	168
Smith,Mallex	40%	167
Hanson,Alen	37%	167
Dyson,Jarrod	40%	166
Quinn,Roman	42%	162
Margot,Manuel	24%	162
Anderson,Tim	22%	161
DeShields Jr.,Delino	32%	156
Dahl,David	26%	154
Barreto,Franklin	20%	148
Jankowski,Travis	33%	147
Engel,Adam	29%	143
Revere,Ben	29%	140
Peraza,Jose	30%	139
Pollock,A.J.	25%	137
Broxton,Keon	34%	137
Fuentes,Reymond	23%	136
Robles,Victor	35%	135
Kiermaier,Kevin	23%	135
Difo,Wilmer	20%	133
Marte,Starling	31%	132
Allen,Greg	27%	129
Reyes,Jose	23%	129
Merrifield,Whit	27%	129
Segura,Jean	23%	129
Altuve,Jose	20%	128
Davis,Rajai	42%	128
Gonzalez,Erik	20%	127
Jones,JaCoby	21%	126
Hernandez,Teoscar	22%	125
Adrianza,Ehire	23%	125
Ellsbury,Jacoby	23%	124
Zimmer,Bradley	31%	124
Acuna,Ronald	29%	122
Bader,Harrison	22%	121

Top Spd, SBO% under 15%

NAME	SBO%	Spd
Hernandez,Cesar	14%	179
Fowler,Dexter	11%	151
Eaton,Adam	12%	147
Marte,Ketel	14%	146
Torreyes,Ronald	5%	144
Beckham,Tim	10%	144
Hechavarria,Adeiny	10%	143
Mahtook,Mikie	10%	143
Blackmon,Charlie	14%	142
Crawford,J.P.	9%	136
Williams,Nick	10%	135
Asuaje,Carlos	6%	134
Sanchez,Yolmer	14%	133
Mancini,Trey	2%	131
LeMahieu,DJ	7%	131
Machado,Dixon	8%	130
Parker,Jarrett	8%	130
Duffy,Matt	11%	130
Gardner,Brett	14%	129
Escobar,Alcides	13%	128
Camargo,Johan	2%	128
Heredia,Guillermo	8%	126
Frazier,Clint	11%	125

BATTER SKILLS RANKING - Batting Average

TOP ct%, 400+ AB

NAME	ct%	BA
Simmons,Andrelton	90	274
Panik,Joe	89	277
Ramirez,Jose	89	308
Brantley,Michael	88	303
Gurriel,Yulieski	88	288
Cabrera,Melky	88	287
Altuve,Jose	88	335
Prado,Martin	87	292
Phillips,Brandon	87	279
Posey,Buster	87	297
Iglesias,Jose	87	264
Inciarte,Ender	87	297
Betts,Mookie	87	286
Span,Denard	87	275
Murphy,Daniel	87	316
Beltre,Adrian	87	298
Molina,Yadier	87	278
Solarte,Yangervis	87	262
Pujols,Albert	86	252
Escobar,Yunel	86	278
Nunez,Eduardo	86	298
Gregorius,Didi	86	271
Andrus,Elvis	85	289
Turner,Justin	85	297
Cano,Robinson	85	284
Lucroy,Jonathan	85	274
Escobar,Alcides	85	258
Reddick,Josh	85	282
Moustakas,Mike	85	269
Lindor,Francisco	84	283
Gordon,Dee	84	297
Kinsler,Ian	84	269
LeMahieu,DJ	84	316
Segura,Jean	84	289
Flores,Wilmer	84	263
Ramos,Wilson	84	260
Pillar,Kevin	84	264
Pollock,A.J.	84	281
Heyward,Jason	84	257
Markakis,Nick	84	273
Arenado,Nolan	83	301
Cozart,Zack	83	271
Wong,Kolten	83	269
Polanco,Jorge	83	263
Franco,Maikel	83	252
Hechavarria,Adeiny	83	261
Harrison,Josh	83	274
Merrifield,Whit	83	274
Mercer,Jordy	83	253
Mauer,Joe	83	289
Rizzo,Anthony	82	284
Bregman,Alex	82	286
Margot,Manuel	82	261
Santana,Carlos	82	257
Parra,Gerardo	82	291
Machado,Manny	82	283
Votto,Joey	82	317
Polanco,Gregory	82	254
Benintendi,Andrew	82	278
Rendon,Anthony	82	285
Seager,Kyle	81	259
Hosmer,Eric	81	295
Bell,Josh	81	265
Cain,Lorenzo	81	297
Jones,Adam	81	271
Cabrera,Asdrubal	81	274

LOW ct%, 400+ AB

NAME	ct%	BA
Gallo,Joey	55	221
Davis,Chris	60	225
Sano,Miguel	60	249
Davidson,Matt	62	220
Judge,Aaron	63	256
Zunino,Mike	63	247
Story,Trevor	64	252
Santana,Domingo	64	268
Moncada,Yoan	64	251
Souza,Steven	65	238
Schwarber,Kyle	65	244
Zimmer,Bradley	66	231
Taylor,Michael	66	243
Chapman,Matt	67	236
Buxton,Byron	67	268
Happ,Ian	68	244
Thames,Eric	68	251
Davis,Khristopher	68	246
Beckham,Tim	68	253
Upton,Justin	69	263
Grichuk,Randal	69	243
Gomez,Carlos	69	252
Williams,Nick	69	260
Stanton,Giancarlo	70	272
Baez,Javier	70	273
Olson,Matt	70	234
DeJong,Paul	70	263
Pham,Thomas	70	267
Duvall,Adam	71	241
Duda,Lucas	71	234
Martinez,J.D.	71	297
Grandal,Yasmani	71	235
Renfroe,Hunter	71	249
Altherr,Aaron	71	256
Myers,Wil	71	256
Miller,Brad	71	241

TOP ct%, 300 or fewer AB

NAME	ct%	BA
Torreyes,Ronald	87	270
Pedroia,Dustin	87	288
Frazier,Adam	86	287
Suzuki,Kurt	86	268
Verdugo,Alex	86	270
Sogard,Eric	86	260
Rivera,T.J.	85	282
Mejia,Francisco	85	256
Suzuki,Ichiro	85	268
Urshela,Giovanny	85	237
Aybar,Erick	85	247
Dyson,Jarrod	84	256
Robles,Victor	84	271
Profar,Jurickson	84	242
Garcia,Adonis	84	247
Tapia,Raimel	84	291
Marte,Ketel	84	267
Martinez,Victor	84	269
La Stella,Tommy	83	255
Narvaez,Omar	83	261
Kelly,Carson	82	237
Barney,Darwin	82	237
Diaz,Aledmys	82	252
Machado,Dixon	82	250
Duffy,Matt	82	267
Toles,Andrew	82	278
Sandoval,Pablo	82	232

TOP ct%, bb% over 9%

NAME	bb%	ct%
Pedroia,Dustin	10	87
Posey,Buster	10	87
Betts,Mookie	9	87
Sogard,Eric	11	86
Turner,Justin	10	85
Lucroy,Jonathan	10	85
Zobrist,Ben	12	85
Profar,Jurickson	10	84
Heyward,Jason	9	84
Markakis,Nick	10	84
La Stella,Tommy	10	83
Cozart,Zack	9	83
Narvaez,Omar	11	83
Wong,Kolten	9	83
Ellsbury,Jacoby	9	83
Mauer,Joe	12	83
Rizzo,Anthony	12	82
Bregman,Alex	9	82
Lowrie,Jed	10	82
Santana,Carlos	14	82
Votto,Joey	19	82
Benintendi,Andrew	10	82
Rendon,Anthony	12	82
Tomlinson,Kelby	10	82
Seager,Kyle	9	81
Hosmer,Eric	9	81
Bell,Josh	10	81
Barnhart,Tucker	10	81
Barnes,Austin	12	81
McCann,Brian	10	81
Winker,Jesse	11	81
Diaz,Yandy	12	81
Eaton,Adam	10	81
Alford,Anthony	11	80
Walker,Neil	11	79
Braun,Ryan	9	79
Gardner,Brett	11	79
Puig,Yasiel	10	79
Hernandez,Cesar	11	79
Crawford,J.P.	12	79

TOP ct%, bb% under 6%

NAME	bb%	ct%
Revere,Ben	5	91
Gurriel,Yulieski	6	88
Cabrera,Melky	6	88
Torreyes,Ronald	4	87
Prado,Martin	6	87
Phillips,Brandon	4	87
Iglesias,Jose	5	87
Molina,Yadier	6	87
Suzuki,Kurt	6	86
Peraza,Jose	4	86
Nunez,Eduardo	5	86
Gregorius,Didi	5	86
Rivera,T.J.	4	85
Mejia,Francisco	5	85
Urshela,Giovanny	4	85
Escobar,Alcides	3	85
Gordon,Dee	4	84
Segura,Jean	5	84
Robles,Victor	5	84
Flores,Wilmer	5	84
Ramos,Wilson	5	84
Pillar,Kevin	5	84
Garcia,Adonis	4	84

Top ct%, GB% over 50%

NAME	GB%	ct%
Revere,Ben	56	91
Simmons,Andrelton	51	90
Aoki,Norichika	59	89
Torreyes,Ronald	54	87
Rojas,Miguel	52	87
Iglesias,Jose	52	87
Escobar,Yunel	56	86
Nunez,Eduardo	52	86
Suzuki,Ichiro	54	85
Aybar,Erick	53	85
Gordon,Dee	58	84
LeMahieu,DJ	54	84
Dyson,Jarrod	52	84
Segura,Jean	55	84
Ramos,Wilson	55	84
Garcia,Adonis	52	84
Mauer,Joe	52	83
Machado,Dixon	55	82
Toles,Andrew	51	82
Tomlinson,Kelby	51	82
Hosmer,Eric	56	81
Bell,Josh	51	81
Diaz,Elias	52	81
Arroyo,Christian	55	81
Winker,Jesse	55	81
Diaz,Yandy	59	81
Eaton,Adam	54	81
Riddle,J.T.	54	81
Arcia,Orlando	53	80
Powell,Boog	51	80
Allen,Greg	58	80
Vazquez,Christian	53	80
Osuna,Jose	55	80
Castro,Starlin	52	80
Peralta,David	52	80
Difo,Wilmer	55	80
Kendrick,Howie	59	79
Jay,Jon	51	79
Braun,Ryan	51	79
Hernandez,Cesar	54	79

Top ct%, GB% under 40%

NAME	GB%	ct%
Ramirez,Jose	40	89
Murphy,Daniel	36	87
Suzuki,Kurt	38	86
Gregorius,Didi	38	86
Rivera,T.J.	39	85
Turner,Justin	33	85
Reddick,Josh	37	85
Moustakas,Mike	37	85
Kinsler,Ian	33	84
Reyes,Jose	38	84
Flores,Wilmer	36	84
Martinez,Victor	40	84
Arenado,Nolan	35	83
Cozart,Zack	39	83
Polanco,Jorge	36	83
Harrison,Josh	40	83
Merrifield,Whit	39	83
Kelly,Carson	39	82
Rizzo,Anthony	39	82
Bregman,Alex	35	82
Lowrie,Jed	34	82
Votto,Joey	40	82
Polanco,Gregory	40	82

POTENTIAL SKILLS GAINERS AND FADERS - Batters

Power Gainers

Batters whose 2017 Power Index (PX) fell significantly short of their underlying power skill (xPX). If they show the same xPX skill in 2018, they are good candidates for more power output.

Power Faders

Batters whose 2017 Power Index (PX) noticeably outpaced their underlying power skill (xPX). If they show the same xPX skill in 2018, they are good candidates for less power output.

BA Gainers

Batters who had strong Hard Contact Index levels in 2017, but lower hit rates (h%). Since base hits come most often on hard contact, if these batters can make hard contact at the same strong rate again in 2018, they may get better results in terms of hit rate, resulting in a batting average improvement.

BA Faders

Batters who had weak Hard Contact Index levels in 2017, but higher hit rates (h%). Since base hits come most often on hard contact, if these batters only make hard contact at the same weak rate again in 2018, they may get worse results in terms of hit rate, resulting in a batting average decline.

PX GAINERS

NAME	PX	xPX
Blash,Jabari	99	168
Descalso,Daniel	99	153
Utley,Chase	99	134
Montero,Miguel	79	132
Pina,Manny	96	131
Cabrera,Miguel	92	125
Ruiz,Rio	72	123
Maxwell III,Bruce	73	122
Santana,Daniel	98	121
Collins,Tyler	95	121
Harrison,Josh	93	120
Kinsler,Ian	94	119
Molina,Yadier	92	118
Martinez,Victor	67	117
Cabrera,Asdrubal	94	115
Albies,Ozhaino	89	113
Parra,Gerardo	86	113
Posey,Buster	85	113
Piscotty,Stephen	85	112
Cano,Robinson	95	111
Merrifield,Whit	94	111
Forsythe,Logan	77	111
Semien,Marcus	96	110
Espinosa,Danny	86	109
Gonzalez,Adrian	78	108
Asuaje,Carlos	63	108
Choo,Shin-Soo	95	107
Ramos,Wilson	97	106
Sucre,Jesus	85	105
Pujols,Albert	75	105
Crawford,Brandon	97	102
Knapp,Andrew	82	102
McCann,James	97	101
Rivera,T.J.	82	101
Cervelli,Francisco	78	101

PX FADERS

NAME	PX	xPX
Camargo,Johan	104	64
Osuna,Jose	110	65
Kiermaier,Kevin	104	70
Bourjos,Peter	101	73
Joseph,Caleb	105	74
Canha,Mark	128	75
Parker,Jarrett	123	79
Herrera,Odubel	114	79
Vargas,Kennys	129	81
Gattis,Evan	113	82
Russell,Addison	113	83
Hicks,John	121	86
Drury,Brandon	119	87
Williams,Nick	119	87
Gonzalez,Marwin	137	94
Holliday,Matt	130	97
Souza,Steven	144	100
Contreras,Willson	136	101
Ramirez,Jose	144	102
Harper,Bryce	161	105
Taylor,Michael	149	109
Rupp,Cameron	151	111
Marisnick,Jake	179	119
Happ,Ian	174	122
Schwarber,Kyle	168	125
Stanton,Giancarlo	205	131
Trout,Mike	181	133
Zunino,Mike	199	141

BA GAINERS

NAME	h%	HctX
Hoskins,Rhys	25	136
Martinez,Victor	28	135
Cabrera,Miguel	29	132
Machado,Manny	27	131
Carpenter,Matt	28	128
Betts,Mookie	27	126
Kinsler,Ian	24	126
Molina,Yadier	29	126
Perez,Salvador	28	123
Smoak,Justin	29	123
Lindor,Francisco	28	122
Bruce,Jay	28	122
Moreland,Mitch	28	120
Flores,Wilmer	28	120
Pujols,Albert	25	120
Utley,Chase	27	120
Pollock,A.J.	29	118
Rizzo,Anthony	28	117
Morales,Kendrys	28	117
Schebler,Scott	25	117
Seager,Kyle	27	117
Hernandez,Enrique	26	116
Suzuki,Kurt	27	116
Encarnacion,Edwin	27	116
Duda,Lucas	24	116
Stanton,Giancarlo	29	114
Longoria,Evan	29	114
Gattis,Evan	28	113
Belt,Brandon	28	113
Santana,Carlos	28	112
Olson,Matt	24	111
Ramos,Wilson	27	111
Descalso,Daniel	29	111
Pearce,Steve	28	110
Sucre,Jesus	28	110
Ramirez,Hanley	27	109
D Arnaud,Travis	25	109

BA FADERS

NAME	h%	HctX
Garcia,Greg	34	50
Gordon,Dee	36	56
Smith,Mallex	35	65
Tapia,Raimel	36	68
DeShields Jr.,Delino	36	69
Hernandez,Cesar	35	71
Difo,Wilmer	34	72
Parker,Jarrett	34	73
Buxton,Byron	34	75
Inciarte,Ender	34	77
Carrera,Ezequiel	36	77
Presley,Alex	38	78
Jay,Jon	37	81
Desmond,Ian	35	82
Spangenberg,Cory	34	84
Pennington,Cliff	35	84
Vazquez,Christian	35	86
Asuaje,Carlos	35	87
Herrera,Odubel	35	90
Taylor,Michael	37	90
Headley,Chase	35	90
Camargo,Johan	37	91
Baez,Javier	35	91
Gamel,Benjamin	34	91
Zunino,Mike	36	92
Reynolds,Mark	35	93
Castro,Starlin	35	93
Williams,Nick	38	94
Nimmo,Brandon	37	94
Freese,David	34	94
Kiermaier,Kevin	34	95
Taylor,Chris	36	95
Segura,Jean	34	96
Altuve,Jose	37	98
Almora,Albert	34	98
Jackson,Austin	39	99
Hosmer,Eric	35	99
Kendrick,Howie	38	99

POTENTIAL SKILLS GAINERS AND FADERS - Pitchers

Dom Gainers

From a pitcher's swinging-strike rate (SwK%), we can establish a typical range in which we would expect to find their Dom (k/9). The pitchers on this list posted a 2017 Dom that was in the bottom of that expected range based on their SwK%. The names above the break line are in the bottom 10% of that range, and are the strongest candidates for Dom gains. The names below the break line are in the bottom 25%, and are also good candidates for strikeout gains.

Dom Faders

From a pitcher's swinging-strike rate (SwK%), we can establish a typical range in which we would expect to find their Dom (k/9). The pitchers on this list posted a 2017 Dom that was in the top of that expected range based on their SwK%. The names above the break line are in the top 10% of that range, and are the strongest candidates for a Dom fade. The names below the break line are in the top 25%, and are also good candidates for a Dom fade.

Ctl Gainers

From a pitcher's first-pitch strike rate (FpK%), we can establish a typical range in which we would expect to find their Ctl (bb/9). These pitchers posted a 2017 Ctl that was in the bottom of that expected range based on their FpK%. The names above the break line are in the bottom 10% of that range, and are the strongest candidates for Ctl gains. The names below the break line are in the bottom 25%, and are also good candidates for Ctl gains.

Ctl Faders

From a pitcher's first-pitch strike rate (FpK%), we can establish a typical range in which we would expect to find their Ctl (bb/9). These pitchers posted a 2017 Ctl that was in the top 10% of that expected range based on their FpK%, making them the strongest candidates for a Ctl fade.

DOM GAINERS

NAME	SwK	K/9
Rusin,Chris	13	7.5
Garcia,Jaime	11	7.4
Nolasco,Ricky	11	7.1
Santana,Ervin	11	7.1
Ramirez,Erasmo	11	7.5
Gibson,Kyle	10	6.9
Claudio,Alex	10	6.1
Vargas,Jason	10	6.7
Conley,Adam	10	6.3
Bailey,Homer	10	6.6
Fulmer,Michael	10	6.2
Ramirez,JC	9	6.4
Straily,Dan	13	8.4
Pineda,Michael	13	8.6
Faria,Jake	13	8.8
Montgomery,Jordan	12	8.4
Musgrove,Joe	12	8.1
Gray,Sonny	12	8.5
Anderson,Tyler	12	8.5
Duffy,Danny	12	8.0
Bundy,Dylan	12	8.1
Manaea,Sean	12	8.0
Miranda,Ariel	12	7.7
Odorizzi,Jake	12	8.0
Andriese,Matt	11	8.0
Keuchel,Dallas	11	7.7
Lackey,John	11	7.9
Boyd,Matt	10	7.3
Chatwood,Tyler	10	7.3
Stroman,Marcus	10	7.3
Pruitt,Austin	10	7.2
Cotton,Jharel	10	7.3
Hamels,Cole	10	6.4
Perdomo,Luis	9	6.5
Richard,Clayton	9	6.9

DOM FADERS

NAME	SwK	K/9
Wood,Travis	6	6.2
Fister,Doug	8	8.3
Jimenez,Ubaldo	9	8.8
Quintana,Jose	9	9.9
Arrieta,Jake	9	8.7
Pivetta,Nick	9	9.5
Gray,Jon	9	9.2
Bauer,Trevor	9	10.0
Morton,Charlie	11	10.0
Hill,Rich	12	11.1
Senzatela,Antonio	7	6.8
Chacin,Jhoulys	8	7.6
Chavez,Jesse	8	7.8
Skaggs,Tyler	8	8.0
Miley,Wade	8	8.1
Hendricks,Kyle	9	8.0
Eickhoff,Jerad	9	8.3
Taillon,Jameson	9	8.4
Gonzalez,Gio	9	8.4
Leiter,Mark	9	8.4
Walker,Taijuan	9	8.4
Fiers,Mike	10	8.6
Wheeler,Zack	10	8.5
Pomeranz,Drew	10	9.0
Samardzija,Jeff	11	8.9
Verlander,Justin	11	9.6
Martinez,Carlos	11	9.5
Petit,Yusmeiro	11	10.0
Nola,Aaron	11	9.9
Peacock,Brad	12	11.0
Lamet,Dinelson	13	11.0

CTL GAINERS

NAME	FpK	BB/9
Quintana,Jose	67	2.9
Gonzalez,Miguel	67	3.2
Vargas,Jason	66	2.9
Wacha,Michael	66	3.0
Stammen,Craig	65	3.1
Cueto,Johnny	64	3.2
Teheran,Julio	64	3.4
Holland,Derek	63	5.0
Montero,Rafael	63	5.1
Cain,Matt	63	3.6
Peacock,Brad	63	3.9
Clevinger,Mike	63	4.5
Foltynewicz,Mike	62	3.4
Wood,Travis	62	4.3
Perdomo,Luis	61	3.6
Bailey,Homer	61	4.2
Wheeler,Zack	61	4.2
Cahill,Trevor	60	4.8
Ray,Robbie	60	3.9
Montgomery,Mike	60	3.8
Pelfrey,Mike	59	4.7
Pivetta,Nick	59	3.9
Lackey,John	65	2.8
Anderson,Tyler	65	2.7
Devenski,Chris	65	2.9
Gsellman,Robert	64	3.2
Biagini,Joe	64	3.2
Taillon,Jameson	62	3.1
Hill,Rich	62	3.3
Moore,Matt	61	3.5
Rodriguez,Eduardo	61	3.3
Miranda,Ariel	61	3.5
Hoffman,Jeff	60	3.6
Adleman,Tim	60	3.8
Fister,Doug	60	3.8
Pomeranz,Drew	60	3.6
Gausman,Kevin	60	3.4
Salazar,Danny	60	3.8
Fiers,Mike	60	3.6

CTL FADERS

NAME	FpK	BB/9
Cobb,Alex	59	2.2
Rusin,Chris	59	2.0
Claudio,Alex	63	1.6
Leake,Mike	63	1.8
Petit,Yusmeiro	64	1.8
Kluber,Corey	64	1.6
Nova,Ivan	64	1.7
Samardzija,Jeff	65	1.4
Faria,Jake	54	3.2
McCullers,Lance	55	3.0
Graveman,Kendall	56	2.7
Davies,Zach	57	2.6
Lively,Ben	59	2.4
Lugo,Seth	59	2.2
Hellickson,Jeremy	59	2.6
Martinez,Nick	60	2.3
Fulmer,Michael	61	2.2
Ramirez,Erasmo	62	2.1
Junis,Jakob	62	2.3
Greinke,Zack	62	2.0
Carrasco,Carlos	63	2.1
Tanaka,Masahiro	64	2.1
Pineda,Michael	65	2.0

PITCHER SKILLS RANKINGS - Starting Pitchers

Top Command (k/bb)			Top Control (bb/9)			Top Dominance (k/9)			Top Ground Ball Rate			Top Fly Ball Rate	
NAME	Cmd		NAME	Ctl		NAME	Dom		NAME	GB		NAME	FB
Kershaw,Clayton	7.8		Tomlin,Josh	0.9		Sale,Chris	11.7		Keuchel,Dallas	63		Griffin,A.J.	53
Tomlin,Josh	7.3		Kershaw,Clayton	1.3		Scherzer,Max	11.5		Perdomo,Luis	61		Miranda,Ariel	5.
Sale,Chris	6.3		Moore,Andrew	1.6		Salazar,Danny	11.4		Stroman,Marcus	60		Santiago,Hector	51
Syndergaard,Noah	6.2		Syndergaard,Noah	1.6		Ray,Robbie	11.0		Richard,Clayton	60		Estrada,Marco	50
Kluber,Corey	5.7		Colon,Bartolo	1.8		Darvish,Yu	10.7		Chatwood,Tyler	58		Moore,Andrew	48
Bumgarner,Madison	5.1		Tanaka,Masahiro	1.8		Kluber,Corey	10.6		Castillo,Luis	58		Straily,Dan	47
Tanaka,Masahiro	5.0		Bumgarner,Madison	1.8		Archer,Chris	10.6		Blackburn,Paul	57		Odorizzi,Jake	47
Pineda,Michael	4.8		Leake,Mike	1.8		Strasburg,Stephen	10.6		Anderson,Brett	57		Adleman,Timothy	46
Carrasco,Carlos	4.7		Sale,Chris	1.8		Buehler,Walker	10.5		McCullers,Lance	57		Cotton,Jharel	46
Scherzer,Max	4.5		Kluber,Corey	1.9		Kershaw,Clayton	10.5		Garcia,Jaime	57		Scherzer,Max	46
Strasburg,Stephen	4.5		Samardzija,Jeff	1.9		Kopech,Michael	10.4		Cahill,Trevor	57		Tropeano,Nicholas	46
deGrom,Jacob	4.4		Nova,Ivan	1.9		McCullers,Lance	10.2		Ross,Tyson	55		Stephens,Jackson	46
Paulino,David	4.4		Pineda,Michael	1.9		Syndergaard,Noah	10.1		Morton,Charlie	55		Fulmer,Carson	45
Greinke,Zack	4.3		Porcello,Rick	1.9		Severino,Luis	10.0		Sanchez,Aaron	54		Bundy,Dylan	45
Samardzija,Jeff	4.3		Pruitt,Austin	2.0		Paulino,David	9.9		Godley,Zachary	53		Kennedy,Ian	45
Honeywell,Brent	4.2		Greinke,Zack	2.1		De Leon,Jose	9.9		Martinez,Carlos	53		Lively,Ben	44
Weaver,Luke	4.1		Eflin,Zach	2.1		deGrom,Jacob	9.9		Gray,Sonny	53		Heaney,Andrew	44
Nola,Aaron	4.0		Carrasco,Carlos	2.1		Lamet,Dinelson	9.9		Leake,Mike	53		Ynoa,Gabriel	44
Severino,Luis	4.0		Junis,Jakob	2.1		Carrasco,Carlos	9.9		Cobb,Alex	52		Verlander,Justin	44
Porcello,Rick	4.0		Zimmermann,Jordan	2.1		Reyes,Alex	9.9		Mahle,Tyler	52		Gohara,Luiz	44
Moore,Andrew	4.0		Weaver,Luke	2.1		Nola,Aaron	9.7		Freeland,Kyle	52		Lamet,Dinelson	44
Paxton,James	4.0		Ynoa,Gabriel	2.1		Gohara,Luiz	9.6		Wood,Alex	52		Farmer,Buck	44
De Leon,Jose	3.8		Honeywell,Brent	2.2		Rodon,Carlos	9.5		Romano,Sal	52		Boyd,Matt	44
Archer,Chris	3.8		DeSclafani,Anthony	2.2		Paxton,James	9.5		Syndergaard,Noah	52		Lopez,Reynaldo	43
Darvish,Yu	3.7		deGrom,Jacob	2.2		Snell,Blake	9.5		Nola,Aaron	51		Rodriguez,Eduardo	43
Maeda,Kenta	3.7		Chen,Wei-Yin	2.2		Glasnow,Tyler	9.4		Graveman,Kendall	51		Adams,Chance	42
Price,David	3.6		Paulino,David	2.2		Peacock,Brad	9.4		Perez,Martin	51		Honeywell,Brent	42
Nova,Ivan	3.6		Cobb,Alex	2.3		Newcomb,Sean	9.3		Gibson,Kyle	51		Shoemaker,Matthew	42
Quintana,Jose	3.6		Suter,Brent	2.3		Verlander,Justin	9.3		Richards,Garrett	51		Peacock,Brad	42
Pruitt,Austin	3.6		Shoemaker,Matthew	2.3		Price,David	9.3		Pelfrey,Mike	50		Gonzalez,Miguel	42
Junis,Jakob	3.5		Blach,Ty	2.3		Maeda,Kenta	9.2		Corbin,Patrick	50		Paulino,David	42

High GB, Low Dom			High GB, High Dom			Lowest xERA			Top BPV, 180+ IP			Top BPV, <150 IP	
NAME	GB	Dom	NAME	GB	Dom	NAME	xERA		NAME	BPV		NAME	BPV
Perdomo,Luis	61	6.4	Castillo,Luis	58	9.0	Kershaw,Clayton	2.78		Kershaw,Clayton	180		Pineda,Michael	139
Richard,Clayton	60	5.9	McCullers,Lance	57	10.2	Sale,Chris	3.04		Sale,Chris	179		Paulino,David	134
Blackburn,Paul	57	4.6	Godley,Zachary	53	9.1	Kluber,Corey	3.06		Kluber,Corey	164		Paxton,James	132
Anderson,Brett	57	5.8	Martinez,Carlos	53	8.8	Syndergaard,Noah	3.07		Scherzer,Max	151		Salazar,Danny	131
Leake,Mike	53	6.3	Wood,Alex	52	8.6	Strasburg,Stephen	3.25		Strasburg,Stephen	150		McCullers,Lance	118
Cobb,Alex	52	6.8	Syndergaard,Noah	52	10.1	Carrasco,Carlos	3.33		Carrasco,Carlos	147		Honeywell,Brent	117
Freeland,Kyle	52	6.4	Nola,Aaron	51	9.7	Severino,Luis	3.35		deGrom,Jacob	141		Buehler,Walker	105
Romano,Sal	52	6.8	Nelson,Jimmy	50	8.9	Scherzer,Max	3.37		Nola,Aaron	140		Stewart,Brock	105
Graveman,Kendall	51	5.6	Wheeler,Zack	50	8.7	McCullers,Lance	3.38		Severino,Luis	139		De Leon,Jose	104
Perez,Martin	51	5.4	Kershaw,Clayton	50	10.5	Nola,Aaron	3.39		Archer,Chris	137		Nelson,Jimmy	102
Gibson,Kyle	51	7.0	Tanaka,Masahiro	48	8.9	deGrom,Jacob	3.46		Bumgarner,Madison	134		Morton,Charlie	101
Pelfrey,Mike	50	5.4	Severino,Luis	48	10.0	Tanaka,Masahiro	3.50		Greinke,Zack	128		Kopech,Michael	99
Covey,Dylan	50	5.3	Gonzalez,Gio	48	8.5	Keuchel,Dallas	3.50		Castillo,Luis	128		Pruitt,Austin	99
Gsellman,Robert	50	5.9	Carrasco,Carlos	48	9.9	Archer,Chris	3.53		Weaver,Luke	121		Richards,Garrett	98
Davies,Zachary	50	6.5	Paxton,James	48	9.5	Castillo,Luis	3.53		Quintana,Jose	116		Ryu,Hyun-Jin	97
Hahn,Jesse	50	5.6	Gray,Jonathan	47	9.0	Salazar,Danny	3.53		Samardzija,Jeff	115		Anderson,Tyler	97
Bettis,Chad	49	6.4	Pineda,Michael	47	9.2	Paxton,James	3.54		Lester,Jon	112		Leiter,Mark	96
Fulmer,Michael	49	6.9	Buehler,Walker	47	10.5	Pineda,Michael	3.56		Cole,Gerrit	109		Junis,Jakob	95
Fister,Doug	49	6.6	Greinke,Zack	47	8.9	Wood,Alex	3.60		Hendricks,Kyle	109		Rodriguez,Eduardo	95
Williams,Trevor	48	6.2	Lester,Jon	46	8.8	Darvish,Yu	3.61		Porcello,Rick	107		Ross,Joe	95
Nova,Ivan	48	6.8	deGrom,Jacob	45	9.9	Greinke,Zack	3.62		Stroman,Marcus	107		Shoemaker,Matthew	95
Cashner,Andrew	48	6.1	Jimenez,Ubaldo	45	8.6	Stroman,Marcus	3.62		Verlander,Justin	106		Matz,Steven	95
Feldman,Scott	48	6.2	Rodon,Carlos	45	9.5	Weaver,Luke	3.66		Martinez,Carlos	105		Andriese,Matt	95
Eovaldi,Nathan	48	6.7	Strasburg,Stephen	45	10.6	Bumgarner,Madison	3.67		Bauer,Trevor	101		Sanchez,Anibal	95
Thompson,Jake	47	6.4	Newcomb,Sean	45	9.3	Ray,Robbie	3.73		Leake,Mike	96		Gohara,Luiz	94
Butler,Eddie	47	4.7	Bauer,Trevor	45	9.1	Godley,Zachary	3.74		Corbin,Patrick	94		Karns,Nathan	93
Gaviglio,Sam	47	6.1	Kluber,Corey	44	10.6	Martinez,Carlos	3.75		Cobb,Alex	91		Rodon,Carlos	92
Blach,Ty	47	4.3	Archer,Chris	44	10.6	Morton,Charlie	3.75		Bundy,Dylan	90		Skaggs,Tyler	90
Nicolino,Justin	46	4.4	Karns,Nathan	44	9.1	Hendricks,Kyle	3.75		Gonzalez,Gio	90		Flaherty,Jack	89
Suter,Brent	46	6.1	Quintana,Jose	44	8.9	Richards,Garrett	3.82		Anderson,Chase	83		Mahle,Tyler	87
Urena,Jose	46	5.8	Pomeranz,Drew	44	9.0	Buehler,Walker	3.83		Arrieta,Jake	82		DeSclafani,Anthony	86

PITCHER SKILLS RANKINGS - Relief Pitchers

Top Command (k/bb)

NAME	Cmd
Jansen,Kenley	10.6
Osuna,Roberto	6.8
Melancon,Mark	5.8
Doolittle,Sean	5.6
Wittgren,Nick	5.2
Kimbrel,Craig	4.9
Petit,Yusmeiro	4.8
Miller,Andrew	4.8
Hildenberger,Trevor	4.7
Otero,Dan	4.6
Cecil,Brett	4.5
Musgrove,Joe	4.5
Reed,Addison	4.5
Pagan,Emilio	4.4
Smith,Joe	4.4
Harris,Will	4.4
Jones,Nate	4.4
Hunter,Tommy	4.4
Green,Chad	4.3
Holder,Jonathan	4.2
Oh,Seung-Hwan	4.2
Madson,Ryan	4.1
Rondon,Hector	4.1
Romo,Sergio	4.0
Swarzak,Anthony	4.0
Giles,Ken	4.0
Brebbia,John	4.0
Rivero,Felipe	3.9
Allen,Cody	3.9
Hand,Brad	3.9
Chapman,Aroldis	3.9

Top Control (bb/9)

NAME	Ctl
Otero,Dan	1.3
Jansen,Kenley	1.3
Melancon,Mark	1.4
Wittgren,Nick	1.5
Osuna,Roberto	1.6
Musgrove,Joe	1.7
Bleier,Richard	1.8
Claudio,Alexander	1.8
Hildenberger,Trevor	1.8
Petit,Yusmeiro	1.8
Doolittle,Sean	2.0
Kintzler,Brandon	2.0
Brebbia,John	2.0
Hunter,Tommy	2.1
Reed,Addison	2.1
Smith,Joe	2.1
Vincent,Nick	2.2
Madson,Ryan	2.2
Oh,Seung-Hwan	2.2
Pagan,Emilio	2.2
Cecil,Brett	2.2
Rusin,Chris	2.3
Duffey,Tyler	2.3
Harris,Will	2.3
Stripling,Ross	2.3
Ramirez,Erasmo	2.3
Jones,Nate	2.3
Romo,Sergio	2.4
Swarzak,Anthony	2.4
Holder,Jonathan	2.4
Rondon,Hector	2.5

Top Dominance (k/9)

NAME	Dom
Kimbrel,Craig	15.1
Betances,Dellin	14.7
Miller,Andrew	14.1
Jansen,Kenley	14.0
Chapman,Aroldis	13.8
Minter,A.J.	13.4
Knebel,Corey	12.6
Boxberger,Brad	12.4
Giles,Ken	12.4
Robertson,David	12.2
Allen,Cody	12.1
Diaz,Edwin	12.0
Yates,Kirby	11.9
Edwards,Carl	11.6
Goody,Nicholas	11.5
Steckenrider,Drew	11.5
Blevins,Jerry	11.5
Kela,Keone	11.3
Hand,Brad	11.2
Kahnle,Thomas	11.2
Holland,Greg	11.2
Barraclough,Kyle	11.2
O Day,Darren	11.1
Davis,Wade	11.0
Diekman,Jake	11.0
Smoker,Josh	11.0
Green,Chad	10.9
Simmons,Shae	10.8
Doolittle,Sean	10.8
Wilson,Justin	10.8
Givens,Mychal	10.8

Top Ground Ball Rate

NAME	GB
Britton,Zach	76
Alexander,Scott	74
Bleier,Richard	69
Ziegler,Brad	65
Smith,Carson	65
Claudio,Alexander	65
Dyson,Sam	65
Hughes,Jared	61
Treinen,Blake	61
Otero,Dan	61
Familia,Jeurys	61
Jeffress,Jeremy	59
Coulombe,Daniel	59
Garcia,Luis	59
Petricka,Jacob	59
Kintzler,Brandon	58
Bowman,Matthew	57
Rusin,Chris	57
Montgomery,Mike	57
Chafin,Andrew	57
Hildenberger,Trevor	57
Strop,Pedro	56
Lorenzen,Michael	55
Melancon,Mark	55
Gregerson,Luke	55
Ramirez,J.C.	54
Peralta,Wandy	54
Biagini,Joe	54
Barnes,Jacob	53
Rodney,Fernando	53
Shaw,Bryan	52

Top Fly Ball Rate

NAME	FB
Clippard,Tyler	52
Doolittle,Sean	52
Barnes,Daniel	51
Wojciechowski,Asher	51
Pagan,Emilio	51
Brebbia,John	50
Leclerc,Jose	50
Buchter,Ryan	49
Goody,Nicholas	49
Fields,Joshua	49
Altavilla,Dan	48
Yates,Kirby	47
Hader,Joshua	47
Sewald,Paul	47
Torres,Jose	46
Vincent,Nick	46
Petit,Yusmeiro	46
Oh,Seung-Hwan	46
Dull,Ryan	46
Jansen,Kenley	45
Rondon,Bruce	44
Strahm,Matt	44
Robles,Hansel	44
Jimenez,Joe	44
Street,Huston	43
Shreve,Chasen	43
Devenski,Christopher	43
Green,Chad	43
Ramirez,Jose	43
Allen,Cody	43
Montas,Frankie	43

High GB, Low Dom

NAME	GB	Dom
Alexander,Scott	74	6.9
Bleier,Richard	69	3.5
Ziegler,Brad	65	5.7
Claudio,Alexander	65	6.1
Dyson,Sam	65	6.3
Hughes,Jared	61	6.3
Otero,Dan	61	5.9
Jeffress,Jeremy	59	7.4
Petricka,Jacob	59	6.5
Kintzler,Brandon	58	5.1
Bowman,Matthew	57	6.7
Rusin,Chris	57	7.0
Montgomery,Mike	57	7.0
Ramirez,J.C.	54	6.1
Peralta,Wandy	54	7.5
Biagini,Joe	54	7.1
Senzatela,Antonio	51	6.5
Fedde,Erick	51	6.8
Castro,Miguel	51	6.0
Triggs,Andrew	50	7.3
Lyles,Jordan	50	6.1
Watson,Tony	49	7.4
Torres,Carlos	46	7.5
Bell,Chadwick	46	6.7
Ramirez,Erasmo	45	7.1
Saupold,Warwick	43	5.8
Belisle,Matt	43	7.5
Jackson,Edwin	41	6.7
Holmberg,David	41	5.0
Bibens-Dirkx,Austin	40	5.2
Despaigne,Odrisamer	40	5.2

High GB, High Dom

NAME	GB	Dom
Smith,Carson	65	10.6
Familia,Jeurys	61	9.3
Strop,Pedro	56	10.3
Gregerson,Luke	55	10.0
Barnes,Jacob	53	9.5
Rodney,Fernando	53	10.2
Shaw,Bryan	52	9.0
Madson,Ryan	52	9.0
Wood,Blake	52	9.5
Smith,Joe	51	9.3
Stripling,Ross	51	8.6
Diekman,Jake	51	11.0
Harris,Will	50	10.1
Cedeno,Xavier	50	9.1
Betances,Dellin	50	14.7
Soria,Joakim	50	9.3
Rivero,Felipe	49	10.4
Liriano,Francisco	49	8.5
Cishek,Steve	49	9.2
Rondon,Hector	48	10.1
Barnes,Matt	48	10.1
Bradley,Archie	48	9.7
Pazos,James	48	10.1
Jones,Nate	48	10.2
Kelly,Joe	48	8.5
Leone,Dominic	47	9.5
Greene,Shane	47	9.0
Miller,Andrew	47	14.1
Drake,Oliver	47	9.8
Herrera,Kelvin	47	8.8
Kahnle,Thomas	47	11.2

Lowest xERA

NAME	xERA
Miller,Andrew	2.35
Jansen,Kenley	2.37
Kimbrel,Craig	2.43
Chapman,Aroldis	2.72
Smith,Carson	2.77
Betances,Dellin	2.83
Britton,Zach	2.83
Simmons,Shae	2.87
Osuna,Roberto	2.96
Giles,Ken	3.10
Robertson,David	3.11
Jones,Nate	3.18
Melancon,Mark	3.18
Minter,A.J.	3.18
Harris,Will	3.20
Rivero,Felipe	3.20
Hand,Brad	3.23
Strop,Pedro	3.26
Gregerson,Luke	3.27
Madson,Ryan	3.29
Kahnle,Thomas	3.30
Smith,Joe	3.31
Familia,Jeurys	3.34
Boxberger,Brad	3.35
Hildenberger,Trevor	3.36
Allen,Cody	3.37
Rondon,Hector	3.38
Diaz,Edwin	3.39
Cecil,Brett	3.44
Iglesias,Raisel	3.50
Otero,Dan	3.50

Top BPV, 10+ Saves

NAME	BPV
Jansen,Kenley	231
Kimbrel,Craig	203
Chapman,Aroldis	176
Osuna,Roberto	173
Giles,Ken	160
Doolittle,Sean	151
Allen,Cody	149
Hand,Brad	148
Diaz,Edwin	144
Rivero,Felipe	143
Melancon,Mark	142
Steckenrider,Drew	135
Parker,Blake	131
Iglesias,Raisel	130
Knebel,Corey	129
Holland,Greg	123
Britton,Zach	120
Davis,Wade	117
Oh,Seung-Hwan	117
Familia,Jeurys	111
Neris,Hector	109
Bedrosian,Cam	108
Vizcaino,Arodys	104
Herrera,Kelvin	104
Colome,Alexander	101
Treinen,Blake	99
Rodney,Fernando	94
Edwards,Carl	94
Belisle,Matt	85
Greene,Shane	82
Barraclough,Kyle	81

Top BPV, <10 Saves

NAME	BPV
Miller,Andrew	199
Minter,A.J.	163
Robertson,David	155
Smith,Carson	155
Betances,Dellin	152
Harris,Will	147
Jones,Nate	146
Cecil,Brett	144
Boxberger,Brad	144
Gregerson,Luke	143
Rondon,Hector	142
Holder,Jonathan	140
Smith,Joe	139
Kahnle,Thomas	139
Hildenberger,Trevor	138
Green,Chad	137
Madson,Ryan	133
Yates,Kirby	132
Swarzak,Anthony	132
Reed,Addison	130
Hunter,Tommy	129
Devenski,Christopher	129
Goody,Nicholas	129
Romo,Sergio	126
Hoyt,James	124
O Day,Darren	124
Feliz,Michael	124
Strop,Pedro	122
Stripling,Ross	122
Middleton,Keynan	121
Blevins,Jerry	121

PRO (Positive Relative Outcomes) Scores - Batters

See page 61 for a detailed explanation of PRO scores. Min 250 PA. Based on 2017 performance.

Best Net Scores

Hitter	Pos.	Neg.	Net
Votto,Joey	54%	46%	8%
Turner,Justin	54%	48%	6%
Carpenter,Matt	50%	50%	1%
Freeman,Freddie	50%	50%	-1%
Avila,Alex	48%	52%	-3%
Cabrera,Miguel	48%	52%	-4%
Mauer,Joe	48%	52%	-4%
Trout,Mike	49%	53%	-4%
Posey,Buster	48%	53%	-5%
Goldschmidt,Paul	48%	54%	-6%
Sogard,Eric	47%	53%	-6%
Judge,Aaron	48%	54%	-6%
Murphy,Daniel	49%	55%	-6%
Barnes,Austin	48%	54%	-6%
Seager,Corey	48%	54%	-6%
Fowler,Dexter	47%	54%	-6%
Castellanos,Nick	47%	53%	-7%
Martinez,Victor	47%	54%	-7%
Martinez,J.D.	47%	55%	-7%
Correa,Carlos	47%	54%	-8%
Lowrie,Jed	47%	55%	-8%
Martinez,Jose	47%	55%	-8%
Choo,Shin-Soo	46%	54%	-8%
Belt,Brandon	47%	55%	-8%
Rendon,Anthony	47%	56%	-9%
Rizzo,Anthony	47%	55%	-9%
Blackmon,Charlie	46%	55%	-9%
Forsythe,Logan	46%	55%	-9%
Encarnacion,Edwin	46%	56%	-10%
Conforto,Michael	46%	56%	-10%
Flowers,Tyler	45%	56%	-10%
Grossman,Robbie	45%	56%	-11%
Pham,Tommy	45%	56%	-11%
Beltre,Adrian	46%	57%	-11%
Arenado,Nolan	46%	57%	-11%
Smoak,Justin	46%	57%	-11%
Utley,Chase	45%	56%	-11%
LeMahieu,DJ	45%	56%	-11%
Frazier,Adam	45%	56%	-11%
Bryant,Kris	45%	57%	-12%
Barnhart,Tucker	44%	55%	-12%
Jaso,John	45%	57%	-12%
Walker,Neil	45%	57%	-12%
Cabrera,Asdrubal	45%	57%	-12%
Bruce,Jay	45%	57%	-12%
Santana,Domingo	44%	56%	-12%
Duda,Lucas	44%	57%	-13%
Lind,Adam	45%	58%	-13%
Cano,Robinson	44%	57%	-13%
Parra,Gerardo	43%	56%	-13%
Cruz,Nelson	44%	58%	-13%
Morrison,Logan	45%	58%	-13%
Kinsler,Ian	46%	59%	-13%
Bour,Justin	45%	58%	-13%
Harper,Bryce	44%	57%	-14%
Cespedes,Yoenis	46%	59%	-14%
Ramirez,Jose	45%	58%	-14%
Lamb,Jake	44%	58%	-14%
McCann,James	44%	58%	-14%
Brantley,Michael	44%	58%	-14%
Thames,Eric	44%	57%	-14%

Worst Net Scores

Hitter	Pos.	Neg.	Net
Engel,Adam	26%	74%	-48%
Torreyes,Ronald	27%	74%	-46%
Saladino,Tyler	30%	71%	-42%
Espinosa,Danny	30%	71%	-41%
Rosales,Adam	30%	71%	-41%
Hamilton,Billy	29%	69%	-40%
Barney,Darwin	30%	70%	-40%
Diaz,Aledmys	32%	71%	-39%
Hedges,Austin	33%	71%	-39%
Anderson,Tim	31%	69%	-39%
Trumbo,Mark	33%	71%	-38%
Desmond,Ian	31%	69%	-38%
Davis,Rajai	32%	70%	-38%
Marisnick,Jake	31%	69%	-38%
Hardy,J.J.	33%	70%	-37%
Davidson,Matt	33%	70%	-37%
Maldonado,Martin	31%	68%	-37%
Goins,Ryan	32%	68%	-37%
Rickard,Joey	33%	69%	-36%
Rupp,Cameron	32%	68%	-36%
Smith,Kevan	32%	68%	-36%
Baez,Javier	32%	68%	-36%
Dyson,Jarrod	31%	67%	-36%
Renfroe,Hunter	34%	70%	-36%
Heredia,Guillermo	32%	68%	-35%
Villar,Jonathan	32%	67%	-35%
Vargas,Kennys	34%	69%	-35%
Smith,Mallex	30%	65%	-35%
Gregorius,Didi	35%	70%	-35%
Napoli,Mike	35%	69%	-34%
Buxton,Byron	33%	67%	-34%
Turner,Trea	34%	67%	-33%
Hundley,Nick	34%	68%	-33%
Pence,Hunter	34%	67%	-33%
Chapman,Matt	36%	69%	-33%
Joseph,Caleb	34%	67%	-33%
Camargo,Johan	35%	68%	-33%
Nunez,Eduardo	35%	67%	-32%
Gordon,Dee	32%	64%	-32%
Castro,Starlin	35%	68%	-32%
Escobar,Alcides	35%	67%	-32%
Plouffe,Trevor	36%	68%	-32%
Owings,Chris	36%	67%	-31%
Duvall,Adam	36%	68%	-31%
Pinder,Chad	35%	66%	-31%
Broxton,Keon	34%	66%	-31%
Young,Chris	37%	68%	-31%
Sandoval,Pablo	37%	68%	-31%
Taylor,Michael	35%	66%	-31%
Valencia,Danny	36%	67%	-31%
Joseph,Tommy	37%	68%	-31%
Spangenberg,Cory	34%	65%	-31%
Holliday,Matt	36%	67%	-31%
Zimmer,Bradley	34%	64%	-31%
Vogt,Stephen	38%	68%	-31%
Difo,Wilmer	34%	64%	-31%
Odor,Rougned	36%	67%	-31%
Lagares,Juan	35%	66%	-31%
Margot,Manuel	35%	66%	-31%
Sanchez,Yolmer	35%	65%	-31%
Leon,Sandy	37%	67%	-30%

Best Positive Scores

Hitter	Pos.
Votto,Joey	54%
Turner,Justin	54%
Carpenter,Matt	50%
Freeman,Freddie	50%
Trout,Mike	49%
Murphy,Daniel	49%
Cabrera,Miguel	48%
Avila,Alex	48%
Goldschmidt,Paul	48%
Mauer,Joe	48%
Posey,Buster	48%
Barnes,Austin	48%
Judge,Aaron	48%
Seager,Corey	48%
Fowler,Dexter	47%
Lowrie,Jed	47%
Martinez,J.D.	47%
Sogard,Eric	47%
Rendon,Anthony	47%
Martinez,Victor	47%
Belt,Brandon	47%
Correa,Carlos	47%
Rizzo,Anthony	47%
Castellanos,Nick	47%
Martinez,Jose	47%
Encarnacion,Edwin	46%
Beltre,Adrian	46%
Blackmon,Charlie	46%
Conforto,Michael	46%
Forsythe,Logan	46%
Kinsler,Ian	46%

Worst Negative Scores

Hitter	Neg.
Engel,Adam	74%
Torreyes,Ronald	74%
Saladino,Tyler	71%
Trumbo,Mark	71%
Hedges,Austin	71%
Diaz,Aledmys	71%
Rosales,Adam	71%
Espinosa,Danny	71%
Davis,Rajai	70%
Gregorius,Didi	70%
Renfroe,Hunter	70%
Barney,Darwin	70%
Davidson,Matt	70%
Hardy,J.J.	70%
Napoli,Mike	69%
Desmond,Ian	69%
Vargas,Kennys	69%
Hamilton,Billy	69%
Rickard,Joey	69%
Anderson,Tim	69%
Chapman,Matt	69%
Marisnick,Jake	69%
Young,Chris	68%
Goins,Ryan	68%
Vogt,Stephen	68%
Rupp,Cameron	68%
Baez,Javier	68%

PRO (Positive Relative Outcomes) Scores - Pitchers

See page 61 for a detailed explanation of PRO scores. Min 200 batters faced. Based on 2017 performance.

Best Net Scores

Pitcher	Pos.	Neg.	Net
Scherzer,Max	73%	29%	44%
Sale,Chris	73%	29%	44%
Kluber,Corey	72%	30%	42%
Kershaw,Clayton	71%	30%	41%
Severino,Luis	70%	31%	39%
Strasburg,Stephen	70%	32%	38%
Castillo,Luis	69%	31%	38%
Keuchel,Dallas	68%	31%	37%
Wood,Alex	68%	33%	35%
Estrada,Marco	70%	35%	35%
Tanaka,Masahiro	68%	34%	34%
Santana,Ervin	68%	35%	33%
Salazar,Danny	67%	34%	33%
Maeda,Kenta	67%	34%	33%
Morton,Charlie	67%	34%	33%
Carrasco,Carlos	67%	34%	33%
Happ,J.A.	67%	34%	33%
Hill,Rich	67%	34%	33%
deGrom,Jacob	67%	34%	33%
Paxton,James	67%	35%	32%
Montgomery,Jordan	67%	35%	32%
Greinke,Zack	67%	35%	32%
Weaver,Luke	66%	34%	32%
Gray,Jon	66%	35%	31%
Pineda,Michael	66%	35%	31%
McCullers,Lance	65%	34%	31%
Duffy,Danny	66%	36%	30%
Samardzija,Jeff	66%	36%	30%
Griffin,A.J.	68%	39%	29%
Straily,Dan	66%	37%	29%
Bumgarner,Madison	66%	37%	29%
Triggs,Andrew	65%	36%	29%
Nola,Aaron	65%	36%	29%
Arrieta,Jake	65%	36%	29%
Anderson,Chase	65%	36%	29%
Lester,Jon	65%	36%	29%
Godley,Zack	64%	35%	29%
Miranda,Ariel	66%	38%	28%
Berrios,Jose	65%	37%	28%
Gray,Sonny	64%	36%	28%
Nelson,Jimmy	64%	36%	28%
Gonzalez,Gio	64%	36%	28%
Hendricks,Kyle	64%	36%	28%
Faria,Jake	65%	38%	27%
Jackson,Edwin	65%	38%	27%
Quintana,Jose	64%	37%	27%
Cole,Gerrit	64%	37%	27%
Anderson,Tyler	64%	37%	27%
Corbin,Patrick	64%	37%	27%
Wacha,Michael	64%	37%	27%
Roark,Tanner	64%	37%	27%
Martinez,Carlos	64%	37%	27%
Lively,Ben	64%	38%	26%
Farmer,Buck	64%	38%	26%
Rodriguez,Eduardo	64%	38%	26%
Garcia,Jaime	63%	37%	26%
Stroman,Marcus	63%	37%	26%
Blackburn,Paul	63%	37%	26%
McCarthy,Brandon	64%	39%	25%
Dickey,R.A.	63%	38%	25%
Chacin,Jhoulys	63%	38%	25%

Worst Net Scores

Pitcher	Pos.	Neg.	Net
Tillman,Chris	54%	48%	6%
Holland,Derek	54%	47%	7%
Garrett,Amir	54%	46%	8%
Anderson,Brett	54%	46%	8%
Bailey,Homer	54%	46%	8%
Norris,Daniel	54%	46%	8%
Conley,Adam	56%	46%	10%
Zimmermann,Jordan	57%	46%	11%
Volquez,Edinson	55%	44%	11%
Ross,Tyson	56%	45%	11%
Glasnow,Tyler	56%	45%	11%
Gibson,Kyle	56%	45%	11%
Perez,Martin	56%	45%	11%
Gossett,Daniel	57%	44%	13%
Feldman,Scott	56%	43%	13%
Stratton,Chris	57%	43%	14%
Cain,Matt	57%	43%	14%
Cueto,Johnny	57%	43%	14%
Harvey,Matt	57%	43%	14%
Miley,Wade	57%	43%	14%
Butler,Eddie	58%	44%	14%
Ross,Joe	57%	42%	15%
Sims,Luke	57%	42%	15%
Ramirez,JC	58%	43%	15%
Cobb,Alex	58%	43%	15%
Nolasco,Ricky	58%	43%	15%
Velasquez,Vince	58%	43%	15%
Kennedy,Ian	58%	43%	15%
Santiago,Hector	60%	45%	15%
Wheeler,Zack	58%	42%	16%
Garza,Matt	58%	42%	16%
Ryu,Hyun-Jin	58%	42%	16%
Kuhl,Chad	58%	42%	16%
Odorizzi,Jake	59%	43%	16%
Eflin,Zach	58%	41%	17%
Junis,Jakob	59%	42%	17%
Urena,Jose	59%	42%	17%
Moore,Matt	59%	42%	17%
Colon,Bartolo	59%	42%	17%
Hamels,Cole	59%	42%	17%
Richard,Clayton	59%	41%	18%
Hahn,Jesse	59%	41%	18%
Jimenez,Ubaldo	60%	42%	18%
Mejia,Adalberto	60%	42%	18%
Shields,James	60%	42%	18%
Hellickson,Jeremy	60%	42%	18%
Chatwood,Tyler	59%	40%	19%
Newcomb,Sean	59%	40%	19%
Gsellman,Robert	59%	40%	19%
Nova,Ivan	59%	40%	19%
Blach,Ty	59%	40%	19%
Pivetta,Nick	60%	41%	19%
Eickhoff,Jerad	60%	41%	19%
Lackey,John	60%	41%	19%
Lugo,Seth	60%	41%	19%
Wainwright,Adam	60%	41%	19%
Porcello,Rick	61%	42%	19%
Boyd,Matt	61%	42%	19%
Perdomo,Luis	60%	40%	20%
Freeland,Kyle	60%	40%	20%
Davies,Zach	60%	40%	20%

Best Positive Scores

Pitcher	Pos.
Scherzer,Max	73%
Sale,Chris	73%
Kluber,Corey	72%
Kershaw,Clayton	71%
Severino,Luis	70%
Estrada,Marco	70%
Strasburg,Stephen	70%
Castillo,Luis	69%
Griffin,A.J.	68%
Tanaka,Masahiro	68%
Wood,Alex	68%
Keuchel,Dallas	68%
Santana,Ervin	68%
Salazar,Danny	67%
Paxton,James	67%
Maeda,Kenta	67%
Morton,Charlie	67%
Carrasco,Carlos	67%
Happ,J.A.	67%
Montgomery,Jordan	67%
Hill,Rich	67%
deGrom,Jacob	67%
Greinke,Zack	67%
Gray,Jon	66%
Weaver,Luke	66%
Pineda,Michael	66%
Straily,Dan	66%
Duffy,Danny	66%
Miranda,Ariel	66%
Bumgarner,Madison	66%
Samardzija,Jeff	66%

Worst Negative Scores

Pitcher	Neg.
Tillman,Chris	48%
Holland,Derek	47%
Norris,Daniel	46%
Zimmermann,Jordan	46%
Bailey,Homer	46%
Anderson,Brett	46%
Garrett,Amir	46%
Conley,Adam	46%
Perez,Martin	45%
Gibson,Kyle	45%
Santiago,Hector	45%
Glasnow,Tyler	45%
Ross,Tyson	45%
Butler,Eddie	44%
Gossett,Daniel	44%
Volquez,Edinson	44%
Miley,Wade	43%
Harvey,Matt	43%
Cueto,Johnny	43%
Kennedy,Ian	43%
Cain,Matt	43%
Velasquez,Vince	43%
Nolasco,Ricky	43%
Feldman,Scott	43%
Cobb,Alex	43%
Ramirez,JC	43%
Stratton,Chris	43%

RISK MANAGEMENT

GRADE "F" in HEALTH

Pitchers	Pitchers	Batters
Anderson,Brett	O Day,Darren	Adrianza,Ehire
Anderson,Tyler	Ottavino,Adam	Ahmed,Nick
Bailey,Homer	Paxton,James	Altherr,Aaron
Bedrosian,Cam	Peacock,Brad	Bird,Gregory
Belisle,Matt	Pelfrey,Mike	Brantley,Michael
Bettis,Chad	Petricka,Jacob	Cervelli,Francisco
Blevins,Jerry	Phelps,David	Choo,Shin-Soo
Boxberger,Brad	Pineda,Michael	D Arnaud,Travis
Cahill,Trevor	Price,David	Duda,Lucas
Cashner,Andrew	Reyes,Alex	Duffy,Matt
Cedeno,Xavier	Richards,Garrett	Hardy,J.J.
Chatwood,Tyler	Rodon,Carlos	Holliday,Matt
Chen,Wei-Yin	Rodriguez,Eduardo	Holt,Brock
Claudio,Alexander	Rondon,Bruce	Jackson,Austin
Cobb,Alex	Ross,Joe	Lagares,Juan
Corbin,Patrick	Ross,Tyson	Lowrie,Jed
Darvish,Yu	Ryu,Hyun-Jin	Maybin,Cameron
Delgado,Randall	Sabathia,CC	Mesoraco,Devin
DeSclafani,Anthony	Sanchez,Aaron	Owings,Chris
Doolittle,Sean	Santiago,Hector	Pence,Hunter
Duffy,Danny	Shoemaker,Matthew	Pollock,A.J.
Eflin,Zach	Simmons,Shae	Prado,Martin
Eovaldi,Nathan	Skaggs,Tyler	Profar,Jurickson
Familia,Jeurys	Smith,Carson	Sandoval,Pablo
Feldman,Scott	Stammen,Craig	Saunders,Michael
Gant,John	Strahm,Matt	Schwarber,Kyle
Garcia,Jaime	Street,Huston	Sogard,Eric
Garza,Matt	Stroman,Marcus	Spangenberg,Cory
Gearrin,Cory	Syndergaard,Noah	Toles,Andrew
Glover,Koda	Thornburg,Tyler	Travis,Devon
Graveman,Kendall	Tomlin,Josh	Tulowitzki,Troy
Gray,Jonathan	Triggs,Andrew	Vazquez,Christian
Griffin,A.J.	Tropeano,Nicholas	Werth,Jayson
Guerra,Junior	Vargas,Jason	Wright,David
Harvey,Matt	Velasquez,Vincent	
Hatcher,Chris	Vizcaino,Arodys	
Heaney,Andrew	Wainwright,Adam	
Hernandez,David	Wheeler,Zack	
Hernandez,Felix	Wood,Alex	
Hill,Rich	Wright,Steven	
Holland,Derek	Zych,Tony	
Hudson,Daniel		
Iwakuma,Hisashi		
Jones,Nate		
Karns,Nathan		
Kela,Keone		
Kershaw,Clayton		
Lyles,Jordan		
Lynn,Lance		
Lyons,Tyler		
Matz,Steven		
McCarthy,Brandon		
McCullers,Lance		
McHugh,Collin		
Miller,Shelby		
Minor,Mike		
Montas,Frankie		
Montero,Rafael		
Moore,Matt		
Morrow,Brandon		
Morton,Charlie		
Nolasco,Ricky		
Norris,Daniel		
Nova,Ivan		

Highest Reliability Grades - Health/Experience/Consistency (Min. Grade = BBB)

CA	POS	Rel
Grandal,Yasmani	2	ABA
Martin,Russell	2	BBA
McCann,Brian	2	BBA
Perez,Salvador	2	ABA
Realmuto,Jacob	2	ABB

1B/DH	POS	Rel
Abreu,Jose	3	AAB
Bell,Josh	3	ABA
Carpenter,Matt	3	BAA
Encarnacion,Edwin	03	AAA
Headley,Chase	35	AAB
Mauer,Joe	3	BAB
Myers,Wil	3	BBA
Reynolds,Mark	3	ABB
Rizzo,Anthony	3	AAB
Valencia,Danny	3	ABB
Votto,Joey	3	BAA

2B	POS	Rel
Asuaje,Carlos	4	ABA
Cabrera,Asdrubal	456	BBB
Castro,Starlin	4	BBB
Hernandez,Cesar	4	BBB
Miller,Brad	4	BBB
Phillips,Brandon	45	AAA

SS	POS	Rel
Anderson,Tim	6	ABA
Bogaerts,Xander	6	AAA
Cabrera,Asdrubal	456	BBB
Crawford,Brandon	6	AAB
Escobar,Alcides	6	AAA
Galvis,Freddy	6	AAA
Gregorius,Didi	6	BAB
Lindor,Francisco	6	AAA
Mercer,Jordy	6	ABB
Polanco,Jorge	6	ABB
Russell,Addison	6	BBA
Seager,Corey	6	AAB
Simmons,Andrelton	6	AAB

3B	POS	Rel
Arenado,Nolan	5	AAB
Bryant,Kris	5	AAB
Cabrera,Asdrubal	456	BBB
Crawford,J.P.	5	ABB
Diaz,Yandy	5	ABA
Donaldson,Josh	5	BAA
Frazier,Todd	5	AAA
Headley,Chase	35	AAB
Lamb,Jacob	5	ABB
Longoria,Evan	5	AAB
Machado,Manny	5	BAB
Phillips,Brandon	45	AAA
Suarez,Eugenio	5	AAB

OF	POS	Rel
Bonifacio,Jorge	9	ABB
Bruce,Jay	9	AAB
Calhoun,Kole	9	AAB
Davis,Khristopher	07	AAB
Duvall,Adam	7	AAA
Eaton,Adam	8	BBB
Gamel,Ben	79	ABB
Gardner,Brett	78	AAB
Gonzalez,Carlos	9	BAB
Granderson,Curtis	789	BAA
Hamilton,Billy	8	BBB
Herrera,Odubel	8	AAA
Inciarte,Ender	8	BAA
Jones,Adam	8	AAA
Markakis,Nick	9	AAA
Mazara,Nomar	79	AAA
Pillar,Kevin	8	AAA
Piscotty,Stephen	9	BBB
Renfroe,Hunter	9	ABB
Rosario,Eddie	7	ABB
Trout,Mike	8	BAB
Yelich,Christian	8	AAB

SP	Rel
Arrieta,Jake	BAB
Dickey,R.A.	BAA
Gonzalez,Gio	BAA
Greinke,Zack	BAB
Hammel,Jason	BAB
Jimenez,Ubaldo	BAA
Leake,Mike	BAA
Lester,Jon	BAA
Miley,Wade	BAA
Ray,Robbie	BBA
Sale,Chris	BAB
Santana,Ervin	BAA
Scherzer,Max	BAA
Archer,Chris	AAA
Bauer,Trevor	AAA
Davies,Zachary	ABA
deGrom,Jacob	AAA
Fiers,Mike	AAA
Maeda,Kenta	AAB
Martinez,Carlos	AAA
Perdomo,Luis	ABA
Porcello,Rick	AAA
Quintana,Jose	AAA
Roark,Tanner	AAA
Samardzija,Jeff	AAA
Straily,Dan	AAB
Teheran,Julio	AAB

RP	Rel
Chavez,Jesse	BBA
Hand,Brad	BBB
Jansen,Kenley	BAA
Johnson,Jim	BBB
Ramos,A.J.	BAB
Rodney,Fernando	BBA
Allen,Cody	AAA
Giles,Ken	ABA
Montgomery,Micha	ABB
Osuna,Roberto	AAA
Ramirez,Erasmo	ABA

RISK MANAGEMENT

GRADE "A" in CONSISTENCY (in order by Rel)

Pitchers (min 120 IP)	Batters (min 400 AB)
Archer,Chris	Duvall,Adam
Bauer,Trevor	Herrera,Odubel
deGrom,Jacob	Jones,Adam
Fiers,Mike	Markakis,Nick
Martinez,Carlos	Mazara,Nomar
Porcello,Rick	Pillar,Kevin
Quintana,Jose	Bogaerts,Xander
Roark,Tanner	Cruz,Nelson
Samardzija,Jeff	Encarnacion,Edwin
Davies,Zachary	Escobar,Alcides
Perdomo,Luis	Frazier,Todd
Dickey,R.A.	Galvis,Freddy
Gonzalez,Gio	Lindor,Francisco
Jimenez,Ubaldo	Phillips,Brandon
Leake,Mike	Anderson,Tim
Lester,Jon	Bell,Josh
Miley,Wade	Grandal,Yasmani
Santana,Ervin	Perez,Salvador
Scherzer,Max	Inciarte,Ender
Ray,Robbie	Carpenter,Matt
Hill,Rich	Donaldson,Josh
Anderson,Tyler	Votto,Joey
Chatwood,Tyler	Myers,Wil
Corbin,Patrick	Russell,Addison
Darvish,Yu	Benintendi,Andrew
DeSclafani,Anthony	Buxton,Byron
Graveman,Kendall	Cespedes,Yoenis
Kershaw,Clayton	Kemp,Matt
McCullers,Lance	Kiermaier,Kevin
McHugh,Collin	Winker,Jesse
Nolasco,Ricky	Albies,Ozhaino
Norris,Daniel	Bregman,Alex
Price,David	Contreras,Willson
Richards,Garrett	Harrison,Josh
Rodriguez,Eduardo	Nunez,Eduardo
Sabathia,CC	Semien,Marcus
Stroman,Marcus	Smith,Dominic
Syndergaard,Noah	
Tomlin,Josh	
Tropeano,Nicholas	
Wood,Alex	
Bumgarner,Madison	
Chacin,Jhoulys	
Eickhoff,Jerad	
Gallardo,Yovani	
Happ,J.A.	
Hendricks,Kyle	
Lackey,John	
Nola,Aaron	
Salazar,Danny	
Strasburg,Stephen	
Tanaka,Masahiro	
Verlander,Justin	
Wacha,Michael	
Walker,Taijuan	
Bundy,Dylan	
Carrasco,Carlos	
Estrada,Marco	
Perez,Martin	
Pomeranz,Drew	
Manaea,Sean	
Urena,Jose	
Farmer,Buck	
Fulmer,Michael	
Giolito,Lucas	
Lamet,Dinelson	
Lopez,Reynaldo	
Miranda,Ariel	
Montgomery,Jordan	
Weaver,Luke	
Williams,Trevor	

TOP COMBINATION OF SKILLS AND RELIABILITY
Maximum of one "C" in Reliability Grade

BATTING POWER (Min. 400 AB)

PX 105+	PX	Rel
Gallo,Joey	219	ACB
Davis,Khristopher	165	AAB
Trout,Mike	159	BAB
Olson,Matt	157	ABC
Davis,Chris	152	BAC
Upton,Justin	151	AAC
Renfroe,Hunter	151	ABB
Donaldson,Josh	148	BAA
Grichuk,Randal	147	BCB
Belt,Brandon	145	CBB
Sanchez,Gary	143	ACB
Arenado,Nolan	142	AAB
Goldschmidt,Paul	141	AAC
Cruz,Nelson	140	AAA
Bryant,Kris	139	AAB
Carpenter,Matt	138	BAA
Duvall,Adam	135	AAA
Bruce,Jay	135	AAB
Contreras,Willson	132	ACA
Myers,Wil	131	BBA
Encarnacion,Edwin	130	AAA
Lamb,Jacob	130	ABB
Dozier,Brian	129	AAC
Souza,Steven	129	CBB
Votto,Joey	128	BAA
Shaw,Travis	128	ABC
Grandal,Yasmani	128	ABA
Castellanos,Nick	127	BAC
Dickerson,Corey	125	BBC
Abreu,Jose	125	AAB
Rizzo,Anthony	125	AAB
Frazier,Todd	124	AAA
Correa,Carlos	123	BBC
Gonzalez,Carlos	121	BAB
Springer,George	121	CAB
Seager,Corey	120	AAB
Rosario,Eddie	119	ABB
Russell,Addison	115	BBA
Turner,Justin	115	BBC
Machado,Manny	113	BAB
Odor,Rougned	113	AAC
Buxton,Byron	113	BCA
Kepler,Max	113	ACB
Baez,Javier	112	ACB
Gyorko,Jedd	112	BCB
Schoop,Jonathan	112	BBC
Bradley,Jackie	111	ABC
Seager,Kyle	111	AAC
Santana,Carlos	111	AAC
Kemp,Matt	110	CAA
Fowler,Dexter	109	CAB
Cron,C.J.	109	BCB
Trumbo,Mark	108	BAC
Williams,Nick	106	ABC
Drury,Brandon	106	ABC
Suarez,Eugenio	106	AAB
Gennett,Scooter	106	ABC
Perez,Salvador	105	ABA

RUNNER SPEED (Min. 400 AB)

Spd 100+	SX	Rel
Hamilton,Billy	188	BBB
Buxton,Byron	183	BCA
Hernandez,Cesar	179	BBB
Albies,Ozhaino	178	ACA
Margot,Manuel	162	BCB
Anderson,Tim	161	ABA
Fowler,Dexter	151	CAB
Eaton,Adam	147	BBB
Inciarte,Ender	142	BAA
Crawford,J.P.	136	ABB
Williams,Nick	135	ABC
Sanchez,Yolmer	133	ACB
Marte,Starling	132	ABC
Cain,Lorenzo	131	BAC
Merrifield,Whit	129	ABC
Gardner,Brett	129	AAB
Altuve,Jose	128	AAC
Escobar,Alcides	128	AAA
Rosario,Eddie	125	ABB
Gamel,Ben	124	ABB
Zimmer,Bradley	124	ACB
Wong,Kolten	124	BCB
Bogaerts,Xander	123	AAA
Grichuk,Randal	122	BCB
Herrera,Odubel	121	AAA
Realmuto,Jacob	121	ABB
Trout,Mike	120	BAB
Galvis,Freddy	120	AAA
Harrison,Josh	119	CBA
Myers,Wil	119	BBA
Andrus,Elvis	119	AAC
Bryant,Kris	118	AAB
Lindor,Francisco	117	AAA
Baez,Javier	117	ACB
Castellanos,Nick	117	BAC
Miller,Brad	115	BBB
Dozier,Brian	114	AAC
Kinsler,Ian	114	AAC
Semien,Marcus	113	CBA
Arenado,Nolan	113	AAB
Nunez,Eduardo	112	BCA
Machado,Manny	111	BAB
Yelich,Christian	111	AAB
Dickerson,Corey	111	BBC
Springer,George	108	CAB
Kepler,Max	108	ACB
Valencia,Danny	108	ABB
Gallo,Joey	108	ACB
Mercer,Jordy	107	ABB
Lamb,Jacob	106	ABB
Gennett,Scooter	105	ABC
Simmons,Andrelton	104	AAB
Odor,Rougned	104	AAC
Gregorius,Didi	103	BAB
Carpenter,Matt	103	BAA
Polanco,Jorge	102	ABB
Souza,Steven	102	CBB
Pillar,Kevin	101	AAA
Goldschmidt,Paul	100	AAC

OVERALL PITCHING SKILL

BPV over 85	BPV	Rel
Jansen,Kenley	231	BAA
Kimbrel,Craig	203	BAC
Sale,Chris	179	BAB
Osuna,Roberto	173	AAA
Kluber,Corey	164	CAB
Giles,Ken	160	ABA
Robertson,David	155	ABC
Betances,Dellin	152	ACB
Scherzer,Max	151	BAA
Allen,Cody	149	AAA
Hand,Brad	148	BBB
Carrasco,Carlos	147	CAA
Diaz,Edwin	144	ACB
Rivero,Felipe	143	BCA
Gregerson,Luke	143	BCA
Rondon,Hector	142	ACA
deGrom,Jacob	141	AAA
Archer,Chris	137	AAA
Reed,Addison	130	ACB
Devenski,Christopher	129	ACB
Greinke,Zack	128	BAB
Holland,Greg	123	BCA
Petit,Yusmeiro	121	ACB
Ray,Robbie	119	BBA
Musgrove,Joe	118	ACA
Shaw,Bryan	117	ACA
Maeda,Kenta	117	AAB
Quintana,Jose	116	AAA
Samardzija,Jeff	115	AAA
Givens,Mychal	115	ACB
Lester,Jon	112	BAA
Porcello,Rick	107	AAA
Martinez,Carlos	105	AAA
Nicasio,Juan	105	ACA
Cishek,Steve	105	BCB
Nelson,Jimmy	102	BAC
Bauer,Trevor	101	AAA
Treinen,Blake	99	ACA
Brach,Brad	98	ACA
Gausman,Kevin	98	CBB
Casilla,Santiago	97	CBB
Wilson,Justin	97	ACA
Leake,Mike	96	BAA
Chavez,Jesse	96	BBA
Rodney,Fernando	94	BBA
Watson,Tony	91	ACA
Marquez,German	90	ACB
Gonzalez,Gio	90	BAA
Fulmer,Michael	89	ACA
Hammel,Jason	89	BAB
Pomeranz,Drew	88	CAA
Manaea,Sean	88	BCA
Ramirez,Erasmo	87	ABA
Johnson,Jim	87	BBB

PORTFOLIO 3 PLAN - Batters

TIER 1 Hitters

Rel BBB+; xBA score 3+; Power OR Speed score 3+

BATTERS	Age	Bats	Pos	MM	REL	MAY	R$
Trout,Mike	26	R	9	4455	BAB	109	$43
Votto,Joey	34	L	3	4255	BAA	102	$33
Arenado,Nolan	27	R	5	4155	AAB	95	$31
Bryant,Kris	26	R	5	4345	AAB	102	$31
Lindor,Francisco	24	B	6	2455	AAA	106	$30
Yelich,Christian	26	L	9	3445	AAB	108	$28
Machado,Manny	25	R	5	3345	BAB	91	$28
Bogaerts,Xander	25	R	6	1435	AAA	87	$27
Rizzo,Anthony	28	L	3	4155	AAB	95	$27
Abreu,Jose	31	R	3	4155	AAB	95	$25
Myers,Wil	27	R	3	4435	BBA	97	$25
Inciarte,Ender	27	L	9	1555	BAA	102	$25
Donaldson,Josh	32	R	5	4255	BAA	102	$25
Cruz,Nelson	38	R	0	4135	AAA	93	$24
Encarnacion,Edwin	35	R	03	4145	AAA	100	$24
Rosario,Eddie	26	L	7	3345	ABB	91	$23
Seager,Corey	24	L	6	4255	AAB	102	$23
Eaton,Adam	29	L	9	2445	BBB	87	$23
Herrera,Odubel	26	L	9	2435	AAA	93	$22
Gardner,Brett	34	L	79	1535	AAB	89	$21
Anderson,Tim	25	R	6	2535	ABA	95	$21
Davis,Khristopher	30	R	70	5235	AAB	95	$21
Hernandez,Cesar	28	B	4	1545	BBB	87	$20
Polanco,Jorge	24	B	6	2335	ABB	85	$19
Realmuto,Jacob	27	R	2	2445	ABB	91	$19
Lamb,Jacob	27	L	5	4235	ABB	85	$19
Longoria,Evan	32	R	5	3235	AAB	83	$19
Gonzalez,Carlos	32	L	8	4245	BAB	91	$18
Pillar,Kevin	29	R	9	1335	AAA	87	$18
Gregorius,Didi	28	L	6	2345	BAB	85	$17
Carpenter,Matt	32	L	3	4145	BAA	89	$17
Simmons,Andrelton	28	R	6	1355	AAB	89	$17
Bruce,Jay	31	L	8	4135	AAB	89	$16
Renfroe,Hunter	26	R	8	4235	ABB	85	$15
Perez,Salvador	28	R	2	3235	ABA	83	$15
Morales,Kendrys	35	B	0	3035	AAB	70	$14
Headley,Chase	34	B	53	2325	AAB	83	$14
Gamel,Ben	26	L	78	1325	ABB	73	$13
Escobar,Alcides	31	R	6	1435	AAA	87	$13
Russell,Addison	24	R	6	3235	BBA	79	$12
Diaz,Yandy	26	R	5	1343	ABA	42	$9
Granderson,Curtis	37	L	987	4223	BAA	46	$8

TIER 2 Hitters

Rel BCC+; 5 PT; xBA, Power, or Speed score 3+ <$20

BATTERS	Age	Bats	Pos	MM	REL	MAY	R$
Hamilton,Billy*	27	B	9	0515	BBB	64	$31
Jones,Adam	32	R	9	2235	AAA	87	$19
Seager,Kyle	30	L	5	3135	AAC	73	$19
Cabrera,Melky	33	B	78	1055	BAC	64	$19
Odor,Rougned	24	L	4	3325	AAC	85	$19
Shaw,Travis	28	L	5	4235	ABC	81	$19
Gennett,Scooter	28	L	4	3245	ABC	81	$19
Polanco,Gregory	26	L	87	2245	BBC	72	$18
Margot,Manuel	23	R	9	2545	BCB	88	$18
Mauer,Joe	35	L	3	1255	BAB	79	$18
Suarez,Eugenio	26	R	5	3125	AAB	70	$18
Zimmer,Bradley	25	L	9	2505	ACB	75	$18
Wong,Kolten	27	L	4	1435	BCB	72	$18
Dickerson,Corey	29	L	70	4145	BBC	77	$17
Santana,Carlos	32	B	3	3245	AAC	85	$17
Winker,Jesse	24	L	8	2145	ACA	73	$17
Kepler,Max	25	L	8	3345	ACB	87	$17
Castro,Starlin	28	R	4	2235	BBB	75	$17
Schebler,Scott	27	L	8	4245	ACC	83	$16
Bradley,Jackie	28	L	9	3235	ABC	75	$16
Flores,Wilmer	26	R	53	3045	ACB	69	$16
Pujols,Albert	38	R	0	1135	AAB	64	$16
Bell,Josh	25	B	3	2145	ABA	76	$16
Duvall,Adam	29	R	7	4125	AAA	80	$16
Phillips,Brandon	37	R	45	1155	AAA	80	$15
Molina,Yadier	35	R	2	1145	BBC	61	$15
Williams,Nick	24	L	8	3325	ABC	75	$15
Mazara,Nomar	23	L	87	2035	AAA	67	$15
Cabrera,Asdrubal	32	B	654	2235	BBB	75	$15
Crawford,Brandon	31	L	6	2135	AAB	70	$15
Markakis,Nick	34	L	8	1035	AAA	60	$15

* Tier 2 players should generally be less than $20. If you pay more, be aware of the extra risk.

TIER 2 Hitters (Cont.)

Rel BCC+; 5 PT; xBA, Power, or Speed score 3+ <$20

BATTERS	Age	Bats	Pos	MM	REL	MAY	R$
Olson,Matt	24	L	3	4235	ABC	81	$14
Frazier,Todd	32	R	5	4125	AAA	80	$14
Calhoun,Kole	30	L	8	2235	AAB	76	$14
Gallo,Joey	24	L	53	5315	ABC	81	$14
Cron,C.J.	28	R	3	3125	BCB	66	$14
Gyorko,Jedd	29	R	5	3135	BCB	66	$13
Grichuk,Randal	26	R	78	4325	BCB	77	$13
Davis,Chris	32	L	3	4005	BAC	58	$13
Galvis,Freddy	28	B	6	1425	AAA	80	$12
Franco,Maikel	25	R	5	3145	ABC	75	$12
Piscotty,Stephen	27	R	8	2135	BBB	64	$12
Drury,Brandon	25	R	4	3045	ABC	69	$11
Crawford,J.P.	23	L	5	1315	ABB	67	$11
Trumbo,Mark	32	R	08	3215	BAC	64	$11
Sanchez,Yolmer	26	B	45	1325	ACB	64	$10
Mercer,Jordy	31	R	6	1135	ABB	61	$10
Grandal,Yasmani	29	B	2	4025	ABA	70	$10

TIER 3 Hitters

Health>"F"; xBA score 3+; Power or Speed score 3+ <$15

BATTERS	Age	Bats	Pos	MM	REL	MAY	R$
Fowler,Dustin	23	L	8	3433	DDB	35	$15
Kendrick,Howie	34	R	7	1353	DBC	34	$15
Smith,Dominic	23	L	3	3035	ADA	63	$15
Chisenhall,Lonnie	29	L	8	4235	CDC	67	$15
Revere,Ben	30	L	7	0553	BCD	39	$14
Kipnis,Jason	31	L	4	3335	DBC	66	$14
Dyson,Jarrod	33	L	9	0533	BDB	35	$14
Peralta,David	30	L	87	2345	DCF	61	$14
Dahl,David	24	L	0	2533	DDF	30	$14
Ellsbury,Jacoby	34	L	9	1543	CBB	43	$14
Ramirez,Hanley	34	R	0	3045	CBF	57	$14
Barnes,Austin	28	R	24	3453	ADF	42	$14
Reyes,Jose	35	B	654	2533	BCA	45	$13
Robles,Victor	21	R	8	2553	AFF	40	$13
Escobar,Eduardo	29	B	50	3235	ACD	68	$13
Gattis,Evan	31	R	20	4043	BCB	36	$13
Pirela,Jose	28	R	7	2345	ADF	66	$13
Panik,Joe	27	L	4	1355	CBD	70	$13
Castillo,Welington	31	R	2	3233	BCB	36	$13
Senzel,Nick	23	R	5	3243	AFF	32	$13
Hechavarria,Adeiny	29	R	6	1535	CBC	74	$12
Morrison,Logan	30	L	3	3135	CBC	63	$12
Aoki,Norichika	36	L	78	1453	BCB	43	$12
Lucroy,Jonathan	32	R	2	1345	BBF	64	$12
Joseph,Tommy	26	R	3	4035	ADF	56	$12
Almora,Albert	24	R	9	2353	ACB	45	$12
Moreland,Mitch	32	L	3	3035	CBC	58	$11
Lind,Adam	34	L	37	3243	ACF	36	$11
Tapia,Raimel	24	L	8	2553	ADB	49	$11
Difo,Wilmer	26	R	64	1533	ADA	41	$11
McMahon,Ryan	23	L	3	4243	ADF	37	$10
Jay,Jon	33	L	79	1343	DDC	28	$10
Hernandez,Teoscar	25	R	7	4333	ACC	43	$10
Smith,Seth	35	L	8	3333	ACA	44	$10
Frazier,Adam	26	L	74	1351	ACB	12	$9
Marte,Ketel	24	B	6	1543	ACD	41	$9
Aguilar,Jesus	28	R	3	4033	ACC	33	$8
Joyce,Matt	33	L	87	4135	ACF	64	$8
Adams,Matt	29	L	3	4033	CDC	29	$8
Pearce,Steve	35	R	7	3033	DDF	21	$8
Brinson,Lewis	24	R	7	2331	ADC	9	$8
Goodwin,Brian	27	L	97	4321	BCC	12	$7
Tomlinson,Kelby	28	R	54	0541	ADA	11	$7
Valaika,Pat	25	R	6	4131	ACC	10	$7
Naquin,Tyler	27	L	9	2331	ADC	9	$7
Mejia,Francisco	22	B	2	1341	AFF	8	$6
Delmonico,Nick	25	L	7	3333	ACB	42	$6
Alford,Anthony	23	R	7	2331	CFF	7	$6
Aybar,Erick	34	B	6	1341	CCB	9	$5
Meadows,Austin	23	L	OF	2441	DFF	8	$5
Caratini,Victor	24	B	2	2341	AFC	10	$5
Torreyes,Ronald	25	R	465	1431	ADB	11	$5
Suzuki,Ichiro	44	L	8	0331	ADD	8	$5
Gonzalez,Erik	26	R	4	2431	ACB	12	$4
Voit,Luke	27	R	3	3031	ADB	8	$4
Romine,Andrew	32	L	495	1331	AFA	9	$4
Presley,Alex	32	L	8	1331	BDB	8	$4
Utley,Chase	39	L	4	2331	BCB	10	$3
Jaso,John	34	L	83	3021	CDB	7	$3
Marte,Jefry	27	R	3	3231	ADA	11	$2
Osuna,Jose	25	R	83	3140	ADA	0	$1

The Mayberry Scores here are recalibrated to the draft pool in order to generate a sufficient number of players. They wil not necessarily match the Mayberry scores on the player pages or on BaseballHQ.com

PORTFOLIO 3 PLAN - Pitchers

TIER 1 Pitchers
Rel BBB+; xERA score 3+ and K/9 score 3+

PITCHERS	Age	Th	MM	REL	MAY	R$
Sale,Chris	29	L	5505	BAB	121	$34
Scherzer,Max	33	R	4505	BAA	127	$33
Jansen,Kenley	30	R	5530	BAA	69	$29
Kimbrel,Craig	30	R	5530	BAC	62	$27
Greinke,Zack	34	R	3305	BAB	97	$25
Osuna,Roberto	23	R	5530	AAA	72	$23
Allen,Cody	29	R	4530	AAA	72	$22
deGrom,Jacob	30	R	3405	AAA	126	$22
Giles,Ken	27	R	4530	ABA	69	$21
Hand,Brad	28	L	4531	BBB	88	$21
Martinez,Carlos	26	R	2305	AAA	106	$17
Archer,Chris	29	R	3505	AAA	133	$17
Quintana,Jose	29	L	2305	AAA	106	$16
Lester,Jon	34	L	2305	BAA	102	$16
Maeda,Kenta	30	R	2303	AAB	46	$14
Gonzalez,Gio	32	L	2305	BAA	89	$13
Ray,Robbie	26	L	2503	BBA	58	$13
Bauer,Trevor	27	R	2305	AAA	93	$11
Rodney,Fernando	41	R	2420	BBA	34	$11
Robertson,David	33	R	4510	ABC	18	$9
Ramos,A.J.	31	R	1520	BAB	32	$5
Nelson,Jimmy	29	R	2301	BAC	12	$2
Johnson,Jim	35	R	1310	BBB	12	$2

TIER 2 Pitchers
Rel BCC+; PT score 3+; xERA or K/9 score 3+   <$20

PITCHERS	Age	Th	MM	REL	MAY	R$
Fulmer,Michael	25	R	2103	ACA	36	$14
Arrieta,Jake	32	R	1205	BAB	79	$13
Porcello,Rick	29	R	1205	AAA	87	$12
Samardzija,Jeff	33	R	2205	AAA	87	$11
Montgomery,Michael	29	L	1103	ABB	36	$8
Leake,Mike	30	R	2005	BAA	76	$7

* Tier 2 players should generally be less than $20. If you pay more than $20, you should be aware of the extra risk.

TIER 3 Pitchers
Health > "F"; xERA score 3+   <$15

PITCHERS	Age	Th	MM	REL	MAY	R$
Miller,Andrew	33	L	5510	DBB	16	$13
Parker,Blake	33	R	3420	ADB	31	$12
Happ,J.A.	35	L	1203	DAA	36	$12
Hamels,Cole	34	L	1203	DAB	34	$11
Salazar,Danny	28	R	3503	DAA	59	$11
Devenski,Christopher	27	R	3511	ACB	35	$11
Herrera,Kelvin	28	R	2320	ACC	24	$11
Reed,Addison	29	R	3311	ACB	30	$10
Steckenrider,Drew	27	R	3520	AFC	30	$10
Greene,Shane	29	R	1321	BCB	40	$10
Cueto,Johnny	32	R	1203	DAB	34	$10
Godley,Zachary	28	R	2303	ADF	40	$9
Taillon,Jameson	26	R	2203	DCB	31	$9
Oh,Seung-Hwan	35	R	1320	ABD	24	$9
Gray,Sonny	28	R	2203	DAB	34	$9
Lackey,John	39	R	1203	DAA	36	$9
Walker,Taijuan	25	R	1203	DBA	34	$9
Madson,Ryan	37	R	4310	DCC	13	$9
Edwards,Carl	26	R	3520	ADB	33	$9
Betances,Dellin	30	R	5510	ACB	18	$8

TIER 3 Pitchers, Continued
Health > "F"; xERA score 3+   <$15

PITCHERS	Age	Th	MM	REL	MAY	R$
Betances,Dellin	30	R	5510	ACB	18	$8
Bradley,Archie	25	R	3411	DDB	25	$8
Green,Chad	27	R	3501	BDC	14	$8
Brach,Brad	32	R	2410	ACA	13	$8
Barraclough,Kyle	28	R	2521	BDB	44	$7
Harris,Will	33	R	4410	DCA	15	$7
Givens,Mychal	28	R	3501	ACB	16	$7
Gausman,Kevin	27	R	1303	CBB	40	$6
Paulino,David	24	R	2403	CDC	37	$6
Minter,A.J.	24	L	4510	AFC	16	$6
Nicasio,Juan	31	R	2310	ACA	12	$5
Soria,Joakim	34	R	3310	DCB	11	$5
Honeywell,Brent	23	R	2301	AFC	10	$5
Wacha,Michael	27	R	1203	DAA	36	$5
Kahnle,Thomas	28	R	4510	ADB	18	$5
Swarzak,Anthony	32	R	2410	BDF	12	$5
Sherfy,Jimmie	26	R	2310	AFC	10	$5
Smith,Joe	34	R	4310	DCB	13	$5
Strop,Pedro	33	R	4400	DCB	0	$5
Feliz,Michael	25	R	3500	CDB	0	$5
Hildenberger,Trevor	27	R	4210	AFF	12	$5
Leone,Dominic	26	R	3410	ADD	13	$4
Pagan,Emilio	27	R	1400	AFD	0	$4
Petit,Yusmeiro	33	R	2301	ACB	12	$4
Gregerson,Luke	34	R	4410	BCA	17	$4
Middleton,Keynan	24	R	2410	ADB	12	$4
Cishek,Steve	32	R	2310	BCB	13	$4
Goody,Nicholas	26	R	2510	ADC	15	$4
Watson,Tony	33	L	2210	ACA	11	$3
Hunter,Tommy	31	R	3300	DDB	0	$3
Musgrove,Joe	25	R	2201	ACA	13	$3
Duffey,Tyler	27	R	2211	ACF	20	$3
Yates,Kirby	31	R	2510	CDF	12	$3
Fields,Joshua	32	R	2400	ADA	0	$3
Kopech,Michael	22	R	2401	AFF	10	$3
Rondon,Hector	30	R	3400	ACA	0	$3
Shaw,Bryan	30	R	3300	ACA	0	$3
Bush,Matt	32	R	2410	BDF	10	$3
Dull,Ryan	28	R	1310	DDB	9	$3
Baez,Pedro	30	R	2410	CCB	12	$2
Morgan,Adam	28	L	2401	ADA	13	$2
Stripling,Ross	28	R	3301	ADB	13	$2
McGee,Jake	31	L	2310	DCC	9	$2
Otero,Dan	33	R	3000	ADC	0	$2
Pressly,Ryan	29	R	2310	DDA	9	$2
Pazos,James	27	L	3400	ADF	0	$2
Maton,Phil	25	R	2310	AFF	9	$2
Ziegler,Brad	38	R	2010	DBB	8	$2
Strickland,Hunter	29	R	1300	ADD	0	$2
Casilla,Santiago	37	R	2310	CBB	11	$2
Romo,Sergio	35	R	2400	DDB	0	$2
Alexander,Scott	28	L	3110	BDD	9	$1
Barnes,Matt	28	R	2400	ADC	0	$1
Hughes,Jared	32	R	1000	CCB	0	$1
Kintzler,Brandon	33	R	1011	DDC	15	$1
Diekman,Jake	31	L	2510	DDA	13	$1
Wilson,Justin	30	L	2500	ACA	0	$1
Hoyt,James	31	R	2410	ADC	14	$1

The Mayberry Scores here are recalibrated to the draft pool in order to generate a sufficient number of players. They will not necessarily match the Mayberry scores on the player pages or on BasebalHQ.com.

DAILY FANTASY INDICATORS

Top OPS v LHP, 2016-2017

Hitter	OPS
Stanton,Giancarlo	1107
Martinez,J.D.	1086
Arenado,Nolan	1080
Beltre,Adrian	1047
Goldschmidt,Paul	1042
Bryant,Kris	1012
Dozier,Brian	1012
Cespedes,Yoenis	1001
Prado,Martin	992
Donaldson,Josh	978
Flores,Wilmer	976
Bregman,Alex	974
Rendon,Anthony	972
Werth,Jayson	972
Tomas,Yasmany	960
Morales,Kendrys	959
Springer,George	957
Trout,Mike	955
Posey,Buster	955
McCutchen,Andrew	952
Braun,Ryan	950
Reyes,Jose	948
LeMahieu,DJ	946
Abreu,Jose	943
Cruz,Nelson	938
Ramos,Wilson	936
Judge,Aaron	934
Upton,Justin	932
Votto,Joey	927
Altuve,Jose	927
Cabrera,Miguel	927
Hundley,Nick	914
Sano,Miguel	906
Suzuki,Kurt	905
Blackmon,Charlie	905
Ramirez,Hanley	904
Ramirez,Jose	903
Cain,Lorenzo	903
Rupp,Cameron	900
Castillo,Welington	898
Cozart,Zack	897

600+ PA, 2016-2017

Top OPS v RHP, 2016-2017

Hitter	OPS
Judge,Aaron	1079
Trout,Mike	1045
Votto,Joey	1041
Freeman,Freddie	1015
Blackmon,Charlie	999
Murphy,Daniel	984
Martinez,J.D.	955
Altuve,Jose	947
Harper,Bryce	946
Donaldson,Josh	942
Rizzo,Anthony	937
Cano,Robinson	922
Bryant,Kris	919
Lamb,Jacob	918
Cruz,Nelson	908
Carpenter,Matt	900
Goldschmidt,Paul	899
Arenado,Nolan	897
Bour,Justin	895
Seager,Corey	890
Ramirez,Jose	886
Encarnacion,Edwin	885
Santana,Carlos	883
Turner,Justin	881
Stanton,Giancarlo	881
Bruce,Jay	878
Hosmer,Eric	876
Yelich,Christian	872
Santana,Domingo	870
Reddick,Josh	869
Belt,Brandon	868
Correa,Carlos	868
Reynolds,Mark	867
Gonzalez,Carlos	861
Pederson,Joc	858
Cespedes,Yoenis	855
Fowler,Dexter	854
Davis,Khristopher	852
Seager,Kyle	851
Moustakas,Mike	850
Beltre,Adrian	850

Top L-R Splits, 2016-2017

Hitter	OPS vL-vR
Prado,Martin	309
McCann,James	300
Werth,Jayson	296
Hundley,Nick	284
Flores,Wilmer	269
Reyes,Jose	265
Morales,Kendrys	255
Gomes,Yan	247
Stanton,Giancarlo	226
Rupp,Cameron	218
Tomas,Yasmany	209
Bregman,Alex	198
Beltre,Adrian	197
Freese,David	188
Dozier,Brian	186
Arenado,Nolan	183
Anderson,Tim	182
McCutchen,Andrew	181
Posey,Buster	180

Top R-L Splits, 2016-2017

Hitter	OPS vR-vL
Pederson,Joc	335
Lamb,Jacob	331
Reddick,Josh	309
Jaso,John	304
Marte,Starling	243
Utley,Chase	241
Cano,Robinson	240
Gonzalez,Adrian	237
Duda,Lucas	230
Span,Denard	223
Aoki,Norichika	208
Vogt,Stephen	203
Benintendi,Andrew	191
Rosario,Eddie	190
Mazara,Nomar	183
Bruce,Jay	179
Gardner,Brett	177
Revere,Ben	174
Gonzalez,Carlos	172

Best Parks - LH HR

Ballpark	Factor
NYY	42%
MIL	31%
CHW	22%
PHI	20%
CIN	19%
COL	17%
ATL	16%
BAL	14%
LA	13%

Best Parks - RH HR

Ballpark	Factor
PHI	24%
NYY	23%
BAL	21%
COL	18%
WAS	14%
CHC	14%
MIN	13%
ARI	11%
CHW	10%

Worst Parks - LH HR

Ballpark	Factor
SF	-47%
BOS	-22%
OAK	-16%
SD	-15%
KC	-15%
MIA	-14%

Worst Parks - RH HR

Ballpark	Factor
SF	-26%
KC	-24%
ATL	-19%
STL	-18%
MIA	-17%
PIT	-17%
OAK	-13%
TAM	-10%
LA	-10%

Consistent High-PQS SP

Pitcher	QC*
Sale,Chris	126
Scherzer,Max	118
Kershaw,Clayton	84
Severino,Luis	78
Kluber,Corey	76
Bumgarner,Madison	58
Verlander,Justin	50
Carrasco,Carlos	48
Godley,Zachary	48
Strasburg,Stephen	48
Nola,Aaron	28
Paxton,James	24
Archer,Chris	22
Samardzija,Jeff	18
Morton,Charlie	16
Gonzalez,Gio	12
Greinke,Zack	12
Cobb,Alex	8
Martinez,Carlos	6

10+ Games Started, 2017

Most DOMinant SP

Pitcher	DOM
Sale,Chris	69%
Kluber,Corey	66%
Severino,Luis	65%
Scherzer,Max	65%
Kershaw,Clayton	56%
Verlander,Justin	55%
Paxton,James	54%
Bumgarner,Madison	53%
Greinke,Zack	50%
Carrasco,Carlos	50%
Nelson,Jimmy	48%
deGrom,Jacob	48%
Strasburg,Stephen	46%
Wood,Alex	44%
Nola,Aaron	44%
Ray,Robbie	43%
Martinez,Carlos	41%
Samardzija,Jeff	41%
Weaver,Luke	40%
Castillo,Luis	40%

Most DISastrous SP

Pitcher	DIS
Worley,Vance	75%
Wood,Travis	71%
Pelfrey,Mike	71%
Tillman,Chris	68%
Freeland,Kyle	68%
Perez,Martin	66%
Adleman,Timothy	65%
Butler,Eddie	64%
Farmer,Buck	64%
Miley,Wade	63%
Koehler,Tom	62%
Harvey,Matt	61%
Bailey,Homer	61%
Colon,Bartolo	61%
Martinez,Nicholas	61%
Ross,Tyson	60%
Sims,Lucas	60%
Griffin,A.J.	60%
Gallardo,Yovani	59%
Volquez,Edinson	59%

Best Parks - Runs

Ballpark	Factor
COL	43%
BOS	16%
ARI	15%
CLE	13%
TEX	12%

Worst Parks - Runs

Ballpark	Factor
HOU	-17%
MIA	-16%
NYM	-10%
LA	-10%
SF	-10%

Note: for Runs, best parks for hitters = worst for pitchers

Consistent Low-PQS SP

Pitcher	QC*	Pitcher	QC*
Worley,Vance	(284)	Perez,Martin	(246)
Wood,Travis	(284)	Harvey,Matt	(244)
Pelfrey,Mike	(274)	Freeland,Kyle	(244)
Tillman,Chris	(272)	Bailey,Homer	(232)
Butler,Eddie	(256)	Covey,Dylan	(232)
Adleman,Timothy	(250)	Guerra,Junior	(228)
Koehler,Tom	(248)	Colon,Bartolo	(222)

Quality-Consistency score

Best Parks - BB

Ballpark	Factor
TEX	8%

Worst Parks - BB

Ballpark	Factor
LA	-11%

Best Parks - Ks

Ballpark	Factor
TB	10%
SEA	9%
PHI	9%

Worst Parks - Ks

Ballpark	Factor
COL	-13%
DET	-8%

Universal Draft Grid

Most publications and websites provide cheat sheets with ranked player lists for different fantasy draft formats. The biggest problem with these tools is that they perpetuate the myth that players can be ranked in a linear fashion.

Since rankings are based on highly variable projections, it is foolhardy to draw conclusions that a $24 player is better than a $23 player is better than a $22 player. Yes, a first round pick is better than a 10th round pick, but within most rounds, all players are pretty much interchangeable commodities.

But typical cheat sheets don't reflect that reality. Auction sheets rank players by dollar value. Snake draft sheets rank players within round, accounting for position and categorical scarcity. But just as ADPs have a ridiculously low success rate, these cheat sheets are similarly flawed.

We have a tool at BaseballHQ.com called the Rotisserie Grid. It is a chart—that can be customized to your league parameters—which organizes players into pockets of skill, by position. It is one of the most popular tools on the site. One of the best features of this grid is that its design provides immediate insight into position scarcity.

So in the *Forecaster*, we have transitioned to this format as a sort of Universal Draft Grid.

How to use the chart

Across the top of the grid, players are sorted by position. First and third base, and second and shortstop are presented side-by-side for easy reference when considering corner and middle infielders, respectively.

The vertical axis separates each group of players into tiers based on potential fantasy impact. At the top are the Elite players; at the bottom are the Fringe players.

Auction leagues: The tiers in the grid represent rough breakpoints for dollar values. Elite players could be considered those that are purchased for $30 and up. Each subsequent tier is a step down of approximately $5.

Snake drafters: Tiers can be used to rank players similarly, though most tiers will encompass more than one round. Any focus on position scarcity will bump some players up a bit. For instance, with the dearth of Elite catchers and the wealth of Elite outfielders, one might opt to draft Gary Sanchez (from the Stars tier) before the Elite level Starling Marte. The reason we target scarce positions early is that there will be plenty of solid outfielders and starting pitchers later on.

To build the best foundation, you should come out of the first 10 rounds with all your middle infielders, all your corner infielders, one outfielder, at least one catcher and two pitchers (at least one closer).

The players are listed at the position where they both qualify and provide the most fantasy value. Additional position eligibility (20 games) is listed in parentheses. Listings in bold are players with high reliability grades (minimum "B" across the board).

Each player is presented with his 7-character Mayberry score. The first four digits (all on a 0-5 scale) represent skill: power, speed, batting average and playing time for batters; ERA, dominance, saves potential and playing time for pitchers. The last three alpha characters are the reliability grade (A-F): health, experience and consistency.

Within each tier, players are sorted by the first character of their Mayberry score. This means that batters are sorted by power; pitchers by ERA potential. If you need to prospect for the best skill sets among players in a given tier, target those with 4s and 5s in whatever skill you need.

CAVEATS and DISCLAIMERS

The placement of players in tiers does not represent average draft positions (ADP) or average auction values (AAV). It represents where each player's true value may lie. It is the variance between this true value and the ADP/AAV market values—or better, the value that your league-mates place on each player—where you will find your potential for profit or loss.

That means **you cannot take this chart right into your draft with you.** You have to compare these rankings with your ADPs and AAVs, and build your draft list from there. In other words, if we project Freddie Freeman as a "Elite" level pick but you know the other owners (or your ADPs) see him as a third-rounder, you can probably wait to pick him up in round two. If you are in an auction league with owners who overvalue players from the Pacific Northwest, and Jean Segura (projected at $27) gets bid past $30, you will likely take a loss should you decide to chase the bidding, especially given the depth of shortstops in 2018.

Finally, this chart is intended as a preliminary look based on current factors. For Draft Day, you will need to make your own adjustments based upon many different criteria that will impact the world between now and then. Daily updates appear online at BaseballHQ.com. A free projections update is available in March at **http://www.baseballhq.com/bf2018**

Simulation League Cheat Sheet
Using Runs Above Replacement creates a more real-world ranking of player value, which serves simulation gamers well. Batters and pitchers are integrated, and value break-points are delineated.

Universal Draft Grid

TIER	FIRST BASE		THIRD BASE		SECOND BASE		SHORTSTOP	
Elite	Goldschmidt,Paul	(4355 AAC)	**Arenado,Nolan**	**(4155 AAB)**	Ramirez,Jose (3)	(3455 ABF)	Turner,Trea	(3545 CBD)
	Votto,Joey	**(4255 BAA)**	**Bryant,Kris**	**(4345 AAB)**	Altuve,Jose	(2555 AAC)	**Lindor,Francisco**	**(2455 AAA)**
	Freeman,Freddie	(4255 CAC)			Gordon,Dee	(0545 ABD)	Andrus,Elvis	(1455 AAC)
Gold	Bellinger,Cody (O)	(4435 ADF)	**Machado,Manny**	**(3345 BAB)**	Dozier,Brian	(4435 AAC)	Correa,Carlos	(4355 BBC)
	Rizzo,Anthony	**(4155 AAB)**	Turner,Justin	(3255 BBC)	Murphy,Daniel	(3255 AAF)	Bregman,Alex (3)	(4455 ADA)
	Abreu,Jose	**(4155 AAB)**			Merrifield,Whit	(2535 ABC)	Segura,Jean	(1545 BAF)
	Myers,Wil	**(4435 BBA)**			LeMahieu,DJ	(1355 AAF)	**Bogaerts,Xander**	**(1435 AAA)**
	Hosmer,Eric	(2255 AAD)						
Stars	**Encarnacion,Edwin**	**(4145 AAA)**	**Donaldson,Josh**	**(4255 BAA)**	Schoop,Jonathan	(3135 BBC)	**Seager,Corey**	**(4255 AAB)**
	Desmond,Ian (O)	(2425 CAC)	Rendon,Anthony	(4245 BBD)	Nunez,Eduardo (3)	(2455 BCA)	Baez,Javier (2)	(3415 ACB)
			Castellanos,Nick (O)	(4145 BAC)	Cano,Robinson	(2055 AAC)	Rosario,Amed	(2525 AFD)
			Beltre,Adrian	(3155 BBC)	Kinsler,Ian	(2335 AAC)	**Anderson,Tim**	**(2535 ABA)**
			Devers,Rafael	(3135 AFF)	Albies,Ozhaino	(1525 ACA)	Owings,Chris (2O)	(2535 FBB)
					Hernandez,Cesar	**(1545 BBB)**	Arcia,Orlando	(1535 ABD)
Regulars	Thames,Eric (O)	(5235 ABF)	Sano,Miguel	(5115 CCC)	Happ,Ian (O)	(4215 AFF)	Story,Trevor	(5325 CBD)
	Hoskins,Rhys (O)	(4145 ADD)	**Lamb,Jacob**	**(4235 ABB)**	Moncada,Yoan	(3505 AFB)	DeJong,Paul (2)	(4135 ADD)
	Carpenter,Matt	**(4145 BAA)**	Shaw,Travis	(4235 ABC)	Odor,Rougned	(3325 AAC)	Gonzalez,Marwin (1O)	(3245 ABF)
	Bour,Justin	(4045 DCC)	Healy,Ryon (1)	(3035 ABD)	Gennett,Scooter	(3245 ABC)	Cozart,Zack	(3345 DCD)
	Belt,Brandon	(4135 CBB)	Seager,Kyle	(3135 AAC)	Taylor,Chris (O)	(3535 ACD)	**Polanco,Jorge**	**(2335 ABB)**
	Smoak,Justin	(4035 ACD)	Moustakas,Mike	(3055 DCB)	Harrison,Josh (3)	(2445 CBA)	**Gregorius,Didi**	**(2345 BAB)**
	Cabrera,Miguel	(3045 BAF)	**Longoria,Evan**	**(3235 AAB)**	**Castro,Starlin**	**(2235 BBB)**	Semien,Marcus	(2425 CBA)
	Mancini,Trey (O)	(3335 ABF)	**Suarez,Eugenio**	**(3125 AAB)**	Villar,Jonathan	(2523 ABF)	**Simmons,Andrelton**	**(1355 ABC)**
	Zimmerman,Ryan	(3235 DBF)	Flores,Wilmer (1)	(3045 ACB)	Wong,Kolten	(1435 BCB)	Peraza,Jose (2)	(0533 ACB)
	Santana,Carlos	(3245 AAC)	Spangenberg,Cory (O)	(2435 FFB)	**Phillips,Brandon (3)**	**(1155 AAA)**		
	Martinez,Jose (O)	(3353 ADF)						
	Gurriel,Yulieski	(2155 ADF)						
	Bell,Josh	**(2145 ABA)**						
	Mauer,Joe	**(1255 BAB)**						
Mid-Level	Olson,Matt	(4235 ABC)	Gallo,Joey (1)	(5315 ACB)	Kipnis,Jason	(3335 DBC)	**Russell,Addison**	**(3235 BBA)**
	Davis,Chris	(4005 BAC)	**Frazier,Todd**	**(4125 AAA)**	Mondesi,Raul	(3503 ADB)	Beckham,Tim	(3425 CDB)
	Bird,Gregory	(4135 FFB)	Chapman,Matt	(4205 ADB)	Drury,Brandon	(3045 ABC)	**Cabrera,Asdrubal (23)**	**(2235 BBB)**
	Reynolds,Mark	**(4123 ABB)**	Escobar,Eduardo	(3235 ACD)	Walker,Neil	(2135 DBB)	**Crawford,Brandon**	**(2135 AAB)**
	Joseph,Tommy	(4035 ADF)	Gyorko,Jedd	(3135 BCB)	**Miller,Brad**	**(2215 BBB)**	Solarte,Yangervis (23)	(2245 CBB)
	Duda,Lucas	(4035 FCC)	Senzel,Nick	(3243 AFF)	Panik,Joe	(1355 CBD)	Reyes,Jose (23)	(2533 BCA)
	McMahon,Ryan	(4243 ADF)	Franco,Maikel	(3145 ABC)	Pedroia,Dustin	(1253 DBB)	**Escobar,Alcides**	**(1435 AAA)**
	Smith,Dominic	(3035 ADA)	Candelario,Jeimer	(3125 ADB)			**Galvis,Freddy**	**(1425 AAA)**
	Cron,C.J.	(3125 BCB)	**Headley,Chase (1)**	**(2325 AAB)**			Hechavarria,Adeiny	(1535 CBC)
	Morrison,Logan	(3135 CBC)	Arroyo,Christian	(2143 AFA)			Iglesias,Jose	(1255 DBB)
	Moreland,Mitch	(3035 CBC)	Perez,Hernan (O)	(1423 ACC)			Difo,Wilmer (2)	(1533 ADA)
	Lind,Adam (O)	(3243 ACF)	Prado,Martin	(1145 FCC)				
	Alonso,Yonder	(2125 CBD)	Crawford,J.P.	(1315 ABB)				
	Valencia,Danny	(2225 ABB)						
Bench	Aguilar,Jesus	(4033 ACC)	Valbuena,Luis (1)	(4025 DCC)	Travis,Devon	(3253 FFB)	Valaika,Pat	(4131 ACC)
	Napoli,Mike	(4003 ABC)	Davidson,Matt	(4005 DCB)	Zobrist,Ben (O)	(2243 BBC)	Pinder,Chad (O)	(3313 BCB)
	Adams,Matt	(4033 CDC)	Dietrich,Derek	(3123 BCB)	Forsythe,Logan (3)	(2223 CBB)	Barreto,Franklin	(2413 ADA)
	Vogelbach,Daniel	(3013 ACB)	Anderson,Brian	(2035 ADC)	Lowrie,Jed	(2133 FCC)	Diaz,Aledmys	(2233 BCF)
	Gonzalez,Adrian	(2043 DBC)	Escobar,Yunel	(1033 DBB)	Descalso,Daniel (O)	(2323 BDD)	Swanson,Dansby	(1315 ADC)
			Diaz,Yandy	**(1343 ABA)**	Sanchez,Yolmer (3)	(1325 ACB)	**Mercer,Jordy**	**(1135 ABB)**
			Freese,David	(1013 BCA)	Frazier,Adam (O)	(1351 ACB)	Marte,Ketel	(1543 ACD)
			Rivera,T.J. (1)	(1141 CDB)	Hanson,Alen (O)	(1521 ACA)	Rojas,Miguel	(1243 CDC)
			Garcia,Adonis	(1241 DCC)	Tomlinson,Kelby (3)	(0541 ADA)	Tulowitzki,Troy	(1013 FCB)
			Cuthbert,Cheslor	(1223 BDC)	Kingery,Scott	(1423 AFF)	Camargo,Johan (3)	(1233 ADD)
							Sogard,Eric (2)	(0231 FFD)
Fringe	Vargas,Kennys	(4021 ACA)	Schimpf,Ryan	(5011 ACF)	Cowart,Kaleb (3)	(2311 ADB)	Hernandez,Enrique (O)	(3223 BDC)
	Carter,Chris	(4101 ACD)	Rodriguez,Sean	(3101 DFF)	Gonzalez,Erik	(2431 ACB)	Adames,Willy	(3311 ACA)
	Voit,Luke	(3031 ADB)	Ruiz,Rio	(1003 ACA)	Utley,Chase	(2331 BCB)	Rosales,Adam	(3201 AFF)
	Walker,Christian	(3121 ABC)	Plouffe,Trevor	(1111 CCB)	Moroff,Max	(2201 ACA)	Torres,Gleyber	(2321 AFF)
	White,Tyler	(3111 ACB)	Sandoval,Pablo	(1021 FDF)	Espinosa,Danny	(2201 ACC)	Urena,Richard	(2051 AFA)
	Jaso,John (O)	(3021 CDB)	Urshela,Giovanny	(1031 ACA)	**Asuaje,Carlos**	**(1223 ABA)**	Motter,Taylor	(1321 ACC)
	Reed,A.J.	(3001 ADD)			Romine,Andrew (3O)	(1331 AFA)	Aybar,Erick	(1341 CCB)
	Marte,Jefry	(3231 ADB)			Barney,Darwin (3)	(1323 ADD)	Adrianza,Ehire	(1411 FFB)
	Osuna,Jose (O)	(3140 ADA)			Garcia,Greg (3)	(1231 ADA)	Tatis Jr.,Fernando	(1401 AFF)
	Hicks,John	(2113 ADC)			Saladino,Tyler (3)	(1413 BDF)	Torreyes,Ronald (23)	(1431 ADB)
	Moran,Colin	(2021 BDD)			La Stella,Tommy	(1141 DFB)	Ahmed,Nick	(1323 FDB)
	Rua,Ryan (O)	(2401 BFD)			Holt,Brock	(0321 FDC)	Goins,Ryan (2)	(1113 ACC)
	Guzman,Ronald	(1311 ADA)					Rodgers,Brendan	(1011 AFF)
	Jones,Ryder	(1301 ADC)					Hardy,J.J.	(1013 FCD)

Universal Draft Grid

TIER	CATCHER		DH		OUTFIELD		OUTFIELD	
Elite					Trout,Mike	(4455 BAB)	Hamilton,Billy	(0515 BBB)
					Blackmon,Charlie	(4455 AAD)		
					Betts,Mookie	(3455 AAD)		
					Marte,Starling	(1535 ABC)		
Gold					Stanton,Giancarlo	(5145 CBF)	Yelich,Christian	(3445 AAB)
					Martinez,J.D.	(5255 DBD)	Buxton,Byron	(3515 BCA)
					Judge,Aaron	(5235 ABF)	Benintendi,Andrew	(3345 ADA)
					Harper,Bryce	(4255 CAF)	Pollock,A.J.	(3555 FCC)
					Pham,Thomas	(4445 CDF)	McCutchen,Andrew	(3245 AAD)
					Braun,Ryan	(4355 CBC)	Cain,Lorenzo	(1535 BAC)
Stars	Sanchez,Gary	(4155 ACB)	Cruz,Nelson	(4135 AAA)	Davis,Khristopher	(5235 AAB)	Brantley,Michael	(2455 FDF)
	Contreras,Willson	(4155 ACA)			Upton,Justin	(4225 AAC)	Kiermaier,Kevin	(2535 DCA)
	Posey,Buster (1)	(1255 AAC)			Springer,George	(4145 CAB)	Herrera,Odubel	(2435 AAA)
					Santana,Domingo	(4225 CCB)	Garcia,Avisail	(2245 CBD)
					Ozuna,Marcell	(3145 AAD)	Inciarte,Ender	(1555 BAA)
					Rosario,Eddie	(3345 ABB)	DeShields Jr.,Delino	(1505 ACD)
					Puig,Yasiel	(3235 CCB)	Gardner,Brett	(1535 AAB)
					Eaton,Adam	(2445 BBB)		
Regulars	Realmuto,Jacob	(2445 ABB)	Pujols,Albert	(1135 AAB)	Schwarber,Kyle	(5125 FDF)	Williams,Nick	(3325 ABC)
	Molina,Yadier	(1145 BBC)			Cespedes,Yoenis	(4145 DBA)	Hicks,Aaron	(3335 DCF)
					Conforto,Michael	(4145 BCD)	Jones,Adam	(2235 AAA)
					Gonzalez,Carlos	(4245 BAB)	Polanco,Gregory	(2245 BBC)
					Dickerson,Corey	(4145 BBC)	Margot,Manuel	(2545 BCB)
					Souza,Steven	(4315 CBB)	Zimmer,Bradley	(2505 ACB)
					Schebler,Scott	(4245 ACC)	Reddick,Josh	(2345 CBC)
					Tomas,Yasmany	(4155 DCC)	Winker,Jesse	(2145 ACA)
					Haniger,Mitch	(4235 CDC)	Choo,Shin-Soo	(2235 FBC)
					Duvall,Adam	(4125 AAA)	Parra,Gerardo	(2153 CCF)
					Bruce,Jay	(4135 AAB)	Pence,Hunter	(2335 FCC)
					Gomez,Carlos	(4325 CCB)	Mazara,Nomar	(2035 AAA)
					Renfroe,Hunter	(4235 ABB)	Cabrera,Melky	(1055 BAC)
					Fowler,Dexter	(3535 CAB)	Acuna,Ronald	(1413 AFF)
					Kemp,Matt	(3145 CAA)	Pillar,Kevin	(1335 AAA)
					Taylor,Michael	(3515 ADC)	Span,Denard	(1355 CBC)
					Kepler,Max	(3345 ACB)	Smith,Mallex	(1523 CCA)
					Bradley,Jackie	(3235 ABC)	Garcia,Leury	(1433 CDB)
					Mahtook,Mikie	(3525 BDD)		
Mid-Level	Gattis,Evan	(4043 BCB)	Morales,Kendrys	(3035 AAB)	Chisenhall,Lonnie	(4235 CDC)	Tapia,Raimel	(2553 ADB)
	Perez,Salvador	(3235 ABA)	Ramirez,Hanley	(3045 CBF)	Grichuk,Randal	(4325 BCB)	Jackson,Austin	(2333 FDD)
	Barnes,Austin (2)	(3453 ADF)	Dahl,David	(2533 DDF)	Broxton,Keon	(4503 ACB)	Markakis,Nick	(1035 AAA)
	Castillo,Welington	(3233 BCB)			Fowler,Dustin	(3433 DDB)	Kendrick,Howie	(1353 DBC)
	Ramos,Wilson	(2045 DCF)			Altherr,Aaron	(3435 FCF)	Ellsbury,Jacoby	(1543 CBB)
	Lucroy,Jonathan	(1345 BBF)			Trumbo,Mark	(3215 BAC)	Gamel,Ben	(1325 ABB)
	Vazquez,Christian	(1243 FFC)			Bautista,Jose	(3115 CAD)	Heyward,Jason	(1235 BAD)
					Peralta,David	(2345 DCF)	Maybin,Cameron	(1533 FBB)
					Calhoun,Kole	(2235 AAB)	Aoki,Norichika	(1453 BCB)
					Robles,Victor	(2553 AFF)	Jay,Jon	(1343 DDC)
					Pirela,Jose	(2345 ADF)	Revere,Ben	(0553 BCD)
					Piscotty,Stephen	(2135 BBB)	Dyson,Jarrod	(0533 BDB)
					Almora,Albert	(2353 ACB)		
					Calhoun,Willie	(2253 ADC)		
Bench	Grandal,Yasmani	(4025 ABA)	Moss,Brandon	(4213 BBB)	Hernandez,Teoscar	(4333 ACC)	Jones,JaCoby	(2403 ADB)
	Chirinos,Robinson	(4113 CFD)	Holliday,Matt	(3123 FCB)	Phillips,Brett	(4513 ACB)	Naquin,Tyler	(2331 ADC)
	Iannetta,Chris	(4013 ADC)	Wright,David	(3221 FFB)	Marisnick,Jake	(4403 ADD)	Alford,Anthony	(2331 CFF)
	Martin,Russell	(3023 BBA)	Duffy,Matt	(1441 FDD)	Pederson,Joc	(4123 BCD)	Bader,Harrison	(2301 ADA)
	Flowers,Tyler	(3013 BDC)	Bauers,Jake	(1321 ABB)	Joyce,Matt	(4135 ACF)	Grossman,Robert	(2123 ACD)
	Hundley,Nick	(3123 BDB)	Martinez,Victor	(1041 CBF)	Granderson,Curtis	(4223 BAA)	Gordon,Alex	(2115 CCC)
	Alfaro,Jorge	(3203 ADA)			Goodwin,Brian	(4321 BCC)	Carrera,Ezequiel	(1523 BDB)
	Castro,Jason	(3213 ACA)			Smith,Seth	(3333 ACA)	Lagares,Juan	(1423 FDA)
	Hedges,Austin	(3113 ADC)			Bonifacio,Jorge	(3223 ABB)	Verdugo,Alex	(1133 ADB)
	Vogt,Stephen	(2033 BCB)			Ervin,Phillip	(3411 ADA)	Rickard,Joey	(1423 CDC)
	D Arnaud,Travis	(2233 FDC)			Pearce,Steve	(3033 DDF)	Quinn,Roman	(1521 DFA)
	Pina,Manny	(2223 ADB)			Parker,Jarrett	(3303 DDA)	Blanco,Gregor	(1511 BDD)
	McCann,Brian	(2233 BBA)			Delmonico,Nick	(3333 ACB)	Heredia,Guillermo	(1123 ADA)
	McCann,James	(2223 BCC)			Frazier,Clint	(3411 ADA)	Powell,Boog	(1311 ADD)
	Suzuki,Kurt	(2143 ACD)			Young,Chris	(3213 CDB)	Jankowski,Travis	(0511 DDB)
	Wieters,Matt	(2123 CCB)			O Neill,Tyler	(3301 ACD)		
	Knapp,Andrew	(2301 BDF)			Davis,Rajai	(2521 ACA)		
	Barnhart,Tucker	(1243 ACB)			Toles,Andrew	(2243 FFA)		
	Cervelli,Francisco	(1223 FCB)			Brinson,Lewis	(2331 ADC)		
	Mejia,Francisco	(1341 AFF)			Allen,Greg	(2521 AFB)		
	Maxwell,Bruce	(1015 ADF)			Fisher,Derek	(2323 ADA)		
Fringe	Murphy,Tom	(4211 CFF)			Blash,Jabari	(4101 BDB)	Fuentes,Reymond	(1521 ADC)
	Rupp,Cameron	(4111 ADB)			Kivlehan,Patrick	(4111 ADB)	Hernandez,Gorkys	(1311 ADA)
	Garver,Mitch	(3221 ADD)			Werth,Jayson	(3113 FCB)	Profar,Jurickson	(1231 FFA)
	Avila,Alex	(3003 DDC)			Saunders,Michael	(3221 FDF)	Hays,Austin	(1111 AFF)
	Gomes,Yan	(3213 CDD)			Cordero,Franchy	(3521 AFB)	Peterson,Jace	(1211 ACA)
	Perez,Roberto	(3011 CFC)			Nimmo,Brandon	(2223 CCB)	Suzuki,Ichiro	(0331 ADD)
	Sanchez,Hector	(3011 DFC)			Meadows,Austin	(2441 DFF)		
	Caratini,Victor	(2341 AFC)			Adams,Lane	(2501 ACB)		
	Joseph,Caleb	(2021 BDF)			Luplow,Jordan	(2211 AFF)		
	Rivera,Rene	(2011 AFC)			Soler,Jorge	(2201 DDA)		
	Herrmann,Chris (O)	(2501 BFF)			Engel,Adam	(2501 ADB)		
	Maldonado,Martin	(2003 ADB)			Garcia,Willy	(2101 ACB)		
	Stassi,Max	(2101 BFB)			Slater,Austin	(1123 BDB)		
	Mesoraco,Devin	(1011 FFD)			Presley,Alex	(1331 BDB)		

Universal Draft Grid

TIER	STARTING PITCHERS				RELIEF PITCHERS			
Elite	Kershaw,Clayton	(5505 FAA)	Sale,Chris	(5505 BAB)				
	Kluber,Corey	(5505 CAB)	Scherzer,Max	(4505 BAA)				
Gold	Strasburg,Stephen	(4505 DAA)	Bumgarner,Madison	(3305 DAA)	Jansen,Kenley	(5530 BAA)	Kimbrel,Craig	(5530 BAC)
Stars	Carrasco,Carlos	(4405 CAA)	Verlander,Justin	(2305 DAA)	Britton,Zach	(5230 DBB)	Hand,Brad	(4531 BBB)
	Severino,Luis	(4405 ABD)			Chapman,Aroldis	(5530 DBB)	Rivero,Felipe	(4431 BCA)
	deGrom,Jacob	(3405 AAA)			Osuna,Roberto	(5530 AAA)	Davis,Wade	(3530 DBA)
	Greinke,Zack	(3305 BAB)			Allen,Cody	(4530 AAA)	Iglesias,Raisel	(3431 DCA)
	Hendricks,Kyle	(2205 BAA)			Giles,Ken	(4530 ABA)	Knebel,Corey	(3531 DCB)
Regulars	Syndergaard,Noah	(5403 FCA)	Weaver,Luke	(3305 ADA)	Melancon,Mark	(4230 DAA)		
	Archer,Chris	(3505 AAA)	Wood,Alex	(3303 FBA)	Diaz,Edwin	(3530 ACB)		
	Castillo,Luis	(3305 ADF)	Cole,Gerrit	(2205 DAB)	Doolittle,Sean	(3530 FCA)		
	Darvish,Yu	(3503 FCA)	Lester,Jon	(2305 BAA)	Holland,Greg	(3530 BCA)		
	Keuchel,Dallas	(3203 DAB)	Martinez,Carlos	(2305 AAA)	Treinen,Blake	(3230 ACA)		
	Nola,Aaron	(3405 DBA)	Price,David	(2303 FAA)	Colome,Alexander	(2230 DAC)		
	Tanaka,Masahiro	(3303 DAA)	Quintana,Jose	(2305 AAA)	Neris,Hector	(2431 ACC)		
Mid-	Paxton,James	(3403 FCB)	Arrieta,Jake	(1205 BAB)	Miller,Andrew	(5510 HBB)		
Level	Salazar,Danny	(3503 DAA)	Berrios,Jose	(1203 ACC)	Familia,Jeurys	(4331 FAB)		
	Stroman,Marcus	(3205 FAA)	Bundy,Dylan	(1305 CCA)	Devenski,Christopher	(3511 ACB)		
	Bauer,Trevor	(2305 AAA)	Duffy,Danny	(1203 FAB)	Parker,Blake	(3420 ADB)		
	Fulmer,Michael	(2103 ACA)	Hamels,Cole	(1203 DAB)	Reed,Addison	(3311 ACB)		
	Gonzalez,Gio	(2305 BAA)	Happ,J.A.	(1203 DAA)	Steckenrider,Drew	(3520 AFC)		
	Maeda,Kenta	(2303 AAB)	Peacock,Brad	(1303 FCB)	Herrera,Kelvin	(2320 ACC)		
	Ray,Robbie	(2503 BBA)	Porcello,Rick	(1205 AAA)	Hill,Rich	(2503 FCA)		
	Richards,Garrett	(2203 FCA)	Sanchez,Aaron	(1103 FBC)	Rodney,Fernando	(2420 BBA)		
	Samardzija,Jeff	(2205 AAA)	Santana,Ervin	(1105 BAA)	Vizcaino,Arodys	(2430 FCA)		
	Anderson,Chase	(1205 DAB)						
Bench	McCullers,Lance	(3403 FCA)	Lackey,John	(1203 DAA)	Betances,Dellin	(5510 ACB)	Swarzak,Anthony	(2410 BDF)
	Godley,Zachary	(2303 ADF)	Lamet,Dinelson	(1403 ADA)	Harris,Will	(4410 DCA)	Belisle,Matt	(1220 FDA)
	Gray,Jonathan	(2303 FBC)	Lynn,Lance	(1205 FBB)	Jones,Nate	(4410 FDA)	Greene,Shane	(1321 BCB)
	Gray,Sonny	(2203 DAB)	Manaea,Sean	(1203 BCA)	Kahnle,Thomas	(4510 ADB)	Montgomery,Michael	(1103 ABB)
	Hernandez,Felix	(2203 FAB)	McHugh,Collin	(1203 FAA)	Madson,Ryan	(4310 DCC)	Oh,Seung-Hwan	(1320 ABD)
	Honeywell,Brent	(2301 AFC)	Montgomery,Jordan	(1203 ACA)	Minter,A.J.	(4510 AFC)		
	Leake,Mike	(2005 BAA)	Nova,Ivan	(1103 FAB)	Robertson,David	(4510 ABC)		
	Morton,Charlie	(2203 FCB)	Pomeranz,Drew	(1303 CAA)	Bradley,Archie	(3411 DDB)		
	Paulino,David	(2403 CDC)	Reyes,Alex	(1403 FFD)	Claudio,Alexander	(3010 FDC)		
	Ryu,Hyun-Jin	(2203 FDC)	Roark,Tanner	(1205 AAA)	Edwards,Carl	(3520 ADB)		
	Taillon,Jameson	(2203 DCB)	Rodriguez,Eduardo	(1303 FCA)	Givens,Mychal	(3501 ACB)		
	Chacin,Jhoulys	(1103 DBA)	Snell,Blake	(1403 ADC)	Green,Chad	(3501 BDC)		
	Clevinger,Michael	(1303 ADC)	Stewart,Brock	(1301 DDC)	Soria,Joakim	(3310 DCB)		
	Cobb,Alex	(1105 FCF)	Teheran,Julio	(1205 AAB)	Barraclough,Kyle	(2521 BDB)		
	Corbin,Patrick	(1205 FBA)	Tomlin,Josh	(1103 FBA)	Bedrosian,Cam	(2420 FDC)		
	Cueto,Johnny	(1203 DAB)	Wacha,Michael	(1203 DAA)	Brach,Brad	(2410 ACA)		
	Davies,Zachary	(1103 ABA)	Walker,Taijuan	(1203 DBA)	Kela,Keone	(2510 FDA)		
	Faria,Jake	(1303 BDB)	Estrada,Marco	(0205 CAA)	Lyons,Tyler	(2311 FDC)		
	Flaherty,Jack	(1201 ADF)	Odorizzi,Jake	(0203 DAB)	Minor,Mike	(2311 FDF)		
	Gausman,Kevin	(1303 CBB)			Nicasio,Juan	(2310 ACA)		
Fringe	Garcia,Jaime	(2203 FAB)			Smith,Carson	(5510 FDC)	Phelps,David	(2400 FCC)
	Kopech,Michael	(2401 AFF)			Boxberger,Brad	(4510 FCD)	Pressly,Ryan	(2310 DDA)
	Nelson,Jimmy	(2301 BAC)			Gregerson,Luke	(4410 BCA)	Ramos,Edubray	(2500 ADC)
	Anderson,Tyler	(1203 FDA)			Hildenberger,Trevor	(4210 AFF)	Romo,Sergio	(2400 DDB)
	DeSclafani,Anthony	(1103 FCA)			Smith,Joe	(4310 DCB)	Rusin,Chris	(2101 DCD)
	Fiers,Mike	(1203 AAA)			Strop,Pedro	(4400 DCB)	Sherfy,Jimmie	(2310 AFC)
	Foltynewicz,Mike	(1203 BCC)			Alexander,Scott	(3110 BDD)	Stammen,Craig	(2201 FDF)
	Gibson,Kyle	(1103 CBB)			Cecil,Brett	(3400 DDB)	Watson,Tony	(2210 ACA)
	Glasnow,Tyler	(1301 BDC)			Cedeno,Xavier	(3300 FDF)	Wilson,Justin	(2500 ACA)
	Gohara,Luiz	(1401 AFF)			Feliz,Michael	(3500 CDB)	Yates,Kirby	(2510 CDF)
	Graveman,Kendall	(1003 FBA)			Hunter,Tommy	(3300 DDB)	Ziegler,Brad	(2010 DBB)
	Hammel,Jason	(1203 BAB)			Leone,Dominic	(3410 ADF)	Barnes,Daniel	(1300 ADF)
	Iwakuma,Hisashi	(1001 FBC)			O Day,Darren	(3510 FCB)	Buchter,Ryan	(1300 ADB)
	Junis,Jakob	(1203 ADB)			Otero,Dan	(3000 ADC)	Clippard,Tyler	(1410 ACB)
	Leiter,Mark	(1201 ADC)			Pazos,James	(3400 ADF)	Dull,Ryan	(1310 DDB)
	Mahle,Tyler	(1103 ADF)			Rondon,Hector	(3400 ACA)	Gearrin,Cory	(1200 FDB)
	Marquez,German	(1203 ACB)			Shaw,Bryan	(3300 ACA)	Hader,Joshua	(1511 ADB)
	Matz,Steven	(1103 FCC)			Stripling,Ross	(3301 ADB)	Hernandez,David	(1300 FDA)
	Pivetta,Nick	(1203 ADF)			Baez,Pedro	(2410 CCB)	Hughes,Jared	(1000 CCB)
	Sabathia,CC	(1203 FAA)			Barnes,Jacob	(2400 BDD)	Johnson,Jim	(1310 BBB)
	Shoemaker,Matthew	(1201 FBB)			Barnes,Matt	(2400 ADC)	Kintzler,Brandon	(1011 DDC)
	Skaggs,Tyler	(1201 FDC)			Blevins,Jerry	(2500 FDB)	Law,Derek	(1210 ADF)
	Woodruff,Brandon	(1203 CDC)			Bush,Matt	(2410 BDF)	McAllister,Zach	(1300 CCB)
	Cashner,Andrew	(0003 FAB)			Casilla,Santiago	(2310 CBB)	Norris,Bud	(1310 DBA)
	Cotton,Jharel	(0203 BDB)			Cishek,Steve	(2310 BCB)	Pagan,Emilio	(1400 AFD)
	Dickey,R.A.	(0103 BAA)			Diekman,Jake	(2510 DDA)	Ramirez,Erasmo	(1101 ABA)
	Eickhoff,Jerad	(0203 DBA)			Duffey,Tyler	(2211 ACF)	Ramos,A.J.	(1520 BAB)
	Giolito,Lucas	(0203 ADA)			Fields,Joshua	(2400 ADA)	Rogers,Taylor	(1210 ADB)
	Heaney,Andrew	(0201 FDF)			Goody,Nicholas	(2510 ADC)	Senzatela,Antonio	(1101 ADB)
	Hellickson,Jeremy	(0103 DAB)			Hendriks,Liam	(2400 CCA)	Sewald,Paul	(1300 ADB)
	Kennedy,Ian	(0203 CAB)			Hoyt,James	(2410 ADC)	Strickland,Hunter	(1300 ADD)
	Kuhl,Chad	(0103 ACB)			Lorenzen,Michael	(2201 DCD)	Tepera,Ryan	(1211 ADB)
	Lively,Ben	(0001 ADF)			Maton,Phil	(2310 AFF)	Triggs,Andrew	(1101 FDC)
	Lopez,Reynaldo	(0203 ADA)			McGee,Jake	(2310 DCC)	Tuivailala,Sam	(1210 ADF)
	Straily,Dan	(0205 AAB)			Middleton,Keynan	(2410 ADB)	Vincent,Nick	(1200 DDB)
	Suter,Brent	(0003 BDB)			Morgan,Adam	(2401 ADA)	Warren,Adam	(1200 DCB)
	Tropeano,Nicholas	(0203 FDA)			Morrow,Brandon	(2310 FDF)	Wittgren,Nick	(1200 DDA)
	Vargas,Jason	(0005 FCD)			Musgrove,Joe	(2201 ACA)	Brebbia,John	(0210 AFF)
	Williams,Trevor	(0003 ACA)			Petit,Yusmeiro	(2301 ACB)	Torres,Jose	(0200 ADF)

Universal Draft Grid

TIER	STARTING PITCHERS				RELIEF PITCHERS			
Below Fringe	Pineda,Michael	(3300 FAA)	Fulmer,Carson	(0100 ADB)	Simmons,Shae	(5510 FFC)	Jackson,Edwin	(0101 DCB)
	Buehler,Walker	(2500 AFF)	Gallardo,Yovani	(0001 DAA)	Chafin,Andrew	(2200 DDA)	LeBlanc,Wade	(0100 BDB)
	De Leon,Jose	(2400 CDF)	Gant,John	(0100 FDB)	Cingrani,Tony	(2400 DDB)	Leclerc,Jose	(0410 BDD)
	Anderson,Brett	(1001 FCC)	Garrett,Amir	(0101 ADF)	Coulombe,Daniel	(2200 ADC)	Lyles,Jordan	(0000 FDC)
	Andriese,Matt	(1201 DCA)	Garza,Matt	(0001 FBA)	Drake,Oliver	(2400 ADC)	Montas,Frankie	(0300 FDC)
	Bailey,Homer	(1203 FDF)	Gaviglio,Sam	(0000 ADA)	Garcia,Luis	(2210 ADB)	Ramirez,J.C.	(0001 CCA)
	Cahill,Trevor	(1201 FDA)	Gonzales,Marco	(0101 CDD)	Grimm,Justin	(2400 BDB)	Ramirez,Jose	(0201 ADB)
	Chatwood,Tyler	(1103 FBA)	Gonzalez,Miguel	(0003 DBB)	Holder,Jonathan	(2400 AFF)	Robles,Hansel	(0300 ADB)
	Chen,Wei-Yin	(1100 FBA)	Griffin,A.J.	(0201 FCB)	Wood,Blake	(2400 BDB)	Rondon,Bruce	(0410 FDC)
	Eovaldi,Nathan	(1101 FCA)	Gsellman,Robert	(0001 DDB)	Altavilla,Dan	(1400 AFC)	Saupold,Warwick	(0000 CDA)
	Fedde,Erick	(1101 BFA)	Guerra,Junior	(0200 FDF)	Alvarez,Jose	(1200 ADA)	Strahm,Matt	(0301 FDA)
	Feldman,Scott	(1001 FCA)	Hahn,Jesse	(0001 DDD)	Barnette,Tony	(1310 BCC)	Street,Huston	(0100 FCF)
	Gossett,Daniel	(1103 ADF)	Harvey,Matt	(0101 FBC)	Biagini,Joe	(1101 ADB)	Torres,Carlos	(0200 ACB)
	Jimenez,Ubaldo	(1303 BAA)	Hoffman,Jeff	(0101 ADD)	Bleier,Richard	(1000 ADB)	Wojciechowski,Asher	(0100 CDD)
	Karns,Nathan	(1301 FCB)	Holland,Derek	(0001 FBB)	Bowman,Matthew	(1100 ADC)	Wood,Travis	(0101 ACC)
	McCarthy,Brandon	(1201 FDB)	Lugo,Seth	(0101 DCB)	Chavez,Jesse	(1201 BBA)		
	Mendez,Yohander	(1101 ADF)	Martinez,Nick	(0001 ADB)	Delgado,Randall	(1300 FCB)		
	Perdomo,Luis	(1003 ABA)	Mejia,Adalberto	(0101 BDC)	Dyson,Sam	(1010 ABC)		
	Pruitt,Austin	(1101 ADD)	Miley,Wade	(0203 BAA)	Glover,Koda	(1200 FDB)		
	Richard,Clayton	(1005 DBB)	Miller,Shelby	(0200 FCC)	Hatcher,Chris	(1300 FDB)		
	Rodon,Carlos	(1401 FBA)	Miranda,Ariel	(0203 ACA)	Hembree,Heath	(1300 BDA)		
	Ross,Joe	(2203 AFF)	Montero,Rafael	(1200 FFF)	Hudson,Daniel	(1401 FCA)		
	Sanchez,Anibal	(2201 DDB)	Moore,Andrew	(1101 ADB)	Jeffress,Jeremy	(1100 ACB)		
	Urias,Julio	(2203 AFF)	Moore,Matt	(1200 FFF)	Jimenez,Joe	(1410 BFF)		
	Velasquez,Vincent	(2201 DDB)	Newcomb,Sean	(1101 ADB)	Kelly,Joe	(1300 DDB)		
	Wainwright,Adam	(1101 FBB)	Nicolino,Justin	(0001 BCA)	Kontos,George	(1200 DCB)		
	Wheeler,Zack	(1301 FDF)	Nolasco,Ricky	(0103 FBA)	Liriano,Francisco	(1303 DAB)		
	Adams,Chance	(0100 ADC)	Norris,Daniel	(0203 FCA)	Martes,Francis	(1401 ADF)		
	Adleman,Timothy	(0100 DCA)	Pelfrey,Mike	(0001 FBB)	Maurer,Brandon	(1300 CCA)		
	Asher,Alec	(0000 ADF)	Perez,Martin	(0003 CAA)	Ottavino,Adam	(1400 FDD)		
	Bettis,Chad	(0003 FCC)	Romano,Sal	(0103 ADF)	Peralta,Wandy	(1211 ADC)		
	Blach,Ty	(0003 ACD)	Ross,Tyson	(0201 FCD)	Petricka,Jacob	(1100 FDD)		
	Blackburn,Paul	(0001 CDA)	Santiago,Hector	(0101 FBB)	Rodriguez,Francisco	(1200 ABC)		
	Boyd,Matt	(0103 ACB)	Shields,James	(0203 DAB)	Romero,Enny	(1400 CDB)		
	Bridwell,Parker	(0003 ADB)	Sims,Lucas	(0300 ADD)	Shreve,Chasen	(1400 BDB)		
	Butler,Eddie	(0000 BDC)	Stephens,Jackson	(0101 ADC)	Smoker,Josh	(1500 CDD)		
	Cole,A.J.	(0101 ADC)	Stephenson,Robert	(0203 ADC)	Thornburg,Tyler	(1300 FDF)		
	Colon,Bartolo	(0003 DAB)	Stratton,Chris	(0103 ADB)	Zych,Tony	(1200 FDB)		
	Conley,Adam	(0103 CCC)	Thompson,Jake	(0001 ADC)	Bell,Chadwick	(0100 ADB)		
	Covey,Dylan	(0000 DDD)	Tillman,Chris	(0103 DAB)	Bibens-Dirkx,Austin	(0000 ADB)		
	Eflin,Zach	(0001 FDD)	Urena,Jose	(0005 BCA)	Castro,Miguel	(0001 BDF)		
	Farmer,Buck	(0103 ADA)	Wright,Steven	(0001 FCB)	Despaigne,Odrisamer	(0001 BCD)		
	Finnegan,Brandon	(0200 DCA)	Ynoa,Gabriel	(0000 BDB)	Feliz,Neftali	(0200 DCC)		
	Fister,Doug	(0103 DBB)	Zimmermann,Jordan	(0003 DBB)	Garcia,Jarlin	(0100 CDA)		
	Freeland,Kyle	(0003 ACC)			Holmberg,David	(0000 ADD)		

SIMULATION LEAGUE DRAFT   TOP 500+

NAME	POS	RAR
Trout,Mike	8	74.6
Votto,Joey	3	61.3
Blackmon,Charlie	8	55.2
Altuve,Jose	4	48.7
Harper,Bryce	9	47.1
Goldschmidt,Paul	3	44.2
Martinez,J.D.	9	43.9
Freeman,Freddie	3	43.8
Arenado,Nolan	5	43.7
Kershaw,Clayton	P	43.2
Stanton,Giancarlo	9	40.3
Correa,Carlos	6	39.0
Bryant,Kris	5	39.0
Kluber,Corey	P	37.5
Strasburg,Stephen	P	35.7
Judge,Aaron	9	35.6
Donaldson,Josh	5	34.7
Scherzer,Max	P	34.5
Murphy,Daniel	4	34.3
Sale,Chris	P	34.2
Bumgarner,Madison	P	33.0
Contreras,Willson	2	31.6
Seager,Corey	6	31.5
Ramirez,Jose	45	30.7
Sanchez,Gary	2	28.9
Hendricks,Kyle	P	28.5
Betts,Mookie	9	28.3
Greinke,Zack	P	28.2
Rizzo,Anthony	3	27.7
Yelich,Christian	8	27.6
Turner,Justin	5	27.4
Rendon,Anthony	5	26.1
deGrom,Jacob	P	25.5
Cespedes,Yoenis	7	25.5
Conforto,Michael	78	25.2
McCutchen,Andrew	8	24.9
Posey,Buster	23	24.8
Keuchel,Dallas	P	24.6
Syndergaard,Noah	P	24.6
Severino,Luis	P	24.5
Ozuna,Marcell	7	24.3
Martinez,Carlos	P	24.3
Braun,Ryan	7	23.3
Bregman,Alex	56	23.3
Upton,Justin	7	23.1
Weaver,Luke	P	23.0
Turner,Trea	6	22.7
Carrasco,Carlos	P	22.6
Wood,Alex	P	22.3
Nola,Aaron	P	22.2
Verlander,Justin	P	21.2
Abreu,Jose	3	21.2
Sanchez,Aaron	P	21.1
Benintendi,Andrew	78	20.9
Springer,George	89	20.8
Stroman,Marcus	P	20.8
Lindor,Francisco	6	20.8
Beltre,Adrian	5	20.7
Paxton,James	P	20.5
Bellinger,Cody	37	20.4
Brantley,Michael	7	20.1
Price,David	P	19.8
Bogaerts,Xander	6	19.1

NAME	POS	RAR
Pham,Thomas	78	19.0
Cruz,Nelson	0	19.0
Miller,Andrew	P	18.9
Castillo,Luis	P	18.7
Jansen,Kenley	P	18.7
Cole,Gerrit	P	18.6
Richards,Garrett	P	18.6
Davis,Khristopher	7	18.4
Carpenter,Matt	3	18.4
Kimbrel,Craig	P	18.2
Dozier,Brian	4	17.9
Gonzalez,Gio	P	17.8
Fowler,Dexter	8	17.6
Anderson,Chase	P	17.5
Hoskins,Rhys	37	17.4
Schwarber,Kyle	7	17.3
Barnes,Austin	24	17.2
LeMahieu,DJ	4	16.8
Tanaka,Masahiro	P	16.6
Peacock,Brad	P	16.6
Quintana,Jose	P	16.5
Pollock,A.J.	8	16.3
Machado,Manny	5	16.3
Encarnacion,Edwin	3	16.2
Fulmer,Michael	P	16.0
Santana,Ervin	P	15.9
Lester,Jon	P	15.6
Berrios,Jose	P	15.6
Britton,Zach	P	15.5
Lamb,Jacob	5	15.2
Happ,J.A.	P	15.2
Cozart,Zack	6	15.2
Giles,Ken	P	15.0
Hosmer,Eric	3	15.0
Winker,Jesse	9	14.9
Darvish,Yu	P	14.8
Archer,Chris	P	14.8
Ray,Robbie	P	14.7
Eaton,Adam	8	14.6
Bour,Justin	3	14.6
Iglesias,Raisel	P	14.5
Story,Trevor	6	14.3
Arrieta,Jake	P	14.2
Montgomery,Michael	P	14.1
Cain,Lorenzo	8	13.9
Lynn,Lance	P	13.8
Santana,Domingo	9	13.7
Zunino,Mike	2	13.6
Harris,Will	P	13.6
Betances,Dellin	P	13.5
Givens,Mychal	P	13.5
Bradley,Archie	P	13.4
Pomeranz,Drew	P	13.4
Reed,Addison	P	13.4
Knebel,Corey	P	13.3
Devenski,Christopher	P	13.2
Lucroy,Jonathan	2	13.1
Allen,Cody	P	13.1
Devers,Rafael	5	13.1
Rivero,Felipe	P	13.0
Cabrera,Miguel	3	13.0
Gray,Jonathan	P	12.9
Green,Chad	P	12.8

NAME	POS	RAR
Ryu,Hyun-Jin	P	12.8
Davis,Wade	P	12.8
Taillon,Jameson	P	12.7
Hill,Rich	P	12.7
Hand,Brad	P	12.5
Steckenrider,Drew	P	12.5
Gonzalez,Carlos	9	12.5
Duffy,Danny	P	12.5
Chapman,Aroldis	P	12.5
Belt,Brandon	3	12.4
Stewart,Brock	P	12.4
Godley,Zachary	P	12.3
Gonzalez,Marwin	367	12.3
DeJong,Paul	46	12.1
Claudio,Alexander	P	11.9
Maeda,Kenta	P	11.8
Rosario,Eddie	7	11.7
McHugh,Collin	P	11.7
Puig,Yasiel	9	11.7
Kahnle,Thomas	P	11.6
Salazar,Danny	P	11.6
Realmuto,Jacob	2	11.3
Robertson,David	P	11.3
Snell,Blake	P	11.3
Cano,Robinson	4	11.2
Santana,Carlos	3	11.2
Castellanos,Nick	59	11.1
Clevinger,Michael	P	11.1
Buxton,Byron	8	11.0
Thames,Eric	37	11.0
Andrus,Elvis	6	11.0
Smith,Carson	P	10.9
Dickerson,Corey	7	10.9
Martinez,Jose	37	10.9
Bauer,Trevor	P	10.8
Diaz,Edwin	P	10.8
Strop,Pedro	P	10.7
Brach,Brad	P	10.6
Minor,Mike	P	10.6
Jones,Nate	P	10.6
Mancini,Trey	37	10.4
Cueto,Johnny	P	10.4
Hamels,Cole	P	10.4
Hughes,Jared	P	10.3
Madson,Ryan	P	10.3
Melancon,Mark	P	10.2
Neris,Hector	P	10.2
Parker,Blake	P	10.2
Castillo,Welington	2	10.2
Nova,Ivan	P	10.1
Manaea,Sean	P	10.0
Gallo,Joey	35	10.0
Gray,Sonny	P	9.9
Porcello,Rick	P	9.8
Familia,Jeurys	P	9.7
Montgomery,Jordan	P	9.7
Leake,Mike	P	9.7
Flaherty,Jack	P	9.7
Gattis,Evan	2	9.6
Tomas,Yasmany	7	9.3
Shaw,Bryan	P	9.3
Herrera,Odubel	8	9.2
Smoak,Justin	3	9.2

NAME	POS	RAR
Hildenberger,Trevor	P	9.0
Honeywell,Brent	P	9.0
Pagan,Emilio	P	9.0
Odorizzi,Jake	P	8.9
Cabrera,Melky	79	8.9
Cobb,Alex	P	8.9
Osuna,Roberto	P	8.8
Lyons,Tyler	P	8.8
Hernandez,Felix	P	8.8
Walker,Taijuan	P	8.8
Bundy,Dylan	P	8.8
Cabrera,Asdrubal	456	8.8
Hunter,Tommy	P	8.7
Otero,Dan	P	8.6
Moustakas,Mike	5	8.5
McCullers,Lance	P	8.5
McAllister,Zach	P	8.4
Suter,Brent	P	8.4
Gausman,Kevin	P	8.4
Swarzak,Anthony	P	8.4
Stammen,Craig	P	8.3
Corbin,Patrick	P	8.3
Gearrin,Cory	P	8.2
Edwards,Carl	P	8.2
Sano,Miguel	5	8.1
Kendrick,Howie	7	8.0
Leone,Dominic	P	7.9
Treinen,Blake	P	7.9
Smith,Joe	P	7.9
Petit,Yusmeiro	P	7.9
Reyes,Alex	P	7.8
Bruce,Jay	9	7.8
Doolittle,Sean	P	7.8
Alexander,Scott	P	7.6
Colome,Alexander	P	7.6
Morton,Charlie	P	7.6
Strickland,Hunter	P	7.6
Stripling,Ross	P	7.6
Bedrosian,Cam	P	7.6
Morgan,Adam	P	7.6
Garcia,Avisail	9	7.6
Chacin,Jhoulys	P	7.5
Hicks,Aaron	78	7.5
Reddick,Josh	79	7.2
Fields,Joshua	P	7.2
Gregerson,Luke	P	7.1
Herrera,Kelvin	P	7.1
Chisenhall,Lonnie	9	7.1
Goody,Nicholas	P	7.0
Chirinos,Robinson	2	7.0
Walker,Neil	4	7.0
Law,Derek	P	7.0
Teheran,Julio	P	7.0
Holland,Greg	P	6.9
Hader,Joshua	P	6.8
Molina,Yadier	2	6.8
Cedeno,Xavier	P	6.7
Vincent,Nick	P	6.7
Boxberger,Brad	P	6.7
Pazos,James	P	6.6
Kiermaier,Kevin	8	6.6
Watson,Tony	P	6.6
Phelps,David	P	6.4

SIMULATION LEAGUE DRAFT   TOP 500+

NAME	POS	RAR	NAME	POS	RAR	NAME	POS	RAR	NAME	POS	RAR
Matz,Steven	P	6.4	Rodriguez,Eduardo	P	4.7	Dull,Ryan	P	3.0	Aoki,Norichika	79	1.2
Yates,Kirby	P	6.4	McCann,Brian	2	4.6	Johnson,Jim	P	3.0	Ottavino,Adam	P	1.2
Baez,Pedro	P	6.3	Hembree,Heath	P	4.6	Senzatela,Antonio	P	2.9	Pina,Manny	2	1.2
Vizcaino,Arodys	P	6.3	Sherfy,Jimmie	P	4.6	Kontos,George	P	2.9	Marquez,German	P	1.2
Inciarte,Ender	8	6.3	Iannetta,Chris	2	4.6	Lamet,Dinelson	P	2.8	Ellsbury,Jacoby	8	1.2
Musgrove,Joe	P	6.2	Blevins,Jerry	P	4.6	Maton,Phil	P	2.8	Valaika,Pat	6	1.1
Belisle,Matt	P	6.2	Zimmerman,Ryan	3	4.6	Mahle,Tyler	P	2.8	Cashner,Andrew	P	1.1
Jackson,Austin	78	6.2	Bradley,Jackie	8	4.5	Gregorius,Didi	6	2.8	Tapia,Raimel	9	1.1
Kemp,Matt	7	6.1	Garcia,Luis	P	4.5	Casilla,Santiago	P	2.7	Romero,Enny	P	1.1
Davies,Zachary	P	6.1	Tuivailala,Sam	P	4.5	Skaggs,Tyler	P	2.7	Hundley,Nick	2	1.1
McMahon,Ryan	3	6.1	Glasnow,Tyler	P	4.4	Buehler,Walker	P	2.7	Reyes,Jose	456	1.0
Grandal,Yasmani	2	6.1	Kintzler,Brandon	P	4.4	Alvarez,Jose	P	2.7	Dyson,Sam	P	0.9
Taylor,Chris	478	6.1	Kopech,Michael	P	4.3	Samardzija,Jeff	P	2.7	Grichuk,Randal	79	0.9
Rusin,Chris	P	6.0	Altherr,Aaron	79	4.3	Shreve,Chasen	P	2.6	Drake,Oliver	P	0.9
Minter,A.J.	P	6.0	Senzel,Nick	5	4.3	Iwakuma,Hisashi	P	2.6	Rodon,Carlos	P	0.8
Bush,Matt	P	6.0	Hernandez,Cesar	4	4.2	Woodruff,Brandon	P	2.5	Pivetta,Nick	P	0.8
Nicasio,Juan	P	6.0	Calhoun,Willie	7	4.2	Granderson,Curtis	789	2.5	Adames,Willy	6	0.8
Simmons,Shae	P	5.9	Caratini,Victor	2	4.2	Kepler,Max	9	2.5	Ramirez,Jose	P	0.8
Nunez,Eduardo	45	5.9	Wacha,Michael	P	4.1	Altavilla,Dan	P	2.5	Moore,Andrew	P	0.8
Myers,Wil	3	5.9	Gurriel,Yulieski	3	4.1	Peralta,Wandy	P	2.5	Andriese,Matt	P	0.7
Feliz,Michael	P	5.8	Ziegler,Brad	P	4.0	Mahtook,Mikie	89	2.4	Panik,Joe	4	0.7
Perez,Salvador	2	5.8	Hendriks,Liam	P	4.0	Avila,Alex	2	2.4	Heaney,Andrew	P	0.7
Barnes,Matt	P	5.8	Garcia,Jaime	P	4.0	Hernandez,Teoscar	7	2.4	Eovaldi,Nathan	P	0.6
Barnes,Jacob	P	5.8	Jones,Adam	8	3.9	Pence,Hunter	9	2.4	Velasquez,Vincent	P	0.6
Ramos,Edubray	P	5.7	O Day,Darren	P	3.9	D Arnaud,Travis	2	2.4	Lively,Ben	P	0.6
Romo,Sergio	P	5.7	Cingrani,Tony	P	3.9	Urias,Julio	P	2.4	Ramirez,J.C.	P	0.6
Haniger,Mitch	9	5.7	Junis,Jakob	P	3.9	Tropeano,Nicholas	P	2.4	Longoria,Evan	5	0.6
Segura,Jean	6	5.6	Renfroe,Hunter	9	3.8	Estrada,Marco	P	2.3	Paulino,David	P	0.6
Roark,Tanner	P	5.6	Joyce,Matt	79	3.7	Zych,Tony	P	2.3	Clippard,Tyler	P	0.5
Cishek,Steve	P	5.5	Jeffress,Jeremy	P	3.7	Smith,Seth	9	2.2	Leclerc,Jose	P	0.5
Rondon,Hector	P	5.5	Kelly,Joe	P	3.7	Barnette,Tony	P	2.1	Biagini,Joe	P	0.4
Peralta,David	79	5.5	Olson,Matt	3	3.6	Guerra,Junior	P	2.1	De Leon,Jose	P	0.4
Hoyt,James	P	5.4	Bleier,Richard	P	3.6	Chen,Wei-Yin	P	2.1	Bell,Josh	3	0.4
Soria,Joakim	P	5.4	Ramirez,Erasmo	P	3.5	Kinsler,Ian	4	2.1	Luplow,Jordan	9	0.4
Wittgren,Nick	P	5.4	Middleton,Keynan	P	3.5	Baez,Javier	46	2.0	Pineda,Michael	P	0.4
Shaw,Travis	5	5.4	Coulombe,Daniel	P	3.5	Almora,Albert	8	2.0	Ross,Joe	P	0.4
Nelson,Jimmy	P	5.4	Holder,Jonathan	P	3.5	Pressly,Ryan	P	2.0	Bird,Gregory	3	0.3
Mauer,Joe	3	5.3	Alford,Anthony	7	3.5	Shoemaker,Matthew	P	2.0	Frazier,Clint	7	0.3
Choo,Shin-Soo	9	5.3	Pedroia,Dustin	4	3.5	Pederson,Joc	8	2.0	Wainwright,Adam	P	0.3
Wilson,Justin	P	5.2	Schebler,Scott	9	3.4	Mejia,Adalberto	P	2.0	Murphy,Tom	2	0.3
Gardner,Brett	78	5.2	Duffey,Tyler	P	3.4	Naquin,Tyler	8	2.0	Jaso,John	39	0.2
Buchter,Ryan	P	5.1	Owings,Chris	469	3.4	Foltynewicz,Mike	P	1.9	Russell,Addison	6	0.2
Barraclough,Kyle	P	5.1	Frazier,Adam	47	3.4	DeSclafani,Anthony	P	1.9	Eickhoff,Jerad	P	0.2
Suzuki,Kurt	2	5.1	Delgado,Randall	P	3.4	Williams,Trevor	P	1.9	Adams,Chance	P	0.1
Warren,Adam	P	5.1	Diekman,Jake	P	3.3	Tomlin,Josh	P	1.9	Alonso,Yonder	3	0.1
Kela,Keone	P	5.1	Morrow,Brandon	P	3.3	Pearce,Steve	7	1.7	Jimenez,Joe	P	0.0
Seager,Kyle	5	5.0	Torres,Jose	P	3.2	Giolito,Lucas	P	1.7	Torres,Gleyber	6	0.0
Kuhl,Chad	P	5.0	Chafin,Andrew	P	3.2	Freeland,Kyle	P	1.7	Valbuena,Luis	35	0.0
McGee,Jake	P	5.0	Garver,Mitch	2	3.2	Martin,Russell	2	1.6	Polanco,Gregory	79	0.0
Ramos,A.J.	P	5.0	Bowman,Matthew	P	3.2	Vogt,Stephen	2	1.6	Polanco,Jorge	6	-0.1
Greene,Shane	P	5.0	Gohara,Luiz	P	3.2	Thornburg,Tyler	P	1.6	Torres,Carlos	P	-0.1
Hernandez,David	P	4.9	Graveman,Kendall	P	3.2	Toles,Andrew	7	1.6	Street,Huston	P	-0.1
Faria,Jake	P	4.9	Ramos,Wilson	2	3.2	Barnes,Daniel	P	1.6	Hatcher,Chris	P	-0.1
Triggs,Andrew	P	4.9	Anderson,Tyler	P	3.2	Rodney,Fernando	P	1.5	Gomez,Carlos	8	-0.2
Cecil,Brett	P	4.9	Knapp,Andrew	2	3.2	Cervelli,Francisco	2	1.4	Robles,Hansel	P	-0.2
Brebbia,John	P	4.9	Sewald,Paul	P	3.1	Phillips,Brett	8	1.4	Fowler,Dustin	9	-0.2
Schoop,Jonathan	4	4.9	Tepera,Ryan	P	3.1	Petricka,Jacob	P	1.3	Calhoun,Kole	9	-0.3
Barnhart,Tucker	2	4.8	Lorenzen,Michael	P	3.1	Travis,Devon	4	1.3	Mejia,Francisco	2	-0.3
Parra,Gerardo	79	4.8	Desmond,Ian	37	3.1	Goodwin,Brian	78	1.3	Suarez,Eugenio	5	-0.4
Sabathia,CC	P	4.8	Span,Denard	8	3.0	Rogers,Taylor	P	1.3	Wheeler,Zack	P	-0.4
Marte,Starling	78	4.8	Glover,Koda	P	3.0	Wood,Blake	P	1.2	Verdugo,Alex	8	-0.4
Lind,Adam	37	4.7	Gennett,Scooter	4	3.0	Flowers,Tyler	2	1.2	Diaz,Yandy	5	-0.5
Oh,Seung-Hwan	P	4.7	Lackey,John	P	3.0	Crawford,Brandon	6	1.2	Drury,Brandon	4	-0.5

2018 CHEATER'S BOOKMARK

BATTING STATISTICS

Abbrv	Term	Formula / Desc.	BAD UNDER	'17 LG AVG AL	'17 LG AVG NL	BEST OVER
Avg	Batting Average	h/ab	235	256	261	280
xBA	Expected Batting Average	See glossary		260	261	
OB	On Base Average	(h+bb)/(ab+bb)	290	320	329	340
Slg	Slugging Average	total bases/ab	350	430	437	450
OPS	On Base plus Slugging	OB+Slg	650	750	766	780
bb%	Walk Rate	bb/(ab+bb)	6%	9%	9%	10%
ct%	Contact Rate	(ab-k) / ab	73%	76%	76%	83%
Eye	Batting Eye	bb/k	0.30	0.40	0.43	0.50
PX	Power Index	Normalized power skills	80	100	100	120
Spd	Speed Score	Normalized speed skills	80	100	100	120
SBO	Stolen Base Opportunity %	(sb+cs)/(singles+bb)		8%	8%	
G/F	Groundball/Flyball Ratio	gb / fb		1.2	1.3	
G	Ground Ball Per Cent	gb / balls in play		43%	44%	
L	Line Drive Per Cent	ld / balls in play		20%	21%	
F	Fly Ball Per Cent	fb / balls in play		36%	35%	
BPV	Base Performance Value	See glossary	20	34	36	55
PRO	Percentage Ratio Outcome	See glossary	-37%	-24%	-24%	-17%
RC/G	Runs Created per Game	See glossary	3.00	4.70	4.94	6.00
RAR	Runs Above Replacement	See glossary	0.0			10.0

Batting statistics do not include pitchers' batting statistics

PITCHING STATISTICS

Abbrv	Term	Formula / Desc.	BAD OVER	'17 LG AVG AL	'17 LG AVG NL	BEST UNDER
ERA	Earned Run Average	er*9/ip	4.75	4.38	4.34	3.00
xERA	Expected ERA	See glossary		3.78	3.72	
WHIP	Baserunners per Inning	(h+bb)/ip	1.50	1.33	1.35	1.15
BF/G	Batters Faced per Game	((ip*2.82)+h+bb)/g	28.0			
PC	Pitch Counts per Start		120	92	91	
OBA	Opposition Batting Avg	Opp. h/ab	280	254	256	235
OOB	Opposition On Base Avg	Opp. (h+bb)/(ab+bb)	350	318	322	290
BABIP	BatAvg on balls in play	(h-hr)/((ip*2.82)+h-k-hr)		296	299	
Ctl	Control Rate	bb*9/ip		3.2	3.4	2.5
hr/9	Homerun Rate	hr*9/ip		1.3	1.2	1.0
hr/f	Homerun per Fly ball	hr/fb		14%	14%	
S%	Strand Rate	(h+bb-er)/(h+bb-hr)		71%	72%	
DIS%	PQS Disaster Rate	% GS that are PQS 0/1	38%	36%		15%

Abbrv	Term	Formula / Desc.	BAD UNDER	'17 LG AVG AL	'17 LG AVG NL	BEST OVER
RAR	Runs Above Replacement	See glossary	-0.0			+10
Dom	Dominance Rate	k*9/ip		8.3	8.4	9.0
Cmd	Command Ratio	k/bb		2.6	2.5	3.3
G/F	Groundball/Flyball Ratio	gb / fb		1.19	1.30	
SwK	Swinging Strike Percentage	swinging strikes/pitches		10.9%	10.8%	11.5%
FpK	First Pitch Strike Percentage	first pitch strikes/batters		60%	60%	63%
BPV	Base Performance Value	See glossary	50	84	83	100
PRO	Percentage Ratio Outcome	See glossary	7%	24%	24%	27%
DOM%	PQS Dominance Rate	% GS that are PQS 4/5		22%	21%	50%
Sv%	Saves Conversion Rate	(saves / save opps)		65%	67%	80%
REff%	Relief Effectiveness Rate	See glossary		66%	67%	80%

NOTES

BASEBALL**HQ**.com

Home page for year-round fanalytic coverage:
www.BaseballHQ.com

For March projections update and any other information related to this book:
www.baseballhq.com/bf2018

For the schedule of dates and cities for our Spring 2018 First Pitch Forums, including registration information:
www.FirstPitchForums.com

Facebook: **www.facebook.com/baseballhq**
Twitter: **www.twitter.com/baseballhq**
HQ staffers on Twitter:
www.twitter.com/BaseballHQ/lists/hq-staff